THE MACMILLAN
COMPACT
ENCYCLOPEDIA

THE MACMILLAN
COMPACT
ENCYCLOPEDIA

MACMILLAN

This encyclopedia contains double-page features in which line drawings, photographs, and linking text are combined to give a cross-curricular approach to the following nine important topics:

ENERGY	pp 184-185
FLIGHT	pp 200-201
HEAT AND COMBUSTION	pp 246-247
MEDIA AND COMMUNICATION	pp 348-349
POLLUTION	pp 430-431
RITUALS	pp 460-461
SPACE TRAVEL	pp 508-509
TIME	pp 540-541
WATER	pp 574-575

Copyright © Market House Books Limited, Aylesbury, 1989, 1990, 1991.

First published 1989 by Pan Books Ltd
This edition published 1991 by the Macmillan Press Ltd
a division of Macmillan Publishers Ltd
Stockton House, 1 Melbourne Place, London WC2B 4LF and Basingstoke
Associated companies in Auckland, Delhi, Dublin, Gaborone,
Hamburg, Harare, Hong Kong, Johannesburg, Kuala Lumpur, Laos,
Manzini, Melbourne, Mexico City, Nairobi, New York, Singapore and Tokyo

British Cataloguing in Publication Data
A CIP catalogue for this book is available from the British Library
ISBN 0-333-56404-9

Compiled and prepared for automatic typesetting by Market House
Books Ltd, Aylesbury
Printed in England by Clays Ltd, St Ives plc

Picture Acknowledgements
Ardea; Sally and Richard Greenhill; Frank Lane Picture Library;
Magnum Photos; Mansell Collection; Network Photographers; Panos
Pictures; Axell Poignant Archive; Popperfoto; Quadrant Picture
Library; Reflex; Science Museum London; Select; Topham Picture Library.

This book has been prepared by Market House Books Ltd, Aylesbury,
for Pan Books Ltd by arrangement with the Macmillan Press.

Editors
Alan Isaacs
Elizabeth Martin

Contributors
John Daintith
Hazel Egerton
Rosalind Fergusson
Robert Hine
Valerie Illingworth
Jonathan Law
David Pickering
Catherine Sandbrook
Catherine Smith
Anne Stibbs
Edmund Wright

Picture Research
Juliet Brightmore

Artwork
Lynn Williams

Adviser
Ian Sandbrook

Notes

1. The extensive use of cross references has made the book virtually self-indexing. Few abbreviations have been used in the text: the only symbol appearing is an asterisk (*) preceding a word to tell the reader that further information on the entry will be found at the article on the word so marked.

2. *Chinese transliterations*
This encyclopedia follows official Chinese practice in using the pinyin system of transliterating Chinese names. Thus, almost all articles appear under the pinyin transliteration of the subject's name. However, the transliteration of the name in the Wade-Giles system (formerly the system most commonly used in the English-speaking world) will also be found in its alphabetical place, where the reader will be cross referred to the pinyin name under which the article appears. The Wade-Giles equivalent (unless the Wade-Giles and pinyin transliterations are almost identical) and, when it exists, the conventional western name, is given in brackets following the pinyin name. A small number of names are so well known in the Wade-Giles or conventional western forms that it has become usual to retain these very familiar spellings. They are Canton, Chiang Kai-shek, China, Chou-En-Lai, Inner Mongolia, Mao Tse-tung, Peking, Sun Yat-sen, Tibet, Yangzte River, Yellow River.

3. *Population figures*
For towns and cities the population figures given refer, wherever possible, to the town or city proper rather than the urban agglomeration of which it forms part.

A

Aachen (French name: Aix-la-Chapelle) 50 46N 06 06E A spa city in W Germany, in North Rhine-Westphalia near the Belgian and Dutch borders. It is an important industrial centre with iron and steel and textile industries. Population (1987): 239 200.

aardvark (Afrikaans: earth pig) A nocturnal African mammal, *Orycteropus afer*, also called ant bear. It is about 1.5 m long, lives in grassland, and has a long snout, large ears, and a thick tail. Its strong claws are used to dig burrows and tear open the mounds of termites, which are picked up with its long sticky tongue.

abacus A calculating device consisting of balls strung on wires or rods set in a frame, probably of Babylonian origin. Its use declined in Europe with the introduction of *Arabic numerals in about the 10th century AD.

Abadan 30 20N 48 15E A city in SW Iran, on an island in the Shatt (river) al-Arab. Much of Iran's oil is brought here by pipeline for refining or exporting. Population (1985 est): 294 068.

abalone A sea snail of rocky coasts, also called ear shell or ormer. Up to 30 cm long, its dishlike shell has a row of holes along the outer edge; water passes over the gills and out through these holes, together with waste products from the body. Abalones have a large muscular foot, which is eaten as a delicacy, and the shells are used as mother-of-pearl (*see* pearl).

abdomen In mammals (including man), the region of the body extending from the lower surface of the diaphragm to the pelvis. The abdomen contains the intestines, liver, pancreas, kidneys, gall bladder, and—in females—the ovaries and womb. In insects and similar animals the abdomen is the rear section of the body, which is usually divided into segments.

Abdullah (1882–1951) Emir of Transjordan (1921–46) and first King of Jordan (1946–51). He fought in the Arab revolt against Turkish rule during World War I. He was assassinated in 1951.

Aberdeen 57 10N 2 04W A city, port, and former county of NE Scotland, the administrative centre of Grampian Region situated on the North Sea coast between the mouths of the Rivers Don and Dee. Aberdeen is an old cathedral city with a university dating from 1494 (King's College). Fishing has always been important, as has the working of local granite. Other industries include shipbuilding, paper making, textiles, chemicals, and engineering. Being close to the North Sea, Aberdeen has become an important service centre for the oil industry. Population (1988): 205 180.

aberration A defect in a lens or mirror that causes blurring or distortion of the image. **Spherical aberration** is caused by rays from the outside of the lens or mirror being brought to a focus at a different point from those nearer to the centre. In **chromatic aberration**, different colours are focused at different points, since the refractive index of glass varies with the wavelength. *See also* astigmatism.

Aberystwyth 52 25N 4 05W A town and resort in Wales, in Dyfed on Cardigan Bay. A college of the University of Wales was established in 1872 and the National Library of Wales, in 1911. Population (1981): 8666.

Abidjan 5 19N 4 00W The former capital (now Yamoussoukro) of Côte d'Ivoire, off the Gulf of Guinea. A small village until developed by the French in the 1920s, it became the capital in 1934. It is now an important port. Population (1984): 1 850 100.

Abominable Snowman A creature, also called Yeti (Tibetan: Snowman), that is believed to live at high altitudes in the Himalayas. There have been no authenticated sightings, but gigantic footprints in the snow have been photographed (which may have other natural causes).

Aborigines The dark-skinned hunters and gatherers who inhabited Australia before European settlement began in 1788. Their culture was simple, but relationships between families and tribes were complex. Aboriginal mythology was generally rich and elaborate and included accounts of creation at the dawn of time, which they call "Dream Time." There are roughly 136 000 people of Aboriginal descent in Australia. The few remaining nomads are threatened by loss of their lands. A movement to protect Aborigines' rights has grown stronger and in 1971 the first Aborigine MP was elected.

abortion The removal of an unborn baby from the womb before it is able to survive outside its mother. An abortion can occur naturally (it is then called a miscarriage), but it can also be performed by a doctor to prevent the birth of a severely deformed or abnormal child or to protect the health of the mother. In the UK it is against the law to perform an abortion after the unborn baby is 24 weeks old, and two doctors must agree that it is necessary.

Aboukir, Battle of (25 July, 1799) The battle in which Napoleon defeated the Ottoman Turks during his occupation of Egypt. The 7000-strong French army defeated the unruly Turkish force of 18 000.

Abraham, Plains of A plateau in E Canada, on the W edge of Quebec citadel. Here Gen James Wolfe defeated the French under Gen Montcalm (13 September, 1759), leading to British control over Canada.

absolute zero The lowest temperature that can theoretically be attained. It is equal to −273.15°C or 0 K. In practice, absolute zero can never be reached, although temperatures of a few thousandths of a degree above absolute zero have been achieved. *See* cryogenics.

absorption 1. A reduction in the energy of a beam of light, a sound wave, etc. 2. *See* adsorption.

abstract art A form of art in which shapes, patterns, and colours are used in place of recognizable objects or people. Tendencies to abstraction can be found in almost any age or school of art, particularly oriental and decorative art. However, the widespread use of *photography in the 20th century to create permanent visual records made painting much less important for this purpose. Artists were therefore encouraged to explore the wider fields of abstraction. In about 1910 Wassily Kandinsky (1866–1944) produced the first abstract watercolour, heralding the free expression of such artists as Jackson *Pollock; in contrast, *cubism led to the geometric abstract style of such painters as Piet *Mondrian and Kasimir Malevich (1878–1935). A particular characteristic of abstract sculpture is the use of such materials as plastic, glass, and steel.

Abu Dhabi. *See* United Arab Emirates.

Abuja 9 10N 7 06E The intended federal capital of Nigeria. Agriculture is the most important activity with some local manufacturing.

Abu Simbel A monumental rock-cut temple complex constructed about 1250 BC by Pharaoh *Ramses II in *Nubia. Four colossal statues of Ramses, each 20 m (66 ft) high, at the entrance were raised to escape flooding by Lake Nasser (1968).

abyssal zone The ocean depths below 1000 m, lying beyond the continental slope (*see* continental shelf). Since no light penetrates to these depths, they contain relatively little marine life and the temperature never rises above 4°C. The ocean depths below 6000 m, the deep-sea trenches, are sometimes classified separately as the **hadal zone**.

Abyssinian cat A breed of short-haired cat, many individuals of which are descendants of one exported to the UK from Abyssinia in the 19th century. They have slender bodies and wedge-shaped heads with large ears. The reddish-brown coat has black or brown markings and the eyes are green, yellow, or hazel. The Red Abyssinian is a rich copper-red.

acacia A tropical or subtropical tree or shrub of which there are over 700 species, particularly abundant in Australia (*see* wattle). Acacias have clusters of yellow or white flowers, produce long flattened pods, and usually have leaves consisting of many small leaflets. In some species the leaflets do not develop and the leafstalks are broad and leaflike. These species are often very spiny. Acacias yield a number of useful products: gums (including *gum arabic), tannins, dyes, and woods suitable for furniture. Many are grown in temperate regions as garden plants.

Académie Française The French literary academy founded by Cardinal de Richelieu in 1634 (incorporated 1635) to preserve the French literary heritage. Its membership is limited at any one time to 40 "immortals," who have included Corneille, Racine, and Voltaire. It is continuously engaged in the revision of the official French dictionary.

Academy, Greek The college founded (c. 385 BC) near Athens by Plato, which continued in various forms until it was broken up by Justinian in 529 AD. It is famed mainly for contributions to philosophy and science.

ACAS (*advisory, conciliation and arbitration service*) A public body set up by parliament in 1975 to work with trade unions and employers to settle disputes and promote industrial peace.

acceleration The rate of change of a body's velocity. Linear acceleration is the rate of change of linear velocity. It is measured in such units as metres per second per second. Angular acceleration is the rate of change of angular velocity and is measured in such units as radians per second per second.

acceleration of free fall (*g*) Formerly called acceleration due to gravity; the acceleration of a falling body when air resistance is neglected. Caused by gravitational attraction between the body and the earth, it varies slightly at different points on the earth's surface. Its standard value is 9.806 metres per second per second.

accelerators Large machines used for accelerating beams of charged particles (electrons, protons, etc.) to very high speeds primarily for research in *particle physics. The particles are accelerated by electric fields either in a straight line, as in the linear accelerator, or in a circle, as in the cyclotron, synchrotron, and synchrocyclotron. The beam is confined to its path by magnetic fields. Particle accelerators are operated by directing the beam of particles at a stationary target or, for greater energy, by colliding two beams of particles together. Accelerators are also used to create artificial isotopes and in *radiotherapy. The first accelerator was a linear accelerator, produced in 1932 by *Cockcroft and Walton.

Accra 5 32N 0 12W The capital of Ghana, a port on the Gulf of Guinea. It is built on the site of three 17th-century trading fortresses founded by the English, Dutch, and Danish. It became the capital of the Gold Coast in 1877. Following the opening (1923) of a railway to the agricultural lands away from the coast it developed rapidly into the commercial centre of Ghana. The University of Ghana was founded in 1948 at Legon, just outside Accra. Population (1984): 974 879.

accumulator A cell or battery that can be recharged by passing a current through it in the direction opposite to that of the discharge current. The most common example is the lead-acid accumulator used in motor vehicles. This consists, when charged, of a positive lead dioxide electrode and a negative spongy lead electrode, both immersed in sulphuric acid with a relative density of 1.20–1.28. During discharge lead sulphate forms on the electrodes and the acid density falls. Nickel-iron (NiFe) accumulators with an electrolyte of 20% potassium hydroxide are also used. Interest in electric cars has stimulated accumulator development in recent years. While lead accumulators will deliver up 8×10^4

joules per kilogram, the newer zinc-air accumulator can produce five times this energy density.

acetylene (or ethyne; C_2H_2) A colourless toxic inflammable gas formed by the action of water on calcium carbide. It is widely used as a starting material for many organic compounds. Because of its high flame temperature (about 3300°C) it is used in oxy-acetylene welding. See also alkynes.

Acheron A river in N Greece, in Greek mythology the chief river of the underworld. In Dante, it is the river across which the souls of the dead are ferried to hell by Charon.

Achilles In Greek mythology, the greatest Greek warrior in the Trojan War. The son of Peleus, King of Thessaly, and Thetis, a sea nymph, he was dipped by his mother in the River Styx as a child, which made his whole body invulnerable except for the heel by which she had held him. After a quarrel with *Agamemnon he ceased fighting until the death of his friend Patroclus at the hand of *Hector. Achilles then slew Hector and was himself later killed by Paris, who shot a poisoned arrow into his heel.

ACID RAIN Sulphur deposits in Europe.

acid rain Rain that contains sulphuric and nitric acids, formed when sulphur dioxide and nitrogen oxides are absorbed from the atmosphere. This form of pollution can result in destruction of fish, crops, and trees, as well as damage to buildings. The oxides are produced mainly by burning fuels in industrial processes and by emissions from car exhausts. Until recently attempts to reduce them have been hampered by absence of international agreement.

acids and bases Acids are chemical compounds containing hydrogen that can be replaced by a metal atom to produce a *salt. They have a sour taste and turn litmus red. When dissolved in water they break down into ions. Hydrochloric acid (HCl), for instance, gives chloride ions and hydrogen ions: $HCl + H_2O \rightarrow Cl^- + H^+ + H_2O$. The hydrogen ion is associated with a water molecule, a combination referred to as a hydroxonium ion (H_3O^+).

Bases are compounds that react with acids to form salts and water. Bases that dissolve in water, known as **alkalis**, produce hydroxide ions

(OH^-). Many are metal hydroxides, such as sodium hydroxide (NaOH). The neutralization of an acid by a base in solution is a reaction in which hydrogen and hydroxide ions combine to give water. See also pH.

Aconcagua, Mount (Spanish name: Cerro Aconcagua) 32 40S 70 02W A mountain in W Argentina, in the Andes, regarded as being the highest point in the W hemisphere. It is of volcanic origin. Height: 6960 m (22 835 ft).

acoustics The branch of physics concerned with the production, transmission reception, properties, and uses of sound. It has several subdivisions. The most important, architectural acoustics, is concerned with the design of concert halls, theatres, etc., so that sounds can be heard in all parts of them with the maximum clarity and the minimum distortion. *Ultrasonics is the study of very high frequency sound. The structure and function of sound sources, such as loudspeakers, and sound receptors, such as microphones, also form part of acoustics. Other fields include speech communication and the design of machines that can understand spoken instructions.

acquired characteristics. See Lamarckism.

acropolis (Greek: high town) In ancient Greek towns, the isolated rocky plateau on which stood the religious and administrative centre of the town and which served as a citadel in time of war. The most famous is the Acropolis of Athens, which is still adorned by remains of buildings erected by Cimon, Themistocles, and *Pericles after the sack of Athens by the Persians (480 BC). These buildings include the Propylaea, *Parthenon, Erectheum, and the reconstructed temple of Athena Nike.

acrylics Synthetic materials produced by *polymerization of acrylonitrile (vinyl cyanide; $CH_2:CHCN$). Acrylic resins are used in paints and plastics, the most common being *Perspex. Acrylic fibre is widely used in textiles, mainly for knitwear, furnishing fabrics, and carpets.

Actaeon A mythological Greek hunter, son of the god Aristaeus and Autonoe, daughter of Cadmus, King of Thebes. Ovid, in his Metamorphoses, relates how Actaeon accidentally caught sight of the goddess Artemis bathing naked and was turned by her into a stag and killed by his own hounds.

actinides A group of related chemical elements in the periodic table ranging from actinium (atomic number 89) to lawrencium (atomic number 103). They are radioactive and include a number of *transuranic elements. Chemically, they resemble the *lanthanides.

actinium (Ac) A highly radioactive metal that occurs naturally in uranium minerals. It is the first of the actinide series of elements and is chemically similar to the lanthanide elements. It was discovered in 1899 by A. L. Debierne (1874–1949). The **actinium series** of radioactive decay is headed by uranium-235, which undergoes a series of alpha and beta decays ending with the stable isotope lead-207. At no 89; at wt (227); mp 1050°C; half-life of ^{227}Ac 21.6 yrs.

Actium, Battle of (31 BC) The decisive land and sea battle that ended the civil war in ancient

Rome. Octavian, later *Augustus (the first Roman emperor), defeated the forces of *Mark Antony and *Cleopatra.

Act of Parliament. *See* parliament.

actuary A mathematician employed by an *insurance company to calculate the cost of policies. The calculations are based on certain risks and eventualities (e.g. sickness, life expectancy). In the UK qualifications are awarded by the Institute of Actuaries through examination.

acupuncture A traditional Chinese system of healing in which thin metal needles are inserted into selected points in the body. The needles are stimulated either by manual rotation or electrically. Acupuncture is used to relieve pain and in China as an anaesthetic for surgical operations. The traditional explanation of its effectiveness, dating back to 2500 BC, relates to balancing the opposing life forces *yin and yang. Recent research in the West suggests that the needles may activate deep sensory nerves, which cause parts of the brain to release endorphins (natural pain killers; *see* encephalins).

Adam, Robert (1728–92) British architect and interior designer, born in Kirkcaldy, Fifeshire, the son of the architect **William Adam** (1689–1748). He evolved a unique style that blended the *rococo and *neoclassicism, although he occasionally used *gothic forms. After visiting Italy (1755–58), Robert, often in collaboration with his brother **James Adam** (1732–94), built many country houses, notably Kenwood House (1768), the interior of Syon House (1769), and Osterley Park (1780). His building of town houses in London, such as Apsley House (1775), led him into severe financial difficulties. In his last years in Edinburgh he produced much of his finest work, for instance Charlotte Square (1791).

Adams, John (1735–1826) US statesman; first vice president (1789–97) and second president of the USA (1797–1801). During the American Revolution he won European support for the North American cause. His term as president was troubled by disputes with his vice president, Thomas *Jefferson, over US policy towards Revolutionary France. Adams was defeated by Jefferson in the election of 1800. His son **John Quincy Adams** (1767–1848) was sixth president of the USA (1825–29). As secretary of state (1817–25) he was largely responsible for the *Monroe Doctrine (1823). His term as president was made difficult by the opposition of Andrew Jackson, who defeated Adams in the presidential election in 1828. From 1831 Adams served in the House of Representatives, where he campaigned vigorously against slavery.

adaptive radiation The process by which a group of similar animals or plants evolves over a long period into a number of different forms. The original group increases in size and spreads to occupy different habitats. It eventually forms several subgroups that differ from each other, each adapted to the particular conditions of its habitat. In time–and if the subgroups differ sufficiently–a number of new species will be formed from the original stock. The Australian marsupials evolved in this way into burrowers,

fliers, flesh-eaters, plant-eaters, and many other different forms.

adder A widely distributed European *viper, *Vipera berus*, about 80 cm long, common in heathland areas. It is usually greyish with a broad black zigzag line along its back and black spots on its sides. Although venomous, its bite is rarely fatal. It is one of the three species of snakes found in Britain. The name adder is also given to a highly venomous Australian snake (death adder) of the cobra family and to some harmless North American snakes.

Addis Ababa 9 02N 38 43E The capital of Ethiopia, on a central plateau 2440 m (8000 ft) above sea level. It is the country's administrative centre and chief market place and its major industries produce cement, tobacco, textiles, and shoes. The headquarters of the Organization of African Unity and the UN Economic Commission for Africa are in Addis Ababa. The National University was established in 1961. Population (1984): 1 412 575.

additive process. *See* colour.

Adelaide 34 56S 138 36E The capital of South Australia, on the Torrens River. Founded in 1837, it is an important commercial centre with a harbour at Port Adelaide. Industries include the manufacture of cars and textiles, oil refining, and electronics. Population (1986): 993 100.

Aden 12 50N 45 03E The main port of Yemen, on the **Gulf of Aden**, which connects the Indian Ocean with the Red Sea. Taken by the British in 1839, Aden was an important coaling station on the route to India through the Suez Canal (opened 1869). It became part of the Federation of Saudi Arabia in 1963 and was the scene of fighting between rival nationalist groups until 1968, when it became the capital of the independent republic of South Yemen, now part of Yemen. Industry centres on the port and an oil refinery. Population (1984): 318 000.

Adenauer, Konrad (1876–1967) German statesman. He was a successful Rhineland politician until the Nazi government forced him out of public life (1934) and imprisoned him (1934, 1944). In 1946 Adenauer re-emerged as chairman of the Christian Democratic Union (CDU) and became the first chancellor (1949–63) of the Federal Republic of Germany. He presided over Germany's economic miracle and did much to restore its international prestige.

adenoids Two masses of tissue at the back of the nose that help to destroy disease-causing microbes in the throat. In children they are normally large. When a person suffers repeated sore throats or a blocked nose the adenoids may be infected and may have to be removed surgically. This operation is often combined with removal of the tonsils, as the tonsils tend to be infected at the same time.

adenosine triphosphate. *See* ATP.

adjutant stork A large carrion-eating *stork, *Leptotilos dubius*, occurring in Asia and similar to the related marabou. It has a white plumage with dark-grey back, wings, and tail, a short neck, and a heavy pointed bill. Its head and neck are naked and a bald pouch hangs from the throat.

Adler, Alfred (1870–1937) Austrian psychiatrist who introduced the concept of the inferiority complex. Initially an associate of Sigmund *Freud, Adler's views diverged from Freud's and by 1911 he had founded his own school. Adler saw people as striving to compensate for feelings of inferiority resulting from physical or social disabilities (*The Neurotic Constitution*, 1912). He regarded sex as an opportunity to express dominance.

Admiral's Cup A sailing competition held every two years by the Royal Ocean Racing Club since 1957. The competition comprises three races in the Solent and two longer races, from Cherbourg to the Isle of Wight and from Plymouth to the Fastnet Rock off Ireland and back (the Fastnet Cup). Three yachts represent each nation.

Admiralty Court. *See* maritime law.

Adonis In Greek mythology, a youth from Cyprus, loved by *Aphrodite for his great beauty. *Zeus decreed that his time should be divided between Aphrodite on earth, Persephone, queen of the underworld, and himself. He was celebrated in many festivals, his death and resurrection representing seasonal change.

adoption The process by which a natural parent's legal rights and duties towards an unmarried minor are transferred to another adult. The Adoption Act (1976), controls the work of adoption societies, the rights of the natural parents, and the adopted child's right to know his original name. Birth control, abortion, and the acceptance of one-parent families has decreased the number of children available for adoption in recent years. However, greater publicity has been given to finding adoptive homes for children with special needs, e.g. older children, children of mixed race, and the handicapped.

adrenal glands Two small pyramid-shaped glands in man and other mammals, one at the upper end of each of the kidneys. The inner part (medulla) of each gland produces the hormones *adrenaline and *noradrenaline, and controlled directly by the nervous system. The outer part (cortex) produces three types of hormones; these regulate the balance of salts and water in the body, the way the body uses starchy foods and sugars, and the activity of the sex glands (*see* corticosteroids). The adrenal cortex is controlled by hormones secreted by the *pituitary gland.

adrenaline (*or* epinephrine) A hormone secreted mainly by the *adrenal glands. Adrenaline increases heart rate, raises blood pressure, and increases the level of glucose in the blood. Its release into the bloodstream is triggered by stress and helps prepare the body for "fight or flight." *See also* noradrenaline.

Adriatic Sea A northern arm of the Mediterranean Sea, extending between Italy and Yugoslavia for about 750 km (466 mi). Its principal ports are Brindisi, Bari, Venice, Trieste, and Rijeka. The Italian coast is flat; the Yugoslav coast rocky with many offshore islands.

adsorption The production of a layer of atoms or molecules of a substance on a solid or liquid surface. The adsorbed atoms or molecules may be strongly held by chemical bonds (**chemi-sorption**), in which case the adsorbed layer is usually only one molecule thick. Adsorption may also occur through weaker physical forces (**physisorption**), often giving rise to several molecular layers. In contrast, **absorption** involves material penetrating into the bulk of a solid or liquid.

adultery Voluntary sexual intercourse between a married person and someone who is not that person's husband or wife. In many countries, including some US states, adultery is a crime; under some systems, such as Islamic law, it may carry the death penalty. Generally, however, it is only a ground for *divorce or separation, as in English law.

Advent (from Latin: *adventus*, coming) The first season of the *church year, leading up to *Christmas. It begins on the Sunday nearest St Andrew's Day (30 Nov). From the 6th century it has been observed as a solemn preparation for celebrating Christ's birth and for his Second Coming.

adventists Several Protestant Christian faiths that stress a belief in the imminent Second Coming of Christ. In the USA adventism began in 1831 with the preaching of William Miller (1782–1849), who predicted the Second Coming for 1843–44, but changed the date when his prediction proved false. In the UK a similar movement was founded in 1832 as the Catholic Apostolic Church. There have been many adventist movements, the Seventh-Day Adventists being the main church today.

advocate In Scotland and in some countries, such as France, having a legal system based on Roman law, a person whose profession is to plead the cases of others in a court of justice. The English version is a *barrister. In Scotland, the **Lord Advocate** is the chief law officer of the Crown, generally the same as the *attorney general in England.

Aegean Sea A section of the NE Mediterranean Sea, lying between Greece and Turkey and containing many islands, including the Cyclades, Dodecanese, and N Sporades.

Aeneas A legendary Trojan leader, son of Anchises and *Aphrodite, and hero of Virgil's *Aeneid*. After the Greek victory in the Trojan War, he sailed away from burning Troy with his family and other survivors and was shipwrecked near Carthage. He fell in love with *Dido but abandoned her to continue his divinely ordained voyage to Italy, where he founded what was to become Rome.

Aeolus The Greek god of the winds and ruler of Aeolia. In Homer's *Odyssey* he gave Odysseus a bag containing unfavourable winds; Odysseus' companions untied it, causing their ship to be blown back to Aeolia. An **aeolian harp** is a wooden resonating box with gut strings; when hung in the open air it produces chords that vary according to the wind pressure.

aerial (*or* antenna) An electrical conductor that transmits and receives radio waves. Waves from a distant source set up a varying *alternating current in the receiving aerial. A transmitting aerial works by the same process in reverse. A modern aerial for UHF (ultra-high frequency) and VHF (very high frequency) radio waves consists of a dipole formed from two metal rods, each measuring about one-quarter of the received or transmitted wavelength. In the **Yagi aerial** named after H. Yagi (1886–1976), a reflector rod is set behind the dipole and several director rods are placed in front of it. This provides a more directional array than the simple dipole and is widely used as a receiving and transmitting aerial for television.

aerobics A method of keeping fit by exercising to stimulate the heart and lungs to work faster, thereby increasing the volume of oxygen available to the body. It involves repetitive and sustained use of the muscles and claims to reduce the resting pulse rate and increase the efficiency of the heart. The system was started in the USA by Dr Ken Cooper for the US forces in the 1970s and subsequently adapted by Jackie Sorensen as a dance and exercise form.

aerodynamics The study of the behaviour and flow of air around such objects as moving vehicles, buildings and bridges, engines, furnaces, as well as aircraft (*see* aeronautics) and missiles.

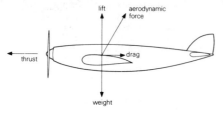

forces acting on aircraft

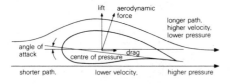

cross-section of aerofoil

AERONAUTICS *The forces acting on an aircraft. The aerofoil cross-section shows how the lift, which keeps it in the air, results from the passage of the aerofoil through the air, causing a lower pressure above it and a higher pressure below it.*

aeronautics The science and history (*see also* aircraft) of flight. An object flying through air is subject to four basic forces: its own weight (vertically downwards as a result of gravity), lift (to counterbalance its weight and keep it in the air), thrust (to force it through the air), and drag (resulting from friction between the body and the air). Birds and insects use their wings to provide both lift and thrust; man, in his heavier-than-air fixed-wing craft, uses an aerofoil to provide the lift and an *internal-combustion engine (propeller or jet) to provide the thrust (*see also* aircraft; gliders; flight). *Helicopters use rotating aero-

foils to provide lift, while *rockets use no lift surfaces, the jet of expanding gas providing both lift and thrust. The use of aerofoils as lift surfaces depends on Bernoulli's theorem. This states that the total energy of a flowing fluid, such as air, remains constant; thus, if the velocity of the fluid increases, its pressure decreases in proportion. An aerofoil is a wing so shaped that (at subsonic speeds) air is accelerated over its rounded leading edge and curved upper surface, causing a reduced pressure above it. A smaller reduction in air velocity on its underside causes a slightly increased pressure below it. The combination of these pressure differences provides the lift. The design of practical aircraft wings has to take into account a number of complex factors, including turbulence in the airflow. At supersonic speeds these forces are somewhat altered (*see* sound barrier) and the aerofoil has to be more swept-back and more streamlined. *See also* airships; balloons.

aerosol A mixture consisting of tiny particles of liquid or solid in a gas. Fog, mist, and smoke are common natural examples. Aerosols can be produced from a huge range of substances, including insecticides, paints, hairsprays, etc. In these, the substance is mixed with an easily liquefied gas (often a fluorinated or chlorinated hydrocarbon) under pressure, which acts as a propellant when the pressure is released. Fears have been expressed that fluorinated hydrocarbons, being lighter than air, could cause chain reactions in the upper atmosphere, which could destroy the *ozone layer. *See* colloid.

Aeschylus (c. 525–456 BC) Greek tragic dramatist, the first of the great trio of Athenian tragedians that included Sophocles and Euripides. He wrote over 80 plays, of which only 7 survive: *The Persians* (472), *Seven against Thebes* (467), the *Oresteia* trilogy (*Agamemnon, Libation Bearers*, and *Eumenides*; 458), *Suppliant Women* and *Prometheus Bound*. His introduction of a second actor, allowing dialogue and action independent of the chorus, and his innovations in costume and scenery, transformed the conventions of drama.

Aesop The supposed author of a collection of Greek fables, said by Herodotus to be a slave from Samos who lived in the 6th century BC. Originating in popular folklore, the fables all have animal characters who are used to illustrate a moral point. The Roman poet Phaedrus popularized them in the 1st century AD, and the French poet La Fontaine wrote more sophisticated versions in the 17th century.

Aesthetic movement A British literary and artistic movement of the late 19th century, summarized in the slogan "art for art's sake." Reacting against the ugliness of industrialism and against the social philosophies of the time, its followers sought to create beauty for its own sake. They were influenced by the *Pre-Raphaelite Brotherhood, formed in 1848, whose emphasis on pure aesthetics was continued by Swinburne, William Morris, and others, culminating in the work of Oscar Wilde, Aubrey Beardsley, and the other contributors to the periodical *The Yellow Book* (1894–97).

Aeth–. For names beginning Aeth *see* Eth–.

Afars and the Issas, French territory of the. *See* Djibouti, Republic of.

Afghan hound A breed of large dog having long legs, large drooping ears, and a very long silky coat. The Afghan probably originated in ancient Egypt and was later used in Afghanistan to hunt leopards and gazelles. Height: 68–73 cm (dogs); 61–66 cm (bitches).

Afghanistan, Democratic Republic of A state in central Asia. The country is mountainous, the Hindu Kush range rising over 6000 m (20 000 ft). The only lower-lying areas are along the River Amu Darya (ancient name: Oxus) in the N and the delta of the River Helmand in the SW. *Economy*: largely agricultural, primarily stock raising (especially of fat-tailed sheep). There has been industrial development in recent years, especially since the discovery of natural gas in the N. Main exports include Persian lambskins, fruit, cotton, wool, carpets, and natural gas (to the Soviet Union). *History*: before the opening up of international sea routes in the 15th century Afghanistan was an important centre on the overland routes across central Asia. For centuries under the rule of different powers, including the Mongol Genghis Khan in the 13th century, it became an independent kingdom in 1747. During the 19th century Afghanistan became involved in the struggle between Britain and Russia for influence in central Asia. After two wars with Britain (1839–42 and 1878–80) it became a buffer state between British India and Russia, with Britain controlling its foreign policy. Independence was achieved in 1921 under the leadership of Amanollah Khan (1892–1960) after the third Afghan War. In 1926 Amanollah declared himself king. He was deposed in 1929; King Zahir came to the throne in 1933. Since World War II there has been friction with Pakistan over the question of an independent Pathan state in Pakistan. In 1973 the monarchy was overthrown by Mohammed Daud, a cousin of King Zahir, and in 1977 a republic was set up with Daud as president. In 1978 he was killed in a military coup and a new government under Nur Mohammed Taraki (1917–79) was set up by the Marxist People's Democratic Party. In 1979, Babrak Karmal came to power with Soviet aid; he was replaced in 1986 by the Soviet-backed Mohammad Najibullah. Soviet military occupation of Afghanistan provoked worldwide condemnation. After nine years of fighting Mujahidin guerrillas, Soviet forces withdrew in 1989: attempts by the Mujahidin to overthrow the government have since failed. Joint official languages: Pushtu and Dari Persian. Official currency: afghani of 100 puls. Area: 657 500 sq km (250 000 sq mi). Population (1986 est): 9 000 000. Capital: Kabul.

Africa The second largest continent in the world. A notable feature of the NE is the *Great Rift Valley, which contains freshwater lakes as well as the continent's highest point, Mount *Kilimanjaro. The principal rivers are the Nile, Niger, Zaïre, and Zambezi. Africa's climate and vegetation vary considerably from the arid desert of the Sahara to the tropical rainforest of the Congo basin. The inhabitants of Africa are principally of Negroid origin, although the Berbers remain dominant in N Africa and the Sahara and there are a few Cushite-speaking peoples in the NE. *History*: Louis *Leakey's finds of hominoid man at Olduvai Gorge are evidence of Africa's long history. The earliest African civilization was established in Egypt in about 3400 BC. From the 7th century AD Arab influence was strong and Islam spread with trade across the Sahara and on the East African coast. Several African kingdoms and empires emerged during this period, notably the Sudanese empires of Ghana, Mali, and Songhai. From the 15th century European exploration and exploitation began, initiated by the Portuguese. Slaves, ivory, and gold were exported from Africa from the 17th to the late 19th centuries. From 1880 to 1912 most of Africa was divided by the European powers, creating new political boundaries; this resulted in long-standing problems (*see also* South Africa, Republic of). In the 1950s there was movement towards independence and Africa now consists of independent nations. Area: about 30 300 000 sq km (11 700 000 sq mi). Population (1984): 537 000 000.

African National Congress (ANC) A Black nationalist movement in S Africa. Founded in 1912 as the South African Native National Congress, the ANC has fought apartheid since 1948, turning to guerrilla activity after being outlawed in 1950. Although Oliver Tambo (1917–) is its official leader, Nelson *Mandela is its symbolic head. It was legalized in 1990 and its leaders have held talks with the South African government.

African violet A flowering plant, *Saintpaulia ionantha*, native to tropical East Africa. 10–15 cm high, the plants have hairy leaves and pink, blue, purple, or white flowers. Many varieties and hybrids are grown as pot plants.

Afrikaner A South African of Dutch or *Huguenot descent. The Afrikaners comprise about 60% of the Republic's White population. Formerly called "Boers" (farmers), they have built up a modern urban society since the 1930s. In the 18th and 19th centuries they led a seminomadic life. Their two independent states, the South African Republic and the Orange Free State, came under British rule after the second *Boer War. Their language, **Afrikaans**, developed from Dutch and together with English has been an official language of South Africa since 1925.

Agadir 30 30N 9 40W A port in SW Morocco, on the Atlantic coast. An earthquake in 1960 destroyed much of the town and killed about 12 000 people. Population (1984): 62 300.

Agamemnon King of Mycenae and commander of the Greek army in the Trojan War. His quarrel with Achilles is the main theme of Homer's *Iliad*. After his return from Troy with *Cassandra he was murdered by his wife Clytemnestra and her lover Aegisthus.

agate A form of chalcedony having concentric bands of colour due to intermittent deposition in rock cavities; the colours, ranging from white, milky blue, yellow, and brown to red, are due to traces of mineral or organic colouring matter. Being hard, it is used for mortars for grinding, and also for ornamental purposes.

agave A plant native to S USA and tropical America, many species of which are widely grown in gardens. Agaves have thick fleshy, sometimes toothed, leaves and a cluster of flowers that—in some species—grows on a tall stalk (up to 12 m high). Growth is slow—it may be 60 or more years before flowers are produced; after flowering the plant dies. Several species are commercially important as a source of fibre, especially *sisal; the fermented juice of others is used as an alcoholic drink (pulque) or distilled to produce spirits (tequila).

Agincourt, Battle of (25 October, 1415) The battle that took place during the *Hundred Years' War at Agincourt (now in the Pas-de-Calais), in which the French were defeated by an English army led by Henry V. The decisive English victory, which owed much to their outstanding archers, was achieved with not more than 1600 dead; the French may have lost as many as 6000 men.

agoraphobia. See phobia.

agouti A rabbit-sized rodent of Central and South American forests. Agoutis have long legs, small ears, and a very short hairless tail. The hair on the rump is often long and brightly coloured and can be erected when the animal is alarmed.

Agra 27 09N 78 00E A city in India, in Uttar Pradesh on the River Jumna. Former capital of the Mogul Empire (1566–69 and 1601–58), it fell to the British in 1803 and from 1835 until 1862 was capital of the North-West Provinces. Notable buildings include the celebrated *Taj Mahal. Population (1981 est): 694 191.

Agricola, Gnaeus Julius (40–93 AD) Roman governor of Britain and father-in-law of his biographer Tacitus. Sent to govern Britain in 78, after holding previous legionary posts there, he followed a policy of romanization, exploration, and expansion before his recall in 84.

agricultural revolution The name given to the changes in agriculture in Britain that took place mainly in the 18th century. The open-field system of strip farming was replaced by larger enclosed fields, hedged and ditched, in which improved agricultural methods and new tools could be used (see Tull, Jethro); the quality of cattle and sheep was improved by scientific stock breeding. This resulted in more food being grown for the increasing industrial population (see industrial revolution), although it meant hardship for those farmers who were forced to move by enclosure.

agriculture The study and practice of farming. Settled farming probably dates back to 10 000 BC, when in many regions of the world man changed from being a hunter and gatherer of food to become a farmer, keeping cattle, goats, sheep, and pigs and growing wheat, barley, rice, etc. This enabled settled communities to evolve and early civilizations to flourish in such regions as the fertile river basins of the Tigris, Euphrates, and Nile. Until the end of the 19th century farming was based on energy derived from man and his draught animals. Some parts of the world still use such traditional methods; however, during the 20th century, especially in developed countries, the tractor has become the main energy source. In this century, too, there has been great success in improving breeds of plants and animals, improving soil fertility (see fertilizers), increasing use of farm machinery, and control of plant and animal pests. These measures have enormously increased the quantity and quality of food produced. See also arable farming; livestock farming.

ai. See sloth.

Aidan, St (c. 600–51 AD) Irish monk and bishop. A monk at *Iona until he became bishop of Northumbria in 635, he founded the monastery at Lindisfarne (see Holy Island), the centre of his extensive missionary activity in N England. His life is described by *Bede in his *Ecclesiastical History*. Feast day: 31 Aug.

AIDS (acquired immune deficiency syndrome) A disease caused by a virus in which certain cells (called T-lymphocytes or T-cells) of the body's immune system are destroyed. This lowers the body's defences against other diseases, which may eventually lead to the death of the patient. The AIDS virus is called human immunodeficiency virus (HIV), and it is passed from person to person in body fluids, particularly in blood and semen. However, many carriers of the virus show no obvious symptoms of disease, or develop AIDS only after several years. In western countries AIDS is still most frequent in homosexual males, intravenous drug users, and haemophiliacs. However, the disease is becoming more common among heterosexual men and women. The virus is transmitted mainly by sexual intercourse and by injections using unsterile needles and syringes. There is as yet no effective treatment or vaccine, so preventive measures are vitally important. These include the use of condoms and restricting the number of sexual partners. About 203 500 cases had been reported worldwide by the end of 1989.

aikido A Japanese martial art, primarily for self-defence by dodging an attacker and leading him in the direction in which his momentum takes him before subduing him without injury.

air. See atmosphere.

aircraft Any machine capable of flying. Aircraft fall into two categories: lighter-than-air machines (see airships; balloons) and heavier-than-air machines. The latter include *helicopters and fixed-wing aircraft, first *gliders and then powered aeroplanes. 19th-century experience of gliding, especially by Otto Lilienthal (1849–96) in Germany, provided the Wright Brothers with the information they needed to build their first powered aircraft in 1907. In 1909 the Frenchman Louis *Blériot flew across the English Channel. By the beginning of World War I, aircraft were sufficiently advanced to be used for reconnaissance and their usefulness as bombers soon became evident. By the end of the war aerial combat had become part of modern warfare. After the war air circuses and flying clubs popularized flying, especially as a means of travelling.

AIRCRAFT (MILITARY)

Sopwith Camel *A highly maneuvrable fighter, first delivered in 1917. Its 130 hp Clerget engine gave it a top speed of 113 mph (181 km/hr).*

Fokker Eindecker E111 *German fighter, in service from 1915. It had a top speed of 83 mph (133 km/hr) and the first machine gun synchronized to fire through the propeller.*

Handley Page 0/400 *The largest World War I bomber. Its twin 360 hp engines enabled it to carry 2000 lbs (907 kg) of bombs.*

Supermarine Spitfire *British fighter. Originally powered by a Rolls-Royce Merlin engine, it later had the Griffon engine, giving it a top speed of 450 mph (724 km/hr).*

Boeing B-29 Superfortress *This enormous US bomber entered the war in 1943 and was used to drop the atom bombs on Japan.*

Messerschmitt 109 *German fighter, designed in 1935. The latest version (the 109G) had an 1800 hp engine enabling it to fly at 430 mph (692 km/hr).*

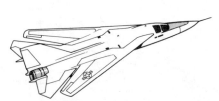

General Dynamics F-111 *US fighter and fighter-bomber, the first warplane to have swing wings (1967). It is powered by a Pratt and Whitney TF30 turbo fan.*

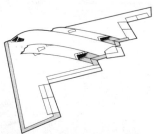

Northrop B2 stealth bomber *US Bomber, publicly revealed in 1989. The most expensive warplane ever developed, costing £350 million each, its revolutionary 'flying wing' design is alleged to make it invisible to enemy radar.*

AIRCRAFT (CIVIL)

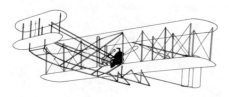

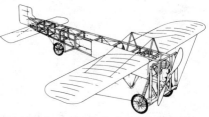

Wright Brothers' Flyer *The first powered flight at Kitty Hawk, North Carolina, on December 17, 1903 lasted 12 seconds.*

Blériot XI. *Louis Blériot's 30-minute flight from Calais to Dover on July 25, 1909 was the first cross-channel flight.*

Handley Page 42E Hannibal *In 1928 the British airline, Imperial Airways, bought eight HP42 aircraft. The 24-seater Hannibal had a top speed of 100 mph (160 km/hr).*

Douglas DC3 *Introduced in 1936, it was widely used in World War II as the Dakota transport. Its Pratt and Whitney 1200 hp engines gave it a maximum speed of 200 mph (320 km/hr).*

Vickers Viscount *Introduced into service in 1950, it was the first successful turboprop airliner. Powered by four engines, it carried 60 passengers.*

De Havilland Comet I *The first jet airliner, it went into service in 1952. Crashes due to metal fatigue caused its withdrawal and in 1958 it was replaced by the Comet IV.*

Boeing 747 *Nicknamed the "jumbo jet" this wide-bodied jetliner, which can carry up to 500 passengers, has been in service with many airlines since 1970.*

Concorde *The first supersonic airliner, it was built by the French and British in cooperation. Powered by four engines, it came into service in 1976.*

In 1924 Imperial Airways was formed in the UK, using Handley Page airliners, and during the 1930s a worldwide network of commercial routes developed. The Atlantic was first flown nonstop from New York to Paris in 1927 by Charles *Lindbergh and by 1939 there was a transatlantic flying-boat service.

By the outbreak of World War II aircraft of all kinds were ready for aerial combat. The British jet-powered Gloster Meteor entered service in 1944, as did the German Messerschmitt Me 262 jet.

By the end of war the *jet engine had been established and it has dominated aircraft design ever since. However, the first postwar civil aircraft used the jet engine to drive propellers (e.g. the Vickers Viscount), the first true jet to enter passenger service being the ill-fated British Comet. The highly successful Boeing 707 (with its four engines in pods suspended below the wings) followed in 1954.

The first supersonic passenger aircraft (SST) to fly was the Soviet Tupolev Tu-144 in 1968. This was followed a year later by the Anglo-French Concorde, which is now in worldwide service. However, long- and medium-range passenger services are likely to be dominated for most of the remainder of this century by the wide-bodied (jumbo) jets, such as the Boeing 747 and the European Airbus. See also aeronautics; flight.

aircraft carrier A naval vessel with a large flat deck for launching and landing warplanes. The first flight from the deck of a ship was made in 1910, and the first true aircraft carrier, HMS *Argus*, was completed for the Royal Navy in 1918, too late for action in World War I. Carriers played a dominant role in World War II, being especially effective in the war against the Japanese. After World War II carriers came to be regarded chiefly as tactical units, although they saw considerable action in the Korean and Vietnam Wars. The USS *Enterprise*, the first nuclear-powered carrier (1961), displaced 76 000 tonnes and steamed more than 432 000 km (270 000 mi) before requiring refuelling. Because of the increased range of aircraft, the enormous cost of carriers, and the ease with which they can be sunk by sophisticated missiles, few are likely to be built in the future. The UK's HMS *Ark Royal* was withdrawn from service in 1979, but a new *Ark Royal* was commissioned in 1985.

air-cushion vehicle. See Hovercraft.

Airedale terrier The largest breed of terrier, originating in Yorkshire. It has a long squarish muzzle, a short tail, and a tan-coloured wiry coat with black back and sides. A powerful and intelligent dog, the Airedale has been used as a guard dog, for hunting, and as a police dog. Height: 58–61 cm (dogs); 56–58 cm (bitches).

airships *Balloons that can be steered and that obtain their thrust from a propeller. The first airship to fly was a French steam-powered machine, designed in 1852 by H. Giffard; however, the first practical airship was the electrically powered *La France* (1884), built by Renard and Krebs. By 1900 German airships, designed by Count Ferdinand von Zeppelin (1838–1917), were leading the field. Between 1910 and 1914

Zeppelins were in extensive passenger service, carrying some 35 000 passengers, without mishap. In World War I these machines were used by the Germans to bomb England. Thereafter, a series of disasters destroyed the credibility of hydrogen-filled airships. The British *R101* caught fire at Beauvais in 1930, the US *Shenandoah* and the *Akron* were lost in 1933, and the German *Hindenberg* was destroyed in 1937. However, the availability of the nonflammable gas helium created a mild revival of interest in the 1980s.

Aix-la-Chapelle. See Aachen.

Ajaccio 41 51N 8 43E The capital of Corsica, a port on the Gulf of Ajaccio. Napoleon I was born here and his home is now preserved as a museum. Tourism is the principal industry. Population (1982 est): 55 279.

Ajax A legendary Greek hero, son of Telamon, King of Salamis. Described in Homer's *Iliad* as great in stature and in courage, he fought *Hector in single combat. He became insane with rage after being defeated by Odysseus in the contest for the armour of the dead *Achilles. *Sophocles' play *Ajax* depicts the hero recovering his sanity, only to be driven by shame to suicide.

Akihito (1933–) Emperor of Japan. He succeeded his father Hirohito in 1989.

Alabama A state in the SE USA, on the Gulf of Mexico. Except for the forested uplands in the NE it consists of an undulating plain, drained by the Alabama and Tombigbee Rivers. The iron and steel industry around the state's largest city, Birmingham, is the most important. Mobile is an important seaport. Cotton remains a principal crop along with peanuts, soya beans, wheat, and maize; the raising of cattle and poultry is also important. *History*: first explored by the Spanish in the 16th century, it passed to the British in 1763. In 1783 it came under US control and with an area to the S added in the Louisiana Purchase (1803) became a state in 1819. New settlers established large cotton plantations based on slave labour and in the US Civil War the state sent most of its White male population to fight against the N. Area: 133 677 sq km (51 609 sq mi). Population (1987 est): 4 148 905. Capital: Montgomery.

alabaster A pure fine-grained form of gypsum. It is white or delicately shaded and often translucent and attractively veined. It has long been worked ornamentally, for carvings, etc., but weathers too easily for external use. The alabaster of Volterra, Tuscany, is well known.

Alamo, the A mission in the USA, in San Antonio, Texas. During the Texas revolution it was defended from 24 Feb until 6 March, 1836, by less than 200 Texan volunteers (including the legendary Davy Crockett), who were all massacred during the onslaught of 4000 Mexican troops led by Santa Anna. Six weeks later a victory at San Jacinto secured Texan independence.

Alaska The largest state in the USA, occupying the extreme NW corner of the North American continent. It is a mountainous volcanic area, rising over 6000 m (20 000 ft) to Mount McKinley, the highest peak in North America. The numerous rivers include the Yukon flowing W into the Bering Sea. Oil production (discovered 1950) is the major industry and there are rich supplies of natural gas. Coal, gold, and copper are mined. Fishing, especially salmon, and forestry are also major industries. Agricultural development is hindered by the short growing season and severe climate. *History*: first settled by Russians, it was under the trade control of the Russian American company until 1867 when it was purchased by the USA. A number of gold rushes in the late 19th century helped to swell the sparse population. It became the 49th state in 1959. Area: 1 518 800 sq km (586 412 sq mi). Population (1987): 537 800. Capital: Juneau.

Alban, St (3rd century AD) The first English martyr. A pagan soldier, he protected a Christian priest and was converted by him. On admitting this to the Roman authorities, he was scourged and beheaded on a site subsequently dedicated to him as the Abbey of St Albans. Feast day: 22 or 17 June. Emblem: a stag.

Albania, Socialist People's Republic of (Albanian name: Shqiperia) A country in SE Europe, occupying part of the Balkan Peninsula on the Adriatic Sea. It consists of a mountainous interior, rising to over 2700 m (9000 ft), with extensive forests and fertile coastal lowlands. *Economy*: mainly agricultural, although industrial development is increasing. There have been recent attempts to develop the rich mineral resources and natural-gas deposits. Main exports include crude oil, bitumen, chrome ore, copper wire, tobacco, fruit, and vegetables. *History*: became independent in 1912 after more than four centuries of Turkish rule. Following a civil war, in which Italy intervened, Albania became a republic in 1925 and a monarchy in 1928, when its president, Ahmed Beg Zogu (1895–1961), was proclaimed as King Zog. After occupation by Italy and Germany during World War II, a republic was set up in 1946 with a communist-controlled assembly. Enver Hoxha (1908–85), as first party secretary, was executive leader from 1946 to 1985. Democratic reform was resisted until 1990, when a multiparty election was promised in 1991. Head of state: Ramiz Alia (1925–). Official language: Albanian. Currency: lek of 100 qintars. Area: 28 748 sq km (11 101 sq mi). Population (1988): 3 080 000. Capital: Tirana. Main port: Durrës.

albatross A large seabird that occurs mainly in southern oceans. It has a stout hooked bill; usually a white or brown plumage, often with darker markings on the back, wings, or tail; and very long narrow wings. There are 14 species: the wandering albatross, *Diomedea exulans*, has the largest wingspan of any bird, reaching up to 3.5 m. Albatrosses can glide for hours over the open sea, feeding on squids and cuttlefish; they come ashore only to breed.

Albee, Edward (1928–) US dramatist. His early one-act plays, notably *Zoo Story* (1958) and *The Death of Bessie Smith* (1960), discuss social tensions using techniques of the *Theatre of the Absurd. His first three-act play, *Who's Afraid of Virginia Woolf?* (1962), which presents the love-hate relationship of an academic couple, was very successful. Later plays include *A Delicate Balance* (1967, Pulitzer Prize), *Seascape*

(1975), and *The Man Who Had Three Arms* (1983).

Albert, Prince (1819–61) Prince Consort of the United Kingdom and younger son of Ernest I, Duke of Saxe-Coburg-Gotha. In 1840 he married his cousin Queen Victoria and became her chief adviser. Although he was initially unpopular, his devotion to duty and his active patronage of the arts, science, and industry eventually won him respect. He is perhaps best remembered for his organization of the *Great Exhibition (1851). He died of typhoid.

Alberta A province of W Canada, mostly on the Great Plains. It consists mainly of a plateau, rising to the foothills of the Rocky Mountains in the SW. The undulating S prairie and parkland further N support profitable ranches and grain farms. Alberta is Canada's largest oil and gas producer and possesses vast coalfields. *History*: first explored in the 18th century, Alberta became Canadian territory in 1869. The arrival of the railway from E Canada (1883) facilitated agricultural settlement, and Alberta became a province in 1905. Area: 644 389 sq km (248 799 sq mi). Population (1986): 2 365 825. Capital: Edmonton.

albinism An inherited disorder in which tyrosinase, one of the enzymes required for the formation of the pigment melanin, is absent. Albinos have abnormally pale skin, fair hair, and pink or light-blue irises. The condition can be eased by the use of spectacles to treat the eye abnormalities common in albinos and by protection of the skin and eyes from direct sunlight. Albinism, which can affect all human races, is also seen in animals.

Albuquerque 35 05N 106 38W A city in the USA, in New Mexico on the Rio Grande. The state's largest city, it is situated in a rich agricultural area and food canning and the manufacture of livestock products are its principal industries. It is the home of the University of New Mexico (1892). Population (1986 est): 366 750.

Alcatraz An island in the USA, in W California in San Francisco Bay. It was the site of a notorious maximum security prison from 1934 until 1962.

alchemy A type of science combining practical *chemistry with mystical views of the universe. Developing independently in China and Egypt, probably before the 3rd century BC, alchemy remained a central branch of science and philosophy in Asia, Europe, and the Islamic lands for over 1500 years. It had three main goals: the elixir of life (to ensure immortality), the panacea (or universal medicine), and the means of turning base metals into gold (*see* philosopher's stone). In China, *Taoism, which sought long life, fostered alchemical experimentation in search of the elixir. In Europe, concentration upon gold-making brought alchemy into disrepute.

Alcibiades (c. 450–404 BC) Athenian general and politician. Brought up by *Pericles, he was the pupil and lover of *Socrates. Alcibiades encouraged Athenian imperialism during the *Peloponnesian War (431–404) until, accused of desecrating monuments in Athens, he defected to Sparta (415). He regained Athenian favour (410) and was a successful commander until defeat, the fault of a junior officer, forced him into exile (406). He was murdered in Phrygia.

Alcock, Sir John (William) (1892–1919) British aviator. He served with the Royal Naval Air Service in World War I and in 1919, accompanied by **(Sir) Arthur Brown** (1886–1948), was the first to fly the Atlantic Ocean. They flew a Vickers-Vimy from St John's, Newfoundland, to Clifden, Co Galway, in 16 hours 27 minutes. A few months later Alcock was killed in a flying accident.

Alcoholics Anonymous A voluntary organization started in the USA in 1934 to help alcoholics. Members, who must genuinely want to stop drinking, help one another by sharing their experiences of alcoholism. There are local groups in over 90 countries, including the UK, which has more than 950 groups. An associated organization, **AL-ANON**, provides support for the close relatives of alcoholics.

alcoholism An illness in which regular heavy drinking leads to dependence on alcohol. Alcoholism causes mood changes, deterioration in personal standards, and periods of memory loss. Continued heavy consumption will eventually lead to cirrhosis of the liver, heart disease, and damage to the nerves. Suddenly ceasing consumption may produce tremors, delusions, and hallucinations. Treatment, which is lengthy and difficult, includes alcohol withdrawal (with drugs to ease the withdrawal symptoms) together with the support of doctors, family, and friends. *See* Alcoholics Anonymous.

alcohols The class of organic compounds that includes *ethanol (ethyl alcohol; C_2H_5OH) and *methanol (methyl alcohol; CH_3OH). Ethanol is the common alcohol found in intoxicating drinks and is often called simply "alcohol." Alcohols contain at least one hydroxyl group and have the general formula ROH, where R is a *hydrocarbon group. They react with *acids to give *esters and water. Primary alcohols oxidize to form *aldehydes and secondary alcohols to form *ketones.

Alcott, Louisa May (1832–88) US novelist. Her first book, *Flower Fables* (1854), was written when she was 16 to raise money for her family. *Hospital Sketches* (1863) recounted her experiences as a nurse in the Civil War. *Little Women* (1868–69), her most famous book, was largely autobiographical. Other works include *An Old-Fashioned Girl* (1870), *Little Men* (1871), and *Jo's Boys* (1886).

Aldeburgh 52 9N 1 35E A small resort in SE England in Suffolk. Once an important port, it is now famous for its annual music festival established in 1948 by Benjamin *Britten, who lived here. Population (1985 est): 3 000.

aldehydes A class of organic chemicals that contain the -CHO group. They are prepared by the oxidation of alcohols and are themselves oxidized to form carboxylic acids. Common aldehydes are formaldehyde (methanal) and acetaldehyde (ethanal).

alder A tree or shrub of the birch family, growing in the N hemisphere. The leaves are roundish and toothed; the flowers grow as separate male and female catkins on the same tree. The fruit is a woody cone containing small winged nuts. The black alder (*Alnus glutinosa*), about 20 m high, is found in wet places throughout Europe and Asia and in N Africa. Its timber is used in general turnery.

alderman In the UK, senior members of the major local authorities, normally elected by the directly elected members, until the Local Government Act (1972) abolished the office as an active rank except in the City of London. The term is taken from the Anglo-Saxon local official – the ealdorman. In the USA, many cities call their local-government officers aldermen but their powers vary from city to city.

Aldermaston 51 23N 1 09W A village in S England, in Berkshire. It is associated with protest marches (1958–63) organized by the *Campaign for Nuclear Disarmament and is the site of the Atomic Weapons Research Establishment. Population (1987 est): 2157.

Alderney (French name: Aurigny) 49 43N 2 12W The third largest of the Channel Islands, separated from France by the dangerous Race of Alderney channel. Its economy is based on dairy farming and tourism. Area: 8 sq km (3 sq mi). Population (1981 est): 2086. Chief town: St Anne.

Aldershot 51 15N 0 47W A town in S England, in Hampshire. It is the chief garrison town and army training centre in the UK. Population (1985 est): 38 000.

Aldrin, Jr, Edwin Eugene (1930–) US astronaut, the second man to walk on the moon. Known as "Buzz", he was an air force pilot during the Korean War before becoming an astronaut in 1963. He undertook a 5½-hour spacewalk in 1966 and was lunar module pilot (under Neil *Armstrong) in Apollo 11 when it made the first moon landing in 1969.

ale. *See* beer.

Aleutian Islands A chain of volcanic Alaskan islands lying between the Bering Sea and the Pacific Ocean, divided politically between the Soviet Union and the USA. The chief settlements are on Unalaska. Russian exploitation of supplies after 1741 greatly reduced the population, but fishing and seal, otter, and fox hunting are now regulated. There are strategic US military stations on the islands and underground nuclear tests have been made (since 1971).

Alexander I (c. 1077–1124) King of the Scots (1107–24), who ruled the highlands while his brother and successor David ruled the lowlands. He was noted for his reform of the Scottish church and his foundation of the monastery of Scone (1114). He aided Henry I of England's campaign against Wales (1114).

Alexander II (1198–1249) King of the Scots (1214–49). Hoping to regain the northern counties of England, he supported the unsuccessful *Barons' War (1215–17) against King John. In 1221 he married Joan, the sister of Henry III of England, and gave up his claims to English territory in 1237, when the present border between England and Scotland was fixed.

Alexander (III) the Great (356–323 BC) King of Macedon (336–323), who between 334 and his death conquered most of the world then known. Alexander, who was a pupil of Aristotle, inherited a plan to invade Persia from his father Philip II; having secured his position in Macedon and Greece, he put this plan into action. In 333 he defeated the Persian king Darius III at Issus; in 332 he destroyed Tyre in his greatest victory. Alexander then proceeded to conquer Egypt and Babylon (331). Moving on to Media and then east into central Asia, he finally embarked on the Indian expedition (327–325). He crossed the River Indus and conquered the Punjab. Forced to turn back by his reluctant army, he died at Babylon shortly after the long return journey.

Alexander III (1241–86) King of the Scots (1249–86). He married (1251) Margaret, daughter of Henry III of England. Under his leadership, the Scots defeated the Norwegians at the battle of Largs (1263) and by the Treaty of Perth (1266) gained the Isle of Man and the Hebrides from Norway.

Alexander of Tunis, Harold, 1st Earl (1891–1969) British field marshal. After distinguished service in World War I, Alexander held command in India. In World War II he commanded the evacuation of British forces from Dunkirk and was the last man to leave France. He became commander in chief in the Middle East (1942) and then, as Eisenhower's deputy, defeated the Germans in N Africa (1943). He ended the war as Allied supreme commander in the Mediterranean and was subsequently governor general of Canada (1946–52) and Conservative minister of defence (1952–54).

Alexandra (1872–1918) The wife from 1894 of *Nicholas II of Russia. A German princess and granddaughter of Queen Victoria, Alexandra fell under the evil influence of *Rasputin. His disastrous domination of her government while Nicholas was supreme commander of the Russian forces in World War I helped to trigger the Russian Revolution and the execution of Alexandra and her family by the Bolsheviks.

Alexandria (Arabic name: al-Iskandariyah) 31 13N 22 55E The chief seaport and second largest city in Egypt, between Lake Mareotis and the Mediterranean Sea. It handles most of Egypt's trade and the chief export is cotton; industries include oil refining and cotton ginning. *History:* founded in 332 BC by Alexander the Great, it remained the Egyptian capital for over a thousand years. It was a Greek and Jewish cultural centre with a famous library. In 30 BC Alexandria fell to the Romans, becoming their most important regional capital. It declined following the removal of the capital to Cairo. It was bombarded by the British in 1882, Pompey's Pillar and Cleopatra's Needles being among the few ancient monuments to escape destruction. Population (1986 est): 2 893 000.

alfalfa A flowering plant, *Medicago sativa,* also called lucerne. Growing to a height of 1 m, it resembles clover, having clusters of small purple flowers. Native to Europe, it is widely grown as forage for cattle and because of its ability to fix nitrogen (*see* legume).

Alfred the Great (849–99) King of Wessex (871–99). He prevented the Danish conquest of England, defeating them at Edington (878) after a campaign of guerrilla warfare based at *Athelney. The legend of the king, travelling in disguise, burning the peasant housewife's cakes, and being severely reprimanded by her, possibly refers to this unsettled period of his life. After his victory he allowed the Danes to keep their conquests in Mercia and East Anglia provided that Guthrum, their king, was converted to Christianity. Alfred built a navy of warships to defend the south coast against further Danish invasions (885–86; 892–96) and protected Wessex with a chain of fortifications. He took London (886), thus gaining control of all England save the Danish areas.

algae A vast group of simple plants (about 25 000 species) that contain the green pigment chlorophyll (and can therefore carry out *photosynthesis) but have no true stems, roots, or leaves. They range from single-celled organisms to the giant seaweeds. Most algae are aquatic, although some live in damp places on land—on rocks, trees, or in soils. A few are parasitic or associate with other organisms (*see* lichens). Reproduction is extremely variable and may be asexual, by cell division, fragmentation, or spore production, and/or sexual, by gamete production. Algae provide a valuable food source for fish and other aquatic animals and many are used as fertilizers and in industry. *See* brown algae, blue-green algae, green algae, red algae.

Algarve The most southerly province of Portugal, bordering on Spain and the Atlantic Ocean. It became a Moorish kingdom in 1140 and was the last stronghold of the Moors in Portugal, being reconquered in 1249. Sparsely populated inland, its fertile coastal belt is densely populated and produces chiefly maize, figs, almonds, and olives; fishing is also important. Tourism is a flourishing industry. Area: 5071 sq km (1957 sq mi). Population (1981): 328 605. Chief town: Faro.

algebra The branch of mathematics that uses symbols to represent unknown quantities. The first work on the subject was written by Diophantus of Alexandria in the 3rd century AD and the name derives from the Arabic *al-jabr,* a term used by the mathematician al-Khwarizmi to mean the addition of equal quantities to both sides of an equation and later adopted as the name for the whole subject. Algebra was used in ancient Babylon, Egypt, and India and brought to Europe by the Arabs. In classical algebra symbols, such as x and y, represent ordinary numbers and the central part of the subject is the study of algebraic equations. Modern, or abstract, algebra is concerned with any system of quantities that obey a particular set of general rules and relationships.

Algeria, Democratic and Popular Republic of A country in N Africa, on the Mediterranean Sea. It consists chiefly of the N Sahara Desert, with the Atlas Mountains in the N and small fertile areas near the coast. The inhabitants, who live almost entirely in the N, are mainly Arabs and Berbers. *Economy*: mainly agricultural although industrialization has proceeded rapidly since independence, financed by the discovery of oil (the main export) and natural gas in the desert areas. *History*: a former province of the Roman Empire, in the 7th century Algeria came under the control of the Arabs, who introduced Islam. Overrun by Turks in the 16th century, it became a pirate state in the 18th century ruled by *deys*, who preyed on Mediterranean shipping. Algeria was annexed by the French in the 19th century and in 1881 the N section became part of Metropolitan France. A war of independence, waged by the Front de Libération nationale (FLN), lasted from 1954 to 1962 when independence was granted by de Gaulle. A republic was set up under Ahmed Ben Bella but was overthrown in 1965 by a Council of Revolution. Col Houari Boumédienne (1925–78) became president; he was succeeded in 1978 by Col Benjedid Chadli (1929–). After riots, a multiparty system was introduced in 1989. Prime minister: Mouloud Hamrouche. Official language: Arabic; French is also widely spoken. Official religion: Islam. Currency: dinar of 100 centimes. Area: 2 381 745 sq km (919 595 sq mi). Population (1988 est): 23 546 000. Capital and main port: Algiers.

Algiers (Arabic name: al-Jaza'ir; French name: Alger) 36 45N 3 05E The capital of Algeria, an important port in the N of the Mediterranean Sea. Its main exports include wine, citrus fruits, and iron ore. The University of Algiers was founded in 1879 and the University of Science and Technology in 1974. *History*: originally founded by the Phoenicians, it was re-established by the Arabs in the 10th century. Overrun by Turks in the 16th century, it became a base for Barbary pirates until taken by the French in 1830. During World War II it was the headquarters of the Allied forces in N Africa. Population (1988): 1 721 607.

algin (sodium alginate) A slimy substance extracted from seaweed. It is used as a thickener in such foods as ice cream and in industrial compounds.

Alhambra A castle on a hilly terrace outside *Granada (Spain), built between 1238 and 1358. It was the last stronghold of the Muslim kings of Granada. Combining citadel and palace, it is an outstanding example of Moorish architecture, with magnificent courts and gardens. The name derives from Arabic *al-hamra*, the red, an allusion to the red stucco used on the walls.

Ali (c. 600–67) The cousin of *Mohammed and his son-in-law by marriage to *Fatimah. Born at Mecca, he was the second, or perhaps the first, person to embrace Islam. He became the fourth caliph in 656, but faced much opposition and was murdered in 661 at Kufa, Iraq. His tomb is honoured at Najaf. According to *Shiite Muslims, Ali was the only lawful successor of Mohammed and only his descendants are recognized as imams.

Ali, Muhammad (Cassius Marcellus Clay; 1942–) US boxer. A gold medallist in the 1960 Olympic Games, he became professional world heavyweight champion (1964). On becoming a Black Muslim he changed his name and was soon afterwards stripped of his title for three years because of his refusal to join the US army. Defeated (1971) by Joe Frazier, he again became champion in 1974 by defeating George Foreman (1949–), losing the title briefly in 1978 to Leon Spinks. His defeat of Spinks later that year made him the only boxer to become world champion three times. In 1980 he was defeated by Larry Holmes in his bid to regain the world title. He now suffers from Parkinson's disease resulting from blows to the brain.

aliphatic compounds Organic chemical compounds that are not *aromatic. They include the *alkanes, *alkenes, and *alkynes as well as some cyclic compounds (cycloalkanes).

alkali. *See* acids and bases.

alkali metals The elements forming group I of the *periodic table: lithium, sodium, potassium, rubidium, caesium, and francium. All are soft, silvery-white *metals with low densities, melting points, and boiling points. In chemical reactions they tend to form positive ions and have a valence of 1. They are highly reactive. The oxides and hydroxides are alkalis.

alkaline-earth metals The elements forming group II of the *periodic table: beryllium, magnesium, calcium, strontium, barium, and radium. They are similar to the *alkali metals in appearance and chemistry, but are harder, have higher melting and boiling points, and are somewhat less reactive. They have a valence of 2. The **alkaline earths** are the oxides of these metals.

alkaloids A group of chemical compounds that are produced by plants and have various effects on the body. Many alkaloids are used as medicinal drugs, including quinine, morphine, and atropine. Others, such as strychnine and coniine (from hemlock), are poisons. Caffeine, nicotine, and LSD are also alkaloids.

alkanes (*or* paraffins) A series of hydrocarbons, which contain only single bonds between the carbon atoms. They have the general formula C_nH_{2n+2}. The first four members of the series methane (CH_4), ethane (C_2H_6), propane (C_3H_8), and butane (C_4H_{10}) are gases, higher members are liquids or waxes. They are obtained from natural gas or oil and have many uses.

alkenes (*or* olefins) Hydrocarbons that contain at least one carbon–carbon double bond in their molecules. The simplest types, with one double bond, have the general formula C_nH_{2n}; ethylene (*or* ethene, C_2H_4) is the first member of this series. The alkenes are more reactive than the *alkanes and are capable of *polymerization. They are obtained from petroleum and are used as starting materials in industrial chemistry.

Al Khalil. *See* Hebron.

alkynes (*or* acetylenes) Hydrocarbons that contain at least one carbon–carbon triple bond in their molecules. The simplest types, with one triple bond, have the general formula C_nH_{2n-2}; acetylene (*or* ethyne, C_2H_2) is the first member of this series. The alkynes are capable of *polymerization, extremely reactive, and difficult to use in large quantities.

Allah (Arabic, probably from *al-ilah*: the god) The Islamic name of God. Allah was worshipped in pre-Islamic Arabia as early as the 3rd century BC. In Mecca he was given special rank as "the god," but lesser tribal gods continued to be worshipped alongside him until *Mohammed proclaimed Allah as the only God, the same God as worshipped by Jews and Christians. He is eternal, the creator of the universe, the judge of men, merciful and kind. His teachings are laid down in the *Koran.

Allahabad 25 57N 81 50E A city in N India, in Uttar Pradesh where the Rivers Ganges and Jumna meet. It is principally an administrative and educational centre; its university was established in 1887. There is an annual religious festival and a much larger one every 12 years. A former centre of the independence movement, it was the home of the Nehru family. Population (1981 est): 619 628.

Allen, Ethan (1739–89) American soldier, who pursued the independence from New York and New Hampshire of the Green Mountain region (now Vermont). Between 1770 and 1775 he commanded the Green Mountain Boys, who helped to capture Fort Ticonderoga (1775), the first American victory in the American Revolution. He was imprisoned by the British (1775–78) and died shortly before Vermont achieved statehood in 1789.

Allen, Woody (Allen Stewart Konigsberg; 1935–) US film actor and director. His films include *Play It Again, Sam* (1972), *Annie Hall* (1977), *Manhattan* (1979), *The Purple Rose of Cairo* (1985), *Hannah and Her Sisters* (1986), and *Crimes and Misdemeanours* (1990).

Allenby, Edmund Henry Hynman, 1st Viscount (1861–1936) British field marshal. After experience in the Boer War, he commanded the Third Army in France in World War I. In 1917, appointed commander in chief of the Egyptian Expeditionary Force against the Turks in Palestine, he captured (9 Dec) Jerusalem (as a "Christmas present" for the British people) and then went on to devastate the Turks at Megiddo (1918). He ended his career as high commissioner in Egypt (1919–25).

allergy An abnormal reaction by the body to certain substances, including pollen, dust, certain foods and drugs, fur, moulds, etc. Normally all foreign substances (antigens) entering the body are destroyed by *antibodies. Allergic people, however, become hypersensitive to certain antigens (called allergens), so that whenever they are encountered in future they stimulate not only the normal antibody reaction but also the abnormal symptoms of the allergy, such as sneezing and skin rashes. Allergic conditions include *hay fever, some forms of *asthma and dermatitis, and urticaria. Treatment includes the use of *antihistamines and corticosteroids and desensitization.

alligator A large broad-snouted reptile related and similar to the *crocodiles. Each side of the jaw contains 17–22 teeth, which are all covered when the mouth is closed. The American alligator (*Alligator mississippiensis*) is mainly black and lives in rivers of the SE USA, reaching a length of 5–6 m; the rare Chinese alligator (*A. sinensis*) of the Yangtze River is smaller. They dig burrows in which they hibernate during cold weather.

Allosaurus A large bipedal *dinosaur of the Jurassic and Cretaceous periods (200–65 million years ago). Up to 11 m long, it had large strong hind limbs, a well-developed tail, small forelegs, and thick protective knobs of bone over the eyes. Although fairly slow, it hunted prey, possibly in groups, and was equipped with sharp claws, powerful jaws, and sharp pointed teeth.

alloy A blend of a metal with other metals or nonmetals. The first alloy was probably *bronze, which was used in Europe in about 2000 BC. *Steel and *brass are the most widely used alloys. Alloys of aluminium are also common, especially in the aircraft industry.

All Saints' Day A Christian feast in honour of all saints, whether known or unknown. In the Eastern Churches it has always been observed on the first Sunday after Pentecost. In the West its date varied until fixed as 1 Nov by Gregory III. *See also* Hallowe'en.

All Souls' Day A Christian feast in the Western Church in honour of all Christians who have died (the "faithful departed"). It is observed on 2 Nov. Requiem masses, containing the *Dies Irae*, are celebrated.

allspice (*or* pimento) A widely used aromatic spice, so named because it combines the flavours of several different spices. It is derived from the powdered dried unripe berries of an evergreen tree, *Pimenta dioca*, which is native to Central America and the West Indies and grows to a height of 9 m.

Almagest. *See* Ptolemy.

almanac A calendar of the months and days of the year containing astronomical and other miscellaneous data. It usually includes information about eclipses, phases of the moon, positions of the planets, times of sunset and sunrise and of high and low tides, as well as religious and public holidays. Modern almanacs include official government publications listing national statistics.

almond A tree, *Prunus amygdalus*, of the rose family native to SW Asia but widely grown in warm regions for its nuts. The edible nuts are produced by a variety called sweet almond; the nuts of the bitter almond yield aromatic almond oil, used as a flavouring. Almond trees grow to a height of 7 m; they have attractive pink flowers and are grown for ornament in cooler regions.

alpaca A shaggy-coated mammal, *Lama pacos*, related to the camel, traditionally domesticated and bred in the South American Andes. Its dark fine high-quality fleece reaches nearly to the ground from its shoulder height of 90 cm and is shorn every two years, each animal yielding about 3 kg. Alpacas thrive at high altitudes, living on damp grassy plateaus.

alphabets Writing systems in which each symbol represents a speech sound (*see* phonetics). The first modern phonetic alphabets were created on the E shores of the Mediterranean around 2000 BC. From this Semitic alphabet all the major alphabets in use today—Roman,

North Semitic				Greek		Etruscan	Latin		Modern Capital
early Phoenician	early Hebrew (cursive)	Moabite	Phoenician	early	classical	classical	early	classical	Roman
K	K	K	K	A	A	A	A		A
9	9	9	9	B	B			B	B
7	1	1	1	1	Γ	>		C	C
△	9	9	9	△	△		▽	D	D
7	7	7	7	3	E	∃	7	E	E
Y	Y	Y	4	7		ʔ	7	F	F
									G
I	⊥	I	I	I	I	‡			
日	日	日	日	日	H	日	日		H
⊕	⊘	⊗	⊗	⊗	⊖	⊙			
⟨	⟨	⟨	⟨	⟨	I	I	I	I	I
									J
↓	⅃	⅄	⅄	⅄	K	⅄	⅄	K	K
L	L	L	L	1	∧	⅃			L
⅄	⅄	⅄	⅄	⅄	M	⅄	⅄		M
⅄	⅄	⅄	⅄	N	N	⅄	⅄		N
≢	≢	≢	≢	☰	⋈				
O	O	O	O	O	0		O		O
?	?	?	?	⅂	Π	⅂	Γ		P
		⅃	⅄	M		M			
		⅄	⅄	⅄		Q			Q
9	Q	⅄	⅄	P	4			R	R
W	W	W	W	⟩	Σ	5	5	S	S
+	X	X	+×	X	T	+			T
					Y	∨	ω		U
									V
									W
				×					X
									Y
									Z

ALPHABETS *The letters of the modern Roman alphabet have developed from the ancient Phoenician syllabary. This script in its Aramaic form was also the ultimate source of the Arabic alphabet and probably of the Brahmi alphabet, from which the many scripts of modern India are derived.*

Greek, Cyrillic, Hebrew, Arabic, and Devanagari—have developed. *See also* International Phonetic Alphabet.

alpha particle The nucleus of a helium-4 atom, consisting of two protons and two neutrons. It is extremely stable and is emitted by some radioactive nuclei in the process known as **alpha decay**, a process that reduces the *mass number of the nucleus by four and its *atomic number by two. An example is the decay of uranium-238 into thorium-234.

Alps The highest mountain range in Europe. It extends some 800 km (497 mi) in an arc roughly E–W through France, Switzerland, Italy, and Austria, and rises to 4807 m (15 771 ft) at Mont Blanc near the W end. Several major rivers rise here, including the Rhône, Rhine, Drava, and Po. Many of the lower slopes are used as pasture in summer, while in winter the Alps are Europe's major skiing area.

Alsace (German name: Elsass) A planning region and former province in NE France, separated from Germany by the River Rhine. It is a fertile agricultural area and has important potassium deposits. *History*: it was often a scene of

conflict between France and Germany. Under Roman occupation from the 1st century AD, it became a Frankish duchy in the 5th century and was part of the Holy Roman Empire from the 10th to the 17th centuries. The French gained control of Alsace in 1648, after the Thirty Years' War, but it was lost to Germany in 1871, after the Franco-Prussian War, and linked with *Lorraine to form the German imperial territory of **Alsace-Lorraine**. This existed until it went back to France in 1919. It came under German control again in World War II and was restored to France in 1945. Area: 8310 sq km (3208 sq mi). Population (1986 est): 1 599 800.

Alsatian dog. *See* German shepherd dog.

Altamira Upper *Palaeolithic cave site in N Spain, recognized in 1879, noted for the 150 magnificent paintings of animals on the cave's ceiling. Bison, painted in red ochre with black manganese manes, tails, and hooves, are the chief species depicted. *See also* Magdalenian.

alternating current (ac) Electrical current that periodically reverses its direction. It is the form of current that is produced when a coil of wire rotates in a magnetic field and, as this is the way in which current is produced in *power stations by electric generators, it is the form of current most widely used in homes, offices, and factories. The electromotive force (emf), E, produced by a generator is equal to $E'\sin\omega t$, where E' is the maximum emf, ω is the angular velocity of rotation, and t is the time. Thus the current has the form of a sine wave, with a frequency $\omega/2\pi$. *See also* electricity supply.

alternation of generations A phenomenon occurring in the *life cycles of many plants and some animals (particularly certain jellyfish and other *coelenterates) in which there is an alternation between two distinct forms (generations); these forms differ from each other in structure, reproduction, and also often in habit. In plants the generation reproducing sexually is called the gametophyte and the asexual generation is the sporophyte. Either form may be the most conspicuous or dominant in a particular species; for example, the gametophyte is dominant in mosses and the sporophyte in flowering plants. Some coelenterates alternate between asexual polyps attached to the seabed and free-swimming sexually reproducing jellyfish.

alternative energy The use of natural energy from the sun, wind, sea, etc. Most countries now rely heavily on fossil fuels (coal, oil, and natural gas) and *nuclear energy. However, reserves of fossil fuels are declining and their use contributes to the *greenhouse effect. The estimates of uranium reserves are also uncertain and there is opposition to the development of nuclear reactors, mainly on the grounds of safety and environmental hazard from waste disposal. Fusion reactors are still very much in the experimental stage. Renewable energy sources, which can never be used up, include *solar power, *wind power, and *wave power; they are being seriously investigated in the UK. *Hydroelectric power is already in use and has limited potential for further expansion. Tidal power is the use of water raised by the tide and collected behind a barrage to generate electricity in a similar way to hydroelectric generation. Geothermal power comes from the heat beneath the earth's crust. In Iceland naturally heated water is taken from rocks near the surface, but opportunities for making use of geothermal energy are rare. Biomass energy, or biogas (methane generated from sewage, refuse, or specially cultivated organisms) is also being utilized, especially on a small scale in some countries.

alternative medicine Forms of treatment of physical and mental illness used as alternatives to those normally used in medicine. Known also as fringe, natural, and unorthodox medicine, it includes such specialties as *osteopathy, *homeopathy, *acupuncture, and *hypnosis, which are recognized and practised by some qualified doctors. Other branches include *chiropractic, naturopathy, herbalism, dietary treatments, the laying on of hands, and self-healing (e.g. by yoga, biofeedback, etc.).

Althing The parliament of Iceland, the oldest in the world, founded in about 930 AD. Since independence in 1944 it has been the country's senior authority. It has 60 members in two houses of equal power.

altimeter A device for measuring height above the ground. A **pressure altimeter** consists of an aneroid *barometer calibrated in metres (or feet) above sea level. A **radio altimeter** consists of a device that measures the time taken for a radio or radar signal to reach the ground and return.

aluminium (Al) A light silvery-white metal discovered by Wöhler in 1827. It is the most common metal in the earth's crust and the main source is *bauxite, an impure hydrated oxide. The metal is obtained by electrolysis of the oxide dissolved in a flux of low melting point with the mineral cryolite. Its most important uses depend on its lightness (relative density 2.70) and good electrical conductivity. It is used in electrical power cables, saucepans, and many industrial applications. Pure aluminium is soft, but its *alloys with copper, magnesium, and other elements have considerable strength. This combined with their low densities makes such alloys important in aircraft construction. Compounds include alum ($K_2SO_4.Al_2(SO_4)_3.24H_2O$) and the oxide ($Al_2O_3$), which occurs naturally as corundum and *ruby and is used as an abrasive, a gem, and in *lasers. The hydroxide ($Al(OH)_3$) is used in glass manufacture and as a cure for indigestion. At no 13; at wt 26.9815; mp 660.4°C; bp 1800°C.

alveolus. See lungs.

alyssum A low-growing herbaceous plant, native to S Europe but widely grown in gardens. Alyssums have small flowers grouped in clusters. Varieties of sweet alyssum (*Alyssum maritimum*), 10–15 cm high, have white or pink flowers and are grown as annuals. Perennial alyssums include *A. saxatile*, which grows to 30 cm high and has yellow flowers.

Alzheimer's disease (*or* presenile dementia) A disease that gradually destroys nerve cells of the brain. It causes speech disturbances, progressive loss of mental faculties, and other symptoms of senility, though it may occur in middle age. Its cause is uncertain; a virus may be responsible, or it may be caused by an inherited genetic disorder. Named after the German neurologist Alois Alzheimer (1864–1915).

amaryllis A perennial herbaceous plant, *Amaryllis belladonna*, also called belladonna lily, native to South Africa but widely cultivated for ornament. Growing from bulbs, it has strap-shaped leaves and a 45 cm long stem bearing a cluster of 5–12 funnel-shaped sweet-scented flowers, usually rose-pink and often veined.

Amazon, River (Portuguese name: Rio Amazônas) The largest river system and the second longest river in the world. Rising as the Río Marañón in the Andes, in Peru, it flows generally W–E to enter the Atlantic Ocean in NE Brazil. Its drainage basin extends over much of Brazil, and parts of Venezuela, Colombia, Ecuador, Peru, and Bolivia. It is deep and wide enough for oceangoing vessels as far as Iquitos, 3700 km (2300 mi) upstream. Destruction of the tropical rain forest in the Amazon basin caused concern in the 1980s. Length: 6440 km (4000 mi). Drainage basin area: about 5 827 500 sq km (2 250 000 sq mi).

Amazons (Greek: breastless ones) A mythical nation of female warriors who were believed by the ancient Greeks to live in Pontus, near the Black Sea. Trained for war and hunting, the Amazons got their name from their habit of removing the right breast to make it easier to draw bows. They intervened in the *Trojan War against the Greeks, but Achilles killed their queen, Penthesilea. At one time they invaded Attica but were defeated by *Theseus, who took their queen Hippolyte captive.

amber A translucent or opaque yellow fossil resin produced by coniferous trees; insects and leaves are often preserved in the mineral, having been trapped on the sticky surface prior to hardening. Found mostly around the S Baltic coast, it is used for beads, ornaments, and varnish.

ambergris A waxy substance found in the intestines of sperm whales. Mainly cholesterol, with fatty oils and steroids, it has a musky scent. It is used in making perfumes.

amboyna A tropical Asian tree, *Pterocarpus indicus*, that reaches a height of about 9 m and yields reddish beautifully grained wood used for furniture.

American eagle. See bald eagle.

American football. See football.

American Indians A diverse group of peoples of North, Central, and South America and the Caribbean Islands. In many respects they resemble the Mongoloid peoples of Asia. However, their physical differences from the Mongoloids suggest other origins. Their ancestors probably arrived in the Americas from Asia via Alaska between 10 000 and 20 000 years ago. They have coarse dark straight hair, yellowish-brown skins, and little body hair. They speak a variety of languages and culturally range from primitive hunters and gatherers to the creators of the *Aztec, *Maya, and *Inca civilizations.

American Revolution (*or* American War of Independence; 1775–83) The conflict in which the 13 colonies of North America gained independence from Britain. American resentment at Britain's strict rule focused in the mid-18th century on taxation. Protests against the Stamp Act (1765) and Townshend Acts (1767) led to the *Boston Tea Party (1773), which caused Britain to impose the harsh Intolerable Acts (1774). The first *Continental Congress met at Philadelphia and, after talks between both sides had failed, the first shots of the war were fired at Lexington and Concord (April, 1775). In the autumn the Americans invaded Canada, taking Montreal and besieging Quebec until forced to withdraw to Ticonderoga in Spring, 1776. On 4 July the second Continental Congress issued the *Declaration of Independence. Gen Howe landed on Long Island in August and defeated the newly appointed American commander in chief, Washington, near White Plains. At the beginning of January, 1777, however, Washington won a victory at Princeton before settling in winter quarters. Britain's hopes for 1777 were based on a plan for Burgoyne to march S from Canada and join forces with Howe at the Hudson River. Burgoyne duly arrived at the Hudson (Aug) but Howe had left New York by sea, landed at Chesapeake Bay, and defeated Washington at the Brandywine, taking Philadelphia (Sept). Burgoyne, meanwhile, was forced to surrender his army at Saratoga, a defeat that proved a turning point by bringing France into the war on the American side. In 1778 the British attacked in the S. Howe's successor, Clinton, took Charleston, South Carolina, and Cornwallis defeated Gates at Camden (1780). In early 1781 the British lost badly at Cowpens (17 Jan) but won, with heavy losses, the battle of Guilford Court House (15 March). Cornwallis now moved into Virginia, establishing a base at Yorktown. There besieged by a Franco-American force under the Comte de Rochambeau (1725–1807) and Washington, on 19 October Cornwallis surrendered. The British navy had been threatened throughout by American privateers and the activities of such commanders as John Paul Jones, but the main threat at sea came from America's European allies–the French, Spanish (from 1779), and Dutch (from 1780), who gained control of the English Channel and threatened invasion. Rodney's success (1782) in the West Indies was not sufficient to reverse the effect of Yorktown but enabled Britain to regain control of the Atlantic. In 1783 Britain agreed to American independence in the Treaty of Paris.

America's Cup A sailing race held traditionally off Newport, Rhode Island (USA), but also elsewhere, in which US yachts are challenged for a cup won by the US *America* off the Isle of Wight in 1851. The USA retained the cup until 1983, when it was won by the Australian entry *Australia II*. The 1987 result was disputed, the cup being awarded to the USA in 1989.

americium (Am) The fourth element after uranium in the *periodic table, first made (1944) by G. T. Seaborg and others by addition of neutrons to plutonium followed by β-decay. It forms the oxide (AmO_2) and is strongly radioactive. At no 95; at wt (243); mp 994°C.

amethyst A gemstone comprising a purple variety of quartz. Its colour is due to impurities, particularly iron oxide. The best crystals are found in Brazil and the Urals. It is used for jewellery.

Amiens 49 54N 2 18E A city in NE France, the capital of the Somme department situated on the River Somme. Known as Samarobriva in pre-Roman times, it was the ancient capital of Picardy. The **Peace of Amiens** (1802), which marked a respite in the Revolutionary and Napoleonic Wars, was signed here. Its fine gothic cathedral survived the damage of both World Wars. An important railway junction, Amiens' industries include textiles, tyres, and chemicals. Population (1982 est): 136 358.

Amin Dada, Idi (c. 1925–) Ugandan politician; president (1971–79). He rose rapidly in the army, becoming commander in 1966. He overthrew Milton Obote (1925–) to become president and in 1972 ordered the expulsion of 80 000 non-Ugandan Asians. He and his government were notorious for their brutality; Amin was overthrown in a Tanzanian-backed coup after which he went into exile.

amines A class of basic organic compounds derived from ammonia (NH_3), in which one (primary amines), two (secondary amines), or three (tertiary amines) of the hydrogen atoms are replaced by organic groups. *See also* amino acids.

amino acids A group of organic acids characterized by having at least one carboxyl group ($-COOH$) and at least one amino group ($-NH_2$). About 20 amino acids comprise the basic constituents of *proteins, the arrangement and types of amino acids determining the structure and hence the function of the protein molecule. Certain essential amino acids cannot be manufactured by the body and must be supplied in the diet. In man these are: arginine, histidine, isoleucine, leucine, lysine, methionine, phenylalanine, threonine, tryptophan, and valine.

Amis, Sir Kingsley (1922–) British novelist and poet, one of the *Angry Young Men. Educated at Oxford, he taught at Swansea and Cambridge universities and in the USA. His first novel, *Lucky Jim* (1954), was a popular success. Later novels include *I Want It Now* (1968), *Ending Up* (1974), *Jake's Thing* (1978), *Stanley and the Women* (1984), *The Old Devils* (1986), which won the 1986 Booker Prize, and *The Folks That Live on the Hill* (1990). He published several volumes of poetry and edited the *Oxford Book of Light Verse* (1978). His son **Martin Amis** (1949–) is the author of such books as *The Rachel Papers* (1974), *Success* (1978), *Money* (1984), *The Moronic Inferno* (1986), and *London Fields* (1989).

Amman 31 57N 35 56E The capital of Jordan. Amman was the capital of the biblical Ammonites, and there are some Greek and Roman remains. In the 20th century the town grew from a small village, and in 1946 it became the capital of independent Jordan. The city has received many refugees from the Arab-Israeli Wars (1948, 1967, and 1973). The university was founded in 1962. Amman is now an important communications centre, with some manufacturing industry. Population (1984 est): 777 500.

ammeter An instrument for measuring electric current. The two most common types are the moving-coil and the moving-iron ammeters. The moving-coil ammeter is more sensitive but will only measure direct current. The moving-iron ammeter will measure both alternating and direct current but is less sensitive and its scale is non-linear. Some modern instruments are electronic and have a digital display.

ammonia (NH_3) A colourless poisonous gas used for the manufacture of fertilizers, nitric acid, explosives, and synthetic fibres. It is made by the *Haber-Bosch process.

ammonite A marine mollusc abundant during the late Palaeozoic and Mesozoic eras, becoming extinct 100 million years ago. Fossil ammonites are common: they have either straight or coiled shells, some up to 200 cm in diameter, containing many chambers. These allowed the animal to remain buoyant while swimming.

amnesia Loss of memory resulting from such causes as head injuries, drugs, hysteria, senility, or psychological illness. The memory loss may be for events before the injury or disease (**retrograde amnesia**) or for events after it (**anterograde amnesia**). Treatment depends on the cause.

Amnesty International An organization, founded by Peter Benenson in the UK in 1961, aiming to defend freedom of speech, opinion, and religion in all parts of the world. Its work consists of campaigns for the release of "prisoners of conscience," against torture, and for human rights and it is concerned for the welfare of refugees. It has some 100 000 members in 75 countries and is funded by voluntary contributions. Amnesty International was awarded the Nobel Peace Prize in 1977.

amniocentesis The removal for examination of a small quantity of the fluid (amniotic fluid) that surrounds an unborn baby in the mother's womb. The specimen may be taken by needle through the wall of the abdomen or, later in pregnancy, the opening of the womb. Tests on the amniotic fluid may reveal the presence of certain diseases or congenital disorders in the baby (e.g. Down's syndrome or spina bifida). If serious abnormality is detected, the possibility of an abortion can be considered. Amniocentesis is routinely offered when there is a family history of congenital disease and usually to pregnant women over 35 years of age.

amoeba A free-living microscopic animal (*see* protozoa). Amoebas occur widely in soil and water and their flexible cells assume various shapes. The common amoeba (*Amoeba proteus*) may be up to 0.5 mm long. Amoebas move by means of broad lobes (pseudopodia), which are also used to engulf food particles and liquids. They reproduce by splitting into two and under unfavourable conditions form cysts with a thick protective wall surrounding the cell. Some amoebas are parasites, including *Entamoeba histolytica*, which causes amoebic dysentery in man.

amount of substance A quantity proportional to the number of particles, such as atoms or ions, in a sample. The constant of proportionality is the reciprocal of the *Avogadro constant. Amount of substance is measured in *moles.

ampere (A) The *SI unit of electric current equal to the current that when passed through two parallel infinitely long conductors placed 1 metre apart in a vacuum produces a force between them of 2×10^{-7} newton per metre of length. Named after A. M. *Ampère.

Ampère, André Marie (1775–1836) French physicist, who was a professor at Bourg and later in Paris. He introduced the important distinctions between electrostatics and electric currents and between current and voltage, demonstrated that current-carrying wires exert a force on each other, and gave an explanation of magnetism in terms of electric currents. **Ampère's law** states that the strength of the magnetic field at any point produced by a current (*I*) flowing through a conductor of length *l* is proportional to Il/d^2 where *d* is the distance between the point and the conductor. The unit of electric current is named after him.

amphetamine A stimulant drug that produces a feeling of alertness and wellbeing, increases muscular activity, and reduces fatigue and appetite. Because of the risk of addiction, particularly when combined with barbiturates ("purple hearts"), amphetamine is now rarely prescribed. It is occasionally used to treat hyperactivity in children. Trade name: Benzedrine.

amphibian An animal belonging to the class *Amphibia*, which contains over 2500 species of frogs, toads, newts, salamanders, and caecilians. Adult amphibians breathe through lungs and live in a wide range of habitats; however they require damp surroundings in order to minimize loss of body fluids through their thin, moist, and usually scaleless skin. Generally amphibians lay their eggs in ponds or rivers, often migrating long distances to do so. The eggs hatch into aquatic tadpoles that breathe using gills and develop into adults by a transformation known as *metamorphosis.

amphiboles A group of rock-forming minerals, mostly complex hydrous ferromagnesian silicates. Hornblende and tremolite are examples. Amphiboles are common in igneous and metamorphic rocks and often occur in fibrous or needle-shaped forms, including some forms of *asbestos.

Amphitrite The Greek goddess of the sea. Poseidon chose her to be his wife when he saw her dancing with her sister Nereids. She rejected him and fled to the island of Naxos, but he sent a dolphin to reclaim her. She bore him three sons, Triton, Rhodos, and Benthesicyma.

amplifier An electronic device for increasing the strength of a varying electric signal (such as the sound signal in radio or the picture signal in television). Originally built with thermionic valves, but now almost exclusively with *transistors, amplifiers are designed to multiply the input (current, voltage, or power) by a specific factor, known as the gain. Often an amplifier consists of several stages, the output from one stage becoming the input to the next stage.

Amritsar 31 35N 74 56E A city in NW India, in Punjab. Founded in 1577 by the fourth guru of the Sikhs, Ram Das, it has become the centre of the Sikh faith. It was the scene of a massacre (1919), in which hundreds of Indian nationalists were killed when fired upon by troops under British control. In 1984 about 1000 people died when the Sikh shrine, the Golden Temple, was fortified by Sikh extremists and stormed by the Indian army. A commercial, cultural, and communications centre, it manufactures textiles and silk. Population (1989 est): 691 837.

Amsterdam 52 21N 4 54E The official capital of the Netherlands, in North Holland province on the Rivers Amstel and IJ. Chartered in 1300, it became the capital in 1808. Linked to the North Sea by canal (1876), it is a major seaport. It is also an important financial and industrial centre, with a famous diamond cutting and polishing trade. Industries include shipbuilding, dairy produce, tobacco, and brewing. The city is mostly built on piles and linked with canals and approximately 1000 bridges. Population (1987): 682 702.

Amundsen, Roald (1872–1928) Norwegian explorer, the first person to reach the South Pole. In 1897 he became first mate on the *Belgica*, which was engaged in Antarctic exploration. After sailing the Northwest Passage in the *Gjöa* (1903–06) he abandoned his plan to reach the North Pole on hearing of Peary's success (1909). He himself beat *Scott to the South Pole in 1911. In 1926 he flew an airship over the North Pole with Umberto Nobile (1885–1928). Amundsen died while searching for Nobile following the latter's airship crash in the Arctic Ocean. A small section of the S Pacific Ocean, bordering on Ellsworth Land in Antarctica, is called **Amundsen Sea** after him.

Anabaptists (from Greek: rebaptizers) Any of various radical religious groups that appeared in several continental countries during the *Reformation. They were called Anabaptists because they rejected infant baptism in favour of baptizing adults. Persecuted by Roman Catholics and Protestants, they were accused of fanaticism, heresy, and immorality. They believed in pacifism, common ownership of goods, and the Second Coming of Christ; they also held radical political views. Their modern descendants, such as the Mennonites, number more than 500 000.

anabolic steroids. *See* androgens.

anabolism. *See* metabolism.

anaconda A nonvenomous South American constrictor snake, *Eunectes murinus*. Up to 10 m long, it is typically dark green with oval black spots and lives in swamps and rivers, feeding on fish and small caymans and also hunting deer, peccaries, and birds along the water's edge.

anaemia A reduction in the number of red cells or in the quantity of red pigment (*see* haemoglobin) in the blood. It may be due to loss of blood, for example after an accident or operation or from chronic bleeding of a peptic ulcer, or lack of iron, which is necessary for the production of haemoglobin. **Haemolytic anaemias** are caused by increased destruction of the red blood cells, as may occur in certain blood diseases (e.g.

sickle-cell disease and thalassaemia) and malaria or because of the presence of toxic chemicals. Anaemia can also result from the faulty production of red cells, such as occurs in **pernicious anaemia** (when it is due to deficiency of *vitamin B_{12}).

anaesthesia A state of insensitivity to pain. Anaesthesia occurs in certain diseases of the nervous system, but is induced artificially for surgical operations. Alcohol and opium derivatives have been used as anaesthetics for centuries, but it was not until the 1840s that the first anaesthetic gases—ether, nitrous oxide, and chloroform —were used to induce **general anaesthesia** (total unconsciousness). This procedure now involves premedication (including administration of sedatives) to prepare the patient for surgery, followed by induction of anaesthesia by injecting a short-acting barbituraté (usually sodium thiopentone). Anaesthesia is maintained by inhalation of an anaesthetic gas (e.g. halothane). **Local anaesthesia** is usually used for dental surgery and also for other minor operations. Procaine and lignocaine are widely used local anaesthetics. **Spinal anaesthesia** (epidural or subarachnoid) produces loss of sensation in a particular part of the body by injecting a local anaesthetic into the space round the spinal cord. It may be used, for example, during childbirth.

Anaheim 33 50N 117 56W A city in the USA, in S California near Los Angeles. It is a major tourist centre, containing the famous Disneyland opened in 1955. Population (1986): 240 730.

analgesics A class of drugs that relieve pain. **Narcotic analgesics**, such as *morphine, are powerful pain killers that act directly on the brain. Some anaesthetics also have analgesic properties. *Aspirin and paracetemol are examples of **antipyretic analgesics**, which also reduce fever. These drugs are not addictive but are less potent than the narcotics.

analog computer. *See* computer.

analytic geometry *See* coordinate systems.

anarchism A political theory arguing for the dismantling of the state and all governmental authority. Most anarchists believe that voluntary cooperation between individuals and groups is not only a fairer and more moral way of organizing society but is also more effective and orderly. Anarchism favours personal freedom and holds that societies in which freedom is limited are unstable. As an influential political force, anarchism was defeated in Russia by communism but survived in Europe, especially in Spain until the end of the Civil War (1939).

Anastasia (1901–?1918) The youngest daughter of *Nicholas II of Russia. Although she was believed to have been executed after the Russian Revolution, a Mrs Anna Anderson (d. 1984) claimed from 1920 that she was Anastasia. In 1961 her claim was officially rejected.

Anatolia. *See* Asia Minor.

anatomy The study of the structure of living organisms. Early studies of human anatomy were made by the Greek physician Galen, in the 2nd century AD, but it was not until the 16th century that dissecting human corpses became acceptable and anatomists—notably Vesalius —made valuable contributions to the science. In the 17th century William *Harvey discovered the circulation of blood and the development of the microscope enabled advances in the detailed structure of the body to be made by such microscopists as Malpighi, Leeuwenhoek, and Swammerdam. In the 20th century anatomy was greatly assisted by the development of the electron microscope, which allowed much finer detail to be studied. Specialized branches of anatomy include embryology (the study of development), *histology (tissues), and *cytology (cells).

Anaxagoras (c. 500–428 BC) Greek philosopher, born at Clazomenae (Asia Minor). In about 480 he moved to Athens, but because of his influence on *Pericles, he was eventually (450) banished on a trumped-up charge of impiety. He believed that the physical universe was made up of an infinite number of substances and that matter was infinitely divisible. He was also the first to explain solar eclipses.

Anaximander (c. 610–c. 546 BC) Greek philosopher, born in Miletus (Asia Minor). He was one of the earliest thinkers to develop theories about the physical universe. He held that it came from something unlimited, not just one particular kind of matter, and maintained that the earth lay unsupported at the centre of the universe. He also discussed the origin of life, holding that it arose in the sea, and that man evolved from some more primitive species.

anchovy A small herring-like fish living in tropical and warm-temperate waters. 10–25 cm long, anchovies have a large mouth extending behind the eye, a small lower jaw, and a pointed snout. They live in large shoals, chiefly in coastal waters, and are widely fished for food and bait.

Andalusia (Spanish name: Andalucía) The southernmost region of Spain, bordering on the Atlantic Ocean and Mediterranean Sea. It occupies chiefly the river basin of the Guadalquivir and is one of Spain's most fertile regions producing citrus fruit, olives, and wine. Under Roman control after the 2nd century BC, the region was invaded in the early 8th century by the Muslims. In the 15th century Castile finally recovered Andalusia from the Muslims. It is popular with tourists, who are attracted by the great Moorish buildings found especially in Córdoba, Seville, and Granada.

Andaman and Nicobar Islands A Union Territory of India, comprising two island groups in the E Bay of Bengal. The Andaman forests support plywood and match industries. Coconuts, rubber, and coffee are also important. The Nicobar Islands 120 km (75 mi) S of the Andaman Islands, produce coconuts, areca nuts, and fish. Area: 8293 sq km (3215 sq mi). Population (1981): 188 254. Capital: Port Blair.

Andersen, Hans Christian (1805–75) Danish author, famous for his fairy tales. The son of a shoemaker, he attempted to become an actor in Copenhagen. A well-wisher enabled him to attend the university there in 1828; he subsequently travelled widely in Europe and wrote novels, plays, and travel books. His international reputation, however, was earned by the 168 fairy tales that he wrote between 1835 and 1872.

Andes (Spanish name: Cordillera de los Andes) A mountain system in W South America. It extends N for about 7250 km (4500 mi) from Cape Horn to the Isthmus of Panama, reaching 6960 m (22 835 ft) at Mount Aconcagua. Its parallel mountain ranges are chiefly of volcanic origin and contain several active volcanoes, including Cotopaxi; earthquakes are common. It is rich in mineral wealth, including gold, silver, platinum, mercury, copper, and lead.

Andorra, Coprincipality of (Catalan name: Valls d'Andorra; French name: Les Vallées d'Andorre) A small principality in the E Pyrenees, between France and Spain. It is mountainous with peaks reaching heights of almost 3000 m (about 9500 ft). Tourism and agriculture (wheat, potatoes, livestock raising, and tobacco) are the principal industries. Andorra pays dues to its overlords of 960 francs to France and 460 pesetas to the bishopric of Urgel in Spain in alternate years. Andorra is a tax haven and has received many immigrants in recent years. Official language: Catalan; French and Spanish are also spoken. Official currencies: French and Spanish currencies are both in use. Area: 465 sq km (179 sq mi). Population (1988): 42 712. Capital: Andorra la Vella.

Andrea del Sarto (Andrea d'Agnolo; 1486– 1530) A leading Florentine Renaissance painter, whose work, through its influence on his pupils Jacopo da Pontormo (1494–1557), Giovanni Battista Rosso (1494–1540), and Giorgio Vasari (1511–74), became a starting point for Tuscan mannerism. Andrea spent most of his life in Florence, producing a series of frescoes in the cloister of the Scalzi and the SS Annunziata. Among his most important paintings are several representing the Holy Family, some portraits, and the *Madonna of the Harpies* (1517; Uffizi).

Andrew, St In the New Testament, one of the 12 Apostles. Originally a fisherman in partnership with his brother Simon Peter, he was a disciple of John the Baptist before following Jesus. Apparently crucified, he is the patron saint of Scotland and Russia. Feast day: 30 Nov.

androgens A group of steroid hormones that influence the development and function of the male reproductive system and determine male secondary sexual characteristics, such as the growth of body hair and deepening of the voice at puberty. The major androgens are testosterone and androsterone, produced by the testes in higher animals and man and also in small amounts by the adrenal glands and ovaries in mammals. Natural and synthetic androgens are used in medicine to treat conditions caused by androgen deficiency. Some synthetic androgens (**anabolic steroids**) promote the growth of muscle and bone and are administered to weakened patients; their use by athletes is generally banned.

anemone A flowering plant of the buttercup family, growing in N temperate regions. The leaves are segmented and the flowers lack true petals (the sepals function as petals). The Eurasian wood anemone (*Anemone nemorosa*), 10–

15 cm high, has white flowers. Many species are cultivated for their brightly coloured flowers.
aneroid barometer. *See* barometer.
angelfish 1. A tropical fish having a narrow oval body, a small mouth, and often an elongated snout. Up to 70 cm long, angelfish are solitary, living around coral reefs. They are usually patterned in a variety of brilliant colours. 2. A South American fish that is often kept in aquariums.

angelica A flowering plant of the carrot family, growing up to 2 m tall and having umbrella-like clusters of white or greenish flowers. The Eurasian species *Angelica archangelica* yields an oil used in liqueur and perfume making, and its stems are steeped in sugar to make candied angelica, used to decorate cakes and pastries.

Angelico, Fra (Guido di Pietro; c. 1400–55) Italian painter of the early *Renaissance, born in Vicchio (Tuscany). In the early 1420s he became a Dominican monk in Fiesole. His order transferred in 1436 to St Mark's Convent, Florence, where he painted several frescoes, including a famous *Annunciation*. From 1445 to about 1450 he painted frescoes in the Vatican but only the *Scenes from the Lives of SS Stephen and Lawrence* has survived. His paintings were all on religious themes and reflected his "angelic" nature (hence his popular name).

angina pectoris Chest pain caused by a reduction in the supply of blood to the heart due to narrowing of the coronary blood vessels supplying the heart. It is usually associated with *atherosclerosis, is brought on by exercise, and can occur before a heart attack. Treatment includes rest and administration of glyceryl trinitrate, drugs to reduce blood pressure, and coronary bypass operations.

anglerfish A small marine fish, also called goosefish, that has a flat body, large head, and wide mouth. The first ray of the spiny dorsal fin is modified to form a "fishing line" ending with a fleshy flap of skin – the "bait," which is often luminous in deepsea species. Fish, invertebrates, and even seabirds are lured and snapped up by the huge mouth.

Angles A Germanic tribe that came from the Angeln district of Schleswig, which together with the *Saxons and *Jutes invaded and conquered most of England during the 5th century AD. England is named after them.

Anglesey (Welsh name: Ynys Môn; Latin name: Mona) A low-lying island off the NW coast of Wales, linked to the mainland by road and rail bridges over the Menai Strait. Now part of Gwynedd, it formed a separate county until local government reorganization in 1974. The chief agricultural activity is sheep rearing. Area: 705 sq km (272 sq mi). Population (1984 est): 68 500. Chief town: Beaumaris.

Anglo-Catholicism A movement that stresses the close relationship of the Church of England with Catholic Christianity. The main source of modern Anglo-Catholicism was provided by the *Oxford Movement. Anglo-Catholics emphasize traditional Catholic practices with regard to the celebration of the Eucharist, clothing, etc.

Anglo-Saxons The Germanic conquerors of Britain during the 5th century AD (*see* Angles; Saxons; Jutes). They first established a number of separate kingdoms, principally *Northumbria, *Mercia, and *Wessex, but eventually England was unified under an Anglo-Saxon dynasty. Kings ruled with the assistance of a witan or council of wise men. Popular government and justice at the local level took the form of hundred courts. They were converted to Christianity as a result of the mission of St *Augustine of Canterbury. The Anglo-Saxons developed a rich art and literature. Their language is also known as Old *English.

Angola, People's Republic of A country in SW Africa, on the Atlantic Ocean. The Cabinda district lies to the N of the River Congo and is separated from the rest of the country by a section of Zaïre. The country consists of a narrow coastal plain and a broad plateau that reaches heights of over 2000 m (6500 ft). The inhabitants are almost all Negroes (mainly of Bantu origin) with small numbers of mixed race. *Economy*: the main crops are sugar cane and coffee. Angola is rich in mineral resources and diamonds have long been an important source of revenue. There is considerable oil production, especially offshore from Cabinda, and hydroelectricity is being harnessed. Main exports include oil, coffee, diamonds, and iron ore. *History*: discovered and settled by the Portuguese in the late 15th century, the area became an overseas province of Portugal in 1951. In 1974 Portugal agreed to independence but civil war broke out; in November, 1975, Portugal granted independence to the "Angolan people" rather than to any one group. The People's Republic of Angola was declared by the MPLA (Popular Movement for the Liberation of Angola), with its capital in Luanda, supported by the Soviet Union and Cuba. The opposition was led by the FNLA (National Front for the Liberation of Angola) and UNITA (National Union for the Total Independence of Angola), backed by South Africa. After 13 years of fighting an uneasy ceasefire was established in 1988. Talks to end the civil war began in 1990. President: Dr José dos Santos. Official language: Portuguese. Official currency: kwanza of 100 lwei. Area: 1 246 700 sq km (481 351 sq mi). Population (1990): 9 978 000. Capital and main port: Luanda.

Angora goat A breed of goat, originating in Turkey, whose long silky hair is regularly sheared and used commercially to make mohair. Mohair is now also obtained from several other goat breeds derived from the Angora.

Angora rabbit A breed of domesticated rabbit, originating in France in the 17th century, of which there are now both English and French varieties. The long wool, which is usually white but can be black or blue, is shorn and spun for use in clothing manufacture (**Angora wool**).

Angry Young Men A group of British novelists and dramatists in the 1950s who were dissatisfied with postwar British society and despised the so-called "Establishment" and its traditional institutions. Many of them came from working-class or lower-middle-class backgrounds. The

phrase "angry young man" was first applied to the dramatist John *Osborne. Among other writers associated with this group were the novelists Kingsley *Amis, John Wain (1925–), and John Braine (1922–86), the dramatist Arnold *Wesker, and the critic Colin Wilson (1931–).

angstrom A unit of wavelength equal to 10^{-10} m (one tenth of a nanometre), named after A. J. Ångström.

Ångström, Anders Jonas (1814–74) Swedish physicist and astronomer. He was a founder of spectroscopy, his work on solar spectra leading to the discovery (1862) of hydrogen in the sun.

Anguilla 18 14N 63 05W A West Indian island in the E Caribbean Sea, in the Leeward Islands. Formerly part of the UK Associated State of St Kitts-Nevis-Anguilla, it became a separate British dependency in December, 1980. Its economy is based chiefly on stock raising, salt production, boatbuilding, and fishing. Area: 90 sq km (35 sq mi). Population (1988): 6700. *See also* St Kitts-Nevis.

angular velocity. *See* velocity.

animal Any living organism belonging to the kingdom *Animalia*. Animals are typically mobile and feed on *plants, other animals, or their remains. Their body *cells lack the rigid cellulose wall of plant cells and they require specialized tissues, such as bone, for protection and support. Because of their activity, animals have specialized organs for sensing the nature of their environment; information from the sense organs is transmitted and coordinated by means of a nervous system. There are over one million species of animals. *See also* life; taxonomy.

animal behaviour. *See* ethology.

animal rights movement A campaign conducted by several organizations in protest against cruelty to animals. Targets of the movement, which developed in the 1970s, include zoos, animal research centres, foxhunts, and those who sell animal products. Some groups, such as the League Against Cruel Sports, favour parliamentary action, while others, such as the Animal Liberation Front, do not disapprove of criminal acts, including the release of research animals, damage to property, and bombings.

anise An annual Mediterranean plant, *Pimpinella anisum*, of the carrot family, growing to a height of up to 75 cm and having umbrella-like clusters of small yellow-white flowers. It is cultivated in subtropical areas for its liquorice-flavoured seeds (aniseed), which are used in cookery and yield an oil used to flavour drinks, etc.

Ankara 39 55N 32 50E The capital of Turkey, in the W central region of the country. Conquered by Alexander the Great in the 4th century BC, it later came within the Roman and Byzantine Empires. It was attacked by Persians and Arabs, and in the 11th century it was defeated by the Turks. It became the capital of modern Turkey in 1923 and since then has expanded considerably; it has three universities including the Middle East Technical University (1956). Population (1985): 2 251 533.

ankylosaur A heavily armoured *dinosaur of the late Cretaceous period, which ended 65 million years ago. Ankylosaurs were low and flat and their backs were covered with hard protective bony plates. *Euoplocephalus* (or *Ankylosaurus*) up to 5 m long, weighed 3 tonnes and its plated tail ended in a large bony knob.

Annapurna, Mount 28 34N 83 50E A massif in NW central Nepal, in the Himalayas. Its highest peak **Annapurna I**, at 8078 m (26 504 ft), was first climbed in 1950 by a French team.

Anne (1665–1714) Queen of England and Scotland (Great Britain from 1707) and Ireland (1702–14). Anne, the last Stuart monarch, was the daughter of the Roman Catholic James II but was herself brought up as a Protestant. Following the overthrow (1688) of James, she supported her Protestant brother-in-law, William III, whose heiress she became. She married (1683) Prince George of Denmark (1653–1708) and was pregnant 18 times by him; none of her five children born alive survived childhood. Anne therefore agreed to the Act of *Settlement (1701), which led to the Hanoverian succession after her death.

Anne (Elizabeth Alice Louise) (1950–) Princess of the United Kingdom, eighth in line to the throne, the only daughter of *Elizabeth II and Prince Philip. In 1973 she married Mark Phillips (1948–), having a son Peter (1977–) and a daughter Zara (1981–) before their separation in 1989. A respected horsewoman, she is president of the Save the Children Fund; in 1987 she was made Princess Royal for her charitable work.

annealing. *See* heat treatment.

annelid worm An invertebrate animal of which there are about 9000 species, widely distributed in salt water, fresh water, and on land. The muscular body is divided into many fluid-filled segments. Annelids include the bristleworms (*see* ragworm; lugworm; fanworm), the earthworms, and the leeches.

Anne of Cleves (1515–57) The fourth wife of Henry VIII of England. The marriage (January, 1540) was arranged to forge an alliance with German Protestant rulers but Henry found Anne unattractive and quickly divorced her (July, 1540).

Annigoni, Pietro (1910–88) Italian painter. One of the most famous 20th-century artists to use the techniques of the Old Masters, Annigoni worked chiefly in tempera and fresco. He is best known for his portraits of President Kennedy (1961) and Queen Elizabeth II (1955 and 1970). In later years he devoted himself to frescoes of the life of Christ in the Church of S Michele Arcangelo, in Ponte Buggianese, near Florence.

annual rings (or growth rings) A pattern of rings visible in a cross section of a tree trunk, produced by different rates of wood growth: the wood produced in spring consists of large cells corresponding to vigorous growth; autumn wood has small cells as growth slows down, and in winter growth ceases. The number of rings gives an estimate of the age of the tree. *See also* dendrochronology.

annuals Plants that complete their life cycle—from germination, flowering, and seed production to death—within one year. Many annuals are planted in flowerbeds (e.g. marigolds) and flower extensively in the summer months. Compare perennials.

annuity A form of pension in which an insurance company makes a series of payments to a person (annuitant) or his or her dependents over a number of years (term), in return for either a lump sum or regular instalments. An immediate annuity begins at once and a deferred annuity after a fixed period. An annuity certain is for a specific number of years. A life annuity is paid from a certain age until death. A perpetuity is unending.

Annunciation In the Bible, the announcement by the angel Gabriel to the Virgin Mary of the coming birth of Christ (Luke 1.26–38). The feast, in full called the Annunciation of the Blessed Virgin Mary, or Lady Day, is celebrated on 25 March.

anodizing A process in which a light metal or alloy, usually aluminium, is covered with a protective layer by oxidation in an electrolytic cell. Usually the cell contains chromic acid; the metal treated is the anode of the cell. A porous layer of oxide is formed, which can be dyed to give a coloured finish.

anorexia nervosa A psychological illness in which the patient, usually an adolescent girl, refuses food over a long period. It often starts with dieting to lose weight, which becomes obsessional: the patient becomes very thin and may—without treatment—starve to death. The causes are complex, often involving disturbances in family relationships. Treatment in hospital may be required, which involves intensive nursing, sedative drugs, and *psychotherapy.

Anouilh, Jean (1910–87) French dramatist. His first play, *The Ermine*, was performed in 1932. He achieved his first success in 1937 with *Traveller without Luggage*. His plays include reworkings of Greek myths (*Antigone*, 1944), social comedies (*Ring Round the Moon*, 1950), and historical dramas (*Becket*, 1959).

Anschluss (German: union; 1938) The union of Austria with Germany. Following the forced resignation of the Austrian chancellor Kurt von Schuschnigg (1897–1977), Nazi forces entered Austria and Schuschnigg was imprisoned. *Anschluss* was declared and confirmed by a national vote.

Anselm of Canterbury, St (c. 1033–1109) Italian theologian and philosopher, Archbishop of Canterbury, and Doctor of the Church. Appointed to the see of Canterbury in 1093, Anselm defended church rights against William II Rufus until he went into exile to Rome in 1097. Recalled by *Henry I in 1100, he eventually reached an uneasy peace with him. He is the leading early scholastic philosopher and is perhaps best known for his argument for the existence of God, which states that God is "that than which nothing greater can be conceived." Feast day: 21 April. Emblem: a ship.

ant An insect related to bees and wasps. There are over 10 000 species. Ants occur in almost all land habitats, are 0.05–25 cm long, and live together in colonies. A colony consists of wingless sterile female workers and a smaller number of fertile males and females that are usually produced by a single queen. The young males and females fly from the nest to mate, after which the males die and the young queens found new colonies. Ant societies range from simple groups of a few individuals to large complex nests comprising millions of ants and sometimes containing other insects taken as slaves to work in the colony. Some ants have stings; others secrete burning acids (such as formic acid) as a defence.

Antakya. See Antioch.

Antananarivo (former name: Tananarive) 18 52S 47 30E The capital of Madagascar. It was occupied by the French in 1895. A cultural centre, it has a university (1961) and two cathedrals. Industries include tobacco and leather goods. Population (1986): 703 000.

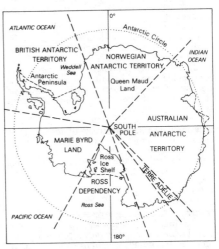

ANTARCTICA *Under the Antarctic Treaty (1959) all political claims were halted and freedom of scientific research in the continent was ensured.*

Antarctica The most southerly continent, surrounding the South Pole. An almost circular ice-covered plateau, it contains the Weddell and Ross Seas and about 90% of the world's ice. The continent's climate is the severest in the world and although it lacks vegetation it has abundant wildlife including whales, seals, and penguins. Scientific stations were established during the International Geophysical Year (1957–58). Some nations (*see* Australian Antarctic Territory; British Antarctic Territory; Norwegian Antarctic Territory; Ross Dependency) have political claims to territory in Antarctica. *History*: in his voyage of 1772–75 Capt James Cook sailed around the continent. The South Pole was reached first by Roald *Amundsen of the Norwegian Antarctic Expedition on 14 December, 1911, and a month later by *Scott of the British

Expedition. Area: about 14 200 000 sq km (5 500 000 sq mi).

Antarctic Ocean The sections of the S Atlantic, Pacific, and Indian Oceans around Antarctica. Except in the height of summer (late Feb to early March), it is covered by drifting pack ice.

Antarctic Treaty (1959) An agreement, signed by Argentina, Australia, Belgium, Chile, France, Japan, New Zealand, Norway, South Africa, the Soviet Union, the UK, and the USA, to keep the Antarctic free of military use for 30 years.

ant bear. *See* aardvark.

anteater A long-tailed animal occurring in tropical South America. It is toothless and has a narrow snout with a long sticky tongue used to pick up ants and termites after tearing open their nests with its powerful claws. The giant anteater (*Myrmecophaga tridactyla*) reaches 1.8 m in length and has grey and black fur and a bushy tail. Two other closely related species are smaller, have long grasping tails, and live in trees (*see* tamandua).

The name anteater is given to several other animals that feed on ants or termites: the pangolins (scaly anteaters), echidnas (spiny anteaters), and *aardvark.

antelope A fast-running hoofed mammal occurring chiefly in Africa but occasionally in Asia. The shoulder height varies from 25 cm (the royal antelope) to 180 cm (the *eland). All male antelopes and some females have horns. *See also* dik-dik; duiker; gazelle; gnu; kudu; waterbuck.

antenna The sensory feeler of insects, crustaceans, and many other arthropods, one or two pairs of which are attached to the head. They are usually jointed threadlike structures containing receptors of sound, smell, touch, and temperature.

anther. *See* stamen.

anthracite. *See* coal.

anthrax A contagious disease of many animals, including farm livestock, that can be transmitted to man. Caused by the bacterium *Bacillus anthracis*, it is usually caught by eating contaminated food. The symptoms often appear suddenly, with a rise in temperature, staggering, difficulty in breathing, convulsions, and death. In horses and pigs a more gradual form may occur, with progressive swelling of the throat and neck resulting in breathing difficulties and choking. In many countries the authorities must be notified of any outbreaks. Treatment is with antibiotics and prevention is by vaccination of herds. Man may develop localized swellings after handling infected carcasses or pneumonia from inhaling the bacterial spores (woolsorters' disease).

anthropoid ape An *ape, such as a gibbon, chimpanzee, orang-utan, or gorilla, that is most closely related to man.

anthropology The scientific study of man. It includes *archaeology, *linguistics, cultural or social anthropology, and physical anthropology. Physical anthropology is concerned with the origins and evolution of man through the examination of his fossil remains, and the study and classification of the races. Cultural anthropology is concerned with the evolution of human society

and culture, including language, and with the comparison of social, linguistic, technical, and behavioural differences.

antiballistic missiles High-speed nuclear weapons used to attack hostile *ballistic missiles. Operated by ground-based radar and computers, they rely for their final attack on their own guidance systems, destroying the target by radiation from their warheads. Short-range versions with low-yield warheads (e.g. US *Sprint*) are designed to seek and destroy targets within the earth's atmosphere; long-range missiles with high-yield warheads operate in space (e.g. US *Spartan*, Soviet *Galosh*).

antibiotics Drugs used to treat infections caused by bacteria or fungi. Some are produced by living moulds and yeasts, and are extracted and purified for use in medicine; others are entirely man-made. Such antibiotics as *penicillin actually kill bacteria, whereas other antibiotics, such as tetracycline and chloramphenicol, simply halt their growth. Yet others are used to treat fungal infections; these include nystatin and griseofulvin. One drawback of antibiotics is that they can cause allergic reactions in the patient. Also, the bacteria may become resistant, so that the antibiotic concerned is no longer effective. Nevertheless, the widespread use of antibiotics since World War II has enabled many bacterial and fungal diseases to be controlled.

antibody A protein produced by certain white blood cells (lymphocytes) that reacts with a particular foreign particle (e.g. a bacterium) that has entered the body. The antibody helps to destroy the foreign particle (known as the **antigen**). If the same bacteria invade the body in future, many more of the same antibodies are produced, enabling the body to destroy the bacteria very rapidly and so resist infection. This provides the basis of *immunity. Antibodies are also responsible for the rejection of foreign tissue or organ transplants. *See also* monoclonal antibody.

anticline *See* fold.

anticoagulants Drugs, such as heparin and warfarin, that interfere with blood clotting. They are used when there has been, or there is a risk of, clots forming in the blood vessels, as after *thrombosis of the leg veins.

anticyclone (*or* high) An area in which the atmospheric pressure is higher than the surrounding air and increases towards the centre. Winds, generally light, circulate around the high pressure centre in a clockwise direction in the N hemisphere and anticlockwise in the S hemisphere. Calm settled weather usually comes with anticyclones in temperate latitudes.

Antietam, Battle of (17 September, 1862) A decisive battle in the US Civil War, which prevented the Confederate capture of Washington, DC. In the last of a series of battles, the advance of the Confederate general Robert E. Lee, was checked at Antietam by the Federal general George B. McClellan (1826–85). The South lost about 10 000 men but McClellan allowed Lee to withdraw into Virginia.

antigen. *See* antibody.

Antigone In Greek mythology, the daughter of *Oedipus and Jocasta, whose story forms the basis of Sophocles' tragedy *Antigone*. When her father was banished from Thebes she accompanied him into exile in Colonus. Her brothers Eteocles and Polyneices killed each other, and although the Theban senate had prohibited the burial of Polyneices, Antigone performed the funeral rites for her brother. She was consequently ordered to be buried alive by Creon, ruler of Thebes, and hanged herself.

Antigua and Barbuda A West Indian country in the E Caribbean Sea, comprising the islands of Antigua, Barbuda, and Redonda. Tourism is the chief source of revenue; sugar and cotton production are also important. *History*: Antigua was discovered by Columbus (1493) and colonized by British settlers in 1632. It formed an associated state within the British Commonwealth from 1967 until gaining independence in 1981. Prime minister: Vere C. Bird. Area: 440 sq km (170 sq mi). Population (1986 est): 81 500. Capital: St John's.

antihistamines Drugs that interfere with the action of histamine, a chemical produced by the body that is responsible for the symptoms of an allergy. Antihistamines are therefore used to treat hay fever, nettle rash, and other allergies. Some antihistamines (e.g. dramamine) are used to prevent travel sickness and others are effective sedatives (drowsiness is a common side effect of many antihistamines).

Antilles The islands of the West Indies, excluding the Bahamas. The group is divided into the Greater Antilles and the Lesser Antilles.

antimatter Matter in which the constituent atoms consist of antiparticles. For every elementary particle (*see* particle physics) there exists an antiparticle that is identical except for certain of its properties, such as electric charge, which are of equal magnitude but opposite in sign. An atom of antimatter would contain a nucleus of antiprotons and antineutrons surrounded by positrons (antielectrons). Although many different antiparticles are known no antimatter has (yet) been detected.

antimony (Sb) A metallic element, occurring in nature as the element and more commonly in the sulphide stibnite (Sb_2S_3). The element exists in two forms: the normal metallic form, which is brittle bluish-white and flaky, and an amorphous grey form. It forms the oxide (Sb_2O_3) by burning in air and the volatile hydride, stibine (SbH_3), which like many antimony compounds is poisonous. Pure antimony is used in making *semiconductors; other uses include addition to lead to increase its hardness in battery plates and as oxides or sulphides in paints, glasses, and ceramics. At no 51; at wt 121.75; mp 630.7°C; bp 1750°C.

Antioch (modern Turkish name: Antakya) 36 12N 36 10E A town in central S Turkey, near the coast and the Syrian border. Founded in 301 BC, it had a large early Christian community, and there are notable Roman mosaics in the Archaeological Museum. Population (1980): 94 942.

antiparticle. *See* antimatter.

antipope Those raised to the papacy in opposition to a lawfully elected pope. Hippolitus, the first of some 40 antipopes, was created in the early 3rd century. During the later Roman Empire and the middle ages most antipopes represented rival factions supporting different political or religious claims. In the 11th and 12th centuries some 14 antipopes were chosen by the Holy Roman Emperors, who resented the Church's growing independence. From 1378, following the *Great Schism, the popes remaining in Avignon (*see* Avignon papacy) under French control were called antipopes. The Council of Pisa (1409) elected a new pope to end the Schism, but he too was regarded as an antipope until unity was restored at the Council of *Constance (1515). There have been no antipopes since the mid-15th century.

antirrhinum A flowering plant native to the Mediterranean region and W North America but widely grown as garden plants. The most common cultivated species is the ornamental snapdragon (*Antirrhinum majus*), 30–80 cm high with brightly coloured two-lipped tubular flowers that are pollinated by large bees.

antitoxin An *antibody produced against a toxin. Toxins are harmful substances that may be produced, for example, by bacteria infecting the body. Antitoxins can be used to treat or prevent specific infections, for example, tetanus.

antlion An insect that resembles a dragonfly and lives only long enough to mate and lay eggs. The predatory larva lives 1–3 years, generally at the bottom of a conical pit in loose sand: any insect that falls into the pit is snapped up with its large jaws, which protrude from the sand.

Antonescu, Ion (1882–1946) Romanian general and politician. A pro-Nazi, he became prime minister (1940), replacing Carol II's government with an oppressive regime. In 1941 he commanded the army in Bessarabia. He was executed for war crimes.

Antonine Wall A Roman frontier defence work 58.5 km (36.5 mi) long, linking the Firths of Forth and Clyde in S Scotland and still surviving in places. It was built about 142 AD by Lollius Urbicus, governor of Britain, for the emperor *Antoninus Pius, and abandoned in 196 AD. A military road linked 29 small forts along a turf wall 3 m (10 ft) high and 4.3 m (14 ft) wide, behind a large ditch. *See also* Hadrian's Wall.

Antoninus Pius (86–161 AD) Roman emperor (138–61). Antoninus was appointed by Emperor Hadrian to his advisory council and adopted as his successor in 138. His reign was generally prosperous; minor campaigns were fought abroad and noted legal reforms were introduced; the *Antonine Wall was built during his reign. He was made into a god after his death.

Antwerp (Flemish name: Antwerpen; French name: Anvers) 51 13N 4 25E A city in Belgium, on the River Scheldt. Antwerp is one of the largest seaports in the world and has important shipbuilding and ship-repairing industries. Other industries include oil refining, diamond cutting, textiles, and electronics. It possesses many fine buildings, including the 14th-century gothic cathedral and the 16th-century Butchers' Hall. There is a large Flemish-speaking population. Population (1989 est): 476 044.

anus. *See* intestine.

ANZAC The *A*ustralian and *N*ew Zealand *A*rmy *C*orps, which served in World War I in Europe and the Middle East. On ANZAC Day, 25 April (the day of the ANZAC landing in Gallipoli in 1915), in Australia and New Zealand the dead of both World Wars are remembered.

aorta. *See* artery; heart.

Aouita, Saïd (1960–) Moroccan middle-distance runner. In 1987 he became the holder of world records in the 2000 m, 5000 m, and 1500 m events.

apartheid (Afrikaans: apartness) The policy of separate development of the White and non-White populations in South Africa. Apartheid, which was introduced by the Afrikaner National Party in 1948, aims to divide South Africa into separate regions for Whites and Blacks. The White minority that governs South Africa has been criticized for this policy and in 1961 South Africa was forced to withdraw from the British Commonwealth. In 1985 non-Whites won limited constitutional rights and marriage between the races was allowed. Increased internal unrest, combined with sporting and financial pressure from outside, led *de Klerk to take steps towards dismantling apartheid.

apatite The commonest phosphorus mineral, of composition $Ca_5(PO_4)_3(OH,F,Cl)$. It is found in small quantities in many igneous rocks and is used in the production of *fertilizers. The enamel of teeth is composed almost entirely of apatite (*see also* fluoridation) and the chief inorganic constituent of bone is hydroxyapatite, $Ca_{10}(PO_4)_6(OH)_2$.

Apatosaurus A huge herbivorous *dinosaur, formerly called *Brontosaurus*, of the late Jurassic period, which ended about 135 million years ago. Up to 21 m long and weighing up to 30 tonnes, it had massive pillar-like legs, a long neck and tail, and lived in swamps, coming ashore to lay eggs. With its nostrils placed high on its head, it was able to stand almost fully submerged.

ape A highly intelligent tailless *primate found in central Africa and S Asia. There are 11 species divided into two groups: the tree-dwelling gibbons and the ground-dwelling great, or anthropoid, apes (*see* chimpanzee; orang-utan; gorilla). Gibbons are often solitary but ground-dwelling apes live in complex societies and all have highly developed means of communication. Some tailless primates of other families are also called apes.

Apennines (Italian name: Appennini) A mountain range in Italy. It extends about 1050 km (652 mi) down the Italian peninsula from the Maritime Alps in the NW to the Strait of Messina in the S. The highest peak is Monte Corno at 2914 m (9560 ft). The Apennines are volcanic in the S (*see* Vesuvius).

aphid An insect, also called a plant louse, that causes serious damage to plants. Small, soft, and often wingless, aphids have long thin antennae (feelers) and weak legs and are usually green (greenfly), red, or brown. There are two thin tubes projecting from the abdomen from which honeydew is secreted. Aphids feed on plant sap, piercing plant tissues with sharp beaklike

mouthparts; they cause curling of leaves, stunt plant growth, and often form galls.

Aphrodite In Greek mythology, the goddess of love, called *Venus by the Romans. According to Homer she was the daughter of Dione and Zeus; Hesiod says that she was born from the foam after *Uranus had been castrated and his genitals thrown into the sea. She was the wife of Hephaestus but had an affair with Ares. Paris' choice of her as the most beautiful of the three goddesses at the wedding feast of Peleus and Thetis (the others were Hera and Athena) caused the *Trojan War. Revered throughout Greece as the personification of spiritual love, she also embodied sensual lust.

Apocrypha (Greek: hidden things) Twelve books taken over by the early Christian Church from the Greek version of the Old Testament but not forming part of the Hebrew Bible. They began as part of the Hellenistic Judaism of Alexandria but were not accepted by strict Jews. In the *Vulgate, most of them are printed with the Old Testament but they are left out or printed as a separate section in Protestant versions of the Bible.

Apollo The Greek god of light, reason, and male beauty. He is also associated with medicine, prophecy, music and poetry, the care of animals and crops, morality, and the maintenance of society. He and his sister *Artemis were the children of *Zeus by Leto. He established his oracle at Delphi after killing Python, its dragon guardian.

Apollo moon programme The US programme to land men on the moon by 1970, announced by President Kennedy in 1961. The programme was under the control of *NASA. A Saturn V rocket launched the Apollo spacecraft towards the moon and, once the craft was in lunar orbit, the lunar module descended to the moon's surface carrying two astronauts. The third astronaut remained in the orbiting craft. At the end of the surface mission the lunar module's descent stage was left on the moon while its ascent stage carried the astronauts back to the orbiting craft. The spacecraft then returned to earth. The astronauts travelled to and from the moon in the command module, the rocket engines for in-flight manoeuvres, fuel cells, etc., being carried in the separate service module, which was discarded just before the craft re-entered the earth's atmosphere.

The first six Apollo missions were unmanned test flights, the next four being manned. Apollo 11 made the first manned lunar landing in July, 1969. Of the six missions that followed, all, except Apollo 13, were highly successful.

Apostles In the New Testament, the 12 men chosen by Jesus as his disciples who, after his death, were to spread his teaching throughout the Roman world. Originally they were: Andrew, Bartholomew (*or* Nathaniel), James son of Alphaeus, James son of Zebedee, John, Jude (*or* Thaddeus), Judas Iscariot, Matthew (*or* Levi), Philip, Simon Peter, Simon the Zealot, and Thomas. After his suicide Judas Iscariot was replaced by Matthias. St Paul is also included among the Apostles because of his claim to having seen Jesus after the resurrection.

Appalachian Mountains A mountain range in the USA. It extends NE–SW from the Mohawk River to Alabama, separating the Mississippi-Missouri lowlands from the Atlantic coastal plain. It consists of a series of mountain ranges and plateaus, including the Allegheny Mountains, the Catskill Mountains, and the White Mountains of New Hampshire. Its highest point is Mount Mitchell, at 2038 m (6684 ft). Coalmining is important and iron ore is also extracted. It also contains the **Appalachian Trail**, the longest continuous footpath in the world.

appendix (*or* vermiform appendix) A thin blind-ended tube, 7–10 cm long, that opens from the end of the large intestine. It has no known function in man and is prone to infection (**appendicitis**), in which case its surgical removal is often required to prevent its rupture. In herbivorous animals (e.g. rabbits and cows) the appendix is large and functions in the digestion of vegetable matter.

Appian Way The road, built about 312 BC by the statesman Appius Claudius, between Rome and Capua. It was the first in the strategic network of Roman roads. A short stretch is still visible near Rome.

apple A deciduous tree or shrub of the rose family, native to N temperate regions and widely cultivated for its rounded fleshy fruits. There are now many varieties of dessert, cooking, and cider apples. Shoots of the required variety are grafted onto other varieties, selected for their hardiness, rapid growth, disease resistance, etc. *See also* crab apple.

Appleton layer. *See* ionosphere.

apricot A tree, *Prunus armenica*, of the rose family, native to China and widely grown in warm temperate countries, especially Spain, for its fruits. It is 6–9 m tall and has white five-petalled flowers and toothed heart-shaped leaves. The hairy-skinned orange-yellow fruits have sweet flesh and smooth stones.

Aqaba 29 32N 35 00E A port in Jordan, on the **Gulf of Aqaba**, a narrow inlet at the NE end of the Red Sea. Aqaba was the Roman stronghold of Aelana. Being Jordan's only port, it has been considerably expanded to handle the export of phosphates. Population (1983 est): 40 000.

aquamarine A pale blue or green variety of beryl. Many fine specimens of this gemstone come from Brazil, Madagascar, and California.

aqueduct A narrow bridge, channel, or conduit designed to enable water to flow at a steady rate over irregular land, such as a valley. Aqueducts were built by the Greeks, but the technique was developed to its highest level of sophistication by the Romans. Impressive Roman examples still survive at Nîmes, Segovia, and Rome.

aquilegia A flowering plant of the buttercup family, commonly known as columbine. Its showy flowers have petals with long honey-secreting spurs. A favourite garden flower, it has been cultivated since the 16th century. Many modern garden hybrids are derived from the Eu-

ropean columbine (*Aquilegia vulgaris*), 40–100 cm high with purple to white flowers.

Aquinas, St Thomas (c. 1225–74) Italian Dominican theologian, scholastic philosopher, and Doctor of the Church, known as *Doctor Angelicus*. Born near Naples, the son of Count Landulf of Aquino, he was educated at the Benedictine school at Monte Cassino and at the University of Naples. Joining the Dominican Order in 1244 in spite of parental opposition, he became a pupil of Albertus Magnus in Paris (1245) and followed him to Cologne in 1248. He was a theological adviser to the papal Curia between 1259 and 1269 and then taught at Paris until 1272, when he was appointed a professor at Naples. He was made into a saint in 1323. His two most influential works are the *Summa contra gentiles* (1259–64), written for the use of missionaries, and the uncompleted *Summa theologica* (1266–73), the first systematic work on Latin theology. Feast day: 7 March.

Aquitaine (Latin name: Aquitania) A planning region in SW France, bordering on the Bay of Biscay. Formerly an administrative region in Roman Gaul, it extended from the Pyrenees N to the River Loire. It became an independent duchy under the Merovingians (7th century). The marriages of Eleanor of Aquitaine to Louis VII of France and then to Henry II of England resulted in rival French-English claims to the territory. Area: 41 408 sq km (15 984 sq mi). Population (1986 est): 2 718 200.

Arab horse An ancient breed of horse originally bred by the Bedouins in Arabia. It is usually grey, chestnut, or bay with a long silky mane and tail, a wedge-shaped head, and an arched neck. The Arab is prized as a riding horse because of its speed, hardiness, and docile temperament. Height: 1.42–1.52 m (14–15 hands).

Arabia A peninsula in the Middle East, forming the SW tip of Asia and bordered by the Red Sea, the Gulf of Aden, the Gulf of Oman, and the Persian Gulf. It consists of Saudi Arabia, Yemen, Oman, the United Arab Emirates, Qatar, Bahrain, and Kuwait. *History*: as remains of irrigation systems show, S Arabia was the site of technologically advanced ancient civilizations. It was conquered briefly by the Persians in 575 AD and later suffered from Mecca by Islam in the 7th century. From the 16th century until World War I the Ottoman Turks held nominal control over much of the peninsula, challenged chiefly by the Wahhabiyah. From the mid-19th century until the late 1960s the UK was the chief foreign presence.

Arabian Desert 1. A desert chiefly in Saudi Arabia, covering most of *Arabia. Area: about 2 300 000 sq km (887 844 sq mi). **2.** A desert in E Egypt between the River Nile and the Red Sea.

Arabian Sea A section of the NW Indian Ocean between Arabia and India. Connected to the Mediterranean Sea by the Red Sea and the Suez Canal, it forms a major shipping route.

Arabic A member of the Semitic group of languages. It is written from right to left. Arabic is the mother-tongue of some 110 million people inhabiting SW Asia (the Middle East) and the countries of N Africa. Arabic can be roughly grouped into three parts: (a) Classical Arabic, the language of the *Koran and the great Arab writers and poets; (b) Modern Literary, or Standard, Arabic, used in the press and broadcasting; and (c) the spoken dialects (vernaculars), which differ from country to country.

Arabic numerals The number symbols 0, 1, 2, 3, 4, 5, 6, 7, 8, 9. They are believed to have originated in India and were introduced into Europe by the Arabs in about the 10th century AD. Compare Roman numerals.

Arab-Israeli Wars. See Israel, State of.

Arab League An organization formed to promote Arab unity and cooperation. Formed in Cairo in 1945, it consisted of those Arab countries that were then independent; others joined on winning independence. Palestine, represented by the PLO, is a member. The League has had some success in the scientific and cultural field but in politics has often been split. In 1979, following the Egyptian-Israeli peace treaty, Egypt was expelled from the League, which moved from Cairo to Tunis: it returned when Egypt was readmitted in 1989.

arable farming The cultivation of plants for food, fibres, vegetable oils, etc. Arable farming is often carried out along with *livestock farming, enabling the farmer to grow his own animal feeds and to make use of animal manures as *fertilizers. Grass is the chief feed for *ruminant livestock and a major arable crop.

Cereal crops are a principal source of food and animal feedstuffs. The major cereals are wheat, barley, rice, and maize with oats, millet, sorghum, and rye grown in smaller quantities.

Beans are grown as a major source of vegetable protein, the most important being soya beans, produced chiefly in China and the USA. Crops grown for their oil content include sunflower, groundnut, linseed, cottonseed, and rape. Modern pesticides and fertilizers, together with better farming equipment, irrigation, and plant breeding have resulted in dramatic increases in crop yields, bringing about a Green Revolution, especially in developing countries.

Arabs A Semitic people originally inhabiting the Arabian peninsula. They are roughly divided into two cultural groups: the nomadic Bedouin tribes and the settled communities of the towns and oases. Wealth from oil has recently led to the development of the towns, but Islam remains a strong force in social customs, particularly in women's role in society. The Arabs appeared as a power in world history early in the 7th century AD, with the rise of Islam, and they carried their language (see Arabic), religion, and culture as far as Spain in the W and Indonesia in the E.

Arachne In Greek mythology, a girl from Lydia who defeated Athena in a tapestry-weaving contest. The jealous goddess destroyed all Arachne's work; she attempted to hang herself, but Athena changed her into a spider.

arachnid Any invertebrate animal of the group that includes the spiders, scorpions, harvestmen, ticks, and mites. There are about 65 000 species, most of which live on land. An arachnid's body is divided into two parts: a combined head and thorax (cephalothorax) and an abdomen. The cephalothorax bears four pairs of legs and a pair of strong pincer-like claws on the head. Arachnids are mostly carnivorous; many secrete poison from specialized glands to kill prey or enemies. Others are parasites, some of which are carriers of disease. Arachnids usually lay eggs, which hatch into immature adults. See arthropod.

Arafat, Yassir (1929–) Palestinian leader. In the 1950s he was one of the founders of al-Fatah and in 1968 became president of the *Palestine Liberation Organization.

Aragon A region and medieval kingdom in NE Spain. A series of conquests during the 11th and 12th centuries brought the Aragonese rule over much of N Spain. Later expansion gave the Aragonese Sicily (1282), Sardinia (1320), and the kingdom of Naples (1442), conquered by Alfonso the Magnanimous (1385–1458). In 1469 Ferdinand the Catholic (1452–1516) married Isabella the Catholic (1451–1504) of Castile; when Ferdinand became king of Aragon in 1479 the two kingdoms were united.

Arakan A state in W Burma, extending along the Bay of Bengal and flanked by the Arakan Yoma, a mountain range rising over 3000 m (1000 ft). The principal industry is the cultivation of rice. There is a large minority of Bengali Muslims in the N. History: a powerful kingdom in the 15th century, it was absorbed into Burma (1783) before passing to Britain (1826–1948). It became a state in 1975. Area: 36 762 sq km (14 191 sq mi). Population (1983): 2 045 891. Capital: Sittwe.

Aral Sea A salt-water lake in the SW Soviet Union in the Kazahk and Uzbek SSRs. Once the fourth largest lake in the world, overuse of its source rivers (the Amu Darya and Syr Darya) for irrigation has reduced its water volume by more than half. It is heavily polluted by agricultural chemicals. Area (including salt flats): about 66 000 sq km (25 477 sq mi).

Aramaic A western branch of the Semitic group of languages. Its 22-letter alphabet is the ancestor of both Hebrew and Arabic alphabets. Aramaic was much used during the late Babylonian empire and was the official language of the Persian Empire under Darius I. It replaced Hebrew as the language of the Jews from about the time of the Exile in 605 BC until long after the rise of Islam.

Ararat, Mount (Turkish name: Ağrı Dağı) 39 44N 44 15E A mountain in E Turkey, near the Soviet and Iranian borders. It is volcanic in origin. Traditionally, Noah's ark came to rest here after the flood (Genesis 8.4). Height: 5165 m (16 946 ft).

Arawak Indians of the Greater Antilles and northern and western areas of the Amazon basin. Their languages are the most widespread of the South American Indian languages and include Goajiro in Colombia, Campa and Machiguenga in Peru, and Mojo and Bauré in Bolivia. They are farmers growing manioc and maize. Prior to the Spanish conquests they were divided into numerous chiefdoms. They were never a warlike people and in the Caribbean area Carib tribes frequently raided Arawak groups and enslaved Arawak women. The tribal gods were the spirits of chiefs represented by idols called zemis, which were housed in temples.

arbor vitae A coniferous tree of the cypress family, native to North America and E Asia. They have scalelike leaves, which densely cover the flattened stems, and small scaly cones, 1–1.8 cm long. The Chinese arbor vitae or cedar (*Thuja orientalis*), which grows to a height of 30 m, is a popular ornamental tree; the giant arbor vitae, or western red cedar (*T. plicata*), of W North America, grows to a height of 40 m and yields a valuable timber.

Arcadia A mountainous region of ancient Greece, in the central Pelopponesus, that was identified in the literature of Greece, Rome, and the Renaissance (e.g. in Sidney's *Arcadia*) as an earthly paradise. It is a modern department.

archaeology The scientific study of the remains of man's past. Archaeology may be supplemented by written records, but it is principally concerned with material evidence for man's social and cultural development. Modern archaeology has numerous specialized branches –classical, industrial, underwater, etc. Before the 19th century, digging was carried out to plunder precious objects from ruins. Realization of the importance of the surroundings in which objects are discovered led to more scientific excavation. Essential techniques include stratigraphy, based on the principle that in any sequence of deposits the uppermost is latest and the lowest earliest, and typology, the study of changes in forms (e.g. of pottery). Methods of dating include radiometric dating, palaeomagnetism, thermoluminescence, varve dating, and *dendrochronology.

Archaeopteryx An extinct primitive bird which lived in the Jurassic period (160–120 million years ago). It resembled a reptile in having numerous teeth, a long bony tail, and claws on the hand, but was feathered and is believed to be the ancestor of modern birds. *Archaeopteryx* lived in dense forests, climbing trees using its claws and gliding down in search of food.

Archangel (Russian name: Arkhangelsk) 64 32N 40 40E A port in the NW Soviet Union, in the RSFSR on the River Dvina, 50 km (30 mi) from the White Sea. Founded in 1584, it was Russia's leading port until the early 18th century. The Soviet Union's largest timber-exporting port, it has timber-processing and shipbuilding industries and also supports a fishing fleet. Population (1987): 416 000.

archery A sport in which generally a number of arrows are shot at a target over a certain distance. The modern bow developed from the medieval longbow, but the skill of shooting arrows from a bow dates back to primitive times. **Target archery** consists of shooting at a target of standard size marked with five or ten scoring zones. Different competitions require different distances and numbers of arrows. **Field archery** consists of shooting at large animal figures bearing scoring rings. In **clout shooting** arrows are shot into the air to fall on a target marked on the ground, while in **flight shooting** the purpose is to achieve the maximum distance. Archery is an amateur sport, governed internationally by the Fédération internationale de Tir à l'Arc (founded 1931).

Archimedes (c. 287–c. 212 BC) Greek mathematician and inventor, regarded as the greatest scientist of classical times. Archimedes was born in Syracuse, Sicily, and studied in Alexandria, afterwards returning to Syracuse, where he remained for the rest of his life. He is best known for his discovery of Archimedes' principle, supposedly in response to the King of Syracuse asking him to determine whether a gold crown had been mixed with silver. Legend has it that he made his discovery while taking a bath and ran through the streets of Syracuse shouting "Eureka!" **Archimedes' principle** states that when a body is partly or wholly lowered into in a fluid its apparent loss of weight is equal to the weight of the liquid displaced. He is also credited with the invention of **Archimedes' screw**, a device for raising water consisting of an inclined helical screw rotated about a central axis in a trough of water, although the device was probably already known to the Egyptians. He was killed by a soldier during the Roman invasion of Syracuse.

architecture The art of designing and constructing buildings that are both useful and attractive. Factors principally influencing an architect are: the use to which the building will be put; the materials, money, and labour available; and contemporary artistic taste. The earliest civilizations built on a monumental scale for their gods or the deified dead (*see* pyramids; ziggurat). Secular architecture reflected the needs of local rulers for security, comfort, and–very important –display. The Greeks were the first to develop the concepts of proportion and harmony that still influence western architectural theory. Roman engineers greatly extended flexibility of design by their use of arches and domes. Medieval European architecture reached its peak in the gothic cathedral but the Renaissance revived interest in the principles of classical architecture. This was followed by a gothic revival at the beginning of the 19th century. In the 20th century technical advances in the use of prestressed concrete influenced modern architecture; while the necessities of engineering increasingly determine a building's appearance, the best modern architects demonstrate that architecture can still survive as an art form.

Arctic Circle The area around the North Pole enclosed by the parallel of latitude 66°32'N. It includes parts of Greenland, the Soviet Union, the USA, Canada, and Scandinavia and extensive areas of ice-covered ocean, notably the Arctic Ocean. The population consists mainly of Eskimos, who live by hunting. *History*: during the 16th century exploration of the Arctic by the Dutch and English began in the search for a Northeast or Northwest Passage to the Far East. In 1725–42 the Russian Imperial Navy carried out exploration. In 1879 a US expedition under G. W. De Long (1844–81) became trapped in the ice while attempting to reach the North Pole and its ship was crushed. Wreckage found off the coast of Greenland having drifted across the Arctic Ocean suggested that a sea route through

ARCHITECTURE

the orders of classical architecture

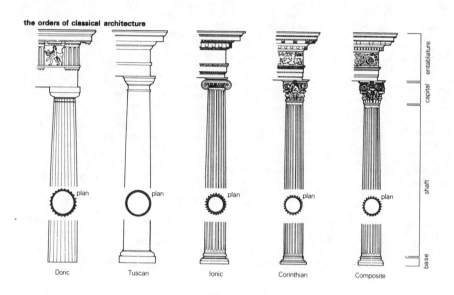

Doric   Tuscan   Ionic   Corinthian   Composite

some terms in classical architecture   **some terms in gothic architecture**

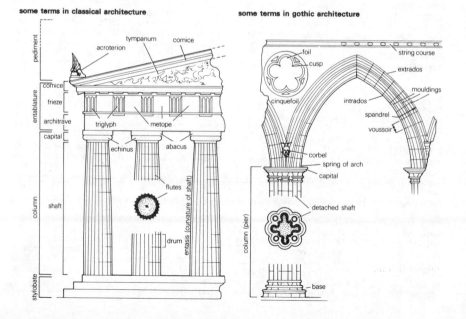

the ice was possible. The Norwegian Fridtjof Nansen in the *Fram* drifted for nearly two years (1893–95) through the ice and proved that the North Pole was within an ice-covered sea. Robert E. Peary was the first to reach the North Pole (1909). Since then extensive mapping and geological and meteorological studies have been carried out; the Soviet Union has been particularly active and, like the USA, has established several drifting scientific stations.

Arctic fox A small fox, *Alopex lagopus*, found throughout tundra regions. It feeds on birds and small mammals, especially lemmings and Arctic hares, and grows a dense woolly coat of fur in winter. There are two varieties: the white fox, which has a white winter coat and a brown summer coat; and the blue fox, which is dark grey in summer and pale grey in winter. Arctic foxes have been farmed commercially for their fur.

Arctic Ocean The world's smallest ocean, almost completely enclosed by North America, Eurasia, and Greenland. Explored since the 17th century, it is covered by ice.

Ardennes A chain of hills in W Europe. It extends through N Luxembourg, S Belgium, and NE France at an average height of about 500 m (1640 ft), separating the Rivers Meuse and Moselle.

are (a) A unit of area in the *metric system equal to 100 square metres. The *hectare is more frequently used than the are.

Ares The Greek god of war, identified by the Romans with *Mars. Son of Zeus and Hera, his popularity never rivalled that of the other Olympian gods. He loved *Aphrodite, by whom he had three offspring, Deimos, Phobos, and Harmonia.

Argentina, Republic of The second largest country in South America. It consists chiefly of subtropical plains and forests (the Gran Chaco) in the N, the fertile temperate pampas in the centre, the Andes in the W, and the semidesert Patagonian plateau in the S. The inhabitants are almost all of European origin, mainly Italian and Spanish, with a very small and dwindling Indian population. *Economy*: chiefly agricultural with stock rearing, especially cattle. The main industries have traditionally been meat processing and packing but there has been recent growth in oil refining, plastics, textiles, and chemicals. Natural-gas deposits have been intensively developed and Argentina is practically self-sufficient in oil. There are plans to increase the use of hydroelectric power and nuclear energy is also being developed. *History*: colonized by the Spanish from 1515 onwards. The country gained its independence in 1816, under José de San Martín, and a new constitution in 1853 marked the end of civil war and unrest. Since the late 19th century Argentina has been ruled mostly by military dictatorships. Most prominent among the rulers since World War II has been Lt Gen Juán *Perón, who came to power in 1946. Following the death (1952) of his popular wife, Eva, he was overthrown in a military revolution (1955). In 1973 he returned to power but died the following year. In 1976 Lt Gen Jorge Rafael Videla (1925–) came to power at the head of a three-man junta

and strong measures were introduced to combat the violence and unrest. Lt Gen Roberto Viola succeeded Videla as president in 1981 but was later removed from office by the military junta, led by Gen Leopoldo Galtieri, who became president in December, 1981. On 2 April, 1982, Argentina launched an invasion of the Falkland Islands but following armed conflict with a task force sent by the UK was forced to surrender on 14 June, 1982; a defeat that forced Galtieri's resignation and later imprisonment. Raúl Alfonsín (1926–) was elected president in 1983 and was succeeded by Carlos Menem in 1989. Official language: Spanish. Official religion: Roman Catholic. Official currency: austral of 100 centavos. Area: 2 777 815 sq km (1 072 515 sq mi). Population (1986 est): 31 060 000. Capital and main port: Buenos Aires.

argon (Ar) A noble gas that occurs in the earth's atmosphere (0.94%). Although previously detected in the sun's atmosphere, it was first isolated in 1894 by Rayleigh and Ramsay, by the distillation of liquid air. Because it is chemically inert, it is used to fill fluorescent lamps and as an inert gas blanket for welding reactive metals. At no 18; at wt 39.948; mp –189.2°C; bp –185.7°C.

Argonauts In Greek mythology, the 50-man crew of Jason's ship *Argo*, on the quest of the *Golden Fleece. It included the shipbuilder Argo, the tireless helmsman Tiphys, the keen-sighted Lynceus, Heracles and his follower Hylas, and even Orpheus and the Dioscuri, Castor and Pollux. During the voyage the Argonauts encountered such perils as the Sirens, the Harpies, the Symplegades (moving rocks that crushed ships) and the bronze giant Talos.

Argos 37 38N 22 43E A town in the NE Peloponnese (S Greece). Belonging in Homeric times to a follower of *Agamemnon, Argos gave its name to the surrounding district (the Argolid). Eclipsed by nearby Sparta after the 6th century BC, Argos remained neutral or the ineffective ally of Athens during the 5th-century struggles between Sparta and Athens. Considerable remains of the city survive.

Ariadne In Greek legend, the daughter of Minos, King of Crete, and Pasiphaë. She helped *Theseus to kill the Minotaur and escape from its labyrinth. He abandoned her on the island of Naxos, where she was found by Dionysus, who married her.

Ariane. See European Space Agency.

Aristarchus of Samos (c. 310–230 BC) Greek astronomer, who maintained that the earth rotates upon its axis and orbits the sun. He made the first attempts to estimate the size and distance from the earth of the sun and the moon.

Aristophanes (c. 450–c. 385 BC) Greek comic dramatist. He wrote about 40 plays, of which 11 survive: *The Acharnians* (425), *The Knights* (424), *The Clouds* (423), *The Wasps* (422), *The Peace* (421), *The Birds* (414), *Lysistrata* (411), *Thesmophoriazusae* (410), *The Frogs* (405), *Women in Parliament* (393), and *Plutus* (388). His plots were satirical fantasies on contemporary topics.

Aristotle (384–322 BC) Greek philosopher and scientist. His father was court physician in Macedonia. Aristotle joined *Plato's Academy at Athens (367–347) but, failing to become head of the Academy at Plato's death, he accepted the protection of Hermeias, ruler of Atarneus in Asia Minor, and married his patron's niece. About 343 Philip of Macedon appointed Aristotle tutor to his son Alexander, then aged 13. After Alexander came to power in 336, Aristotle founded the *Lyceum at Athens (a research community with library and museum). When Alexander died in 323 BC, anti-Macedonian reaction forced Aristotle to withdraw to Chalcis, where he died. Aristotle wrote over 400 books; those that survive (about one-quarter), edited by Andronicus of Rhodes about 40 BC, are apparently notes for his students' use, not intended for general publication.

arithmetic The branch of mathematics that deals with numbers, measurement, and calculation. The fundamental operations of arithmetic are addition, subtraction, multiplication, and division. Other operations include finding square and cube roots, raising a number to a power, and taking logarithms. Arithmetic is also concerned with fractions and the various number systems, such as the decimal system and the binary system.

arithmetic progression (*or* arithmetic sequence) An ordered collection of numbers in which successive terms have a constant difference, for example, 1, 4, 7, 10, 13 . . . .

Arizona A state in the SW USA. It falls into two natural regions: in the NE lies part of the Colorado Plateau, an area of dry plains and ridges, and in the S and W is an area of desert basins and gentle valleys, drained by the Gila and Salt Rivers. The Colorado River flows through the Grand Canyon in the NW of the state. Inadequate water supplies have long been a problem and a number of major irrigation projects have been built. Most of the population lives in towns in the S and W. Manufacturing (electrical, communications, aeronautical, and aluminium products) is the major industry. The state produces over half of the USA's copper as well as gold, silver, oil, and timber. Tourism is an important source of revenue. The main crops are cotton, vegetables, and citrus fruits; livestock is also important. It has the largest Indian population in the USA; the main tribes are the Navajo, Hopi, and Apache. *History*: inhabited by Indians as early as 25 000 BC, the area was explored by the Spanish in the 16th century. Following the Mexican War, Arizona, then part of New Mexico, was handed over to the USA (1848). It was swept by Apache wars until 1877 and became a state in 1912. Area: 295 023 sq km (113 909 sq mi). Population (1987 est): 3 469 000. Capital: Phoenix.

Arkansas A state in the S central USA, lying W of the Mississippi River. It consists chiefly of the largely forested uplands of the N and W, descending to the Mississippi alluvial plain in the E and the West Gulf coastal plain in the S. The **Arkansas River** (2335 km; 1450 mi) bisects the state from W to E. The state is no longer primari-

ly agricultural although the Mississippi Plain provides fertile land; soya beans and rice have replaced cotton as the major crop. There are major lumbering, petroleum, and gas developments around Smackover and El Dorado and coal deposits in the Arkansas River Valley. The state produces 90% of US bauxite. Manufactures include electronic equipment and wood products. *History*: explored by the Spanish and French in the 16th and 17th centuries, it formed part of the Louisiana Purchase by the USA in 1803. It became a state in 1836, withdrew from the Union in 1861, and was readmitted in 1868. Area: 137 539 sq km (53 104 sq mi). Population (1986 est): 2 372 000. Capital: Little Rock.

Arkwright, Sir Richard (1732–92) British inventor and industrialist, who invented a spinning frame powered by water, the so-called water frame (patented in 1769). Arkwright subsequently mechanized other spinning processes and his mills were vandalized by spinners put out of work by the new factory system.

Armada, Spanish The fleet of 130 ships sent by Philip II of Spain in 1588 to invade England. After indecisive encounters with the English fleet led by Howard of Effingham, under whom Sir John Hawkins held command, the Armada anchored off Calais only to be scattered by English fireships during the night of 28 July. A major battle off Gravelines followed, in which the Armada was defeated. It suffered further losses in storms as it escaped round Scotland and Ireland, arriving in Spain with 86 ships. The defeat was a major blow to Spain, which had claimed divine authority for its crusade against Protestant England. The battle is also remembered for the famous incident in which Sir Francis *Drake is traditionally supposed to have refused to set sail until he had finished the game of bowls he was playing at Plymouth Hoe.

armadillo A mammal that lives in open country in the southern USA and South America. Armadillos have a covering of jointed bands or horny plates that enables them to roll themselves into a ball for protection. They have long-clawed toes for burrowing, simple peglike teeth, and feed on insects and other invertebrates. Armadillos range in size from the giant armadillo (*Priodontes giganteus*), about 120 cm long, to the rare pink fairy armadillo (*Chlamyphorus truncatus*), 12 cm long.

Armenian Soviet Socialist Republic A densely populated and mountainous republic in the S Soviet Union. Industry includes food processing, metallurgy, and chemicals. The rich mineral deposits include copper, lead, and zinc. The raising of livestock is the chief agricultural activity. *History*: the region formed the E part of the historic area inhabited by the Armenians, a people with an ancient culture, language, and literature of their own. It was acquired by Russia in 1828. The Russian province declared its independence in 1918 but it subsequently formed part of the Transcaucasian Soviet Federated Republic. It became a separate republic in 1936. In 1988 an earthquake killed 25 000 people. There have also been violent ethnic disturbances over the disputed *Nagorno-Karabakh territory. Area: 29 800 sq km (11 490 sq mi). Population (1988): 3 360 000. Capital: Yerevan.

armour Defensive equipment used as a protection in warfare. Body armour (helmet, breast-

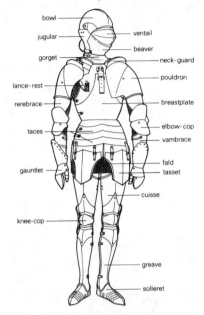

bowl
jugular
gorget
lance-rest
rerebrace
taces
gauntlet
knee-cop
ventail
beaver
neck-guard
pouldron
breastplate
elbow-cop
vambrace
fald
tasset
cuisse
greave
solleret

ARMOUR *The skill of the European armourer reached its height in the late 15th and early 16th centuries, when suits of plate armour were made to cover the entire body.*

plate, greaves) was used in Bronze Age Greece. The Romans used heavier armour for both men and horses. In the early Middle Ages chainmail was widely used but after about 1300 plate armour, often magnificently decorated and encasing the whole body, was worn by knights on horseback. With the use of *gunpowder, body armour was gradually discarded, although in World War I metal helmets were revived as a protection from shrapnel.

Armstrong, Louis (1900–71) US Black jazz trumpeter and singer, known as "Satchmo." Born in New Orleans, he learned to play the cornet in his youth. His career took him to Chicago, where he made many recordings (some of them with Earl Hines), which earned him a worldwide reputation.

Armstrong, Neil Alden (1930–) US astronaut, the first man to walk on the moon. A navy pilot during the Korean War, he worked for NASA, (1955–71) and became an astronaut in 1962. He was commander of Apollo 11 (1969). As he stepped onto the moon he said "That's one small step for a man, one giant leap for mankind."

Arnhem 52 00N 5 53E A city in the E Netherlands, the capital of Gelderland province. In World War II a large airborne landing of British

troops attempted to secure a bridgehead over the River Rhine here to enable the Allies to invade Germany. The attempt failed with heavy casualties in the ensuing battle (17–27 September, 1944). A railway junction, its industries include engineering and pharmaceuticals. Population (1987): 127 671.

Arno, River A river in central Italy. Rising in the Apennines, it flows mainly W through Florence and Pisa to the Ligurian Sea. It burst its banks in 1966 causing disastrous floods in Florence. Length: 240 km (150 mi).

Arnold, Thomas (1795–1842) British educator. Appointed headmaster of Rugby (1828), Arnold reformed the school and launched the prefectorial system, which came to characterize English public schools. Arnold's piety was infectious, and Rugby became noted for "muscular Christianity." *Tom Brown's Schooldays* provides a record of Arnold's achievement. His son **Matthew Arnold** (1822–88) was a poet and critic. He worked as a government inspector of schools from 1851 to 1886. His critical works include *Essays in Criticism* (1865; 1888) and *Culture and Anarchy* (1869).

aromatic compound A type of cyclic organic compound that includes *benzene and compounds obtained from benzene. Aromatic compounds contain a ring structure and are thus fairly stable, tending to undergo substitution reactions rather than addition reactions. The explanation for the stability of the benzene ring lies in a model in which the carbon atoms are joined by single bonds and the extra six valence electrons are free to move around the ring in a delocalized orbital. Aromatic compounds were originally distinguished from *aliphatic compounds because of the distinctive properties of benzene compounds, many of which have a fragrant odour.

Arp, Jean (Hans) (1887–1966) French sculptor and poet. He was one of the founders of the dada movement (1916) and later associated with the surrealist movement in Paris. Arp experimented with arrangements of torn coloured papers, designed according to chance, and produced numerous painted wood reliefs.

arquebus. *See* musket.

arrest The forcible detention of a person to enforce obedience to the law. In England, a person may be arrested on a magistrate's warrant to answer to a criminal charge, or for a civil offence, such as contempt of court. He may also be arrested if he commits, or is clearly about to commit, a crime. In theory any citizen can make an arrest and is bound to do so if a felony or breach of the peace is committed in his presence, but in practice most valid arrests are made by the police or other law-enforcement officers, who can make arrests without warrants.

arrowroot A plant, *Maranta arundinacea*, native to Guyana but widely cultivated in the West Indies for the fine starch that is extracted from its underground fleshy tubers and used in cooking. The plant is about 1.5 m high and has short-stalked white flowers and broad-bladed leaves with long narrow sheaths.

Arrow War. See Opium Wars.

arsenic (As) A brittle metal-like element that occurs in nature in a variety of forms: as the element itself, as the sulphides realgar (As_2S_2) and orpiment (As_2S_3), as sulpharsenides, such as arsenopyrite (FeSAs), and as arsenates. The element occurs in several forms and was known to the ancients. Arsenic has important uses in the semiconductor industry. Arsenic and its common compounds are extremely poisonous. Compounds include the white oxide (As_2O_3), the gaseous hydride arsine (AsH_3), and arsenates, some of which are used as insecticides. At no 33; at wt 74.9216; mp 817°C (28 atm); sublimes 613°C.

arson At common law, maliciously setting fire to something, including buildings, vehicles, etc. As a distinct offence, arson was replaced in English law by the Criminal Damage Act (1971), which covers all types of criminal damage (the destruction or damage of property belonging to another). Criminal damage committed by fire is still, however, charged as arson.

Art Deco The style of design predominant in the decorative arts of the 1920s and 1930s. The name derives from the 1925 Exposition Internationale des Arts Décoratifs in Paris. In deliberate contrast to *Art Nouveau, Art Deco was characterized by emphatic geometrical lines and shapes, vibrant colour schemes, and the use of man-made substances, such as plastic. Influenced by the Bauhaus, Art Deco was practised by René Lalique (1860–1945) and Romaine de Tirtoff Erté (1892–), among others. It was debased by shoddy mass production, but interest in it rekindled late in the 1960s.

Artemis In Greek mythology, the daughter of Zeus and Leto and twin sister of Apollo. Settled in *Arcadia, she and her band of Oceanids and nymphs spent their time hunting. Artemis banned love and punished all who disobeyed. *Actaeon was killed for watching her bathe and *Orion for touching her. Despite this severity she was protectress of both animal and human young. Ephesus was the most famous centre of her worship. She was associated with the moon and identified by the Romans with *Diana.

Artemis, Temple of One of the Seven Wonders of the World, built at Ephesus in 356 BC. The deity worshipped here was the many-breasted fertility goddess called Diana of the Ephesians in Acts 19.28, rather than the classical *Artemis.

arteriosclerosis The loss of elasticity in the walls of arteries. It is also a synonym for *atherosclerosis.

artery A thick-walled blood vessel that carries oxygen-rich blood away from the *heart to supply all the tissues and organs of the body. The largest is the aorta, which leads directly from the heart and descends into the abdomen, giving rise to all the other arteries of the body. In middle age the lining of the arteries commonly becomes thickened by *atherosclerosis.

artesian well A well sunk into an aquifer (a water-saturated rock layer) that is confined between two layers of impermeable rock. Water flows upwards through the well under pressure. The aquifer reaches the surface and receives rainfall where the water table is higher than the site of the well, resulting in the required head of pressure.

arthritis Inflammation of one or more joints, causing pain, swelling, and restriction of movement. Many different diseases can cause arthritis, the most important of which are *osteoarthritis, rheumatoid arthritis, and *gout. **Rheumatoid arthritis**, which is more common in women, usually affects the hands and feet and often also the hips, knees, and shoulders. The membrane lining the joint becomes inflamed, resulting in damage to the cartilage over the joint with consequent pain and deformity. It is diagnosed by a blood test (the blood contains the rheumatoid factor) and X-rays. Treatment usually includes pain-relieving and anti-inflammatory drugs; some patients benefit from gold salts and steroids, while severe cases may require surgical replacement of the affected joint(s).

arthropod An invertebrate animal of which there are about a million species (i.e. 75% of all known species). There are about 12 classes, the most important of which are *arachnids, *crustaceans, *insects, *centipedes, and *millipedes. An arthropod's body is divided into segments and is covered with a hard outer skeleton (cuticle) that is shed periodically to allow the body to grow. Jointed legs and other appendages are used for swimming, walking, feeding, respiration, reproduction, etc. Young arthropods often go through *metamorphosis to reach the adult form. Many are harmful—as pests, parasites, or carriers of disease—but others are beneficial to man, as pollinators of plants, food sources, predators of pests, and decomposers of organic wastes.

Arthurian legend The medieval stories and poems concerning the legendary British king Arthur and his knights. Arthur first appears in the *Historia Regum Britanniae* of Geoffrey of Monmouth. In the legend, he is the son of Uther Pendragon, was born at Tintagel in Cornwall, became king of Britain at 15, and won a number of famous victories. He married Guinevere and held court at Caerleon in Wales (or, in some versions, at Camelot, which may have been near South Cadbury, Somerset). Involved in a war at Rome, he left his kingdom in the charge of his nephew Modred, who betrayed him and abducted Guinevere. Arthur returned to Britain and defeated Modred but was himself wounded. He was taken to the Isle of Avalon (the Celtic paradise, associated with Glastonbury) to be healed. Succeeding writers added new episodes: the Anglo-Norman poet Wace (c. 1100–c. 1175) introduced the knights of the Round Table, Layamon (early 13th century) added magical elements, and Chrétien de Troyes focused on the quest of the *Holy Grail. Other characters were the magician Merlin and the sorceress Morgan le Fay (Arthur's sister). Sir Thomas Malory's *Morte d'Arthur* (c. 1470) was the culmination of the medieval tradition, although Tennyson's *Idylls of the King* (from 1842) and T. H. White's *The Once and Future King* (1958) are later versions.

artichoke A thistle-like plant, *Cynara scolemus*, of the daisy family, also known as globe artichoke, native to central and W Mediterranean regions and widely grown in warm temperate areas for its nutty-tasting immature flower heads. The hairy indented straplike leaves, 1 m long, arise each year from the base of the short stems, which bear purplish flowers. *See also* Jerusalem artichoke.

Articles of Confederation The first constitution of the USA (written 1776–77, adopted 1781), which was replaced by the Constitution of 1789. The leaders of the American Revolution feared the abuses of a strong central government and adopted a federal system that guaranteed each state its "sovereignty, freedom, and independence." The *Continental Congress could not collect taxes but could wage war and borrow and issue money.

artificial insemination The artificial introduction of semen into the vagina of a female at or shortly after ovulation. Although practised in the 14th century by Arab horse breeders, the techniques were developed largely for livestock in the Soviet Union during the early 20th century. Semen collected from a single male can be stored at low temperatures for months before being used to fertilize many females. This has resulted in dramatic breed improvements and the control of venereal disease. Artificial insemination is also used in human medicine; for an infertile husband, semen is obtained from an anonymous donor (artificial insemination donor–AID). Semen may be provided by the husband in cases of impotence (artificial insemination husband–AIH). When the wife is infertile the husband's semen may be used to artificially inseminate a surrogate mother. This woman gives birth to the child and must then be prepared to give up all claims on it to the natural father and his wife. In 1985 commercial surrogacy became illegal in the UK. *See also* test-tube baby.

artificial intelligence (AI) The design of computer programs to perform tasks that involve intelligence when carried out by human beings. Tasks performed by AI include playing games like chess, understanding language and speech, making plans, proving theorems, and detecting objects.

artificial kidney. *See* dialysis.

artillery *Firearms with a calibre (internal diameter) in excess of 20 mm, used to bombard enemy positions, provide cover, etc. Early guns were classed by weight of the projectile fired, e.g. 12-pounder. Modern weapons are identified by calibre: light (below 120 mm), medium (121–160 mm), heavy (161–210 mm), and super or very heavy (above 211 mm). Gun projectiles have flat trajectories (flight paths), while mortars and howitzers have high trajectories, with correspondingly short ranges. Artillery rockets deliver more explosive further, without needing heavy launchers. Modern electronic equipment enables artillery fire to score a direct hit with near certainty on any visible target; as guns may be targets artillery is now usually remote controlled.

Art Nouveau A decorative style of art occurring in Europe and America in the 1890s and early 1900s. It is characterized by designs of foliage and shapes linked by wavy lines. In Britain it is associated with the *Arts and Crafts movement of William *Morris, the designs of Charles Rennie Mackintosh (1868–1928), and the graphic work of Aubrey *Beardsley. On the Continent leading examples are the Parisian metro designs of Hector Guimard (1867–1942), the extravagant Barcelona flats and hotels of Antonio Gaudi (1852–1926), and the Belgian stores and houses of Victor Horta (1861–1947).

Arts and Crafts movement An English 19th-century aesthetic movement derived from William *Morris and his Pre-Raphaelite associates, whose firm was founded (1861) to produce handmade furnishings. The movement revived the principles of medieval craftsmanship and respect for materials. It culminated in the establishment of the Century Guild for Craftsmen (1882) and the Arts and Crafts Exhibition Society (1888). It helped to create the emerging *Art Nouveau style.

arum (*or* arum lily) A tropical African plant, *Zantedeschia aethiopica*, widely grown for its flowers. It has arrow-shaped leaves and each "flower" consists of a cone of tiny yellow flowers surrounded by a white funnel-shaped petal-like part called a spathe. The related bog arum, or wild calla (*Calla palustris*), grows in swamps of N temperate and subarctic regions. It has heart-shaped leaves and small flowers enveloped in a white spathe.

Arundel 50 51N 0 34W A market town in SE England, in West Sussex on the River Arun. Its 11th-century castle (mainly rebuilt in the 19th century) is the seat of the Dukes of Norfolk. Other notable buildings include the 19th-century Roman Catholic cathedral. Population (1981): 2235.

Aryans Peoples speaking Indo-European, Indo-Iranian, or Indo-Aryan languages. It has been claimed that all the Indo-European peoples originated from an Aryan people who spread out from a common homeland into Europe and N India. Indo-Aryan-speaking peoples certainly invaded and settled in N India between 2000 BC and 1000 BC. They were tribal herdsmen who later became farmers. The earliest literature of India, the Vedas, written in *Sanskrit, contains hymns, spells, and details of Aryan rituals.

ASA rating The American Standards Association measure of the sensitivity or speed of photographic *film. A film rated at 200 is twice as fast (i.e. needs half the exposure time) as 100 ASA film. General-purpose films have speeds between 50 and 160 ASA. High-speed films for indoor photography and poor light are rated between 200 and 1000 ASA.

asbestos A fibrous form of certain silicate minerals, including serpentine and, in particular, some of the *amphiboles. Asbestos is heat-resistant, chemically inert, and has a high electrical resistance; it has therefore a wide industrial application. The fibres are spun and woven or made into blocks. The main producers are Canada, the Soviet Union, and Brazil. **Asbestosis** is a disease caused by breathing air contaminated with asbestos fibres. It affects the air sacs of the lungs, which become thickened and scarred, causing breathlessness: patients are liable to develop lung cancer and the use of asbestos is now discouraged except in controlled circumstances.

Ascension 7 57S 14 22W A rocky island in the S Atlantic Ocean, a dependency of St Helena. It has little vegetation and was uninhabited until 1815. A British telecommunications centre, it is also a US air base and space research station. Area: 88 sq km (35 sq mi). Population (1985): 1708. Chief settlement: Georgetown.

Ascension In the Christian calendar, the day on which it is believed Christ ascended into Heaven. Since the 4th century it has been celebrated 40 days after Easter.

Asclepius (or Aesculapius) In Greek mythology, a son of *Apollo and the god of medicine. He was instructed by the centaur *Chiron in hunting and medicine. When he restored Hippolytus to life as a favour to Artemis, Zeus became angry and struck him dead with a thunderbolt. The sick, believing in Asclepius' power to cure them through dreams, came to sleep in his temples, the chief of which were at Epidaurus and on the island of Cos.

ascorbic acid. See vitamin C.

Ascot 51 25N 0 41W A village in S England, in Berkshire. The construction of its famous racecourse was ordered by Queen Anne in 1711. Traditionally the sovereign opens the Royal Ascot meeting in June. Population (1983 est): 13 234, with Sunningdale.

ASDIC. See echo sounding.

ash A tree of the olive family, native to the N hemisphere. Many species yield a pale-yellow wood of commercial importance and others are widely grown in parks, streets, etc. Reaching a height of 30 m, ashes have leaves made up of pairs of oval or lance-shaped leaflets, small inconspicuous flowers, and winged fruits ("ash keys"). Most species are deciduous, including the European ash (Fraxinus excelsior). See also mountain ash.

Ashcroft, Dame Peggy (1907–) British actress. She made her debut at the Birmingham Repertory Theatre in 1926. Her most notable performances include Juliet in 1935, Hedda Gabler in 1954, and more recent roles in plays by Pinter and Beckett. She won an Oscar for her performance in the film A Passage to India (1984).

Ashdown, Paddy (Jeremy John Dunham) (1941–) British politician, leader of the Social and Liberal Democratic Party (1988–). He entered parliament in 1983 after service in the Commandos and the Special Boat Section. A former diplomat, he succeeded David Steel as leader of the party.

Ashes A mock trophy awarded to the winning team in cricket Test matches between England and Australia. It began with the first Australian victory (1882), when an obituary for English cricket in the Sporting Times ended with the words: "The body will be cremated and the ashes taken to Australia." In 1883 the victorious English captain was presented with an urn (now kept

in the pavilion at *Lord's cricket ground) containing the ashes of the stumps used in the match.

Ashkenazim Jews of German or Eastern European origin, as opposed to *Sephardim. They have a distinct tradition of pronouncing Hebrew, as well as other customs, and until this century they mostly spoke Yiddish. The first Ashkenazy synagogue in London was founded in 1690.

Ashmolean Museum A museum in Oxford, housing paintings and archaeological collections. The collection was donated to Oxford University in 1675 by Elias Ashmole (1617–92) and put on public display in 1683. Now in the neoclassical building (1845) of Charles Robert Cockerell (1788–1863), it includes Italian Renaissance paintings and English 19th-century works.

Ashton, Sir Frederick (William Mallandaine) (1904–88) British ballet dancer and choreographer, born in Ecuador. He joined the Sadler's Wells Ballet in 1935, became an associate director in 1952, and was director of the Royal Ballet from 1963 to 1970. His works included Cinderella (1948), Ondine (1958), La Fille mal gardée (1960), and many ballets choreographed for Margot Fonteyn.

Ashur The oldest Assyrian capital (modern Qalat Sharqat) on the River Tigris in Iraq. Named after its guardian sun-god, Ashur became capital of the rising *Assyrian empire (14th century BC) to which it gave its name. With its later cocapitals *Nimrud and *Nineveh it was destroyed in 612 BC. First excavated in 1903, Ashur's ruins include major temples and a *ziggurat.

Ash Wednesday In the Christian calendar, the first day of *Lent, which is so named from the custom, probably dating from the 8th century, of marking the foreheads of the congregation with ashes as a sign of penitence.

Asia The largest continent in the world, it occupies about one-third of the dry land. Extending W to the Ural Mountains, it is separated from the continent of Africa by the Red Sea and bounded on the N by the Arctic Ocean. It includes the islands of Indonesia, Japan, the Philippines, and Taiwan. It contains the world's highest point (Mount *Everest) and also its lowest (the *Dead Sea). Its great central mass of mountains and plateaus has historically formed a major barrier between N and S Asia. Vast alluvial plains border the major rivers, including the Rivers Ganges, Mekong, and Ob and the Yangtze and Yellow Rivers. It contains about half of the world's total population. There are three main population groups: Negroid (in the Philippines), Mongoloid (including the Chinese, Japanese, and Koreans), and Caucasoid (including the Arabs, Afghans, and Pakistanis). All the world's major religions originated in Asia, only Christianity and Judaism spreading W to any great extent. Others include Hinduism (with the largest following), Buddhism, Islam, Confucianism (in China), and Shintoism (in Japan). Agriculture is the chief occupation, employing about two-thirds of the total population. Asia also has important mineral resources, notably the oil and natural-gas deposits of the Arab states. Area: 44 391 162 sq km (17 139 445 sq mi). Population (1984): 2 778 000 000.

Asia Minor (*or* Anatolia) The westernmost part of Asia between the Black Sea and the Mediterranean Sea, now mostly occupied by Turkey. Between 2000 BC and 1000 BC, Asia Minor was the centre of the *Hittite empire. After the Hittites' collapse (12th century BC) central and W Asia Minor were dominated by Phrygia, which was most powerful in the 8th century, when the Assyrian Empire conquered SE Asia Minor. Phrygia fell to Lydia in the 6th century but in 546 Cyrus the Great established Achaemenian control over Asia Minor. In 333 it was conquered by Alexander the Great and after his death, during the *Hellenistic age, the S was fought over by the Seleucids and the Ptolemies. Asia Minor came under Roman control in the 2nd and 1st centuries BC, forming part of the *Roman Empire and then the *Eastern Roman (subsequently Byzantine) Empire. Conquered by the Seljuq Turks in the 11th century AD and overrun by the Mongols in the 13th, Asia Minor became part of the Ottoman Empire during the 14th and 15th centuries.

asp An aggressive European *viper, *Vipera aspis*, that lives in dry habitats. About 60 cm long, it is grey-brown to coppery brown with dark bars or zigzags, grey, yellowish, or blackish underparts, and a yellow patch under the tail tip. The snout is upturned into a small spike. The asp that killed Cleopatra was probably the Egyptian cobra (*Naja haje*).

asparagus A plant of the lily family that is widely cultivated in temperate and subtropical regions for its young edible shoots, which are cooked and eaten as a luxury vegetable. Several African species are ornamental, including the **asparagus fern**, which produces attractive feathery sprays of branchlets and is a popular house plant.

aspen A poplar tree having slender flattened leafstalks, so that the leaves tremble in the faintest breeze. The European aspen (*Populus tremula*), which grows to a height of 25 m, has rounded toothed leaves. Its soft white wood is used for matches and paper pulp.

asphalt A black highly sticky or solid *hydrocarbon compound, used in road construction and the manufacture of roofing materials. It is obtained from the distillation of certain crude oils and from surface deposits (asphalt lakes), which occur naturally after the lighter components of a crude oil reservoir have evaporated.

asphodel A Mediterranean lily-like plant with white or yellow flowers. In Greek mythology, the asphodel said to grow in the Elysian fields was *Asphodeline lutea*, which has yellow flowers. The asphodel of the early English and French poets was probably the daffodil. The bog asphodel (*Narthecium ossifragum*), of NW Europe, grows in swampy regions. It grows to a height of 30 cm and has a head of small yellow flowers.

aspidistra A plant of the lily family, native to E Asia but commonly grown as a hardy pot plant for its long ornamental leaves. It may occasionally produce small purple bell-shaped flowers.

aspirin Acetylsalicylic acid: a drug widely used to treat mild pain, such as headache and toothache. It also relieves inflammation and is therefore helpful in the treatment of rheumatoid arthritis, and it reduces fever. Aspirin may also be used in the treatment of heart-attack victims. In some people aspirin may cause bleeding from the stomach and it is no longer used for children. *See also* analgesics.

Asquith, Herbert Henry, 1st Earl of Oxford and (1852–1928) British statesman and Liberal prime minister (1908–16). Asquith's government introduced important social reforms, including noncontributory old-age pensions (1908 budget) and the National Insurance Act (1911); it ended the veto power of the House of Lords with the 1911 Parliament Act. After the outbreak of World War I Asquith headed a Liberal-Conservative government (1915–16). He remained leader of the Liberal Party until 1926. His second wife **Margot Asquith** (1865–1945) wrote an outspoken *Autobiography* (1922). His children by his first marriage included **Lady Violet Bonham-Carter, Baroness Asquith** (1887–1969), who was president of the Liberal Party Organization (1944–45).

ass A small fast-running mammal related to the horse and native to Africa and Asia. Asses are about 200 cm long, weighing up to 250 kg, and have characteristically long ears. The Asiatic wild ass (*Equus hemionus*) has a grey or tan hide, a dark bristly mane, and a dark stripe along the back. The African wild ass (*E. asinus*) is the ancestor of the domestic donkey. *See also* mule.

Assad, Hafiz al- (1928–) Syrian statesman; president (1971–). In 1966, following the coup in Syria by the radical Ba'athists, he became minister of defence. In 1970 he led a coup by the military wing of the *Ba'ath party and was elected president the following year.

Assassins (Arabic: hashish eaters) A sect of the Ismaili. In Persia and Syria in the 12th and 13th centuries they were notorious for their practice of stabbing opponents, especially Muslims. It was commonly believed that the stabbings were carried out while they were under the influence of the drug hashish, hence their name.

Assisi 43 04N 12 37E A town in central Italy, in Umbria. It is the birthplace of St *Francis of Assisi, who founded the Franciscan Order in 1209, and is the site of a Franciscan convent, which has two gothic churches containing frescoes by Giotto. Population (1989 est): 24 567.

Assyrian Empire An ancient kingdom on the Upper Tigris (now N Iraq), where the Assyrians (named after their god Ashur) settled in about 2500 BC, coming under the influence of Babylon. Ashur-uballit I (c. 1365–c. 1330) laid the foundations of the Empire, which was extended by Tiglath-pileser I (1120–1074), who conquered the city of Babylon. A new era of conquest was begun by Ashurnasirpal II (883–859). The Assyrian Empire was extended to Syria and Palestine under Shalmaneser III (858–824) and Assyrian power reached its height under Tiglath-pileser III (745–727). Nineveh, the capital, fell to Media and Babylon in 612.

Astaire, Fred (Frederick Austerlitz; 1899–1987) US dancer and film star. He began his career as a music-hall dancer. His best-known films are the 1930s musicals in which he partnered Ginger Rogers. These include *Top Hat* (1935), *Follow the Fleet* (1936), and *Shall We Dance* (1937). His later costars included Judy Garland, Leslie Caron, and Audrey Hepburn.

astatine (At) A short-lived radioactive *halogen. Its longest-lived isotope, ^{210}At, has a half-life of 8.3 hours. Small amounts exist in nature as a result of the radioactive decay of uranium and thorium. At no 85; at wt (210); mp 302°C; bp 337°C.

aster A flowering plant of the daisy family, native to N temperate regions and widely grown as garden plants. Usually 60–100 cm tall, they have flowers with blue, red, or white rays and a central yellow disc. Michaelmas daisies, with small purple flowers, are also types of aster.

asteroid. *See* minor planet.

asthma A disorder in which breathlessness and wheezing are aggravated by certain stimuli, which cause the air passages (bronchi) to become constricted. Bronchial asthma may be an allergic reaction (*see* allergy), it may occur as a result of a chest infection, or it may be brought on by exertion, certain drugs, or strong emotion. The most common treatment is by means of drugs that relax and widen the air passages, usually in the form of aerosol inhalers.

astigmatism A form of *aberration that can occur in mirrors and lenses (including the eye). It results when the curvature is different in two mutually perpendicular planes; rays in one plane may then be in focus while rays in the other are out of focus. It is corrected in the eye by the use of cylindrical lenses.

Astor, Nancy Witcher, Viscountess (1879–1964) British politician, who was the first woman MP to sit in the House of Commons (1919–45). An American by birth, she championed the causes of women's rights and education, representing the constituency that was formerly that of her husband **Waldorf, 2nd Viscount Astor** (1879–1952). An MP from 1910 to 1919, Astor was owner (1919–45) of the *Observer* newspaper.

Astrakhan 46 22N 48 04E A port in the Soviet Union, in the SE RSFSR on the River Volga. The city was an important trading centre, declining after the Revolution. Astrakhan fur, from the Karakul lamb of central Asia, was first brought to Russia by Astrakhan traders. More than half the population is employed in fishing or allied occupations. Population (1987): 509 000.

astrology The study of the positions of the heavenly bodies and their presumed influence upon human affairs. Astrology developed in *Babylonia and then passed to Greece, India, China, and the Islamic lands. In medieval Europe astrologers had a respected role in public and personal life. The two branches of astrology are "natural" (concerned mainly with observations and theory) and "judicial" (foretelling events by means of a horoscope).

astronomer royal An eminent British astronomer appointed by the sovereign on the advice of the prime minister. Until 1971 the astronomer royal was also head of the Royal Observatory (formerly at Greenwich now at Herstmonceux). The first holder was John Flamsteed appointed in 1675, when the Observatory was founded. The present holder is Prof. Arnold Wolfendale.

astronomical unit (AU) A unit of length equal to the mean distance between the earth and the sun (1.495 × 10^{11} metres, 92.9 × 10^6 miles).

astronomy The study of celestial bodies. One of the most ancient of the sciences, naked-eye astronomy flourished in China, Babylonia, Egypt, and classical Greece (*see* Aristarchus of Samos; Ptolemaic system).

After ancient Greek culture declined interest in astronomy was the preserve of the Arabs for many centuries. European interest in the heavens, transmitted from the Arabs through Spain, reawakened in the 16th century with the work of *Copernicus and Tycho *Brahe, who were able to separate the science of astronomy from *astrology. But it was not until 1609 that Galileo's refracting *telescope enabled the sky to be investigated in any detail; in 1671 Newton devised the more effective reflecting telescope. These devices provided the means for measuring the positions of planets, stars, etc., more accurately and for studying their motion. In the 19th century, the use of spectroscopy (*see* spectrum) provided the basis for the new sciences of *astrophysics and astrochemistry.

Until the 1930s all observations of the heavens were made by observing the light that passed through the earth's atmosphere. Jansky's discovery (1932) that radio waves are emitted by celestial bodies marked the beginnings of *radio astronomy.

The advent of high-altitude balloons and rockets and then artificial satellites orbiting above the atmosphere has revolutionized astronomy. Carrying special detecting equipment they have enabled the radiation from space that is absorbed by the atmosphere—gamma rays, X-rays, ultraviolet, and most wavelengths of infrared radiation—to provide information, for example, on the birth of stars and the more violent cosmic phenomena. In addition planetary probes, such as the two *Voyager craft, have greatly increased our knowledge of many members of the solar system.

astrophysics The study of the physical and chemical processes and characteristics associated with celestial objects. It is based on theories developed in astronomy, physics, and chemistry and on observations of the radiation emitted by the objects. Originally only studies at optical and then at radio and infrared wavelengths were made, but with the recent advent of rockets and artificial satellites, sources of X-rays, gamma rays, and ultraviolet radiation can also be observed. *See also* cosmology.

Asunción 25 15S 57 40W The capital of Paraguay, an important port in the S on the River Paraguay. Founded in 1536, it was for a time the centre of the Spanish settlements in the area. The National University was founded in 1890 and the Catholic University in 1960. Industries include flour milling, food processing, and textiles. Population (1984): 729 307.

Aswan (*or* Assuan; Greek name: Syene) 24 05N 32 56E A city in S Egypt, on the River Nile. Some ruins of the ancient city of Syene remain. The **Aswan High Dam** and earlier **Aswan Dam** are nearby. The High Dam was begun in 1960 and financed by the Soviet Union; it was completed in 1970. It is about 5 km (3 mi) long and 100 m (328 ft) high; its reservoir, Lake Nasser, extends for about 560 km (350 mi) behind the dam. Since its construction the famous annual Nile floods have been controlled and water is available for irrigation and for hydroelectric power. About 7 km (4 mi) downstream is the Aswan Dam (completed 1902); 2 km (1.2 mi) long and 54 m (177 ft) high, this provides irrigation water. Population (1986 est): 195 700.

Asyut (*or* Assiut; ancient name: Lycopolis) 27 14N 31 11E The largest city in Upper Egypt, on the River Nile. It is an important commercial centre and is renowned for its handicrafts and its textile industries. Below the city the Asyut barrage provides water for irrigation. It has a university (1957). Population (1986 est): 291 300.

Atalanta A swift-footed huntress of Greek mythology. Hippomenes (or Meilanion), on her promise to marry any man who could outrun her, raced with her. Given three of the Hesperides' golden apples by *Aphrodite, which he dropped to distract her, he won the race and married her.

Atatürk, Kemal (Mustafa Kemal; 1881–1938) Turkish statesman, who was the chief founder of modern Turkey; president (1923–38). Born in Salonika, he entered the army and distinguished himself in World War I. After the war he opposed the Treaty of Versailles and as president of the provisional government organized the defeat of the Greek invasion of Asia Minor (1920). In 1922 the Ottoman sultan was overthrown and Mustafa Kemal became the first president of Turkey. From then until his death he worked to make Turkey a modern state independent of the church. He took the surname Atatürk (Father of the Turks) in 1934.

Athelney, Isle of A small area in Somerset, at the point where the Rivers Tone and Parrett join. It was formerly an island, isolated by marshes. Alfred the Great built a small fortification here in 878 as a base for his campaign against the Danes.

Athelstan (d. 939) King of England (925–39), succeeding his father Edward the Elder; he was crowned King of Mercia in 924. He defeated a Scottish invasion force in 937 and is also known for six surviving legal codes.

Athena (*or* Pallas Athena) The virgin Greek goddess of war and of wisdom, the protectress of Athens which is named after her. Born from the head of Zeus, fully armed with a javelin, she was his favourite child. In the Trojan War she constantly aided the Greeks. She also helped Heracles in his labours and guided Perseus on his expedition against the Gorgons. She is identified with the Roman Minerva.

Athens (Modern Greek name: Athínai) 37 59N 23 42E The capital of Greece, situated on a plain in the SE of the country. It is the administrative, cultural, and economic centre of the country and adjoins its port and industrial sector, *Piraeus. The many remains of ancient Athens are on the Acropolis. Crowned by the *Parthenon, it also contains the Ionic Erechtheum, the Propylaea (a gateway), and the tiny temple of Athena Nike. To the NW, the recently restored Agora (market), contains the Theseum (5th century BC), probably the best-preserved ancient temple. To the N and E lies modern Athens. *History*: there is evidence of settlements dating back to the 3rd millennium BC. Athens probably first rose to fame under Pisistratus and his sons in the 6th century BC. Around 506 Cleisthenes established a democracy for the free men of Athens. During the following century it became the leading Greek city state, defeating the Persians with the aid of its powerful navy (*see* Greek-Persian Wars). The Long Walls, connecting the city to Piraeus, and the Parthenon date from this period. Under Pericles, it reached a peak of intellectual brilliance with the philosophy of Socrates and the drama of Aeschylus, Sophocles, and Euripides. Defeated by Sparta in the *Peloponnesian War (431–404), it recovered slowly, regaining its intellectual supremacy with such figures as Plato, Aristotle, and Aristophanes. Defeated by Philip of Macedon in 338 BC, it came under the rule of Rome in the 2nd century BC. It continued to prosper and, despite being overrun by Germanic tribes in the 4th century AD, remained academically important until Justinian closed the schools of philosophy in 529. The city fell to the Crusaders in 1204 and was under Turkish occupation from 1456 until 1833, when it became the capital of the newly independent kingdom of Greece. Population (1981): 885 136.

atherosclerosis (*or* atheroma) Patchy thickening of the lining of arteries caused by the deposition of fatty material and fibrous tissue. This tends to obstruct the blood flow and may result in *thrombosis, leading to a heart attack or a stroke. In the western world atherosclerosis is common in adults: its cause is believed to be associated with a diet high in animal fats (*see* cholesterol), cigarette smoking, and obesity.

athletics Sports that involve running, walking, throwing, and jumping competitions. They are divided into track and field events. At international level the track events include races over 100 m, 200 m, 400 m, 800 m, 1500 m, 5000 m, and 10 000 m; the 110 m and 400 m hurdles (*see* hurdling); the 4 × 100 and 4 × 400 m relay races; the 3000 m steeplechase; the *marathon; and the 20 km walk (*see* walking). The standard field events are *high jump, *long jump, *triple jump, *pole vault, *shot put, *discus throw, *hammer throw, and *javelin throw. In addition there are the *decathlon (for men), the modern pentathlon, and the *pentathlon (for women). The governing body is the International Amateur Athletic Federation.

Atlanta 33 45N 84 23W A city in the USA, the capital of Georgia, situated at the foot of the Appalachian Mountains. Founded in 1837 and partly destroyed by Gen Sherman in 1864, it is now the industrial, administrative, transportation, and cultural centre of the SE USA. Population (1986): 421 910.

Atlantic, Battle of the. *See* World War II.

Atlantic Ocean The world's second largest ocean, extending between Antarctica, America, Europe, and Africa. Its major currents include the *Gulf Stream crossing it W–E. Its floor is rich in minerals, oil and gas now being exploited. The Mid-Atlantic Ridge rises above sea level as islands, such as the Azores. The youngest ocean, the Atlantic was formed when the continents now surrounding it split apart 200 million years ago.

Atlantis In Greek legend, a large island civilization in the Atlantic beyond the Pillars of Hercules (Straits of Gibraltar), which, according to Plato's dialogues the *Timaeus* and *Critias*, was destroyed by earthquake. The story, transmitted to the Greeks by the Egyptians, may refer to a violent volcanic eruption (c. 1450 BC) on the island of Thera in the Cyclades N of Crete.

Atlas In Greek mythology, the brother of Prometheus and son of the Titan Iapetus and the nymph Clymene. As a punishment for his part in the revolt of the Titans against the Olympians he was forced to hold up the pillars separating heaven from earth. From the 16th century this was commonly depicted in the frontispieces of books of maps, which thus came to be called atlases.

Atlas Mountains A mountain system in NW Africa, extending generally NE from the Atlantic coast of Morocco to Tunisia. It consists of several mountain chains and plateaus and rises to 4165 m (13 664 ft) at Mount Toubkal in the Moroccan Great Atlas range.

atmosphere (meteorology) The gaseous envelope surrounding the earth or any other celestial body. The earth's atmosphere is composed of nitrogen (78.08%), oxygen (20.95%), argon (0.93%), and carbon dioxide (0.03%), together with small proportions of other gases and variable amounts of water vapour. In the lowest layer of the earth's atmosphere, the **troposphere**, air temperature decreases as height increases. The thickness of this layer varies from about 7 km (4.5 mi) to about 28 km (17.5 mi) at the equator. It is here that most of our weather—winds, rain, etc.—occurs. In the **stratosphere**, which goes up to about 50 km (31 mi), temperature is fairly constant. The *ionosphere lies in the layer above the stratosphere. The outermost layer, from about 400 km (248 mi), is called the **exosphere**. From 100 km (62 mi) upwards the oxygen breaks up into atoms. There is little nitrogen above 150 km (93 mi). The atmosphere protects the earth from excessive radiation and cosmic particles and is important in maintaining the heat balance of the earth. The pressure of the atmosphere at sea level is 101 325 pascals (1013.25 millibars). *See also* ozone.

atom. *See* atomic theory.

atomic bomb. *See* nuclear weapons.

atomic clock A highly accurate clock in which the process used to keep the time changing at an extremely steady rate actually occurs within certain atoms or molecules. The caesium clock is an example.

atomic energy. *See* nuclear energy.

Atomic Energy Commission A US agency established in 1946 to control the production of nuclear weapons and atomic energy.

atomic mass unit (amu) A unit of mass equal to one-twelfth of the mass of an atom of carbon-12 ($1.660\,33 \times 10^{-27}$ kg). Atomic weights (relative atomic masses) are based on this unit. The unit is also called the dalton (after John *Dalton).

atomic number (Z) The number of protons in a nucleus of an atom. It determines the position of the element in the *periodic table and, in a neutral atom, is equal to the number of electrons surrounding the nucleus. It is also known as proton number.

atomic theory The theory that an atom is the smallest particle of an element that can take part in a chemical reaction. The idea was suggested over 2300 years ago (*see* Democritus). It was only taken seriously in the early 19th century, when John *Dalton used it to explain how elements combine in simple proportions. The structure of the atom was first investigated by Lord *Rutherford, who discovered that it consisted of a heavy positively charged core (the *nucleus) surrounded by *electrons. Niels Bohr based his theory (the Bohr atom) on this model but the modern concept of the atom was finally worked out by Schrödinger and others. *See also* particle physics.

Almost all of the atom's mass lies in the nucleus, which consists of positively charged *protons and neutral *neutrons of almost equal mass (the mass of the electron is only 1/1836 that of the proton). The number of electrons in a neutral atom is equal to the number of protons in the nucleus, as the charge on the proton is equal but opposite to that of the electron. The electrons can be thought of as existing in a series of shells around the nucleus, each shell linked to a particular energy level. The chemical behaviour of an atom is largely determined by the number of electrons in its outermost shell, as atoms are most stable when they have no partly filled shells. This is often achieved by chemical combination. *See also* chemical bond.

atomic weight. *See* relative atomic mass.

ATP (adenosine triphosphate) An energy-rich compound with an important role in the living processes of organisms. On its formation from ADP (adenosine diphosphate) in the body's cells, ATP incorporates a large amount of energy that, on release, is used by cells to manufacture proteins, carbohydrates, etc., and to provide energy for muscle contraction and similar processes.

atropine A medicinal drug, extracted from deadly nightshade, that acts on certain nerves of the autonomic nervous system. It is used during anaesthesia to decrease lung secretions, which lowers the risk of chest infections following operations, and to treat asthma, diarrhoea, colic, peptic ulcers, and parkinsonism. It also causes the pupil of the eye to widen and speeds up the heart rate.

There is no simple way to illustrate an atom:

  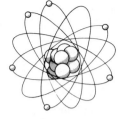 

by the 19th century it was regarded as a minute solid billiard ball;

with the work of Rutherford between 1906 and 1914 and Bohr in 1913 it was depicted as a miniature solar system with a central nucleus and orbiting electron;

Sommerfeld's refinements of quantum theory in 1916 led to a model with precessing elliptical orbits and spinning electrons;

by 1926 Schrödinger's wave mechanics had been published, based on de Broglie's dual wave – particle concept of electrons. The atom is now regarded as a nucleus surrounded by a "haze" of probabilities that electrons will occur in certain positions.

ATOMIC THEORY

Atropos. *See* Fates.

Attenborough, Sir Richard (1923–) British film actor, director, and producer. A talented character actor, he appeared in such films as *Loot* (1969) and *10 Rillington Place* (1971). As director, his films include *A Bridge Too Far* (1977), *Gandhi* (1982), and *A Chorus Line* (1985). His brother **Sir David Attenborough** (1926–) is a naturalist and broadcaster, whose television series include *Life on Earth* (1978), *The Living Planet* (1983), and *Trials of Life* (1990).

Attica A region of ancient E central Greece. According to Greek legend the 12 towns of Attica were united by Theseus into a single state, which was dominated by Athens by the 5th century BC.

Attila (c. 406–53) King of the Huns (434–53), known as the Scourge of God. After murdering his brother and coruler, Bleda, he extended his possessions in central Europe and attacked (441–43) the eastern frontier of the Roman Empire. In 451 he invaded Gaul and suffered his only defeat, at the battle of the Catalaunian Plains. His campaigns in Italy (452) caused much destruction. The pope paid him to spare Rome and Attila died shortly afterwards.

Attlee, Clement (Richard), 1st Earl (1883–1967) British statesman; Labour prime minister (1945–51). A barrister by profession, Attlee taught at the London School of Economics (1913–23). He was elected MP for Limehouse in 1922 and was leader of the Labour Party (1935–55) and deputy prime minister of the wartime coalition government (1942–45). As the first postwar prime minister he introduced the welfare state, nationalized major industries, and granted independence to India.

attorney general The chief law officer of the Crown in England and Wales and its representative in the courts. He is legal adviser to the government and the House of Commons, of which he is always a member and to which he is answerable, and is head of the English bar. He advises on the drafting of Acts of Parliament. With his junior, the director of public prosecutions, he prosecutes crimes in the sovereign's name.

aubergine A spiny plant, *Solanum melongena*, native to S Asia and also known as eggplant. Related to the potato, it is commonly grown in warmer regions for its white, yellow, or purple fruit, which is eaten as a vegetable. The plant grows to a height of 60–110 cm.

aubrietia (*or* aubrieta) A trailing plant of the mustard family, native to mountainous areas of E Europe and W Asia and commonly grown in rock gardens. It has small purple, red, or pink flowers.

Auckland 36 55S 174 47E The largest city and port in New Zealand, on North Island. Founded in 1840, it was the capital of New Zealand until 1865. The University of Auckland was established in 1882 and there are two cathedrals (Roman Catholic and Anglican). The city is connected with the mainly residential North Shore by the Auckland Harbour Bridge (1959). Auckland is a major industrial centre with engineering, food processing, shipbuilding, and chemical industries. Population (1988): 841 700.

Auden, W(ystan) H(ugh) (1907–73) British poet. His early volumes, beginning with *Poems* (1930) and *Look, Stranger!* (1936), established him as a leading left-wing poet of the 1930s. He also wrote verse dramas with Christopher *Isherwood, with whom he went to the USA in 1939. He became a US citizen in 1946, returning to England while he was professor of poetry at Oxford (1956–61). He wrote several opera libretti, notably for Stravinsky's *The Rake's Progress* (1951).

Aughrim, Battle of (12 July, 1691) The final defeat of the main army of the former King James II of England by the army of William III in Ireland. It was the most disastrous battle in Irish history, with 7000 Jacobite dead. It is still celebrated, together with the battle of the Boyne, by Ulster Unionists on its anniversary (*see also* Orange Order).

Augsburg 48 21N 10 54E A city in S Germany, in Bavaria where the Rivers Wertach and Lech meet. It is a major industrial centre; its manufactures include textiles, chemicals, cars, aircraft, and printing machinery. Many of its historic buildings, including the 10th-century cathedral, survived the bombardment of World War II. *History*: founded by the Romans in 15 BC, it was an imperial free city from 1276 and became an important banking and commercial centre in the 15th and 16th centuries. Notable assemblies were held in Augsburg in 1530 (the **Augsburg Confession**) and 1555, when the **Peace of Augsburg**, establishing the coexistence of Catholicism and Lutheranism, was issued. Population (1987): 246 700.

Augustine of Canterbury, St (died c. 604) Italian churchman, the first Archbishop of Canterbury. Chosen by Pope Gregory I to convert England to Christianity in 596, he converted Ethelbert I of Kent and successfully established Canterbury as the leading religious centre. Feast day: 26 or 27 May.

Augustine of Hippo, St (354–430 AD) North African theologian; Father and Doctor of the Church, born at Tagaste. After studying at Carthage, he became a Manichaean, but under the influence of St Ambrose, Bishop of Milan, he converted to Christianity in 386. On his return to Africa, he lived as a monk until he was ordained at Hippo in 391. He became Bishop of Hippo in 396 and died there during a Vandal siege. His *The City of God*, a defence of Christianity in 22 books, and his spiritual autobiography, *The Confessions*, are the most important books written by an early Father of the Church. **Augustinians** are members of religious orders that follow the Rule of St Augustine. Feast day: 28 Aug.

Augustus (*or* Octavian; 63 BC–14 AD) The first Roman emperor, who restored the greatness of the Roman world following the disintegration of the Republic. Born Gaius Octavius, he was the great-nephew and adopted son of Julius Caesar. After Caesar's assassination in 44, Augustus (now Gaius Julius Caesar Octavianus; *or* Octavian) came to an agreement with *Mark Antony and in 43 they formed the second Triumvirate with Lepidus. Lepidus was forced to retire in 36 and Augustus' relations with Mark Antony failed to withstand Antony's abandonment of his wife Octavia (Augustus' sister) for *Cleopatra. Antony's defeat at Actium in 31 allowed Augustus to establish his authority at the head of an oppressive government known as the principate. In 27 he was proclaimed Augustus (sacred). With the military assistance of Agrippa, and later of his own stepson Tiberius, he secured and then expanded the Empire. In 4 AD he named Tiberius his heir. Augustus was made a god after his death.

auk A stout-bodied seabird occurring in the N hemisphere and having a black and white plumage and short pointed wings. *Puffins, *razorbills, *guillemots, and the extinct flightless great auk (*Pinguinus impennis*) are all species of auk.

aurora A display of changing coloured light seen high in the earth's atmosphere, often taking the form of red or green streamers. Aurorae occur predominantly in polar regions when energetic charged particles from the sun become trapped in the earth's magnetic field. The rapidly moving particles interact with atoms and molecules in the upper atmosphere and cause them to emit light.

Auschwitz. *See* Oświęcim.

Austen, Jane (1775–1817) British novelist. She was the daughter of a clergyman and lived an outwardly uneventful life with her family in the south of England, settling in Chawton in Hampshire in 1809. Her six major novels are *Sense and Sensibility* (1811), *Pride and Prejudice* (1813), *Mansfield Park* (1814), *Emma* (1815–16), *Northanger Abbey* (1818), and *Persuasion* (1818).

Austerlitz, Battle of (2 December, 1805) The battle in which Napoleon's 68 000-strong army defeated almost 90 000 Russians and Austrians led by Mikhail Kutuzov (1745–1813). It took place near Austerlitz (now Slavkov u Brna, Czechoslovakia). Napoleon's great victory forced the Austrians to make peace with France by the Treaty of Pressburg and the Russian army to return to Russia.

Australia, Commonwealth of A country in the S Pacific, comprising the whole of the smallest continent and the island of Tasmania to the SE. External territories include Norfolk Island, Christmas Island, the Cocos (Keeling) Islands, and the *Australian Antarctic Territory. Much of the country has a hot dry climate and a large part of the vast central plains are desert or semidesert. The most fertile areas are in the E, along the coastal plains, and in the extreme SW. The Great Barrier Reef lies off the tropical NE coast and the highest mountains, rising over 2000 m (7000 ft), are in the Great Dividing Range, which runs parallel to the E coast. The Murray River and its tributaries in the SE form the main river system. The inhabitants are very largely of European, especially British, origin but there are about 100 000 Aborigines and people of mixed race living in the interior. Since World War II the population has increased dramatically, largely as a result of immigration. *Economy*: the main crops are cereals, sugar cane, and fruit. Livestock, particularly sheep and cattle, is also important. Since the 1960s, however, there has been marked growth in iron and steel products. Mining is now of vital importance, especially the extraction of coal, iron, bauxite, uranium, copper, lead, and zinc; about 70% of the oil used in Australia is now produced there. The main exports are wool, meat, cereals, sugar, iron ore, and nonferrous ores. *History*: the country was inhabited by the Aborigines, immigrants from SE Asia, for approximately 20 000 years before the arrival of the Europeans, beginning with the Portuguese in the 16th century and the Dutch in the early 17th century. In 1770 Captain Cook claimed the fertile E coast for Britain, which was first used as a penal colony. Civilian settlements were established further to the N and W towards the interior, eventually reaching the far side of the Blue Mountains in 1813. Colonies were developed in Tasmania, Western Australia, Victoria, South Australia, and Queensland. By 1829 the whole continent was a British dependency. The discovery of gold in Victoria in 1851 attracted large numbers of immigrants. In 1901 the six colonies were federated to form the Commonwealth, becoming an independent dominion of the British Empire. In 1911 the Australian Capital Territory and the Northern Territory were added to the

Commonwealth. In 1978 the Northern Territory achieved self-government although the federal government retained control over uranium. Australia is a member of the British Commonwealth; constitutional links between Australia and the UK ceased in 1986. Prime minister: Robert Hawke. Official language: English. Official currency: Australian dollar of 100 cents. Area: 7 686 884 sq km (2 967 283 sq mi). Population (1988 est): 16 500 000. Capital: Canberra. Main port: Sydney.

Australian Antarctic Territory The area of Antarctica claimed by Australia. It includes all the land lying S of latitude 60°S and between longitudes 45°E and 160°E, excluding Terre Adélie. Several research stations are sited here.

Australian Capital Territory An administrative division of SE Australia. It was created in 1911 from the Limestone Plains region of New South Wales as a site for *Canberra, the capital of Australia. Jervis Bay was transferred to the territory in 1915 for development as a seaport. It is the site of the Australian Academy of Science, the Royal Military College, and the Royal Australian Naval College (at Jervis Bay). Area: 2432 sq km (939 sq mi). Population (1985): 253 085.

Australian Rules. *See* football.

Australopithecus A fossil manlike creature of the late Pliocene and Pleistocene eras of S and E Africa. Although small in brain size, their skeletons were more like those of modern man than of apes. They walked erect, were vegetarians, and used primitive tools. They are now thought not to have been the direct ancestors of modern man, having split off from the *Homo* evolutionary line some 4 million years ago. There were several species, including *A. afarensis* and *A. robustus*, which probably lived at the same time as early forms of man. Significant fossil finds of *Australopithecus* have been made by Louis and Richard Leakey at Olduvai and Lake Turkana. *See* Homo.

Austria, Republic of (German name: Österreich) A country in central Europe, on the N side of the Alps. A large part of the country is mountainous but the E area consists of lower hills and plains, with the River Danube flowing through the NE. Most of the inhabitants are German but there are minorities of Croats, Slovenes, and others. *Economy*: although agriculture and forestry are important, there is considerable heavy industry, based particularly on iron and steel. Hydroelectric power is a valuable source of energy. Main exports include iron and steel, machinery, paper and paper products, wood, and textiles. *History*: Austria has a long history going back to the Celtic settlements of the early Iron Age. The area was part of the Roman Empire from 15 BC until the 5th century AD when it was overrun by Germanic tribes. In succeeding centuries it was occupied in turn by Slavs and Magyars from whom it was taken in 955 by the Holy Roman Emperor Otto I. Leopold of Babenberg founded the first Austrian dynasty. In 1282 the *Habsburgs acquired Austria, which was to become the centre of their vast empire. In 1526 Bohemia and Hungary were

united under the Austrian Crown. The Austrian Empire continued to hold a predominant position in Europe until the middle of the 19th century when its power was lessened by successive defeats, especially in the *Austro-Prussian War. In 1867 the Habsburgs formed the Dual Monarchy of *Austria-Hungary, under the Emperor Francis Joseph. The assassination of the Archduke Francis Ferdinand by Serbian nationalists in 1914 was the immediate cause of World War I. In 1918 Austria became a republic. It was annexed by Nazi Germany in 1938 (*see* Anschluss). After World War II it was occupied jointly by the Allies, regaining its independence as a republic in 1955. Franz Vranitsky (1937–) succeeded Fred Sinowatz as chancellor in 1986. Austria applied to join the EC in 1989. President: Kurt Waldheim. Official language: German. Currency: schilling of 100 groschen. Area: 85 853 sq km (32 375 sq mi). Population (1987 est): 7 575 732. Capital: Vienna.

Austria-Hungary, Dual Monarchy of The Habsburg monarchy from 1867 to 1918, established in response to Hungarian nationalism. The empire of Austria and the kingdom of Hungary each had its own laws, parliament, and ministries but were united by the monarch (Emperors *Francis Joseph and then *Charles), minister for foreign affairs and minister for war, and by the twice-yearly meetings of representatives of each parliament. The Dual Monarchy disappeared in 1918 with the proclamation of an Austrian republic.

Austrian Succession, War of the (1740–48) The war between Austria and Prussia, in which Britain supported Austria and France and Spain were allied to Prussia. It was brought about by the disputed succession of Maria Theresa to the Austrian lands. The war was begun by *Frederick the Great of Prussia, who took over the Austrian province of Silesia in 1740. The war was ended by the Treaty of Aix-la-Chapelle, at which Prussia obtained the greater share of Silesia.

Austro-Prussian War (*or* Seven Weeks' War; 1866) A war between German states led respectively by Austria and Prussia. The Prussian victory was an important landmark in Bismarck's plan for uniting Germany under Prussian leadership.

autism A rare and severe mental illness that starts in early childhood. Autistic children do not form normal personal relationships but they can become emotionally attached to things. They do not communicate normally and they are very upset by tiny changes in their familiar surroundings. Most, but not all, are mentally retarded. Autism can be caused by brain damage and can also be inherited. Lengthy specialized education is usually necessary for autistic children.

auto-da-fé (Portuguese: act of faith) The public ceremony at which persons convicted of crimes by the *Inquisition in Portugal, Spain, and their colonies were sentenced. Punishment of victims, including the burning of heretics, was the responsibility of the state authorities. The first *auto-da-fé* was held in Seville in 1481 and the last, in Mexico in 1815.

autogiro An aircraft with large horizontal freely rotating blades to obtain lift. It differs from the *helicopter in that a propeller provides forward motion, which in turn causes the rotation of the unmotorized horizontal blades.

automation The use of electronic devices controlled by a computer in mechanical processes that would otherwise be controlled by human operators. It has had a great effect in such fields as steel and chemical manufacture. Telecommunications (automatic telephone exchanges), transport (navigation, railway signals), and mining also employ automated systems.

autopsy (necropsy *or* postmortem) The dissection and examination of a dead body. An autopsy is performed when the cause of death is uncertain: it may provide further information on a poorly understood disease or evidence of criminal involvement. Except for sudden death or death due to obscure causes, permission for autopsy must be granted by the relatives.

autumnal equinox. *See* equinox.

autumn crocus A European plant, *Colchicum autumnale*, of the lily family, also called meadow saffron. It has narrow strap-shaped leaves, up to 30 cm long, and a single purple-blue crocus-like flower, which appears in autumn after the leaves have died. The drug colchicine, extracted from the corms, is used in the treatment of gout and in genetic research. *Compare* crocus.

auxin An organic substance, produced within a plant, that stimulates, inhibits, or modifies growth of the plant. Auxins are sometimes known as plant hormones. The main auxin is indoleacetic acid (IAA). Auxins are responsible for a variety of effects, for example shoot curvature, leaf fall, and fruit growth. Synthetic auxins, such as 2,4-dichlorophenoxyacetic acid (2,4-D), are used as weedkillers for broad-leaved weeds.

Avalon. *See* Arthurian legend.

Avebury 51 27N 1 51W A village in S England, in Wiltshire, on the site of a large complex of Neolithic and early Bronze Age stone circles, banks, and ditches. The principal circle, with its ditch and outer bank, encloses over 12 hectares (30 acres); within it are two smaller ones. Nearby is *Silbury Hill.

Avignon 43 56N 4 48E A town in SE France, the capital of the Vaucluse department on the River Rhône. Famous landmarks include the 14th-century papal palace (*see* Avignon papacy) and the 12th-century bridge, of which only four arches remain. A popular tourist centre, Avignon trades in wine and has chemical, soap, and cement industries. Population (1983): 88 650.

Avignon papacy (1309–77) The period during which the popes resided in Avignon (France) rather than Rome. The papal court was established in Avignon by Clement V, who, like the six popes who followed in Avignon, was French. English and German criticism of French dominance over the papacy eventually forced its return to Rome under Gregory XI. Shortly afterwards the division in the Church known as the *Great Schism occurred, largely because of the

increased power acquired by the cardinals during the Avignon papacy (*see also* antipope).

avocado A tree, *Persea americana*, up to 18 m tall, native to Mexico and Central America but now extensively cultivated in Florida, California, and South Africa for its fruit. These fruits —avocado pears—may reach a weight of 2 kg: they have a green to dark-purple skin, a fatty flesh rich in fat, protein, and vitamins A and B, and a single hard seed.

avocet A wading bird having long slender legs and a long thin upcurved bill used to skim the surface of mud or water in search of small invertebrates. The Eurasian avocet (*Recurvirostra avosetta*), 50 cm long, has a black-and-white plumage and is protected in Britain.

Avogadro, Amedeo, Conte di Quaregna e Ceretto (1776–1856) Italian physicist, who became professor of physics at the University of Turin. He developed *Gay-Lussac's theory that equal volumes of gases contain equal numbers of particles, establishing the difference between atoms and molecules. Because he made this vital distinction the theory is now known as **Avogadro's hypothesis**. His name is also remembered in the **Avogadro number** (*or* Avogadro constant), the number of molecules in one mole of substance (it has the value $6.022\,52 \times 10^{23}$ mol^{-1}). Avogadro's work was not acknowledged until *Cannizzaro brought it to public notice in 1854.

Avon A county of SW England, bordering on the Severn estuary. It was formed in 1974 from parts of NE Somerset and SW Gloucestershire. It consists mainly of low-lying basin, rising to the Cotswold Hills in the NE and the Mendip Hills in the S. The River Avon flows W into the Severn estuary. Dairy farming is the chief agricultural activity. Industry, including engineering, printing, chemicals, tobacco processing, and aircraft manufacture, is concentrated in the Bristol area. Avonmouth is a major port. There is a thriving tourist industry, notably at Weston-super-Mare and Bath. Area: 1337 sq km (516 sq mi). Population (1988 est): 954 300. Administrative centre: Bristol.

Avon, (Robert) Anthony Eden, 1st Earl of (1897–1977) British statesman; Conservative prime minister (1955–57). Foreign secretary from 1935 to 1938, he resigned in opposition to Neville Chamberlain's policy of appeasement. At the beginning of World War II he was secretary for war and then (1940–45; 1951–55) foreign secretary. He succeeded Churchill as prime minister and following Nasser's nationalization (1956) of the *Suez Canal and an Israeli attack on Egypt, joined France in an offensive against Egypt. Egypt retained control of Suez and Eden resigned shortly afterwards. He became Earl of Avon in 1961.

Avon, River The name of several rivers in the UK, including: **1.** A river in central England, flowing SW from Northamptonshire to the River Severn at Tewkesbury. Length: 154 km (96 mi). **2.** A river in SW England, flowing S and W from Gloucestershire to the Severn estuary at Avonmouth. Length: 120 km (75 mi). **3.** A river in S England, flowing S from Wiltshire to the English Channel. Length: 96 km (60 mi).

Axis Powers The coalition of Germany, Italy, and Japan that opposed the Allied Powers in *World War II. It developed from agreements going back to 1936 and led to the Tripartite Pact (1940).

axolotl A salamander, *Ambystoma mexicanum*, occurring in Mexican lakes. It reaches a length of 25 cm, has a long tail and weak limbs, breathes by means of gills, and is typically dark brown. Adult axolotls resemble the larvae, there being no *metamorphosis.

Ayatollah   Ruholla   Khomeini. *See* Khomeini, Ayatollah Ruholla.

Ayckbourn, Alan (1939–) British dramatist. He gained his first London success with *Relatively Speaking* (1967). His later comedies include *Absurd Person Singular* (1973), the trilogy *The Norman Conquests* (1974), *Season's Greetings* (1980), and *Body Language* (1990), all based on observation of middle-class life. He directs a repertory theatre in Scarborough.

Ayers Rock A vast rock, the largest in the world, in Australia, in SW Northern Territory. It is 335 m (1099 ft) high and 10 km (6.25 mi) in circumference. Its red colour varies according to atmospheric changes and the position of the sun.

Aylesbury 51 50N 0 50W A market town in S central England, the administrative centre for Buckinghamshire. It has food-processing, printing, engineering, and light industries. Population (1985 est): 50 000.

Ayub Khan, Mohammad (1907–74) Pakistani statesman; president (1958–69). He became defence minister in 1954. Following President Iskander Mirza's coup in 1958 Ayub Khan became chief martial law administrator and then overthrew Mirza to become president. He negotiated (1966) the ceasefire agreement with Shastri following the India-Pakistan war of 1965. He was forced to resign following civil unrest in East Pakistan.

azalea A deciduous shrub that is similar and closely related to rhododendrons. Growing to a height of up to 2 m, azaleas are native to North America and S Asia but widely cultivated. The funnel-shaped flowers are of various colours.

Azerbaidzhan Soviet Socialist Republic A constituent republic in the S Soviet Union, on the Caspian Sea. Most of the population are Shiite Muslims. Oil and gas are the most important industries. *History*: the region was acquired by Russia from Persia in the early 19th century, proclaimed its independence in 1918, but subsequently formed part of the Transcaucasian Soviet Federated Socialist Republic; it became a separate republic in 1936. In the late 1980s Armenian claims to *Nagorno-Karabakh led to civil war and the arrival (1990) of Soviet troops. Area: 86 600 sq km (33 430 sq mi). Population (1987 est): 6 800 000. Capital Baku.

Azores (Portuguese name: Açôres) 38 30N 28 00W Three groups of volcanic islands in the N Atlantic Ocean, in Portugal. The chief islands include São Miguel, Terceira, Faial, and Flores. Settled by the Portuguese in the 15th century, they were previously uninhabited. The site of US air bases, they produce fruit, tobacco, and wine. Area: 2300 sq km (888 sq mi). Population (1986 est): 253 500. Capital: Ponta Delgada, on São Miguel.

Aztecs A Nahuatl-speaking people who ruled an empire in central and S Mexico before their defeat by Hernán Cortés in the 16th century. They had an advanced civilization centred on their capital Tenochtitlán and other cities. They constructed large palaces and temples in which they worshipped many gods, especially Huitzilopochtli to whom they sacrificed human victims. The last of their kings was *Montezuma.

B

Babbage, Charles (1792–1871) British mathematician and inventor. In an attempt to produce more accurate mathematical tables, Babbage developed the idea of a mechanical computer that could store information. Although he never completed the machine, it was the forerunner of the modern computer.

baboon A large Old World monkey of African and Asian grassland. Baboons are 95–185 cm long including the tail (45–70 cm) and have a shaggy mane and a long doglike face with large teeth. They feed on insects, small vertebrates, and vegetable matter. They live in well-organized troops containing 40–150 individuals arranged in a social hierarchy according to age and sex.

Babylon The capital of ancient Babylonia, positioned on the River *Euphrates S of modern Baghdad. Its first period of prominence was about 2150 to 1740 BC, under a dynasty of which Hammurabi was the most illustrious member. Subse-

quently, rising *Assyrian power threatened Babylonian independence, though some Babylonians, such as Nebuchadnezzar I (reigned c. 1146–1123), temporarily reversed the trend. Sacked in 689 BC by the king of Assyria, Sennacherib (d. 681 BC), Babylon was rebuilt from 625 BC onwards, especially during the reign (c. 605–562) of *Nebuchadnezzar II. The remains of this city were excavated (1899–1917) by the German archaeologist Robert Koldewey (1855–1925). In 539 BC Babylon surrendered to Cyrus the Great of Persia (d. 529 BC); by 275 BC few inhabitants remained. *See also* Hanging Gardens; ziggurat.

Babylonia The area of *Mesopotamia on the alluvial plain on the lower reaches of the River Euphrates, which was controlled by ancient *Babylon. Before about 2000 BC approximately the same area was known as *Sumer, of which *Ur was the capital.

Bacchanalia The Roman form of the Greek religious ceremonies in honour of Bacchus (*see* Dionysus). The cult reached Rome from S Italy in the 2nd century BC. Originally involving only women, Bacchic worship included wild rituals and secret orgies. In 186 BC a decree of the Senate prohibited Bacchanalia in Rome.

Bacchus. *See* Dionysus.

Bach, Johann Sebastian (1685–1750) German composer and keyboard player, the greatest member of a large musical family. He became a chorister in Lüneburg and in 1703 a violinist at the Weimar court, later becoming organist there. In 1707 he married his cousin Maria Barbara Bach (1684–1720); after her death he married Anna Magdalena Wilcken (1701–60). Among his greatest works are the *St John Passion* (1723), the *St Matthew Passion* (1729), and the *Mass in B minor* (1733–38), as well as over 200 cantatas. His pieces for orchestra include violin and harpsichord concertos and the *Brandenburg Concertos* (1721). For the harpsichord and clavichord he composed a collection of 48 preludes and fugues entitled the *Well-Tempered Clavier* (Part I, 1722; Part II, 1744) and the *Goldberg Variations* (1742). Bach's music did not become widely known until Mendelssohn revived it.
Of Bach's 20 children, 3 sons became famous musicians. His eldest son **Wilhelm Friedemann Bach** (1710–84) studied in Leipzig and became church organist in Dresden (1733–46) and subsequently in Halle (1746–64). He ended his life in poverty, leaving cantatas, concertos, and symphonies.
His third son **Karl Philipp Emanuel Bach** (1714–88) became musician to Frederick the Great in Berlin and subsequently director of the main church in Hamburg. He developed a new style of composition in his symphonies, concertos, and keyboard music that became the basis of the classical style.
J. S. Bach's 11th son **Johann Christian Bach** (1735–82), called the English (or London) Bach, studied in Berlin and after holding posts in Italy became music master to the British royal family. He composed 13 operas, as well as concertos, church music, and piano pieces.

bacillus Any rod-shaped bacterium. Some belong to the genus *Bacillus*: these are spore-forming species including parasites of plants and animals. *B. anthracis* was first shown to cause anthrax in livestock by Robert Koch (1843–1910).

backgammon A board game for two players that was known in ancient Mesopotamia, Greece, and Rome and in medieval England (as "the tables"). Each player has 15 pieces, which are moved round the 24 chevrons (points) marked on the board, the number of points moved being indicated by the throws of two dice. From their starting positions the players move in opposite directions. Each tries to bring all his pieces into the last quarter (his home board), after which he can remove them from the board.

background radiation Low-intensity radiation naturally present on the earth. It results either from the bombardment of the earth by *cosmic rays or from naturally occurring radioactive substances in the earth's crust.

Bacon, Francis (1909–) British painter, born in Dublin of English parentage. Self-taught, he was assured a place in British art with his *Three Studies* (of figures for the base of a Crucifixion). Another of his well-known paintings is *Study after Velázquez* (1951), a version of Velázquez's portrait of pope Innocent X.

Bacon, Francis, 1st Baron Verulam, Viscount St Albans (1561–1626) English lawyer and philosopher. He was called to the Bar in 1582 and became an MP in 1584. Under James I (reigned 1603–25) Bacon became attorney general (1613) and Lord Chancellor (1618). In 1621, however, he was found guilty of bribery and corruption, fined £40,000, and banished from office. In 1597 he published his first group of *Essays*; further such writings appeared in 1625. *The Advancement of Learning* (1605) presented a new classification of sciences and was expanded in the *De augmentis scientiarum* of 1623. In *Novum organum scientiarum* (1620) he argued in favour of the scientific method of induction. His other works include a *History of Henry VII* (1622) and the *New Atlantis* (1626), which describes his ideal state.

Bacon, Roger (c. 1214–c. 1292) English monk, scholar, and scientist, called Doctor Mirabilis for his wide-ranging skills and learning. In three books written for Pope Clement IV he attempted to record the current state of knowledge; other works prophesied aeroplanes, microscopes, steam engines, and telescopes.

bacteria Microscopic single-celled organisms found wherever life is possible. Generally 0.0001–0.005 mm long, they may be spherical (coccus), rodlike (*see* bacillus), or spiral-shaped (spirillum) and often occur in chains or clusters of cells. True bacteria have a rigid cell wall, which may be surrounded by a slimy capsule, and they often have long whiplike flagella for locomotion and short hairlike pili used in a form of sexual reproduction. A few bacteria can use simple chemical substances, including carbon dioxide from the atmosphere, to manufacture their own nutrients, but most require a source of carbon derived from living organisms (i.e. organic carbon) plus other nutrients for growth. Some bacteria can reproduce every 15 minutes, leading to rapid population growth.
The most important role of bacteria is in decomposing dead plant and animal tissues and releasing their constituents to the soil (*see* carbon cycle). Nitrogen-fixing bacteria in the soil or sea convert atmospheric nitrogen gas to nitrites and nitrates, which can then be used by plants (*see* nitrogen cycle). Cheese making and fermentation reactions depend on bacteria. Bacteria also play an important part in animal digestion, especially in ruminants. However, certain (pathogenic) species may cause disease while others, such as *Salmonella*, can cause *food poisoning.

bacteriophage (*or* phage) A *virus that infects a bacterium. 25–800 nanometres in size, phages may be spherical, filamentous, or tadpole-shaped with a head and tail. They consist of a protein coat surrounding a core of nucleic acid (either DNA or RNA) that carries the genes of the virus and is inserted into the bacterium. The viral genes then use the protein-synthesis apparatus of the bacterium to produce new phages, which are released from the bacterium, usually causing its destruction.

Baden-Powell, Robert Stephenson Smyth, 1st Baron (1857–1941) British general and founder of the Boy Scouts (*see* Scout Association). He achieved fame through his defence of Mafeking in the *Boer War (1899–1900). Using the experience of character training he had gained overseas, he founded the Boy Scouts in 1908 and, with his sister Agnes, the Girl Guides in 1910.

Bader, Sir Douglas (1910–82) British fighter pilot. After losing his legs in a flying accident (1931), Bader argued himself back into the RAF at the start of World War II. Becoming a national hero, he was finally shot down and imprisoned by the Germans, who only prevented his escape by taking away his artificial legs. In 1976 he was knighted for his work for the disabled.

badger A nocturnal burrowing mammal of the *weasel family. The largest species is the Eurasian badger (*Meles meles*), about 90 cm long, with short strong legs, long coarse greyish hair on the body, and a black and white striped head. It lives in a complex system of burrows (a set) and feeds on insects, rodents, worms, berries, etc.

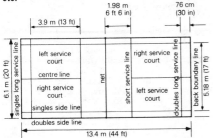

BADMINTON *The dimensions of the court. The top of the net at the centre is 5 ft (1.5 m) above the floor.*

badminton An indoor court game for two or four players, played with rackets and a shuttlecock of nylon or cork and feathers. It originated in about 1870 and may have first been played in the park of Badminton House, in the village of Badminton (Avon). It is a volleying game (the shuttles do not bounce) and points are scored only by the serving side. If the serving side fails to make a good return the service changes (in doubles games both partners serve before their opponents). A game is usually played to 15 points (women's singles go to 11 points).

Baghdad 33 20N 44 26E The capital of Iraq, on the River Tigris near the centre of the country. Built by the caliph Mansur in the 8th century, it was a centre of commerce, learning, and religion until sacked by the Mongols in 1258. It became the capital of independent Iraq (1927) and has three universities (1947, 1957, and 1963). Population (1985): 4 648 609.

bagpipes A reed-pipe instrument of ancient origin, found in many countries. Air is forced into a windbag either by the mouth (Scottish bagpipes) or by a bellows (Northumbrian pipes). By pressing the bag under his arm the player pushes air into the sounding pipes, which consist of one to three drones (each sounding a single note) and a chanter pipe. Bagpipes are regarded as the national instrument of Scotland, having been introduced to the British Isles in the 13th century.

Bahamas, Commonwealth of the A state consisting of about 700 islands in the West Indies, off the SE coast of Florida. The principal islands, which are mainly low lying, include New Providence (with the capital Nassau), Grand Bahama, Abaco, Eleuthera, Andros, and Watling Island (San Salvador). The majority of the population is of African descent. *Economy*: tourism accounts for over 50% of revenue and employment. Efforts are now being made to develop agriculture and fisheries. Main exports include cement, petroleum products, chemicals, and fish. *History*: in 1492 Columbus made his first landing in the W hemisphere on the island of San Salvador. The islands became a British crown colony in 1717. In 1973 it attained full independence within the Commonwealth. Prime minister: Lynden Oscar Pindling (1930–   ). Official language: English. Official currency: Bahamian dollar of 100 cents. Area: 13 864 sq km (5353 sq mi). Population (1986): 235 000. Capital and main port: Nassau.

Bahia. *See* Salvador.

Bahrain, State of An independent sheikdom in the Arabian Gulf, occupying a low-lying group of islands between Saudi Arabia and the Qatar Peninsula. The inhabitants are mainly Arabs. *Economy*: almost totally dependent upon oil. A large refinery processes local oil and much larger amounts coming from Saudi Arabia by pipeline. *History*: the islands were under Portuguese rule from 1521 until 1602, and during parts of the 17th century Iran had control, eventually being expelled by the Khalifa family, who have ruled the area for most of the time since. It was a British protected state from 1861 until 1971 when full independence was declared by the emir, Sheik Isa ibn Sulman al-Khalifa (1933–   ). Bahrain became a member of OPEC in 1970. Official language: Arabic; English is also widely spoken. Official religion: Islam. Official currency: Bahrain dinar of 1000 fils. Area: 660 sq km (255 sq mi). Population (1987): 416 275. Capital and main port: Manama.

Bainbridge, Beryl (1934–   ) British novelist and playwright. Born in Liverpool, she worked as an actress before writing such novels as *The Dressmaker* (1973), *Injury Time* (1977), and *An Awfully Big Adventure* (1989) and the collection of short stories *Mum and Mr Armitage* (1985). Her plays include *It's a Lovely Day Tomorrow* (1977) and *Evensong* (1986).

Baird, John Logie (1888–1946) Scottish electrical engineer, who invented an early television system. In 1924 he first succeeded in transmitting the outline of shapes, although his 240-line television system was not adopted by the BBC.

Baird also pioneered the use of radar and fibre optics.

Bakhtaran (former name: Kermanshah) 34 19N 47 04E A town in W Iran, with a large Kurdish population. Population (1986): 565 544.

Baku 40 22N 49 53E A port in the S Soviet Union, the capital of Azerbaidzhan SSR on the Caspian Sea. The old town is a maze of narrow streets and ancient buildings, including a 17th-century palace. It is the oldest centre of Soviet oil production. In 1990 it was a focus for violent ethnic unrest. Population (1987): 1 741 000.

Bala, Lake (Welsh name: Llyn Tegid) The largest natural lake in Wales, in E Gwynedd. The town of Bala lies at its N end. Length: 6 km (4 mi).

Balaclava, Battle of (25 October, 1854) An indecisive battle between Russian and British-Turkish forces in the *Crimean War. It was made famous by Tennyson's poem "Charge of the Light Brigade". The battle was notorious for the heavy British casualties caused by misunderstanding between Lord *Raglan, the British commander in chief, and Lord Lucan (1800–88), the cavalry commander. The courageous Light Brigade charged Russian artillery at the end of a narrow valley and of its 673 men, 113 were killed.

balalaika A Russian plucked instrument of the guitar family, having a long fretted fingerboard, a triangular body, and three wire strings that are plucked with a plectrum. Small versions are held like a guitar and the larger ones balanced on the floor like a double bass.

balance A sensitive device for comparing two masses, consisting of a beam pivoted at its centre (usually on a knife edge) with pans hanging from each of its ends. The material of unknown mass is placed in one pan and weights of known mass are placed in the other. A pointer indicates when the beam is horizontal and the whole device is enclosed in a glass case to avoid draughts and temperature changes. A standard balance will weigh to the nearest 0.0001 g, while extremely sensitive **microbalances** can be used to weigh objects with a mass of only 1 microgram.

balance of payments The difference between a country's income and its expenditure abroad. It consists of 2 accounts: the current account records the country's **balance of trade** earnings or losses on visible goods and invisible earnings on such items as insurance, transport, tourism, and some kinds of government spending. The capital account records all long- and short-term capital flows, both in the public and private sectors. If the current and capital accounts added together show a loss, the country will be in debt.

balance of power An agreed rule of action which seeks to make sure that no nation or group of nations becomes too dominant. Practised by Greek city states, the rule was adopted in Europe in the alliance system of 15th-century Italy and by the Congress of Vienna at the start of the 19th century. In the 20th century the League of Nations and the UN have both tried to keep the peace, but it is the possession of nuclear weapons that has prevented major war.

Balanchine, George (Georgy Melitonovich Balanchivadze; 1904–83) US ballet dancer and choreographer, born in Russia. He worked for Diaghilev's Ballets Russes in Europe from 1924 and went to the USA in 1933, becoming artistic director of the New York City Ballet. His ballets include *Firebird* (1950) and *Don Quixote* (1965).

bald eagle A large sea *eagle, *Haliaetus leucocephalus*, also called the American eagle; it is the national emblem of the USA and an endangered species. It is dark brown with a white head and tail and has a prominent curved beak and unfeathered legs.

Baldwin, James Arthur (1924–87) US Black novelist, essayist, and dramatist. His first novel, *Go Tell It on the Mountain* (1953), is based on his experience of poverty and religion in Harlem, New York City, where he was born. He lived in Paris from 1948 to 1957, when he returned to the USA as an active civil-rights campaigner. His works include novels, such as *Giovanni's Room* (1956) and *Just Above My Head* (1979), two plays, and collections of essays.

Baldwin of Bewdley, Stanley, 1st Earl (1867–1947) British statesman, who was Conservative prime minister (1923–24, 1924–29, 1935–37), when he dealt with the *General Strike (1926) and Edward VIII's abdication (1936). Baldwin was criticized for failing to condemn Italy's conquest of Ethiopia and his reluctance to rearm in the face of Germany's military build-up.

Balearic Islands A group of islands in the W Mediterranean Sea comprising a Spanish province. It includes the chief islands of *Majorca, *Minorca, *Ibiza, and Formentera, together with several islets. The islands were conquered by Aragon from the Moors in the 14th century. Area: 5014 sq km (1936 sq mi). Population (1982): 669 101. Capital: Palma, on Majorca.

Balfour Declaration (1917) The decision of the British Government, made known in a letter of 2 Nov from the British foreign secretary, Arthur Balfour (1848–1930), to Lionel, Baron Rothschild (1868–1937), the chairman of the British Zionist Federation, to support the establishment of a national Jewish home in Palestine. Arab hopes in Palestine, however, prevented the British Government from fulfilling the promise of the Declaration, which was abandoned in 1939.

Bali An Indonesian island off E Java. Mountainous and volcanic, it has southern fertile plains that produce chiefly rice. *History*: Hindu since the 7th century AD, Bali resisted the 16th–17th century spread of Islam through Indonesia. Dutch rule began in 1908. In the 1965–67 Indonesian purge of communists 40 000 people were killed. Area: 5558 sq km (2146 sq mi). Population (1981 est): 2 469 930. Chief town: Denpasar.

Balkans An area in SE Europe consisting of present-day Greece, Albania, Yugoslavia, Bulgaria, part of Romania, and the European part of Turkey. Part of the Roman empire from the 2nd century BC and of the Eastern Roman (Byzantine) Empire from the 5th century AD, the Balkans were ruled by the Ottoman Turks from the 15th to the 19th century, when independence was granted (*see also* Balkan Wars). All the Balkan states, except Greece, became communist after *World War II.

Balkan Wars (1912–13) In the first Balkan War (1912–13) the Balkan League (Bulgaria, Serbia, Greece, and Montenegro) defeated Turkey. In the final Treaty of London, Turkey lost all its European possessions except E Thrace. In the second Balkan War (1913) the victors fought over their gains in Macedonia, from most of which Bulgaria was excluded by the Treaty of Bucharest; Turkey regained Thrace.

Ballesteros, Severiano (1957–) Spanish golfer. His first major win was the Dutch Open Championship (1976). Subsequent victories include three British Open Championships (1979, 1984, and 1988) and the Barcelona Open Championship (1985).

ballet A dramatic art in which dancing and mime, accompanied by music, combine to tell a story or evoke a mood. Ballet developed from the formal dances of French court entertainments, notably under Louis XIV. In the 18th century ballet established itself in the public theatre but still as a feature of *opera or other forms of drama. Dancing on the tips of the toes (*sur les pointes*) was introduced early in the 19th century, which saw the heyday of romantic ballet. Modern ballet arose in the early 20th century when Fokine and *Diaghilev (*see also* Ballets Russes) combined the polished technique of the imperial Russian dancers with the naturalism encouraged by the American Isadora *Duncan. Since World War II choreographers have created new ballets inspired by folk dance, jazz, and even gymnastics.

Ballets Russes A Russian ballet company (1909–29) founded in Paris by *Diaghilev. It gave the West its first opportunity to see Russian imperial dancers and fostered the most avant-garde talents of the period, greatly influencing the subsequent development of ballet. Its choreographers included Fokine, Massine, *Balanchine, and *Nijinsky, who was also one of its principal dancers. *Ravel and *Stravinsky composed music for several of its ballets.

Balliol, John (c. 1250–1314) King of the Scots (1292–96), chosen by Edward I of England. In 1295 he rebelled against English domination and was defeated by Edward at Dunbar (1296) and overthrown. His son **Edward Balliol** (d. 1364) became King of the Scots in 1332, after invading Scotland, supported by Edward III of England. An uprising against Balliol was put down by Edward (1333), who kept the Scottish lowlands, but internal opposition forced Balliol's abdication in 1356.

ballistic missiles Rocket-powered nuclear missiles that are propelled to desired altitudes and then follow an unpowered flight path towards their target. Their accuracy is calculated as a probability (e.g. 45–60%) of landing within a stated radius about their target (*Circular Error of Probability*). Intercontinental ballistic missiles (ICBMs) are capable of reaching any point

on the surface of the earth. Both the USA and the Soviet Union possess large numbers of these, some of which (MIRVs—multiple independently targeted re-entry vehicles) have up to ten separate warheads. *See also* antiballistic missiles.

balloons Lighter-than-air craft, consisting of a bag of gas that is able to rise and float in the air. If it is not tethered to the ground it flies where the wind blows it. The first successful balloon flight, man's first aerial voyage, was made in 1783 by the *Montgolfier brothers' hot-air balloon; it flew 9 km across Paris. Two years later a hydrogen balloon designed by J. A. C. Charles flew across the Channel. The popular sport of **ballooning** uses a hot-air balloon carrying propane gas to heat the air within the bag. The height record for a manned balloon is 30 480 m (D. Simons, US Air Force, 1957). The first crossing of the Atlantic Ocean by helium balloon was achieved in 1978, and by hot-air balloon in 1987, by Richard Branson.

Balmoral Castle The principal country residence of the British monarch in Scotland, situated in SW Aberdeenshire by the River Dee. It was bought by the royal family in 1848 and rebuilt in the 1850s.

balsa An evergreen tree, *Ochroma pyramidale*, native to Central and South America, also called corkwood. About 12 m tall, it is the source of an extremely light pale-coloured wood, which is widely used for corks, canoes, floats, etc.

Baltic Sea A section of the Atlantic Ocean in N Europe, bounded by Denmark, Norway, Sweden, Finland, the Soviet Union, Poland, Germany. To the W, it leads into the Little Belt, the Great Belt, and the Sound, and to the E, the Gulfs of Bothnia, Finland, and Riga. It has very low salt content and it can freeze sufficiently to hinder navigation.

Baltimore 39 25N 76 40W A city in the USA, in Maryland at the mouth of the Patapsco River. Established in 1729, it was named after the first Baron Baltimore who founded Maryland. It was the starting point of the USA's first railway (1827). Baltimore contains a number of universities; in the 1980s considerable rebuilding in the port area has revitalized the city. Industries include steel, food processing, oil refining, and chemicals. Population (1987): 745 900.

Baluchistan A province in W Pakistan, on the Arabian Sea and the Iranian and Afghani borders. Mostly rough arid highlands, it is inhabited by pastoral Pathans, Baluchs, and other peoples. The NW deserts are practically uninhabited but the coastal plain and E lowlands support cereals and herbs. *History*: on trade routes from India to the Middle East, Baluchistan has flourished since ancient times. Britain won control in the 19th century; in 1947 it became part of Pakistan. Area: 347 190 sq km (134 050 sq mi). Population (1985 est): 4 908 000. Capital: Quetta.

Balzac, Honoré de (1799–1850) French novelist. A lawyer's clerk, he wrote popular novels under several different names. In 1828, bankruptcy forced him to turn to writing; *Les Chouans* (1829) was his first successful novel, and in the next 20 years he added over 40 novels

to the series *La Comédie humaine*. In these novels, which included *Eugénie Grandet* (1833), *Le Père Goriot* (1834), and *La Cousine Bette* (1846), he developed new techniques of realism.
Bamako 12 40N 7 59W The capital of Mali, a port in the S on the River Niger. A centre of Muslim learning under the medieval Mali Empire, it had dwindled to a small village by the end of the 19th century. It became the capital of the French Sudan in 1905. Population (1981): 620 000.

bamboo A treelike plant of the grass family, native to tropical and subtropical regions, particularly SE Asia. From an underground stem (rhizome) arise hollow woody jointed stems, which may reach a height of 40 m in some species. These are used for building, etc., while the young shoots are eaten.

Banaba. *See* Ocean Island.

banana A palmlike plant of the Old World tropics, grown for its fruit. The "trunk," up to 9 m high, is composed of the overlapping bases of the leaves, which are often 3 m or more long. The tip of the flowering stem bears male flowers; clusters of female flowers, further up the stem, develop into seedless fruits, up to 30 cm long, without being fertilized. (All cultivated bananas are sterile: the plants are propagated from suckers arising from the underground rhizome.) Varieties called plantains are cooked and eaten when still green in Africa and the Caribbean.

Bandar Seri Begawan (former name: Brunei Town) 4 56N 114 58E The capital of Brunei, a port in the NE near the mouth of the Brunei River. Population (1984): 54 000.

bandicoot A ratlike *marsupial mammal occurring in Australia (including Tasmania) and New Guinea. About the size of rabbits, bandicoots are mainly carnivorous, eating insects, worms, and grubs.

Bandung 6 57S 107 34E A city in Indonesia, in W Java. Its chief industries are chemicals, quinine, plastics, metal processing, and textiles. It has two universities and a nuclear research centre (1964). Population (1981): 1 400 000.

Bangalore 12 58N 77 35E A city in S India, the capital of Karnataka. Founded in the 16th century, it fell to the British in 1791. Its modern industries include aircraft assembly, machine tools, and electronics. Population (1983): 2 914 000.

Bangkok (Thai name: Krung Threp) 13 44N 100 30E The capital and main port of Thailand, in the SW near the mouth of the River Chao Phraya. It became a royal city and the capital in 1782. It is the centre of most of the country's industry and commerce and it has eight universities. Population (1987): 5 609 352.

Bangladesh, People's Republic of A country in the Indian subcontinent on the delta of the Rivers Ganges and Brahmaputra. *Economy*: Its large population, mostly Bengali, is largely occupied in agriculture, rice being by far the most important crop. Bangladesh produces 50% of the world's raw jute, its main export. Fishing is also important. *History*: the area formed part of the kingdom of Bengal, and its conquest by the Afghans in the 12th century led to the growth of the

Islamic religion. It was part of British India from 1857 until 1947 when it became a province of Pakistan (East Pakistan). Civil war broke out in 1971, Indian forces coming to the aid of the Bengalis. In 1972 East Pakistan achieved independence as Bangladesh and became a member of the Commonwealth; Sheikh Mujibur Rahman (1920–75) became prime minster. In 1974 floods and famine led to political unrest and terrorism and in 1975 Mujib was assassinated in a military coup. Gen Ziaur Rahman took power in 1976 and was elected president in 1978; he was assassinated in 1981. The military, led by Lt Gen Hussain Mohammed Ershad, took power in March 1982, and in 1983 Ershad became president; political unrest led to his resignation in 1990. Official language: Bengali. Official religion: Islam. Official currency: taka of 100 paisa. Area: 142 797 sq km (55 126 sq mi). Population (1987): 104 100 000. Capital: Dhaka. Main port: Chittagong.

Bangui 4 23N 19 20E The capital of the Central African Republic, a port in the SW on the Ubangi River. Founded in 1889, its main exports are cotton and coffee. Population (1985 est): 473 817.

Banjul (name until 1973: Bathurst) 13 20N 16 38W The capital of The Gambia, a port in the W at the mouth of the River Gambia, founded by the British in 1816. Population (1983): 44 188.

Bank of England The British central bank, which was nationalized in 1946. It was originally set up in 1694 by a group of London merchants to lend money to William III. Since the mid-19th century it has been the only bank allowed to issue banknotes. The Bank is responsible for paying for the national debt, holding the country's gold reserves, and carrying out the government's monetary policy.

bankruptcy The legal process by which the property of a person who cannot pay his debts is shared out among those to whom he owes money. In England the bankruptcy law was originally for protecting those who were owed money, but since the reign of Queen Anne it also aims to protect the person who is bankrupt by ending his obligation to repay most of his past debts. The Bankruptcy Act (1914) and the Insolvency Acts (1976, 1986) set out the circumstances in which a person may be made bankrupt, what portion of his property is to be distributed, and the order in which creditors are paid. When applied to a company, bankruptcy is known as liquidation.

Bannister, Sir Roger (Gilbert) (1929–) British doctor and middle-distance runner, who on 6 May, 1954, was the first man to run a mile in under 4 minutes (3 minutes 59.4 seconds).

Bannockburn 56 06N 3 55W A village in Scotland, in the Central Region. 1.5 km (1 mi) NW is Scotland's most famous battlefield, where in 1314 Robert the Bruce, King of the Scots, defeated the English under Edward II, who had come to relieve the besieged Stirling Castle. Population (1981): 6068.

Banting, Sir Frederick Grant (1891–1941) Canadian physiologist, who, with C. H. Best (1899–1978), discovered a technique for the successful isolation of the hormone *insulin from pancreatic tissue in 1921, enabling *diabetes to be treated. Banting was awarded a Nobel Prize (1923).

Bantu A large subgroup of African languages of the *Niger-Congo group spoken over the whole of the S half of Africa by about 60 million people. It includes Zulu, Xhosa, and Kongo; perhaps the most widely known representative is *Swahili, the language of Tanzania and the most widely used of E Africa.

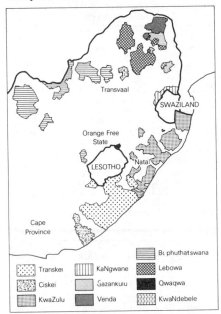

Transvaal

SWAZILAND

Orange Free State

LESOTHO   Natal

Cape Province

KwaZulu

Transkei   KaNgwane   Bophuthatswana
Ciskei   Gazankulu   Lebowa
KwaZulu   Venda   Qwaqwa
                    KwaNdebele

BANTU HOMELANDS *The areas designated as Black African territories in South Africa are dispersed over the E and N parts of the Republic.*

Bantu Homelands (*or* Bantustans) The areas of South Africa set aside for the Black populations, comprising just over 13% of the land area. Acts of parliament in 1913 and 1936 prohibited Blacks from holding land in White areas. Limited self-government was to be granted to the Bantustans; the Transkei was the first to receive this (1963); it was granted full independence in 1976. Bantustan policy has been opposed by African leaders (in particular Chief Buthelezi).

banyan A tropical Asian tree, *Ficus benghalensis*, related to the fig and reaching a height of 30 m. Supporting aerial roots, which grow down to penetrate the soil, subsequently give rise to thorny branches of their own.

baptism A ceremony in which a new member is introduced into a religious group. It occurs in many religions and involves the use of water as a symbol of purification from sin. In the Christian Church, it is a *sacrament performed in the name of the Father, the Son, and the Holy Spirit. Both the *Baptists and the modern descendants

of the *Anabaptists practise adult baptism, but most other Churches prefer infant baptism.

Baptists Protestant Christians who baptize, by dipping the whole body into water, only those old enough consciously to accept the Christian faith. "General Baptist" Churches, were founded in 1612 by John Smyth (c. 1554–1612) and Thomas Helwys (c. 1550–c. 1616), while "Particular Baptist" Churches, founded in 1633 by Calvinists, believed that salvation was only for a particular few. Both movements joined to become the Baptist Union in 1891. The first Baptist Church in America was established at Providence, Rhode Island, by Roger Williams in 1639.

bar A unit of pressure equal to 10^5 pascals. The commonly used unit is the millibar (one-thousandth of a bar).

Barbados, State of An island state in the West Indies, E of the Windward Islands. Most of the population is of African descent. *Economy*: sugar cane is the main crop, and tourism is important. The discovery of offshore oil and natural gas has assisted the growth of small industries. *History*: a British colony from 1627 until 1966, it became a fully independent state within the Commonwealth. Prime minister: Erskine Sandiford (1937–   ). Official language: English. Official currency: Barbados dollar of 100 cents. Area: 430 sq km (166 sq mi). Population (1987 est): 256 000. Capital and main port: Bridgetown.

Barbary A region in N Africa stretching from Egypt to the Atlantic Ocean that is named after the *Berbers. In ancient times it consisted of Mauritania, Numidia, Africa, Propria, and Cyrenaica. It was successively conquered by the Romans, Vandals, Arabs, Turks, Spaniards, French, and Italians. Between the 16th and 18th centuries, Barbary was notorious for its pirates, who caused havoc in the Mediterranean.

Barbary ape A large monkey, *Macaca sylvana*, that is the only species of macaque found in N Africa. Barbary apes are tailless and roam in bands over the forest floor, feeding on seeds, leaves, insects, etc. There is a colony in Gibraltar.

barbel A long slender freshwater fish that is related to *carp and occurs in clear fresh waters of Asia, Africa, and Europe. It has four fleshy threadlike appendages (barbels) near its mouth, which detect prey while exploring the river bed. The European species *Barbus barbus* is usually 30–50 cm long.

barbiturates A class of drugs that act by depressing the activity of the brain. Short-acting barbiturates, such as thiopentone, are used to induce *anaesthesia. Medium-acting barbiturates, such as pentobarbitone, are used as sleeping tablets. Small doses of long-acting barbiturates, such as phenobarbitone, are used as sedatives to relieve anxiety and to control epilepsy. As barbiturates are habit-forming their use is now severely limited.

Barcelona 41 25N 2 10E A city in NE Spain, in Catalonia on the Mediterranean Sea. Manufactures include locomotives, aircraft, textiles, and electrical equipment. It has many educational establishments including the University

Bardeen, John

54

founded in 1430. *History*: founded by the Carthaginians, it was taken by the Moors in 713 AD and by Charlemagne in 801 AD. In 1137 Catalonia and Aragón united and Barcelona became the capital, rivalling Genoa and Venice as a leading European port. During the 19th century it became important through its cotton industry. It was the seat of the Republican government during the Spanish Civil War (1936–39). In 1939 Barcelona fell to Gen Franco and the Republican government finally surrendered. The 1992 Olympic Games will be held here. Population (1986): 1 694 064.

Bardeen, John (1908–91) US physicist, who shared the 1956 Nobel Prize for his part in the invention of the transistor (with W. B. *Shockley and W. H. *Brattain) while working at the Bell Telephone Laboratories in 1948. He also shared the 1972 Nobel Prize for his work on the theory of superconductivity (with L. N. Cooper and J. R. Schrieffer).

Bardot, Brigitte (1934–) French film actress. Her films include *And God Created Woman* (1956), *Vie privée* (1961), *Viva Maria* (1965), and *Shalako* (1968). She became probably the best-known sex symbol of the 1960s.

Barebones Parliament The assembly, also known as the parliament of saints, called by Oliver *Cromwell in July, 1653. It consisted mainly of merchants and lesser gentry, "godly men" chosen by the congregations, and was named after one of them, Praisegod Barebone (c. 1596–1679).

Barenboim, Daniel (1942–) Israeli pianist and conductor, who studied in Salzburg, Paris, and Rome. He made his debut in London in 1955. In 1967 he married the cellist Jacqueline du Pré, with whom he gave recitals. He conducted the Orchestre de Paris (1975–89) and directs the Chicago Symphony Orchestra (1989–).

Barents Sea A section of the Arctic Ocean between Eurasia and Svalbard. It covers part of the Eurasian continental shelf and is rich in fish. It is named after the Dutch navigator Willem Barents (1550–97).

barium (Ba) A silvery reactive metal that resembles calcium in its behaviour. It was discovered in 1808 by Sir Humphry *Davy and occurs naturally as barytes ($BaSO_4$) and witherite ($BaCO_3$). The sulphate is used as a white pigment in paint and, because it does not transmit X-rays, is used in X-ray diagnosis. All soluble barium compounds are poisonous, the carbonate being used as rat poison. At no 56; at wt 137.34; mp 725°C.

bark The dead outer layer of the stems and roots of woody plants, which protects the inner tissues. Antiseptic deposits, such as tannins, give the colour. Bark may include layers of insulating *cork, which is responsible for the characteristic ridges and patterns on some tree trunks. Small breathing pores (called lenticels) in the bark are conspicuous in many of the smooth-barked trees. Bark is a source of cinnamon, quinine, and various other products.

bark beetle A hard cylindrical wood-boring beetle, also called an engraver beetle. It is usually less than 6 mm long, coloured red-brown or black, and causes considerable damage to trees. It burrows an elaborate system of tunnels underneath the bark to lay eggs that develop into burrowing larvae. Certain species also transmit diseases and can be serious economic pests.

barley A cereal grass that produces its grain in four rows, two-rows, or six-rows. Over 165 million tonnes of grain are harvested annually in temperate, subtropical, and subarctic regions. It is used in the brewing industry, as an animal feed, and to produce pearl barley.

Bar Mitzvah (Hebrew: son of the commandment) The ceremony marking the introduction of a Jewish boy into the adult community at the age of 13.

Barnabas, St In the New Testament (Acts), a Christian Apostle of the 1st century. After going with St Paul to preach in Cyprus (his birthplace), he clashed with him and they parted company. He is traditionally regarded as the founder of the Cypriot Church. Feast day: 11 June.

barnacle A marine *crustacean that usually lives attached to rocks, ships, etc. It filters food particles from the water with long feathery appendages, which protrude from the chalky shell. Goose barnacles are attached by means of a stalk; others, including the acorn barnacle, are unstalked. Barnacles are *hermaphrodite; their larvae swim about in the sea but later settle and become fixed to a surface by means of a cement-like substance secreted by their antennae.

Barnardo, Thomas John (1845–1905) British doctor and philanthropist. In 1867 Barnardo founded the first of his famous homes at Stepney, London, to care for poor children. Over a hundred homes exist in the UK, with others in Australia and New Zealand.

barn owl A widely distributed owl with a heart-shaped face, long feathered legs, and usually a reddish plumage with pale underparts. The common barn owl (*Tyto alba*), 30–45 cm long, nests in old barns and hunts for small rodents.

Barnsley 53 34N 1 28W A town in N England, in South Yorkshire on the River Dearne. Principally a coalmining centre, Barnsley's other industries include glass manufacture, engineering, etc. Population (1981): 73 646.

barometer An instrument for measuring atmospheric pressure. In the mercury barometer, atmospheric pressure forces mercury from a reservoir into a vertical evacuated glass tube marked with a scale. The height of the mercury column is directly proportional to the atmospheric pressure. In the aneroid barometer, variations in the atmospheric pressure on the lid of an evacuated metal box cause a pointer to move round a dial. The aneroid barometer is less sensitive than the mercury barometer but it is smaller and more convenient to use.

Barons' Wars 1. (1215–17) The civil war between King John of England and his barons. John's failure to honour the *Magna Carta led the barons to offer the English Crown to the future Louis VIII of France, who invaded England. Many of the barons' grounds for complaint were removed by John's death and the reissue of the Magna Carta but war continued until the barons' defeat at Lincoln and Sandwich (1217). **2.**

(1264–67) The civil war between Henry III of England and his barons led by Simon de *Montfort, following Henry's rejection of the Provisions of Oxford. He was captured at the battle of Lewes (1264) and England was controlled by de Montfort until his death at Evesham (1265). Fighting continued until the royalist capture of the Isle of Ely in 1267.

baroque In architecture, a style dominant in European Roman Catholic countries in the 17th and early 18th centuries. Beginning in Italy as a reaction against classicism, it was characterized by curved and broken lines and ornate decoration (which led to *rococo). English architects, such as *Wren and *Vanbrugh, were influenced by it.
In art, the baroque was a style that developed from Italian mannerism.
In music, the compositions of the 17th and early 18th centuries, from Monteverdi to Bach, are frequently called baroque music.

barracuda A fish found in all tropical seas and caught for food and sport. Its body is up to 1.8 m long and bears two dorsal fins. Barracudas occur in shoals and feed voraciously on other fish; the larger species are considered dangerous to man.

Barrie, Sir James (Matthew) (1860–1937) British dramatist and novelist. The son of a Scots weaver, he came to London as a freelance writer in 1885. After two successful novels about Scottish rural life he wrote mostly for the theatre. His best-known plays are *The Admirable Crichton* (1902), *Peter Pan* (1904), which has also remained a popular children's book, and *Dear Brutus* (1917).

barrow A prehistoric burial mound, also called a tumulus or cairn. From about 2000 BC earth barrows, concealing stone or timber passages and burial chambers, were built all over Europe for the burial of warrior chiefs. Long barrows, such as at West Kennet (S England), were used for Neolithic multiple burials. Round barrows were more usual in Bronze Age cultures. Barrows continued in use in Iron Age Europe, and as late as the 7th century AD.

Barry, Sir Charles (1795–1860) British architect. Barry worked in both classical and gothic styles. In 1836 he won the competition to rebuild the Houses of Parliament (*see* Palace of Westminster), which, assisted by Augustus Pugin (1812–52), he designed in the gothic manner. He also designed the Reform Club (1837) in London.

Bartók, Béla (1881–1945) Hungarian composer. Bartók studied and taught at the Budapest Academy of Music, where he and Zoltan Kodály (1882–1967) undertook research into Hungarian folksong. In 1940 he went to live in the USA, where he died in poverty. A virtuoso pianist, he composed three piano concertos, *Mikrokosmos* (1926–37), and other piano works. His stage works include the opera *Duke Bluebeard's Castle* (1911) and the ballet *The Miraculous Mandarin* (1919). His six string quartets and *Music for Strings, Percussion, and Celesta* (1936) were more experimental. His most popular work is the *Concerto for Orchestra* (1943).

Bartolommeo, Fra (Baccio della Porta; c. 1472–1517) Florentine Renaissance painter. After training under Cosimo Rosselli (1439–1507), he became a supporter of Savonarola, whose death moved him to join the Dominican monastery of S Marco (1500) and abandon painting until 1504. His religious works include *St Mark* and the *Pietà* (both Palazzo Pitti, Florence).

baryon *See* particle physics.

Baryshnikov, Mikhail (Nikolayevich) (1948–) Soviet-born ballet dancer. A leading dancer with the Kirov Ballet (1967–74), he defected to the West in 1974 joining the American Ballet Theatre (ABT) (1974–78) and becoming artistic director (1980–90). His film appearances include *Turning Point* (1978) and *White Nights* (1986).

basalt The most common type of volcanic rock, typically dark, heavy, and fine textured. Three broad groups of basalt are recognized: alkali basalt, high-alumina basalt, and tholeiite.

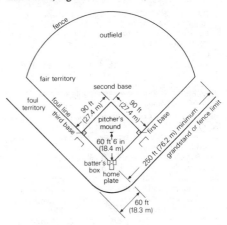

BASEBALL *The dimensions of the field.*

baseball A nine-a-side bat-and-ball game that evolved from rounders, played mainly in the USA, Japan, and Latin America. The object for each team while batting is to score as many runs as possible and while fielding to prevent the other team from doing so. A team bats until three players are out; one turn at bat for both teams constitutes an inning, of which there are usually nine in a game. The pitcher, standing at the pitcher's mound, throws the ball to the batter, standing at home plate, who tries to hit it into fair territory and run. He scores a home run by making a complete circuit of the bases (first, second, third, and home). A player may be struck out (if he misses the ball or hits it into foul territory in each of three attempts), caught out, tagged out (if he or the base he is running towards is touched by a player with the ball), or put out by being hit by a batted ball while running.

Basel

Basel. *See* Basle.

bases. *See* acids and bases.

Basic A computer language developed in the USA in the 1960s. Designed principally for use by inexperienced programmers, it is one of the easiest languages to learn and is widely used, in more recent versions, in personal *computers.

Basie, Count (William B.; 1904–84) US Black jazz pianist and band leader. He became famous for his distinctive "big band" style and recorded many albums, including *Atomic Mr. Basie* and *Straight Ahead.*

basil An annual plant of the mint family, native to India and cultivated widely as a pot herb. Sweet basil (*Ocimum basilicum*), up to 30 cm high, has toothed leaves and small white or bluish flowers.

Basildon 51 34N 0 25E A town in SE England, in Essex. Created as a new town in 1949 from several townships, its industries include engineering, printing, tobacco, and other light industry. Population (1985 est): 160 000.

basilica 1. A Roman public meeting hall. In imperial times, many had a layout similar to the Basilica of Maxentius in Rome: rectangular ground plan, colonnaded aisles, entrance porch (narthex), and windows in the upper storey (clerestory). 2. A Christian church based on a similar plan (e.g. S Giovanni in Laterano in Rome).

basilisk 1. A tropical American lizard that lives in trees. Up to 60 cm long, it has a narrow body, a long whiplike tail, and a flat lobe protruding from the back of its head. It has long hind legs with lobed toes fringed with scales, enabling it to run over the surface of water. 2. A legendary snakelike serpent of ancient Greece and Rome whose glance was believed to be fatal to all living things except the weasel.

Basingstoke 51 16N 1 05W A town in S England, in Hampshire. Its manufactures include agricultural machinery, scientific instruments, and leather goods. It is also developing as a warehousing and distribution centre for southern England. Population (1984 est): 80 000.

basketball A five-a-side court game invented in the USA (1891) by James Naismith (1861–1939). The object is to toss or put an inflated ball into the opponents' basket, a net mounted 3.05 m (10 ft) above the floor on a backboard. Players use only their hands, passing the ball or dribbling it by bouncing, and they may not run with it. A professional game has 4 12-minute quarters. Five substitutes are allowed to each side. The premier professional basketball league is the National Basketball Association in the USA (founded in 1949).

Basle (French name: Bâle; German name: Basel) 47 33N 7 36E The second largest city in Switzerland, on the River Rhine where the French, German, and Swiss borders meet. A Roman fort originally occupied the site. Industries include chemicals, pharmaceuticals, and engineering. The Bank for International Settlements was established here in 1929. Population (1987): 171 700.

Basque A non-Indo-European language spoken by some 500 000 Basque people of the W

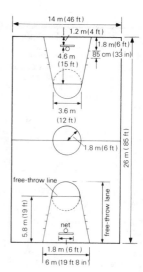

BASKETBALL *The dimensions of the court.*

Pyrenean areas of Spain and France. The Basques are strongly Roman Catholic and traditionally had some freedom of government of their own region, forming an independent government (1936–37) at the time of the Spanish Civil War. Nationalism is still strong and the Basque Separatist movement is still active.

Basra 30 30N 47 50E A town in SE Iraq, on the Shatt (river) al-Arab. It is linked by rail and river steamer to Baghdad; the modern port (Al Ma'qil) was constructed by the British during World War I. Population (1985 est): 616 700.

bass A bony fish that resembles the perch. The sea basses include the common European bass (*Dicentrarchus labrax*). This species can grow up to 1 m long and has a grey or blue back with a white or yellowish belly. Freshwater bass, belonging to a different family, are found in North America.

Bassano, Jacopo (Jacopo *or* Giacomo da Ponte; c. 1517–92) Italian painter of the Venetian school, born in Bassano, the son of a painter. He was one of the earliest painters of country subjects, e.g. *Pastoral* (Lugano); his religious works include *Adoration of the Kings* (National Gallery, Edinburgh).

basset hound A breed of dog originating in France. It has a long body with very short legs and a narrow face with drooping ears and a mournful expression. They were formerly popular hunting dogs. Height: 33–38 cm.

bassoon A musical instrument of the woodwind family. Its conical tube is about 2.5 m (8 ft) long and is bent back on itself. It has a metal crook into which a double reed is inserted. With a range of about three and a half octaves above B flat below the bass stave, it is used for melodic as well as bass parts.

Bass Strait A channel separating the mainland of Australia from Tasmania. It has valuable oil and natural gas deposits. Length: 290 km (180 mi). Maximum width: 240 km (150 mi).

Bastille A fortress in Paris, It was built in about 1370 to protect the wall around Paris against English attack and became a state prison under Cardinal de *Richelieu. The storming of the Bastille on 14 July, 1789, is regarded as the beginning of the *French Revolution.

Basutoland. *See* Lesotho, Kingdom of.

bat A flying mammal found in most temperate and tropical regions. There are two groups: the fruit bats, which are vegetarians and occur in Old World tropical and subtropical regions, and the smaller insect-eating bats. Both groups may also feed on pollen, nectar, blood, and small animals. The wings are extensions of skin that are supported between the forelimb (with its very long fingers), the hind limbs, and the tail. Insectivorous bats have poor vision and use echolocation for navigation and catching prey, whereas fruit bats have large eyes adapted for night vision.

Bateson, William (1861–1926) British biologist, whose experiments on inheritance helped found the science of genetics. His results (1905–08) supported the findings of Gregor *Mendel published in 1865 although he refused to accept the chromosome theory proposed by T. H. Morgan.

Bath 51 23N 2 22W A city in SW England, in Avon on the River Avon. It was an early Roman centre known as Aquae Sulis because of its hot natural springs. The Roman baths have survived and are considered the best Roman remains in the UK. Bath became fashionable as a spa town in the 18th century when many of the finest buildings were built, including the Royal Crescent and the Assembly Rooms. Bath Abbey, mainly 16th-century, lies in the town centre. Population (1981): 79 965.

Bath, Order of the A British order of knighthood, formed by George I in 1725 to take the place of Knights of the Bath, traditionally founded by Henry IV in 1399. It consists of the sovereign, knights and dames grand cross (GCB), knights and dames commanders (KCB), and companions (CB). Its name comes from the bathing ceremony that was the main part of the ceremony of admission to the original order.

Bathurst. *See* Banjul.

batik Cloth, traditionally cotton, dyed by a special method. An ancient Indonesian craft, batik involves the repeated application of melted wax, later removed, to protect parts of the material from the dye.

Baton Rouge 30 30N 91 10W A city in the USA, the capital of Louisiana situated on the Mississippi River. It is a major deepwater port with oil and sugar refineries. Population (1987 est): 242 184.

battered baby syndrome Injuries inflicted on babies or young children by their parents. Battering commonly takes the form of facial bruises, cigarette burns, head injuries (often with brain damage), and fractured bones. The parents are often emotionally disturbed or have themselves suffered from physical abuse in infancy. A care order is often necessary to safeguard a child from further abuse.

Battle 50 55N 0 29E A town in S England, in East Sussex. It was the scene of the battle of Hastings (1066) in which Harold II was defeated by William the Conqueror, who built Battle Abbey to commemorate his victory. Population (1989): 5800.

Baudelaire, Charles (1821–67) French poet. He inherited his father's fortune in 1842 and lived extravagantly until what was left of the money was placed in trust by his family (1844). In 1852 he discovered Edgar Allan *Poe, publishing several translations of his works (1856–65). His only volume of poetry, *Les Fleurs du mal* (1857, revised 1861), contained several erotic poems, which led to his being convicted for obscenity. He became paralysed as a result of venereal disease and died in Paris soon after.

Baudouin I (1930–) King of the Belgians (1951–), succeeding his father Leopold III. He was interned by the Nazis in World War II. In 1960 he married Fabiola de Mora y Aragón (1928–).

Bauhaus A German school of design founded in 1919 at Weimar and closed by the Nazis in 1933. From 1925 to 1932 it was housed at Dessau in a building designed by *Gropius (its director until 1928), itself a work of great influence. The Bauhaus sought to bring all the arts together and to develop a practical style appropriate for the industrial 20th century. *See also* Kandinsky; Klee.

bauxite The chief ore of aluminium. It is formed by the weathering of aluminium-rich rocks and consists mainly of hydrated aluminium oxide.

Bavaria (German name: Bayern) The largest *Land* of Germany, bordering on Austria and Czechoslovakia. Predominantly agricultural, the main crops are rye, wheat, and barley. *History*: a duchy and later a kingdom ruled by the Wittelsbachs from 1180 to 1918, it then became a republic. Area: 70 547 sq km (29 232 sq mi). Population (1987): 10 553 000. Capital: Munich.

Bax, Sir Arnold Edward Trevor (1883–1953) British composer. His tone poems, such as *Tintagel* (1917) and *The Garden of Fand* (1916), and his seven symphonies remain his most popular works. He was Master of the King's Music from 1941 until his death.

bay A Mediterranean evergreen tree, *Laurus nobilis*. It can reach a height of 20 m, has aromatic dark-green lance-shaped leaves, small yellowish flowers, and blackish berries. The leaves are used to season food. *See* laurel.

Bayeux 49 16N 0 42W A town in NW France, in the Calvados department on the River Aure. The 11th-century Bayeux tapestry (69 m long, depicting the Norman conquest) is exhibited in a former seminary and there is a fine 13th-century cathedral. Industries include dairy foods and plastics. Population (1982 est): 15 237.

Bay of Pigs (Spanish name: Bahía de los Cochinos) A bay on the SW coast of Cuba where on 17 April, 1961, about 1200 Cuban exiles attempted to invade the country. Hoping to overthrow Fidel *Castro, and supported by the US *Central Intelligence Agency, the invasion was unsuccessful largely because it lacked sufficient US military backing.

bayonet A blade that may be attached to the muzzle of a firearm. The bayonet, which is thought to have originated in the early 17th century in Bayonne (France), replaced the pike. Bayonets were used in both World Wars.

Bayreuth 49 27N 11 35E A town in S Germany, in Bavaria. It is famous as the home of Richard Wagner, who designed its Festival Theatre (1872–76), where his operas are performed annually. Population (1984 est): 71 800.

BBC. See British Broadcasting Corporation.

BCG (bacille Calmette Guérin) A vaccine consisting of a weakened form of the tuberculosis bacterium, which is injected to give partial protection against tuberculosis. A successful vaccination produces a lump at the injection site.

Beaconsfield, Benjamin Disraeli, 1st Earl of. See Disraeli, Benjamin.

beagle A breed of dog originating in the UK. It has a deep chest, strong shoulders, and drooping ears. Beagles have long been used as hunting hounds; more recently, they have become popular household pets. Height: 33–40 cm.

bean The seed or fruit of certain herbs, shrubs, or trees of the family Leguminosae. See broad bean; carob; French bean; haricot bean; Lima bean; mung bean; runner bean; soya bean.

bear A large heavy mammal of the order Carnivora, found in Europe, Asia, and America. Bears have a shaggy coat and a short tail and walk flat on the soles of their broad feet. They can stand erect and most of them are vegetarian. Newly born bears are very small (about the size of rats), blind, and toothless. See black bear; brown bear; polar bear.

bearbaiting A blood sport formerly popular in Britain and Europe. A bear, sometimes blinded, was chained to a bear pit or bear garden and dogs were let loose to attack it. **Bullbaiting** used bulls in a similar way. Both bearbaiting and bullbaiting were made illegal in the UK in 1835.

bearded tit. See reedling.

bearded vulture. See lammergeier.

Beardsley, Aubrey Vincent (1872–98) British illustrator of the periodicals The Yellow Book and The Savoy and of several books, including Wilde's Salome and Pope's Rape of the Lock, who achieved notoriety with his grotesque and erotic imagery. His curved lines, characteristic of *Art Nouveau, contrast with dense areas of black ink.

beating the bounds A traditional ceremony that takes place in several English towns and villages on Ascension Day. Primarily a religious event, it evolved during the reign of Elizabeth I, and developed from the earlier ceremonies of Rogationtide. A priest leads those present round the parish boundaries offering prayers for the harvest while young boys beat the boundary stones with sticks. A similar Scottish ceremony is called riding the marches.

Beatitudes In the New Testament, the eight blessings with which Jesus opened the Sermon on the Mount (Matthew 5.3–12). They describe such Christian virtues as meekness, mercy, and purity of heart (e.g. "Blessed are the meek: for they shall inherit the earth."). The word comes from the Latin of the *Vulgate, beati sunt (blessed are).

Beatles A British rock group, which achieved worldwide popularity during the 1960s. The Beatles appeared at the Cavern Club in Liverpool in 1962 and subsequently recorded "Love Me Do" and "She Loves You," which became top of the Hit Parade in 1963. By this time the group consisted of George Harrison, John Lennon, Paul McCartney, and Ringo Starr; they toured the USA successfully, made two films, and were awarded MBEs in 1965. In 1970 they disbanded to pursue separate careers.

Beatrix (1938–) Queen of the Netherlands since the abdication (1980) of her mother Queen Juliana. Her marriage (1966) to the West German Claus von Amsberg (1926–) caused some controversy.

beats Variations in the intensity of sound when two pure notes of nearly equal frequency are heard. The effect is similar to that of interference. At certain times, the amplitudes of the waves add together to give a maximum and, at intermediate times, they tend to cancel each other out. The ear hears this as a regular change in intensity (or loudness). The frequency of the beats is equal to the difference in the frequencies of the two notes.

Beaufort scale A scale of wind speed devised in 1805 by Admiral Sir Francis Beaufort (1774–1857).

Beauvais 49 26N 2 05E A market town in N France, in the Oise department. Its fine cathedral (begun 1227) was damaged during World War II and the factory in which the famous Gobelin tapestries had been made since the 17th century was completely destroyed. Population (1982 est): 54 147.

Beauvoir, Simone de (1908–86) French novelist and essayist. The constant companion of Jean-Paul *Sartre, whom she met in 1929, her books include The Blood of Others (1948), The Second Sex (1953), The Coming of Age (1973), and All Said and Done (1975).

beaver A large aquatic *rodent, Castor fiber, of Europe, Asia, and North America. Over 1 m long, beavers have a dark sleek waterproof coat and a broad flat tail used for balance and swimming. They build a "lodge" of sticks and mud, with dams above and below, using their large incisor teeth to cut wood. During the summer they feed on vegetation; in winter they eat bark.

Beaverbrook, Max(well) Aitken, 1st Baron (1879–1964) British newspaper owner and politician, born in Canada. In 1919 he took over the Daily Express, in 1921 he founded the Sunday Express, and in 1929 bought the Evening Standard (London). In World War I he served in Lloyd George's War Cabinet as minister of information (1918) and in Churchill's World War II Cabinet as minister of aircraft production (1940–41).

Beaufort number	description of wind	wind speed	
		knots	metres per second
0	calm	<1	0.0– 0.2
1	light air	1– 3	0.3– 1.5
2	light breeze	4– 6	1.6– 3.3
3	gentle breeze	7–10	3.4– 5.4
4	moderate breeze	11–16	5.5– 7.9
5	fresh breeze	17–21	8.0–10.7
6	strong breeze	22–27	10.8–13.8
7	near gale	28–33	13.9–17.1
8	gale	34–40	17.2–20.7
9	strong gale	41–47	20.8–24.4
10	storm	48–55	24.5–28.4
11	violent storm	56–63	28.5–32.6
12	hurricane	≥64	≥32.7

BEAUFORT SCALE

Bechuanaland. *See* Botswana, Republic of.
Becker, Boris (1967–) German tennis player. In 1985, aged 17, he became the youngest player ever to win the men's singles at Wimbledon, which he also won in 1986 and 1989.
Becket, St Thomas à (c. 1118–70) English churchman. The son of a London merchant, Becket became chancellor to Henry II in 1154 and archbishop of Canterbury in 1162. After quarrelling with Henry he refused to swear allegiance to the Constitutions of *Clarendon and was exiled to France (1164–70). Subsequent attempts to resolve the dispute failed and on 29 December, 1170 he was murdered in Canterbury Cathedral by Henry's Knights. He was made a saint in 1173.
Beckett, Samuel (1906–89) Irish novelist, dramatist, and poet. After studying at Trinity College, Dublin he settled in Paris in 1937. He wrote in both French and English. His plays, which include *Waiting for Godot* (1954), and his prose works, such as *Malone Dies* (1956) and *How It Is* (1964), treat human existence with a pessimism tempered by desperate humour. His later works, such as *Breath* (1972) and *Not I* (1973), are notably brief and concentrated. He won the Nobel Prize in 1969.
becquerel (Bq) The *SI unit of activity of a radioactive substance equal to the number of disintegrations occurring in one second. Named after Antoine Henri *Becquerel.
Becquerel, (Antoine) Henri (1852–1908) French physicist, who was professor at the Conservatoire des Arts et Métiers in Paris. He discovered radioactivity (1896) by chance, on finding that invisible rays from uranium salts could affect a photographic plate even through a light-proof wrapper. For his research on these radiations, Becquerel shared the Nobel Prize (1903) with his associates Pierre and Marie *Curie.
bedbug A flat wingless blood-sucking insect, about 5 mm long. In temperate regions *Cimex lectularius* is the species that most commonly attacks man, hiding by day in bedding, furniture, etc., and becoming active at night.
Bedchamber Crisis (1839) The issue in British politics over Queen Victoria's ladies of the bedchamber. After the resignation of Lord Melbourne, a Whig, Peel attempted to form a Tory ministry and asked Victoria to dismiss her Whig ladies. She refused and Melbourne remained in office until his government fell in 1841, when Victoria agreed to the dismissal of three ladies.
Bede, St (c. 673–735 AD) English historian, known as the Venerable Bede. After 682 he lived at the monastery of Jarrow in Northumberland. His *Ecclesiastical History of the English People* (c. 731), written in Latin and later translated into English, is an important source for British history, especially the early Anglo-Saxon period (5th–8th centuries). He was the author of many grammatical, scientific, and historical works. Feast day: 27 May.
Bedford 52 08N 0 29W A town in S England, the administrative centre of Bedfordshire on the River Ouse. John *Bunyan was born nearby and spent 12 years in Bedford gaol. Population (1983 est): 89 200.
Bedfordshire A county in the South Midlands of England. It is chiefly low lying, rising to the Chiltern Hills in the SW, and is drained by the Great Ouse River. Agricultural products include wheat and vegetables. The chief industries are centred on Luton, Dunstable, and Bedford. Area: 1235 sq km (477 sq mi). Population (1986 est): 525 900. Administrative centre: Bedford.
Bedlington terrier A breed of dog originating in Bedlington, N England, in the early 19th century. It has long legs and a long narrow face and is a popular sporting dog locally. The thick coat may be blue or sandy. Height: about 40 cm.
Bedouin The wandering *Arab tribes of the Syrian and Arabian deserts. Their economy is based on camels, sheep, and goats. Courageous fighters, the Bedouin played an active role in the early Arab conquests, but are now under pressure to take up a settled existence.
bee An insect (10–30 mm long) related to ants and wasps. Bees feed on pollen and nectar and are important pollinators of flowers. In some species the sting is barbed, remaining in the wound. Most solitary bees nest in soil, hollow trees, or wall cavities. Some, however, tunnel into wood (the carpenter bee) or construct nests using earth (the mason bee) or leaves (the leafcutter bee). The female lays one or more eggs in a nest that is then sealed. The social bees live in communities organized into castes—workers (infertile females), drones (males, developed from unfertilized eggs), and a queen (a fertile fe-

male). Colonies are established in trees, walls, or cliffs (*see also* honeybee).

beech A deciduous tree native to N temperate regions, occasionally reaching a height of 40 m. Beeches have smooth grey bark. The leaves are oval, pointed, and toothed, the flowers are unisexual and inconspicuous, and the fruits are nutlike seeds enclosed in husks (beechnuts or mast). The common beech of Europe and Asia is *Fagus sylvatica*, the timber of which is used for furniture and flooring.

Beecham, Sir Thomas (1879–1961) British conductor. He used his inherited fortune for the advancement of English musical life. He championed the works of Richard Strauss, Sibelius, and particularly Delius, whose friend and biographer he became. He founded the London Philharmonic Orchestra (1932) and the Royal Philharmonic Orchestra (1947).

beekeeping (*or* apiculture) The rearing of colonies of honeybees in hives, usually for their honey or *beeswax. Sheets of wax in wooden frames (starter combs) are hung inside the hive. Onto these the bees build wax cells that they fill with honey and seal. When a frame is full it is removed, the honey is extracted, and the comb is reused. A colony makes about 32 kg of honey in a summer, but 14 kg of this is needed by the bees for food during the winter; following a bad summer they must be fed sugar syrup. About 10 000–20 000 bees survive the winter; during the spring, when a colony has increased to over 50 000, a large group is likely to leave the hive (i.e. it swarms). The beekeeper collects the swarm and puts it into an empty hive.

beer and brewing Beer is an alcoholic drink made from fermented malt flavoured with hops. Brewing is the process of making beer. Barley, or other grain, is first allowed to germinate, the resulting product, the malt, being dried (kilned), ground, and heated with water (mashed). Starch in the grain is converted into soluble carbohydrates by enzymes in the malt. The resulting sweet liquid, the wort, is boiled with hops to concentrate the wort and utilize the bitter flavour of the hops. The wort is then filtered and cooled ready for fermentation. Yeast is added and the carbohydrates in the wort are converted into alchohol. The liquid is drained and stored. Beer was drunk in ancient Egypt and has been enjoyed in a great many countries ever since. Ale was originally a stronger drink than beer, brewed without hops. Now it usually means any beer although ale is sometimes reserved for stronger brews fermented at higher temperatures. **Mild** beer is made with fewer hops than **bitter** and a darker malt is used to add colour. **Lager** is traditionally a light beer matured over a long period at low temperature. **Stout** is made from a blend of roasted barley and malts.

beeswax A substance produced by bees to build honeycombs. It is collected by heating the honeycomb in water (after removing the honey) so that the floating wax can be separated after it solidifies on cooling. Beeswax (melting point 61–69°C) is used in high-quality polishes, etc.

beet A herbaceous plant, *Beta vulgaris*, native to Europe and the Mediterranean region. Several varieties are widely cultivated in temperate areas, the most important of which is the sugar beet. The root of the red or garden beet yields beetroot, while the mangel-wurzel is an important fodder.

Beethoven, Ludwig van (1770–1827) German composer, born in Bonn. His father, a court musician, attempted to make money by presenting him as a child prodigy. He settled in Vienna in 1792 after studying there with Haydn. At the age of 30 he began to go deaf, an experience that increased his loneliness and eccentricity, but did not stop him composing. About 600 of Beethoven's works survive, among them 9 symphonies, 5 piano concertos, 1 violin concerto, 16 string quartets, 10 violin and piano sonatas, 32 piano sonatas, 2 ballets, 2 masses, the opera *Fidelio* (1805–14), and about 200 song settings. His last most intense works include the *Missa Solemnis* (1818–23), the ninth symphony (1817–23), and the experimental late string quartets.

beetle An insect belonging to the largest order (*Coleoptera*; about 278 000 species) of the animal kingdom. The forewings are specialized as hard structures (called elytra), which cover the functional hindwings when these are not being used for flying. The elytra and the thick cuticle protect the beetle against enemies and enable aquatic species to trap a store of air. Many beetles are serious pests of crops, timber, textiles, etc.; others are useful by eating insect pests or by speeding up the process of decomposition.

beetroot. *See* beet.

begonia A tropical plant with fleshy leaves that is widely grown as a house or garden plant for its brightly coloured flowers. The underground parts are long-lived and may be roots or rhizomes.

Behan, Brendan (1923–64) Irish playwright. His first play, *The Quare Fellow* (1954), and his autobiography, *Borstal Boy* (1958), were based on his years of detention and imprisonment for Irish Republican Army (IRA) activities. His best-known play was *The Hostage* (1956).

behaviour therapy A method of treating psychological problems by assuming that they are the result of faulty learning. It was developed mainly by H. Eysenck. Sometimes conditioning is used to teach new behaviour, such as better ways of relating to other people, or to eliminate undesirable behaviour, such as excessive drinking. It includes treatment for phobias, in which repeated exposure to the feared object or situation gradually reduces the subject's fear of it.

Beiderbecke, Bix (Leon Bismarck B.; 1903–31) US jazz cornetist and pianist. He played with Louis Armstrong and in the band of Paul Whiteman (1891–1967), becoming a jazz legend; his early death was caused by alcoholism.

Beijing. *See* Peking.

Beirut 33 52N 35 30E The capital of the Lebanon, situated on the E Mediterranean Sea. After centuries of Turkish domination, it was held by the French from World War I until 1941, when it became the capital of the newly independent Lebanon. It was badly damaged in the civil war (1975–76) and in 1982 when Israeli forces besieged the city and forced the Palestine Liberation Organization to leave. It was subsequently the scene of violent clashes between various religious factions until the private militias left the city in 1990. Population (1982 est): 1 100 000.

Belau, Republic of (name until 1981: Palau or Pelew) A group of islands in the W Pacific Ocean, constituting a UN Trust Territory. Self-government was achieved in 1981. President: Ngiratkel Etpison. Area: 476 sq km (184 sq mi). Population (1988 est): 14 106.

Belfast 54 40N 5 50W The capital of Northern Ireland, a seaport situated where the River Lagan enters Belfast Lough. The principal buildings include the City Hall (1906) and Parliament Buildings (1932) at Stormont. *History*: large-scale growth of Belfast came with the expansion of the linen-making and shipbuilding industries in the 19th century; it became a city in 1888. The Parliament of Northern Ireland sat in the city from 1921 to 1972. Recently conflict between Protestant and Roman Catholic communities has intensified. The British army has maintained a presence in Belfast since August, 1969. Population (1987 est): 303 800.

Belgian Congo. *See* Zaïre, Republic of.

Belgium, Kingdom of (French name: Belgique; Flemish name: België) A country in NW Europe, on the North Sea. It is generally low lying except for the Ardennes in the SE. The main rivers are the Scheldt and the Meuse, which are linked by an extensive network of inland waterways. The population is divided between the French and the Flemish, with other small minorities. *Economy*: highly industrialized, with coal and iron resources supporting considerable heavy industry. Agriculture and food processing are important. In 1948 Belgium and Luxembourg joined with the Netherlands to form the *Benelux Economic Union. Belgium is also a member of the EC. *History*: the area was part of the Roman Empire until about the end of the 2nd century AD, when it was invaded by Germanic tribes. In medieval times the cities of Ghent, Bruges, and Ypres rose to virtual independence and economic prosperity through the wool industry. After being occupied by France during the Napoleonic Wars, Belgium was joined to the Netherlands in 1815. Following an uprising, it became independent in 1830, and the National Congress elected Prince Leopold of Saxe-Coburg as King of the Belgians in 1831. In spite of efforts to remain neutral it was attacked and occupied by Germany in both World Wars. When the Germans invaded in 1940, King Leopold III surrendered immediately but the government struggled on in exile in London. In 1950 the king was persuaded to abdicate in favour of his son, Baudouin. The main political problem since World War II has been tension between the French-speaking Walloons in the S and the Flemish-speaking community in the N. The loss in 1960 of the Belgian Congo, now Zaïre, had an adverse effect on Belgium's economy. Prime minister: Wilfried Martens. Official languages: French, Flemish, Dutch, and German. Official currency: Belgian franc of 100 centimes. Area: 30 513 sq km (11 778 sq mi). Population (1988 est): 9 888 000. Capital: Brussels. Main port: Antwerp.

Belgrade (Serbo-Croat name: Beograd) 44 50N 20 30E The capital of Yugoslavia and of Serbia, situated in the NE where the Rivers Danube and Sava meet. It became the Serbian capital in the early 15th century. It later suffered Turkish and Austrian occupations but again became capital of Serbia in the late 19th century and of Yugoslavia after World War I. It was occupied by the Germans in World War II and has expanded considerably in the years since. Population (1981): 1 407 073.

Belize, Colony of (name until 1973: British Honduras) A country in Central America between Mexico and Guatemala. The country is generally low lying, rising to the Maya Mountains in the SW. The population is of African, Spanish-American, and Mayan Indian descent, with other small minorities. *Economy*: mainly agricultural; the combined value of sugar and citrus exports have exceeded that of timber since the early 1960s. *History*: once an important Mayan settlement, Belize was discovered by Columbus in 1502 but the first European occupation was an independent settlement of British woodcutters, which held out against the Spanish throughout the 17th century. In 1862 it became a British colony under Jamaica, becoming an independent colony in 1884; it attained self-government in 1964 and was granted full independence in 1981. Prime minister: George Price. Official language: English; Spanish is also widely spoken. Official currency: Belize dollar of 100 cents. Area: 22 963 sq km (8867 sq mi). Population (1987 est): 176 000. Capital: Belmopan.

Belize City 17 29N 88 10W The chief port of Belize, on the Caribbean coast. It was formerly capital of Belize but following a severe hurricane (1961), Belmopan, which became capital in 1970, was constructed inland. The main exports are timber, coconuts, and maize. Population (1987 est): 48 400.

Bell, Alexander Graham (1847–1922) Scottish-born US scientist and inventor. He went to Canada in 1870 and to the USA in 1873, where he became professor of vocal physiology at Boston University. Bell's work in telegraphy and telephony led to the invention of the telephone, which he patented in 1876, demonstrated at American exhibitions, and had in commercial use by 1877.

belladonna. *See* deadly nightshade.

belladonna lily. *See* amaryllis.

Bellerophon In Greek mythology, the grandson of Sisyphus and son of Glaucus, King of Corinth. Sent by Iobates, King of Lycia, to kill the *Chimera, he was able to carry out his task by flying above the dragon on Pegasus, a winged horse.

Bellini, Jacopo (c. 1400–c. 1470) Venetian painter, who was a pupil of Gentile da Fabriano. Although his few surviving paintings obey the decorative conventions of Byzantine and Gothic art, his two sketchbooks (British Museum and Louvre) reveal a remarkable understanding of perspective. They influenced his son-in-law Andrea Mantegna and his two sons, who both trained under him. The eldest, **Gentile Bellini**

(c. 1429–1507), is best known for his portraits and procession scenes. *The Procession in St Mark's Square* (Accademia, Venice) depicts his native city with realism. Gentile's brother **Giovanni Bellini** (c. 1430–1516) was an important influence on Venetian art, especially through his pupils *Titian and *Giorgione. His paintings included several altarpieces, such as *Madonna and Saints* (S Zaccaria, Venice) and portraits, such as *Doge Loredano* (National Gallery, London).

Bellini, Vincenzo (1801–35) Italian opera composer. Of his 11 operas, *La somnambula* and *Norma* (both 1831) and *I Puritani* (1835) remain popular, although they require singers of outstanding ability.

Belloc, (Joseph-Pierre) Hilaire (1870–1953) British poet and essayist. Born in France, he served as a Liberal MP from 1906 to 1910. His works include light verse, such as *Cautionary Tales* (1907), essays, biographies, and satirical novels, often illustrated by his friend G. K. *Chesterton. A Roman Catholic, he vigorously opposed the socialism of G. B. *Shaw and H. G. *Wells.

Bellow, Saul (1915–) Canadian-born US novelist, the son of poor Russian Jewish immigrants. His first novel, *Dangling Man* (1944), was influenced by *existentialism. His later novels, such as *Mr Sammler's Planet* (1970), *Humboldt's Gift* (1975), and *The Dean's December* (1982), are ironic studies of urban Jewish intellectuals. He published *Him with His Foot in his Mouth* in 1986; in 1976 he won the Nobel Prize.

Belmopan 17 12N 88 00W The capital of Belize, on the River Belize about 80 km (50 mi) inland from Belize City, which it succeeded as capital in 1970 after the latter was damaged by a hurricane in 1961. Population (1989 est): 3700.

Belorussian Soviet Socialist Republic (Belorussia *or* White Russia) A constituent republic in the W central Soviet Union. The majority of its inhabitants are Belorussians, an Eastern Slav people. Formed in 1919, it was badly devastated in World War II. It has a separate seat in the UN. Area: 207 600 sq km (80 134 sq mi). Population (1987): 10 100 000. Capital: Minsk.

beluga 1. A giant *sturgeon, *Huso huso*, up to 8.4 m long, that occurs in the Caspian and Black Seas and the River Volga of E Europe. It is a highly prolific egg producer and the source of the best caviar. 2. *See* white whale.

bends. *See* decompression sickness.

Benedictines The monks and nuns belonging to the Roman Catholic Order of St Benedict (OSB), a union of independent abbeys, which follow the Rule of St Benedict of Nursia (c. 480– c. 550). They were responsible for preserving the learning of the ancient Greeks and Romans after the fall of the Roman Empire. The liqueur Bénédictine is named after the order and is made at Fécamp, France.

benefit of clergy The development in England of the 12th-century church law that criminous clerks (criminal clerics) should not be tried by both Church and state courts. Henry II established that all clerics had the right to be tried only in Church courts. These could not give the death sentence. Bad use was made of this privi-

lege in the middle ages and although limited during the Reformation it was not finally abolished until the early 19th century.

Benelux The customs union formed by Belgium, the *Netherlands, and *Lux*embourg in 1948. It was the first free-trade market in Europe. All three countries are now members of the *EEC, which has similar aims.

Beneš, Edvard (1884–1948) Czechoslovak statesman. In 1918 Beneš helped Tomáš Masaryk to found Czechoslovakia and became foreign minister, playing an important role in the League of Nations. In 1935 he became president but spent World War II as president of a government in exile in London, returning to Czechoslovakia in 1945. He resigned the presidency in 1948, when Czechoslovakia became a communist state.

Bengal A region of the Indian subcontinent, in the NE on the Bay of Bengal around the Ganges and Brahmaputra deltas; it is divided between India and Bangladesh. *History*: the centre of Buddhist (8th–12th centuries), Hindu (11th–13th centuries), and Islamic dynasties, Bengal became the base for British expansion through India. It was divided between India and Pakistan at independence (1947).

Bengal, Bay of The shallow NE limb of the Indian Ocean, between the Indian subcontinent on the W and Burma and the Andaman and Nicobar Islands on the E. Shipping and coastal life are dominated by the NE winter monsoon and the SW summer monsoon.

Ben-Gurion, David (David Gruen; 1886–1973) Israeli statesman and first prime minister (1948–53, 1955–63). In 1917 he joined the British Army's Jewish Legion to free Palestine from Ottoman control (achieved in 1918) and to establish a Jewish home in Palestine. In 1920 he founded the General Federation of Labour (the Histadrut) and in 1930, the Israeli Workers' Party (Mapai). He led the Zionist effort to establish a Jewish state (achieved 1948). After resigning as prime minister in 1963, he was leader of the opposition party, the Rafi, until his retirement in 1970.

Benin, People's Republic of (name until 1975: Dahomey) A country in West Africa, on the Gulf of Guinea. Flat forests and swamps in the S rise to plateaus in the centre and to mountains in the N. The population is mainly Fon and Yoruba in the N and Somba and Bariba in the S. *Economy*: chiefly agricultural, cotton has been introduced in the N and coffee in the S, and these provide the main exports. Offshore oil has been found and hydroelectric schemes are being planned. *History*: the powerful Aja kingdom of Dahomey was a centre of the slave trade in the 17th century but was conquered by the French in 1893 and became part of French West Africa. Dahomey attained self-government in 1958 and became an independent republic within the French Community in 1960. A series of military coups followed, in the last of which (1972) Brig Gen Mathieu Kérékou (1933–) seized power. In 1974 he established a Marxist-Leninist state. Moves towards democracy began in 1990. Official language: French. Official currency: CFA (Communauté financière africaine) franc of 100 centimes. Area: 112 600 sq km (43 464 sq mi). Population (1987 est): 4 153 000. Capital: Porto Novo. Main port: Cotonou.

Benn, Anthony (Neil) Wedgwood (1925–) British Labour politician, a leader of the party's left wing. The 2nd Viscount Stansgate from 1960, he gave up his title in 1963, the first person to do so under the Peerage Act (1963). He was minister of technology (1966–70), for industry (1974–75), and for energy (1975–79). He lost his parliamentary seat in the 1983 general election but won a by-election at Chesterfield in 1984.

Bennett, (Enoch) Arnold (1837–1931) British novelist. The son of a solicitor in Newcastle-under-Lyme, he published his first novel, *A Man from the North*, in 1898 and lived in Paris from 1902 to 1912. His best-known novels are about life in the Potteries area of Staffordshire, where he grew up. They include *Anna of the Five Towns* (1902), *The Old Wives' Tale* (1908), and *Clayhanger* (1910).

Ben Nevis 56 48N 5 00W The highest mountain in the British Isles, in the Highland Region of Scotland, in the Grampians. Height: 1343 m (4406 ft).

Bentham, Jeremy (1748–1832) British philosopher, pioneer of utilitarianism. From a wealthy middle-class background, he studied law, but preferred theory to practice and in 1776 published *A Fragment on Government*. In 1789 *Principles of Morals and Legislation* presented utilitarianism. He retired to the country in 1814 and wrote on politics and ethics until his death.

Benz, Karl (Friedrich) (1844–1929) German engineer and car manufacturer. In 1885 he built the first car to be driven by an internal-combustion engine. The Benz Company merged with Daimler in 1926 to form Daimler-Benz, the makers of Mercedes-Benz cars.

Benzedrine. See amphetamine.

benzene (or benzol; C_6H_6) A colourless highly flammable liquid. It is the simplest *aromatic compound, its molecules consisting of a ring of six carbon atoms each with a hydrogen atom attached. Benzene is obtained from *oil and from *coal tar. It is widely used in the chemical industry.

benzodiazepines A class of tranquillizing drugs that act by depressing specific areas of the brain. They include diazepam (Valium) and chlordiazepoxide (Librium), which are used as sedatives to relieve anxiety. Nitrazepam (Mogadon) is used as a sleeping pill. Both nitrazepam and diazepam are habit forming.

Beowulf An Anglo-Saxon epic poem preserved in a late 10th-century manuscript. Probably composed in the 8th century by a Christian poet sympathetic to pagan ideals, it mentions historical events of early 6th-century Scandinavia. In the first part the hero, Beowulf, kills the marauding monster, Grendel; in the second part, Beowulf, now king of the Swedish tribe of Geats, slays a dragon and seizes its hoard of treasure.

berberis A widely distributed deciduous or evergreen spiny shrub. The small yellow or orange flowers usually grow in clusters and the fruits are red or blue berries. Some species are grown as garden plants. Berberis is involved in a rust disease of wheat and is therefore outlawed in some areas.

Berbers A Muslim people occupying parts of N Africa (Morocco, Algeria, Tunisia, and nearby regions) and speaking a non-Semitic language. Before the introduction of Arabic speech in the 7th century AD, Berber languages were spoken over the whole of the area and are still spoken by an estimated ten million people; Morocco is still mainly Berber in population.

Berg, Alban (1885–1935) Austrian composer. A friend and pupil of *Schoenberg, he adopted atonality and used *serialism. His greatest works are the operas *Wozzeck* (1915–21) and *Lulu* (1928–35), *Lyric Suite* (for string quartet; 1925–26), and a violin concerto (1935).

bergamot A tree, *Citrus bergamia*, closely related to the orange. An essence (oil of bergamot) extracted from the rind of its fruit is used in perfumery, for which it is grown in S Italy and Sicily. The name is also given to two plants of the mint family: *Mentha citrata*, which yields an extract similar to oil of bergamot, and *Monarda citriodora* (lemon bergamot), sometimes used in a tealike beverage.

Bergen 60 23N 5 20E A seaport and second largest city in Norway, situated in the SW. Founded about 1070 AD, it became the chief commercial city and the country's capital (12th–13th centuries). It had connections with Hanseatic merchants (14th–18th centuries). It was rebuilt after damage by fire in 1702, 1855, and 1916 and by bombing during World War II. It exports fish products and base metals. Population (1989): 209 000.

Bergman, Ingmar (1918–) Swedish film and stage director. His films include *The Seventh Seal* (1956), *Wild Strawberries* (1957), *Persona* (1966), *Scenes from a Marriage* (1974), *Autumn Sonata* (1978), and *Fanny and Alexander* (1982).

Bergman, Ingrid (1915–82) Swedish actress. She went to Hollywood in 1939 and became an international film star, appearing in such films as *Casablanca* (1942), *Gaslight* (1944), and numerous other major films, her last being *Autumn Sonata* (1978).

Bergson, Henri (1859–1941) French philosopher and psychologist, one of the greatest thinkers of his time. He discussed free will and determinism in such works as *Matière et mémoire* (1896) and *L'Evolution créatrice* (1907). He won the Nobel Prize for Literature in 1927.

beriberi A disease caused by deficiency of *vitamin B_1 (thiamine). It is common in areas where the staple diet is polished rice, i.e. rice with the husks removed (thiamine occurs mainly in the rice husks). Dry beriberi affects the nerves, causing muscular weakness and pain. Wet beriberi is probably the result of combined protein malnutrition and thiamine deficiency: it causes accumulation of fluid and swelling of the limbs, leading eventually to heart failure. Treatment consists of providing a diet with adequate thiamine and vitamin supplements.

Bering Sea A section of the N Pacific Ocean between the Soviet Union, Alaska, and the Aleutian Islands. Navigation is difficult, with storms and a partial ice covering in winter. The NE continental shelf contains oil and gas, as yet unexploited. The channel connecting the Bering Sea with the Arctic Ocean is the **Bering Strait**.

Berkeley, George (1685–1753) Irish bishop and idealist philosopher. In *A New Theory of Vision* (1709), *Principles of Human Knowledge* (1710), and *Three Dialogues between Hylas and Philonous* (1713), he argued that the material world exists only in the mind.

Berkeley, Sir Lennox Randal Francis (1903–89) British composer. He studied under Nadia Boulanger and taught at the Royal Academy of Music from 1946 to 1968. Berkeley's works include the *Serenade for Strings* (1939), *Four Poems of St Teresa* for contralto and strings (1947), and the fourth symphony (1978).

berkelium (Bk) A synthetic *transuranic element first produced by Seaborg at the University of California at Berkeley in 1949. The longest-lived isotope (^{249}Bk) has a half-life of 314 days. At no 97; at wt (247).

Berkshire A county of S England. It consists mainly of lowlands rising to the Berkshire Downs in the N. It is predominantly agricultural; industries include paints, plastics, and pharmaceutical goods at Slough and light engineering and horticulture at Reading; the Atomic Research Establishment is at Aldermaston. Area: 1256 sq km (485 sq mi). Population (1987 est): 740 600. Administrative centre: Reading.

Berlin 52 31N 13 20E The capital city and a *Land* of Germany, in the NE of the country on the River Spree. *History*: founded in the 13th century, it was an important member of the Hanseatic League. It became the capital of the Hohenzollern Electors of Brandenburg and grew in importance with their increasing power, becoming the capital of Prussia in the 18th century and of the German Empire in 1871. Badly damaged in World War II, it was occupied by the four major powers after the defeat of Germany. In 1948 Berlin became two separate administrative units: Soviet-controlled **East Berlin** and **West Berlin**, formed from the US, UK, and French zones. The Soviet Union blockaded the city for almost a year (*see* Berlin airlift). From 1949–90 East Berlin was the capital of East Germany: West Berlin remained an enclave within East Germany, administratively linked with West Germany. In 1961 the Berlin wall was built to stop the flow of refugees from E to W. Demolition of the wall began in 1989, and Berlin became capital of the reunited Germany in 1990. It is a major industrial and cultural centre. Population (1989): 3 409 737.

Berlin airlift (1948–49) An operation by the Allies (the US, the UK, and France), to supply isolated West Berlin with the necessities of life after the Soviet Union cut off all rail, road, and water links with the city in an attempt to force the Allies to give up their rights there. The airlift continued until the blockade was lifted as a result of a temporary stoppage of exports from the E European states.

Berlioz, (Louis) Hector (1803–69) French Romantic composer and conductor. His first successful work, the *Symphonie Fantastique* (1830–

31), was influenced by his love for his future wife, the Irish actress, Harriet Smithson (1800–54). His dramatic symphony *Harold in Italy* (1834) and choral symphony *Romeo and Juliet* (1839) were popular successes. The oratorio *The Childhood of Christ* (1850–54) was his last major success, for his two-part opera *The Trojans* (1856–59) was not performed complete in his lifetime. He was the author of a famous essay on orchestration and a volume of memoirs.

Bermuda A British crown colony, comprising some 300 coral islands (of which 20 are inhabited), in the W Atlantic Ocean. The largest island is Bermuda (*or* Great Bermuda), while smaller ones include Somerset, Ireland, and St George. Approximately three-quarters of the population is Black. *Economy*: tourism and agriculture are the main activities. *History*: visited by the Spanish navigator Juan de Bermudez in 1515, the islands were first settled in 1609 by British colonists shipwrecked there on the way to Virginia. They became the responsibility of the British Crown in 1684 and became self-governing in 1968 but demands for independence have grown; the governor was assassinated in 1973 and there was serious rioting in December, 1977. Governor: Sir Desmond Langley. Prime minister: Sir John Simon. Official language: English. Official currency: Bermuda dollar of 100 cents. Area: 53 sq km (20 sq mi). Population (1986): 59 000. Capital: Hamilton.

Bermuda Triangle The most notorious of several geographic regions, all lying roughly between 30° and 40° of latitude, in which numerous ships and aircraft have vanished without trace. The Triangle covers about 3 900 000 sq km (1 500 000 sq mi) between Bermuda, Florida, and Puerto Rico. No generally satisfactory explanation of these disappearances has been suggested, but the powerful currents may explain the lack of wreckage.

Bern (French name: Berne) 46 57N 95 58W The capital of Switzerland, on the River Aare. Founded as a military post in the 12th century, it joined the Swiss Confederation in 1353 and became the capital in 1848. It has considerable industry and contains the headquarters of several international organizations. Population (1987): 136 500.

Bernadette of Lourdes, St (1844–79) French peasant girl, who in 1858 claimed to have had 18 visions of the Virgin Mary at a grotto near Lourdes. At 20 she became a nun. She was made a saint in 1933 and her shrine is a place of pilgrimage. Feast day: 18 Feb or 16 April.

Bernadotte, Jean Baptiste Jules (c. 1763–1844) French marshal, who was King of Sweden (1818–44) as Charles XIV John, founding the present Swedish royal house. Rising from the ranks he became a marshal under Napoleon with whose support he was adopted as heir by the dying Charles XIII of Sweden. Turning against Napoleon, Bernadotte contributed to his defeat at Leipzig (1813). In 1814 he forced Denmark to hand over Norway to the Swedish monarchy.

Bernese Oberland (*or* Bernese Alps) A section of the Alps in SW Switzerland, 105 km (65 mi) long, between the Rivers Rhône and Aare.

Its mountain peaks include the Eiger and the Finsteraarhorn and it is a popular area for mountain climbing.

Bernhardt, Sarah (Sarah Henriette Rosine Bernard; 1844–1923) French actress. Plays in which she gave worldwide performances include *Phèdre* (1879), *La Dame aux camélias*, and *L'Aiglon* by Edmond Rostand. She was also manager of several theatres in Paris and opened the old Théâtre des Nations as the Théâtre Sarah Bernhardt.

Bernini, Gian Lorenzo (1598–1680) Italian *baroque sculptor and architect, born in Naples, the son of a sculptor. His first major sculptures were for Cardinal Scipione Borghese and included *Apollo and Daphne* (1622–24; Borghese Gallery, Rome). Encouraged by Urban VIII, he extended his talents into architecture, major works being his decoration of the tomb of St Peter (1624–33) and the piazza and colonnade (1656–67) of St Peter's, Rome. Later sculptures included fountains for Roman piazzas and such portrait busts as *Louis XIV* (1665; Versailles).

Bernoulli's principle The principle of conservation of energy applied to the flow of a liquid or gas. If the effects of friction are neglected the total energy of the flow at any point in a pipe is equal to the sum of the kinetic energy due to the flow velocity, the gravitational potential energy due to height, and the energy of pressure in the fluid itself. Bernoulli's theorem states that the sum of these three components is constant throughout a flow system. Named after Daniel Bernoulli (1700–82).

Bernstein, Leonard (1918–90) US conductor, composer, and pianist. From 1958 to 1969 he was musical director and conductor of the New York Philharmonic Orchestra. His works, including symphonies, choral works, and songs, often contain jazz and folk elements. His musicals, such as *On the Town* (1944) and *West Side Story* (1957), have been widely popular.

Berthollet, Claude Louis, Comte (1748–1822) French chemist and physician. He introduced bleaching by chlorine; he also showed that ammonia consists of hydrogen and nitrogen. Berthollet, working with *Lavoisier, developed a new system of chemical terms. He travelled to Egypt as scientific adviser to Napoleon, who made him a senator and a count.

Bertolucci, Bernardo (1940–) Italian film director. Many of his films are strongly influenced by Marxism, notably *Before the Revolution* (1965) and the epic *1900* (1977). He achieved his greatest commercial successes with *Last Tango in Paris* (1972) and *The Last Emperor* (1988).

beryl A mineral consisting of beryllium alumino-silicate, found principally in or close to granites. It occurs as crystals up to one metre in length and is white, pale blue, or green. Aquamarine and emerald are types of beryl used as gems.

beryllium (Be) A light (relative density 2.34) alkaline-earth metal that was discovered in 1828 by F. Wöhler and A. Bussy (1794–1882) independently. Its salts are highly toxic and require careful handling. It occurs in nature in such minerals as *beryl and phenacite (Be_2SiO_4). X-rays can pass through it and so it is used as windows on X-ray tubes. Alloys of beryllium and copper are extensively used and the oxide (BeO), having a high melting point (2530°C), is used as a ceramic. At no 4; at wt 9.0122; mp 1278°C; bp 2450°C.

Berzelius, Jöns Jakob, Baron (1779–1848) Swedish chemist, whose main work was the discovery of atomic compositions of chemical compounds. He discovered the elements selenium (1817), silicon (1824), and thorium (1828) and established the atomic and molecular weights of more than 2000 elements and compounds. He introduced the current method of writing chemical formulae and the use of oxygen as a reference standard for atomic weights.

Bessarabia A region in the SW Soviet Union, largely in the Moldavian and Ukrainian SSRs and with a predominantly Moldavian population. The main activity is agriculture and food processing. *History*: the region was colonized by the Greeks and later fell successively to the Romans, Huns, Magyars, Mongols, and Turks, passing to Russia in 1812. In 1918 Bessarabia declared its independence, later voting for union with Romania. In 1940 Romania handed Bessarabia over to the Soviet Union. Area: about 44 300 sq km (17 100 sq mi).

Bessemer process A steelmaking process invented by Sir Henry Bessemer (1813–98) in 1855. A long cylindrical vessel (Bessemer converter) is filled with molten pig iron; air, introduced through holes in the bottom of the converter, is blown through the hot iron to oxidize the carbon, silicon, and manganese impurities. Phosphorus is removed by reaction with the converter's lining. Carbon, in the form of spiegel, is then added to give *steel of the required carbon content. It has now been largely replaced by the basic-oxygen process, in which high-pressure oxygen is blown onto the metal (pig iron and scrap) through a water-cooled lance in a furnace resembling a Bessemer converter.

beta decay A type of radioactive decay in which the nucleus of an atom emits either an *electron (originally called a beta particle) or an antiparticle of an electron, a positron. An antineutrino accompanies the electron and a *neutrino accompanies the positron. Since the nuclear charge changes by one in both cases, the nucleus is converted into the nucleus of another element.

betatron A type of particle *accelerator used for producing very high energy electrons. The electrons are accelerated round a circular path by means of a large pulsed magnetic field. Electron energies up to 300 MeV have been produced.

betel A mixture of the boiled dried seeds (**betel nuts**) of the areca, or betel palm (*Areca catechu*), and the leaves of the betel pepper (*Piper betle*), which is chewed with lime in India.

Betelgeuse An immense remote yet conspicuous red supergiant, over 500 light years distant, that is the second brightest star in the constellation Orion. It is a variable star with its magnitude ranging, usually, from 0.3 to 0.9 over a period of about 5.8 years.

Bethlehem 31 42N 35 12E A town on the West Bank of the River Jordan, near Jerusalem. The Church of the Nativity was built in 326 over the cave that is the presumed birthplace of Jesus Christ. Population (1984): 20 000.

Betjeman, Sir John (1906–84) British poet. He published his first book of poetry in 1933. His verse autobiography, *Summoned by Bells* (1960), reflected the nostalgia and gentle social satire characteristic of his other poems. He took a keen interest in Victorian and Edwardian architecture. He was poet laureate from 1972.

Bevan, Aneurin (1897–1960) British Labour politician, A brilliant speaker, Nye Bevan clashed with the Labour Party in 1939 over its complacent attitude towards Hitler. He edited the socialist *Tribune* from 1940 to 1945. As minister of health (1945–51), he launched the National Health Service. He was also minister of labour in 1951.

Beveridge, William Henry Beveridge, 1st Baron (1879–1963) British economist, writer, and academic. Beveridge became an authority on unemployment. His best-known work was the *Report on Social Insurance and Allied Services* (1942), the so-called **Beveridge Report**, which created the welfare state.

Bevin, Ernest (1881–1951) British politician and trade-union leader. Bevin formed, and was general secretary (1921–40) of, the Transport and General Workers' Union and in 1937 became chairman of the TUC. In 1940 he became minister of labour, serving in Churchill's war cabinet. He was foreign secretary (1945–51) in the postwar Labour Government, when he helped to form NATO.

bezique A card game, usually for two players, that became popular in France about 1860. Two packs of 32 cards are used (standard packs with the cards from two to six removed). Each player is dealt eight cards; the next card indicates the trump suit and the rest form the stockpile. The object is to score points by collecting melds (certain combinations of cards) and to take tricks containing brisques (aces and tens). Play continues until one player's score reaches 1000 or 1500.

Bhopal 23 17N 77 28E A city in India, the capital of Madhya Pradesh. Notable buildings include the unfinished Taj-ul-Masjid, the largest mosque in India. Bhopal's varied manufactures include vehicle parts and cotton textiles. In 1984 over 2000 people died after poisonous isocyanate gas escaped from the US-owned Union Carbide factory. Population (1981): 672 000.

Bhutan, Kingdom of (Bhutanese name: Drukyul) A small country in the E Himalayas, between India and Tibet. It is entirely mountainous, rising over 7300 m (21 900 ft) in the N. Over half the population are of Tibetan origin, known as Bhutias, with minorities of Nepalese in the S and Indians in the E. *Economy*: mainly agricultural; forests cover almost 70% of the land and hydroelectricity is being developed. *History*: in 1865 part of S Bhutan was annexed by the British. In 1910 Britain agreed not to interfere in Bhutan's internal affairs and in 1910 Sir Ugyen Wangchuk was elected the first hereditary maharaja (now referred to as king). Since 1969 power

has been divided between the king, the Council of Ministers, the National Assembly, and the monastic head of Bhutan's lamas. Head of state: King Jigme Singye Wangchuk (1955–). Official language: Dzongkha Bhutanese. Official currency: ngultrum of 100 chetrums. Area: 46 600 sq km (18 000 sq mi). Population (1988): 1 400 000. Capital: Thimphu.

Bhutto, Zulfikar Ali (1928–79) Pakistani statesman; president (1971–73) and then prime minister (1973–77). He formed the Pakistan People's Party in 1967 and became president after East Pakistan became independent as Bangladesh. Overthrown by a military coup, he was defeated in the subsequent election and sentenced to death (1978) for conspiring to murder a political opponent. He was executed a year later. His daughter, **Benazir Bhutto** (1953–), leader of the Pakistan People's Party, served as prime minister (1988–90).

Biafra The eastern region of the Federal Republic of Nigeria (1967–70) inhabited by the Ibo people. In an attempt to protect the interests of the Ibo people against the dominant Hausa, Lieut Col Odumegwu Ojukwu (1933–) declared independence. The federal government refused to recognize the new state and attacked it. Large numbers of the Ibo were killed, and they surrendered on 15 January, 1970.

biathlon 1. An athletic event first included in the Winter Olympic Games in 1960; competitors ski 20 km (12.5 mi) with rifles and ammunition and at each of four points along the course take five shots at 150 m (164 yd). 2. An athletic event consisting of running 4000 m (2.5 mi) and swimming 300 m (328 yd), introduced in 1968 by the Modern Pentathlon Association of Great Britain as a preparation for the full modern pentathlon.

Bible (Greek *biblia*, books) The collected books of the *Old Testament, the *New Testament, and the *Apocrypha. The Hebrew Old Testament was definitively accepted as rule of faith by the rabbinical council of Jamnia (90– 100 AD), although most of the books had been accepted much earlier. The New Testament rule of faith was also established gradually but had essentially its present form by the 3rd century AD. To Christians it represented the complete fulfilment of the prophecies of the Old Testament. Both Jews and Christians originally regarded their scriptures as divinely inspired, and therefore correct in every particular; this belief, however, has for many people been eroded by the development of science from the 17th century onwards. The oldest complete manuscript of the Old Testament dates from the 11th century AD, but there are earlier versions of partial texts (*see also* Dead Sea Scrolls). The earliest incomplete parts of the New Testament date from the 2nd century AD. *Translations*: the first translation of the Bible is the Latin *Vulgate of St Jerome. Major English versions are: the version prefaced by Wycliffe (1382–88), the last manuscript Bible written before the introduction of printing; the New Testament (1525) by Tyndale; the Bible of Miles Coverdale; the Great Bible (1539), supervised by Coverdale with the support of Thomas Cromwell; the Geneva (*or*

Breeches) Bible; the Bishops' Bible (1568); the Douai Bible; the King James (*or* Authorized) Version; the *Revised Version* (1881–95); the *Revised Standard Version* (1946–57), a modernization of the King James Version; and *The New English Bible* (1961–70).

bicycles Light two-wheeled vehicles, the wheels of which are moved by cranks attached to pedals operated by the rider. Bicycles developed in the 19th century from a two-wheeled hobbyhorse, known as the dandy-horse or celeripede. Around 1840 a Scotsman, Kirkpatrick Macmillan, applied the dandy-horse principle to models with pedals. The first true bicycles, with rotary cranks on their front wheels, went into production in Paris in 1865. Nicknamed "boneshakers," they popularized cycling as a pastime. To increase efficiency the front wheel was gradually made larger, resulting in the highly popular ordinary (*or* pennyfarthing) bicycle. Then came the so-called safety bicycle (1876), which had a chain and sprocket drive to the rear wheel and was essentially the same as the modern bicycle. Pneumatic rubber tyres (1889), a freewheeling mechanism (1894), and variable gears (1899) were later improvements.

Racing first became popular in France, where the earliest race was held (1868).

Biddle, John (1615–62) English religious leader, founder of Unitarianism (*see* Unitarians). While a schoolmaster he wrote his *Twelve Arguments* against the deity of the Holy Ghost, for which he was imprisoned in 1645. Although his followers began to meet openly from 1652, he was arrested and banished under Cromwell and finally died in prison in London.

bigamy The offence of marrying a person while being married to another. Defences include an honest and reasonable belief in the death of the original marriage partner, or that the first marriage was not valid. Although a person would not be guilty of bigamy in such cases, the second marriage will still not be valid.

big-bang theory A cosmological theory (*see* cosmology), first proposed in the 1920s, that all the matter and radiation in the universe originated in an immense explosion about 10 to 20 thousand million years ago. As the universe so created expanded, the initially high temperature decreased, enabling hydrogen and helium to form. This matter eventually interacted to form *galaxies. The theory also predicts that the radiation formed shortly after the explosion should by now have cooled to about three kelvin. This is indeed the temperature of the background radiation detected in 1965 at microwave frequencies, and now considered strong evidence for the big-bang theory.

Big Ben The 14-ton bell in the clock tower of the Palace of Westminster (London), named after Sir Benjamin Hall (1802–67), commissioner of works when the clock was installed (1859). Both the clock and the tower itself are also known by this name.

bighorn A mountain sheep, *Ovis canadensis*, of North America. Bighorns range in size from the small Nelson's bighorn to the largest Rocky Mountain bighorns, which stand 100 cm at the shoulder.

Bihar A state in N India, bordering on Nepal. The densely populated rural Ganges plain in the N produces rice, sugar cane, pulses, and vegetables. The S Chota Nagpur plateau yields minerals, including much of the world's mica. *History*: the centre of N Indian civilization from 1500 BC, it was the scene of the early development of Buddhism and Jainism. Area: 173 876 sq km (67 116 sq mi). Population (1981): 69 823 154. Capital: Patna.

Bikini Atoll 11 35N 165 20E An atoll in the central Pacific Ocean in the Marshall Islands. It was the site of US atomic and hydrogen bomb tests (some underwater) from 1946 to 1958.

Biko, Steven. *See* Black Consciousness.

Bilbao 43 15N 2 56W A port in N Spain, the largest city in the Basque Provinces on the River Nervión. One of Spain's chief ports, its exports include iron ore, lead, and wine. Population (1986): 378 221.

bilberry A deciduous shrub, *Vaccinium myrtillus*, of the heath family, 30–60 cm high, also known as blaeberry, huckleberry, and whortleberry. It is found on acid moors and mountains in N Europe and N Asia. The green angular stems bear small pointed leaves that turn red in autumn. The globular pink flowers develop into blue berries, which may be eaten raw or cooked.

bile A greenish alkaline fluid secreted by the liver and stored in the gall bladder. Contraction of the gall bladder, which is triggered by a hormone released from the first part of the small intestine (duodenum) in the presence of food, causes the bile to be expelled through the common bile duct into the intestine. Bile is composed of a mixture of bile salts (which helps digest fatty foods) and bilirubin (a breakdown product of the blood pigment *haemoglobin).

bilharziasis. *See* schistosomiasis.

billiards A game for two players using cues and balls on a table. In **English billiards** the table measures 12 × 6 ft (3.6 × 1.8 m) and has six pockets (holes round the edges of the table); points are scored using three balls 2 in (5.2 cm) in diameter. The white and the white-with-a-spot balls are cue balls, one for each player. A cannon, in which the cue ball strikes both the other balls, scores two points; a winning hazard, in which the cue ball pockets another ball, scores two points (white) or three (red); a losing hazard, in which the cue ball is pocketed after striking another ball, scores two points (off white) or three (off red). A turn (*or* break) lasts until the player fails to score. **Carom billiards** is played on a smaller table with no pockets and scoring is by cannons (*or* caroms). **Bar billiards** is played on a small table with a timing device and holes in the surface, into which balls are potted off each other until the time runs out. *See also* snooker.

Bill of Rights 1. (1689) An act of parliament that included the Declaration of Rights, the conditions on which the English throne was offered to William and Mary in 1689 (*see* Glorious Revolution). It reduced royal power, barred Roman Catholics from the throne, and guaranteed freedom of speech. **2.** (1791) The first ten amendments to the US *Constitution, described by Jefferson as "what the people are entitled to against every government on earth." They include freedom of press, speech, and religion and the right to a fair and public trial.

binary star Two stars moving around the same point but in different orbits, each under the gravitational attraction of the other. Possibly 50% of stars are members of binary or other multiple systems. The components of a **visual binary** can be distinguished by telescope whereas a **spectroscopic binary** can only be detected by spectroscope measurements, the components usually being very close. In an **eclipsing binary** one component passes alternately in front of and then behind the other, causing the combined brightness to fluctuate.

binary system A number system that uses only two digits 0 and 1. Numbers are expressed in powers of 2 instead of powers of 10, as in the decimal system. In binary notation, 2 is written as 10, 3 as 11, 4 as 100, 5 as 101, 8 as 1000, and so on. *Computers calculate in binary notation. *See also* bit.

binding energy The energy released when protons and neutrons bind together to form an atomic nucleus. The mass of a nucleus is always less than the sum of the masses of the constituent protons and neutrons. The missing mass is converted into the binding energy according to *Einstein's law $E = mc^2$.

bindweed A widely distributed climbing plant. Bindweeds twine their stems around other plants for support and can be persistent weeds. The leaves are large and arrow-shaped and the conspicuous white, pink, or yellow flowers are funnel-shaped. *See also* convolvulus.

binoculars A portable optical instrument used for magnifying distant objects. It consists of two telescopes fixed side by side, one for each eye, inside which there are a number of lenses and usually prisms. These allow a focused and enlarged image to be produced the right way up within the short length of each telescope.

binomial nomenclature A system devised by *Linnaeus in the 18th century for the scientific naming of plants and animals, each species being identified by two Latin names—the name of the genus (written with an initial capital letter) followed by the name of the species. The specific name may be followed by the author's name, usually abbreviated. Thus the wolf is *Canis lupus* L (for Linnaeus).

binomial theorem The theorem, discovered by *Newton in 1676, that the quantity $(a + n)^n$, where n is an integer, can be expanded in a series: $(a + b)^n = a^n + na^{n-1}b + [n(n-1)a^{n-2} b^2]/2! + [n(n-1)(n-2)a^{n-3}b^3]/3! + \ldots + b^n$ where, for example, 3! (called factorial three) is $3 \times 2 \times 1$.

biochemistry The scientific study of the chemical composition and reactions of living organisms. Discovering the complex sequence of reactions involved in the digestion of food, the utilization of energy, the manufacture of new tissues, etc., gives us an understanding of an organism's metabolism. Biochemists are also concerned with the role of *genes, *hormones, and

*enzymes in starting and controlling metabolic reactions.

biodegradable substances Materials that can be broken down by such processes as decomposition by fungi and bacteria—and can therefore be reused by living organisms. Substances that are **nonbiodegradable**, such as plastics, persist in the environment, causing pollution.

bioengineering (*or* biomechanics) The application of biological and engineering principles to the design and manufacture of equipment for use in conjunction with biological systems. Examples include artificial limbs, heart pacemakers, life-support systems for astronauts, etc.

biogas *See* alternative energy.

biological control The control of pests by the use of living organisms. The controlling agent is usually a predator, parasite, or disease of the pest organism. For example, the virus disease myxomatosis was introduced into Australia and Britain to control the rabbit population. Recent methods of controlling insect pests include the release of sterile males to mate among the population. Biological control avoids the environmental pollution of chemical pesticides.

biological warfare The use of disease-causing microorganisms as weapons. In World War I, the Germans infected Allied cavalry horses with bacteria causing the disease glanders. Although biological warfare is now officially banned by the major powers, research continues in developing new and more deadly strains of such organisms as the plague bacterium (*Pasteurella pestis*) and the smallpox virus. Such organisms could be delivered in the warhead of a missile. Alternatively, they could be added to the enemy's water or food supplies.

bioluminescence The production of light by living organisms, including certain bacteria, fungi, and various animals (e.g. fireflies and glowworms). In some the luminescence is due to symbiotic light-producing bacteria.

bionics The study of living systems in order to design man-made systems based on similar principles. It assumes that most living creatures have adapted in the best possible way to their environments. The applications of bionics include the design of a ship's propeller modelled on a fish's tail.

biotechnology The industrial use of microorganisms to produce large quantities of products useful to man. Examples are the manufacture of bread, cheese, beer, vinegar, etc., utilizing fermentation processes of bacteria and yeasts, and of antibiotics using moulds. Other valuable medical products, including insulin and vaccines, have been produced on a large scale by techniques of *genetic engineering.

biotin. *See* vitamin B complex.

birch A deciduous tree or shrub of the N hemisphere. Birches grow up to 25 m and have smooth grey bark, that peels off in strips. The glossy leaves are usually triangular, with toothed edges. The flowers are male and female catkins producing tiny winged nuts. Birch wood, especially that of the Eurasian silver birch (*Betula pendula*), is used for turned articles.

bird A warm-blooded animal of which there are about 8600 species, adapted for flight by having fore limbs modified as wings and a body covering of feathers. Birds have a light skeleton with hollow bones and a large keel-shaped breastbone providing attachment for the powerful flight muscles. The jaws are elongated into a horny bill (teeth are absent or reduced). Birds have good eyesight and colour vision and most are active by day. Many communicate by means of song and some undergo long seasonal migrations. Birds are of great economic importance to man. The eggs and flesh of poultry provide food and wildfowl and game birds are hunted for sport. Other species are pests, for example by damaging crops. Modern birds include both flying and flightless species (ratites); the largest group includes the songbirds. *See also* ornithology.

bird of paradise A bird, 30–65 cm long, occurring in New Guinea and neighbouring islands. The male is usually brightly coloured, with long tail feathers and ornamental plumes, and performs an acrobatic display to attract the dull-coloured female. Their feathers are much prized and were formerly exported for use in ladies' hats.

bird of prey A bird that hunts other animals for food, also called raptor. Birds of prey are divided into the nocturnal hunters, comprising the owls, and those that hunt by day, comprising the eagles, falcons, hawks, secretary bird, and the vultures. Live prey is normally taken but the vultures specialize in feeding on carrion. Birds of prey are characterized by their strong hooked bills for tearing flesh, clawed talons, and powerful flight with a high-speed dive onto prey.

bird's nest fern An Old World tropical fern, *Asplenium nidus*, that has a dense rosette of upward-pointing leaves, 60–120 cm long, with a central hollow forming a nest in which humus collects. The plant is grown for ornament.

bireme. *See* ships.

Birendra Bir Bikram Shah Dev (1945–) King of Nepal (1972–), following the death of his father Mahendra, whose policies he undertook to follow. He married (1970) Aishwarya Rajya Laxmi Devi Rana.

Birkenhead, F(rederick) E(dwin) Smith, 1st Earl of (1872–1930) British Conservative politician. A barrister, Birkenhead entered parliament in 1906. As attorney general (1915–19) he was famous for his prosecution of Sir Roger Casement and while lord chancellor (1919–22) he introduced major land-law reforms. He was secretary for India (1924–28).

Birmingham 52 30N 1 50W A city in central England, in the West Midlands. Britain's second largest city, it is a centre of engineering and metalworking. It possesses two universities, Aston University (1966) and Birmingham University (1900), an art gallery (1874–81), a symphony orchestra, a ballet company, and a repertory theatre founded in 1913. Among postwar developments are a modern shopping complex centred on the Bull Ring (to be redeveloped shortly), where a market has been held since ancient times, and the National Exhibition Centre (1976) at Bickenhill. Population (1985): 1 008 000.

Birmingham 33 30N 86 55W A city in the USA, in Alabama. Settled in 1813, it is the state's largest city and the main industrial centre of the South. It has an important iron and steel industry. Population (1986): 277 510.

birthstone In *astrology, a gemstone associated with a particular date of birth. The wearing of one's birthstone as a lucky charm started with the ancient belief that certain gems had supernatural powers. The modern list of birthstones is usually: January–garnet; February–amethyst; March–bloodstone; April–diamond; May –emerald; June–pearl; July–ruby; August –sardonyx; September–sapphire; October –opal; November–topaz; December–turquoise.

Biscay, Bay of (French name: Golfe de Gascogne; Spanish name: Golfo de Vizcaya) An inlet of the Atlantic Ocean, off the coast of W France and N Spain. It is comparatively deep and has rough seas. Width: about 320 km (199 mi).

bisexuality. *See* homosexuality.

Bismarck, Otto Eduard Leopold, Prince von (1815–98) Prussian statesman; first chancellor of the German Empire (1871–90). A conservative, known as the Iron Chancellor, Bismarck came to power after the collapse of the *Revolution of 1848. After victory in the *Franco-Prussian War (1870–71) William I of Prussia accepted the imperial crown and Bismarck became chancellor of the new German Empire. He came into conflict (the Kulturkampf) with the Roman Catholic Church and, abroad, presided over the Congress of Berlin (1878) and formed the Triple Alliance with Austria and Italy. Losing the support of William II, Bismarck resigned in 1890.

Bismarck Archipelago A group of volcanic islands in the SW Pacific Ocean, in Papua New Guinea. It includes New Britain, New Ireland, and the Admiralty Islands. Area: 49 658 sq km (19 173 sq mi). Population (1980 est): 314 308.

bismuth (Bi) A dense white brittle metal, similar in properties to tin and lead. It is obtained as a by-product when other metals are purified and also from the sulphide (Bi_2S_3) and the oxide (Bi_2O_3). It has unusual properties, having low thermal and electrical conductivity, and decreasing in volume on melting. It is used to make low-melting alloys. At no 83; at wt 208.9808; mp 271.3°C; bp 1560°C.

bison Either of two massive hoofed mammals. The North American bison (*Bison bison*) was once abundant on the plains, numbering about 30 million, but is now found only on reserves: by 1990 there were only some 500 specimens. Over 150 cm at the shoulder and weighing up to 1000 kg, it has a shaggy mane and low-slung head with incurved horns. The smaller European bison (*B. bonasus*), also called wisent, is now found only in zoos.

Bissau 11 50N 15 37N The capital and chief port of Guinea-Bissau, on the Geba estuary. Founded by the Portuguese in 1687, it became capital of Portuguese Guinea in 1941. Population (1988): 125 000.

bit A binary digit, either 0 or 1. Groups of bits are used within a computer to represent numbers, letters, etc. Changing one of the bits changes the number, letter, etc. It is thus the smallest unit of information in computer memory.

bittern A bird related to the herons, occurring throughout the world in swamps and reedbeds. The European bittern (*Botaurus stellaris*) is a solitary bird, about 70 cm long, with a yellow-brown dark-streaked plumage that provides excellent camouflage. The little bittern (*Ixobrychus minutus*) is only 34 cm long with buffish-white wing patches.

bitumen The tarry residue left after *distillation of oil, lignite, or coal, consisting almost entirely of a mixture of carbon with large *hydrocarbon molecules. Its principal uses are in roadmaking and binding cement.

bivalve Any *mollusc that has two hinged shell plates (valves), including *clams, *mussels, *oysters, and scallops. Bivalves inhabit both salt and fresh water. Most bivalves are of separate sexes but some are hermaphrodite. Some hermaphrodite bivalves, including oysters, incubate the fertilized eggs.

Bizet, Georges (Alexandre César Léopold B.; 1838–75) French composer. In 1855 he produced his first major work, the symphony in C major. Among his best-known works are the incidental music to Alphonse Daudet's play *L'Arlésienne* (1872) and the opera *Carmen* (1873–74).

Black and Tans The soldiers recruited by the British Government to fight the IRA in Ireland in 1920–21. Their name comes from their uniform, khaki with black caps and belts. They acted with great severity and were hated by the Irish.

black bear The native bear of North American forests, *Ursus* (or *Euarctos*) *americanus*. American black bears grow to a weight of 150 kg; they climb well and eat berries, pine cones, and grass as well as small animals. The name is also used for the Himalayan black, or moon, bear, *Selenarctos thibetanus*, which inhabits forests of central and E Asia and has a white V-shaped mark on its chest.

black beetle. See cockroach.

blackberry (*or* bramble) A prickly scrambling shrub, *Rubus fruticosus*, of the rose family, occurring throughout Europe. The stems, up to 5 m long, root wherever they touch the ground. The dark-green leaves usually consist of five oval toothed leaflets and the pinkish-white flowers are borne in terminal clusters. The fruits, each of which consists of several small berries joined together, are eaten raw or cooked.

blackbird A songbird, *Turdus merula*, that is one of the commonest European birds, particularly in urban areas. The male, about 25 cm long, is black with a bright-yellow bill and eye ring; the larger female is dark brown with a dark bill. Blackbirds feed chiefly on worms and other invertebrates but will also eat scraps.

black body A body that absorbs all the electromagnetic radiation falling upon it, thus producing no reflection. (In practice no body

reaches this ideal.) When heated it emits radiation (black-body radiation) having a range of wavelengths. The intensity reaches a maximum at a particular wavelength, which depends only on the temperature of the body.

blackcap A European *warbler, *Sylvia atricapillus*. About 14 cm long, it has an olive-brown plumage with paler underparts and a darker cap (black in the male and reddish-brown in the female). Blackcaps feed chiefly on insects but –before migrating–they eat fruit to build up energy reserves.

Black Consciousness The recognition by minority Black communities throughout the world of their identity, history, and culture, as distinct from that of Whites. Political and social movements contributing to the development in the USA of Black Consciousness have included the National Association for the Advancement of Coloured People, and the later Black Muslims. In South Africa the Black Consciousness Movement was led by **Steven Biko** (d. 1977), whose death from extensive injuries while in police detention provoked worldwide concern.

Black Country, the An industrial area of central England. Situated N of Birmingham, it consists largely of the S Staffordshire coalfield. It gained its name from the grime produced by intense industrialization in the 19th century.

blackcurrant A shrub, *Ribes nigrum*, of the gooseberry family, native to most of Europe and N Asia and widely cultivated. The stems and three-lobed leaves emit a characteristic smell. The drooping clusters of greenish bell-shaped flowers develop into edible black berries.

Black Death The worst outbreak of plague of the medieval period. Starting in the Far East, it spread through Europe and England in May, 1348. Estimates of death rates vary from 20% to more than 50%. The outbreak had a deep effect not only on population growth but also upon rural society and the economy as a whole. Further outbreaks followed in the 1350s and 1370s.

black hole A celestial "object" that has undergone such total gravitational collapse that no light can escape from it. Once a collapsing object's radius has shrunk below a critical value (the Schwarzschild radius) it becomes a black hole; for a star, this radius is about 10 km or less. The surface having this radius is called the event horizon of the black hole. The object will continue to contract until compressed to an infinite density at a single central point–a singularity. Black holes of immense mass are now thought to exist at the centres of certain galaxies, possibly including our own, and to be the powerful sources of energy in *quasars. They could be up to a thousand million times the mass of the sun.

Black Hole of Calcutta A small cell (5.5 m × 4.5 m) in which over one hundred British soldiers were said to have been confined overnight in 1756, less than 25 men surviving. The outrage was committed by the Nawab of Bengal, who, objecting to the fortification of Calcutta by the East India Company, defeated the British garrison.

Black Mountains A mountain range in SE Wales, in Powys, mainly in the Brecon Beacons

National Park. It rises to 811 m (2660 ft) at Wann Fach.

Blackpool 53 50N 3 03W A resort in NW England, on the Lancashire coast, famous for its Tower (modelled on the Eiffel Tower), Pleasure Beach, and illuminations. Population (1987): 144 100.

Black Prince, Edward the. See Edward, the Black Prince.

Black Rod An official of the House of Lords, first appointed in 1522. He keeps order in the House and when the monarch delivers a speech, summons members of the Commons by knocking on their door with his black rod.

Black Sea An inland sea bounded by Bulgaria, Romania, the Soviet Union, and Turkey; it is connected to the Mediterranean Sea via the Bosporus in the SW and to the sea of Azov in the N. Fresh water from the Rivers Danube and Dnepr helps to keep its salt content low.

black swan The only Australian *swan, Cygnus atratus. Almost 1 m in length, both sexes have a pure black plumage, red bill, and a trumpeting call.

blackthorn (or sloe) A thorny shrub, Prunus spinos, of the rose family, forming dense thickets, up to 4 m high, in many parts of Europe and Asia. The clusters of white flowers usually appear before the leaves, which are oval and toothed. The bitter-tasting blue-black stone fruits are used to flavour sloe gin.

black widow A venomous *spider, also called button or redback spider, found in tropical and subtropical regions. The female of the North American species Latrodectus mactans, has a shiny black body, 25 mm long, with red markings on the abdomen. (The male is about 6 mm long and usually killed and eaten by the female after mating.) The bite is serious but rarely fatal.

bladder In anatomy, any hollow organ containing fluid, especially the urinary bladder, into which urine drains from the *kidneys.

bladderwort A *carnivorous aquatic plant. Most bladderworts are submerged beneath the water with finely divided leaves bearing small bladders, which trap tiny aquatic animals by a trapdoor mechanism triggered by sensitive hairs. The two-lipped tubular flowers protrude above the water.

Blake, Robert (1599–1657) English admiral. A Parliamentarian in the Civil War, Blake became one of *Cromwell's most successful commanders and in 1650 destroyed Prince Rupert's Royalist fleet. In the first Dutch War, Blake was largely responsible for the English victory and sank 16 Spanish ships at Santa Cruz off Tenerife (1657). He died while returning to Plymouth.

Blake, William (1757–1827) British poet, painter, and engraver. His poems, the texts of which he engraved and illustrated, include Songs of Innocence (1789), Songs of Experience (1794), various "Prophetic Books," Milton (1808), and Jerusalem (1820). His watercolours for The Book of Job (1826) and Dante's Divine Comedy (1827) were inspired by his visions and engravings in the style of Michelangelo. Although unrecognized by his generation, except by a few friends, he was a forerunner of Romanticism.

Blantyre (or Blantyre-Limbe) 15 46S 35 00E The largest city in Malawi, in the Shire Highlands. In 1956 it was linked with the nearby town of Limbe, a major railway centre, and is Malawi's chief industrial centre. Population (1985 est): 355 200.

Blarney 51 56N 8 34W A village in the Republic of Ireland, in Co Cork. Blarney Castle contains the famous Blarney Stone, which is kissed in order to receive the gift of "blarney" or smooth talk. Population (1985 est): 1500.

blast furnace A furnace used in the smelting of ore. In steel making, iron ore, coke, and limestone are poured in at the top of a vertical furnace and a blast of hot air is blown in at the bottom to burn the coke. Molten iron is drawn off at the bottom. A glassy waste, called slag, is also produced.

bleaching The whitening, lightening, or removing of colour by chemical treatment or exposure to sunlight. Most bleaching agents are oxidizing agents, which convert a pigment into an oxidized colourless form. Examples are hydrogen peroxide, hypochlorites, and **bleaching powder** (calcium hypochlorite, calcium chloride, and calcium hydroxide). In some processes reducing agents, such as sulphur dioxide, are used.

Blenheim, Battle of (13 August, 1704) The battle won by the Duke of *Marlborough and Prince Eugene of Savoy (1663–1736) against the French army in the War of the *Spanish Succession. It was fought at Blenheim (now Blindheim) on the River Danube and **Blenheim Palace** at Woodstock (Oxfordshire) was built (1705–25) by *Vanbrugh for Marlborough by a grateful parliament.

blenny A small fish related to the perch, found among rocks in shallow waters of tropical and temperate seas. Blennies have an elongated scaleless body with a blunt nose. Many have small tentacles on their heads.

Blériot, Louis (1872–1936) French aviator. Beginning his career as a motorcar engineer he was the first to fly the English Channel (1909), from Calais to Dover, in a monoplane. He later became a manufacturer of aircraft.

Bligh, William (1754–1817) British admiral. He accompanied *Cook on his second voyage round the world and in 1787 was sent to Tahiti on the Bounty to collect examples of the breadfruit tree. Setting sail for home, his crew mutinied, leaving Bligh and 18 officers aboard a small boat without maps. He eventually reached safety. In 1805 he was made governor of New South Wales.

blight A severe disease of plants caused by pests, fungi, or other agents. Symptoms commonly include spotting followed by wilting and death. The notorious potato blight that devastated Ireland in the mid-19th century was caused by the fungus Phytophthora infestans.

blindworm. See slowworm.

Bliss, Sir Arthur Edward Drummond (1891–1975) British composer. Director of music at the BBC (1942–44), Bliss was knighted in 1950 and was Master of the Queen's Music (1953–75). His works include A Colour Symphony (1922), music for the film The Shape of Things *to Come* (1935), the opera *The Olympians* (1948–49), and a cello concerto (1970).

Bloch, Felix (1905–83) US physicist, born in Zurich, who moved to the USA when Hitler came to power. He developed the nuclear magnetic resonance technique for which he shared the Nobel Prize (1952) with E. M. Purcell. During World War II he worked on the development of the atomic bomb. In 1954 he became the first director of *CERN.

Bloemfontein 29 07S 26 14E The judicial capital of South Africa and the capital of the Orange Free State. Founded in 1846, it is an important agricultural centre and new gold mines have been opened nearby. Population (1989 est): 240 000.

Blondin, Charles (Jean-François Gravelet; 1824–97) French acrobat and tightrope walker. In 1859 he walked across a tightrope suspended over Niagara Falls and later repeated the feat several times.

blood The red body fluid consisting of a watery plasma in which are suspended various blood cells—the red cells (*see* erythrocyte) and several kinds of white cells (*see* leucocyte). It also contains platelets—small particles involved in blood clotting. Blood acts as a means of transporting oxygen, carbon dioxide, digested food, hormones, waste materials, salts, and many other substances to and from the tissues. An average adult has about 70 millilitres of blood per kilogram of body weight (i.e. about 5 litres in an average man). Blood is present in all animals with a circulatory system: its functions are similar to that of human blood although its composition varies. *See also* blood clotting; blood groups; circulation of the blood.

blood clotting The mechanism by which blood is converted from a liquid to a solid state to prevent loss of blood after injury. The process involves chemical reactions between soluble proteins (clotting factors) in the blood in the presence of platelets, resulting in the formation of a fibrous protein (fibrin), which forms the basis of the blood clot. *See also* thrombosis.

blood fluke A parasitic flatworm that causes the disease schistosomiasis in many parts of the world. The flukes are carried by freshwater snails and enter their human hosts to inhabit blood vessels, feeding on blood and causing the symptoms of the disease.

blood groups The different types of blood, classified on the basis of the presence of certain proteins on the surface of the red cells. These surface proteins are genetically determined and act as antigens (*see* antibody), being recognized by the body's immune system. The major system of blood grouping is the ABO system, discovered in 1900 by Karl Landsteiner (1868–1943). It consists of four groups: A, B, AB, and O. Group A cells carry the A antigen and the plasma contains *antibodies against B antigen (anti-B antibodies); similarly, group B cells carry the B antigen, and anti-A antibodies are present in the plasma. Transfusion of blood between these groups causes destruction of the donor blood cells (*see* blood transfusion). Group O blood contains neither antigen and can therefore be used in

transfusions to people of groups A and B. Group AB blood contains neither anti-A nor anti-B antibody: people of this blood group can accept both A and B blood during transfusion. *See also* rhesus factor.

bloodhound A breed of dog with a keen sense of smell, originating from the Mediterranean area and widely used for tracking. It has a large head with long drooping ears and wrinkled skin around the eyes. Height: 63–69 cm (dogs); 58–64 cm (bitches).

blood pressure The pressure that blood exerts on the walls of the arteries, due to the pumping action of the heart. Blood pressure is at its lowest between heartbeats (i.e. at diastole) and at its highest when the ventricles of the heart are contracting (i.e. systole). It is recorded, using a sphygmomanometer, as the height in millimetres of a column of mercury (mmHg). Blood pressure varies but a healthy adult might have a systolic pressure of about 120 mmHg and a diastolic pressure of 80 mmHg, expressed as 120/80. *See also* hypertension.

blood transfusion Usually the transfer of blood from a **blood bank** to a person who has suffered extensive loss of blood; for example, during surgery or following an accident. Some people (e.g. Jehovah's Witnesses) object to transfusion on religious grounds. The blood is stored in the bank at 4°C and should be used within 3–4 weeks. The *blood group of the recipient must match that of the donor.

Bloody Assizes. *See* Jeffreys of Wem, George, 1st Baron.

Bloomsbury group A group of English writers and artists of the 1910s and 1920s who met in private houses in Bloomsbury, London. The group included the writers Virginia *Woolf, E. M. *Forster, and Lytton Strachey, the art critics Clive Bell (1881–1964) and Roger Fry, and the economist J. M. *Keynes. Most of them had studied at Cambridge University and were influenced by G. E. Moore's *Principia Ethica* (1903).

bluebell One of several plants having bell-shaped blue flowers. In England the bluebell is *Endymion non-scriptus*, of the lily family; up to 50 cm high, it grows from a bulb. In Scotland the name is applied to the harebell.

blue fox. *See* Arctic fox.

blue-green algae Organisms formerly classified as algae but now usually regarded as bacteria. They contain a blue pigment (phycocyanin), in addition to the green chlorophyll. Reproduction is asexual. They occur on moist surfaces and in the soil, where they contribute to *nitrogen fixation. Aquatic blue-green algae are a constituent of plankton.

blue gum. *See* eucalyptus.

Blue Mountains A mountain range in Australia, in New South Wales. Part of the Great Dividing Range, it reaches 1180 m (3871 ft) at Bird Rock and contains the Blue Mountains National Park.

Blue Riband of the Atlantic An award for the fastest crossing of the Atlantic by a recognized shipping route, excluding powerboats or purpose-built vessels. First awarded in 1838, the title has been held by many famous passenger liners, notably the *Queen Mary* (1938–52) and the *United States* (from 1952), which won it with a time of 3 days, 10 hours, and 40 minutes. Since 1933 the Hales Trophy has been awarded to holders of the Riband. In 1990 the British *Hoverspeed Great Britain* reduced the record to 3 days, 7 hours, and 54 minutes, but its eligibility has been disputed.

blues A type of US folk music that evolved from the Negro spirituals and work songs of the 1860s. The first published blues were "Memphis Blues" (1912) by W. C. Handy (1873–1958) and Jelly Roll Morton's "Jelly Roll Blues" (1915). The blues influenced the development of jazz and rock music and stimulated composers, such as George Gershwin. Famous blues singers include Bessie Smith.

bluetit A European tit, *Parus caeruleus*, with a blue crown and wings, a yellow breast, and white face. Bluetits feed chiefly on insect larvae.

blue whale The largest living whale, *Balaenoptera musculus*, growing to over 30 m and weighing over 150 tonnes. They are nearing extinction due to overhunting.

Blunt, Anthony. *See* Maclean, Donald.

boa A snake belonging to the constrictor family, occurring in Old and New World regions. 20–760 cm long, boas are usually green or yellowish with a camouflaging pattern. They kill their prey by biting and then crushing.

Boadicea (Latin name: Boudicca; d. 61 AD) Queen of the Iceni. Her husband Prasutagus ruled in what is now Norfolk (England). At his death in 60, Roman officials maltreated Boadicea and her daughters. She led the Iceni into rebellion, sacking Colchester, London, and St Albans. The Roman governor Suetonius Paulinus defeated the rebels at or near Fenny Stratford. Boadicea committed suicide.

boar, wild A Eurasian wild pig, *Sus scrofa*, once common in European forests. Up to 1.5 m long and 1 m high at the shoulder, it has a rough greyish bristly coat and the males have four tusks. The wild boar is the ancestor of domestic pigs.

Boat Race An annual rowing race on the River Thames between Oxford and Cambridge Universities, first held in 1829 at Henley. The present course of 6.8 km (4.25 mi) from Putney to Mortlake was established in 1845. By 1990 Cambridge had won 69 races and Oxford 66, with one dead heat (1877).

bobcat A short-tailed cat *Felis rufa*, resembling a lynx, found in North America. About 90 cm long, it is brown with greyish markings and has large ears.

bobsledding The sport of racing bobsleds (also called bobsleighs or bobs), which was developed by British sportsmen at St Moritz (Switzerland) in the late 19th century. A bobsled is a steel-bodied toboggan with two pairs of runners, the front pair steerable, holding two or four people. The bobsleds slide down a narrow chute some 1500 m (1640 yd) long with high walls, reaching over 130 km per hour (81 mph).

Boccaccio, Giovanni (1313–75) Italian writer and poet. Son of a merchant of Florence, he wrote *Filocolo*, a prose romance, *Filostrato*,

which supplied the plot of Chaucer's *Troilus and Criseyde*, and *Teseida*, the source of Chaucer's *Knight's Tale*. Between 1348 and 1353 he wrote the *Decameron*, a collection of a hundred stories told by a party escaping from plague-stricken Florence in 1348. In later life he chiefly wrote scholarly works in Latin and lectured on Dante's *Divine Comedy*.

Bodensee. *See* Constance, Lake.

Bodleian Library The major library of Oxford University, first established in 1409 and restored and enlarged by Sir Thomas Bodley from 1598 to 1602. Since 1610 it has been entitled to receive a free copy of every book published in Britain; it contains well over 2.5 million volumes.

Boeotia A region of central Greece, N and W of Attica. Its rich central plains are surrounded by hills and mountains. The dozen or so city states that shared the territory formed a federal state dominated by *Thebes in 446 BC.

Boer Wars (*or* South African Wars) The wars fought against the British by the Boers or *Afrikaners of South Africa. In the first (1880–81) the Boers of the Transvaal under Kruger rebelled against British rule. After massively defeating the British garrison at Majuba Hill, the Transvaal won back its independence under the Pretoria Convention. In the second Boer War (1899–1902) the Boer forces were at first successful, besieging Ladysmith, Mafeking, and Kimberley. They suffered defeats during 1900 but were able to hold off the British under *Kitchener and F. S. Roberts (1832–1914). The British devastated the countryside, rounded up Boer women and children, of whom some 20 000 died in concentration camps, and finally defeated the Boers, who lost their independence in the Peace of Vereeniging (1902).

Boethius, Anicius Manlius Severinus (c. 480–524 AD) Roman statesman and philosopher. A noble, he became chief minister under Theodoric. His love of Roman traditions earned Theodoric's displeasure, and Boethius was imprisoned, tortured, and eventually executed. His translations of Aristotle and essays on music and mathematics were standard texts in medieval Europe but his most famous work is *The Consolation of Philosophy*, written while he was in prison.

Bogarde, Dirk (Derek van den Bogaerde; 1921–) British film actor of Dutch descent. His major performances were *The Damned* (1969), *Death in Venice* (1970), and *Providence* (1978). He is also the author of the autobiographical *A Postilion Struck by Lightning* (1977), *Snakes and Ladders* (1978), and *An Orderly Man* (1983) as well as the novels *A Gentle Occupation* (1980) and *Voices in the Garden* (1981).

Bogart, Humphrey (1899–1957) US film actor. His films include *Casablanca* (1942), *To Have and Have Not* (1944), in which Lauren Bacall (1924–), whom he subsequently married, made her screen debut, *The Big Sleep* (1946), and *The African Queen* (1951).

Bogotá, Santa Fé de 4 38N 74 15W The capital of Colombia, on a fertile central plateau of the E Andes at an altitude of 2640 m (8600 ft).

Founded by the Spanish in the early 16th century on the site of the conquered Indian settlement of Bacatá, it became capital of New Grenada. Population (1985): 4 185 174.

Bohemia (Czech name: Čechy; German name: Böhmen) An area and former province (1918–49) of W Czechoslovakia. It consists chiefly of a plateau enclosd by mountains. It is the most industrialized part of Czechoslovakia; agriculture and mining are also important. *History*: Bohemia derives its name from the Boii (the first known inhabitants), who were displaced by the Czechs (1st-5th centuries AD). Bohemia became part of the greater Moravian empire in the 9th century. It was most powerful during the reign of the Přemyslid Otakar II (1230–78; reigned 1253–78). The Přemyslid dynasty came to an end with the assassination of Wencelas III (1289–1306; reigned 1305–06) and John of Luxembourg was subsequently elected king (1310). The golden age of Bohemia was established by his son Charles I (Emperor Charles IV).

Bohr, Niels Henrik David (1885–1962) Danish physicist, who worked with J. J. *Thomson at Cambridge and *Rutherford at Manchester. He made an immense contribution to atomic theory by combining Rutherford's nuclear model with Planck's quantum theory. The model of the atom (the Bohr atom), in which a central nucleus is surrounded by electrons was improved by Sommerfeld but is the basis for modern atomic theory. Bohr later worked at Los Alamos on the bomb, after escaping from German-occupied Denmark. A supporter of atomic energy for peaceful uses, he organized the first Atoms for Peace Conference in 1955.

Boise 43 38N 116 12W A city in the USA, the capital and largest city of Idaho. The centre of a gold rush in 1862, it has timber, food-processing, and agricultural industries. Population (1984 est): 107 188.

boletus A mushroom whose cap bears a series of vertical tubes (instead of gills), in which the spores are formed. Most grow near trees and they are generally edible or harmless (*see* cèpe), except Satan's boletus (*B. satanas*), which is poisonous. This species has a short stalk and a grey cap 10–20 cm in diameter.

Boleyn, Anne (c. 1507–36) The second wife (from 1533) of Henry VIII and the mother of Elizabeth I. When Henry tired of her she was accused of treason through committing adultery and executed.

Bolingbroke, Henry St John, 1st Viscount (1678–1751) English statesman and philosopher. A Tory MP, he became secretary of war (1704–08). As a supporter of the *Jacobites, he fled to France after his dismissal (1714) by George I, where he helped to organize the Fifteen Rebellion. He also wrote *Reflections upon Exile* and *Reflections Concerning Innate Moral Principles*. Returning to England in 1725, he became the opponent of Robert *Walpole. In 1735 he returned to France.

Bolívar, Simón (1783–1830) South American soldier, known as the Liberator. The son of a wealthy Venezuelan creole family, his travels in Europe led to a lasting admiration for the ideas of the Enlightenment. He returned to Latin America in 1807 and devoted the rest of his life to its liberation from Spain. In 1813 he seized Caracas but after defeat in 1814 went into exile until 1817. His victory at the battle of Boyacá (1819) achieved the liberation of New Granada (renamed Colombia). Bolivar became its president and, after liberating Venezuela and Quito (Ecuador) in 1821, organized a federation of three newly independent states. Latin America was finally freed of the Spanish by campaigns in Peru, Alto Peru taking the name Bolivia in his honour. His dream of a united Andean republic was defeated by political bickering.

Bolivia, Republic of An inland country in South America consisting of low plains in the N and E, crossed by the Madre de Dios, Bené, and Mamoré river systems. In the W, ranges of the Andes rise to over 6400 m (21 000 ft) and the Altiplano, a plateau averaging about 3900 m (13 000 ft), contains Lakes Titicaca and Poopó. Most of the population, which is of mixed Indian and Spanish descent, lives at altitudes of over 3000 m (10 000 ft). *Economy*: tinmining remains the principal industry. Other minerals include zinc, lead, antimony, and copper. The main crops are sugar cane, potatoes, maize, rice, and wheat. *History*: ruins near Tiahuanaco indicate a pre-Inca civilization (the Aymaras) going back to the 10th century. The area later became part of the Inca Empire and was conquered by the Spanish in the 16th century, when it became known as Alto Peru. Soon after the Spanish conquest the discovery of tin and silver led to great prosperity. In 1776 it became part of the viceroyalty of Buenos Aires. After a long war it gained its independence with the help of Simón Bolívar (after whom it is named) in 1825 and became a republic with Antonio José de Sucre (1795–1830) as first president. Political unrest and violent changes of government continued through the 19th century into the 20th; in 1971 a military coup brought Gen Hugo Banzer Suárez to power; he was overthrown in a coup in 1978. By 1985 Bolivia had the highest rate of inflation in the world and massive foreign debts. President: Jaime Paz Zamora. Official languages: Spanish, Quechua, and Aymara. Official currency: boliviano. Area: 1 098 580 sq km (424 160 sq mi). Population (1988 est): 7 000 000. Capital: La Paz (legal capital: Sucre).

boll weevil A brownish *weevil, *Anthonomus grandis*, also called cotton boll weevil. Originally a native of the New World tropics, it is now a major insect pest of cotton crops in the W hemisphere. The female lays a single egg within each cotton boll, which thus fails to develop.

Bologna 44 30N 11 20E A city in N Italy, the capital of Emilia-Romagna. The site dates from Etruscan times; the Emperor Charles V was crowned here in 1530. Regarded as Italy's gastronomic centre, its industries include engineering and food processing. Population (1987): 427 240.

Bologna, Giovanni da. *See* Giambologna.

Bolsheviks One of the two separate groups into which the Russian Social Democratic

Workers' Party split in 1903 in London (the other was the Mensheviks). The Bolsheviks, which means those in the majority, were led by *Lenin, who believed that the revolution must be led by a single party of professional revolutionaries. The Bolsheviks came to power in the *Russian Revolution (1917).

Bolshoi Ballet The principal Russian ballet company, based at the Bolshoi Theatre in Moscow. It developed from a dancing class established by the Moscow orphanage in the late 18th century and moved into its present premises in 1856 after fire had destroyed the first Bolshoi Theatre. It first appeared in London in 1956 and has since become one of the world's leading ballet companies.

Bolt, Robert Oxton (1924–) British dramatist. His plays include *A Man for All Seasons* (1960), a study of Sir Thomas More. He has written screenplays for such films as *Lawrence of Arabia* (1962) and *The Mission* (1988).

Bolton 53 35W 2 26W A town in NW England, in Greater Manchester. Traditionally a cotton-spinning town, Bolton also manufactures textile machinery and chemicals. Population (1985): 261 000.

Bombay 18 56N 72 51E A city in India, the capital of Maharashtra and the country's main seaport on the W coast. The city occupies a group of islands joined by causeways. Its natural harbour, 11 km (7 mi) wide, is the focus of most of India's international trade. The Tata hydroelectric system powers much of Bombay's industry, which includes cotton textiles, food processing, and oil refining. The population is mainly Hindu but there are large Muslim, Christian, and Jewish minorities. *History*: handed over to the Portuguese in 1534, it passed to Charles II of England in 1661 and to the British East India Company in 1668. The railways, the opening of the Suez Canal, and land reclamation led to expansion in the 19th century. Population (1981): 8 227 000.

Bombay duck A fish, *Harpodon nehereus*, found in the estuaries of N India, where it is widely used for food. It has a grey or brown body, about 40 cm long, with small dark speckles and large fins.

bone A rigid tissue that forms most of the skeleton of higher animals and man. Most bones have a central cavity filled with *marrow. The strength of bone is due to fibres of the protein collagen. Bone also contains bone salts, chiefly calcium salts (*see* apatite). Bone tissue is formed by the activity of bone cells (osteoblasts), which become enclosed in the tissue when they have ceased to function. Bone formation starts in the embryo. Most bones (including the long bones) develop from cartilage and the process is complete at birth. Membrane bones (e.g. the skull bones) are formed directly in connective tissue, the process being completed after birth (hence the gap (called a fontanelle) in a newborn baby's skull).

bongo An antelope, *Boocerus euryceros*, of African forests. About 120 cm high at the shoulder, bongos are red-brown with white body stripes and markings on the head. The male has spi-

ralled horns up to 100 cm long. Bulls are solitary; cows and calves live in small herds.

Bonington, Chris (Christian John Storey B.; 1934–) British mountaineer, author, and photographer. He is famous especially for the first British ascent of the N face of the Eiger (1962) and his ascent of Everest in 1985.

Bonn 50 43N 7 07E A city in NW Germany, in North Rhine-Westphalia on the River Rhine. The old part of the town contains the cathedral (12th–13th centuries) and Beethoven's birthplace (now a museum). It passed from France to Prussia in 1815 and was the capital of West Germany (1949–90); following reunification the seat of government remained (temporarily) in Bonn. Population (1986): 290 800.

Bonnard, Pierre (1867–1947) French painter. Originally a lawyer, he attracted attention with his lithographs, *Aspects of the Life of Paris* (1895), and illustrations for Verlaine's book *Parallèlement* (1900). After 1900 his paintings of interiors, landscapes, and bathing women were treated increasingly with dazzling colour and light.

Bonnie Prince Charlie. *See* Charles Edward Stuart, the Young Pretender.

bonsai An ordinary shrub or tree, such as a conifer or flowering cherry, that is trained to grow only to about 60 cm high. The technique was first practised in China over 700 years ago. It was later perfected by the Japanese and has now spread to the W hemisphere. Both branches and roots of potted cuttings are trained and pruned. The trees may take ten years to acquire an aged appearance, and some live 300–400 years.

booby A large tropical seabird related to the gannets and having a large head, a long tapering bill, and a wedge-shaped tail. 65–85 cm long, boobies typically have a white plumage with brown markings and dive to catch fish.

Booker Prize An annual prize of £15,000 for a work of British, Irish, or Commonwealth fiction. It was set up in 1969 by the British engineering company Booker McConnell and the Publishers' Association, on the lines of the French Prix Goncourt. Since 1971 it has been run by the National Book League. Recent winners include Kingsley Amis (1986), Penelope Lively (1987), Peter Carey (1988), and A. S. Byatt (1990).

bookworm Any insect that damages books by gnawing the bindings and boring holes in the paper. Bookworms include silverfish, booklice, moth and beetle larvae, etc.

Boole, George (1815–64) British mathematician, who applied the methods of algebra to logic. By replacing logical operations by symbols, Boole showed that the operations could be used to give logically correct results. His method, known as Boolean algebra or symbolic logic, led to mathematics being given a logically consistent foundation. The subject was further developed by G. Frege, B. A. W. *Russell, and A. N. Whitehead.

boomerang A curved hand-thrown wooden missile used by Australian Aborigines to kill game or as a weapon of war. The angled shape and the spin given to the missile when thrown enables them to return to the thrower if they miss their target. Up to 75 cm (30 in) long, they can travel a distance of 45 m (50 yd).

Booth, William (1829–1912) British preacher and founder of the *Salvation Army. He was born in Nottingham and became a Methodist preacher. He established a mission in Whitechapel in 1865. The reluctance of established churches to accept his slum converts led to the foundation of the Salvation Army (1877).

Bophuthatswana A *Bantu Homeland in South Africa, consisting of several separate areas. The majority of the population is Tswana. *Economy*: chiefly agriculture, especially livestock. Mineral resources include chrome, platinum, asbestos, and iron. *History*: in 1972 it became the first Bantu Homeland to receive self-government under the Bantu Homelands Constitution Act (1971). It was granted independence in 1977, but this is recognized only by South Africa. President and prime minister: Chief Lucas Mangope (1923–). Official currency: South African rand. Area: 38 261 sq km (14 769 sq mi). Population (1984 est): 1 420 000, of whom 65% lived in South Africa. Capital: Mmabatho.

borage A widely grown annual Mediterranean herb, *Borago officinalis*. Up to 60 cm high, with terminal clusters of small blue flowers with backward-pointing petals, borage is used in herbal remedies, beverages, etc.

Bordeaux (Latin name: Burdigala) 44 50N 0 34W A city in SW France, the capital of the Gironde department on the River Garonne. It is a major seaport and wine centre. Industries include shipbuilding, engineering, and oil and sugar refining. *History*: an important centre under the Romans, it became the capital of Aquitania (*see* Aquitaine) but declined following the collapse of the Roman Empire. It flourished once again under English rule (1154–1453). It was the seat of the French government for a brief period in 1914 and again in 1940. Population (1983): 221 500.

Borders Region An administrative region in SE Scotland, bordering on England. It was created under local government reorganization in 1975 from the counties of Berwick, Roxburgh, Peebles, Selkirk, and the SW part of Midlothian. The region consists chiefly of uplands descending E to the Merse lowlands. It is predominantly agricultural. Area: 4672 sq km (1804 sq mi). Population (1988 est): 102 592. Administrative centre: Newtown St Boswells.

border terrier A breed of working dog originating in the border region of England and Scotland. It has a deep narrow body, triangular forward-falling ears, and a short strong muzzle. Weight: 6–7 kg (dogs); 5–6 kg (bitches).

bore A tidal flood wave occurring in certain river estuaries and travelling upstream several kilometres at great speed. It occurs about the times of full and new moon, when the spring flood tide brings sea water into an estuary more quickly than it can travel up the river.

Borgia, Cesare (c. 1475–1507) Duke of the Romagna and captain general of the armies of the Church. The illegitimate son of Pope Alexander VI, Borgia became Archbishop of Valencia and a cardinal. He surrendered his cardinalship to marry the sister of the King of Navarre and to become captain general of the Church. He won the Romagna in three campaigns (1499–1502) but was forced to give it up after Alexander's death (1502). He escaped from imprisonment and died working for the Navarrese king. His sister **Lucrezia Borgia** (1480–1519) was married three times by her father Alexander VI to further his political aims. Her third husband Alfonso (1486–1534) became Duke of Este and she presided over a distinguished court at Ferrara.

Born, Max (1882–1970) British physicist, born in Germany. He shared the 1954 Nobel Prize with W. Bothe for his work in statistical mechanics. With *Heisenberg he developed matrix mechanics. Born was professor of natural philosophy at Edinburgh University from 1936 to 1953.

Borneo A mountainous island SE of Peninsular Malaysia, in the Greater Sunda Islands. During the 19th century Borneo was settled and divided by the Dutch and British. It now consists of the Indonesian territory of Kalimantan, the Malaysian states of Sabah and Sarawak, and the British-protected sultanate of *Brunei. The chief population groups are the coastal Malays and indigenous Dyaks. It possesses valuable resources of oil, coal, and gold. Area: 750 000 sq km (290 000 sq mi).

Borodin, Aleksandr Porfirevich (1833–87) Russian composer. A professor of chemistry, he produced two symphonies (1867 and 1876), the tone poem *In the Steppes of Central Asia* (1880), three string quartets, and the opera *Prince Igor* (completed by *Rimsky-Korsakov and Glazunov in 1890).

boron (B) A nonmetallic element first obtained in pure form (1808) by Sir Humphry Davy. It has two forms: an impure brownish noncrystalline powder and pure brown crystals. The main source, kernite ($Na_2B_4O_7.4H_2O$), is mined in California. Boron is used in semiconductors and in hardened steel. The isotope boron-10 absorbs neutrons: boron carbide (B_4C) and boron alloys are used as neutron absorbers in the control rods and shielding of nuclear reactors. Borax ($Na_2B_4O_7.10H_2O$), is used in glass manufacture. At no 5; at wt 10.81; mp 2300°C.

borough A unit of local government that developed in Anglo-Saxon England. In the UK, county boroughs were set up by the Local Government Act (1888) but were wound up by the Local Government Act (1972). Boroughs remain the units of local government in *London (outside the City).

Borstal system An English system of punishment established by the Prevention of Crime Act (1908) for offenders aged between 15 and 21. The name comes from the prison at Borstal near Rochester, Kent, where the system was introduced. It was abolished by the Criminal Justice Act (1982).

borzoi A breed of large dog originating in Russia, also called Russian wolfhound, and used originally for hunting wolves. A swift runner, it has a long silky coat. Height: about 70 cm.

Bosch, Carl (1874–1940) German chemist, who developed the Haber process for the conversion of atmospheric nitrogen into ammonia, so that it could be used industrially. This *Haber-Bosch process has been widely used to make nitrates for explosives and fertilizers.

Bosch, Hieronymus (Jerome van Aeken; c. 1450–c. 1516) Dutch painter. He was born in 's Hertogenbosch (hence his name), where from 1486 he belonged to the Roman Catholic Brotherhood of Our Lady. The often unexplained symbolism of his half-animal half-human creatures and devils was inspired by contemporary proverbs. Among his major works are *The Haywain* (El Escorial) and *Garden of Earthly Delights* (Prado).

Bosnia and Hercegovina A constituent republic of Yugoslavia. It is primarily agricultural. *History*: part of ancient Illyria, the region was inhabited by Slavs from the 7th century AD onwards and later came under the control of Hungary. It became an independent kingdom in the late 14th century and annexed Hercegovina but fell to the Turks in 1463. In 1908 it was annexed to Austria-Hungary; Serbian opposition to this led to the assassination of Archduke Francis Ferdinand, precipitating World War I. Area: 51 129 sq km (19 737 sq mi). Population (1986): 4 360 000. Capital: Sarajevo.

Bosporus (Turkish name: Karadeniz Boğazi) A strait (narrow channel) separating Europe and Asia and connecting the Black Sea with the Sea of Marmara. It is spanned by one of the world's longest suspension bridges. Length: about 30 km (19 mi). Width: about 0.6–4 km (0.4–2.5 mi).

Boston 42 20N 71 05W A city in the USA, the capital of Massachusetts. An important port and financial and educational centre, it is the site of Boston University (1869), Northeastern University (1898), and Harvard Medical School. *History*: founded in 1630 by Puritan Englishmen, it became a centre of opposition to the British prior to the American Revolution (*see* Boston Tea Party). Population (1986): 573 600.

Boston Tea Party (1773) An action carried out by a group of American radicals to express their hostility to Britain before the American revolution. Objecting to the import of cheap tea enforced by the Tea Act to rid the East India Company of its surplus stocks, they threw a cargo of tea into Boston harbour. Britain reacted by introducing the Intolerable Acts. *See also* Stamp Act.

Boston terrier A breed of dog originating in the USA from crosses between bulldogs and terriers. It is compactly built with a short square muzzle and a short tail. Height: about 38 cm.

Boswell, James (1740–95) Scottish writer, the biographer of Samuel *Johnson. Son of an Edinburgh lawyer, he first met Johnson in 1763. He travelled widely on the Continent from 1764 to 1766, meeting Voltaire and Rousseau. The biography, published in 1791, was widely acclaimed.

Bosworth Field, Battle of (22 August, 1485) The battle fought near Market Bosworth, Leicestershire, in which Henry Tudor defeated Richard III, thereby ending the Wars of the *Roses. Rich-

ard was killed in the battle and Henry became the first *Tudor monarch, as Henry VII.

botany The scientific study of plants. Scientific botany dates from the 4th century BC, with the studies of the ancient Greeks–notably Theophrastus and Dioscorides. The basic principles of modern plant classification were laid down by John Ray at the end of the 17th century, and by the middle of the 18th century *Linnaeus had published his works on the naming and classification of plants, which established the principles of *taxonomy still in use. The invention of the microscope in the 16th century enabled detailed studies of plant structure, while the 18th century saw important advances in plant physiology with the discovery of *photosynthesis. Botany in the 20th century has been revolutionized by advances in physiology, biochemistry, and breeding techniques, enabling a scientific approach to be made to horticulture, *agriculture, and forestry.

Botany Bay An inlet of the Tasman Sea, in SE Australia. It was the site of Capt *Cook's first landing in Australia (1770) and is now surrounded by the suburbs of Sydney. Area: about 42 sq km (16 sq mi).

Botha, Pieter Willem (1916–) South African statesman; prime minister (1978–84) and president (1984–89). Although a strict supporter of *apartheid, he presided over the new constitution of 1984, which allowed some non-Whites limited political power.

Botham, Ian Terence (1955–) British cricketer. A brilliant all-rounder, he played for Somerset (1973–86), Worcestershire (1987–), Queensland (1987–88), and England (1977–), captaining the side (1980–81). Known for his unruly behaviour, he held a record number of test wickets (until 1988) and has scored over 3000 runs in test matches.

Bothnia, Gulf of A shallow section of the Baltic Sea, between Sweden and Finland. It remains frozen for about five months of the year. Area: about 117 000 sq km (45 200 sq mi).

Bothwell, James Hepburn, 4th Earl of (c. 1535–78) The third husband of Mary, Queen of Scots. He was almost certainly responsible for the murder of her second husband Darnley in 1567. Following their defeat at Carberry Hill, Bothwell escaped to Denmark, where he died, insane, in captivity.

bo tree An Indian tree, *Ficus religiosa*, up to 30 m high, also called the peepul or pipal. It has heart-shaped leaves and globular purple fruits. Related to the fig, the bo tree is sacred to Buddhists, as Buddha sat beneath one when he attained enlightenment.

Botswana, Republic of (former name until 1966: Bechuanaland) A Commonwealth country in the centre of S Africa, lying between the Rivers Zambezi and Molopo. It is largely an arid plateau, with the Kalahari Desert in the S and W. The River Okavango in the N is important for irrigation. The majority of the population, consisting mainly of the Bantu-speaking Tswana group, lives along the E border. The original inhabitants, the Bushmen, are now a small minority. *Economy*: chiefly agricultural. Minerals, including coal and diamonds discovered in the 1960s, are being developed. *History*: the area became the British Protectorate of Bechuanaland in 1885 and was annexed to the Cape Colony in 1895. It later became a British High Commission Territory, gaining internal self-government in 1965 and full independence in 1966. Until 1980 it was under the democratic rule of Sir Seretse Khama (1921–80). Head of state: Dr Quett Masire. Official language: English; the main African language is Tswana. Official currency: pula of 100 thebe. Area: 575 000 sq km (222 000 sq mi). Population (1988 est): 1 211 816. Capital: Gaborone.

Botticelli, Sandro (Alessandro di Mariano Filipepi; c. 1445–1510) Florentine *Renaissance painter, called by his brother's nickname, meaning "little barrel." His chief patrons were the Medici, for whom he produced illustrations for Dante's *Divine Comedy* and allegorical paintings, such as *Primavera*, *Birth of Venus* (both Uffizi), and *Mars and Venus* (National Gallery, London). In 1481–82 he worked on frescoes for the Sistine Chapel, in the Vatican.

bottlenose A grey-blue *dolphin, *Tursiops truncatus*, growing to 4 m. Bottlenose dolphins are popular in dolphinariums and are used for research into the social behaviour of whales.

botulism A rare and serious form of *food poisoning caused by eating foods containing the toxin produced by the bacterium *Clostridium botulinum*. The toxin can affect the centres of the brain that control the heart and breathing, and may result in death. The bacterium thrives in improperly preserved foods but is destroyed in cooking.

Boucher, François (1703–70) French *rococo painter. Born in Paris, the son of a lacemaker, he was chiefly influenced by *Watteau. He worked for Louis XV, and Madame de Pompadour, whom he painted (National Gallery of Scotland). He became director of both the Gobelins tapestry factory (1755) and the French Academy (1765).

Boudicca. *See* Boadicea.

Bougainville A volcanic forested island in the SW Pacific Ocean, the largest of the *Solomon Islands and a province of Papua New Guinea. Copra, cocoa, timber, and tortoise shell are exported. Area: about 10 360 sq km (4000 sq mi). Population (1980): 109 000. Chief town: Kieta.

bougainvillea A tropical South American shrub widely grown for ornament in warm regions. The shrub climbs by means of hooked thorns and bears numerous showy "flowers" for most of the year. The coloured parts are actually large petal-like bracts, which surround the small inconspicuous flowers.

Boulez, Pierre (1925–   ) French composer and conductor, a pupil of Messiaen, he was influenced by Schoenberg, Webern, and Cage. He has used *serialism in such works as *Structures I and II* (for two pianos; 1951–52 and 1956–61) and has set poems by René Char and Mallarmé.

Boulogne-sur-Mer 50 43N 1 37E A port and resort in N France, in the Pas-de-Calais. It was severely damaged in World War II. It is the

country's main fishing port and has a ferry service to England. Population (1983): 48 500.

Bourbons A European dynasty that started in Bourbonnais (now Allier, central France). In 1272 Agnès Bourbon married the sixth son of Louis IX. The first Bourbon king of France was Henry IV (reigned 1589–1610) and Bourbons continued to rule until the *French Revolution (1792). The present pretender to the French throne is Henry, Count of Paris (1908–   ). The Bourbon Louis XIV's grandson became (1700) Philip V of Spain, where the Bourbons ruled almost continuously until the abdication of Alfonso XIII in 1931. His grandson *Juan Carlos was restored to the Spanish throne in 1975. In Naples and Sicily Bourbons ruled between 1734 and 1860.

Bournemouth 50 43N 1 54W A resort in S England, in Dorset. It has its own symphony orchestra. Population (1985 est): 145 000.

Bowdler, Thomas (1754–1825) British doctor and editor. His *Family Shakespeare* (1818) dropped all words "which cannot with propriety be read aloud in a family." He similarly "bowdlerized" Gibbon's *Decline and Fall of the Roman Empire* (1826).

bowerbird A songbird found in Australasian forests. 22–35 cm long, it is related to the bird of paradise. Males court females by building dome-shaped bowers with twigs, moss, etc., often decorating them with feathers and shells.

Bowie, David (David Jones; 1947–   ) British pop singer. His albums include *Ziggy Stardust* (1972), *Heroes* (1977), and *Let's Dance* (1983). He has also acted in films, notably *The Man Who Fell to Earth* (1976).

bowling (*or* tenpin bowling) A game in which two players compete by attempting to knock down standing pins with rolling balls. The ten pins, 38.1 cm (15 in) high and each weighing about 1.5 kg (3.5 lb), are placed in a triangle (frame) 18.29 m (20 yd) distant at the end of a wooden lane. The balls, which have a thumb hole and two finger holes, have a maximum circumference of 68.5 cm (27 in) and a maximum weight of 7.26 kg (16 lb). Ten frames comprise a game.

bowls A game in which biased bowls ("woods") are rolled towards a smaller one (the "jack"). **Flat green bowls** is played on a level grass surface 40–44 yd (36.6–40.2 m) square. Matches are usually played between two sides of four, each player using two bowls; a contest consists of three to six matches played together. The jack is rolled onto the green by the first player and is followed by the other bowls in turn, the object being to position them as near the jack as possible. **Crown green bowls** is played, mainly in N England, on a green 30–60 yd (27.4–54.9 m) square and sloping up to a central area raised 6–12 in (15–30 cm). Matches are usually singles lasting until one player reaches a score of 21.

box A small evergreen tree, *Buxus sempervirens*, native to Africa, S Europe, and S England. The leaves are small and glossy and being slow growing, box is widely grown as hedges that can be clipped into ornamental shapes.

boxer A breed of working dog originating in Germany. It has a powerful frame with long straight legs and a broad muzzle. Height: 56–61 cm (dogs); 53–58 cm (bitches).

Boxer Rising (1900) A rebellion in China so called because the rebels belonged to a secret society named the Fists of Righteous Harmony. They opposed the western presence in China and, wearing yellow sashes, marched on Peking, killing and pillaging as they went. The rebellion was eventually suppressed by an international force.

boxing Fist-fighting between men wearing gloves in a roped-off ring. Organized boxing in modern times began in 18th-century England. The modern boxing rules, which established the use of gloves, are the **Queensberry Rules**, drawn up under the Marquess of Queensberry (1844–1900) and published in 1867. In professional boxing the ring is 14 × 20 ft (4 × 6 m) square. The weight limits for professional boxers are: flyweight, 112 lb (50.8 kg); bantamweight, 118 lb (53.5 kg); featherweight, 126 lb (57.2 kg); lightweight, 135 lb (61.2 kg); light welterweight, 140 lb (63.5 kg); welterweight, 147 lb (66.7 kg); light middleweight, 154 lb (69.8 kg); middleweight, 160 lb (72.6 kg); light heavyweight, 175 lb (79.4 kg); heavyweight, unlimited. A bout consists of up to 15 3-minute rounds, separated by 1-minute intervals. A fight may be decided on points (marks awarded by the judges after each round), by disqualification, or by knockout (defined as being unable to rise within ten seconds). Great medical concern has recently been expressed regarding the danger to health of this sport. The present heavyweight champion is Mike Tyson (1966–) of New York.

Boycott, Geoffrey (1940–) British cricketer who captained Yorkshire (1970–78) and played for England (1964–74, 1977–81). He was banned from test cricket (1982–85) for playing in an unofficial tour of South Africa.

Boyle, Robert (1627–91) British scientist born in Ireland. His *The Skeptical Chymist* (1661), pointed out differences between elements, compounds, and mixtures and dismissed the Aristotelian idea of the four elements. His work on gases led to *Boyle's law (1663).

Boyle's law At constant temperature, the pressure of unit mass of a gas is inversely proportional to its volume. This law is only approximately true for real gases. A gas that obeys Boyle's law exactly is called an ideal gas. Named after Robert *Boyle.

Boyne, Battle of the (1 July, 1690) The victory of William III of England over the former King James II in Ireland. The battle was fought at the River Boyne, N of Dublin, where James hoped to halt the Williamites' advance southwards. The battles of the Boyne and of Aughrim are still celebrated by Ulster Unionists on the latter's anniversary, 12 July.

Boyoma Falls (former name: Stanley Falls) A series of seven cataracts in NE central Zaïre, on a 100-km (62-mi) stretch of the River Lualuba, where it becomes the Zaïre River.

Boy Scouts. *See* Scout Association.

bracken (*or* brake) A widely distributed fern, *Pteridium aquilinum*. Its black underground rhizome grows extensively, producing aerial fronds,

up to 5 m high, with stalks bearing triangular blades made up of branches of paired leaflets. Spore capsules occur in brownish clusters (sori) on the underside of the leaflets. The roots have been used in tanning and the fronds in thatching and as fodder.

Bradbury, Malcolm (1932–) British novelist and critic, whose novels include *The History Man* (1975), *Rates of Exchange* (1983), and *Cuts* (1988).

Bradbury, Ray (1920–) US science-fiction writer. His novels include *Fahrenheit 451* (1953) and *Death is a Lonely Business* (1986). His collections of stories include *The Golden Apples of the Sun* (1953).

Bradford 53 48N 1 45W A city in N England, in West Yorkshire near Leeds. It is the foremost wool textile town in the UK. In 1985 56 people died when a grandstand at Bradford City's football ground caught fire. Population (1989): 466 000.

Bradman, Sir Donald George (1908–) Australian cricketer, who was the most successful batsman of his era (1928–48). He scored 117 centuries in 338 first-class innings and in Test matches averaged 99.94 runs. His best score was 452 not out (1929–30). As Australian captain (1936–48) he never lost a series; on retirement (1949) he became an administrator of the game.

Braemar 57 01N 2 34W A village in NE Scotland, in Grampian Region on Clunie Water (a tributary of the River Dee). It is a resort and the scene of the annual Highland games.

Bragança (*or* Braganza) The ruling dynasty of Portugal from 1640 to 1910 and of Brazil from 1822 to 1889. The family was descended from Alfonso, illegitimate son of John I (1357–1433; reigned 1385–1433) and 1st Duke of Bragança. The first Bragança king was John IV (1604–56; reigned 1640–56) and the last was Manuel II (1889–1932; reigned 1908–10), who was removed from the throne, after which Portugal became a republic. When Brazil became independent (1822), it was ruled by two members of the family, Pedro I (1798–1834; reigned 1822–31) and Pedro II (1825–91; reigned 1831–89), before becoming a republic (1889).

Bragg, Sir William Henry (1862–1942) British physicist, who worked in Australia from 1886 to 1908. His early research is described in *Studies in Radioactivity* (1912). With his son **Sir (William) Lawrence Bragg** (1890–1971) he discovered the law of X-ray diffraction that bears their name. Together they wrote *X-rays and Crystal Structure* (1915) and were jointly awarded the Nobel Prize for 1915.

Brahe, Tycho (1546–1601) Danish astronomer, who made accurate astronomical instruments enabling him to revise existing astronomical tables. King Frederick II had two observatories built for him, where he worked from 1580 to 1597. A supporter of *Copernicus' theory that the planets revolve round the sun, he believed the earth to be immovable. After Frederick's death, he moved to Prague, where *Kepler became his student.

Brahma The creator god of later Vedic religion. Arising from the cosmic Golden Egg, he

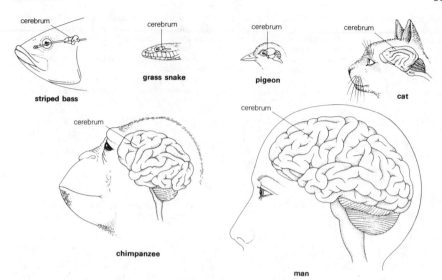

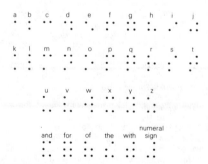

BRAIN *The brains of these representative vertebrates (drawn to the same scale) show a progressive increase in the size and complexity of the cerebrum. In humans this development is such that the cerebrum covers or encloses all the other parts of the brain.*

starts off the recurring process of the creation and destruction of the world. His four heads and arms represent the four *Vedas, castes, and yugas (ages of the world). Brahma represents the creative side of the supreme gods in the trimurti triad but since the 7th century his worship has been replaced by that of Siva and *Vishnu.

Brahman (cattle). *See* zebu.

Brahmaputra River A river in S Asia. Rising in SW Tibet as the Tsangpo, it flows generally E across the Himalayas before turning S into the Assam Valley of NE India as the Dihang. From here, as the Brahmaputra, it flows WSW across NE India to join the River *Ganges N of Gaolundo Ghat. Length: 2900 km (1800 mi).

brahmin (*or* brahman) The first of the four major Hindu castes, that of the priests, they alone are able to perform the most important religious tasks, to study and recite the scriptures. Since in India spiritual and non-spiritual knowledge are virtually inseparable, brahmins frequently have considerable intellectual and political power.

Brahms, Johannes (1833–97) German composer, born in Hamburg. Brahms moved to Vienna in 1863 and later became musical director of the Gesellschaft der Musikfreunde (Society of Friends of Music; 1872–75). His main orchestral works comprise four symphonies, two piano concertos, a violin concerto, and a concerto for violin and cello. His choral works include *A German Requiem* (1868) and the *Alto Rhapsody* (1869). He wrote a large quantity of chamber music and composed much piano music and many songs.

Braille, Louis (1809–52) French teacher, who, blinded by an accident at the age of three, published a system of writing that allows the blind to read by touch. Modern Braille consists of 63 characters, each of which is made up of one to six raised dots.

brain The enlarged part of the central nervous system that lies within the skull of higher animals. Ensheathed by three membranes (meninges), it is the principal organ for controlling and coordinating bodily activities, besides being the seat of intelligence and memory. The hindmost part of the brain, joining the *spinal cord, is the medulla oblongata: this ascends to the pons, which joins the midbrain. These parts, together called the brainstem, control breathing and heartbeat and regulate the level of consciousness. They also convey information to and from the cerebrum. The cerebellum, connected to the brainstem, ensures the coordination of movements. The upper end of the brainstem is connected to the most highly developed part of the

BRAILLE *The alphabet.*

brain–the cerebrum. This consists of two cerebral hemispheres joined by a tract of nerve fibres. Its surface is intricately folded and is made up of an outer layer of nerve cell bodies (grey matter) and an inner mass of nerve fibres (white matter). The cerebrum is largely responsible for understanding language, thought, and the voluntary control of movements. The hemispheres differ in function: one hemisphere controls the dominant side of the body (normally the left hemisphere in right-handed people) and that hemisphere controls speech. The nondominant hemisphere specializes in analysing how things are arranged in space. Deep within the cerebrum and brainstem lie cavities (ventricles) filled with cerebrospinal fluid. The brain of vertebrate animals is similar but less highly developed than the human brain; in lower animals a collection of ganglia (nerve cell bodies) functions as the brain.

brambling A finch, *Fringilla montifringilla*, 14.5 cm long, that breeds in Asia and N Europe and migrates south in winter. It has a brown-speckled plumage with white wing bars and orange underparts but in winter the male has a black head and back.

Bran A legendary Celtic god-king of Britain, whose story is told in the *Mabinogion*. A giant, he once waded across the Irish sea. His severed head lived on for some 80 years, giving good advice before being finally buried in London to protect Britain from invasion. It was dug up by King Arthur, who believed that the country was better protected by the valour of individuals.

Brancusi, Constantin (1876–1957) Romanian sculptor, he moved to Paris in 1904. His stone and metal sculptures, such as the *Sleeping Muse* series beginning in 1906 and the *Birds* variations (1912–40), are both simple and abstract. In contrast, his wood sculptures, such as the *Prodigal Son* (1915), use distinctive forms inspired by African art.

Brandenburg A *Land* and former electorate in E Germany. The region was conquered by the Germans between the 10th and 12th centuries and in 1157 Albert (I) the Bear became elector of Brandenburg. Under Frederick William, the Great Elector (1640–88), Brandenburg gained rule over Prussia and became a leading German power. In 1701 the Elector of Brandenburg became Frederick I of Prussia. The present city of Brandenburg was the capital of this state. After World War II some eastern parts of Brandenburg became Polish. It was reinstated as a *Land* in 1990.

Brandenburg Gate A ceremonial gateway in Berlin, built (1789) in the neoclassical style by the architect C. G. Langhans (1732–1808). Situated at the W end of Unter den Linden, it became the symbol of the modernized city.

Brando, Marlon (1924–) US film actor, influenced by the "method" technique of acting of the New York Actors' Studio in the 1950s. His films include *A Streetcar Named Desire* (1951), *On the Waterfront* (1954), *The Godfather* (1972), and *Apocalypse Now* (1979).

Brandt, Willy (1913–) German statesman; chancellor of West Germany (1969–74). In Nor-

way from 1933, he was a leader of the resistance movement against the Nazis throughout World War II. A member of the Social Democratic Party from 1931, he was its chairman from 1964 to 1987. As chancellor he agreed treaties with Russia, Poland, and East Germany and in 1971 was awarded the Nobel Peace Prize. He resigned the chancellorship when it was revealed that one of his aides was an East German spy.

brandy A spirit obtained from fermented grape juice (wine) or other fruit juices. The best types of wine brandy are stored in oak casks until fully developed and named after the Cognac and Armagnac districts of France. Marc (French) or grappa (Italian) brandy is made from the refermented grape pips, skins, and stems left after pressing for wine. VSOP–very superior old pale –brandy is usually 20–25 years old.

Brandywine, Battle of the (11 September, 1777) A battle during the *American Revolution. Sir William Howe (1729–1814), advancing on Philadelphia, encircled Gen George *Washington's troops in an attempt to cut off the city. Howe crossed the Brandywine Creek, defeated Washington's surprised troops, and subsequently occupied Philadelphia.

Braque, Georges (1882–1963) French painter, who with *Picasso developed cubism. Notable among Braque's innovations were the use of lettering in compositions, e.g. *The Portuguese* (1911; Basle), mixing paint with sand to produce interesting textures, and papiers collés (paper pasted on canvases).

Brasília 16 0S 48 10W The capital and a federal district of Brazil, situated on the central plateau. It was built in 1960, the chief designer being Lúcio Costa and the principal architect, Oscar Niemeyer (1907–). Its fine modern buildings include the National Congress Building and the cathedral. Population (1980): 411 305.

brass An alloy of copper and zinc. Brasses containing less than 36% zinc are ductile when cold, those with more than 36% zinc are harder. It does not rust but exposure to sea water causes a loss of zinc. This is partially prevented by the addition of tin (1%) in Naval Brass, sometimes with about 0.05% of arsenic.

brass instruments Wind instruments made of brass. The *French horn, *trumpet, *trombone, and *tuba are used in orchestras; brass bands also include *bugles and *cornets. Brass instruments have either a cup-shaped or cone-shaped mouthpiece, the shape of which influences the tone quality, as does the type of bore, which may be conical (horn) or cylindrical (trumpet). A brass instrument plays the harmonic series of notes natural to its length; additional notes are produced by the use of crooks, slides, or valves.

Bratislava (German name: Pressburg; Hungarian name: Pozsony) 48 10N 17 10E The third largest city in Czechoslovakia, the capital of the Slovak Republic on the River Danube. It was the capital of Hungary (1526–1784). Notable buildings include the gothic cathedral (13th century), where many of the kings of Hungary were crowned. Oil, piped from the Soviet Union via the Friendship Oil Pipeline, is refined here. Population (1986): 417 000.

Brattain, Walter Houser (1902–87) US physicist, who shared the 1956 Nobel Prize for his part in the invention of the transistor (with W. B. *Shockley and John *Bardeen).

Braun, Eva (1910–45) The mistress and finally the wife of Adolf Hitler. Their relationship probably began in 1933 and they were married shortly before their suicides on 30 April, 1945.

Brazil, Federal Republic of (Portuguese name: Brasil) A country comprising almost half the area of South America. The N of the country is dominated by the *Amazon basin with its tropical rain forests. The land rises to the Guiana Highlands in the N and the Brazilian Highlands in the S, with large stretches of grassland in between. The population is largely of European descent, with a small and dwindling Indian minority. Most of the inhabitants live along the coast; the building of *Brasília was an attempt to draw the population away from the overcrowded coastal areas. *Economy*: mainly an agricultural country, the chief crops are sugar cane, manioc, maize, rice, and beans. Brazil was formerly the world's largest producer of coffee. Livestock breeding has increased and Brazil is now ahead of Argentina as a cattle producer. Brazil is exceptionally rich in mineral resources; the iron-ore reserves are estimated to be the largest in the world. Recently large deposits of phosphates have been discovered there, as well as uranium, manganese, gold, and copper. 90% of power comes from hydroelectric sources. There is now an agreement with West Germany, based on Brazil's uranium deposits, to build eight nuclear power stations. *History*: claimed by the Portuguese in 1500, it became a Portuguese settlement. During the Napoleonic Wars the Portuguese court was transferred to Brazil and in 1815 it was made a kingdom. In 1822 independence was declared by Pedro I (1798–1834), son of John VI of Portugal. In 1889 his son Pedro II (1825–91) was deposed and Brazil became a republic. From 1930 to 1945 it was ruled by the benevolent dictator Getúlio Vargas (1883–1954). Less stable governments followed; in 1964 Gen Humberto Castelo Branco (1900–67) came to power in a military coup. In 1967 Marshal Artur da Costa e Silva (1902–69) was elected president, being replaced in 1969 by a junta comprising the three heads of the armed forces. Fernando Collor de Mello (1949–) became president in 1990. Official language: Portuguese. Official currency: cruzeiro. Area: 8 511 965 sq km (3 286 000 sq mi). Population (1988 est): 144 300 000. Capital: Brasília. Main port: Rio de Janeiro.

Brazil nut The seed of a tall forest tree, *Bertholletia excelsa*, up to 45 m high, native to tropical South America. The tree produces fluffy flowers that develop into woody fruits, each containing 12–24 seeds (the nuts).

brazilwood An evergreen South American tree, *Caesalpinia brasiliensis*, of the pea family. The leaves consist of paired leaflets and the orange flowers develop into seed pods. The tree yields a very hard wood used for cabinetwork.

brazing. *See* solder.

Brazzaville 4 07W 15 15E The capital of the People's Republic of Congo, situated on the Zaïre River opposite Kinshasa (Zaïre). Founded in the 1880s, it became capital of French Equatorial Africa in 1910. During World War II it was the centre of the Free French forces in Africa. It became capital of the newly independent Republic of Congo in 1960. Population (1984): 585 812.

breadfruit The starchy fruit of a tropical tree *Artocarpus communis*. When roasted it forms a staple part of the diet in the Pacific islands. The tree grows to a height of 30 m and has shiny indented leaves. The large round fruits have a thick rind and develop from long female catkins.

bream A food and game fish, *Abramis brama*, related to the *carp and occurring in European lakes and slow-moving rivers. Its deep body, 30–70 cm long, is bluish grey or brown above and silvery below. *See also* sea bream.

Bream, Julian Alexander (1933–) British guitarist and lutenist, whose repertoire includes arrangements of baroque and Renaissance pieces as well as works written for him by Britten and Henze.

breathalyzer A roadside test used by the police to estimate the amount of alcohol in the breath, which reflects the level of alcohol in the blood. In the UK a suspected driver blows into a balloon through a tube containing potassium dichromate crystals. When the balloon is inflated (i.e. sufficient breath has been examined), if the colour change extends beyond a line marked on the tube, the driver has an alcohol level above the legal limit (80 mg per 100 millilitres of blood). He is then taken to a police station to have a blood or urine test. Electronic devices largely replaced the traditional breathalyzer in the 1980s.

Brecht, Bertolt (1898–1956) German dramatist and poet. He first studied medicine and was converted to Marxism in 1928. *Die Dreigroschenoper* was an adaptation of John Gay's *The Beggar's Opera*, with music by Kurt Weil. In 1933 he moved to Scandinavia and the USA (1941–47). During these years he wrote *Galileo* (1938), *Mother Courage* (1939) and *The Caucasian Chalk Circle* (1949). In 1949 he returned to East Berlin and founded his Berliner Ensemble Company.

Breeches Bible. *See* Bible.

breeder reactor. *See* fast reactor.

Bremen The smallest *Land* of Germany, comprising the cities of Bremen (population: 522 000) and Bremerhaven (population: 132 200) enclosed by the *Land* of Lower Saxony. Area: 404 sq km (156 sq mi). Population (1987): 654 500.

bremmstrahlung Electromagnetic radiation emitted by a charged particle, such as an electron, when it is slowed down on passing close to a nucleus. The particle loses energy as a result. *Cosmic rays lose energy as bremmstrahlung on entering the earth's atmosphere.

Breslau. *See* Wrocław.

Brest (name until 1921: Brest-Litovsk; Polish name: Brześć nad Bu-giem) 52 08N 23 40E A port in the W Soviet Union, in the Belorussian

SSR. It is a major industrial centre. Population (1987): 238 000.

Brest 48 23N 4 30W A port and naval base in NW France, in the Finistère department on the Atlantic Ocean. A German U-boat base in World War II, it was almost entirely destroyed by Allied bombing. Industries include fishing, chemicals, and clothing. Population (1983): 166 500.

Brethren Members of the Protestant Brethren Churches. The largest, called the Church of the Brethren, was founded in Germany in the early 18th century. Persecution forced its members to emigrate to America, where they became known as "Tunkers," "Dunkers," or "German Baptists." They do not drink alcohol or fight in wars and they practise adult baptism by dipping the whole of the body in water three times.

Brétigny, Treaty of (1360) The treaty that ended the first phase of the *Hundred Years' War. Never fully effective, it promised a ransom of £500,000 for John II of France (1319–64; reigned 1350–64; captured at Poitiers in 1356) and granted territories, including Aquitaine, to Edward III of England. In return, Edward was to give up his claim to the French throne.

Bretton Woods Conference (1944) A conference held at Bretton Woods, New Hampshire (USA), at which the USA, UK, and Canada established a system of international financial rules, which led to the setting up of the *International Monetary Fund (IMF) and the International Bank for Reconstruction and Development (World Bank). Each country agreed to keep its currency within 1% of a value fixed for gold and to back the IMF in bridging any temporary payments imbalances. In 1971 the US government ceased to fix the value of dollars in gold, and the system collapsed.

brewing. *See* beer and brewing.

Brezhnev, Leonid Ilich (1906–82) Soviet statesman; secretary of the Soviet Communist Party (1964–82) and president of the Soviet Union (1977–82). Brezhnev, a metallurgist, was a political leader in the Red Army during World War II. He and *Kosygin forced Khrushchev to resign in 1964.

briar A shrubby rambling rose with arching prickly stems, found in hedgerows and scrub in many parts of Europe. An example is the sweet briar, or eglantine (*Rosa rubiginosa*), with pink flowers.
Briar is also the name of a shrubby white-flowered plant (*Erica arborea*), the roots of which are used for making briar pipes.

bricks A building material in the form of a rectangular block usually measuring 225 × 112 × 75 mm. They are normally made from clay and baked or fired in a kiln at about 900°C. Water is driven off, organic matter becomes oxidized, and some of the clay minerals fuse and fill the gaps between the clay particles. Iron oxide gives the brick its reddish colour. London stock bricks are yellowish on account of the sand and alumina they contain. Bricks are laid in various patterns, known as bonds.

bridge A card game that developed from whist. **Straight bridge** was first played in Britain

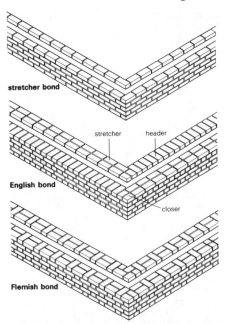

BRICKS *The factors of cost, strength, and decorative effect influence a bricklayer's choice of bond for a particular task.*

about 1880; having overtaken whist in popularity, about 1911 it was displaced by its descendant, **auction bridge**, in which the opposing pairs of partners competed to decide the trump suit. By 1929 **contract bridge**, which had developed in the USA, was popularized by Ely Culbertson (1891–1955). Two pairs of partners bid to name the trump suit (or to play without a trump suit) and "contract" to win a particular number of tricks above the six tricks of the "book." A game consists of 100 points, with each spade or heart trick counting 30, each diamond or club 20, and for a bid in no trumps 40 for the first trick and 30 for subsequent tricks. Only the tricks contracted for in the bidding are counted towards game; extra points are awarded separately for "honours" (ace to ten of trumps), overtricks, and for slams (when the partners have bid for and won all the tricks or all but one trick in a hand). Penalty points are awarded to the opponents for undertricks. The side winning two games in a row two games out of three wins the rubber, which counts as either 500 or 700 extra points.

Bridges, Robert Seymour (1844–1930) British poet, who worked as a doctor until 1882. Several volumes of lyrics came before the long philosophical poem, *The Testament of Beauty* (1929). He also produced an edition of the poems of his friend Gerard Manley *Hopkins. He was made poet laureate in 1913.

Bridgetown 14 05N 59 35W The capital of Barbados, a port in the SW on Carlisle Bay, founded in 1628. Population (1983 est): 7466.

Bridgewater Canal A waterway constructed in 1759–61 by James Brindley (1716–72) from Worsley to Manchester (later extended to Liverpool) for transporting coal. The first British canal, it is constructed on an aqueduct across the Irwell Valley.

Brighton 50 50N 0 10W A resort in S England, on the East Sussex coast. Originally a fishing village, its growth began with the development of sea bathing in the 1750s and the patronage of the Prince Regent (later George IV), who had the Royal Pavilion redesigned by John *Nash in oriental style. Other notable features include the Lanes (famous for their antique shops) and the boating marina (completed in 1979). Population (1981): 146 134.

brill An edible flatfish, *Scophthalmus rhombus*, related to *turbot, that occurs in European coastal waters. Its smooth body is sandy with light and dark spots above.

brimstone A lemon-yellow butterfly, *Gonopteryx rhamni*, found in Europe, N Africa, and parts of Asia. Adults hibernate, flying early in spring. The next generation emerges in June or later, the caterpillars feeding on buckthorn.

Brisbane 27 30S 153 00E The third largest city in Australia, the capital and chief port of Queensland. Exports include wool, meat, mineral sands, and wheat. Notable buildings include Parliament House (1869), two cathedrals, the Observatory (1829) built by convicts, and the Queen Elizabeth II Stadium built for the 1982 Commonwealth Games. Population (1988): 1 180 400.

bristletail A slender wingless insect, 5–20 mm long, that has two or three long tail bristles. Most bristletails live in damp sheltered places and feed on plant detritus. *See also* silverfish.

Bristol 51 27N 2 35W A port and industrial city in SW England, the administrative centre of Avon. A major port in the 17th and 18th centuries, it traded mostly with the Americas and prospered greatly from the slave trade. Its docks at Avonmouth and Portishead (including the modern Portbury dock) are still active. Nearby is the Avon Gorge, spanned by Brunel's Clifton Suspension Bridge (1832–64). Population (1988): 377 700.

Bristol Channel An inlet of the Atlantic Ocean in the UK, between South Wales and SW England. It forms an extension of the Severn Estuary and has the greatest tidal range in England. Length: about 137 km (85 mi).

British Antarctic Territory A British colony established in 1962 that consists of the South Orkney and South Shetland islands and a part of the Antarctic. It is used as a base for the British Antarctic Survey stations.

British Broadcasting Corporation (BBC) A broadcasting authority in the UK. The BBC was first set up as a private company in 1922 and was made into a public corporation under royal charter in 1927; it is responsible to parliament and is politically neutral and independent. It runs two national television stations, five national radio stations, and a number of local radio stations. It relies on income from television licences as it is not permitted to carry advertising. The BBC provides external services in 38 languages, for which it receives a subsidy from the government.

British citizenship A new form of citizenship introduced on 1 January 1983 by the British Nationality Act (1981). It is acquired by birth in the UK to a parent who is either a British citizen or a settled resident there, by descent, by registration, or by naturalization. With two other new forms, British Dependent Territories citizenship and British Overseas citizenship, it replaced the single form of citizenship of the UK and Colonies created by the British Nationality Act (1948).

British Columbia The westernmost province of Canada, on the Pacific Ocean. It is bounded by the Rocky Mountains in the E and the Coast Range in the W. The main rivers (the Fraser, Kootenay, Thompson, and Columbia) and their tributaries are swift flowing and there are many lakes and waterfalls. Forests cover over 55% of the surface. There are rich mineral resources; gold, silver, lead, zinc, copper, coal, and oil are all produced. Only a small area is farmed, and half the population lives in the Lower Mainland. *History*: the area was visited by Captain Cook (1778) and a British colony established on Vancouver Island (1849) spread to the mainland when gold was discovered (1858). It became part of Canada in 1871, and the transcontinental railway (1885) encouraged development. Area: 930 528 sq km (359 277 sq mi). Population (1986): 2 883 367. Capital: Victoria.

British Council An institution set up in 1934 and made into a corporation by royal charter in 1940. The Council's chief aims are to promote a knowledge of the UK abroad, to promote the teaching of English, and to encourage cooperation between the developing countries and the UK.

British Council of Churches A body, set up in 1947, of representatives of the major Churches in Britain and Ireland except the Roman Catholic Church (although this sends observers to meetings). The recommendations it makes to member Churches are designed to bring about unity and joint action. It founded Christian Aid and is an Associate Council of the World Council of Churches.

British Guiana. *See* Guyana, Cooperative Republic of.

British Honduras. *See* Belize, Colony of.

British Indian Ocean Territory A British colony established in 1965 consisting of the Chagos Archipelago, the largest island of which is Diego Garcia, which Mauritius claimed to own. Aldabra, Farquhar, and Desroches were returned to the Seychelles in 1976. Although the islands are at present leased to companies that run copra plantations, they were acquired as a base for military activities. There is no permanent population.

British Legion. *See* Royal British Legion.

British Library The national library, formed in 1973 from the British Museum Library, founded in 1753, and other collections, and kept mainly in the *British Museum. Until 1989 it received a copy of every book published in Britain and contains over 18 million volumes. New premises are being prepared.

British Museum The national museum founded in 1753 to house the private collection of Sir Hans *Sloane. It now occupies Sir Robert Smirke's neoclassical building (1847) in Bloomsbury, London. Its collections include Egyptian mummies, the Elgin Marbles, and the Rosetta Stone. The natural history exhibits were transferred to a building (designed by Alfred Waterhouse (1830–1905) and built 1873–80) in South Kensington, known as the Natural History Museum.

British Standards Institution (BSI) An institution founded in 1901 (renamed in 1931). Its function is to establish minimum standards of quality for various products and to avoid duplication of design, sizes, and patterns. Products that conform to BSI standards bear the Kite mark as a symbol of quality. The BSI works in association with the International Organization for Standardization.

British thermal unit (btu) A unit of energy equal to 1055.06 joules. It was formerly defined as the amount of heat required to raise the temperature of 1 lb of water through 1°F.

Britons The native-born inhabitants of Britain before the Anglo-Saxon settlements. They spoke languages of the Brythonic branch of the *Celtic language family. At the Roman conquest (1st century AD) Britain was divided into tribal kingdoms with a common Celtic culture.

Brittany (Breton name: Breiz; French name: Bretagne) A planning region and former province in NW France. It consists of a peninsula between the Bay of Biscay and English Channel. It was part of ancient Armorica and in 56 BC was conquered by Julius Caesar. During the 5th–6th centuries AD Celts from Britain migrated here to escape the Anglo-Saxon invasion. It finally became part of France in 1532. Area: 27 184 sq km (10 494 sq mi). Population (1986 est): 2 764 200.

Britten, (Edward) Benjamin, Baron (1913–76) British composer. A pupil of Frank Bridge, he spent the years 1939–42 in the USA and subsequently founded the English Opera Group (1947) and the Aldeburgh Festival (1948). He wrote many leading roles in his operas for his lifelong friend, the tenor Sir Peter Pears. Among Britten's works are the operas *Peter Grimes* (1945), *Billy Budd* (1951), and *Death in Venice* (1973); the orchestral works *Variations on a Theme by Frank Bridge* (1937) and the *Cello Symphony* (1964); choral works, such as the *Spring Symphony* (1949) and *A War Requiem* (1962); and many chamber works.

brittle star A marine invertebrate animal, also called sand star or serpent star, related to starfish (*see* echinoderms). It has a small dislike body with five long fragile arms, used for locomotion.

Brno (German name: Brünn) 49 12N 16 40E The second largest city in Czechoslovakia, formerly the capital of the province of Moravia. A fortified town in the middle ages, it contains the Spilberk fortress, an Austrian political prison (1621–1857). Brno is now an important industrial centre. Population (1986): 385 000.

broad bean An annual plant, *Vicia faba*, 60–150 cm tall, with a ribbed stem and grey-green leaves. The flowers have white petals and dark-purple blotches. The large pod has a woolly lining surrounding large flat edible beans, for which the plant is cultivated. *See also* bean.

broadbill A brightly coloured bird of tropical African and Asian forests. It is about 12 cm long with a large head, partly joined toes, and a very broad short bill. Most species eat insects.

Broads, the A low-lying area mainly in Norfolk but extending into Suffolk. It consists of shallow lakes, believed to have originated as medieval peat diggings, linked to the Rivers Bure and Yare and their tributaries. They now provide boating and fishing facilities.

broccoli A cultivated variety of wild cabbage with a stout upright stem and a loose cluster of flower heads at the top, grown in temperate and cool regions. Sprouting broccoli has purple or white flowers. Calabrese or green sprouting broccoli is an Italian variety, often with fused parallel stems. Both are eaten as vegetables.

bromine (Br) A dense reddish-brown liquid element, discovered by A. J. Balard (1802–76) in 1826. It is obtained from sea water and other natural salt solutions. The liquid element changes readily into a vapour, which has a pungent smell similar to that of chlorine with severe irritating effects. Compounds include silver bromide (AgBr), used in photography. At no 35; at wt 79.904; mp –7.2°C; bp 58.78°C.

bronchi. *See* lungs.

bronchitis Inflammation of the air passages (bronchi) leading to the lungs. Acute bronchitis is often due to a virus infection. Chronic bronchitis is common in middle-aged men in the UK, being aggravated by cigarette smoking. Irritation of the mucus-secreting glands in the bronchi results in a persistent cough, with the production of large amounts of sputum. The patient is breathless and liable to chest infections. Treatment consists of the prompt management of any chest infection.

Brontë sisters Three British novelists, daughters of the rector of Haworth, an isolated village in Yorkshire. After attending a local boarding school, **Charlotte Brontë** (1816–55) and **Emily Brontë** (1818–48) rejoined their sister **Anne Brontë** (1820–49) at home. Their early writings depicted the imaginary kingdoms of Angria and Gondal. All the sisters worked for brief periods as governesses and teachers to help pay off the debts of their alcoholic artist brother, **Patrick Branwell Brontë** (1817–48). In 1846 the sisters published *Poems by Currer, Ellis, and Acton Bell* and in 1847, under the same names, the novels *Jane Eyre* (by Charlotte), *Wuthering Heights* (by Emily), and *Agnes Grey* (by Anne). In 1848 Emily died of tuberculosis, as did Anne in 1849. Charlotte published *Shirley* (1849) and *Villette* (1853). She married her father's curate in 1854 and died in pregnancy a year later.

Brontosaurus. *See* Apatosaurus.

Brontotherium An extinct North American hoofed mammal, a type of titanothere that lived between 38 and 26 million years ago. Standing

bronze 86

2.5 m at the shoulder, it had a large skull with a pair of bony horns.

bronze An alloy of copper and (4–11%) tin. Because it melts between 900°C and 1000°C, about the temperature of an ordinary wood fire, it was one of the first metals to be used for making weapons and utensils, being known around 2000 BC in Britain. It is harder than pure copper. *See also* gun metal.

Bronze Age The cultural phase during which metallurgical technology, based first on copper (in the Chalcolithic period) and then on bronze, replaced the stone technology of the *Neolithic period. In Eurasia the development of international trade, literacy, the plough, and the wheel took place during this phase, which began at varying dates according to locality (the earliest being about 6500 BC in Anatolia); it gave way to the *Iron Age in about 1000 BC. In Africa, iron, discovered about 800 BC, replaced stone without an intervening Bronze Age. In the Americas, copper, discovered about 100 AD, was followed rapidly by iron.

Bronzino, Il (Agnolo di Cosimo; 1503–72) Florentine mannerist painter (*see* mannerism). His religious and allegorical works, such as *Venus, Cupid, and Folly* (National Gallery, London), were influenced by *Michelangelo. As court painter to Cosimo I de' Medici he painted many portraits, including *Eleanor of Toledo and Her Son Giovanni* (Uffizi).

Brooke, Rupert (Chawner) (1887–1915) British poet. His scholarship, charm, and good looks gained him many influential friends in literary circles. He received a naval commission in 1914 but died of blood poisoning on a hospital ship in the Aegean, without having seen action. The idealistic patriotism of his wartime poetry, *1914 and Other Poems* (1915), made him a national hero.

broom A deciduous shrub, *Sarothamnus scoparius* (or *Cytisus scoparius*), of the pea family. 60–200 cm high, it has shiny green five-angled stems and small pointed compound leaves. The bright-yellow flowers are clustered at the ends of the twigs. Broom is found in heaths and woodland glades in Europe. It is poisonous to livestock but is often grown as an ornamental.

Brown, Sir Arthur. *See* Alcock, Sir John.

Brown, Capability (Lancelot B.; 1716–83) British landscape gardener, who carried on the work of William Kent. Abandoning the formal continental style, Brown's gardens, as for example at Blenheim Palace (1765), sought to imitate nature, establishing an English style of park. He was also an architect, designing houses and garden buildings. His nickname arose because he frequently told his patrons that their grounds had "capabilities" for landscaping.

Brown, Ford Madox (1821–93) British painter, born in Calais. Influenced by the Pre-Raphaelites, he painted chiefly historical themes, although his most famous paintings, *Work* (Manchester) and *The Last of England* (Birmingham), are of contemporary subjects.

Brown, John (1800–59) US abolitionist, who raided the Federal Arsenal at Harpers Ferry, Virginia, in an attempt to establish a slave refuge

and a base for promoting slave uprisings. He was captured and executed for treason; he is the hero of the song "John Brown's Body."

Brown, Robert (1773–1858) Scottish botanist, who in 1831 first recognized the *nucleus as a basic part of cells. Four years earlier, while observing a solution of pollen grains in water under a microscope, he discovered the continuous random movement of the grains, now known as the **Brownian movement**. Although Brown was unable to exlain it, it is now known to be due to collisions between the atoms and molecules of the fluid with the particles.

brown algae Algae that contain a brown pigment (fucoxanthin) in addition to and sometimes masking the green chlorophyll. Brown algae include all the larger seaweeds, such as wracks and kelps. Many show an *alternation of generations.

brown bear A large shaggy mostly brown bear, *Ursus arctos*, of the N hemisphere. There are many races and subspecies–the reputedly ferocious grizzly bear (*U. arctos horribilis*), of N Canada and Alaska, reaches a length of 2.5 m and a weight of 550 kg; the Alaskan Kodiak bear –a giant grizzly–is the largest living land carnivore, reaching a length of 2.8 m and a weight of 760 kg.

Browning, Robert (1812–89) British poet. The son of a bank clerk, he wrote several verse dramas and dramatic monologues, including the famous "My Last Duchess" (1842). The poem cycle *The Ring and the Book* was his last major work. His wife **Elizabeth Barrett Browning** (1806–61) was also a poet. A spinal injury when she was 15 made her a lifelong semi-invalid. She met Robert Browning in 1845 and in 1846 she defied her domineering father and eloped with Browning to Italy. Here she wrote her most famous work, *Sonnets from the Portuguese* (1850). She later became involved in Italian politics, the abolition of slavery, and spiritualism.

Browning Automatic Rifle (BAR) A gas-operated automatic *rifle designed in 1917 by John Moses Browning (1855–1926). Used throughout the US army until the Korean War, it weighed over 8.6 kg (19 lbs).

Brubeck, Dave (1920–) US jazz pianist, who studied music with Darius Milhaud and Arnold Schoenberg. Brubeck formed a quartet in 1951. One of his most famous pieces is "Take Five."

Bruce, Robert. *See* Robert (I) the Bruce.

brucellosis (*or* undulant fever) An infectious disease of farm animals caused by the bacterium *Brucella abortus*. Symptoms include fever weakness, cough, joint pain, and sometimes swelling of the lymph nodes. The antibiotic tetracycline usually cures the disease, which can be contracted by man from contaminated milk.

Bruch, Max (1838–1920) German composer, best known for his first violin concerto (1868) and *Kol Nidrei* (1880) for cello and orchestra, based on a Jewish hymn.

Bruckner, Anton (1824–96) Austrian composer. A professor at the Vienna conservatoire (1871–91), he was granted a pension and apartments in the Belvedere palace in Vienna in 1891, where he worked on his ninth (unfinished) symphony (1887–96). His symphonies had a mixed reception during his lifetime and were frequently performed in shortened versions. Bruckner also composed choral and chamber music and a *Te Deum* (1881–84).

Brueghel the Elder, Pieter (*or* Bruegel; 1525–69) Flemish painter, popularly called Peasant Brueghel, whose patrons included Cardinal de Granvelle (1517–86). Influenced by *Bosch in such works as the macabre *Triumph of Death* (Prado), in 1563 he settled in Brussels, where he executed his best-known works, e.g. *Peasant Wedding* (Kunsthistorisches Museum, Vienna), and a landscape series entitled the *Labours of the Months*. Many of his paintings were copied by his eldest son **Pieter Brueghel the Younger** (?1564–?1638). His younger son **Jan Brueghel the Elder** (1568–1625) is noted for his flower and landscape paintings.

Bruges (Flemish name: Brugge) 51 13N 3 14E A town in NW Belgium. It was the capital of Flanders in the 12th century and during the 13th and 14th centuries it became the centre of the Hanseatic League. It has many fine gothic buildings, including the 14th-century cathedral, the Church of Notre Dame and the Market Hall (13th–15th centuries) with its famous belfry. It is linked by canal to many European ports. Population (1989 est): 120 000.

Brummell, George Bryan (1778–1840) British dandy, known as Beau Brummell. He was a prominent member of fashionable society and a close friend of the Prince Regent, later George IV. After becoming bankrupt he fled to France and died in an asylum.

Brunei, State of A small sultanate in NW Borneo, consisting of two separate areas, bounded by the Malaysian state of Sarawak. The people are mainly Malays, while about a quarter of the population are Chinese or other minorities. *Economy*: dominated by oil since the discovery of the Seria oilfield in 1929 and the later offshore oilfields. A deepwater port and a natural-gas liquefaction plant have recently been built. Agriculture is being encouraged. *History*: a powerful state in the 16th century controlling the whole of Borneo, it became a British protected state in 1888. Since 1962 the sultan has ruled by decree. In 1967 Hassanal Bolkia Mu'izzuddin Waddaulah (1946–) succeeded his father as sultan. Internal self-government was achieved in 1971 and full independence in 1983. Official language: Malay; Chinese and English are also widely spoken. Official religion: Islam. Official currency: Brunei dollar of 100 cents. Area: 5800 sq km (2226 sq mi). Population (1988 est): 226 300. Capital and main port: Bandar Seri Begawan.

Brunel, Isambard Kingdom (1806–59) British engineer, whose most famous works were the Clifton suspension bridge (1864) and his ships the *Great Western* (1837), the *Great Britain* (1843), and the *Great Eastern* (1858). Much of his work was done for the Great Western Railway, for which he built over 1600 km of track. His father **Sir Marc Isambard Brunel** (1769–1849) was also an engineer. Born in France, he worked in New York after fleeing the French Revolu-

tion. He moved to England in 1799, where he became famous for his tunnelling shield, which allowed tunnels to be dug below water. His tunnel under the River Thames from Rotherhithe to Wapping took from 1825 to 1842 to complete.

Brunelleschi, Filippo (1377–1446) Italian Renaissance architect, who began his career as a goldsmith. His most famous construction is the dome of Florence cathedral (1430s). The Ospedale degli Innocenti (1419–26) is often regarded as the first architectural expression of the Renaissance.

Brunswick (German name: Braunschweig) 52 15N 10 30E A city in N Germany, in Lower Saxony on the River Oker. It was the capital of the former duchy of Brunswick. Notable buildings include the castle and the romanesque cathedral (both 12th-century), the old town hall (14th-15th centuries), and the ducal palace (1768–69). Population (1989 est): 254 851.

brush turkey A megapode bird, *Alectura lathami*, occurring in rain forests of New Guinea and E Australia. It is 65–70 cm long with a black plumage and builds a huge nest of fermenting plant material.

Brussels (French name: Bruxelles) 50 51N 4 22E The capital of Belgium, situated on the River Senne. The headquarters of the EC and NATO, it has many fine buildings including the 15th-century gothic town hall, the 13th-century Maison du Roi, the 18th-century Palais de la Nation (parliament building), and the Royal Palace. *History*: settled by the French in the 7th century AD, it developed into a centre of the wool industry in the 13th century. It became the capital of the Spanish Netherlands in the 15th century and later of the Austrian S Netherlands. In 1830 it was chosen as capital of the new kingdom of Belgium. Population (1988 est): 970 346.

Brussels sprout A variety of wild cabbage cultivated for its large edible buds in Europe and the USA. The stout shoots, up to 80 cm high, have curly leaves arranged spirally up the stem; the large buds grow in the angle between the leaf bases and the stem.

Brutus, Marcus Junius (?85–42 BC) Roman soldier, who supported Pompey against Caesar in the civil war, was pardoned by Caesar and made governor of Cisalpine Gaul (46). He subsequently joined the conspiracy to murder Caesar (44) and committed suicide after his defeat by Antony at Philippi (42).

bryony Either of two unrelated Eurasian plants. **Black bryony** (*Tamus communis*) is a herbaceous climber with heart-shaped leaves. The bell-shaped yellow flowers are borne in separate male and female clusters. The fruits are scarlet berries. **White bryony** (*Bryonia dioica*) is a perennial climbing herb with lobed leaves. Greenish male and female flowers occur on separate plants and produce poisonous scarlet berries.

bryophyte A small flowerless green plant of the division *Bryophyta* (about 25 000 species), comprising the liverworts and *mosses. The plant body is either separated into stems and leaves or is a flat branching structure (thallus). Bryophytes lack true vascular (conducting) tissues and roots (the rootlike rhizoids serve mainly for anchorage). They show *alternation of generations: the plant itself is the sexual (gametophyte) phase, which bears male and female sex organs (antheridia and archegonia, respectively). Fertilization of an egg cell results in the development of a spore capsule – the asexual (sporophyte) phase – which remains attached to the gametophyte. The spores germinate to form new plants.

bubonic plague. *See* plague.

Buchan, John, 1st Baron Tweedsmuir (1875–1940) British novelist. *Prester John* (1910) was the first of a series of lively adventure novels that included *The Thirty-Nine Steps* (1915), in which his character Richard Hannay first appeared. Director of Information during World War 1, he was made governor general of Canada in 1935.

Bucharest (Romanian name: Bucureşti) 44 25N 26 07E The capital of Romania, in the SE on a tributary of the Danube. It became capital of Wallachia in 1659 and capital of Romania in 1862. It was badly damaged by German bombing in World War II. Population (1980 est): 1 861 007.

Buckingham, George Villiers, 1st Duke of (1592–1628) He replaced Robert Carr, Earl of Somerset, in the favour of James I of England (1615), becoming Earl of Buckingham (1617), Lord High Admiral (1619), and Duke of Buckingham (1623). His attempt to arrange the marriage of Prince Charles to the daughter of the Spanish king failed (1623); he was assassinated after his unsuccessful expedition to relieve the Huguenots at La Rochelle (1627). His son **George Villiers, 2nd Duke of Buckingham** (1628–87) was a member of the Cabal group of ministers under Charles II. After his father's death he was brought up in the royal family, with whom he went into exile after the royalist defeat in the Civil War (1651). He became a privy councillor at the Restoration. Also a playwright, he wrote the satirical *The Rehearsal* (1671).

Buckingham Palace The London residence of the British monarch. It was built about 1705 for the Duke of Buckingham, becoming a royal residence in 1761. It was completely redesigned by Nash for George IV, although its main façade was not added until 1913.

Buckinghamshire A county of England, bordering on Greater London. The land rises gently N from the River Thames to the Chiltern Hills before descending to the fertile Vale of Aylesbury. It is mainly agricultural; industry includes the manufacture of furniture at High Wycombe. Area: 1878 sq km (725 sq mi). Population (1987 est): 621 900. Administrative centre: Aylesbury.

buckwheat A herbaceous plant of the dock family. Up to 60 cm tall, it has arrow-shaped leaves and clusters of densely packed small pink or white flowers. Buckwheats are native to Asia but widely cultivated for their seed, used as a cereal substitute.

Budapest 47 33N 19 03E The capital of Hungary, situated in the N of the country on the River Danube. Most of Hungary's industry is sited here. *History*: from the 14th century the fortress of Buda, on the W bank of the Danube, was the seat of the Magyar kings. After occupation by the Turks, it came under Habsburg rule in the 17th century. In 1872 it united with Pest, on the E bank, to form the city that became the capital of Hungary in 1918. Population (1985): 2 104 000.

Buddha, title of **Gautama Siddhartha** (c. 563–c. 483 BC) Indian prince, whose teachings formed the basis of *Buddhism. The son of Suddhodana and his queen, Maya, in Kapilavastu (Nepal), Gautama was reputed to have been an exceptional child. At the age of 16 he married his cousin Princess Yasodhara, who some 13 years later bore him a son, Rahula. Soon after this Gautama, renouncing his life of indolence, abandoned his family and set out to seek solutions to the problems of human existence. After six years of asceticism he concluded that austerity was no solution, and sought enlightenment within himself. According to tradition, he achieved this seated beneath a banyan tree, in a village now called Buddh Gaya, in Bihar (his title, *Buddha*, is Sanskrit for the Awakened One). He devoted the rest of his life to teaching the principles of this enlightenment. He died at Kusinagara in Uttar Pradesh.

Buddhism The religion founded in NE India in the 6th century BC by Gautama Siddhartha (the *Buddha). His followers seek to copy his example of perfect morality, wisdom, and compassion, eventually reaching a state of enlightenment. According to Buddhist teaching, all worldly things are illusion and impermanent, including the self. The central beliefs of Buddhism are based on the Buddha's Four Noble Truths, the last of which is the Eightfold Path by which enlightenment may be reached and the individual self put out of existence in *nirvana. Buddhism has developed into many schools (*see* Zen Buddhism). It has more than 500 million followers in Sri Lanka, Nepal, Japan, and elsewhere.

buddleia A widespread tree or shrub with small four-petalled flowers clustered in dense heads. Many species are grown as ornamentals, especially *Buddleia davidii* (butterfly bush), 4–5 m high, the long purple flower heads of which attract butterflies; and *B. globosa*, which has round orange flower heads.

budgerigar A small parakeet, *Melopsitticus undulatus*, occurring in large flocks in Australia. It is 19 cm long and has a green and yellow plumage. Since its introduction to Britain in 1840 it has become a popular cagebird. Selective breeding has produced birds of many colours.

Buenos Aires 34 50S 58 37W The capital of Argentina situated on the Río de la Plata estuary. The financial, commercial, and industrial centre of the country, its chief exports are beef and wool. It possesses a national library and a famous opera house (the Teatro Colón). *History*: founded in 1580, it became capital of the newly created viceroyalty of the Río de la Plata in 1776 and of the new Republic of Argentina in 1880. Population (1980 est): 2 922 800.

buffalo A large African hoofed mammal, *Syncerus caffer*, also called Cape buffalo. Weighing over 700 kg and measuring 110–150 cm at the shoulder, buffaloes have massive curved horns and a smooth black coat. They live in large herds in grassy areas where both tree cover and water are available. *Compare* bison; water buffalo.

Buffalo   42 52N 78 55W A city in the USA, in New York state on Lake Erie and the Niagara River. It is linked to New York City by the New York State Barge Canal (formerly Erie Canal). Population (1986): 324 820.

Buffalo Bill.   *See* Cody, William F(rederick).

Bug, River   1. (*or* Western Bug) A river in E central Europe, rising in the Soviet Union and flowing NW as part of the border between the Soviet Union and Poland to the River Vistula. Length: 724 km (450 mi). 2. (*or* Southern Bug) A river in the SW Soviet Union, rising in the W Ukraine and flowing SE to the Dnieper estuary on the Black Sea. Length: 853 km (530 mi).

Buganda   A former kingdom in East Africa, now comprising an administrative region of Uganda bordering on Lake Victoria.

bugle   A high-pitched brass instrument with a wide conical tube, a cup-shaped mouthpiece, and a small bell. It lacks valves and so can only play a single harmonic series of notes (usually beginning with C). Formerly much used for military signalling, it is now used on ceremonial occasions.

Bukhari, al-   (810–70 AD) Muslim scholar. After extensive travels, he collected more than 600 000 traditional records (the Hadith) of the prophet Mohammed. The resulting collection is revered by Muslims as second in authority only to the Koran.

Bulawayo   20 10S 28 43E The second largest city in Zimbabwe. It was founded in 1894 by the British, near to Lobengula, the centre of the Ndebele tribe. The city is the country's chief industrial centre. Population (1982): 414 800.

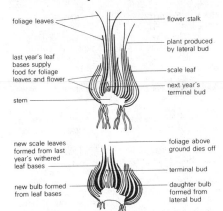

foliage leaves

flower stalk

plant produced by lateral bud

last year's leaf bases supply food for foliage leaves and flower

scale leaf

next year's terminal bud

stem

new scale leaves formed from last year's withered leaf bases

foliage above ground dies off

terminal bud

new bulb formed from leaf bases

daughter bulb formed from lateral bud

BULB *A section through a daffodil bulb in spring (above) and summer (below) to show growth cycle.*

bulb   A specialized underground stem of certain perennial herbaceous plants, for example onions and tulips, that serves as an overwintering organ. Food is stored in overlapping fleshy leaves or leaf bases, borne on a very short stem, and is used to produce one or more plants the following season.

Bulganin, Nikolai Aleksandrovich   (1895–1975) Soviet statesman; prime minister (1955–58). Bulganin became (1944) a member of Stalin's war cabinet and in 1947, defence minister. As prime minister, Bulganin participated in the attempt to oust Khrushchev in 1957 and was subsequently dismissed.

Bulgaria, People's Republic of   A country in SE Europe, in the E Balkans on the Black Sea. The low-lying Danube basin in the N rises to the Balkan Mountains in the centre; further S the Rhodope Mountains reach heights of almost 3000 m (10 000 ft). The inhabitants are mainly Bulgars, with minorities of Macedonians, Turks, and Gipsies. *Economy*: industrialization has proceeded rapidly since World War II. Coal, iron, and other minerals are mined and hydroelectricity and nuclear energy contribute to power supplies. Oil and natural gas have been found offshore in the Black Sea. Agriculture has been mechanized and organized on a cooperative basis. Bulgaria is a member of *COMECON. *History*: following the invasion of the Bulgars in the 7th century AD, Bulgaria became a significant power in SE Europe. Under Turkish rule in 1396, Bulgaria became independent in 1908. In 1944 it was occupied by the Soviet Union; power was seized by the left-wing Fatherland Front, which formed a pro-Soviet government that declared war on Germany, its former ally. In 1946 a People's Republic was proclaimed. The Communist Party lost power in 1989 and free elections were held in 1990. Official language: Bulgarian. Official currency: lev of 100 stotinki. Area: 110 912 sq km (42 823 sq mi). Population (1988): 8 973 600. Capital: Sofia. Main port: Varna.

bull (from Latin: *bulla*, seal)   Originally, the seal attached to papal edicts (the Pope's proclamation), it later referred to the documents themselves, now only to important ones. Making statements about Church teachings, they are named by their opening phrase, for example *Pastor Aeternus* (Eternal Father; 1870).

bulldog   A breed of dog originating in England, where it was used in bull- and bearbaiting. It has a compact rounded body with short sturdy legs and a short tail. The relatively large head has an undershot jaw and loose folds of skin. Weight: 25 kg (dogs); 23 kg (bitches).

bullfighting   The national spectator sport of Spain, it is also popular in parts of France and Latin America; mounted bullfighting, in which the bulls are not killed, is practised in Portugal. At a Spanish *corrida de toros* (bullfight) three matadors kill two bulls each. Following the initial ceremonial procession the first bull enters the ring. The first passes are made by the *banderilleros* (assistants) with their capes to attract the bull's attention. The matador then makes his first series of passes with his cape, controlling the bull's charge. During the next stage, the matadors make the bull charge at a mounted picador, who uses a lance to stab the bull's neck, so that it lowers its head. This procedure is repeated up to three times. During the following stage the neck muscle is further weakened by pairs of barbed sticks (*banderillas*) thrust into it by the *banderilleros*. In the final stage the matador performs a series of passes with his *muleta* (a small red cape folded over a stick) to weaken the bull until he can sever its aorta with his sword.

bullfinch A woodland finch, *Pyrrhula pyrrhula*, of N Eurasia. It is about 14 cm long and has a grey back, a pinkish breast, and black head. Bullfinches strip buds and flowers from trees and shrubs and are often regarded as pests.

bullfrog A large frog, *Rana catesbiana*, of North America. Dull green with a slightly warty skin, bullfrogs grow to about 20 cm and can jump up to 2 m. Females are larger than males. Other large frogs—*Pyxicephalus adspersus* in Africa and *Rana tigrina* in India—are also called bullfrogs.

bull mastiff A breed of dog resulting from crosses between bulldogs and mastiffs. It is sturdily built with a short broad muzzle and folds of skin surrounding the face. The short coat is redbrown. Height: 63–68 cm (dogs); 61–66 cm (bitches).

bull terrier A breed of dog originating in the UK from crosses between bulldogs and terriers. It is strongly built with a courageous temperament. Height: 48–56 cm. (Miniature bull terriers must not exceed 36 cm in height.)

bulrush A widely distributed herbaceous plant, *Scirpus lacustris*, of the sedge family growing in ponds, rivers, etc. 1–3 m high, it has cylindrical leafless stems bearing branched clusters of small reddish-brown flowers. The name is also applied to the reedmace; the biblical bulrush is the papyrus.

bumblebee A social bee found mainly in temperate regions. Bumblebees, 15–25 mm long, are usually black with yellow or orange bands. They live in colonies containing 100–400 workers in the summer. Their life cycle is like that of the honeybee, although only young fertilized queens survive the winter.

Bunker Hill, Battle of (17 June, 1775) A battle of the *American Revolution actually fought on Breed's Hill (next to Bunker Hill) in Charlestown, near Boston. The Americans defended the hill from two British attacks but Sir William Howe (1729–1814) displaced them at the third attempt.

Bunsen, Robert Wilhelm (1811–99) German chemist. He did not invent the laboratory gas burner known as the **Bunsen burner** although he did popularize it. Working with Kirchhoff, Bunsen developed spectroscopy, using a Bunsen burner to heat the substance. In 1860 they used the technique to discover the elements *rubidium and *caesium.

bunting A sparrow-like bird related to the finches. Buntings are 12–20 cm long and usually have a brownish or greyish plumage. The yellowhammer and the snow bunting are examples.

Buñuel, Luis (1900–83) Spanish film director whose films, made mainly in France and Mexico, include *Un Chien andalou* (1928), *Viridiana* (1961), and *That Obscure Object of Desire* (1977).

Bunyan, John (1628–88) British writer. Son of a tinker, he fought in the parliamentary army during the Civil War. After being converted to religion, he became the leader of a group of Baptists in Bedford and in 1660 he was imprisoned for preaching without a licence. During his 12 years in prison he wrote his spiritual autobiography, *Grace Abounding* (1666), and began his imaginative allegory *The Pilgrim's Progress* (1678).

Burgess, Anthony (John Burgess Wilson; 1917–   ) British novelist and former teacher of English literature. His books include *A Clockwork Orange* (1962), *Inside Mr Enderby* (1963), *Nothing like the Sun* (1964), *Napoleon Symphony* (1974), *Earthly Powers* (1980), *The Kingdom of the Wicked* (1985), *Little Wilson and Big God* (1988), and *Any Old Iron* (1989).

Burgess, Guy. See Maclean, Donald.

Burghley, William Cecil, Lord (1520–98) English statesman; close adviser to Elizabeth I. He served both Somerset and Northumberland under Edward VI and outwardly supported Roman Catholicism under Mary I. His realistic attitude is evident in Elizabeth's religious settlement (*see* Reformation). He influenced Elizabeth's pro-Protestant foreign policy and helped to prepare for the Spanish invasion (*see* Armada, Spanish). He secured the execution of Mary, Queen of Scots. He was succeeded as royal adviser by his son **Robert Cecil, 1st Earl of Salisbury** (c. 1563–1612), who arranged the accession of James VI of Scotland to the English throne as James I (1603). As lord treasurer (1608–12), he was James' chief adviser.

Burgundy A region in France, E of the Rivers Rhône and Saône. A Scandinavian people occupied the region in the 4th century AD, establishing a kingdom that was conquered by the Franks in 534. The NW part of the region became a duchy in the 9th century, passing to the French Crown in the mid-14th century. Population (1986 est): 1 607 200.

Burke, Edmund (1729–97) British political philosopher. An MP from 1765, he became a Rockingham Whig. He attacked George III's exalted view of the monarch's political role in the pamphlet *Thoughts on the Cause of the Present Discontents* (1770) and blamed the unrest in the American colonies on British misgovernment. An opponent of democracy, he argued in favour of responsible aristocratic government. His books include *Reflections on the Revolution in France* (1790) and *A Philosophical Enquiry into the Origin of Our Ideas of the Sublime and Beautiful* (1757).

Burkina Faso (name until 1984: Upper Volta) A landlocked country in West Africa. It consists mainly of a large low-lying area, crossed by the River Volta. The population is almost entirely African, the largest groups being the Mossi and Fulani. *Economy*: chiefly agricultural. Production of crops is being increased by improved water supplies. Some minerals, including manganese, have been found. *History*: the area was occupied by powerful Mossi states from the 14th century. It became part of the French protectorate of Soudan in 1898 and in 1919 the separate protectorate of Upper Volta was formed. In 1932 it was divided between Niger, Ivory Coast, and Soudan but was brought back together in 1947.

In 1958 Upper Volta became a republic, gaining full independence in 1960. A military coup in 1966 brought Lt Col (later Gen) Sangoulé Lamizana (1916–) to power; he was overthrown in 1980. In 1983, after another military coup, Capt Thomas Sankara became head of state; he was killed in 1987 during a further coup under Capt Blaise Compaoré(1951–). In 1985 territorial disputes led to armed conflict with neighbouring Mali. Official language: French. Official currency: CFA (Communauté financière africaine) franc of 100 centimes. Area: 274 002 sq km (105 764 sq mi). Population (1988 est): 8 530 000. Capital: Ouagadougou.

Burma, Socialist Republic of the Union of (Official name from 1989: Union of Myanmar) A country in SE Asia, on the Bay of Bengal. A narrow plain running N-S rises to the Arakan Mountains and the Chin Hills in the W and the Shan Plateau in the E. The majority of the population, concentrated in the delta of the River Irrawaddy, is Burmese but there are several minorities, including the Shan, Karen, Chachin, and Chin peoples. *Economy*: primarily agricultural, the main crop is rice. Almost half the land is under forest. There is some mining, especially of lead and zinc, and all industry is nationalized. Foreign trade is carried out through government trading organizations, the main exports being rice, rubber, jute, and timber. *History*: by the 13th century the Burmese had a civilization based on Hinayana Buddhism. Following defeat by the Mongols in 1287, the area was ruled by the Shans and the Mons. The rule of the Burmese Alaungpaya in the 18th century began a period of increased prosperity. After successive wars it came under British rule in 1885 as part of British India. In 1937 it attained limited self-government and was separated from India. In 1948 it became a republic outside the Commonwealth. In 1962 its parliamentary democracy was overthrown in a military coup by Gen U Ne Win (1911–), who formed (1974) a one-party socialist republic, of which he was president until 1981. He was succeeded by Gen San Yu (1919–) but remained the effective ruler. In 1988, amid calls for democratic reform, Maung Maung was elected president but replaced within weeks by Gen Saw Maung after a military coup. Martial law was imposed. Elections were held in 1990 but the military refused to hand over power. Official language: Burmese. Official currency: kyat of 100 pyas. Area: 678 000 sq km (261 789 sq mi). Population (1988 est): 39 840 000. Capital and main port: Rangoon.

Burmese A language of the Tibeto-Burman branch of Sino-Tibetan, spoken by 20 million people in Burma, where it is the official language. Written in an alphabet that came from the Pali script of India, Burmese literature dates from the 11th century AD.

Burmese cat A breed of short-haired cat originating from an Asian hybrid imported into the USA in 1933. The Burmese has a small head with large ears and greenish-yellow eyes and usually a dark-brown or silver coat.

Burne-Jones, Sir Edward Coley (1833–98) British Pre-Raphaelite painter and designer. After meeting *Rossetti (1856) he abandoned his studies at Oxford for an art career, Typical of his romantic paintings is *King Cophetua and the Beggar Maid* (Tate Gallery). More influential were his designs for stained glass and tapestries, often for the firm of William *Morris.

Burns, Robert (1759–96) Scottish poet. Son of a poor farmer in Ayrshire, Burns became the Scottish national poet. *Poems, Chiefly in the Scottish Dialect* (1786) won him immediate fame; from 1786 until 1788 he was a leading figure in Edinburgh society. His return to farming was a failure and from 1789 he worked for the excise service. His poems range from love lyrics to broad humour, as in "Tam o'Shanter" (1788), and scathing satire, as in "The Twa Dogs" (1786). He collected and wrote numerous songs. **Burns Night** (25 Jan) commemorates his birth.

Burton, Richard (Richard Jenkins; 1925–84) British actor, born in Wales. He first achieved success in Shakespearean roles, but from the 1950s acted almost entirely in films. These included *Look Back in Anger* (1959), *Becket* (1964), and *Who's Afraid of Virginia Woolf?* (1966). His two marriages to Elizabeth Taylor were highly publicized.

Burton-upon-Trent 52 49N 1 36W A town in central England, in E Staffordshire on the River Trent. Formerly a cotton-spinning town, its brewing tradition dates back to brewing by the Benedictine monks of Burton Abbey (founded 1002). Population (1988): 57 740.

Burundi, Republic of A small inland country in central Africa, bordering on Lake Tanganyika. It consists chiefly of high plateau along the Nile-Congo dividing range, descending to the Great Rift Valley in the W. Most of the population belongs to the Hutu, a Bantu tribe, but the rulers are Tutsi and there are other tribal minorities. *Economy*: mainly subsistence agriculture; coffee is the main export and tea is also being developed. Minerals have been found. *History*: the area became part of German East Africa in 1890 and from 1919 it was administered by Belgium. It became independent in 1962. In 1966 the hereditary Mwami Mwambutsa IV was deposed by his son, Mwami Ntare V. In the same year, following a military coup, Capt (later Lt Gen) Michel Micombero (1940–83) set up a republic with himself as president. In 1972 he assumed absolute powers and fighting broke out in which thousands were killed. In 1976 Micombero was overthrown in a coup and Jean-Baptiste Bagaza (1946–) became president. In 1987 Maj Pierre Buyoya overthrew Bagaza and became head of state; the following year the longstanding rivalry between the Hutu and the Tutsi led to further massacres. Official languages: French and Kirundi. Official currency: Burundi franc of 100 centimes. Area: 27 834 sq km (10 759 sq mi). Population (1988 est): 5 130 000. Capital: Bujumbura.

burying beetle A strong beetle, also called a sexton beetle, occurring in N temperate regions. Burying beetles are 1.5–35 mm long and many have black and orange markings. They feed and lay their eggs on the dead bodies of small animals, which they first bury: the larvae use the same food source.

Bury St Edmunds 52 15N 0 43E A market town in E England, in Suffolk. Its ruined abbey was built as a shrine to St Edmund, last King of

East Anglia (martyred in 870 AD). Population (1989): 32 000.

Bush, George (Herbert Walker) (1924–) US statesman; Republican vice president (1981–88); president (1989–). Ambassador to the UN (1971–72), he was subsequently director of the CIA (1976–77). In 1991 he authorized military action against Iraq in the Gulf War.

bushbaby A small nocturnal mammal, related to the loris, found in African forests. They are 27–80 cm long including the tail (15–40 cm). The common bushbaby (*Galago senegalensis*) has soft dense greyish fur and a long bushy tail. They live in small groups.

bushel A unit of capacity equal to 8 gallons or 2219.36 cubic inches in the UK and 2150.42 cubic inches in the USA. In the USA it is used for dry capacity only not liquid capacity.

bushmaster A pit viper, *Lachesis muta*, occurring in scrub and forests of Central and South America. The longest venomous snake (its venom can be fatal) of the New World, it reaches a length of 1.8 m and is brownish pink with dark diamond-shaped blotches.

bushrangers Outlaws in the Australian outback in the late-18th and 19th centuries. They robbed farmsteads and stagecoaches, murdered, and plundered, but while some were ruthless, others shared their gains with the poor. The most famous is probably Ned *Kelly.

bustard A large bird, related to cranes, occurring in grasslands of the Old World and having long legs adapted for running. Bustards have a long stout neck, broad wings, and a grey or brown mottled plumage. The great bustard (*Otis tarda*), 120 cm long and weighing 14 kg, is the largest European land bird.

butadiene (H_2C:CHHC:CH_2) A colourless gas that burns readily and is made from *butanes and butenes. It is used in making synthetic rubbers.

butane (C_4H_{10}) A colourless gaseous *alkane that burns readily. It is used in the manufacture of synthetic rubber. Under pressure it forms a liquid, used as a fuel.

butcherbird. *See* shrike.

Bute A Scottish island in the Firth of Clyde, in Strathclyde Region separated from the mainland by the Kyles of Bute. The island serves Glasgow as a holiday resort. Area: 121 sq km (47 sq mi). Population (1981): 7733. Chief town: Rothesay.

Butler, Samuel (1835–1902) British novelist. Son of a clergyman, he rejected his family and religion in 1859 to emigrate to New Zealand. In 1864 he returned wealthy and turned to literature. *Erewhon* (1872), which made him famous, satirizes Victorian ideals. The autobiographical *The Way of All Flesh* (1903) describes his liberation from his family background.

butterflies and moths Insects belonging to the order *Lepidoptera* (about 100 000 species), distributed worldwide. The adults have two pairs of wings, which are often highly coloured and patterned; the wingspan ranges from 4 mm to up to 300 mm. They all undergo a metamorphosis in four stages: egg, larva (*see* caterpillar), pupa (chrysalis), and adult (imago). The caterpillars feed mainly on plants, in some cases becoming serious crop pests; the adults feed mainly on nectar and other plant juices using a long tubular organ (proboscis) and may aid plant pollination in the process. Butterflies generally are active by day and rest with their wings vertical; moths, which are mainly nocturnal, generally rest with their wings horizontal. Antennae (feelers) are smooth and club-shaped in butterflies and plumed or feathery in moths.

butterfly bush. *See* Buddleia.

butterwort A *carnivorous plant found in the N hemisphere and South America. 12–15 cm high, it has a rosette of yellow-green leaves covered with sticky glands, on which insects are trapped, and a single funnel-shaped violet or pink flower.

Buxton 53 17N 1 55W A spa in the Peak District of Derbyshire on the River Wye. Its mineral waters were first used by the Romans. During the 1970s Buxton Opera House, built in 1903 and formerly used only as a theatre and cinema, was restored to its original condition. Population (1981): 20 797.

buzzard A hawk with broad wings, a rounded tail, and brown plumage. Buzzards hunt for small mammals, reptiles, etc., and soar gracefully. The common Eurasian buzzard (*Buteo buteo*), is 55 cm long; the migrating rough-legged buzzard (*B. lagopus*) is distinguished by its feathered legs.

buzz bomb. *See* V-1.

Byng, John (1704–57) British admiral who, in 1756, failed to relieve Minorca, then under attack by the French, and retreated to Gibraltar. He was made a scapegoat and shot for failing to do his duty–or, in Voltaire's satirical view, as a warning to his colleagues ("pour encourager les autres").

Byrd, William (?1543–1623) English composer, who, in spite of being a Roman Catholic, became organist of Lincoln Cathedral and subsequently of the Chapel Royal (1572). His compositions include Catholic masses and motets, Anglican services, anthems, and keyboard music.

Byron, George Gordon, Lord (1788–1824) British poet. Born with a clubfoot, he became a leading figure in London society, after the publication of *Childe Harolde's Pilgrimage* (1812). His many lovers included his half-sister Augusta Leigh and Lady Caroline Lamb (*see* Melbourne, Viscount). His marriage (1815) to Annabella Milbanke lasted one year. Byron then left England to stay near Geneva with *Shelley. In Italy in 1818 he began writing the satire *Don Juan*. He died in Greece while training troops at Missolonghi, involved in the Greek struggle for independence.

Byzantine Empire. *See* Eastern Roman Empire.

Byzantium. *See* Istanbul.

C

Cabal   Five ministers of Charles II of England who dominated politics from 1667 to about 1674. They were Sir Thomas Clifford (1630–73), Lord Ashley (later 1st Earl of Shaftesbury), the 2nd Duke of *Buckingham, the Earl of Arlington (1618–85), and the Earl of Lauderdale (1616–82).

cabbage   A flowering plant, *Brassica oleracea* var. *capitata*, widely cultivated as a vegetable. The short stem bears a round heart, up to 25 cm in diameter, of tightly compressed leaves. All cabbages and many related vegetables, including the cauliflower and Brussels sprout, are derived from the wild cabbage, a plant native to coastal regions of W Europe.

cabbage white butterfly   A white butterfly whose caterpillars eat cabbages and related vegetables. The species are the large white (*Pieris brassicae*), the green-veined white (*P. napi*), and the small white (*P. rapae*).

cabinet   A committee of the ministers of government. In the UK the cabinet originated in the 16th-century cabinet council, a committee of the *Privy Council. Cabinet power was increased by William III's recognition that his ministers should be chosen from the dominant political group in parliament and by the emergence in the 18th century of the *prime minister. Cabinets now consist of some 20 leading ministers, from either house of parliament.

cable TV   A system of television broadcasting in which signals are sent by cables instead of by radio waves. Developed in 1949 to improve reception in areas in which aerials were unsatisfactory, cable TV was first widely adopted in the USA in the 1970s. A commercial cable TV system in the UK was debated in the early 1980s, with limited services being tested in selected areas.

Cabot, John (Italian name: Giovanni Caboto; c. 1450–c. 1499) Italian explorer. He settled in England in about 1484 and under Henry VII's patronage discovered Cape Breton Island (which he thought to be Asia) in 1497. He set out on a second voyage in 1498 and appears to have died at sea. His son **Sebastian Cabot** (c. 1476–1557) was a map-maker to Henry VIII. In Spanish service he explored the coast of South America (1525–28).

cacao.   *See* cocoa and chocolate.

cachalot.   *See* sperm whale.

cactus   A perennial flowering plant growing chiefly in the drier regions of tropical America and the West Indies. Size and shape vary widely; the larger species may grow to a height of 10 m or more, while many of the small species are grown as house plants. Cacti have several features aimed at preventing water loss—their leaves or shoots are reduced to spines, they have thick waxy outer layers, and many possess thick water-

storing stems. The flowers are large and brightly coloured.

caddis fly   A mothlike insect, also called sedge fly. Caddis flies—1.5–40 mm long, with long antennae—are found in cool damp places and feed on nectar. The omnivorous larvae (called caddis worms) live in flowing fresh water, often in portable cases constructed from sand, stones, pieces of leaf, etc.

Cádiz   36 32N 6 18W A city and seaport in SW Spain, in Andalusia on the Gulf of Cádiz. It was founded by Phoenician merchants (c. 1100 BC). Following the discovery of America it prospered as a base for the Spanish treasure fleet; the harbour was burned by Sir Francis Drake in 1587. Population (1986): 154 051.

cadmium (Cd)   A soft dense metal, discovered in 1817 by Friedrich Strohmeyer (1776–1835). Cadmium occurs naturally as the mineral greenockite (CdS) and in zinc, copper, and lead sulphide ores. It is chemically similar to lead. It is used in the control rods of nuclear reactors, in light meters, television-tube phosphors, batteries, in low-melting-point alloys to make solders, and in special low-friction alloys for bearings. At no 48; at wt 112.40; mp 320.9°C; bp 765°C.

Caen   49 11N 0 22W A city and port in NW France, the capital of the Calvados department on the River Orne. Situated at the centre of an agricultural and horse-breeding area, Caen has iron, silk, and leather industries. Population (1983 est): 117 453.

Caerleon   51 37N 2 57W A town in South Wales, in S Gwent on the River Usk. A Roman legionary fortress (Isca) was built here (c. 75 AD). Its amphitheatre is the best preserved in Britain. Caerleon is also associated with *Arthurian legend. Population (1981): 6711.

Caernarfon (English name: Caernarvon) 53 08N 4 16W A town in North Wales, the administrative centre of Gwynedd on the Menai Strait. Caernarfon is a tourist centre, market town, and small port. Its castle (built by Edward I in 1284) is the likely birthplace of Edward II, the first Prince of Wales, and was the scene of the investiture of Prince *Charles as Prince of Wales in 1969. Population (1981): 9506.

Caerphilly   51 35N 3 14W A market town in South Wales, in Mid Glamorgan. Situated in a coalmining area, it is best known for Caerphilly cheese (originally made here) and its castle, the largest in Wales. Population (1981): 42 736.

Caesar, (Gaius) Julius (100–44 BC) Roman general and statesman, born of a noble family, he allied himself with the popular party by his marriage in 84 to *Cinna's daughter Cornelia. After her death in 68, he married Pompeia, whom he divorced in 62, and in 59 he married Calpurnia. During the 60s Caesar joined *Pompey and *Crassus in the first *Triumvirate (60), becoming consul (59), and then governor of Gaul. Caesar's domination of Gaul (58–50), and his campaigns in Britain (55, 54), made him a popular hero. When the Triumvirate ended (50), the Senate asked Caesar to resign his armies. He refused and, crossing the River Rubicon into Italy (49), began the civil war. Caesar defeated Pompey at *Pharsalus (48) and spent the following winter in Alexandria with *Cleopatra, who became his lover. He later defeated the remnants of Pompey's party at Thapsus (46) and Munda (45), after which he returned to Rome as dictator. On the Ides of March (15 March, 44), Caesar was assassinated by republicans, including *Brutus and *Cassius, who feared he would make himself king.

Caesar wrote outstanding accounts of his campaigns in Gaul (*De bello gallico*) and the civil war (*De bello civili*).

Caesarean section A surgical operation in which a baby is delivered through an incision made in the abdominal wall and the womb, so called because Julius Caesar was said to have been born in this way. Caesarean section is usually employed when the baby is abnormally positioned in the womb or is too large to pass through the birth canal.

caesium (Cs) The most reactive alkali metal. It was discovered by Bunsen and Kirchhoff in 1860 and occurs naturally in the mica lepidolite and as pollucite, $(Cs,K)AlSi_2O_6.nH_2O$. It is used in photoelectric cells. At no 55; at wt 132.905; mp 28.40°C; bp 690°C.

caffeine (or theine; $C_8H_{10}O_2N_4$) The substance in coffee and tea that acts as a stimulant. In its pure form it is white and crystalline.

Cage, John (1912–) Avantgarde US composer. His works include *4 minutes 33 seconds* (1954), silence in three movements for any instrument(s), and *Apartment Building 1776* (1976).

Cagney, James (1899–1986) US actor. He began making films in the 1930s, after working in vaudeville, and became famous for his portrayals of tough gangsters. His films include *Public Enemy* (1931) and *The Roaring Twenties* (1939).

Caicos Islands. See Turks and Caicos Islands.

Cainozoic era. See Cenozoic era.

cairn. See barrow.

Cairngorm Mountains A mountain range in NE Scotland, in Grampian Region, forming a N extension of the Grampians. Its highest peaks include Ben Macdhui at 1309 m (4296 ft) and Braeriach at 1296 m (4252 ft). The area is popular for winter sports, centred on Aviemore.

cairn terrier A breed of small dog originating in the Scottish Highlands, where it was used to flush game from cover. The colour varies from red, sandy, or mottled grey to almost black. Height: about 25 cm.

Cairo (Arabic name: El Qahira) 80 01N 31 14E The capital of Egypt, situated in the N of the country on the E bank of the River Nile. It is the largest city in Africa. Population (1986 est): 6 325 000. See also Giza, El.

caisson disease. See decompression sickness.

Calabria A mountainous region occupying the southern "toe" of Italy. Crotone is the main industrial centre. Area: 15 080 sq km (5822 sq mi). Population (1987 est): 2 145 724. Capital: Catanzaro.

Calais 50 57N 1 52E A port in N France, in the Pas-de-Calais department. It produces lace, tulle, and other textiles. *History*: besieged and captured by the English under Edward III in 1346, Calais remained in English hands until 1558. Population (1983 est): 78 819.

calceolaria A perennial plant, related to the antirrhinum, native to temperate South America. The plants grow to a height of 30–70 cm and bear brightly coloured slipper-shaped flowers.

calcium (Ca) A reactive metal, first obtained in pure form by Sir Humphry *Davy in 1808. It occurs in nature as calcite ($CaCO_3$), *fluorite (CaF_2), and *gypsum ($CaSO_4.2H_2O$) and is an essential part of shells, bones, and teeth. The element is obtained from the molten chloride ($CaCl_2$). At no 20; at wt 40.08; mp 839 ± 2°C; bp 1484°C.

calculus Mathematical techniques, developed by *Newton and *Leibniz, based on the concept of infinitely small changes in continuously varying quantities. For example, velocity (v), the rate of change of position, is said to be the derivative of position (x) with respect to time (t); written $v = dx/dt$, where dt is a vanishingly small time interval and dx is the distance the body travels in this time. If x is a known function of t, values for v at any time can be obtained by calculating the derivative of (differentiating) this function with respect to time. Similarly, the derivative of the velocity (or the second derivative of position) at any instant gives its acceleration (a), i.e. $d^2x/dt^2 = dv/dt = a$. The **differential calculus** is the system of rules for making such calculations. On a graph, the derivative of a function is the gradient of the curve at any point. The **integral calculus** is concerned with the same process in reverse. If velocity is a continuously varying function of time, the change in position over a time interval is calculated by adding together the products of v and dt for each of the infinitessimally small intervals of time (dt) that make up the interval. As with differential calculus, the calculation of integrals follows general rules. On a graph, the area between the curve of a function and the horizontal axis is the integral of the function over the specified interval.

Calcutta 22 35N 88 21E A city in India, the capital of West Bengal on the River Hooghly. It is a major industrial centre and the most important seaport on the E coast of India. Jute manufacturing is the main industry, while engineering, cotton textiles, and chemicals are also important. The city centre contains many imposing buildings. Calcutta was founded in 1692 as a trading post for the British East India Company. Population (1981 est): 9 165 650.

calendar Any system for determining the length and divisions (days, weeks, and months) of a year. Calendars are usually based on the earth's orbital period around the sun (a year), although in some systems the moon's orbital period around the earth (a month) is used. Since the seasons recur after each tropical *year (which contains 365.2422 days), the average length of the calendar year should be as close as possible to that of the tropical year. This is achieved by using leap years, which contain one more day than the usual calendar year.

In the **Julian calendar**, introduced by Julius Caesar, a period of three years, each of 365 days, was followed by a leap year of 366 days. The average length of the year was therefore 365.25 days. Since this was over 11 minutes longer than the tropical year, an extra day appeared about every 128 years. This was amended by the **Gregorian calendar**, introduced in 1582 by Pope Gregory XIII; it was made law in Britain and its colonies in 1752, and is now in almost worldwide use. Leap years are restricted to century years divisible by 400 (e.g. 1600 and 2000) and any other year divisible by four. This reduces the average length of the calendar year to 365.2425 days.

Calgary 51 05N 114 05W A city in W Canada, in Alberta. It is the centre of Canada's petroleum industry and the distribution and farming centre of S Alberta. The Calgary Stampede, a famous rodeo, takes place annually. Population (1986): 636 104.

calico A simple woven cotton fabric that originated as a printed fabric from Calicut, India. It is used mainly for dresses.

California The third largest state in the USA, on the W coast. It consists of a narrow coastal plain rising to the Coast Range, with the fertile central valleys of the Sacramento and San Joaquin Rivers, deserts in the S, and the Sierra Nevada Mountains in the E. It is the most populous and prosperous state in the USA. Oil and natural gas are exploited along with cement, sand and gravel, and borate. Aircraft and ship construction are important as are food processing and wine production. The state also produces fruit, cotton, sugar beet, beef cattle, and turkeys. *History*: first discovered by the Spanish (1542) it remained under their control until it was handed over to the USA (1848), when gold was discovered, leading to a rapid population increase. California became a state in 1850. Area: 411 013 sq km (158 693 sq mi). Population (1987 est): 27 662 900. Capital: Sacramento.

californium (Cf) A synthetic *transuranic element first produced in 1950. Californium-252 is used as a neutron source in instruments for determining moisture contents and discovering precious metals. At no 98; at wt (251).

Caligula (Gaius Caesar; 12–41 AD) Roman emperor (37–41), son of Germanicus Caesar and Agrippina the Elder. Succeeding Tiberius, he initially enjoyed great popularity but his subsequent tyrannical and extravagant behaviour brought allegations of madness and led to his assassination.

calla. *See* arum.

Callaghan, (Leonard) James, Baron (1912–) British statesman; Labour prime minister (1976–79). He entered parliament in 1945 and was chancellor of the exchequer

(1964–67), resigning in protest against Harold *Wilson's devaluation of the pound, and then home secretary (1967–70) and foreign secretary (1974–76). He became prime minister when Wilson resigned; defeated in 1979, he remained party leader until 1980.

Callas, Maria (Maria Kalogeropoulos; 1923–77) US-born soprano of Greek parentage. She possessed a brilliant coloratura voice and fine acting ability. From 1950 she was prima donna of La Scala, Milan.

Calliope In Greek legend, goddess of epic poetry and the chief of the nine *Muses. She was loved by Apollo; her children included Hymen, Ialemus, and *Orpheus.

Callisto. *See* Galilean satellites.

calorie A unit of heat now being replaced by the *joule. Formerly defined as the amount of heat required to raise the temperature of 1 gram of water through 1°C, the calorie is now defined as 4.1868 joules. The kilocalorie or Calorie (with a capital "C") is equal to 1000 calories.

Calvary A hill beyond the walls of Jerusalem where Christ was crucified. The Hebrew name is Golgotha (a skull). Its precise location is unknown but traditionally is taken as the spot within the Church of the Holy Sepulchre, where St Helena discovered a supposed relic of the Cross in 327 AD.

Calvin, John (1509–64) French Protestant reformer, founder of *Calvinism. He studied law and theology before settling in Basle in 1536, where he published his influential *Institutes*. During a visit to Geneva in 1536 he met the Protestant reformer, Guillaume Farel (1489–1565), who persuaded him to stay. Their efforts to organize the Reformation in the city resulted in their exile (1538). Calvin then preached in Strasbourg, but was invited back to Geneva in 1541, remaining there as its virtual dictator until his death.

Calvinism The Christian teaching of John *Calvin, much of it published in his work *The Institutes*. Reformed Churches that are not Lutheran, including the state Churches of Holland and Scotland (*see* Presbyterianism) are based on Calvinism. Calvin stresses the supreme power of God and man's corruption without God's grace. Like Luther, Calvin believed that faith must be based on Scripture alone, that justification could only be achieved through faith, and that men had no freedom of choice. Unlike Luther, he believed that the chosen ones were predestined for salvation and the rest for damnation; he also believed that the church should control the state.

calx. *See* phlogiston theory.

Camargue, la The Rhône delta area in S France, between the river channels of the Grand Rhône and the Petit Rhône. Once chiefly marshy, much land has been reclaimed enabling bulls and horses to be reared. Rice is also grown. Area: about 560 sq km (215 sq mi).

Camberwell beauty A butterfly, *Nymphalis antiopa*, occurring in temperate Eurasia and in North America, where it is called mourning cloak because of its sombre coloration: purple wings with cream edges. The adults hibernate and the caterpillars feed on various trees.

cambium A layer of cells in woody plants that is responsible for producing additional *xylem and *phloem tissue, bringing about an increase in girth. The cambium also produces bark and protective callus tissue after injury. *See also* meristem.

Cambodia (former name: Kampuchea) A country in SE Asia, in the Indochina Peninsula on the Gulf of Thailand. It consists mainly of an alluvial plain drained by the River Mekong and enclosed by mountains. Most of the inhabitants are Khmers, with small minorities of Vietnamese and Chinese. *Economy*: predominantly agricultural, the staple crop being rice. Production has been severely reduced by the recent political upheavals and there is little industry. Cambodia is rich in forests, and phosphates, gemstones, and gold are produced. There is an abundance of freshwater fish. Exports include rubber and dried fish. *History*: the kingdom of Funan (1st–6th centuries AD) was conquered by the Buddhist *Khmers. Following the collapse of their empire in the 15th century, Cambodia was attacked by the Thais and Vietnamese. It became a French protectorate in 1863 and part of *Indochina in 1887. In 1949 it achieved self-government as a member of the French Union, gaining full independence in 1953. Under Prince *Sihanouk Cambodia was used as a base by North Vietnamese (communist) forces (*see* Vietnam War). He was deposed (1970) by Gen Lon Nol (1913–85), who was supported by the USA. Shortly afterwards US and South Vietnamese troops invaded the renamed Khmer Republic to support Lon Nol against the communist Khmer Rouge guerrillas. In the ensuing civil war the Khmer Rouge emerged victorious in 1974. The Khmer Rouge Government, led by Pol Pot (1925–   ), attempted to reshape the country's economy by driving the Cambodians out of the towns and killing some three million of them. The Vietnamese invaded the country in 1978; Pol Pot was overthrown and a People's Revolutionary Council was set up. In 1982 the Khmer Rouge, with two other exiled Cambodian factions, formed the Coalition Government of Democratic Kampuchea (CGDK), which has a seat at the UN. Guerrilla attacks by CGDK forces have continued, even after the Vietnamese withdrew in 1989, and in 1990 both sides agreed to consider the involvement of UN peace-keeping forces to end the fighting. Prime minister: Hun Sen (1951–   ). Official language: Khmer; French is widely spoken. Official currency: riel of 100 sen. Area: 181 000 sq km (71 000 sq mi). Population (1985 est): 6 232 000. Capital and main port: Phnom Penh.

Cambrian Mountains A mountain system in Wales, extending N–S and including Snowdonia, Plynlimon, and the Black Mountains.

Cambrian period The earliest geological period of the *Palaeozoic era. It began about 590 million years ago and lasted at least 70 million years, lying between the Precambrian and Ordovician periods. Rocks of this period are the first to contain a large number of fossils, including primitive forms of most invertebrates living today. The Cambrian period is divided into Lower, Middle, and Upper.

Cambridge 52 12N 0 07E A city in E England, the administrative centre of Cambridgeshire on the River Cam (*or* Granta), a tributary of the Great Ouse. The city is dominated by its university (*see* Cambridge, University of). Cambridge has electronics, scientific, and printing industries. It is also an important market centre for East Anglia. Its many historic university buildings, its famous Backs (lawns sloping down to the river), and Bridge of Sighs make it a popular tourist centre. Population (1983): 100 500.

Cambridge 42 22N 71 06W A city in the USA, in Massachusetts on the Charles River opposite Boston. A famous educational centre, it is the site of Harvard University (1636) and the Massachusetts Institute of Technology (MIT). Industries include printing and publishing. Population (1980): 95 322.

Cambridge, University of One of the oldest universities in Europe. The oldest college, Peterhouse, dates from 1284. King's College was founded in 1441 and its chapel (built 1446–1515 in the perpendicular gothic style) is a distinctive landmark. The largest college, Trinity, was founded by Henry VIII in 1546. The first college for women, Girton, opened in 1869 (although it was not at first located at Cambridge).

Cambridgeshire A county of E England. It consists chiefly of low-lying fenland, crossed by the Rivers Ouse and Nene. It is predominantly agricultural, producing cereals, fruit, and vegetables. Area: 3409 sq km (1316 sq mi). Population (1986 est): 635 200. Administrative centre: Cambridge.

camel A hoofed mammal used for riding, as pack animals, and as a source of milk, meat, wool, and hides. The one-humped Arabian camel is about 2 m high and generally brown. The dromedary is a long-legged breed of Arabian camel developed for racing and riding. The heavier two-humped Bactrian camel is native to central Asian steppes, where wild herds still exist. Adapted to living in sandy deserts, camels can close their nostrils, have heavy protective eyelashes, and horny knee pads for kneeling. Camels can replace rapidly the water that is lost from the body, drinking up to 60 litres of water at a time. Fat (not water) is stored in the hump, which shrinks when food is scarce.

camellia An evergreen shrub or tree related to the tea plant and native to India, China, and Japan. Several species are grown as ornamentals. Up to 9 m high, they have oval leaves and large white, pink, or red flowers.

Camelot The legendary capital of King Arthur's kingdom (*see* Arthurian legend). Cadbury Camp, near Yeovil, and Winchester are among the places identified with it.

Camembert 48 52N 0 10E A village in NW France, in the Orne department. Camembert is famous for the creamy cheese named after it.

camera, photographic A device for producing a photographic image. Basically, a camera consists of a light-tight box containing a lens and a *film or plate on which an image can be formed under the action of (usually) light. The light coming through the lens is focused on the film by adjusting the distance between the film and the lens. A picture is taken by opening the shutter over the lens to expose the film. The diameter of the opening (aperture) in front of the lens is measured by its *f-number. The brightness of the image, the shutter speed, and lens aperture determine the light available to record the image.

camera, television A camera for live transmission of moving pictures. The image is focused onto a screen in the electronic camera tube. It is scanned in horizontal lines, fast enough to appear as a continuous moving picture to the human eye; in most cameras, the image is scanned 25 to 30 times per second. The brightness of light at each point of the image is made into an electrical signal, which is strengthened before being transmitted. *See also* television.

Cameroon, United Republic of (French name: République du Cameroun) A country in West Africa, on the Gulf of Guinea. Hot swampy coastal plains rise to forested plateaus in the centre and to the Adamwa Highlands in the N. The main river is the Sanaga. The population consists of over a hundred ethnic groups, the most numerous being the Bamileke. *Economy*: chiefly subsistence agriculture; the main cash crop is coffee. Hydroelectricity is used for aluminium smelting, which is the chief industry. Oil was discovered in 1973 and provides half the country's revenue. *History*: in 1884 the German protectorate of Kamerun was established and after World War I it was divided into the French and British Cameroons. The French Cameroons became independent as the Federal Republic of the Cameroon in 1960. In 1961 the S British Cameroons joined Cameroon and the N joined Nigeria. President: Paul Biya (1933–). Official languages: French and English. Official currency: CFA (Communauté financière africaine) franc of 100 centimes. Area: 475 442 sq km (183 530 sq mi). Population (1988 est): 11 082 000. Capital: Yaoundé. Main port: Doula.

camomile (*or* chamomile) A scented branching European herb, *Anthemis nobilis* (or *Chamaemelum nobile*), of the daisy family. An infusion of the daisy-like flowers (camomile tea) is used as a tonic.

Campaign for Nuclear Disarmament (CND) An organization formed in 1958 to campaign for Britain's nuclear disarmament. In the late 1950s and early 1960s, led by Canon John Collins (1905–82) and Bertrand *Russell, it organized large demonstrations, including the Aldermaston marches. It revived in the early 1980s amid new fears of nuclear war but membership declined in the late 1980s with lessening of East–West tensions. Chair: Marjorie Thompson.

campanula A herbaceous plant, often known as bellflower, native to N temperate zones and tropical mountains. 15–120 cm high, they bear blue, pink, or white bell-shaped flowers. Some species, including the Canterbury bell (*Campanula medium*), are grown as garden plants.

Campbell, Sir Malcolm (1885–1948) British motor engineer, who broke the land-speed rec-

ord nine times between 1924 and 1935 and the water-speed record three times between 1937 and 1939. He was the first man to exceed 483 km per hour (300 mph; 1935). His son **Donald Malcolm Campbell** (1921–67) also set land- and water-speed records, including a 648.7 km per hour (403.1 mph) land-speed record at Lake Eyre (1964). He was killed in an attempt to break his own water-speed record on Coniston Water. The speed at which he crashed, 527.9 km per hour (328 mph), was an unofficial record. His daughter **Gina Campbell** (1948–) broke the women's water-speed record in 1984.

Campbell, Mrs Patrick (Beatrice Stella Tanner; 1865–1940) British actress. Her stage successes included plays by Shakespeare and Ibsen. She created the role of Eliza Doolittle in *Pygmalion* by her friend George Bernard Shaw.

Campbell-Bannerman, Sir Henry (1836–1908) British statesman; Liberal prime minister (1905–08). Campbell-Bannerman's government granted the Transvaal and Orange River Colony responsible government and passed the Trades Disputes Act (1906), which gave trades unionists greater freedom to strike. Resigning shortly before his death, he left his successor Asquith a strong and united Liberal Party.

Camp David The retreat in the Appalachian Mountains, Maryland, of the president of the USA. It was here that Anwar Sadat and Menachem Begin agreed in September, 1978, to a framework for establishing peace in the Middle East. This agreement, arranged by President Jimmy Carter, laid the foundations for the peace treaty between Israel and Egypt signed in March, 1979.

Camus, Albert (1913–60) French novelist, who was linked with *existentialism. Born in poverty in Algiers, he won a school scholarship and studied philosophy at university. During World War II he edited *Combat*, a journal of the French Resistance. Camus published several collections of essays and plays, and three novels, notably *The Outsider* (1942), *The Plague* (1947), and *The Rebel* (1953). In 1957 he won the Nobel Prize.

Canaan An area roughly corresponding to modern Israel, W Jordan, and S Syria, known from the Bible as the land promised by God to the Israelites before the Exodus.

Canada, Dominion of A country occupying the entire northern half of the North American continent (except for Alaska). More than half of Canada consists of the Canadian Shield, at the centre of which lies the Hudson Bay lowlands. The Western Cordillera, which is partly made up of the Coast Mountains and the Rocky Mountains, runs parallel to the Pacific coast and contains Mount *Logan, Canada's highest peak. Between the Rocky Mountains and the Canadian Shield lie the Interior Lowlands (consisting of prairies, plains, and the Mackenzie Lowlands). The SE region of Canada is dominated by the St Lawrence River and the *Great Lakes and is the most densely populated area in the country. The population is mainly of British and French descent. *Economy*: the numerous manufacturing industries (mainly in Ontario and Quebec) include paper, iron and steel, motor vehicles, and food processing. As well as iron ore, the rich mineral resources include asbestos, nickel, zinc, molybdenum, uranium, silver, and gold. Oil production has increased considerably since the discovery of large oilfields in Alberta and natural gas is also produced. Agriculture is important, with cereals in the Prairie Provinces and considerable fruit growing in British Columbia and Ontario. Other industries include fishing, forestry, and the fur trade. Main exports include oil, wheat, wood pulp, and paper. *History*: there is evidence of Viking settlement in the NE around 1000 AD. In 1497 John Cabot reached Newfoundland and Nova Scotia, the first being claimed for England in 1583. In 1534 Jacques Cartier explored the Gulf of St Lawrence and in 1608 Champlain established the first permanent settlement at Quebec. Known as New France, this became a royal province in 1663. The fur trade was of extreme importance and in 1670 the English set up the *Hudson's Bay Company. By 1696 the French and English were in open conflict: in 1713 the Treaty of Utrecht gave Acadia (present-day Nova Scotia), Newfoundland, and Hudson Bay to Britain. After the Seven Years' War, during which Gen Wolfe defeated the French under Gen Montcalm (1759), the Treaty of Paris (1763) gave Canada to Britain. By the British North America Act (1867) a confederation of Lower Canada (Quebec), Upper Canada (Ontario), Nova Scotia, and New Brunswick was established. Manitoba joined the confederation in 1870, British Columbia in 1871, and Prince Edward Island in 1873. Alberta and Saskatchewan were created from the NW Territories in 1905. In 1931 Canada became an independent constitutional monarchy in the British Commonwealth. In 1982 a new constitution for Canada was signed by Elizabeth II. Prime minister: Brian Mulroney. Official languages: English and French. Official currency: Canadian dollar of 100 cents. Area: 9 976 169 sq km (3 851 809 sq mi). Population (1987): 25 963 000. Capital: Ottawa. Main port: Montreal.

Canada balsam A transparent resin obtained from fir trees. It is used as an adhesive in optical instruments because its refractive index is similar to that of glass.

Canada goose A large goose, *Branta canadensis*, that breeds in Canada and Alaska, migrating in flocks to the southern USA for the winter. It is 60–100 cm long and has a black head and neck, white throat, dark-brown back, and pale underparts. The Canada goose has been introduced into parts of Europe.

Canadian Shield. *See* shield.

Canaletto (Antonio Canal; 1697–1768) Venetian painter, famous for his views of Venice. He trained under his father, a theatrical-scenery painter, before visiting Rome (1719–20), where he designed opera sets. In England (1746–55), he painted views of London. His early work, painted in the open air, was considerably freer than his later much more architectural painting, for which he used mechanical drawing instruments.

canals Man-made open water channels. Conveyance canals carry water for irrigation, power, or drainage. Navigation canals carry ships and often connect two natural waterways. Canals have been dug from ancient times. The Grand Canal in China, started in 109 km (620 mi) long by the 8th century. Some modern ship canals achieve spectacular reductions in voyage distances, especially the *Suez Canal (completed in 1869) and the *Panama Canal (1914). Others include the Corinth Canal (1893), the Kiel Canal (1895), and the St Lawrence Seaway (1959) connecting the Great Lakes.

canary A small songbird, *Serinus canarius*, of the finch family, native to the Canary Islands, Madeira, and the Azores. Wild canaries have an olive-green plumage with yellow to grey underparts streaked with black. Popular as cagebirds since the 15th century, they have been bred both for their musical song and attractive plumage —usually pure yellow but sometimes white or striped.

Canary Islands (Spanish name: Islas Canarias) A group of Spanish volcanic islands in the Atlantic Ocean, close to NW Africa. Since 1927 they have constituted two provinces: Las Palmas (including the islands of Fuerteventura, Gran Canaria, and Lanzarote) and Santa Cruz de Tenerife (including the islands of Ferro, Gomera, La Palma, and *Tenerife). The islands became Spanish possessions in the 15th century. Fruit is grown for export and tourism is also a major source of revenue. Total area: 7270 sq km (2807 sq mi). Population (1986 est): 1 442 500.

Canaveral, Cape (name from 1963 until 1973: Cape Kennedy) A barrier island in the USA, in E central Florida separated from the mainland by lagoons. It is the site of operations by NASA at the Kennedy Space Center.

Canberra 35 15S 149 10E The capital of Australia, in the Australian Capital Territory on the Molonglo River. Formally inaugurated in 1927, it is the home of the National University (1946). Population (1986 est): 285 800.

cancer A group of diseases caused by the abnormal division of cells to form tumours that invade and destroy the tissues in which they arise. Such tumours are described as malignant: their cells spread to set up secondary tumours at other sites in the body (this spread is called metastasis). The cause of cancer remains uncertain, although exposure to certain substances (*see* carcinogen) and certain viruses will produce it. In the western world the breasts, colon, lungs, bronchi, prostate gland, and stomach are common sites for cancer. *Leukaemia is a form of cancer affecting the blood-forming tissues. Treatment may include anti-cancer drugs, radiotherapy, and surgery.

Cancer (Latin: Crab) A constellation in the N sky, lying on the *zodiac between Leo and Gemini. It contains the star cluster Praesepe.

candela (cd) The *SI unit of luminous intensity equal to the intensity, in a given direction, of a source that emits radiation of frequency 540 × 10^{12} Hz and of which the radiant intensity in that direction is 1/683 watt per steradian.

Candia. *See* Iráklion.

candidiasis An infection caused by a yeast (*Candida albicans*). Popularly known as thrush, it affects the mouth and vagina most frequently; it may develop after treatment with certain antibiotics and with diseases and drugs that reduce the natural ability of the body to overcome such infections. Candidiasis is cleared readily by antibiotics.

Candlemas The Christian feast of the Purification of the Virgin Mary and the Presentation of Christ in the Temple (Luke 2.22–38), which is observed on 2 Feb. It is so called because of the distribution of candles, symbolizing Christ's appearance as the "light of the world."

Canea (Greek name: Khaniá) 35 31N 24 01E The capital of Crete, on the Gulf of Khaniá. The island's main port, it exports leather, olives, olive oil, and fruit. Population (1981): 47 804.

cannabis The resin (hashish) or crushed leaves and flowers (marihuana, "grass," or "pot") obtained from certain species of *hemp. The drug is eaten or inhaled and produces a variety of effects on the mind. These include wellbeing and a distorted sense of time. Occasionally feelings of anxiety and apprehension are experienced. The long-term effects of cannabis use may affect memory and cause progression to "hard" drugs.

Cannae, Battle of (216 BC) The battle, fought at the village of Cannae in Apulia (SE Italy), in which *Hannibal and the Carthaginians killed almost 50 000 Romans. It is the worst Roman defeat on record.

Cannes 43 33N 7 00E A resort in S France, in the Alpes-Maritimes department on the French Riviera. Its development as a fashionable resort dates from 1834; an annual film festival is held here. Population (1983 est): 70 302.

cannibalism The practice of eating human flesh, either as food or for ceremonial or magical purposes. In ceremonial cannibalism certain parts of a defeated enemy may be eaten in order to absorb his strength and courage or to prevent his spirit taking revenge. The word comes from the *Arawak word for the *Carib Indians among whom it was common. Ceremonial cannibalism was practised also by the New Zealand Maoris, the Fijian islanders, in Polynesia, in parts of Africa, in New Guinea, and among some North American Indian peoples.

Canning, George (1770–1827) British statesman; foreign secretary (1807–09, 1822–27) and Tory prime minister (1827). An MP from 1793, he held office under Pitt. He became foreign secretary in 1807 but resigned in 1809 in opposition to the management of the Napoleonic Wars by the secretary for war, Castlereagh. He again became foreign secretary after Castlereagh's suicide before briefly becoming prime minister. His son **Charles John, Earl Canning** (1812–62) was governor general of India (1856–62).

cannon An early form of *artillery that fired stones, cast-iron or wrought-iron balls. It was used primarily until 1670 as a siege gun. A 14th-century invention (by the German monk, Berthold Schwarz), early cannon were made of wrought-iron rods welded together, covered in lead, and wrapped with iron bands. After 1500 cannon made in England were moulded into shape by casting. Modern cannons include guns, *mortars, and *howitzers.

canonization The process of making a dead person into a *saint. In the Roman Catholic Church this is done by a formal declaration of the pope after a long investigation. Beatification, by which the Church allows a person to be given the title "Blessed," comes before canonization and depends on evidence of genuine miracles and the person's exceptional virtue. The Church then puts the case for the canonization and appoints the *Promotor Fidei* (Latin: promoter of the faith, popularly known as the devil's advocate) to oppose it; the process is completed after proof of further miracles.

canon law The laws of Christian Churches. They include regulations governing the clergy, the Church courts, matters of worship and Church teachings, and so on. In the 12th century Gratian (died c. 1179) produced his *Decretum*, a collection of rules that the Roman Catholic Church adopted. The *Decretum* was included in a later collection, the Corpus Juris Canonici, which in 1917 was revised to form the Codex Juris Canonici, the present Roman Catholic code of law. The law of the Church of England was mainly contained in the early-17th-century *Book of Canons*, but new laws were introduced in the 1960s.

Cantabrian Mountains (Spanish name: Cordillera Cantábrica) A mountain range in N Spain extending E–W along the Atlantic coast and rising to 2648 m (8868 ft).

Canterbury 51 17N 1 05E A city in SE England, in Kent on the River Stour. The cathedral (11th–15th centuries), where Thomas *Becket was martyred in 1170, is the seat of the Archbishop and Primate of the Anglican Church. The University of Kent (1960) overlooks the city. Population (1984): 39 000.

Canterbury, Archbishop of The chief bishop of the Anglican Communion of churches, called Primate of All England. The first of the line was St *Augustine of Canterbury. After the royal princes he is higher in rank than the Lord Chancellor and the other peers and signs himself with his Christian name and the Latin shortened form of Canterbury, for example "Robert Cantuar." The present (103rd) Archbishop (since 1991) is George Leonard *Carey.

Canterbury bell. *See* campanula.

Canterbury Plains A low-lying area of New Zealand, on E central South Island bordering on the Pacific Ocean. It is the most densely populated area of South Island and is important for raising lambs and producing cereals, fodder crops, and vegetables. Area: about 10 000 sq km (4000 sq mi). Chief town: Christchurch.

Canton (Chinese names: Guangzhou *or* Kuang-chou) 23 08N 113 20E A port in S China, the capital of Guangdong province on the Zhu Jiang (Pearl River) delta. Densely populated, it is the commercial and industrial centre of S China; industries include steel, shipbuilding, paper, textiles, and the manufacture of machinery and chemicals. Population (1986): 3 290 000.

Cantonese. *See* Chinese.

Cantor, Georg (1845–1918) Russian mathematician. Cantor's family moved in 1856 to Germany, where he spent the rest of his life. He was the first mathematician to set the concept of infinity on a rigorous mathematical foundation. His ideas were viciously attacked, by Leopold Kronecker (1823–91) in particular. He broke down in 1884 under the strain and died in a mental asylum.

Canute II (*or* Cnut; c. 994–1035) Danish King of England after defeating *Edmund Ironside (1016). He became King of Denmark (1019) and of Norway (1028). He defended England from Viking attacks (1017, 1026, 1028) and subjected Malcolm II of Scotland (1028). According to legend, he proved to flatterers the limits of his powers by demonstrating his inability to prevent the waves coming in.

canyon A deep narrow valley with steep sides found mainly in arid areas. Canyons are often formed by rivers cutting into soft rock in arid areas. The lack of rainfall hinders weathering and maintains the steep slopes. The largest and best-known canyon is the *Grand Canyon (USA).

capacitance The ability of an electrical component (a capacitor) to store charge. It is measured in *farads and defined as the ratio of the stored charge in coulombs to the potential difference in volts across the component.

Cape Cod A sandy peninsula in the USA, in Massachusetts between Cape Cod Bay and the Atlantic Ocean. A popular summer resort area, it also produces cranberries and asparagus. Length: 105 km (65 mi).

Cape Horn (Spanish name: Cabo de Hornes) The most southerly point in South America, at the S end of Horn Island, Chile. It is notorious for its stormy weather.

Cape of Good Hope A headland in South Africa, at the SW extremity of Cape Province. It was discovered (1488) by Dias, who named it the Cape of Storms.

Cape Province (official name: Cape of Good Hope Province; Afrikaans name: Kaapprovinsie) The largest province in South Africa, in the extreme S of the African continent. It consists chiefly of plateaus separated by mountain ranges. The SW produces most of South Africa's fruit and vegetables for export and has many vineyards; sheep and cattle rearing is extensive. Diamonds and copper are the chief minerals. *History*: first settled by the Dutch (1652), it was handed over to Britain in 1814, becoming known as the Cape Colony. In 1910 the colony became a province in the Union of South Africa. Area: 646 332 sq km (400 762 sq mi). Population (1986): 4 901 261. Capital: Cape Town.

caper A bramble-like spiny shrub, *Capparis spinosa*, native to drier regions of S Europe. The pickled flower buds are the capers used in cooking.

capercaillie The largest European grouse, *Tetrao urogallus*, of Eurasian coniferous forests, where it feeds on pine buds and needles. The

male, almost 100 cm long, is black with a blue-green gloss and red wattles above the eyes. The smaller female is brown with black and white markings.

Cape Town (Afrikaans name: Kaapstad) 33 56S 18 28E The legislative capital of South Africa and capital of Cape Province, on the Atlantic Ocean. Founded by Jan van Riebeeck in 1652 as a supply post for the Dutch East India Company, it is the oldest White settlement in South Africa. Cape Town is a major port; its industries include oil refining, chemicals, motor vehicles, and textiles. Population (1980): 213 830.

Cape Verde, Republic of (Portuguese name: Cabo Verde) A country occupying a group of ten islands and five islets in the N Atlantic Ocean, off the coast of West Africa. The majority of the population is of mixed African and European descent. *Economy*: mainly subsistence agriculture. Fish are the main export. *History*: the Cape Verde Islands were settled by the Portuguese in the mid-15th century, becoming a Portuguese colony in the 19th century and gaining full independence in 1975. Head of state: President Mascarenhas Monteiro. Official language: Portuguese. Official currency: Cape Verdean escudo of 100 centavos. Area: 4033 sq km (1557 sq mi). Population (1988 est): 331 000. Capital: Praia. Main port: Mindelo.

capital A structure used to join a column to the part of the building it supports. In classical architecture there are five orders of columns with strictly defined types of capital, of varying degrees of ornateness, for each (*see* orders of architecture). In romanesque and gothic architecture, the type of capital used depended mainly on the skill and taste of the masons involved.

capital-gains tax A UK tax, introduced in 1965, on the profit gained by disposing of an item of property by sale or gift (and until 1971 on death). It applies to stocks and shares (except some government stocks), to homes that are not the owner's only residence, and to all other saleable items of property with some exceptions (e.g. cars, assets sold for less than £6,000). It does not apply to gains from gambling or life assurance policies. The rate of tax is 30% on the gain, but the first £5,000 of a person's gains in any year are not counted.

capitalism An economic and political system that developed following the industrial revolution. The main features of the system are uncontrolled free markets, profit, and unrestricted public ownership of shares (capital). If the system is allowed to develop without restriction it creates certain problems (*see* laissez-faire). This has led western countries to restrict capitalism by substantial government regulation. Communist countries have followed the doctrines of Karl Marx (*see* Marxism), which favours the central management of the economy by the government.

capital punishment The punishment of a convicted criminal by execution. In 18th-century Britain over 200 offences carried the death penalty, including minor theft and forgery. In 1868 public executions were abolished and by the

Homicide Act (1957) only certain kinds of murder remained punishable by death (murder committed in the course of theft, in resisting arrest, etc.). In 1965 the death penalty was abolished for all forms of murder, but treason remains a capital crime.

Capone, Al (1899–1947) US gangster, born in Italy, who dominated the Chicago underworld of organized crime in the late 1920s. He was imprisoned in 1931 for income-tax evasion.

Capri, Island of (Latin name: Capreae) An Italian island at the SW entrance to the Bay of Naples. It has been a popular resort since Roman times. The Blue Grotto, a cavern accessible only by sea, is a notable feature. Area: about 13 sq km (5 sq mi). Population (1981 est): 7489.

Capricorn (astrology). *See* zodiac.

capsicum A flowering plant of the potato family, native to Central and South America. The fruits of some species are the *chillies and peppers used in cookery. Sweet peppers, up to about 10 cm long, have a mild taste and are eaten raw or cooked. They are usually green but may be red or yellow. Dwarf varieties are grown for ornament.

capsule In botany, a type of dry *fruit that releases its seeds through pores, teeth, or slits: an example is the poppy capsule. The term also refers to the spore-producing structures of mosses and liverworts and the slimy envelope surrounding some bacterial cells. In zoology, it is the layer of connective tissue surrounding some organs, for example the kidney.

capuchin monkey A long-tailed South American monkey. Capuchins are 70–90 cm long including the tail (40–50 cm) and live in large troops in the treetops, feeding chiefly on fruit.

Capuchins A Roman Catholic order of friars founded in 1525. They are reformed *Franciscans, named after the pointed hood they wear in imitation of St Francis. They were almost suppressed in 1542, but became an important force during the Counter-Reformation, being recognized in 1619 as one of the three independent branches of the Franciscan order.

capybara The largest living rodent, *Hydrochoerus hydrochaeris*. Resembling giant guinea-pigs, up to 1.25 m long and 50 cm high, capybaras graze on river banks in Central and South America, living in groups. They have short yellowish-brown hair and partially webbed feet.

car The search for a self-propelled vehicle to replace the horse began seriously at the beginning of the 18th century. Joseph Cugnot (1725–1804) in 1770 used a steam engine to drive a gun tractor and in 1808 Richard Trevithick built a working steam carriage. Neither of these vehicles was very practical. A smaller more efficient power source was needed. This was eventually provided by two German engineers, Nikolaus *Otto and Gottlieb *Daimler, who in 1876 patented the Otto-cycle *internal-combustion engine. In 1885, another German, Karl *Benz, used a version of this engine to power a tricycle. By 1890 both Daimler and Benz were selling motorized dog carts, while in France by the end of the century Panhard, Comte Albert de Dion, Georges

Bouton, and Peugeot were all selling cars. In the USA, Henry Ford built his first car in 1896. In the UK, however, the development of the motor car was slowed down by the law, introduced in 1865 and repealed in 1896, which insisted that cars must be preceded by a man carrying a red flag. Henry *Royce, dissatisfied with imported cars, decided to build his own. In partnership with C. S. Rolls, he sold his first Rolls-Royce Silver Ghost in 1907.

By the start of World War I, some 130 000 cars were registered in the UK. Motoring was expensive, however. In the early 1920s a family Ford or Austin, cost about £500. It was not until 1925, when Ford brought the price of his Model T down to $290 in the USA, that many more people could enjoy motoring. During the 1930s the price of cars steadily dropped until 1939 when an Austin 7 cost about £100. Since World War II a model has had to sell a million vehicles to be a commercial success. The pollution and congestion caused by the modern car has led to widespread concern.

Caracas 10 35N 66 56W The capital of Venezuela, situated near the N coast and linked by road to its port, La Guaira. It was founded by the Spanish as Santiago de León de Caracas in the 16th century. Population (1987): 1 246 677.

carat 1. A unit of weight for precious stones equal to 0.200 grams. 2. A measure of the fineness of gold equal to the number of parts of gold by weight in 24 parts of the alloy. Thus 18-carat gold contains 18/24ths pure gold.

Caratacus (*or* Caractacus; 1st century AD) King of the Catuvellauni; son of *Cunobelinus (Cymbeline). Caratacus organized resistance to the Roman invasion of 43 AD. Defeated, he fled first to Wales then to the north British queen, Cartimandua, who betrayed him. He was pardoned by Emperor Claudius but died in exile.

Caravaggio (Michelangelo Merisi; 1573–1610) An Italian *baroque painter, whose nickname derives from his birthplace. In Rome he painted scenes of the life of St Matthew in S Luigi dei Francesi. He designed numerous altarpieces, some of which were condemned for depicting sacred figures as peasants. Caravaggio is noted for his dramatic *Supper at Emmaus* (National Gallery, London).

caraway A perennial flowering plant, *Carum carvi*, of the carrot family, native to N temperate regions from Europe to the Himalayas. The stem grows to 25–60 cm and terminates in clusters of white flowers. The fruit is an oblong capsule containing the caraway seeds, used in cookery.

carbohydrate One of a large group of chemical compounds containing the elements carbon, hydrogen, and oxygen and having the general formula $C_x(H_2O)_x$. Green plants manufacture carbohydrates—such as *sugars and *starch —during *photosynthesis and their cell walls consist largely of carbohydrates—mainly *cellulose. Hence carbohydrates are the primary source of food energy for animals. *Glycogen is a carbohydrate energy reserve found in animals, while chitin is a structural carbohydrate occurring in arthropods.

CAR

Benz 8hp *1600 of these "horseless carriages" were sold between 1898 and 1900. Described as the first reliable car offered to the public, its twin-cyclinder 1570 cc engine gave it a top speed of 18 mph (29 km/hr).*

Rolls-Royce Silver Ghost *First built in 1907 (and continuing in production until 1927) it quickly established itself as "the best car in the world." Its 7-litre 6-cylinder engine gave it a top speed of 65 mph (105 km/hr).*

Ford Model T *15 million of this first mass-produced car (nicknamed the "Tin Lizzie") were made between 1908 and 1927. Its 4-cylinder, 2898 cc engine gave it a top speed of 40 mph (64 km/hr).*

Bugatti Royale *Made to compete with the Rolls-Royce, this 13-litre 8-cylinder car cost over £5000 in 1927 – too much for even its intended royal customers. Six were sold. In 1987 one survivor was sold for £5.5 M.*

Volkswagen *Nicknamed "the Beetle," this 1937 German design by Ferdinand Porsche was still selling in the 1970s, making it the best selling car ever made. Its air-cooled slow-revving rear engine increased from 1131 to 1600 cc over the years.*

MG TC *This post-war British sports car (1946-55) was little changed from the TA model first built in 1937. The TC had a 1250 cc engine.*

Buick *This 1949 US car represented a release from wartime restrictions and set the trend for a generation of large American cars.*

Mini *The best selling British car ever made. Designed by Alec Issigonis, the Mini was introduced in 1959 and is still selling. Its frontwheel drive, transverse engine, and 10-inch wheels make it an extremely roomy car for its size.*

Citroen BX *This 1987 French 1900 cc diesel-powered model has a top speed of 103 mph (166 km/hr) and claims a fuel consumption of 61.4 mpg at 56 mph (90 km/hr). It also features Citroen's self-levelling hydropneumatic suspension.*

carbolic acid. *See* phenols.

carbon (C) A chemical element that is unique in the number and variety of its compounds. The element occurs in two forms: *graphite, which is a soft greyish mineral, and *diamond, the hardest substance known. Charcoal and *coke are also composed of carbon. The number of carbon compounds results from the ability of carbon to form single, double, and triple bonds with itself and other elements and to form chains and rings. At no 6; at wt 12.011; sublimes at $3367 \pm 25°C$.

carbon cycle (biology) The process by which carbon (in the form of carbon dioxide) in the atmosphere is taken up by plants during *photosynthesis and transferred from one organism to the next in a *food chain, i.e. the plants are eaten by herbivorous animals that are themselves eaten by carnivores. At various stages carbon is returned to the environment with the release of carbon dioxide at *respiration and through decay.

carbon dioxide (CO_2) A colourless odourless gas that does not burn. It is present (about 0.03% by volume) in air, being produced by *combustion of carbon compounds and by *respiration. Industrially, CO_2 is made from chalk or limestone and is used as a coolant in nuclear reactors, as a refrigerant, in fire extinguishers, and in "fizzy" drinks.

Carboniferous period A geological period of the *Palaeozoic era occurring about 370–280 million years ago between the Devonian and Permian periods. During the period the great quantity of land plants led to the formation of the world's major *coal deposits. *Amphibians became more common and by the end of the period some *reptiles had evolved. The Carboniferous is divided into Lower and Upper (Mississippian and Pennsylvanian).

carbon monoxide (CO) A colourless odourless gas that burns readily. It is produced by the incomplete *combustion of carbon compounds. CO is highly poisonous, combining with red blood cells and preventing them from carrying oxygen. It is present in the exhaust fumes of internal-combustion engines.

carborundum A dark crystalline compound (silicon carbide) manufactured by heating silica (sand) with carbon (coke). It is used as an abrasive and as a material for lining furnaces, etc.

carboxylic acids. *See* fatty acid.

carburettor The device in a petrol engine that converts the liquid petrol into a vapour and mixes it with air in the correct proportions. The carburettor also contains a choke to make the petrol-air mixture richer for cold starting, a throttle valve (which controls the speed of the engine) and an air filter. In some petrol engines the carburettor is replaced by a *fuel-injection system.

carcinogen An agent that causes cancer. Chemical carcinogens include tar (as produced by cigarettes) and certain dyes. Large doses of radiation and the polyoma virus are also known to cause cancer, particularly leukaemia.

cardamon A perennial herb, *Elettaria cardamomum*, of the ginger family, native to India. 1.5–3 m tall, it has large leaves, green and purple veined flowers, and small capsules filled with hard seeds. The spice cardamon consists of whole or ground dried fruit or seeds. It is cultivated in India, Sri Lanka, and Guatemala.

Cardiff (Welsh name: Caerdydd) 51 30N 3 13W The capital of Wales and the administrative centre of South Glamorgan and Mid Glamorgan, situated at the mouth of the River Taff. At the centre of the city lies the Norman castle, rebuilt in the 1870s. Cardiff Arms Park is the home of Welsh rugby. *History*: originally a small Roman fort, it received its first royal charter in 1581. Cardiff's prosperity was based on coal from the valleys to the N of the city. Cardiff was chosen as the capital of Wales in 1955. Population (1988 est): 283 900.

Cardigan, James Thomas Brudenell, 7th Earl of (1797–1868) British cavalry officer. In 1854, during the Crimean War, he led the fatal charge of the Light Brigade at *Balaclava, made famous by Tennyson. The woollen garment known as a cardigan was named after him.

cardinals, college of (*or* Sacred College) The body of the people of highest rank next to the pope in the *Roman Catholic Church. Developing from the parish priests and deacons of the city of Rome, the present membership of 125 was established under John XXIII and Paul VI. Cardinals are chosen by the pope, who invests them with the red hat symbolic of their rank. They assist the pope as a privy council and elect the pope from among their own number.

Carey, George Leonard (1935–) British churchman; Archbishop of Canterbury (1991–). He was formerly Bishop of Bath and Wells (1987–91).

cargo cults Religious cults found chiefly in Melanesia since the late 19th century. Their followers believe that a new paradise will be heralded mainly by the arrival of a supernatural cargo of goods brought by spirits, who are variously viewed as gods, ancestors, or White foreigners.

Carib An American Indian people of the Lesser Antilles and northern South America, after whom the Caribbean was named. The island Caribs were warriors and cannibals, who before the arrival of the Spaniards expelled the *Arawak Indians from the Lesser Antilles, enslaving the women and eating the men. The mainland Caribs were less aggressive.

Caribbean Sea A section of the Atlantic Ocean, between the West Indies, E Central America. Area: 2 718 200 sq km (1 049 500 sq mi). Maximum depth: 7686 m (25 216 ft).

caribou. *See* reindeer.

caries Cavities in the teeth caused by bacterial erosion of the enamel and dentine. The bacteria feed on sugar from the diet: the sugar and bacteria become attached to the teeth to form plaque; acid formed by bacterial breakdown of the sugar causes the caries. *See also* fluoridation.

Carlisle 54 54N 2 55W A city in NW England, the administrative centre of Cumbria on the River Eden. Once a Roman military centre (Luguvallum) and important fortress in the border wars with the Scots, it has a 12th-century cathedral and a castle (11th-13th centuries). Industries include flour milling, food processing, textiles, and agricultural engineering. Population (1981 est): 71 503.

Carlow (Irish name: Ceatharlach) A county in the E Republic of Ireland, in Leinster. Chiefly low lying, it rises to mountains in the E. Agriculture is intensive producing barley, wheat, and sugar beet. Area: 896 sq km (346 sq mi). Population (1986): 40 948. County town: Carlow.

Carlyle, Thomas (1795–1881) Scottish historian and essayist. *Sartor Resartus*, a blend of fiction, philosophy, and autobiography, was published in 1836 and was followed by his major work, *The French Revolution*, in 1837.

Carmelites A Roman Catholic religious order founded in the mid-12th century by St Berthold (died c. 1195), who established a monastery at Mount Carmel (N Israel). With the collapse of the Crusader kingdoms (*see* Crusades), the order moved to Europe. The original strict rule was relaxed and in 1452 an order of Carmelite nuns was started. In the 16th century the order was reformed by St *Teresa of Ávila stressing a life of contemplation.

Carnap, Rudolf (1891–1970) German-born philosopher. A founder of the *Vienna Circle, he was professor of philosophy at Vienna, Prague, Chicago, and California Universities.

carnation A perennial cultivated ornamental plant derived from the clove pink (*Dianthus caryophyllus*), growing to 40–60 cm and having variously coloured double flowers. Hardy border carnations are suitable for outdoor cultivation, while the perpetual flowering varieties grow under glass.

Carnivora An order of mammals adapted for hunting and eating flesh. Carnivores have strong jaws with pointed canine teeth. They are the major predators and most species are terrestrial. Carnivores include dogs, wolves, foxes, bears, raccoons, pandas, weasels, mongooses, and cats.

carnivorous plant A plant that obtains at least some of its nutrients by the digestion of insects and other small animals. *Butterworts and *sundews trap and digest insects by means of the sticky secretions produced by glands in the leaves. The *Venus flytrap traps its prey between hinged leaves with marginal teeth. Another common method of capture and digestion is by means of liquid-filled "pitchers" into which the insects fall (*see* pitcher plant).

carob The horn-shaped edible fruit pod of the carob tree, *Ceratonia siliqua*, an evergreen native to the Mediterranean region. The pods, sometimes known as algaroba or St John's bread, contain a sugary pulp and are used for fodder. The seeds are believed to have been the original carats of jewellers. Carob is also widely used as a substitute for chocolate.

Carolina. *See* North Carolina; South Carolina.

Caroline of Brunswick (1768–1821) The wife of George IV of the United Kingdom. After their separation (1796), he forbade her to see their child Charlotte. When George became king (1820), his attempt to divorce Caroline failed owing to popular support for her but she was prevented from attending the coronation (1821).

carp An omnivorous freshwater fish, *Cyprinus carpio*, native to Asia but widely introduced elsewhere and raised for food. It has an elongated body, usually about 35 cm long, with large scales, greenish or brownish above and paler below, and a long dorsal fin.

Carpathian Mountains A mountain range in Czechoslovakia, Poland, Hungary, the Soviet Union, and Romania. They form a rough semicircle about 1450 km (90 mi) long (including the Transylvanian Alps, which are also known as the **Southern Carpathians**). The highest peak is Mount Gerlachovka, at 2663 m (8737 ft), in NE Czechoslovakia.

carpel The female organ of a flower, consisting of the stigma, style, and ovary. After fertilization, each carpel may ripen to produce a fruit containing one or more seeds. *See also* pistil.

Carroll, Lewis (Charles Lutwidge Dodgson; 1832–98) British writer and mathematician. He lectured in mathematics at Oxford University from 1855 to 1881. The children's classic, *Alice's Adventures in Wonderland* (1865), was written for the young Alice Liddell, the daughter of the head of his Oxford College. It and the sequel, *Through the Looking-Glass* (1872), combine fantasy, logic, and nonsense. He also wrote nonsense verse, notably *The Hunting of the Snark* (1876).

carrot A biennial flowering plant, *Daucus carota*, found from Europe to India. The stem grows to 30–100 cm and bears a head of white flowers. *Daucus carota sativus*, the cultivated carrot, is grown as an annual, and produces the familiar edible root.

Carte, Richard D'Oyly. *See* D'Oyly Carte, Richard.

Carter, Jimmy (James Earl C.; 1924–) US statesman; Democratic president (1977–81). Carter left his family peanut farming for politics and was governor of Georgia from 1970 to 1974. He brought about the peace treaty between Egypt and Israel (1979).

Cartesian coordinates. *See* coordinate systems.

Carthage (Punic name: *Kart-Hadasht*, New City) An ancient city of N Africa, near modern Tunis. Traditionally founded 814 BC by *Dido and exiles from *Tyre, Carthage rapidly became leader of the *Phoenician trading cities of N Africa, waging intermittent war with the Greeks of Marseilles and Sicily. From 264 BC Carthage fought the three *Punic Wars with *Rome, her former ally, and was totally destroyed (146 BC). Refounded by Julius *Caesar (45 BC), Carthage became, in turn, the capital of Roman Africa, the capital of the *Vandal kingdom (439–533 AD), and a Byzantine outpost, until destroyed by the Muslims in 697 AD.

Carthusians A Roman Catholic religious order founded in 1084 by St Bruno and taking its name from the location of the first community, La Grande Chartreuse, near Grenoble. Although originally without a written rule, the Carthusians led a strict life of fasting, solitude, and silence. The French monks are noted for the liqueur Chartreuse, which they make.

Cartier, Jacques (1491–1557) French navigator. In 1534, under the patronage of Francis I, he sailed in search of the *Northwest Passage and explored the coast of N Canada and Newfoundland. The next year he sailed up the St Lawrence as far as what became Montreal.

Cartier-Bresson, Henri (1908–   ) French photographer and pioneer of photojournalism. His photographs, collected in such books as *The Decisive Moment* (1952) and *Europeans* (1955), concentrate on ordinary people. As a film maker, he worked with Jean *Renoir in the late 1930s and returned to this medium in the 1960s.

cartilage A flexible supportive body tissue consisting chiefly of a *polysaccharide–chondroitin sulphate–in which elastic or collagen fibres may be embedded. Cartilage lines the ends of bones where they form joints and also provides the skeleton of the nose, ear, and parts of the throat (larynx) and air passages. A tough cartilage forms the discs between the bones of the spine.

Cartwright, Edmund (1743–1823) British inventor and industrialist, In 1785 he invented a power loom and then set up a factory in Doncaster for weaving and spinning yarn. Four years later he invented a machine for combing wool. In 1793 his business failed but parliament recognized his achievements in 1809 with an award of £10,000.

caryatid A carved column in the shape of a draped female figure that first appeared in Greek architecture around 500 BC. The most notable are on the Erechtheum on the *Acropolis of Athens. Caryatids were infrequent in Roman architecture but were revived in 19th-century classicism.

Casablanca (Arabic name: Dar-el-Beida) 33 39N 7 35W A port and largest city in Morocco, on the Atlantic coast. First established by the Portuguese (1515), it was taken by the French in 1907. It has major industries and fishing and tourism are also important. Population (1984): 2 600 000.

Casals, Pablo (Pau C.; 1876–1973) Spanish cellist, conductor, and composer. Casals revolutionized the style and technique of cello playing and excelled as an interpreter of Bach's six suites for unaccompanied cello and of the major cello concertos.

Casanova, Giovanni Giacomo, Chevalier de Seingalt (1725–98) Italian adventurer. He lived in many European cities, working at different times as a violinist, a spy, and a librarian. His adventures, which included many romantic conquests, are recorded in his memoirs, of which the first complete edition was published in 1960.

casein The major protein present in milk. Casein is easily digested and contains a good balance of essential *amino acids. Cheese consists largely of insoluble para-casein, formed from casein by the action of enzymes. Casein is also used industrially to make thermoplastics (e.g. knife handles).

cashew A tree, *Anacardium occidentale*, native to tropical America and cultivated widely in the tropics. It grows to about 12 m and has red flowers. The fruit is a kidney-shaped nut that develops at the end of a hanging pear-shaped re-

ceptacle. The edible kernel–the cashew nut–is extracted after the fruit is roasted.

Caspian Sea The largest inland sea in the world, bounded by Iran and the Soviet Union and fed chiefly by the River Volga. Its surface is 28.5 m (93.5 ft) below sea level. The chief ports are Astrakhan and Baku, both in the Soviet Union. Sturgeon and seals are caught here and oil and gas extracted. Area: about 370 000 sq km (142 827 sq mi).

Cassandra A legendary Trojan prophetess, daughter of King Priam of Troy. After she had refused to submit to Apollo's advances, he condemned her prophecies to eternal disbelief. When Troy fell she was taken by Agamemnon, with whom she was later murdered.

cassava A shrubby flowering plant, *Manihot esculentus* (or *M. utilissimus*), of the spurge family, also known as manioc, native to tropical America. Many varieties–divided into two groups, sweet and bitter cassavas–are cultivated in the tropics for their starchy tuberous roots. These can be processed into tapioca, ground to produce manioc or cassava meal (Brazilian arrowroot), used as fodder, or eaten as a vegetable.

cassiopeium. *See* lutetium.

cassiterite The only commercial ore of tin, consisting of tin(II) oxide. It is found in certain igneous rocks and as alluvial deposits. It is brown or black.

Cassius Longinus, Gaius (d. 42 BC) Roman general. Cassius supported *Pompey until Pompey's defeat by Julius Caesar at *Pharsalus. He was then pardoned by Caesar but joined the conspiracy to assassinate him in 44. Outlawed, Cassius committed suicide after defeat in the battle of *Philippi.

cassowary A large flightless bird occurring in rain forests of Australia and New Guinea. The largest cassowary (*Casuarius casuarius*) is 150 cm tall and has a black plumage, two red throat wattles, and a blue head. Cassowaries have powerful legs, each having a long sharp claw.

Castagno, Andrea del (Andrea di Bartolo de Simone; c. 1421–57) Italian *Renaissance painter, who was born near Castagno but settled in Florence. His major frescoes depict the *Last Supper* and the *Passion* (Sta Apollonia, Florence). Later works include the portrait of *Niccolò da Tolentino* (Duomo, Florence).

castes Groups of people within a society, divided by family, wealth, occupation, etc.; positions are fixed and mobility from one caste to another is prevented by ritual systems. In the Hindu caste system of India there are four main divisions: brahmins (priests), ksatriyas (warriors), vaisyas (merchants), and sundras (serfs). Outside these groups are the "outcastes" or "untouchables".

Castile A former kingdom in central Spain. Originally a district at the foot of the Cantabrian Mountains, Castile expanded in the 9th and 10th centuries, becoming a united country. In 1035 it became a kingdom and in 1230 was united with the kingdom of León, with Castile dominating. In 1479 Spain was virtually united following the marriage of *Isabella of Castile to *Ferdinand the Catholic and Castile became the political and administrative centre of Spain.

cast iron A form of iron containing between 2.5% and 4.5% of carbon by weight. The carbon makes it hard and brittle and it tends to crack under tension. Cast iron is made by casting *pig iron (i.e. heating it and shaping it in a mould) and adjusting its composition to improve the strength.

castle A fortified defensive building, from the Latin *castellum*, a small fortified place. The castle underwent many changes as more powerful weapons were developed. In the early middle ages it consisted of a building on a mound of earth surrounded by a wooden fence (the motte and bailey castle), a design later copied in stone. The simplest stone castle, such as the White Tower in London, is called a keep or donjon. Later designs became more complicated, involving extensive outworks of battlemented towers and walls (curtain walls), for example Caernarfon Castle in Wales.

Castlereagh, Robert Stewart, Viscount (1769–1822) British statesman, born in Ulster; foreign secretary (1812–22). An MP in the Irish parliament (1780), he became Viscount Castlereagh in 1796, when his father Robert Stewart (1739–1821) became 1st Marquess of Londonderry. Appointed chief secretary for Ireland in 1798, he resigned in 1801, when George III rejected Catholic Emancipation. His policies as secretary for war (1807–09) were attacked by Canning, with whom Castlereagh fought a duel. As foreign secretary he played an important role at the Congress of *Vienna (1814–15).

Castor and Pollux Twin heroes of classical mythology, also known as the Dioscuri. Pollux was immortal, the son of *Zeus and *Leda; Castor was mortal, the son of Tyndareus and Leda. When Castor died, Pollux asked Zeus to allow them to remain together. Transformed into the Gemini constellation, they were the patrons of mariners.

castor oil A pale yellow viscous oil extracted from the seeds of the *castor-oil plant. It is used as a *laxative and in the manufacture of plastics.

castor-oil plant A flowering plant, *Ricinus communis*, of the spurge family, up to 12 m high, native to tropical Africa and Asia. It is cultivated for its seeds, from which *castor oil is extracted, and as an ornamental shrub, up to 2 m high.

castration Removal of the testes (in the male) or ovaries (in the female). In medicine, castration may be performed in cases of cancer of the testes: it always produces sterility but—unless done before puberty—need not cause impotence. Farm animals and pets are castrated to make them more docile and prevent breeding.

Castro (Ruz), Fidel (1926–) Cuban statesman; president (1976–). The son of a sugar planter, Castro opposed the dictator Fulgencio Batista (1901–73). In 1953 he led an unsuccessful attack on the Moncada barracks and was imprisoned until 1955. In 1956 he invaded Cuba from Mexico with a small armed band, with which he finally defeated government troops, entering Havana in 1959. Castro established a socialist government, which the USA attempted to overthrow. As a result, Cuba became dependent on the Soviet Union. *See also* Bay of Pigs.

cat A carnivorous mammal belonging to the family *Felidae* (36 species). Most cats have sheathed claws and sharp canine teeth to kill their prey. Their acute vision, sense of smell, and hearing are adaptations for hunting stealthily, often at night. With no natural enemies, the kittens (or cubs) are born blind and toothless and learn hunting techniques through play.
The wide range of different breeds of domestic cat (*Felis catus*), including *Persian, *Siamese, and *Abyssinian, are thought to have been developed from the African wildcat, or cafer cat, and possibly the European *wildcat. Wild species range in size from the *tiger to the tiny South African black-footed cat (*F. nigripes*).

catabolism. *See* metabolism.

catacombs Underground cemeteries, especially those containing early Christian graves. The earliest and biggest catacombs are in Rome, particularly those of St Calixtus and St Sebastian along the *Appian Way. Most catacombs consist of narrow passages into the walls of which the burial niches were cut. With the acceptance of Christianity they fell into disuse, although some remained as centres of pilgrimage.

Catalan A *Romance language spoken by about five million people in Catalonia and the Balearic Islands in Spain, Andorra, and the Roussillon region of France. It is closely related to Spanish and to the Occitan language (*see* Provençal) of France.

Catalonia (Spanish name: Cataluña; Catalan name: Catalunya) A mountainous region of NE Spain, on the Mediterranean Sea. The main crops are cereals, olives, and grapes. It is also highly industrialized. *History*: united with Aragon in 1137 and Castile in 1497, Catalonia has maintained a strong separatist tradition. In 1932 an autonomous government was established and this lasted throughout the Civil War (1936–39), in which Catalonia was on the Republican side. The Catalan government was restored in 1977. Area: 31 932 sq km (12 329 sq mi). Population (1986 est): 6 057 200. Capital: Barcelona.

catalysis The speeding up of a *chemical reaction by a substance (catalyst) that is not itself consumed in the reaction. The reverse reaction is also accelerated. Catalysis is used extensively in industrial chemical processes. In living organisms *enzymes are catalysts for biochemical reactions.

catamaran A fast sailing vessel with two identical hulls, rigidly fastened parallel to one another, and, usually, a single mast with two triangular sails. The modern catamaran is based on a native canoe-like vessel of the SW Pacific.

cataract (ophthalmology) Opaque areas that form in the lens of the eye resulting in blurred vision. They are caused by the deposition of small crystals or changes in the composition of the lens substance. Cataracts are a common cause of blindness in the elderly; certain diseases, such as poorly controlled diabetes mellitus, can also lead to cataracts. Cataracts are treated by surgical removal of the lens and the use of

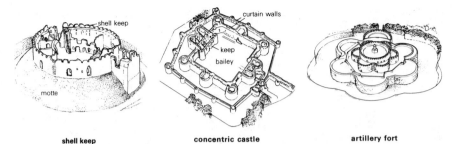

shell keep   concentric castle   artillery fort

CASTLE *The early medieval shell keep gave way to the massive fortifications of the 14th and 15th centuries, which were in turn superseded by the artillery fort with its low walls and sweeping lines of fire.*

appropriate spectacles or the implantation of a plastic lens.

caterpillar The larva of *butterflies and moths. Soft-bodied and wingless, caterpillars have a head and 13 body segments with 3 pairs of true legs and 5 pairs of abdominal prolegs, which aid in locomotion. They feed on leaves or plant sap and some species are serious crop pests. Caterpillars show a wide variety of camouflaging colours and shapes.

Catesby, Robert. *See* Fawkes, Guy.

catfish A bony *fish with a stout scaleless body, 4–450 cm long, a broad flat head, and long whisker-like barbels. Freshwater catfish, sometimes called bullheads, occur worldwide; marine catfish inhabit tropical and coastal waters.

cathedral The principal church of an ecclesiastical area (diocese), governed by a bishop or an archbishop. The name comes from Latin *cathedra*, bishop's seat. Generally larger than other churches, cathedrals, such as *St Peter's Basilica, Rome, *St Paul's Cathedral, London, and *Notre-Dame de Paris, contain some of their country's finest works of art.

Catherine (II) the Great (1729–96) Empress of Russia (1762–96), who gained the throne in a coup in which her husband, Emperor Peter III (1728–62; reigned 1762), was murdered. Catherine's reign marked the growth of Russia as a result of her successful wars against the Turks (1768–74, 1787–92) and the dividing of Poland (1772, 1793, 1795). She had to abandon her plan to free the serfs in the face of opposition from their masters. Of her many lovers, only Potemkin influenced her government.

Catherine de' Medici (1519–89) Regent of France (1560–63) during the childhood of her second son, Charles IX, and virtual ruler until his death (1574). The daughter of Lorenzo de' Medici, Duke of Urbino, she married Henry II of France in 1533. Intent on defending royal authority during the *Wars of Religion, she argued in favour of tolerance for the *Huguenots but later supported the Catholics. She was largely responsible for the *St Bartholomew's Day Massacre. Her influence waned during the reign of her third son *Henry III.

Catherine of Aragon (1485–1536) The first wife (1509–33) of Henry VIII of England and the mother of Mary I. Failing to bear him a son, she was divorced by Henry, who argued that their marriage was invalid because Catherine was the widow of his brother Arthur. The pope's refusal to accept their divorce led to the English *Reformation.

cathode The negative electrode of an electrolytic cell, valve, etc. It is the electrode by which the electrons enter the system.

cathode-ray tube (CRT) A vacuum tube that converts electrical signals into visible form by projecting a beam of electrons onto a fluorescent screen. It is an essential component of the television receiver, computer screen, and the cathode-ray oscilloscope (CRO). The electron beam is moved back and forth across the screen, its intensity being varied by input signals as it moves. In a television tube the beam intensity varies to form the light and dark regions of the picture.

Catholic emancipation A campaign in Britain and Ireland to gain full civil and political rights for Roman Catholics. In the late 18th century several acts were passed in their favour, but Catholics were still not allowed to be represented in parliament. The opposition of the Tory establishment and the monarchy continued until O'Connell's efforts achieved the Catholic Emancipation Act of 1829.

Cato the Elder (Marcus Porcius C.; 234–149 BC) Roman statesman, who wrote the first history of Rome. Cato as censor (184) passed laws against luxury and sponsored improvements in public works.

Cato the Younger (Marcus Porcius C.; 95–46 BC) Roman politician; the great-grandson of Cato the Elder and an opponent of Julius Caesar. Caesar, with *Pompey and *Crassus, created the first *Triumvirate (60) in part to silence Cato's opposition to their ambitions. Supporting Pompey in the civil war in an attempt to save the Republic, Cato escaped after Pompey's death to Utica, in Africa. There, on hearing of Caesar's victory at *Thapsus, he committed suicide.

cattle *Ruminant mammals native to Eurasia and Africa. Modern domestic cattle are probably descended from the auroch, an extinct European wild ox. They vary in body shape, size, and colour according to breed but are generally 90–110 cm high at the shoulder and weigh 400–900 kg. Cattle are primarily used for milk and meat production (*see* livestock farming).

Catullus, Valerius (c. 84–c. 54 BC) Roman poet. Born in Verona, he became the leading member of a group of poets in Rome. 116 poems survive, including the 25 lyrics to a married woman named Lesbia.

Caucasian languages. *See* Northeast Caucasian; Northwest Caucasian; South Caucasian.

Caucasoid A race or group of races and peoples originally inhabiting Europe, North Africa, and the Near East. They are characterized by very pale to dark brown skins, straight to curly hair, narrow high-bridged noses, plentiful body hair, and a high frequency of Rh-negative blood type.

Caucasus Mountains (Russian name: Kavkaz) Two mountain ranges in the SW Soviet Union extending NW–SE between the Black Sea and the Caspian Sea and separated by the River Kura: the **Great Caucasus**, some 1000 km (621 mi) long, to the N and the **Little Caucasus**, about half that length, along the Turkish border. Their highest point is Mount Elbrus.

cauliflower A variety of wild *cabbage cultivated as a vegetable in Europe and the USA. The stem bears a white heart, up to 25 cm in diameter, surrounded by leaves.

Cavaliers The royalist party during the English *Civil War. After the *Restoration of the monarchy (1660) the name was kept by the court party and was given to the parliament that sat from 1661 to 1679. The cavaliers wore elaborate dress, with lace ruffles, feathers, and velvet, in contrast to the sober dress of the *Roundheads.

Cavan (Irish name: Cabhán) A hilly county in the NE Republic of Ireland, in Ulster, drained chiefly by the River Erne, it has lakes and drumlins. Agriculture produces oats, potatoes, and dairy products. Some small industries exist in the towns. Area: 1890 sq km (730 sq mi). Population (1986): 53 881. County town: Cavan.

Cavell, Edith (1865–1915) British nurse. From 1907 she worked at a training centre for nurses in Brussels. She was executed by the Germans in 1915 for helping Allied soldiers to escape from German-occupied Belgium. Before she died she is supposed to have said "I realize that patriotism is not enough. I must have no hatred or bitterness towards anyone."

Cavendish, Henry (1731–1810) British physicist; grandson of the Duke of Devonshire, from whom he inherited a fortune. He discovered hydrogen and investigated its properties. He also identified the gases in the atmosphere and showed that water is a compound. The first to measure accurately the universal gravitational constant, he used it to calculate the mass of the earth.

caves Underground hollows, usually opening onto the surface. In limestone regions, where most caves occur, many constitute part of a system of natural underground drainage. These caves are connected by subterranean streams. These caves are formed by the slow solution of limestone by slightly acidic rain water. The other main type of cave is that eroded from the base of a cliff by the sea. Such caves are located at some point of weakness in an otherwise resistant rock. Fin-

gal's Cave in the Scottish Hebrides is a spectacular cavern in columnar basalt, the sea forming its floor.

caviare A Russian delicacy, eaten as an hors d'oeuvre, which consists of sturgeon's roe, salted and freed from fat. Beluga roe is considered the best, although caviare is also obtained from other types of sturgeon. Real caviare is extremely expensive, but a substitute, lumpfish roe, is relatively inexpensive.

Cavour, Camillo Benso di, Count (1810–61) Italian statesman who unified Italy in 1861. In 1852 he formed his first government under *Victor Emmanuel II of Sardinia-Piedmont. Cavour accepted an alliance with France and Britain during the Crimean War and agreed a further alliance with France at Plombières in 1859 to remove Austria from Italy. He resigned when France came to terms with Austria but became prime minister again in 1860, arranging the union of Sardinia-Piedmont with Parma, Modena, Tuscany, and the Romagna.

cavy A small South American *rodent, the ancestor of the domestic guinea pig. Cavies are mainly nocturnal and live in groups in scrub and grassland, digging burrows and feeding on vegetation.

Cawnpore. *See* Kanpur.

Caxton, William (c. 1422–91) The first English printer. A cloth merchant, Caxton lived in Bruges from 1446 until 1470, when he moved to Cologne. There he learned the technique of printing and produced the first printed book in English, *Recuyell of the Historyes of Troye* (1475). On returning to England (1476), he printed a long and varied list on his press at Westminster, including Chaucer's *Canterbury Tales* (1478) and an encyclopedia, *The Myrrour of the Worlde* (1481).

Cayenne 4 55N 52 18W The capital and main Atlantic port of French Guiana, in the NW of the Île de Cayenne. Founded by the French in 1643, it served as a French penal settlement (1854–1938). Cayenne pepper derives its name from a plant grown in the area. Population (1982): 38 091.

cayman (*or* caiman) An amphibious reptile, related to the alligator, occurring in rivers of Central and South America. 1.2–4.5 m long, it feeds on fish, birds, and insects.

Cayman Islands A British colony in the Caribbean Sea, consisting of three low-lying coral islands (Grand Cayman, Little Cayman, and Cayman Brac) lying about 320 km (200 mi) NW of Jamaica. The population is of mixed African and European descent. The Cayman Islands are a tax haven and tourist centre. The main exports are turtle products and tropical fish. *History*: discovered in 1503 by Columbus, who named them Las Tortugas because of the abundance of turtles. Formerly attached to Jamaica, they gained limited self-government in 1959, becoming a colony in 1962. Official language: English. Official currency: Jamaican dollar of 100 cents. Area: 260 sq km (100 sq mi). Population (1987 est): 22 900. Capital and main port: Georgetown.

CBE. *See* Order of the British Empire.
CBI. *See* Confederation of British Industry.
Ceanannus Mór. *See* Kells.
cedar A conifer of the pine family, native to the Mediterranean and Himalayas. Cedars usually grow to 40 m high. Their needle-like leaves grow in tufts of 10–40 on short spurs and their cones are barrel-shaped. The best-known species are the *deodar, the Atlas cedar (*Cedrus atlantica*), and the cedar of Lebanon (*C. libani*).
Ceefax. *See* teletext.
Celebes. *See* Sulawesi.
celeriac A variety of cultivated *celery, also known as turnip-rooted or knob celery, grown for its globular edible root. The root, up to 15 cm in diameter, tastes like celery.
celery The cultivated form of wild celery, or smallage (*Apium graveolens*), a biennial herb of the carrot family, native to Europe, India, and Africa. Many varieties of cultivated celery have been developed for their edible leafstalks (up to 30 cm long). Traditionally, the green varieties are blanched to tenderize the tissues.
celesta A small keyboard instrument, the quiet bell-like tone of which is produced by hammers striking steel plates hung over wooden resonators. Invented about 1880, it was used by Tchaikovsky in his ballet *Casse-Noisette*.
celestial sphere The large imaginary sphere at the centre of which lies the earth and on the inner surface of which can be projected the stars and other celestial bodies. The directions of these bodies, as seen from earth, are measured in terms of their angular distances from certain points and circles on the celestial sphere. These circles include the **celestial equator**, where the earth's equatorial plane meets the celestial sphere. The reference points include the **celestial poles**, where the earth's axis meets the celestial sphere.
cell The basic unit of living matter. It produces energy, makes new molecules from raw materials, and undergoes division to form new cells. All plants and animals are composed of cells, the average size of which ranges from 0.01 to 0.1 mm; the simplest organisms (bacteria, protozoa, etc.) consist only of a single cell. The fundamental importance of cells was first recognized by the biologists Schleiden and Schwann in 1838–39. All cells (except those of bacteria and blue-green algae and mammalian red blood cells) possess a *nucleus, containing the genetic material, and cytoplasm, containing structures (organelles) specialized for different functions (*see* Golgi apparatus; lysosome; mitochondria; ribosome). The cells of the body not involved in reproduction (called somatic cells) divide by *mitosis to produce daughter cells identical to themselves. The reproductive cells divide by *meiosis to produce special sex cells (gametes), which take part in sexual reproduction. The basic difference between plant and animal cells is that plant cells have a rigid cellulose cell wall and chlorophyll for *photosynthesis (*see* chloroplast).
Cellini, Benvenuto (1500–71) Florentine goldsmith and sculptor, famous for his autobiography (1558–62). Cellini worked as a medallist

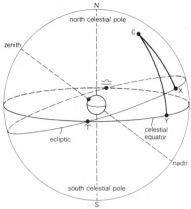

T first point of Aries; vernal equinox
≏ first point of Libra; autumnal equinox
C celestial object
ΥY right ascension of C (in hours counterclockwise from Υ)
ΥX celestial longitude of C (in degrees counterclockwise from Υ)
YC declination of C
XC celestial latitude of C

CELESTIAL SPHERE

and craftsman for the papacy in Rome, the Medici in Florence, and Francis I in France. The famous gold saltcellar (Kunsthistorisches Museum, Vienna) was made for Francis. His *Perseus* (Loggia dei Lanzi, Florence) is his best-known sculpture.
cello (full name: violoncello) A musical instrument of the *violin family, held between the knees and supported at its lower end by an adjustable pin. It has an extensive range above its lowest note (C two octaves below middle C). Its four strings are tuned C, G, D, A. It emerged as a solo instrument in the 18th and 19th centuries.

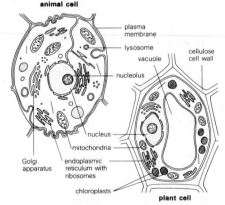

CELL *Plant and animal cells are basically similar but plant cells are supported by cellulose cell walls and contain the green pigment chlorophyll within chloroplasts.*

celluloid A highly flammable material made from cellulose nitrate and camphor. It was the first commercially made plastic, introduced over a hundred years ago.

cellulose ($C_6H_{10}O_5)_n$ A *carbohydrate that is present in the cell walls of plants and consists of linked glucose units. It can be made from wood pulp and is used to manufacture rayon and cellulose-acetate plastics. Cellulose has an important role in the human diet as dietary *fibre.

Celsius scale The official name of the centigrade temperature scale. It was devised by the Swedish astronomer Anders Celsius (1701–44), who originally designated zero as the boiling point of water and 100° as the freezing point. The scale was later reversed. Celsius temperature, t, is defined by the equation $t = T - 273.15$, where T is the *thermodynamic temperature. Each degree Celsius is equal to one *kelvin.

Celtic languages A branch of the Indo-European language family formerly widespread in W Europe. It is divided into: Gaulish and Insular Celtic. The Gaulish languages are now extinct, being replaced in early medieval times by *Romance, Germanic, and other languages. Insular Celtic can be divided into a Goidelic branch (including *Manx and *Gaelic) and a Brythonic branch (including Welsh, *Cornish, and Breton).

Celts A people who occupied a large part of Iron Age Europe. They were known to the Greeks as Keltoi and to the Romans as Gauls. There were numerous Celtic tribes and chiefdoms sharing a culture that can be traced back to the Bronze Age of central Europe (c. 1200 BC). See also Druids.

cement A powdered mixture of calcium silicates and aluminates. On mixing with water it sets into a hard mass. **Portland cement** and similar materials are made by heating limestone with clay and grinding the product. Portland cement was invented by a British stonemason, Joseph Aspdin (1799–1855), and named after the stone quarried at Portland, Dorset, which it resembles. It is used in *mortars and in *concrete.

Cenozoic era (or Cainozoic era) The most recent geological era, beginning about 65 million years ago and following the *Mesozoic era. It includes both the *Tertiary and *Quaternary periods. During this era the mammals developed and became increasingly abundant, after the extinction of most of the reptiles dominant in the Mesozoic; the Cenozoic is sometimes known as the age of mammals.

centaur In Greek legend, a creature half-human and half-horse, living in the mountains of Thessaly and descended from Ixion, King of the Lapiths. They were defeated by the Lapiths in a battle after their unruly behaviour at the wedding of Ixion's son. See also Chiron.

centigrade scale. See Celsius scale.

centipede An *arthropod with long antennae and a slender flattened body of 15–181 segments. The first segment bears a pair of poison claws and nearly all the remaining segments bear a single pair of legs (compare millipede). Tropical centipedes can grow up to 280 mm long. Centipedes are found under stones, etc., during the day and at night prey on earthworms and insects. They lay eggs or produce live young.

Central African Federation. See Rhodesia and Nyasaland, Federation of.

Central African Republic (name from 1976 until 1979: Central African Empire) A country in central Africa, consisting mainly of a plateau lying at about 900 m (3000 ft). The dense forests in the S are drained by the River Ubangi, an important channel of communication. The population belongs to the Banda or Baya tribes. Economy: chiefly subsistence agriculture, although uranium and diamonds have been mined. The main exports are cotton and coffee. History: as Ubangi-Shari it was one of the four territories of French Equatorial Africa and from 1958 had internal self-government as a member of the French Community. It gained independence as the Central African Republic, becoming (1960–79) an empire under Jean-Bédel Bokassa. Head of state: President Kolingba. Official language: French; Sango is the national language. Official currency: CFA (Communauté financière africaine) franc of 100 centimes. Area: 625 000 sq km (241 250 sq mi). Population (1988 est): 2 860 000. Capital: Bangui.

Central America An isthmus of S North America, extending from the Isthmus of Tehuantepec to the NW border of Colombia and comprising an area of 596 000 sq km (230 000 sq mi). It consists of Belize, Costa Rica, El Salvador, Guatemala, Honduras, Nicaragua, and Panama, together with four Mexican states.

Central Criminal Court (The Old Bailey) The *Crown Court having the power to try all offences committed in the City of London and Greater London. The recorder of London and common serjeant are its permanent judges and judges of the Queen's Bench Division also sit.

Central Intelligence Agency (CIA) A US government department established in 1947 to coordinate US intelligence operations. It is not permitted to operate within the USA.

Central Region An administrative region in central Scotland, created under local government reorganization in 1975 from the counties of Clackmannan, most of Stirling, S Perth, and part of West Lothian. It consists of the lowland plain of the Rivers Forth and Teith rising to uplands in the N and S. Agriculture includes cattle and dairy farming in the W and arable and livestock farming in the E. Industry is important with coalmining and oil refining. Tourism thrives, especially around the Trossachs. Area: 2518 sq km (971 sq mi). Population (1987 est): 272 077. Administrative centre: Stirling.

centre of gravity A fixed point through which the resultant gravitational force on a body always passes.

centrifugal force. See centripetal force.

centripetal force A force on a moving body causing it to move in a curved path. An object is made to move in a circle by a centripetal force directed towards the centre. It has an acceleration towards the centre of v^2/r, where v is the object's velocity and r the radius of the circle.

The centripetal force is necessary to overcome the object's tendency to move in a straight line and appears to be balanced by an equal **centrifugal force** directed radially outwards.

ceorl The free peasant (as distinct from the slave) of Anglo-Saxon England. Economic pressures led to a worsening of the ceorl's position, and eventually he was absorbed amongst the unfree *villeins.

cèpe An edible mushroom, *Boletus edulis*. Common in temperate woodlands from August to November, it has a stout stalk and a brown to white hemispherical cap 6–20 cm in diameter.

Cepheid variable A luminous supergiant star the brightness of which varies regularly. The period between successive instants of maximum brightness depends on the *luminosity of the star. By measuring the period and the average brightness, a Cepheid's distance can be determined. *See also* variable stars. Cepheids occur in ours and other galaxies and are a means of measuring distances of galaxies up to about 20 million light years away.

ceramics Any nonmetallic material made by heat treatment into useful articles. The main categories are heavy articles of baked clay, such as bricks and tiles, materials that can withstand high temperatures, such as furnace linings, sintered articles, such as abrasives, and domestic products made from earthenware, stoneware, or *porcelain.

Cerberus In Greek legend, the monstrous dog who guarded the entrance to the underworld, usually portrayed as having three heads and a dragon's neck and tail. The final task of *Heracles was to overpower this monster.

cereals Grasses cultivated for their high yields of grain, which constitutes a major item in the diet of man and livestock. Wheat, rice, and maize are the most important cereals, but barley, oats, rye, and millet are also widely cultivated. *See also* arable farming.

cerebellum. *See* brain.

cerebral palsy Damage to the developing brain resulting in uncoordinated movements, muscular weakness, and paralysis (an affected child is called a spastic). The brain damage may be caused by injury during birth, insufficient oxygen before, during, or immediately after birth, or a viral infection. In some cases intelligence is affected. Treatment includes appropriate physiotherapy and special education; speech therapy may also be needed.

cerebrospinal fluid The fluid that surrounds the brain and spinal cord. It is produced by special blood vessels inside the brain and is reabsorbed by special bunches of veins. It acts as a shock absorber and support for the central nervous system.

cerebrum. *See* brain.

Ceres (astronomy) The largest *minor planet, 1003 km in diameter, and the first to be discovered (in 1801 by Piazzi). It orbits the sun every 4.6 years between 2.55 and 2.98 astronomical units from the sun.

Ceres (mythology). *See* Demeter.

cerium (Ce) The most abundant *lanthanide element, discovered in 1803 by Berzelius and

others. It is used as a catalyst and for polishing. At no 58; at wt 140.12; mp 799°C; bp 3426°C.

CERN (European Laboratory for Particle Physics; formerly Organisation (previously Conseil) européenne pour la Recherche nucléaire) A W European organization founded in 1954 to carry out nuclear research. Its headquarters are in Geneva.

Cervantes, Miguel de (1547–1616) Spanish novelist. In 1569 he went to Italy and fought at Lepanto in 1571. Returning to Spain in 1575, he was captured by pirates and imprisoned for five years. After 1580 he held several jobs in the civil service while writing his novel, *La Galatea* (1585), and several plays. *Don Quixote* (Part I, 1605; Part II, 1615), his novel about a self-deluding knight and cunning squire, Sancho Panza, won him fame but little reward.

Ceylon. *See* Sri Lanka, Democratic Socialist Republic of.

Cézanne, Paul (1839–1906) French postimpressionist painter. After studying law for two years, he was encouraged by his friend Emile *Zola to settle in Paris (1861). His early paintings failed to find favour and in 1872 he turned to *impressionism, a period represented by *The Suicide's House* (Louvre). Seeking more solidity he abandoned impressionism. Living mainly in Provence, he painted portraits, e.g. *The Card Players* (Louvre), still lifes, landscapes, and a series of *Bathers*.

c.g.s. system A metric system of units based on the centimetre, gram, and second. It has been replaced for scientific purposes by *SI units.

Chablis 47 49N 3 48E A village in central France, in the Yonne department, famous for the white wine named after it.

Chad, Republic of (French name: Tchad) A country consisting mainly of semidesert in N central Africa. The land rises from Lake Chad in the SW to the Tibesti Mountains in the N, reaching heights of about 3400 m (11 000 ft). The majority of the population (concentrated in the S) is Sara, a Bantu people; the nomadic peoples of the N are largely Muslims. *Economy*: mainly subsistence agriculture with livestock and fishing. The exports are cotton and meat. *History*: one of the four territories of French Equatorial Africa, it had internal self-government as a member of the

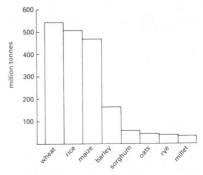

CEREALS *World production of cereals (1989).*

French Community from 1958, gaining independence in 1960. Since 1963 there has been ethnic unrest in the N. In 1990 the government was overthrown and the new president, Idriss Deby, promised democratic reform. Official language: French. Official currency: CFA (Communauté financière africaine) franc of 100 centimes. Area: 1 284 000 sq km (495 624 sq mi). Population (1987 est): 5 241 000. Capital: N'djamena (formerly Fort Lamy).

Chadwick, Sir James (1891–1974) British physicist, who worked at Cambridge with *Rutherford before discovering the *neutron in 1932; by studying the radiation produced by beryllium when bombarded with alpha particles, Chadwick was able to show that it consisted of neutrons. He was awarded the 1935 Nobel Prize.

chaffinch A *finch, *Fringilla coelebs*, about 15 cm long, common in woods and parks in Europe, W Asia, and N Africa. The male chaffinch has a chestnut back, pinkish breast, greyish-blue crown, and conspicuous white wing bars. The female has a duller plumage with a green back.

Chagall, Marc (1887–1985) Russian-born Jewish painter and printmaker. After studying in St Petersburg (1907–10), he visited Paris (1910), where he painted some of his best-known works, such as *Me and the Village* (1911; New York). His childlike distorted and sometimes inverted figures and objects influenced the surrealists. Moving to France (1922), he illustrated Gogol's *Dead Souls* and La Fontaine's *Fables*. During World War II he lived in the USA, where he designed ballet sets and costumes; he subsequently worked on mosaics and tapestries for the Israeli Knesset (1966).

Chagos Islands. *See* British Indian Ocean Territory.

Chain, Sir Ernst Boris (1906–79) British biochemist, born in Germany, who—with Lord *Florey at Oxford—isolated and purified penicillin. For their work, Chain, Florey, and Sir Alexander *Fleming (the discoverer of penicillin) were awarded a Nobel Prize (1945).

chain reaction A series of reactions in which the product of each reaction sets off further reactions. In a nuclear chain reaction each nuclear fission is brought about by a neutron ejected by a previous fission. For example, the fission of a uranium-235 nucleus produces either two or three neutrons each of which can bring about the fission of another uranium-235 nucleus. Chain reactions are the source of energy in *nuclear reactors and *nuclear weapons.

chalcedony A minutely grained sometimes fibrous *silica mineral. The numerous varieties include carnelian (red); agate, onyx, and sardonyx (banded); jasper (red or brown); and chert and flint (grey or black). The last two occur in limestones; others occur mainly in veins and volcanic rock.

Chalcidice (Modern Greek name: Khalkidhikí) A peninsula in NE Greece. It ends in three promontories, the northernmost of which contains Mount Athos; these are mostly wooded and mountainous. Area: 2945 sq km (1149 sq mi). Population (1981): 79 036.

chalcopyrite The principal ore of copper, sometimes called copper pyrites, $CuFeS_2$. It is yellow with a greenish streak.

Chaldea (*or* Chaldaea) The region of S Babylonia in which the new Babylonian empire was established by Nabopolassar (d. 605 BC) in 625 in the last years of the Assyrian empire. At its height under *Nebuchadnezzar II (reigned 604–562), the Chaldean empire, centred on the rebuilt city of Babylon, dominated the Middle East until overthrown by the Achaemenians in 539.

chalk A sedimentary rock, a white fine-grained variety of *limestone (calcium carbonate). Coccoliths (the remains of extinct unicellular organisms) are the main constituents of chalk although other invertebrate remains are included. Chalk is characteristic of the Upper *Cretaceous period in W Europe. Pieces of flint are often found in chalk; these are formed from the remains of silica-containing organisms.

chamberlain An officer appointed by a monarch, nobleman, or corporation to perform ceremonial duties. The chamberlains of medieval England were financial officers of great political importance. The chamberlain was succeeded by the Lord Chamberlain, who is responsible for the administration of the royal household. Until 1968 he also licensed plays for public performance.

Chamberlain, Joseph (1836–1914) British politician, who was mayor of Birmingham (1873–76), and became a Liberal MP in 1876. In 1886 he split the Liberal Party because of Gladstone's support of Irish Home Rule. In 1895 he became colonial secretary in the Conservative Government. His reputation grew during the *Boer War but his commitment to imperial preference caused a rift in the Conservative ranks, which led to his resignation (1903) and contributed to the election of the Liberals in 1906. His eldest son **Sir (Joseph) Austen Chamberlain** (1863–1937) became a Liberal-Unionist MP in 1892. He was chancellor of the exchequer (1919–21) and then foreign secretary (1924–29), when he presided over the *Locarno Pact; he was awarded the Nobel Peace Prize (1925). Joseph's son by his second marriage **(Arthur) Neville Chamberlain** (1869–1940) was a Conservative MP and prime minister (1937–40) of the National Government. His appeasement of the fascist powers and three visits to Hitler in 1938 resulted in the *Munich Agreement, which recognized Germany's possession of the Sudetenland. Claiming to have brought "peace for our time" he did buy time to rearm, but was forced by Hitler's invasion of Czechoslovakia to abandon appeasement. He declared war after Hitler's attack on Poland but resigned in May, 1940, when he joined Churchill's cabinet.

chamber music Music written to be played in the intimacy of a room rather than a large hall. In the baroque period chamber sonatas were distinguished from church sonatas and in the late 18th century Haydn, Mozart, and Beethoven established the piano trio (violin, cello, and piano), the duo sonata (one instrument and piano), and the string quartet (two violins, viola, and cello) as the main chamber music forms. Chamber music has been written for other combinations of players, including the woodwind quintet (oboe, flute, clarinet, horn, and bassoon), the clarinet quintet (clarinet and string quartet), and the piano quintet (piano and string quartet).

chameleon An African tree-dwelling lizard characterized by its ability to change its skin colour. 17–25 cm long, chameleons have a narrow body, a sticky tongue that can be extended to catch insects, and bulging eyes that can move independently. Some species have a helmet-shaped head or conspicuous horns. They may be green, yellow, or brown, often with spots, and change colour by concentrating or dispersing the pigment in their skin cells.

chamois An agile *ruminant, *Rupicapra rupicapra*, of mountainous regions in Europe and SW Asia. Chamois grow to about 75 cm high and have narrow horns with backward-pointing hooked tips. The soft skin is used for cleaning glass, although chamois leather is now usually derived from sheep and goats.

chamomile. *See* camomile.

champagne A sparkling wine, produced around Reims and Épernay, NE France from black (*pinot noir*) and white (*pinot chardonnay*) grapes. Addition of sugar syrup determines whether it will be sweet (*sec*) or dry (*brut*) champagne.

Champagne A former province in NE France, now part of the planning region of **Champagne-Ardenne.** It began to produce the sparkling *champagne at the end of the 17th century.

Chancery, Court of In English law, the court in which the system of *equity developed in the 15th century, as the personal court of the king's chief law officer, the Lord Chancellor, in which he dealt with cases for which the *common law could not provide a remedy. In 1875 it was joined to the Supreme Court of Judicature; it survives as the Chancery Division of the High Court.

Chandigarh 30 43N 76 47E A Union Territory and modern (1953) city in NW India, on the Haryana–Punjab border. The joint capital of both states, it was planned by *Le Corbusier in 30 rectangular sectors for housing, government, and industry. Punjab University was established here in 1947. Area: 114 sq km (44 sq mi). Population (1981 est): 451 610.

Chandler, Raymond (1888–1959) US novelist. Educated at Dulwich College, England, he returned to the USA and worked in business before starting to write detective stories in the 1930s. The detective Philip Marlowe features in all his nine novels, including *The Big Sleep* (1939) and *The Long Goodbye* (1954).

Chang Jiang. *See* Yangtze River.

Channel Islands (French name: Îles Normandes) A group of islands in the English Channel, off the coast of NW France. They comprise *Jersey (the largest), *Guernsey, *Alderney, and *Sark. Since the Norman conquest (1066) they have been a dependency of the British Crown. During World War II they were the only British territory to come under German oc-

cupation. Tourism is important but the islands are also noted for their early agricultural and horticultural produce. The Jersey and Guernsey breeds of cattle are world famous. Area: 194 sq km (75 sq mi). Population (1986): 144 494.

Channel tunnel (*or* Chunnel) A tunnel linking Britain with France. First suggested to Napoleon in 1802, digging was started by two private companies in 1882. The government intervened on security grounds and the scheme was abandoned in 1883. In 1964 the two governments revived the project and in the early 1970s work again started, to be abandoned on economic grounds in 1974. Work upon a high-speed rail tunnel began in 1987, with construction of the tunnel to be completed in 1993.

chanterelle An edible mushroom, *Cantharellus cibarius*, occurring in temperate woodlands. It is funnel-shaped and yellow with the gills clearly visible and measures 3–10 cm across the cap. The flesh is regarded as a delicacy if cooked slowly.

Chantilly 49 12N 2 28E A town in France, in the Oise department near the Forest of Chantilly. Once renowned for its lace making, Chantilly is famous for its racecourse and the Grand Château's art collection. Population (1982 est): 10 208.

Chaos In earliest Greek mythology, the goddess representing the primeval emptiness from which evolved Night, Erebus (darkness), Tartarus (the underworld), and Eros (desire).

Chaplin, Charlie (Sir Charles C.; 1889–1977) US film actor, born in Britain. Recruited by the Keystone Studio while touring the USA with Fred Karno's pantomime company in 1913, he gained immediate success with his portrayals of the tramp, a pathetic figure dressed in baggy trousers and a bowler hat. From 1918 he wrote and directed his own films, including *The Gold Rush* (1924), *City Lights* (1931), and, following the introduction of sound, *Modern Times* (1936) and *The Great Dictator* (1940). Accused of having communist sympathies, he left the USA in 1952 to live in Switzerland. He was awarded an Oscar in 1973 and was knighted in 1976.

char A food and game fish related to the *trout, found in Arctic coastal waters and fresh waters of Europe and North America. Its torpedo-shaped body, about 30 cm long, is green with yellow spots above and silvery or bright red below.

Chardin, Jean-Baptiste-Siméon (1699–1779) French painter of still lifes and domestic interiors after the Dutch tradition, e.g. *The Housewife* (Louvre) and *The Young Schoolmistress* (National Gallery, London).

Charlemagne (c. 742–814) King of the Franks (771–814). The son of Pepin the Short, he conquered the Saxon tribes (772–81) and became King of Lombardy (773). In 778 he campaigned in NE Spain, where at Roncesvalles his champion Roland, later the hero of the *Chanson de Roland*, was killed. In 800, having conquered most of western Christendom, he was crowned emperor of the West by Pope Leo III.

Charles (Philip Arthur George) (1948–) Prince of Wales and heir-apparent to the throne of the United Kingdom as the eldest son of Elizabeth II. After studying at Trinity College, Cambridge (1967–70), he served in the RAF and the Royal Navy before undertaking public duties. In 1981 he married Lady Diana Spencer (1961–). Their first child, Prince William Arthur Philip Louis of Wales was born in 1982 and their second, Prince Henry Charles Albert David, in 1984.

Charles I (1600–49) King of England, Scotland, and Ireland (1625–49), succeeding his father James I. His first three parliaments (1625; 1626; 1628–29) were dominated by hostile Puritans. Charles resorted to imposing taxes without parliamentary consent and ruled without parliament from 1629 to 1640. His attempt to introduce *Laud's Anglican prayer book in Presbyterian Scotland led to the Bishops' Wars (1639–40), the financial demands of which forced Charles to summon the Short Parliament (April–May 1640). The *Long Parliament, summoned in November following Charles' defeat by the Scots, demanded far-reaching reforms. Charles attempted to arrest five members of the House of Commons and in April 1642 the *Civil War broke out. After his defeat at Naseby (1645), his cause was lost and he surrendered to the Scots at Newark in 1646. Charles was found guilty of treason and beheaded (30 January, 1649).

Charles (II) the Bald (823–77) Holy Roman Emperor (875–77) and, as Charles I, King of France (843–77). After the death of his father Louis I, civil war broke out between Charles and his three older brothers. By 843 Charles had gained by the Treaty of Verdun the western Frankish territories, which eventually became France.

Charles II (1630–85) King of England, Scotland, and Ireland (1660–85). He fought with his father, Charles I, in the *Civil War and, after his father's execution (1649), was crowned by the Scots. Defeated by Cromwell (1651), he was forced into exile. After the fall of the Protectorate (1659), George Monck arranged the *Restoration of the monarchy and Charles became king. In 1662 he married Catherine of Braganza. At first dependent on the Earl of *Clarendon (1609–74), Charles was forced to dismiss his adviser (1667) after the failure of the Dutch War of 1665–67 and replaced him with the *Cabal. His Roman Catholic sympathies became clear with his Declaration of Indulgence (1672), which dropped the laws against Dissenters and Roman Catholics. Parliament responded with the Test Act (1673) preventing Dissenters and Roman Catholics from taking office, which together with the unpopular Dutch War of 1672–74 destroyed the Cabal. Fear of Roman Catholicism coupled with Catherine's childlessness, came to a head with the *Popish Plot (1678), which spread rumours of a Catholic plot to murder Charles and place his Roman Catholic brother and heir, later James II, on the throne. Charles resisted subsequent parliamentary attempts to exclude James from the succession and from 1681 ruled without parliament. On his deathbed he acknowledged his Roman Catholicism.

Charles (V) the Wise (1337–80) King of France (1364–80) during the Hundred Years' War with England. As regent (1356–60) for his father John II, Charles suppressed the peasants' revolt known as the Jacquerie (1358). Between 1369 and 1375 he regained most of the territory lost to England by the disastrous Treaty of Brétigny (1360).

Charles V (1500–58) Holy Roman Emperor (1519–56). Charles inherited Burgundy and the Netherlands (1506) from his father Philip of Burgundy (1478–1506); he became King of Spain and Naples (1516) on the death of his maternal grandfather Ferdinand II of Aragon and Holy Roman Emperor on the death of his paternal grandfather Maximilian I. Charles' possessions provoked warfare with Francis I of France (1494–1547; reigned 1515–47): in 1525, having defeated Francis at Pavia, Charles briefly took the French king prisoner and in 1527, in response to an alliance between France, the papacy, Venice, and Milan, Charles' troops sacked Rome. Their contest for European control ended inconclusively with the Treaty of Crépy (1544). The emergence of the *Reformation in 1521 led Charles to preside over the Diet of Worms, which condemned *Luther. His subsequent attempts to make peace with the Protestants failed and in 1546 Charles took up arms against the Protestant Schmalkaldic League, defeating it at Mühlberg (1547). In 1551, however, two German Protestant rulers allied with Henry II of France and Charles was forced to accept Protestant demands. Exhausted by the problems of his Empire, Charles retired to a Spanish monastery, dividing his possessions between his son, who became *Philip II of Spain, and his brother, Emperor Ferdinand I (1503–64).

Charles (VI) the Well-Beloved (1368–1422) King of France (1380–1422). Conflict for the regency, following his attacks of insanity (from 1392) led to civil war between the Armagnacs and the Burgundians. In 1415 Henry V of England defeated the French at *Agincourt. After further campaigns Henry married (1420) Charles' daughter Catherine of Valois (1401–37) and was named as regent of France and Charles' heir.

Charles VI (1685–1740) Holy Roman Emperor (1711–40), who issued the Pragmatic Sanction (1713) to secure the succession of his daughter *Maria Theresa to his Austrian possessions. His claim (1700) to the Spanish throne gave rise to the War of the *Spanish Succession (1701–14), in which he was unsuccessful. In 1716–18 and 1736–39 he fought the Turks; he lost the War of the Polish Succession (1733–38).

Charles VII (1403–61) King of France (1422–61). He suffered losses to the invading English and their Burgundian allies until 1429 when, with *Joan of Arc, he regained Orleans. By 1453, he had driven the English from all of France, except Calais. *See also* Hundred Years' War.

Charles VII (1697–1745) Holy Roman Emperor (1742–45) during the War of the *Austrian Succession. The Elector of Bavaria (1726–45), Charles joined the alliance against Maria

Theresa when she claimed the Austrian inheritance. He was elected emperor in opposition to Maria Theresa's husband Francis (subsequently Emperor Francis I).

Charles IX (1550–74) King of France (1560–74) during the *Wars of Religion. His mother *Catherine de' Medici dominated his reign and was largely responsible for the *Saint Bartholomew's Day Massacre of Huguenots that Charles ordered in 1572.

Charles X (1757–1836) King of France (1824–30). Charles lived abroad after the French revolution, returning at the Bourbon restoration (1815), when he became leader of the ultraroyalist party. His reactionary rule led to his overthrow (1830) and he fled to England.

Charles Edward Stuart, the Young Pretender (1720–88) The son of the Old Pretender, *James Edward Stuart. Known as Bonnie Prince Charlie, in 1745 he landed in Scotland, rallied his *Jacobite supporters and marched S to claim the English throne. After withdrawal to Scotland, he was defeated at Culloden (1746), but escaped to exile in Europe.

Charles's law For a gas at constant pressure, its volume is directly proportional to its *thermodynamic temperature. The law is closely approximated in gases above their critical state. An alternative statement is that gases expand by 1/273 of their volume at 0°C for every 1°C rise in temperature. Named after Jacques Charles (1746–1823).

Charleston 38 23N 81 40W A city in the USA, the capital of West Virginia. It was the home (1788–95) of Daniel Boone. Industries include chemicals, glass, and paints. Population (1985 est): 59 371.

Charleston 32 48N 79 58W A city in the USA, in South Carolina near the Atlantic coast. Founded in 1670, the first (1861) military action of the US Civil War took place here. A major port, its manufactures include fertilizer, paper, and steel. Population (1988 est): 80 900.

Charleston A ballroom dance of the 1920s named after Charleston, South Carolina, where it had been a popular dance in the early 1900s. It became a national craze following the Black musical *Runnin' Wild* (1923) with its syncopated rhythms, and toe-in steps.

Charleston, Battles of Two battles of the *American Revolution fought at Charleston, South Carolina. In the first (1776) the Americans drove back the British, whose invasion of the South was thus delayed. In the second the Americans surrendered (12 May, 1780) Charleston after a 45-day siege.

Charlton, Bobby (Robert C.; 1937–) British Association footballer, who played for Manchester United (1956–73) and also for England (106 times scoring 49 goals). He was a member of the England team that won the 1966 World Cup.

Charon In Greek legend, the ferryman who carried the souls of the dead over the Rivers Styx and Acheron to the underworld. Only the correctly buried dead were taken. A coin placed in the mouth of the corpse was his payment.

Chartism A British working-class movement for political reform, centring on the London Working Men's Association (LWMA). Founded in June, 1836 by William Lovett (1800–77), the LWMA drew up a People's Charter (1838) of six points: the right to vote for all males, the secret ballot, equal electoral districts, abolition of property qualifications for MPs, payment of MPs, and annual general elections. Their Charter with 1.2 million signatures was rejected by parliament (1839), as were their two later petitions (1842, 1848). Chartism lost support in the 1840s because of rivalry between its leaders, Lovett and Feargus O'Connor (1794–1855), reviving trade, and greater prosperity. The movement had died by the end of the decade.

Chartres 48 27N 1 30E A town in N central France, the capital of the Eure-et-Loire department on the River Eure. The principal market town of the Beauce region its gothic cathedral (begun c. 1194) has 13th-century stained glass. Population (1983 est): 38 715.

Charybdis See Scylla and Charybdis.

Chatham, 1st Earl of. See Pitt the Elder, William.

Chaucer, Geoffrey (c. 1342–1400) English poet, who visited Europe as a soldier and diplomat, held positions in the customs service, and received pensions from Richard II and Henry IV. His poems *The Book of the Duchess* and *The Parliament of Fowls* were inspired by the French tradition of the dream poem. Chaucer also wrote a mock version of Dante's *Divine Comedy* in *The House of Fame* and used Boccaccio's poem *Il filostrato* as the basis for *Troilus and Criseyde*. His best-known work is *The Canterbury Tales*, a collection of stories told by a group of pilgrims travelling from London to Canterbury.

Cheddar 51 17N 2 46W A village in SW England, in Somerset, famous for its cheese and for the caves and rare limestone flora of the **Cheddar Gorge**, a pass through the Mendip Hills. Population (1983): 3994.

cheese A dairy product made from milk solids (curd), separated from the liquid (whey) by coagulating milk with rennet or some other enzyme. The curd is then salted, pressed into blocks, and left to mature. Cheese is a rich source of protein and calcium. It contains fat but little carbohydrate since most of it is removed with the whey.

cheetah A large *cat, *Acinonyx jubatus*, of Africa and SW Asia, also called hunting leopard. It has a reddish-yellow coat with black spots and grows to about 2 m in length. The fastest mammals, sprinting at up to 110 km per hour (70 mph), they run down their prey.

Chekhov, Anton Pavlovich (1860–1904) Russian dramatist and short-story writer. He studied medicine at Moscow University and developed as a writer after graduating in 1884. Suffering from tuberculosis, he bought a farm at Melikhovo in 1892 and, after 1897, lived at Yalta in the Crimea. His first play, *The Seagull* (1896), failed at first but succeeded triumphantly when revived in 1898 by Stanislavsky's Moscow Art Theatre. His major plays—*Uncle Vanya* (1897),

The Three Sisters (1901), and *The Cherry Orchard* (1904)–were written for this company.

Chelsea A residential district in the Greater London borough of Kensington and Chelsea, on the N bank of the River Thames. It is noted for the Chelsea Royal Hospital for old soldiers (Chelsea Pensioners), designed by *Wren and completed in 1692.

Cheltenham 51 54N 2 04W A town in SW England, in Gloucestershire. A fashionable spa town in the 18th century, it is famous for its schools (Cheltenham College, a boys' public school, and Cheltenham Ladies' College) and racecourse. Population (1984): 86 400.

chemical bond The force that holds the atoms together in a molecule or the ions together in a crystalline solid. In **covalent bonds**, atoms are held together by sharing pairs of electrons in their outer shells (*see* atomic theory). In the **electrovalent** (*or* ionic) **bond** an outer electron is transferred from one atom to another so that ions are formed. The electrostatic force between the ions holds the molecule or crystal together. **Coordinate** (*or* dative) **bonds** are covalent bonds in which both electrons are donated by the same atom.

chemical reaction A process in which one or more chemical substances change to other substances. Chemical reaction involves rearrangement of electrons between reacting species to form different molecules.

chemical warfare The use of toxic substances to kill or disable personnel, pollute food or water supplies, etc. Chlorine, phosgene, and mustard gas were used in World War I. Chemical weapons range from the relatively humane *tear gas to the lethal *nerve gases.

chemisorption. *See* adsorption.

chemistry The scientific study of matter, especially the changes and interactions it can undergo. *Aristotle's view that matter was composed of four elements (earth, air, fire, water) persisted from the 4th century BC until it was demolished by Robert *Boyle in his *Skeptical Chymist* (1661). The modern concept of an *element was provided by Boyle, who also correctly distinguished between elements, compounds, and mixtures. The explanation of the structure of compounds in terms of the elements was developed by such 18th-century chemists as *Cavendish, *Priestley, and *Lavoisier. *Dalton's atomic theory, produced at the beginning of the 19th century, led to further advances. However, it was not until the beginning of the 20th century that the work of J. J. Thomson and Rutherford (*see* atomic theory) enabled the electronic theory of *valence to emerge, making sense of the work of Newlands and *Mendeleyev in ordering the elements into the *periodic table. **Inorganic chemistry** is concerned with the study of all these elements (except carbon) and their compounds and interactions. **Organic chemistry** is the study of the enormous number of compounds of carbon. **Physical chemistry** is concerned with the application of physics to a more exact assessment of the structures of compounds and the laws that control chemical reactions.

Chemnitz (name 1953–90: Karl-Marx-Stadt) 50 49N 12 50E A city in SE Germany, on the River Chemnitz. Formerly a textile centre, it became famous for machine construction in the 19th century. Population (1990 est): 300 000.

chemoreception The reception by an organism of chemical stimuli. In man and other air-breathing vertebrates, the chemicals in food, etc., are sensed by taste buds on the tongue and walls of the mouth, while airborne chemicals are detected by smell (olfactory) receptors in the lining of the nasal passages (*see also* pheromone). Both smell and taste organs are present in fish; worms and other lower animals have only a general sensitivity to chemicals over the body surface. Chemoreception is used by animals for locating and identifying other organisms, food sources, etc.

chemotherapy The treatment of disease by drugs. Coined by Paul *Ehrlich, chemotherapy originally referred to chemicals used to treat infectious diseases (e.g. salvarsan for syphilis) and was later expanded to include antibiotics. It now usually refers to the treatment of cancer by drugs as distinct from X-rays (*see* radiotherapy).

Chequers (*or* Chequers Court) A country house in S England, in Buckinghamshire near Princes Risborough. Dating from 1565, it has been the official country residence of British prime ministers since 1921, when it was given to the nation by Arthur Hamilton, 1st Viscount Lee of Fareham (1868–1947).

Cherbourg 49 38N 1 37W A seaport in NW France, in the Manche department on the Cotentin Peninsula. Cherbourg has civil and military docks and large shipbuilding yards. Formerly an important transatlantic port, Cherbourg still has a cross-channel service to Southampton. Population (1982 est): 30 112.

Cherenkov, Pavel Alekseievich (1904–) Soviet physicist, who in 1934 discovered **Cherenkov radiation**, the blue-white light produced by the atoms of a medium through which a charged particle is passing at more than the speed of light. Three years later the effect was explained by James Franck (1882–1964) and Igor Tamm (1895–1971). The three physicists shared the 1958 Nobel Prize.

Chernobyl 51 17N 30 15E A town in the SW Soviet Union, in the Ukrainian SSR. In 1986 the nuclear reactor here exploded, causing the deaths of 31 people at the time and 220 people later and the release of a radioactive cloud causing fallout in many parts of the world. *See* nuclear power.

Cherokee A North American Indian people of the hill country of E Tennessee and North Carolina, speaking an Iroquoian language. They lived in farming towns of 30 to 60 log cabins.

cherry A tree of the rose family, of N temperate regions, having small fruits surrounding a stone containing a seed. Cherry trees produce clusters of white or pinkish flowers, and some varieties are grown only for ornament. Sour cherries include the morello, whose dark-red fruits are used in jams and liqueurs. Sweet dessert cherries arose from the gean (*Prunus avium*), native to Eurasia and N Africa. Found in woods and hedges, it grows to 25 m. Fruits of cultivated forms vary from pale yellow to dark red.

cherubim and seraphim Supernatural beings who are the two highest orders of angels in the heavenly hierarchy. The seraphim are described by Isaiah (Isaiah 6.2–7) as six-winged attendants upon God's throne. The cherubim are traditionally shown as winged heads.

chervil An annual herb, *Anthriscus cerefolium*, of the carrot family. 30–50 cm high, it is grown for its leaves for salads and seasonings. Its white flowers grow in clusters. A native of central, E, and S Europe, it grows on waste ground throughout Europe, the Americas, N Africa, and New Zealand.

Cherwell, Viscount *See* Lindemann, Frederick Alexander, 1st Viscount Cherwell.

Chesapeake Bay The largest inlet on the USA's Atlantic coast, bordering on Virginia and Maryland. Length: approximately 320 km (200 mi).

Cheshire A county in NW England, bordering on Wales. It consists chiefly of the low-lying Cheshire Plain rising to the Pennines in the E. It is predominantly agricultural. Industries include chemicals and textiles. Area: 2322 sq km (897 sq mi). Population (1987 est): 951 900. Administrative centre: Chester.

Cheshire, (Geoffrey) Leonard, Group Capt (1917–   ) British philanthropist. In the RAF during World War II, he won the Victoria Cross. His horror at the atomic bombing of Nagasaki led him to found the Cheshire Foundation Homes for the incurably sick, of which there are 222 in 44 countries. He married (1959) **Sue, Baroness Ryder** (1923–   ), who founded the Sue Ryder Foundation for the Sick and Disabled of All Age Groups.

chess A board game for two players, each of whom controls 16 pieces. The the object of the game is to force the opponent's king into a position from which it cannot escape. A player attempts to weaken his opponent by capturing his pieces (other than the king). The game is complicated with a vast literature devoted to its tactics and strategy. 2nd century chess pieces demonstrate the game's antiquity. Well known to 5th-century Hindus, it reached Europe, via Persia and Arabia, in the 10th century. The rules have hardly changed since the 16th century, although the identities of some of the pieces have. Since 1922 the rules have been controlled by the Fédération internationale des Échecs (FIDE), which has also organized world championships since 1946. *See* p. 118.

Chester 53 12N 2 54W A city in NW England, the administrative centre of Cheshire on the River Dee. It was a Roman fortress (Deva) and a medieval walled city and port (the walls remain intact and there are many half-timbered buildings). Its cathedral dates from the 11th century. Chester is a commercial and railway centre, with clothing and metallurgical industries. Population (1988): 58 500.

Chesterfield 53 15N 1 25W A town in N central England, in Derbyshire. Its 14th-century parish church has a famous crooked spire. Chesterfield's industries include engineering, iron founding, chemicals, glass, and pottery. Population (1988 est): 72 000.

Chesterton, G(ilbert) K(eith) (1874–1936) British essayist, novelist, and poet. His detective stories, beginning with *The Innocence of Father Brown* (1911), were highly successful. With Hilaire Belloc, who he met in 1900, he was an opponent of the socialism of G. B. Shaw and H. G. Wells. Converted to Roman Catholicism in 1922, he wrote a number of religious books, such as *St Francis of Assisi* (1923). Other books include *Dickens* (1906) and *The Victorian Age in Literature* (1913) as well as the fictional works *The Napoleon of Notting Hill* (1904) and *The Man Who Was Thursday* (1908).

chestnut A tree, *Castanea sativa*, of the beech family, also called sweet or Spanish chestnut, bearing large brown edible nuts inside prickly burs. Native to Europe and N Africa and widely grown, it reaches a height of 30 m. The leaves are toothed and pointed and the flowers grow in yellow catkins, 10–12 cm long. *Compare* horse chestnut.

Chevalier, Maurice (1888–1972) French singer and actor. An entertainer in Parisian revues, he went to Hollywood in the 1930s and starred in many successful musical films, including *Love Me Tonight* (1932), *Love in the Afternoon* (1957), and *Gigi* (1958).

Cheviot Hills A range of hills in the UK. They extend along the border between Scotland and England, mainly in Northumberland, reaching 816 m (2677 ft) at The Cheviot.

chevrotain A small deerlike animal, also called mouse deer, of SE Asia. Measuring 20–33 cm at the shoulder, their brownish coats have white underparts; some species have white stripes or spots. They are not true deer, lacking antlers; males have enlarged upper canine teeth that form tusks.

Cheyenne An Algonkian-speaking North American Indian people of the Plains region. They lived in what is now Minnesota but wars between the tribes forced them to abandon farming and become wandering buffalo-hunters in the Plains. The northern branch was present at the battle of the Little Bighorn (1876).

Cheyenne 41 08N 104 50W A city in the USA, the capital and largest city of Wyoming. It is an agricultural trading centre. Population (1988 est): 50 600.

Chiang Ch'ing. *See* Jiang Qing.

Chiang Ching-kuo. *See* Chiang Kai-shek.

Chiang Kai-shek (or Jiang Jie Shi; 1887–1975) Nationalist Chinese soldier and statesman. He took part in the overthrow of the *Qing dynasty in 1911 and in 1925 became leader of the Guomindang (Nationalist People's Party). Originally allied with the communists (*see* China), the Nationalists began fighting the communists in 1927; following Japan's defeat in World War II civil war again broke out. Chiang was forced to flee to *Taiwan in 1949, where he established the Republic of China. His son **Jiang Jing Guo** (or Chiang Ching-kuo; 1910–   ), prime minister (1971–78) and president (1978–88) studied in the Soviet Union and married a Russian. On returning to China in 1937, he joined the Guomindang, fleeing with his father to Taiwan in 1949.

CHESS

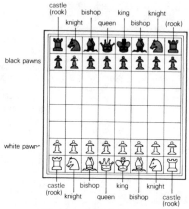

The chessboard ready for play. A white square is always on the player's right. The queen always starts on a square of her own colour.

BLACK

	a	b	c	d	e	f	g	h	
8	QR1 QR8	QN1 QN8	QB1 QB8	Q1 Q8	K1 K8	KB1 KB8	KN1 KN8	KR1 KR8	**8**
7	QR2 QR7	QN2 QN7	QB2 QB7	Q2 Q7	K2 K7	KB2 KB7	KN2 KN7	KR2 KR7	**7**
6	QR3 QR6	QN3 QN6	QB3 QB6	Q3 Q6	K3 K6	KB3 KB6	KN3 KN6	KR3 KR6	**6**
5	QR4 QR5	QN4 QN5	QB4 QB5	Q4 Q5	K4 K5	KB4 KB5	KN4 KN5	KR4 KR5	**5**
4	QR5 QR4	QN5 QN4	QB5 QB4	Q5 Q4	K5 K4	KB5 KB4	KN5 KN4	KR5 KR4	**4**
3	QR6 QR3	QN6 QN3	QB6 QB3	Q6 Q3	K6 K3	KB6 KB3	KN6 KN3	KR6 KR3	**3**
2	QR7 QR2	QN7 QN2	QB7 QB2	Q7 Q2	K7 K2	KB7 KB2	KN7 KN2	KR7 KR2	**2**
1	QR8 QR1	QN8 QN1	QB8 QB1	Q8 Q1	K8 K1	KB8 KB1	KN8 KN1	KR8 KR1	**1**
	a	b	c	d	e	f	g	h	

WHITE

Chess notations. In the algebraic notation each square is referred to by a file letter a–h and a rank number 1–8. In the descriptive notation the files bear the names of the piece on the first rank. The ranks are counted 1–8 away from the player.

The king, weak and vulnerable, moves only one square at a time (in any direction). The name of the game is a corruption of the Persian word for king–shah.

The queen, the most powerful piece, moves any distance in any direction. Originally known as the counsellor, its present name and moves were adopted in the 15th century.

The castle or rook moves any distance vertically or horizontally. Originally represented as a chariot (Arabic: rukh), it is known in many languages as a castle or tower (French: tour).

The knight, the only piece to jump over other pieces, moves one square horizontally and two vertically or two horizontally and one vertically. Usually represented by a horse's head, it is sometimes known as the horse (as it was in the Arabic version).

The bishop moves in any direction diagonally. In the Hindu and Arabic games the piece was called an elephant. In the European games the piece has acquired a variety of identities: a bishop in English, a jester (fou) in French, a runner (Laufer) in German, but still an elephant (slon) in Russian.

The pawn moves forward one square (or two on its first move). In Arabic it was a foot-soldier, the English word deriving from the Latin pes, pedis. In some European languages the piece is called a peasant (e.g. German: Bauer).

chiaroscuro (Italian: light-dark) The overall pattern of light and shade in a picture. Controlled chiaroscuro was an important element of *Renaissance composition, while strong contrasts of light and shade were a main feature of *baroque painting. Chiaroscuro is displayed to supreme effect in the etchings of *Rembrandt and *Whistler.

Chicago 41 50N 87 45N A city and major port in the USA, in Illinois on Lake Michigan. The third largest city in the country, its manufactures include iron and steel, textiles, and chemicals and there are large grain mills and meat-packing plants. The first of its skyscrapers was built in 1887; the Sears Tower (1974) is the world's tallest office building, 443 m (1454 ft). *History*: founded in 1803, it became a city in 1837. In 1871 it was almost completely destroyed by fire. Population (1986): 3 009 530.

Chichén Itzá A Maya city in N Yucatán (Mexico), it was the centre of a wide area under Toltec influence from the late 10th to the 13th centuries. Remains include El Castillo (a pyramidal temple mound), an astronomical observatory, and a cenote (natural well), in which sacrificial objects have been found.

Chichester 50 50N 0 48W A market town in S England, the administrative centre of West Sussex. Chichester has Roman remains and a cathedral dating from the 11th century. Other buildings include a 16th-century octagonal market cross and the Festival Theatre (1962). Population (1981): 24 189.

chickenpox A common infectious virus disease. Usually contracted in childhood, it normally gives an immunity that lasts for life. At the end of the incubation period (about a fortnight) the patient develops a fever and an irritating rash. Small raised spots appear on the chest and spread over the body, face, and limbs. The spots become reddened blisters, which dry and flake off, usually in less than a week. The patient is infectious until the last blister has flaked off. *See also* shingles.

chick pea An annual plant, *Cicer arietinum*, of the pea family, up to 40 cm high, with whitish flowers and edible pealike seeds. Probably native to W Asia, it is the chief pulse of India, where cooked seeds are called dhal.

chicory A perennial herb, *Cichorium intybus*, of the daisy family, 30–120 cm high, with blue flowers. The ground roots yield chicory, a coffee additive, while the leaves are used in salads. A native of Eurasia and N Africa, it is widely cultivated. *See also* endive.

chiffchaff A woodland *warbler, *Phylloscopus collybita*, about 10 cm long, with a grey-green plumage and whitish underparts. It occurs in Europe and W Asia during the summer and winters in S Europe and Africa. It can be recognized by its "chiff-chaff" call.

chigger. *See* harvest mite.

Chihuahua A breed of dog originating from an ancient Mexican breed and developed in the USA. Its coat is either smooth and glossy or long and soft. Height: about 13 cm.

Children's Crusade (1212) A strange episode of the *Crusades, in which some 50 000 children set out from France and Germany to capture Jerusalem. None reached their destination and few returned home, most being sold into slavery.

Chile, Republic of A country in South America, extending in a narrow strip along the W coast of the S half of the continent. It includes many islands and half of Tierra del Fuego. The country is dominated by the Andes, which are separated from a lower coastal range by a central valley. The majority of the population is of mixed Spanish and Indian descent. *Economy*: based chiefly on the export of minerals, notably copper and iron ore. Coal, oil, and natural gas are also produced. The main crops are wheat, sugar beet, potatoes, and maize and there is an expanding wine industry. Fruit and forest production is growing and there are government attempts to promote the dairy industry. *History*: when Magellan sailed through (1520) the strait named after him, S Chile was occupied by Mapuche Indians, who continued to control the region until the 19th century. A Spanish colony was founded at Santiago in 1541 and Chile was attached to the viceroyalty of Peru. The revolt against Spain began in 1810, but victory over the Spaniards was achieved only in 1817 with the help of the Argentine liberator José de *San Martin. In 1818 the Republic of Chile was established under Bernardo O'Higgins. Head of state: President Patricio Aylwin. Official language: Spanish. Official currency: Chilean peso of 100 centavos. Area: 741 767 sq km (286 397 sq mi). Population (1988 est): 12 683 000. Capital: Santiago. Main port: Valparaiso.

chilli A tropical American variety of *capsicum, also called red pepper. The elongated hot-tasting red fruits, 2–3 cm long, are used, fresh or dried, in cooking and are also an essential ingredient of curry powder and tabasco sauce.

Chiltern Hills A chalk ridge in S central England. It extends NE from the Goring Gap in the Thames Valley, reaching 255 m (852 ft) at Coombe Hill. Many of its hills are covered with beech woods.

Chiltern Hundreds Since the mid-18th century, if an MP wishes to resign (which he may not do directly), he applies for a stewardship of the Chiltern Hundreds, which disqualifies him from membership of the Commons.

Chimera A legendary Greek fire-breathing monster with a lion's head, a goat's body, and a serpent's tail. After ravaging Lycia she was killed by Bellerophon. The name now applies to any fantastic imaginary creation.

chimpanzee An ape, *Pan troglodytes*, of West African forests. Chimpanzees are 100–170 cm tall and live in small groups, mostly on the ground, feeding chiefly on fruit and leaves. They communicate by facial expressions and calls and possess considerable intelligence, often using tools (such as branches).

Ch'in. *See* Qin.

China, People's Republic of A country in E Asia, ranging from the low-lying and densely populated plains of the NE to the high peaks of the Tibetan Plateau in the W. China proper falls into three natural regions around the three main rivers: the Yellow River in the N, the Yangtze in the centre, and the Xi Jiang in the S. Over 90% of the inhabitants are Han Chinese. *Economy*: mainly dependent upon agriculture, producing rice in the S, wheat and millet in the N, and livestock, especially pigs. Cotton is grown in the N and tea in the S. Coal is the major source of power. China has been self-sufficient in oil since 1973. Iron ore is the most important mineral deposit and China is the main world producer of tungsten ore. Exports include farm produce, textiles, and minerals. *History*: China is one of the world's oldest civilizations, going back over nearly 4000 years. The first important recorded dynasty was the Shang in the valley of the Yellow River (18th-12th centuries BC). From the 12th to the 3rd centuries BC the *Zhou spread S and E. Under the *Qin, in the 3rd century BC, the first Great Wall was built. Technological advances occured under the *Han dynasty (3rd century BC to the early 3rd century AD) and with the *Tang dynasty (7th-10th centuries) China reached the high point of its civilization. It was followed by the Song (10th-13th centuries), the *Mongol (13th-14th centuries), the *Ming (14th-17th centuries), and the *Qing, which lasted until 1912. British efforts to open up the country to free trade led to the Opium War in 1839 and to the opening of treaty ports (and also to the transfer of Hong Kong). Later trade was established with several European countries and Chinese opposition included the Taiping Rebellion (1851-64) and the Boxer Rebellion (1899-1900). In 1911 a revolution led by Sun Yat-sen ousted the Qing and a republic was set up. The 1920s saw the rise of the Guomindang (Nationalist People's Party) under Gen Chiang Kai-shek and the foundation of the Chinese Communist Party in 1921. In 1926 relations between them broke down and a struggle began that continued until after World War II, during which part of the country was occupied by Japan. In 1949 the Guomindang was defeated by the communists and a People's Republic was set up by *Mao Tsetung. Chiang Kai-shek retreated to *Taiwan. Since Mao's death (1976) Deng Xiao Ping (1904-) has been the dominant political figure. A period of liberalization was followed by military suppression of protests, including a massacre of students in Tiananmen Square, Peking, in 1989. Since 1971 China has had a seat at the UN. Official language: Mandarin Chinese. Official currency: yuan of 10 chiao and 100 fen. Area: 9 597 000 sq km (3 704 400 sq mi). Population (1988): 1 072 200 000. Capital: Peking. Main port: Shanghai.

china clay A mineral deposit consisting mainly of kaolin, a hydrous aluminium silicate. It is used for making high-grade china and porcelain and in many industrial processes, including paper making.

chinchilla A rodent widely bred for its valuable long soft blue-grey fur. Measuring 30-50 cm long, wild chinchillas are found high in the Andes. The name 'chinchilla' is also given to a breed of rabbit, with thick bluish fur, and a breed of

long-haired cat whose white fur is tipped with black, giving it a silvery lustre.

Chinese A language or group of languages of the Sino-Tibetan family spoken in E Asia. There are many different dialects of Chinese, including Mandarin, Min, Kan, Hakka, Hsiang, Wu, and Cantonese (or Yüeh). One dialect cannot be understood by the speaker of another. In China there have been attempts recently to standardize the language, using Mandarin as a basis. Many Chinese words, otherwise identical, have quite distinct meanings according to how the voice is pitched. Words are usually of one syllable. The language is written in pictorial symbols, which enables them to be understood by speakers of any dialect. There are as many as 40 000 of these of which 10 000 are in common use.

Chinese lantern plant A hardy ornamental plant, *Physalis alkekengi*, of the potato family, also called bladder cherry or winter cherry. A native of S and central Europe, it grows to a height of 20-60 cm. The edible fruit is enclosed in a reddish inflated calyx resembling a lantern.

Chinese water deer A very small deer, *Hydropotes inermis*, most common along the banks of the Yangtze River in China. Only 50 cm high at the shoulder, with a pale-brown coat and short tail, it has no antlers; the male's upper canine teeth are elongated into tusks.

Ch'ing. *See* Qing.

chinoiserie Decorative art and architecture that used Chinese motifs and was popular in the late 17th and 18th centuries. The fashion was inspired by Chinese porcelain, lacquer, etc., imported into Europe in the 17th century. Examples of chinoiserie in England include the *willow pattern, combining Chinese elements into a new design, and the interior of the Brighton Royal Pavilion.

Chinook A North American Indian people of the NW Pacific coast of the USA. The Chinook were salmon fishers and traders along the lower Columbia River. Chinook Jargon, a combination of Chinook, *Nootka, and other Indian languages mixed with English and French words, became the trading language of the entire W coast of America.

chipmunk A ground *squirrel of North America and Asian forests. Chipmunks are 15-30 cm long and have a black and white striped back and strong feet and claws for digging. They live in burrows; in the winter they feed on a store of nuts and dried fruit carried under ground in their large cheek pouches.

Chippendale, Thomas (1718-79) British cabinetmaker, famous for his elegant furniture designs, especially his chairs. His illustrated collection of rococo furniture designs, *The Gentleman and Cabinet Maker's Director* (1754), was influential, although his later neoclassical styles are considered the finest. His son, also **Thomas Chippendale** (died c. 1822), continued the business.

Chippewa. *See* Ojibwa.

Chiron In Greek legend, a *centaur, son of Cronos and the sea nymph Philyra. He was revered for his wisdom and knowledge of medicine. After being accidentally wounded by Heracles he bequeathed his immortality to Prometheus and was transformed into the constellation Sagittarius.

Chittagong 22 20N 91 48E A city and major port in Bangladesh, on the Indian Ocean. It is the second most important industrial centre in the country. Population (1986): 1 750 000.

chive A European perennial plant, *Allium schoenoprasum*, related to the onion. It has small white elongated bulbs and produces clumps of thin tubular leaves and rounded heads of small bluish or lilac flowers on long stalks. The leaves are used for seasoning and garnishing foods.

chlordiazepoxide. *See* benzodiazepines.

chlorine (Cl) A greenish poisonous *halogen gas, discovered in 1774 by C. W. Scheele. It is found only in compounds, especially common salt (NaCl), sylvite (KCl), and carnallite ($KMgCl_3.6H_2O$). Chlorine is liberated by the electrolysis of brine. Chlorine gas is reactive and combines directly with most elements. It is used as a disinfectant for drinking-water supplies and swimming pools and in the manufacture of many compounds. At no 17; at wt 35.453; mp −100.98°C; bp −34.6°C.

chloroform (*or* trichloromethane; $CHCl_3$) A colourless liquid that changes readily into a gas. It is made by reacting *bleaching powder with acetone, acetaldehyde, or ethanol. Its main use is now in the manufacture of *fluorocarbons but it is also used as a solvent and as an anaesthetic.

chlorophyll A green pigment present in organisms capable of *photosynthesis. There are various kinds of chlorophyll: higher plants possess chlorophylls *a* and *b*, located in *chloroplasts. The chlorophylls absorb red and blue light, trapping light energy for photosynthesis.

chloroplast A structure within a plant cell in which the process of *photosynthesis takes place. It is bounded by a membrane and contains the green pigment *chlorophyll. Chloroplasts vary greatly in shape and number within a cell; they are most numerous in the leaves.

chocolate. *See* cocoa and chocolate.

cholera A serious infection of the intestine caused by the bacterium *Vibrio cholerae*, which is transmitted in drinking water contaminated by faeces of a patient. Epidemics of cholera occur in regions where sanitation is poor. Cholera causes severe vomiting and diarrhoea; untreated, this can lead to fatal dehydration. Treatment consists of replacing the lost body fluid and salts by injections. Vaccinations against cholera provide only temporary immunity.

cholesterol A compound derived from steroids and found in many animal tissues. Cholesterol is manufactured chiefly by the liver and its derivatives are found in cell membranes, bile, blood, and gallstones. High levels of cholesterol in the blood are associated with an increased risk of heart disease, as a result of fatty deposits in the walls of arteries. *See also* atherosclerosis.

Chopin, Frédéric (François) (1810–49) Polish composer and pianist of French descent. He studied in Warsaw but later settled in Paris, where he lived with the novelist George *Sand from 1838 to 1847. A fervent nationalist, much of his music was influenced by Polish folk music.

His piano compositions include 2 concertos, 3 sonatas, 24 preludes, and many waltzes, nocturnes, polonaises, and studies. He also wrote a cello sonata, a piano trio, and songs.

Chordata A phylum (major group) of animals that includes the vertebrates and several smaller more primitive groups. They are distinguished by a hollow dorsal nerve cord; a rodlike *notochord that forms the basis of the skeleton; and paired gill slits in the wall of the pharynx behind the head, although in vertebrates these are apparent only in embryos.

chorea Involuntary jerky movements caused by disease of part of the brain. Huntington's chorea, named after the US physician James Huntington (1850–1916), is a hereditary disease causing mental deterioration. Sydenham's chorea, formerly known as St Vitus's dance and named after the English physician George Sydenham (1624–89), is often associated with rheumatic fever in children. It can be treated with sedatives.

choreography The art of composing *ballet and other theatrical dances. The most comprehensive system for recording dance steps is that devised by the Hungarian dancer Rudolph Laban (1829–1958), known as Labanotation. The choreographer is usually a professional dancer, who teaches the dancers each step of the ballet.

Chota Nagpur. *See* Bihar.

Chou. *See* Zhou.

Chou En-lai (*or* Zhou En Lai; 1898–1976) Chinese communist statesman; prime minister (1949–76) and foreign minister (1949–58). Chou led workers in the 1927 general strike in Shanghai, after which he fled to Nanchang, where he helped to organize an uprising. In 1932 he became political commissar to the Red Army and during the *Sino-Japanese War (1937–45) his reputation grew. After the establishment in 1949 of the People's Republic of China, he gained worldwide prominence as a diplomat.

chough A large black songbird, *Pyrrhocorax pyrrhocorax*, of the crow family, about 37 cm long, with red legs and a long red down-curved bill. It occurs in the Alps, Spain, and a few sea cliffs around Britain.

chow chow A breed of dog originating in China more than 200 years ago. The chow has a compact body and—unusually—a blue-black tongue. The thick coat forms a mane around the neck and shoulders and the tail is held well over the back. Height: 46–51 cm.

Chrétien de Troyes (12th century AD) French poet, author of the earliest romances dealing with the *Arthurian legend. He was a member of the court of Marie, countess of Champagne, to whom his romance *Lancelot* was dedicated. His romances include *Perceval* (or *Conte del Graal*), in which the *Holy Grail appears in a literary work for the first time.

Christadelphians A religious movement founded in Brooklyn, New York, in 1848 by John Thomas (1805–71), an English immigrant. The group rejects much standard Christian teaching, including the Trinity, the existence of Christ before the Incarnation, and the immortality of the soul.

Christchurch 43 33S 172 40E A city in New Zealand, on E South Island. Founded in 1850, it has a gothic-style cathedral (completed in 1901) and many fine parks. Industries are primarily associated with the rich agriculture of the *Canterbury Plains; these include meat processing, tanning, chemicals, and flour milling. Population (1988): 300 700.

Christian Aid A British organization founded in 1949 by the *British Council of Churches to direct the use of donations made to assist the Third World. Christian Aid, which makes no distinctions as to race, religion, or politics, supports development programmes in agriculture, health, and education, giving relief aid in emergencies.

Christian Democrats Political parties having programmes based on Christian principles and generally of a conservative nature. The German **Christlich-Demokratische Union** (Christian Democratic Union; CDU), was founded in West Germany in 1945. Since 1982 it has been the main party in the coalition government led by Helmut Kohl. In Italy the **Democrazia Cristiana** (Christian Democratic Party; DC), founded in 1943 as the successor to the Partito Popolare Italiano (Italian Popular Party), has dominated government since 1945. Other Christian Democratic parties are found in Austria, Belgium, France, Norway, and Spain.

Christianity The religious faith based on the teachings of *Jesus Christ, which had its origin in *Judaism. Its believers hold that Jesus is the Messiah whose coming was foretold in the Old Testament. It began as a movement within Judaism. Chiefly through the work of St Paul, Christianity spread rapidly through the Roman Empire, despite persecutions under Nero and later emperors. Christian belief was at first taught by the Apostles by word of mouth; however, the need for a written record of Jesus' life and teaching was soon fulfilled by the *Gospels. When Constantine became emperor (312), the power of bishops and scriptures been accepted. When Constantine established his new capital, Constantinople, there was a gradual separation between the Eastern *Orthodox Church and the Western *Roman Catholic Church. Western Christianity, under the Bishop of Rome who was held to be St Peter's successor, spread vigorously. The Orthodox Church became increasingly isolated. The two Churches formally separated in 1054. The Western Church led by the Pope reached the peak of its influence in the 13th century under Pope Innocent III. In the later middle ages increasing nationalism and the greater powers of non-church rulers weakened the unity of the papacy and *Holy Roman Empire. By the 16th century the Church was unable to prevent the divisions caused by the *Reformation. Some reformers, such as the followers of Martin *Luther and the English Church, were quite conservative, while the Calvinists, based in Geneva, were considerably more radical. The Reformation and the Roman Catholic response to it, the *Counter-Reformation, encouraged the spread of Christianity throughout the world. The total number of Christians has been estimated at more than 944 million, or approximately 24% of the world population.

Christian Science A religious movement founded by Mary Baker *Eddy. Having been influenced by P. P. Quimby (d. 1866), a spiritual leader, she developed a set of principles of faith healing based on Christ's healing powers, which she explained in *Science and Health* (1875). The First Church of Christ, Scientist, opened in Boston, Massachusetts, in 1879. The movement spread throughout the world; by 1990 there were 2700 churches. The emphasis of the movement is on healing, primarily of sin and secondarily of disease.

Christie, Dame Agatha (1890–1976) British author of detective fiction and playwright. She introduced her most famous character, the Belgian detective Hercule Poirot, in *The Mysterious Affair at Styles* (1920); he met his end in *Curtain* (1975). In all, she wrote over 50 detective stories, many of which feature her other well-known fictional detective, Miss Jane Marple. Several stories, including *Murder on the Orient Express* (1934) and *Death on the Nile* (1937), have been filmed, and her play *The Mousetrap* (opened 1952) holds the record for a London run.

Christmas The Feast of the birth of Christ. In the West it has been celebrated on 25 Dec since 336 AD, partly in order to replace the non-Christian sun worship on the same date. In the East, both the Nativity and *Epiphany were originally celebrated on 6 Jan, but by the end of the 4th century 25 Dec was accepted by almost everyone, although the Armenian Church still celebrates Christmas on 6 Jan. Many Christmas customs can be traced back to non-Christian origins.

Christmas Island An island in the Indian Ocean, SW of Java. It became a territory of the Commonwealth of Australia in 1958. The only commercial activity is phosphate mining. Area: 135 sq km (52 sq mi). Population (1986 est): 2000.

Christmas Island (*or* Kiritimati) A large coral atoll in the W central Pacific Ocean, in Kiribati in the Line Islands. British and US nuclear tests were held here between 1957 and 1962. It has coconut plantations. Area: 359 sq km (139 sq mi). Population (1985): 1737.

Christmas rose A species of *hellebore, about 35 cm tall, native to central and S Europe and Asia Minor. It is grown in gardens for its attractive white or pink winter-flowering blossoms.

Christopher, St (3rd century AD) Christian martyr of Syria. According to legend, he carried a child across a river where he was working as a ferryman. The child grew heavier and he learned that it was in fact Christ and he was thus carrying the weight of the world. He is the patron saint of travellers. Feast day: 25 July.

chromium (Cr) A hard grey transition metal, discovered in 1798 by Louis Nicolas Vauquelin (1763–1829). It occurs principally as chromite ($FeCr_2O_4$). The metal is obtained from the oxide (Cr_2O_3). The chief uses of chromium are in *electroplating steel and in making alloys. All chromium compounds are coloured and the most widely used, other than the oxide, are chromates (for example K_2CrO_4) and dichromates ($K_2Cr_2O_7$), which are used as oxidizing agents and in the dyeing industry. At no 24; at wt 51.996; mp 1857 ± 20°C; bp 2482°C.

chromosome One of the threadlike structures that carry the genetic information (see gene) of living organisms and are found in the nuclei of their cells. Chromosomes consist of *DNA with associated *RNA and proteins. Before cell division, the threads contract and thicken and each chromosome can be seen as two identical threads (chromatids) joined at the centromere. The chromatids later separate to become the daughter chromosomes (see mitosis). A normal human body cell has 46 chromosomes comprising 22 matched pairs (called autosomes) and two *sex chromosomes. A human sperm or egg cell has half this number of chromosomes (see meiosis). Abnormal numbers or parts of chromosomes often lead to abnormalities.

Chronicles, Books of Two Old Testament books covering the history of Judah from the Creation to the end of the Babylonian exile (538 BC). Special emphasis is given to the building of the Temple at Jerusalem. They were probably written in the 4th century BC and originally formed a continuous history with the books of Ezra and Nehemiah.

chrysalis The *pupa of most *butterflies and moths.

chrysanthemum A plant or shrub of the daisy family, native to Eurasia, Africa, and North America. The wild ancestors of the horticultural chrysanthemums were probably Japanese and Chinese species. Chrysanthemums have colourful single or double long-lasting flower heads. The different varieties may bloom at any time from early spring to autumn.

chub One of several freshwater fish related to the *carp, found in Europe and North America. The European chub (Leucixus cephalus) has a plump elongated body, usually 30–40 cm long, and is dark blue or green above and silvery below.

Churchill, Lord Randolph Henry Spencer (1849–95) British Conservative politician; third son of the 7th Duke of Marlborough and the father of Sir Winston *Churchill. He entered parliament in 1874 and led the group of Tory Democrats known as the Fourth Party. After serving as secretary for India (1885–86), he was briefly chancellor of the exchequer, when his budget was not accepted by the prime minister, Lord *Salisbury, because Churchill wished to reduce funds for the armed forces. He married (1874) Jeanette (Jennie) Jerome (1854–1921), an American.

Churchill, Sir Winston (Leonard Spencer) (1874–1965) British statesman and author. The son of Lord Randolph *Churchill, he served as a war correspondent in the second Boer War before becoming a Conservative MP in 1900. In 1904 he joined the Liberals and subsequently served as president of the Board of Trade (1908–10), home secretary (1910–11), and first lord of the admiralty (1911–15). In 1915, during World War I, he rejoined the army and served in

France. In 1917 he became minister of munitions, supporting the development of the *tank. Churchill lost his parliamentary seat in 1922 but was re-elected in 1924, becoming chancellor of the exchequer in Baldwin's government. From 1929 he was out of office until the outbreak of World War II, when he became first lord of the admiralty and then, in 1940, prime minister of a coalition government. During *World War II, his remarkable speeches and outstanding qualities as a leader made him a symbol of British resistance to tyranny throughout the free world. He was largely responsible for Britain's victorious alliance with the Soviet Union and the USA (1941) but came to view Soviet communism as a future threat. Churchill's coalition government was defeated in 1945 but he returned as Conservative prime minister in 1951, serving until his resignation in 1955. His writings include The Second World War (1948–54) and A History of the English-Speaking Peoples (1956–58); he won the 1953 Nobel Prize for Literature.

Church of England The state-recognized church in England, which combines Protestant elements and the principles of the English Church established by St *Augustine, the first Archbishop of Canterbury. Christianity was probably introduced in Britain during the Roman occupation in the 2nd century AD. Before the mission of St Augustine (597), the Church in Britain was dominated by Celtic missionaries from Ireland and Scotland. There were disagreements between the Celtic Church and Rome, and after the Synod of *Whitby ruled in Rome's favour, the English Church remained under the Pope's power until the *Reformation. Under Henry VIII, the king was recognized as being Supreme Head of the Church. The two bases of Anglican teaching and worship are the Book of *Common Prayer, introduced in the reign of *Edward VI, and the *Thirty-Nine Articles, published under Elizabeth I, who was expelled from the Church by the pope (1570). By the 19th century three parties had developed within the Church: the Low Church or Evangelical group, which stresses the Protestant tradition; the High Church group (see Anglo-Catholicism); and a Liberal group favouring adaptation to modern ideas. The two provinces of the Church are the archbishoprics of Canterbury (see Canterbury, Archbishop of) and York (see York, Archbishop of), each of which is divided into bishoprics. Church affairs are supervised by the General Synod (established 1970 to replace the Church Assembly); its decisions depend on parliamentary approval. Church property is administered by the Church Commissioners for England (established 1948). See also Lambeth Conferences; latitudinarianism.

Church of Scotland The state-recognized Church in Scotland. The Scottish Church separated from Rome in 1560, largely under the influence of John *Knox. The argument between Episcopalians who recognized bishops and Presbyterians, who did not, continued until the reign of William of Orange, who established Presbyterian Church in 1690.

CIA. *See* Central Intelligence Agency.

cicada A plant-eating insect of warm and tropical regions. Cicadas are 20–50 mm long and have large membranous wings. Males produce loud noises by vibrating two membranes at the base of the abdomen (stridulation). Cicadas usually inhabit trees and the females lay eggs in the wood. The larvae drop to the ground and burrow to feed on plant juices from roots. After 1–17 years they emerge as adults.

Cicero, Marcus Tullius (106–43 BC) Roman statesman. Elected consul in 63 BC, his execution of the Catiline conspirators without trial lost him support and he was exiled in 58 BC for 18 months. During the civil war he supported Pompey against Caesar. After the assassination of Caesar in 44 BC he made a series of attacks on Antony, the *Philippics*, for which he was later arrested and killed. The greatest of Roman speakers, he also wrote essays on the art of speaking and philosophical works.

CID. *See* Criminal Investigation Department.

cider An alcoholic drink made from fermented apple juice. In England cider is produced mainly in the West Country, from apples grown specifically for cider making. Sweet cider has a large amount of unfermented sugar, dry cider little sugar, and rough cider is dry cider with some acetic acid.

Cimon (died c. 450 BC) Athenian general and politician. He opposed *Themistocles' hostile policy towards the Spartans, believing Persia was the common Greek enemy, and in about 466 he scored a great victory against the Persians. His opponents, including *Pericles, caused him to be ostracized (461) but after his return to Athens, Cimon agreed a truce with Sparta (c. 450) and died fighting the Persians in Cyprus.

cinchona A tree of the South American Andes, cultivated widely in the tropics, especially India, for its bark. This yields powerful medicinal drugs, including *quinine. Cultivation has lost importance since the development of similar synthetic drugs lacking side-effects.

Cincinnati 39 10N 84 30W A city in the USA, in SW Ohio on the Ohio River. Founded in 1788, it developed as a meat-packing centre in the 19th century. Today it is an important inland port and major manufacturing centre. Population (1986): 369 750.

cinema The first motion picture shown to a public audience was made in 1895 by the French brothers Louis and Auguste Lumière, whose equipment was developed from the inventions of Thomas *Edison. The first commercial success was the American film *The Great Train Robbery* (1903). Influential pioneers of the silent cinema included D. W. *Griffith, Mack Sennett, and Charlie *Chaplin in the USA, F. W. Murnau (1889–1931) in Germany, and *Eisenstein in Russia. The success of Al *Jolson's *The Jazz Singer* (1927), which had a synchronized musical score, marked the end of the era of silent films; colour film was introduced in the 1930s. Between 1930 and 1945 the cinema industry in the USA was largely controlled by the giant Hollywood studios MGM and Paramount. The decline in cinema audiences from the late 1940s because of

the rival attraction of television caused the break-up of the Hollywood system, and since World War II some of the most significant developments in the cinema have been achieved by directors elsewhere. Prominent British directors included Carol *Reed and Sir Alfred *Hitchcock; continental directors include *Fellini, Antonioni, *Bergman, and *Buñuel.

cineraria A herbaceous perennial pot plant of the daisy family, developed from *Senecio cruentus* of the Canary Islands. It has handsome, sometimes brilliantly coloured, daisy-like flowers.

Cinna, Lucius Cornelius (d. 84 BC) Roman politician. Expelled from Rome by his opponent Sulla (87), Cinna returned with Marius and captured Rome. He tried to restrain Marius' brutal revenge on their opponents and as consul (86–84) restored order. He was killed in a mutiny shortly before Sulla's return to Italy.

cinnabar (moth) A moth, *Callimorpha jacobaeae*, of Europe and Asia. Both the adults (scarlet and black) and the caterpillars (striped black and yellow) taste bad: their warning coloration discourages predators. The caterpillars feed on ragwort and have been used to control this weed.

cinnabar (ore) A bright red mineral consisting of mercury sulphide, the chief ore of mercury. It occurs in volcanic rocks. Spain, the Soviet Union, Italy, and Mexico are the main producers.

cinnamon An evergreen tree, *Cinnamomum zeylanicum*, of the laurel family. 7–10 m high, it is native to Sri Lanka and cultivated widely in the tropics, the bark of its twigs being peeled off and rolled up to form the spice cinnamon.

Cinque Ports An association of five English ports (Sandwich, Dover, Hythe, New Romney, Hastings) in Kent and Sussex formed during the 11th century to defend the Channel coast. After the Norman conquest they were given considerable privileges in return for providing the main part of the navy. Winchelsea and Rye were added to their number. The Lord Warden of the Cinque Ports survives as an honorary post.

Circe Legendary Greek sorceress, who had the power to transform men into beasts. Odysseus, who visited her island of Aeaea on his voyage from Troy, was protected by the herb moly, and forced her to restore his men to human form.

circle A closed curved line, every point on which lies at the same distance, called the radius, from the centre. Its diameter is any straight line joining two points on the circle and passing through the centre. The ratio of the distance around any circle (the circumference) to its diameter is equal to the number π (*see* pi). The area of a circle, radius r, is πr^2.

circulation of the blood By supplying the tissues with blood, the circulatory system enables the transport of oxygen, nutrients, etc., and the removal of waste products. Oxygen-rich blood is pumped out of the *heart into the aorta and then, via the arteries, to all the tissues of the body. Here oxygen is removed, and deoxygenated blood returns, through the veins, to the heart. This blood is then pumped to the lungs, where it is reoxygenated, and returned to the heart to repeat the circuit. The circulation of the blood was first discovered by William *Harvey in 1628.

circumcision   The removal of all or part of the foreskin. In many primitive societies circumcision usually forms part of a ceremony introducing youths into adulthood. Among some Islamic peoples it is performed just before marriage; Jewish babies are circumcised in a religious ceremony when they are eight days old. Its origin is unknown but it has hygienic advantages, especially in hot climates. It is also carried out for medical reasons in certain circumstances.

cirque (or corrie)   A rounded rock basin with steep sides, often containing a lake or small glacier. Common in glaciated mountain ranges, cirques form through weathering and the movement of ice and debris.

cirrhosis   Destruction of the cells of the liver followed by their replacement with fibrous tissue, which eventually produces symptoms of liver failure (e.g. jaundice, swelling of the legs and abdomen, and vomiting of blood). Cirrhosis may be caused by *alcoholism, *hepatitis, obstruction of the bile duct, and heart failure, but often the cause is not known. Treatment depends on the cause.

cirrocumulus cloud (Cc)   A high *cloud with a mottled appearance composed of ice crystals; it is sometimes known as "mackerel sky."

cirrostratus cloud (Cs)   A high thin veil of *cloud composed of ice crystals, visible as a halo around the sun or moon.

cirrus cloud (Ci)   A high detached *cloud occurring above 6000 m (20 000 ft), composed of ice crystals and appearing wispy and fibrous. It is usually associated with fine weather.

Cistercians   An order of Roman Catholic monks founded by St Robert of Molesme (c. 1027–1111) as a stricter branch of the *Benedictine order. The mother house at Cîteaux, France, from which the order took its name, was founded in 1098. In the 17th century the order was reformed into two groups: the monks of the Strict Observance (*Trappists) and those of the Common Observance.

Citizens' Advice Bureaux, National Association of (CAB)   A British organization with over 1000 branches throughout the UK that provides free and confidential advice to anyone on any subject. Their trained staff (mostly volunteers) is equipped to advise on such matters as state benefits, debt problems, and housing.

citric acid   An organic compound that occurs in plant and animal tissues and is involved in the series of metabolic reactions called the *Krebs cycle. A commercial preparation of citric acid is used to flavour foods.

citron   A *citrus fruit, Citrus medica. The tree, 2–3 m high, was originally from the Far East. It was introduced into the Mediterranean region in about 300 BC; this remains the main centre of commercial cultivation. The rough yellowish sour fruits are used to make candied peel.

citrus fruits   An important group of tropical and subtropical fruits originating in SE Asia. Citrus trees are small evergreens with five-petalled, usually white, flowers. The fruits are rich in vitamin C, citric acid, and pectin (used in jam making). The most important are the *orange, *lemon, *lime, *grapefruit, *citron, bergamot, and *tangerine.

city states   Independent self-governing districts, each consisting of a town and its surrounding countryside. In ancient Greece there were several hundreds of city states, of which Athens was the largest.

Ciudad Juárez   31 42N 106 29W A city in N Mexico, on the Rio Grande. Its importance is due to its location on the US border and as a marketing centre for cotton. Population (1980): 567 365.

civet   A solitary nocturnal catlike mammal related to genets and mongooses. The African civet (Viverra civetta) is about 1.2 m long with coarse greyish spotted fur. Mainly carnivorous, civets also eat fruit and roots. The secretion of their anal glands is used in perfumes to make other scents last longer.

civil engineering   The branch of *engineering that deals with the design and construction of buildings, roads, railways, dams, canals, etc. The term was first used in 1750 by John Smeaton (1724–92) to distinguish his work from that of the military engineers.

civil law   The group of laws which cover the rights of private individuals and their relationships with each other rather than with the state. It is also called private law, as distinguished from public law and *criminal law. The term is also used of legal systems which came from *Roman law, as opposed to *common law systems. For example, in civil law court decisions cannot be used to influence the decision of later similar cases. English-speaking countries generally use common law, although the law of Scotland is more closely related to civil law.

civil list   In the UK, the sum given annually from the Consolidated Fund to the monarch and his or her marriage partner and children (except the Prince of Wales, who receives the income of the Duchy of Cornwall) to meet their expenses. The list was introduced in 1689, became law in 1697, and in 1830 all government expenses were removed from it. Originally when the monarch came to the throne, parliament voted a fixed sum to be paid annually but it may now be increased by Treasury order.

civil rights   The individual's rights to liberty, equality of treatment, education, etc., under the law and protected by the state. In countries with a written *constitution, such as the USA, they form part of the constitution. In England there have been a number of unsuccessful attempts to set out these rights, which are still only protected by the general law. See also Bill of Rights; human rights.

Civil War, English (1642–51)   The war between Charles I and parliament, which led to the execution of the king (1649) and the establishment of Oliver Cromwell's *Protectorate (1653). The Civil War was the result of a conflict between king and parliament that came to a head in the events of the *Long Parliament (summoned in 1640). Charles rejected parliament's Nineteen Propositions in June, 1642, and on 22

Aug he started military action at Nottingham. The first battle, at Edgehill, ended without a clear outcome but during 1643 the royalists (*or* *Cavaliers) gained ground in the N and W. The parliamentarian (*see* Roundheads) negotiation of the Solemn League and Covenant with the Scots led to its victory at *Marston Moor (1644); the formation of the *New Model Army led to the clear defeat of Charles at *Naseby (1645). In 1646 Charles surrendered to the Scots at Newark and the first Civil War was brought to an end. He was handed over to parliament in January, 1647, but was seized by the army in June. He escaped to the Isle of Wight and in December reopened negotiations with the Scots. The second Civil War followed (1648), with royalist uprisings in Wales and Kent, ending with Cromwell's defeat of the Scots at Preston in August. In the following year, Charles was tried and executed and the *Commonwealth was established by the Rump Parliament. The Civil War ended when Cromwell took power in Ireland (1649–50), defeated Charles' heir (later Charles II) at Dunbar (1650), and won a victory against the Scots at Worcester in 1651.

Civil War, US (1861–65) The struggle between the Federal government of the USA and the 11 *Confederate States in the South. The war developed because of the wide division between the farming slave-owning South and the industrialized North. When Abraham Lincoln, who was opposed to slavery, was elected president the southern states under Jefferson Davis withdrew, and war broke out when the Confederates opened fire on Fort Sumter, South Carolina. The opening campaigns in Virginia led to the Confederate victory at the first battle of Bull Run (July, 1861). Early in 1862 the Confederate Stonewall Jackson led a brilliant campaign in the Shenandoah Valley but on 4 May the Federal Army of the Potomac under George B. McClellan captured Yorktown and defeated Robert E. Lee's force in the Seven Days' battles (25 June–1 July). In August the Confederates scored a victory at the second battle of Bull Run and Lee pushed N into Maryland. Defeated at *Antietam (Sept), the Confederates were then victorious at Fredericksburg (Dec). In Tennessee, meanwhile, the Confederate success at Shiloh (6–7 April) was followed by a defeat at Stones River (31 Dec–2 Jan). In 1863, following his victory at Chancellorsville, Virginia (1–5 May), Lee began his second invasion of the N, only to be defeated at *Gettysburg (July). In the W, Federal troops under Ulysses S. Grant attacked Vicksburg, Mississippi, which fell on 4 July, and, after defeat at Chickamauga (19–20 Sept), won the victory of Chatanooga (23–25 Nov). In 1864 Grant, by now the Federal general in chief, advanced against Lee, whom he met in a battle with no clear outcome at *Cold Harbor (June). Sherman, who held the Federal command in the W, took Atlanta (Sept) before making his historic March to the Sea. After capturing Savannah in September, Sherman moved N through the Carolinas and on 9 April, 1865, Lee surrendered at Appomatox Court House. By 2 June the Federal victory was complete.

clairvoyance. *See* extrasensory perception.

clam A *bivalve mollusc with two equal shells and a muscular burrowing foot. Burrowing clams live buried in sand and mud, mainly in shallow coastal waters; they feed by taking in water through a tube (siphon) extended into the water. The largest burrowing clam is the geoduck (*Panopea generosa*), weighing up to 5 kg, while the giant clam (*Tridacna gigas*) can exceed 250 kg.

clan A group of people descended from a common ancestor. Clans are important in primitive societies, as in the pre-18th-century Scottish Highlands. The Scottish clans, until they were suppressed after the *Jacobite rebellions of 1715 and 1745, controlled different territories and were frequently rivals. The members of a clan wore particular clothing (*see* Highland dress) and often carried the name of its founder preceded by Mac (son of), e.g. MacDonald. The clan chiefs are still officially recognized.

Clare (Irish name: Chláir) A county in the W Republic of Ireland, in Munster situated between Galway Bay and the Shannon estuary. It consists of a low-lying central plain rising E to mountains and W to the limestone area of the Burren. Agriculture is the chief occupation. Area: 3188 sq km (1231 sq mi). Population (1986): 91 343. County town: Ennis.

Clare, John (1793–1864) British poet, the self-educated son of a farm labourer in Northamptonshire. His first book, *Poems Descriptive of Rural Life and Scenery* (1820), brought him fame. Three further volumes, including his best-known work, *The Shepherd's Calendar* (1827), were less successful. In 1837 he became insane and in 1841 was confined to a lunatic asylum in Northampton, where he wrote some of his best poems.

Clarendon, Edward Hyde, 1st Earl of (1609–74) English statesman and historian. He served as the king's chancellor of the exchequer during the English Civil war and went into exile in 1646. At the Restoration (1660) he became Lord Chancellor and gave his name to the Clarendon Code of anti-Nonconformist legislation. His daughter Anne married the future James II. Criticized for the sale of Dunkirk to France (1662) and for his handling of the second Dutch War (1664–67), the *Cabal brought about his fall. Forced again into exile, he completed his massive *History of the Rebellion and Civil Wars in England* (1702–04).

Clare of Assisi, St (1194–1253) Italian nun, founder of the "Poor Clares." Influenced by the teaching of St *Francis of Assisi, she gave up all her possessions and followed him. St Francis established a community of women with Clare as abbess in 1215. They lived in absolute poverty without even shared property. She was made a saint in 1255. Because of an incident in which she saw mass celebrated at a distance, she was proclaimed patron saint of television in 1958. Feast day: 12 Aug.

clarinet A cylindrical woodwind instrument with a single reed. It is a transposing instrument in B flat or A existing in several sizes and has a range of three and a half octaves. Music for the B flat clarinet is written one tone higher than it sounds. The clarinet did not become a regular member of the orchestra until the late 18th century.

classicism The aesthetic qualities of the arts and literature of ancient Greece and Rome, which served as ideals for various later European artistic movements. These qualities include harmony and balance of form, clarity of expression, and emotional restraint. The Italian Renaissance of the 15th and 16th centuries was the first and most general attempt to revive these qualities in the arts. In literature, Renaissance interpretations of Aristotle's *Poetics* influenced writers all over Europe in the 17th and 18th centuries. Towards the end of the 18th century there was a general reaction against rigid neoclassicist doctrines.

Classics In *flat racing in England, five annual races (*see* Derby; Oaks; One Thousand Guineas; St Leger; Two Thousand Guineas) for three-year-old horses only.

Claudius I (10 BC–54 AD) Roman emperor (41–54). Claudius came to power in the chaos that followed the murder of his nephew Emperor *Caligula. His rule was generally efficient: he extended the Empire, taking part in the invasion of Britain (43), but the influence over him of freed men and of his third wife Valeria Messalina angered the Senate. Agrippina the Younger, his niece and fourth wife, was suspected of his murder.

Clausius, Rudolf Julius Emanuel (1822–88) German physicist, who in 1854 developed the idea of *entropy and used it in a statement of the second law of thermodynamics. He also contributed to the development of the *kinetic theory of gases and suggested that electrolysis involved the conversion of molecules into charged particles.

clavichord A keyboard instrument, popular from the 15th to the 18th centuries and revived in the mid-20th century. Its delicate tone is produced by small brass plates fixed to the end of each key, which strike the strings.

clavicle The collar bone. There are two clavicles, each running from the upper end of the breastbone to form a joint with the shoulder blade. They brace the shoulders and help to support the arms.

clay A type of earth that has plastic properties when wet and hardens and cracks when dry. It consists of fine rock particles (less than 0.004 mm in diameter). The principal minerals present in clays are hydrous silicates, mainly of aluminium and magnesium.

Clay, Cassius. *See* Ali, Muhammad.

clay-pigeon shooting. *See* shooting.

cleavage The repeated division of a fertilized egg cell (zygote) to produce a ball of cells that forms the blastula.

clef (French: key) The symbol placed at the beginning of a musical stave to indicate the pitch of the notes. The treble clef, a decorative G, indicates that the second line up of the stave is the G above middle C; the bass clef, an archaic F, indicates that the fourth line up is the F below middle C. The C clef can be set on any of the lines of the stave to establish it as middle C.

cleft palate An abnormality in which there is a cleft, or slit, in the roof of the mouth (palate). It is caused by failure of the left and right halves of the palate to fuse during embryonic development. It may be associated with a harelip. The cleft can be repaired surgically at 16 to 18 months of age.

clematis A woody climbing plant of the buttercup family, widely distributed in temperate regions. There are many garden varieties, grown for their showy flowers, usually purple, pink, or white.

Clemenceau, Georges (1841–1929) French statesman; prime minister (1906–09, 1917–20). As a member of the chamber of deputies from 1876 to 1893, he became known as the Tiger for his attacks on other politicians. As prime minister he strengthened ties with Britain. During World War I he attacked the government for defeatism until becoming prime minister for the second time, when he led France to victory.

Cleopatra VII (69–30 BC) Queen of Egypt (51–48, 47–30). Cleopatra was coruler with her brother Ptolemy XIII (61–48), who overthrew her in 48. Restored by Caesar, she accompanied him to Rome and supposedly gave birth to his son Caesarion. After Caesar's murder, Cleopatra returned to Egypt and in 41 she met Antony. In 37 he abandoned his wife Octavia and lived with Cleopatra, who bore him three sons. Antony's brother-in-law Octavian defeated Antony and Cleopatra at *Actium in 31 and in 30 they both committed suicide.

Cleopatra's Needles A pair of ancient Egyptian obelisks carved in the reign of Thutmose III (c. 1475 BC) at Heliopolis. They were moved by *Augustus Caesar to Alexandria in 12 BC. In 1878, one was set up on the Victoria Embankment, London, the other in Central Park, New York.

Cleveland 41 30N 81 41W A city in the USA, in Ohio on Lake Erie. It is a major Great Lakes port and the largest city in Ohio. One of the country's leading iron and steel centres, its other industries include oil refining, food processing, and the manufacture of motor vehicles. Population (1986): 535 830.

Cleveland A county in NE England, bordering on the North Sea. It was created in 1974 from parts of SE Durham and NE Yorkshire. It consists chiefly of lowlands rising to the Cleveland Hills in the S. The main river, the Tees, flows NE. Industry includes chemicals, iron and steel, and engineering. Area: 583 sq km (255 sq mi). Population (1987 est): 554 500. Administrative centre: Middlesbrough.

Cleveland Bay A breed of horse developed in the Cleveland region of N Yorkshire, England. It is reddish brown (bay) with black mane, tail, and legs. Formerly a pack and coach horse, Clevelands are now used mainly for crossing with Thoroughbreds to produce showjumpers. Height: 1.57–1.68 m (15½–16½hands).

climate The average weather conditions of an area measured over a long period of time. Climate is influenced first by latitude, which determines the amount of solar radiation received by an area. Second, the distribution of land and sea will affect climate as the land heats and cools far more rapidly than the sea. Ocean currents will also modify a region's climate (*see* Gulf Stream). The third factor is the altitude and geographical features of an area; temperature will fall with increased altitude and hills and mountain barriers force clouds to rise and produce rainfall.

clipper ship A fast sailing vessel developed in the 19th century for international commerce, so called because it clipped short the time required for a given passage. Clipper ships did not carry a large cargo.

clitoris. *See* penis.

Clive of Plassey, Robert, Baron (1725–74) British soldier and colonial administrator, who established British supremacy in India. He joined the East India Company in 1743 and made his name by capturing Arcot (1751). In 1757 he recaptured Calcutta from the Nawab of Bengal, whom he then defeated at Plassey. This assured the East India Company control of Bengal, of which Clive was virtual ruler until 1760. He was appointed governor and commander in chief of Bengal in 1764, remaining in office until 1767. He was subsequently named in an inquiry into the East India Company's affairs, was cleared (1773), but committed suicide shortly afterwards.

cloaca The chamber at the rear of the body in vertebrate animals (except the placental mammals), into which the digestive, urinary, and genital tracts open. Faeces, urine, and eggs or sperm are discharged through its vent to the outside.

clock A device for measuring the passage of time. Clockwork has two essential components: an energy store (a raised weight or a coiled spring) and an escapement that regulates the release of energy from the store. The earliest recorded escapement was in a giant Chinese astronomical clock (c. 1090 AD). Early European clocks (called turret clocks from their usual position in church towers) recorded time by striking on the hour, but the 14th-century Italian family of Dondi introduced dials. The use of mainsprings from about 1500 enabled portable clocks (*see also* watch) to be made. Accuracy was greatly increased in the 17th century by the anchor escapement (1671) and pendulums (*see* Huygens). In the 20th century clocks regulated by the natural vibrations of atoms (*see* atomic clock) have been developed.

clone A group of genetically identical organisms produced from a single parent cell by asexual division of that cell–for example by vegetative reproduction in plants or parthenogenesis in animals. Gene clones (identical copies of a gene) are produced by *genetic engineering.

closed shop A place of work in which all employees are required to be members of one or more particular trade unions. Closed shops are usually allowed by the employer, whose collective bargaining position may be made simpler if the union (or unions) can speak for the whole workforce.

clothes moth A small moth whose larvae feed on clothes, carpets, blankets, etc. Adults general-

ly have a wingspan of 12–25 mm and are pale grey-brown in colour. They prefer dark places. Pesticides, dry cleaning, and man-made fibres have reduced their damaging effects.

Clotho. *See* Fates.

cloud A mass of minute water droplets or ice crystals, or a combination of both, produced by the *condensation of water vapour in the atmosphere. When the droplets grow rain, sleet, snow, etc., may occur. Clouds are usually divided into ten principal forms. The high clouds, normally above 5000 m (16 000 ft), are *cirrus, *cirrostratus, and *cirrocumulus. The medium clouds at 2000–5000 m (6500–16 000 ft) comprise altocumulus and altostratus. Below this level the low clouds are *stratus, *stratocumulus, and *nimbostratus. Some clouds grow vertically and cannot be classified solely by height; these are chiefly *cumulus and cumulonimbus.

cloud chamber A device, invented by C. T. R. *Wilson, used for studying the properties of ionizing particles. It contains a saturated vapour that can be cooled very quickly. If an ionizing particle then passes through the chamber drops of liquid condense along its trail, thus making the trail visible.

clouded leopard A large nocturnal forest *cat, *Neofelis nebulosa*, of SE Asia, Borneo, Sumatra, and Java. It is 120–190 cm long including its tail (60–90 cm) and has a greyish or yellowish coat with black markings.

clove An aromatic evergreen Indonesian tree, *Eugenia caryophyllata*, of the myrtle family, growing to a height of 12 m. The dried flower buds are used as spice. Clove oil is distilled from the buds, stalks, and leaves for use in medicine and as artificial vanilla.

clover An annual or perennial plant of the pea family. Clovers, which occur mainly in N temperate regions, have leaves divided into three leaflets and dense heads of flowers. They are valuable as fodder plants and for their nitrogen-fixing ability (*see* nitrogen fixation). Alsike (*Trifolium hybridum*), red clover (*T. pratense*), and crimson clover (*T. incarnatum*) are three widely grown species.

clubmoss A perennial mosslike *pteridophyte plant, also called ground pine, found mainly in tropical and subtropical forests and mountainous regions. It has a creeping stem with wiry branches, densely covered with needle-like leaves. The spore capsules occur at the base of special leaves (sporophylls), which are often arranged in conelike clusters (strobili).

Cluny 46 25N 4 39E A town in E France, in the Saône-et-Loire department. Its famous Benedictine abbey (founded 910 AD) became the centre of the Cluniac order, which was widely influential in Europe (c. 950–c. 1130). Population (1982 est): 4734.

cluster of galaxies A group of *galaxies that are physically linked by gravity. Most galaxies are members of a cluster: our own Galaxy belongs to the Local Group. The densest clusters contain a thousand or more galaxies. Neighbouring clusters are loosely grouped into **superclusters.**

Clwyd A county of NE Wales, bordering on the Irish Sea and the Dee estuary. It was created under local government reorganization in 1974 from Flintshire, most of Denbighshire, and E Merionethshire. It is mainly hilly with fertile valleys. Tourism is important. Area: 2425 sq km (936 sq mi). Population (1989 est): 402 800. Administrative centre: Mold.

Clyde, River A river in W Scotland. Rising in SE Strathclyde Region, it flows NW through Glasgow and S of Clydebank to enter the Atlantic Ocean at the Firth of Clyde. Length: 170 km (106 mi).

Clydesdale A breed of draught horse developed in the Clydesdale region of Scotland in the 18th century. It has a compact body with strong legs and feet and may be bay, brown, black, or chestnut. Height: about 1.75 m (17 hands).

CND *See* Campaign for Nuclear Disarmament.

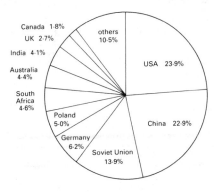

COAL *World production (1989).*

coal A mineral deposit containing carbon and used as a fuel and raw material for the chemical industry. Coal is formed from fossil vegetable matter. The plant remains are changed from a peatlike material into lignite (brown coal), sub-bituminous and bituminous coal, semian-thracite, and anthracite. During this process the percentage of carbon present increases and the moisture decreases; anthracite is about 90% carbon. Most coal was formed in the *Carboniferous period.

Coal has been mined in Britain since Roman times but on a small scale until the industrial revolution. From about 1800 coal was being heated to high temperatures to produce *coal gas and *coke. By the middle of the 19th century, there was interest in the by-products (coal tar, ammonia, and pitch) of coal gas production. The chemistry of the constituents of coal tar developed into the study of organic chemistry, and the use of *aromatic compounds from coal tar led to the development of the dyestuffs and explosives industries. In the 20th century these products also became the foundation of the plastics industry. During the 1920s and 1930s processes were also developed (mainly in Germany) for converting coal into oil. *Natural gas has now largely re-

placed coal gas and petrochemicals (*see* oil) have to a considerable extent replaced coal tar as sources of organic raw materials.

coal gas A gas consisting mainly of hydrogen (50%) and methane (30%), with some carbon monoxide (8%) and other gases. It is obtained by heating coal to 1000°C. Coal gas was formerly supplied to homes for heating and cooking, but it has now been largely replaced by *natural gas.

Coal Measures. *See* Carboniferous period.

coastguard A force formed by some countries during the 19th century to prevent smuggling. In Britain it now deals mainly with lifesaving and maritime safety through a network of coast-watching stations and provides a weather-forecasting service.

Coast Mountains A mountain range of W Canada, extending from the US border 1600 km (1000 mi) N into Alaska. Very rugged, it rises steeply from the Pacific coast. It includes Canada's largest mountain mass and a long glacier belt. Mount Waddington at 3978 m (13 260 ft) is the highest point.

cobalt (Co) A transition metal similar to iron and noted for its deep-blue colour when present as a salt in glass, tiles, and pottery. It was discovered by G. Brandt (1694–1768) in 1735 and occurs as cobaltite (CoAsS) and in copper, nickel, iron, silver, and lead ores. Cobalt is mined chiefly in Zaïre and Canada. It is used in the manufacture of cutting steels and magnets. The isotope ^{60}Co is a strong source of gamma rays and is used in radiotherapy (the **cobalt bomb**) and in industry. At no 27; at wt 58.9332; mp 1495°C; bp 2870°C.

Coblenz. *See* Koblenz.

cob nut. *See* hazel.

Cobol (*co*mmon *b*usiness *o*riented *l*anguage) A computer-programming language used mainly for business applications.

cobra A highly venomous snake occurring in warm regions of Africa and Asia and able to expand its neck ribs to form a hood. The king cobra (*Ophiophagus hannah*) of S Asia, over 3.6 m long, is the largest venomous snake; it preys chiefly on other snakes. The common Indian cobra (*Naja naja*), used by snake charmers, is 1.7 m long.

coca A Peruvian tree, *Erythroxylon coca*, cultivated in Java, South America, and Sri Lanka for its leaves, which—when dried—yield cocaine. Coca leaves have been chewed for centuries in South America for their effect in relieving fatigue and hunger; prolonged use can cause addiction and mental and physical damage.

cocaine An alkaloid ($C_{17}H_{21}O_4N$) derived from *coca leaves and also made synthetically. It was the first drug to be used as a local anaesthetic, but it has largely been replaced by safer drugs for this purpose (e.g. procaine). However, it is still used in pain-killing mixtures for treating people with fatal illnesses (e.g. cancer). Cocaine is an addictive stimulant. *See also* anaesthesia.

cochineal A natural red dye obtained from the dried bodies of certain female scale insects, especially *Dactylopius coccus* of Mexico. It has now been largely replaced by synthetic dyes, but continues to be used for colouring foodstuffs and cosmetics.

cochlea. See ear.

cockatiel A small Australian *cockatoo, *Nymphicus hollandicus*, of interior grasslands. It is 32 cm long and has a grey plumage with white wing patches, a yellow head and crest, and reddish ear patches.

cockatoo A parrot found throughout Australia, Malaysia, and the Philippines. Cockatoos are usually white, often with a pink or yellow blush, although some species are black; all have a long crest that can be erected.

cockchafer A European beetle, *Melolontha melolontha*, also called maybug, that is very destructive to plants. Up to 35 mm long, it is black with reddish-brown legs and wing cases and has a loud buzzing flight. The larvae, which attack plant roots and cause the most damage, are also called white grubs or rookworms.

Cockcroft, Sir John Douglas (1897–1967) British physicist, who shared the 1951 Nobel Prize with Ernest *Walton for their development in 1932 of the first particle *accelerator, which was used for accelerating protons to split an atomic nucleus (of lithium). In World War II he worked on the atom bomb and in 1946 became director of the Atomic Energy Research Establishment at Harwell.

Cockerell, Sir Christopher Sydney (1910–) British engineer and inventor of the *hovercraft. Having worked on radar in World War II, he filed his first patent for an air-cushion vehicle in 1955. The first practical hovercraft, the SR.NI, was launched in 1959.

cocker spaniel A breed of gundog, thought to be of Spanish origin. It is compact with short legs, a short tail, and a square muzzle. The long flat silky coat is usually black, red, or cream, either plain or mottled. Height: 39–41 cm (dogs); 38 cm (bitches).

cockfighting A blood sport in which two or more gamecocks fight against each other, often to the death. Illegal in Britain since 1849, it is still widespread in certain parts of the world. The cocks are equipped with steel or bone spurs on their legs and set against each other in a cockpit.

cockle A *bivalve mollusc with rounded and ribbed shell valves, 1–23 cm in diameter. Cockles burrow in sand or mud, straining food particles from water drawn in through protruding siphons (tubes). The European cockle (*Cardium* (or *Cerastoderma*) *edule*) is edible.

cockroach A nocturnal insect with a black or brown flat body, 12–50 mm long, long antennae, and leathery forewings. Cockroaches seldom fly; they feed on plant and animal materials and can be household pests.

cocoa and chocolate Foods derived from the seeds of the cacao tree (*Theobroma cacao*), native to tropical America and cultivated mainly in West Africa. The tree is pruned and woody pods, 23–30 cm long, grow directly from its trunk. The pods contain seeds (cocoa, or cacao, beans), which are fermented and dried before export. Manufacturing is carried out mainly in the importing countries, where the beans are shelled, roasted, and ground. From them cocoa powder and chocolate are made. Cocoa butter, a fat re-

tained in chocolate but removed from cocoa powder, is a rich source of food energy.

coconut The fruit of the coconut palm, *Cocos nucifera*; one of the most important tropical crops. Up to 25 m high, the tree bears a crown of giant feather-like leaves. The coconuts take a year to ripen and have a thick fibrous husk. The hollow core contains coconut milk; the white kernel is eaten raw or dried to yield copra, from which coconut oil is extracted for use in soaps, synthetic rubbers, and edible oils. The residual coconut cake is used as a livestock feed and the husk fibre (coir) is used for matting, etc.

Cocos Islands (or Keeling Islands) Two Australian coral atolls in the E Indian Ocean. First settled in 1826, they were under Australian administration from 1955 and became part of Northern Territory in 1984. Copra is produced and there is an important meteorological station. Area: 13 sq km (5 sq mi). Population (1986): 616.

Cocteau, Jean (1889–1963) French poet and artist. He made his name with the novel *Les Enfants terribles* (1929) and sketches written for *Diaghilev's ballet company, such as *Parade* (1917). In World War I he served as an ambulance driver and became acquainted with *Picasso, *Modigliani, and other leading painters and writers. His work includes poetry (*L'Ange Heurtebise*, 1925), plays (*Orphée*, 1926), and films (*Le Sang d'un poète*, 1929; and his own *Les Enfants terribles*, 1950).

cod A carnivorous fish, *Gadus morhua*, of temperate N Atlantic waters that is commercially fished for food and liver oil. Up to 1.8 m long, it is generally dark grey with spots and has a whisker-like barbel on its lower jaw.

codeine A pain-relieving drug (see analgesic). It is a derivative of morphine but is less toxic and less addictive. The combination of aspirin and codeine is a stronger pain killer than either of the two drugs used separately. Codeine also reduces coughing and is therefore often added to cough mixtures.

Code Napoléon The organized collection of the *civil law of France. Drawn up by a commission set up by *Napoleon I when he was first consul, the code—properly called the *Code Civil* —was brought into force in 1804. It and the other codes produced later under Napoleon's administration served as a model for civil law codes elsewhere.

Cody, William F(rederick) (1846–1917) US showman, known as Buffalo Bill. An army scout and Pony Express rider, he gained his nickname by supplying the men working on the Union (later Kansas) Pacific Railway with buffalo—killing 4280 in eight months (1867–68). In 1883 he began touring the USA and Europe with his Wild West Show.

Coe, Sebastian (1956–) British middle-distance runner. A gold medallist in the 1500 m race at the 1980 and 1984 Olympics, he has held world records at distances of 800 m, 1000 m, and the mile.

coelacanth A primitive bony fish. Once thought to have been extinct for 60 million years, several living individuals have been found since the discovery, in 1938, of the first coelacanth of modern times off the coast of SE Africa. It has a heavy body, up to 1.5 m long, with limblike fins, and crawls on the bottom, feeding on other fish.

coelenterate Any one of a large group of aquatic invertebrate animals, including *hydra, *jellyfish, *sea anemones, *corals, etc. There are two different generations of the life cycle (*see* alternation of generations; polyp; medusa) and either or both may occur. The body cavity has a single opening (mouth) and stinging cells (nematocysts) are used for defence or catching prey.

coeliac disease A disease in which the small intestine is abnormally sensitive to gliadin (a component of the protein *gluten, found in wheat). It results in inability of the cells of the intestine to digest or absorb food. The symptoms include diarrhoea, stunted growth, and general ill health. The condition is treated by a gluten-free diet.

coelom The body cavity of many animals. In mammals (including man) the coelom of the embryo is divided into three cavities, which become occupied by the lung, heart, and intestines. In the fully developed mammal the coelom is reduced to the virtually nonexistent spaces between the membranes lining the heart (the pericardium), the lungs (the pleura), and the intestines (the peritoneum).

coenzyme A nonprotein substance that associates with certain enzymes and is essential for the proper functioning of these enzymes. *ATP is a major coenzyme.

coffee The seeds (called beans) of certain tropical evergreen trees, which yield a stimulating drink. *Coffea arabica* is the most widely grown coffee tree, producing the best quality beans. *C. canephora* is more disease resistant, longer living, and can be grown at lower altitudes. *C. liberica*, of still lower quality, is grown in Malaysia and Guyana. The coffee beans are usually fermented, then sun-dried before export. The main coffee-producing areas are South and Central America, Jamaica, East Africa, and Mysore in India.

Cognac 45 42N 0 19W A town in W France, in the Charente department. Under French law, the name Cognac may only be applied to brandy produced in a certain area around the town. Population (1982 est): 20 995.

coke A fuel consisting mainly of carbon. It is made by heating coal in the absence of air and is produced as a by-product of *coal gas. Coke is used in *blast furnaces and other industrial processes as well as for domestic heating.

cola. *See* kola.

Colchester 51 54N 0 54E A market town in SE England, in Essex on the River Colne. Founded by Cymbeline (Cunobelinus) in about 10 AD, Colchester was an important Roman town (Camulodunum); the Roman walls remain in part and there is a Norman castle. Essex University (1961) is nearby. Colchester's industries include engineering and printing. Population (1981 est): 81 945.

colchicine. *See* autumn crocus.

Cold Harbor, Battles of Two battles in the US *Civil War fought near Richmond, Virginia, the Confederate capital. In the first (27 June,

1862) the Confederate general, Robert E. *Lee defeated the Federal forces under George B. McClellan (1826–85), both sides suffering heavy losses. In the second (3–12 June, 1864), the Federal advance on Richmond under Ulysses S. *Grant was temporarily stopped when he met Lee's forces.

Colditz 51 08N 12 49E A town in Germany, on the River Mulde. Its castle, built on a cliff above the town, was used as a top-security prisoner-of-war camp during World War II.

Cold War The hostility between the USA and the Soviet Union, and their respective allies, following World War II. The term was first used in 1947 by the US politician Bernard Baruch (1870–1965). Fear of nuclear war prevented military action, and the Cold War was fought on economic, political, and ideological fronts. It was at its strongest in the 1950s, but had given way by the 1970s to more relaxed relations and was formally ended in 1990 following political changes in E Europe.

Coleridge, Samuel Taylor (1772–1834) British poet and critic. In 1795 he met William *Wordsworth and their joint publication of *Lyrical Ballads* (first edition 1798) marked an important break with 18th-century poetry. His finest poems, such as *Kubla Khan* (1797) and *The Rime of the Ancient Mariner* (1797–98), were written at this time, but his personal life was troubled by his marriage, his poverty, and his increasing opium addiction. His subsequent work included the critical *Biographia Literaria* (1817).

coleus A plant of the deadnettle family originating in the Old World tropics. Many cultivated varieties are grown as house plants for their variegated leaves.

colitis Inflammation of the large intestine (the colon), causing abdominal pain and diarrhoea (sometimes with the passage of blood). Colitis can be caused by bacterial infection (e.g. dysentery) or by *Crohn's disease. In ulcerative colitis the colon becomes ulcerated, and may require surgery in severe cases.

collagen A structural protein that is the main component of the white fibres of *connective tissue. It is strong and resists stretching, and is found in tendons and ligaments and also in skin, bone, and cartilage.

collar bone. *See* clavicle.

collective farms Farming groups, found especially in communist countries. Collectivization was started in the Soviet Union by Stalin. The farms and equipment belong to the state, which decides what is to be grown, but farmworkers, in surrounding villages, pay rent for their homes and are allowed to have their own garden plots and livestock; profits are shared in collective farms while in state farms workers receive wages. Collectivization was introduced into China in 1955 and is also used in Israel (*see* kibbutz).

collie A breed of dog originating in Scotland, widely used as a sheepdog. The rough-coated collie has a long dense coat and bushy tail; the smooth-coated variety has a shorter smooth coat; and the bearded collie has a long coat with a shaggy beard. Height: 56–61 cm (dogs); 51–56 cm (bitches).

Collingwood, Cuthbert, 1st Baron (1750–1810) British admiral. He fought at the battles of the Glorious First of June (1794) and Cape St Vincent (1797) during the *Revolutionary and Napoleonic Wars. After Nelson's death at *Trafalgar (1805) he succeeded to his command and was eventually buried alongside him in St Paul's Cathedral.

colloid A system in which minute particles (larger than molecules) remain suspended in a liquid, solid, or gaseous medium. If the particles are solid and the medium is liquid the colloid is known as a **sol** (e.g. milk). If both are liquid the colloid is an **emulsion** (e.g. mayonnaise). If the particles link together, with the medium circulating through the meshwork, the colloid is called a **gel** (e.g. a photographic emulsion). *See also* aerosol.

Cologne (German name: Köln) 50 56N 06 57E A city in W Germany on the River Rhine. It is the site of a university (1388) and the largest gothic cathedral in N Europe (founded 1248). Population (1987): 914 300.

Colombia, Republic of A country in NW South America, on the Pacific Ocean and the Caribbean Sea. The majority of the population is of mixed Spanish and Indian descent. *Economy*: the chief product is coffee, which accounts for over half the total exports. Gold, silver, copper, lead, and mercury are mined and Colombia is a rich source of platinum and emeralds. There are also large reserves of oil, coal, and natural gas. *History*: inhabited by Indians before the Spanish colonization of the 16th century. In 1819 Simón Bolívar secured the independence of Greater Colombia, which included what are now Panama, Venezuela, and Ecuador. This lasted until 1830 when Venezuela and Ecuador broke away; Panama became independent in 1903. Head of state: President Virgilio Barca Vargas (1921–). Official language: Spanish. Official religion: Roman Catholic. Official currency: Colombian peso of 100 centavos. Area: 1 138 914 sq km (456 535 sq mi). Population (1986): 29 956 000. Capital: Bogotá. Main port: Barranquilla.

Colombo 6 55N 79 52E The capital and main port of Sri Lanka, on the W coast at the mouth of the River Kelani. Colombo has one of the largest artificial harbours in the world. Population (1984): 643 000.

Colombo Plan An agreement, signed in Colombo (Ceylon) in 1951, designed to encourage economic development in the countries of S and SE Asia. It now has 26 members—20 countries within the region and Australia, Canada, Japan, New Zealand, the UK, and the USA.

colon. *See* intestine.

colophony. *See* resin.

Colorado One of the Mountain States in the W central USA. Most of the population lives in the Colorado Piedmont, between the Rocky Mountains and the Great Plains. Industries include chemicals, military equipment, and food products. Colorado also produces molybdenum, coal, and oil. Tourism, especially winter sports, is of growing importance. *History*: explored by

the Spanish, part of Colorado was acquired by the USA in the Louisiana Purchase (1803) and part from Mexico in 1848. Following the discovery of gold (1859), it became a territory in 1861 and a state in 1876. Area: 269 998 sq km (104 247 sq mi). Population (1986 est): 3 267 118. Capital: Denver.

Colorado potato beetle A brown and yellow striped beetle, *Leptinotarsa decemlineata*, about 10 mm long. Both the adults and larvae eat potato leaves: the larvae also attack the tubers. It is native to W North America but has spread eastwards, throughout Europe, to become a serious pest of potato crops everywhere.

Colorado River A river in the W USA, rising in the Rocky Mountains and flowing SW through Colorado, Utah, and Arizona (where it passes through the *Grand Canyon) to the Gulf of California in Mexico. It is extensively used for irrigation and as a source of hydroelectric power. Length: 2320 km (1440 mi).

Colosseum An amphitheatre in Rome, it was begun (c. 70 AD) by the emperor *Vespasian. It is an elliptical building, four storeys high, 188 m (617 ft) long, and 156 m (512 ft) wide. It could seat 47 000 people and was used for gladiatorial and wild-beast fights.

Colossians, Epistle of Paul to the A New Testament book written by the Apostle Paul about 60 AD to the church in Colossae in W Asia Minor.

Colossus of Rhodes A gigantic statue of the sun god Helios by the harbour of Rhodes. Cast in bronze by Chares of Lindos about 280 BC and standing about 31 m (100 ft) tall, it was one of the *Seven Wonders of the World. An earthquake destroyed it 50 years after its completion.

colour The sensation produced when light of different *wavelengths falls on the human eye. The visible spectrum is usually split into seven major colours: red, orange, yellow, green, blue, indigo, and violet, in order of decreasing wavelength (from about 6.5×10^{-7} m for red light to 4.2×10^{-7} m for violet). A mixture of all these colours in equal proportions gives white light. Other colours are produced by varying the proportions or omitting components. Coloured pigments, dyes, and filters absorb certain wavelengths, transmitting or reflecting the rest. Thus a red book illuminated by white light absorbs all the components of white light except red, which is reflected. This is a subtractive process, the final colour being that remaining after absorption of the others. Combining coloured lights is an additive process. A mixture of the whole spectrum gives white light, as will a mixture of lights of three *primary colours.

colour blindness The inability to distinguish certain colours, the most common of which is red-green colour blindness. Colour blindness is usually an inherited and incurable condition; a trait carried by the X-chromosome, it is far more common in men than women. Occasionally colour blindness may be due to disease of the retina.

colour television. *See* television.

Colt revolver A *revolver with a five-shot cylinder rotated and locked in line with the single barrel by cocking the weapon. Invented by the

US engineer Samuel Colt (1814–62) in 1835, it became the .45 calibre Frontier Peacemaker (1873) and the standard .45 US army and navy revolver, remaining in service until 1945.

Columba, St (c. 521–597 AD) Irish missionary ordained in 551. He founded churches in Ireland before setting up a monastery on Iona. From here, Christianity was spread to Scotland. Feast day: 9 June.

Columbia 34 00N 81 00W A city in the USA, the capital of South Carolina. An important commercial centre, its industries include textiles, plastics, and machinery. Fort Jackson (a major US Army post) is adjacent to the city. Population (1986): 93 020.

columbine. See Aquilegia.

columbium. See niobium.

Columbus 39 59N 83 03W A city in the USA, the capital of Ohio on the Scioto River. A major industrial and commercial centre of a rich agricultural area. Population (1986): 566 030.

Columbus, Christopher (1451–1506) Italian navigator, who discovered America. Born in Genoa, he became a pirate and in 1476 was shipwrecked off Portugal, where he settled. His plan to reach the East by sailing westwards was rejected by the Portuguese king (John the Perfect) but was supported by Ferdinand and Isabella of Spain. On 3 August, 1492, he set sail in the *Santa Maria*, landing on Watling Island (now San Salvador Island, in the Bahamas) in October. On his second voyage (1493–96) he discovered Guadeloupe, Puerto Rico, and Jamaica. His third voyage (1498–1500) achieved the discovery of Trinidad and the mainland of South America but ended in disaster: in 1499, following a revolt against him, command. Sent back to Spain in chains, he was released on arrival and shortly afterwards set off on his last voyage (1502–04). From this he returned ill and disheartened, dying not long afterwards in Valladolid.

column. See orders of architecture.

Comanche A North American Indian people of the southern Plains. They speak a language of the Uto-Aztecan group, closely related to *Shoshoni. They migrated to this area from Wyoming in the 18th century. They often attacked white men in Texas until they agreed to settle in Oklahoma in 1867.

combustion A chemical reaction in which a substance combines with oxygen, producing heat and light. The principal overall reactions are the oxidation of carbon to carbon dioxide and the oxidation of hydrogen to water (C + $2H_2 + 2O_2 \rightarrow CO_2 + 2H_2O$).

COMECON. See Council for Mutual Economic Assistance.

Comédie-Française The French national theatre, founded in 1680 and reconstituted in 1803 by Napoleon. It is organized as a cooperative society, owned by its members. Despite its strong emphasis on tradition, it has produced many of France's most original actors.

comet A small body moving in an elongated orbit around the sun. A typical comet consists of a small nucleus of ice and dust surrounded by a luminous cloud of gas and dust, the coma. Tails of gas and of dust only appear when a comet is near the sun; they point away from the sun and may be millions of kilometres long. **Short-period comets** (such as *Halley's comet) have orbital periods of less than 150 years. The remainder have much longer periods. A comet eventually breaks up to produce a stream of particles around its orbit.

Comintern. See International.

commedia dell'arte An Italian form of theatre that flourished throughout Europe from the 16th to the 18th centuries. It was performed by professional actors who made up comic and often vulgar stories, usually concerning romantic problems. The standard characters included *Harlequin, Pantaloon, and the lover Inamorato.

commensalism A relationship between two individuals of different species in which one (the commensal) lives with the other (the host), from which it derives food, shelter, or transport. The association neither harms nor benefits the host. Certain barnacles attached to whales provide an example. See also symbiosis.

commercial banks Institutions that offer a deposit, transfer, and loan service to companies and private individuals. In the UK, the commercial banks (or high-street banks) are public limited companies (joint-stock banks), most of which amalgamated during the 19th century to emerge from World War I as the big five: Barclays Bank, Lloyds Bank, Midland Bank, National Provincial Bank, and Westminster Bank (in 1968 the last two merged to form the National Westminster Bank). Others include the Royal Bank of Scotland and the Trustee Savings Bank. These are now facing competition from the building societies in personal banking.

common law The part of the law of England and of most English-speaking countries that was originally unwritten and based on the common customs of the country. Common law developed on the principle of judicial precedent, by which a decision on a case would have to be taken into account when deciding a similar case. It differs from the law established by Acts of Parliament, called statute law, from *equity, administered by the Court of *Chancery, and from the *civil law of most European countries.

Common Market. See European Community.

Common Prayer, Book of The official form of service of the Church of England. After the Reformation, Thomas *Cranmer and others set out an order of worship in English. The first Prayer Book was published under Edward VI in 1549; a more Protestant revision appeared in 1552. The Roman Catholic Queen Mary abolished the Prayer Book; when Elizabeth I came to the throne it was used again, but then abolished by the Puritans. The 1662 version, established by the Act of Uniformity, is still in use; a revised version was accepted in 1928. The 1980 *Alternative Service Book*, in modern English, is now preferred by the Church.

Commons, House of. See parliament.

Commonwealth (1649–53) The period in English history between the execution of Charles I and the establishment of the *Protectorate, or sometimes until the *Restoration in 1660 (this period is also called the Interregnum).

Commonwealth (British)   A loose association of 50 independent nations once under the rule of the government of the UK (*see* Empire, British). The Commonwealth of Nations was established by the Statute of Westminster (1931), based on the principles, stated at the 1926 Imperial Conference, of member states' independence, equality, and loyalty to the Crown. After World War II it became the Commonwealth, with the following states still members: Antigua and Barbuda, Australia, the Bahamas, Bangladesh, Barbados, Belize, Botswana, Brunei, Canada, Cyprus, Dominica, The Gambia, Ghana, Grenada, Guyana, India, Jamaica, Kenya, Kiribati, Lesotho, Malawi, Malaysia, Malta, Mauritius, New Zealand, Nigeria, Pakistan, Papua New Guinea, St Kitts-Nevis, St Lucia, Seychelles, Sierra Leone, Singapore, Solomon Islands, Sri Lanka, Swaziland, Tanzania, Tonga, Trinidad and Tobago, Uganda, the UK, Vanuatu, Western Samoa, Zambia, and Zimbabwe; Nauru, Tuvalu, Maldives, and St Vincent and the Grenadines are special members and are not represented at the meetings of Commonwealth heads of government; there are in addition a number of associated states and dependent territories. Commonwealth heads of government meet every two years.

communications satellite   An unmanned artificial satellite by which long-distance television broadcasting, telephone communications, and computer links are achieved. Radio signals are sent from one transmitting station to the satellite, where they are amplified and retransmitted to ground receiving stations.

The first active satellite was the US Telstar 1, launched in 1962. Telstar was in a low elliptical orbit and only visible for a short portion of its orbit. A communications satellite is now usually placed in a geostationary orbit, a circular orbit about 36 000 km above the earth's equator with a period of 24 hours in which it appears to remain nearly stationary in the sky.

Various organizations have been set up to provide worldwide communications; notably **Intelsat** (International Telecommunications Satellite Organization), which was founded in 1964 and now has over 100 member countries. **Direct broadcast satellites** can be picked up by domestic aerials without amplification at ground stations.

communism   A movement based on the joint ownership of all property. *The Communist Manifesto* (1848) of Marx and Engels set out a plan in which the capitalist system of private ownership is replaced by a communist society in which capital is communally owned. This process has several stages: the revolutionary overthrow of the middle classes (*see* Marxism), a temporary period when the people are ruled by a dictator (*see* Leninism), and the preparatory stage of *socialism.

In the second half of the 19th century several social democratic parties in Europe were influenced by Marxist theories, although they later aimed to reform capitalism (hence the term "reformist") rather than overthrow it. The exception was the Russian Social Democratic Labour Party, which

finally demolished the Tsar's administration in the Revolution of November, 1917. In 1918 this party became the Communist Party of the Soviet Union.

After the success of the Russian Revolution many socialist parties in other countries became communist parties, owing loyalty of varying degrees to the Soviet Communist Party (*see* International). In 1944–46 the Soviet army helped to establish communist administrations in several E European countries. In 1949 the communists in China overthrew the Nationalists and started the People's Republic of China. In 1989 the Communist parties in Poland, Hungary, Czechoslovakia, Bulgaria, Romania, and East Germany renounced their monopoly of power; the Soviet Communist Party followed suit in 1990. Communist parties in W Europe have affected elections in France and Italy. In the UK, the Communist Party (founded in 1920) claims some 7500 members.

Communism Peak (Russian name: Pik Kommunizma)   38 59N 72 01E The highest mountain in the Soviet Union, in the Pamirs in the S near the Afghan and Chinese borders. Height: 7495 m (24 589 ft).

community   In ecology, a group of living organisms that occupies a particular habitat. The plants and animals of a community are closely associated with each other in various ecological relationships: for example, they depend on one another for food (*see* food chain). The size and composition of the community depend on the nature of the habitat and its climate; it may show seasonal changes, or change gradually from year to year (*see* succession). *See also* ecology.

community service   A form of sentence introduced in the UK by the Criminal Justice Act (1972). It requires an offender to work for a set number of hours for the community instead of being imprisoned or fined. In the UK the offender must be aged 17 or over, have given his consent, and have committed no violence.

Como   45 48N 09 05E A city and resort in N Italy, in Lombardy on Lake Como. Known as Comum in Roman times, it has a 15th-century marble cathedral and a gothic town hall. Como has several industries, including the famous silk factories. Population (1989): 94 634.

Comoros, Federal and Islamic Republic of the   A country consisting of a group of islands in the Indian Ocean, between the Madagascar and the African mainland. The main islands are Grand Comoro, Anjouan, and Mohéli. The population is of mixed African and Arab descent. *Economy*: almost entirely agricultural. Sugar cane was formerly the main crop but vanilla and perfume plants are now increasing. *History*: became a French colony in the 19th century. At first joined to Madagascar, the Comoros became a separate French overseas territory in 1947. In a referendum in 1974 the majority voted in favour of independence, except for the island of Mayotte, which remains French. In 1976 the independence of the three islands was recognized by France. Official languages: French and Arabic; Swahili is also used commercially. Official currency: CFA franc of 100 centimes. Area: 1862 sq km (719 sq mi). Population (1987 est): 422 500. Capital and main port: Moroni.

compact disc A 120 mm metal disc covered in plastic, used for recording digital information. Data is represented by tracks cut in the disc and is read by a laser beam. Applications include the high fidelity *recording of sound and high capacity read-only memory (**CD-ROM**) for computers.

Companions of Honour, Order of the (CH) British order of chivalry, instituted in 1917. It consists of the sovereign and not more than 65 men and women who have made distinguished contributions to the nation.

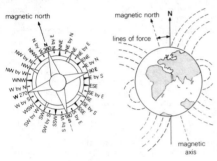

magnetic compass

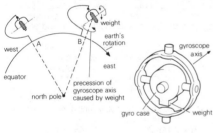

gyro compass

COMPASS *In the magnetic compass, the needle lines up with the earth's magnetic field. In the gyrocompass a spinning gyroscope is suspended on three mutually perpendicular frames. The axis of spin of a free gyroscope shifts round as the earth rotates: as the axis of the gyrocompass moves from the horizontal at position A to position B, a weight pulls it downwards. The gyroscopic effect causes the axis to shift round at right angles to the gravitational force (precess) and describe a circle around the N-S direction. With damping the gyroscope axis settles down pointing N.*

compass A device for determining the direction of magnetic north. The magnetic compass, which has been in use since the 2nd century BC, consists of a magnetic needle balanced on a point, the S end of the magnet indicating the direction of magnetic N. Compensation must be made for magnetic N not being in the same direction as geographic N in most longitudes and

for any ferrous objects near the compass. A more sophisticated compass, used on larger vessels and in aircraft, is the **gyrocompass**, which employs the effect of the earth's rotation on the orientation of a spinning object's axis of rotation.

Compiègne 49 25N 2 50E A town in N France, in the Oise department on the River Oise. Joan of Arc was captured here by the English in 1430. The Armistice (1918) was signed in a railway coach in the forest of Compiègne ending World War I as was the agreement made between the Pétain government and Hitler in 1940. Population (1983): 37 250.

complex numbers Quantities that consist of a real *number and an imaginary number. They may be written in the form $a + ib$, where a and b are real numbers and $i = \sqrt{-1}$. A complex number $a + ib$ may be thought of as a pair of ordered numbers (a,b) similar to a pair of Cartesian coordinates (x,y) (*see* coordinate systems). Then (a,b) can be regarded as a point on a plane called the complex plane or Argand diagram in which the real axis is taken as horizontal and the imaginary axis as vertical.

Composite order. *See* orders of architecture.

comprehensive schools Secondary schools attended by children of all abilities. In the UK the widespread introduction of comprehensive schools was started in 1965 by the Labour Government and by 1977 some 70% of the secondary-school population attended comprehensives. By 1986 this had risen to 85.4%, with only 3% in *grammar schools.

Compton, Arthur Holly (1892–1962) US physicist, who in 1923 discovered the **Compton effect** (increase in wavelength of electromagnetic radiation when scattered by free electrons). He shared the 1927 Nobel Prize with C. T. R. *Wilson.

computer A device for processing information at high speeds, by electronic methods. The principles behind the modern computer were conceived by Charles *Babbage in the 19th century. The first practical machines were built in Britain and the USA during World War II. Developments in information theory and the invention of the *transistor resulted in the computer revolution of the next 20 years. In the 1970s, advances in integrated circuits using silicon chips led to the development of *minicomputers and then *microcomputers.

A **digital computer** processes information in the form of groups of binary numbers (*see* bit), which are represented by the on and off positions of electronic switches. The sequence of operations it performs on this information is controlled by a *program, and the suite of programs that enables a computer to perform useful functions is called its *software. The physical equipment, or **hardware**, of a computer generally has three main components: the central processing unit (CPU), main memory, and devices that enable information to be fed into the machine, display it in a readable form, or act as auxiliary memory. Input, formerly by punched tape or cards, is now by keyboard at a visual display unit (VDU) or by methods of automatic data capture, such as optical character recognition (OCR).

Output is by printout on paper, VDU, or magnetic disc or tape. Developments, such as *compact discs and CPUs that work much faster by using optical rather than electrical impulses, promise to increase the power of computers. The laser printer has transformed the quality of the printed output. The **transputer**, which harnesses several microprocessors in parallel, offers microcomputer users the computing speed that is currently only available on large mainframe computers.

An **analog computer** deals with continuously varying physical quantities, such as current or voltage. They are used mainly for simulation or monitoring and in industry or scientific research. Sometimes they act alongside a digital computer (a combination known as a **hybrid computer**).

Comte, Auguste (1798–1857) French philosopher. Called the founder of sociology, he coined the term, although similar work had been done before him. His principal work is *Cours de philosophie positive* (6 vols, 1830–42).

Conakry (*or* Konakry) 9 25N 13 56W The capital of Guinea, a port on Tombo Island, linked to the mainland by a causeway. It was founded by the French in 1884 and became capital of French Guinea in 1893. Population (1983): 705 280.

concerto A musical composition for one or more solo instruments and orchestra, usually in three movements (a *sonata form movement, a slow movement, and a rondo finale). In the late 18th century Mozart and Beethoven perfected the form in their piano concertos; 19th-century composers treated it more freely, developing the violin concerto; and in the 20th century concertos have been written in a number of different styles.

conch A heavy-shelled marine *snail. Conch shells have a roughly triangular outer whorl with a broad lip and can be 2–35 cm long.

Concorde. *See* aircraft.

concrete A building material that was used by the Romans but in its modern form followed the invention of Portland *cement in 1824. Concrete consists of a mixture of Portland cement and an aggregate of sand, gravel, and stones. When water is added, hydration reactions cause the cement to harden around the aggregate. **Reinforced concrete**, invented in France in 1850, uses steel bars (usually up to 50 mm in diameter) to increase its tensile strength. In **prestressed concrete** the concrete is maintained in a state of compression by stretching the steel reinforcing wires (usually 6 mm in diameter) and keeping them in a state of tension after the concrete has set.

condensation 1. A change of physical state from a gas or vapour to a liquid. Condensation occurs in buildings when warm moist air comes in contact with cold surfaces, such as windows and uninsulated walls. 2. A type of organic chemical reaction in which two molecules combine to form a larger molecule with elimination of a smaller molecule, such as water or methanol.

conditioned reflex A *reflex learnt by associating a particular stimulus with a normal stimulus. In *Pavlov's experiments with dogs, the normal stimulus causing salivation (i.e. food) was paired with a different stimulus (a ringing bell) so often that eventually the bell by itself caused the dogs to salivate. *See also* conditioning.

conditioning The process by which animals (and humans) alter their behaviour by learning that two events are related in some way. For example, an action may be rewarded or punished, which thus either encourages or discourages the behaviour. *See also* conditioned reflex.

condor A huge South American vulture, *Vultur gryphus*, found high in the Andes. It is black with a white ruff, bare pink head and neck, and has a wingspan of 3 m. It feeds chiefly on carrion. The very rare Californian condor (*Gymnogyps californianus*) is smaller with a bare yellow head and red neck.

conduction 1. (thermal) The transfer of heat from a region of high temperature to one of lower temperature, without the transfer of matter. It occurs when kinetic *energy is transferred by collisions between atoms and molecules in gases, liquids, and nonmetallic solids. In metals the energy is transferred by collisions between the free electrons and the ions of the lattice. 2. (electrical) The passage of an electric current through a substance. In metals, which are the best conductors, it results from the passage of free electrons moving in one direction under the influence of an electric field. In an electrolyte it is due to the passage of positive ions in one direction and negative ions in the other. In gases it is due to positive ions flowing in one direction and electrons in the other. In *semiconductors it results from the passage of electrons in one direction and positive holes in the other.

cone (botany) The structure (strobilus) that bears the reproductive organs (sporophylls) in some primitive plants (clubmosses, etc.) and conifers. In conifers both male and female cones are produced: the familiar woody cones of pines, etc., are female with overlapping woody structures called bract scales, which bear the sporophylls in their clefts.

Coney Island 40 35N 73 59W A resort in the USA, in New York City on the S shore of Long Island. With its amusement parks and beach it attracts many tourists.

Confederate States The 11 southern states of the USA that withdrew from the Union (1860–61), bringing about the US *Civil War: South Carolina, Georgia, Texas, Virginia, Arkansas, Tennessee, North Carolina, Mississippi, Florida, Alabama, and Louisiana.

Confederation of British Industry (CBI) The employers' association in the UK. The CBI represents the employers in talks with the government and the Trades Union Congress on prices and incomes policies and sets out industry's views on economic and financial matters.

confirmation A Christian ceremony that completes the introduction of a member into the Church. In the Eastern Orthodox Church, it is administered by a priest immediately after baptism and followed by Holy Communion; in the West, it is given by a bishop–in the Roman Catholic Church not before the seventh birthday and usually at the age of 11 or 12, and in the Anglican Churches after the child has learnt the catechism.

Confucius (Kong Zi *or* K'ung-fu-tzu; c. 551–479 BC) Chinese philosopher, the founder of Confucianism. A minor official, he was promoted to ministerial rank, becoming famous for his effective policies. When the ruler refused to heed his advice, he left (c. 496) and spent many years wandering from court to court. Most of the works supposedly by him are later collections but the *Analects (Lun Yu)* is probably a genuine collection of his sayings. The teaching of **Confucianism** is contained in five books. Retaining the concept of a divine will (*ming*), Confucianism emphasizes man's duty to his fellows, according to precise rules. It was the official religion of China until the Cultural Revolution (1966–68).

Congo, People's Republic of the (name until 1960: Middle Congo) A country in W central Africa, bordering on the Zaïre River. The uplands give way to plains in the NE. The population is chiefly Bantu. *Economy*: largely agricultural, with some minerals, including lead, zinc, and gold; oil was discovered in 1969. *History*: in the 15th century the Portuguese established trading relations with the Congo kingdom. In the 19th century the French explorer Pierre de Brazza (1852–1905) established the colony of Middle Congo, which in 1910 became one of the four territories of French Equatorial Africa. In 1958 it attained internal self-government as a member of the French Community and in 1960 became independent as the Republic of Congo. Official language: French. Official currency: CFA (Communauté financière africaine) franc of 100 centimes. Area: 342 000 sq km (132 018 sq mi). Population (1988 est): 2 266 000. Capital: Brazzaville. Main port: Pointe-Noire.

Congo, Republic of. *See* Zaïre, Republic of.

Congo River. *See* Zaïre River.

Congregationalism A form of church government in which central power is rejected and each congregation is independent. Congregationalist groups were active during the Reformation, and in England the Independents, as they were known, were strong during the Commonwealth, having opposed Charles I. Congregationalism spread to America, where it grew fast. In England, the United Reformed Church was founded in 1972 by the union of the Congregationalists with the Presbyterians.

Congress The law-making body of the USA set up by the *constitution (1789) and consisting of the Senate, the upper house, and the House of Representatives, the lower house. The Senate serves as a check on the larger House of Representatives, with which it has equal law-making responsibility as well as powers to approve treaties and confirm appointments. Each state in the Union is represented by two senators. There are 435 seats in the House of Representatives, shared among the states according to population.

Congreve, William (1670–1729) British dramatist. Educated in Ireland, he returned to England in 1688 to study law but, supported by

*Dryden, entered the literary world instead. The comedies *Love for Love* (1695) and *The Way of the World* (1700) are his best-known plays.

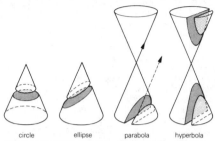

CONIC SECTION *The circle, ellipse, parabola, and hyperbola are produced by slicing through the cone.*

conic sections Geometrical figures produced by the intersection of a plane and a cone. If the plane cuts the cone at right angles to its axis the figure is a *circle. If the plane is tilted slightly an *ellipse is formed. If the plane is tilted further, until it lies parallel to the side of the cone, the figure is a *parabola. Tilted more, the figure becomes a *hyperbola, which has two branches because the plane also intersects another cone the vertex of which touches the vertex of the first cone.

conifer A *gymnosperm tree of the colder temperate zones. Nearly all conifers are evergreen (larches are exceptions), with simple needle-like or scalelike leaves. The reproductive organs are typically borne in separate male and female *cones, usually on the same tree, and produce winged seeds that are dispersed by wind (the yew and juniper are exceptions). Conifers also include the pines, cedars, spruces, firs, cypresses, and sequoias.

Coniston Water A lake in NW England, in Cumbria in the Lake District. World water-speed records were established here by Sir Malcolm Campbell (1939) and his son Donald Campbell (1959). Length: 8 km (5 mi).

conjugation The process by which exchange of genetic material occurs in certain lower organisms by means of a connecting tube between the two "mating" individuals. In ciliate protozoa and certain algae it is a type of sexual reproduction, involving a cytoplasmic bridge (protozoa) or a conjugation tube (algae). In bacteria the connection between "male" and "female" cells is by means of special hairs (pili) or cell-to-cell bridges.

conjunction An alignment of two celestial bodies in the solar system, usually the sun and a planet, when the angular distance between them as seen from earth (i.e. the angle planet-earth-sun) becomes zero.

conjunctivitis Inflammation of the conjunctiva—the membrane that covers the surface of the eye and lines the eyelids. Known as pinkeye, it is marked by itching, redness, and watering of the eye. It may be caused by allergy, bacterial infection, or irritation.

Connacht (or Connaught) A province and ancient kingdom of the NW Republic of Ireland. It consists of the counties of Galway, Leitrim, Mayo, Roscommon, and Sligo. Area: 17 122 sq km (6611 sq mi). Population (1986): 430 726.

Connaught. See Connacht.

Connecticut A state in the NE USA, in New England. It is one of the most densely populated states in the USA. Yale University at New Haven is the most famous of its large number of universities. History: one of the original 13 colonies in the USA, it was first explored by the Dutch in the early 17th century. The first settlement was by English colonists from the Massachusetts Bay Colony (1633–35). Area: 12 973 sq km (5009 sq mi). Population (1983 est): 3 138 000. Capital: Hartford.

connective tissue The tissue that supports, binds, or separates the specialized tissues and organs of the body. Connective tissue consists of a pastelike ground substance of polysaccharide and protein in which are embedded white collagen fibres, yellow elastic fibres, and various cells (including fibroblasts, which produce the ground substance and the fibres). The amount of collagen determines the toughness of the tissue. Specialized connective tissue includes fatty tissue, blood, bone, and cartilage.

Connemara An area in the W Republic of Ireland, in Co Galway bordering on the Atlantic Ocean. It contains many lakes, peat bogs, and the Twelve Bens, a group of quartzite mountains.

conquistador (Spanish: conqueror) One of the Spanish conquerors of the Indians of Central and South America in the first half of the 16th century. They were driven by a desire to find fame and gold and to serve the Roman Catholic Church. The most famous were Hernán *Cortés and Francisco *Pizarro.

Conrad, Joseph (Teodor Josef Konrad Watęcz Korzeniowski; 1857–1924) Polish-born British novelist, who knew no English before he was 20. Orphaned at the age of 11, he went to Marseilles in 1874, where he became a sailor. Conrad published his first novel, Almayer's Folly, in 1895. His seagoing experiences influenced his fiction and his own outlook. His major novels include Lord Jim (1900), Nostromo (1904), and Under Western Eyes (1911).

Conservative Party A UK political party that grew out of the Tory party in the 1830s under the leadership of Sir Robert *Peel. When he abolished the *Corn Laws (1846) there was a split in the party, with the Peelites later joining the Liberal Party. Under the leadership of *Disraeli the Conservatives developed a clear philosophy, combining support for the monarchy, the Empire, and the Church of England. Under *Salisbury and then Balfour the party was almost continuously in power from 1886 to 1905 and again, under Bonar *Law, *Baldwin, Neville *Chamberlain, and *Churchill, from 1922 to 1945. After the Labour landslide of 1945 it returned to power led by Churchill (1951–55), Eden (1955–57), Macmillan (1957–63), Home (1963–64), Heath (1970–74), Thatcher (1979–90), and Major (1990–). The party is commit-

ted to encouraging free enterprise and individualism.

Consols. See gilt-edged security.

Constable, John (1776–1837) British landscape painter. After working for his father, he trained in London at the Royal Academy schools. He painted the Suffolk countryside, Hampstead Heath, and Salisbury Cathedral with a particular concern for changing weather conditions, as in his Haywain (1821; National Gallery, London) and Dedham Vale (1828; National Gallery, Edinburgh).

Constantine the Great (?285–337 AD) Roman emperor in the West (312–24) and sole emperor (324–37). The son of Constantius (c. 250–306), Constantine was acclaimed as his father's successor by his troops at York but did not secure his position until he defeated his rival Maxentius (d. 312). He became sole emperor after defeating the Eastern emperor Licinius (c. 270–325; reigned 311–24). Constantine was the first Roman emperor to adopt Christianity. In 313 he issued the Edict of Milan, which established toleration of Christians, and in 325 summoned the Council of *Nicaea. He was baptized on his deathbed.

Constantinople. See Istanbul.

constellations The 88 areas into which the N and S hemispheres of the sky are now divided. Each star, galaxy, or other celestial body lies within, or sometimes overlaps, the boundaries of one of the constellations and is often named in terms of this constellation. The constellations originally had no fixed limits but were groups of stars forming a distinctive pattern.

constitution The principles by which a country is governed, defining the powers of those who make laws and those who carry them out. The UK has an unwritten constitution consisting of some statutes (laws established, by Acts of Parliament), much *common law, and a good deal of custom. In many countries, the constitution is written. The US constitution was drawn up in 1787. It contains 7 articles and 27 amendments of which 10 make up the *Bill of Rights (1791). Since 1791, the American Constitution has been altered to include the abolition of slavery (13), the right to vote for all (15), and *prohibition of liquor (18).

constrictor A nonvenomous snake occurring in tropical regions that kills by coiling its muscular body around its prey and squeezing until it suffocates. They often have claws, which are vestigial limbs. Boas and pythons are types of constrictor.

constructivism A movement in abstract sculpture, architecture, and design, which was launched in Russia by the Realist Manifesto (1920) of the brothers Naum Gabo (1890–1977) and Antoine Pevsner (1886–1962) with the aim of freeing contemporary art from political overtones. The movement made use of modern materials, such as plastic and steel.

consuls The two magistrates who held complete non-military and military power under the *Roman Republic. They were elected annually by the Comitia Centuriata and were at the head of the Senate. Under the Empire they were chosen by the emperor and held office for only two to four months, after which they held the post in name only.

contact lenses A removable form of lens worn directly against the eye to replace spectacles or to protect the eye in some corneal disorders. Originally made of glass, modern plastic lenses can be hard (corneal), gas permeable (allowing oxygen to permeate the cornea), or soft (hydrophilic). At first the lenses may irritate the eyes, but most people can adapt to them with time.

contempt of court An act or failure to act that tends to weaken the authority of a court or lessen the chances of a fair trial. Examples include insulting a presiding judge, failing to obey a court order, or publishing matters on which the court is to decide. A person found in contempt may be fined or imprisoned.

continent One of the major land masses of the earth: Asia, Africa, North America, South America, Europe, Australia, and Antarctica.

continental drift The theory, first set out in 1912 by Alfred Wegener, that the continents are slowly drifting (*see also* plate tectonics). Wegener's work was based on similarities in geological structures, the plant and animal life, and coastal outlines of different continents. Recently changes in the earth's magnetic field have provided firmer evidence. It is believed that about 200 million years ago a supercontinent (Pangaea) began to break up and the fragments drifted apart until the continents reached their present positions. It is possible that continents have been joining together and breaking up throughout the earth's history.

continental shelf The area of sea floor adjacent to the continents, dipping gently from the shoreline to a depth of about 200 m. At this depth, the continental slope begins, dipping more steeply to the ocean bottom. Shelves tend to be wider off low-lying regions than mountainous regions; the average width is about 70 km.

contraception The prevention of unwanted pregnancy, also known as birth control and family planning. The rhythm method and coitus interruptus are the most simple but least reliable. In the former intercourse is avoided around the middle of the menstrual cycle, when release of the egg (ovulation) is most likely; in the latter the penis is withdrawn before ejaculation. Barrier methods include the condom (or sheath), which is worn over the penis, and the diaphragm, which is fitted over the entrance (cervix) of the womb and should be used with a spermicidal jelly (which kills sperm). More reliable is the intrauterine device (IUD)—a loop or coil inserted into the womb. In some women, however, it causes heavy menstrual bleeding or recurrent infection. Since the 1960s, the most efficient means of preventing pregnancy has been 'the pill' (*see* oral contraceptive), but this, too, may produce side effects. Recently developed methods include the use of a soft polythene sponge soaked with spermicide, which is inserted into the vagina and gives 24-hour protection; a morning-after pill for women; and implants of progestogen (synthetic *progesterone), which are inserted under the

skin and give long-term protection. *See also* sterilization.

contract In law, a promise or bargain, which can be enforced, usually written but sometimes spoken. Something of value, called "consideration," must be exchanged in return for the promise, although it need not be of the same value. Breach of contract, meaning failure to carry out the promise, may result in the offender having to pay for the loss of the other party.

convection The transfer of heat within a fluid (a gas or liquid) by means of motion of the fluid. Convection may be natural or forced. In natural convection, the fluid flows by virtue of the warmer part being less dense than the cooler part. Thus the warmer fluid rises and the colder fluid sinks under the influence of gravity. In forced convection, some external cause, such as a fan, drives colder fluid into a warmer one, or vice versa.

Convocations of Canterbury and York The assemblies of the clergy of the two provinces of the Church of England. Dating from at least the 8th century, they were originally assemblies of bishops only. They were later divided into two houses, an upper house made up of diocesan bishops and a lower house made up of certain lower clergy. The extent of their powers varied, but essentially they had the right to tax themselves and managed to keep this right until after the Restoration. From 1717 to 1852, however, they were prevented from dealing with questions of business and held only formal meetings. In 1969 many of their powers were taken on by the General Synod of the Church of England.

convolvulus A widely distributed twining plant with bell-shaped flowers. The Eurasian bindweed (*Convolvulus arvensis*) has persistent roots and rapidly growing stems. Some species are cultivated in gardens; others have medicinal (purgative) properties.

cony. *See* hyrax; pika.

Cook, Captain James (1728–79) British navigator and mapmaker. He joined the Royal Navy (1755) and served in the *Seven Years' War (1756–63). His observations on the eclipse of the sun in 1766 were presented to the Royal Society, which gave him command of an expedition to Tahiti. The expedition set sail in the *Endeavour* in 1768 and observed the passage of Venus across the sun; Cook went on to discover New Zealand and the E coast of Australia, returning to England in 1771. On his second voyage (1772–75), in the *Resolution*, he sailed round the Antarctic, charting Easter Island and discovering New Caledonia, the South Sandwich Islands, and South Georgia Island. On his return he received the Royal Society's Copley Medal for his work on diet (on avoiding scurvy). On his third voyage (1776–79) he was killed by Hawaiians.

Cook, Mount (Maori name: Aorangi) 43 37S 170 08E The highest mountain in New Zealand, in South Island in the Southern Alps. Height: 3764 m (12 349 ft).

Cook Islands A group of scattered islands in the SE Pacific Ocean, a New Zealand dependency. The chief islands are Rarotonga, Atiu, and Aitutaki. Fruit, copra, and mother-of-pearl are exported. Area: 241 sq km (93 sq mi). Population (1986): 17 185. Capital: Avarua.

coolabar A *eucalyptus tree, *Eucalyptus microtheca*, growing to 25 m, common inland in W Australia. The wood, which is grey outside but deep red within, is also called jinbul, moolar, blackbox, and dwarf box.

Coolidge, John Calvin (1872–1933) US statesman; Republican president (1923–29). His presidency followed the scandals associated with Warren Harding (1865–1923) but Coolidge's honesty was never questioned. He did little to control the stock market and to prevent the 1929 financial crash.

Cooper, Gary (Frank James C.; 1901–61) US film actor, best known for his Hollywood westerns, including *The Virginian* (1929), *The Westerner* (1940), and *High Noon* (1952).

cooperative societies Societies that make, buy, or sell produce, either without profit or with profits shared among members or shareholders. The cooperative movement began in the early 19th century to avert the hardship caused by competition. Cooperative societies in agriculture, in which machinery is shared and produce is sold jointly, are common in both the advanced and developing countries. In the UK the largest cooperative is the Cooperative Wholesale Society (CWS).

coordinate systems Geometrical systems that locate points in space by a set of numbers, the coordinates of the point.
In **Cartesian coordinates**, devised by René *Descartes, a point is located by its distance from intersecting axes. In a plane (two dimensions) there are two axes and in space (three dimensions) there are three. Usually the axes are at right angles to each other.
Polar coordinates denote position by distance and direction, using a fixed point, called the origin, and a fixed line, called the polar axis. The polar coordinates are the length, r, of the radius of the circle centred at the origin and passing through the point, and the angle, θ, between this radius and the polar axis. In three dimensions, **spherical polar coordinates** are used. The radius of a sphere centred at the origin and the two angles it makes with the polar axis define the point.

coot An aquatic bird of the *rail family, with lobed toes, which dives to feed on small animals and aquatic plants. The European coot (*Fulica atra*) occurs throughout the Old World and is 37 cm long with black plumage and a white bill.

Copenhagen (Danish name: København) 55 40N 12 35E The capital and chief port of Denmark, on the E coast of Sjælland. Notable buildings include the 17th-century Charlottenborg Palace (now the Royal Academy of Arts) and Christiansborg Palace (now the parliamentary and government buildings). *History*: settled in 900 AD, it became capital of Denmark in 1443. In 1801 the Danish fleet was destroyed by Nelson at the battle of Copenhagen. In 1728, and again in 1795, it was badly destroyed by fire. Population (1988): 619 985.

Copernicus, Nicolaus (1473–1543) Polish astronomer, who developed the modern theory of the solar system. After studying mathematics

and music at Cracow and Bologna, Copernicus became interested in calculating planetary positions. He noticed that by using a system in which the earth revolved round the sun, instead of *Ptolemy's system in which the earth was at the centre of the universe, these calculations were easier to make. His book *De revolutionibus orbium coelestium* was published in 1543.

Copland, Aaron (1900–90) US composer, teacher, and pianist. He is best known for the ballets *Billy the Kid* (1938), *Rodeo* (1942), and *Appalachian Spring* (1944). Other works include a jazz piano concerto (1927), *Fanfare for the Common Man* (1942), and a *Piano Fantasy* (1950) using *serialism.

copper (Cu) A reddish-brown metal, known from prehistoric times and named after the island of Cyprus, which was the principal source in Roman times. It occurs as the element, the sulphide chalcopyrite ($CuFeS_2$), the carbonate malachite ($CuCO_3.Cu(OH)_2$), and in other minerals. It is mined in Zambia, Zaïre, Chile, Australia, New Guinea, and elsewhere. Copper is extracted by *smelting and *electrolysis. It is important because of its good electrical (second only to silver) and thermal conductivity. Copper wire is widely used in the electrical industry and copper pipes are used in plumbing. It is contained in *brass and *bronze and other alloys. At no 29; at wt 63.546; mp 1083°C; bp 2595°C.

copra. See coconut.

Coptic Church The largest Christian Church in Egypt, which traces its history to St *Mark. As a result of its Monophysite beliefs, condemned at the Council of Chalcedon (451), the Coptic Church became isolated from other Christian groups. The Muslim conquest of Egypt in 642, together with language and cultural differences, widened the division. The Church suffered some persecution under Arab rule. In 1741 a number of Copts entered the Roman Catholic communion, becoming the Uniat Coptic Church. Alexandria, important in the early Church, remains the seat of the head of the Coptic Church. The Copts are in fellowship with the Armenian and Syrian (Orthodox) Churches.

copyright law The law protecting the sole right of anyone who creates or publishes original literary, dramatic, and artistic works to reproduce them and to make use of them. The protection in England lasts for 50 years after the death of the owner of the copyright. Copyright is different from a patent in that it cannot exist in an idea, but only in its expression.

coral A sedentary marine animal belonging to a class of *coelenterates. They are found in all oceans, feeding mainly on small animals. Reproduction can be asexual (by budding) or sexual, the eggs being fertilized in the water. The stony (or true) corals secrete an external skeleton of calcium carbonate. **Coral reefs** are slowly produced by succeeding colonies of stony corals, at temperatures above 20°C. The skeletons of some corals are used as gemstones.

coral snake A burrowing venomous snake that preys on other snakes. Most species are ringed with red, black, and yellow or white. Coral snakes occur in America, SE Asia, and Africa.

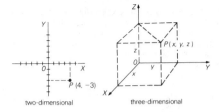

cartesian coordinates

two-dimensional   three-dimensional

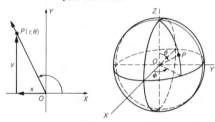

polar coordinates

two-dimensional   three-dimensional

COORDINATE SYSTEMS *In two-dimensional Cartesian coordinates a point P is located by giving its* x- *and* y- *coordinates, in this case 4 and -3 (always given in this order, as shown). In three-dimensional Cartesian coordinates* P *is located in terms of three axes. In polar coordinates* P *is located by a radius* r *and an angle* θ. *In three dimensions a second angle,* φ, *is required.*

cor anglais A double-reeded musical instrument, the alto member of the oboe family. It is a transposing instrument, the notes sounding a fifth lower than written. It has a range of two and a half octaves from the E below middle C.

Corbusier, Le. *See* Le Corbusier.

Córdoba 37 53N 4 46W A city in S Spain, in Andalusia on the River Guadalquivir. It became the capital of Moorish Spain in 756 AD and by the 10th century was Europe's largest cultural centre. Its immense Moorish cathedral (8th–10th centuries) was originally a mosque. Population (1986): 304 826.

Corfu (Latin name: Corcyra; Modern Greek name: Kérkira *or* Kérkyra) A Greek island in the NE Ionian Sea. It has belonged to many powers, including Venice (1386–1797) and Britain (1815–64). The local produce includes olives and fruit; tourism is important. Area: 641 sq km (250 sq mi). Population (1981): 97 102. Chief town: Corfu.

corgi One of two breeds of working dog originating in SW Wales. The Cardigan Welsh corgi has a long tail, rounded ears, and a shortish coat, which may be brown or black and tan; the Pembroke Welsh corgi has a short tail, pointed ears, and a finer coat of red, fawn, or black and tan. Height: 30 cm (Cardigan); 25–30 cm (Pembroke).

coriander An annual plant, *Coriander sativum*, of the carrot family. 20–70 cm high, it has

small pink or white flowers. Probably native to the Mediterranean, its seeds are used as a spice.

Corinth (Greek name: Kórinthos) 37 56N 22 55E A port in S Greece. *History*: a settlement before 3000 BC, it became the second largest city state after Athens. Rivalry between the two led to the *Peloponnesian War. Destroyed by the Romans in 146 BC, Corinth was later revived as a Roman colony (44 BC). Population (1981): 22 495.

Corinthian order. *See* orders of architecture.

Corinthians, Epistles of Paul to the Two New Testament books written by the apostle Paul to the Christian Church at Corinth in about 57 AD. In the first he answers questions on practical matters, for example marriage and celibacy, the resurrection of the dead, and the *Eucharist. In the second he defends himself against his opponents at Corinth.

Coriolis force A *force required to account for the motion of a body as seen by an observer in a rotating frame of reference. For example, a shell shot from a gun at the centre of a rotating table appears to an outside observer to travel in a straight line. To an observer on the table it appears to have a curved path. The Coriolis force is required to account for this apparent tangential acceleration. Named after the French physicist Gaspard de Coriolis (1792–1843).

cork Tissue that forms the outer layer of *bark in woody plants. The cork oak (*Quercus suber*) is cultivated in Portugal and SW Spain as the source of commercial cork. The cork is stripped from the tree every 8–10 years.

Cork (Irish name: Corcaigh) The largest county in the Republic of Ireland. Mountains in the W extend eastwards intersected by valleys, notably that of the River Blackwater. Its coastal inlets include Bantry Bay and Cork Harbour. Agriculture and fishing are important. Area: 7459 sq km (2880 sq mi). Population (1986): 279 427. County town: Cork.

Cork (Irish name: Corcaigh) 51 54N 8 28W The second largest city in the Republic of Ireland and county town of Co Cork. The settlement grew up around a monastery (founded by St Finbarr in the 6th century AD); its buildings include the Protestant and Catholic cathedrals and the university. An industrial and trading centre, it has a fine harbour. Population (1986): 133 196.

corm A fleshy underground stem base of certain perennial herbaceous plants that acts as an overwintering structure. Growth the following season occurs by one or more buds.

cormorant A long-necked waterbird, related to gannets, found on most coasts and some inland waters. 50–100 cm in length, cormorants are glossy black and have webbed feet and a long hook-tipped bill.

cornea The transparent outer layer of the eyeball. Corneal grafts have been used successfully using tissue from donors to treat diseases of the cornea; since the cornea has no blood supply the graft cannot be rejected by antibodies in the patient's blood.

cornet A trumpet-like valved brass instrument, with cup-shaped mouthpiece and conical bore. Pitched in B flat, it has a range of two and a half octaves from the E below middle C.

cornflower An annual plant, *Centaurea cyanus*, of the daisy family, growing to about 75 cm high, found widely as a weed in fields. Flowers are bright blue.

Cornish A *Celtic language of the Brythonic group which used to be spoken in Cornwall and Devon, but became extinct in about 1800.

Corn Laws The laws that controlled (1360–1846) the import and export of corn to guarantee farmers' incomes. They were disliked by the working classes, because they kept the price of bread high, and by the manufacturers, who argued that little money was left for buying manufactured goods. The Anti-Corn Law League was led by Richard Cobden (1804–65) and John Bright (1811–89). In 1846 Sir Robert *Peel's government abolished them.

cornucopia A decorative motif from Greek antiquity denoting abundance and wealth. It consists of a goat's horn filled with fruit and flowers.

Cornwall (Celtic name: Kernow) The most southwesterly county of England, including the Isles of *Scilly. It consists mainly of hills rising to Bodmin Moor in the E. Agriculture and tourism are important but tinmining has declined. Area: 3546 sq km (1369 sq mi). Population (1987 est): 453 100. Administrative centre: Truro.

Cornwall, Duchy of A private estate of some 130 000 acres, mostly in Cornwall, Devon, and Somerset, belonging to the eldest son of the sovereign.

corona The outer layer of a star's atmosphere. The sun's **inner corona** lies above the chromosphere and consists of rapidly moving electrons. Its temperature reaches about 2 000 000 °C some 75 000 km above the visible solar surface (the *photosphere). The sun's **outer corona** extends for millions of kilometres and consists of comparatively slow-moving dust particles. *See also* solar wind.

coronary heart disease The most common form of *heart disease in the western world. It is caused by *atherosclerosis (fat deposits) of the coronary arteries, which reduces the blood flow to the heart. This may lead to the formation of a blood clot in these arteries—**coronary thrombosis**. The patient experiences sudden pain in the chest (*see* angina pectoris) and the result may be a heart attack (*see* myocardial infarction). The disease is associated with smoking, lack of exercise, high-fat diets, high blood pressure, and middle age; it is commoner in men. **Coronary bypass surgery** (using blood vessels from the leg to bypass blockages in the coronary arteries) has been very successful.

coroner In England and Wales, an officer of the Crown appointed by a county council to inquire into a death by violence, in suspicious circumstances, or in prison. Coroners, who are barristers, solicitors, or doctors, may be helped by a jury of 7 to 11 people. If the jury reaches a verdict of manslaughter or murder the coroner can commit the accused for trial. A coroner also inquires into cases of *treasure trove. In Scotland, the coroner's duties are carried out by the procurator fiscal.

Corot, Jean Baptiste Camille (1796–1875) French landscape painter, whose misty landscapes were highly praised in the 1850s. More popular today are his open-air sketches, small landscapes, and figure studies.

corporation tax A tax imposed on the profits of a company on a yearly basis. In the UK, the rate of tax is announced by the chancellor of the exchequer in his budget. From 1988 it was 35% (25% for small companies).

Corpus Christi, Feast of (Latin: body of Christ) A Christian feast honouring the institution of the *Eucharist, observed in the West on the second Thursday after *Whit Sunday. It is not generally observed by Protestant Churches.

Corpus Juris Civilis. *See* Roman law.

Correggio (Antonio Allegri; c. 1494–1534) Italian Renaissance painter, born at Correggio, near Modena. He worked chiefly in Parma, where he decorated the Camera di S Paolo, the domed vaulting of S Giovanni Evangelista, and the cathedral with frescoes.

Corsica (French name: Corse) An island in the Mediterranean Sea, a region of France. It is mountainous and largely covered with *maquis*, dense scrub vegetation. Agriculture produces fruit, olives, vegetables, and tobacco; tourism is also important. *History*: under Genoese control from the 14th century, it was sold to France in 1768. During World War II it came under Italian occupation but was liberated by the French in 1943. Area: 8680 sq km (3367 sq mi). Population (1984): 244 600. Capital: Ajaccio.

Cortés, Hernán (1485–1547) Spanish conquistador. In Hispaniola and Cuba from 1504, he led an expedition to Mexico in 1519 and reached Tenochtitlán, the capital of the Aztec Empire. In Cortés' absence the Aztecs launched an attack on Tenochtitlán, forcing the Spaniards' retreat—the *noche triste* (night of sorrows). Cortés eventually rebuilt his forces and destroyed Tenochtitlán (1521) and the Aztec Empire, founding New Spain. After further expeditions he died in poverty in Spain.

cortex The outer tissues of an animal or plant organ. In plants the cortex is situated between the *epidermis and the conducting tissues of stems and roots. Its cell walls may contain corky and woody materials or silica, providing strength, and also stored food, usually starch. In animals the outer tissue of the *adrenal gland, the cerebrum, and the *kidney is called the cortex.

corticosteroids Steroid hormones secreted by the cortex of the adrenal glands (or synthetic drugs with similar properties). One group —called glucocorticoids (e.g. cortisone, prednisolone, and dexamethasone)—control the way the body uses carbohydrates, fats, and proteins. They are used as drugs to treat allergic conditions, inflammatory disorders, autoimmune diseases, and some cancers. Another group—the mineralocorticoids (e.g. aldosterone, fludrocortisone)—control the body's salt and water balance.

corundum A mineral consisting mainly of aluminium oxide, additional minerals giving a variety of colours. Sapphire is a blue variety containing iron and titanium; ruby contains chromium. Corundum being the second hardest mineral to diamond is used as an abrasive.

Corunna. *See* La Coruña.

corvette A small manoeuvrable warship, used during World War II by the Royal Navy for escorting ships threatened by submarines. In the days of sail, the corvette, smaller than a frigate, was a sloop rigged as a ship. Those that remained after World War II were renamed antisubmarine frigates in 1959.

Cos (Modern Greek name: Kos) A Greek island in the Dodecanese. It was a member of the Delian League and the home of Hippocrates. It produces fruit, silk, and tobacco. Cos lettuce originally came from here. Area: 282 sq km (109 sq mi). Population (1981): 20 350.

cosmic rays A continuous stream of high-energy *protons, that bombard the earth from space. They collide with atomic nuclei in the earth's atmosphere producing large numbers of elementary particles, known as secondary radiation. Some cosmic rays originate from the sun but most come from outside the solar system.

cosmology The study of the origin, evolution, and structure of the universe. Two simple but incorrect cosmological models are the flat earth draped by a canopy of stars and the earth-centred (geocentric) universe, the *Ptolemaic system. More accurate theories emerged as instruments were developed to study the heavens (*see* astronomy). The model now most widely accepted is the *big-bang theory.

Cossacks A people of S and SW Russia descended from Tatars and escaped slaves from Poland, Lithuania, and Muscovy. They set up a number of self-governing communities, which were given special privileges by Russian or Polish rulers in return for military service. Known for their horsemanship, the Cossacks slowly lost their independence as Russia expanded in the 17th and 18th centuries. Many fled Russia after the Revolution (1918–21) and collectivization (*see* collective farms) absorbed remaining Cossack communities.

Costa Rica, Republic of A country in Central America between Nicaragua and Panama. It includes the island of Cocos, 483 km (186 mi) to the SW. The Caribbean lowlands rise to a central plateau, with volcanic peaks reaching 3819 m (12 529 ft). The inhabitants are mainly Spanish, with a dwindling Indian population. *Economy*: the main crops are coffee, bananas, and sugar (the principal export). Almost 75% of the land is forested; minerals include gold, haematite, and sulphur. *History*: discovered by Columbus in 1502, it became a Spanish colony in 1540. It was part of the captaincy general of Guatemala until gaining independence in 1821. From 1824 until 1838 it formed part of the Central American Federation. Official language: Spanish. Official religion: Roman Catholic. Official currency: colon of 100 centimos. Area: 50 900 sq km (19 653 sq mi). Population (1988): 2 816 558. Capital:

San José. Main ports: Limón (on the Caribbean) and Puntarenas (on the Pacific).

cot death The death of a baby, usually occurring overnight in its cot, from an unidentifiable cause. Some 20% of infant deaths in the UK are cot deaths. The causes may include virus infections or allergic reactions.

Côte d'Ivoire, Republic of (Name until 1986: Ivory Coast) A country in West Africa, on the Gulf of Guinea. Swamps and tropical forests give way to savanna on higher land to the N. The population includes Baule, Bete, Senufo, and Malinke. *Economy*: livestock is important as well as coffee, maize, yams, and other tropical plants. *History*: explored by the Portuguese in the late 15th century, the area was disputed by several nations before becoming a French colony in 1893. It became part of French West Africa in 1904 and an overseas territory in 1946. Self-governing from 1958, it became independent in 1960. President: Félix Houphouët-Boigny. Official language: French. Official currency: CFA (Communauté financière africaine) franc of 100 centimes. Area: 322 463 sq km (124 470 sq mi). Population (1988 est): 11 634 000. Capital: Yamoussoukro. Main port: Abidjan.

cotoneaster A shrub of the rose family, native to N temperate regions of the Old World widely grown for its red berries. Some species are evergreen. *Cotoneaster horizontalis* is a popular ground and wall cover.

Cotonou 6 24N 2 31E The chief city in Benin, on the Gulf of Guinea. A deepwater port, it is the nation's main commercial centre. Population (1982 est): 487 020.

Cotopaxi 0 40S 78 28W The world's highest active volcano, in N central Ecuador, in the Andes. Height: 5896 m (19 457 ft).

Cotswold Hills A range of limestone hills in SW central England, mainly in Gloucestershire, noted for its picturesque towns and villages.

cotton A herbaceous plant of the mallow family, native to tropical and subtropical regions. Usually 1–2 m high, cotton plants bear whitish flowers and produce seed pods (bolls), which burst when filled with the soft masses of fibres. The bolls are harvested mechanically and the fibres separated from the seeds (ginning) and cleaned and aligned (carding), ready for spinning into yarn. Cotton cloth is widely used in garments, furnishings, etc. The seeds are crushed to yield cottonseed oil, used in margarines, soaps, etc., and the residue is used as a livestock feed.

cotyledon The seed leaf: the first leaf or leaves of the embryo in seed-bearing plants (gymnosperms and angiosperms). They may act as a food store within seeds, providing the embryo plant with sufficient energy to germinate. Flowering plants with one cotyledon are classified as *monocotyledons; those with two as *dicotyledons. *See* germination.

couch grass A grass, *Agropyron repens*, also known as quack grass or twitch, native to Europe and naturalized in other N temperate regions. 30–120 cm high, it is a persistent weed.

cougar A red-brown *cat, *Felis concolor*, of North and South America, also called puma, mountain lion, and catamount. It is 1.5–3 m long and has a powerful leap.

coulomb (C) The *SI unit of electric charge equal to the quantity of electricity transferred by a current of one ampere in one second. Named after Charles de Coulomb (1736–1806), French physicist.

Coulomb's law. *See* electric charge.

Council for Mutual Economic Assistance (COMECON) An economic association founded by several communist countries in 1949. Its current members are the Soviet Union, Bulgaria, Czechoslovakia, Hungary, Mongolia, Poland, Romania, and Cuba.

Council of Europe An association of European states, founded in 1949, that is committed to defending parliamentary democracy and to encouraging the economic and social progress of its members. Its seat is in Strasbourg.

COUNTERPOINT *An example of counterpoint from J. S. Bach's Fantasia in C minor.*

counterpoint The art of combining two or more melodic lines simultaneously in music. The use of counterpoint continued beyond the end of the polyphonic period.

Counter-Reformation A movement within the *Roman Catholic Church that opposed the Protestant *Reformation. It lasted from the middle of the 16th to the middle of the 17th century, and resulted in the emergence of the *Jesuits, the Council of *Trent, the extension of the *Inquisition, and a revival of Catholic spirituality.

country and western A type of US popular music that evolved from the hillbilly ballads of the Appalachian Mountains and the cowboy songs of the West. The singer is accompanied by the guitar and other stringed instruments. Influenced by other styles of popular music, country and western has its own offshoots, such as bluegrass.

county A geographical unit of local government. In the UK the name was originally applied by the Normans to the Anglo-Saxon shire. The Local Government Act (1972; effective 1974) joined together some old counties, established new ones, and placed a variety of public services in the hands of elected county councils. The Local Government (Scotland) Act (1973) created nine new regions and three island areas. Northern Ireland has 6 counties but administration is carried out by 26 district councils.

courgette A variety of marrow, also called zucchini, eaten when small and immature (up to 15 cm long). Mature courgettes resemble ordinary marrows.

coursing A blood sport dating back to 1500 BC, in which game (usually hare) is pursued by hounds (usually greyhounds). A meeting is presided over by a mounted umpire. Hounds are judged on points for their speed, for overtaking each other, and for forcing the quarry to turn.

The British coursing season is from September to March; its main event is the Waterloo Cup, staged in February at Altcar, Lancashire.

court-martial A court, consisting of commissioned officers in the army, navy, or air force, assembled to try a member of the services for an offence against military discipline or ordinary law. An offender can still be tried by ordinary courts, which must take into account any punishment imposed by the court-martial.

courts of law Assemblies in which the law is applied. In England and Wales *civil law is applied by the County Courts and the High Court of Justice, while *criminal law is applied by the Magistrates' Courts and the Crown Court. Appeals from the civil courts go to the civil division of the Court of Appeal and those from the criminal courts go from Magistrate's Courts to the Crown Court and from the Crown Court to the criminal division of the Court of Appeal. Two or more judges of the High Court, when sitting together, may make up a Divisional Court, which hears appeals on points of law from Magistrates' Courts and Crown Courts. The Divisional Court can either (1) order the lower court to continue its hearing while directing how the law should be applied or (2) allow or dismiss the appeal itself. The House of Lords is the Supreme Court of Appeal in both criminal and civil cases. The High Court of Justice and the Court of Appeal together with the Crown Court form the Supreme Court of Judicature.

The County Courts are responsible for most civil law actions. Divorce petitions start in the County Courts but are transferred to the High Court if defended. The High Court of Justice consists of the *Chancery, Queen's Bench (including the Admiralty Court and the Commercial Court), and Family Divisions.

A criminal case comes first before a Magistrates' Court (*see* justice of the peace), which is responsible for less serious cases (e.g. traffic offences) but commits more serious cases for trial at the Crown Court. The Crown Court, which was created in 1971 to replace the Courts of Assize and Courts of Quarter Session, is organized in six areas (Midland and Oxford, North Eastern, Northern, South Eastern, Wales and Chester, and Western). A Crown Court sits in London as the *Central Criminal Court (Old Bailey).

In Scotland the supreme court for civil cases is the Court of Session, established in 1532, and the supreme court for criminal cases is the High

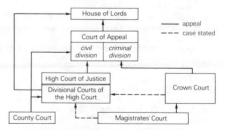

COURTS OF LAW

Court of Judiciary. Appeals from the former go to the House of Lords and from the latter to a tribunal of three judges of the High Court of Justiciary.

Cousteau, Jacques Yves (1910–) French naval officer and underwater explorer. He shared in the invention of the aqualung (1943) and invented a way of using television under water. In 1945 he founded the Undersea Research Group of the French navy at Marseilles and In 1950 became commander of the research vessel *Calypso*. He is famous for such films as *The Silent World* (1953) and *The Living Sea* (1963) and his ecological campaigns.

covenant A fixed agreement between two parties in which each promises to do something for the other (*see also* deed). In the Old Testament, the covenant between God and Israel forms the basis of the Jewish religion. In return for obedience to the Law (the Ten Commandments) as given to Moses, the Israelites were promised a special relationship with God as the chosen people.

Covenanters Scottish Presbyterians who in the 16th and 17th centuries promised to defend their church. The National Covenant of 1638 was signed by thousands of Scottish Presbyterians after Charles I's attempt to introduce the English Prayer Book. Their opposition came to a head in the Bishops' Wars. In the English *Civil War the Covenanters joined the parliamentarians in 1643 in return for the promise of church reform (the Solemn League and Covenant). After the Restoration (1660) they were persecuted until Presbyterianism was recognized by the State in Scotland after the Glorious Revolution (1688).

Covent Garden The principal English opera house (the Royal Opera House). The first theatre on the site was opened in 1732, the present building, dating from the 1850s, is the home of both the Royal Opera and the Royal Ballet Company. It takes its name from a square (originally a convent garden) onto which it backs, which was laid out in 1631 by Inigo *Jones. London's fruit and vegetable market occupied the square until 1973, when it moved to Nine Elms (Wandsworth) and the square became a shopping precinct.

Coventry 52 25N 1 30W A city in England, in the West Midlands. Heavily bombed during World War II, the city centre was almost entirely rebuilt. Its cathedral, designed by Sir Basil Spence, was opened in 1962 and retains the ruins of the old cathedral, which was bombed in 1940. Population (1984 est): 314 100.

Coward, Sir Noel (1899–1973) British dramatist, composer, and actor. *The Vortex* (1924) established his reputation but *Hay Fever* (1925) and *Blithe Spirit* (1941) are his best-known plays. He also contributed to revues, musicals, and films, notably *In Which We Serve* (1942) and *Brief Encounter* (1946).

Cowes 50 45N 1 18W A town in S England, on the Isle of Wight. It is a resort and yachting centre. Population (1981): 19 663.

cowpea An annual African plant, *Vigna unguiculata*, grown for food in tropical areas. The dried seeds of the short erect plant are eaten in Africa and America; the tall climbing plant, grown in SE Asia, has long pods eaten young.

Cowper, William (1731–1800) British poet. With John Newton he published *Olney Hymns* in 1779. "John Gilpin's Ride" (1783), a comic ballad, and "The Task" (1785), on rural themes, were both successful. His mental instability led to several suicide attempts.

cowpox A contagious virus disease of cattle that can be caught by man. Edward *Jenner used fluid from cowpox blisters to produce the first effective smallpox vaccine.

cowrie A marine snail found in warm seas. 1– 15 cm long, cowries have glossy shells with inrolled lips and feed at night on small animals. The shell of the tropical money cowrie (*Cypraea moneta*), about 3 cm long, is used as currency in Africa and India.

cowslip A perennial spring-flowering Eurasian herb, *Primula veris*, growing to a height of 20 cm. Related to the primrose, it has yellow flowers.

coyote A wild *dog, *Canis latrans*, of Central and North American grassland, also called prairie wolf. Coyotes are about 120 cm long, including the bushy tail (30 cm), and have yellowish fur.

coypu A South American aquatic rodent, *Myocaster coypus*. About 60 cm long (excluding a long hairless tail), it has webbed hind feet. They are farmed for the underfur of the belly, known as nutria.

crab A *crustacean with a wide body covered by a hard carapace. They have a pair of pincers and four pairs of legs for walking (typically sideways) or swimming. They are carnivores and most species are marine.

crab apple A tree, *Malus sylvestris*, 2–10 m high: one of the species from which cultivated *apples have been developed. A native of Europe and Asia, it is sometimes grown for ornament.

Crabbe, George (1754–1832) British poet, doctor, and cleric, born in Aldeburgh, Suffolk, scene of many of his poems. *The Village* (1783) a realistic portrayal of rural life, was followed by *The Borough* (1810) and *Tales of the Hall* (1819).

Crab nebula An expanding mass of gas, lying about 6000 light years distant in the constellation Taurus. It is the remnant of a *supernova, observed in 1054. Within the nebula lies the **Crab pulsar**, rotating with a period of 0.033 seconds.

Cracow. See Kraków.

Craig, Edward Henry Gordon. See Terry, Ellen.

crake A small shy bird belonging to the *rail family, commonly found in marshes. The Eurasian spotted crake (*Porzana porzana*) is 23 cm long and has a red ring at the base of the bill.

Cram, Steve (1960–) British middle-distance runner. He won the world championship 1500 m title in 1982–83 and set several new world records, including the mile and 2000 m (both 1985) and 1500 m.

Cranach the Elder, Lucas (Lucas Müller; 1472–1553) German artist, sometimes called the Reformation painter, because he painted Luther and other Reformation leaders. He is also noted for his nudes, e.g. *Adam and Eve* (Courtauld Institute, London).

cranberry A low evergreen shrub of the heather family, bearing red berries and growing in boggy areas of Europe, N Asia, and North America. The berries are used for jams and jellies.

crane (bird) A long-legged bird occurring in Old World regions and North America. Up to 140 cm tall with a wingspan of over 200 cm, cranes are grey to white with black wingtips. Northern species are migratory.

cranefly A harmless fly, also called daddy longlegs. Craneflies are 6–75 mm long with long delicate legs and wings. The larvae generally occur in water or rotting vegetation. However some –the leatherjackets–are plant pests.

cranesbill A widely distributed herbaceous plant of the geranium family, usually having pink or purple flowers. It takes its name from the slender beaklike carpels. The meadow cranesbill (*Geranium pratense*), a perennial up to 60 cm high, has blue flowers.

Cranmer, Thomas (1489–1556) Anglican churchman. He became Archbishop of Canterbury in 1532, following his support of Henry VIII's divorce dispute with the pope. He is remembered for his contributions to the Prayer Books of 1549 and 1552. Under Queen Mary he was tried as a heretic and burned at the stake.

Crassus, Marcus Licinius (c. 115–53 BC) Roman politician, nicknamed *Dives* (wealthy). Crassus suppressed Spartacus' revolt (71) and joined Pompey and Caesar in the first Triumvirate (60). He was killed during an invasion of Parthia.

crayfish A freshwater *crustacean, also called crawfish and crawdad. It has a small lobster-like body, 25–75 mm long, and feeds on plant and animal material. Some species are edible.

Crécy, Battle of (26 August, 1346) The first land battle of the *Hundred Years' War, fought in N France, in which the English, led by *Edward III, defeated the French under Philip VI.

Cree An Algonkian-speaking North American Indian people. They lived by hunting and trapping in small wandering bands. The Plains Cree moved into the Plains and took up the buffalo-hunting culture.

creeds Formal statements of the main Christian beliefs, repeated as part of the communion service in many Churches. The two most widely used are the Apostles' Creed (probably 3rd century AD) and the Nicene Creed, probably a revision by the Council of Constantinople (381) of the creed proclaimed at the Council of *Nicaea (325). Another creed used in the Anglican Church is the Athanasian Creed, probably dating from the 5th century.

Creek A North American Indian people divided into the Muskogee of Georgia and the Hitchiti of Alabama. They tattooed their bodies heavily. A group of Creek towns fought the whites who were intruding into their territories in the 18th and early 19th centuries. On their defeat in the 1830s they were removed to Oklahoma.

Cremona 45 08N 10 01E A town in N Italy, in Lombardy. It has a 12th-century cathedral and a 13th-century palace. From the 16th to the 18th centuries it was famous for the manufacture of violins. Population (1981): 80 758.

creole 1. Originally a White person born in Spanish America during the colonial period (16th to 18th centuries). 2. A person of mixed blood living in the Caribbean area or in Latin America. 3. A dialect based on French, English, or Dutch, spoken especially in the West Indies as a mother tongue.

creosote A substance obtained from tar. The creosote used for preserving wood is obtained from *coal tar and is a brownish mixture of aromatic hydrocarbons and *phenols. Creosote made from wood tar is a mixture of phenols and is used in pharmacy.

cress A plant of the mustard family the leaves of which are used in salads, especially garden cress, or peppergrass (*Lepidium sativum*). The seedlings are eaten, often with those of white mustard (*Sinapis alba*). *See also* watercress.

Cretaceous period A geological period of the Mesozoic era, between about 135 and 65 million years ago. The dinosaurs and other giant reptiles, as well as the ammonites and many other invertebrates, became extinct at the end of the Cretaceous.

Crete (Modern Greek name: Kríti) The largest of the Greek islands, in the E Mediterranean Sea. It is generally mountainous, rising over 2400 m (7874 ft). The economy is based primarily on agriculture and tourism. *History*: colonized probably in the 6th millennium BC from Asia Minor, Crete was very powerful during the Middle Minoan period (c. 2000–c. 1700 BC; *see* Minoan civilization). Relics include the palace at *Knossos. It fell to Rome (67 BC), Byzantium (395 AD), and the Muslims (826). In 1204 it was sold to the Venetians. It fell to Turkey in 1669 and officially became part of Greece in 1913. Area: 8332 sq km (3217 sq mi). Population (1981): 502 165. Capital: Canea.

cretinism The condition resulting from a deficiency of thyroid hormone, which is present from birth. Affected children are mentally retarded dwarfs with coarse skin and facial features. Cretinism is treated with injections of thyroxine.

Crick, Francis Harry Compton (1916–) British biophysicist, who (with James D. *Watson) proposed a model for the molecular structure of *DNA (1953). Following this breakthrough, Crick studied protein synthesis. He shared a Nobel Prize (1962) with Watson and Maurice *Wilkins.

cricket (sport) An 11-a-side bat-and-ball team game, in which the object is to score the most runs. It developed in England among shepherds using their crooks as bats; its rules were laid down in 1744 and the game is played almost entirely in the UK and its former empire. Presided over by two umpires, it is played on a grass pitch 22 yd (20.12 m) long having at each end a wicket of three stumps supporting two bails. The members of one team take turns to bat in pairs, one defending each wicket. Each player bats un-

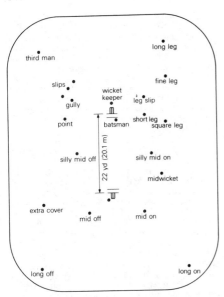

CRICKET *The pitch, showing the usual fielding positions (for a right-handed batsman).*

til he is bowled, caught, stumped, run out, or judged lbw (leg before wicket). The members of the other team field, some taking turns to bowl. After every over of six balls (sometimes eight in Australia) the bowler changes, the new bowler bowling from the other wicket. A match consists of one or two innings and may last for a few hours or up to six days. International cricket is played mainly in Test matches between England, Australia, the West Indies, New Zealand, India, Pakistan, and Sri Lanka. In England first-class cricket chiefly involves the 18 professional first-class county teams. *See also* Ashes.

cricket (zoology) An insect resembling a grasshopper but with longer antennae. The males stridulate (i.e. make a chirping noise) by rubbing the front wings together. Crickets have black or brown flattened bodies, 3–50 mm long, with long tail appendages (cerci) and short forewings (they do not fly). The females lay their eggs in soil or crevices.

Crimea (Russian name: Krym) A peninsula and autonomous region (*oblast*) in the SW Soviet Union. It is mainly flat but rises to 1545 m (5069 ft) in the S. Iron ore is mined here and wheat, tobacco, and wine are produced. *History*: colonized by Greeks in the 6th century BC, the Crimea was invaded by Goths, Huns, and others; in 1239 it became a territory of the Tatars. This was overthrown by Turks in 1475, and the area was annexed by Russia in 1783. Area: about 27 000 sq km (10 423 sq mi). Population (1983): 2 277 000. *See also* Crimean War.

Crimean War (1853–56) The war between Russia, on one side, and Britain, France, the Ottoman (Turkish) Empire, and (from 1855) Sardinia-Piedmont, on the other. Caused by Rus-

sia's ambitions to expand in the Balkans, the war came to a head in the year-long siege of Sevastopol and the battles of *Balaclava and *Inkerman. The Russians eventually evacuated the port in September, 1855, and peace was reached at Paris (1856). Over 250 000 men were lost by each side, many from disease in the appalling hospitals of the Crimea. The British Government sent Florence *Nightingale to inspect those at Scutari, where she improved conditions.

Criminal Investigation Department (CID) The investigative department of police forces in the UK. A CID was created at Scotland Yard in 1878, based on the detective branch that had been in existence since 1842. All UK police forces now have their own CIDs, and all who join must first have served as uniformed officers.

criminal law The body of law deciding on the acts and circumstances that amount to a crime (a wrong against society prohibited by law) and the punishment for crimes. In England criminal law is derived mainly from *common law, although statute law (law established by Acts of Parliament) has strongly influenced its development. Most crimes involve both an act (*actus reus*) and an intention (*mens rea*) but in some, including most motoring offences, no intention is involved. *Insanity, infancy (children under the age of ten), or duress (threats) may excuse a crime. However, if the offender intends to do what he does, not knowing it to be against the law, the crime may not be excused. In England all criminal cases appear first before a Magistrates' Court and may then be committed to the Crown Court (*see* courts of law).

Crippen, Hawley Harvey (1862–1910) US murderer. He poisoned his wife in London and then attempted to escape to the USA with his mistress. He was arrested on board ship (following one of the first uses of shore to ship radio) and returned to England, where he was hanged.

critical mass The mass of fissile substance that is just capable of sustaining a *chain reaction within it. Below the critical mass, too many of the particles that might have induced a reaction escape.

Croatia (Serbo-Croat name: Hrvatska) A constituent republic of NW Yugoslavia. It is chiefly mountainous, descending to plains in the NE, and primarily agricultural. *History*: settled by the Croats in the 7th century AD, the region was successively controlled by Hungary, Turkey, and Austria until the formation of the kingdom of the Serbs, Croats, and Slovenes (later Yugoslavia) in 1918. Croatia was proclaimed an independent state in 1941 and rejoined Yugoslavia in 1945. Area: 56 538 sq km (22 050 sq mi). Population (1986 est): 4 665 000. Capital: Zagreb.

Croatian. *See* Serbo-Croat.

Crockett, Davy (1786–1836) US frontiersman. As a colonel in the Tennessee militia and member of Congress he fought for Texas in its struggle for independence from Mexico and was killed at the *Alamo.

crocodile A reptile distinguished from alligators and caymans by having a more pointed snout and fewer teeth, the fourth tooth of the lower jaw remaining visible when the mouth is closed. Crocodiles occur chiefly in tropical fresh waters although the estuarine crocodile (*Crocodylus porosus*), which reaches a length of 6 m, occurs in coastal waters of SE Asia and Australia. Crocodiles, alligators, and caymans, known collectively as crocodilians, are amphibious and mainly nocturnal carnivores. The ears and nostrils can be closed by valves when under water. The female builds a nest of mud or vegetation in which over a hundred shelled eggs may be laid.

crocodile bird An African riverbank bird, *Pluvianus aegyptius*, that feeds on parasites picked from crocodiles. It is 23 cm long and is black with white markings.

crocus A low-growing plant of the iris family, native to Mediterranean regions and widely planted in gardens. Growing from corms, there are spring-flowering species with white, yellow, blue, or purple flowers, and autumn-flowering species with purple flowers. An Asian species (*Crocus sativus*) is the source of *saffron. Compare autumn crocus.

Croesus (died c. 546 BC) The last king of *Lydia (c. 560–c. 546 BC), famous for his wealth. He conquered the Greek cities on the coast of Asia Minor but was defeated by the Persian king Cyrus (II) the Great (d. 529) in 546. According to legend, Croesus was saved by Apollo from execution by Cyrus.

Crohn's disease An inflammatory disorder of the intestinal tract, named after the US physician B. B. Crohn (1884–1983). Symptoms include abdominal pain and diarrhoea. Patients are treated with drugs; some cases require surgery.

Cro-Magnon A prehistoric race of men. Skeletal remains were found (1868) at Cro-Magnon (SW France) and similar bones have been found at other European sites. They first appeared about 35 000 years ago. The Cro-Magnon were tall and broad-faced; they hunted and produced the earliest known examples of cave art (*see* Lascaux). *See also* Homo.

Crompton, Samuel (1753–1827) British inventor of the spinning mule (1779). It was able to produce yarn of a higher quality and at a greater speed than had previously been possible. Crompton sold his idea for very little money but in 1812 he was awarded a parliamentary grant of £5,000.

Cromwell, Oliver (1599–1658) English soldier and statesman; Lord Protector of England (1653–58). Cromwell was MP for Huntingdon in the parliament of 1628–29 and a critic of Charles I in the *Long Parliament, summoned in 1640. After the outbreak of the *Civil War he raised a troop of cavalry, which became known as the Ironsides (formed 1643), and fought at Edgehill (1642). He held command at *Marston Moor (1644) and helped to form the *New Model Army under Fairfax, which with Cromwell as second in command defeated Charles at *Naseby (1645). When the second Civil War ended in Charles' defeat (1648), Cromwell signed the king's death warrant. After the establishment of the Commonwealth he ruthlessly dominated Ireland (1649–50) and defeated

Charles' heir at Dunbar (1650) and Worcester (1651). In 1653 he expelled the Rump of the Long Parliament and following the failure of the *Barebones Parliament the *Protectorate was established. As Lord Protector, Cromwell established Puritanism but permitted religious toleration. He ended the first Dutch War, allied with France against Spain (gaining Dunkirk), and conquered Jamaica (1655). He refused the crown in 1657. He was succeeded as Lord Protector by his son **Richard Cromwell** (1626–1712), who was forced to abdicate in 1659.

Cromwell, Thomas, Earl of Essex (c. 1485–1540) English statesman, who made the English Church independent of Rome (*see* Reformation). He entered Wolsey's service in 1514, became an MP in 1529 and chancellor of the exchequer in 1533. He gained Henry's divorce from Catherine of Aragon by Acts that made the king head of the English Church. Between 1536 and 1540 he organized the dissolution of the monasteries, but his arrangement of Henry's disastrous marriage to Anne of Cleves led to his execution for treason.

Cronus A Greek god, the youngest of the Titans. He ruled the universe after castrating his father Uranus. He swallowed all the children he fathered by his sister Rhea except Zeus, for whom a stone was substituted. Zeus was reared secretly in Crete and eventually overthrew Cronus.

croquet A ball-and-mallet game that probably developed from *paille-maille*, a French game played by the 13th century. It is played on a grass lawn, ideally 35 × 28 yd (32 × 25.6 m), with an arrangement of six hoops and one peg. Two to four players follow a set course through the hoops, each using a coloured ball, the winner being the first to hit the peg with his ball. If a player's ball hits (roquets) another ball, the player may croquet this ball by placing his own ball next to it and striking his own ball so that the opponent's ball is also moved; the object is to advance his own ball towards the peg and to drive his opponent's ball off course.

Crosby, Bing (Harry Lillis C.; 1904–77) US popular singer. He achieved worldwide fame during the 1930s and 1940s with such hits as *White Christmas* (1942). He starred in many films, often with Bob *Hope, and also in his own radio and television shows.

crossbill A finch, 14.5–17 cm long, whose unique cross-tipped bill is specialized for extracting seeds from unopened cones. The common crossbill (*Loxia curvirostra*) of Eurasia and North America feeds on spruce seeds. The male is red and the female grey-green.

crossbow A short bow mounted on a stock, used in Europe throughout the middle ages. Crossbows were drawn by hand, a belt hook, or a winch. The bolt or *quarrel* was short, iron-tipped, and capable of penetrating armour. Slower and less accurate than the *longbow, it could be fired from behind cover.

crosses As a symbol, the cross is found in the art of several ancient cultures. One of the earliest Egyptian picture-writing symbols is the cross-shaped ankh (*crux ansata*), the symbol of life. As

ankh   Greek   Latin   tau

St Andrew's   Celtic   papal   Maltese

CROSSES *As a Christian symbol the cross was popularized by Constantine the Great and came into wide use in the 4th century.*

the symbol of Christ's crucifixion the cross had several forms. The Latin cross is the common form in the Western Church; others include the tau cross (or cross of St Anthony) and the cross of St Andrew. In European art and Western Churches, the crucifixion is usually shown with a Latin cross. The Greek cross or cross of St George is the traditional form in use in Orthodox Churches. The cross has influenced countless aspects of religious ceremony, including the cross-shaped plan of churches. On a shield in *heraldry, it is given various elaborated forms; a familiar example is the Maltese cross, the badge of the *Hospitallers and, in Britain, of the St John Ambulance Association.

croup   An acute infection of the respiratory tract, usually caused by viruses, resulting in inflammation and obstruction of the larynx (voice box). Croup occurs most commonly in children under five years of age; symptoms include difficulty in breathing. Treatment consists of steam inhalations and sedatives; severe cases may require surgery.

crow   A large songbird typically having a black plumage and a stout bill. Its food includes carrion and it has a distinctive harsh call. A typical species is the carrion crow (*Corvus corone*), about 46 cm long, but the family also includes the *rooks, *ravens, *choughs, *jays, and *jackdaws.

crown colony   A territory that is under the direct legal control of the UK. Most crown colonies have now been granted independence: the most important one remaining is *Hong Kong.

Crown Court.   *See* courts of law.

crown jewels   Royal insignia and regalia and the personal jewellery inherited or acquired by a sovereign. The British Crown Jewels, now kept in the Tower of London, were mainly amassed after the Restoration, the earlier set having been destroyed under Cromwell. Those used for coronations include a replica of St Edward's crown, the Sword of State, the Orb, and the Sceptre. Those used for other state occasions include the

Imperial State Crown and another Sword of State.

Crown land   Land that belongs to the UK monarch and is managed by the Crown Estate Commissioners. The profits from the land do not go to the monarch, as all income was given up by George III in 1760 in exchange for the income provided by the *civil list.

crown-of-thorns starfish   A reddish spiny starfish, *Acanthaster planci*, up to 45 cm across, with 12–19 arms. With the destruction of its chief predator, the Pacific triton (*Charonia tritonis*), by shell collectors, it has spread throughout the South Pacific.

cruiser   A fast heavily armed warship, smaller than a battleship but larger than a *destroyer and designed for a larger cruising radius. Cruisers with nuclear power to allow them to travel very great distances have replaced most of the battleships in the world's major navies.

Crusades   The military expeditions organized in western Christendom mainly to take back the Holy Places of Palestine from Muslim occupation. In the first Crusade (1095–99) Jerusalem was captured and the Kingdom of Jerusalem, the County of Edessa, Antioch, and Tripoli were created. The fall (1144) of Edessa inspired the unsuccessful second Crusade (1147–48) and the capture of Jerusalem by *Saladin in 1187 led to the inconclusive third Crusade (1189–92), led by *Philip II Augustus of France, Emperor *Frederick I Barbarossa, and *Richard (I) the Lionheart of England. The fourth Crusade (1202–04) plundered Constantinople (1204). The four Crusades of the 13th century failed to recover lost ground and Acre, the last foothold of the West in Palestine, was lost in 1291. *See also* Children's Crusade.

crustacean   Any *arthropod of a class that includes the *barnacles, *woodlouse, *shrimps, *lobsters, *crabs, etc. The head bears two pairs of antennae (feelers) and three pairs of jaws; the head and thorax together are usually covered by a hard carapace. The numerous pairs of legs are modified for different functions. Most crustaceans are aquatic, breathing by means of gills. The larvae pass through several stages (*see* metamorphosis) to reach the adult form.

cryogenics   The production, effects, and uses of very low temperatures, usually from −150°C down to almost *absolute zero. Cryogenic effects include changes in electrical properties, such as *superconductivity, and changes in mechanical properties, such as superfluidity (*see* superfluid). Cryogenics has been applied to food preservation, surgery, and life-support systems in space.

Crystal Palace   A building designed by Joseph Paxton (1801–65) to house the *Great Exhibition of 1851. The Crystal Palace, which had an area of 69 892 sq m (772 289 sq ft), was built in Hyde Park, London, of prefabricated glass and iron. It was later dismantled and reassembled at Sydenham in SE London but burnt down in 1936.

crystals   Solids that have a regular geometrical shape because the constituent atoms, ions, or molecules are arranged in an ordered repeating pattern, known as a crystal lattice. There are seven crystal systems. Crystal structures are studied by a variety of techniques, including *X-ray diffraction and electron microscopy. **Crystallography** is concerned with the study of the structure and properties of crystals.

Cuba, Republic of A country in the Caribbean Sea, off the S coast of Florida. It consists of two main islands, Cuba and the Isla de Pinos, together with over 1500 small islands. On the island of Cuba fertile plains rise to mountains in the centre and SE and hills in the NW. The population is mainly of European origin, with large African and mixed minorities. *Economy*: state controlled, it is dependent upon its sugar crop. Tobacco is another important export crop. Mineral resources include nickel (the second largest export). *History*: discovered by Columbus in 1492, it was a Spanish colony until 1898; after three years of US occupation Cuba became a republic (1901). In 1940 Fulgencio Batista (1901–73) took Cuba into World War II on the Allied side. He was overthrown in *Castro's second socialist revolt (1959), after which Cuba moved closer in its international relations to the Soviet Union. In 1961 a US-supported invasion of Cuban exiles was defeated at the *Bay of Pigs and in 1962 the Soviet installation of missile bases in Cuba resulted in a US naval blockade. The crisis was resolved when the Soviet Union agreed to remove the bases. Head of government and first secretary of the Cuban Communist Party: Fidel Castro Ruz. Official language: Spanish. Official currency: Cuban peso of 100 centavos. Area 148 124 sq km (46 736 sq mi). Population (1988 est): 10 462 000. Capital and main port: Havana.

cubism A style of painting and sculpture originating in the works of *Picasso and *Braque in about 1907. It started as an attempt to represent a solid form in two dimensions. Volume was suggested by combining several viewpoints of an object into a complex of geometrical shapes. Cubism was the principal influence on the evolution of *abstract art.

cuckoo A bird occurring worldwide and ranging from 16–70 cm in length. The European cuckoo (*Cuculus canorus*), grey with white barring, lays its eggs in the nests of other birds, which rear its young.

cuckoopint A perennial European plant, *Arum maculatum*, also called lords-and-ladies. 30–50 cm tall, it has a cylindrical cluster of tiny flowers, which protrudes from a funnel-shaped petal-like bract (spathe). The flowers give rise to poisonous red berries.

cuckoo-spit insect. *See* froghopper.

cucumber An annual vine, *Cucumis sativus*, widely cultivated since ancient times. The long green juicy fruits, up to 60 cm long, are eaten raw, cooked, or pickled (*see* gherkin).

Cuernavaca 18 57N 99 15W A city and resort in S central Mexico. It is the site of Cortés' palace, a Franciscan cathedral (1529), and a university (1939). Population (1980): 232 355.

Culloden Moor A moor in N Scotland, in the Highland Region near Inverness. In 1746 it was the scene of the last land battle to be fought in Britain, in which the Young Pretender, Charles

Edward Stuart, was defeated by the Duke of Cumberland.

Culpeper, Nicholas (1616–54) English herbalist, physician, and astrologer. In 1649 he published a translation of the official London Pharmacopoeia. This was followed by his famous *Complete Herbal* (1653).

Cultural Revolution, Great Proletarian (1966–68) A political movement launched in China by Mao Tse-tung to strengthen revolutionary attitudes. Many leading officials were dismissed and the formal educational system was abolished. Many universities were closed and young people, called into service as *Red Guards, attacked Party officials and destroyed cultural objects.

Cumbria A county in NW England, bordering on the Irish Sea. It was created in 1974 from Westmorland, Cumberland, and parts of NW Lancashire and NW Yorkshire. It includes the *Lake District. Agricultural activity includes sheep, dairy, and arable farming. New industries are replacing the traditional ones of coal, iron, and steel. Atomic energy establishments exist at Sellafield and Calder Hall. Area: 6809 sq km (2628 sq mi). Population (1987 est): 486 900. Administrative centre: Carlisle.

cumin An annual herb, *Cuminum cyminum*, of the carrot family. Up to 30 cm high, it has small whitish flowers. Native to the Mediterranean, is cultivated in Europe, India, and China for its bitter fruits, which are used in curry powders, to flavour liqueurs, etc.

cumulus cloud (Cu) A low type of *cloud having a heaped appearance and developing vertically from a flat base. They are produced by the upward movement of large masses of air. **Cumulonimbus cloud** is heavy and dense, extending vertically to about 6000 m (20 000 ft), and is associated with thunderstorms. Its upper part often spreads out to form an anvil shape.

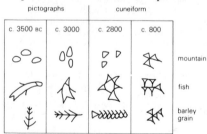

CUNEIFORM *The wedge-shaped strokes of cuneiform writing developed gradually from pictographs.*

cuneiform The oldest writing system of which records survive, used to represent a number of ancient Near Eastern languages. The name comes from the wedge-shaped marks (Latin *cuneus*, a wedge) made by the imprint of a pointed instrument in soft clay. By the 3rd millennium BC cuneiform pictures (pictographs) had developed into groups of wedge-shaped imprints. Probably invented by the Sumerians not later than 3100 BC, cuneiform spread to other language groups in the area. By 100 BC, however, it had largely been replaced by the North Semitic writing system that was used to represent the Aramaic language.

Cunobelinus (*or* Cymbeline; died c. 42 AD) British ruler (c. 10–c. 42) of the Catuvellauni tribe. Their lands embraced much of SE England after they overcame the Trinovantes. He founded Colchester (c. 10).

Cupid The Roman god of love, identified with the Greek Eros, and lover of Psyche. He is usually portrayed as a winged boy shooting arrows of love.

cupronickel An alloy of 75% copper and 25% nickel (by weight) that is not damaged by the action of moisture, air, or chemicals. In the UK the Coinage Act (1946) substituted cupronickel coinage for silver alloy; the four cupronickel coins now in circulation are the 5p, 10p, 20p, and 50p pieces.

Curaçao A West Indian island, the largest in the Netherlands Antilles. Discovered in 1499, it was settled by the Spanish before being colonized by the Dutch in 1634. The refining of oil from Venezuela is of major importance; other industries include the production of Curaçao liqueur and calcium-phosphate mining. Area: 444 sq km (173 sq mi). Population (1983): 165 011. Chief town: Willemstad.

curare A resinous substance obtained from certain South American trees, used as an arrow poison by South American Indians. Curare causes muscular contraction; curare-like compounds (e.g. tubocurarine) are injected during general anaesthesia to relax muscles.

Curia, Roman. *See* Roman Curia.

Curia Regis The King's Court of early medieval Europe, which fulfilled all the functions of royal government. From its departments developed the public government offices, such as, in England, the Chancery and the Exchequer, as well as the courts of law and parliament.

curie (Ci) A unit of activity of a radioactive isotope equal to 3.7×10^{10} disintegrations per second. Named after Pierre *Curie. The curie has recently been replaced by the becquerel (Bq), where $1 \text{ Ci} = 3.7 \times 10^{10} \text{ Bq}$.

Curie, Marie (1867–1934) Polish chemist, renowned for her research into *radioactivity. Born Marya Sklodowska, she emigrated to France and married (1895) **Pierre Curie** (1859–1906), a French physicist. Marie Curie noticed in 1898 that one particular uranium ore produced a surprisingly large amount of radiation. Realizing that the radiation was caused by a new element, she and her husband spent four years isolating one gram of radium salt from eight tons of the ore. The Curies, together with Henri Becquerel, were awarded the 1903 Nobel Prize for Physics and, for her discovery of radium and polonium, she won the 1911 Nobel Prize for Chemistry. Pierre Curie discovered the *piezoelectric effect (1880) and showed that ferromagnetism reverts to paramagnetism (*see* magnetism) above a certain temperature, now known as the **Curie point** (1895). He was killed in a road accident; she died as a result of the radiation to which she had been exposed. Their daughter **Irène Joliot-Curie**

(1896–1956) married the French physicist **Frédéric Joliot** (1900–59) in 1926. They were awarded the 1935 Nobel Prize for Chemistry for producing radioactivity artificially.

curium (Cm) An artificial *transuranic element discovered by Seaborg and others in 1944 and named after Marie and Pierre Curie. All 13 isotopes are radioactive. Curium is a silvery reactive metal. Its compounds include the oxides (CmO_2, Cm_2O_3) and halides (CmF_3, $CmCl_3$). At no 96; at wt (247); mp 1340 ± 40°C.

curlew A streaked brown or grey bird with a long neck and long curved bill. Curlews breed in inland subarctic regions and migrate south in winter to marshes and mudflats. The common Eurasian curlew (*Numenius arquata*) is almost 60 cm long and ranges from Britain to central Asia.

curling A target game played on ice with stones fitted with handles, played since at least the early 16th century and strongly associated with Scotland. Two teams of four players take it in turns to slide two curling stones, each up to 36 m (39 yd), along the ice towards the "house," a series of circles within one another at the end of the rink. A team scores one point for each stone finishing nearer the centre of the house than any of its opponents'.

currant 1. One of several species of related shrubs of the gooseberry family. Some are cultivated for their fruit, for example *blackcurrant and *redcurrant, and others, such as the *flowering currant, are grown as ornamentals. 2. The dried berry of a small seedless grape, grown in the Mediterranean region and used in cooking.

currawong An Australasian songbird, about 50 cm long, usually black (sometimes with white markings) with a long hook-tipped bill. They feed on insects, small mammals, and birds and frequently destroy fruit crops.

cuscus A cat-sized *marsupial mammal found in forests of NE Australia, New Guinea, and nearby islands. Cuscuses have a prehensile tail and climb slowly around trees at night, eating mainly leaves and fruit.

Cushing's disease A disorder resulting from excess *corticosteroid hormones in the body, named after H. W. Cushing (1869–1939). The symptoms include obesity, loss of minerals from the bones, and reddening of the face and neck. It may be caused by a tumour of the pituitary gland or the adrenal gland or by prolonged therapy with high doses of corticosteroids: the treatment depends on the cause.

custard apple A small tree so called because of the custard-like flavour of its fruits. The common custard apple (*Annona reticulata*), 5–8 m high and widely grown in the West Indies, produces reddish many-seeded fruits, 8–12 cm in diameter.

Custer, George A(rmstrong) (1839–76) US cavalry general. After earning distinction in the Civil War, he commanded the Seventh Cavalry against the Indians. Sent to round up Sioux and Cheyenne forces under Chief *Sitting Bull in S Dakota's Black Hills in 1876, he and his force of about 260 were massacred at the *Little Bighorn (Custer's Last Stand).

cuttlefish A marine mollusc, related to the squid, found in temperate coastal waters. 2.5–90 cm long, the body is supported by an internal chalky shell–the cuttlebone–which gives buoyancy. When alarmed, the animal emits an inky fluid.

Cuyp, Aelbert Jacobsz (1620–91) Dutch landscape painter. He was born in Dordrecht, the son of **Jacob Gerritsz Cuyp** (1594–1651), a portrait and landscape painter. Aelbert's paintings are distinguished by their golden light, one fine example being *Herdsmen with Cows by a River* (National Gallery, London).

cyanocobalamin. *See* vitamin B complex.

Cybele An Asiatic earth goddess identified by the Greeks with *Rhea. The centre of her worship was Phrygia, whence her cult spread to Athens and later to Rome. She represented the powers of nature and was a protectress of wild animals. Her priests were eunuchs known as Corybantes.

cybernetics The study of communication and control between men, machines, and organizations. The human ability to adapt and make decisions is imitated in the design of computer-controlled systems. Cybernetics has also been used as a link between the physical and life sciences, for instance in using information theory to explain how messages are transmitted in nervous systems and in genetic processes.

Cyclades (Modern Greek name: Kikládhes) A group of some 220 Greek islands in the S Aegean Sea, including Ándros, Delos, Íos, Míkonos, Melos, Náxos (the largest), Páros, and Syros. Total area: 2578 sq km (995 sq mi). Population (1981): 88 458. Capital: Hermopolis (on Syros).

cyclamen A perennial plant of the primrose family, native from the European Mediterranean to Iran and widely cultivated as house and garden plants. All cyclamens produce corms but most can be grown from seed. They have drooping flowers with red, pink, or white petals.

cyclone An area of relatively low atmospheric pressure. In the N hemisphere wind circulates in an anticlockwise direction around its centre, in the S hemisphere it is clockwise. Except in the tropics, cyclones are now usually referred to as *depressions or lows. Tropical cyclones include *hurricanes and *typhoons.

cyclops A very small freshwater crustacean so named because its single eye recalls that of the giant Cyclops in Greek mythology.

cyclotron A type of particle *accelerator in which charged particles are accelerated in an outward spiral path inside two hollow D-shaped conductors (called dees) placed back to back. The maximum energy of the particles is about 25 MeV.

Cymbeline. *See* Cunobelinus.

Cynics The followers of the Greek moral philosopher *Diogenes of Sinope, who were active from the early 3rd century BC. They rejected the pursuit of worldly wealth and success and believed that basic human needs can be very simply satisfied.

cypress A conifer native to S Europe, E Asia, and North America and widely planted for orna-

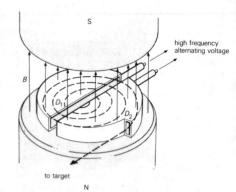

CYCLOTRON *The charged particles are accelerated in the two D-shaped conductors* (D_1 *and* D_2), *which are supported in the magnetic field B.*

ment and timber. Cypresses have tiny scalelike leaves and rounded cones, 1–4 cm in diameter. The Italian or funeral cypress (*Cupressus sempervirens*) is 25–45 m high. Lawson's cypress (*Chamaecyparis lawsonii*) is a related tree widely grown in gardens. *See also* swamp cypress.

Cyprus, Republic of (Greek name: Kypros; Turkish name: Kıbrıs) An island state in the E Mediterranean Sea. A central plain rises to the Kyrenia Range in the N, and in the SW the Troödos Massif rises over 1800 m (6000 ft). Most of the population is Greek or Turkish, the former being in the majority. *Economy*: mainly agricultural. Mineral resources include iron pyrites, asbestos, chromite, and copper ores. Exports include wine, citrus fruits, potatoes, and metals. *History*: there was already a Greek colony on Cyprus almost 4000 years ago. It was conquered by Egypt in the 6th century BC and later formed part of the Persian, Macedonian, Roman, Byzantine, and Arab empires. In 1489 it became a Venetian dependency. In 1571 it was conquered by the Turks and in 1878 it came under British administration. In the 1930s Greek Cypriots began advocating Enosis (Union with Greece), and in 1955 a Greek Cypriot organization (EOKA), led by Archbishop *Makarios and Gen Grivas, began guerrilla warfare against the British. Cyprus became a republic in 1960 and a member of the Commonwealth in 1961. There were fierce clashes between the Greek and Turkish communities in the 1960s and in 1974 Turkey invaded the island. In 1975 the Turks set up the Turkish Federated State of Cyprus in the N, with Rauf Denktash as president. On the death of Makarios in 1977, Spyros Kyprianou (1932–) was elected president. In 1988 he was succeeded by Giorgios Vassiliou (1931–). Official languages: Greek and Turkish; English is also widely spoken. Official currency: Cyprus pound of 1000 mils. Area: 9251 sq km (3572 sq mi). Population (1988 est): 689 000. Capital: Nicosia. Main port: Limassol.

Cyrano de Bergerac, Savinien (1619–55) French writer and dramatist. He wrote a comedy, *Le Pédant joué* (1654), tragedies, and two sa-

tirical romances. He was noted for his comically long nose as well as his chivalrous nature.
Cyrenaica A region of E Libya, inhabited mainly by tribesmen of the Senussi. From early times Cyrenaica was colonized or conquered by Greeks, Egyptians, Romans, Vandals, Arabs, Turks, and Italians successively. It was united with Libya in 1951.
Cyrillic alphabet The alphabet used for Russian, Belorussian, Ukrainian, Bulgarian, Serbian, and various other languages of the Soviet Union. It was developed from a Greek alphabet of the 9th century AD and is thought to have been invented by the Greek brothers, St Cyril (c. 827–69 AD) and St Methodius (c. 825–49 AD). It originally consisted of 43 letters, but modern versions have about 30.
cystic fibrosis A hereditary disease affecting the mucus-secreting and sweat glands. Symptoms, which appear in early childhood, are due to the production of thick mucus, which obstructs the pancreatic duct, intestinal glands, and air passages. Patients suffer from recurrent chest infections. Treatment includes antibiotics, physiotherapy, a low-fat high-protein diet, and the administration of pancreatic enzymes. The defective gene responsible has now been identified and located.
cytology The study of the structure and function of cells. The light microscope enabled the *nucleus (with its chromosomes) and other structures of cells to be observed. More recent developments have included the use of more powerful microscopes (e.g. phase-contrast and electron microscopes), improved techniques of cell separation and analysis (often automated), new labelling and staining methods (e.g. using antibodies and radioisotopes), and tissue culture. Cytological tests enable the diagnosis of many diseases, including cancer.

cytoplasm. *See* cell.
Czech A West Slavonic language spoken by nine million people in W Czechoslovakia. It is the official language of this area and is written in the Latin alphabet.
Czechoslovakia (Czech and Slovak Federative Republic) A country in central Europe. Totally surrounded by land, it is mainly wooded and mountainous. The population is about two-thirds Czech and almost a third Slovak. *Economy*: since 1961 the emphasis has shifted from heavy to light industry. Agriculture is organized in collectives and state farms and the principal crops include sugar beet, wheat, potatoes, and barley. Forestry is also important. *History*: Czechoslovakia was created, under Tomáš *Masaryk and Edvard *Beneš, in 1918 following the collapse of the Austrian Empire. By 1939 Hitler's Germany had taken control of all Czechoslovakia. Following the war Ruthenia was handed over to the Soviet Union, and some three million Germans were expelled from Czechoslovakia. By 1948 the Communist Party was in power and Czechoslovakia was closely allied with the Soviet Union. In 1968 the liberal reforms initiated by Dubček provoked a Soviet invasion. This was followed by the repressive regime of Gustáv Husák (1913–). In 1989 the Communist regime fell and was replaced by a socialist government under Václav Havel. Official languages: Czech and Slovak. Official currency: koruna of 100 haléřů. Area: 127 877 sq km (49 365 sq mi). Population (1988 est): 15 723 000. Capital: Prague.
Częstochowa 50 49N 19 07E A city in S Poland. It has a monastery that was defended against the Swedes in the Thirty Years' War and to which Roman Catholics make pilgrimages. Population (1985): 247 000.

D

dab A flatfish found in N Atlantic and N Pacific waters. The European dab, *Limanda limanda*, is an important food fish.
dabchick A small *grebe, *Tachybaptus ruficollis*, of Europe, S Asia, and Africa. It has a brown back, pale underparts, and a chestnut breast and cheeks. It feeds on small fish.
dace A slender fish belonging to a group that includes chub, roach, minnow, etc. The European dace (*Leuciscus leuciscus*) is silvery coloured, and lives in fast-flowing streams and rivers.
Dachau 48 15N 11 26E A town in S Germany, in Bavaria. It was the site of a Nazi concentration camp (1933–45). Population (1984 est): 33 200.
dachshund A breed of brownish or black dogs originating in Germany, where they were developed to pursue badgers. The two varieties—standard and miniature—may be long-haired, smooth-haired, or wire-haired.
dada A European art and literary movement, beginning in Zürich in 1916, which rejected tradi-

tional artistic criteria. Much of its ideology was transmitted in poetry periodicals. The effect in graphic art is shown in the collages of *Ernst and Schwitters and the ready-mades of *Duchamp, who exported dada to the USA. Dada petered out in the 1920s.

daddy longlegs. *See* cranefly.
Daedalus A legendary Greek craftsman and sculptor, said to have built the labyrinth for King *Minos of Crete. Minos imprisoned him but he created wings for himself and his son Icarus and flew away; **Icarus** was killed when the sun melted his wings but Daedalus reached Sicily safely.
daffodil A perennial European plant, *Narcissus pseudonarcissus*, widely grown as a garden bulb. It has narrow leaves and yellow flowers, each with a trumpet-shaped central crown surrounded by six segments.

Daguerre, Louis-Jacques-Mandé (1789–1851) French inventor of the daguerreotype. Working with Joseph Niepce (1765–1833), who had produced the first permanent photographic image (the heliograph), Daguerre succeeded during the 1830s in producing a photograph by focusing light onto a copper plate that had been coated with a silver salt. Daguerreotypes were widely made in the mid-19th century.

dahlia A herbaceous perennial tropical American plant of the daisy family, originally cultivated as a food for its tubers but now grown for ornament. The coloured flowers, single or double, come in a variety of shapes and sizes.

Dahomey. *See* Benin, People's Republic of.

Dáil Éireann The assembly of elected representatives of the Republic of Ireland. It is the more important house in the National Parliament, the other house being the Seanad Éireann (the Senate). The 144 members are elected by *proportional representation, at least every 5 years. The president (the nominal head of state) summons and dissolves the Dáil on the advice of the prime minister.

Daimler, Gottlieb (Wilhelm) (1834–1900) German inventor, whose early internal-combustion engines (1883) were soon sufficiently light and efficient to power machines; in 1890 he founded a company to manufacture motor *cars.

Dairen. *See* Lüda.

dairy products Products derived from milk. Separation of milk by centrifugation yields skimmed milk and cream. Churning the cream disrupts the fat globules, removes water, and produces butter, containing over 80% fat, and buttermilk. Cream is sold in various stages of concentration; other less concentrated forms include evaporated milk (containing about 65% water) and condensed milk (about 26% water). Yogurt (*or* yoghurt) is produced by adding bacteria, principally of the genera *Streptococcus* and *Lactobacillus*, to whole milk. The acid they produce during incubation coagulates the milk. *See also* milk; cheese.

daisy A herbaceous plant, native to Eurasia, with flowers consisting of a central yellow disc surrounded by white or purple petal-like florets. Many species are grown as garden plants. The common wild Eurasian daisy is *Bellis perennis*, a perennial up to 6 cm high, common in grasslands and lawns.

Dakar 14 45N 17 08W The capital and main port of Senegal, on Cape Verde peninsula, and the country's main industrial centre. Population (1984): 671 000.

Dakota. *See* North Dakota; South Dakota.

Dalai Lama The title of the spiritual and political ruler of Tibet and head of the Gelukpa Buddhists. Chosen by oracles, he is regarded as incapable of error. The 14th Dalai Lama went into exile in India in 1959; he was awarded the Nobel Peace Prize in 1989.

Dali, Salvador (1904–89) Spanish surrealist painter. He joined the Paris surrealists (1929) and, inspired by Freudian theories, painted startling dream images with photographic realism. While living in New York (1940–55), he turned

to religious subjects and became a Roman Catholic.

Dalian. *See* Lüda.

Dallas 32 47N 96 48W A city in the USA, in NE Texas on the Trinity River. The discovery of oil in E Texas during the 1930s and the introduction of the aircraft and electronics industries during World War II has enabled it to become the state's second largest city and the commercial centre of the SW. Population (1986): 1 003 520.

Dalmatia A coastal belt in W Yugoslavia, mainly in Croatia bordering on the Adriatic Sea. Predominantly mountainous, it has a thriving tourist industry. The chief towns are Zadar, Split, and Dubrovnik.

Dalmatian dog A breed named after Dalmatia, on the Adriatic coast, from where they were exported to the UK. Dalmatians were formerly used as carriage dogs. The short sleek coat is white with black or liver (brown) spots.

dalton. *See* atomic mass unit.

Dalton, John (1766–1844) British chemist who developed the *atomic theory of matter and *Dalton's law of partial pressures.

Dalton's law of partial pressures The total pressure exerted by a certain volume of a gaseous mixture is equal to the sum of the pressures (called partial pressures) exerted by each gas, if it alone occupied the same volume. Named after John *Dalton.

dam A barrier across a river for diverting the flow of water; raising the water level for navigation; storing water for irrigation, industrial use, or water control; and providing a source for *hydroelectric power. Gravity dams, usually made of concrete, have a flat vertical face upstream. They are no longer used for the largest dams. Arch dams consist of curved concrete structures presenting their convex faces upstream. They can be much less massive than gravity dams and are therefore cheaper.

Daman and Diu A Union Territory in W India, formerly (until 1987) part of Goa, Daman, and Diu. Diu is an island off the coast of Gujarat. Area: 456 sq km (176 sq mi). Population (1981): 1 082 117. Chief town: Daman.

Damascus 33 30N 36 19E The capital of Syria, in the SE of the country close to the Lebanese border. Under Ottoman rule from 1516 until 1918, Damascus was taken by the French (1920) and became capital of independent Syria in 1941. The Great Mosque and the Gate of God are notable buildings. Population (1987): 1 292 000.

damask rose An Asian rose, *Rosa damascena*, about 1.5 m high, with spicy-scented pink and white flowers. It is the main source of attar of roses—the rose oil used as the base of many perfumes.

Damocles Legendary courtier of Dionysius I of Syracuse in the 9th century BC. Dionysius seated him at a banquet beneath a sword suspended by a single hair, thus illustrating the insecurity of human life, irrespective of wealth or power.

damselfly   A slender delicate insect, closely related to the *dragonflies. It has similar habits but is smaller.

damson   The plumlike fruit of *Prunus damascena*, a slender twisted tree of the rose family found across the N hemisphere. It has small white flowers that develop into purple fruits.

Dan, tribe of   One of the 12 *tribes of Israel. It claimed descent from Dan, the son of Jacob by his concubine Bilhah. Its territory lay N of the Sea of Galilee and its city of Dan was situated at the northernmost point of the Hebrew settlement.

dandelion   A common perennial weed, *Taxacum officinale*, of the daisy family, with jagged toothed leaves and a solitary flower head of bright-yellow florets. The seeds have parachutes of fine white hairs and are dispersed by wind.

Danelaw   The area of Anglo-Saxon England E of Watling Street from the River Tees to the River Thames within which Danish laws and customs were observed from the late 9th to the late 11th centuries.

Daniel   (6th century BC) An Old Testament prophet and Jewish exile in Babylon, believed to have written **The Book of Daniel**, the first six chapters of which relate to supernatural episodes under Kings Nebuchadnezzar and Belshazzar.

Danish   The official language of Denmark, spoken by about five million people. It belongs to the East Scandinavian branch of the North Germanic languages. It is closely related to other Scandinavian languages which all developed from the same original language.

Dante Alighieri   (1265–1321) Italian poet. Born in Florence, his involvement in the political struggle between the propapal Black Guelfs and the democratic White Guelfs led to his exile (c. 1301) from Florence. Dante's works include the love poem *La vita nuova* (c. 1292), the epic poem *The Divine Comedy* (c. 1307), and two essays on spoken Italian.

Danube, River   The second longest river in Europe after the River Volga. Rising in the Black Forest in Germany, it flows mainly ESE across central and SE Europe to enter the Black Sea in Romania. Major cities along its course include Vienna, Budapest, and Belgrade. Length: 2850 km (1770 mi).

Danzig.   *See* Gdańsk.

daphne   (botany) A Eurasian shrub, many species of which are grown. Its small bell-shaped flowers occur in clusters. Species include the deciduous mezereon (*Daphne mezereum*), with reddish flowers and red berries, and the evergreen spurge laurel (*D. laureola*), with greenish flowers and black berries.

Daphne   (Greek mythology) A mountain nymph who rejected Apollo and, to escape him, was transformed by Gaea into a laurel tree. Apollo made the laurel a symbol of honour and victory.

Daphnia.   *See* water flea.

Daphnis   In Greek legend, a Sicilian shepherd who, punished with blindness for infidelity, consoled himself by inventing pastoral poetry and song.

Dardanelles   (Ancient name: Hellespont)   A narrow channel separating European and Asian Turkey and connecting the Sea of Marmara with the Aegean Sea. It was the scene of a campaign in *World War I. Length: 60 km (37 mi); width: 1.5–6.5 km (1–4 mi).

Dar es Salaam   6 48S 39 12E The capital and main port of Tanzania, on the Indian Ocean. Founded in 1862, it was capital of German East Africa (1891–1916) and of Tanganyika (1916–64). It is an important commercial and industrial centre. Population (1985): 1 394 000.

Darjeeling   27 02N 88 20E A town in India, in West Bengal near the Himalayas. It is a tourist resort and a major tea-growing centre. Population (1981): 57 603.

Darling, Grace   (1815–42) British heroine, daughter of a lighthouse keeper in Northumberland, who in 1838 helped her father rescue five people from a shipwreck (*Forfarshire*).

Darling River   A river in E Australia, rising in the Great Dividing Range and flowing generally SW across New South Wales before joining the Murray River at Wentworth. Length: 2740 km (1702 mi).

Darlington   54 31N 1 34W A town in NE England, in Durham. The Stockton–Darlington freight railway (1825) was the world's first railway. Darlington has engineering and construction industries. Population (1989): 99 200.

Darnley, Henry Stuart, Lord   (1545–67) The second husband of Mary, Queen of Scots, and father of James I of England. He married Mary, his cousin, in 1565. He was involved in the murder of her secretary David Riccio (1566) and was himself murdered, probably by *Bothwell.

darter   A slender bird of tropical and subtropical inland waters. About 88 cm long, brownish with white markings, males have plumes on the head. They have pointed bills for catching fish underwater.

Dartmoor   A moorland area of England, in SW Devon. A national park since 1951, it consists of a granite upland rising to tors (rocky hills), the highest of which is High Willhays at 621 m (2039 ft). Its historic remains include stone circles and Bronze and Iron Age settlements. A major tourist attraction, it is also used for military training. Area: 945 sq km (365 sq mi).

Dartmouth   50 21N 3 35W A port and resort in SW England, in Devon on the Dart estuary. The Royal Naval College (1905) is situated here. Population (1981): 6298.

Darwin   12 23S 130 44E A city in Australia, the capital and chief port of the Northern Territory. It had to be largely rebuilt after a cyclone in 1974. Population (1986): 66 131.

Darwin, Charles Robert   (1809–1882) British naturalist, who developed the concept that living things evolve by means of natural selection (*see* Darwinism). Darwin sailed with HMS *Beagle* on an expedition to South America and the Pacific (1831–36). He made detailed observations of the geology and natural history of the region. In 1859 he published his findings in *Origin of Species by Means of Natural Selection*. His views aroused bitter controversy because they conflicted with the Bible. This led to the debate at Oxford in 1860 between Darwin's supporters, led by T. H. Huxley, and Bishop Samuel Wilberforce. Huxley's arguments won the day. In *The Descent of Man* (1871), Darwin applied his theories to mankind. His grandfather **Erasmus Darwin** (1731–1802) was a physician noted for his radical views, especially on biology.

Darwinism The theory of the *evolution of living things based on the work of Charles *Darwin. Darwin observed that (1) there are individual variations in any group of organisms; (2) the size of the group remains constant although more offspring are produced than are necessary to maintain it. He concluded that the forces acting on the group–competition, disease, climate, etc.–resulted in the survival of those best fitted to the environment, a process he called **natural selection**. The offspring of the survivors would inherit their parent's advantageous features. With time–in a gradually changing environment –this process would result in a change in the characteristics of the entire group (or population), and ultimately the evolution of new *species. Darwin's theory was modified by later discoveries in genetics; for example, the source of the variation observed by Darwin is based mostly on *mutations. The modern version of his theory is known as **neo-Darwinism**.

dasyure A small carnivorous *marsupial mammal found in Australia and New Guinea. Dasyures are nocturnal and good climbers. See also Tasmanian devil.

data processing The production and storage of information by means of computers. In batch processing, data is grouped and coded before processing. In on-line processing each user feeds data into the system continuously. Most large organizations now use data-processing techniques extensively. The Data Protection Act (1984) came into force in November 1985 and seeks to protect the freedom of the individual.

date A *palm tree, *Phoenix dactylifera*, native to N Africa and SW Asia cultivated for its fruits. Male and female flowers grow on separate trees, the female flowers developing into large clusters of fruits. The trunk yields timber and the leaves are used for weaving, etc.

dating. See helium dating; potassium-argon dating; radiocarbon dating; rubidium-strontium dating; uranium-lead dating.

Daumier, Honoré (1808–79) French cartoonist, painter, and sculptor. He produced numerous documentary pictures, such as *Rue Transnonain*. After 1835 he worked for *Charivari*, satirizing the professions and other targets. His paintings include *The Third Class Railway Carriage*.

dauphin From 1350 until 1830 the title of the heirs to the French Crown. The Dauphiné, which was a province of SE France, was bought by the future Charles V in 1350. After becoming king (1364), he gave the Dauphiné and its accompanying title to his son. After this every heir to the throne was called dauphin.

David (d. 962 BC) King of Israel (c. 1000–962). His successes against the Philistines, including the slaying of Goliath, aroused Saul's jealousy and he became an outlaw. After the death of Saul and his son Jonathan, David was proclaimed King of Hebron and then of all Israel. He conquered Jerusalem, making it the nation's capital, finally defeated the Philistines, and united the tribes of Israel. His reign was troubled by the revolt of his son Absalom, who was eventually defeated and killed. David was succeeded by Solomon, his son by Bathsheba. According to the Jewish prophets, the Messiah must be a descendant of David.

David I (1084–1153) King of the Scots (1124–53). He recognized Matilda as successor to Henry I of England, and invaded N England (1138) after Stephen had seized the throne. Stephen defeated him in the battle of the Standard (1138), near Northallerton. David founded or refounded over a dozen monasteries.

David, St (*or* St Dewi; c. 520–600 AD) The patron saint of Wales and first abbot of Menevia (now St David's). He was also a missionary and the founder of many churches in Wales. Feast day: 1 March.

David ap Gruffudd (d. 1283) The brother of *Llywelyn ap Gruffudd, after whose death (1282) David claimed the title Prince of Wales. He was executed by Edward I for leading the Welsh in rebellion against him.

da Vinci, Leonardo. See Leonardo da Vinci.

Davis, Bette (Ruth Elizabeth D.; 1908–89) US film actress. From the 1930s to the 1950s she gave intense performances in such films as *Jezebel* (1938), *Dark Victory* (1939), and *All About Eve* (1950). In recent years she has played elderly eccentric or neurotic women.

Davis, John (*or* J. Davys; c. 1550–1605) English navigator. He went on three voyages in search of the *Northwest Passage (1585, 1586, 1587), passing through the strait named after him to Baffin Bay. In 1592, seeking the Magellan Strait, he discovered the Falkland Islands.

Davis, Miles (1926–) US jazz trumpeter and composer, one of the creators of cool jazz. His albums include *Miles Ahead* and the innovatory *Kind of Blue.*

Davis, Steve (1957–) British snooker player. He won the world professional championship in 1981, 1983, 1984, and 1987–1989.

Davy, Sir Humphry (1778–1829) British chemist and inventor of the miner's safety lamp (1815). Davy began his career by discovering the value of nitrous oxide as an anaesthetic. For this work he was invited to join the Royal Institution in London, where his most important work was the discovery of potassium in 1807 and sodium, calcium, barium, magnesium and strontium in 1808. He employed the young Michael *Faraday as his assistant.

Day Lewis, C(ecil) (1904–72) British poet and critic. He was a leading left-wing poet of the 1930s but his later verse was more lyrical. He was appointed poet laureate in 1968. As "Nicholas Blake" he wrote a series of detective stories.

DBE. See Order of the British Empire.

DDT (dichlorophenyltrichloroethane) An *insecticide now banned in the UK and restricted in most of Europe as it accumulates in *food chains causing serious environmental hazards.

deadly nightshade (*or* belladonna) A perennial plant, *Atropa belladonna*, of the potato family, native to Eurasia. It has purple or greenish bell-shaped flowers. The shiny black berries taste sweet but contain a deadly poison. The plant is a source of a variety of medicinal drugs.

Dead Sea A lake in E Israel and W Jordan. It is fed by the River Jordan and, having no outlet, has a high salt content and supports no life. Area: 1050 sq km (401 sq mi).

Dead Sea Scrolls A group of *Hebrew and *Aramaic rolls of handwritten documents found in caves near Khirbat *Qumran, on the Dead Sea. The first were discovered in 1947; the 500 different documents, dating from 250 BC to 70 AD, may have formed the library of an *Essene community, which was hidden during the Jewish revolt (66–70 AD). They include texts of many Old Testament books, commentaries, and material relating to that community.

Dean, Forest of An ancient royal forest in W England, in Gloucestershire between the Rivers Severn and Wye.

Dean, James (James Byron; 1931–55) US film actor who trained at the Actors' Studio, and became a cult hero for his generation. His films were *East of Eden* (1954), *Rebel without a Cause* (1955), and *Giant* (1955), released following his death in a car crash.

death The permanent ending of all bodily functions in an organism. With modern mechanical ventilators the heartbeat may be maintained long after "natural" breathing has stopped as a result of irreversible brain damage. Death is therefore now defined on the basis of brain function: when the parts of the brain that control breathing and other vital reflexes have ceased to function the patient is said to be brain dead.

death cap A highly poisonous mushroom, *Amanita phalloides*, fairly common in and near deciduous woodlands. Its cap is usually pale greenish yellow. The stalk is white or greenish white, with a baglike sheath (volva) at its base.

death's-head moth A *hawk moth, *Acherontia atropos*, with a wingspan of 125 mm, found in Europe, Africa, and Asia. Its body has markings resembling a skull and crossbones, hence the name.

Death Valley A desert area in the USA, in SE California, and the hottest and driest part of North America. The plants and animals that survive the harsh conditions are of interest to scientists. In 1933 it was declared a national monument.

deathwatch beetle A widely distributed wood-boring beetle, *Xestobium rufovillosum*, about 7 mm long, that damages buildings and furniture. It lays eggs in crevices in wood, which the larvae tunnel through reducing it to powder. The pupae make knocking sounds striking their heads against the walls of their burrows.

debenture stock A document setting out the conditions on which a sum of money is lent to a company with a fixed rate of interest. A **secured debenture** is one in which company property is used as security for the loan, either a particular item of property (fixed charge) or all the property (floating charge). An **unsecured debenture** has

no such security, but the holders of the debenture can force the company into liquidation (*see* bankruptcy) if their debenture is not repaid on the due date and they come before other shareholders in having their money repaid. An **irredeemable debenture** is never repaid, being bought only for the interest.

de Broglie, Louis Victor, 7th Duc (1892–1987) French physicist, who won the 1929 Nobel Prize for his theory that elementary particles have associated waves, known as **de Broglie waves**. The theory was confirmed by the subsequent observation of *electron diffraction and forms the basis of *wave mechanics.

Debussy, Claude (Achille) (1862–1918) French composer. He spent most of his life in Paris; his most famous works include *Prélude à l'après-midi d'un faune* (for orchestra; 1892–94), the opera *Pelléas et Mélisande* (1892–1902), *La Mer* (three symphonic sketches; 1903–05), a string quartet, and a sonata for flute, viola, and harp.

Decadents A group of late-19th-century French symbolist poets and their contemporaries in England. They aimed to create a literature liberated from all moral and social responsibilities. Poets linked with the movement included *Rimbaud, *Verlaine, and *Mallarmé in France, and Arthur Symons and Oscar *Wilde in England. *See also* Aesthetic movement.

decathlon An athletic competition for men, consisting of ten events over two days. On the first are 100 m sprint, long jump, shot put, high jump, and 400 m sprint; on the second are 110 m hurdles, discus throw, pole vault, javelin throw, and 1500 m run. Competitors score for performances in each event, the winner gaining the highest total. World record: 8847 points (1984) by Daley Thompson (Great Britain).

Decembrists. *See* Dekabrists.

decibel (dB) A unit used to compare two power levels on a logarithmic scale. Two power levels P and P_0 differ by n decibels when $n = 10 \log_{10} P/P_0$. The unit is often used to express a sound intensity in which case P_0 is usually taken as the intensity of the lowest audible note of the same frequency as P.

deciduous plants. *See* evergreen plants.

decimal system The number system in common use, having a base 10 and thus using ten separate numerals, 0 through to 9. It also involves the use of a decimal point to express numbers less than one, as in 0.25. The decimal system was invented by the Hindus and adopted by the Arabs in the 9th century (*see also* mathematics). Use of the decimal point did not occur until the early 18th century. Decimalization of currency systems was introduced by France after the Revolution and followed by most other European and American countries, except for Britain, which did not decimalize until 1971. *See also* metric system.

Declaration of Independence (4 July, 1776) The declaration, adopted by the 13 colonies of North America, that announced their independence from Great Britain. Written by Thomas *Jefferson between 11 June and 2 July and revised before adoption, the Declaration lists complaints and states principles of government and is one of the most important proclamations in the history of western politics.

Declaratory Act. *See* Stamp Act.

declination. *See* magnetic declination; right ascension.

decompression sickness (*or* caisson disease) A hazard to pilots and underwater divers caused by too rapid a return to normal atmospheric pressure. At high pressures (e.g. underwater) gas can be carried in the blood. A rapid return to normal pressure causes nitrogen (the main component of air) to form bubbles in the blood, interrupting the blood supply to the tissues, producing joint pain (the bends), general discomfort, and breathing problems (the chokes). Decompression sickness is prevented by placing the patient in a special chamber at high pressure and gradually reducing the pressure to normal.

Decorated The style of gothic architecture predominant in England between 1300 and 1370. In contrast to *Early English, Decorated is characterized by complex flowing patterns, especially in window tracery. Roof vaults were ribbed and the double curved arch with elaborate ornamentation became common.

Dee, River The name of three rivers in the UK. **1.** A river in NE Scotland, flowing E to the North Sea at Aberdeen. Length: 140 km (87 mi). **2.** A river in North Wales and NW England, rising in Gwynedd and flowing E and N through Llangollen and Chester to the Irish Sea. Length: 112 km (70 mi). **3.** A river in S Scotland, flowing S to the Solway Firth. Length: 80 km (50 mi).

deed In law, a document in writing, signed, sealed, and delivered, which hands over ownership of property to another or commits the maker to a particular action. It may be between two people or groups of people, or it may involve one person or group only (deed poll). A deed does not need to have the same conditions as a *contract.

deer A *ruminant mammal living mainly in the N hemisphere, although a few are found elsewhere. Nearly all deer have bony antlers that are shed every year. Deer range in size from the *elk to the small South American pudu. Most deer live in herds but some, such as the *muntjac, are solitary.

deerhound A long-established British breed of dog, formerly used for hunting deer. It has a deep-chested long body with long legs and a long tapering head with small ears. The wiry coat is usually blue-grey but may be shades of brown or fawn.

defamation In law, a false statement about another person that tends to damage his reputation. It is called libel if made in a permanent form (e.g. in newspapers) and slander if made by spoken words. Both types of defamation are dealt with by *civil law, although libel may be a crime if it is intended to cause a breach of the peace. Everyone who repeats or publishes a libellous statement may be taken to court by the person libelled. A statement judged to be a fair comment on a matter of public interest cannot count as defamation.

deflation A government action to slow down the economy, with the aim of easing *inflation or cutting down on imports and thus helping the *balance of payments. Both restriction on borrowing and increased taxation can be used to deflate the economy.

Defoe, Daniel (1660–1731) British novelist, economist, and journalist. His early career as a merchant ended in bankruptcy in 1692. He worked as a journalist and informer for both Whigs and Tories and suffered imprisonment (1702) for one of his pamphlets. From 1704 to 1713 he wrote most of the thrice-weekly *Review* himself. His famous novels were written late in his career, *Robinson Crusoe* in 1719 and *Moll Flanders* and *Colonel Jack* in 1722.

defoliant A chemical applied to foliage in order to cause shedding of leaves. Defoliants are used to aid mechanical harvesting of cotton and also in *chemical warfare.

Degas, (Hilaire Germain) Edgar (1834–1917) French painter and sculptor. Early portraits and history paintings led in the mid-1860s to contemporary scenes, particularly of ballet and racecourses. His pastels of women at their toilet are among his finest works. He exhibited with the impressionists but was little influenced by them.

de Gaulle, Charles André Joseph Marie (1890–1970) French general and statesman; president (1958–69). A supporter of mechanized warfare during the 1930s, he was promoted early in World War II to general (1940). He opposed the Franco-German armistice, becoming leader of the Free French in London. In 1958 he was summoned from retirement to deal with the crisis in Algeria, where French settlers were in revolt. He became president of the new Fifth Republic in 1959 and achieved Algerian independence by 1962. He subsequently pursued his vision of a Europe free of US influence, refusing to sign the *Nuclear Test-Ban Treaty (1963) and withdrawing France from NATO (1966). He was also opposed to UK membership of the EEC. At home his position was weakened by the student and industrial unrest of May, 1968, and in 1969 he resigned.

De Havilland, Sir Geoffrey (1882–1965) British aircraft designer and manufacturer, who produced some of the first jet-propelled aircraft. During both World Wars he designed several military aircraft, including the Mosquito of World War II.

deism A system of belief that, in contrast to *theism, takes God as the philosophical beginning, not as a personal God who reveals himself to his creatures. Deism was an anti-Christian movement in England in the late 17th and early 18th centuries that rejected the Scriptures. Deism, often tending towards atheism, had more influence on German and French thinkers, including *Voltaire, than in England.

Dekabrists (*or* Decembrists) Members of an unsuccessful anti-Tsarist revolt in December, 1825, following the death of Alexander I. They were members of various secret organizations formed after the Napoleonic Wars by people who had been military officers, and who had become discontented with Russia's government which opposed reform.

de Klerk, F(rederik) W(illem) (1937–) South African statesman; president (1989–). Having served in several ministerial posts, he succeeded P. W. Botha as president.

Delacroix, Eugène (1798–1863) French Romantic painter, influenced by *Rubens, and *Constable. His paintings were often inspired by Dante, Shakespeare, and Byron, and by contemporary events, e.g. *Massacre at Chios* (1824) and *Liberty Leading the People* (1830).

De la Mare, Walter (1873–1956) British poet and novelist. Among his best-known works are the poem "The Listeners" (1912), the fantastic novel *Memoirs of a Midget* (1921), and the collections *Come Hither* (1923) and *Love* (1943).

Delaunay, Robert (1885–1941) The earliest French painter in the abstract style. His first major works represented the Eiffel Tower (1910–11) in cubist style but in his series of *Discs* (1912–13) he pioneered orphism (which he called *simultaneisme*), a style in which colour alone was the subject matter.

Delaware The second smallest state in the USA. It occupies part of the low-lying ground of the Atlantic coastal plain with higher ground in the NW. It is one of the most industrialized states; Wilmington contains the administrative centres of several large chemical companies. *History*: the Swedes founded the first permanent settlement, Fort Christiana (now Wilmington), in 1638. Delaware was subsequently captured by the Dutch (1655) and the English (1664). It became part of Pennsylvania in 1682 and shared a governor with that colony until 1776. It was the first of the original 13 states of the USA. Area: 5328 sq km (2057 sq mi). Population (1987): 644 000. Capital: Dover.

Delft 52 01N 4 21E A town in the W Netherlands, in South Holland province. Since the late 16th century it has been famous for its pottery and porcelain known as delftware. Population (1987): 87 736.

Delhi 28 40N 77 14E The capital of India, situated between the Ganges and Indus on the W bank of the River Jumna. It consists of Old Delhi, built in 1639 on the site of cities dating from the 15th century BC, and New Delhi, which replaced Calcutta as the capital of British India in 1912. The old and new cities with the surrounding area comprise the Union Territory of Delhi, an administrative unit of some 1418 sq km (553 sq mi). The massive Red Fort of Old Delhi contains the Imperial Palace (1638–48) of Shah Jahan, and the Jami Masjid (Principal Mosque). New Delhi was designed chiefly by Sir Edwin Lutyens. Population (1990): 6 220 406.

Delian League A group of Greek city states formed in 478 BC during the *Greek-Persian Wars under the leadership of Athens. Members met on the sacred island of Delos. The League was broken up after Athens' defeat (404) in the Peloponnesian War but was revived in defence against Sparta in 378, lasting until the defeat (338) of Athens and Thebes at Chaeronea.

deliquescence The process in which some crystalline substances, such as calcium chloride

($CaCl_2$), absorb water from the atmosphere to such an extent that they dissolve. Deliquescent substances are used in several industries to provide dry atmospheres.

Delius, Frederick (1862–1934) British composer of German descent. Largely self-taught, he was influenced by Debussy and Grieg. His works include *Paris, the Song of a Great City* (1899), *Appalachia* (1902), *On Hearing the First Cuckoo in Spring* (1912), and *North Country Sketches* (1913–14). Delius became blind in 1925 but continued to compose with the help of Eric Fenby (1906–87).

Della Robbia, Luca (1400–82) Florentine Renaissance sculptor. Working first in marble, Luca produced the relief *Cantoria* (1431–38) for the Duomo, Florence. Subsequently he specialized in enamelled terracotta sculptures.

Delos (Modern Greek name: Dhílos) 37 23N 25 15E A Greek island in the S Aegean Sea, one of the Cyclades. It was of great importance in antiquity (*see* Delian League), and many ancient temples and other buildings have been excavated. Area: 3 sq km (1 sq mi).

Delphi A village in central Greece. In antiquity, it was the principal sanctuary and oracle of *Apollo. The oracle's advice about religion, morality, commerce, and colonial projects, spoken by a priestess in a trance, was widely sought by individuals and the Greek states. As traditional beliefs declined after the 4th century BC the oracle lost influence. It was closed by the Christian emperor, Theodosius (390 AD).

delphinium An annual or perennial garden plant of the buttercup family, native to the N hemisphere, with tall spikes of deep-blue flowers. Cultivated varieties have single or double flowers in shades of blue, pink, purple, or white.

delta A fan-shaped accumulation of sediment deposited at the mouth of a river, where it flows into a sea or lake. It forms when the river is slowed down on meeting the sea or lake, resulting in a reduction of the amount of soil, etc., that it can transport. Deltas (e.g. the Nile Delta) are often cultivated but tend to flood.

Demeter A Greek corn goddess and mother goddess, sister of *Zeus. She was worshipped at Eleusis, whose people helped her in her search for her daughter *Persephone, abducted to the underworld. In gratitude she instructed them in agriculture and religion. She was identified with the Roman goddess Ceres.

de Mille, Cecil B(lount) (1881–1959) US film producer and director. His best-known films were epics based on biblical themes, notably *The Ten Commandments* (1923; remade 1956), *The King of Kings* (1927), and *Samson and Delilah* (1949).

democracy A form of government in which people either rule themselves, as in ancient Athens, or elect representatives to rule, as in most modern democracies. Elections must be held regularly, be secret, and provide a choice of candidates; the elected assembly must also be free to make laws and to criticize government policy. Modern democratic ideas come from 18th-century *utilitarianism. Some argue that, in a modern democracy, the country is governed by a small select group which, although voted into power, allows the voters to take little part.

Democratic Party One of the two major political parties in the USA (*compare* Republican Party). Starting from Jefferson's Republican Democrats in 1792, it became the Democratic Party during the presidency (1829–37) of Andrew Jackson. In 1860, just before the Civil War, the Democrats split over the issue of *slavery into northern and southern groups and the party, dominated by southern Democrats, was overshadowed until it won back northern support in the 1880s. With F. D. Roosevelt's *New Deal programme in the 1930s, the Democrats were again seen as a progressive party. Notable Democratic presidents include Woodrow Wilson, F. D. Roosevelt, and J. F. Kennedy.

Democrats. *See* Social and Liberal Democratic Party.

Democritus (c. 460–370 BC), Greek philosopher and scientist. His atomism, was developed from Leucippus. Democritus wrote also on cosmology, biology, perception, music, and ethics.

demography The study of the sizes, distribution, and composition of human populations, using the methods of *statistics to obtain the information. It includes analysis of birth, death, and marriage rates for whole populations or groups within them.

Demosthenes (384–322 BC) Athenian statesman who attacked Philip of Macedon's imperial ambitions in Greece in speeches called the *Philippics* (351, 344, 341) and promoted an Athenian alliance with Thebes against Philip. This was defeated by Philip at Chaeronea (338), assuring Macedonian supremacy in Greece. After the death of Philip's son, Alexander the Great (323), Demosthenes again encouraged a Greek revolt. Condemned to death by Alexander's successors, Demosthenes committed suicide.

demotic script A form of Egyptian hieroglyphic writing. Pictorial hieroglyphics became less realistic from about 2500 BC until in the 7th century BC they developed into the cursive script called demotic. This continued in common use until the 5th century AD. *See also* Rosetta Stone.

dendrochronology (*or* tree-ring dating) An archaeological dating technique based on the *annual rings of trees. Variations in ring widths have been shown to correspond to rainfall and temperature variations and thus very old tree trunks can give a record of past climates. Any construction incorporating timber can be dated by comparing the timber-ring patterns with a specimen of known age.

dendrology. *See* tree.

denim A coarse cloth, named after the French fabric *serge de Nîmes*. It is made of cotton, often mixed with nylon, and usually dyed blue. Originally popular for work garments, denim became fashionable for jeans and other casual clothes in the 1970s.

Denis, St (3rd century) The patron saint of France. Of Italian birth, he was sent to Gaul as a missionary and there became the first Bishop of Paris. He was martyred under the Emperor Valerian. His shrine is in the Benedictine abbey at St Denis near Paris. Feast Day: 9 Oct.

Denmark, Kingdom of (Danish name: Danmark) A country in N Europe, between the Baltic and the North Seas. It consists of the N section of the Jutland peninsula and about a hundred inhabited islands. *Greenland and the *Faroe Islands are part of the Danish kingdom. *Economy*: agriculture is important; however, since World War II industry has predominated. Furniture, textiles, porcelain, etc., are valued for their design and exports include agricultural products, fish, machinery, and metals. *History*: Viking kingdoms occupied the area from the 8th to the 10th century, when Denmark became a Christian monarchy under Harald Bluetooth. His grandson, Canute, ruled over Denmark, Norway, and England, forming the Danish Empire, which was dissolved soon after his death. The Peace of Copenhagen (1660) concluded a long period of conflict between Denmark and Sweden. It then became an absolute monarchy until 1849, when a more liberal government was formed. During World War II Denmark was occupied by Germany but a resistance movement aided the Allied victory. Iceland, which had previously been united with Denmark, became independent in 1944. In 1973 Denmark joined the EC. Head of state: Queen Margrethe II (1940–). Prime minister: Poul Schlüter (1929–). Official language: Danish. Official religion: Evangelical Lutheran. Official currency: krone of 100 øre. Area: 43 074 sq km (16 631 sq mi). Population (1988 est): 5 082 000. Capital and main port: Copenhagen.

density The mass of unit volume of a substance. In *SI units it is measured in kilograms per cubic metre; water has a density of 1000 kg m^{-3} at 4°C. **Relative density** (formerly called "specific gravity") is the density of a substance divided by the density of water at 4°C. The density of a gas (vapour density) is often expressed as the mass of unit volume of the gas divided by the mass of the same volume of hydrogen at standard temperature and pressure.

dentistry The branch of medicine concerned with the teeth. It involves the repair, extraction, and replacement of teeth; the correction of badly positioned teeth (orthodontistry); the care of the gums and other structures supporting the teeth; and the surgical repair of fractures or abnormalities of the jaws. *See also* fluoridation.

Denver 39 45N 105 00W A city in the USA, the capital of Colorado on the South Platte River. Founded in 1858 during the Colorado gold rush, Denver is the financial, administrative, and industrial centre for a large agricultural area. Population (1986): 505 000.

deodar A tall *cedar, *Cedrus deodara*, native to the Himalayas widely planted in parks in temperate regions. It has young branches that droop down and large barrel-shaped cones.

deoxyribonucleic acid. *See* DNA.

depreciation The loss in value of goods as a result of wear and tear, going out of use, etc. For example, a machine that costs £10,000 and is expected to last ten years depreciates at the rate of £1,000 a year. A firm must set aside a certain sum each year to account for depreciation.

depression (economics) A period during the *trade cycle in which there is insufficient demand for goods. Profits, and therefore investment, are correspondingly low and high unemployment occurs (see Depression). Governments since World War II have adopted deficit financing policies to counter depressions, but the combination of depression and *inflation in the 1970s led to a revival of *monetarism.

depression (meteorology) A *cyclone in the midlatitudes; also called a low or a disturbance. Frequently accompanied by *fronts, depressions move towards the NE in the N hemisphere and towards the SE in the S hemisphere. They are characterized by unsettled weather and are the main source of rainfall in the lowland areas of the midlatitudes.

depression (psychiatry) Severe and persistent misery. It can be a normal reaction to distressing events, such as bereavement (reactive depression). Sometimes, however, it is out of all proportion to the situation or may have no apparent external cause (endogenous depression): it can then be a sign of mental illness. In manic-depressive psychosis the depression is severe and leads to extremes of despair and guilt. In depressive neurosis the symptoms are less extreme but may still lead to suicide. Treatment with antidepressant drugs is often effective and psychotherapy is helpful. Severe cases may need *electroconvulsive therapy.

Depression The period, also called the Slump, that began in the USA in 1929, when share prices fell so disastrously that thousands were made bankrupt. Overseas trade almost stopped, industrial production dropped, millions in industrialized countries were unemployed, and agricultural countries were made poor. Roosevelt's *New Deal (1934) brought Americans hope of recovery, but Britain, despite giving up free trade to protect its industries, never regained its commercial importance. In Germany the Depression contributed to the rise of the Nazis.

De Quincey, Thomas (1785–1859) British essayist and critic. He lived largely by journalism, writing numerous essays on various subjects. His autobiographical *Confessions of an English Opium Eater* first appeared in 1822.

Derain, André (1880–1954) French postimpressionist painter. In his bold designs, particularly in his Thames paintings (1905–06), he developed *fauvism, but after 1907 he came under the influence of *Cézanne and painted in a cubist manner. He later reverted to a traditional style after studying the Old Masters. He produced notable scenery and costumes for the *Ballets Russes.

Derby A flat race for three-year-old horses, run over 2.4 km (1.5 mi) at Epsom in early June. The most important of the English Classics, it was started (1780) by the 12th Earl of Derby.

Derby 52 55N 1 30W A city in central England, in Derbyshire on the River Derwent. Derby is an important engineering centre (with Rolls-Royce aero engines) and has large railway workshops. Population (1985 est): 215 000.

Derbyshire A county in N central England consisting of lowlands in the SE rising to the *Peak District in the NW. The main rivers are the Derwent, Trent, Dove, and Rother. Sheep and dairy farming are important with industrial activity centred on the coalfield in the E and SW. Area: 2631 sq km (1016 sq mi). Population (1987 est): 918 700. Administrative centre: Matlock.

dermatology. See skin.

Derwent, River The name of several rivers in England, including: **1.** A river in N central England, flowing SE from N Derbyshire to the River Trent. Length: 96 km (60 mi). **2.** A river in N England, flowing S from the North York Moors to join the River Ouse between Selby and Goole. Length: 92 km (57 mi). **3.** A river in NW England, flowing N and W from the Borrowdale Fells in Cumbria to the Irish Sea. Length: 54 km (34 mi).

desalination The removal of salt from sea water, usually to irrigate arid regions, especially if *solar power can be used as an energy source. Methods commonly employed are evaporation of the sea water, the condensed vapour forming relatively pure water, and freezing of the sea water, which produces pure ice.

Descartes, René (1596–1650) French philosopher and mathematician. After a Jesuit education and military service, he settled in Holland. Descartes' *Discourse on Method* (1637) introduced themes which he developed in his greatest work, the *Meditations* (1641). Asking "How and what do I know?" he arrived at his famous statement "Cogito ergo sum" ("I think, therefore I am"). From this he proved to his own satisfaction God's existence (he was a Roman Catholic) and hence the existence of everything else. He believed that the world consisted of two different substances—mind and matter (the doctrine of Cartesian dualism). Descartes also contributed to geometry (see coordinate systems) and optics. He held that mathematics was the supreme science.

desert An area with a mean annual rainfall below 250 mm (10 in) and limited vegetation. Deserts may occur in areas of high atmospheric pressure, such as the *Sahara, or near the W coast of continents cooled by cold ocean currents (e.g. the *Kalahari Desert). They are also found in continental interiors where mountain barriers restrict rainfall, such as the *Gobi Desert. Many deserts are characterized by stony scrublands, occasional rock uplands, and some shifting sand dunes. The wind is an important agent of erosion and the rain, falling as violent downpours, is capable of moving large amounts of debris.

desertification The process by which dry areas become deserts. Removal of the topsoil, by man or erosion by wind, water, or drying out, results in a reduction in the ground's ability to hold water, which can cause crops to fail and famine. Bad farming practices and the cutting of trees for firewood helped to create the Dust Bowl in the USA and have caused deserts in Africa, Australia, and SW Asia to advance by several kilometres each year. The process is controlled by careful management of surface cover and climate.

desert rat. *See* jerboa.

desman A small aquatic mammal native to Europe and Asia and related to the moles. They have webbed hind feet, live in burrows in river banks, and feed on invertebrates and fish.

Des Moines 41 35N 93 35W A city in the USA, the capital of Iowa. Founded in 1843, it is an important industrial and commercial centre. Population (1980): 371 800.

destroyer A fast armed naval vessel that is smaller than a *cruiser, has a displacement of about 3000 tonnes, and is 110–150 m (330–450 ft) long. They are used against submarines, in convoys, and in "hunter-killer" groups consisting of one *aircraft carrier and up to six destroyers.

detached retina A condition in which the retina—the light-sensitive layer at the back of the eye—becomes separated from the layer beneath it. It happens slowly and painlessly and the patient loses part of his vision. It is caused by injury or inflammation and is most common in very short-sighted people. Detached retina is treated surgically, by using a laser beam to weld the retina in place.

detergents Chemicals used for cleansing. Although the term includes *soaps it is usually applied just to *surfactants. Such detergents have large molecules, typically composed of a hydrocarbon oil-soluble part and a water-soluble part. These compounds are thus able to promote the solution of oil, grease, etc., in water. Household detergents may also contain water softeners, bleaches, and fabric brighteners.

determinism The philosophical theory that every event has a cause and that all events are decided by physical laws. Applied to human actions, the concepts of determinism and of *free will seem to contradict each other. If intentions and reasons for doing things are decided beforehand and if actions are predictable, this contradicts the idea that a person can freely choose his actions and is responsible for his choice. However, some philosophers believe that determinism and free will can exist together.

Detroit 42 23N 83 05W A city and port in the USA, in Michigan on the Detroit River. Founded in 1701, it is the fifth largest city in the USA. It is dominated by the motor-vehicle industry, its other industries including chemicals, steel, and oil refining. Population (1986): 1 086 220.

deuterium (D; *or* heavy hydrogen ^{2}H) An *isotope of *hydrogen having a nucleus consisting of one proton and one neutron. It occurs naturally in hydrogen (0.0156%). Heavy water (deuterium oxide; D_2O) is used in *nuclear reactors as a moderator. *See also* thermonuclear reactor. At no 1; at wt 2.014.

Deuteronomy The fifth book of the Old Testament, said to be by Moses, although this is widely questioned. It is a series of addresses by Moses to the Israelites immediately before the occupation of the Promised Land of Canaan (Palestine), and includes the Ten Commandments.

De Valera, Eamon (1882–1975) Irish statesman; prime minister (1932–48, 1951–54, 1957–59) and president (1959–73). A commandant in the 1916 *Easter Rising, he escaped execution

and in 1917 was elected to the British parliament and became the president of *Sinn Féin. From 1919 to 1922 he was president of the newly declared Irish Republic but rejected the terms of the Anglo-Irish treaty of 1921 (*see* Home Rule). In 1926 he founded *Fianna Fáil.

de Valois, Dame Ninette (Edris Stannus; 1898–) British ballet dancer and choreographer, born in Ireland. During the 1920s she worked with Diaghilev's Ballets Russes. In 1931 she founded the Sadler's Wells Ballet, the company that became the *Royal Ballet in 1956 and that she directed until 1963.

devaluation A downward change in the value of one country's currency in terms of other currencies. A country that devalues makes its exports cheaper and its imports more expensive; thus devaluation should help correct a *balance of payments deficit by increasing the volume of exports and decreasing the volume of imports.

Devil. *See* Lucifer.

devil ray. *See* manta ray.

devil's coach horse A large carnivorous European beetle, *Staphylinus olens*. If threatened it curls its abdomen upwards and releases an offensive odour.

devolution Handing over of political powers from a central government to regional governments. Growing nationalism in Scotland and Wales led to two devolution bills in the House of Commons in 1976. However, in a referendum in March, 1979, in Wales there was an absolute majority against devolution; in Scotland a small majority favoured devolution but not the 40% required for the bill to become law.

Devon A county of SW England, bordering on the Atlantic Ocean in the N and the English Channel in the S. It consists mainly of the mid-Devon plain, rising to *Dartmoor in the SW and *Exmoor in the NE. The chief rivers are the Dart, Exe, and Tamar. Tourism and agriculture are important while industry is concentrated around Exeter and Plymouth, a major naval base. Area: 6712 sq km (2591 sq mi). Population (1988): 1 021 100. Administrative centre: Exeter.

Devonian period A geological period of the Upper Palaeozoic era between the Silurian and Carboniferous periods, about 415 to 370 million years ago. It is divided into seven stages, based on invertebrate fossil remains, such as corals. The rocks containing these fossils were marine deposits but the period also shows continental deposits (Old Red Sandstone). Fossils from these rocks include fish, plants, and freshwater molluscs.

dew The *condensation of moisture on the ground or objects near the ground, especially at night. It occurs when the air near the ground falls to a temperature, called the **dew point**, at which it becomes saturated and the vapour present condenses into droplets.

Dewar flask A flask, used to store a substance at constant temperature. The space between its double glass walls is evacuated to prevent heat loss by *conduction and the inside wall is silvered to prevent radiation; the flask is stoppered to avoid evaporation. Also known as the

Thermos flask, it was invented by Sir James Dewar (1842–1923).

Dewey Decimal Classification An international system for classifying books, originated in 1873 by the US librarian Melvil Dewey (1851–1931) for the Amherst College Library. Books are divided according to subject into ten groups, each group having a hundred numbers; principle subdivisions within each group are divided by ten; with the use of decimal numbers further subdivisions can be generated.

dextrose. *See* glucose.

Dhaka (name until 1984: Dacca) 23 42N 90 22E The capital of Bangladesh, situated in the SE of the country, on the Burhi Ganga River. It is a riverport and commercial and industrial centre. The capital of the Bengal province of the Mogul Empire in the 17th century, it came under British rule in the 18th century and upon independence in 1947 was made capital of East Pakistan. Population (1984 est): 3 600 000.

diabetes One of several diseases, the most common of which is **diabetes mellitus** (*or* sugar diabetes), in which the body is unable to utilize sugars due to a deficiency of the pancreatic hormone *insulin. Symptoms include thirst, weight loss, and a high level of glucose in the urine and in the blood (hyperglycaemia). Treatment is based on a controlled diet, often with insulin injections or pills to reduce the sugar in the blood. **Diabetes insipidus** is a rare disease due to a deficiency of the pituitary hormone vasopressin, which regulates water balance in the body. The patient produces large quantities of urine and is always thirsty. It is treated with the hormone.

Diaghilev, Sergei (Pavlovich) (1872–1929) Russian ballet impresario. The outstanding success of his season of Russian ballet (1909) resulted in the organization of a permanent company (1911), known as the *Ballets Russes, which Diaghilev directed until his death.

dialect The language of a particular district or group. The difference between language and dialect is not clear, but the speakers of the dialects of a language usually understand each other. Dialects develop as a result of geographical separation: slightly differing versions of one original language develop in different places within a generation or so of the time of separation. Social factors also affect dialect development. In English, for example, the medieval dialect of London has developed into a socially important class dialect spoken in most parts of Britain (*see* received pronunciation).

dialectical materialism The official philosophy of *Marxism, developed by Marx and Engels. It is based on **historical materialism**, explained in the *Communist Manifesto*, an account of history based on economy: for every system of production there is an appropriate organization of class and property. While economic forces continually develop production systems, the class and property structure remains unchanged, causing tension between economic forces and social relations, which continues until the final socialist society is developed.

dialysis A process, discovered by Thomas Graham (1804–69), for separating large and small molecules in solution by diffusion through a semipermeable membrane. Different molecules in a solution diffuse at different rates, large molecules being almost completely blocked by a semipermeable membrane, whereas small molecules are not. Dialysis is used in kidney machines, or dialysers, which take over the function of diseased kidneys by filtering waste material from the blood leaving behind proteins, blood cells, and other large particles.

diamond The hardest known mineral, comprising a variety of crystalline *carbon, formed under intense heat and pressure. Diamonds are mined in S Africa, Siberia, and Namibia; over 80% are used industrially, mainly for cutting and grinding tools, the others being used as gems. One of the largest diamonds discovered is the Cullinan diamond. Many industrial diamonds are produced synthetically from *graphite subjected to very high temperatures and pressures.

Diana The Roman goddess identified with the Greek Artemis, associated with women and childbirth and with the moon. She is usually represented as a virgin huntress armed with bow and arrows.

diaphragm 1. In anatomy, a dome-shaped sheet of muscle that separates the thorax (chest cavity) from the abdomen. The diaphragm is attached to the spine, lower ribs, and breastbone and contains a large opening through which the oesophagus (gullet) passes. It plays an important role in producing breathing movements (*see* respiration). 2. *See* contraception.

diarrhoea The frequent passing of liquid stools. It is a symptom, not a disease; causes include anxiety, infection or inflammation of the intestines, impaired absorption of food, and side effects of drugs. It can be eased by the use of drugs but proper treatment must aim at eliminating the cause.

diaspora (Greek: dispersion) Jewish communities outside the land of Israel since they were forced into exile (6th century BC). The most important centres of the diaspora were, in the ancient world, Babylonia and Egypt; in the middle ages, Spain and France; and in early modern times, E Europe. In the late 19th century many Jews left Russia and Poland, and the Nazi *holocaust destroyed many old European communities. The main centre is now the USA, with some six million Jews.

diastole. *See* blood pressure; heart.

diatoms Microscopic algae that occur as single cells or colonies in fresh water and oceans (forming an important constituent of *plankton) and also in soil. They have silicon-rich cell walls (called frustules) composed of two halves that fit together. Fossilized frustules form a porous rock called diatomaceous earth (*or* kieselguhr), used in filters, abrasives, etc.

diazepam. *See* benzodiazepines.

Dickens, Charles (1812–70) British novelist. He began his writing career by contributing to popular magazines, achieving sudden fame with *The Pickwick Papers* (1837), which he followed with *Oliver Twist* (1838) and *Nicholas Nickleby* (1839) and the very successful *Old Curiosity Shop* (1840–41); like all his novels, these first appeared in monthly instalments. *David Copperfield* (1849–50) was a strongly autobiographical work, portraying Dickens' father as Mr Micawber. His later novels, from *Bleak House* (1853) to the incomplete *Edwin Drood* (1870), were increasingly pessimistic; *Great Expectations* (1860–61) and *Our Mutual Friend* (1864–65) develop most fully Dickens' radical view of society.

dicotyledons The larger of the two main groups of flowering plants, which includes hardwood trees, shrubs, and many herbaceous plants (*compare* monocotyledons). Dicots have two seed leaves (cotyledons) in the embryo, the flower parts are arranged in fours or fives (or multiples), and the leaves have a pattern of veins.

dictionaries. *See* lexicography.

Diderot, Denis (1713–84) French philosopher and writer. With *Voltaire, Diderot helped create the *Enlightenment, mainly through the *Encyclopédie*, which he edited after 1750 (*see* Encyclopedists).

Dido In Greek legend, the daughter of a king of Tyre, who fled to Africa when her husband was murdered; there she founded *Carthage. According to legend she burnt herself to death on a funeral pyre to avoid marriage to Iarvas of Numidia; in *Virgil's *Aeneid* she killed herself after being abandoned by her lover *Aeneas.

dielectric A substance that acts as an electrical insulator. When a voltage is applied across a dielectric placed between two metal plates, the electric charge on the plates increases. Dielectrics, such as air, ceramics, or wax, are therefore used to increase the electrical *capacitance of devices.

Dieppe 49 55N 1 05E A port and resort in N France, in the Seine-Maritime department on the English Channel. Population (1989): 38 000.

Diesel engine. *See* internal-combustion engine.

diet, imperial. *See* Reichstag.

dietetics The study of the principles of nutrition enabling dieticians to advise on diets to maintain health and for patients with various diseases. A balanced diet should contain foods with adequate amounts of carbohydrates, fats, proteins, minerals, and vitamins—as well as dietary *fibre.

Dietrich, Marlene (Maria Magdalene von Losch; 1904–) German film actress and singer. Her image of sultry beauty was developed by the Austrian-born director Josef von Sternberg (1894–1969) in such films as *The Blue Angel* (1930), *Blonde Venus* (1932), and *Shanghai Express* (1932).

diffraction The spreading or bending of light waves as they pass the edge of an object or aperture. The irregular boundary of the shadow of an object cast on a screen by a small light source is an example of diffraction. A similar effect occurs with sound waves. *See also* interference.

diffusion **1.** The mixing of gases or liquids by means of the random thermal motion of the molecules (or other particles). The rates at which gases diffuse are inversely proportional to their densities (Graham's law). Diffusion also occurs between certain solids; for example gold will

slowly diffuse into lead. **2.** The scattering of a beam of light on reflection from a rough surface or on transmission through such materials as frosted glass.

digestion The process by which food is converted into substances that can be absorbed by the *intestine. The process begins with the chewing and mixing with saliva of food in the mouth, and continues with the action of digestive enzymes secreted by the *stomach, duodenum, and *pancreas. Rhythmic contractions of the intestinal wall (called peristalsis) ensures mixing of enzymes and food and propulsion of food along the intestine. The products of digestion include amino acids, various sugars, and fat molecules; these are absorbed by the intestine into the bloodstream.

digital computer. *See* computer.

digitalis A preparation obtained from the dried leaves of foxglove plants. Digitalis is purified to give various drugs that are used to improve the action of the heart.

digital mapping The production of a map using a computer. The points and lines that make up the map are turned into computer data, which is stored on magnetic tapes. A print of all or part of the map can then be produced or it may be displayed on a visual display unit. Changes can be simply made without the whole map having to be redrawn. In the UK the *Ordnance Survey began converting its large-scale maps to digital data in 1973.

digital recording. *See* recording of sound.

Dijon 47 20N 5 02E A city in France, the capital of the Côte-d'Or department on the Burgundy Canal. The former capital of Burgundy, it is the site of the palace of the Dukes of Burgundy and has a cathedral (13th–14th centuries). It is famous for its mustard. Population (1983): 150 500.

dik-dik A small African antelope found in the undergrowth of forested areas. Dik-diks are generally solitary and only the males have horns.

dilatation and curettage (D and C) An operation in which the neck (cervix) of the womb is dilated (widened) and the lining of the womb is scraped out. D and C may be performed for a variety of reasons, including the removal of any membranes remaining in the womb after a miscarriage, removal of cysts or tumours, removal of a specimen of tissue for examination in various disorders, and for ending a pregnancy.

dill An annual or biennial European herb, *Anethum graveolens*, of the carrot family. 60 cm high, the stem bears feathery leaves and clusters of small yellow flowers, producing hard flat fruits. The leaves and fruits are used to flavour fish, pickled cucumbers, etc.

D'Indy, Vincent (1851–1931) French composer, the pupil and biographer of Franck and the cofounder of the Paris Schola Cantorum (1894). He was influenced by Wagner and wrote a number of orchestral works, including the *Symphony on a French Mountaineer's Song* (1886), as well as operas and chamber music.

dingo An Australian wild dog introduced from Asia. It has a tan-coloured coat. It is nocturnal and generally solitary.

Dinka A people of the Nile basin region of the Sudan. Warlike and independent, the Dinka move with their cattle from dry-season pastures by the rivers to wet-season settlements, where they grow millet. There are many independent tribes.

dinosaur An extinct reptile that was the dominant land-dwelling animal during the Jurassic and Cretaceous periods (200–65 million years ago). Dinosaurs first appeared about 225 million years ago, ranging in size from about 60 cm to such mighty creatures as *Diplodocus*. The carnivorous dinosaurs included the bipedal *Allosaurus* and *Tyrannosaurus*; the herbivores included the bipedal *Iguanodon*, the horned *Triceratops*, and *Stegosaurus*. All dinosaurs died out at the end of the Cretaceous period, along with the *ichthyosaurs, *pterosaurs, and *plesiosaurs. Why this happened is still not certain, but they were probably unable to adapt to changes in the climate and to the effects of a rise in the sea level, which flooded their coastal habitats.

Diocletian(us), Gaius Aurelius Valerius (245–313 AD) Roman emperor (284–305). He gained power after success in the army. In 293 he established the tetrarchy to govern the Empire in a time of civil strife: the Empire was divided into East and West, with each ruled by an emperor. Diocletian ruled in the East with the aid of Galerius, abdicating in 305.

diode. *See* semiconductor diode; thermionic valve.

Diogenes of Sinope (412–322 BC) The founder of the philosophical sect of the *Cynics. Diogenes claimed, in contrast to most Greek thinkers, total freedom for the individual. Unlike modern anarchists, he saw no need for rebellion to assert independence, which he thought he already had. His disregard for convention made him the subject of many stories.

Dionysus (*or* Bacchus) The Greek god of wine, originally a vegetation god. He was the son of Semele (daughter of Cadmus) by Zeus. A common theme of many Dionysian legends is his revenge on people who refused to accept his divinity.

Dioscuri. *See* Castor and Pollux.

diphtheria An acute bacterial infection affecting the nose, throat, or larynx. Virtually eliminated in the West by extensive immunization, it is still found in Africa and India. The disease can be cured using penicillin and antitoxin.

Diplodocus An amphibious dinosaur of the Jurassic period (200–136 million years ago) and the largest vertebrate ever to live on land, reaching a length of 27 m. It had a narrow body with massive pillar-like legs, a long neck with a tiny head, and a long tail. It fed on soft vegetation in swamps and shallow lakes.

dipper An aquatic songbird of Eurasia and America found near mountain streams, diving into the water to search for insects and small fish. The Eurasian white-breasted dipper (*Cinclus cinclus*) is about 17 cm long.

Dirac, Paul Adrien Maurice (1902–84) British physicist. In 1928 he introduced a general summary of quantum theory, into which he later incorporated *relativity and predicted the existence of antiparticles. He shared the 1933 Nobel Prize with Schrödinger.

discount houses Financial institutions in the UK that act as an agent between the *commercial banks and the Treasury.

discus throw A field event in athletics. The circular discus is made of wood and metal, the men's weighing 2 kg (4.4 lb) and the women's 1 kg (2.2 lb). It is thrown as far as possible with one hand from within a circle 2.5 m (8.2 ft) in diameter. World record: men: 74.08 m (1986) by Jürgen Schult (East Germany); women: 76.80 m (1988) by Gabriele Reinsch (East Germany).

disinfectant A substance or process that kills germs or prevents them multiplying. Carbolic acid (phenol) was introduced in the 1870s by Joseph *Lister; it and its derivatives are still used in cleaning materials and in skin disinfectants. Chlorine and such compounds as sodium hypochlorite kill bacteria and also some viruses. Other chemical disinfectants include hydrogen peroxide (H_2O_2), iodine (I_2), and formaldehyde (HCHO). Dry heating to 140°C for about 3 hours will kill all disease-causing germs. Boiling water and ultraviolet light are also effective disinfectants.

Disney, Walt (1901–66) US film cartoonist. His most famous character, Mickey Mouse, was designed in 1928. His films include cartoon features, such as *Snow White and the Seven Dwarfs* (1938), *Pinocchio* (1939), and *Bambi* (1943), nature documentaries, and such films as *Treasure Island* (1950) and *Mary Poppins* (1964). His *Fantasia* (1940) used colourful images and cartoons to accompany classical music. He opened Disneyland, an amusement park, in California in 1955. Similar parks opened in Florida (Walt Disney World; 1971), Tokyo (1985), and Paris (1992).

Disraeli, Benjamin, 1st Earl of Beaconsfield (1804–81) British statesman; Conservative prime minister (1868, 1874–80). Becoming an MP in 1837, Disraeli was critical of Peel's Conservative Government (1841–46) and opposed the repeal of the *Corn Laws. He was three times chancellor of the exchequer in Derby's governments (1852, 1858–59, 1866–68) and was largely responsible for the 1867 *Reform Act. He succeeded Derby in February, 1868, but lost office in the autumn election, to the Liberals under Gladstone. Under Disraeli's second term the Conservative Party policies included upholding the monarchy, Empire, and Church of England, while sponsoring social reform. In 1875 he bought Britain a major stake in the Suez Canal and in 1876 made Queen Victoria Empress of India. Also a writer, Disraeli's novels include *Vivien Grey* (1826), *Coningsby* (1844), and *Sybil* (1845).

distillation A method of purifying or separating the components of a liquid by boiling the liquid and condensing the vapour. It is used for separating liquids from solids or a mixture of liquids with different boiling points (fractional distillation). Distillation is used in refining petroleum, in the production of alcoholic spirits, and in extracting pure water from sea water.

dittany A perennial European plant, *Dictamnus albus*, also known as the gas plant, it gives off an aromatic oil. Dittany produces a drooping spike of white or pink flowers. Family: *Rutaceae*. The name is also used for other plants.

Diu. *See* Daman and Diu.

diuretics A class of drugs that increase the excretion of urine by the kidneys. They are used to treat diseases (such as heart failure) in which fluid accumulates in the tissues and also in the treatment of high blood pressure.

diver A large aquatic bird of the N hemisphere, also called loon. Divers breed on lakes and ponds and winter in mild coastal regions. They have pointed wings and black and white plumage; they dive to catch fish, frogs, etc.

dividend A share in the profits of a company paid to shareholders. The rate of dividend is declared at the company's annual general meeting and will reflect the preceding year's profit.

divine right of kings A political principle claiming that monarchs are responsible only to God and that their subjects owe them unquestioning obedience. The theory started in the middle ages and was most fully developed in the 16th and 17th centuries, especially in England under the Stuart kings and in France under Louis XIV.

Divisional Court. *See* courts of law.

divorce The legal process by which a marriage is ended. Until the Matrimonial Causes Act (1857), which established a Divorce Court, divorce in England was possible only by special Act of Parliament. The High Court and county courts (*see* courts of law) now deal with divorce. Since 1971, the only ground for divorce has been that the marriage has broken down for good. The person who applies for the divorce (the petitioner) must show that the other person (the respondent) has (1) committed adultery, (2) behaved in such a way that the petitioner cannot reasonably be expected to live with him or her, (3) deserted the petitioner for two years, (4) lived separate and apart from the petitioner for two years and agrees to the divorce, or (5) lived separate and apart from the petitioner for five years. If the couple can't agree, the court decides on the custody of the children under 16 and the financial arrangements.

Diwali An important Hindu festival held during October or November in honour of *Lakshmi, goddess of wealth (or in Bengal, Kali). Lamps are also lit in honour of Rama. In *Jainism the festival commemorates the death of their saint Mahavira.

Djakarta. *See* Jakarta.

Djibouti, Republic of (name until 1977: the French Territory of the Afars and the Issas) A small country in NE Africa, on the Gulf of Aden at its entrance to the Red Sea. Consisting of a rocky coastal plain rising to a plateau, the inhabitants are Somalis (chiefly Issas) and Afars, with Arabic and European minorities. *Economy*: centres on Djibouti (a free port since 1949), which is linked by rail to Ethiopia and handles about half of that country's trade. *History*: it became a French colony (French Somaliland) in 1896 and an overseas territory in 1967. Independence was granted in 1977 as Djibouti with Hassan Gouled Aptidon (1916–) as its first president. Official languages: Hamitic languages of Somali. Official

currency: Djibouti franc of 100 centimes. Area: 21 783 sq km (8409 sq mi). Population (1988 est): 484 000. Capital and chief port: Djibouti.

DNA (*or* deoxyribonucleic acid) The chief ingredient of the *chromosomes, DNA is necessary for the organization and functioning of living cells.

The molecular structure of DNA was proposed by J. D. *Watson and F. H. *Crick in 1953. It consists of a double helix of two nucleic acid strands coiled around each other. Each strand carries a sequence of the four chemical bases: adenine (A), guanine (G), cytosine (C), and thymine (T). The bases on one strand are joined by hydrogen bonds to the bases on the other, like the rungs of a ladder. The rungs always connect the same pairs of bases: A always binds with T and G with C. Before the cell divides, the rungs of the ladder break and the two strands separate. Each then acts as a 'blueprint' for the cell to manufacture new complementary strands. The result is two identical copies of the original helix. This property of self-replication enables DNA to duplicate the genes of an organism during the cell divisions of growth (*see* mitosis) and the production of germ cells for the next generation (*see* meiosis).

Dnepr, River (*or* R. Dnieper) The third longest river in Europe, in the W Soviet Union. Rising in the Valdai Hills, NE of Smolensk, it flows mainly SE through Belorussia and the Ukrain to the Black Sea. Length: 2286 km (1420 mi).

Dnepropetrovsk (name from 1787 until 1796 and from 1802 until 1826: Ekaterinoslav) 48 29N 35 00E A large industrial city in the SW Soviet Union, in the Ukrainian SSR on the River Dnepr. It produces iron and steel. Population (1987): 1 182 000.

Dobermann pinscher A breed of dog developed by Louis Dobermann in Germany in the late 19th century. It has a powerful body with a short tail and a long muzzle. The short smooth coat is black, or blue-grey with tan markings. Dobermanns are used as police and guide dogs.

dock A plant (usually perennial) of temperate regions. It has a deep root and large lance-shaped leaves. The greenish flowers produce small nutlets. Dock leaves are the traditional antidote to nettle stings.

Dodecanese A group of some 20 Greek islands in the SE Aegean Sea, including Cos, *Rhodes (the largest), and Pátmos. Taken from Turkey by Italy in 1912, they passed to Greece in 1947. Total area: 2719 sq km (1050 sq mi). Population (1981): 145 071. Capital: Rhodes.

Dodgson, Charles Lutwidge. *See* Carroll, Lewis.

dodo A large flightless bird, *Raphus cucullatus*, that lived on Mauritius but was extinct by 1681. It had a grey plumage, tiny wings, and a large head with a hooked bill.

Dodoma 6 10S 35 40E A town in E central Tanzania. It replaced Dar es Salaam as the capital in 1983. Population (latest est): 45 703.

dog A carnivorous mammal belonging to the family *Canidae*. The modern domestic dog (*Canis familiaris*) probably evolved from wolves and was first domesticated over 10 000 years ago.

DOG

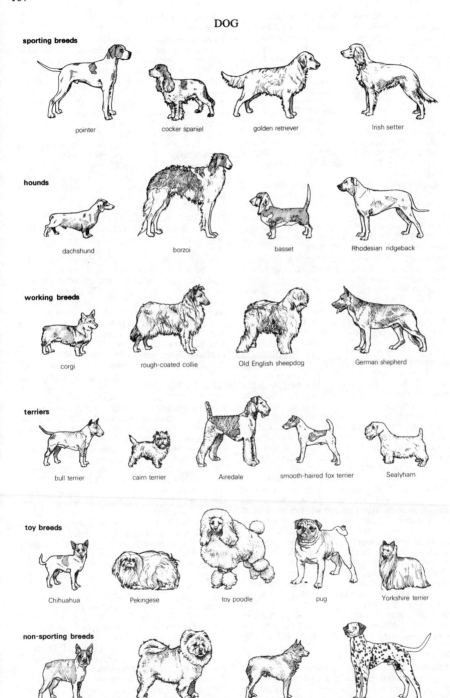

sporting breeds

pointer   cocker spaniel   golden retriever   Irish setter

hounds

dachshund   borzoi   basset   Rhodesian ridgeback

working breeds

corgi   rough-coated collie   Old English sheepdog   German shepherd

terriers

bull terrier   cairn terrier   Airedale   smooth-haired fox terrier   Sealyham

toy breeds

Chihuahua   Pekingese   toy poodle   pug   Yorkshire terrier

non-sporting breeds

Boston   chow chow   shipperke   Dalmatian

They have sharp teeth, strong jaws, and keen hearing and smell. Their intelligence led to their use by man as sporting dogs, working dogs, and household pets. There are up to 400 breeds.

doge The title of the chief magistrate of Venice from about 697 AD to the fall of the Venetian Empire in 1797. Elected for life, he had considerable power until 1172, when he became little more than a figurehead. The present richly decorated **Doge's Palace** originated in the early 14th century.

dogfish A small *shark. The brown-spotted dogfish, *Scyliorhinus stellaris* and *S. canicula* are commonly found in Mediterranean and British coastal waters. They are edible and purchased as "rock salmon."

Dogger Bank A vast sandbank in the central North Sea, 17–36 m (55–120 ft) below water. It is a major fishing ground.

dog rose A shrubby rose, *Rosa canina*, with arching stems and pink or white flowers, that grows in woods, hedges, and roadsides of Europe, North Africa, and SW Asia.

dogwood A shrub of the N hemisphere. It has pointed leaves with curved veins and clusters of four-petalled flowers. The fruit is a berry. The common European dogwood (*Cornus sanguinea*) has white flowers and black berries.

Doha 25 15N 51 36E The capital of Qatar, on the E coast. Population (1983 est): 190 000.

Dohnányi, Ernö (Ernst von D.; 1877–1960) Hungarian composer and pianist. He spent his last years in the USA. He was greatly influenced by Brahms, who praised his early works. His best-known composition is the *Variations on a Nursery Theme* (for piano and orchestra; 1913), based on the tune known in England as "Baa Baa Black Sheep."

Dolby system An electronic device for reducing the hiss in sound reproduction, particularly in *tape recorders. Invented by Ray Dolby (1933–), it selectively boosts the higher frequencies in the sound in quiet passages before recording, to drown the hiss produced by the tape, and reduces them when playing back.

doldrums The equatorial belt within which the *trade-wind zones converge. Winds are light and variable but the strong upward movement of air caused by the convergence produces frequent thunderstorms, heavy rains, and squalls.

Dollfuss, Engelbert (1892–1934) Austrian statesman; chancellor (1932–34). His chancellorship was increasingly strained by his inability to control the Austrian Nazis or to cooperate with the Social Democrats. He was assassinated in July during an unsuccessful attempt by the Nazis to seize power.

dolmen (Breton: table stone) A prehistoric tomb made of huge stone slabs set upright and supporting a stone roof. Widely distributed in *Neolithic Europe, dolmens were often covered by a *barrow.

dolomite A mineral consisting of colourless or grey calcium magnesium carbonate, $CaMg(CO_3)_2$. Rocks containing over 15% magnesium carbonate are called dolomites, those containing less are magnesian *limestones, and those containing both dolomite and calcite are dolomitic limestones.

Dolomites (Italian name: Alpi Dolomitiche) A section of the Alps in NE Italy. Composed of dolomitic limestone, they are characterized by their steep-sided rocky peaks.

dolphin A toothed agile *whale with a streamlined body up to 4.5 m long. Dolphins live in groups and feed mainly on fish. They are intelligent creatures with well-developed abilities for communicating with each other. The common dolphin (*Delphinus delphus*), which grows to 2.1 m, is blue-black with a white belly and striped body. *See also* bottlenose; porpoise.

Domesday Book (1086) The survey of England ordered by William I to work out the extent of his own possessions and the value for taxation purposes of the estates of his tenants in chief. Parts of N and NW England and some towns, including London and Winchester, were left out. Royal commissioners collected, shire by shire, details about each *manor, naming its present owner and its owner under Edward the Confessor, changes in its size since Edward's reign, the numbers of its inhabitants and the services or rents they owed, and the numbers of its ploughteams, mills, and fisheries. The survey, in two volumes, is now in the Public Record Office.

Domingo, Placido (1941–) Spanish tenor, educated in Mexico. He sings a wide range of roles but specializes in Puccini and Verdi, starring in film versions of *La Traviata* in 1983 and *Otello* in 1986.

Dominica, Commonwealth of An island country in the West Indies, the largest of the Windward Islands. It is of volcanic origin and very mountainous. The population is mainly of African descent. *Economy*: chiefly agricultural. *History*: discovered by Columbus in 1493, it was alternately French then British before becoming British in 1783. It became self-governing in 1967 and an independent republic within the British Commonwealth in November, 1978. President: Clarence A. Seignoret. Official language: English. Official currency: East Caribbean dollar of 100 cents. Area: 728 sq km (289 sq mi). Population (1987): 94 191. Capital: Roseau.

Dominican Republic A largely mountainous country in the Caribbean Sea, occuping the E two-thirds of the island of Hispaniola (Haiti occupies the W third). The population is mainly mixed African and European. *Economy*: chiefly agricultural. Mining and industry are being developed. *History*: a Spanish colony following discovery in 1492 by Columbus, the E was handed over, 1795–1809, to the French, who had colonized the W. The E gained independence from Spain in 1821. It was held by Haiti from 1822 until 1844, when the Dominican Republic was founded. US occupation (1916–22) was followed by the establishment (1930) of Trujillo's 30-year dictatorship. Following Trujillo's assassination the elected president, Juan Bosch, was deposed (1963) in a military coup. President: Joaquín Balaguer. Official language: Spanish. Official currency: Dominican Republic peso of 100 centavos. Area: 48 442 sq km (18 700 sq mi).

Population (1987 est): 6 708 000. Capital and main port: Santo Domingo.

Dominicans (Latin *Ordo Praedicatorum*: Order of Preachers) A Roman Catholic order of friars, also known as Black Friars, or (in France) Jacobins, founded by St Dominic (c. 1170–1221). Living by begging much of the time, the friars were teachers and preachers. Among their scholars was St Thomas *Aquinas. They defended orthodox practices in the *Inquisition. There are two orders of Dominican nuns.

Don, River A river in the SW Soviet Union, flowing mainly S to the Sea of Azov. A canal links it to the River Volga. Length: 1981 km (1224 mi).

Donatello (Donato de Nicolo di Betti Bardi; c. 1386–1466) Florentine sculptor. A pioneer of the Renaissance, he broke with tradition in his lifelike marble sculptures and developed a form of relief sculpture creating perspective. Working in bronze he produced *David* (c. 1430–35; Florence), the influential monument in Padua known as the *Gattamelata* (1447–53), and the high altar for S Antonio, Padua (1446–50).

Donbass. *See* Donets Basin.

Donegal (Irish name: Dún Na Ngall) A county in the N Republic of Ireland, in Ulster bordering on the Atlantic Ocean. Chiefly mountainous, it has a rugged indented coastline. Area: 4830 sq km (1865 sq mi). Population (1986): 129 428. County town: Lifford.

Donets Basin (*or* Donbass) An industrial region in the SW Soviet Union, in the Ukrainian SSR. It is the major coal-producing and steel-manufacturing area in the country, the major city being Donetsk. Area: about 25 900 sq km (10 000 sq mi).

Dönitz, Karl (1891–1980) German admiral. A U-boat commander in World War I, in World War II he developed the "pack" system of submarine attack. In 1943 he became grand admiral and then commander in chief of the German navy. He was appointed chancellor after Hitler's death and was imprisoned (1946–56) for war crimes.

Donizetti, Gaetano (1797–1848) Italian composer of operas. His 75 stage works rely more on coloratura display than on dramatic effect. They include *Lucia di Lammermoor* (1835) and *Daughter of the Regiment* (1840).

Don Juan The aristocratic libertine of European literature. In Tirso de Molina's play *El burlador de Sevilla* (1630) he kills the father of his latest victim; he mockingly invites the old man's statue to dinner, and it drags him off to hell. Subsequent versions include *Molière's *Don Juan* (1665), *Mozart's *Don Giovanni* (1787), *Byron's (*Don Juan*, 1819–24) and G. B. *Shaw's (*Man and Superman*, 1903).

donkey A domesticated *ass more commonly used for pulling or carrying loads than for riding. *See also* mule.

Donne, John (1572–1631) English metaphysical poet. He became an Anglican priest in 1615 and was appointed Dean of St Paul's in 1621. His poetry, almost all written before his ordination, combines passions for God (e.g. *La Corona*; 1607) and women with intellectual wit.

Doppler effect The apparent change in frequency of a wave caused by relative motion between the source and the observer. When the source and the observer approach each other, the apparent frequency increases; when one is travelling away from the other, the apparent frequency decreases. An example is the change in pitch of a train whistle as it passes a station. The effect can also be observed as a shifting of the wavelength of light from a receding star towards the red end of the spectrum; this is known as the *redshift. Named after Christian Doppler (1803–53), Austrian physicist.

Dorchester 50 43N 2 26W A market town in S England, the administrative centre for Dorset on the River Frome. Population (1985): 14 000.

Dordogne, River A river in SW France. Rising in the Auvergne Mountains, it flows SW and W to enter the Gironde estuary NNE of Bordeaux. It is important for hydroelectric power and has famous vineyards along its lower course. Length: 472 km (293 mi).

Doré, (Paul) Gustave (Louis Christophe) (1832–83) French illustrator, painter, and sculptor, born in Strasbourg. He established his popularity in the 1850s with illustrations of Rabelais' books and Balzac's *Contes drôlatiques*. These were followed by grotesque illustrations to Dante, Cervantes, Tennyson, etc. His scenes of poverty in *London* influenced Van Gogh.

Dorians Iron Age Greek conquerors of the S Aegean region (c. 1100–1000 BC). Moving southward from Epirus and SW Macedonia, they brought about the final collapse of the Bronze Age *Mycenaean civilization. They settled chiefly in the Peloponnese.

Doric order. *See* orders of architecture.

dormancy A period during which the living processes of a plant, animal, or reproductive body (e.g. seeds) are reduced, enabling them to survive unfavourable environmental conditions. Dormancy may be triggered by changes in temperature, daylength, and availability of water, etc. *See also* hibernation.

dormouse A climbing rodent of Eurasia and Africa. The common dormouse (*Muscardinus avellanarius*) is reddish, about 6 cm long with a bushy tail. It feeds at night on nuts and seeds, hibernating during winter.

Dorset A county of SW England, bordering on the English Channel. It consists chiefly of lowlands, crossed by ranges of hills. The chief rivers are the Frome and the Stour. Agriculture is predominant. Tourism is important, notably in Bournemouth and Weymouth. Area: 2634 sq km (1017 sq mi). Population (1988 est): 655 700. Administrative centre: Dorchester.

Dortmund 51 32N 07 27E A city in NW Germany, in North Rhine-Westphalia in the *Ruhr. It is a port on the Dortmund–Ems Canal and a major industrial and brewing centre. Population (1986): 569 800.

dory. *See* John Dory.

Dos Passos, John (1896–1970) US novelist. He served as an ambulance driver in World War I and worked as a war correspondent in Spain, Mexico, and the Near East. His major work, the trilogy *U.S.A.* comprises *The Forty-Second Par-*

allel (1930), *1919* (1932), and *The Big Money* (1936).

Dostoievski, Fedor Mikhailovich (1821–81) Russian novelist. He lived in W Europe from 1867 to 1871, plagued by his epilepsy and compulsive gambling. He returned to Russia in 1871 and became relatively prosperous, stable, and conservative. His major novels, in which he explored moral and political themes, are *Crime and Punishment* (1866), *The Idiot* (1868–69), *The Possessed* (1869–72), and *The Brothers Karamazov* (1879–80).

dotterel A small Eurasian *plover, *Eudromias morinellus*, that nests in tundra regions and migrates to the Mediterranean and SW Asia for the winter. It has a broad white eye stripe, a grey breast, and a russet belly.

Douai Bible The Roman Catholic version of the Bible in English, translated from the *Vulgate by Roman Catholic scholars from Oxford, who had fled to Europe during the reign of Elizabeth I and who were members of the English College at Douai. The New Testament was published at Reims in 1582 and the Old Testament at Douai in 1609–10. Its language influenced the translators of the *King James Version.

Douala 4 04N 9 43E The largest city in Cameroon, on the River Wouri estuary. A deepwater port and the chief export point of the country, it is also a major West African industrial centre. Population (1985): 852 700.

double bass The lowest-pitched musical instrument of the violin family. Its four strings are tuned in fourths (E, A, D, G). It has a range of over three octaves, from the E an octave below the bass stave and is used in symphony orchestras and jazz bands (usually by plucking).

Douglas 54 09N 4 29W The capital of the Isle of Man, on the E coast. It is a port and resort, its buildings including the House of Keys (parliament house), the Manx Museum, and a casino. Population (1986): 20 368.

Douglas fir A conifer, *Pseudotsuga menziesii*, of the pine family, native to W North America and cultivated for ornament and its timber, used for poles, masts, etc. 60–90 m high. It has flexible needles and cylindrical cones.

Douglas-Home, Sir Alec. See Home of the Hirsel, Alec Douglas-Home, Baron.

Doulton English pottery works, originally at Lambeth (London), specializing in salt-glazed stoneware. Brown stoneware vessels with moulded portrait and landscape decoration were typical of the period to 1850. From 1856 unique studio pottery in coloured glazes was produced, using wood-fired kilns.

Dounreay The site in N Scotland, on the N coast of the Highland Region, of the world's first experimental fast-breeder reactor.

Douro, River (Spanish name: Duero) A river in SW Europe. Flowing W from N central Spain, it forms part of the border between Spain and Portugal before entering the Atlantic Ocean at Oporto. Length: 895 km (556 mi).

dove. See pigeon.

Dover 51 08N 1 19E A port in SE England, in Kent on the Strait of Dover. An ancient Cinque Port, it is the UK's chief ferry and hovercraft port for the Continent. Population (1981): 32 843.

Dowding, Hugh Caswall Tremenheere, 1st Baron (1882–1970) British air chief marshal, who was head of the RAF Fighter Command in 1940. His genius in coordinating early warning radar, pilots, and equipment played a major role in winning the Battle of Britain.

Dow-Jones Index An average of the prices on the New York Stock Exchange of 30 industrial shares, calculated each day by Dow Jones and Co., first devised in 1897.

Dowland, John (1563–1626) English composer and lutenist. He specialized in writing songs with lute accompaniment.

Downing Street A London street adjoining Whitehall. No 10 is the official residence of the prime minister; the chancellor of the exchequer resides at No 11. It was named after the English statesman Sir George Downing (1623–84).

Down's syndrome A disease in which a baby's cells have one extra chromosome, named after J. L. H. Down (1828–96), English physician. Affected children are mentally retarded and because they resemble orientals, were formerly called mongols. Usually cheerful and loving, Down's children, with special education, can live relatively normal lives. Down's syndrome can be detected during pregnancy (*see* amniocentesis).

Doyle, Sir Arthur Conan (1859–1930) Scottish author, creator of the detective Sherlock Holmes. Conan Doyle first studied medicine, his Holmes being inspired by an Edinburgh lecturer. His many Holmes stories, which began with *A Study in Scarlet* (1887) are related by Dr John H. Watson. Conan Doyle also created the brilliant Professor Challenger in *The Lost World* (1912) but he valued most his historical novels, such as *The White Company* (1890).

D'Oyly Carte, Richard (1844–1901) British theatre impresario and manager. He produced most of the comic operas of Gilbert and Sullivan. He opened the Savoy Theatre, London, in 1881 to house these productions.

Drabble, Margaret (1939–) British novelist. Most of her novels concern the moral and emotional problems of women in modern society. They include *The Millstone* (1965), *The Ice Age* (1977), and *The Radiant Way* (1987).

Draco (7th century BC) Athenian lawgiver. His legal system was so harsh that "draconian" has since been used to describe any strict or cruel law. Draco's code prescribed the death penalty for most offences.

Dracula, Count A Transylvanian vampire, the central character of Bram Stoker's gothic novel *Dracula* (1897) and many horror films. The name, meaning "demon," was applied to Vlad IV the Impaler, a 15th-century Walachian prince on whom the character was based.

dragonfly A coloured insect that has a long body, large eyes, and transparent veined wings (spanning up to 180 mm). Both adults and freshwater nymphs are carnivores, eating insect pests.

dragoon European mounted soldier of the 16th and 17th centuries who could fight as a light cavalryman (*see also* hussars) or as an infantryman. Named after the muzzle-loading carbine they carried, they were originally used as an arm of the infantry. By the 18th century most light cavalrymen were called dragoons (or carabiniers).

drag racing 1. A form of *motor racing that began in the USA. It is held in heats of two cars on a straight strip a quarter of a mile (402 m) long. Using a standing start, races depend heavily on acceleration. Speeds have exceeded 400 km per hour (250 mph) in specially constructed light powerful vehicles. 2. A form of motorcycle racing organized in the same way.

Drake, Sir Francis (1540–96) English navigator and admiral. Drake's first important voyages were trading expeditions to the West Indies and in 1567 he accompanied Sir John *Hawkins (a relative) to the Gulf of Mexico. In 1578 he became the first Englishman to navigate the Straits of Magellan intending, with Elizabeth I's consent, to raid the Pacific coast. Alone out of five ships, his *Golden Hind* sailed N but unable to find a way back to the Atlantic Ocean crossed the Pacific Ocean, returning home in 1580 via the Cape of Good Hope. Drake crowned his career by helping to defeat the Spanish *Armada (1588), pausing only to complete a game of bowls on Plymouth Hoe.

Drakensberg Mountains (or Quathlamba) The chief mountain range in S Africa, extending from Cape Province (South Africa) along the E border of Lesotho to Swaziland, reaching 3482 m (11 425 ft) at Thaba Ntlenyana.

draughts (US name: checkers) A board game for two players, developed in 12th-century Europe from an ancient Egyptian game. Each player has 12 discs (black for one, white or red for the other) placed on the 12 black squares at the opposite ends of a chessboard. The pieces move only on the black squares and black always starts. A piece is moved diagonally forwards onto an empty neighbouring square. If the next square is occupied by one of the opponent's pieces but the square beyond that is empty, the playing piece must jump onto the empty square, removing the opponent's piece. A further jump must be made from there if possible (in the same turn). If a piece reaches the opposing back line it becomes a "king" (a second piece is placed on top of it) and may then move forwards or backwards. The winner is the player who takes or prevents all his opponent's pieces from moving.

Dravidian languages A language family of about 20 languages spoken in S India. The major languages are *Tamil (also spoken in Sri Lanka), Kanarese (or Kannada), Telugu, Malayalam, and Tulu.

Dresden 51 5N 13 41E A city in SE Germany, on the River *Elbe, the capital of Saxony. One of the world's most beautiful cities before its devastation by bombs in 1945, it has since been rebuilt. Dresden is a centre of culture, light industry, and market gardening. Population (1986): 519 737.

Dresden porcelain. *See* Meissen porcelain.

dressage The training of a riding (or carriage) horse to make it responsive to its rider (or driver). Originally a training for military charges, the present, more humane, methods developed in the 18th century. In *haute école*, a horse is taught to perform intricate leaps and movements. Dressage competitions consist of a series of complex set movements.

Dreyfus, Alfred (1859–1935) French Jewish army officer. Unjustly accused of revealing state secrets to the Germans in 1894 Dreyfus, the victim of antisemitism, was sent for life to Devil's Island. After agitation by Émile Zola the case was reopened in 1898 and following a retrial in 1899, Dreyfus was pardoned but not completely cleared until 1906.

dromedary. *See* camel.

drone. *See* bee.

Drosophila A small *fruit fly that feeds on rotting or damaged fruit, etc. Some species, especially *D. melanogaster*, are used in laboratory studies of heredity.

drugs Substances that alter the functioning of the body. Medicinal drugs are widely used for the treatment and prevention of disease. The wide range of drugs available for this purpose includes anaesthetics (*see* anaesthesia), *analgesics, *antibiotics, *diuretics, hormonal drugs, and *tranquillizers. Some drugs, many of which are addictive (*see* narcotics), are taken for the pleasurable effects they produce. Strict controls exist to restrict this misuse.

Druids Ancient Celtic priests, respected as teachers and judges. They worshipped nature gods, believed in immortality of the soul and *reincarnation, and taught astronomy. Their main religious ceremony involved the sacred oak tree. They sacrificed humans, usually criminals, on behalf of the dying. In Gaul and Britain they were wiped out by the Romans, but in Ireland they survived until the arrival of Christian missionaries.

drupe A fruit with a stone, such as a cherry, plum, or peach. The fruit wall (pericarp) develops into three layers: an outer skin (epicarp), succulent flesh (mesocarp), and a stone (endocarp) containing the seed.

Drury Lane Theatre The oldest theatre in London, first opened in 1663. The present building (1813) has housed every form of dramatic production. Its early managers included David *Garrick and R. B. *Sheridan.

Druses (or Druzes) Members of a religious sect living mainly in Syria, the Lebanon, and Israel. Druses are not generally accepted as Muslims. Their scriptures are based on the Bible, the Koran, and on Sufi writings (*see* Sufism).

Dryden, John (1631–1700) English poet and critic. He welcomed the Restoration, writing several plays for the reopened theatres, for example *Marriage à la Mode* (1673) and *All for Love* (1677). His verse satires include *Absalom and Achitophel* (1681) and *MacFlecknoe* (1682).

dry rot The decay of timber caused by fungi, especially *Serpula lacrymans*. Spores germinate in timber having a moisture content of over 20% and the fungus appears whitish on the surface. The timber becomes crumbly and the infection may spread to adjoining dry timbers. Treatment is by removal of infected timbers and application of fungicide to the remaining parts. *Compare* wet rot.

Dubai. *See* United Arab Emirates.

Du Barry, Marie Jeanne Bécu, Comtesse (?1743–93) The last mistress of *Louis XV of France from 1768 until his death (1774), when she was banished from court. She was guillotined during the French Revolution.

Dublin (Irish name: Baile Átha Cliath) 53 20N 6 15W The capital of the Republic of Ireland, on Dublin Bay. An important commercial and cultural centre, it is also the largest manufacturing centre and the largest port in the Republic. Its industries include whiskey distilling, brewing, clothing, glass, and food processing. Population (1986): 502 337.

Dublin (Irish name: Baile Átha Cliath) A county in the E Republic of Ireland, in Leinster bordering on the Irish Sea. Chiefly low lying, it rises in the S to the Wicklow Mountains and is drained by the River Liffey. Area: 922 sq km (356 sq mi). Population (1986): 1 020 796. County town: Dublin.

Dubrovnik (Italian name: Ragusa) 42 40N 18 07E A port and tourist resort in S Yugoslavia, in Croatia on the Adriatic coast. Population (1985): 35 000.

Duchamp, Marcel (1887–1968) French artist. His first success was *Nude Descending a Staircase* (1912; Philadelphia), influenced by *cubism and futurism. This was followed by his controversial ready-made objects, for example a urinal, first shown in New York. He lived in New York after 1915 and became leader of its *dada art movement. His best-known work is the glass and wire picture of *The Bride Stripped Bare by Her Bachelors, Even* (1915–23; Philadelphia).

duck A small waterbird related to geese and swans, found in salt and fresh waters throughout the world except Antarctica. They are adapted for swimming and diving, having a dense waterproofed outer plumage with a thick underlayer of down. The long bill has internal horny plates for sifting food. The 200 species of duck mostly live in groups; many are migratory and strong fliers. Dabbling ducks feed at the surface of the water, diving ducks forage in deeper water.

duck-billed platypus A primitive aquatic egg-laying mammal, *Ornithorhynchus anatinus*, of Australia and Tasmania. Platypuses have webbed feet and a broad flat toothless beak. The female lays two eggs and after incubation suckles the tiny young.

Duero, River. *See* Douro, River.

Dufy, Raoul (1877–1953) French painter. His early influences were *impressionism and then *fauvism. He later developed an individual style in lively racecourse and regatta scenes, notable for the way forms are drawn sketchily over areas of thinly applied colour.

dugong A marine herbivorous mammal, *Dugong dugon*, of the Indo-Pacific region. Dugongs, also known as sea cows, have blue-grey rough skin and a bristly snout; the males have short tusks. Their forelimbs are flippers and they lack hind limbs, having a flattened tail for swimming.

duiker A small nocturnal African antelope that lives in bush or forest. Both sexes usually have smooth backward-pointing horns and often a distinct stripe along the back.

Dukas, Paul (1865–1935) French composer, teacher, and critic. He is best known for his orchestral scherzo *The Sorcerer's Apprentice* (1897). His works also include the opera *Ariane et Barbe-Bleue* (1907).

dulcimer A musical instrument consisting of a shallow resonating box with strings stretched over two moveable bridges. It is played with two small hammers and is much used in European and Asian folk music.

dulse An edible purplish-red seaweed, *Rhodymenia palmata*, found on N Atlantic coasts. A red alga, it has flat leathery lobed fronds.

Dumas, Alexandre (1802–70) French novelist and dramatist, often called Dumas *père*. He is noted for his historical romances, including *The Count of Monte Cristo* (1844–45), *The Three Musketeers* (1844), and *The Black Tulip* (1850).

His son **Alexandre Dumas** (1824–95), Dumas *fils* is best-known for the novel *La Dame aux camélias* (1848), the basis of Verdi's opera *La Traviata*.

Du Maurier, George (Louis Palmella Busson) (1834–96) British cartoonist and novelist, born in Paris, who contributed cartoons to *Punch* and other magazines. His novel *Trilby* (1894) is based on his life as a student in Paris. His granddaughter **Dame Daphne Du Maurier** (1907–89) wrote romances, usually set in Cornwall, including *Rebecca* (1938) and *My Cousin Rachel* (1951).

Dumfries and Galloway Region An administrative region in SW Scotland, bordering on the Solway Firth. Formed in 1975 from the counties of Dumfries, Kirkudbright, and Wigtown, it is predominantly agricultural and consists of uplands and moors in the N descending to coastal lowlands in the S. Area: 6369 sq km (2460 sq mi). Population (1989 est): 147 036. Administrative centre: Dumfries.

Duncan I (d. 1040) King of the Scots (1034–40). His claim to the throne was challenged by Macbeth, by whom he was murdered.

Duncan, Isadora (1878–1927) US dancer. She lived mostly in Europe, where she gained a reputation for both her innovative modern dancing and her flamboyant lifestyle.

Dundee 56 28N 3 00W A city and port in E Scotland, the administrative centre of Tayside Region on the Firth of Tay. It is known chiefly for the manufacture of jute goods and also provides supplies and services for the North Sea oil industry. Population (1988 est): 174 255.

Dunedin 45 52S 170 30E A port in New Zealand, in SE South Island at the head of Otago Harbour. Founded by Scottish Presbyterians in 1848, it has two cathedrals (Anglican and Roman Catholic) and the University of Otago (the oldest in the country, founded in 1869). Population (1989): 116 000.

Dunfermline 56 04N 3 29W A town in E Scotland, in Fife Region on the Firth of Forth. Several Scottish kings, including *Robert the

Bruce, are buried in the 11th-century abbey. Population (1981): 52 057.

dung beetle A *scarab beetle, usually small and dark, that has the habit of rolling dung into balls, which serve as a food source for both the adults and larvae.

Dunkirk (French name: Dunkerque) 51 02N 2 23E A port in N France, in the Nord department on the Strait of Dover. During *World War II Allied troops were successfully evacuated from its beaches (1940) following the fall of France. Dunkirk is an industrial centre and has an oil refinery and naval shipbuilding yards. Population (1983): 83 760.

Dun Laoghaire 53 17N 6 08W A port in the E Republic of Ireland, in Co Dublin. It is the terminus of a ferry service from Holyhead, Wales. Population (1981): 54 496.

dunlin A common *sandpiper, *Calidris alpina*, that breeds in far northern regions, ranging south to N Britain. It has a bill with a curved tip and a black and red-brown plumage that changes to grey in winter.

Dunlop, John Boyd (1840–1921) Scottish inventor, who is credited with inventing the pneumatic tyre (1887). Dunlop began to produce his tyres commercially in 1890. Initially for bicycles, they later contributed greatly to the development of motor cars.

dunnock A shy songbird, *Prunella modularis*, also called hedge sparrow. About 14 cm long, it has a dull-brown plumage with a greyish throat and breast. It has a fine sharp bill and feeds on insects.

Duns Scotus, John (c. 1260–1308) Scottish-born Franciscan philosopher, who, with Roger *Bacon and *William of Ockham, carried on a controversy against *Aquinas. Contradicting Aquinas, Duns Scotus held that what makes one thing distinct from another is its essential properties rather than its accidental properties. Although nicknamed the Subtle Doctor by contemporaries, he suffered Renaissance ridicule.

Dunstan, St (924–88 AD) English churchman. Appointed Abbot of Glastonbury in 943, he rebuilt its monastery and revived English monasticism. The chief minister under Kings Eadred and Edgar, he became Bishop of Worcester (957), Bishop of London (959), and Archbishop of Canterbury (960). Feast day: 19 May.

duodenal ulcer. *See* peptic ulcer.

duodenum. *See* intestine.

Durban 29 53S 31 00E The main seaport in South Africa and the largest city in Natal, on the Indian Ocean. Population (1985): 982 075.

Dürer, Albrecht (1471–1528) German *Renaissance painter, engraver, and woodcut designer. He was influenced by Italian artists but his woodcuts of the *Apocalypse* (1498) are still *gothic in style. Paintings include the *Self-Portrait* as Christ (1500) and *Adoration of the Magi* (1504). He made his famous engravings, including *Knight, Death, and the Devil*, in the period 1512–19.

Durham 54 47N 1 34W A city in NE England, the administrative centre of Co Durham on the River Wear. It has a Norman cathedral and an 11th-century castle. Population (1986): 39 600.

Durham A county in NE England, bordering on the North Sea. It consists chiefly of undulating lowlands, rising W to the uplands of the Pennines and is drained by the Rivers Wear and Tees. Agriculture includes sheep and dairy farming. Coalmining, formerly of major importance, is concentrated in the E. Area: 2436 sq km (964 sq mi). Population (1987 est): 598 700. Administrative centre: Durham.

durmast A Eurasian oak, *Quercus petraea*, up to 40 m tall. It has long-stalked oval leaves with rounded lobes and hairy undersides and unstalked conical acorns (hence its other name —sessile oak). Its durable wood is used for furniture, construction work, and boat building and the bark for tanning.

Durrell, Lawrence George (1912–90) British novelist and poet. His best-known work is *The Alexandria Quartet*, comprising *Justine* (1957), *Balthazar* (1958), *Mountolive* (1958), and *Clea* (1960). His later work includes the novels *Tunc* (1968) and *Nunquam* (1970) and a further quintet. His brother **Gerald Malcolm Durrell** (1925–) is a naturalist and popular writer, famous for such books as *My Family and Other Animals* (1956).

durum. *See* wheat.

Düsseldorf 51 13N 6 47E A city in NW Germany, capital of North Rhine-Westphalia on the River Rhine. A port and major commercial and industrial centre of the *Ruhr, its main industry is iron and steel. Population (1987): 561 200.

Dutch The national language of the Netherlands, belonging to the West Germanic language group. In Belgium it is one of the two official languages and is known as Flemish (*or* Vlaams). It has many local variations. It comes from Low Franconian, the speech of the Salic Franks, who settled in this area.

Dutch East Indies. *See* Indonesia.

Dutch elm disease A serious disease, first described in the Netherlands in 1919, that reached epidemic proportions in Britain in the 1970s, killing millions of elm trees. The fungus responsible, *Ceratocystis ulmi*, blocks the vessels that carry water to the leaves, which wilt and eventually die. The disease is carried by *bark beetles. Protective measures can be taken but are too expensive for widespread use.

Dutch Guiana. *See* Suriname.

Duvalier, François (1907–71) Haitian politician, known as Papa Doc; president (1957–71). His secret police, the Tonton Macoutes, eliminated opposition and used Negro nationalism and voodoo to maintain popular sympathy. In 1964 he became president for life. His son **Jean-Claude Duvalier** (1951–), known as Baby Doc, succeeded him, but had to flee to France after an uprising in 1986.

Dvořák, Antonín (1841–1904) Czech composer. He wrote his famous ninth symphony, entitled "From the New World", while director of the National Conservatory in New York, 1892–95. Besides the symphonies he wrote concertos for piano, violin, and cello, orchestral tone poems, chamber music, piano music, and songs. His Czech nationalism is particularly evident in his famous *Slavonic Dances* for piano duet (1878–86).

dyeing The process of permanently changing the colour of a material. Natural dyes, such as *madder and indigo, have been known since 3000 BC. Mauveine, the first synthetic dye, was discovered in 1856 by W. H. Perkin. Most modern dyes are *aromatic compounds. To dye fibres, the material is immersed in an aqueous solution containing the dye, so that the dye molecules adhere to the fibres. An inorganic chemical (the mordant) may be added to make the dye less soluble once it has adhered to the fibre. Dyes used without a mordant are called **direct dyes**. **Vat dyes**,used on cotton fibres, are insoluble in water, but are applied in reduced soluble form and then reoxidized.

Dyfed The largest county of Wales, in the SW bordering on the Irish Sea. It was created in 1974 from the former counties of Cardiganshire, Carmarthenshire, and Pembrokeshire. It consists mainly of undulating uplands and coastal plains (extensive in the S). Although predominantly agricultural, new industries are being introduced and a major oil refining area has developed at Milford Haven. Area: 5765 sq km (2227 sq mi). Population (1987 est): 343 200. Administrative centre: Carmarthen.

Dylan, Bob (Robert Allen Zimmerman; 1941–) US singer and songwriter. He spoke for the protest movement of the 1960s with such folk albums as *The Times They Are A-changin'* (1964) but later adopted a more modern style.

dynamics. *See* mechanics.

dynamite An explosive solid consisting of 75% nitroglycerine and 25% kieselguhr, a porous form of silicon dioxide (SiO_2). It was invented in 1866 by *Nobel. Nitroglycerine alone is very sensitive to shock. The kieselguhr makes it safe to handle. Dynamite is used for blasting, particularly under water.

dynamo. *See* electric generator.

dyne The unit of force in the *c.g.s. system equal to the force that will give to a mass of one gram an acceleration of one centimetre per second per second.

dysentery An infection of the large bowel causing painful diarrhoea; the faeces often contain blood and mucus. It may be caused either by bacteria of the genus *Shigella* (bacillary dysentery) or by amoebae (amoebic dysentery). It can occur wherever there is poor sanitation, but amoebic dysentery is much more common in tropical countries.

dysprosium (Dy) A *lanthanide element discovered in 1886. It forms the oxide (Dy_2O_3) and halides (for example DyF_3). At no 66; at wt 162.50; mp 1412°C; bp 2335°C.

E

eagle A large bird of prey related to the hawks found in mountainous regions of the world. Eagles have a large hooked bill and strong feet and are typically brown. With a wingspan of 1.3–2.4 m, they can soar for long periods searching for food. *See also* bald eagle; golden eagle.

ealdorman The chief royal official of the Anglo-Saxon shire who presided over the shire court, carried out royal orders, and collected the military tax. Ealdormen later became hereditary earls, and their duties were taken up by the sheriffs.

ear The organ of hearing and balance in vertebrate animals. Sound waves are transmitted through the external auditory meatus and cause the eardrum (tympanic membrane) to vibrate. These vibrations are transmitted through the ear ossicles to the fenestra ovalis, which leads to the inner ear. The Eustachian tube connects the middle ear to the back of the throat (pharynx), enabling the release of pressure that builds up in the middle ear. The cochlea contains special cells that convert the sound vibrations into nerve impulses, which are transmitted to the hearing centres of the brain. The inner ear also contains the organs of balance: three semicircular canals, each registering movement in a different direction.

Earhart, Amelia (1898–1937) US aviator, who was the first woman to fly solo across the

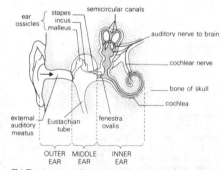

EAR *A vertical section through the human ear shows its internal structure; the middle and inner ears are embedded in the bone of the skull. The arrow indicates the direction of sound waves entering the ear.*

Atlantic (1932) and Pacific (1935) Oceans. She died on an attempted flight around the world.

Early English The style of gothic architecture predominant in England in the 13th century, characterized by narrow pointed windows and arches.

175

earth The third planet from the sun, at an average distance of 149.6 million km (93 million mi). Its diameter at the equator is 12 756 km (7926 mi), slightly less at the Poles. It orbits the sun in 365.26 days, and makes one rotation on its axis every 23.93 hours. The earth is believed to be about 4600 million years old. It consists of an inner core of solid iron, surrounded by an outer core of molten iron. Surrounding this is the solid mantle which is separated from the crust by the Mohorovičić discontinuity. The crust consists of basaltic oceanic crust surmounted by less dense granitic continental crust (see basalt; granite). The crust varies in thickness from 5 km under the oceans to 60 km under mountain ranges. The most abundant elements in it are oxygen (47%) and silicon (28%). 70.8% of the earth's surface is ocean. The greatest ocean depth is over 11 000 m (36 000 ft), in the Marianas Trench; the greatest height of land is 8848 m (29 028 ft), at Mount Everest. See also atmosphere.

earthquake A series of shocks felt at the earth's surface, ranging from mild tremblings to violent oscillations, resulting from the breakup of brittle rocks within the earth's crust and upper mantle. The *Richter scale is used for comparing earthquake magnitudes. Most earthquakes occur in certain regions (seismic zones); these include a zone around the Pacific, the Alpine-Himalayan belt, and the midocean ridges. See plate tectonics.

earthworm An *annelid worm found in soil all over the world. Earthworms feed on rotting vegetation, pulling the dead leaves down into their burrows and improving the fertility of the soil. Each body segment has four pairs of bristles for gripping the surface as the worm moves.

earwig A nocturnal usually herbivorous insect found in Europe and warm regions. It has a dark slender body and a pair of pincers (cerci) at the end of the abdomen. At rest, the membranous semicircular hindwings are covered by short leathery forewings.

Eastbourne 51 00N 0 44W A resort in S England, on the East Sussex coast near Beachy Head, where the South Downs reach the sea. Population (1981): 77 608.

Easter The feast celebrating Christ rising from the dead. It was associated by the early Church with the Jewish *Passover. At the Council of Nicaea in 325 AD, it was agreed that Easter would be linked to the full moon on or following the spring *equinox and might thus fall on any Sunday between 22 March and 25 April. See also Good Friday; Lent.

Easter Island (or Rapanui) 27 05S 109 20W A Chilean volcanic island in the S Pacific Ocean. It is famed for its tall stone sculptures. The population is of Polynesian origin. Area: 166 sq km (64 sq mi). Population (1982 est): 1867. Chief settlement: Hanga-Roa.

Eastern Roman Empire (or Byzantine Empire) The Roman territories E of the Balkans separated from the western Roman Empire by Diocletian in 293 AD. Under Constantine the Great the Empire became Christian. Constantinople (previously Byzantium; now Istanbul) was declared the capital in 330 AD. The Eastern Empire survived until Constantinople fell to the Ottoman Turks in 1453.

Easter Rising (1916) An armed revolt mainly in Dublin against the British Government. Patrick Pearse, a leader of the Irish Republican Brotherhood, and James Connolly with his Citizen Army, a total of 2000 men, proclaimed the establishment of the Irish Republic. Serious street fighting followed with the government using artillery. The rebels gave in and some 15 of the leaders were executed.

East Germany. See Germany.

East India Company 1. (British) A commercial company that was made into a corporation in 1600 to trade in East Indian spices. After Robert *Clive's victories in the Seven Years' War (1756–63) against the French East India Company (founded 1664), it virtually governed British India. Its powers were then limited by a series of Government of India Acts (1773–1830). The Company ceased to exist in 1873. 2. (Dutch) A commercial company founded in 1602 to encourage Dutch trade in the East Indies. By the late 17th century, its main concern was the government of *Java.

East Sussex A county of SE England, formerly part of Sussex, bordering on the English Channel. It consists mainly of undulating land with the South Downs, drained by the River Ouse, in the S. It is predominantly agricultural. Coastal resorts include Brighton and Eastbourne. Area: 1795 sq km (693 sq mi). Population (1987 est): 698 000. Administrative centre: Lewes.

ebony The valuable wood of several tropical evergreen trees from India and Mauritius. Hard, dark, and heavy, it is used for furniture, inlaying, etc.

Eboracum (or Eburacum). See York.

EC. See European Community.

echidna A primitive Australian egg-laying mammal, also called spiny anteater. It is about 45 cm long, has long spines, and digs for ants, picked up with its sticky tongue. The egg is incubated in a pouch on the female's belly, in which the young echidna suckles at a teat.

Echidna In Greek legend, a monster, half woman and half serpent. By the monster Typhon she gave birth to many other legendary monsters, including Cerberus, Scylla, and the Sphinx.

echinoderm A marine invertebrate animal of which the *starfish, *sea urchins, and *sea cucumbers are different types. Echinoderms usually have a skin-covered skeleton of hard protective plates, often bearing spines. Small saclike fluid-filled organs (tube feet) are used in locomotion, breathing, feeding, etc.

Echo In Greek legend, a nymph deprived of speech by Hera and able to repeat only the final words of others. Her hopeless love for *Narcissus caused her to fade away until only her voice remained.

echolocation A method by which certain animals can locate objects by emitting sounds and detecting the echo. Insect-eating bats use echolocation to locate their prey when hunting on the wing. Toothed whales and porpoises emit brief clicks, enabling them to pick out very small objects.

echo sounding The use of sound waves to measure the depth of the sea or to detect other vessels or obstacles. The device consists of a source of ultrasonic pulses and an electronic circuit to measure the time taken for the pulse to reach the target and its echo to return. The device was developed by the Allied Submarine Detection Investigation Committee in 1920 and was known as ASDIC. The name was changed to sonar (*so*und *na*vigation and *r*anging) in 1963.

eclipse The passage of an astronomical body into the shadow of another. A **lunar eclipse** occurs when the moon enters the earth's shadow at full moon. The gradual obscuring of the moon's surface is seen wherever the moon is above the horizon. A **solar eclipse** occurs at new moon, but only when the moon passes directly in front of the sun. The moon's shadow moves rapidly across the earth. Observers in the outer shadow region (the penumbra) will see a **partial eclipse**, with part of the sun hidden. Observers in the inner (umbral) region of the shadow will see a **total eclipse**, in which the sun's disc is obscured; the *corona can, however, be seen.

ecology The scientific study of organisms in their natural environment, including the relationships of different species with each other and the environment. A *community of organisms and their habitat is called an **ecosystem**. Ecologists predict the effects of human activities (e.g. farming, industry) on ecosystems, enabling wildlife to be conserved.

economics A social science concerned with the production of goods and services, their distribution, exchange, and consumption. **Microeconomics** is concerned with the problems facing individuals and firms, while **macroeconomics** is concerned with the regulation of national economies by governments. In the western democracies problems centre upon the control of *inflation, unemployment, and the *balance of payments, as well as the encouragement of economic growth. *See also* monetarism.

ecosystem. *See* ecology.

Ecuador, Republic of A country in NW South America, lying on the Equator. It consists chiefly of a coastal plain in the W, separated from the tropical jungles of the Amazon basin by the Andes. The population is largely of Indian and mixed race. *Economy*: mainly agricultural, the main cash crops being bananas, coffee, and cocoa. Valuable hardwoods are produced and fishing is important. Ecuador is now South America's second largest oil producer (Venezuela being the first). *History*: the Andean kingdom of Quito had already been conquered by the Incas when the Spanish established a colony in 1532. It gained independence in 1821 and in 1822 joined Gran Colombia under Bolívar. In 1830 it became the independent republic of Ecuador. Head of state: President Rodrigo Borja Cevallos. Official language: Spanish; the main Indian language is Quechua. Official currency: sucre of 100 centavos. Area: 270 670 sq km (104 505 sq mi). Population (1986): 9 640 000. Capital: Quito. Main port: Guayaquil.

Eddy, Mary Baker (1821–1910) US religious leader, founder of *Christian Science. Mrs Eddy was much influenced by the spiritual leader Phineas Parkhurst Quimby (1802–66). She published her beliefs in *Science and Health* (1875) and in 1879 founded the Church of Christ, Scientist, in Boston.

Eddystone Rocks 50 10N 4 16W A dangerous group of rocks off the coast of SW England, in the English Channel. The lighthouse built by John Smeaton (1759) was replaced in 1882.

edelweiss A common alpine plant, *Leontopodium alpinum*, of the daisy family, often grown in rock gardens. About 15 cm high, it has woolly leaves and tiny yellow flowers.

Eden, Anthony. *See* Avon, (Robert) Anthony Eden, 1st Earl of.

Edgar (c. 943–75) The first king of a united England (959–75). Edgar promoted a monastic revival, encouraged trade by reforming the currency, and improved naval defence.

Edgar the Aetheling (c. 1050–c. 1130) The grandson of Edmund II Ironside (Aetheling means royal prince). His claim to the English throne was rejected in 1066 owing to his youth and ill health. In 1068 and 1069 he led revolts against William I but came to terms with him in 1074.

Edinburgh 55 57N 3 13W The capital of Scotland and administrative centre of the Lothian Region, situated in the E centre of the country on the Firth of Forth. The castle stands on steep basalt cliffs in the old town. The Royal Mile extends E from the castle rock to the Palace of Holyrood House (begun c. 1500). The new town contains fine Georgian architecture. The annual Edinburgh International Festival was founded in 1947. Population (1988 est): 433 480.

Edison, Thomas Alva (1847–1931) US inventor. His most famous invention, the electric light bulb, was constructed in 1879. By 1881 Edison had built a generating station and was supplying electricity to over 80 customers. Among his other 1300 inventions were the gramophone, motion pictures, and improvements to *Bell's telephone.

Edmonton 53 34N 113 25W A city in W Canada, the capital of Alberta on the North Saskatchewan River. Population (1986): 785 465.

Edmund I (921–46) King of England (939–46), who expelled the Norse king Olaf from Northumbria (944).

Edmund II Ironside (c. 981–1016) The son of Ethelred II of England, defeated by Canute at Ashingdon (1016) in the struggle for the throne.

Edward I (1239–1307) King of England (1272–1307), succeeding his father Henry III. He married (1254) *Eleanor of Castile. He subdued Wales, on which he imposed the English system of administration. Later he tried to assert his authority over Scotland but died while on his way to fight Robert Bruce (*see* Robert I).

Edward II (1284–1327) King of England (1307–27), succeeding his father Edward I. He became the first English Prince of Wales (1301) and married (1308) Isabella of France (1292–1358). His reign was troubled by his extravagance, his military disasters in Scotland, notably at Bannockburn (1314), and the unpopularity of his favourites, Piers Gaveston (d. 1312) and Hugh le Despenser (1262–1326). Isabella and her lover Roger de Mortimer murdered him.

Edward III (1312–77) King of England (1327–77), succeeding his father Edward II. He assumed power in 1330 after imprisoning his mother Isabella of France (1292–1358) and executing her lover Roger de Mortimer. Through his mother he claimed the French throne, thus starting (1337) the *Hundred Years' War.

Edward IV (1442–83) King of England (1461–70, 1471–83) during the Wars of the *Roses. He married (1464) Elizabeth Woodville. The Yorkist leader, he was crowned after defeating the Lancastrians at Mortimer's Cross and Towton (1461). He was forced from the throne (1470) by the Earl of *Warwick but regained it after defeating the Lancastrians at Tewkesbury (1471).

Edward V (1470–?1483) King of England (1483), succeeding his father Edward IV. His uncle, the Duke of Gloucester, imprisoned Edward and his brother Richard in the Tower of London and had himself crowned as Richard III. The two boys, known as the Princes in the Tower, were probably murdered in 1483.

Edward VI (1537–53) King of England (1547–53), succeeding his father Henry VIII. Effective power was held by the Duke of Somerset until 1550, when the Duke of *Northumberland seized power. A fervent Protestant, Edward encouraged the *Reformation in England.

Edward VII (1841–1910) King of the United Kingdom (1901–10), succeeding his mother Queen Victoria. He married (1863) Alexandra of Denmark. A popular king, he ably represented Britain abroad.

Edward VIII (1894–1972) King of the United Kingdom (1936), succeeding his father George V. He abdicated on 11 December, 1936, in order to marry (1937) the twice-divorced Mrs Wallis Simpson (1896–1986). He became Duke of Windsor and subsequently lived in France.

Edward, the Black Prince (1330–76) Prince of Wales and the eldest son of Edward III. He won victories against France in the *Hundred Years' War and his nickname may refer to the black armour he was said to have worn at Crécy (1346).

Edward the Confessor (c. 1003–66) King of England (1042–66), nicknamed for his piety and his foundation of a new Westminster Abbey (1065). Edward's childlessness led ultimately to the Norman conquest. He was made a saint in 1161.

Edward the Elder (d. 924) King of England (899–924), succeeding his father Alfred the Great. He defeated the Danes (918), taking East Anglia, and also conquered Mercia (918) and Northumbria (920).

Edward the Martyr (c. 963–78) King of England (975–78), succeeding his father Edgar. Murdered at Corfe Castle, he was made a saint in 1001.

Edwin (c. 585–633) King of Northumbria (616–33), who became overlord of all English kingdoms S of the Humber, except for Kent. He

and his people converted to Christianity (627). He was killed in battle against Penda of Mercia.

EEC. See European Economic Community.

eel A snakelike bony *fish found worldwide. Most species live in the sea, mainly in shallow waters, and feed on other fish. The freshwater eels migrate to the sea to breed and the young eels (elvers) return to rivers and streams. See also electric eel.

EFTA. See European Free Trade Association.

egg (or ovum) The female reproductive cell (see gamete), which—when fertilized by a male gamete (sperm)—develops into a new individual. Animal eggs are surrounded by yolk. Some animals lay eggs; in others the eggs develop inside the mother's body. Eggs that are laid (e.g. birds' eggs) contain a large yolk since the developing embryo depends on the yolk for nourishment. In most mammals, on the other hand, the egg is nourished by the mother's blood and thus has little yolk. See also ovary.

eggplant. See aubergine.

egret A white bird related to the *heron. The great white egret (*Egretta alba*) has long silky ornamental plumes in the breeding season.

Egypt, Arab Republic of A country in NE Africa, extending into SW Asia. Most of the country consists of desert–the *Sinai Peninsula, the Eastern Desert, and the Western Desert, the population being concentrated along the fertile Nile Valley. *Economy*: modern irrigation schemes, such as the *Aswan High Dam, have led to an increase in the production of cotton, the chief cash crop and there has been considerable expansion of industry since the 1950s. Oil was discovered in 1909 and in recent years production has greatly increased. Egypt's archaeological remains make tourism important. *History*: ancient Egypt was ruled by 30 successive dynasties of *pharoahs from about 3100 BC until 343 BC. The famous *pyramids were built in the period c. 2686–c. 2160. Notable rulers included *Thutmose III and *Ramses (II) the Great. Alexander the Great conquered Egypt in 332. On his death Egypt was acquired by the Macedonian Ptolemy I Soter. The Ptolemies ruled until the suicide of *Cleopatra VII in 30 BC, when Egypt passed under Roman rule. In 395 AD, Egypt became part of the Byzantine (Eastern Roman) Empire. The Arabs conquered Egypt in 642, after which it was governed by a series of caliphs under whom Islam was introduced. It was ruled by the Mamelukes from 1250 until 1517, when it was conquered by the Ottoman Turks. In 1798 Napoleon established a French protectorate over Egypt, which in 1801 was overthrown by the British and Ottomans. In 1869 the opening of the Suez Canal gave Egypt greater international significance. From 1882 the British dominated Egyptian government. In 1914, on the outbreak of World War I, Egypt became a British protectorate until independence under King Fu'ad I was granted in 1922. In 1936 his son Farouk signed a treaty of alliance with Britain, which retained rights in the Suez Canal zone. The immediate postwar period saw the first Arab-Israeli War (1948–49) and a military coup

(1952) that overthrew the monarchy (1953) and brought *Nasser to power (1954); he nationalized the Suez Canal in 1956. In 1958 Egypt, Syria, and subsequently North Yemen formed the *United Arab Republic, a name retained by Egypt until 1971. In the Six Day War with Israel (1967) Egypt lost the Sinai peninsula, which was partly regained in 1973. In 1970 Nasser was succeeded by Sadat. In 1979 Egypt and Israel signed a peace treaty. Sadat was assassinated by Islamic extremists in 1981; he was succeeded as president by Hosni Mubarak (1929–   ). Official language: Arabic. Official religion: Islam. Official currency: Egyptian pound of 100 piastres. Area: 1 000 000 sq km (386 198 sq mi). Population (1987 est): 49 280 000. Capital: Cairo. Main port: Alexandria.

Ehrlich, Paul   (1854–1915) German bacteriologist. Ehrlich investigated acquired immunity to disease in animals and, with Emil Behring (1854–1917), he prepared a serum against diphtheria. In 1910 he announced the discovery of an arsenic compound (Salvarsan) for treating syphilis. Ehrlich shared a Nobel Prize (1908) with I. I. Metchnikov (1845–1916).

eider   A large sea duck, *Somateria mollissima*, of far northern sea coasts. About 55 cm long, males are mostly white with a black crown, belly, and tail; females are mottled dark brown. The soft breast feathers of the female are the source of eiderdown.

Eiffel Tower   A metal tower in Paris, built for the 1889 Centennial Exposition by the French engineer Alexandre-Gustave Eiffel (1832–1923). The 300 m (984 ft) tower was the highest building in the world until 1930.

Eiger   46 34N 8 01E A mountain in central S Switzerland, in the Bernese Oberland. Its difficult N face was first climbed successfully in 1938. Height: 3970 m (12 697 ft).

Eindhoven   51 26N 5 30E A town in the S Netherlands, in North Brabant province. Population (1987): 190 962.

Einstein, Albert   (1879–1955) German physicist who became a US citizen in 1940. While working at the Patent Office in Berne, Switzerland, Einstein did research in theoretical physics and in 1905 published four highly original papers. One gave a mathematical explanation of the *Brownian movement, the second explained the *photoelectric effect, the third announced his special theory of *relativity, and the fourth related mass to energy. In 1916 he extended the theory of relativity to the general case. He received the 1921 Nobel Prize for Physics. Einstein was lecturing in California when Hitler came to power in 1933. Being Jewish, he decided to remain in the USA and spent the rest of his life at the Institute for Advanced Study in Princeton. Although in 1939 he warned Roosevelt that Germany might make the first atom bomb, Einstein took no part in its manufacture and became a postwar supporter of nuclear disarmament.

Éire.   *See* Ireland, Republic of.

Eisenhower, Dwight D(avid)   (1890–1969) US general and statesman; Republican president (1953–61). In World War II he was commander of US troops in Europe (1942), of Allied

forces in N Africa and Italy (1942–43), and then supreme commander of Allied forces in Europe (1943). He commanded the forces in the D-Day invasion of Normandy. In 1951 he became supreme commander of NATO. A popular president, "Ike" introduced social welfare programmes but his administration was marred by the anticommunist campaign of Joseph *McCarthy.

Eisenstein, Sergei   (1898–1948) Russian film director. His films, which include *Battleship Potemkin* (1925), *Alexander Nevsky* (1938), and *Ivan the Terrible* (1942–46), used advanced film techniques.

eisteddfod   A Welsh assembly in which there are competitions for prizes in literature, music, and drama. Originating in medieval times, the tradition later declined but was revived as the chief national cultural festival during the 19th century.

Ekaterinburg.   *See* Sverdlovsk.

Ekaterinodar.   *See* Krasnodar.

Ekaterinoslav.   *See* Dnepropetrovsk.

eland   A large horned antelope of African plains. The common eland (*Taurotragus oryx*) is light brown with thin vertical white stripes towards the shoulders and a black-tufted tail.

elastomer   A material that can be deformed and will revert to its original shape. *Rubber, a natural elastomer, has many applications. However, synthetic elastomers of styrene-butadiene, polybutadiene, polyisoprene, *silicones, etc., are widely used.

Elba   An Italian island in the Tyrrhenian Sea. Napoleon I was exiled here (1814–15) following his abdication. Area: 223 sq km (86 sq mi). Population (1984 est): 28 907.

Elbe, River   (Czech name: Labe)   A river in central Europe, flowing mainly NW from N Czechoslovakia to the North Sea at Hamburg. It is connected by various canal systems to the Rivers Weser, Rhine, and Oder. Length: 1165 km (724 mi).

El Cid   (Rodrigo Díaz de Vivar; c. 1040–99) Spanish warrior. A servant of Alfonso VI of Castile, he was exiled by the king in 1079 and became a soldier of fortune. Always loyal to his king, he was returned to favour and became ruler of Valencia.

elder   A shrub or tree of temperate and subtropical areas. The cream-coloured flowers can be used in tea or wine. The red or black berries are used in wine, jams, and jellies.

Eldorado   (Spanish: the golden one) A legendary Indian ruler in Colombia who coated himself in gold dust before bathing in a lake. The name was later applied to a region of great wealth. The 16th-century conquest of South America was hastened by expeditions seeking Eldorado, notably those of Francisco *Pizarro (1539) and Jiménez de Quesada (1569–72).

Eleanor of Aquitaine   (c. 1122–1204) The wife first (1137–52) of Louis VII of France and then (1154–89) of Henry II of England. Henry imprisoned her (1174–89) for involvement in their sons' rebellion against him. After Henry's death she helped to have them crowned as Richard I (1189) and John (1199).

Eleanor of Castile (1246–90) The wife (from 1254) of Edward I of England. Edward erected the **Eleanor Crosses** (e.g. Charing Cross) wherever her body rested on its way from Nottinghamshire, where she died, to her funeral in London.

electoral college An indirect voting system used in the US for electing the president and vice president. Each state chooses by popular vote a number of electors (the number of its representatives plus its two senators) to send to an electoral college. All the electors promise to vote for the presidential candidate with the highest popular vote in the state. Thus the elected president has a bigger majority in the college than he would have had by vote throughout the country.

Electra In Greek legend, the daughter of Agamemnon and Clytemnestra. She helped her brother Orestes escape after the murder of Agamemnon and later helped him to kill Clytemnestra and her lover Aegisthus.

Electra complex. *See* Oedipus complex.

electric charge A property of *electrons, *protons, and other particles (*see* particle physics). The magnitude of the charge is always 1.6021×10^{-19} coulombs, but it can be either positive or negative. Like charges (e.g. two positive charges) repel each other and unlike charges attract each other. The force (F) between charges q_1 and q_2 a distance d apart is given by Coulomb's law, $F = q_1 q_2 / 4\pi\varepsilon_0 d^2$, where ε_0 is the electric constant. On a large scale, charge results from an excess or deficiency of electrons compared to the protons in the nuclei of a substance.

electric eel An eel-like freshwater fish, *Electrophorus electricus*, that occurs in NE South America. Up to 3 m long, it has electric organs (modified muscle tissue) in the tail, which produce electric shocks capable of killing prey and of stunning a man.

electric field The lines of force surrounding an electric charge. The field strength at any point is inversely proportional to the square of the distance of that point from the charge (Coulomb's law). Another charge placed in this field experiences a force proportional to the field strength and to the magnitude of the introduced charge. The force is attractive if the charges are opposite and repulsive if they are alike.

electric generator A device for converting mechanical energy into electricity. A simple electromagnetic generator, or dynamo, consists of a conducting coil rotated in a magnetic field. Current induced in this coil is fed to an external circuit by slip rings in an alternating-current generator (an alternator) or by a commutator, which rectifies the current, in a direct-current generator. Most *power stations use generators to produce three-phase alternating current, i.e. there are three windings on each generator, producing three separate output voltages. For transmission there are three conductor wires with a common neutral wire, but for homes, etc., the supply is split into single phases.

electricity The phenomena that arise as a result of *electric charge. Electricity has two forms: *static electricity, which depends on stationary charges, and current electricity, which consists of a flow of charges, specifically *elec-trons. Current electricity was first demonstrated by *Volta in 1800 and investigated by *Ampère during the next 25 years.

electricity supply The system that generates, transmits, and distributes electric power. *Power stations are interconnected by transmission lines to form a grid. Grid-control centres monitor the load from factories, homes, etc., varying supply when necessary, keeping it at a constant voltage and frequency. The cheaper-to-run nuclear and coal-fired stations run continuously to provide the base load. Less economic stations that are easier to start up and shut down supply the peak demand. The grid voltage is reduced at substations for area distribution and further reduced at local substations to the UK domestic supply voltage of 240 volts.

electric motor A device that converts electrical energy into mechanical energy. Electric motors depend on the principle that a current-carrying conductor in a magnetic field experiences a force and that two electromagnets placed together are forced apart. The simplest motor uses this principle to turn a single coil of wire (the armature or rotor) between the poles of a permanent magnet. Practical motors use a stationary winding (stator) in place of a permanent magnet. Most motors work on an alternating-current (ac) supply. In the induction motor, current is fed to the stator, which induces a current in the rotor; interaction between the magnetic field of the stator and the induced rotor current causes the rotor to rotate. In the synchronous ac motor, current is also fed to the rotor (through slip rings) and the rate of rotation is proportional to the supply frequency. In a dc motor current is fed to the rotor through a commutator. *See also* linear motor.

electric ray A fish, also called torpedo *ray, found mainly in shallow waters of warm and temperate regions. Electric organs (modified muscle tissue) on each side of the head produce electric shocks used in defence and food capture.

electrocardiography Examination of the electrical activity of the heart. As the heart contracts, impulses pass through electrodes attached to the skin to a recording apparatus (electrocardiograph). The recording itself, called an electrocardiogram (ECG), aids in the diagnosis of heart disease.

electroconvulsive therapy (ECT) A treatment for mental disorders, such as certain types of *depression, in which an electric current is passed through the brain in order to cause a convulsion. The convulsion is greatly reduced by giving an anaesthetic and drugs to relax the muscles. It is now being replaced by drug therapy.

electroencephalography The measurement of the electrical activity of the brain. Brain waves are recorded in the form of a tracing—an electroencephalogram (EEG)—from electrodes on the scalp. Electroencephalography is used to diagnose diseases of the brain.

electroluminescence. *See* luminescence.

electrolysis The chemical changes produced by passing an electric current through electrodes in a liquid (electrolyte) containing ions; the positive ions drift towards the negative electrode

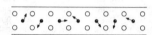

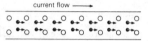

Atoms consist of electrons, protons, and neutrons. The electrons cluster round the central nucleus of protons and neutrons.

Electrons have a negative electric charge — protons are positively charged. The charges are equal but opposite.

Similar charges repel each other, opposite charges attract each other. These are the forces harnessed to make electricity.

An electrical current consists of a flow of electrons in one direction. But in many atoms, such as helium, they are tightly bound to the nucleus. To flow as a current electrons have to be free.

In a metal wire some of the electrons are free to move about between the metal ions (atoms that have lost an electron). Normally they move about at random and no current flows.

When the majority of electrons flow in one direction this is an electric current. 1 ampere is equivalent to a flow of 6×10^{18} electrons per second.

There are two main methods of making electrons flow to generate a current.

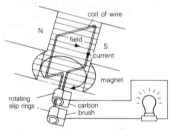

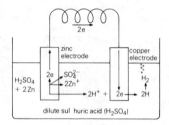

One method is to subject them to a changing magnetic field—this is the principle of the dynamo. If a coil of wire is rotated between the poles of a magnet, the electrons are forced round the coil. This is the power-station method; coal or oil is burned to raise steam to drive a turbine, which rotates the coils.

The other way is to make use of a chemical reaction in an electric cell to dissociate the electrons from their atoms and molecules. The separated charges then flow in opposite directions as a result of the forces between them. This is how a battery works. The sulphuric acid dissolves the zinc electrode producing 2 electrons, a sulphate ion (SO_4^{2-}), 2 zinc ions (Zn^+), and 2 hydrogen ions (H^-).

ELECTRICITY

(cathode) and the negative ions towards the positive electrode (anode). At the electrodes, the ions may give up their charge and form molecules or the atoms of the electrode may ionize and pass into solution. Electrolysis is used to electroplate metals and in the manufacture of chemicals.

electromagnet. *See* magnet.

electromagnetic field A region in which electric and magnetic forces act without physical contact (action at a distance). The link between electricity and magnetism was explained by *Faraday in terms of a field of force, which is distorted by the presence of a current-carrying conductor or by another magnet. *Maxwell developed the theory that electricity and magnetism are different manifestations of the same phenomenon (the electromagnetic field), magnetism being the result of relative motion of *electric fields.

electromagnetic induction The production of voltage in an electrical conductor when it is in a changing magnetic field or if it moves in relation to a steady magnetic field. The direction of the induced *electromotive force opposes the change or motion causing it. Since a current-carrying conductor itself induces a magnetic field, if

the current changes, **self-inductance** occurs, opposing the current change. **Mutual inductance** occurs between two adjacent conductors that carry changing currents.

electromagnetic radiation *Waves of energy associated with electric and magnetic fields. The two fields vibrate perpendicularly to each other and to the direction in which the wave travels. In free space the waves travel at a velocity of 2.9979×10^8 metres per second, known as the speed of light (symbol: c). Their *wavelength, λ, and *frequency, f, are related by the equation $\lambda f = c$. Those with the highest frequencies are known as *gamma radiation; in descending order of frequency the **electromagnetic spectrum** includes *X-rays, *ultraviolet radiation, visible *light, *infrared radiation, *microwaves, and *radio waves. Electromagnetic radiation exhibits its typical wave properties, such as *refraction and *interference but it can also be regarded as a stream of massless particles called *photons.

electromotive force (emf) The electrical *potential difference or voltage between two points in an electric circuit. It causes the movement of charge that constitutes an electric current.

electron A negatively charged elementary particle with mass $9.109\,56 \times 10^{-31}$ kilogram. Electrons are responsible for all electrical and magnetic effects and for most chemical processes. An electric current passing through a metal consists of a flow of electrons; a current of 1 ampere is equivalent to a flow of 6×10^{18} electrons per second.

electronics The study of devices that utilize the movement of *electrons and other charged particles. Originating with the *thermionic valves and their use in radios and record players, it expanded rapidly during World War II to include radar, missile guidance, and *computers. The replacement of thermionic valves by *transistors, and later by *integrated circuits has resulted in more compact and reliable equipment. The impact of electronics has been immense, as its developments include television, communications satellites, and computerization.

electronic tagging A method of monitoring the movements of persons convicted of certain offences as an alternative to prison. The offender wears a microchip device emitting a signal to a transmitter attached to a telephone. If the offender moves out of a 75-metre (250-ft) range, the telephone sends a message to the controlling computer.

electron microscope A type of *microscope in which a beam of electrons is used to produce an image of a tiny object. Typically an electron microscope can resolve (distinguish) two points 10^{-9} metre apart and produce magnifications of up to a million.

electroplating Depositing a layer of one metal on another by making the object to be plated the cathode in an electrolytic bath (*see* electrolysis). Metals used for electroplating include silver (*see* silverplate), gold, chromium, and nickel.

elementary particles. *See* particle physics.

elements Substances that cannot be broken down into simpler fragments by chemical means. A sample of an element contains atoms that are chemically identical, since they have the same *atomic number but they may consist of a mixture of *isotopes. Over 100 elements are known, of which about 90 occur naturally, the rest being produced in nuclear reactions. *See also* periodic table.

elephant A mammal with tough grey skin and a muscular trunk—an extension of the nose and upper lip. The upper incisor teeth are ivory tusks. The African elephant (*Loxodonta africana*) is the largest land mammal, standing 3–4 m high at the shoulder. The smaller Indian elephant (*Elephas maximus*) is used for transport and heavy work. The extinct *mammoths were related to elephants.

elephantiasis A tropical disease caused by chronic infection with nematode worms, called filariae, which block the lymphatic channels and cause swelling of the legs and scrotum (or vulva).

elephant seal A large Antarctic seal, *Mirounga leonina*. The male grows to over 6 m; females to about 3 m. The smaller elephant seal (*M. angustirostris*) lives off the W coast of North America.

African elephant

Indian elephant

ELEPHANT *The African elephant can be distinguished from the smaller Indian species by its larger ears, flatter forehead, smooth skin, and concave back.*

Elgar, Sir Edward (1857–1934) British composer of choral works, two symphonies, concertos for violin and cello, and chamber music. His best-known works are the *Dream of Gerontius* (1900), the *Enigma Variations* (1899), and the *Pomp and Circumstance* marches (1901–30).

Elgin Marbles Ancient Greek marble friezes, from the *Parthenon, sold to the British Museum in 1816 by Lord Elgin for £35,000. He acquired them from the Turks occupying Athens, who were using the Parthenon for target practice. The British government has refused to return them to Greece.

El Greco (Domenikos Theotokopoulos; 1541–1614) Greek-born painter who worked mainly in Spain. He trained in Venice under Titian and in 1577 moved to Spain, settling in Toledo. His later paintings of saints and his masterpiece, *The Burial of Count Orgaz* (1586–88), feature bold colours and elongated figures.

Elijah An Old Testament prophet, possibly 9th century BC. He attacked the cult of Baal among the Israelites (1 Kings 18) and successfully maintained the worship of Jehovah as the one god.

Eliot, George (Mary Ann Evans; 1819–80) British novelist, noted for her depiction of provincial English society. She wrote the novels *Adam Bede* (1859), *The Mill on the Floss* (1860), *Silas Marner* (1861), *Middlemarch* (1871–72), and *Daniel Deronda* (1876).

Eliot, T(homas) S(tearns) (1888–1965) Poet and dramatist, born in Missouri and naturalized British (1927). His major poems were *The Waste Land* (1922) and *Four Quartets* (1935–41) and his verse dramas include *Murder in the Cathedral* (1935), *The Cocktail Party* (1949), and *The Elder Statesman* (1958). He was awarded the Nobel Prize in 1948.

Elizabeth I (1533–1603) Queen of England and Ireland (1558–1603), daughter of Henry VIII and Anne *Boleyn. Her devotion to England made her one of its greatest monarchs. Her religious compromise (1559–63) established Protestantism in England (*see* Reformation). England won a great naval victory in 1588 by destroying the Spanish *Armada. Elizabeth never married and was called the Virgin Queen.

Elizabeth II (1926–) Queen of the United Kingdom (1952–), and head of the Commonwealth. She married Prince *Philip in 1947; their four children are Prince *Charles, the Princess Royal (*see* Anne), the Duke of *York, and Prince Edward (1964–).

Elizabeth the Queen Mother (1900–) The widow of George VI, whom she married in 1923, and mother of *Elizabeth II and Princess *Margaret.

elk The largest deer, *Alces alces*, found in forests of N Eurasia and also in N North America, where it is called a moose. Up to 2 m high, elks have a curved muzzle and a short neck. The coat is brown and males grow large antlers.

Ellice Islands. *See* Tuvalu.

Ellington, Duke (Edward Kennedy E.; 1899–1974) US Black jazz musician. In New York he established a group of musicians that remained the core of his band for 30 years. Ellington concentrated on composing large-scale works for jazz orchestra.

ellipse A closed curve like an elongated *circle (*see* conic sections). The sum of the distances from any point on the circumference to each of two fixed points, known as the foci, is a constant.

elm A tree of N temperate regions. Up to 40 m high, elms have oval pointed toothed leaves, small reddish flowers, and rounded winged nuts. Elms are widely planted for shade and ornament and for their strong durable timber. Species include the English elm (*Ulmus procera*) and the Eurasian wych elm (*U. glabra*). *See also* Dutch elm disease.

El Salvador, Republic of A country in Central America, on the Pacific Ocean. Narrow coastal lowlands rise to a fertile plateau enclosed by volcanic mountains. There are frequent earthquakes. *Economy*: mainly agricultural, coffee and cotton being the main crops. *History*: the Aztec population was conquered by the Spaniards in 1526. The region formed part of the Central American Federation (1823–38) and in 1841 became an independent republic. The repressive regime of Gen Carlos Humberto Romero (1924–) was overthrown in 1979. In 1984 José Napoléon Duarte, a US-supported Christian Democrat, was elected president; he was defeated in the 1989 election by Alfredo Cristiani. El Salvador is a member of the OAS, the Organization of Central American States, and the Cen-

tral American Common Market. Official language: Spanish. Official religion: Roman Catholic. Official currency: colón of 100 centavos. Area 21 393 sq km (8236 sq mi). Population (1985 est): 5 480 000. Capital: San Salvador. Main port: Acajutla.

Elsinore. *See* Helsingør.

Ely 52 24N 0 16E A city in E England, in Cambridgeshire on the River Ouse. The Isle of Ely is an area of higher ground surrounded by fenland. Ely has an 11th-century cathedral. Population (1983 est): 11 030.

Elysium (*or* Elysian Fields) In Greek mythology, the fields on the banks of the River Oceanus where those favoured by the gods live in eternal happiness. In Roman mythology Elysium is part of the underworld.

Emancipation Proclamation (1863) The proclamation issued by President Abraham *Lincoln that freed slaves in the rebellious southern states of the USA. The 13th Amendment abolished *slavery throughout the nation (1865).

embolism The sudden blocking of an artery by a blood clot or other material from another part of the body. A clot most commonly forms in the leg and lodges in the arteries of the lung–a **pulmonary embolism**. A clot from the heart may lodge in the brain, causing a *stroke. *See also* thrombosis.

embryo An animal or plant in its earliest stages of development. In vertebrates the embryonic stage lasts from the first division of the fertilized egg until the animal hatches from the egg or is expelled from the womb. A human embryo is called a *fetus from the eighth week of pregnancy. In plants, the embryo lies within the *seed. **Embryology** is the study of the development of embryos.

emerald A green variety of *beryl, highly valued as a gem. The finest specimens come from Muzo, Colombia.

Emerson, Ralph Waldo (1803–82) US essayist and poet, a leading exponent of *transcendentalism. He published *Nature*, in 1836 and expressed his humanism in *Representative Men* (1850) and *The Conduct of Life* (1860).

emery A granular greyish rock composed of *corundum with magnetite, hematite, or spinel. It is used as an abrasive.

Empedocles (c. 490–430 BC) Sicilian Greek philosopher. He founded the doctrine that earth, air, fire, and water make up the world, and that love and strife (attraction and antipathy) govern their distribution.

emperor penguin A *penguin, *Aptenodytes forsteri*. 1.2 m tall, it is the largest seabird and has a blue-grey plumage with a black head, a white belly, and orange patches on the neck.

emphysema A disease of the lungs involving destruction of tissue and enlargement of the air spaces. Commonly caused by cigarette smoking, it is often accompanied by chronic *bronchitis and breathlessness.

Empire, British Britain's overseas possessions from the 16th to early 20th centuries. Permanent settlements in North America–in Virginia, Maryland, and New England–were

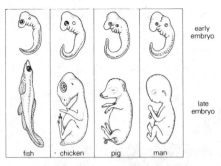

early embryo

late embryo

fish · chicken pig man

various vertebrate embryos *The different species are hard to distinguish in the early stages of development; later they develop individual characteristics.*

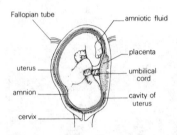

Fallopian tube — amniotic fluid

placenta

uterus — umbilical cord

amnion — cavity of uterus

cervix

human embryo *A few weeks before birth this fetus is practically fully formed.*

EMBRYO

established in the early 17th century. The American colonies were lost in 1783 (*see* American Revolution). *Canada and *India were secured by victories in the *Seven Years' War (1756–63). With the Napoleonic Wars in the early 19th century Britain gained possessions in the West Indies (Trinidad, Tobago, St Lucia), Mauritius, Ceylon, and, in Africa, the Cape (*see* South Africa). What are now Sierra Leone, Ghana, and Nigeria were gained in the late 18th century, and African settlements continued in the 19th century. The first Australian colonists were prisoners: New South Wales was settled in 1778, Tasmania in 1803, and Queensland in 1824. New Zealand was controlled by the British from 1840, Hong Kong from 1841, and Burma from 1886. In the mid-19th century, the self-governing colonies in Canada, Australia, New Zealand, and South Africa received responsible government, whereby governors were advised by local ministers. In 1907 Canada, Australia, and New Zealand (and in 1910 South Africa), by now federated, became dominions. The *Commonwealth of Nations was established in 1931, after which Britain's other colonies gradually achieved full independence.

Empire style The neoclassical style in the decorative arts developing during the Napoleonic empire (1804–14). It was inspired by classical Greek, Roman, and Egyptian models (*see* neoclassicism) and reflected contemporary interest in archaeology (e.g. *Pompeii). Shapes tended to be plain but *caryatids were used as supports.

The grandiose **Second Empire style** was the official architectural style of the French Government under Emperor Napoleon III (1852–70). It became popular throughout Europe and America.

emu A large flightless long-legged Australian bird, *Dromaius novaehollandiae*, found in open plains and forests. It has a dark-brown hairlike plumage with a naked blue spot on each side of the neck, and can run at high speeds.

emulsion. *See* colloid.

enamel A glaze that is fused onto the surface of metal. Enamelled gold jewellery dating back to the 13th century BC has been found. Enamel is generally made from melted sand, soda potash, and red lead stained with a metal oxide. It is spread on the metal object, which is then placed in a furnace to fuse the enamel with the metal. Painted enamels are applied after the ground enamel has been fired. Painted enamelwork is particularly associated with Limoges (15th and 16th centuries) and England (18th century).

encephalins (*or* enkephalins) Pain-relieving substances found in parts of the brain and spinal cord. These and similar compounds are called **endorphins**. The pain-relieving effects of acupuncture may be due to the release of the body's encephalins.

encephalitis Inflammation of the brain, usually resulting from a virus infection. The patient is often drowsy and fevered and has a bad headache. There is no specific treatment for viral encephalitis but the patient usually recovers.

Encke's comet A *comet with a period (established by the German astronomer J. F. Encke; 1791–1865) of 3.3 years (decreasing by 2.5 hours/revolution) that has been closely studied during its numerous appearances.

Encyclopedists The French intellectuals who contributed to *Diderot's monumental *Encyclopédie*, published in 33 volumes between 1751 and 1777. Over 200 scholarly experts, including *Voltaire and *Rousseau, contributed articles.

endive A plant, *Cichorium endivia*, of the daisy family, probably native to S Asia and N China and cultivated widely. Its shiny leaves are either curled and narrow, used for salads, or broad, used for cooking. *See also* chicory.

endocrine glands Ductless glands: glands that produce and secrete *hormones directly into the bloodstream. They include the *pituitary, *thyroid, *adrenal, and *parathyroid glands and parts of the *pancreas (the islets of Langerhans). The study of the endocrine glands in health and disease is called **endocrinology**.

endorphins. *See* encephalins.

Endymion In Greek legend, a beautiful youth who was put into an everlasting sleep by Selene, goddess of the moon, so that she could enjoy his beauty forever.

energy A property of a system that enables it to do work, i.e. to move the point of application of a force. *Kinetic energy is energy of motion, whereas *potential energy is stored energy. Other forms of energy include thermal energy (the kinetic energy of the atoms and molecules in a body), chemical energy (the potential energy stored in the

Exhaustible Most of the world's energy comes from fossil fuels – coal, oil, and natural gas. These fuels are buried beneath the land or the sea in exhaustible deposits. Once they have been used up, other forms of energy will have to be found for powering motor vehicles and aircraft. Estimates of known stocks vary, but most experts agree that the diminishing reserves will be exhausted within the next few hundred years, although new deposits of oil and coal are continuously being discovered.

Coal Most easily burnt in stationary installations like power stations, coal is essential for making coke, used to extract iron from its ores, and to make steel. It is the hardest and the most dangerous fuel to extract from the earth.

Oil Oil burns and expands, producing a large volume of gas which drives cars and aircraft engines. It is a source of many important chemicals.

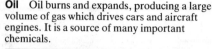

Enormous quantities of oil are wasted by idling engines in the world's many traffic jams.

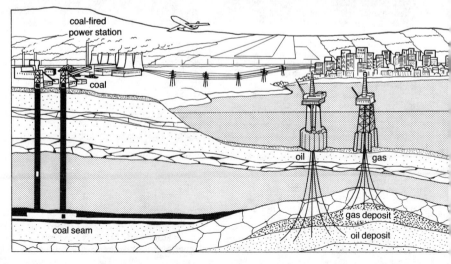

coal-fired power station

coal

oil

gas

gas deposit

oil deposit

coal seam

Renewable Unlike fossil fuels and uranium, some energy supplies are inexhaustible. The sun indirectly controls the weather and the winds, which power wind generators, and the hydrological cycle, which provides hydroelectric and wave power. It is also a source of direct solar energy.

Nuclear All nuclear power stations now in use depend on the fission of uranium fuels. They provide only 5.6% of the world's energy. Although reserves of uranium in the earth's crust are exhaustible, estimates suggest that stocks will not be depleted for many centuries. In the future, nuclear fusion, based on deuterium fuels, may become feasible. The supply of fuel for this type of power station is virtually unlimited, as about 15 hydrogen atoms in every thousand consist of deuterium and water is 11% hydrogen (by weight).

Water Falling water is an important source of energy, schemes utilizing reservoirs and dams providing some 6.6% of the world's energy. This is the hydroelectric station at Hoover Dam, Colorado, in the USA.

Wind Large aerogenerators are a practical source of economic renewable energy.

Other renewable energy sources are the tides and geothermal energy. The tides derive their energy from the gravitational forces between the moon and earth. Geothermal energy comes from the heat of the earth's core (magma) and from radioactive decay in the crust. Currently about 0.1% of the earth's energy is supplied by tapping hot rocks beneath the surface.

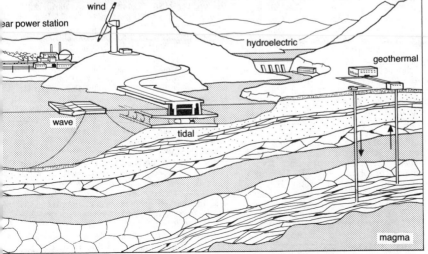

wind

ear power station

hydroelectric

geothermal

wave

tidal

magma

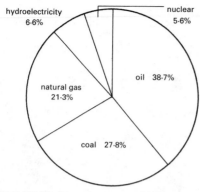

ENERGY *World primary sources (1989).*

chemical bonds between atoms), nuclear energy (the potential energy stored in the atomic nucleus), and radiant energy (the energy associated with electromagnetic waves). Energy is now measured in joules (SI units).

Energy sources: the combustion of wood and fossil fuels (coal, oil, natural gas) is a process long known to man. The *industrial revolution and the later advent of motorized transport brought huge increases in the demand for fossil fuels, which now provide nearly 88% of total world energy consumption. Concern about the exhaustion of fossil fuel reserves and their effect on the environment (*see* greenhouse effect) is directing attention to alternative energy sources as well as *nuclear energy.

Engels, Friedrich (1820–95) German socialist who worked with Karl *Marx. He introduced Marx to British economic conditions and the working-class movement. Among other works he wrote the *Condition of the Working Class in England in 1844* (1845). After Marx's death, he edited the last volume of *Das Kapital* (1885).

engineering The scientific design, creation, and use of structures and machines. *Civil engineering is involved with the design of bridges, dams, buildings, etc., whereas mechanical engineering is concerned with machinery and engines. Other important branches of engineering are electrical engineering, aeronautical engineering, and chemical engineering.

England The largest political division and the centre of government of the *United Kingdom. It consists of two main zones: the lowlands, which extend across the Midlands, the SE, East Anglia, and the Fens, and the highlands of the Pennines and the Lake District in the N and the granite uplands of Dartmoor and Exmoor in the SW. The chief rivers are the Thames and the Severn. *Economy:* the development of industry has been a major contributor to England's wealth. North Sea oil and gas are important. The main English coalfields are in the East Midlands, Yorkshire, and Northumberland and Durham. The decline of heavy industry (including shipbuilding) has led to high levels of unemployment in the North and Merseyside. Advanced technology has expanded rapidly in recent years. Agri-

culture is important, with dairy farming dominant in the W and livestock rearing (especially sheep and cattle) in the N and SW. The major crops, mainly from the E and SE, are cereals, potatoes, and sugar beet. *History:* historical records begin with the Roman occupation, from 43 AD until the early 5th century. Christianity was introduced in the 4th century, and *Anglo-Saxons ruled England from the 5th to early 11th centuries. From 1016 to 1042 the English were ruled by the Danish kings *Canute and *Hardecanute. The *Norman conquest (1066) established a new dynasty of Norman kings, who were succeeded by the *Plantagenets (1154–1485). The 16th century, under the *Tudors, saw the establishment of Protestantism in England (*see* Reformation), the formal union of England and Wales (*see* Union, Acts of), and, under Elizabeth I, a significant development in overseas exploration and trade. The Tudors were succeeded by the *Stuarts in 1603. The *Civil War ended with Charles I's execution (1649) and the establishment of republican government. The Stuart *Restoration (1660) followed the fall of Oliver Cromwell's *Protectorate. The 18th century saw union with Scotland (1707); following union with Ireland in 1801, England, Wales, Scotland, and Ireland became the United Kingdom of Great Britain and Ireland. With the *industrial revolution the UK evolved from an agricultural to an industrial economy. The 19th century also saw the heyday of the British *Empire and colonial rivalry with Germany, which resulted in *World War I. After *World War II a *Labour government began a programme of *nationalization. From 1951 to 1964 government was in the hands of the *Conservatives but Labour was then returned (1964–70; 1974–79). In 1979 Margaret *Thatcher began another long term of Conservative government, which continued under John *Major from 1990. Area: 130 360 sq km (50 332 sq mi). Population (1986 est): 47 254 000. Capital: London.

English A West Germanic language spoken in Britain, the USA, Canada, New Zealand, Australia, and many other parts of the world. It is the world's most widely used language. Its history may be divided into three periods: Old English (c. 450–1100 AD); Middle English (1100–1500), when the influence of French after the Norman conquest brought new vocabulary and sound patterns; and Modern English (from 1500), which was much influenced by the speech of London.

English Channel (French name: La Manche) An arm of the Atlantic Ocean in NW Europe, between England and France. It is one of the busiest shipping lanes in the world. *See also* Channel tunnel.

engraving A method of producing a printing plate by carving the design onto a metal or wood plate. **Intaglio engraving** includes *etching, in which the printed impression pulls ink from inside the carved grooves. **Relief engraving** includes *woodcut, in which the carved-away areas are not inked.

Enlightenment (*or* Age of Reason) An 18th-century philosophical movement in Europe, characterized by scientific inquiry and the use of reason. It arose during the 17th century, when such scholars as Newton, Locke, Pascal, and Descartes questioned accepted beliefs. In France philosophers attacked established religion and the Enlightenment beliefs in individual liberty and equality were expressed in the work of *Voltaire, *Rousseau, and others. The movement came to an end with the French Revolution.

entellus. See langur.

entropy A measure of the disorder of a system, used in *thermodynamics. Thus a solid has less entropy than a liquid since the constituent particles in a solid are more ordered. The change in entropy of a reversible system is equal to the energy it absorbs divided by the thermodynamic temperature at which it is absorbed. The entropy of a closed system never decreases during a thermodynamic process.

enzymes A group of proteins that act as biological catalysts, i.e. they speed up (or slow down) the rate of chemical reactions in living organisms. Because each enzyme catalyses a specific reaction, it is the enzymes that determine the function of the cell.

Eocene epoch. See Tertiary period.

eohippus An extinct ancestor of the *horse that lived during the Eocene epoch, 60–40 million years ago. About 28 cm tall, it had four toes on the forefoot and three on the hindfoot.

ephemeris (Greek: diary) A reference manual, usually published annually, that is used in astronomical observation and navigation. It lists the predicted positions of the sun, moon, and planets in the forthcoming year and also gives times of eclipses and similar information.

Ephesians, Epistle of Paul to the A New Testament book that started as a circular letter from the Apostle Paul to churches in Asia Minor. Written about 60 AD, it stresses the equality of Jewish and non-Jewish Christians.

Ephesus An ancient Greek city and trading centre on the Ionian coast of *Asia Minor. In Roman times it was rivalled only by *Alexandria as a commercial centre. It was sacked by the *Goths in 262 AD. See also Artemis, Temple of.

Epicureanism A philosophical movement founded by Epicurus around 300 BC in Athens. He taught that the highest good was to seek pleasure, to avoid pain, and to have peace of mind.

Epicurus (341–270 BC) Greek philosopher and founder of the school of *Epicureanism. His surviving works are few and fragmentary but his philosophy influenced *Lucretius.

Epidaurus A city state of ancient Greece, situated across the Saronic Gulf from Athens. Its sanctuary of *Asclepius was famous in antiquity for its medical cures. The 4th-century BC theatre (part of the temple complex) is still used for plays.

epidemiology The science that investigates where and why diseases occur. Epidemiologists study how infectious diseases are spread (in epidemics) or why certain noninfectious diseases (e.g. cancers) are linked to a particular environment or way of life.

epidermis The outermost layer of cells in animals and plants. In higher animals (including mammals) it forms the outer layer of the skin.

epididymis. See testis.

epidural. See anaesthesia.

epiglottis A leaf-shaped flap of cartilage at the root of the tongue that prevents food and fluid from entering the windpipe during swallowing.

epilepsy A disease involving fits or sudden loss of consciousness: sufferers include Julius Caesar and Byron. In grand mal epilepsy the patient suddenly loses consciousness and has convulsions for a few minutes. Petit mal is a mild form seen in children, who lose consciousness for a few seconds without falling over. All forms are treated with anticonvulsant drugs.

epinephrine. See adrenaline.

Epiphany (or Twelfth Day) A Christian feast celebrated on 6 Jan. In Eastern Orthodox Churches it celebrates the baptism of Jesus. In the Western Church it celebrates Christ showing himself (Greek: epiphancia) to the non-Jews when the *Magi came to Bethlehem. **Twelfth Night** is the night before Epiphany, devoted to festivities.

epiphyte One plant that grows on another for support. Epiphytes are not parasites: some obtain nourishment from decaying plant remains and many obtain water by developing aerial roots.

epistemology The study of the nature, basis, and limits of knowledge. One of the three main branches of *philosophy, it is essential to all philosophical enquiry.

Epistles The 21 books of the *New Testament written as letters, by Paul (13), John (3), Peter (2), James and Jude. In many Churches, the Epistle is the first of two passages of Scripture (usually from the New Testament Epistles) read at the celebration of the *Eucharist, the second being the *Gospel.

epoch. See geological time scale.

epoxy resin A type of synthetic *resin containing the –O– atom (epoxy group). Viscous liquids that set to hard solids on the addition of curing agents, they are used as adhesives.

Epstein, Sir Jacob (1880–1959) British sculptor of US birth. After 1912, working in London, he experimented with avantgarde sculpture, provoking criticism with such works as *Genesis* (1931). However, his busts of Einstein (1933) and Vaughan Williams (1950) were more favourably received. His last works included *Christ in Majesty* (1957) for Llandaff Cathedral and *St Michael and the Devil* (1958) for Coventry Cathedral.

equator The circle around the earth at latitude 0°, lying midway between the poles in a plane at right angles to the earth's axis. It is 40 076 km (24 902 mi) long and divides the N from the S hemisphere.

Equatorial Guinea, Republic of A small country in W central Africa, on the Gulf of Guinea. It consists of mainland Río Muni and the islands of Bioko (formerly Macías Nguema) and Pagalu (formerly Annóbon) and several smaller islands. The inhabitants are mainly

*Fang, Fernandinos, and Bubi (descendants of slaves from West Africa), who inhabit Bioko. *Economy*: chiefly agricultural. *History*: a Spanish colony, the area became two Spanish provinces in 1959 and gained independence in 1968. In 1979 the life president Francisco Macías Nguema (1924–79) was executed in a coup led by Lt Col Teodoro Obiang Nguema Mbasogo. Official language: Spanish. Official currency: CFA (Communauté financière africaine) franc of 100 centimes. Area: 28 051 sq km (10 831 sq mi). Population (1988 est): 336 000. Capital and main port: Malabo (formerly Santa Isabel).

equinox Either of the two points at which the ecliptic intersects the celestial equator (*see* celestial sphere). The ecliptic represents the apparent annual path of the sun around the celestial sphere. The sun crosses the celestial equator from S to N at the **vernal** (*or* spring) **equinox**, usually on 21 March. It crosses from N to S at the **autumnal equinox**, usually on 23 Sept.

equity The rules developed by the Court of *Chancery to give a fair result when the *common law failed. The rules of equity developed by the same method as the common law, i.e. taking into account past rulings when deciding similar cases. The two systems were united in 1875 when the High Court of Justice was established. Now all courts administer both systems, equity being the stronger in conflict with the common law. *See also* courts of law.

era. *See* geological time scale.

Erasmus, Desiderius (1466–1536) A Renaissance Christian thinker and writer, born at Rotterdam, who taught all over Europe. His many works include *Encomium Moriae* (*Praise of Folly*; 1509), written for Thomas *More and the first translation of the Greek New Testament.

erbium (Er) A *lanthanide element that forms an oxide (Er_2O_3) and halides (e.g. $ErCl_3$). It is added to phosphors, glasses, and alloys. At no 68; at wt 167.26; mp 1529°C; bp 2510°C.

Erevan. *See* Yerevan.

ergocalciferol. *See* vitamin D.

ergot A disease caused by the fungus *Claviceps purpurea*, which affects cereals causing a black fungal body to develop instead of grain. Bread made with diseased grain causes **ergotism**, with gangrene of the fingers and toes.

Erie, Lake The fourth largest of the *Great Lakes in North America. Linked with Lake Ontario via the Welland Ship Canal, it forms part of the St Lawrence Seaway system, but closes to navigation during winter. Area: 25 718 sq km (9930 sq mi).

Eris A Greek goddess personifying strife. She threw a golden apple inscribed "To the Fairest" among the gods, which Aphrodite, Hera, and Athena claimed. *Paris chose Aphrodite as the recipient because she offered him the most beautiful wife. This Judgment of Paris, explains the origin of the *Trojan War.

Eritrea A province in Ethiopia (since 1962), bordering on the Red Sea. Locusts and water shortage limit agricultural production. Political discontent developed into civil war during the 1970s and continued into the 1980s.

ERNIE. *See* premium bond.

Ernst, Max (1891–1976) German artist, who founded (1919) the Cologne *dada movement. He excelled in collage and became a surrealist in Paris. In 1941 he moved to the USA.

Eros (mythology) The Greek god of love, the son of Aphrodite, usually portrayed as a winged youth with bow and arrows and identified with the Roman Cupid.

Erse. *See* Gaelic.

erythrocyte (*or* red blood cell) A disc-shaped blood cell, about 0.007 mm in diameter, that lacks a nucleus and contains the pigment *haemoglobin, which transports oxygen from the lungs to the tissues. *See also* anaemia.

escape velocity The velocity required by a projectile to enable it to escape from the gravitational field of a celestial body. For the earth the escape velocity is 11 200 metres per second.

eschatology (Greek *eschatos*: last) The part of the study of Christianity concerned with last things, often summed up as death, judgment, heaven, and hell.

Escorial, El A square granite palace near Madrid built (1563–84) for Philip II. It houses a magnificent collection of books and paintings.

Esdras, Books of Two books of the *Apocrypha claiming to be by Ezra.

Esfahan. *See* Isfahan.

Eskimo A Mongoloid people of the Arctic region of North America and Greenland who hunt seals, whales, etc., with harpoons. Fishing is also important. Some construct half-buried earth shelters or use snow-covered skin tents, others use igloos.

Eskimo-Aleut languages A language group, sometimes included in the American Indian group. It consists of two different languages: Eskimo, spoken in Greenland and in many *dialects along the N coast of Canada, and Aleut, in the *Aleutian Islands.

ESP. *See* extrasensory perception.

Esperanto An international language invented by a Polish philologist, L. L. Zamenhof (1859–1917), in 1887, it is spoken by over 100 000 people. Grammatically it is entirely regular, and its pronunciation is true to its spelling.

Essen 51 27N 6 57E A city in W Germany, in North Rhine-Westphalia near the River Ruhr. It has a 9th-century cathedral. It is the administrative centre of the *Ruhr. Population (1987): 615 400.

Essenes An ancient Jewish group active between the 2nd century BC and the 2nd century AD in Palestine. The *Dead Sea Scrolls may have come from an Essene community. *See* Qumran.

essential oils Substances, such as lavender oil, with a characteristic scent produced by aromatic plants. They are used in perfumes, food flavourings, and medicines.

Essex A county of E England, bordering on the North Sea. It is a low lying county in which agriculture is important. Industry is located mainly in the SW. Southend-on-Sea and Clacton are resorts and Harwich is a ferry port. Area: 3674 sq km (1419 sq mi). Population (1987 est): 1 521 800. Administrative centre: Chelmsford.

Essex, Robert Devereux, 2nd Earl of (?1566–1601) English soldier and courtier to Elizabeth I. He commanded an expedition (1591–92) sent to aid Henry IV of France and in 1593 became a privy councillor; he took part in the sack of Cádiz (1596). Dismissed (1600) after failing to suppress an Irish rebellion, he was executed for raising a riot in London.

estate A right over land (all of which in England belongs to the Crown), either: (1) freehold tenure, in which the right is for a period that cannot be decided by anyone other than the holder and for the use of which no payment is made, except for rates; (2) leasehold tenure, in which a tenant holds an estate from a landlord for a fixed period.

Este An Italian princely family coming from Lombard, which under **Obizzo II** (1264–93) gained control of Ferrara, Modena, and Reggio. Ferrara became part of the papal states in 1598. The **Villa d'Este**, at Tivoli, near Rome, was designed (1550) for Cardinal Ippolito II d'Este (1509–72).

esters Organic compounds produced by the reaction of an alcohol with an acid, with the elimination of water; they have the general formula R.CO.OR'. The lighter ones have a pleasant smell and are used in perfumes, etc.

Esther The queen of the Persian King Ahasuerus, who according to **The Book of Esther** in the Old Testament stopped a plot to massacre Persian Jews, which is remembered in the Jewish feast of *Purim.

Estonian A language of the Baltic-Finnic branch of the Finno-Ugric division of the *Uralic language family. It is spoken by Estonians.

Estonian Republic (*or* Estonia) A republic in the NW Soviet Union with many lakes and numerous islands in the Baltic Sea. Estonia was handed over to Russia in 1721. Rebellions led to independence, recognized by Russia in 1920. It was assigned to the Soviet Union by the Nazi-Soviet Pact (1939) and became an SSR in 1940. The independence movement gained strength in the 1980s, fostering fears of Soviet intervention. Area: 45 100 sq km (17 410 sq mi). Population (1987): 1 556 000. Capital: Tallinn.

etching A method of making prints from a metal plate covered with an acid-resistant substance, on which a design is drawn with a needle. The plate is then placed in acid, the exposed lines being eaten away. These recessed lines retain ink and the design is transferred to the paper by rolling under pressure.

ethane (C_2H_6) A colourless gas, the second member of the *alkane series. It occurs in *natural gas.

ethanol (*or* ethyl alcohol; C_2H_5OH) A colourless flammable liquid present in alcoholic drinks. It is prepared by *fermentation or by hydrating *ethene and is used as a solvent and to make other chemicals.

Ethelbert (c. 552–616 AD) King of Kent, who became overlord of all England south of the Humber. He wrote the first surviving English code of laws and received *Augustine's mission to spread Christianity.

Ethelred I (d. 871 AD) King of England (866–71), in whose reign the Vikings launched an invasion of England. Ethelred died after his victory at Ashdown, leaving his brother *Alfred the Great to fight on.

Ethelred the Unready (968–1016) King of England (978–1016). Forced to pay tributes (Danegeld) to Danish raiders, he was driven into exile by King Sweyn of Denmark in 1013 but returned after Sweyn's death (1014).

ethene (*or* ethylene; C_2H_4) A colourless flammable gaseous *alkene. It is obtained from petroleum and is used to make *polythene (polyethylene).

ether Any organic compound with the general formula R–O–R', formed by the *condensation of two alcohols. Ethoxyethane, $C_2H_5OC_2H_5$, known as ether, is a volatile liquid used as an anaesthetic and solvent.

ethics One of the three branches of *philosophy, it seeks to establish standards by which to judge human actions. While it formerly aimed to guide behaviour, now it tries to discover how decisions between right and wrong are made. See also hedonism; rationalism; utilitarianism.

Ethiopia, People's Democratic Republic of (former name: Abyssinia) A country in NE Africa, on the Red Sea. It consists of deserts in the SE and NE and a central plateau, crossed by river valleys (including that of the Blue Nile). The population consists of many ethnic groups. *Economy*: agriculture is chiefly at subsistence level and has worsened recently as a result of drought and serious crop failures. *History*: according to legend, the rulers of Ethopia were descended from Solomon and the Queen of Sheba. In the 4th century Ethiopia became the first Christian country in Africa, followed by centuries of struggles (especially with Muslims) and internal divisions. Only in the 19th century was the country reunited. In 1936 Addis Ababa was conquered by Italy and the emperor, *Haile Selassie, fled to England. Ethiopia then formed part of Italian East Africa. In 1941 the Allies liberated Ethiopia and Haile Selassie returned, but was deposed in 1974 by a provisional military government. After 1977, the government became known as the Derg (Provisional Military Administrative Council) with Mengistu Haile Mariam (1937–) as president. Since the late 1970s there have been repeated struggles between the government and rebel forces in *Eritrea, Tigré, and the *Ogaden area. Droughts in 1982, 1984, 1987, 1989, and 1990 led to famine, in which foreign aid was hampered by internal strife. See also Falashas. Official language: Amharic; English is widely spoken. Official religion: Ethiopian Orthodox (Coptic). Official currency: birr of 100 cents. Area: 1 000 000 sq km (386 000 sq mi). Population (1986 est): 46 000 000. Capital: Addis Ababa. Main port: Massawa.

ethnology The comparative study of contemporary cultures, also called cultural *anthropology. Ethnography is the descriptive study of culture.

ethology The study of animal behaviour, founded in the 1930s by the work of Konrad *Lorenz and Niko Tinbergen (1907–88).

ethyl alcohol

Ethologists investigate how animals sense and respond to signals or stimuli (whether from other animals, from their own bodies, or from the environment) and what their response means to other animals. Ethologists also investigate the interaction between inherited behaviour (instinct) and that shaped by experience (learning).

ethyl alcohol. *See* ethanol.

Etna, Mount 37 45N 15 00E A volcano in E Sicily. The first recorded eruption was in 476 BC and significant eruptions this century have occurred in 1928, 1949, and 1971. Height: 3263 m (10 705 ft).

Eton 51 31N 0 37 W A town in SE England, in Berkshire opposite Windsor on the River Thames. Eton College, the famous public school, was founded by Henry VI in 1440. Population (1983 est): 3473.

Etruscans The ancient inhabitants of Etruria (now Tuscany) in central Italy. From the 8th to the 5th centuries BC their cities, forming a political association, dominated the region, but after 396 they were absorbed by the Romans. Their non-Indo-European language is still largely untranslated.

etymology The study in which words are traced back to their earliest forms. Most English words come either from Proto-Germanic or from Latin and French, with some scholarly words taken from Greek. In the past 200 years English has borrowed words from every part of the world.

eucalyptus A widely cultivated tropical or subtropical evergreen tree of the myrtle family, native to Australia. Also known as gum trees, they can be 90–100 m high. The grey bark is smooth and the leaves are long and narrow. Eucalyptus trees are important sources of timber, also yielding oils used in perfumery, etc.

Eucharist (Greek *eucharistia*: thanksgiving) The main *sacrament and central act of worship of Christian Churches. Also known as Holy Communion and the Mass, its origin is described in the Synoptic *Gospels. At the Last Supper, Christ blessed and shared the bread and wine to represent his death on the cross, leading to mankind's salvation.

Euclid (c. 300 BC) Greek mathematician. His book *Elements* summarized all known geometry from a few simple rules. Geometry obeying Euclid's rules is known as Euclidean geometry; all other kinds are called non-Euclidean.

Eugénie (1826–1920) The influential wife (1853–73) of *Napoleon III of France, several times acting as his regent. After the fall of the Empire (1870) she retired to England.

euphonium Brass instrument with a wide conical bore, a cup-shaped mouthpiece, four valves, and a range of about three and a half octaves above the B flat below middle C.

Euphrates, River A river in SW Asia, rising in E Turkey and flowing SE through Syria into Iraq. 190 km (118 mi) from the Persian Gulf, it joins the River Tigris to form the Shatt al-Arab. Length: 2700 km (1678 mi).

EURATOM. *See* European Atomic Energy Community.

Eureka Stockade (1854) A rebellion against strict government laws in which the miners of Ballarat in Victoria (Australia) stockaded themselves into the Eureka goldfield. They were defeated by government forces, about 25 miners and 5 troopers being killed.

eurhythmics A system of teaching music by developing the student's physical response to rhythm. Devised by Émile *Jaques-Dalcroze (1865–1950) in about 1905, it has been used in physical education and *ballet and modern dance training.

Euripides (c. 480–406 BC) Greek dramatist, the third (after *Aeschylus and *Sophocles) of the three major writers of Attic tragedy. Of approximately 90 plays, 19 survive, including the tragedies *Medea* (431), *Hippolytus* (428), *Electra* (415), *The Trojan Women* (415), *The Bacchae* (405), and *Iphigenia at Aulis* (405).

Europe A continent bordering on the Arctic Ocean (N), the Atlantic Ocean (W), and the Mediterranean Sea (S). A central plain, extending from the Ural Mountains to the Atlantic Ocean comprises two-thirds of the continent. It rises in the S to a series of mountain systems (e.g. the Pyrenees, Alps, Apennines, Carpathian Mountains), and in the N to the mountainous region of Scandinavia and Scotland. The chief rivers flow from the Valdai Hills (e.g Volga, Don, Dnieper) or the Alps (e.g. Danube, Rhine, Rhône, Po). Its four **climatic zones** are characterized by mild winters, cool summers, and rain all the year round (NW); mild winters, hot summers, and chiefly spring and autumn rain (Mediterranean); cold winters, warm summers, and chiefly summer rain (Central Europe); and very cold winters (E Europe). Coalfields occur, especially in the UK, Germany, France, Belgium, and the Soviet Union; oil and natural-gas reserves are found in the Soviet Union, Romania, Albania, and beneath the North Sea. Iron-ore and nickel, tin, and manganese are found mostly in the Soviet Union, but nonmetallic minerals occur widely. Most of the nations in Europe speak an *Indo-European language. Christianity is the dominant religion. National conflict culminated in the two World Wars. After World War II a split developed between the communist countries of E Europe, dominated by the Soviet Union, and the countries of W Europe. *See also* European Community. Area: about 10 400 000 sq km (4 000 000 sq mi). Population (1985): 492 000 000.

European Atomic Energy Community (EURATOM) An international organization founded in 1958 by the Treaty of Rome (1957) to encourage and develop the peaceful uses of atomic energy in Europe. In 1967 EURATOM and the European Coal and Steel Community merged with the EEC.

European Community (EC) An organization of W European states created—as the European Economic Community (EEC; Common Market) —by the Treaty of Rome (1957) to encourage economic cooperation and common development with the aim of economic, and some political, unity. Agreements have been reached on removing customs duties between members, fixing import

taxes from nonmembers, and working towards free movement of labour, services, and capital. The original members were Belgium, France, Italy, Luxembourg, the Netherlands, and West Germany. In 1973 the UK, Denmark, and the Republic of Ireland joined; Greece joined in 1981 and Spain and Portugal in 1986. In 1985 Greenland left after gaining home rule from Denmark. In 1967 the *European Atomic Energy Community and the European Coal and Steel Community merged with the EEC. The EEC put into effect a Common Agricultural Policy (CAP) in 1962 and a Common Fisheries Policy (1983). In 1988 the first EC passports were issued in the UK. In 1992 an internal market for capital, goods, services, and labour will be launched.
The Commission of the European Communities is in Brussels and consists of one or two members appointed by each member country; it advises and carries out the policies of the Council of Ministers, consisting of ministers from member governments. The heads of government meet triannually as the European Council. The European Parliament sitting in Strasbourg and Luxembourg alternately is consulted on annual budgets. Members are (since 1979) elected by direct vote in the member countries and sit as political groups (e.g. Christian Democrats, Socialists).

European Free Trade Association (EFTA) An association of six states (Austria, Finland, Iceland, Norway, Sweden, and Switzerland) founded in 1960 to encourage free trade of industrial goods between members. In 1984 free trade was established between the EC countries and the EFTA countries.

European Space Agency (ESA) An organization responsible for Europe's space programme, formed in 1975. The 11 full-member nations include the UK. All ESA *satellites were launched by NASA before completion of the ESA launcher **Ariane**, the first successful launching of which took place in 1979.

europium (Eu) A *lanthanide element, used in television-tube phosphors. At no 63; at wt 151.96; mp 822°C; bp 1597°C.

Eurydice In Greek legend, a dryad, the wife of *Orpheus. She died of a snake bite. Orpheus descended to the underworld to recover her but lost her forever when he violated the condition of her release and turned to look at her before emerging.

euthanasia (Greek: easy death) The illegal taking of life to relieve suffering. **Voluntary euthanasia** includes both taking life (e.g. by drugs) and withholding life-supporting treatment (passive euthanasia). With **compulsory euthanasia** the responsibility for deciding to end a life (e.g. of a deformed baby) rests on society.

eutrophication The pollution of lakes by sewage, fertilizers washed from the land, and industrial wastes (inorganic nitrates and phosphates). These compounds stimulate the growth of algae, reducing the oxygen content in the water, and so killing animals with a high oxygen requirement.

Evans, Dame Edith (1888–1976) British stage and film actress. Her long career included

many celebrated performances in Shakespearean roles and in classic comedies such as *The Rivals* and *The Importance of Being Earnest*.

Evelyn, John (1620–1706) English author, best known for his *Diary*, a detailed personal record of the years 1641–1706.

evening primrose A flowering plant of the fuchsia family. 90–100 cm tall, native to the Americas but widespread in Europe. The yellow flowers open in the evening.

Everest, Mount 27 59N 86 56E The highest mountain in the world, on the Nepal–Tibet border in the Himalayas. The summit was first reached by (Sir) Edmund *Hillary and Sherpa *Tenzing Norgay on 29 May, 1953, in an expedition led by Col John Hunt. Height: 8848 m (29 028 ft).

evergreen plants Plants whose foliage is retained throughout the year. The leaves are produced and shed at different times all the year round. Most conifers are evergreen. **Deciduous plants** produce leaves that are all shed before winter. Deciduous trees generally occur in temperate regions in which there are seasonal fluctuations in climate.

Evert, Chris(tine) (1954–) US tennis player who was Wimbledon singles champion in 1974, 1976 and 1981. She won the US singles title 1975–78, 1980, and 1982.

evolution In biology, the process by which the first and most primitive of living organisms have developed into the plant and animal life known today. Until the 18th century it was generally believed that each group of organisms was separately created by God. The first theory of evolution was published by Lamarck, in 1809 (*see* Lamarckism), who believed in the inheritance of acquired characteristics. A more satisfactory theory was put forward by Charles *Darwin and A. R. *Wallace in 1858: they proposed that new species arose by a process of natural selection (*see* Darwinism). Later work has supported Darwin's theory, which is now generally accepted.

Excalibur King Arthur's magic sword. In one legend Arthur succeeds in drawing it from a stone, thereby proving his claim to the English throne. In another he receives it from the Lady of the Lake, to whom it is thrown back at his death. *See also* Arthurian legend.

excitation In physics, the raising of a system from its lowest energy level (the ground state) to a higher energy level (the excited state). The term is usually confined to atoms, molecules, ions, and nuclei and is most frequently caused by the absorption of a *photon.

excommunication The shutting out of a Christian from the community of the Church for bad conduct. In the early Church, stopping people from receiving the *sacraments was frequently used as a means of punishment, and in the middle ages the pope used it to apply political pressure against monarchs. It is still used by the Roman Catholic Church as a form of punishment.

Exeter 50 43N 3 31W A city in SW England, the administrative centre of Devon on the River Exe. It has a 13th-century cathedral and an ancient Guildhall. Population (1983 est): 101 800.

existentialism A philosophical movement developed by *Sartre after World War II from the philosophy of *Kierkegaard. Sartre's existentialism allows individuals freedom in an otherwise meaningless universe. But a man is responsible for his effect on others, though only *his* existence is real to him and he is ultimately his own judge. Sartre explained existentialism chiefly in *Being and Nothingness* (1943).

Exmoor A high moorland and national park of SW England, extending from NE Devon into W Somerset, reaching 520 m (1707 ft) at Dunkery Beacon. It supports heather, bracken, and grass and is grazed by hardy Exmoor ponies, red deer, and sheep. Parts are now being ploughed. Area: 686 sq km (265 sq mi).

Exodus (Greek: going out) The second book of the Old Testament, traditionally by Moses, but probably composed between the 9th and 4th centuries BC. It refers to possible events in the 15th century BC that led to the departure of the Israelites from slavery in Egypt and their journey to Mount Sinai, where they received the Ten Commandments.

exorcism The religious practice of driving out evil spirits by prayers and other ceremonies. Still available in some Churches to expel evil spirits that supposedly possess people, it may only be performed by a priest with a bishop's permission.

exosphere. *See* atmosphere.

expanding universe The theory that the universe is expanding was proposed by Edwin Hubble (1889–1953) in 1929 from the *redshift of light from distant galaxies, which arises from the recession of the galaxies from us (and from each other). The expansion can be explained by the *big-bang theory.

explosives Substances that produce a large volume of gas very suddenly, the energy of which can be used for industrial or military purposes. **Chemical explosives** include *TNT, *nitroglycerin, *dynamite, and *gelignite. Modern high explosives are often in the form of water gels, which are plastic, water resistant, and easy to handle safely. *See also* nuclear weapons.

exposure meter A device for measuring the intensity of light falling on a *camera, and thus for determining the exposure time and lens *f-number needed to suit the conditions. The aperture and shutter speed can then be set manually or sometimes automatically.

expressionism A movement in modern art, the aim of which was to convey the crude force of human emotion. The chief exponents were Die Brücke and Der Blaue Reiter groups in Germany.

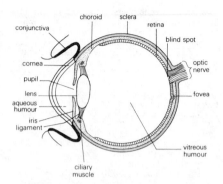

EYE *The structure of the human eye is revealed in this section. The blind spot, where the optic nerve leaves the eye, contains no visual cells and is therefore insensitive to light. The fovea is the area of acutest vision.*

extortion In law, a wrongdoing committed by a holder of public office who, using his office, takes from another money or valuables. It was abolished in England by the Theft Act (1968) and is now covered by *blackmail.

extrasensory perception (ESP) Obtaining information by means other than the senses. Clairvoyance (knowledge of distant events and hidden objects), telepathy (transferring thoughts), and precognition (knowledge of future events) are the three main forms of ESP, evidence for which is inconclusive.

extrusive rock. *See* igneous rock.

eye The organ of sight. The human eyeball has a white outer layer (sclera), except at the front, where it is replaced by the transparent cornea. A membrane (the conjunctiva) covers the white of the eye and lines the eyelids. Light entering the eye is refracted by the cornea and passes through the watery aqueous humour and the opening (pupil) in the *iris to the lens. The iris controls the amount of light entering the eye. The shape of the lens can be adjusted by the ciliary muscles to focus the image through the vitreous humour onto the *retina. Light-sensitive cells in the retina send impulses to the brain via the optic nerve. *See also* longsightedness; ophthalmology; shortsightedness.

Eyre, Lake A shallow salt lake of NE South Australia. It is normally dry except during the rainy season when heavy rains are fed into the lake. Area: about 9100 sq km (3500 sq mi).

F

Fabergé, Peter Carl (1846–1920) Russian goldsmith and jeweller. He designed elegant *objets d'art* and was famous for his jewelled Easter eggs containing gifts made for the tsars.

Fabian Society A society, named after *Fabius Maximus, formed in London in 1884 to promote socialist ideas and establish a socialist state in Britain. Members included George Bernard *Shaw and Sidney and Beatrice *Webb. The Fabians helped to found the Labour Party and continue to press the cause of socialism.

Fabius Maximus, Quintus (d. 203 BC) Roman general of the second *Punic War. Appointed dictator after *Hannibal's defeat of the Romans at Trasimene in 217, Fabius attempted to wear Hannibal down by avoiding pitched battles.

facsimile transmission. *See* fax.

Factory Acts UK parliamentary Acts that control conditions of work in factories. The early Factory Acts (1802, 1819, 1833) were mainly concerned with the employment of children after the *industrial revolution. Ashley (later Lord Shaftesbury) was largely responsible for the Acts of 1844 and 1847, which achieved the ten-hour day. Welfare in factories is now controlled by the Factories Act (1961) and the Health and Safety at Work Act (1974).

Faeroe Islands (*or* Faroe Islands) A Danish group of 22 self-governing islands in the N Atlantic Ocean, between the Shetland Islands and Iceland, the chief ones being Strómó, Østeró, and Vaagó. Fishing and fish processing are important. Area: 1400 sq km (540 sq mi). Population (1988 est): 46 000. Capital: Thorshavn, on Strómó.

Fahd bin Abdul Aziz (1923–) King of Saudi Arabia (1982–). Son of Khalid Ibn Abdul Aziz, he became king after his father's death.

Fahrenheit scale A temperature scale in which the temperature of melting ice is taken as 32 degrees and the temperature of boiling water as 212 degrees. Named after the German physicist Gabriel Daniel Fahrenheit (1686–1736).

faience Tin-glazed earthenware made in France. The technique originated in Faenza, Italy (hence the full name *porcellana di Faenza*), but Italian potters were using it in France in the 16th century. Centres of production during the 17th and 18th centuries were Lyons, Marseilles, Moustiers, Nevers, and Rouen.

Fairbanks, Douglas (Julius Ullman; 1883–1939) US film actor. With D. W. Griffith, Charlie Chaplin, and his wife Mary Pickford he founded United Artists Corporation in 1919. His films include *The Mark of Zorro* (1920) and *The Black Pirate* (1926). His son, the actor **Douglas Fairbanks Jr** (1909–), played similar roles, such as *The Prisoner of Zenda* (1937).

Fair Isle 59 32N 1 38W A sparsely inhabited island in the North Sea, off the N coast of Scotland between the Orkney and Shetland Islands. It is famous for its knitted goods with intricate patterns. Area: 16.5 sq km (6 sq mi).

fairy penguin The smallest of the *penguins, *Eudyptula minor*, about 30 cm tall. It is the only penguin commonly occurring on Australian coasts.

Faisal I (1885–1933) King of Iraq (1921–33). He played an important part in the Arab revolt against the Turks during World War I. After the war he was briefly King of Syria before the French occupation (1920). In 1921 the British installed him as king in Iraq.

Faisal Ibn Abdul Aziz (1905–75) King of Saudi Arabia (1964–75). He ruled Saudi Arabia from 1958, although his brother Saud (1902–69) did not abdicate until 1964. His reign saw Saudi Arabia become an important oil-producing country. He was assassinated by his nephew.

faith healing (*or* spiritual healing) The curing of illness by means apparently unexplained by science. The temple of *Asclepius at *Epidaurus was a famous faith-healing centre in ancient Greece. Christ is credited with several miraculous cures.

Falabella The smallest breed of pony, developed by the Falabella family in Argentina using Shetland pony stock. Height: 38–76 cm.

Falange Española The Spanish Fascist party (*see* fascism), created in 1933 by José António Primo de Rivera (1870–1936). In 1937 *Franco merged the Falange with the various Nationalist parties to create the National Movement, which became Spain's only legal party after the Civil War.

Falashas An Ethiopian tribe who practise an early form of *Judaism. In early 1985 the Israelis organized a secret airlift of over 7000 Falashas to Israel from famine-stricken Ethiopia.

falcon A ground-nesting widely distributed bird of prey having long pointed wings and a notched hooked bill. It kills small birds in flight with its claws or seizes small mammals from the ground. *See also* gyrfalcon; kestrel; merlin; peregrine.

falconry (*or* hawking) The sport of hunting small animals or birds with falcons, eagles, etc. It was practised in Asia from the 8th century BC and was popular in Europe from medieval times to the 17th century. The birds are trained to sit hooded on the gloved fist and, by the use of a lure (an imitation bird with meat attached), to hunt and kill (but not retrieve).

Falkland Islands (Argentine name: Islas Malvinas) An island group and British crown colony in the S Atlantic Ocean: the main islands are East and West Falkland; its dependencies to the SE are *South Georgia and the South Sandwich group. The population is of British origin. Sheep farming is the main occupation. *History*: first landed on by Capt John Strong in 1690, they became a British colony in 1833. Argentina has long laid claim to the group and on 2 April, 1982, invaded the islands. A task force sent by the UK recaptured them on 14 June. Area: 12 173 sq km (4700 sq mi). Population (1986): 1916. Capital: Stanley.

Falla, Manuel de (1876–1946) Spanish composer. Influenced by Spanish folksong, his music includes ballet scores *Love the Magician* (1915) and *The Three-Cornered Hat* (1919), *Nights in the Gardens of Spain* (1909–15), and a concerto for harpsichord and chamber ensemble.

Fallopian tubes. *See* ovary.

fallout Radioactive particles deposited from the atmosphere after a nuclear explosion. Large particles are deposited within a radius of a few hundred kilometres during the first few hours. Tropospheric fallout may occur anywhere along the same line of latitude as the explosion during the first week. Particles drawn high into the stratosphere can cause fallout for several years. *See also* radiation sickness.

fallow deer A *deer, Dama dama*, native to Mediterranean forests. About 90 cm high, fallow deer are brown with white spots in summer, becoming greyish in winter; males have flattened antlers.

Famagusta 35 07N 33 57E A port in Cyprus, on the E coast. Founded in the 3rd century BC, it did not develop until the 13th century AD, when Christians fled here from Palestine. It was largely evacuated following the Turkish invasion of N Cyprus (1974). Population (1985): 19 428.

family planning. *See* contraception.

Fang A Bantu people of West Africa consisting of a number of tribes in N Gabon, Equatorial Guinea, and S Cameroon.

Fangio, Juan Manuel (1911–) Argentinian motor-racing driver, who was world champion a record five times (1951, 1954–57).

fanworm A marine *annelid worm, also called peacock or feather-duster worm. Fanworms build a parchment-like tube, up to 45 cm long, from which emerges a feathery crown of tentacles that trap food particles.

FAO. *See* Food and Agriculture Organization.

farad (F) The *SI unit of electrical *capacitance equal to the capacitance of a capacitor that, if charged with 1 coulomb (C), has a potential difference of 1 volt (V) across its plates, i.e. 1 F = 1 C V⁻¹. Named after Michael *Faraday.

Faraday, Michael (1791–1867) British chemist and physicist. In 1813 he became assistant to Sir Humphry *Davy at the Royal Institution, succeeding Davy as professor of chemistry (1833). After discovering electrolysis (1832) he worked out the laws that control it. He discovered the connection between electricity and magnetism and, independently of Joseph Henry (1797–1878), first showed that electromagnetic induction was possible. He produced the first electrical generator (1831) and transformer (1832).

farce A type of comic play usually including peculiar situations, improbable coincidences,

and exaggerations of character and action. Many were written in the late 19th century, by *Feydeau and Labiche in France and *Pinero in England.

Farnborough 51 17N 0 46W A town in S England, in Hampshire. The Royal Aircraft Establishment, the UK's chief aeronautical research centre, is situated here and there are annual air displays. Population (1987 est): 42 800.

Faroe Islands. *See* Faeroe Islands.

Farouk I (1920–65) The last king of Egypt (1936–52). His inability to prevent British intervention in Egyptian affairs, and defeat in the first Arab-Israeli War (1948–49), led to his overthrow.

fascism A 20th-century political movement that originated in Italy in 1919 under *Mussolini. Fascism rejected ideas of individual freedom and equality, held some nations or races superior to others, and put all power in the hands of a cult figure. In Germany Hitler added hatred of the Jews to fascist militarism and anticommunism. World War II destroyed Mussolini's and Hitler's fascism, but Franco's fascist rule in Spain survived almost 40 years.

Fassbinder, Rainer Werner (1946–82) German film director whose realistic films include *The Bitter Tears of Petra von Kant* (1972), *Fear Eats the Soul* (1974), *Despair* (1978), and *The Marriage of Maria Braun* (1979).

Fatah, al- (Arabic: the victory) A Palestinian organization, also known as the Palestine National Liberation Movement, established in the late 1950s. Led by Yassir *Arafat, al-Fatah began guerrilla warfare against Israel in the mid-1960s. It split into factions in the 1980s.

Fates In Greek mythology, three goddesses who determine human destinies. The daughters of Zeus and Themis (goddess of justice), they are: Lachesis, who assigns a person's position at birth; Clotho, who spins out the thread of their existence; and Atropos, who cuts the thread at death.

fathom A unit used to express depths of water, equal to six feet.

Fatimah (d. 632) The daughter of *Mohammed. She married *Ali and was the mother of his sons, Hasan and Husayn, from whom most of the Shiite *imams were descended. The Fatimid caliphs claimed descent from her.

fats and oils Substances that occur widely in animals and plants as an energy store and as insulating material. Fats and oils are used in making soaps, margarines, cooking oils, paints, etc. Fats are solid at 20°C but oils are liquid; natural fats and oils are *lipids, whereas mineral oils are hydrocarbons (*see* oil).

fatty acid (*or* carboxylic acid) An organic acid containing one or more carboxyl (–COOH) groups. They combine with glycerol to form the main constituent of *fats and oils. The hard animal fats contain a high proportion of saturated fatty acids (i.e. containing no double bonds); soft fats, such as vegetable and fish oils, contain more unsaturated fatty acids (containing one or more double bonds). When eaten, unsaturated fatty acids involve less risk of heart disease than saturated acids.

Faulkner, William (1897–1962) US novelist. *Sartoris* (1929) was the first of his stories set in the fictitious Yoknapatawpha County, based on his native Mississippi. His major novels include *The Sound and the Fury* (1929) and *Absalom, Absalom!* (1936). He was awarded the Nobel Prize in 1949.

fault A fracture in the rocks of the earth's crust, the rocks on each side being displaced either vertically, horizontally, or obliquely. Faulting occurs as a result of accumulated strain in the rocks, usually at plate margins (*see* plate tectonics). *See also* rift valley.

Fauré, Gabriel (Urbain) (1845–1924) French composer and organist. His works include the well-known *Requiem* (1886–87), incidental music for Maeterlinck's play *Pelléas and Mélisande* (1898), the opera *Pénélope* (1913), the orchestral *Pavane* (1887), and songs.

Faust A legendary medieval German scholar and magician who sold his soul to the Devil in exchange for knowledge and power. He has has inspired numerous literary works, notably by *Marlowe (1592), *Goethe (1808, 1832), and Thomas *Mann (1947), as well as musical works, including an opera by *Gounod.

fauvism A movement in French painting at the turn of the century, characterized by the use of strong colours (the name comes from the French *fauves*, wild beasts). Under the leadership of *Matisse, fauvists included *Dufy, *Braque, and *Rouault.

Fawkes, Guy (1570–1606) English conspirator, a Roman Catholic convert who joined Robert Catesby (1573–1605) in the Gunpowder Plot to blow up James I and parliament. The conspirators were informed upon and Fawkes was discovered (5 November, 1605) with the gunpowder in a cellar of the Palace of Westminister. He was executed. Nov 5 continues to be celebrated with fireworks and the burning of "guys".

fax (*or* facsimile transmission) A method of sending images (text or pictures) by a telecommunications link. Most fax transmissions are sent through the normal telephone network. The document is scanned optically to break it into a pattern of dots, which are transmitted as electrical pulses. The receiving device reconstructs the image from this information and prints it out on light-sensitive paper. Recent advances in technology have made it cheap and reliable, and it is now in widespread use.

FBI. See Federal Bureau of Investigation.

Federal Bureau of Investigation (FBI) The organization within the US Department of Justice that carries out investigations into possible breaches of federal law, especially those related to security. Founded as the Bureau of Investigation in 1908, it became the FBI in 1935. It had an important role in the campaign against organized crime in the 1930s and also in the anticommunist activities of Joseph *McCarthy in the 1950s. More recently it has had successes against the Mafia.

feldspars The most important group of rock-forming minerals and the major constituents of *igneous rocks. There are four components of feldspars: anorthite (calcium plagioclase, $CaAl_2Si_2O_8$); albite (sodium plagioclase, $NaAlSi_3O_8$); orthoclase (potassium feldspar, $KAlSi_3O_8$); and celsian (barium feldspar, $BaAl_2Si_2O_8$, which is rare).

Felixstowe 51 58N 1 20E A resort in E England, in Suffolk on the North Sea. It has developed rapidly as a container port, with ferry services to Rotterdam and Zeebrugge. Population (1985 est): 20 858.

Fellini, Federico (1920–) Italian film director, whose work includes *La strada* (1954), *8½* (1963), *Roma* (1972), *Casanova* (1976), *Intervista* (1987), and *The Voice of the Moon* (1990).

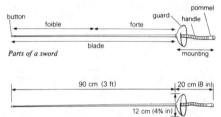

Parts of a sword

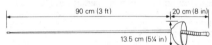

Foil *The foil weighs a maximum of 17.6 oz (500 g). Its blade is quadrangular and very flexible.*

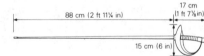

Épée *The épée weighs a maximum of 27.2 oz (770 g). Its blade is triangular and stiffer than that of the foil.*

Saber *The saber weighs a maximum of 17.6 oz (500 g). Its blade is a flattened V-shape.*

FENCING

fencing The sport of combat with a sword, of which there are three main forms: foil, épée, and sabre. Bouts are fought on a *piste*, or marked-out area. The winner is the first to score five hits (for men) or four (for women) in six minutes (for men) or five (for women).

Fenians Members of a secret Irish-American revolutionary society, the Irish Republican Brotherhood (IRB), formed in 1858 by James Stephens (1825–1901). The IRB was replaced by the IRA.

fennec A nocturnal desert *fox, *Fennecus zerda*, of Africa and the Middle East, which is sandy-coloured and has large pointed ears.

fennel A strong-smelling herb, *Foeniculum vulgare*, of the carrot family, native to S Europe. The feathery leaves and the seeds (which taste of aniseed) are used to flavour food. The leafstalks of Florence, or sweet, fennel (*F. dulce*) are eaten as a vegetable or in salads.

Fens, the A low-lying highly fertile area in E England, extending across parts of Cambridgeshire, Lincolnshire, Norfolk, and Suffolk. Once waterlogged, the Fens are now virtually all drained.

fenugreek A herb, *Trigonella foenumgraecum*, of the pea family, native to the Mediterranean. The seeds are used to flavour curry and chutney.

Ferdinand (V and II) the Catholic (1452–1516) King of Castile as Ferdinand V (1474–1504) and of Aragon as Ferdinand II (1479–1516). He ruled Castile jointly with his wife *Isabella I of Castile. As King of Aragon he united Castile and Aragon, adding Granada in 1492. The introduction of the Inquisition (1480) and the expulsion of the Jews (1492) aimed to strengthen both church and monarchy.

Ferdinand VII (1784–1833) King of Spain (1808, 1814–33). In 1808 Ferdinand was forced by Napoleon to abdicate but returned to the throne in 1814. His repressive policies caused a liberal uprising (1820) and the establishment of a liberal government until 1823, when it was overthrown with French help.

Fermat, Pierre de (1601–65) French mathematician who founded *number theory and, with Blaise *Pascal, probability theory.

fermentation The process by which microorganisms and tissues obtain energy in the absence of oxygen. The fermentation of carbohydrates by yeasts to form alcohol is the basis of making wines and beers. Other types of fermentation produce lactic acid, as in the souring of milk by bacteria.

Fermi, Enrico (1901–54) US physicist, born in Italy. For his work in Italy on the bombardment of uranium by thermal neutrons he was awarded the 1938 Nobel Prize. He moved in 1938 to the USA, where he achieved the first controlled nuclear chain reaction and helped in developing the atom bomb.

fern A leafy *pteridophyte plant of which there are about 15 000 species, mostly found in shady damp regions, especially in the tropics. The life cycle shows *alternation of generations. The fern plant itself is the asexual (sporophyte) generation, which has a creeping underground stem (rhizome) and feathery fronds. Asexual spores, produced in clusters on the underside of the leaflets, develop into the sexual (gametophyte) generation—a tiny heart-shaped plant producing egg and sperm cells. The fertilized egg cell develops into a new sporophyte plant.

ferret A domesticated form of *polecat, *Mustela putorius*, that is slightly smaller than the European polecat and lighter in colour (sometimes albino). Ferrets are used to drive rats and rabbits from their burrows.

ferromagnetism The property of a material, such as iron, cobalt, nickel, and their alloys, that enables it to become a permanent magnet, i.e. ferromagnetic materials placed in a *magnetic field develop a strong internal field, some of which is retained when the external field is removed.

fertilization The union of a male and a female sex cell (*gamete), which is the essential process of sexual reproduction. The resulting cell, called a zygote, develops to form a new individual, in which half the chromosomes (and genes) are from the male parent and half from the female. In self-fertilization both gametes are produced by the same individual; in cross-fertilization they derive from different individuals.

fertilizers Substances added to soils to improve plant growth. Traditional fertilizers include manure, bone meal, and dried blood. Artificial fertilizers include phosphates, potash, and nitrates, which are added in different proportions to suit individual crop requirements. Artificial fertilizers have been of immense benefit in improving crop productivity, although their excessive use can lead to *pollution.

Fès (*or* Fez) 34 05N 5 00W A city in N Morocco. In the 14th century it became a major centre for commerce and Islamic learning. Its Qarawiyin Mosque is the oldest in Africa and contains a university (859 AD). Population (1982): 448 823.

fescue A grass native to temperate regions of the N hemisphere. It grows in tufts. Meadow fescue (*Festuca pratensis*) is used for livestock fodder; sheep's fescue (*F. ovina*) grows on mountains and in dry and exposed soil.

fetishism 1. In *anthropology, the practice of using charms magically, found among W African tribes and in the West Indies. 2. In *psychiatry, the abnormal condition in which sexual satisfaction is obtained by using such objects (fetishes) as articles of clothing, rubber objects, leather, etc.

fetus (*or* foetus) The developing baby in the womb from the beginning of the ninth week of pregnancy until birth (*see* embryo). The fetus is protected by a series of membranes enclosing amniotic fluid and is connected to the mother's bloodstream through the *umbilical cord and *placenta.

feudalism The medieval system by which property was granted by the king to a lord (tenant in chief) in return for military or other service and loyalty. The tenants in chief might in turn grant part of their land to inferior tenants in return for their service. Feudalism originated in 9th-century France and became the basis of medieval society, politics, and law, with tenants maintaining local armies and administering private justice. From the 12th century its importance declined wherever the king's power increased; in England it was formally abolished in 1661.

Feydeau, Georges (1862–1921) French playwright, famous for his many farces, written between 1881 and 1916. They include *The Lady from Maxim's* (1889), *Hotel Paradiso* (1894), and *A Flea in Her Ear* (1907).

Fez. See Fès.

Fianna Fáil (Irish: Soldiers of Destiny) Political party in the Irish republic, founded in 1926 by Eamon *De Valera from moderate *Sinn Féin members. The ruling party in the years

1932–48, 1951–54, 1957–73, 1977–81, Jan 1982–Dec 1982, and 1987– , its leaders have been De Valera (until 1959), Sean Lemass (until 1966), Jack Lynch (until 1979), and Charles *Haughey.

fibre (*or* dietary fibre) The constituent of the human diet that is not digested. It consists of the cell walls of plants, including cellulose. It is present in wholewheat cereals, root vegetables, nuts, and fruit and is considered helpful in preventing constipation, obesity, diabetes mellitus, and colonic cancer.

fibreglass (glass fibre *or* spun glass) Glass drawn into fine threads. It is woven into curtain material; made into glass wool for insulation; woven into coarse mats for filters; and used in reinforcing moulded plastics for boats, etc.

fibre optics The use of thin flexible glass fibres for transmitting light. The light inside the fibre is totally internally reflected and travels through the fibre with little loss of intensity. Glass fibres are used in the transmission of information in the form of light pulses and for examining otherwise inaccessible places, for example in medical diagnosis.

fibres Threadlike substances of natural or man-made origin. *Wool and *silk are the most widely used animal fibres. Vegetable fibres include *cotton, *flax, *hemp, *jute, and *sisal. Carbon fibres, *fibreglass, and *asbestos are formed from mineral substances. Man-made fibres include **modified natural fibres**, such as *rayon, and **synthetic fibres**, which include *polyesters, *nylon, and *acrylics.

fiddler crab A small burrowing *crab, 25–30 mm long. The brightly coloured male has an enlarged claw. Fiddler crabs are found on salt marshes and beaches of tropical and temperate regions.

field In physics, a region of space in which certain bodies exert a force on similar bodies, when they are not in contact. For example, an electrically charged body exerts a force (attractive or repulsive, depending on polarity) on other charged bodies and a magnetized body has a magnetic field around it. A field is often represented by lines of force to indicate the direction in which the force acts.

Fielding, Henry (1707–54) British novelist and dramatist. He wrote about 25 plays, mostly satirical and topical comedies, between 1728 and 1737. His major novels include *Joseph Andrews* (1742), the ironical *Jonathan Wild* (1743), and *Tom Jones* (1749).

fieldmouse A nocturnal *mouse, *Apodemus sylvaticus*, of Europe and Asia. About 9 cm long, with an 8-cm tail, it has a brown coat with white underparts and feeds on seeds.

Field of the Cloth of Gold (1520) The meeting near Calais of Henry VIII of England and Francis I of France. Francis hoped for English support against Emperor Charles V, with whom, however, Henry later formed an alliance.

Fields, Gracie (Dame Grace Stansfield; 1898–1979) British entertainer who began in Lancashire as a music-hall singer and comedian and made several films during the 1930s. She lived for many years in Capri.

Fields, W. C. (William Claude Dukenfield; 1880–1946) US film actor. In *The Bank Dick* (1940), *My Little Chickadee* (1940), and other films, he exploited his eccentricity.

fife A small side-blown *flute, pitched in B flat and used in military fife-and-drum bands.

Fife Region An administrative region in E Scotland, bordering on the North Sea. It consists of a lowland peninsula between the Firths of Forth and Tay. Area: 1305 sq km (504 sq mi). Population (1988 est): 344 717. Administrative centre: Glenrothes.

Fifteen Rebellion. *See* Jacobites.

fig A tree or shrub, *Ficus carica*, of the mulberry family, probably native to W Asia. It has large leaves and tiny flowers. The fleshy pear-shaped structure that contains the flowers develops into the edible fig after fertilization.

fighting fish An aggressive fish found in SE Asia and the Malay Archipelago. The Siamese fighting fish (*Betta splendens*) is greenish and about 6.5 cm long.

fig marigold A plant, also called mesembryanthemum, found in warm regions, especially South Africa, and widely cultivated in gardens. Fig marigolds have large brilliantly coloured daisy-like flowers and figlike fruits.

Fiji, Republic of A country in the S Pacific Ocean consisting of some 800 islands (only 106 inhabited); the largest are Viti Levu and Vanua Levu. *Economy*: chiefly agricultural, sugar cane being the main crop. Tourism is important. *History*: discovered by the Dutch explorer Tasman in 1643, the islands were handed over to Britain in 1874. Fiji became independent within the British Commonwealth in 1970. In 1987 Fiji left the Commonwealth after a military coup. President: Ratu Sir Penaia Ganilau. Prime minister: Ratu Sir Kamisese Mara. Official language: English. Official currency: Fiji dollar of 100 cents. Area: 18 272 sq km (7055 sq mi). Population (1987): 726 000. Capital and main port: Suva.

film A flexible strip of cellulose acetate, or similar plastic, coated with a light-sensitive emulsion. A black-and-white photographic emulsion usually consists of gelatin containing suspended crystals of silver bromide or chloride. After the film has been exposed in a *camera the exposed crystals are reduced to black deposits of fine silver particles when treated with the chemicals in the developer, giving a reversed (or negative) image. Bathing the film in sodium thiosulphate (hypo) or other fixers enables the unchanged silver salts to be washed away with water. The sensitivity (speed) of film is usually quoted as an *ASA rating. *See also* photography.

films. *See* cinema.

filter A device that allows some things to pass through it but not others. For example, a paper or *fibreglass filter is used to remove solid particles from a liquid or gas. Such filters are used in air-conditioning units, water purification, etc. In optics, coloured filters are used to select light with a certain range of wavelengths.

finch A songbird occurring in most regions of the world except Australia. Finches have hard conical bills used to crack open seeds, although they also feed on buds and fruit. Species include the *bullfinch, *chaffinch, and *brambling.

Fine Gael (Irish: Tribe of Gaels) Irish political party, founded in 1933 by William Cosgrave. It was the senior member of ruling alliance parties in Ireland (1948–51, 1954–57, 1973–77, 1981–Jan 1982, and Dec 1982–87), led by John Costello, Liam Cosgrave, and Dr Garret Fitzgerald. It is more conservative than the rival *Fianna Fáil.

arch   whorl   loop

FINGERPRINT *Loops are the commonest form of pattern (c. 65%), followed by whorls (c. 30%), and then arches (c. 5%).*

fingerprint The impression made by the ridges on the fingertips. Taking fingerprints to identify criminals was introduced into the UK in 1901, largely as a result of the work of Sir William Herschel (1833–1917) and Sir Edward Henry (1859–1931). The print is taken by inking the fingers and thumbs and then rolling them on paper. Fingerprints left at the scene of a crime may be recorded photographically. Scotland Yard has a library of over two million prints of known criminals. Recently, **genetic fingerprinting** has been introduced, based on the individual characteristics of a person's blood, semen, etc.

Finisterre, Cape 42 52N 9 16W The most westerly point in Spain, on the Atlantic coast.

Finland, Republic of (Finnish name: Suomi) A country in N Europe, with S and W coastlines on the Baltic Sea. Over 10% of the area consists of lakes, which, with rivers and canals, provide a network of inland waterways. *Economy*: agriculture, especially cereals and dairy produce, is important. Extensive forests provide for the timber and paper industries. Hydroelectricity provides the main source of power. *History*: conquered by Sweden in the 12th century AD, Finland became a grand duchy in the 16th century. In the 18th century the SE was occupied by Russia and in 1809 the rest was handed over to Russia. It became independent in 1917, following the Russian Revolution, and a republic two years later. During World War II it was invaded by Soviet forces and forced to give certain territories to the Soviet Union. A treaty of friendship between the two countries was signed in 1948. President: Dr Mauno Henrik Koivisto (1923–   ). Official languages: Finnish and Swedish. Official currency: markka of 100 pennia. Area: 305 475 sq km (117 913 sq mi). Population (1987): 4 942 000. Capital and main port: Helsinki.

Finnic A group of *Finno-Ugric languages. Finnic includes Finnish, Estonian, and Lapp.

Finno-Ugric languages A large group of languages of the *Uralic family, spoken by more than 20 million people in in Scandinavia, E Europe, and W Asia. They can be divided into Ugric (*Hungarian and Ob-Ugric) and *Finnic.

fiord. *See* fjord.

fins Organs of locomotion and balance in fish and some other aquatic animals. The fins of fish are supported by bony or cartilaginous fin rays. The tail (or caudal) fin is often used for propulsion and the dorsal and anal fins used for balancing. The paired pectoral fins, just behind the gills, and pelvic fins, further back, are generally used for steering.

fir A coniferous tree of the pine family. Mostly native to N temperate regions, they are also called silver firs, as many species have leaves that are silvery underneath. Firs have blunt needles and erect stout cones. The European silver fir (*Abies alba*) is grown for its timber: it reaches a height of 50 m.

firebrat A primitive wingless insect, *Thermobia domestica*. A *bristletail found in buildings worldwide, it prefers warm places, such as bakery ovens, where it feeds on starchy materials.

fireclay A soft clay often occurring beneath coalseams; it is possibly fossil soil or earth in which swamp plants grew. Because they are heat-resistant, fireclays are used to line furnaces, etc.

firefly A widely distributed nocturnal beetle that emits a greenish light—often as short flashes —from an organ on the abdomen (*see* bioluminescence). The wingless females and larvae are called glowworms.

Firenze. *See* Florence.

Fire of London (2–5 September, 1666) The fire that started in a baker's shop in Pudding Lane and destroyed four-fifths of the City. More than 13 000 buildings, including the medieval St Paul's Cathedral, were burnt to the ground. Sir Christopher *Wren played a major part in the rebuilding. The **Monument**, which he designed in 1671, stands close to Pudding Lane to commemorate the Fire.

fireworks Devices that produce coloured flames or smoke and small explosions. Gunpowder rockets and fire crackers were first used in ancient China for military purposes and for celebrations. The explosive, usually gunpowder, is coloured by metallic salts: sodium salts for yellow, barium for green, strontium for red, and copper for blue. Metal filings are added for sparks and aniline dyes provide coloured smokes.

firn (*or* névé) A stage in the transformation of fresh snow to glacier ice. Compaction and recrystallization of the snow increases its density and it becomes firn. Further compaction transforms firn to glacier ice.

Fischer-Dieskau, Dietrich (1925–   ) German baritone. He is renowned for his performances of songs and of a wide range of operatic roles.

Fischer-Tropsch reaction A chemical reaction that enables liquid fuels and other hydrocarbons to be produced from coal. It was invented by F. Fischer (1852–1948) and H. Tropsch (1839–1935) in 1925 and was used in Germany during World War II.

fish A cold-blooded aquatic vertebrate; over 30 000 species occur worldwide in seas and fresh waters. They have streamlined bodies covered with scales and *fins used for swimming and balancing. Oxygen is obtained from water by *gills in the wall of the mouth cavity, although a few species can also breathe air (*see* lungfish). **Cartilaginous fishes** (including sharks and rays) have a skeleton of cartilage, and **bony fishes** (all other types) have a bony skeleton. Most fish feed on other fish and invertebrates, although some eat plants. Large numbers of small eggs are laid and are usually fertilized in the water. Fish are a major source of food and other products, such as fishmeal, oil, and glue.

fish hawk. *See* osprey.

fission (physics). *See* nuclear energy.

Fitzgerald, Edward (1809–83) British poet. His famous *Rubaiyat of Omar Khayyam* (1859) was a free adaptation of the 12th-century Persian original.

Fitzgerald, Ella (1918–) US Black jazz singer. Her many albums include *Hello Love, Duke Ellington's Song Book,* and the *Gershwin Song Books.*

Fitzgerald, F(rancis) Scott (Key) (1896–1940) US novelist. His autobiographical first novel, *This Side of Paradise* (1920), was highly successful. After 1924 Fitzgerald lived on the French Riviera, where his wife Zelda suffered from schizophrenia, later (1930) being sent to an asylum. Fitzgerald declined into alcoholism. His other works include *The Beautiful and the Damned* (1922), *The Great Gatsby* (1925), and *Tender is the Night* (1934).

Fitzgerald, Garret (1926–) Irish statesman; prime minister of Ireland (1981–87). He was leader of the Fine Gael party from 1977 to 1987 and was responsible for passing the Anglo-Irish agreement in 1985.

Fiume. *See* Rijeka.

fives A British court game that developed in different forms at Eton, Rugby, and Winchester public schools. It is played with gloved hands by two or four players on a three- or four-walled court, each side returning the ball in turn to certain areas of wall.

fjord (*or* fiord) A narrow sea inlet between mountains, especially in Norway. Usually U-shaped, fjords are glaciated valleys that have been flooded by the sea.

flag A Eurasian iris, *Iris pseudacorus* (yellow flag), growing in marshes and ditches. Up to 1.2 m high, it has yellow flowers and bladelike leaves. The sweet flag (*Acorus calamus*) is related to the cuckoo pint. Native to Asia and North America, it is widely found at the edges of ponds, rivers, etc. About 1 m high, it has yellow flowers.

flagella Long threadlike structures that project from the surface of a cell, used for locomotion or the production of water currents. Flagella occur in protozoa, sperms, sponges, and also in bacteria (in a simpler form).

flageolet 1. A musical instrument similar to the *recorder but with two thumb holes on the underside and a head fitted with a slender ivory mouthpiece containing a sponge to absorb condensation. 2. A variety of *haricot bean with pale green seeds.

Flamboyant In French gothic architecture, the major style during the 15th century. Similar to the earlier English Decorated style, Flamboyant takes its name from its elaborate curves and flamelike patterns, especially in windows. St Maclou, Rouen (begun 1432), is a fine example.

flamenco Spanish music of Moorish influence developed by gipsies in Andalusia. It consists of a song accompanied by dancing, in which men perform toe and heel tapping steps (*zapateados*) and women rely on graceful movements. Flamenco guitar playing includes tapping the body of the guitar with the fingers.

flamingo A wading bird occurring in large flocks on saltwater lakes in warm regions. Flamingos have a long neck, a broad wingspan, and white plumage, tinged with pink. They sieve algae, diatoms, etc., from mud using filters in their bills.

Flaminius, Gaius (d. 217 BC) Roman popular leader, an advocate of the plebeians' rights. In 220, as consul, he built the Flaminian Way, Rome's road to N Italy. Elected in 217 as leader against *Hannibal, he was defeated and killed at Trasimene.

Flamsteed, John (1646–1719) English astronomer, who established a national observatory at Greenwich and was appointed the first astronomer royal in 1675. His star catalogue gave the positions of more than 3000 stars.

Flanders A historic region in Europe that now comprises the provinces of East Flanders and West Flanders in Belgium and parts of N France and the Netherlands. After the 12th century it became a major industrial centre, cloth being especially important. During World War II the Battle of Flanders (10 May–2 June, 1940) resulted in the Allied withdrawal from *Dunkirk.

flash point The lowest temperature at which a liquid produces enough vapour to ignite on the application of a small flame under specified conditions.

flatfish A group of carnivorous bony *fish that includes the *halibut, *plaice, *sole, and *turbot. Flatfish lie on sandy bottoms of coastal waters; the upper surface of the flattened body is coloured to blend with their surroundings and both eyes occur on the upward-facing side of the head.

flat racing Horse racing without jumps, usually over distances between 0.8 km (0.5 mi) and 2.4 km (1.5 mi). *Thoroughbred horses are used, mainly as two- and three-year-olds. Weight handicaps are used in most races. The most important races are the English *Classics, the US Triple Crown, and the French Prix de l'Arc de Triomphe.

flatworm A flat-bodied wormlike animal. Some flatworms are free-living (planarians) but the majority are parasitic (*see* fluke; tapeworm). They range in size from 1 mm to 15 m. Many are hermaphrodite.

Flaubert, Gustave (1821–80) French novelist. His first controversial novel, *Madame Bovary* (1856), was followed by *Salammbô* (1862), *L'Education sentimentale* (1870), *La Tentation de*

Birds and insects fly by flapping their wings.
Downstroke of bird's wings

Man first rose into the air in 1783 – in the Montgolfier brothers' hot air balloon.

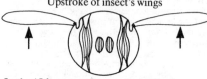

Upstroke of insect's wings

In the 15th century Leonardo da Vinci designed a human wing-flapping machine. It does not work – because man is too heavy.

A century later Otto Lilienthal built the first glider.
It closely resembled the modern hang glider.

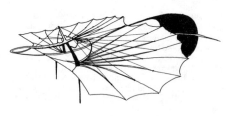

Aircraft have transformed 20th century life both in peace and war.

Rescue

Crop spraying

Flying doctor

Troops and cargo transport

War and destruction

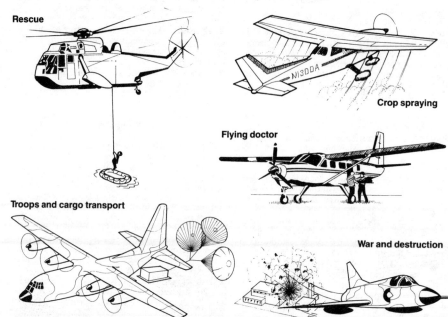

Gliders and swooping birds make use of the same principle. A wing-shaped object (aerofoil) moving through the air creates a lift force. The longer path the air has to travel over the upper part makes the air accelerate with a consequent reduction in pressure. The flatter underside makes the air move more slowly and the pressure rises. The high pressure below and the lower pressure above gives the wing the lift it needs to counter its weight.

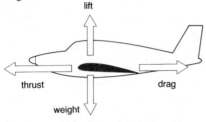

To move the wing through the air requires thrust. The Wright brothers built a light internal-combustion engine to drive a propeller for the first powered flight (1903). The petrol engine and propeller were the only method of producing thrust, until the jet engine first flew in 1941. Now all large aircraft are jet-propelled.

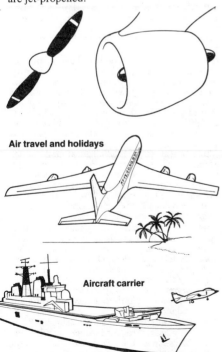

Air travel and holidays

Aircraft carrier

Birds can fly enormous distances in annual migrations. The Arctic tern holds the record; it flies 17 600 km each year from the Antarctic to its breeding ground in the Arctic.

Birds navigate by using the sun and polestars as constant references. In cloud a bird relies on the earth's magnetic lines of force, which are vertical at the magnetic poles and can be envisaged as forming a grid around the earth. The bird can maintain its direction by sensing the angles made by its body with these lines of force. The homing pigeon's navigating ability enabled it to be used by man as a message carrier from the earliest times.

Bats navigate and catch insects by means of echolocation – similar to radar. Their large ears can pick up echoes of high-pitched sounds reflected from distant objects.

Saint Antoine (1874), and the short stories in *Trois contes* (1877).

flax A plant of the N hemisphere with narrow leaves and blue flowers, whose stem fibres are used to make linen, fine paper, etc. The seeds produce *linseed oil.

flea A small wingless bloodsucking insect with legs modified for jumping. Fleas have irritating bites and move from host to host; some species carry serious diseases. Two widely distributed species are the human flea (*Pulex irritans*) and the oriental rat flea (*Xenopsylla cheopis*), which transmits bubonic plague and typhus to humans.

Flémalle, Master of (c. 1378–1444) One of the founders (with the *van Eyck brothers) of the Flemish school of painting. He is usually identified as Robert Campin. His works display the realistic details from everyday life that characterize the Flemish school.

Fleming, Sir Alexander (1881–1955) British microbiologist, who discovered *penicillin. In 1928 Fleming noticed that a mould contaminating a bacterial culture had destroyed the bacteria. He identified the mould but could not identify the antibiotic. This was later achieved by Lord *Florey and Sir Ernst *Chain, with whom Fleming shared the 1945 Nobel Prize.

Fleming, Sir John Ambrose (1849–1945) British electrical engineer, who constructed (1904) the first radio valve (*see* semiconductor diode). This led to the invention of the triode two years later by Lee De Forest (1873–1961), which heralded the age of radio.

Flemings Inhabitants of N and W Belgium who speak Flemish, a dialect of *Dutch, and seek to maintain their cultural identity. They number approximately 5 500 000. Like the Dutch they are descended from the Salic Franks, a Germanic people, who settled the area during the 3rd and 4th centuries AD. *See* Walloons.

fleur-de-lys A heraldic device, which has three petals turned outwards, resembling the bearded iris. It was the coat of arms of the French monarchy from the middle ages.

flight The ability to travel through the air. By the end of the 19th century it was clear that men were too heavy and too weak to fly like birds and insects. Aerofoils (*see* aeronautics) and the *internal-combustion engine, products of the 20th century, were required to enable *aircraft to become everyday means of travel. See pages 200–201.

flint A variety of *chalcedony. It is a hard grey mineral and breaks leaving sharp edges (hence its Stone Age use for tools and weapons). It occurs in chalk and as pebbles in river gravels, etc.

flint glass A highly refractive glass, also known as lead glass and crystal glass. It is used in high-quality glassware and in lenses.

Flodden, Battle of (9 September, 1513) The battle in which the English under Thomas Howard, Earl of Surrey (1443–1524), defeated the Scots under *James IV at Flodden Edge, Northumberland. The Scots had invaded England after allying with France against Henry VIII.

Florence (Italian name: Firenze) 43 47N 11 15E A city in Italy, the capital of Tuscany on the River Arno. Its buildings include the 13th-century cathedral of Sta Maria del Fiore. The Ponte Vecchio (1345) across the Arno connects the *Uffizi gallery to the Palazzo Pitti (now an art gallery). *History*: an early Roman colony, it had developed as a centre of trade by the 12th century. It flourished financially and culturally (14th–16th centuries) under the *Medici family. Following a period of Austrian rule in the 18th century, Florence became part of the kingdom of Italy in 1861 and was the provisional capital (1865–71). Population (1987): 421 299.

Florey, Howard Walter, Baron (1898–1968) Australian pathologist, who, working with Sir Ernst *Chain, isolated *penicillin and produced the pure drug in large quantities. In 1941 they conducted the first clinical trials, proving its value in combating bacterial infections. Florey shared the 1945 Nobel Prize with Chain and the discoverer Sir Alexander *Fleming.

Florida A state in the SE of the USA, between the Atlantic Ocean and the Gulf of Mexico. Tourism, based on its subtropical climate, is important, with many resorts, such as Palm Beach. The John F. Kennedy Space Center is at Cape Canaveral. Florida produces some 75% of the USA's citrus fruits. *History*: under Spanish rule from 1513, it was handed to the British in 1763 but returned to Spain after the American Revolution. It passed to the USA in 1819, becoming a state in 1845. It supported the Confederates during the US Civil War. Area: 151 670 sq km (58 560 sq mi). Population (1988 est): 12 262 425. Capital: Tallahassee.

flounder A European *flatfish, *Platichthys flesus*. It has a greenish or brownish mottled upper surface and is an important food and game fish.

flour The powdered grain of wheat or other cereals, used in baking bread. When the two proteins in wheat, glutenin and gliadin, are mixed with water they form gluten, which permits the dough to expand and retain the carbon dioxide resulting from fermentation of the yeast in bread dough. Different types of flour are made by varying the percentage of flour separated from the wheat. The principal commercial flours are whole wheat (100%), wholemeal and stone-ground (92%), wheatmeal (80–90%), and white flours (70–72%). Whole wheat and wholemeal flour retain more of the bran (the outer skin of the wheat grain) than white flour and are a good source of dietary *fibre. Self-raising flour is plain flour with the addition of raising agents.

flower The reproductive organ of flowering plants, essential for the production of seeds and fruits. It contains *stamens producing pollen (male gametes) and *carpels containing the female gametes. These are surrounded and protected by the petals and sepals, which in many plants secrete *nectar to attract insects and birds for pollination. Wind-pollinated flowers are small and inconspicuous.

flowering currant A garden shrub, *Ribes sanguineum*, native to North America and smelling of blackcurrants. Its clusters of pink flowers appear in early spring, before the maple-shaped leaves.

flowering quince. See japonica.

flowering rush A freshwater plant, *Butomus umbellatus*, native to Eurasia but common throughout temperate regions. A popular garden plant, it has long leaves and a cluster of pinkish flowers at the tip of a stalk.

fluid mechanics The study of the mechanical properties of fluids, i.e. gases and liquids. Hydrostatics is concerned with fluids at rest and hydrodynamics (or fluid dynamics) with fluids that are flowing. *Hydraulics deals with the practical applications of these sciences. Two important aspects of hydrodynamics are the conservation of energy in fluid flow and the distinction between streamline and turbulent flow. See also aerodynamics.

fluke A parasitic *flatworm that is typically leaf-shaped. They may live on the outer surface or inside the body. Some flukes spend their entire life cycle with the same host, while others have up to four different hosts, passing early larval stages in various invertebrates.

fluorescence. See luminescence.

fluorescent lamp A lamp that uses fluorescence (see luminescence) as its source of light. It consists of a glass tube containing a low-pressure gas, such as mercury vapour, through which a current is passed causing collisions between the free electrons and atoms of the gas. *Ultraviolet radiation emitted by the atoms strikes a phosphor coating on the inner surface of the tube, causing the phosphor to emit visible light.

fluoridation The addition of fluoride (usually sodium fluoride) to drinking water to reduce dental *caries (tooth decay), especially in children. The fluoride combines with a natural substance (apatite) in the tooth enamel to form fluoroapatite, which has a greater resistance to bacterial decay.

fluorine (F) A reactive pale-yellow gaseous element belonging to the *halogen group. It was first isolated by H. Moissan in 1886 and occurs as *fluorite (CaF_2) and cryolite (Na_3AlF_6). It is prepared by electrolysis of potassium hydrogen fluoride (KHF_2) solution in dry hydrofluoric acid (HF) and is important in the nuclear-power industry. See also fluoridation; fluorocarbons. At no 9; at wt 18.9984; mp $-219.62°C$; bp $-188.14°C$.

fluorite (or fluorspar) A mineral consisting of calcium fluoride (CaF_2). It occurs in hydrothermal veins, often in ore deposits, and in some igneous rocks. Most fluorite is used in iron and steel making; it is also used as a source of fluorine and in the ceramic and glass industries.

fluorocarbons Synthetic compounds of carbon and fluorine (sometimes also containing atoms of other halogens). They are resistant to chemical attack and are nontoxic and nonflammable. They are used as refrigerants, anaesthetics, and high-temperature lubricants. Polytetrafluoroethene (Teflon) is used for nonstick coatings in cooking utensils. **Chlorofluorocarbons** (CFCs), containing both fluorine and chlorine, have been used as propellants for aerosols, although this use is being restricted as they can lead to reactions in the upper atmosphere that can lead to depletion of the *ozone layer. See also pollution.

fluorspar. See fluorite.

flute A woodwind instrument of ancient origin. The modern side-blown flute (in which a column of air is made to vibrate by blowing across an oval mouth hole) and the *recorder are members of the same family. Originally made of wood, most flutes are now metal. The modern orchestral flute is about 0.6 m (2 ft) long and has a range of three octaves above middle C.

flux (physics) The net amount of a directional quantity passing through a surface area at right angles to the surface. A flux describes phenomena that involve forces or the flow of energy, such as electric flux, magnetic flux, and luminous flux.

fly An insect of which there are over 85 000 species. The adults have only two wings (the front pair), the hind pair being reduced to balancing organs. Most species feed on plant juices or the blood of mammals. The larvae—often called maggots—feed on plant and animal refuse or are parasites. Bloodsucking species, such as *mosquitoes and *tsetse flies, may transmit such diseases as malaria, sleeping sickness, and yellow fever. The housefly (*Musca domestica*) can spread such diseases as typhoid and dysentery by contaminating food. Blowflies, which include bluebottles, can be pests of sheep and cattle. The name fly is also used for various other flying insects.

fly agaric A poisonous (but rarely fatal) mushroom, *Amanita muscaria*, found in most woodlands. Its cap is red with white scales and the stalk is white. It was formerly used as a fly killer, hence its name.

flycatcher A small songbird that feeds on insects. It has a small bill surrounded by stiff bristles and delicate legs used for perching. Typical flycatchers include the grey-and-brown European spotted flycatcher (*Muscicapa striata*) and the black-and-white pied flycatcher (*Ficedula hypoleuca*).

Flying Doctor Service of Australia, Royal A scheme begun in 1928 at Cloncurry, Queensland, to transport doctors to patients in remote areas. The development of a Morse radio transmitter-receiver made long-range consultation and emergency treatment easier. The service is free.

Flying Dutchman A legendary ship haunting the sea around the Cape of Good Hope. Its captain, driven back from the Cape by a storm, swore a blasphemous oath to round it or be forever damned. The story inspired Wagner's opera (1843) of the same name.

flying fish A fish that swims just below the surface in warm seas. If disturbed it jumps from the water by beating the tail and glides through the air using winglike pectoral fins.

flying fox A fruit *bat ranging from Africa to Australia. Flying foxes have foxlike heads and a wingspan of up to 1.5 m.

flying lizard A lizard of SE Asia, having large folds of brightly coloured skin between the legs supported by ribs that are spread out when the lizard jumps from a tree.

flying snake A slender snake occurring in S Asia and the East Indies. By launching themselves from trees into the air and flattening their belly scales they can glide short distances.

flying squirrel A nocturnal *squirrel occurring in SE Asia, North America, and Eurasia. Flying squirrels have a flap of loose skin from elbow to knee that is stretched tight by extending the legs, enabling them to glide from branch to branch.

Flynn, Errol (1909–59) Australian actor. He played the handsome adventurous hero in such Hollywood films as *Captain Blood* (1935), *Gentleman Jim* (1942), and (as John Barrymore) *Too Much Too Soon* (1958).

flytrap. *See* Venus flytrap.

f-number The ratio of the focal length of a camera lens to the diameter of the shutter opening (aperture). For example, f-8 means that the focal length is eight times the aperture. The smaller the f-number, the greater the illumination of the film.

Foch, Ferdinand (1851–1929) French marshal. In World War I he was responsible for halting the German advance at the Marne and the Allied victory at Ypres (1915). After the Somme offensive (1916), he became chief of the general staff (1917). In 1918, as Allied commander in chief, he forced the Germans back to the Rhine, effecting their defeat.

foetus. *See* fetus.

fog A cloud near the ground, within which visibility is less than 1 km (0.6 mi). Fog is the result of the *condensation of water on particles in the lower air, usually through the cooling of air to below its *dew point; it often occurs in industrial areas.

föhn A warm dry wind that descends down the leeward side of mountains. It occurs in the Alps, the Rocky Mountains (where it is known as the **chinook**), and the Andes. In winter it can cause avalanches by thawing snow.

Fokine, Michel (Mikhail F.; 1880–1942) Russian ballet dancer and choreographer. From 1909 he worked with Diaghilev's Ballets Russes in Paris, choreographing such ballets as *The Firebird* (1910) and *Petrushka* (1911). He became a US citizen in 1932.

fold A buckling of sedimentary rock strata by compression. Large-scale folding produces mountain ranges when two continental plates collide (*see* plate tectonics) and the sediment along their margins is compressed and folded. A simple upfold is called an anticline and a downfold, a syncline.

folic acid. *See* vitamin B complex.

Folies-Bergère A Parisian theatre opened in 1869, famous for its revues featuring scantily clad dancing girls.

folk dance A form of dance developed from ritual dances used in religious worship and to invoke fertility of the land. They have influenced other forms of dances, notably court dancing, 18th- and 19th-century ballroom dances, and *ballet. In England the most popular types are country dancing and the Morris dance.

Folkestone 51 5N 1 11E A resort and port in SE England, in Kent, with Channel crossings to Boulogne. Population (1983 est): 44 200.

folklore The social, material, and oral culture of primitive societies. The social culture includes festivals, dances, and religious rites; the material culture comprises architecture and arts and crafts; the oral culture includes songs, tales, and proverbs.

folk music Music developed from a communal tradition rather than composed by an individual. Examples are Irish ballads, cowboy songs, lullabies, work songs, and love ballads.

follicle-stimulating hormone. *See* gonadotrophin.

Fonda, Henry (1905–82) US film actor and director, whose films include *The Grapes of Wrath* (1940), *War and Peace* (1956), *Twelve Angry Men* (1957), which he directed, and *On Golden Pond* (1981), which earned him an Oscar and also starred his daughter **Jane Fonda** (1937–). Her other films include *Klute* (1971), *Julia* (1977), and *Old Gringo* (1990).

Fontainebleau 48 24N 2 42E A town in N central France, in the Seine-et-Marne department. The 16th-century Royal Palace was largely built by Francis I. Fontainebleau was the headquarters of NATO from 1954 to 1966. Population (1982): 18 753.

Fonteyn, Dame Margot (Margaret Hookham; 1919–91) British ballet dancer, who was a member of the Sadler's Wells company and the Royal Ballet from 1934 to 1959. She performed with most leading US and European companies, often with Rudolf *Nureyev.

Foochow. *See* Fuzhou.

Food and Agriculture Organization (FAO) A specialized agency of the *United Nations set up in 1945 in Rome to supervise international efforts to increase food production and improve the management of forests.

food chain A means of describing how living organisms feed on each other. Most commonly, green plants are at the base of a chain; they are eaten by herbivores, which in turn may be consumed by carnivores. Different food chains are often interconnected to form a **food web**. Other food chains are based on decomposers—organisms that feed on remains of plants and animals.

food poisoning An illness, usually with vomiting and diarrhoea, caused by food contaminated by bacteria (e.g. *Salmonella). Some bacteria produce toxins (poisons) within the body, notably *Clostridium* bacteria, which cause *botulism, the most severe form of food poisoning.

fool's gold. *See* pyrite.

foot-and-mouth disease An infectious virus disease affecting cattle, sheep, goats, pigs, and many wild animals. Symptoms include fever, blisters in the mouth and on the foot, with excessive salivation and lameness. Recovery occurs in 95% of cases but production of offspring and milk yield is reduced. Control is by slaughter of infected animals. The disease must be notifed to the authorities in many countries.

football A field game developed in the 19th century and played throughout the world, the

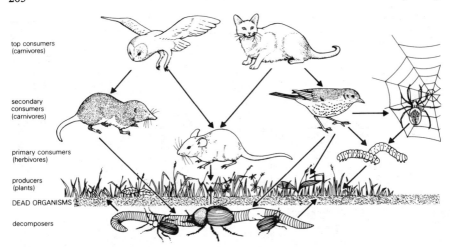

top consumers (carnivores)

secondary consumers (carnivores)

primary consumers (herbivores)

producers (plants)

DEAD ORGANISMS

decomposers

FOOD CHAIN *The feeding relationships between some plants and animals of a meadow habitat are simplified in this food web; in practice many more links and various other organisms are involved.*

object of which is to score goals with an inflated ball.

American football is played with an oval ball on a field marked out as a gridiron. There are 22 players on the field. The game progresses in downs, or periods when the offensive team is advancing the ball towards the goal by passing or running with it. A touchdown, in which the ball is taken across the opponents' goal line, scores six points; a conversion after a touchdown, in which the ball is taken over the goal line again from scrimmage or is kicked between the goalposts, scores respectively two points or one point; a field goal (kicked from anywhere on the field) scores three points. Players wear protective clothing.

Association football (*or* soccer) dates back to the founding in England of the Football Association (1863). It is an 11-a-side game played with a round ball weighing 14–16 oz (396–453 g) and having a circumference of 27–28 in (69–71 cm). The traditional positions of the players are: goal-keeper; two backs; three half-backs; and five forwards; however, in a modern line-up there are only strikers, midfield players, and defenders. Players compete for the ball and try to kick or head the ball into the opponents' goal. Only the goalkeeper may use his hands, and then only in his penalty area. The game is governed internationally by the Fédération internationale de Football association (FIFA).

Australian Rules is an 18-a-side game played with an oval ball measuring 22.75 by 29.5 in (57.2 by 73.6 cm), with which players may run as long as they bounce it every 9 m (10 yd). The ball must be punched rather than thrown. There are four goalposts without crossbars at each end. A goal, kicked between the two inner posts, scores six points; a behind, kicked between an inner and an outer post, scores one point.

Rugby football uses an oval ball that is kicked or passed by hand. The game was first played at

Rugby School, England, according to tradition in 1823. In 1871 the Rugby Football Union was formed, but its ban on professionalism led in 1893 to the formation of the separate Rugby League (then called the Northern Union). **Rugby Union football** (*or* rugger) is a 15-a-side amateur game played throughout the world. The ball is 11–11.25 in (27.9–28.6 cm) long. A try, in which the ball is touched down behind the opponents' goal line, is worth four points; a goal (a try "converted" by kicking the ball over the crossbar of the goalposts), a further two points; a penalty goal and a drop goal each score three points. A scrum, in which the forwards of both teams battle for the ball in a tight mass, is used to restart the game after minor infringements. **Rugby League football** is a 13-a-side game with slightly different rules and scoring in which professionalism is allowed; it is played mainly in N England.

force The agency that changes either the speed or the direction of motion of a body (symbol: *F*). It is a *vector quantity defined as the product of the mass of the body and the acceleration produced on it. Force is measured in newtons. *See also* centripetal force; Coriolis force.

Ford, Ford Madox (Ford Hermann Hueffer; 1873–1939) British novelist, grandson of the Pre-Raphaelite artist Ford Madox Brown. Among his 80 or more novels and books of criticism and memoirs are the novels *The Good Soldier* (1915) and *Parade's End* (1924–28), a tetralogy.

Ford, Gerald R(udolph) (1913–) US statesman; Republican president (1974–77) following Nixon's resignation.

Ford, Henry (1863–1947) US car manufacturer, who founded the Ford Motor Company in 1903 and in 1912 introduced the assembly line to manufacture the famous Model T, 15 million of which had been produced by 1928.

FOOTBALL

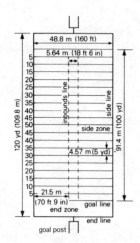

American football

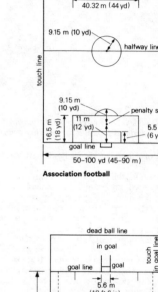

Association football

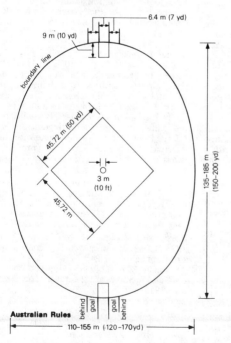

Australian Rules

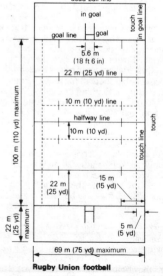

Rugby Union football

FOOTBALL *Dimensions of pitches.*

Foreign and Commonwealth Office The UK government department that is responsible for presenting and furthering the interests of the UK abroad; it was formed in 1968 when the Foreign Office and the Commonwealth Office merged and is headed by the secretary of state for foreign and commonwealth affairs.

Foreign Legion A French military force formed in 1831 to serve in France's African colonies. Its soldiers are international but its officers are usually French. The headquarters are at Aubagne, near Marseille.

forest Land covered with trees and undergrowth. Over 20% of land is forest, providing oxygen, timber, and habitats for wildlife. Northern coniferous forests consist largely of pine, spruce, and firs. In temperate regions forests consist primarily of deciduous trees, especially oak, ash, elm, beech, and sycamore. In Mediterranean climates, the trees include the evergreen oaks. Broad-leaved evergreens are also found in New Zealand and South America, together with southern conifers. Tropical forests contain tall evergreen trees, with many climbing vines and *epiphytes. The major rain forests are in the Amazon and Orinoco river basins, with others in Africa and SE Asia.

Forestry, the cultivation of forests, is of major economic importance. The felling of many tropical rain forests for timber and to clear land for farming could damage the Earth's climate and atmosphere.

Forester, C(ecil) S(cott) (1899–1966) British historical novelist who created Horatio Hornblower, a British naval officer of Napoleonic times, in a series of novels beginning with *The Happy Return* (1937).

forget-me-not A plant that grows in temperate regions. It has long spikes of small blue flowers. Several species are grown as garden plants.

formic acid (*or* methanoic acid; HCOOH) A colourless corrosive liquid *fatty acid with a pungent smell. It is used in textile finishing and chemical manufacture. Its name comes from the Latin *formica*, ant, whose sting is due to the secretion of formic acid.

Formosa. *See* Taiwan.

Forster, E(dward) M(organ) (1879–1970) British novelist, whose works include *Where Angels Fear to Tread* (1905), *The Longest Journey* (1907), *A Room with a View* (1908), *Howard's End* (1910), and *A Passage to India* (1924).

forsythia A of shrub of the olive family, native to E Europe and Asia and widely grown for shrubs and hedges. The four-petalled yellow flowers appear before the leaves.

Forth, River A river in SE Scotland, rising on the NE slopes of Ben Lomond and flowing 104 km (65 mi) E through Stirling to Alloa. The river then expands into the **Firth of Forth** extending 82 km (51 mi) in length and 31 km (19 mi) wide at its mouth. It is spanned by the cantilever iron Forth Rail Bridge (designed in the 1880s by Benjamin Baker) and a road bridge (1964).

Fort Knox 37 54N 85 59W A military base in the USA, in N Kentucky. Established in 1917, it is the site of the US Depository, which contains US gold reserves. Population (1989 est): 38 277.

Fort Lamy. *See* N'djamena.

Fortran (*formula translation*) A computer-programming language, widely used among scientists and engineers.

Fortuna The Roman goddess of good luck, usually portrayed on a ball or wheel, indicating her changeability, and holding a cornucopia from which she distributes her favours. She is identical with the Greek Tyche.

Fort Worth 32 45N 97 20W A city in the USA, in NE Texas near Dallas, centre of the N Texas industrial area. Population (1989): 459 000.

Forty-five Rebellion. *See* Jacobites.

forum A Roman marketplace. The forum was the civic centre of the town, containing all the main temples and public buildings.

Fosse Way A Roman road from Exeter through Cirencester to Lincoln. It marked the frontier in the first phase of the Roman conquest of Britain (c. 47 AD). Its characteristically straight course is now followed partly by the modern A429.

fossil The remains or traces of a plant or animal, usually preserved in *sedimentary rock. It may be the organism itself that is preserved, usually chemically altered; alternatively it may have dissolved leaving an impression (mould) or a cast. Examples of fossils are whole mammoths preserved in ice, insects preserved in amber, and coal (the carbonized remains of extinct swamp plants). The study of fossils is called *palaeontology.

fossil fuels The mineral fuels *coal, *oil, and *natural gas that occur in rock formations and supply nearly 90% of world *energy needs. They were formed from the remains of vegetation (coal) and living organisms (oil and gas), millions of years old, buried under subsequent deposits and later subjected to heat and pressure.

Foucault pendulum A long pendulum with a heavy bob. It demonstrates the earth's rotation since its plane of oscillation slowly rotates. It was invented by Jean Foucault (1819–68) and first demonstrated in 1851 in Paris.

Fountains Abbey A ruined *Cistercian abbey near Ripon, Yorkshire. Founded in 1132, it became the leading Cistercian community in England and had great wealth prior to its dissolution (1539) at the *Reformation.

fowl, domestic A form of the red *jungle fowl, *Gallus gallus*, native to Asian forests. It was first domesticated about 4000 years ago for use in religious ceremonies and used by the Romans for food. Since the 19th century, many breeds and varieties have been developed.

fowl pest An infectious virus disease affecting domestic fowl and certain other birds. Symptoms include a fall in egg production, loss of appetite and energy, laboured breathing, and nasal discharge. In the UK any outbreak must be reported. Vaccination confers immunity after 10–14 days.

fox A carnivorous mammal related to the *dog. Foxes have pointed ears, short legs, and bushy tails. Generally nocturnal, they are stealthy hunters. The most familiar is the red fox (*Vulpes vulpes*), found in woodland and increasingly in suburban gardens. Some species are spe-

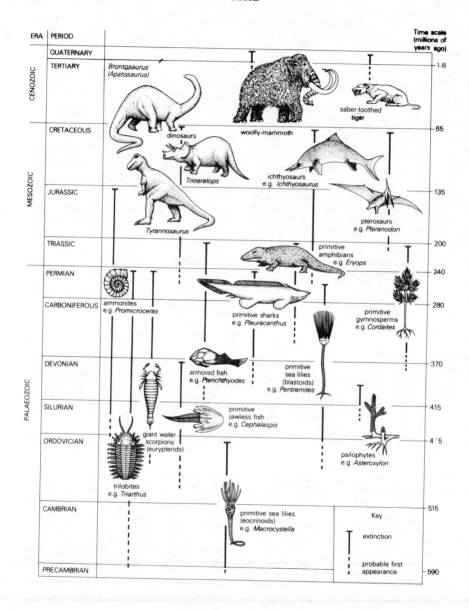

FOSSIL *Some extinct animals and plants from past geological ages.*

cialized for life in difficult habitats, such as the *Arctic fox and the *fennec.

Fox, Charles James (1749–1806) British Whig politician; the first British foreign secretary (1782). He entered parliament (1768) as a supporter of Lord *North but opposed his American policy. He joined North again in a coalition that briefly took office under the Duke of Portland (1738–1809) in 1783. Fox was dismissed from the privy council in 1798 for opposing war with Revolutionary France.

Fox, George (1624–91) English religious leader, founder of the *Quakers. A Puritan by upbringing, Fox became dissatisfied with state control of the church. In 1646 he had a personal revelation and thereafter preached a gospel of love. He was frequently imprisoned for his beliefs.

foxglove A flowering plant, *Digitalis purpurea*, native to W Europe. Foxgloves have large leaves and tall spikes of bell-shaped purple, yellow, or white flowers. The dried leaves contain *digitalis.

foxhound A breed of dog used for foxhunting. Developed in England, it is strongly built, with a short coat coloured black, tan, and white. Height: 56–63 cm.

foxhunting A sport in which mounted huntsmen pursue a fox with a pack of 20 to 30 *foxhounds. It has been organized in the UK since the 18th century. Hunt officials, dressed in scarlet coats, are the master of foxhounds, who directs the hounds, and one or more whippers-in, who help to control them. Hunting has many opponents (notably the League against Cruel Sports) and Oscar Wilde described it as "the unspeakable in pursuit of the uneatable".

fox terrier A sturdy breed of dog, either smooth-haired or wire-haired, developed in England for hunting foxes and badgers. The coat is mainly white with black and tan markings. Height: 37–39 cm.

fracture The breaking of a bone, either by accident or in bones weakened by disease. Fractures are treated by lining up the ends of the broken bone and ensuring they cannot move until they have grown together. Sometimes, however, it is necessary to pin fractures surgically.

Fragonard, Jean Honoré (1732–1806) French *rococo painter whose light-hearted subjects include *The Swing* and *The Progress of Love*. Dutch influence is apparent in his landscapes and portraits. He died in obscurity.

France, Anatole (Jacques Anatole François Thibault; 1844–1924) French novelist, whose intervention in the *Dreyfus case (1897) marked the beginning of his commitment to socialism and, during his final years, communism. His novels include *L'Ile des pingouins* (1909) and *Les Dieux ont soif* (1913). He was awarded the Nobel Prize in 1921.

France, Republic of A country in W Europe, bordering on the English Channel in the N, the Atlantic Ocean in the W, and the Mediterranean Sea in the S. It includes the island of Corsica and several overseas regions and territories (including Martinique, Guadeloupe, French Guiana, French Polynesia, and New Caledonia). The principal rivers are the Seine, the Loire, and the Rhône. *Economy*: agriculture and the wine industry are important, with major industrial developments since World War II. *History*: as the ancient *Gaul, it was conquered by Julius Caesar in the 1st century BC. From the 3rd to the 5th centuries, it was overrun by Goths, Vandals, and *Franks (from whom the name France is derived). Charlemagne (reigned 768–814) and his Carolingian dynasty ruled in France until 987, when Hugh Capet became the first Capetian king. During the 10th century Norsemen (Vikings) established themselves in what became Normandy; in 1066 the Normans invaded England. Conflict between France and England culminated in the *Hundred Years' War (1337–1453). The Capetians were succeeded by the Valois dynasty (1328–1589), and the start of rivalry with Spain for domination of Europe. During the *Wars of Religion the first *Bourbon, Henry IV, came to the throne (1589). During the 17th century Cardinal de *Richelieu and his successor, Cardinal Mazarin, were responsible for France becoming the supreme European power. During the reign (1643–1715) of *Louis XIV France reached the peak of its brilliance. The incompetence of the later Bourbon kings precipitated the *French Revolution in 1789. The First Republic was proclaimed (1792) and Louis XVI was guillotined (1793) (*see* Revolutionary and Napoleonic Wars). In 1799 *Napoleon Bonaparte became first consul and, in 1804, emperor. By 1808 he had brought most of Europe under his power but in 1815 he was finally defeated at *Waterloo. The Bourbons were restored until 1830, when the July Revolution brought Louis Philippe to the throne. Overthrown in the *Revolution of 1848, the monarchy was replaced by the Second Republic of which Louis Napoleon became president; in 1852 he proclaimed himself emperor as *Napoleon III. France was defeated in the *Franco-Prussian War and Napoleon was overthrown in 1870. The subsequent Third Republic lasted until 1940. Early in World War II France fell to Germany and a puppet government was established at Vichy, while *de Gaulle led the Free French in London. In 1944 France was liberated and de Gaulle established a provisional government that gave way (1946) to the Fourth Republic. War in Indochina and the crisis in Algeria led to the fall of the Fourth Republic (1958); de Gaulle, as president of the Fifth Republic, instituted firm government. In 1969 he resigned after strikes and student revolts. Mitterrand's election (1981) made him the first socialist to become president in 35 years; proportional representation was introduced for subsequent elections. Official language: French. Official currency: franc of 100 centimes. Area: 543 814 sq km (209 912 sq mi). Population (1988): 55 840 000. Capital: Paris. Main port: Marseille.

Francis Ferdinand (1863–1914) Archduke of Austria and heir apparent to his uncle, Emperor *Francis Joseph. His assassination (28 June, 1914) by a Serbian nationalist at Sarajevo precipitated *World War I.

Francis Joseph (1830–1916) Emperor of Austria (1848–1916) and King of Hungary

(1867–1916). His long reign led to the establishment of the Dual Monarchy of *Austria-Hungary. In 1879 he allied with the German Empire and in 1882 with Italy, forming the *Triple Alliance. His ultimatum to Serbia, following the assassination of Archduke *Francis Ferdinand (1914), led to *World War I.

Francis of Assisi, St (Giovanni di Bernardone; c. 1182–1226) Italian friar born in Assisi. He renounced worldly life in 1205 to live in poverty and devote himself to prayer. He founded the *Franciscans in 1209. He is often portrayed in paintings in the countryside among animals and birds. He was made a saint in 1228. Feast day: 4 Oct.

Francis Xavier, St (1506–52) Spanish *Jesuit missionary. While studying in Paris (1523–34) he met St *Ignatius of Loyola and helped him found the Jesuit order. From 1541 he worked in the Indies, India, and Japan. Feast day: 3 Dec.

Franciscans An order of friars founded in 1209 by St *Francis of Assisi. His rule imposed poverty on the members and the order. In the early 14th century the order split over how strictly the rule should be followed. It survived, however, and has remained important in the Roman Catholic Church.

francium (Fr) The heaviest alkali metal, a radioactive element discovered in 1939 by Perey. The longest-lived isotope ^{223}Fr has a half-life of 22 minutes. At no 87; at wt (223).

Franck, César Auguste (1822–90) Belgian composer who settled in Paris in 1834. Franck was influenced by Bach and also developed "cyclic form," the use of the same theme in more than one movement of a work. His compositions include *Symphonic Variations* (for piano and orchestra; 1885), a symphony (1886–88), a violin sonata (1886), and a string quartet (1889).

Franco, Francisco (1892–1975) Spanish general and dictator from 1939 until his death. He became chief of the General Staff in 1935 and on 18 July, 1936, staged a military uprising against the Republican Government that led to the *Spanish Civil War. By 1939, with help from Hitler and Mussolini, he had defeated the Republicans and become a ruthless dictator. Franco's government, in which the National Movement (*see* Falange Española) was the only political party, maintained neutrality throughout World War II. Excluded from the UN in 1945, Spain's isolation was ended in the 1950s, when Franco's anticommunism made him an attractive ally.

Franco-Prussian War (1870–71) A war between France and Prussia. France under Napoleon III declared war, fearing Bismarck's proposals to make a relative of William I of Prussia the king of Spain. The French army was soon defeated at the battle of *Sedan. Napoleon was exiled and the Third Republic was established. At the Treaty of Frankfurt France gave up Alsace and Lorraine to the newly established German Empire.

frangipani A tropical American tree, *Plumeria rubra*, cultivated throughout the tropics. It has tapering leaves and round clusters of fragrant pink, reddish-purple, white, or yellow flowers, used to make perfume.

Frank, Anne (1929–45) German Jewish girl, who died in a German concentration camp. Her diary, written while hiding from the Nazis in Amsterdam in 1942–43, became a symbol of Jewish resistance and courage following its publication in 1947.

Frankfurt am Main 50 06N 8 41E A city in W Germany, in Hessen on the River Main. A major commercial centre, it is famed for its annual book fair. It was the seat of the imperial elections (9th to 18th centuries) and coronations (1562–1792) of the Holy Roman emperors. Population (1990): 622 500.

frankincense (*or* olibanum) A *resin obtained chiefly from the tree *Boswellia carteri*, which grows in the Middle East. It burns with a fragrant odour and has been known since ancient times; it is still used as an *incense, in fumigants, and in perfumes.

Franklin, Benjamin (1706–90) US diplomat, scientist, and author. His experiments with electricity, especially the episode in which he flew a kite during a thunderstorm, established the electrical nature of thunderstorms and led him to invent the lightning conductor. In the disputes that led to the American Revolution he represented Pennsylvania's case to Britain (1757–62, 1766–75) and helped frame the Declaration of Independence (1775). As a diplomat he enlisted French help for the colonies and later negotiated peace with Britain (1783).

Franks A Germanic people, who invaded Roman *Gaul between the 3rd and 5th centuries AD. One of the Frankish tribes, the Salian Franks, gained control of most of Gaul under their ruler Clovis (d. 511). The Carolingians, including *Charlemagne, ruled the Franks from 751 until 843. The western Frankish kingdom was the core of France.

Franz Josef Land (Russian name: Zemlya Frantsa Iosifa) A group of about 85 icebound Soviet islands in the N Barents Sea. They were discovered in 1873 by Austrians and annexed by the Soviet Union in 1926. Total area: about 20 700 sq km (79 905 sq mi).

Fraser River The chief river of British Columbia in Canada. Rising near Mount Robson, it flows through mountain gorges and empties into the Strait of Georgia near Vancouver. Length: 1370 km (850 mi).

fraud In law, deception, by words or action or by not revealing facts where there is a duty to do so, for financial gain. To prove fraud it is necessary to show that the deception was made (1) knowingly, (2) without belief in its truth, or (3) without concern whether it was true or not.

Frederick (I) Barbarossa (c. 1123–90) Holy Roman Emperor (1152–90; crowned 1155). A long struggle with the papacy ended with his excommunication in 1160. His warring against the Lombard cities was ultimately unsuccessful; they regained their independence in 1183. He established his authority in Poland, Hungary, Bohemia, and Burgundy.

Frederick II (1194–1250) Holy Roman Emperor (1220–50) and, as Frederick I, King of Sicily (1198–1250). As leader of the fifth Crusade (1228–29) he captured Jerusalem but opposed papal policy and was excommunicated in 1227, 1239, and 1245.

Frederick (II) the Great (1712–86) King of Prussia (1740–86). He liberalized the Prussian legal code and introduced economic and social reforms. His conquest of Silesia (1740) caused the War of the *Austrian Succession (1740–48), after which his possession of the region was confirmed. His victory in the *Seven Years' War (1756–63) confirmed the military supremacy of Prussia.

freehold. *See* estate.

freemasonry A secret society for men, based on brotherly love, faith, and charity. It developed from the medieval stonemasons' guilds. Modern freemasonry began with the establishment (1717) in England of the Grand Lodge, to which over 8000 lodges belong. Its ceremonies, based on Old Testament stories, demand a vow of secrecy as well as a belief in God. In 1738 masons were excommunicated by the pope, since when Catholics have never accepted the principles of masonry. It is banned in E Europe.

freesia A South African plant of the iris family, cultivated commercially. Growing from corms, they have sword-shaped leaves and clusters of scented flowers of various colours. Most cultivated varieties are hybrids of *Freesia refracta* (with yellowish flowers) and *F. armstrongii* (purple flowers).

freestyle wrestling. *See* wrestling.

Freetown 8 20N 13 05W The capital and main port of Sierra Leone, on the Atlantic coast. It was founded in the late 18th century as a refuge for freed slaves and was capital of British West Africa (1808–74), becoming the capital of Sierra Leone in 1961. Population (1985): 469 776.

free verse Poetry without regular metre or form that depends on the rhythms of natural speech. The original French term, *vers libre*, was coined during the 1880s by poets who wished to emphasize rhythm as the essential principle of poetry.

free will In philosophy and theology, the ability of man to choose his own destiny, as opposed to the idea that everything that happens to him is inevitable. Philosophers are concerned to discover how free will affects the way man lives, as compared to *determinism.

freeze drying A method of drying foods for preservation in which the food is rapidly frozen under low pressure. Any water present freezes and then changes directly to water vapour under the low pressure.

Fremantle 32 07S 115 44E A major seaport in Western Australia, SW of Perth at the mouth of the Swan River. Kwinana, an important industrial complex with oil and nickel refineries and bulk-grain facilities, is nearby. Population (1986): 24 010.

French A Romance language spoken in France, Canada, Belgium, Switzerland, and elsewhere. It is the official language of 21 countries. Standard French, based upon a Parisian dialect, has been France's official language since 1539. It

has replaced most northern dialects, known collectively as *langue d'oïl*, and the Occitan dialects of S France known as *langue d'oc* (*see* Provençal). During the 17th century the *Académie Française and the publication of a standard dictionary (1680) quickly made the language stable.

French bean A plant, *Phaseolus vulgaris*, of the pea family, also called kidney bean, probably native to South America. It has heart-shaped leaves and white flowers. The plants are grown for their beans, usually eaten in the pod. *See also* haricot bean.

French Community An association of states, consisting of France and its former colonies, established by the Fifth Republic (1958). It includes Guadeloupe, Guiana, Martinique, Mayotte, La Réunion, St Pierre and Miquelon, Southern and Antarctic Territories, French Polynesia, New Caledonia, and Wallis and Futuna.

French Guiana A French overseas region on the NE coast of South America. A narrow coastal belt rises to a mountainous interior, covered in forest. *History*: it was settled in the 17th century, when the French, Dutch, Portuguese, and English competed for possession. In 1817 it was secured by France, who established penal colonies, including one on Devil's Island. The French Guianese have had full French citizenship since 1848. Area: about 91 000 sq km (34 740 sq mi). Population (1988 est): 90 500. Capital: Cayenne.

French horn An orchestral brass transposing instrument, developed from the hunting horn. It consists of a coiled tube with a wide bell and a cup-shaped mouthpiece. In the 18th century crooks of tubing were inserted to enable it to change a key. In the 19th century valves were fitted giving the horn in F a complete range of about three octaves above B below the bass stave.

French Polynesia A French overseas territory in the S Pacific Ocean consisting of several island groups. The most important of these are the Gambier Islands, the Society Archipelago, the Tuamotu Archipelago, the Tubuai Islands, and the Marquesas Islands. Area: about 4000 sq km (1500 sq mi). Population (1988 est): 191 400. Capital: Papeete.

French Republican calendar The calendar adopted (1793) in France during the Revolution and kept until 1806, when the Gregorian *calendar was reintroduced. The year began on 22 Sept (the foundation date of the Republic) and had 365 days divided into 12 months of 30 days each. The remaining 5 days were festivals, an extra one being added in a leap year.

French Revolution The overthrow of the incompetent government of the French Bourbon kings. In 1789 Louis XVI was forced to summon the *States General but when the nobility attempted to dominate proceedings, the commons formed its own National Assembly. Riots followed, the *Bastille was stormed, and the Assembly proclaimed the Declaration of the *Rights of Man. Feudalism was abolished and in September, 1791, the king accepted a new constitution. However, his lack of cooperation eventually led to the proclamation of a republic and in January, 1793, Louis was executed. The moderate republican Girondins were ousted by the extremist Jacobins and power passed to the Committee of Public Safety. Under *Robespierre the Committee conducted a *Reign of Terror in which thousands were executed. His extremism brought his downfall (1794). Napoleon's coup d'état (1799) brought the Revolution to an end.

French Somaliland. *See* Djibouti, Republic of.

French Sudan. *See* Mali, Republic of.

frequency The number of cycles completed by a vibrating system in unit time, usually one second (symbol: v or f). The unit of frequency is the *hertz. The angular frequency, ω, is related to the frequency by the equation $\omega = 2\pi f$ and is measured in radians per second.

frequency modulation. *See* modulation.

fresco A classical and Renaissance method of wall decoration in which pigments dissolved in water were applied to the wet lime-plastered surface of a wall, making the colours a permanent part of the wall. Up to about 1500 the design was sketched onto the plaster surface and detailed colour was applied in layers of different pigments. Subsequently the composition was drawn on sheets of paper, later applied to the wall, and the design pricked through with a stylus or with charcoal dust forced through the stylus holes. Fresco painting was revived in the 20th century by the Mexican muralist *Rivera.

Freud, Sigmund (1856–1939) Austrian pioneer of psychoanalysis. Freud studied medicine and, in 1882, joined a psychiatric clinic in Vienna. His theory that neuroses were rooted in suppressed sexual desires and sexual experiences of childhood aroused great controversy. In *The Interpretation of Dreams* (1899), he analysed the content of dreams in terms of unconscious desires. In 1902 Freud established a circle in Vienna, which later (1910) became the International Psycho-Analytical Society. However, many of its members, including Carl *Jung and Alfred *Adler, resigned over disagreements. Freud moved to London in 1938. His books include *The Psychopathology of Everyday Life* (1904), *Totem and Taboo* (1913), and *Beyond the Pleasure Principle* (1920).

Freyja (*or* Freya) The Norse goddess of love and fertility, the sister of Frey, the god of sunshine, rain, and fertility. She is the Norse counterpart of Venus and is the leader of the *Valkyries.

friction A force exerted at the boundary between two solids or fluids that slows down motion between them. With two solids in contact, the rolling friction arising when an object rolls over a surface is less than the friction arising from two surfaces sliding over each other, which accounts for the effectiveness of wheels and ball bearings.

Friedman, Milton (1912–) US economist, known for his theories on monetary supply, which contradict those of *Keynes. His published work, which argues for the free market economy, includes *A Theory of the Consumption Function* (1957) and *Capitalism and Freedom* (1962). He won the 1976 Nobel Prize.

Friendly Islands. *See* Tonga, Kingdom of.

friendly societies Voluntary self-help associations the members of which regularly contribute to central funds that provide financial help in times of illness, old age, or death. First formed in the 17th century, the societies inspired many other self-help and insurance schemes.

Friends of the Earth A British environmental pressure group. Established in 1971, it campaigns through demonstrations, public meetings, and parliament. Targets have included motorway projects, whaling, and industrial pollution (including nuclear power plants). The organization also has branches in 25 countries.

Friesian cattle A breed of black-and-white cattle originating from the province of Friesland in the Netherlands. They were exported to North America by early settlers and there developed as Holstein-Friesians. They are high-yielding milk producers and crosses, especially with a Charolais or Hereford bull, give good beef.

frigate bird A seabird occurring in tropical and subtropical oceanic regions, also called man-of-war bird. 80–115 cm long, it has narrow wings, a hooked bill, and a forked tail. Males are black with an inflatable red throat sac in the breeding season; females are brownish with white underparts.

Frisian A West Germanic language formerly spoken along the coastal region of Holland as far as Schleswig in Germany. It is now mainly spoken in Friesland province in Holland and certain offshore islands including Heligoland. It is the language closest to English.

Frisian Islands A chain of islands in the North Sea extending along the coast of, and politically divided between, the Netherlands, Germany, and SW Denmark. The chain comprises three main groups: the West, North, and East Frisian Islands.

fritillary (botany) A plant of the lily family that grows from a bulb and has bell-shaped drooping flowers. The European snake's head (*Fritillaria meleagris*) has reddish flowers. The crown imperial (*F. imperialis*), native to N India, has a cluster of red flowers at the top of a tall (120 cm) stem, topped by a tuft of leaves.

fritillary (zoology) A widely distributed butterfly, usually brown or orange marked with black.

Friuli-Venezia Giulia A region in the extreme NE of Italy. It was formed in 1947, incorporating Trieste in 1954, and has limited self-government. There is farming throughout the region. Area: 7850 sq km (3031 sq mi). Population (1987 est): 1 210 242. Capital: Trieste.

frog A tail-less *amphibian that spends most of its life on land, feeding on insects, and only returns to water to breed. The European frog (*Rana temporaria*) grows to 10 cm; it is greenish with black markings.

froghopper A small jumping insect that feeds on plant juices. Eggs are laid on stems or roots and the *nymphs remain stationary until adult. They often protect themselves against predators by a covering of white froth ("cuckoo spit"). For this reason they are often known as cuckoo-spit insects and spittlebugs.

front In meteorology, the boundary between two air masses of different temperatures. Where the air masses converge the warm air, being lighter, rises and slopes over the cold air. *Depressions are associated with fronts.

frost A weather condition that occurs when the temperature falls below 0°C (32°F). It is recognized by the icy deposit that forms but if the air is very dry this will not occur. In weather forecasting grades of severity of frost are distinguished as slight (−0.1 to −3.5°C), moderate (−3.6 to −6.4°C), severe (−6.5 to −11.5°C), and very severe (below −11.5°C). A distinction is made between ground frost, measured at grass level, and air frost, measured at a height of 1.4 m (4 ft).

Frost, Robert Lee (1874–1963) US poet. He became famous with the publication of *A Boy's Will* (1913) and *North of Boston* (1914).

frostbite Damage to part of the body, usually a hand or foot, resulting from exposure to extreme cold. The blood vessels to the affected limb are narrowed so that little blood (and therefore essential oxygen) reaches it. This may lead to loss of sensation, ulcers, and eventually gangrene. Initial treatment is gently to warm the affected part.

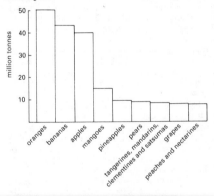

FRUIT *World production of fruit (1989).*

fruit The fertilized ovary of a flower, which contains the seed (or seeds). The variation in the structure of fruits reflects the different means they have evolved to ensure dispersal of the seeds. Fleshy fruits, for example, are usually eaten by animals, the seeds passing out with their faeces. Animals can also carry hooked or sticky fruits on their bodies. Seeds dispersed by wind are usually very light: they are either forcibly ejected from their fruits, for example from the *capsule of a poppy, or they remain attached to the fruit, for example the winged fruits of sycamores and ash trees. Most people use the word 'fruit' to mean fleshy edible fruits, many of which are grown commercially.

fruit fly A small fly the larvae of which feed on fruit. The Mediterranean fruit fly (*Ceratitis capitata*) is a pest of almost all succulent fruits. *See also* Drosophila.

Frunze (name until 1925: Pishpek) 42 53N 74 46E A city in the SW Soviet Union, the capital of Kirghiz SSR on the River Chú. Industries include the manufacture of agricultural machinery, textiles, and food. Population (1985 est): 604 000.

Fry, Christopher (C. Harris; 1907–) British dramatist. His verse plays include *A Phoenix Too Frequent* (1946), *The Lady's Not for Burning* (1948), and *Venus Observed* (1950).

Fuchs, Klaus Emil Julian (1911–88) British physicist and spy, born in Germany. During World War II he worked on atomic bomb research in Britain and in 1950 was found guilty of having passed secrets to the Soviet Union since 1943. He was released from prison in 1959 and emigrated to East Germany.

Fuchs, Sir Vivian (Ernest) (1908–) British explorer. He led the Commonwealth Trans-Antarctic Expedition: with help from Sir Edmund *Hillary he covered and surveyed 3500 km (2173 mi) between 24 November, 1957, and 2 March, 1958. He was director of the Falkland Islands Survey (British Antarctic Survey from 1962) from 1947 to 1950 and from 1960 until 1973.

fuchsia A widely cultivated shrub of the willowherb family, mostly native to tropical America. The plants have pink, red, or purple drooping flowers; each flower has four long coloured sepals surrounding the shorter petals, below which the stamens and stigma protrude.

fuel cell A device that converts the energy of a chemical reaction directly into an electric current. In the simplest type oxygen and hydrogen are fed through separate porous nickel plates into an electrolytic solution. The gases combine to form water and thus set up a potential difference between the plates. Fuel cells are distinguished from *accumulators in that the latter need to be recharged and do not consume their chemicals. They may have uses in electric road vehicles and in space vehicles.

fuel injection The pumping of a spray of fuel directly into the cylinders of an *internal-combustion engine. This is necessary in the case of continuous-combustion engines, such as rocket motors and *gas turbines. In Diesel engines fuel injection is used and in modern petrol engines it is increasingly used to replace the *carburettor as it gives a more even fuel distribution.

fugue A piece of music, generally having three or four parts (*or* voices), in which each part enters in turn with a statement of the main theme (*or* subject). After stating the subject each voice continues with the secondary theme (*or* countersubject). At the climax the voices are overlapped in close succession (*stretto*).

Fujiwara The most distinguished of Japan's noble families, with considerable political and economic power, notably between the 9th and 12th centuries.

Fujiyama (English name: Mount Fuji) 35 23N 138 42E The highest mountain in Japan, it is a dormant volcano in S central Honshu. Long regarded as a symbol of Japan, it has a Shinto shrine. Height: 3776 m (12 388 ft).

Fukuoka 33 39N 130 21E A port in Japan in N Kyushu on Hakata Bay. Kyushu University was established in 1910. Industries include textiles and shipbuilding. Population (1987): 1 182 000.

Fulani A Muslim people scattered over a large area of W Africa from Lake Chad to the Atlantic coast. They are of mixed Negroid and Berber origin. In N Nigeria many adopted the *Hausa language and culture and in the early 19th century established a Muslim empire in which they were the select ruling group.

Fuller, Richard Buckminster (1895–1983) US inventor and architect. His Dymaxion house (1928) and car (1933; improved version 1943) were designed to reduce waste and environmental pollution. His chief contribution was the geodesic dome, a lightweight and cheap structure of interlocking rods that can span large areas.

Fuller, Roy (Broadbent) (1912–) British poet and novelist. His early poetry was concerned with social and political themes; his more recent volumes, including *Buff* (1965) and *New Poems* (1968), are more personal and philosophical. His novels include *Image of a Society* (1956).

fulmar A North Atlantic seabird, *Fulmarus glacialis*, related to the *petrels. It is about 46 cm long and dark grey above with white underparts.

Funchal 32 40N 15 55W The capital of the Madeira Islands, on the S coast of Madeira, and a popular tourist resort. Population (1984): 44 111.

functionalism (architecture) The doctrine, associated with the *international style, that the more fitted to its purpose a building is, the more beautiful it will be. Developed under Louis Sullivan in the 1890s, it was supported by *Le Corbusier. Functionalism led to a severe style; its dominance faded after 1930.

fundamental constants Any of several constants that appear in physical equations, especially the speed of *light (c), *Planck's constant (h), the charge (e) and mass (m_e) of the *electron, and the fine structure constant (α). The latter is defined as $e^2/2hc\varepsilon_0$, where ε_0 is the electric constant; its value is approximately $1/137$. These constants are regarded as fundamental as their values determine the magnitude of many physical effects. Other constants sometimes taken as

fundamental include the electric constant, the magnetic constant, the Boltzmann constant, and the gravitational constant.

fundamentalism A religious movement among some US Protestants, which started after World War I. It insists on the literal truth of the Bible and of such traditional teachings as the Virgin Birth and Christ rising bodily from the dead. It rejects scientific knowledge, such as the theory of *evolution, that do not agree with the Bible.

fungi A group of organisms usually regarded as plants and including mushrooms, mildews, moulds, yeasts, etc. All fungi lack chlorophyll and therefore cannot manufacture their own food by *photosynthesis. Some feed on dead organic matter; others are parasites. The body of most fungi consists of a network of branching threadlike structures (hyphae), forming a mycelium. Sexual reproduction results in the formation of spores, which may be produced in a structure called a fruiting body: this is the visible part of mushrooms. Other fungi consist of single cells, which can reproduce asexually by simple division. Fungi are found worldwide. Some bring about decomposition of dead organic matter; others (e.g. *Penicillium* and *Streptomyces*) are a source of *antibiotics. Many parasitic fungi cause diseases or destroy timber (*see* dry rot). Some fungi associate with algae to form *lichens.

furlong A unit of length equal to 220 yards (1/8 mile), used in horseracing.

furze. *See* gorse.

Fushun 41 51N 123 53E A city in NE China, in Liaoning province. Its industries are based on its oil-shale and coal deposits. Population (1986): 1 240 000.

fusion (physics). *See* nuclear energy.

Futuna Islands. *See* Wallis and Futuna.

Fuzhou (Fu-chou *or* Foochow) 26 10N 119 20E A port in SE China, the capital of Fujian province. An ancient capital, it was the centre of foreign trade from the 10th to the 19th centuries. Population (1986): 1 190 000.

Fyns (German name: Fünen) The second largest Danish island, situated between the Little Belt and the Great Belt. Area: 3481 sq km (1344 sq mi). Population (1987): 453 483.

G

gabbro A dark-coloured coarse-grained *igneous rock formed by the crystallization at depth of basalt magma.

Gaberones. *See* Gaborone.

Gable, Clark (1901–60) US film actor, whose films include *It Happened One Night* (1934), *Gone with the Wind* (1939), and *The Misfits* (1961).

Gabon (official name: Gabonese Republic) A country in West Africa. *Economy*: timber was formerly the most important resource, now mineral

wealth forms the basis of the economy. *History*: formerly a centre of the slave trade, it was settled by the French in the 19th century, becoming part of French Equatorial Africa in 1910. It gained self-government in 1958 and independence in 1960. A one-party political system was instituted in 1967; in the 1980s an underground group known as the *morena* led the opposition. President: Omar Bongo (Albert Bernard B.; 1935–). Official language: French; Bantu languages are widely spoken. Official currency: CFA (Communauté financière africaine) franc of 100 centimes. Area: 267 000 sq km (103 089 sq mi). Population (1988 est): 1 226 000. Capital and main port: Libreville.

gaboon viper A venomous *puff adder, *Bitis gabonica*, occurring in African forests. Up to 2 m long, it has hornlike projections on its snout and is patterned with rectangles and triangles. It feeds on small animals.

Gaborone (former name: Gaberones) 24 45S 25 55E The capital of Botswana. The seat of government was transferred here from Mafeking in 1965. Population (1988 est): 110 973.

Gaddafi, Moammar al- (*or* Qaddafi; 1942–) Libyan colonel and statesman. In 1969 he led a revolt that overthrew the monarchy and in 1970 became chairman of the Revolutionary Command Council. His nationalist and Islamic socialism restructured Libyan society.

gadolinium (Gd) A *lanthanide element named after the Finnish chemist J. Gadolin (1760–1852). It is used in television-tube phosphors. At no 64; at wt 157.25; mp 1313°C; bp 3233°C.

Gaea (*or* Gaia) A Greek goddess personifying the earth. The wife and mother of Uranus (Heaven), by whom she bore the *Titans, the Cyclops, and the Gigantes, she incited the revolt of the Titans against him.

Gaelic A language of the Goidelic group of *Celtic languages. Irish Gaelic is the official language of Eire, spoken in Ireland as a first language by approximately 100 000 people and as a second language by around 700 000. An offshoot is Scottish Gaelic (*or* Erse), spoken in NW Scotland.

Gagarin, Yuri Alekseevich (1934–68) Soviet cosmonaut, who on 12 April, 1961, became the first person to orbit the earth reaching a height of about 301 km (187 mi). He died in a plane crash.

Gaia. *See* Gaea.

Gainsborough, Thomas (1727–88) One of the great British portrait and landscape painters. His *Countess Howe* (Kenwood House, London) and the *Blue Boy* (San Marino, California) were influenced by Van Dyck, while his landscapes were influenced by the Dutch painters *Ruisdael and Meindert Hobbema and later by *Rubens, particularly the *Harvest Wagon* (Barber Institute, Birmingham).

Gaitskell, Hugh (Todd Naylor) (1906–63) British politician; leader of the Labour Party (1955–63). At the 1960 party conference his "Fight, and fight, and fight again" speech against unilateral nuclear disarmament reunited the party, after the 1959 election defeat.

galago. *See* bushbaby.

Galahad In *Arthurian legend, the son of *Lancelot and Elaine, and in some versions the only knight to succeed in the quest of the *Holy Grail.

Galápagos Islands (Spanish name: Archipiélago de Colón) A group of 12 main islands and several smaller ones in the Pacific Ocean, W of and belonging to Ecuador. Visited by Charles *Darwin in 1835, they contain many unique species, including the Galápagos giant tortoise (*Tes-*

tudo elephantopus). Area: 7428 sq km (2868 sq mi). Population (1986 est): 8000.

galaxies Huge assemblies of stars, gas, and dust, bound together by *gravitation. **Spiral galaxies** are flattened systems with spiral arms containing interstellar gas and dust from which stars can form. **Elliptical galaxies** are roughly spherical with no internal structure and very little interstellar matter. **Irregular galaxies** are small and shapeless, with a high content of interstellar matter.

Galaxy (*or* Milky Way system) The spiral *galaxy to which the sun belongs. It contains about a hundred thousand million stars, mostly in its two spiral arms, the sun lying about 33 000 light years from the centre. It possibly has a *black hole at the galactic centre.

Galen (129–c. 199 AD) Greek physician and scholar, whose ideas dominated medicine until the Renaissance. Galen showed the role of the ureter in kidney and bladder function and that arteries carry blood, although his views on blood circulation were mistaken. Galen also wrote on philosophy, law, and mathematics.

galena A grey soft metallic mineral consisting of lead sulphide, found mainly in ore veins. Galena is the main lead ore and often contains silver.

Galicia 1. A medieval kingdom in NW Spain. Colonized by the *Visigoths, it became a subkingdom of Castile in the late 11th century. 2. A province in E Europe, divided between Poland and the Soviet Union after World War II.

Galilean satellites The four largest *satellites of *Jupiter—Io, Europa, Ganymede, and Callisto—discovered by *Galileo (1610) and studied in detail by the US *Voyager probes (1979).

Galilee A district of N Israel, bordering the River Jordan, associated with the early ministry of Jesus Christ, Crusader battles, and Jewish settlement after the fall of Jerusalem (70 AD). Zionist settlements (*see* Zionism), begun in 1892, became part of Israel in 1949.

Galilee, Sea of (Sea of Tiberias; Lake of Gennesaret; Lake Kinneret) A lake in NE Israel, mainly fed by the River Jordan; its surface is 209 m (686 ft) below sea level. It was the scene of many episodes in the life of Christ. Area: 166 sq km (64 sq mi).

Galileo Galilei (1564–1642) Italian physicist and astronomer. Born in Pisa, he demonstrated that the rate of fall of a body is independent of its mass by dropping weights from the Leaning Tower. In 1609 Galileo designed a telescope and used it to discover sunspots and Jupiter's satellites. His book *Dialogue on Two World Systems* (1632) denounced the *Ptolemaic system of astronomy in favour of *Copernicus' system. As the Roman Catholic Church had condemned Copernicus' work in 1616, Galileo was forced by the Inquisition to deny his views and placed under house arrest for the rest of his life.

Galla A people of Ethiopia numbering about 10 million and making up about 40% of the population. They spread from the SE region during the 16th century. Their language belongs to the Hamito-Semitic family.

gall bladder A saclike organ (7-10 cm long) that stores *bile (gall) from the liver. Substances in the bile may form crystals and lead to gallstones, which may block the bile duct leading to the intestine or cause gall bladder infections (cholecystitis).

Gallic Wars (58-51 BC) The campaigns in which Julius Caesar took possession of Transalpine *Gaul (France). Caesar's concern for Italian security led him to interfere in the wars between Gallic tribes. Caesar's own account of the Gallic Wars has survived.

gallinule A widely distributed bird related to the *rails, found on semistagnant water edged by dense vegetation. They have green or purple plumage for camouflage. About 30-45 cm long, they have slender toes enabling them to run over floating vegetation. *See also* moorhen.

Gallipoli (Turkish name: Gelibolu) 40 25N 26 41E A seaport in Turkey, on the NE coast of the Dardanelles. Strategically important for the defence of Istanbul, the town had to be rebuilt after the Gallipoli campaign (*see* World War I). Population (1980): 14 721.

gallium (Ga) A metallic element discovered in 1875 by Lecoq de Boisbaudran. **Gallium arsenide** (GaAs) is a *semiconductor widely used in electronic devices. At no 31; at wt 69.72; mp 29.78°C; bp 2403°C.

gallon An Imperial unit of volume now defined in the UK as 4.546 09 cubic decimetres (roughly 4.55 litres). It was formerly the volume occupied by ten pounds of distilled water. The US gallon is equal to 0.832 68 British gallons.

Galloway. *See* Dumfries and Galloway Region.

gallstones. *See* gall bladder.

Galsworthy, John (1867-1933) British novelist and dramatist. *The Man of Property* (1906) began the series *The Forsyte Saga*, chronicling the decline of a rich English family. His plays include *The Silver Box* (1906).

galvanized steel Steel coated with zinc to prevent corrosion. The zinc may be deposited by electroplating or spraying the steel with molten zinc or by coating it with zinc powder and heating it.

galvanometer An instrument for measuring small electric currents, named after Luigi Galvani. In the moving-coil galvanometer, a current passing through a coil of wire suspended in a magnetic field causes it to rotate to an extent proportional to the current. In the moving-magnet instrument the magnet is suspended in the earth's magnetic field and deflection is caused by a current passing through the surrounding coil.

Galway (Irish name: Contae Na Gaillimhe) A county in the W Republic of Ireland, in Connacht. It extends to Connemara (an area of moors and bogs) in the W. Offshore islands include the Aran Islands. Cattle and sheep rearing are important. Area: 5939 sq km (2293 sq mi). Population (1986): 178 180. County town: Galway.

Gama, Vasco da (c. 1469-1524) Portuguese navigator. In 1497, he continued Bartolomeu Dias' search for the route to India. He rounded the Cape of Good Hope and crossed to Calicut (1498). Received with hostility by the Indians, he withdrew. In 1502 his expedition to establish Portugal's influence in the Indian Ocean returned with considerable booty. Some 20 years later he went back to India as viceroy and died there.

Gambia, Republic of The A country in West Africa, surrounded by Senegalese territory. *Economy*: overwhelmingly agricultural, producing groundnuts and rice. Development plans include an oil refinery and the exploitation of tourism. *History*: the English established a trading settlement on James Island in 1661. The area was administered by the British from 1807 until independence in 1965. It became a republic within the Commonwealth in 1970. Close ties with Senegal were reinforced with the formation of the Senegambia Confederation in 1982. Official language: English. Official currency: dalasi of 100 butut. Area: 10 689 sq km (4125 sq mi). Population (1988 est): 788 163. Capital and main port: Banjul.

Gambia, River A river in West Africa. Rising in Guinea, it flows NW through Senegal and The Gambia to the Atlantic Ocean. Length: 1126 km (700 mi).

gamboge (*or* camboge) A brownish brittle gum-resin obtained from various SE Asian trees of the genus *Garcinia* that turns yellow when powdered. It is used as an artist's pigment and as a strong purgative.

gamete A reproductive cell—either male or female—produced in the sex organs of plants or animals and containing half the number of *chromosomes present in a body (somatic) cell. On *fertilization the new individual therefore has a complete set of chromosomes, half from each parent. The female gamete (*see* egg) is large, contains abundant cytoplasm, and cannot move by itself. The male gamete (*see* pollen; sperm) has little cytoplasm and possesses some means of propulsion.

gametophyte. *See* alternation of generations.

gamma globulin. *See* globulin.

gamma radiation Highly energetic *electromagnetic radiation emitted by certain radioactive substances or produced in certain nuclear reactions; its wavelength is between 10^{-10} and 10^{-14} metre.

Gandhi, Indira (1917-84) Indian stateswoman and daughter of *Nehru; prime minister (1966-77; 1980-84). In 1975 she was accused of electoral corruption and was defeated in the elections of 1977 by Morarji Desai but returned to power in 1980. She was assassinated in 1984 by Sikh members of her bodyguard. Her elder son **Rajiv Gandhi** (1942-   ) succeeded her as prime minister (1984-89).

Gandhi, Mohandas Karamchand (1869-1948) Indian nationalist leader. Mahatma ("Great Soul") Gandhi was born in W India and went to England in 1888 to study law, moving in 1893 to South Africa to practise. A champion of the rights of the Indian community in South Africa, he introduced noncooperation with the civil authorities (satyagraha), which he continued after his return to India (1914). There he became leader of the *Indian National Congress and was imprisoned (1922–24) for civil disobedience and again in 1930 for defying the government's salt monopoly. In 1942 the British Government offered India complete independence after the war in exchange for cooperation in winning it. In reply Gandhi demanded that the British should withdraw immediately from India. The British responded by gaoling Gandhi and the other Congress leaders until 1944. Gandhi played a crucial part in the independence talks and accepted the establishment of Pakistan, undertaking a fast in an attempt to halt the conflict in Bengal. His attempted reconciliation between Hindus and Muslims caused a Hindu fanatic (Nathuram Godse) to assassinate him. Ghandi is regarded by many as a saint and the supreme Indian leader.

Gandzha. *See* Kirovabad.

Ganesa One of the main Hindu gods, shown as having an elephant's head on a human body. His father *Shiva beheaded him, but then replaced his human head with that of the first creature he found.

Ganges, River (*or* Ganga) The great river of N India and the most sacred for Hindus. Formed in the Himalayas, it flows E to the Brahmaputra River, continuing as the River Padma, which is emptied into the Bay of Bengal by the world's largest delta. Length: 2507 km (1557 mi).

Gang of Four. *See* Jiang Qing.

gangrene Death of tissues, which usually results from narrowing of the blood vessels of the legs by *atherosclerosis or because of diabetes. In wet gangrene the tissues become infected. Improving the blood flow to the limbs by surgery or by rest is the usual treatment, although in the worst cases amputation may be necessary.

gannet A seabird found throughout the world (tropical gannets are called *boobies.) The North Atlantic gannet (*Sula bassana*), also called solan goose, reaches 90 cm in length. It is white with black wingtips and has a wedge-shaped tail. Gannets feed on fish and nest on rocky islands and cliffs.

Ganymede (astronomy). *See* Galilean satellites.

Ganymede (mythology) In Greek legend, a Trojan prince of great beauty carried off by Zeus to be his cupbearer.

Gaoxiong (*or* Kao-hsiung; Japanese name: Takao) 22 36N 120 17E A city in SW Taiwan, the second largest on the island and its leading port. Under Japanese occupation (1895–1945) it became an important naval base. Population (1987): 1 300 000.

gar A freshwater bony *fish, also called garpike, found in America. Gars have a slender body, up to 3.5 m long, and feed mainly on smaller fish.

Garbo, Greta (Greta Gustafson; 1905–90) Swedish actress, working mostly in the USA. Films in which she played tragic heroines include *Grand Hotel* (1932), *Anna Karenina* (1935), and *Camille* (1936). As a comedienne she excelled in *Ninotchka* (1939).

García Lorca, Federico (1898–1936) Spanish poet and dramatist. He won international fame with *Gipsy Ballads* (1928). His masterpiece

is the trilogy of folk tragedies *Blood Wedding* (1933), *Yerma* (1934), and *The House of Bernarda Alba* (1936). He was shot by Nationalist partisans in the Spanish Civil War.

Garda, Lake (Latin name: Lacus Benacus) A lake in central N Italy, sheltered on the N by the Alps. Area: 370 sq km (143 sq mi).

gardenia A shrub or tree of the madder family, native to tropical and subtropical Africa and Asia. Many are richly scented and used in perfumes and tea. *Gardenia jasminoides* is a popular pot plant.

garfish. *See* needlefish.

Garibaldi, Giuseppe (1807–82) Italian soldier. Influenced by the patriot Mazzini, he joined an attempted republican revolution in Sardinia-Piedmont (1834) and was forced to flee to South America. He returned to join the *Revolution of 1848. Following another period of exile, he supported the unification movement led by Cavour and Victor Emmanuel II of Sardinia-Piedmont (*see* Risorgimento). In 1860 he set out from Genoa on the Expedition of a Thousand, achieving the conquest of Sicily and Naples. He also fought for the French in the Franco-Prussian War (1870–71).

Garland, Judy (Frances Gumm; 1922–69) US singer and film actress, who began performing at the age of five in vaudeville. Her films included *The Wizard of Oz* (1939), *Meet Me in St Louis* (1944), and *A Star is Born* (1954). Her daughter **Liza Minnelli** (1946–) is also a singer and actress, best known for her role in *Cabaret* (1972).

garlic A widely cultivated plant, *Allium sativum*, of the onion family, native to Asia. Its leafless flower stem grows to a height of 60 cm. Its pungent bulb is widely used in cooking.

garnet A group of minerals with varying compositions. Garnets occur chiefly in metamorphic rocks. They are used as abrasives and flawless crystals are semiprecious stones (usually red).

Garonne, River A river in SW France. Rising in the central Pyrenees, it enters the Atlantic Ocean by the Gironde estuary. Length: 580 km (360 mi).

garpike. *See* gar.

Garrick, David (1717–79) English actor who began his long theatrical career with a performance as Richard III in 1741. As manager of the Drury Lane Theatre from 1747 to 1776, he introduced many innovations in production.

Garter, Order of the A British order of knighthood, traditionally founded in 1348 by Edward III for himself and 25 knights companions. Its motto *Honi soit qui mal y pense* (shame be his who thinks badly of it), supposedly the words of Edward III on tying to his leg a garter dropped by a lady, is written on the blue garter worn by the knights on the left leg. The order's chapel is St George's Chapel, Windsor. The 25 knights are appointed by the sovereign; since 1987 women have been eligible.

Gascony A former duchy of SW France. After Roman rule Gascony was conquered by the Visigoths and then by the Franks. It fell to Aquitaine in 1052 and England in the 12th century. It was regained by the French at the end of the Hundred Years' War (1453).

gases Substances that distribute themselves evenly throughout a closed container. The temperature, pressure, and volume of a gas are fairly accurately described by the *gas laws and the *kinetic theory of gases. *Compare* liquids; solids.

Gaskell, Elizabeth Cleghorn (1810–65) British novelist. In 1832 she married a Unitarian minister and settled in Manchester, the setting of her novel, *Mary Barton* (1848). Other novels include *Cranford* (1853) and *North and South* (1855). She wrote the first biography of her friend Charlotte Brontë (1857).

gas laws Relationships between the thermodynamic temperature (T), pressure (p), and volume (V) of a gas. The simplest laws are *Boyle's law ($p \propto 1/V$) and *Charles's law ($V \propto T$), which are combined in the ideal gas equation: $pV = nRT$, where R is the gas constant (8.314 J K^{-1} mol^{-1}) and n is the number of *moles present. Real gas does not obey this equation exactly and later gas laws attempt to correct it. *See* Van der Waals' equation.

gastric juice A mixture of hydrochloric acid, protein-digesting enzymes, and mucus produced by glands in the lining of the stomach.

gastric ulcer. *See* peptic ulcer.

gastroenteritis Infection of the stomach and intestines, usually due to infection or food poisoning. Gastroenteritis normally causes diarrhoea and vomiting; it is dangerous in babies.

gas turbine A form of *internal-combustion engine consisting of a compressor, a combustion chamber, and a turbine. Air is fed under pressure from the compressor to the combustion chambers, where a fuel, such as paraffin is burnt; the hot gases then drive the turbine, which in turn drives the compressor. Power is supplied either in the form of thrust from a jet (*see* jet engine) or rotation of the turbine shaft.

GATT. *See* General Agreement on Tariffs and Trade.

Gatwick 51 08N 0 11W A village in SE England, 43 km (27 mi) S of London, in Surrey. It is the site of one of London's subsidiary airports.

Gauguin, Paul (1848–1903) French postimpressionist painter. He gave up stockbroking (1883) to become a full-time painter. He visited Martinique in 1887 and stayed with *Van Gogh in Arles in 1888. Seeking the inspiration of a primitive civilization, he moved to Tahiti (1891), where such paintings as *Nevermore* were influenced by native superstitions.

Gaul An ancient region of Europe, divided by the Romans into Transalpine Gaul (the area bound by the Rhine, Alps, and Pyrenees) and Cisalpine Gaul (N Italy). Celtic tribes settled in Transalpine Gaul from about 1500 BC and in Cisalpine Gaul after 500 BC. The Gauls spread south to Rome, which they sacked in 390. In 121 the Romans took possession of S Transalpine Gaul, which they called Gallia Narbonensis, and between 58 and 50 Caesar conquered the rest of Gaul. Roman Gaul prospered until the barbarian invasions in the 5th century.

Gauss, Karl Friedrich (1777–1855) German mathematician. His greatest contributions were in the fields of probability, number theory, complex numbers, algebra, and electricity and magnetism.

Gautier, Théophile (1811–72) French Romantic poet and critic. Influenced by Victor *Hugo, his early writings include *Poésies* (1830) and *Les Jeunes-France* (1833). *Emaux et camées* (1852) embody his belief in art.

gavial (*or* gharial) A long-snouted reptile, *Gavialis gangeticus*, related to the *crocodile; it occurs in N Indian rivers and is sacred to Hindus. 4–5 m long, it catches fish.

Gawain In Arthurian legend, a knight of the Round Table, the nephew of King Arthur and the son of King Lot of Norway and the Orkneys. He was known for his purity and courage.

Gay, John (1685–1732) British poet and dramatist. A friend of Pope, Swift, and other members of the Scriblerus Club, his *Fables* (1727, 1738) were the most successful of his satirical poems. His best-known work is *The Beggar's Opera* (1728), a blend of satire and Italian opera.

Gay-Lussac, Joseph Louis (1778–1850) French chemist and physicist. He discovered boron (1808) and the law that gases combine in a simple ratio by volume (**Gay-Lussac's law**). He also discovered *Charles's law independently of Charles and published his results first.

Gaza Strip A strip of coastal territory, 50 km (30 mi) long, on the SE corner of the Mediterranean Sea. Following the Arab-Israeli Wars it has changed hands several times; it has been under Israeli military occupation since 1967. Under the Camp David agreement (1979), self-government for the area was planned, but violent protests by Palestinian refugees against Israeli occupation continue to occur. Population (1988): 564 000.

gazelle A slender antelope of Africa and Asia. 50–90 cm high, gazelles are distinguished by horizontal stripes on the face. In most species both sexes have horns.

GBE. *See* Order of the British Empire.

GCSE (*or* General Certificate of Secondary Education) An examination for 16-year-old schoolchildren in the UK. Introduced in 1988 to replace GCE O-level and CSE, it is intended to have a more practical base and to give greater weight to continuous assessment of coursework than its predecessors.

Gdańsk (German name: Danzig) 54 22N 18 41E A port in N Poland. It is an industrial centre with shipbuilding, metallurgy, and chemical industries. Population (1985): 467 000.

GDP (gross domestic product). *See* gross national product.

Gdynia 54 31N 18 30E A port in N Poland. Originally a fishing village, it became Poland's main shipbuilding centre and naval base. Population (1985): 243 000.

gean. *See* cherry.

gecko A slender nocturnal widely distributed lizard ranging from 3 to 35 cm long. Many have toe pads with microscopic hooks enabling them to cling to smooth surfaces. They feed on insects and have well-developed vocal cords. The tokay (*Gekko gecko*) of E Asia is a large arboreal gecko.

Geelong 38 10S 144 26E A city and major port in Australia, in S Victoria. Wool, wheat, and oil are the principal exports. Population (1986): 139 792.

Geiger counter A device that counts ionizing particles. It consists of a metal cylinder containing low-pressure gas and a wire anode. Ionizing particles passing through a window at one end induce discharges, which are counted by a suitable circuit. Named after the German physicist Hans Geiger (1882–1945).

gel. See colloid.

gelada A large *monkey, *Theropithecus gelada*, of Ethiopian mountains. 120–150 cm long including the tufted tail (70–80 cm), it has brown hair and two bare patches on the chest. Geladas feed on roots, leaves, and fruit.

gelatin A protein derived from bones and skins. In solution it forms a gel that becomes fluid as the temperature rises and solidifies on cooling. It is used in the food industry, in drugs, and in photographic emulsions.

Geldof, Bob (1952–   ) Irish rock musician, who became involved in fund raising for the starving in Africa. He organized a concert (Band Aid) held simultaneously in the UK and the USA in 1985, which generated unprecedented donations. He received an honorary knighthood in 1986.

gelignite A high explosive consisting of nitroglycerin, cellulose nitrate, potassium nitrate, and woodpulp.

Gell-Mann, Murray (1929–   ) US physicist, who won the 1969 Nobel Prize for his work on elementary particles. In 1953 he introduced the idea of strangeness. He also originated the theory of unitary symmetry and the concept of quarks (see also particle physics).

Gemini (Latin: Twins) A conspicuous constellation in the N sky near Orion, lying on the *zodiac between Cancer and Taurus. The brightest stars are Pollux and Castor.

gemsbok. See oryx.

gene A unit of the hereditary material of an organism that provides the genetic information necessary to fulfil a single function. The term was coined by W. L. Johannsen (1857–1927) in 1909. A gene is a section of *DNA (or *RNA) corresponding to a single message in the *genetic code. Most of a cell's genes are carried on the *chromosomes.

General Agreement on Tariffs and Trade (GATT) A set of trade agreements, in operation from January, 1948, deciding on customs duties for international trading. Members agree to reduction of trade restrictions, on condition that home producers do not suffer losses. There are more than 80 member countries. The secretariat of GATT, which is a specialized agency of the *United Nations, is in Geneva.

General Strike (1926) A national strike in Britain's major industries, lasting from 3 to 12 May. It began when the Trades Union Council (TUC) called out its members in support of the miners, who had refused to accept a reduction in wages. The government under Stanley *Baldwin kept essential services going until the TUC called off the Strike.

Genesis The first book of the Bible, said to be by Moses. It tells the story of the creation, the fall of Adam, the Flood, the scattering of the nations at Babel, and introduces God's *covenant with the Israelites.

genet A carnivorous mammal of Africa and Europe. Genets range in size from the 50-cm Abyssinian genet to the 100-cm African giant genet. They have retractile claws, long tails (up to 50 cm), foxlike heads, and pale fur with dark spots or stripes. Genets hunt birds and small mammals at night.

genetic code The means by which information for the organization and function of living cells is carried by *DNA and *RNA molecules. The genetic code was unravelled in the 1960s by the work of *Crick, M. W. Nirenberg (1927–   ), Har Gobind Khorana (1922–   ), and others. They found that the basic symbol of the code was a sequence of three consecutive bases of the DNA molecule. The code seems to apply to all species.

genetic engineering Alteration of the genetic basis of organisms, usually bacteria, in order to obtain gene products of use to humans. Usually, a sequence of desirable genes is inserted into the DNA of a host bacterium. This altered DNA (or recombinant DNA) then directs the bacterial cell to produce the desired gene product (for example, insulin or interferon). In 1988 it became possible for scientists to patent new forms of animal life created by such processes.

genetics The study of heredity and variation in living organisms, founded on the work of Gregor *Mendel. In 1953 *DNA was shown to carry the genes in chromosomes that determine the characteristics inherited by an organism. Genetics is important in plant and animal breeding and in understanding inherited diseases. See also genetic engineering.

Geneva (French name: Genève; German name: Genf) 46 13N 6 09E A city in SW Switzerland, in which banking and international finance are important. International organizations, including the International Red Cross and the World Health Organization, have headquarters here. Population (1987): 160 900.

Geneva Bible An English translation of the Bible published in 1560 by Puritan exiles in Geneva. It is also called the Breeches Bible because of the use of the word in the translation of Genesis 3.7.

Geneva Conventions International agreements covering the care of civilians and wounded troops in wartime. Inspired by the International *Red Cross, the agreements also cover assistance for forces at sea, the treatment of prisoners of war, and the protection of civilians. Most states accept the conventions.

Genghis Khan (c. 1162–1227) The founder of the Mongol empire. Originally called Tamujin, he adopted the title Genghis Khan (Emperor of All) in 1206 after uniting the nomadic Mongol tribes and destroying Tatar power. Organizing his horsemen into mobile squadrons called *ordus* (hence "hordes"), he breached the Great Wall and captured Peking but failed to conquer China completely, although he crushed resistance in Afghanistan, Persia, and S Russia. After his death his son Ogadai (1185–1241) carried out the empire's organization.

Gennesaret, Lake of. *See* Galilee, Sea of.

Genoa (Italian name: Genova) 44 24N 08 56E A port in NW Italy. A major maritime city during the middle ages, it is still Italy's chief port. Population (1987): 722 026.

Gent. *See* Ghent.

gentian A flowering plant with about 400 species, including many alpine perennials. The blue bell-shaped flowers enliven many rock gardens.

Gentile da Fabriano (Niccolo di Giovanni; c. 1370–1427) Florentine painter of the international gothic style. His frescos for the Doge's Palace, Venice, and the Lateran Basilica, Rome, have perished but the *Adoration of the Magi* (Uffizi) shows his style.

geocentric system. *See* Ptolemaic system.

geochemistry The study of the chemical composition of the earth, the abundance of the *elements, and their distribution in the earth's rocks and minerals. In the earth's crust, oxygen (47%), silicon (28%), and aluminium (8%) are the most abundant elements.

geochronology The dating of geological events, rocks, sediments, and organic remains. *Radiocarbon dating gives an actual date BP (before present). Relative dating establishes the order of events using fossil evidence, pollen analysis, etc.

Geoffrey of Monmouth (c. 1100–54) English chronicler. His work, *Historia Regum Britanniae*, was the source for most medieval literature concerned with the Arthurian legend.

geography The study of the earth's surface as man's environment. Modern geography was founded in the early 19th century by the German scholars Humboldt and Ritter. Physical geography includes geomorphology (the study of the landforms), biogeography (the study of soils and the distribution of animals and plants), and climatology (*see* climate). The main branches of human geography are historical geography (change in an area over a period), economic geography, urban geography, and political geography.

geological time scale A time scale covering the earth's history. The largest divisions are eras (Palaeozoic, Mesozoic, and Cenozoic); these are subdivided into periods. The Tertiary and Quaternary periods are further subdivided into epochs; epochs consist of several ages, and ages can be divided into chrons. A number of eras together is an eon.

geology The study of the earth. The branches are historical (including geochronology, stratigraphy, and palaeontology); physical (including geomorphology, geophysics, petrology, mineralogy, crystallography, and geochemistry); and economic (the distribution of important rocks and minerals).

geomagnetic field The earth's magnetic field. The magnetic poles do not coincide with the geographic poles, and their positions vary with time. Complete reversals of the earth's magnetic field have occurred in the past. The three **magnetic elements** of the earth's field are the

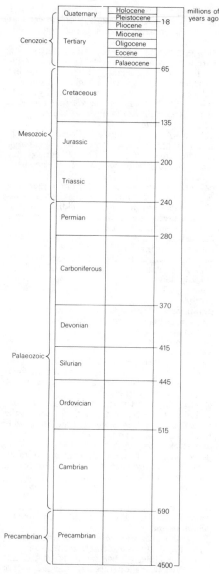

GEOLOGICAL TIME SCALE

*magnetic dip, the *magnetic declination, and the horizontal field strength.

geometry A branch of mathematics concerned with the properties of space and shapes. In Euclidean geometry the space corresponds to common ideas of physical space.

geophysics The study of the physical forces acting on the earth. Important branches of geophysics are seismology, geomagnetism, vulcanology, natural radioactivity, and gravitation.

George I (1660–1727) The first Hanoverian King of Great Britain and Ireland (1714–27) and Elector of Hanover (1698–1727). He divorced his wife for infidelity (1694) and imprisoned her for 32 years. A successful soldier and a shrewd diplomat, he never learnt English and left government to his ministers.

George II (1683–1760) King of Great Britain and Ireland and Elector of Hanover (1727–69). In the War of Austrian Succession he fought at Dettingen (1743), the last British king to appear in battle. He was a patron of musicians, notably Handel.

George III (1738–1820) King of Great Britain and Ireland (1760–1820) and Elector (1760–1815) and King (1815–20) of Hanover. He shared with Lord *North the blame for the loss of the American colonies but then backed William *Pitt the Younger as prime minister (1783–1801). He was permanently insane by 1811, after which the Prince of Wales (later George IV) acted as regent.

George IV (1762–1830) King of the United Kingdom and of Hanover (1820–30). He secretly married a Roman Catholic, Maria Fitzherbert, in 1785 but the marriage was invalid and in 1795 he married *Caroline of Brunswick. His extravagance undermined the monarchy.

George V (1865–1936) King of the United Kingdom (1910–36), second son of Edward VII, whose heir he became on the death (1892) of his elder brother Albert Victor. In 1893 George married *Mary of Teck.

George VI (1895–1952) King of the United Kingdom (1936–52). Second son of George V, he succeeded to the throne when Edward VIII abdicated. He married (1923) Lady Elizabeth Bowes-Lyon (*see* Elizabeth the Queen Mother).

George, St The patron saint of England and of soldiers, portrayed slaying a dragon to rescue a maiden (probably from the *Pegasus myth). His cult was brought to England by Crusaders returning from Palestine, where he was believed to have been martyred during Diocletian's rule. Feast day: 23 April.

George Cross The highest British award for non-military bravery, awarded since 1940. A silver cross engraved with *For Gallantry*, its recipients include the island of Malta (1942). The **George Medal**, the second highest award for non-military bravery, was also instituted in 1940.

Georgetown (*or* Penang) 5 26N 100 16E A city and chief port in NW Peninsular Malaysia, the capital of Penang state. Population (1980): 250 578.

Georgetown 6 46N 58 10W The capital and main port of Guyana. Founded by the British in 1781, it was later occupied by the French and the Dutch. Population (1985 est): 200 000.

Georgia A state on the SE coast of the USA. Agriculture is important; poultry and peanuts have replaced cotton as the major crops. *History*: named after George II, it was founded in 1732. Settlement expanded after the American Revolution; a Confederate state in the US Civil War, it suffered damage during Gen Sherman's March to the Sea (1864). Area: 152 488 sq km (58 876 sq

mi). Population (1987 est): 6 222 000. Capital: Atlanta.

Georgian The language spoken by the Georgian peoples of the USSR Turkey, and Iran. It belongs to the Kartvelian or *South Caucasian group and its written form comes from Aramaic with Greek influences. It has a literature dating from the 5th century AD. It is the official language of the Georgian SSR.

Georgian style A style of British architecture associated with the reigns of George I to George IV (1714–1830). Dominated by Palladianism and *neoclassicism, it was characterized by the symmetrical use of sash windows and the restrained use of classical features.

geostationary orbit. *See* communications satellite.

geothermal energy Heat produced in the earth's interior. Volcanoes, geysers, and hot springs are all sources, although only geysers and springs can be conveniently used. About 0.1% of the world's energy is currently geothermal.

geranium 1. A widely cultivated flowering plant of the genus *Pelargonium*, grown for its showy flowers or ornamental or scented leaves. 2. A flowering plant of the genus *Geranium*, such as cranesbill and herb Robert.

gerbil A small rodent native to Africa and Asia. Ranging in size from 5–20 cm, gerbils have long hind legs. They spend the day in underground burrows, feeding at night on seeds, etc.

German A West Germanic language, which is the official language of Germany and Austria and one of the four languages of Switzerland. High German, the written form, developed from dialects of the highland areas of Germany and Austria. Old High German was spoken before 1100 AD, then Middle High German became the standard. Modern High German developed from the 16th-century dialect of Luther. Low German exists only in a spoken form in N Germany and comes from Old Saxon and Middle Low German speech.

germanium (Ge) A brittle grey-white metalloid, discovered by C. A. Winkler (1838–1904) in 1886. It is present in coal and is concentrated in chimney soot and flue dusts of zinc smelters, from which it is obtained. The element is a *semiconductor but now rarely used in electronics. At no 32; at wt 72.59; mp 937.4°C; bp 2830°C.

German measles A common contagious disease known medically as rubella. Caused by a virus, it produces a pink rash. A woman infected in early pregnancy may give birth to a malformed child; for this reason immunization of girls is encouraged.

German shepherd dog (*or* Alsatian) A breed of large dog originating in Germany. It has a coarse coat that can range in colour from white to black. Easily trained, they are used as guard dogs and guide dogs. Height: 61–66 cm (dogs); 56–61 cm (bitches).

Germany A country in central Europe, formerly (until 1990) comprising the German Democratic Republic (East Germany) and the Federal Republic of Germany (West Germany). Germany is divided into 16 *Länder* (German *Land*, state). The chief rivers are the Rhine, Danube, Ems, Weser, Oder, and Elbe. *Economy*: rapid reconstruction of industry followed World War II, making it the most prosperous country in W Europe. Mineral resources include coal, lignite, iron ore, lead and zinc, and potash. Agriculture has declined but the wine and forestry industries are important. The economy of former East Germany was run in co-operation with the Soviet Union until reunification. *History*: The region was occupied by German tribes from about 500 BC and came into conflict with the Romans from the 2nd century BC. Overrun by the Huns in the 4th and 5th centuries AD, it was dominated by the *Franks from the 6th century. After the failure of the Frankish dynasty medieval Germany was ruled by hereditary dynasties claiming the title Holy Roman Emperor. In the 13th century the first *Habsburg emperor was elected. In the later middle ages the power of the princes was challenged by the *Hanseatic League. The 16th and 17th centuries were dominated by religious strife; the *Reformation began in 1520. In the 17th century the Hohenzollern Electors of Brandenburg acquired Prussia, which became the dominant German state. In 1806 the Holy Roman Empire was brought to an end by Napoleon. The post-Napoleonic German confederation was dominated by Austria and Prussia. Prussian power increased further with victory in the *Austro-Prussian War (1866), and the *Franco-Prussian War (1870–71). In 1871 Bismarck created the German Empire. The late 19th and early 20th centuries saw industrialization and the rise of Germany as a colonial power, Defeated in 1918 in *World War I, the Empire was replaced by the *Weimar Republic. *Hitler rose to power in the early 1930s; his aggressive foreign policy led to *World War II. Following Germany's defeat and disgrace the country was divided into the German Democratic Republic and the Federal Republic of Germany.

The **German Democratic Republic** (GDR; German name: Deutsche Demokratische Republik), lying to the E of the Harz Mountains, was formed from the Soviet-occupied zone of Germany following World War II, it became independent in 1954, with membership of COMECON and the Warsaw Pact and (from 1973) a seat in the UN. The capital was East Berlin. In 1953 riots, particularly in East Berlin, were suppressed by Soviet troops, but the flow of refugees to West Germany continued until 1961, when the *Berlin Wall was erected.

The **Federal Republic of Germany** (German name: Bundesrepublik Deutschland), W of the Harz Mountains, was formed from the British-, French-, and US-occupied zones following World War II; it became fully independent in 1955. The capital was transferred to Bonn, although West Berlin remained in the Federal Republic.

Monetary union and the dismantling of border controls between the two German states took place in July 1990 and reunification was achieved in Oct 1990. Germany is a member of NATO. President: Richard von Weizsächer (1920–). Chancellor: Helmut Kohl. Official language: German. Official currency: Deutsche Mark of 100 Pfennige. Area: 356 798 sq km (137 746 sq mi). Population (1986): 77 705 746. Capital: Berlin (the

seat of government remains in Bonn pending further discussions). Main port: Hamburg.

germination The process by which an embryo plant within a seed is transformed into a plant with roots, stem, and leaves. Water, warmth, and oxygen stimulate germination, which begins with the emergence of the root (radicle) and is followed by the shoot (plumule). Energy is provided by the *cotyledons (seed leaves), which either remain below ground (broad bean) or form the first leaves of the seedling (marrow).

Gershwin, George (Jacob Gershvin; 1898–1937) US composer and songwriter. His jazz-inspired orchestral works include *Rhapsody in Blue* (1924) and *An American in Paris* (1928). The opera *Porgy and Bess* (1935) is still widely performed. His brother **Ira Gershwin** (1896–1983) wrote the lyrics to many of his songs.

Gestapo (German: *Geheime Staatspolizei*, secret state police) The *Nazi secret police formed in 1933 under Göring. Administered from 1936 by the *SS, the two organizations were responsible for carrying out the atrocities committed by the Germans in Europe.

Getty, J(ean) Paul (1892–1976) US businessman, who lived in the UK. He made his fortune in oil, becoming a millionaire at the age of 22. He founded the J. Paul Getty Museum at Malibu, California.

Gettysburg, Battle of (1–3 July, 1863) The most significant battle of the US *Civil War, fought in Pennsylvania as part of the Confederacy's second invasion of the North. After three days the Confederates withdrew; the North lost 23 000 men and the South 25 000. The **Gettysburg Address** was delivered (19 November, 1863) by President Abraham Lincoln at Gettysburg battlefield.

geysers Jets of hot water and steam issuing from holes in the earth's crust, found in volcanically active regions. They occur when water within the crust becomes superheated and suddenly boils. Cones of sinter (deposits of silica) frequently build up around the vents.

Ghana, Republic of A country in West Africa, on the Gulf of Guinea. *Economy*: chiefly agricultural. The main crop is cocoa; gold and diamonds are mined, as well as manganese, bauxite, and limestone. Hydroelectricity and off-shore oil mining are being developed. *History*: from the middle ages several kingdoms flourished in the area. In 1472 the Portuguese and others set up trading posts and it became the British colony of the Gold Coast in 1874. In 1957, with the British part of Togo, it became independent as Ghana, the name of a medieval N African empire. In 1960 it became a republic within the Commonwealth; there have been several military coups, in the last of which (1981) Fl Lt Jerry Rawlings (1942–) came to power. Official language: English. Official currency: cedi of 100 pesawas. Area: 238 305 sq km (92 010 sq mi). Population (1988 est): 13 812 000. Capital: Accra. Main port: Takoradi.

gharial. *See* gavial.

Ghats Two mountain ranges lying along the W and E coasts of India. The **Western Ghats**, extend about 1500 km (932 mi) N of Bombay to Cape Comorin and rise to 2693 m (8840 ft). They are used for tea planting. The **Eastern Ghats** extend about 1400 km (880 mi) from Cuttack to the Nilgiri Hills.

Ghent (Flemish name: Gent; French name: Gand) 51 02N 3 42E A city and port in Belgium at the junction of the Rivers Scheldt and Lys. Population (1988 est): 232 620.

gherkin A West Indian vine, *Cucumis anguria*, grown for its edible fruit, 2.5–7.5 cm long, used when young for pickling. Family: *Cucurbitaceae* (gourd family).

Ghiberti, Lorenzo (c. 1378–1455) Florentine Renaissance sculptor who won the competition for the relief sculptures for the north doors of the Baptistry of the Florentine Duomo. Finished in 1424, these New Testament scenes, mainly in the international gothic style, were followed by Old Testament scenes in the Gates of Paradise (1425–52). At the same time he wrote *I commentarii*, including histories of art and an autobiography.

Ghirlandaio, Domenico (Domenico di Tommaso Bigordi; 1449–94) Florentine painter of the early *Renaissance. He worked on a fresco (1481–82) in the Sistine Chapel and the fresco series (1486–90) in Sta Maria Novella, Florence. *Old Man and Boy* (Louvre) is an example of his portraiture.

Giacometti, Alberto (1901–66) Swiss sculptor and painter, influenced first by *cubism and later by *surrealism, particularly in his construction of sticks, glass, wire, etc., entitled *The Palace at 4 am*. After 1935 his work was characterized by spindly elongated human figures.

Giambologna (Giovanni da Bologna *or* Jean de Boulogne; 1529–1608) Italian mannerist sculptor of Flemish birth. Working with Medici encouragement from 1557 in Florence, he produced fountains and small bronze statues. His works include *Samson and a Philistine* (1567; Victoria and Albert Museum).

Giant's Causeway 55 14N 6 32W A promontory in N Northern Ireland, in Antrim, consisting of several thousand six-sided columns of basalt, formed by an outpouring of lava into the sea. According to legend it was a bridge for the giants to cross between Ireland and Scotland.

giant star A large luminous star that has used up the normal source of energy in its core (hydrogen), and must obtain energy from other nuclear fusion reactions. *See also* red giant.

gibberellins A group of organic compounds that stimulate plant growth. First isolated from the fungus *Gibberella fujikuroi*, over 30 gibberellins are now known. They stimulate the growth of leaves, stems, flowers, and fruit and break the dormancy of seeds and tubers.

gibbon A small *ape of S Asia. 45–65 cm long, gibbons have long arms and hooked fingers used to swing through trees. They feed on fruit and leaves and have a whooping call.

Gibbon, Edward (1737–94) British historian. His ironic treatment of Christianity in The

History of the Decline and Fall of the Roman Empire (1776–88) aroused contemporary controversy.

Gibbons, Grinling (1648–1721) English wood carver and sculptor, born in Rotterdam. Patronized by Charles II, he produced the choir stalls and organ screen in St Paul's Cathedral.

Gibbons, Orlando (1583–1625) English composer and organist. His best-known madrigal is "The Silver Swan" and he contributed pieces to *Parthenia* (1611), the first printed collection of keyboard music in England.

Gibraltar A British crown colony at the southern tip of Spain. The isthmus from the Spanish mainland rises sharply to the 427 m (1400 ft) limestone Rock of Gibraltar. *Economy*: mainly tourism and services to shipping. *History*: settled by the Moors in 711 AD, Gibraltar was taken by Castile in 1462, becoming part of united Spain. It was captured in 1704 by the British and ceded by the Treaty of Utrecht (1713). It became an important British naval base; Spain closed its frontier with Gibraltar (1969–85) and still wishes to repossess it despite opposition from its inhabitants. Official languages: English and Spanish. Official currency: Gibraltar pound of 100 pence. Area: 6.5 sq km (2.5 sq mi). Population (1987 est): 29 000.

Gibraltar, Strait of A narrow channel, 13 km (8 mi) at its narrowest, between Gibraltar and Africa, joining the Atlantic Ocean and the Mediterranean Sea.

Gibson Desert A desert in Western Australia, consisting of a vast area of active sand dunes and desert grass. Area: 220 000 sq km (85 000 sq mi).

Gide, André (1869–1951) French nove t and critic. A homosexual, he married (1895) his cousin Madeleine Rondeaux, the inspiration of two works, *The Immoralist* (1902) and *Strait Is the Gate* (1909). Other novels include *The Vatican Cellars* (1914) and *The Counterfeiters* (1926). His *Journal* is a major autobiography. He won the Nobel Prize in 1947.

Gielgud, Sir (Arthur) John (1904–) British actor, noted for his speaking voice, his performances in Shakespearean productions, and his many films.

Gilbert, William (1544–1603) English physicist and physician to Elizabeth I. His *De magnete* (1600) recorded the discovery of magnetic dip. He also coined such terms as *electricity* and *magnetic pole*.

Gilbert, Sir William Schwenk (1836–1911) British comic dramatist. He published the comic verses *Bab Ballads* (1869) while studying law. In 1870 he met Arthur *Sullivan, for whom he wrote the libretti for 14 popular operas.

Gilbert Islands. *See* Kiribati, Republic of.

gills The respiratory organs of aquatic animals: specialized thin-walled regions of the body surface through which dissolved oxygen is taken into the blood and carbon dioxide released into the water. The gills of fish lie in gill slits on each side of the gullet. The gills of molluscs (e.g. mussels) and fanworms have hairlike cilia that trap food particles in the water flowing over the gills. The external gills of amphibian larvae (tadpoles) are feathery structures projecting from the body wall.

gilt-edged security Securities issued by the UK government that pay a fixed interest rather than a dividend. Most are issued in units of £100.

gin A spirit distilled usually from grain flavoured with juniper berries (the name is derived from the Dutch *jenever*, juniper). It is generally drunk with tonic water, vermouth, etc.

ginger A plant, *Zingiber officinale*, native to SE Asia and widely grown for its underground stems (rhizomes), used as a spice.

ginkgo A deciduous Chinese tree, *Ginkgo biloba*, also called maidenhair tree, that is the only remaining representative of *gymnosperm trees that flourished in the Carboniferous period (370–280 million years ago). Growing to 30 m, it has yellow fruits containing edible kernels.

ginseng An extract of the forked roots of either *Panax quinquefolium* or *P. schinseng*, of the ivy family. It is used, especially in the Far East, for its supposed aphrodisiac and life-prolonging properties.

Giorgione (c. 1477–1510) Italian painter of the Venetian school. He trained under Giovanni *Bellini and worked with *Titian. His portraits, e.g. *Laura* (Vienna), influenced many Venetian painters.

Giotto (Giotto di Bondone; c. 1266–1337) Italian *Renaissance painter and architect. The fresco series of St Francis, in S Francesco, Assisi, is thought to be an early work. He also painted frescoes in the Arena Chapel, Padua and in Sta Croce, Florence. In 1334 he became architect of the city and surveyor of Florence Cathedral.

Gipsies A wandering people whose native language is *Romany. "Gipsy" comes from "Egyptian," but they probably began in India. One group is thought to have moved through Egypt and another through Europe reaching NW Europe during the 15th and 16th centuries. They live by seasonal work, selling things, and fortune telling. Frequently persecuted, half a million were killed by the Nazis.

giraffe A hoofed *mammal, *Giraffa camelopardalis*, of African grasslands. Measuring 3 m at the shoulder, with a neck 2.5 m long, giraffes are marked with brown blotches on a buff background. They feed on leaves.

Girl Guides Association An association founded by Robert and (his sister) Agnes *Baden Powell in 1910 to encourage the physical, mental, and spiritual development of girls. The three classes of members are Brownie Guides (for girls aged between 7 and 10), Guides (10–15), and Ranger Guides (14–20). Its counterpart for boys is the *Scout Association.

giro A system for transferring money. It started in Austria in 1883 and the British National Giro was set up by the Post Office in 1968, becoming independent as Girobank plc in 1988. All accounts are held at the Giro Centre (in Bootle, Lancashire), which transfers money from one account to another on receipt of a form. In bank giro, accounts are held at bank branches.

Gironde, River An estuary used by oceangoing vessels in SW France, on the Bay of Biscay, formed where the Rivers Garonne and Dordogne meet near Bordeaux. Length: 72 km (45 mi).

Gish, Lillian (1899–) US actress, who began as a child on stage with her sister **Dorothy Gish** (1898–1968). Both acted for D. W. *Griffith in silent films, including *The Birth of a Nation* (1916) and *Intolerance* (1916).

Giulio Romano (Giulio Pippi; c. 1499–1546) Italian mannerist painter, who was a pupil of *Raphael, whom he assisted in the decoration of the Vatican apartments. In 1524 he settled in Mantua, where he designed the Palazzo del Tè.

Giza, El (*or* al-Jizah) 30 01N 31 12E A city in N Egypt, forming a suburb of Cairo. Nearby are the great pyramids of Khafre, *Khufu, and Menkaure and the Sphinx. Population (1985): 1 608 000.

glacier A mass of ice and *firn lying on land and moving downwards from its source. **Cirque glaciers** are contained in depressions on mountain slopes or valley heads. **Valley glaciers** are contained within existing valleys, originating from cirque glaciers or from an icesheet. Where a glacier emerges from a valley onto a lowland area, a lobe-shaped **piedmont glacier** results. **Glaciation** is the action of glacier ice on the land surface. The main landforms resulting from glaciation include U-shaped valleys and *cirques.

gladiators The slaves, prisoners of war, condemned criminals, or volunteers who fought to the death in amphitheatres for the entertainment of the ancient Roman people. Fights between gladiators began as part of funeral games but their popularity was soon so great that statesmen sponsored shows to increase their political prestige.

gladiolus A flowering plant of the iris family, native to Europe, Africa, and the Mediterranean regions and widely cultivated. Growing from a corm, the flowering stem reaches a height of 1.2 m, with funnel-shaped flowers.

Gladstone, W(illiam) E(wart) (1809–98) British statesman; Liberal prime minister (1868–74, 1880–85, 1886, 1892–94). Elected to parliament in 1832, he was at first a Tory and supported the Peelites in the repeal of the *Corn Laws, after which the Peelites joined the Whigs (shortly to be termed Liberals). As chancellor of the exchequer (1852–55, 1859–66) Gladstone reduced taxes and government spending. His first ministry split off the Irish Church (1869) and introduced the Education Act (1870), the first Irish Land Act (1870), and the Ballot Act (introducing secret voting). Defeated in the 1874 election, he resigned but became an MP again and prime minister in 1880. His second ministry achieved a second Irish Land Act (1881) and further parliamentary reform (1884) but its failure to save *Gordon from Khartoum led to Gladstone's resignation. During his last ministries he supported Irish *Home Rule but both his Home Rule bills were rejected (1886, 1893).

gland An organ specialized to manufacture a chemical substance (secretion) for use by the body. Humans and higher animals have two kinds of glands. The *endocrine glands lack ducts and release their secretions (hormones) into the bloodstream. The exocrine glands (e.g. salivary and sweat glands) have ducts through which their products are secreted. Plants also have glands, which secrete a variety of products including latex, resin, nectar, and tannin.

Glasgow 55 53N 4 15W The largest city in Scotland, the administrative centre of Strathclyde Region on the River Clyde. Glasgow has engineering, textile, chemical, and brewing industries. Population (1987 est): 715 621.

glasnost A policy of increased freedom in social and cultural matters introduced in the Soviet Union by Mikhail *Gorbachov in 1986. A Russian word meaning openness, *glasnost* was adopted by the Soviet government in conjunction with *perestroika* (meaning progress), which heralded a new (though still limited) flexibility in the organization of the economy of the USSR, and facilitated the improvement of relations with the West.

glass A hard brittle substance, usually transparent, that behaves as a solid although it has many of the properties of a liquid. Glass was known in the 3rd millennium BC but glassblowing was not invented until about 100 BC (in Syria) and windows were not in use until about 100 AD. Ordinary soda glass, used for windows, etc., consists of silica (sand), sodium carbonate, and calcium carbonate (limestone). Flint glass, used for crystal glassware, contains silica, potassium carbonate, potassium nitrate, and lead oxide. Heat-resistant glass also contains borates and alumina; optical glass contains additional elements to control the refractive index. See also fibreglass.

glass snake A widely distributed legless lizard that feeds on insects, lizards, etc. Unlike true snakes, they have ears, eyelids, and rigid jaws. When attacked, they shed their tail.

Glastonbury 51 09N 2 43W A market town in SW England, in Somerset. Here by tradition Joseph of Arimathea founded England's first Christian church; Glastonbury is also the reputed burial place of King Arthur. Population (1981): 6773.

glaucoma An eye disease caused by raised pressure inside the eye. Acute glaucoma results in pain, disturbed vision, and blindness. Chronic glaucoma—one of the commonest causes of blindness—comes on slowly and painlessly. Both types can be controlled by eye drops.

Glazunov, Aleksandr Konstantinovich (1865–1936) Russian composer and a pupil of Rimsky-Korsakov. Glazunov's works, which were influenced by Wagner and Liszt rather than by Russian music, included eight symphonies, concertos, ballets, and string quartets.

Glencoe A glen in W Scotland, in the Highland Region. It was the scene of the massacre of the Macdonalds by the Campbells and English (1692).

Glendower, Owen (Welsh name: Owain Glyndwr; c. 1359–c. 1416) Welsh rebel. Allying with Henry IV's opponents, Glendower controlled most of Wales by 1404 but was subsequently defeated and turned to guerrilla warfare. He disappeared in 1416.

Glenn, John (1921–) US astronaut, who on 20 February, 1962, became the first American to orbit the earth. He later entered politics, becoming a senator in 1974.

gliders Light fixed-wing engineless aircraft that are launched by a winch or catapult or by being towed by a car or aircraft. Once airborne a glider is lifted by warm air currents. The height record is 14.1 km (P. F. Bikle; 1961) and the distance record 1460.8 km (H. W. Grosse; 1972). Pioneered by Otto *Lilienthal, gliders were used in World War II, notably in the ill-fated Arnhem expedition. Since the 1920s gliding has been a popular sport, controlled in the UK by the British Gliding Association (1924). See also hang-gliding.

Glinka, Mikhail Ivanovich (1804–57) Russian composer. He composed the first truly Russian opera *Ivan Susanin* (*A Life for the Tsar*; 1836), piano music, songs, and a second opera *Russlan and Ludmilla* (1842).

global warming. See greenhouse effect.

globe artichoke. See artichoke.

globefish. See puffer.

Globe Theatre An Elizabethan theatre, in Southwark, in which most of Shakespeare's plays were first produced. A cylindrical wooden building open to the sky, it was built in 1599, burnt down in 1613, rebuilt in 1614, and finally demolished in 1644. A reconstructed Globe Theatre is to be opened in the Bankside area of London in 1992.

globulin A type of protein that is generally insoluble in water. Globulins of the blood include the immunoglobulins (antibodies), which are manufactured by the animal to combat infections. Newborn mammals receive these immunoglobulins in their mother's milk. Other globulins occur in eggs, nuts, and seeds.

glockenspiel (German: bell play) A tuned percussion instrument having a keyboard-like arrangement of steel bars played with two small hammers. It has a range of two and a half octaves above bottom G of the bass stave but the notes sound two octaves higher.

Glomma, River (Norwegian name: Glåma) A river in SE Norway and the longest river in Scandinavia. It flows S from a small lake SE of Trondheim to enter the Skagerrak at Fredrikstad. Length: 588 km (365 mi).

Glorious Revolution (1688) The overthrow of James II of England and the establishment of his daughter Mary and her husband William of Orange on the throne. The opposition to James' policies, which favoured Catholics, sought William's armed intervention. James, offering no resistance, fled to France.

glottis. See larynx.

Gloucester 51 53N 2 14W A market town in W England, the administrative centre of Gloucestershire on the River Severn. First developed under the Romans (Glevum) it is noted for its cathedral. Population (1983 est): 92 200.

Gloucestershire A county of W England, bordering Wales. It consists of three regions: the Cotswold Hills, the Severn Valley, and the Forest of Dean. It is predominantly agricultural. Area: 2638 sq km (1019 sq mi). Population (1987 est): 522 200. Administrative centre: Gloucester.

glowworm. *See* firefly.

gloxinia An ornamental plant, *Sinningia speciosa*, native to Brazil, with large bell-shaped velvety flowers. Many hybrids are grown as pot plants.

Gluck, Christoph Willibald (1714–87) German composer. He composed the operas *Orfeo ed Euridice* (1762) and *Alceste* (1767) and over 40 dramatic works.

glucose (*or* dextrose) A simple sugar ($C_6H_{12}O_6$) that performs a vital role in the processes of organisms. Carbohydrates (such as starch) in food or tissue reserves are broken down to glucose, which is transported to cells to provide energy (*see* glycolysis). Glucose levels in blood are regulated by the hormones *insulin and glucagon.

gluten A protein mixture derived from wheat. In bread making, dough rises because the gluten in wheat flour expands, trapping the carbon dioxide in an elastic network. *See also* coeliac disease.

glutton. *See* wolverine.

glycerol (*or* glycerine; $CH_2OHCHOHCH_2OH$) A colourless syrupy liquid with a sweet taste. It is made from fats and oils or by fermentation and is used in explosives, cosmetics, and antifreeze solutions.

glycogen A starchlike carbohydrate found in animal tissues as a reserve energy source. It consists of branched chains of *glucose molecules and breaks down to glucose under the influence of hormones.

glycolysis The chemical reactions occurring in living cells by which glucose is partially broken down to provide usable energy in the form of *ATP. Only a small amount of the available energy is released, the rest being released via the *Krebs cycle.

Glyndebourne An estate near Lewes, in East Sussex, home of the annual Glyndebourne Festival of opera. The opera house was built by John Christie (1882–1962) in 1934 for his wife, the opera singer Audrey Mildmay (1900–53).

GMT. *See* Greenwich Mean Time.

gnat A two-winged *fly, the males of which fly in dancing swarms. Gnats include the less harmful mosquitoes, the craneflies, winter gnats, and several other species.

gneiss A coarse-grained *metamorphic rock consisting of bands of quartz and feldspar alternating with bands of micas and amphiboles.

Gnosticism A religious movement of the early Christian era that was attacked by Church Fathers. Believing in *gnosis* (Greek: knowledge)—a special revelation from God, which would ensure their salvation, they influenced *Manichaeism.

GNP. *See* gross national product.

gnu A large antelope, also called wildebeest, of African plains. Up to 140 cm high, it is grey with a black mane, and a black-tufted tail.

Goa The 25th state of India, formerly part of Goa, Daman, and Diu. It has many fine examples of Portuguese colonial architecture. Area: 3702 sq km (1429 sq mi). Population (1989): 1 007 749.

Goa, Daman, and Diu. *See* Daman and Diu.

goat A hoofed *ruminant related to sheep. Goats are 60–85 cm tall and have hollow horns. Wild goats, found in mountainous regions, live in herds. First domesticated over 10 000 years ago, goats still provide milk, meat, and hides. *See also* ibex.

Gobelins, Manufacture nationale des A French state-controlled tapestry factory, founded in Paris as a dyeworks in the 15th century by Jean and Philibert Gobelin. Manufacturing tapestries from 1529, it was incorporated by Henry IV in 1607. Since 1826 carpets have also been made.

Gobi Desert A desert of SE Mongolia and N China. On a plateau 900–1500 m (2950–4920 ft) high, it is rocky and has salt marshes. It is rich in prehistoric remains. Area: about 1 295 000 sq km (500 000 sq mi).

goby A tropical fish with an elongated body, two dorsal fins, and a suction disc formed from fused pelvic fins. Most are 5–10 cm long, although *Pandaka pygmaea* is the smallest vertebrate at under 13 mm long.

Godavari, River A river in central India, sacred to Hindus. Rising in the Western Ghats, it flows ESE to the Bay of Bengal. Length: 1500 km (900 mi).

Godesberg (*or* Bad Godesberg) 50 41N 7 10E A spa in W West Germany, in North Rhine-Westphalia on the River Rhine; since 1968 a district of Bonn. Population (1979 est): 73 512.

Godiva, Lady (d. ?1080) The English woman who, according to the chronicler Roger of Wendover (d. 1236), rode naked through the streets of Coventry to persuade her husband Leofric, Earl of Mercia, to reduce his taxes. Peeping Tom, ignoring Godiva's request that the townspeople remain indoors, was struck blind.

Godthåb. *See* Nuuk.

Godunov, Boris (Fedorovich) (c. 1551–1605) Russian statesman and tsar (1598–1605), who rose to power under *Ivan the Terrible and became regent for Fyodor I. After Fyodor's death (1598), Godunov was elected tsar.

Godwin Austen, Mount. *See* K2.

godwit A long-legged long-billed migratory bird, related to plovers and sandpipers, that breeds in N Europe, N Asia, and North America. The black-tailed godwit is 40 cm long.

Goebbels, (Paul) Joseph (1897–1945) German Nazi politician, appointed minister of propaganda by Hitler in 1933. He managed a vast machine for the control of public information with a cynical disregard for truth. He killed his wife and six children before committing suicide during the collapse of the Third Reich.

Goethe, Johann Wolfgang von (1749–1832) German poet and statesman. His discovery of Shakespeare inspired an epic drama, *Götz von Berlichingen* (1773) but he made his name with the autobiographical novel *The Sorrows of Young Werther* (1774). The Duke of Saxe-Weimar, at whose court he served, made him prime minister (1775–85). At Weimar he fell in love with Charlotte von Stein, who inspired some of his greatest poetry. A visit to Italy (1786–88) influenced such plays as *Iphigenia on Tauris* (1787) and *Torquato Tasso* (1790). After the novel *Wilhelm Meister's Apprentice Years* (1795–96) he published the first part of the drama *Faust* (1808). He published *Wilhelm Meister's Journeyman Years* in 1829 and the second part of *Faust* shortly before his death.

Gog and Magog In Revelation and other books of the Bible, attendant powers of Satan. In British folklore they are the survivors of a race of giants destroyed by Brutus, legendary founder of Britain. Statues depicting them are located in the Guildhall, London.

Gogol, Nikolai Vasilievich (1809–52) Russian novelist and dramatist. Two volumes of stories based on his Ukrainian childhood won him acclaim from *Pushkin and other writers. To escape the controversy aroused by his satirical play *The Government Inspector* (1836) he went to Rome, where he wrote *Dead Souls* (1842), attacking Russian feudalism. In his last years he became a religious maniac.

Goiânia 16 43S 49 18W A city in central Brazil, the capital of Goiás state. Founded in 1933 to replace the old capital, it serves a cattle-raising and coffee-growing area. Population (1985): 928 046.

Goidelic languages. *See* Celtic languages.

goitre Swelling in the neck caused by enlargement of the thyroid gland. This may be due to lack of iodine (required for thyroid hormone) in the water supply: the gland enlarges to increase production of the hormone. A goitre may also occur when the thyroid is overactive or underactive.

Golan Heights A range of hills in SW Syria, under Israeli administration. Of great strategic importance, they were stormed by Israeli forces in June, 1967, when most local people fled. Jewish settlements have since been established.

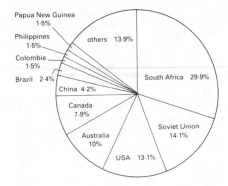

GOLD *World production (1989).*

gold (Au) A dense yellow metal valued since ancient times. It occurs as the element and in compounds with tellurium, in rock veins and alluvial deposits. It alloys with other metals, is a good conductor of heat and electricity, and is chemically unreactive. The major uses are for jewellery, electrical contacts, and as a currency

standard (*see* gold standard). Purity is measured in *carats. At no 79; at wt 196.967; mp 1064.43°C; bp 2966°C.

Gold Coast. *See* Ghana.

goldcrest A songbird, *Regulus regulus*, occurring in coniferous woodland of N Europe and Asia and feeding on insects. About 9 cm long, it has a green plumage and an orange crest.

golden eagle A large brown *eagle, *Aquila chrysaetos*, occurring in mountainous regions of North America, Europe, and Asia. 70–85 cm long with a wingspan of up to 230 cm, it catches small mammals and gamebirds.

goldeneye A diving *duck, *Bucephala clangula*, that breeds in N Europe and Asia and winters in southerly regions. It is 41–45 cm long; males are black and white with a greenish head and a white patch on the cheek; females are grey with white markings and a brown head.

Golden Fleece The fleece of a sacred winged ram, which *Jason and the *Argonauts set out to recover. Athamas, King of Thebes, had two sons, Prhixus and Helle, by his first wife Nephele. His second wife, Ino, hated her stepsons and plotted their death. They escaped across the sea on the golden ram and, having reached Colchis, sacrificed the ram to Zeus and hung the fleece in a grove sacred to Ares, where it was guarded by a dragon.

golden retriever A breed of dog whose ancestors included labradors, setters, and spaniels. The dense wavy coat is gold or cream; they are used as gun dogs, guide dogs, and police dogs. Height: 56–61 cm (dogs); 51–56 cm (bitches).

goldenrod A plant of the daisy family, up to 2.5 m tall and mostly native to North America. The stem bears heads of yellow flowers. Canadian goldenrod (*Solidago canadensis*) is often grown in gardens.

goldfinch A *finch, *Carduelis carduelis*, found in Europe and Asia. About 12 cm long, it has wings with a broad yellow stripe, a black-and-white tail and head, and a red face. Flocks of goldfinches are called charms.

goldfish A freshwater fish, *Carassius auratus*, also called golden carp, of E Asian origin. It is naturally greenish or grey and up to 30 cm long. However, over 125 ornamental varieties have been bred with a red-gold coloration.

Golding, Sir William (1911–) British novelist. His novel, *Lord of the Flies* (1954), concerns a group of schoolboys on a desert island who revert to savagery. Other novels include *Rites of Passage* (1980), which won the 1980 Booker prize, *The Paper Men* (1984), *Close Quarters* (1987), and *Fire Down Below* (1989). He was awarded the Nobel Prize in 1983.

Goldsmith, Oliver (1730–74) Anglo-Irish writer. Born in Ireland, he arrived in London in 1756. A friend of Johnson and Boswell, he was a compulsive gambler. His works include the poem *The Deserted Village* (1770), the novel *The Vicar of Wakefield* (1776), and the play *She Stoops to Conquer* (1773).

gold standard A monetary system in which paper money was converted on demand into gold. Gold reserves were a fixed proportion of the value of banknotes issued. Rates of exchange

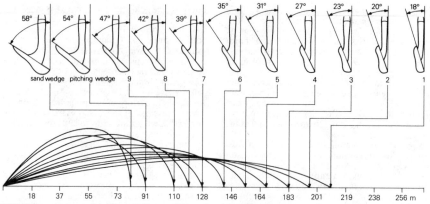

GOLF *Irons are numbered according to the angle of the face; the greater the angle of inclination, the higher the ball is hit into the air. Thus a good player, under normal conditions, knows the range of each iron. The Number One wood (driver) is used from the tee for the maximum distance and the putter is used on the green.*

between countries were fixed by their currency values in gold. Imbalances in international trade were automatically corrected by the gold standard. A country in debt would have lower gold reserves and would therefore have to reduce its money supply. Imports would be reduced and the lowering of prices would boost exports. The gold standard was finally abandoned in 1931. *See also* International Monetary Fund.

Goldwyn, Samuel   (S. Goldfish; 1882–1974) US film producer, born in Poland. In 1916 he cofounded Goldwyn Pictures, which became Metro-Goldwyn-Mayer (MGM) in 1924. His films include *Wuthering Heights* (1939) and *Guys and Dolls* (1955).

golem   In medieval Jewish folklore, an automaton brought to life by a charm. They were supposed to have been used as servants by rabbis.

golf   A club-and-ball game for two or four players that probably began in Scotland. A standard course is usually between 4572 m (5000 yd) and 6400 m (7000 yd) and is divided into 18 holes (9 on a small course), each of which is between 90 m (100 yd) and 540 m (600 yd) long. A "hole" comprises the flat starting point, called the "tee," a strip of mown grass about 27–90 m (30–100 yd) wide, called the "fairway," and a smooth putting green with a hole, diameter 10.8 cm (4.25 in), roughly at its centre. There are obstacles around the course, such as trees, ditches, and sand bunkers. The object of the game is to hit the rubber-cored ball from each tee into each hole with as few strokes as possible ("par" for a hole is the standard number of strokes needed by a first-class player; one stroke less than par is called a "birdie," and an "eagle" is two strokes less). To achieve this a player has a set of clubs of which there are three basic types: woods, irons, and putters.

Golgi apparatus (*or* Golgi complex)   A structure in the cytoplasm of nearly all cells, composed of stacks of flattened sacs bounded by membranes and usually fluid-filled sacs (vesicles). Discovered by the Italian biologist Camillo

Golgi (1843–1926), it is thought to function in the manufacture of certain secretory products, which are then packaged into the vesicles and transported within the cell.

Golgotha.   *See* Calvary.

goliath beetle   A large African beetle, *Goliathus giganteus*, that has the largest body of all the insects, measuring about 96 mm in length. It is white with black stripes.

goliath frog   The largest known living frog, *Rana goliath*, which grows up to 35 cm long and inhabits deep river pools in Africa. Its bones are supposed to have magical properties.

gomuti   A palm tree, *Arenga pinnata* (or *A. saccharifera*), also called sugar palm, occurring in SE Asia. The sap yields palm sugar and the fermented juice (palm wine) is distilled to produce arrack. A form of sago is obtained from the pith and the leaf fibres are used to make ropes.

gonadotrophin   One of several hormones that control the activity of the testes and ovaries (the gonads) in mammals. The pituitary gland produces three gonadotrophins: luteinizing hormone (LH), which (in females) stimulates ovulation and *oestrogen production by the ovaries and (in males) the production of *androgens by the testes; follicle-stimulating hormone (FSH), which promotes ovulation and sperm production; and *prolactin, which triggers milk secretion. The placenta produces chorionic gonadotrophin: measurement of human chorionic gonadotrophin (HCG) in the urine is a widely used pregnancy test.

Goncourt, Edmond de   (1822–96) French writer, who with his brother **Jules de Goncourt** (1830–70) produced histories of France, art criticism, and novels, notably *Germinie Lacerteux* (1864) and *Madame Gervaisais* (1869). Their *Journal* records literary life from 1851 to 1895. They founded the Académie Goncourt, which awards the annual literary prize, the Prix Goncourt.

Gondwanaland   The supercontinent in the S hemisphere believed to have existed prior to 200 million years ago. It probably consisted of South America, Africa, Australia, Antarctica, Arabia, and India. *See also* Laurasia; continental drift.

gonorrhoea An acute sexually transmitted infection caused by a bacterium (the gonococcus). Symptoms in men are discharge from the penis and a burning pain on passing urine. Women may have discharge from the vagina and pain on urinating. Gonorrhoea can be treated with penicillin.

Good Friday The Friday before *Easter, when Christ's crucifixion is commemorated. It is a fast day, and in the Roman Catholic Church the Mass is not celebrated. In the Anglican Church Holy Communion is rarely held.

Good Hope, Cape of. *See* Cape of Good Hope.

goose A large long-necked waterbird related to ducks and occurring in the N hemisphere. Having short bills and webbed feet, they feed on grass, roots, etc., and fly in characteristic V-formations. The breeds of domesticated goose are probably descended from the *greylag goose. *See also* Canada goose.

gooseberry A fruit bush, *Ribes uva-crispa* (or *R. grossularia*), widely cultivated for its hairy prickly berries used for preserves and in desserts.

goosefish. *See* anglerfish.

gopher. *See* souslik.

Gorbachov, Mikhail Sergeevich (1931–) Soviet statesman; general secretary of the Soviet Communist Party (1985–) and president (1988–). He became a member of the Politburo in 1980; he introduced the reforming policies of *glasnost and perestroika and reduced tension with the West. He created a new Congress of People's Deputies but came under pressure from Baltic nationalists and radical reformers.

Gordian knot A knot tying the yoke and beam of the chariot of Gordius, a legendary king of Phrygia. According to legend, whoever could undo the knot would become the ruler of Asia. In 333 BC Alexander the Great is said to have cut the knot with his sword.

Gordon, Charles George (1833–85) British general, who served in the Crimean War and then in China and Egypt. He was governor of the Sudan (1877–80); in 1884 he returned to the Sudan to evacuate Europeans and Egyptians, following al *Mahdi's revolt. Besieged for ten months in Khartoum, he was murdered two days before relief arrived.

Gordon Riots (1780) Anti-Roman Catholic riots in London encouraged by Lord George Gordon (1751–93), who opposed the Roman Catholic Relief Act (1778). The riots were crushed; Gordon was arrested but was not found guilty of treason.

Gorgons In Greek legend, three underworld monsters: the sisters Stheno, Euryale, and *Medusa. They were usually portrayed as having snakes for hair and boars' tusks for teeth.

gorilla The largest living *ape, *Gorilla gorilla*, of African forests. Male gorillas can grow to 1.8 m and weigh 300 kg. They walk on their feet and knuckles, feeding on plants and fruit. Troops, led by a dominant male, are generally not aggressive. The race of mountain gorillas is very rare.

Göring, Hermann Wilhelm (1893–1946) German Nazi politician. He served in the air force in World War I and became a Nazi in 1922, taking command of Hitler's Brownshirts. He was president of the Reichstag in 1932 and became air minister of Germany and prime minister of Prussia from 1933. He established the *Gestapo and directed the development of the Luftwaffe; in 1936 he was given charge of preparing the economy for war. Hitler declared Göring his successor in 1939 but expelled him from the party shortly before the Nazi collapse. Condemned to hang at Nuremburg, he committed suicide before the execution.

Gorki, Maksim (Aleksei Maksimovich Peshkov; 1868–1936) Russian novelist. His early life is described in his trilogy *Childhood* (1913–14), *In the World* (1915–16), and *My Universities* (1923). His other works include *Mother* (1906) and *The Lower Depths* (1906). He lived in exile (1906–13, 1921–28) before returning to Russia as a supporter of Stalin.

Gorkii (Gorki *or* Gorky; name until 1932: Nizhnii Novgorod) 56 20N 44 00E An industrial city in the central Soviet Union, on the Rivers Oka and Volga, renamed in 1932 in honour of Maksim *Gorki. Population (1987): 1 425 000.

gorse (*or* furze) A spiny shrub, *Ulex europaeus*, of the pea family native to Europe, up to 4 m high, with yellow scented flowers. The fruit is a black pod that splits explosively to release the seeds.

goshawk A large powerful grey *hawk, *Accipiter gentilis*, ranging throughout forests of the N hemisphere and formerly used in falconry. It is 60 cm long with a wingspan of 130 cm.

Gospels (Old English: good news) The four New Testament accounts of Christ's life, by *Matthew, *Mark, *Luke, and *John. The first three, known as the Synoptic Gospels, report approximately the same synopsis of the events. The fourth Gospel, John, emphasizes the divinity of Christ. *See also* Bible; New Testament.

Gossaert, Jan (c. 1478–c. 1532) Flemish painter, whose popular surname, Mabuse, was taken from his birthplace Maubeuge. Working in the Renaissance style, his sculptural nudes against Italian architectural backgrounds include *Neptune and Amphitrite* (Berlin). He was noted for his treatment of hands.

Göteborg (English name: Gothenburg) 57 45N 12 00E An ice-free port in SW Sweden, at the mouth of the River Göta. Sweden's second city, it expanded with the opening of the Göta Canal (1832), linking Göteborg with Stockholm. Population (1987): 431 521.

Gothenburg. *See* Göteborg.

gothic art and architecture The styles flourishing in Europe from the mid-12th to the end of the 15th centuries. "Gothic" was originally a derogatory term used by Renaissance artists to describe the destruction of classical art by the Goths. In church architecture, gothic design includes the rib and shaft ceiling, the pointed arch, and the flying buttress. It was first seen in France in the cathedrals of *Notre-Dame (begun 1163) and Chartres (begun c. 1194). In England it was divided into three phases: *Early English

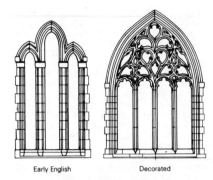

Early English   Decorated

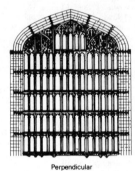

Perpendicular

GOTHIC ART AND ARCHITECTURE *In England the three phases of gothic architecture are characterized by distinctive window designs.*

(c. 1200–c. 1300; e.g. Lincoln Cathedral), *Decorated (c. 1300–70; e.g. Exeter Cathedral), and *Perpendicular (c. 1370–1540; e.g. Winchester Cathedral). Gothic sculpture, like the architecture it adorned, developed a stylized elegance. Gothic painting was first seen in manuscript illumination; its use in panel and manuscript painting came with the international gothic style of the early 15th century. The style was also the foundation of the **gothic revival** of the 19th century, as in such buildings as the Houses of Parliament in London.

gothic novel A type of English novel, popular in the late 18th and early 19th centuries, characterized by mystery, terror, and pseudomedieval –"gothic"–settings. Examples include Horace Walpole's *Castle of Otranto* (1765) and Matthew Gregory Lewis' *The Monk* (1796).

Goths Germanic peoples from Scandinavia (Gotland) who had moved into the Ukraine by the end of the 2nd century AD, before invading the Roman Empire N of the Danube and spreading into the Balkans. Their empire was destroyed by the *Huns in the late 4th century and their two groups, the *Ostrogoths and *Visigoths, separated.

Gotland (Gothland *or* Gottland) The largest of the Swedish islands, in the Baltic Sea. Long disputed between Denmark and Sweden, it was finally handed over to Sweden in 1645. Area:

3140 sq km (1225 sq mi). Population (1987): 56 269, including its associated islands. Capital: Visby.

Göttingen 51 32N 9 57E A city in central Germany. With its university and the Max Planck Association for the furtherance of science, it is an educational centre. Population (1990 est): 134 269.

Gounod, Charles François (1818–93) French composer. His most successful works were the operas *Faust* (1852–59) and *Romeo and Juliet* (1864). He also composed much sacred music.

gourd The fruit of a number of tropical plants of the cucumber family, whose woody shells are used as containers. Other gourds are grown as ornamentals.

gout Arthritis caused by the presence of uric acid crystals in the joints. The big toe and knee are commonly affected and cause great pain. It may lead to damage to the joint unless treated with substances (e.g. allopurinol) that stop the formation of uric acid.

Goya (y Lucientes), Francesco (Jose) de (1746–1828) Spanish painter. After studying in Italy, he settled in Madrid (1775), where he painted scenes of Spanish life for the royal tapestry factory and unflattering portraits of the royal family. Among his best-known paintings are *Maja Clothed, The Shootings of 3 May 1808,* and *Satan Devouring His Children* (all Prado).

Goyen, Jan Josephszoon van (1596–1656) Dutch landscape painter and etcher whose landscapes often featured large expanses of sky.

Gozzoli, Benozzo (Benozzo di Lese; 1420–97) Florentine painter. His major works are the frescoes of the *Journey of the Magi* (Palazzo Medici-Riccardi, Florence), noted for their detailed landscapes and portraits of his contemporaries.

Grace, W(illiam) G(ilbert) (1848–1915) British cricketer, who captained England in 13 Test matches. In his long career (1865–1908) he scored 54 896 runs, including 126 centuries, and took 2876 wickets.

Graces In Greek mythology, the three daughters of Zeus and Hera, representing beauty, grace, and charm. They were named Aglaia, Euphrosyne, and Thalia.

gradient A measure of the inclination of a slope, often expressed as the rise in height divided by the length of the slope, i.e. the sine of the angle of the slope. Mathematically the gradient is the ratio of the vertical rise to the horizontal distance covered, i.e. the tangent of the angle.

Graf, Steffi (1969–) German tennis player who was Wimbledon singles champion in 1988 and 1989.

grafting 1. (horticulture) The transfer of part of one plant, usually a shoot or a bud, onto another plant, usually to obtain new plants (vegetative propagation), particularly for fruit trees and roses. The transplanted piece (the scion) is fastened to the recipient plant (the stock): the wound tissue formed binding the graft together. 2. (surgery). *See* transplantation.

Grahame, Kenneth (1859–1932) British writer, known for the children's classic, *The*

Wind in the Willows (1908), adapted as a play, *Toad of Toad Hall* (1929), by A. A. *Milne.

Graiae In Greek legend, three goddesses personifying old age, the sisters and protectors of the *Gorgons. They shared one eye and one tooth. *Perseus stole the eye in order to take the Gorgons by surprise.

Grainger, Percy Aldridge (1882–1961) Australian-born composer and pianist. A friend of Grieg and Delius, he studied English folksong. His compositions include the "clog dance" *Handel in the Strand* (1913).

gram (g) A unit of mass equal to 1/1000 of a *kilogram.

grammar schools Secondary schools in the UK providing an academic education between the ages of 11 or 12 and 18. Grammar schools, established in the middle ages, originally prepared students for university or for jobs requiring a knowledge of Latin. After World War II, the demand for places forced them to restrict entry by an eleven-plus examination. Most grammar schools have now been replaced by *comprehensive schools, those that remain selecting by a twelve-plus exam.

gramophone. *See* recording of sound.

Grampian Region An administrative region in NE Scotland, created under local government reorganization in 1975. It includes the Cairngorm and Grampian Mountains in the SW. Agriculture, tourism, and fishing are important. Area: 8708 sq km (3361 sq mi). Population (1988): 497 450. Administrative centre: Aberdeen.

Grampians A range of mountains in the Grampian and Tayside Regions of Scotland. Its chief summits include Ben Nevis at 1343 m (4406 ft) and Ben Macdhui at 1309 m (4296 ft).

Grampians A mountain range in Australia. It extends SW from Victoria, reaching 1166 m (3827 ft) at Mount William.

grampus A small toothed *whale, *Grampus griseus*, also called Risso's dolphin. About 3.7 m long, grey with a pale belly, they migrate towards the Poles in summer and the equator in winter.

Granada 37 10N 3 35W A city in S Spain, in Andalusia. Formerly the capital of the kingdom of Granada, it includes many Moorish buildings (notably the Alhambra). Population (1986): 280 592.

granadilla. *See* passionflower.

Gran Chaco A plain in S central South America that caused the Chaco War between Paraguay and Bolivia (1932–35). Area: 780 000 sq km (300 000 sq mi).

Grand Banks A section of the North American continental shelf in the N Atlantic Ocean, an important fishing ground. Area: about 1 280 000 sq km (494 000 sq mi).

Grand Canal (Chinese name: Da Yunhe) The world's longest canal, in E China, extending about 1600 km (1000 mi) N–S from Peking to *Wuhan.

Grand Canyon A gorge in the USA, in Arizona, designated the **Grand Canyon National Park** in 1919. Length: 451 km (280 mi). Width: 6–29 km (4–18 mi). Greatest depth: over 1.5 km (1 mi).

grand mal. *See* epilepsy.

Grand National Steeplechase A *steeplechase, run in March at Aintree near Liverpool (England) over 30 assorted obstacles. It was first run in 1839.

granite A coarse-grained *igneous rock of acid composition, containing quartz, feldspar and mafic (dark-coloured) minerals. Most granites crystallize from magma in igneous intrusions (batholiths), but some are produced by granitic fluids rising from great depths.

Gran Paradiso 45 33N 7 17E The highest mountain in Italy, in the Alps. Height: 4061 m (13 323 ft).

Grant, Cary (Archibald Leach; 1904–86) US film actor, born in England. His films include *Holiday* (1938), *The Philadelphia Story* (1940), *To Catch a Thief* (1955), and *North By Northwest* (1959).

Grant, Ulysses S(impson) (1822–85) US general and Republican president (1869–77). As supreme commander of the Federal armies (1864–65) he defeated the Confederates, the great losses to his own side earning him the nickname Grant the Butcher. As president, he supported attempts to give Blacks the vote.

grape The fruit of the grape vine (*Vitis vinifera*), native to N Asia but widely cultivated. The fruit is used to make wine, brandy, and liqueurs or eaten fresh or dried (as raisins, sultanas, and currants).

grapefruit A tree, *Citrus paradisi*, 6–12 m high, cultivated in the tropics and subtropics. Its yellow-skinned fruits are widely eaten and used to make drinks. *See* citrus fruits.

grape hyacinth A flowering plant of the lily family, native to the Mediterranean region and widely grown as spring bulbs. The flowers grow in a cluster at the tip of a stalk, up to 15 cm high.

graphite A greyish flaky form of carbon, found in many metamorphic rocks, used as a lubricant, in pencil leads, for electrical purposes, and as a moderator in nuclear reactors. It has often been called plumbago or black lead, since it was formerly mistaken for lead.

graphology The study of a person's handwriting to reveal personality traits. Intuitive graphologists rely on an overall impression of the writing. More analytical graphologists are concerned with specific aspects (curvature, ornamentation, size and slope of letters, etc). The study has no scientific background.

grass A plant of the family *Poaceae* (or *Gramineae*), with 6000–10 000 species, found worldwide. Grasses are *monocotyledons; their leaves consist of a sheath and a long narrow blade. The flowering stems (culms) bear inconspicuous flowers. The fruit (the grain) is known as a caryopsis. Cereal grasses (wheat, barley, etc.) and sugar cane are important foods.

Grass, Günter (1927–) German writer. *The Tin Drum* (1959) established him as a moral spokesman for his generation. Other novels include *Dog Years* (1963), *The Meeting at Telgte* (1981), *Headbirths or The Germans are Dying Out* (1982), and *The Rat* (1986).

grasshopper A jumping insect with about 5000 species. 24–110 mm long, they produce sound by rubbing the hind legs against the front wings. Some species can fly (see locust).

grass snake A nonvenomous snake, *Natrix natrix*, also called water snake, occurring throughout Europe. 75–95 cm long, it has a green back with two rows of black spots, vertical black bars along its sides, and a yellow neck patch. It eats fish and small mammals.

Gravenhage, 's. *See* Hague, The.

Graves, Robert (Ranke) (1895–1985) British poet, critic, and novelist. *Goodbye to All That* (1929) recounts his experiences in World War I. His other writings include poems and the novels *I Claudius* (1934) and *Claudius the God* (1934).

gravitation An attractive force between all bodies that possess mass. It was first described by Sir Isaac *Newton in a law stating that the force between two bodies is directly proportional to the product of their masses and inversely proportional to the square of the distance between them. The constant of proportionality is called the universal **gravitational constant**, *G*, which has the value 6.673×10^{-11} N m^2 kg^{-2}.

gravitational collapse The sudden collapse of the core of a *star when its energy runs out, i.e. when thermonuclear fusion ceases. The internal gas pressure can no longer support the star's weight and the result may be a *supernova explosion. The gravitational pull of the remains of the star causes it to contract, producing a *white dwarf, *neutron star, or *black hole.

gray (Gy) The *SI unit of absorbed dose of ionizing radiation equal to the energy in joules absorbed by one kilogram of irradiated material.

Gray, Thomas (1716–71) British poet. His most famous poem is *Elegy Written in a Country Churchyard* (1751), a classical meditation on the graves of the villagers of Stoke Poges, Buckinghamshire.

grayling A troutlike fish with a silvery body, up to 50 cm long, and a sail-like dorsal fin. Graylings live in fresh waters and feed on aquatic insects. They are important food and game fish.

Gray's Inn. *See* Inns of Court.

Graz 47 05N 15 22E The second largest city in Austria, the capital of Styria. Its buildings include a cathedral (1438–62) and a clock tower (1561). Population (1981): 243 166.

Great Artesian Basin The largest area of artesian water in the world, it extends S from Queensland into South Australia and New South Wales. Area: 1 750 000 sq km (676 250 sq mi).

Great Barrier Reef The largest coral reef in the world, off NE Australia. 2012 km (1250 mi) long, its exotic plant and animal life makes it popular with tourists.

Great Bear. *See* Ursa Major.

Great Bear Lake A lake in N Canada, on the Arctic Circle that is frozen eight months of the year. Area: 31 792 sq km (12 275 sq mi).

Great Britain *England, *Scotland, and *Wales, excluding the Isle of Man and the Channel Islands. With Northern Ireland it forms the United Kingdom. Area: 229 523 sq km (88 619 sq mi). Population (1986 est): 55 196 400.

great circle A circle on the surface of a sphere formed by a plane passing through the centre of

that sphere. On the earth, meridians of longitude are half great circles; the equator is also a great circle.

Great Dane A breed of large dog originally bred in Germany for hunting boar. Height: 76 cm minimum (dogs); 71 cm minimum (bitches).

Great Dividing Range (Great Divide *or* Eastern Highlands) The E highlands of Australia. It extends for about 3700 km (2300 mi) from Cape York Peninsula to the Grampians of Victoria, reaching 2230 m (7316 ft) at Mount *Kosciusko.

Greater Antilles The four largest West Indian islands, in the N Caribbean Sea, comprising Cuba, Hispaniola, Jamaica, and Puerto Rico.

Greater Manchester A metropolitan county of NW England, created in 1974 from SE Lancashire and parts of NE Cheshire and SW Yorkshire. Area: 1285 sq km (496 sq mi). Population (1987 est): 2 580 100. Administrative centre: Manchester.

Great Exhibition (1851) A display of the products of industrial Britain and Europe, planned by Prince Albert and held in the *Crystal Palace in Hyde Park, London.

Great Glen (*or* Glen More) A rift valley extending across N Scotland from Fort William to Inverness. The Caledonian Canal was constructed along its length.

Great Lakes Five large lakes along the US-Canadian border: Lakes *Superior, *Michigan, *Huron, *Erie, and *Ontario. They form part of the *St Lawrence Seaway.

Great Ouse River (*or* R. Ouse) A river in E England, rising in Northamptonshire and flowing NE to the Wash. Length: 257 km (160 mi).

Great Plains An extensive area in North America extending from the Mackenzie River Delta in Canada to the Rio Grande in the S. Length: about 4828 km (3000 mi). Average width: about 644 km (400 mi).

Great Rift Valley (*or* East African Rift System) A rift valley that extends from the Jordan Valley in Syria along the Red Sea into Ethiopia and through Kenya, Tanzania, and Malawi into Mozambique. Length: about 6400 km (4000 mi).

Great Salt Lake A salt lake in the USA, in NW Utah in the Great Basin. Its area has fluctuated from less than 2500 sq km (1000 sq mi) to over 5000 sq km (2000 sq mi).

Great Schism (1378–1417) The split in the Roman Catholic Church following the election of two rival popes to replace Gregory XI. Urban VI was elected but his attempt to reform the College of Cardinals caused them to elect an *antipope at Avignon, Clement VII. The Schism ended with the Council of Constance (1414–18) and the election of Martin V in 1417.

Great Trek The movement of Dutch settlers (Afrikaners) in South Africa northwards from the Cape (1835–45). The so-called Voortrekkers, under such leaders as Andries Pretorius (1799–1853), moved away from British rule in search of farmland that they could administer themselves. They established the Transvaal and the Orange Free State.

Great Victoria Desert A desert of Western and South Australia consisting of sand hills and salt marshes. Area: 323 750 sq km (125 000 sq mi).

Great Wall of China   A fortification in N China. Stretching from the Yellow Sea N of Peking nearly 2400 km (1500 mi) inland, it was begun in 214 BC as a defence against nomads, but was rebuilt in the 15th and 16th centuries. About 9 m (30 ft) high, it has numerous watch towers along its length.

grebe   A bird with short wings, a small tail, and partially webbed feet; it is found in rivers and lakes worldwide. Grebes are grey or brown, usually with white underparts, and many have coloured crests and ear tufts that can be erected for display in the breeding season.

Greece, Republic of (Greek name: Ellás)   A country in SE Europe, occupying the S section of the Balkan Peninsula. Numerous islands lie to the S, E, and W; the largest is *Crete. Economy*: since the 1970s industry has replaced agriculture as the main source of revenue. Mineral resources, include lignite, bauxite, and iron ore. Tourism is also important. *History*: the collapse of the *Mycenaean civilization (c. 1200 BC) was followed by the rise of the Greek city states and establishment of colonies overseas. The 5th century BC was dominated by the unsuccessful attempt of the Persians to annex Greece and the Peloponnesian War between Athens and Sparta. Sparta's subsequent supremacy lasted until its defeat by Thebes (371). Greece fell to Philip of Macedon in 338 and became part of the empire of his son, Alexander the Great. After the last Macedonian War (171–168) Rome dominated Greece until 395 AD, when Greece became part of the Byzantine Empire. In the middle ages Greece was invaded by the Franks, Normans, and the Latin Crusaders. By 1460 control had passed to the Ottoman Turks who remained, apart from a Venetian occupation (1686–1715), until independence was achieved in 1829. In 1832 a Bavarian prince became king as Otto I (1815–67); he was deposed in 1862 and succeeded by a Danish prince as George I (1845–1913). Greek demands for Crete failed in a disastrous war with Turkey (1897), but succeeded in the Balkan Wars (1912–13). In 1917 Greece entered World War I on the Allied side, subsequently losing Smyrna to Turkey. In 1924 Greece became a republic until George II was restored in 1935. In World War II the German occupation (1941–44) was followed by civil war that lasted until 1949. Union with Cyprus dominated the 1950s. A military coup (1967) deposed Constantine II and democratic government was not reintroduced until 1975. Greece became a member of the EC in 1981. Head of state: President Constantine Karamanlis. Prime minister: Constantine Mitsotakis. Official language: Greek. Official religion: Greek Orthodox. Official currency: drachma of 100 lepta. Area: 131 986 sq km (50 960 sq mi). Population (1988 est): 10 018 000. Capital: Athens. Main port: Piraeus.

Greek language   An Indo-European language spoken chiefly in Greece and the E Mediterranean islands. Ancient Greek had many dialects, the main groupings being Ionic, Aeolic, and Doric. The Attic dialect, which became the language of classical Greece developed from Ionic. In the 4th century BC a new dialect (*koine*) developed, which became the language of *Hellenistic Greece and the New Testament. Modern Greek has two forms: Katharevusa (purified tongue) used in official publications, and Demotic, for speech, poetry, and fiction.

Greek Orthodox Church   The *Orthodox Church in Greece. The Church in Greece dates from the 1st century and St Paul's activities, especially at Corinth. After *Constantine's acceptance of Christianity in the early 4th century, Greece became one of the main Christian centres under the patriarchate of Constantinople. It is now a self-governing Church.

Greek-Persian Wars   A series of conflicts between the Greeks and Persians. Persian invasions of Greece began in 499 BC, when the Greek cities of Ionia revolted against their Persian overlords and were crushed by Darius I. In 490 the Persians were defeated by the Athenians at Marathon. Darius died in 486 and in 480 Xerxes I crossed the Hellespont with a large force. The Greeks and Persians fought at Thermopylae, where the Spartans (under Leonidas I) heroically held the pass. Xerxes now attacked Attica and Athens was abandoned. At the battle of Salamis the Persians were defeated by the Greek fleet commanded by Themistocles and were again defeated at Plataea (479). By 449 the Persians gave up hope of overcoming Greece.

green algae   *Algae of the division *Chlorophyta* (about 6000 species), that are green, owing to the presence of the pigment chlorophyll. They range from unicellular plants to complex seaweeds. They are aquatic (mainly freshwater) or terrestrial in moist areas.

green belt   An area of open land surrounding a town to prevent uncontrollable urban development. In 1935 the London County Council planned a London green belt, realized in the Green Belt Act (1938) and the Town and Country Planning Act (1947). Since the 1950s, however, planners have preserved only the more desirable areas of the countryside, permitting urban development elsewhere.

Greene, (Henry) Graham   (1904–   ) British novelist. A Roman Catholic convert (1927), he is concerned with questions of morality in his novels, including *Brighton Rock* (1938), *The Power and the Glory* (1940), *The Human Factor* (1978), *Monsignor Quixote* (1982), and *The Captain and the Enemy* (1988). His literary thrillers include *The Ministry of Fear* (1943), *The Third Man* (1950), and *Our Man in Havana* (1958). Other works are film scripts and a biography, *Getting to Know the General* (1984).

greenfinch   A Eurasian *finch, *Carduelis chloris*, about 14 cm long with a green body. The male has a yellow breast and both sexes have yellow wing flashes.

greenfly.   *See* aphid.

greengage   A widely cultivated bush or small tree, *Prunus italica*, related to the *plum, probably native to Asia Minor. It bears green fruits, used in preserves and for canning.

Greenham Common   A US airbase near Newbury in England, which became the first UK site for cruise missiles. A protest camp set up in 1981 by women failed to prevent the installation of the missiles in 1983. Protesters finally left in 1991.

greenhouse effect An effect in which radiation from the sun is transmitted through the atmosphere to the earth's surface, where it may be reradiated as longer wavelength infrared radiation. As some of this infrared is absorbed by carbon dioxide in the atmosphere, a heating effect occurs (**global warming**). A similar effect occurs in greenhouses. *See also* pollution.

Greenland (Danish name: Gro/nland; Greenlandic name: Kalaallit Nunaat) A large island off NE North America. Lying chiefly within the Arctic Circle, it is mostly covered by an ice cap, from which many glaciers emerge, breaking off to form icebergs along the coast. *Economy*: fishing is the chief occupation. Sheep are reared in the SW. Lead and zinc have been mined since the early 1970s; uranium is present. *History:* the Norwegian Eric the Red discovered (c. 986 AD) the island, which he named Greenland to attract settlers. A Danish colony from 1721, it became part of Denmark in 1953. In 1979 it gained self-government under Danish sovereignty. Prime minister: Mr Jonathan Motzfeldt (1939–). Official language: Greenland Eskimo. Official currency: Danish krone of 100 øre. Area: 2 175 600 sq km (840 000 sq mi). Population (1987): 53 733. Capital: Nuuk.

Greenpeace movement An international group founded in 1971 to campaign against nuclear power, dumping nuclear waste, and commercial whaling and sealing. Its direct action has sometimes led to confrontation; in 1985 a Greenpeace vessel was sunk in New Zealand, killing one crew member.

Green Revolution. *See* agriculture; arable farming.

green turtle A large greenish marine turtle, *Chelonia mydas*, used to make turtle soup. Up to 1 m long and weighing up to 140 kg, they occur in warm Atlantic coastal waters. An endangered species, the green turtle can now only be used to make soup if it is farmed.

Greenwich A borough of E Greater London, on the S bank of the River Thames. The Greenwich Royal Hospital, designed by *Wren, became the Royal Naval College in 1873. Wren also designed the original *Royal Greenwich Observatory. Population (1987 est): 216 600.

Greenwich Mean Time (GMT) The local time at Greenwich, London, located on the 0° meridian (*see* latitude and longitude), from which the standard times of different areas of the globe are calculated, 15° longitude representing one hour in time. It was replaced by Coordinated Universal Time (UTC) in 1986.

Greenwich Village A residential section of New York City (USA), in Manhattan. It became popular with authors and artists early in the 20th century.

Gregorian calendar. *See* calendar.

Gregorian chant The official liturgical plainchant of the Roman Catholic Church, dating from the time of Pope *Gregory I. It consists of single unaccompanied melodic lines sung to flexible rhythms.

Gregory I, St (c. 540–604 AD) Pope (590–604), known as Gregory the Great. He made peace with the Lombards, reformed the papal states, and sponsored *Augustine (of Canterbury) in his mission to England. He also introduced *Gregorian chant. Feast day: 3 Sept.

Gregory VII, St (Hildebrand; c. 1021–85) Pope (1073–85). He asserted the independence of the Church from lay control but created opposition in France and Germany, where Emperor *Henry IV declared his overthrow (1076). After being excommunicated, Henry submitted to Gregory at Canossa (1077) but then appointed Wibert, Archbishop of Ravenna, antipope (1080), invaded Italy, and captured Rome (1084). Gregory was rescued by Norman troops but was forced to flee. Feast day: 25 May.

Grenada An island country in the West Indies, in the Windward Islands. It also includes some of the Grenadine Islands. *Economy*: largely agricultural, the chief products are cocoa, fruit, sugar, and nutmeg (the main export). *History*: discovered by Columbus in 1493, it was colonized by the French and handed over to the British in 1763. In 1974 it became independent within the Commonwealth. In March, 1979, the government of Sir Eric Gairy (1922–) was overthrown in a coup led by Maurice Bishop (1944–83). Following an uprising in 1983, during which Bishop was killed, the USA invaded the country to protect US interests. Prime minister: Ben Jones. Official language: English. Official currency: East Caribbean dollar of 100 cents. Area: 344 sq km (133 sq mi). Population (1987 est): 92 000. Capital: St George's.

Grenadine Islands A chain of West Indian islets, extending for about 100 km (60 mi) between St Vincent and Grenada and administratively divided between the two.

Grenoble 45 11N 5 43E A city in SE France. The capital of the Dauphiné until 1341, now a tourist centre of the French Alps. Population (1982): 159 503.

Grey, Lady Jane (1537–54) As great-granddaughter of *Henry VII, the Duke of *Northumberland had her proclaimed Queen of England (1553) when Edward VI died. Mary, the rightful heiress, had popular support and Jane abdicated after nine days. She was executed for treason with her husband Lord Guildford Dudley.

greyhound An ancient breed of dog used for hare coursing and racing. It has a slender streamlined body with long legs. Greyhounds can reach speeds of 70 km per hour. Height: 71–76 cm (dogs); 68–71 cm (bitches).

greylag goose A *goose, *Anser anser*, occurring in Europe and Asia. 75–87 cm long, it has an orange bill and is dark grey above with pale wings and pink legs.

Grieg, Edvard Hagerup (1843–1907) Norwegian composer, whose works include the *Lyric Pieces* (1867–1901), a piano concerto (1868), incidental music to Ibsen's play *Peer Gynt* (1876), chamber music, and many songs.

griffin An eastern mythological creature with the head and wings of an eagle, the body of a lion, and often a serpent's tail.

Griffith, D(avid) W(ark) (1875–1948) US film director and pioneer. His films include *The Birth of a Nation* (1915), *Intolerance* (1916), and *Isn't Life Wonderful* (1924).

griffon A breed of dog originating in Belgium and descended from terriers. It has a square body and a large head; the tail is shortened (docked). Weight: 2–5 kg.

griffon vulture A large *vulture, *Gyps fulvus*, 100 cm long that occurs in mountainous regions of S Europe, South Africa, and Asia. It is grey with darker wingtips and a white head.

Grimm Two brothers, German linguists and folklorists. After working on medieval German texts, **Jakob Grimm** (1785–1863) and **Wilhelm Grimm** (1786–1859) published in 1812–14 their collection of folktales as *Kinder- und Hausmärchen*. The *Deutsche Grammatik* (1819, 1822) contains observations on sound changes in Indo-European languages, known as **Grimm's law**.

Grimsby 53 35N 0 05W A seaport in NE England, in Humberside. Formerly a fishing port, it now relies on other industries. Population (1987 est): 89 900.

grizzly bear. *See* brown bear.

Gromyko, Andrei (1909–89) Soviet diplomat; foreign minister (1957–85) and president of the Soviet Union (1985–88). He influenced Soviet foreign policy for over forty years.

Groningen A province in the Netherlands, bordering the North Sea. Low lying, it is intensively cultivated. Area: 2350 sq km (900 sq mi). Population (1988): 556 757. Capital: Groningen.

Gropius, Walter (1883–1969) German architect. His factory at Alfeld (1911) is a pioneer of the international modern style of architecture. As director of the *Bauhaus (1919–28) he influenced contemporary German design but moved to America to escape the Nazis.

Grossglockner 47 05N 12 44E The highest mountain in Austria, in the Alps. The Grossglockner Road (1930–35) rises to 2576 m (7852 ft). Height: 3797 m (12 457 ft).

gross national product (GNP) A measure of the total annual production of a country, including net income from abroad. GNP can be calculated on income, production, or expenditure. **Gross domestic product** (GDP) is GNP excluding net income from abroad and gives some indication of the strength of domestic industry. **Net national product** makes a provision for *depreciation, i.e. the using up of the country's capital stock.

ground beetle A long-legged beetle with 25 000 species. Dark or with a metallic sheen, they are from 2 to 85 mm long. Most are nocturnal.

ground elder A European plant, *Aegopodium podagraria*, of the carrot family, also called goutweed, bishop's weed, or herb Gerard, common as a garden weed. 49–100 cm tall, it has small white flowers. The leaves may be eaten as a salad.

groundhog. *See* marmot.

groundnut The fruit of *Arachis hypogea*, of the pea family, also called peanut or earthnut, widely cultivated in the tropics. The plant is 30–45 cm high, with yellow flowers. After fertiliza-

tion the pod ripens underground. The seeds (nuts) are eaten and used as a source of oil.

group therapy A treatment for mental illness (*see* psychotherapy) in which several patients meet together to understand their problems, usually with the help of a therapist. It can provide support in overcoming a common problem (such as alcoholism).

grouse A game bird, 30–88 cm long, found in the N hemisphere. Grouse are mostly ground-living, with short wings and feathered legs. They are noted for their courtship displays (called *leks*). They include the black grouse (*Lyrurus tetrix*), red grouse (*Lagopus lagopus scoticus*), and *capercaillie of N Europe; the *ptarmigans; and the North American ruffed grouse (*Bonasa umbellus*) and sage grouse (*Centrocercus urophasianus*). In Britain the grouse-shooting season is from 12 Aug to 10 Dec.

growth hormone (*or* somatotrophin) A protein hormone produced by the pituitary gland that stimulates the manufacture of protein, mobilizes fat reserves, increases glucose levels in the blood, and affects mineral metabolism. Lack of it in children causes dwarfism.

Grozny 43 21N 45 42E A city in the S Soviet Union. It is one of the country's richest oil-producing areas. Population (1987): 404 000.

Grünewald, Matthias (Mathis Gothardt; d. 1528) German painter. His crucifixions, notably the *Isenheim Altarpiece* (Colmar, France), are brightly coloured and influenced 20th-century German expressionists (*see* expressionism).

grunt A small fish that produces piglike grunts. It has a colourful elongated body and occurs in warm coastal waters.

Guadalajara 20 30N 103 20W The second largest city in Mexico, at an altitude of 1650 m (5413 ft). Founded by the Spanish (1530), it is a communications centre. Population (1980): 2 244 715.

Guadalcanal 9 30S 160 00E The largest of the Solomon Islands, in the S Pacific Ocean. During World War II the first major US offensive against the Japanese took place here (1942–43). Area: 6475 sq km (2500 sq mi). Population (1987 est): 71 300. Chief settlement: Honiara.

Guadalquivir, River The main river of S Spain. It flows WSW to the Gulf of Cádiz and is navigable for oceangoing vessels as far as Seville. Length: 560 km (348 mi).

Guadalupe Hidalgo (name from 1931 until 1971: Gustavo A. Madero) 19 29N 99 07W A city in Mexico, a NE suburb of Mexico City. The Basilica of the Virgin of Guadalupe, built after an Indian's vision of the Virgin Mary here in 1531, is a place of pilgrimage. The Treaty of Guadalupe Hidalgo, ending the Mexican War, was signed here. Population (1980): 370 524.

Guadeloupe A French overseas region in the West Indies. It comprises two main islands, Grande Terre and Basse Terre, together with the island dependencies of Marie Galante, La Désirade, Îles des Saintes, St Barthélemy, and the N part of St Martin. The economy is based on sugar cane. Area: 1702 sq km (657 sq mi). Population (1988 est): 336 300. Capital: Basse-Terre.

Guam   13 30N 144 40E A US island in the West Pacific Ocean, the largest of the Mariana Islands. Spanish from 1565 to 1898, it was occupied by the Japanese (1941–44). A naval and air base, it was important during the Vietnam War. Area: 450 sq km (210 sq mi). Population (1984 est): 115 756. Capital: Agaña.

Guangzhou.   *See* Canton.

Guarani   A group of South American Indians of Paraguay and neighbouring areas, who speak languages of the Tupian group. Few now retain their original culture, based on hunting and cannibalism.

Guatemala, Republic of   A country in Central America, on the Pacific Ocean, with a small outlet on the Caribbean Sea. *Economy*: the main crops are coffee, sugar, bananas, and cotton. Minerals include zinc, lead, and nickel. Oil was discovered in 1974. *History*: archaeological evidence suggests pre-Spanish civilizations, especially Maya and Aztec. Part of the Spanish captaincy general of Guatemala (1524–1821), which included most of Central America, it formed the nucleus of the Central American Federation until 1839, when it became independent. Recently democratic government has alternated with military dictatorship, accompanied by political unrest. President: Jorge Serrano. Official language: Spanish. Official religion: Roman Catholic. Official currency: quetzal of 100 centavos. Area: 108 889 sq km (42 042 sq mi). Population (1987 est): 8 990 000. Capital: Guatemala City. Main port: Puerto Barrios.

Guatemala City   14 38N 90 22W The capital of Guatemala, situated in the S of the country and founded in 1776. Population (1988 est): 1 500 000.

guava   A tropical American tree, *Psidium guajava*, of the myrtle family, about 10 m tall. Its white flowers develop into yellow pear-shaped fruits containing many small seeds. Guava fruits, rich in vitamin C, are widely eaten.

Guayaquil (*or* Santiago de Guayaquil)   2 13S 79 54W The largest city and chief port of Ecuador, on the River Guayas. Population (1987): 1 572 615.

gudgeon   A freshwater fish, *Gobio gobio*, related to *carp, found in Europe and N Asia. Its slender greenish body, up to about 20 cm long, has a row of blackish spots along each side. It is used as food and bait.

guelder rose   A small tree or shrub, *Viburnum opulus*, of the honeysuckle family, found throughout Eurasia. 4–5 m high, it has clusters of white flowers, in which the outer flowers are sterile and the smaller inner ones are fertile. The fruits are red berries. The cultivated form is called snowball tree.

guenon   A *monkey of African forests, they are 83–160 cm long including the tail (50–88 cm) and move in troops. The mona monkey (*C. mona*) is a strikingly marked guenon.

Guercino (Giovanni Francesco Barbieri; 1591–1666) Italian painter. His masterpiece, the ceiling frescos in the Casino Ludovisi, Rome, were commissioned by Pope Gregory XV in 1621.

Guericke, Otto von (1602–86) German physicist, who in 1650 invented the air pump. He staged a demonstration in which two teams of horses failed to separate a pair of large hemispheres (called the Magdeburg hemispheres after his home town) placed together from which the air had been pumped out. When air was admitted to the hemispheres they fell apart.

Guernica 43 19N 2 40W A historic Basque town in N Spain, on the Bay of Biscay. Its destruction by German planes supporting the Nationalists on 27 April, 1937, during the Spanish Civil War, is depicted in a painting by Picasso. Population (1989): 16 378.

Guernsey 49 27N 2 35W The second largest of the Channel Islands, in the English Channel. Agriculture and horticulture are important, especially dairy farming (the Guernsey cattle originated here). It is also a finance and tourist centre. Area: 63 sq km 24.5 sq mi). Population (1986): 55 482. Capital: St Peter Port.

Guevara, Che (Ernesto G.; 1928–67) Argentine revolutionary, who became the hero of left-wing youth in the 1960s. A doctor by training, he joined *Castro's invasion of Cuba (1956) and after Castro's victory, influenced Cuba's procommunist foreign relations and directed the land-reform policies. He was killed attempting to organize a revolt in Bolivia.

guide dogs   Dogs specially trained to guide the blind. The first training schools were established in Germany (1911–18) and the British Guide Dog Association was founded in 1931. The most suitable breeds for training are German Shepherd dogs (Alsatians), Labradors, and golden retrievers.

Guildford 51 14N 0 35W A city in SE England, in Surrey on the River Wey. A market and residential town, its buildings include Guildford Cathedral (founded in 1936, designed by Sir Edward Maufe). Population (1981): 56 652.

guilds (*or* gilds)   Associations formed in medieval Europe originally to further some social or religious purpose. Merchant guilds were created in many towns in the 11th century to organize local trade and became a force in local government. Craft guilds, confined to trades, were formed from the 12th century. The *livery companies of London are descended from the craft guilds.

guillemot   A bird, *Uria aalge*, occurring in coastal regions of the N hemisphere. It is 40 cm long and has brown plumage with a white belly and wing stripe; it feeds on fish and worms.

guillotine   A beheading device consisting of two vertical posts and a horizontal knife that is dropped onto the victim's neck. Invented by Joseph Ignace Guillotin (1738–1814), it was introduced in France in 1792, during the French Revolution.

Guinea, Republic of   A country on the coast of West Africa. *Economy*: the chief crops are rice and palm oil and nuts, as well as coffee and fruits. The principal minerals are diamonds, iron ore, and bauxite (alumina is the principal export). *History*: the N formed part of Ghana from the 5th to the 8th centuries AD and of the Mali empire in the 16th century. In 1849 the French established a protectorate over part of Guinea, which became part of French West Africa in 1895. In 1958 French Guinea became independent. The army took over in 1984. President: Col Lansana Conté. Official language: French and the languages of eight ethnic groups. Official currency: syli of 100 cauris. Area: 245 857 sq km (95 000 sq mi). Population (1988 est): 6 533 000. Capital and main port: Conakry.

Guinea-Bissau, Republic of (name until 1974: Portuguese Guinea) A small country on the coast of West Africa. *Economy*: the principal crops are groundnuts (the main export), rice, and palm oil. Bauxite deposits have also been discovered. *History*: explored by the Portuguese in the mid-15th century, the area became a centre of the slave trade. It became a Portuguese colony in 1879 and an overseas province of Portugal in 1951. In 1974 it became independent. After a coup in 1980, constitutional rule returned in 1984, with Maj João Bernardo Vieira as elected head of state. Official language: Portuguese; Crioulo is widely spoken. Official currency: Guinea-Bissau peso of 100 centavos. Area: 36 125 sq km (13 948 sq mi). Population (1988 est): 932 000. Capital: Bissau.

guinea fowl An African bird related to pheasants and turkeys. About 50 cm long, domesticated guinea fowl are descended from the helmet guinea fowl (*Numida meleagris*), which has a large bony crest, red and blue wattles, and a grey plumage.

guinea pig A domesticated rodent, *Cavia porcellus*, descended from the *cavy. Originally bred for food, they are now popular pets. They should be fed on grain, roots, and hay.

guinea worm A parasitic *nematode worm, *Dracunculus medinensis*, that is a serious parasite of man in Africa, India, and the Middle East. The larvae are carried by water fleas often present in drinking water. When swallowed by humans, they burrow into the tissues causing ulcers on the feet and legs.

Guinevere In *Arthurian legend, the wife of King Arthur. Malory's *Morte d'Arthur* (1485) describes her abduction by Modred and her adulterous love for *Lancelot.

Guinness, Sir Alec (1914–   ) British actor, who established his reputation in repertory in the late 1930s. His many films include *Oliver Twist* (1948), *Kind Hearts and Coronets* (1949), *The Bridge on the River Kwai* (1957), and *Star Wars* (1977).

guitar A plucked stringed instrument of Moorish origin, which came to Europe via Spain. The modern Spanish guitar has a flat back, a round sound hole, a fretted fingerboard, and six strings tuned chiefly in fourths. It has a range of over three octaves from the E below the bass stave. Music for it is written an octave higher than it sounds.

Guiyang (*or* Kuei-yang) 26 35N 106 40E A city in S China, the capital of Guizhou province. Population (1986): 1 380 000.

Gujarat A state in W India, on the Arabian Sea SE of Pakistan. Cotton, tobacco, peanuts, and other crops are raised. Area: 116 024 sq km (44 788 sq mi). Population (1984): 34 085 799. Capital: Gandhinagar.

Gujarati An Indo-Aryan language spoken by 20 million people in Gujarat and Maharashtra in India. It is related to Rajasthani, uses a version of Devanagari script, and has a rich literature.

Gulf States The nations situated on the Persian Gulf. They are Oman, United Arab Emirates, Qatar, Bahrein, Saudi Arabia, Kuwait, Iraq, and Iran.

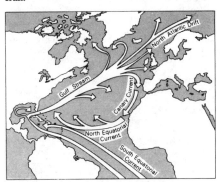

GULF STREAM

Gulf Stream A major ocean current flowing from the Florida Strait parallel to the North American coast as far as the Newfoundland banks. It bears NE across the Atlantic as the North Atlantic Drift, branching into two main directions, one flowing N towards Spitsbergen and the other S to form the Canary Current. The warm water benefits the climate of NW Europe.

Gulf War 1. (1980–88) An indecisive conflict in the Persian Gulf, between Iran and Iraq, which started with an Iraqi invasion of Iran shortly after the Iranian revolution in pursuit of claims over border territory. Peace was achieved by a UN peacekeeping force. **2.** (1991) A war between Iraq under Saddam Hussein and a US-led multinational force, precipitated by Iraq's invasion of Kuwait (2 Aug 1990) and refusal to comply with UN resolutions demanding its withdrawal. Iraq responded to coalition bombing (starting 17 Jan 1991) by missile attacks on Israel and Saudi Arabia. On 24 Feb 1991 the attack by coalition ground forces overwhelmed the Iraqi troops in Kuwait by 26 Feb. Two days later a ceasefire left the Iraqi army destroyed.

gulfweed Tropical brown algae, also called rockweed or sea holly, which forms floating masses of seaweed in the Sargasso Sea. *Sargassum natans* is a common species.

gull A seabird of coastal regions worldwide and also found inland. Up to 75 cm long, gulls are typically grey and white with long pointed wings. Some gulls feed on fish but most are scavengers.

gullet. See oesophagus.

gums Sticky *carbohydrates exuded by plants. **Gum arabic** (*or* gum acacia) is obtained from trees of the genus *Acacia*. **Gum tragacanth** is extracted from shrubs of the genus *Astragalus*. They are used as adhesives and in sweets and cosmetics.

gum tree. See eucalyptus.

gun metal A type of *bronze containing about 90% copper and sometimes a little zinc, originally used for making cannons. Admiralty gun metal (88% copper, 10% tin, 2% zinc) is used in shipbuilding.

gunnel An eel-like fish found in N Atlantic and N Pacific coastal waters. The rock gunnel (*Pholis gunnellus*), also called butterfish, is 30 cm long and brownish with black spots along the dorsal fin.

gunpowder An explosive mixture of saltpetre (potassium nitrate), sulphur, and powdered charcoal. Invented by the Chinese many centuries before its description by Roger *Bacon in the 13th century it has had a profound effect on human conflict.

Gunpowder Plot. *See* Fawkes, Guy.

Guomindang (*or* Kuomintang) The National People's Party of *Taiwan (Republic of China), started in 1912. It formed an alliance with the new Chinese Communist Party (CCP) in 1924. From 1925, the Guomindang was led by *Chiang Kai-shek and with the CCP had gained control of most of China by 1926. A break between the two parties (1927) led to civil war. After Japan's defeat in World War II, renewed civil war ended with communist victory in 1949 and the Guomindang exiled in Taiwan.

guppy A freshwater fish, *Lebistes reticulatus*, native to N South America and the West Indies. Up to 4 cm long, they are brightly coloured and popular aquarium fish.

Gurkhas Soldiers of Nepalese origin who have served in the British Army since 1815. The name comes from that of the ruling dynasty of Nepal.

gurnard A carnivorous bottom-dwelling fish, also called sea robin, found in temperate and tropical seas. It has a tapering body, up to 70 cm long, a large armoured head, and produces sound by vibrating its swim bladder.

guru In *Hinduism, an honoured spiritual teacher who personally instructs and guides the follower. In Tibetan Buddhism the guru embodies the Buddha himself. In *Sikhism, guru is the title of the first ten spiritual leaders (*see* Nanak).

Gutenberg, Johann (c. 1400–c. 1468) German printer, who invented movable metal type. In 1448 he received the financial backing of Johann Fust (1400–66) and by 1455 had produced his 42-line Bible (the Gutenberg Bible). Fust sued Gutenberg in 1455 for repayment of his loan and Gutenberg was forced to give up his machinery.

gutta percha A leathery material obtained from the latex of various trees, especially the SE Asian genus *Palaquium*. Once used as an insulator, it has now been replaced by synthetics.

Guyana, Cooperative Republic of (name until 1966: British Guiana) A country in the NE of South America, on the Atlantic Ocean. *Economy*: the main crops are rice and sugar. Minerals include gold and diamonds, but bauxite is now more important. *History*: explored by the Spanish in 1499, settlements were founded by the Dutch in the 17th century, and it became British Guiana in 1831. In 1961 it gained self-government. In 1966, as Guyana, it became independent within the Commonwealth. It is also a member of CARICOM. It became a Cooperative Republic in 1970. President: Desmond Hoyte. Official language: English. Official currency: Guyana dollar of 100 cents. Area: 210 000 sq km (83 000 sq mi). Population (1987): 812 000. Capital and main port: Georgetown.

Gwalior 26 12N 78 09E A city in India, in Madhya Pradesh. It developed around its 6th century fortress. Population (1989): 539 015.

Gwent A county of SE Wales, on the English border, created under local government reorganization in 1974. It is drained by the Rivers Wye, Usk, Monnow, Ebbw, and Rhymney. Area: 1376 sq km (532 sq mi). Population (1986 est): 441 800. Administrative centre: Newport.

Gwyn, Nell (1650–87) English actress. Originally an orange seller in Drury Lane, she became Charles II's mistress, bearing him two sons. "Let not poor Nellie starve," are said to have been his last words.

Gwynedd A county of NW Wales, bordering on the Irish Sea, created under local government reorganization in 1974. It is predominantly mountainous, rising to 1086 m (3563 ft) in Snowdon. Area: 3868 sq km (1493 sq mi). Population (1987 est): 236 300. Administrative centre: Caernarfon.

gymnastics Exercises to develop balance, strength, and coordination. In ancient Greece gymnasia were used to train men for public games. The modern sport developed in 19th-century Germany and Sweden, becoming a regular part of school curricula in Europe and increasing in popularity as a spectator sport after the medals awarded to Olga Korbut (1972) and Nadia Comaneci (1976) in the Olympics.

gymnosperms A group of seed plants in which the seeds are borne naked, often in *cones, rather than enclosed in a fruit. Gymnosperms include the *conifers, *ginkgo, and various extinct trees.

gynaecology The branch of medicine and surgery concerned with diseases of women, particularly those affecting the reproductive system. **Obstetrics** deals with pregnancy, childbirth, and the period immediately after delivery.

Gypsies. *See* Gipsies.

gypsophila A slender plant of the pink family, native to the Mediterranean area. Up to 1.5 m high, they have clusters of white or pink flowers.

gypsum A whitish mineral consisting of hydrated calcium sulphate found in clays, shales, and limestones. Rock gypsum is often red-stained, granular, and found in layers. *Alabaster is a pure fine-grained translucent form. Gypsum is used in the manufacture of cement, rubber, paper, plaster of Paris, and blackboard chalk.

gypsy moth A moth, *Lymantria dispar*, distributed throughout the N hemisphere. Males are brownish and females white. The larvae are a serious pest.

gyrfalcon The largest *falcon, *Falco rusticolus*, which breeds in N Europe, Asia, and North America. It is 60 cm long and its plumage varies from white to grey with black barring. It hunts rodents, birds, etc.

gyrocompass. *See* compass.

H

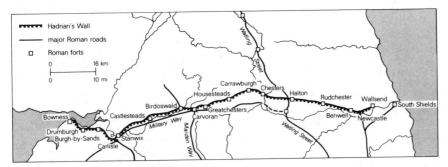

HADRIAN'S WALL *One of the largest Roman remains in the UK.*

Haakon VII (1872–1957) The first King of Norway (1905–57) following the restoration of Norwegian independence. In 1896 he married Maud (d. 1938), the daughter of Edward VII of the UK. His refusal to abdicate during the German occupation (1940–45) encouraged Norwegian resistance.

Haarlem 52 23N 4 38E A city in the W Netherlands, the capital of North Holland province. A major centre for bulbs, it is noted for its cathedral. Population (1987): 149 099.

habeas corpus (Latin: have the body) A remedy against being unlawfully taken prisoner. A court issues a writ ordering the person holding the prisoner to produce him and to agree to whatever the court directs. The writ may be used to test whether an imprisonment is legal but not to appeal against a lawful conviction.

Haber-Bosch process A method for producing ammonia from atmospheric nitrogen and hydrogen. The gases are passed over an iron catalyst at 500°C under pressure. The process was devised by Fritz Haber (1868–1934) and adapted by Carl Bosch (1874–1940).

Habsburgs (*or* Hapsburgs) The most prominent European dynasty from the 15th to 20th centuries. The family started in Switzerland in the 10th century. In 1273 Rudolph I (1218–91) was elected Holy Roman Emperor, establishing possession of Austria, Carniola, and Styria. The Habsburgs held the title again from 1438 to 1740 and from 1745 to 1806. In 1516 *Charles V inherited the Spanish Crown, which he left to his son, *Philip II; his Austrian possessions went to his brother, Ferdinand I (1503–64). The Spanish branch ruled until 1700; the Austrian Habsburgs became emperors of Austria in 1804 and of *Austria-Hungary (1867–1918).

hadal zone. *See* abyssal zone.

haddock A carnivorous food fish, *Melanogrammus aeglefinus*, related to *cod, that usually

occurs in N Atlantic coastal waters. It is up to 1 m long, greyish above and silvery below.

Hades (*or* Pluto) The Greek god of the dead; also the underworld he ruled. He was the brother of Zeus and Poseidon and husband of *Persephone, whom he abducted. The souls of the dead were ferried to Hades across the River Styx by *Charon.

Hadrian (76–138 AD) Roman emperor (117–38). His foreign policy was defensive (he sponsored the building of *Hadrian's Wall in Britain) but he subdued a Jewish revolt (132–35) with severity.

Hadrian's Wall The N frontier of Roman Britain for 250 years. Begun in 122 AD it was designed by the Emperor *Hadrian to hold back the Scottish tribes, and stretched from Tyne to Solway. It comprised ditch, stone and turf wall (incorporating forts), road system, and "vallum" (earthworks marking the military area). Substantial portions still stand.

hadron *See* particle physics.

haematite (*or* hematite) The principal ore of iron, iron(III) oxide (ferric oxide), varying in colour from red to black. It contains over 70% iron.

haemoglobin A substance, contained within red blood cells (*see* erythrocyte), consisting of a protein (globin) combined with an iron-containing pigment (haem). Haem combines with oxygen to form oxyhaemoglobin, which gives blood flowing through the arteries its red colour and enables oxygen to be transported around the body. Oxygen is released at the tissues and the pigment acquires a bluish tinge in the veins.

haemophilia A hereditary disease in which the blood does not clot properly due to absence of one of the clotting factors. The disease is restricted to males but is transmitted through the mother. If an affected person (a haemophiliac) cuts himself seriously he may bleed to death without transfusions of blood plasma.

haemorrhoids (*or* piles) Swollen veins inside the passage leading to the anus, which may enlarge sufficiently to hang outside the anus, causing bleeding and itchiness; in severe cases they are surgically removed or injected with a sclerosing agent to make them shrivel up.

Ha-er-bin (English name: Harbin) 45 45N 126 41E A port in NE China, the capital of Heilongjiang province on the Songhua River. A trading centre, it was a haven for refugees from the Russian Revolution (1917). Population (1986): 2 630 000.

hafnium (Hf) A ductile metal, first detected in zircon (ZrSiO$_4$) in 1923 and named after the Latin (Hafnia) for Copenhagen, where it was discovered. It is chemically similar to zirconium. The ability of hafnium to absorb neutrons is used to control nuclear reactors. Compounds include the chloride (HfCl$_4$), the oxide (HfO$_2$), the carbide (HfC), and the nitride (Hf$_3$N$_4$). At no 72; at wt 178.49; mp 2150°C; bp 5400°C.

hagfish A fishlike animal 40–80 cm long, related to the *lamprey. They occur near the sea bottom in cold regions. Hagfishes may develop either male or female sex organs after hatching.

Haggard, Sir H(enry) Rider (1856–1925) British writer. His government service in South Africa provided the background for his novel *King Solomon's Mines* (1885). *She* (1887) is his best known romance.

haggis A traditional Scottish dish, eaten especially on Burns' Night (25 Jan), made from minced sheep's heart, liver, lungs, onion, oatmeal, and seasoning, stuffed into a sheep's stomach.

Hague, The (Dutch name: 's Gravenhage *or* Den Haag) 52 05N 4 16E The seat of government of the Netherlands and capital of South Holland province. The International Court of Justice is located here. Notable buildings include the 13th-century Binnenhof, in which the government is housed. Population (1987): 445 127.

Haifa 32 49N 34 59E A manufacturing town in NE Israel, on the Mediterranean coast by Mount Carmel. It was the scene of fighting in the 1948–49 Arab-Israeli conflict. Population (1986): 223 400.

Haig, Douglas, 1st Earl (1861–1928) British field marshal, who commanded the British Expeditionary Force in France during World War I. Under the supreme command of *Foch, Haig directed the final victorious assault on the Hindenburg line.

hail The ice pellets that fall from cumulonimbus clouds (*see* cumulus cloud), and originate as ice particles around which layers of ice freeze.

Haile Selassie I (1892–1975) Emperor of Ethiopia (1930–36, 1941–74). In 1936 he fled to England after the Italian invasion, but was restored by the Allies in 1941. He was a prominent figure in international affairs before being overthrown by a military coup.

Hailsham, Quintin McGarel Hogg, Baron (1907–) British lawyer and Conservative politician; Lord Chancellor (1970–74, 1979–87). From 1959 to 1963 he was minister for science and technology. In 1950 he succeeded his father **Douglas McGarel Hogg, 1st Viscount Hailsham**

(1872–1950), Lord Chancellor (1928–29, 1935–38), but disclaimed his viscountcy in 1963 when bidding unsuccessfully for the Conservative leadership. In 1970 he became a life peer.

Hainan Island A Chinese island separated from the mainland by **Hainan Strait**. Sparsely populated, it is one of China's least developed regions. Rubber and timber are produced and iron ore and other minerals are mined. Area: 33 991 sq km (13 124 sq mi). Population (1986 est): 6 000 000. Capital: Haikou.

Hainaut (Flemish name: Henegouwen; French name: Hainault) A province in SW Belgium, bordering on France. It contains coalfields and iron and steel works. Area: 3997 sq km (1466 sq mi). Population (1986): 1 274 034. Capital: Mons.

Haiti, Republic of A country in the Caribbean Sea, occupying the W third of the island of Hispaniola. *Economy*: the main crops are coffee (the principal export), sugar, rice, bananas, and sisal. *History*: the island was discovered by Columbus in 1492 and became a Spanish colony. The E part was handed over to France in 1697, becoming the most prosperous French colony. In 1804 Haiti gained independence; a period of unrest was followed by union with the rest of the island (1822–44). After a series of coups Dr François *Duvalier came to power in 1957 and was succeeded in 1971 by his son, Jean-Claude Duvalier. In 1986 this regime fell in a military coup, and after several brief military regimes Father Jean-Bertrand Aristide was elected president in 1991. Official language: French; Creole is widely spoken. Official religion: Roman Catholic. Area: 27 750 sq km (10 700 sq mi). Population (1988 est): 6 096 000. Capital and main port: Port-au-Prince.

hake A fish related to *cod that occurs in European, African, and American coastal regions. Its body, up to about 1 m long, is grey above and lighter below.

Haldane, Richard Burdon, 1st Viscount (1856–1928) A Liberal MP (1885–1911) until becoming a peer, he was secretary for war (1905–12) when he formed the Territorial Force (*see* Territorial Army). Becoming Lord Chancellor in 1912 he was dismissed in 1915, accused of being pro-German. He wrote a study of *relativity, *The Reign of Relativity* (1921) and helped to found the London School of Economics (1895). His brother **John Scott Haldane** (1860–1936) was a physiologist, who improved mine safety by demonstrating the poisonous effects of carbon monoxide. J. S. Haldane's son **John Burdon Sanderson Haldane** (1892–1964) was a geneticist, working especially on evolution and population genetics. A Marxist, he edited the communist *Daily Worker* (London) during the 1930s.

half-life The time taken for half the atoms in a sample of a radioactive isotope to decay. A very active isotope may have a half-life of only a millionth of a second, whereas some have half-lives of millions of years.

halibut A *flatfish up to about 2 m long, found in N Atlantic coastal waters. The eyed side is mottled brownish.

Halifax 53 44N 1 52W A town in N England, in West Yorkshire on the River Calder, with a strong wool textile tradition. Carpets and worsteds are manufactured as well as machine tools and textile machinery. Population (1981): 87 488.

Halifax 44 38N 63 35W A city and port in E Canada, the capital of Nova Scotia. Founded as a British naval base (1749), its industries include shipbuilding, oil refining, and food processing. Population (1986): 113 577.

Hall, Sir Peter (1930–) British theatre director, who ran the Royal Shakespeare Company (1960–68) and the National Theatre Company (1973–1988).

Halle 51 30N 11 59E A city in central Germany, on the River Saale. The birthplace of Handel. Its industries include sugar refining and coalmining. Population (1986): 234 768.

Hallé, Sir Charles (Karl Hallé; 1819–1895) German conductor, who settled in Britain in 1848 and in 1857 established a series of concerts in Manchester, for which he founded and conducted the **Hallé Orchestra.**

Halley, Edmund (1656–1742) British astronomer. The first to realize that *comets have periodic orbits, he identified (1705) a particular comet, now known as **Halley's comet**, as having a period of 76 years (appearing 1986, 2062, etc.). He was appointed astronomer royal to succeed *Flamsteed (1720).

hallmarks Marks stamped onto British gold or silver objects as a guarantee of purity. Each article has the mark of the assay office, an assay mark to indicate quality, a date mark, the sovereign's head (1784–1890), and the maker's mark. Gold articles also have a mark to indicate purity in *carats.

Hallowe'en 31 Oct, the eve of All Saints' Day. The name comes from All Hallows (hallowed or holy) Eve. Before Christianity came to Britain, 31 Oct was the eve of New Year, when the souls of the dead were thought to revisit their homes. Customs include the shaping of a demon's face from a hollow turnip or pumpkin, in which a candle is then placed.

hallucination A false sensation (affecting any of the senses) of something that is not there. It may be a result of mental illness, especially psychosis, the commonest forms being hearing voices and seeing visions. Drugs, epilepsy, brain disease, and sensory deprivation can also cause it.

halogens The elements forming group VII of the *periodic table: fluorine, chlorine, bromine, iodine, and astatine. In chemical reactions they tend to form negative ions or covalent bonds and they have a valence of 1. All are reactive, particularly fluorine and chlorine. They produce salts on contact with metals ("halogen" means salt-yielding).

Hals, Frans (c. 1581–1666) Dutch painter born in Antwerp, who worked mainly in Haarlem. Apart from his *Laughing Cavalier* (1624; Wallace Collection, London), he is best known for his group portraits. Later works include *Lady-Governors of the Almshouse at Haarlem* (1664; Frans Hals Museum, Haarlem).

hamadryas A small *baboon, *Papio hamadryas*, of NE Africa and Saudi Arabia. 100–140 cm long including the tail, they have silvery mane (very long in males), pinkish face, and red buttocks. They were sacred animals in ancient Egypt.

Hamburg 53 33N 10 00E A city and port in N Germany, on the Rivers Elbe and Alster. A leading commercial centre, it has a university (1919), art gallery, and opera house (1678). Industries include shipbuilding and engineering. Population (1987): 1 571 300.

Hamelin (German name: Hameln) 52 06N 9 21E A town in N Germany, in Lower Saxony on the River Weser. Its many Renaissance houses include the Ratcatcher's House (1602–03), associated with the legendary Pied Piper. Population (1984): 56 000.

Hamilcar Barca (died c. 229 BC) Carthaginian general and Hannibal's father. Commander in Sicily during the first *Punic War, he agreed peace in 241. After suppressing rebellious mercenaries in Carthage, he invaded Spain. He was drowned after the siege of Helice.

Hamilton 43 15N 79 50W A city and port in central Canada, in S Ontario on Lake Ontario. Canada's main centre for the iron and steel, vehicle, and machinery industries, it is also a financial and educational centre. Population (1986): 306 728.

Hamilton 37 46S 175 18E A city in New Zea-

A typical hallmark, from an article assayed in London in 1796.

London   Birmingham

A leopard's head introduced in 1300 (crowned between 1478 and 1821).   *An anchor introduced in 1773.*

Sheffield   Glasgow

The crown introduced in 1773.   *A tree embellished with bell, bird, and fish, introduced in 1681.*

Edinburgh   Dublin

The castle introduced in mid-16th century. The thistle was introduced in 1759.   *The crowned harp introduced in mid-17th century. In 1731 the figure of Hibernia was added.*

marks of some other halls

Chester   Newcastle-on-Tyne   York

Norwich   Exeter

HALLMARKS *A set of typical hallmarks and the marks of the different assay offices.*

land, in N North Island on the Waikato River. It serves a farming and lumbering region. The University of Waikato was established in 1964. Population (1988): 103 500.

Hamilton, Emma (c. 1761–1815) The mistress of Horatio *Nelson, by whom she had a daughter, Horatia (1801–81). After Nelson's death (1805), Lady Emma ran into debt and fled to Calais (1814), where she died. She was formerly the mistress of Charles Greville (1749–1809) and then of his uncle Sir William Hamilton (1730–1803), whom she married in 1791.

Hammarskjöld, Dag (Hjalmar Agne Carl) (1905–61) Swedish international civil servant. As deputy foreign minister (1951–53) he headed the Swedish delegation to the UN, of which he became secretary general in 1953, dealing with the Suez crisis (1956) and the civil war in the Congo (1960). He died in a plane crash and was awarded the Nobel Peace Prize posthumously in 1961.

hammerhead shark A shark, up to 4.5 m long, whose head is flattened and extended on either side into two hammer-shaped lobes, which bear the eyes and nostrils. Found in warm and temperate seas, they feed primarily on fish.

Hammerstein II, Oscar (1895–1960) US lyricist and librettist, who with Richard Rodgers wrote *Oklahoma!* (1943), *Carousel* (1945), *South Pacific* (1949), *The King and I* (1951), and *The Sound of Music* (1959).

hammer throw A field event for men in athletics. The hammer is an iron or brass sphere weighing 16 lb (7.26 kg) attached to a wire handle and grip. It is thrown with both hands within a circle 7 ft (2.13 m) in diameter. World record: 86.74 m (1986) by Yuri Sedykh (Soviet Union).

Hammett, Dashiell (1894–1961) US novelist. He worked as a private detective before writing such detective stories as *The Maltese Falcon* (1930) and *The Thin Man* (1932).

Hampshire A county of S central England, bordering on the English Channel. The chief rivers, the Test and Itchen, drain into the Solent, which separates the Isle of *Wight from the mainland. It is predominantly agricultural; industries, centred on Southampton, include shipbuilding and oil refining, with naval bases at Portsmouth and Gosport. Tourism is important in the *New Forest and coastal resorts. Area: 3772 sq km (1456 sq mi). Population (1989 est): 1 542 900. Administrative centre: Winchester.

Hampton Court A palace on the River Thames near London. Built by Cardinal Wolsey, it was given in the 1520s to Henry VIII, who made substantial alterations; in the 1690s *Wren made further alterations for William III.

hamster A small *rodent, *Cricetus cricetus*, native to Europe and W Asia. It has a red-brown coat with white patches. The golden hamster (*Mesocricetus auratus*), a domestic pet, is thought to be descended from a single family found at Aleppo, Syria, in 1930.

Han (206 BC–220 AD) A Chinese dynasty founded by the general Liu Bang (*or* Liu Pang; 256–195 BC), who overthrew the Qin dynasty. Its power was strengthened by the emperor Wu Di (157–87 BC; reigned 140–87), who conquered a vast empire. Paper was invented by the Han Chinese, who also produced porcelain. The dynasty was overthrown in 8 AD but later restored for a second period, known as the Later Han (23–220 AD).

Handel, George Frederick (1685–1759) German composer, born in Halle. In 1710 he became kapellmeister to the Elector of Hanover but did not return there after visiting England in 1712. He subsequently became music master to the Prince of Wales and director of the Royal Academy of Music on its foundation in 1720. His Italian operas, such as *Alcina* (1735), were successfully produced in London; from 1739 he turned from opera to oratorio, producing such masterpieces as *Saul* (1739), *Israel in Egypt* (1739), and *Messiah* (1742). Other works include the *Water Music* (1717), *Music for the Royal Fireworks* (1749), sonatas, organ concertos, harpsichord suites, and anthems. He became blind in 1751 and is buried in Westminster Abbey.

Hangchow. *See* Hangzhou.

hang-gliding Gliding using a large cloth wing on a light metal framework from which the pilot hangs in a harness, holding a horizontal control bar. The first hang-glider was built by Otto Lilienthal, but the first of the modern design was the sail-wing invented by Frances Rogallo (1912–). Hang-gliding became popular in the late 1960s. A powered hang-glider first crossed the Channel in 1979.

Hanging Gardens of Babylon Gardens in the palace of Nebuchadnezzar II (604–562 BC) on the E side of Babylon. One of the Seven Wonders of the World, they were built on stone arches and watered from the Euphrates by a mechanical system.

Hangzhou (Hang-chou *or* Hangchow) 30 18N 120 07E A city in E China, the capital of Zhejiang province on Hangzhou Bay, an inlet of the East China Sea. It was the capital (1132–1276) of the Southern Song dynasty. Population (1986): 1 250 000.

Hankou (*or* Hankow). *See* Wuhan.

Hannibal (247–c. 183 BC) Carthaginian general. Appointed commander in Spain in 221, he deliberately started the second *Punic War at Rome. In 218 he crossed the Alps in winter, using elephants and losing about 10 000 of his 35 000 men. For two years he devastated Italy, but lost ground in the face of *Fabius' guerrilla tactics. Recalled to defend Carthage after Scipio Africanus' invasion of Africa, Hannibal was defeated at Zama (202). He committed suicide to avoid capture by the Romans.

Hanoi 20 57N 105 55E The capital of Vietnam, situated in the NE on the Red River. The capital of the Vietnamese empire from the 11th to 17th centuries, it was occupied by the French in 1873 and became the capital of French Indochina. Following the Japanese occupation in World War II, it became the capital of the Democratic Republic of Vietnam. Population (1983 est): 2 674 400.

Hanover (German name: Hannover) 52 23N 9 44E A city in N Germany, the capital of Lower Saxony on the River Leine. An industrial centre, products include machinery, textiles, and motor vehicles. *History*: in 1638 Hanover became the capital of the future electorate and kingdom of Hanover. In 1714 Elector George Louis became George I of Great Britain (*see* Settlement, Act of). The Kings of Great Britain were Electors (later Kings) of Hanover until 1837. Population (1986): 506 400.

Hansard The official reports of debates in the UK *parliament, so named since 1943 after **Luke Hansard** (1752–1828) and his son **Thomas Curson Hansard** (1776–1833) who printed it until 1890 when the HM Stationery Office took it over.

Hanseatic League An association of N German trading towns (the Hanse) formed in the 13th century. By the mid-14th century, it had become powerful and conducted a number of trade wars with Denmark and England. Thereafter, its influence declined, being finally dissolved in 1669.

Hanuman In Hindu mythology, a monkey god and one of the main characters in the *Ramayana*.

Hanyang. *See* Wuhan.

Hapsburgs. *See* Habsburgs.

hara-kiri Ceremonious suicide used by Japanese *samurai to avoid shame. It involved cutting one's stomach open with a dagger before decapitation by the sword of another samurai. It is now illegal.

Harare (name until 1982: Salisbury) 17 50 S 31 02 E The capital of Zimbabwe. Founded in 1890, it was the capital of the Federation of Rhodesia and Nyasaland (1935–63). It has two cathedrals and is the centre of a tobacco-growing area. Population (1987 est): 863 100.

Harbin. *See* Ha-er-bin.

Hardanger Fjord A fjord in SW Norway, S of Bergen, penetrating inland from the North Sea for 110 km (68 mi).

Hardecanute (*or* Harthacanute; c. 1019–42) The last Danish King of England (1040–42), succeeding his illegitimate half-brother Harold I Harefoot, and King of Denmark (1035–42). He destroyed Worcester after a riot against his tax collectors.

Hardy, Thomas (1840–1928) British novelist and poet. His novels, set in his native Dorset (called Wessex in his books), include *The Return of the Native* (1878), *The Mayor of Casterbridge* (1886), and *Tess of the D'Urbervilles* (1891). After the public outrage caused by the alleged immorality of *Jude the Obscure* (1895) he published mainly verse. He was awarded the OM in 1910.

hare A widely distributed mammal related to the *rabbit but larger, with long black-tipped ears. They live in the open, are mainly nocturnal, and feed on grass and bark.

harebell A flowering plant, *Campanula rotundifolia*. Growing to 60 cm, it has blue bell-shaped flowers.

Hare Krishna movement (Sanskrit: hail Krishna) A religious community, the International Society for Krishna Consciousness (ISK-CON), founded in New York in 1966 on Hindu principles by Swami Prabhupada (1895–1977).

Members are vegetarian, must not gamble, commit adultery, or use drugs. They dress in saffron robes and the men have shaved heads.

Hargreaves, James (d. 1778) Englishman from Blackburn who invented the spinning jenny (1764), a machine enabling several threads to be spun together. After local spinners, believing their jobs were threatened, broke up his machines, Hargreaves set up (1768) a small mill in Nottingham.

haricot bean A variety of *French bean used as a vegetable or canned as baked beans.

Harlech 52 N 4 07W A historic town in NW Wales, in Gwynedd on Cardigan Bay. It has a ruined castle. Population (1989 est): 1313.

Harlem 40 49N 73 57W A residential district of New York City, USA, in Manhattan. It is a political and social focus for Blacks.

Harlequin A character of the *commedia dell'arte, who began as a comic servant but developed into the lover of Columbine and the central figure of the harlequinade, dressed in a diamond-patterned costume, masked, and carrying a wooden club.

harmonica The mouth organ: the smallest member of the reed organ family; invented by Sir Charles Wheatstone (1802–75) in 1829. Notes are obtained by blowing or sucking rows of parallel reeds.

harmonium A keyboard instrument of the reed organ family, patented in 1848 by Alexandre Debain (1809–77) in Paris. Its reeds vibrate when air is blown past them by foot-operated bellows (*see* organ).

harmony The combining of musical notes into chords. Before about 1650 composers made use of polyphony; between about 1650 and about 1900 (the **harmonic period**) a system of harmony evolved based on diatonic chords (*see* scale), consisting of three notes sounded simultaneously; a note of the key of the composition and the notes a third and a fifth above it. A **harmonic progression** consists of a particular sequence of chords, especially one leading (*or* modulating) into another key. In the early 20th century Schoenberg invented *serialism as a substitute for harmony.

Harold I Harefoot (d. 1040) Danish King of England (1037–40). The illegitimate son of Canute, he became king while Hardecanute, Canute's legitimate son, was in Denmark. Before Hardecanute could overthrow him, Harold died.

Harold II (c. 1022–66) The last Anglo-Saxon King of England (1066). He crushed the forces of his brother Tostig (d. 1066) and Harold III Hardraade of Norway (1015–66) at Stamford Bridge (1066) but was killed in the battle of *Hastings by the army of *William the Conqueror.

harp A plucked stringed instrument of ancient origin. The modern orchestral harp is triangular with about 45 strings stretched between the soundbox and the neck. The pillar contains a mechanism enabling each string to be raised by one or two semitones by means of pedals. The harp has a range of six and a half octaves from the B below the bass stave.

Harpies In Greek mythology, malicious spirits originally conceived as winds but later portrayed as birds of prey with ugly women's faces.

harpsichord A keyboard instrument with strings plucked by quills. The tone can be changed by the addition of stops, which sound strings an octave below or above the note played. It was widely used in the 16th to 18th centuries. *See also* spinet; clavichord.

harquebus (*or* arquebus). *See* musket.

harrier A long-legged widely distributed *hawk, about 50 cm long, and usually brown with a long tail. They feed on frogs, mice, and other small animals.

Harris. *See* Lewis with Harris.

Harrogate 54 00N 1 33W A town and spa in N England, in North Yorkshire, that is a resort and trade centre. Population (1987 est): 69 270.

hartebeest A long-faced fawn coloured antelope, *Alcelaphus busephalus*, of African plains. About 120 cm high, hartebeests have lyre-shaped horns.

Hartford 41 45N 72 42W A city in the USA, the capital of Connecticut and one of the leading insurance centres in the world. Population (1980): 136 392.

Hartlepool 54 41N 1 13W A port in NE England, in Cleveland. Originally a fishing port and medieval walled town, Hartlepool's industries include engineering and timber working. Population (1988 est): 90 000.

Harvard classification system A system, introduced in the 1890s by astronomers at the Harvard College Observatory (USA), by which stars are classified into seven spectral types: O, B, A, F, G, K, and M, in order of decreasing temperature. There are 10 subdivisions for each spectral type, indicated by a digit (0–9) placed after the letter.

Harvard University The oldest university in the USA (founded 1636), located at Cambridge, Massachusetts and named after the clergyman John Harvard (1607–38). The associated women's college, Radcliffe College, dates from 1879.

harvestman A widely distributed *arachnid, also called harvest spider. It has an undivided body, 1–22 mm long, and long legs. They feed on insects and plant materials.

harvest mite A *mite, also called chigger and scrub mite. Its larvae are parasites of man and other vertebrates, feeding on skin and causing inflammation.

Harvey, William (1578–1657) English physician to James I and Charles I. His discovery of blood circulation, published in *On the Motion of the Heart and Blood in Animals* (1628), aroused controversy, but was accepted by his death.

Harwich 51 57N 1 17E A seaport in E England, in Essex on the estuary of the Rivers Stour and Orwell. It has passenger services to Scandinavia and the Continent. Population (1988 est): 15 543.

Haryana A state in N India, mostly in the fertile Upper Ganges plain. It produces cereals, cotton, sugar, and oilseeds. There is some light industry. Area: 44 222 sq km (17 070 sq mi). Population (1981): 12 850 902. Capital: Chandigarh.

Harz Mountains A mountain range extending about 90 km (56 mi) across Germany W of Halle. The highest peak is the Brocken.

hashish. *See* cannabis.

Hasidism A Jewish movement, founded by the Ba'al Shem Tov (c. 1700–60). A blend of *kabbalah and simple piety, Hasidism spread throughout the Jewish communities of E Europe in the 18th and 19th centuries. Many European communities were destroyed in the *holocaust, but some still thrive in America and Israel.

Hassan II (1929–) King of Morocco (1961–). Educated in France, Hassan maintains dictatorial rule in Morocco. He introduced some reforms in 1971 and has pressed Moroccan claims to the Western Sahara.

Hastings 50 51N 0 36E A town on the S coast of England, in East Sussex. Formerly the chief of the Cinque Ports, it has a ruined castle built by William I. Population (1981): 74 803.

Hastings, Battle of (14 October, 1066) The battle at Senlac Hill (*see* Battle), near Hastings, in which William, Duke of Normandy, claiming the English throne, defeated Harold II of England. Harold's death enabled William to conquer England (*see* Norman conquest).

hatchetfish A carnivorous hatchet-shaped fish, up to 10 cm long. Deepsea hatchetfish are related to *salmon but the freshwater or flying hatchetfish of South America are related to *carp.

Hathaway, Anne (c. 1556–1623) The wife of William *Shakespeare. Born at Shottery, near Stratford, she married Shakespeare in 1582 and bore him three children. Her cottage may still be seen in Stratford.

Haughey, Charles (1925–) Irish statesman; prime minister of Ireland (1979–81, 1982, 1987–). He has been president of the Fianna Fáil party since 1979 and has also served in several ministerial posts.

Hausa A people of NW Nigeria and S Niger, numbering about nine million. Their language belongs to the Chadic subgroup of the Hamito-Semitic family. Mainly Muslim, they live in small settlements and grow maize, etc.

Havana (Spanish name: La Habana) 23 00N 82 30W The capital of Cuba, a port in the NW. It exports sugar, cotton, and tobacco. *History*: the original settlement was on the S coast, but the inhabitants moved to the city's present site in 1519. It became the capital of Cuba in the late 16th century. Population (1986 est): 2 014 800.

Havel, Václav (1936–) Czech dramatist and statesman. A leading dissident, he became president of Czechoslovakia after the fall of the Communist regime in 1989.

Hawaii (former name: Sandwich Islands) A state in the USA, occupying a chain of over 20 volcanic islands in the central Pacific Ocean. These include the islands of Hawaii (the largest), Maui, Oahu, Kauai, and Molokai. The main crops are sugar and pineapples; manufactures include oil and chemicals. There are many US military bases and tourism is important. *History*: first discovered by Capt Cook in 1778, Hawaii remained a kingdom until becoming a republic in 1893. It was annexed by the USA in 1894; the

Japanese attack on Pearl Harbor in 1941 precipitated the entry of the USA into World War II. Hawaii became a state in 1959. Area: 16 641 sq km (6425 sq mi). Population (1987 est): 1 082 000. Capital: Honolulu.

Haw-Haw, Lord. *See* Joyce, William.

hawk A bird of prey of which there are over 200 species, ranging from small *sparrowhawks to the 100 cm-long harpy eagle; they have powerful gripping feet and highly developed eyesight. *Compare* falcon.

Hawke, Robert (James Lee) (1929–) Australian statesman; Labour prime minister (1983–). He was president of the Australian Council of Trade Unions (1970–80) before becoming president (1973–78) and leader (1983–) of the Labour Party.

Hawking, Stephen William (1942–) British physicist. Despite suffering from a progressive nervous disease since the 1960s, he described the particle emission of black holes (1974) and showed that general relativity supports the big-bang theory. His *A Brief History of Time* (1987) was a popular bestseller.

Hawkins, Sir John (1532–95) English navigator. The first (1562) to transport slaves from West Africa to the Spanish West Indies. In 1577 he became treasurer of the navy, introducing reforms that contributed to the defeat of the *Armada (1588). He died at Puerto Rico on an expedition with Drake. His son **Sir Richard Hawkins** (c. 1562–1622) served against the Armada and in a subsequent expedition was seized by the Spanish and imprisoned (1594–1602).

hawk moth A moth, also called sphinx moth or hummingbird moth, of which there are about 1000 species. They have large bodies and rapidly beat their small wings hovering over flowers and sipping nectar.

hawksbill turtle A small sea turtle, *Eretmochelys imbricata*, that feeds on algae, fish, etc., and is 40–55 cm long. Its shell is used as tortoiseshell.

Hawksmoor, Nicholas (1661–1736) English baroque architect, who trained with *Wren and *Vanbrugh. His buildings include Easton Neston (1702), All Souls', Oxford (1729), and St Anne's, Limehouse (1714).

hawthorn A thorny shrub or tree with lobed leaves, white flowers, and yellow or red fruits. The European common hawthorn, or may (*Crataegus monogyna*), is found in hedgerows and has red fruits (haws).

Haydn, Franz Joseph (1732–1809) Austrian composer, born in Rohrau. A cathedral chorister in Vienna at the age of eight, he subsequently worked as a freelance musician. In 1761 he became kapellmeister to the Esterházy family, a post he retained for the rest of his life, visiting London in 1791 and 1794. Haydn's compositions include piano sonatas, piano trios, string quartets, masses, concertos, 104 symphonies, operas, and the oratorios *The Creation* (1798) and *The Seasons* (1801).

hay fever An *allergy to pollen, which leads to sneezing, a streaming nose, and inflamed eyes. Treatment involves taking *antihistamines or, in severe cases, steroids.

hazel A hardy shrub or tree up to 12 m high, cultivated for its edible nuts, also called cob nuts. The male flowers are yellow catkins; each female flower develops into a nut.

Hazlitt, William (1778–1830) British critic and essayist. The son of a Unitarian minister, he expressed his opinions brilliantly in such collections as *Lectures on the English Poets* (1818) and *The Spirit of the Age* (1825).

hearing aid A device used by the partially deaf to increase the loudness of sounds. A simple form is the ear trumpet, whose conical shape increases the sound pressure at the ear. Modern electronic aids consist of a microphone, an amplifier, and an earphone in a tiny capsule.

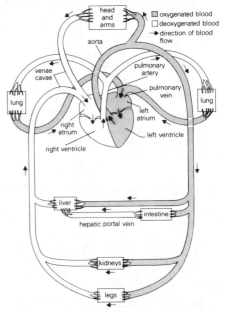

HEART *In man and other mammals the right and left chambers of the heart are completely separate from each other. This ensures that oxygenated and deoxygenated blood do not mix and enables oxygen-depleted blood to receive a fresh supply of oxygen from the lungs before circulating to the rest of the body.*

heart A muscular organ that pumps blood around the body. In mammals it has four chambers—the left and right atria enlarge to receive oxygen-rich blood from the lungs and oxygen-depleted blood from the rest of the body, respectively (this is called diastole). Contraction of the heart (called systole) starts in the atria, forcing blood into the two ventricles. The left ventricle then contracts to force blood into the aorta, which leads to all the other arteries. The right ventricle pumps blood into the pulmonary artery and lungs, where it receives oxygen. Valves between the atria and ventricles and at the entrance to each artery prevent backflow. The heartbeat is maintained by the electrical activity of special-

Communication   Torches and smoke signals have been a means of communication since humans learnt how to make fire.

Pottery   As soon as humans had mastered the use of fire they were able to bake pottery. This began about 7000 BC, in the Neolithic age. Quite sophisticated pottery vessels like this one, were being made in central Europe in 3000 BC.

Metallurgy   This copper-headed axe (c. 3000 BC) was probably made from a lump of copper metal, hammered and softened over an open fire. Smelting copper ores and adding tin to make bronze soon followed. Thus fire enabled humans to enter the Bronze Age.

An iron Hittite dagger (c. 2500 BC). Copper melts at 1083° C, a temperature reached easily in an open wood fire. To reach the melting point of iron (1539° C), a forced-draught (blast) furnace is needed. The Hittites in the second millenium BC were the first iron smelters.

War   The atom bomb dropped on Hiroshima in 1945 provided the world with its first evidence that fire could be made not only by combustion but also by nuclear fission. This form of energy is now used to generate about 5% of the world's electricity.

Chronology

500 000 BC	Man-made fire believed to have existed
7000 BC	Used by Neolithic man for cooking, pottery, and agriculture

6000 BC	Neolithic	Smoke signalling
5000 BC		
4000 BC	Bronze Age	Fire worship
3000 BC		
2000 BC	Iron Age	
1000 BC		

460 BC	Emendocles gives fire as one of the four elements
1000 AD	
1250	Gunpowder invented
1450	Canon invented
1696	Savery's steam engine invented
1876	Otto's internal-combustion engine invented
1938	Whittle's jet engine invented
1945	First atom bomb explodes

Industrial revolution   Hero of Alexander (100 AD) invented the first steam-driven device by boiling water over fire. The first workable steam engine was built by Savery in 1696 using this principle. Newcomen, whose engine is seen here, and Watt made practical external-combustion engines that operated factory machinery and powered the industrial revolution. They also drove the first railway locomotives and steamships.

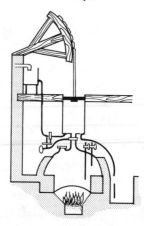

Religion Since the discovery of fire, humans have been able to move into colder climates, changing their way of life in many ways. Its importance made it a religious symbol. The Assyrians, for example (c. 3000 BC), like many others, worshipped a fire god. For Christians it has been regarded as a purifier – heretics were purified by being burnt at the stake.
Bishops Latimer and Ridley are here about to be burnt at the stake in 1555.

Transport Otto's internal-combustion engine – with its fire enclosed in metal cylinders – revolutionized transport, replacing the horse with the motor car and enabling the Wright brothers to produce the first powered aircraft (1903). Forty years later, the jet engine transformed air transport and brought it within the reach of a vast holiday-making public.

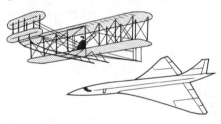

Fire as a hazard Many cities have been devastated by fire – London in 1666 (seen here) and Chicago in 1871 – are but two examples.

The alchemical Mystical and confused, the alchemists of 15th and 16th centuries sought a philosopher's stone to convert base metals into gold. Symbolic descriptions of this stone describe it as the union of fire and water or of male and female – depicted here as a combination of opposites when placed in fire.

The phlogiston theory Put forward in 1669 by Johann Becker, it regarded substances as a mixture of calx and phlogiston. When the substance burnt, the phlogiston was set free, leaving the calx (ashes). A significant step forward in analytical thinking, it was nevertheless proved wrong by Lavoisier's discovery of the role of oxygen in combustion (1778).

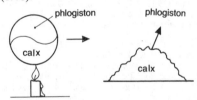

The modern theory When heat is produced in a chemical reaction, it is often evolved slowly, enabling it to be absorbed by the environment as soon as it is produced. If it is evolved rapidly, it cannot be absorbed and the temperature of the reacting substances rises sharply. This causes the emission of heat and light in the phenomenon called fire. Most combustion reactions are oxidations of carbon (wood, coal, etc.) and hydrogen (hydrocarbons, fuels, etc.) as in the equations:

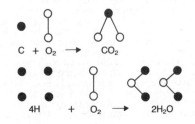

$$C + O_2 \rightarrow CO_2$$

$$4H + O_2 \rightarrow 2H_2O$$

ized cells within the heart (*see* pacemaker). The muscle of the heart is supplied with blood by the coronary arteries. *Atherosclerosis of these arteries may lead to a heart attack (*see* coronary heart disease; myocardial infarction).

heartsease. *See* pansy.

heat The form of energy that is transferred (*see also* heat transfer) from one body or region to another at a lower temperature. The amount of heat gained or lost by a body is equal to the product of its *heat capacity and the temperature through which it rises or falls. Heat is now usually measured in joules. When the temperature of substances rises rapidly as a result of a chemical reaction (especially an oxidation reaction) the heat evolved cannot always be absorbed by the environment. This can cause flame and combustion to occur (see pages 246–247).

heat capacity The amount of heat needed to raise the temperature of a body through one kelvin. It is measured in joules per kelvin. For a gas, the heat capacity may be measured under conditions of either constant pressure or constant volume. *See also* specific heat capacity.

heath An evergreen shrub of the heather family, also called erica, that has spikes of bell-shaped or tubular flowers. Dwarf heaths grow on acid peaty soils, such as moorlands.

Heath, Edward (Richard George) (1916–   ) British statesman; Conservative prime minister (1970–74), who took the UK into the EC (1973). He entered parliament in 1950 and became minister of labour in 1959. He was Lord Privy Seal (1960–63) and secretary of state for industry (1963–64), succeeding (1965) Douglas-Home as leader of the Conservative Party. His Industrial Relations Act (1971) was twice challenged by miners' strikes. Defeated in both the elections of 1974 (February, October), he stood down as party leader in 1975.

heather (*or* ling) An evergreen shrub, *Calluna vulgaris*, up to 60 cm high, with pinkish bell-shaped flowers. It grows on acid soils of heaths, moors, etc.

Heathrow (*or* London Airport) 51 28N 0 27W The world's busiest airport, the chief UK terminal situated in the Greater London borough of Hounslow. Opened in 1946, it has an underground railway connection from central London (since 1977).

heat pump A device that extracts heat from one substance at a low temperature and supplies it to another at a higher temperature, by consuming energy. Heat pumps can be used to extract low temperature heat from rivers, etc., for space- and water-heating units. *See also* refrigeration.

heat transfer The transfer of energy between two bodies or regions as a result of a temperature difference. The methods of transfer are: *convection, *conduction, and *radiation. In convection the heat is transferred by a hotter region flowing into a colder region. In conduction, the heat is transferred by direct contact. In radiation the transfer is by *infrared or *microwaves.

heat treatment The process of heating a metal to a temperature below its melting point and then cooling it in order to change its physical properties. Metals are made up of tiny crystals

(grains). Their hardness, strength, and ductility is determined by the concentration and distribution of irregularities (dislocations) in the crystal lattice. Heating creates and redistributes dislocations, relieving any internal stresses, making the metal softer (known as annealing). Dislocation movement is restricted by boundaries between grains and by impurities. Because both the impurity distribution and the grain structure are affected by heating and the rate of cooling, so also is the metal's strength. Rapid cooling of steel (quenching) by immersion in water hardens it, leaving it brittle. Slow cooling makes it ductile.

heavy water Deuterium oxide (D_2O), water containing the isotope of hydrogen with mass number 2. Less reactive than normal water, it has a relative density of 1.1; its boiling point is 101.42°C. It is present to an extent of 1 part in 5000 in natural water and it is used as a moderator and coolant in some nuclear reactors.

Hebrew A *Semitic language, written from right to left, in an alphabet of 22 letters; vowels are shown by marks attached to the letters. The oldest works of Hebrew literature are those preserved in the *Bible (Old Testament). Hebrew continued to be a literary language throughout the middle ages, being revived in the late 19th century as a spoken language, particularly in Palestine. In 1948 it became an official language of Israel.

Hebrides, the About 500 islands off the W coast of Scotland, subdivided into the Inner and Outer Hebrides, separated by the Minch. The chief islands of the Outer Hebrides include Lewis with Harris and the Uists; those of the Inner Hebrides include Skye, Mull, Islay, and Jura. The main occupations are fishing, and crofting.

Hebron (Arabic name: Al Khalil) 31 32N 35 06E A town in the S of the *West Bank of the River Jordan. One of the oldest cities in the world, it is the traditional burial place of Abraham. Population (1984 est): 75 000.

hectare (ha) A unit of area in the *metric system equal to 100 ares or 10 000 square metres. 1 ha = 2.471 acres.

Hector In Greek legend, the eldest son of Priam, King of Troy, and the husband of Andromache. He fought Ajax in single combat, killed Patroclus, and was killed in revenge by *Achilles.

Hecuba In Greek legend, the wife of Priam, King of Troy, and mother of *Hector. She was captured by the Greeks after the fall of Troy.

hedgehog A nocturnal prickly-coated mammal. The European hedgehog (*Erinaceus europaeus*) grows up to 30 cm long and has brown and cream spines and grey underfur. It feeds on small animals.

hedge sparrow. *See* dunnock.

hedonism The theory that pleasure is the greatest good. *Utilitarianism is the most important modern form of hedonism. *Compare* Epicureanism.

Hegel, Georg Wilhelm Friedrich (1770–1831) German philosopher. His first major work, *The Phenomenology of Mind*, was published in 1807, the *Encyclopedia of the Philosophical Sciences* in 1817, and *The Philosophy of Right* in 1821.

Heidegger, Martin (1889–1976) German philosopher, whose main work was *Sein und Zeit* (*Being and Time*; 1927). As rector of Freiburg University (1933–34) he supported Hitler, which has damaged his reputation.

Heidelberg 49 25N 08 42E A city in SW Germany, in Baden-Württemberg on the River Neckar. It has a ruined castle and the oldest university in Germany (1386). It has some industry. Population (1988): 137 850.

Heisenberg, Werner Karl (1901–76) German physicist, who, with *Schrödinger, was the main architect of quantum mechanics. In 1927 Heisenberg created matrix mechanics, to explain the structure of the hydrogen atom. In the same year he put forward the Heisenberg uncertainty principle (that there is always an uncertainty in simultaneous measurements of the position and momentum of a particle), for which he was awarded the Nobel Prize in 1932. During World War II he was in charge of Germany's unsuccessful attempts to make an atom bomb. After the war he became director of the Max Planck Institute for Physics in Göttingen.

Hejaz (Name from 1981: Western Province) A province in Saudi Arabia, bordering on the Red Sea. The largest town is Jidda. Hejaz, formerly independent, joined Najd in a dual kingdom in 1926, and both became part of Saudi Arabia in 1932. Area: about 350 000 sq km (135 107 sq mi). Population (1985): 3 043 189.

Helen In Greek legend, the daughter of Zeus and *Leda, famed for her supreme beauty. She married Menelaus, King of Sparta, but later fled to Troy with *Paris, thus causing the *Trojan War.

Helena, St (c. 248–c. 328 AD) Roman empress, mother of Constantine the Great. A Christian from 313, she made a pilgrimage to the Holy Land (c. 326), where according to tradition, she rediscovered the cross used at the crucifixion. Feast day: 18 Aug. Emblem: the cross.

Helgoland (*or* Heligoland) 54 09N 7 52E A German island in the North Sea, in the North Frisian group. Handed over to Britain in 1814, it was transferred to Germany in 1890, becoming a German naval base during both World Wars. Area: about 150 ha (380 acres).

helicopter An aircraft that obtains both its lift and its thrust from aerofoils (rotors) rotating about a vertical axis (*see* aeronautics). The first successful helicopter was made in 1939 by Igor *Sikorsky in the USA. Helicopters can rise and drop vertically, hover, and move backwards, forwards, and sideways by control of the pitch of the rotors. They have been developed for rescue services, police observation, and passenger services.

Heliopolis An ancient Egyptian city near Cairo dedicated to the sun god Re. *Cleopatra's Needles came from here.

heliotrope A herb or shrub having heads of blue or white flowers. Many cultivated varieties are used as garden plants.

helium (He) The lightest *noble gas, first detected in 1868 by Janssen (1838–1904) as a line in the spectrum of the sun. The term is derived from Greek *helios*, sun. It is used for filling balloons, as a gas shield in arc welding, and in breathing mixtures used by divers. At no 2; at wt 4.0026; mp −272.2°C; bp −268.9°C. *See also* alpha particles.

helium dating A method of dating rocks, fossils, etc., by measuring the amount of helium in the form of *alpha particles trapped in the sample by the radioactive decay of uranium-235, uranium-238, or thorium-232.

hell In Christian belief, the place in which the souls of the wicked are imprisoned. Some Christians believe that hellfire, described in the Book of Revelation, is real; others that it represents the misery of being deprived of God. *Compare* purgatory.

hellebore A poisonous plant of the buttercup family, of Europe and W Asia. The stinking hellebore (*Helleborus foetidus*) grows to 30–50 cm and bears clusters of purple-edged green flowers. *See also* Christmas rose.

Hellen In Greek mythology, the grandson of Prometheus and ancestor of the Greeks, who called themselves the Hellenes and their country Hellas after him. The subgroups of the Hellenes, the Aeolians, Dorians, Ionians, and Achaeans, were named after his sons and grandsons.

Hellenistic age The period, between the death of *Alexander the Great (323 BC) and *Augustus becoming Roman emperor (27 BC), when Greek culture spread throughout the Mediterranean.

Hellespont. *See* Dardanelles.

Hellman, Lillian (1905–84) US dramatist. Her plays include *The Little Foxes* (1939) and *The Searching Wind* (1944). Her memoirs include *An Unfinished Woman* (1969), *Pentimento* (1973), and *Scoundrel Time* (1976).

Helmand, River (R. Helmund *or* R. Hilmand) A river in Afghanistan, rising in the E of the country and flowing SW then N to enter the lake of Halmun Helmand on the Afghan-Iranian border. Length: 1400 km (870 mi).

Helmholtz, Hermann Ludwig Ferdinand von (1821–94) German physicist and physiologist. In physiology, he developed T. *Young's theory of colour vision (now known as the Young-Helmholtz theory), published in his *Physiological Optics* (1856). He also contributed to the development of thermodynamics.

Helpmann, Sir Robert (1909–86) Australian ballet dancer and choreographer. He went to England in 1933, working with the Sadler's Wells Ballet until 1950. He became artistic director of the Australian Ballet in 1955. His ballets include *Comus* (1942) and *Hamlet* (1942).

Helsingfors. *See* Helsinki.

Helsingør (*or* Elsinore) 56 03N 12 38E A seaport in Denmark, in NE Sjælland on the Sound opposite Helsingborg in Sweden. It contains the fortress of Kronborg (1580), made famous in Shakespeare's *Hamlet*. Population (1987): 56 618.

Helsinki (Swedish name: Helsingfors) 60 13N 24 55E The capital of Finland, a port in the S on the Gulf of Finland. Industries include metals, textiles, and paper. It has an 18th-century cathedral. It replaced Turku as capital of

Finland (then under Russian rule) in 1812. Population (1990 est): 492 800.

Hemel Hempstead 51 46N 0 28W A market town in SE England, in Hertfordshire. Industries include aircraft components, electronic and photographic equipment, and paper. Population (1986 est): 81 000.

Hemingway, Ernest (1899–1961) US novelist. After World War I he moved to Paris. His first novel, *The Sun Also Rises* (1926), was followed by *A Farewell to Arms* (1929), *To Have and Have Not* (1937), *For Whom the Bell Tolls* (1940), *The Old Man and the Sea* (1952), and *Islands in the Stream* (1970). He won the Nobel Prize in 1954. Subject to depressions after leaving his home in Cuba in 1960, he committed suicide.

hemiplegia. *See* paralysis.

hemlock 1. A poisonous Eurasian plant, *Conium maculatum*, of the carrot family. It grows in damp places to a height of 2 m and has purple-spotted stems and white flowers. It was the means by which Socrates died. 2. A coniferous tree of the pine family, native to S and E Asia and North America. The narrow leaves are grouped in two rows along the stems and the cones are brown.

hemp A plant, *Cannabis sativa*, of the mulberry family, native to central Asia. It grows to a height of 5 m, bears yellow flowers, and is cultivated in many regions for its fibre. The flowers, bark, twigs, and leaves contain a narcotic resin (*see* cannabis).

Hengist and Horsa Legendary leaders of the first Anglo-Saxon settlers in Britain. According to the Anglo-Saxon Chronicle (late 9th century AD) Horsa was killed in 455 AD and his brother Hengist ruled over Kent from 455 to 488.

Henley-on-Thames 51 32N 0 56W A town in S central England, in Oxfordshire on the River Thames. It is a residential town with an annual Royal Regatta (first held in 1839). Population (1984 est): 10 976.

henna A shrub, *Lawsonia inermis*, occurring in India and the Middle East. Up to 2 m high, it has fragrant white-and-yellow flowers. The powdered leaves are used for giving hair a reddish tint.

henry (H) The *SI unit of inductance equal to the inductance of a closed circuit such that a rate of change of current of one ampere per second produces an induced e.m.f. of one volt. Named after the US physicist Joseph Henry (1797–1878).

Henry I (1069–1135) King of England (1100–35). The youngest son of *William (I) the Conqueror, he succeeded his brother William Rufus, in spite of the claims of his eldest brother Robert II Curthose, Duke of Normandy. He reformed the legal and administrative systems, especially the Exchequer, and waged several campaigns against Louis VI of France, Fulk V, Count of Anjou, and Norman rebels.

Henry II (1133–89) King of England (1154–89). The son of Matilda and Geoffrey of Anjou and the grandson of Henry I, Henry succeeded Stephen. Married (1152) to *Eleanor of Aquitaine, he ruled an empire that stretched from the River Tweed to the Pyrenees. In spite of frequent

warfare and his quarrel with Thomas *Becket, he maintained control over his possessions until shortly before his death.

Henry II (1519–59) King of France (1547–59); the husband from 1533 of *Catherine de' Medici. He concluded the war against the Emperor *Charles V at Cateau-Cambrésis (1559). His persecution of the Huguenots led to the *Wars of Religion.

Henry III (1207–72) King of England (1216–72), succeeding his father John. Henry's failure to observe the Provisions of *Oxford, which he was forced to accept to placate baronial discontent, led to Simon de *Montfort's rebellion (*see* Barons' Wars).

Henry III (1551–89) King of France (1574–89) during the *Wars of Religion. Forced to flee Paris after an uprising (1588), he allied with the Huguenot Henry of Navarre (the future *Henry IV). He was assassinated while besieging Paris.

Henry IV (1366–1413) King of England (1399–1413); the eldest son of *John of Gaunt. As Henry Bolingbroke, he seized the throne from Richard II. Although successful in wars against Richard's supporters and the Welsh, the costs of these wars and resultant taxation led to struggles between king and parliament for control of royal spending.

Henry IV (1553–1610) The first Bourbon King of France (1589–1610), who restored peace and prosperity following the *Wars of Religion. A Protestant, he succeeded his mother to the throne of Navarre in 1572 and married Margaret of Valois. In 1576 he became a *Huguenot (Protestant) leader in the Wars of Religion. He succeeded to the French throne by becoming a Roman Catholic, but in 1598 he granted the Huguenots freedom of worship by the Edict of *Nantes.

Henry V (1387–1422) King of England (1413–22); the eldest son of Henry IV. He resumed the *Hundred Years' War, winning the battle of *Agincourt (1415), and by 1420, in alliance with Burgundy, controlled much of N France. He married Catherine of Valois.

Henry VI (1421–71) King of England (1422–61; 1470–71), succeeding his father Henry V. He married *Margaret of Anjou in 1445. His inability to govern led to the Wars of the *Roses. Overthrown and imprisoned by the Yorkists (1461), he was briefly restored to power (1470–71). He founded Eton College (1440) and King's College, Cambridge (1447).

Henry VII (1457–1509) King of England (1485–1509). As Henry Tudor, Earl of Richmond, he defeated Richard III at *Bosworth (1485) and his marriage (1486) to Richard's niece Elizabeth of York united the Houses of *Lancaster and *York, effectively ending the Wars of the *Roses. His rule was noted for its harsh taxes, efficient administration, and growing prosperity.

Henry VIII (1491–1547) King of England (1509–47), who began the English *Reformation. In 1512 his army thwarted a Scottish invasion at *Flodden. His desire to make England a notable European power was pursued from 1515 by his Lord Chancellor, Cardinal *Wolsey.

From 1527 Henry unsuccessfully sought the pope's annulment of his marriage to *Catherine of Aragon. He blamed Catherine's failure to produce a son on the fact that his marriage to her was against the Church's laws as she was his brother's widow. Only in 1533, after Thomas *Cromwell made Henry supreme head of the English Church, and therefore independent of Rome, could the king divorce Catherine and marry Anne *Boleyn. In 1536 Anne was executed for adultery; Henry then married Jane *Seymour, who died shortly after giving birth to the future Edward VI (1537). His marriage to *Anne of Cleves ended in divorce; shortly afterwards Henry married Catherine *Howard, who was executed in 1542, and finally, in 1543, Catherine *Parr, who outlived him.

Henry the Navigator (1394–1460) Portuguese patron of explorers; the fourth son of John I. He won a military reputation at the capture of Ceuta (1415) in N Africa. Becoming governor of the Algarve (1419) he set up a school of navigation at Sagres. Under his direction Madeira, the Azores, and the Cape Verde Islands were colonized and the W coast of Africa was explored.

hepatitis Inflammation of the liver, most commonly caused by viruses. The two main types are infectious hepatitis, usually caught by ingesting the virus from food or drink, and serum hepatitis, caught mainly from dirty hypodermic needles or blood products. The patient usually has a fever, loses his appetite, and later develops *jaundice.

Hepburn, Katharine (1909–) US actress. She made several films with Spencer *Tracy; her other films include *The African Queen* (1952); also *The Lion in Winter* (1968) and *On Golden Pond* (1981), for which she received Academy Awards.

Hepplewhite, George (d. 1786) British furniture designer and cabinetmaker, who established a business in London. His neoclassical furniture is a simplified version of the designs of Robert *Adam. It is characterized by straight tapering legs and heart- or oval-shaped chairbacks filled with openwork designs.

Hepworth, Dame Barbara (1903–75) British sculptor. A friend of Henry *Moore, she was also influenced by *Brancusi and *Arp. Her abstract carving in wood and stone created massive shapes broken by holes with wires stretched across their openings. She received the DBE in 1965.

Hera In Greek mythology, the daughter of Cronus and Rhea and the sister and wife of Zeus. She was worshipped as a goddess of women and marriage and is identified with the Roman *Juno.

Heracles (*or* Hercules) A Greek legendary hero, the son of Zeus and Alcmene. After killing his wife and children in a fit of madness, he performed the Twelve Labours as penance: he killed the Nemean lion and the *Hydra of Lerna, captured the Hind of Ceryneia and the Boar of Erymanthus, cleaned the Augean stables, chased away the Stymphalian birds, captured the Cretan bull and the horses of Diomedes, stole the girdle of Hippolyte, captured the oxen of Gery-

on, stole the apples of the Hesperides, and finally captured and bound *Cerberus in Hades.

Herakleion. *See* Iráklion.

heraldry A system of patterns and pictures (devices) on shields originally used to identify individuals when wearing armour. These coats of arms became hereditary in Europe in the early 12th century. They were also used as *seals. In England heraldry is controlled by the College of Arms. The Court of the Lord Lyon has a similar function in Scotland. Coats of arms comprise the shield, a helmet with a crest, a mantling (stylized drapery behind the shield), a wreath, and a motto. The shield bears the heraldic signs (charges); from these heralds can determine the genealogy of the bearer. See p. 252.

herbs and spices The fresh or dried parts of aromatic or pungent plants used in food, drink, medicine, and perfumery. Herbs are generally the leaves of temperate plants and include *basil, *bay leaves, *marjoram, *mint, *parsley, and *thyme. Most spices derive from tropical plants; they are usually dried and may be obtained from the root (e.g. *ginger), bark (e.g. *cinnamon), flower (e.g. *clove), seed pod (e.g. *chilli), or, most commonly, from the seed itself (e.g. *coriander, *cumin, *pepper).

Hercegovina. *See* Bosnia and Hercegovina.

Herculaneum An ancient Italian city near *Naples in Italy. It was destroyed by the same eruption as *Pompeii (79 AD). Much remains buried beneath solidified volcanic mud, which makes excavation there very difficult.

Hercules. *See* Heracles.

hercules beetle A giant green and black *scarab beetle, *Dynastes herculeus*, occurring in Central and South America. The male may reach a length of 15 cm, nearly two-thirds of which is taken up by an enormous pair of horns.

Hereford 52 04N 2 43W A city in W England, in Hereford and Worcester on the River Wye. Hereford deals mainly in agricultural produce; it has given its name to a famous breed of beef cattle. The cathedral was begun in 1079. Population (1988 est): 49 000.

Hereford and Worcester A county of W England, bordering Wales. It was created in 1974 from the former counties of Herefordshire and Worcestershire. The chief rivers are the Wye in the W and the Severn in the E. It is predominantly agricultural, with soft fruit and vegetables grown in the Vale of Evesham. Industries include engineering, chemicals, and food processing. Area: 3927 sq km (1516 sq mi). Population (1989 est): 671 000. Administrative centre: Worcester.

Hereward the Wake (11th century) Anglo-Saxon thegn, who led a raid on Peterborough Abbey (1070) as a protest against William I's appointment of a Norman abbot. He took refuge on the Isle of Ely until its capture by William (1071) forced him to flee.

hermaphrodite (*or* bisexual) A plant or animal possessing both male and female reproductive organs. Such organisms may show cross- or self-*fertilization: the latter method is particularly common when the chance of finding a

tinctures

METALS

FURS

or
(gold)

argent
(silver)

ermine

vair

potent

divisions of fields

per
pale

per
fess

per
cross

parts of the escutcheon

middle
chief

dexter
chief

sinister
chief

fess
point — A C B — honour
point

dexter G
flank — K H L — sinister
flank

nombril — I

dexter D E — sinister
base

F

middle base

COLORS

azure
(blue)

gules
(red)

sable
(black)

vert
(green)

purpure
(purple)

per
bend

per
saltire

per
chevron

HERALDRY *The terminology of heraldry, of which a few terms are illustrated, reveals the science's French origins.*

mate is remote. Hermaphroditism rarely occurs in humans.

Hermes In Greek mythology, the messenger and herald of the gods and the guide of travellers. He was regarded as the god of riches, good luck, and dreams. He was usually portrayed wearing a cap and winged sandals and carrying a golden staff. The son of Zeus and Maia, he is identified with the Roman *Mercury.

hermit crab A widely distributed *crab with a soft unprotected abdomen that lives in portable hollow objects, such as snail shells, for protection. Hermit crabs are usually found in sandy or muddy-bottomed waters.

hernia The condition in which an organ or tissue protrudes through a weak spot in the wall that normally contains it. The most common types are the inguinal hernia (popularly called a rupture) in the groin and the hiatus hernia in the chest. Hernias should usually be surgically repaired or they may become painful and cut off from their blood supply (strangulated).

Hero and Leander Legendary lovers whose story was recounted by the Greek poet Musaeus (4th or 5th century AD). Hero was a priestess of Aphrodite at Sestos and Leander swam to her each night across the Hellespont from Abydos. After a stormy night Hero found her lover's drowned body and in despair drowned herself.

Herod (I) the Great (c. 73–4 BC) King of Judaea (37–4); the son of Antipater the Idumaean (d. 43 BC). Supported by Mark Antony, he became the Romans' king in Judaea. A Jew of Arab origins, he retained power by control of the religious establishment and rigorous suppression of opposition. He ordered the massacre of the infants of Bethlehem.

Herod Antipas (21 BC–39 AD) Tetrarch (governor) of Galilee (4–39 AD) after the division of the realm of his father *Herod the Great. He divorced his wife to marry his niece Herodias, for which he was criticized by John the Baptist. Herodias persuaded her daughter Salome to ask for John's head in return for dancing at Antipas' birthday celebration and John was executed.

Herodotus (c. 484–c. 425 BC) Greek historian. Born at Halicarnassus, he was exiled for political reasons and moved to Samos, then to Athens and finally to Thurii in S Italy. His account of the wars between Greece and Persia in nine

books contained much incidental information gathered on his travels.

heroin (*or* diamorphine) A pain-killing *narcotic drug with a stronger action than *morphine, from which it is made. Heroin is used to relieve patients suffering from painful terminal illness. Because the regular use of heroin leads to addiction, its use in medicine is carefully controlled and its nonmedical use by drug abusers is illegal.

heron A wading bird occurring on lakes and rivers worldwide. 75–150 cm long, herons have long legs, broad wings, and variable plumage. They catch fish and insects with their long pointed bill. *See also* egret.

herpes A virus of which there are several forms. Herpes zoster causes *chickenpox in children and *shingles in adults. Herpes simplex causes cold sores. Herpes simplex II causes the sexually transmitted genital herpes, which produces painful blisters in the genital area.

Herrick, Robert (1591–1674) English poet. He was ordained in 1623 and served as rector of Dean Prior, Devonshire, from 1630 to 1646 and again after the Restoration. The majority of his poems, collected in *Hesperides* (1648), are short lyrics.

herring An important food fish, *Clupea harengus*, found mainly in cold waters of the N Atlantic and the North Sea. It has a slender silvery blue-green body, up to about 40 cm long, and swims in large shoals. Herrings are eaten fresh, pickled, and smoked. In the UK, smoked herring are known as kippers, and are produced mainly in Scotland.

herring gull A large grey and white *gull, *Larus argentatus*, occurring around coasts in the N hemisphere. Adults are 57 cm long and have pink legs; the bill is yellow with a red spot on its lower part.

Hertford 51 48N 0 05W A market town in SE England, the administrative centre of Hertfordshire on the River Lea. Industries include printing, brewing, and brush manufacturing. Population (1981): 21 412.

Hertfordshire A county of S England, bordering on Greater London. Arable farming, producing barley for the brewing industry, dairy farming, market gardening, and horticulture are important. Industries include paper and printing at Watford, and tanning. Area: 1634 sq km (632 sq mi). Population (1987 est): 986 800. Administrative centre: Hertford.

hertz (Hz) The *SI unit of frequency equal to one cycle per second. Named after Heinrich *Hertz.

Hertz, Heinrich Rudolf (1857–94) German physicist, who first produced and detected *radio waves (1888). *Maxwell's equations had predicted the existence of *electromagnetic radiation over a wide range of frequencies but, until Hertz's discovery, radio-frequency radiation was unknown.

Heseltine, Michael (1933–) British Conservative politician; secretary of state for the environment (1979–83; 1990–); secretary of state for defence (1983–86). In 1990 his unsuccessful bid for the leadership of the party led to the fall of Margaret Thatcher.

Hess, Rudolf (1894–1987) German Nazi politician. Hess joined the Nazi Party in 1920, becoming deputy party leader (1933). After his unsuccessful secret mission to Scotland to arrange a separate peace with Britain (1941) he was imprisoned until 1946, when he was convicted at the Nuremberg war trials and sent to Spandau prison, where he ultimately committed suicide.

Hesse (German name: Hessen) A *Land* in central Germany. Formed in 1945, it consists of the former duchies of Hesse-Darmstadt and Nassau. It is chiefly agricultural, producing potatoes, sugar beet, and wheat. Industry, concentrated in the S, includes publishing and the manufacture of machinery and chemicals. Iron ore, salt, and coal are mined. Area: 21 112 sq km (8150 sq mi). Population (1987): 5 552 000. Capital: Wiesbaden.

Hesse, Hermann (1877–1962) German novelist and poet, living in Switzerland from 1911. He worked as a bookseller until publication of his first novel, *Peter Camenzind* (1904). His interest in Indian mysticism and in psychology was reflected in *Siddharta* (1922). His other novels include *Steppenwolf* (1927), *Narziss und Goldmund* (1930), and *The Glass Bead Game* (1943); he was awarded a Nobel Prize (1946).

Heyerdahl, Thor (1914–) Norwegian ethnologist, who led the *Kon-Tiki expedition (1947). In 1969–70 he attempted to cross the Atlantic Ocean from Morocco to South America in a papyrus boat—the *Ra*; he reached Barbados, showing the possibility of Egyptian influence on the Precolumbian civilization of America.

Hiawatha The legendary chief of the Onondaga tribe of American Indians, who was said to have formed the *Iroquois League. His story is the subject of Longfellow's *Song of Hiawatha* (1855).

hibernation A state of *dormancy in winter experienced by many fish, amphibians, reptiles, and mammals of temperate and Arctic regions: by hibernating the animal avoids death by heat loss, freezing, or food scarcity. During hibernation the body temperature drops almost to that of the surroundings and the animal lives on its reserve of body fat until it awakens in the spring.

hibiscus A tropical or subtropical plant, shrub, or tree of the mallow family. Several species are cultivated for their showy five-petalled flowers; two popular shrubs, up to 3 m high, are

the Chinese *Hibiscus rosa-sinensis* (rose of China), which has red, pink, or yellow flowers, and the Syrian *H. syriacus* (rose of Sharon), which has pink, blue, or white flowers.

Hick, Graeme (1966–) British cricketer, born in Zimbabwe, who played for Zimbabwe (1983–84) and Worcestershire (1984–). In 1990 he became the youngest player to score 50 first-class centuries.

hickory A tree of the walnut family, native to E North America and Asia and cultivated for timber, nuts, and ornament. Hickories grow to a height of about 30 m. Pecan nuts come from a species of hickory.

eye   to fly   old age

HIEROGLYPHICS *A picture was used to represent objects, related ideas, and sounds.*

hieroglyphics Originally, an Egyptian system of picture writing in use from about 3000 BC to 300 AD; the word now means any picture or *ideographic writing system. The Egyptians used hieroglyphics largely for inscriptions on monuments. The characters are careful reproductions of people, animals, and objects.

hi-fi. See high-fidelity sound systems.

high-fidelity sound systems (*or* hi-fi) Systems of recording and reproducing sound in which the quality of the reproduced sound is as close as possible to that of the original source. Total distortion in such a system must be less than 2%, the frequency response must be constant between 20 and 20 000 hertz, and the system must be able to play stereophonic or quadraphonic recordings.

high jump A field event in athletics in which jumpers compete to clear a horizontal bar. A competitor is allowed three attempts at a height and is eliminated if he fails to clear it. World records: men: 2.44 m (1989) by Javier Sotomayor (Cuba); women: 2.09 m (1987) by Stefka Kostadinova (Bulgaria).

Highland dress The traditional male costume (since the 17th century) of the Scottish Highlands. It consists of the tartan kilt (a wrapover skirt pleated at the back) and plaid (a cloak worn over one shoulder). Accessories include the sporran (a goatskin pouch), cap, kilt pin, and dagger (worn in the right sock). Highland dress was banned for civilian wear (1746–82) following the Jacobite rebellions. **Tartan** is a woollen cloth with a design of cross stripes. The tradition of each clan having its own tartan probably dates from the 17th century.

Highland Games Scottish athletics meetings, usually professional, held in the Highlands. Events include such Scottish sports as caber tossing, and there are also competitions in highland dancing and playing the bagpipes. The most famous meeting, the Braemar Games, can be traced back to the 8th century AD.

Highland Region   An administrative region in N Scotland, created in 1975 under local government reorganization from the N part of Argyll, Caithness, Inverness, Nairn, Ross and Cromarty, and Sutherland. It includes part of the Inner Hebrides. Sheep farming is the main agricultural activity. Industries associated with North Sea oil are developing and aluminium smelting, pulp and paper production, and distilling are all important. Area: 25 425 sq km (9814 sq mi). Population (1989): 205 000. Administrative centre: Inverness.

High Wycombe   51 38N 0 46W A town in SE England, in Buckinghamshire. It has a long tradition of furniture making and also produces paper, precision instruments, and clothing. Population (1981): 60 516.

Hildebrand.   *See* Gregory VII, St.

Hillary, Sir Edmund (Percival)   (1919–) New Zealand mountaineer and explorer. In 1953 he and *Tenzing Norgay were the first to reach the summit of Mount Everest, for which achievement he was knighted. From 1984 to 1989 he was New Zealand High Commissioner in Delhi.

Hilliard, Nicholas   (1547–1619) English portrait miniaturist. He trained as a jeweller, later becoming court painter to Elizabeth I and James I. Many of his portraits are in the royal collection at Windsor Castle. He wrote a *Treatise on the Art of Limning* (c. 1600).

Himachal Pradesh   A state in NW India, in the W Himalayas beside Tibet's border. Most of the inhabitants are Pahari-speaking Hindus who farm grains, potatoes, maize, and livestock. Area: 55 673 sq km (21 490 sq mi). Population (1989): 4 280 818. Capital: Simla.

Himalayas   The highest mountain system in the world. They extend about 2400 km (1550 mi) along the N Indian border, reaching 8848 m (29 028 ft) at Mount *Everest. The region is disputed by China, India, and Pakistan.

Himmler, Heinrich   (1900–45) German Nazi politician, infamous head of the *SS. Joining the Nazi Party in 1925, he became head of the SS in 1929. From 1936 he also directed the Gestapo and supervised the extermination of Jews in E Europe. After the Nazi collapse he was captured by the Allies and committed suicide.

Hindemith, Paul   (1895–1963) German composer and viola player. He studied in Frankfurt am Main, where he led the opera orchestra (1915–23). His music was banned by the Nazis in 1933; he moved to Turkey and in 1939 went to the USA. His compositions include the opera *Cardillac* (1926), the ballet *Nobilissima Visione* (1938), and much *Gebrauchsmusik* (German: utility music).

Hindenburg, Paul von Beneckendorff und von   (1847–1934) German general in World War I, who with Erich Ludendorff (1865–1937) won a great victory at Tannenberg (1914). In 1916 Hindenburg became commander in chief and directed the German retreat to the **Hindenburg line** (fortified defence on the Western

Front). He became president in 1925 and was re-elected in 1932.

Hindi   The national language of India, spoken by approximately 134 million people. It is an Indo-Aryan language, showing strong *Sanskrit influence in its written form but with a much simpler grammar.

Hinduism   The religious beliefs and customs of about 400 million inhabitants of India and parts of neighbouring countries. It includes extremely varied traditional beliefs and practices developed over the past 5000 years. One of its main beliefs is that one's actions in life lead to *reincarnation at a higher or lower level of life (*see* karma). The aim of the religion is to be released from this cycle of rebirth and to return to the final unchanging reality (Brahman). Release may be sought through good works, devotion to a particular god, such as *Krishna, or through various types of meditation. The main gods are Brahma, Vishnu, and Shiva, together known as the *Trimurti. *See also* Vedanta.

Hindustani   An Indo-Aryan language that originated in the dialect of the Delhi district. The *Moguls and the British encouraged its use as a main language throughout India. *Urdu and *Hindi are the literary forms developed from it.

hip   The part of the body where the legs are joined to the trunk. The skeleton of the hip consists of the *pelvis and the part of the spine (the sacrum) to which it is attached. The hip joint –between the pelvis and femur (thigh bone)–is a common site for arthritis: in severe cases the whole joint may be replaced by an artificial one.

Hippocrates   (c. 460–c. 377 BC) Greek physician and founder of the Hippocratic school of medicine, which greatly influenced medical science until the 18th century. His followers believed that health was governed by the balance of four body fluids, or humours: phlegm, blood, black bile, and yellow bile. The Hippocratic Oath, taken by medical students, was probably not written by Hippocrates.

hippopotamus   A large hoofed mammal, *Hippopotamus amphibius*, of tropical Africa. About 150 cm high at the shoulder and weighing around 3.5 tonnes, hippos have dark-brown skin and tusks up to 60 cm long. They spend the day in rivers or waterholes, emerging at night to graze on surrounding pasture.

Hirohito   (1901–89) Emperor of Japan (1926–89), having previously been regent for five years after his father Yoshihito (1879–1926) had been declared insane. He married (1924) Princess Nagako Kuai. Ruling as divine emperor until Japan's defeat in World War II, he became no more than a constitutional monarch under the 1946 constitution.

Hiroshima   34 23N 132 27E A city in Japan, in SW Honshu on the delta of the River Ota. A former military base and important seaport, it was largely destroyed (6 August, 1945) by the first atomic bomb to be used in warfare; over 130 000 people were killed or injured. Population (1987): 1 034 000.

Hispaniola   The second largest West Indian island, in the Greater Antilles. It is politically divided between the *Dominican Republic and the

Republic of *Haiti. Area: 18 703 sq km (29 418 sq mi).

histamine A substance that is released from body tissues after injury or in an allergic reaction, such as asthma or hay fever. Its effects can include inflammation and breathing difficulties; *antihistamine drugs are given to lessen these.

histology The study of tissues. Originally histology was limited to the study of tissues by light microscopy, but the development of the more powerful electron microscope, and other modern techniques, has enabled the details of very fine structures to be revealed. *See also* cytology.

history The story of the past. The earliest historians were the ancient Greeks, among whom *Herodotus, *Thucydides, and *Xenophon were outstanding. Notable Roman historians include *Sallust, *Cicero, *Livy, and *Tacitus. Early Christian history writing (historiography) was influenced by Jewish historians and in medieval times consisted largely of bare records of events, such as those of *Bede. Early Renaissance scholars (*see* humanism) took a more critical approach, which led to the outstanding work of *Machiavelli in the early 16th century. The 18th-century *Enlightenment included a more fundamental study of the pattern of change in human societies, reflected in the work of Edward *Gibbon. In the 19th century history was established as an academic discipline in the universities; widely read British historians of the 19th century include *Macaulay and *Carlyle. The scope of historiography has greatly widened in the 20th century under the influence of sociology, anthropology, and psychiatry, and new techniques, such as the use of computers to analyse statistics, have been introduced.

Hitchcock, Sir Alfred (1899–1980) British film director. Working almost entirely in Hollywood from 1940, he specialized in complex thrillers with an atmosphere of tension and suspense. His films include *Notorious* (1946), *Strangers on a Train* (1951), *Psycho* (1960), and *The Birds* (1963).

Hitler, Adolf (1889–1945) German dictator, born in Austria. He became president of the *Nazi Party in 1921 and two years later staged an unsuccessful coup–the Munich Putsch –against the Bavarian Government. During a brief imprisonment he wrote most of *Mein Kampf* (*My Struggle*), setting out his political philosophy of the superiority of the Aryan race, the guilt of the Jews for Germany's defeat in World War I, and a violent anticommunism. In the late 1920s and early 1930s Hitler's powers as a speaker and his propaganda machine brought the Nazis increasing support. In 1933 he became chancellor; following *Hindenburg's death in 1934 he assumed the title of Führer (leader). He started his fanatical persecution of the Jews by the establishment of concentration camps and launched a massive rearmament programme. By invading Austria (1938) and then Czechoslovakia and Poland (1939) Hitler started *World War II. In the face of Allied victory he committed suicide with Eva *Braun in the bunker of the chancellory in Berlin.

Hittites An *Indo-European people who appeared in Anatolia (*see* Asia Minor) around 2000 BC. By 1340 BC they had emerged as a major power. Their king was believed to be the representative of god on earth and became a god himself on death. Their language is known from *cuneiform tablets and inscriptions.

HMSO. *See* Stationery Office, Her Majesty's.

hoatzin A primitive bird, *Opisthocomus hoazin*, that occurs in tropical South American swamps and feeds on flowers and fruit. It is 65 cm long and has a small head with a wispy crest and a long tail. Its plumage is streaked brown with yellowish underparts.

Hobart 42 54S 147 18E A city in Australia, the capital and chief port of Tasmania on the Derwent River estuary. Industries include zinc refining and food processing; the chief exports are apples, wool, timber, and dairy produce. The University of Tasmania was established here in 1890. Population (1986): 175 082.

Hobbes, Thomas (1588–1679) English political philosopher. The breakdown of English political and social order in the 1640s inspired him to develop his own political theory. *Leviathan* (1651) argues that because people are basically selfish they need to be ruled by an absolute sovereign, whose function is to enforce public order.

Hobbs, Jack (Sir John Berry H.; 1882–1963) British cricketer. One of the world's greatest batsmen, he played for Surrey and for England in 61 Test matches. During his career (1905–34) he scored 61 237 runs and 197 centuries. He was the first cricketer to be knighted (1953).

Ho Chi Minh (Nguyen That Thanh; 1890–1969) Vietnamese statesman, who led Vietnam in its struggle for independence from the French. Living in France (1917–23), he joined the French Communist Party in 1920. In Canton (1924), where he formed the Association of Young Vietnamese Revolutionaries (Thanh Nien), the forerunner of the Indochinese Communist Party (1930). Returning to Vietnam in 1941, he formed the *Viet Minh, which waged the long and ultimately victorious war against the French (1945–54; *see* Indochina). In 1954 Vietnam was divided into North Vietnam, of which Ho became president, and South Vietnam. In 1959 he extended support to the *Viet Cong guerrilla movement in the South (*see also* Vietnam War).

Ho Chi Minh City (name until 1976: Saigon) 10 46N 106 43E A city in S Vietnam, on the River Saigon. It is the major commercial and industrial centre of the S, with shipbuilding, metalworking, textile, and chemical industries. An ancient Khmer town, it was the capital of French Indochina (1887–1902); during the *Vietnam War it was the capital of South Vietnam. Population (1985): 3 500 000.

hockey An 11-a-side field game for men and women, the object of which is to score goals. It has been played in various forms for at least 4000 years and is an Olympic sport. Each member of the team carries a curved stick for hitting the ball. See p. 256. *See also* ice hockey.

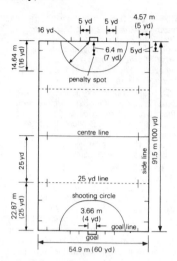

HOCKEY *The dimensions of the pitch.*

Hockney, David (1937–) British painter, printmaker, and draughtsman. After studying at the Royal College of Art (1959–62), he travelled widely in the USA, where he developed his realistic but witty style, his favourite subjects being figure studies and swimming pools. He has also designed stage sets and illustrated books.

Hoffman, Dustin (1937–) US film actor. He made his reputation in the films *The Graduate* (1967) and *Midnight Cowboy* (1969). He was awarded Oscars for his performances in *Kramer vs Kramer* (1980) and *Rain Man* (1989). Other films include *Lenny* (1974) and *Tootsie* (1982).

Hogarth, William (1697–1764) British painter and engraver. He established his reputation with the paintings and engravings of *A Harlot's Progress* (1731–32). He excelled in moralizing social satires in such series as *A Rake's Progress, Industry and Idleness*, and the paintings of *Marriage à la Mode* (Tate Gallery).

Hogg, Quintin. *See* Hailsham, Quintin McGarel Hogg, Baron.

Hokkaido (former name: Yezo) The second largest and northernmost of the four main islands of Japan. Main industries are coalmining, agriculture, and fishing. *History*: the Japanese began to settle on the island in the 16th century; it became administratively self-governing in 1885. Area: 78 508 sq km (30 312 sq mi). Population (1986): 5 678 000. Capital: Sapporo.

Holbein the Younger, Hans (c. 1497–1543) German painter. Settling in England in 1532, he painted portraits of merchants before becoming court painter and designer to Henry VIII (1536). His portrait of Henry VIII in a wall painting (destroyed) for Whitehall Palace became the model for other paintings of the king. His other paintings include *Christina, Duchess of Milan* (National Gallery, London), *Anne of Cleves* (Louvre), and *The Ambassadors* (National Gallery, London). His father **Hans Holbein the Elder**

(c. 1465–1524) was also a painter, whose major work is the *S Sebastian Altar* (Alte Pinakothek, Munich).

hole. *See* semiconductor.

Holiday, Billie (Eleanor Gough McKay; 1915–59) US Black jazz singer, known as "Lady Day." She was discovered in Harlem by Benny Goodman and made her first recording in 1933. She subsequently sang with the bands of Count Basie and Artie Shaw. Addiction to heroin caused her death.

holistic medicine An approach to medical treatment in which all aspects of the patient's life are taken into account in understanding and curing his disease, as opposed to merely treating his symptoms. A basic principle of *alternative medicine, it is gaining acceptance among orthodox doctors.

Holland The low-lying NW region of the Netherlands. A county of the Holy Roman Empire from the 12th century, Holland later came under Burgundy and then under Spain. After the 16th-century *Revolt of the Netherlands against Spanish rule, Holland became the chief province of the independent United Provinces of the Netherlands. The kingdom of the *Netherlands is still commonly called Holland.

holly A widely distributed tree or shrub. The evergreen English holly (*Ilex aquifolium*) grows to a height of 15 m and has spiny dark-green leaves and small white flowers; the female flowers develop into red berries. It is widely cultivated for hedging and used for Christmas decorations. *See also* maté.

hollyhock A plant, *Althaea rosea*, of the mallow family, native to China but widely cultivated. Up to 3 m high, it bears large white, yellow, or red flowers.

Hollywood 34 00N 118 15W A NW suburb of Los Angeles, in California in the USA. Founded in the 1880s, it has been the centre of the US film industry since 1911. Population (1987): 130 219.

holmium (Ho) A metallic lanthanide element, discovered in 1879 by P. T. Cleve (1840–1905) and named after his native city, Stockholm. Holmium occurs in rare-earth minerals, such as monazite ($CePO_4$). It forms an oxide (Ho_2O_3) and halides (HoX_3), but has few uses. At no 67; at wt 164.9304; mp 1474°C; bp 2695°C.

holocaust The extermination of European *Jews by the Nazis (1939–45). Some six million Jews from many countries, approximately two-thirds of European Jewry, were killed in Auschwitz and other concentration camps.

Holocene epoch The present, or Recent, epoch in *geological time, including the last 10 000 years from the end of the Pleistocene, after the last major *Ice Age. At the beginning of the Holocene the rise in sea level resulting from the melting of the ice isolated Britain from the rest of Europe.

holography A method of producing a three-dimensional image without using a camera. A *laser beam is split into two using a semitransparent mirror; one beam falls directly onto a photographic film or plate and the other is reflected by the object onto the film. The two beams form *interference patterns on the film,

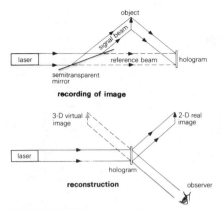

HOLOGRAPHY *A three-dimensional image formed by two beams of light is recorded as an interference pattern on a single plate. The two images, giving a 3-D effect, are reconstructed by shining two similar beams through the hologram.*

which is called a hologram. To reconstruct the image, light from the same kind of laser is shone onto the hologram. Two three-dimensional images can be seen; one is a real image, the other a virtual image. As the head is moved, the image alters.

Holst, Gustav (Theodore) (1874–1934) British composer and teacher. He taught at the Royal College of Music, Morley College, and St Paul's Girls' School, for whose string orchestra he wrote the *St Paul's Suite* (1913). Among his most famous compositions are the choral work *The Hymn of Jesus* (1917), *Egdon Heath* (1927), and the orchestral suite *The Planets* (1914–16).

Holy Grail In medieval legend, a vessel or dish having supernatural power. By the 12th century it was associated with the chalice used by Christ at the Last Supper and later given to *Joseph of Arimathea. The writer Chrétien de Troyes combined the grail legend with the *Arthurian legend, and the knightly quest for the Holy Grail is an important theme in many Arthurian romances.

Holyhead 53 20N 4 38W A port and resort in North Wales in Anglesey, Gwynedd, on Holy Island. It has steamer services to Dun Laoghaire in the Republic of Ireland. Population (1988 est): 13 000.

Holy Island (*or* Lindisfarne) 55 41N 1 48W An island, in NE England off the NE coast of Northumberland. Its monastery was founded by St Aidan (635 AD).

holy orders The ranks of ordained ministers in Christian Churches. The major orders are bishop, priest, deacon, and (in the Roman Church) subdeacon. Ordination is considered a *sacrament by the Orthodox and Roman Catholic Churches.

Holy Roman Empire The empire that replaced the western *Roman Empire of ancient times. The institution dates from 800, when *Charlemagne was crowned emperor of the

West by Pope Leo III. Centred on Germany and Austria, it also included areas of E France and N Italy. In 962 the imperial title passed to the German kings, who kept it until the Empire was abolished in 1806. The Empire was weakened by the Protestant *Reformation in the 16th century, the *Thirty Years' War in the 17th century, and the rise of Prussia. It was finally broken when Napoleon conquered imperial territories in the early 19th century.

Holyrood House A palace in Edinburgh, which is the Scottish residence of the British monarch. A medieval building, it was substantially modified in the classical style from 1671 onwards by Sir William Bruce (d. 1710).

Holy Spirit (*or* Holy Ghost) In Christianity, the third person of the *Trinity, with the Father and the Son. In St John's Gospel the Holy Spirit is seen as the "Paraclete" or Comforter; in Acts, the descent of the Holy Spirit upon the Apostles is described. In art, the Holy Spirit is usually symbolized by a dove.

Home of the Hirsel, Alec Douglas-Home, Baron (Alexander Frederick D.-H.; 1903–) British statesman; Conservative prime minister (1963–64). He was an MP (1931–45, 1950–51) before becoming the 14th Earl of Home. He was foreign secretary (1960–63) and then succeeded Macmillan as prime minister, renouncing his peerages. Following the Conservative electoral defeat (1964) he resigned the party leadership (1965). He received a life peerage in 1974.

homeopathy The system of treating illness developed by the German physician Samuel Hahnemann at the end of the 18th century and based on the principle of "like cures like." To treat a particular disease homeopathists prescribe small doses of a drug that in larger quantities would cause the symptoms of the disease in a healthy person.

Homer (8th century BC) Greek epic poet, presumed author of the *Iliad* and *Odyssey*. He is believed to have lived in Ionia in Asia Minor and according to legend was blind. The *Iliad* concerns the Trojan War; the *Odyssey* relates the various adventures of *Odysseus during his voyage home from the Trojan War to his kingdom of Ithaca.

Home Rule An Irish political movement to give Ireland its own law-making body responsible for home affairs. Founded in 1870, the Home Rule movement gained strength in parliament under the leadership of *Parnell from 1880. The Home Rule bills of 1886 and 1893 were defeated; in 1914 the third Home Rule bill was passed but put off while World War I lasted. An altered act was passed in 1920 providing separate parliaments for northern and southern Ireland. This was accepted by the north but rejected by the south, which in 1922 became completely self-governing as the Irish Free State.

homing instinct. *See* migration, animal.

hominid A member of the family *Hominidae*, which includes human beings and a number of extinct forms, known only from fossil remains (*see* Homo).

Homo A genus (taxononomic group) of hominids who have a large brain, stand upright,

HOMO

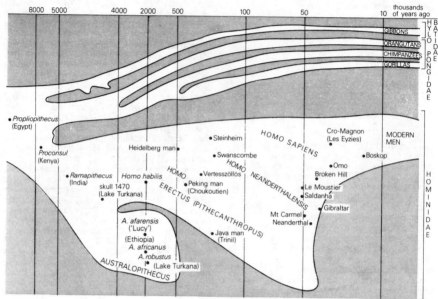

evolution of Homo sapiens *The picture of man's evolution is constantly changing as new fossil evidence comes to light. The fossil Propliopithecus represents the apparent divergence of the gibbons (Hylobatidae), great apes (Pongidæ), and humans (Hominidæ) from the monkeys, but palaeontologists are still debating many of the other classifications and relationships shown on this chart.*

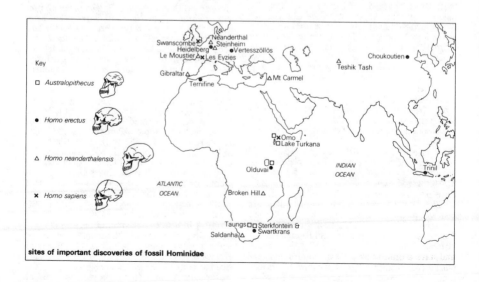

sites of important discoveries of fossil Hominidae

walk on two feet, have a thumb capable of a precision grip, and the ability to make and use tools. The only existing species is *Homo sapiens* (human beings). The extinct species *Homo erectus*, from which *Homo sapiens* may be descended, first appeared more than one million years ago. *Neanderthal man also belongs to the genus *Homo*, as does *Cro-Magnon man. See also Australopithecus.

homosexuality   Sexual attraction or relations between persons of the same sex. Homosexuality in women is known as lesbianism. Many European countries have in recent years relaxed their laws concerning homosexuality. Contemporary movements, such as Gay Liberation, aim to alleviate social problems of homosexuals in a predominantly heterosexual society.

Honduras, Republic of   A country in Central America, with a N coastline on the Caribbean Sea and a short S one on the Pacific Ocean. *Economy*: mainly agricultural, the chief crops are bananas and coffee (the principal exports). Almost half the land is forested, with valuable hardwoods and pine. Fishing is important. The mineral resources include gold, silver, lead, tin and zinc, and mercury. *History*: the area was a centre of Mayan culture from the 4th to the 9th centuries AD. Discovered by Columbus in 1502, it became part of the Spanish captaincy general of Guatemala. It gained independence from Spain in 1821 and then formed part of the Central American Federation (1823–38). Military rule lasted from 1972 to 1982, when Roberto Suazo Córdova became president; he was succeeded in turn by José Azcona Hoya (in 1986) and Rafael Leonardo Callejas (in 1990). Official language: Spanish. Official currency: lempira of 100 centavos. Area: 112 088 sq km (43 227 sq mi). Population (1986 est): 4 300 000. Capital: Tegucigalpa.

honesty   A European plant, *Lunaria annua*, of the mustard family. Up to 1 m high, it has purple or white flowers and is often grown in gardens for its ornamental flat papery seed heads.

honey   A sweet thick yellow syrup made by *honeybees from nectar. Honey consists of about 70% sugars, 18% water, and small amounts of minerals, pollen, and wax.

honeybee   A social *bee, also called hive bee. The best-known species is *Apis mellifera*, native to Europe but reared worldwide for its *honey and *beeswax. The members of a colony form well-defined groups (castes), each with specific tasks. The 50 000–80 000 workers (sterile females) attend to nest building, food gathering, and brood care. The queen lays her eggs in wax chambers (cells). Larvae hatching from fertilized eggs become females; those fed on protein-rich "royal jelly" throughout their development become queens. Drones (males) hatch from unfertilized eggs.

honeyeater   A songbird occurring chiefly in SE Asia and Australasia. They are 10 to 35 cm long and have a drab plumage with wattles or naked patches on the face. The slender bill is downcurved and the long tongue, which can be extended, has a central trough, through which

nectar is drunk, and a brushlike tip for collecting pollen and small insects.

honeysuckle   A shrub or twining plant with clusters of tubular, often sweet-scented, flowers. The common European honeysuckle (*Lonicera periclymenum*), also called woodbine, is a trailing shrub with yellowish flowers. Some species are cultivated as ornamentals, including the fragrant climbing honeysuckle (*L. japonica*).

Hong Kong   A British crown colony lying off the S coast of China. It consists of the island of Hong Kong, the mainland peninsula of Jiulong, the New Territories, and Stonecutters Island. *Economy*: owing to its strategic position and fine natural harbour, it is an important port and banking centre. The export of manufactured goods has become increasingly important since World War II and the textile and clothing industry accounts for over half the total domestic exports. *History*: the island was transferred from China to Britain at the end of the first Opium War (1842); Jiulong was added in 1860, and in 1898 the New Territories were granted on a 99-year lease. The return of the colony to Chinese control in 1997 was agreed between Britain and China in 1984. Official language: English; Cantonese is widely spoken. Official currency: Hong Kong dollar of 100 cents. Area: 1031 sq km (398 sq mi). Population (1986): 5 431 200. Capital and main port: Victoria.

Honolulu   21 19N 157 50W A city in the USA, the capital of Hawaii on SE Oahu in the central Pacific Ocean. It is the site of three universities and of Iolani Palace, the former royal residence. *Pearl Harbor is still an important naval base. Population (1986): 372 300.

Honshu   The largest of the four main islands of Japan, situated between the Pacific Ocean and the Sea of Japan. Most of Japan's major ports and cities are here, although agriculture is also important; rice, fruit, cotton, and tea are grown. Mineral wealth includes oil, zinc, and copper. The traditional industry is silk but the many modern industries include shipbuilding, iron and steel, chemicals, and textiles. Area: 230 448 sq km (88 976 sq mi). Population (1986): 97 283 000. Chief town: Tokyo.

Hooch, Pieter de   (1629–c. 1684) Dutch painter. Working in Delft, Leiden, and Amsterdam, he excelled in small paintings, such as *The Pantry* (Rijksmuseum, Amsterdam), depicting household tasks or dark interiors that open into sunlit rooms.

Hooke, Robert   (1635–1703) British physicist and instrument maker. In 1660 he discovered **Hooke's law**, which states that for an elastic body, the stress is directly related to the strain. Many of his microscope studies were published in *Micrographia* (1665).

Hook of Holland   (Dutch name: Hoek van Holland)   51 59N 4 07E A port in the SW Netherlands, in South Holland province at the North Sea end of the Nieuwe Waterweg (New Waterway). A ferry service operates from here to Harwich, England.

hookworm   A parasitic *nematode worm that lives in the intestine of animals and man. About 1 cm long, hookworms attach themselves to the gut lining and feed by sucking blood and body fluids.

hoopoe A bird, *Upupa epops*, of S Europe, S Asia, and Africa. 28 cm long, it has a long down-curved bill, pink-brown plumage with black and white barred wings, a long tail, and a long black-tipped crest.

Hoover, Herbert (Clark) (1874–1964) US statesman; Republican president (1929–33). As secretary of commerce (1921–29) he was chairman of commissions that began construction of the Hoover Dam (named after him) and the St Lawrence Seaway.

hop A climbing plant, *Humulus lupus*. Native to Eurasia, where it grows to a length of 3–6 m in hedges and thickets, it is widely cultivated for its pale yellow-green female flowers ("cones"), which are used in brewing to flavour beer.

Hope, Bob (Leslie Townes Hope; 1903–) US comedian, born in Britain. He starred in a number of popular films during the 1940s, including *Road to Zanzibar* (1941) and other "Road" films in which he partnered Bing *Crosby. He has also acted as compère of the Academy Award presentations.

Hopkins, Gerard Manley (1844–89) British poet. He was converted to Roman Catholicism in 1866 and ordained as a Jesuit priest in 1877. "The Wreck of the Deutschland" and "The Windhover" are among his best-known poems, which were published posthumously in 1918.

Horace (Quintus Horatius Flaccus; 65–8 BC) Roman poet. He became a leading poet under the emperor Augustus and acquired a farm near Rome, celebrated in his poetry. His *Odes* and his more informal *Satires* and verse *Epistles* vividly portray contemporary Roman society.

hormone A substance that is secreted into the blood in small quantities to cause a response in a particular organ or tissue of the body. Hormones are produced and secreted by *endocrine glands under the control of the nervous system or in response to changes in the chemical composition of the blood. Hormones regulate such processes as digestion, growth, and reproduction. The study of hormones is called endocrinology.

hornbeam A tree of N temperate regions. The common Eurasian hornbeam (*Carpinus betulus*) has smooth grey bark, oval pointed leaves with prominent veins, and small nuts. It is planted for ornament and for its hard fine-grained timber.

hornbill A bird occurring in tropical regions of Asia and Africa. 38–150 cm long, hornbills are distinguished by their huge bill, often bearing a large bony helmet; they feed on fruit and berries.

hornblende A black or greenish-black mineral of the *amphibole group. It consists mainly of silicates of sodium, calcium, magnesium, and iron.

hornet A social *wasp, *Vespa crabro*, that is common throughout Europe and has spread to North America and elsewhere. 35 mm long, it is tawny-yellow with brown markings and nests in hollow trees. It feeds chiefly on insects, nectar, and fruit juices and its painful sting can be dangerous to man.

hornpipe A traditional British dance, originally accompanied by a wooden pipe. It is popular with sailors as it requires no partners and little space.

horoscope. *See* astrology.

horse A hoofed mammal, *Equus caballus*, domesticated worldwide for pulling and carrying loads, riding, and sport. The earliest horse is believed to have been *eohippus, which is thought to have originated in North America and spread to Asia. Later, larger forms evolved in which the central toe became enlarged as the hoof. The many breeds of modern horse range in size from the tiny *Falabella to the massive *Shire horse and are measured in hands (1 hand = 4 in = 10.16 cm) to the top of the shoulders (withers). Horses mature at 3½–5 years of age and the lifespan is usually 20–35 years. Mares have a pregnancy (gestation period) lasting 11 months, producing usually a single foal.

horse chestnut A broad spreading tree, *Aesculus hippocastanum*, native to SE Europe and widely planted in parks and streets. It grows to a height of 25 m, producing large leaves and white flowers; the green spiny fruits ripen to release large brown shiny seeds (conkers).

horsepower (hp) A unit of power equal to 550 foot-pounds per second (745.70 watts). It was devised by James *Watt, who found that a strong horse could raise a weight of 150 pounds 4 feet in 1 second.

horseradish A plant, *Armoracia rusticana*, of the mustard family, probably native to SE Europe and W Asia and widely cultivated. Growing to a height of 125 cm, it has thick fleshy pungent roots from which horseradish sauce is made.

horseshoe crab A nocturnal marine *arthropod, also called king crab, that lives in the coastal waters of E North America and E Asia. It has a hinged body, up to 50 cm long, covered by a brown horseshoe-shaped shield (carapace) and a long tail spine. It usually burrows in sand, feeding on worms and thin-shelled molluscs.

Horus The Egyptian sun-god, usually portrayed as a falcon or with a falcon's head. He was the son of *Osiris and *Isis. The pharaohs were regarded as the incarnations of Horus.

hospice movement A movement that provides care for the terminally ill. Hospices specialize in easing the physical and mental distress of the patients and providing support for their families. Most modern hospices are modelled on St Christopher's Hospice, founded in London in 1967 by Dame Cicely *Saunders.

hospital An institution for diagnosing diseases and treating the sick. In medieval Europe many hospitals were founded by monastic orders and orders of knighthood. St Bartholomew's (1123) and St Thomas's (1207) in London date back to this period. In the UK, during the 18th and 19th centuries, many new voluntary hospitals were founded by wealthy individuals and staffed by doctors who gave their services free. Municipal hospitals with paid medical staff arose alongside the voluntary hospitals; both systems were nationalized by the National Health Service Act (1946). Since then all Nation-

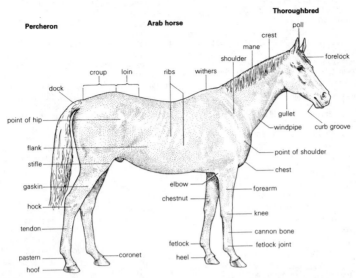

HORSE *Points of the horse.*

al Health hospitals have provided free services. In 1988 plans to create self-governing hospitals servicing both the NHS and private patients were announced. *See also* National Health Service.

Hospitallers (Order of the Hospital of St John of Jerusalem)   A religious order of knighthood that began as a hospital for pilgrims to Jerusalem (c. 1070) and during the *Crusades took on a military function. Immensely wealthy, the Hospitallers were the great rivals of the *Templars. After the fall of Acre (1291) they established themselves in Cyprus, Rhodes, and Malta.

hosta   A garden plant of the lily family, native to China and Japan. It is grown chiefly for its variegated leaves, but also produces attractive purplish or white funnel-shaped flowers.

hot spring   A spring from which hot water flows continuously from deep within the earth's crust. Like *geysers, hot springs normally occur in volcanically active areas.

Hotspur.   *See* Percy, Sir Henry.

Houdini, Harry   (Erich Weiss; 1874–1926) US magician. His ability to escape from handcuffs, straitjackets, and locked containers, even when under water, gained him an international reputation.

Houston   29 45N 95 25W A city in the USA, the main port in Texas. Founded in 1836, it expanded rapidly following the building of a canal (1912–14), linking it to the Gulf of Mexico, and the development of coastal oilfields. Today it is one of the world's major oil and petrochemical centres. Population (1986): 1 728 910.

hovercraft (*or* air-cushion vehicle)   A shiplike vehicle equipped with powerful horizontal blowers capable of lifting it off a surface so that it rides on a cushion of air, which is contained within a rubber skirt. It can navigate on almost

any surface and is moved forward at high speed by vertical propellers. The first hovercraft was built by Christopher *Cockerell in 1959. Hovercraft are used as ferries between England and France and elsewhere.

hoverfly   A fly, also called a flowerfly or syrphid fly, that resembles bees and wasps but does not sting. The larvae of many hoverflies scavenge for food in decaying organic matter or the nests of ants, termites, or bees.

Howard, Catherine   (c. 1520–42) The fifth wife (1540–42) of Henry VIII of England. She was beheaded for treason when Henry learnt of her premarital love affairs.

Howard, John   (c. 1726–90) English prison reformer. Horrified by conditions in Bedford gaol, which he inspected while high sheriff of Bedfordshire, Howard campaigned for sanitary improvements and wages for gaolers. An act of 1774 achieved his aims.

Howard, Leslie   (Leslie Howard Stainer; 1890–1943) British actor of Hungarian descent. He became famous for his performances as the romantic leading man in both British and US films, including *The Scarlet Pimpernel* (1935), *Pygmalion* (1938), and *Gone with the Wind* (1939). He was killed when the aeroplane in which he was travelling was shot down by German aircraft in 1943.

Howard, Trevor   (1916–88) British actor. After working in the theatre in the 1930s he concentrated on films, including *Brief Encounter* (1946), *The Third Man* (1949), *Mutiny on the Bounty* (1962), *Ryan's Daughter* (1970), and *Conduct Unbecoming* (1975).

Howe, Sir (Richard Edward) Geoffrey (1926–) British Conservative politician; chancellor of the exchequer (1979–83); foreign secretary (1983–89). He became deputy prime minister in 1989 but resigned in 1990, contributing to the fall of Margaret Thatcher.

howitzer A low-velocity *artillery firearm with a shorter barrel and a larger bore than a gun but a smaller bore and longer barrel than a *mortar. Often mounted on carriages, they were widely used in World War I. The word comes from the Dutch *houwitzer*, catapult.

howler monkey A large *monkey of Central and South American forests. Howlers are 115–180 cm long including the tail (58–91 cm) and are named after their loud voices. They have beards over their enlarged throats and tails that can hold onto branches, etc.

Hoyle, Sir Fred (1915–) British astronomer, who with H. Bondi (1919–) and T. Gold (1920–) proposed the steady-state theory of the universe. His other theoretical studies have mainly been concerned with stellar evolution. He is also one of the foremost science writers.

Hsi-an. See Xi An.

Hsi Chiang. See Xi Jiang.

Hsiung-nu. See Xiong Nu.

Huancayo 12 05S 75 12W A city in W Peru, the chief commercial centre of the central Andes. It has a cathedral and a university (1962). Population (1981): 321 549.

Huang Hai. See Yellow Sea.

Huang Ho. See Yellow River.

Huddersfield 58 39N 1 47W A town in N England, in West Yorkshire where the Rivers Colne and Holme meet. It is one of the major wool textile towns of West Yorkshire. Population (1981): 123 888.

Hudson, Henry (d. 1611) English navigator, whose first two attempts to navigate a *Northeast Passage to China were unsuccessful. On a third voyage he sailed some 240 km (150 mi) down what came to be called the Hudson River. His fourth voyage (1610–11) took him to what is now Hudson Bay, where his men mutinied and cast him adrift; nothing more was heard of him.

Hudson Bay A shallow bay in N central Canada, linked to the Atlantic Ocean by Hudson Strait and to the Arctic Ocean by Foxe Channel. Frozen during winter, in summer it carries grain ships from W Canada to Europe.

Hudson River A river in the NE USA, flowing from the Adirondack Mountains to New York Bay. A commercial waterway, it is linked by canals with the *Great Lakes and the *St Lawrence Seaway. Length: 492 km (306 mi).

Hudson's Bay Company A fur-trading company, formed in 1670, that was given settlement and trading rights in Canada. In 1870 it sold its territories to Canada but remained a fur-trading agency.

Hue 16 28N 107 35E An ancient city in central Vietnam, on the Huong estuary. It is a commercial and industrial centre. Population (latest est): 165 865.

Hughes, Howard (Robard) (1905–76) US aviator, film producer, and businessman. After founding the Hughes Aircraft Company he broke the landplane speed record in 1935, at 352 mph. His films include *Hell's Angels* (1930) and

The Outlaw (1944). From 1950 he lived in seclusion.

Hughes, Ted (1930–) British poet. His first volume, *The Hawk in the Rain* (1957), contained poems concerned with the natural world. The poems in *Crow* (1970) and subsequent volumes use violent language and subject matter. He became poet laureate in 1984.

Hugo, Victor (Marie) (1802–85) French poet, dramatist, and novelist. His leadership of the Romantic movement was confirmed by the success of his drama *Hernani* (1831). During the 1840s he became increasingly involved in republican politics; after the coup by the future Napoleon III he went to the Channel Islands (1851–70). His later works included the poems *Les Contemplations* (1856) and the novel *Les Misérables* (1862).

Huguenots French Protestants, mostly followers of *Calvin. Their name comes from the Swiss-German *Eidgenoss*, confederate. Soon a strong national minority, their rivalry with the Roman Catholic nobles led to the *Wars of Religion (1562–94). The Edict of Nantes (1598) guaranteed them freedom of worship but after its withdrawal (1685) over 250 000 emigrated.

Hull (official name: Kingston-upon-Hull) 53 45N 0 20W A city in NE England, the administrative centre of Humberside, situated on the Humber estuary. Hull serves as a port for much of the North and Midlands. Its industries include chemicals and engineering as well as fish-related industries. Population (1981): 268 302.

humanism 1. The intellectual movement that formed the inspiration of the *Renaissance. Humanist scholars, such as *Erasmus, studied classical Greek and Roman authors, concentrating on human achievements. 2. A 20th-century philosophical view that denies the existence of God, stressing the importance of human welfare.

human rights The 20th-century idea that all human beings, irrespective of race, sex, or class should have equal civil, political, and economic rights. The UN Universal Declaration of Human Rights (1948), although it cannot be enforced in law, led to various later agreements, such as the Covenants on Civil and Political Rights and on Economic, Social, and Cultural Rights (1966), accepted by 35 states.

Humber An estuary in N England, flowing from the Rivers Ouse and Trent to the North Sea past the ports of Hull, Immingham, and Grimsby. The **Humber Bridge** (opened 1981) is the world's longest single-span suspension bridge (main span 1410 m; 4626 ft). Length: 64 km (40 mi).

Humberside A county in NE England, bordering on the North Sea. Created in 1974 from N Lincolnshire and parts of the East and West Ridings of Yorkshire, it produces cereals, root crops, and livestock. Fishing industries at Hull have declined; industrial activities include iron and steel manufacture and petrochemicals. Area: 3512 sq km (1356 sq mi). Population (1987 est): 846 500. Administrative centre: Hull.

Humboldt Current (or Peru Current) An ocean current flowing N off the Peruvian coast of South America. It is a cold current rich in plankton and the fish that feed on them, giving rise to Peru's fishing industry.

Humboldt Glacier The largest known glacier in the N hemisphere, in NW Greenland. At its end in Kane Basin it is 100 km (60 mi) wide and 91 m (300 ft) high.

Hume, David (1711–76) Scottish philosopher and historian. In *A Treatise of Human Nature* (1739–40) he claimed that impressions have more force than ideas. Hume favoured a psychological approach to philosophy. His *History of England* (1754–62) was a bestseller.

humidity A measure of the amount of water vapour in the atmosphere. Absolute humidity is the number of kilograms of water vapour per cubic metre of air. Relative humidity is the ratio of the absolute humidity at a given temperature to the maximum humidity without precipitation at that temperature, expressed as a percentage.

hummingbird A brightly coloured American bird, 5.5–20 cm long, with a slender bill for feeding on nectar, insects, etc. Hummingbirds produce a hum by rapidly vibrating their wings during flight or hovering.

Humperdinck, Engelbert (1854–1921) German composer. He assisted Wagner with the score of *Parsifal* in 1880–81. Of his many operas only *Hänsel und Gretel* (1893) is still popular.

humus The black organic matter in soil formed from decomposing plants and animals. It is rich in carbon, nitrogen, phosphorus, and sulphur, which maintain soil fertility, and improves water absorption and soil workability.

Hundred Years' War (1337–1453) A war between England and France arising from Edward III's claim to the French throne. The Treaty of *Brétigny (1360) recognized English successes at Sluys (1340), *Crécy (1346), and Poitiers (1356). Subsequently the war was interspersed with frequent truces. Henry V of England was recognized as heir to the French throne after his victory at *Agincourt (1415), but this was reversed by 1453, when the French (inspired by *Joan of Arc) had expelled the English from France, except Calais.

Hungarian A language of the *Finno-Ugric branch of the *Uralic family, spoken by 14 million people mainly in Hungary, where it is the official language. It uses a slightly altered Latin alphabet and has borrowed many words from surrounding languages. *See also* Magyars.

Hungary, Republic of (Hungarian name: Magyar Köztársasag) A country in central Europe. It lies mainly in the basin of the middle Danube. *Economy*: the main crops are cereals, fruit, and vegetables. The only mineral is bauxite. All industries are owned by the state. *History*: the Magyars settled in the Danube area in the 9th century AD. In the 11th century St *Stephen I converted the country to Christianity and became the first Hungarian king. Hungary was conquered by the Turks in 1526 and in the 17th century it became part of the Habsburg Empire. In 1867 Hungary gained self-government as part of the Dual Monarchy of *Austria-Hungary. In 1918 Hungary became a republic but, after a short period of communist rule, a constitutional monarchy was formed. After World War II it became a republic again and in 1949 the communists gained control. In 1956 an uprising was crushed by Soviet forces; in 1989 a multiparty democracy was instituted. President: Arpad Goncz. Official language: Hungarian (Magyar). Official currency: forint of 100 fillér. Area: 93 035 sq km (35 911 sq mi). Population (1987): 10 622 000. Capital: Budapest.

Huns A Mongolian people, who overran much of SE Europe in the late-4th and 5th centuries. United under *Attila, the Huns invaded Greece, Gaul, and finally Italy (452). The death of Attila (453) broke up their empire and they were defeated by an alliance of tribes at Nedao (455).

Hunt, William Holman (1827–1910) British painter, who helped to found the *Pre-Raphaelite Brotherhood. His symbolic paintings include *The Light of the World* (Keble College, Oxford) and *The Scapegoat* (Port Sunlight), inspired by a visit to Syria and Palestine (1854).

Hurd, Douglas (Richard) (1930–) British Conservative politician; foreign secretary (1989–). After service overseas with the Foreign Office, he became an MP in 1974, secretary of state for Northern Ireland (1984–85), and home secretary (1985–89). He also writes political thrillers.

hurdling A track event in athletics in which sprinters jump ten hurdles. Distances are 110 m and 400 m for men and 100 m for women. For the 110 m the height of the hurdles is 106.7 cm (3.5 ft), for the 400 m it is 91.4 cm (3 ft), and for the 100 m 84 cm (2.75 ft). Racers are not normally disqualified for knocking hurdles over.

hurdy-gurdy A stringed instrument sounded by a rosined wheel, turned by the right hand, and stopped by keys played by the left hand; there are two drone strings. Popular in medieval times, it survives in parts of Europe.

hurling (*or* hurley) An Irish 15-a-side stick-and-ball field game similar to *hockey. The ball is hit or carried through the air with a broad curved stick, the hurley (Gaelic word: *caman*), and may be caught in the hand. A goal, hit under the crossbar, scores three points; a hit above the bar scores one.

Huron, Lake The second largest of the Great Lakes, situated between the USA and Canada, and an important shipping route. Area: 59 570 sq km (23 000 sq mi).

hurricane 1. A tropical *cyclone with wind speeds in excess of 64 knots (32.7 m per second) that occurs around the Caribbean Sea and Gulf of Mexico. The centre (eye) of a hurricane is an area of light winds around which strong winds and rain bands spiral. 2. Any wind reaching force 12 on the *Beaufort scale.

husky A breed of sturdy dogs used for pulling sledges in Arctic regions. The Siberian husky has small erect ears, a long muzzle, and a brushlike tail. The dense double-layered coat provides insulation against the climate. Height: 51–63 cm.

hussars Light-cavalry regiments starting in Hungary in the 15th century and used in other European countries. Their uniform included the dolman, a cloak worn hanging from the left shoulder. The name has been adopted by some armoured units.

Hussein (ibn Talal) (1935–) King of Jordan (1952–), who succeeded his mentally ill father Talal. Hussein led Jordan into the 1967 Arab-Israeli War. In 1970 he crushed the al-Fatah guerrillas in the fighting of "Black September" but in

1974, under pressure from other Arab countries, accepted the claims of the Palestine Liberation Organization to the West Bank of the River Jordan.

Hussein, Saddam (1937–) Iraqi statesman; president of Iraq (1979–). He repressed such groups as the Kurds and led Iraq into both *Gulf Wars, the second (1991) following his annexation of Kuwait.

Hussites The followers of the Bohemian religious reformer, Jan Hus (1372–1415), who opposed the use of Latin in services and demanded a reformed church. In spite of crusades led by the Holy Roman Emperor Sigismund, the Hussites remained undefeated until the Council of *Basle in 1433. The more moderate Hussites, the Utraquists, survived until the 17th century.

Huston, John (1906–87) US film director. His first film as director was *The Maltese Falcon* (1941); subsequent films included *The Treasure of the Sierra Madre* (1948), *The African Queen* (1951), *Annie* (1982), and *Prizzi's Honour* (1985).

Huygens, Christiaan (1629–95) Dutch astronomer and physicist, who discovered Saturn's rings (1656), invented the pendulum clock, and designed the lenses called a Huygens eyepiece. His wave theory of light explained double refraction.

hyacinth A flowering plant of the lily family, native to the Mediterranean and tropical Africa. Growing from bulbs, the plants have bell-shaped flowers, varying from white to deep purple, and are widely grown as pot plants.

hybrid The offspring resulting from the mating of two unrelated individuals. Hybrids are often generally fitter than either parent, a phenomenon called hybrid vigour (or heterosis), used by plant breeders to produce plants with higher yields and improved resistance to disease.

Hyderabad 17 22N 78 26E A large city in India, the capital of Andhra Pradesh on the River Musi. Formerly the capital of the princely state of Hyderabad, it is the site of Osmania University (1918). Manufactures include bus and railway equipment and pharmaceuticals. Population (1981): 2 528 000.

Hydra In Greek legend, a monster with many heads who grew two more whenever one was cut off. It was killed by *Heracles.

hydra A freshwater *coelenterate consisting of solitary flexible *polyps, 10–30 mm long, with the mouth at the top surrounded by 6–10 tentacles. Usually attached to stones or vegetation, they feed on small animals.

hydrangea A widely planted shrub native to Asia and America. The white, pink, or blue flowers change colour according to the acidity of the soil.

hydraulics The application of *fluid mechanics to design problems involving the flow of water in pipes, rivers, etc., and the construction of dams, reservoirs, and hydroelectric power stations. Mechanical applications include the design of hydraulic presses, *turbines, etc.

hydrocarbons Compounds containing carbon and hydrogen. Saturated hydrocarbons are classified as *alkanes; unsaturated hydrocarbons include *alkenes and *alkynes. *Aromatic hydrocarbons include *benzene.

hydrochloric acid A solution in water of the colourless gas hydrogen chloride (HCl). It is made by the action of sulphuric acid on salt or by the recombination of hydrogen and chlorine from the electrolysis of sea water. Concentrated hydrochloric acid contains about 40% HCl by weight and is a clear fuming corrosive liquid. The acid in the human stomach is dilute hydrochloric acid (0.4%).

hydroelectric power Electricity generation using the *energy of falling water to turn a *turbine connected to an alternator. Water from high-level reservoirs is led to the power station. The higher the reservoir, the less water is needed for the same output. Hydroelectric power is, therefore, a cheap source in mountainous areas with high rainfall. Hydroelectric power stations can have an output of 10 000 megawatts but in the UK most produce less than 100 MW.

hydrofoil A ship the hull of which is raised out of the water by foils as its speed increases. The foils provide lift by functioning as aerofoils (*see* aeronautics), enabling the drag to be reduced so that the speed can increase far above that of a normal ship of the same weight. The first hydrofoil was built in 1906 by Enrico Fortanini (1848–1930). Modern craft use a large V-shaped foil, to provide stability, or small totally submerged foils, which support the hull on streamlined struts. Propulsion is by propeller or by water jet. Hydrofoils of 150 tonnes are in use in many parts of the world, including a cross-Channel service.

hydrogen (H) The lightest gas, recognized as an element by Cavendish in 1766 and named by Lavoisier after water (Greek *hudro*). Hydrogen makes up about 75% of the mass of the universe. It is the simplest element, its nucleus consisting of one proton. Its heavier isotopes are *deuterium (D or ^{2}H) and *tritium (^{3}H). It occurs as the diatomic gas (H_2), water (H_2O), in many organic compounds, and in all *acids and alkalis. The gas is used as a rocket fuel, in welding, and in chemical manufacture. It combines (explosively) with oxygen to form water and can be obtained from water by electrolysis. At no 1; at wt 1.00797; mp $-259.14°C$; bp $-252.87°C$.

hydrogen bomb. *See* nuclear weapons.

hydrology The study of the occurrence and movement of water on the earth's surface. The **hydrological cycle** is the cyclic movement of water from the sea by evaporation and from plants by transpiration into the atmosphere and back, via precipitation. It has many applications, such as flood control, domestic and industrial water supply, and hydroelectric power.

hydrophobia. *See* rabies.

hyena (*or* hyaena) A doglike mammal that hunts in packs, feeding on carcasses and young animals. There are three species: the African spotted hyena (*Crocuta crocuta*); the Asian

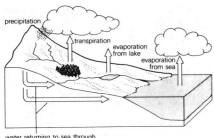

water returning to sea through
streams, rivers, and underground flow.

HYDROLOGY *The hydrological cycle.*

striped hyena (*Hyaena hyaena*); and the brown
hyena (*H. brunnea*) of South Africa, also called
strandwolf.

hygrometer An instrument that measures the
relative *humidity of the atmosphere. In
mechanical hygrometers, a material (usually
human hair) is used, the length of which varies
with the humidity; the variations are transformed into the movement of a pointer along a
scale. The wet-and-dry bulb hygrometer consists
of two thermometers, one having its bulb covered by a moist cloth. The cooling caused by
evaporation from this bulb depends on atmospheric moisture, thus the difference between the
two thermometer readings can be related by
standard tables to the relative humidity.

hymn A song praising god or a saint, often in a
verse. Hymns have been part of Christian worship since the end of the 4th century. During the
middle ages polyphonic settings became common but after the Reformation Lutheran cho-
rales became the basis of the German and English hymn traditions.

hyperbola The curve, or pair of curves,
formed by a *conic section and defined by the
equation $x^2/a^2 - y^2/b^2 = 1$, where a and b are
constants. Its two parts have a common axis and
are separated by a minimum distance $2a$ along
this axis. As it goes out to *infinity, the curve
becomes increasingly close to two straight lines,
called asymptotes.

hypermetropia. *See* longsightedness.

hypertension High *blood pressure, which
can be caused by kidney disease, hormonal dis-

orders, and some other diseases; for most cases,
however, no cause can be found (called essential
hypertension). Usually there are no symptoms;
untreated hypertension may lead to heart failure,
kidney failure, cerebral haemorrhage, and blindness.

hypnosis A means of placing a person in a
trance by the repeated suggestion of the hypnotist. Those capable of being hypnotized can become insensitive to pain, regress to childhood, or
carry out the hypnotist's instructions. First used
to treat patients by *Mesmer in the 18th century,
it was developed (and given its name) by James
Braid (1795–1860). Used to treat certain disorders of the mind and some addictions (e.g. smoking), it is not widely accepted by doctors.

hypothalamus The part of the *brain that coordinates the functions of the autonomic *nervous system. It is particularly involved with the
control of body temperature, regulating how
much is eaten and drunk, and the emotions. It
also releases *neurohormones affecting other organs, especially the *pituitary gland.

hypothermia Lowering the body temperature. It occurs in old people and young babies
living in poorly heated rooms. If the body temperature falls too low internal changes may occur, otherwise gentle warming enables the patient to recover. In heart surgery it is induced
deliberately.

hyrax An African *mammal belonging to the
order *Hyracoidea* (6 species), also called cony.
30–60 cm long, hyraxes are related to hooved
mammals, having hooflike toes and a two-
chambered stomach. They live in small colonies
in trees or rocks, being active at twilight.

hyssop A plant, *Hyssopus officinalis*, native to
S Europe, Asia, and Morocco. Formerly cultivated as a medicinal herb, it grows to a height of
60 cm, and has blue flowers along the stem.

hysterectomy The surgical removal of the
womb, usually when it contains fibroids–benign
tumours that cause heavy menstrual periods.
Other conditions requiring hysterectomy include
cancer of the womb or the cervix. Sexual activity
is not affected by the operation, but no further
pregnancies are possible.

I

Ibadan 7 23N 3 56E The second largest city in
Nigeria. Population (1983 est): 1 060 000.

Iberians A Bronze Age agricultural people of
S and E Spain in the 1st millennium BC. Their
non-Indo-European language, which was replaced by Latin, is known from a variety of inscriptions.

ibex A rare wild *goat, *Capra ibex*, found in
mountainous regions of Europe, Asia, and N Af-

rica. About 85 cm high, ibexes have backward-
curving horns up to 65 cm long and their coat is
brownish-grey.

ibis A long-necked wading bird, related to the
spoonbills, occurring in warm regions. 55–
75 cm long, ibises have a slender bill and the face
and neck lacks feathers. The sacred ibis is an
example.

Ibiza (Iviza *or* Ivica) One of the Balearic islands and a tourist centre. Area: 541 sq km (209 sq mi). Population (1986): 45 000. Chief town: Ibiza.

Ibn Saud (c. 1880–1953) The first King of Saudi Arabia (1932–53). With the military help of the Arabian tribesmen, al-Ikhwan, he extended his territory from the Sultanate of Najd to include much of Arabia by 1924; the name Saudi Arabia was adopted in 1932.

Ibo (*or* Igbo) A people of SE Nigeria who speak Igbo, a language of the Kwa subgroup of the *Niger-Congo family. Cultivators of yams and cassava, they traditionally lived in scattered village clusters. *See also* Biafra.

Ibsen, Henrik (1828–1906) Norwegian playwright and poet. From 1864 to 1891 he lived in Italy and Germany, with occasional visits to Norway. His fame grew with *Brand* (1865) and *Peer Gynt* (1867). In his social plays, *A Doll's House* (1879), *Ghosts* (1881), and *An Enemy of the People* (1882) he dealt with topical issues. *The Wild Duck* (1884) and *Hedda Gabler* (1890) dealt with the problems of individuals, while *The Master Builder* (1892), *John Gabriel Borkman* (1896), and *When We Dead Awaken* (1899), involved autobiographical themes.

Icarus (astronomy) A *minor planet (about 1 km diameter) with the smallest perihelion (0.19 astronomical units). It passed 600 000 km from earth in 1968.

Icarus (mythology). *See* Daedalus.

Ice Age One of several periods in which ice spread towards the earth's equator, caused by falling temperatures. The most recent of these was the *Pleistocene epoch ending about 10 000 years ago, during which four major ice advances occurred. Other ice ages occurred in Permo-Carboniferous times about 250 million years ago and in Pre-Cambrian times about 500 million years ago.

iceberg A large mass of ice in the sea, most of which is submerged. Originating on land, many result when ice breaks away from glaciers. In the N hemisphere icebergs originate chiefly from Greenland; in the S hemisphere most come from the Antarctic.

ice hockey A six-a-side game played with stick and puck on an ice rink. It developed from field hockey and was first played by Englishmen on the frozen Kingston Harbour, Ontario (c. 1860). It is widely played in the USA, the Soviet Union, Sweden, Czechoslovakia, Germany, and Finland.

Iceland, Republic of (Icelandic name: Island) An island country in the N Atlantic, S of the Arctic Circle, off SE Greenland. It consists largely of uninhabited volcanic plateau and glaciers; most of the population live around the coast. *Economy*: the main exports are fish products and aluminium. Hydroelectricity and geothermal power (from geysers and thermal springs) are important. *History*: the Vikings reached Iceland about 874 AD; by the 10th century it had become independent, with its own parliament, the Althing, the oldest in the world. In 1264 it came under Norwegian rule and passed to the Danish Crown in 1381. In 1918 it became independent under the Danish Crown, becoming a republic in 1944. Official language: Icelandic. Official religion: Evangelical Lutheranism. Official currency: króna of 100 aurar (100 old króna = 1 new króna introduced 1981). Area: 103 000 sq km (39 758 sq mi). Population (1989): 253 482. Capital and main port: Reykjavik.

Icelandic A North Germanic language of the Western Scandinavian subgroup, developed from Old Norse. The official language of Iceland.

Iceni A tribe that lived in SE England (now Norfolk and Suffolk). Under *Boadicea (60 AD) their revolt against Roman rule was brutally suppressed.

ice plant A succulent plant, *Cryophytum crystallinum*, covered in glistening hairs. Native to South Africa, it is widely grown as a pot plant.

ice skating A recreation and sport that includes speed skating (racing) and two events judged on style—figure skating (a freestyle performance to music, either singly or in pairs) and ice dancing. *See also* ice hockey.

ichneumon A widely occurring insect, typically about 12 mm long, resembling and related to wasps. Parasitic upon other insects, they control many insect pests.

ichthyosaur An extinct dolphin-like reptile that lived in the Mesozoic era but was most abundant in the Jurassic period (200–135 million years ago). 1–12 m long. It had flexible paddle-like limbs, a large tail fin, and a triangular dorsal fin.

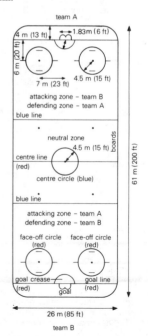

ICE HOCKEY *The dimensions of the rink.*

icon   A painted or mosaic image of Christ or a saint, found in Byzantine and Orthodox churches. Icons are characterized by their symbolic and stylized approach to perspective, colour, etc.

Iconium.   *See* Konya.

Idaho   A state in the NW USA, dominated by the N Rocky Mountains. It is primarily agricultural but is also rich in minerals, producing silver and antimony. *History*: first settled in the early 19th century, it became a state in 1890. Area: 216 412 sq km (83 557 sq mi). Population (1986 est): 1 003 000. Capital: Boise.

ide.   *See* orfe.

idealism   Any philosophical doctrine that assumes the real world exists only in the mind. Philosophers who have held idealist views include *Berkeley, *Kant, *Hegel, and *Plato.

ideographic writing systems (*or* ideography) Writing systems in which each idea is represented by a symbol; they probably came from pictographic systems, with symbols representing abstract ideas added to those representing concrete things. Languages such as Chinese use ideographic writing systems.

igloo   A temporary dome-shaped dwelling made from blocks of snow by Eskimos between the Mackenzie River delta and Labrador in N Canada. The blocks are cut with a long knife and the joints filled with snow. The igloo is entered by a semicylindrical passageway about three metres long.

Ignatius Loyola, St   (1491–1556) Spanish founder of the *Jesuits. After reading (1521) the life of Christ while recovering from a war wound, he visited the Holy Land (1523) and studied theology in Spain and in Paris. There, in 1534, with St *Francis Xavier he became a monk. Ordained in 1537, he moved to Rome, where he founded the Society of Jesus with the approval of Pope Paul III in 1540. Feast day: 31 July.

igneous rock   One of the three major categories of rock (*compare* metamorphic rock; sedimentary rock) consisting mostly of crystalline rocks cooled directly from *magma. Silica is the dominant chemical constituent of igneous rocks. Examples include *obsidian, *granite, and dolerite.

iguana   A lizard found in N and S America; there are desert-dwelling, tree-dwelling, and amphibious species. The green common iguana (*Iguana iguana*), 1.8 m long (including the tail 1.3 m), has a spiny crest along the back; males have a hanging fold of skin beneath the throat. The marine iguana (*Amblyrhynchus cristatus*) of the Galapagos is the only lizard that feeds in the sea. *See also* basilisk.

iguanodon   A large herbivorous dinosaur that lived in the Jurassic and Cretaceous periods (200–65 million years ago). About 5 m tall, it stood on two hind legs and had a heavy balancing tail.

Illinois   A group of Algonkian-speaking North American Indian tribes of Wisconsin, Illinois, Missouri, and Iowa. Their villages were of rush-mat-covered dwellings, each housing several families. Men hunted forest game while women cultivated corn. Much reduced by intertribal wars, they eventually scattered.

Illinois   A state in the USA, in the Midwest. Approximately half its population is in the Chicago area, the area to the S being rural. Illinois is a major producer of soya beans, corn, beef, and dairy products. Manufacturing and coalmining are also important. *History*: it originally formed part of the French province of Louisiana but was handed over to Britain (1763). It came under US control (1783), becoming a territory in 1809 and a state in 1818. Area: 146 075 sq km (56 400 sq mi). Population (1987 est): 11 582 000. Capital: Springfield.

illuminated manuscripts   Manuscripts of gospels, prayers, etc., decorated with designs in watercolour and gold leaf. First practised by monastic scribes in the early middle ages, the art is exemplified in the 8th-century Book of Kells and the later Duke of Berry's book of hours by the de Limburg brothers (active c. 1400–c. 1416).

Illyria   The Adriatic coastal region W of the Balkans. Inhabited from the 10th century BC by warlike tribes, Illyria constantly harassed Macedonia and Epirus. Illyria became the Roman province of Illyricum in 167 BC.

imaginary number.   *See* complex numbers.

Immaculate Conception   The belief of the Roman Catholic Church that the Virgin Mary was conceived free from original sin. It was opposed by such theologians as St Bonaventure and St Thomas Aquinas but was proclaimed as dogma in 1854 by Pope Pius IX.

immunity   The resistance of the body to infection, especially resistance due to *antibodies. Babies have passive immunity from antibodies transferred from the mother's blood through the placenta. Active immunity involves the formation of antibodies after exposure to an antigen (bacteria that invade the body during an infection are antigens). The two different kinds of immune response produced by antibodies involve: white blood cells called T-lymphocytes (produced by the *thymus), which produce cells with antibody bound to their surface and are responsible for such reactions as graft rejection; B-lymphocytes, which produce cells that release free antibody into the blood.

Immunization is the production of immunity by an injection containing antibodies against specific diseases (e.g. tetanus and diphtheria), which provides temporary passive immunity, or by *vaccination, which produces the longer lasting active immunity.

impala   A common antelope, *Aepyceros melampus*, of central and S African savanna. About 100 cm high, impalas have a red-brown coat and white underparts; males have lyre-shaped horns.

impeachment   A prosecution brought in the UK by the House of Commons as prosecutor and tried by the House of Lords as judge, especially against a minister of the Crown for a serious public offence. In the USA impeachments are brought by the House of Representatives and tried by the Senate.

impedance   A measure of the ability of a circuit to resist the flow of an alternating current. It is given by $Z = R + iX$, where Z is the impedance, R is the *resistance, X is the *reactance, and i = $\sqrt{-1}$. Impedance and reactance are measured in *ohms.

Imperial War Museum A museum in S London founded in 1917 to collect military equipment, uniforms, and art, relating mainly to the World Wars.

Impressionism A French art movement that took its name from Monet's painting *Impression: Sunrise* (1872; Musée Marmottan, Paris), shown at the first of the eight impressionist exhibitions between 1874 and 1886. The leading impressionists were *Monet, *Pissarro, *Sisley, and *Renoir; they aimed to capture fleeting effects of light and weather with dabs of bright colour.

Imprinting A rapid and irreversible form of learning that takes place in some animals in the first hours of life. It was first described by Konrad *Lorenz in geese. *See also* ethology.

Incarnation The Christian doctrine, stated in the Gospel of St John and St Paul's Epistle to the Colossians, that the second person of the *Trinity took human form. Although in other religions gods temporarily appear in human form, in Christianity the union of the divine and human in Christ is permanent.

Incas A *Quechua-speaking South American Indian people of the Peruvian Andes. From their capital, Cuzco, they ruled an empire from Ecuador to Chile in the 15th century. It was destroyed in the 16th century by the Spaniards. *See also* Machu Picchu.

incense A mixture of gums (especially gum benzoin) burnt for its smell (*see also* frankincense), used in religious ceremonies in ancient Egypt, Greece, and Rome as well as in Jewish ceremonies. In the Book of Revelation it is a symbol of the prayers of saints; its use in Christian worship began in the 6th century and continues in Orthodox and Roman Catholic churches.

incest Forbidden sexual relations between close relatives. The forbidding of incest makes good scientific sense: children born to parents who are blood relatives can have serious genetic abnormalities (recessive genes becoming dominant).

Inchŏn 37 30N 126 38E A city in NW South Korea, Seoul's main seaport on the Yellow Sea. Population (1985): 1 387 475.

incunabula Books printed in the early days of modern printing (before 1500) after the invention of movable type by *Gutenberg. N European incunabula used a heavy type known as black letter; Italian books used a lighter roman typeface.

Independence Day The US national holiday on the anniversary of the adoption of the *Declaration of Independence by the Continental Congress on 4 July, 1776.

indexation. *See* price index.

India, Republic of (Hindi name: Bharat) A country in S Asia. Bordering on Pakistan, China, Nepal, Bhutan, and Burma, it comprises 25 states and 7 Union Territories. The chief religions are Hinduism (83% of the population) and Islam (11%). *Economy*: 70% of the workforce is engaged in agriculture; rice, pulses, cereals, tea, jute, cotton, and tobacco are the main crops.

Mineral resources include coal, iron ore, manganese, bauxite, mica, and ilmenite. Oil is produced from the Arabian Sea. India has nuclear power. *History*: the *Indus Valley was the site of a civilization for a thousand years before the invading Aryans established theirs (c. 1500 BC). From this civilization Hinduism emerged as India's religion. The Mauryan Empire followed (c. 320 BC–c. 185 BC), which unified most of India. Hindu culture flourished (4th–6th centuries AD) in the N under the Gupta dynasty although persistent Muslim raids on the N culminated in a Muslim sultanate based on Delhi (1129), under which India was again unified. A later Muslim invasion resulted in the *Mogul Empire (established 1526). The British *East India Company (founded 1600) developing its interests in India fought with French traders in the 18th century; with Robert Clive's victory at Plassey (1757), power shifted from the East India Company to the British Government. Political unrest under British government led to the *Indian Mutiny (1857–59), after which there was greater Indian involvement in government; in 1919 a parliament was created. The nationalist movement (*see* Indian National Congress), under the leadership of Mahatma *Gandhi, demanded home rule, which was conceded by Britain in 1947 on condition that a separate Muslim state should be established. The subsequent creation of *Pakistan (1947) involved violent upheavals in which 500 000 people were killed and trouble between Hindus and Muslims persisted. India became a sovereign state in 1950, with the addition of former French and Portuguese territories (1956 and 1961) and Sikkim (1975). Indira *Gandhi (prime minister 1966–77, 1980–84) in 1984 suppressed a Sikh movement demanding self-government for the Punjab, being later assassinated by Sikhs in her bodyguard; she was succeeded by her son, Rajiv Gandhi; in 1990 he was succeeded by Chandra Shekhar. Official languages: Hindi and English. Official currency: Indian rupee of 100 paise. Area: 3 287 590 sq km (1 269 072 sq mi), including Jammu and Kashmir. Population (1986): 783 940 000. Capital: New Delhi.

Indiana A state in the USA, forming part of the Mississippi Basin. It produces soya beans, cereals, and vegetables. Coal and building stone are also exploited. *History*: explored by the French in the 17th century, it became British in 1763, passing to the USA in 1783. Increased settlement followed the defeat of the Indians (1794) and Indiana became a state in 1816. Area: 93 993 sq km (36 291 sq mi). Population (1988 est): 5 575 000. Capital: Indianapolis.

Indianapolis 39 45N 86 10W A city in the USA, the capital of Indiana. It is the scene of annual speedway races, including the **Indianapolis 500**, first held in 1911. Population (1986 est): 719 820.

Indian corn. *See* maize.

Indian languages Languages of differing origins spoken in the Indian subcontinent. The two major language families are the *Indo-European and the *Dravidian. The Indo-European is divided into the *Iranian subgroup (Baluchi and Pashto spoken on the NW borders of India) and

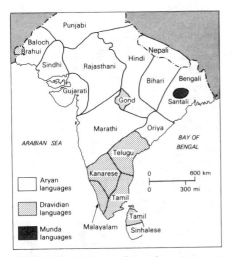

INDIA *The distribution of major language groups in the Indian subcontinent.*

the Indo-Aryan subgroup, including *Hindustani; *Hindi, the official national language; Rajasthani, Punjabi, *Gujarati, and Sindhi in the west; Bengali and Bihari in the east; and Kashmiri. Most of S India is covered by the Dravidian family. In addition there are scattered languages of the Munda group in the NE, and languages of *Sino-Tibetan origins are spoken in the Himalayas.

Indian Mutiny (1857–59) A revolt of about 35 000 sepoys (Indian soldiers serving the British East India Company). It began when the rebels massacred Europeans at Meerut in May, 1857, and then captured Delhi. Under Colin Campbell (1792–1863), the British regained Delhi in Sept; by July, 1858, the revolt had largely been controlled.

Indian National Congress The political party, founded in 1885, that governed India after independence in 1947. Under Mahatma *Gandhi, it recommended noncooperation with the British after 1917, refusing to support Britain in World War II without being promised Indian independence. The party was led by Jawarhalal *Nehru from 1951 to 1964, by Lal Bahadur Shastri (1904–66) until 1966, and then by Mrs Indira *Gandhi until her assassination in 1984, when the leadership passed to her son Rajiv Gandhi.

Indian Ocean The ocean that extends between Asia, Africa, Australia, and Antarctica. Lying within the tropical and temperate zones, its floor is rich in minerals.

Indicator A substance used to indicate through changes in colour, fluorescence, etc., the presence of another substance or the completion of a chemical reaction. For example, litmus is red in the presence of acids but blue in the presence of alkalis.

Indium (In) A silvery metal, named after the indigo line in its spectrum. It is used in making transistors and low-melting alloys. At no 49; at wt 114.82; mp 156.6°C; bp 1450°C.

Indochina The area of SE Asia comprising present-day Burma, Thailand, Malaya, Vietnam, Cambodia, and Laos. The French formed the Union of Indochina in 1887. Following World War II, when the Japanese occupied all Indochina, there was fighting between nationalists (*see* Viet Minh) and the French until 1954, when the *Geneva Conference ended French control over the area.

Indo-European languages The largest language family of the world, sometimes called Indo-Germanic. Spoken throughout Europe and in India, Iran, and parts of the Soviet Union, the family includes Germanic; Italic; Indo-Iranian; *Celtic; Baltic; Slavic (*see* Slavonic); Albanian; *Greek; Armenian; Tocharian; and Anatolian.

Indonesia, Republic of (name from 1798 until 1945: Dutch East Indies) A country in SE Asia, consisting of a series of islands extending E–W for some 5150 km (3200 mi) in the Pacific and Indian Oceans. The main, mostly volcanic, islands are Sumatra, Java and Madura, Bali, Sulawesi, Lombok, the Moluccas, and Timor together with part of Borneo (Kalimantan), and Irian Jaya (the W half of New Guinea). *Economy*: mainly agricultural, including rice, rubber, palm oil, copra, sugar cane, and coffee. *History*: in the 16th century it was occupied successively by the Portuguese, the British, and the Dutch; ruled by the Dutch East India Company (1602–1798), it then became a colony of the Netherlands. After Japanese occupation during World War II, it became a republic in 1945 under the leadership of Dr Sukarno, being granted independence in 1949–50. A military coup in 1966 under Gen Suharto established a military dictatorship. Official language: Bahasa Indonesia. Official currency: rupiah of 100 sen. Area: 1 903 650 sq km (735 000 sq mi). Population (1987): 172 250 000. Capital and main port: Jakarta.

Indore 22 42N 75 54E A city in India, in Madhya Pradesh. Formerly the capital of the princely state of Indore, it is a trading centre. Population (1981): 827 000.

Indra The principal Hindu god of the Vedic period (c. 1500–1200 BC), god of war and storm (shown wielding a thunderbolt). He slew the dragon Vritra, releasing the water and light to create the universe.

Indri The largest Madagascan woolly lemur, *Indri indri*. Up to 70 cm long, it is grey and black, with long hind legs and a doglike head. It lives in treetops and has a loud howling cry.

Indulgence In the Roman Catholic Church, being let off penalties for sins already forgiven by God in the sacrament of penance. Started in the early Church, indulgences in the later middle ages came to have a financial value, which led to widespread misuse and was one of the causes of Luther's attack on the Church at the Reformation. Their sale was prohibited in 1567.

Indus, River A river in S central Asia. Rising in Tibet in the Himalayas, it flows through Kashmir, then across Pakistan to its delta near Karachi on the Arabian Sea. The Indus Valley contained one of the earliest organized cultures (c. 2500–1700 BC). Length: 2900 km (1800 mi).

industrial revolution The process that transformed Britain and other countries from agricultural to industrial economies. It began in Britain in about 1750 with inventions in the textile industry (*see* *Hargreaves, *Arkwright, and *Crompton) in which small units were replaced by factories housing the new machinery. After the invention of the steam engine these factories were put up near coalfields. As a result industrial towns sprang up creating an industrial working class, who were expected to endure poor living and working conditions. By the mid-19th century British industrial methods had spread to continental Europe and the USA, laying the foundations for further industrial developments in the 20th century.

inert gases. *See* noble gases.

inertia A property of a body that causes it to resist changes in its velocity or, if stationary, to resist motion. In linear motion, mass is a measurement of a body's inertia (*see* mass and weight); in rotation about an axis, inertia is given by the body's *moment of inertia.

inertial guidance A means of guiding a missile by the use of on-board instruments (gyroscopes and computers). There is no communication with its destination or point of departure.

infallibility A dogma of the Roman Catholic Church, first stated in 1870, which says that the pope cannot make mistakes in defining the Church's teaching in matters of faith and morals when speaking *ex cathedra* (Latin: from the throne).

infection Illness caused by bacteria, viruses, fungi, or protozoa. Examples of bacterial infections include pneumonia and whooping cough. Viruses cause influenza and measles (among others); malaria and sleeping sickness result from protozoan infection, and fungi cause ringworm. Infectious diseases are the commonest cause of sickness. Infections may be caught by direct contact with an infected person, contact with a human or animal carrier or contaminated objects, and contact with infected droplets produced by coughing and sneezing. *Antibiotics are used to treat a wide range of infections although with viral diseases they only prevent secondary bacterial infections (*see also* vaccination).

infinity In mathematics, a quantity larger than any that can be specified. The symbols $+\infty$ and $-\infty$ are read as "plus infinity" and "minus infinity" respectively. They indicate infinitely large positive and negative values.

inflation A general increase in prices resulting from excessive demand for goods (demand-pull inflation), increased prices by sellers even when demand has not increased (cost-push inflation), or an expansion of the money supply (monetary inflation). **Deflation** is the opposite process and causes a reduction in both output and employment. Attempts to control inflation have included: control of wages and prices (prices and incomes policy), increased taxation, reduced government spending, a controlled money sup-

ply, and an increased bank rate. *Compare* depression.

inflorescence A group of flowers borne on the main stalk of a plant. In one type, called a racemose (or indefinite) inflorescence, the tip of the main stem continues to grow and flowers arise below it. Examples are foxglove and wheat. A cymose (or definite) inflorescence is one in which a flower is produced at the tip of the main stem, which then ceases to grow. Examples are buttercup and stitchwort.

infrared radiation Electromagnetic radiation with wavelengths between about 750 nanometres and 1 millimetre. In the electromagnetic spectrum it lies between the red end of visible light and microwaves. It was discovered in 1800 by William Herschel (1738–1822).

infrared telescope A reflecting *telescope for detecting and studying infrared radiation from space. Semiconductor detectors are used, and these (and in some cases parts of the telescope) must be cooled to very low temperatures. Infrared telescopes are normally sited at high altitudes to reduce infrared absorption by the atmosphere or are carried on satellites.

Ingres, Jean-Auguste-Dominique (1780–1867) French painter. Many of his historical and mythological paintings aroused criticism but his *Vow of Louis XIII* (Cathedral, Montauban) established him as an opponent of *Romanticism. He is noted for his portraits and his nudes, e.g. *Valpinçon Bather* (Louvre).

initiation rites Ceremonies performed when a child reaches adulthood or when joining certain professions or associations. During this period adolescents among primitive peoples are often educated in the duties of adulthood.

initiative. *See* referendum and initiative.

ink cap A *mushroom in which an inky fluid drips from the cap after the spores have been released. The common ink cap (*Coprinus atramentarius*) usually grows at the base of trees; it has a brownish cap, 3–7 cm high, and a whitish stalk.

Inkerman, Battle of (5 November, 1854) A battle of the *Crimean War, in which the French and British defeated the Russians at Inkerman, near Sevastopol. The Russians lost about 12 000 men, the British and French about 3500.

Inner Temple. *See* Inns of Court.

Innsbruck 47 17N 11 25E A city in W Austria, the capital of the Tirol on the River Inn. It is a popular tourist centre. Population (1981): 117 287.

Inns of Court Assocations with the sole right to give the rank of barrister-at-law, known as "calling to the Bar." For the English bar, the Inns are the Honourable Societies of Lincoln's Inn (established 1310), Middle Temple (1340), Inner Temple (1340), and Gray's Inn (1357). Most barristers' offices (known as chambers) in London are in one of the Inns.

inorganic chemistry. *See* chemistry.

Inquisition (*or* Holy Office) An institution of the Roman Catholic Church designed to fight heresy and moral offences, formally instituted (1231) by Pope Gregory IX. Secret trials and torture were used. Fines and penances were imposed on those who confessed; those who refused were imprisoned or executed. The Inquisition was revived in Spain in 1478 against Jews and Muslims. The growth of Protestantism also led to the establishment (1542) of a Roman Inquisition by Pope Paul III, which numbered *Galileo among its victims. In 1965 it was renamed the Sacred Congregation for the Doctrine of the Faith with the task of maintaining discipline.

insanity In law, a loss of reason caused by disease of the mind, making a person not responsible for his acts. If a jury finds a person committed an act as charged but was insane, it must return a verdict of not guilty by reason of insanity. According to **M'Naghten's Rules** a person is insane if he was unaware of the nature or quality of his act or did not know it was morally wrong.

insect An invertebrate animal, 0.2–350 mm long, of which there are about a million species accounting for 83% of all animal life. An insect's body is divided into the head, which bears a pair of antennae; the thorax, with three pairs of legs; and the abdomen. The majority of insects lay eggs, which go through a series of changes (metamorphosis) to reach the adult stage. Insects can be predators, parasites, scavengers, and can also spread disease. Others are useful in pollinating crops or killing pests, while some produce useful substances, such as honey, beeswax, and silk. See also arthropod. See p. 272.

insecticides Substances used to kill insects. Originally, strong poisons, such as arsenic compounds and cyanides, were used but these were dangerous to humans and livestock. They were replaced by synthetic organic substances, beginning with *DDT in 1945. **Contact insecticides** are applied directly to the insects, while **residual insecticides** are sprayed on surfaces that the insects touch. Insecticides can cause environmental *pollution. See also biological control.

insectivorous plant See carnivorous plant.

instinct 1. A complex pattern of behaviour determined by heredity, which is not greatly altered by the experience of the individual. Birdsong and the behaviour of social insects (such as bees) are examples. 2. An innate drive, such as hunger or sex, that urges an individual towards a particular goal.

insulin A protein hormone secreted by the islets of Langerhans in the *pancreas. It stimulates the uptake of glucose and amino acids from the blood by the tissues. First isolated in 1921 by *Banting and Best, insulin's molecular structure was revealed by Sanger and Hodgkin. A deficiency of insulin causes *diabetes mellitus.

insurance A method of providing money to make up for a misfortune or loss that may not occur. Events that must occur, such as death, are provided for by assurance. In the UK and some other countries some insurance is provided by the government (see National Insurance). Other types of insurance are undertaken by insurance companies or by *Lloyd's. The public does not deal directly with the underwriters (insurers) but arranges insurance through a broker, who works for a commission. The insurance premium (cost to the insured) is calculated by the insurer's *actuary on the basis of the probability that the risk will occur.

integrated circuit (IC) A complete electronic circuit of *transistors, diodes, etc., contained in a *semiconductor wafer. Since the 1970s computers have enabled ICs to become smaller and more complex. A silicon chip (or microchip) is covered with circuits, and computer-controlled microscopic probes search out the best points for connections for each specific device.

intelligence The ability to reason and to learn from experience. Intelligence is thought to depend both on inherited abilities (nature) and on the surroundings in which a person is brought up (nurture). Jean Piaget greatly contributed to our understanding of intellectual development. The first **intelligence tests** were devised by Alfred Binet in 1905 to give an **intelligence quotient** (IQ); the average IQ is 100 and over 95% of the population come between 70 and 130. However, some now believe that intelligence can be expressed only through speech and writing (and therefore cannot be tested).

intelligence service The government department responsible for obtaining information about the military and economic capabilities and political intentions of another country (intelligence) and for blocking a foreign country from obtaining such information (counterintelligence). In 1909 and 1912 respectively the army's Directorate of Military Operations organized MO-5 (counterintelligence) and MO-6 (intelligence), which became MI(Military Intelligence)-5 (the Security Service) and MI-6 (the Secret Intelligence Service). In the USA the services are the *Central Intelligence Agency and the *Federal Bureau of Investigation (counterintelligence); in the USSR the agency is the *KGB.

Intelsat. See communications satellite.

interest The money charged for the use of a loan. The principal (P) is the amount of the loan; the term (t), the time in years for which the money is lent; and the rate (r), the annual percentage rate of interest. In simple interest, the lender is paid $Prt/100$ in interest and repaid P after t years. In compound interest, the interest each year is not paid to the lender but is added to the principal, so after t years the lender is paid $P(1 + r/100)^t$.

interference A wave phenomenon in which two waves combine either to reinforce each other or to cancel each other out, depending on their relative phases. The pattern of light and dark strips so produced is called an **interference pattern** (or interference fringe). Interference was discovered in 1801 by Thomas *Young and provided strong evidence for the wave theory of light.

interferon A protein that appears in the blood plasma during viral infections: it is released from infected cells and inhibits the growth of the viruses. Interferon plays an important role in *immunity because it can enter uninfected cells and make them immune to all viral infections. It was discovered in 1957 by a British virologist, Alick Isaacs (1921–67).

INSECT

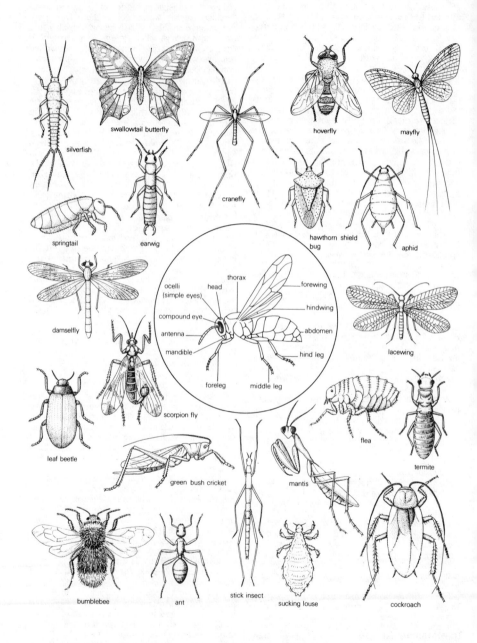

INSECT *The structure of a typical insect (centre), with representatives from all the principal insect orders.*

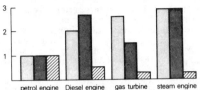

petrol engine   Diesel engine   gas turbine   steam engine

INTERNAL-COMBUSTION ENGINE *Esti-
mates of cost, weight, and pollution for various
types of internal-combustion engine compared to a
steam engine.*

internal-combustion engine An engine in
which the fuel is burnt inside the engine rather
than in a separate furnace (*see* steam engine). Examples include all piston engines, *jet engines,
and *rockets. The first practical internal-combustion engine was patented by N. *Otto in
1876, and it is the Otto-cycle petrol engine that
still powers most road vehicles. A simpler but
less efficient petrol engine is the two-stroke, used
where low power is required. The main alternative to the petrol engine is the Diesel engine,
based on a cycle invented by the German engineer Rudolf Diesel (1858–1913), which is heavier and more expensive than the petrol engine.
The *gas turbine uses continuous combustion.
Jet engines based on the gas turbine are used
widely in aircraft.

International An association of socialist or labour parties formed to encourage the spread of
socialism or communism. The **First International**
was founded in London in 1864 as the International Working Men's Association. Karl *Marx
became its leader but it failed to make any political changes. Its last meeting was held in 1876 in
Philadelphia.
The **Second International** was founded in Paris
in 1889 with headquarters in Brussels. Its leaders
included Ramsay *MacDonald. At the outbreak
of World War I, the organization collapsed.
The **Labour and Socialist International** was
founded in Vienna in 1921 with the object of creating a socialist commonwealth. It ended after
Hitler's invasion in 1939.
The **Third International** (*or* Comintern), an organization of world Communist Parties, was
founded by Lenin in March, 1919, to encourage
worldwide working class revolution. Stalin dissolved the International in 1943.
The **Fourth International**, founded by *Trotsky
in Mexico City in 1937, opposed Stalin and the
Third International.
The **Socialist International**, founded in London
in 1951, believes in parliamentary democracy
and opposes communism.
**International Bank for Reconstruction and
Development** (IBRD) A specialized agency of
the *United Nations, known as the World Bank,
with headquarters in Washington, DC. It finances development in member countries by

lending to governments. It was set up by the 1944
*Bretton Woods agreements.
International Brigades A volunteer army recruited during the Spanish Civil War (1936–39)
by the Comintern to aid the Republicans against
Franco. It consisted of some 20 000 volunteers,
of which about 60% were communists; it was disbanded in 1938.
International Court of Justice The court set
up by the UN to judge disputes between states.
Sitting in The Hague, it consists of 15 judges,
each from a different state, elected by the UN
General Assembly. Judgments are enforced by
application to the UN Security Council.
International Date Line A line following the
180° meridian, deviating to avoid some land areas. The date immediately E of the line is one day
earlier than to the W since 180°E is 12 hours
ahead of *Greenwich Mean Time and 180°W is
12 hours behind.
International law The rules that decide the legal relationship between states (public), or the
method of resolving disputes between individuals in different legal systems (private). Public international law, also called the law of nations, is
administered by the *International Court of Justice. Private international law, also called conflict of laws, decides which country's laws should
apply.
International Monetary Fund (IMF) A specialized agency of the *United Nations, with
headquarters in Washington, DC, set up by the
1944 *Bretton Woods agreements to stabilize exchange rates and facilitate international trade.
International Phonetic Alphabet (IPA) An
expanded Roman alphabet, developed by the International Phonetic Association in the late 19th
century. It has a symbol for every sound used in
language and is used in dictionaries.
international style An architectural style of
the 20th century. Originating with such architects as *Gropius, *Wright, and *Le Corbusier,
the style evolved from the materials and advanced technology produced by industrialization. It is characterized by the use of concrete,
often roughcast, and asymmetric cubic forms.
Interpol (*Inter*national Criminal *Poli*ce Organization) An association of about 120 national
police forces formed in 1923 to provide a means
of international cooperation in the prevention of
crime. It organizes the exchange of police information and the arrest of accused persons abroad.
Interregnum. *See* Commonwealth.
intestine The part of the digestive tract that
extends from the stomach to the anus. The small
intestine, which includes the duodenum, jeju-
num, and ileum, is the main site of digestion and
absorption of food. The large intestine, the colon, caecum, rectum, and anus, is concerned with
absorbing water from digested food and forming
faeces.
intra-uterine device (IUD). *See* contraception.
introversion (*or* intraversion) Interest in one-
self rather than in the outside world: it is the opposite of extroversion. Introverts are reflective
and highly susceptible to permanent *conditioning.

intrusive rock. See igneous rock.

Inverness 57 27N 4 15W A city in N Scotland, the administrative centre of the Highland Region, at the head of the Moray Firth. It has a 19th-century cathedral and castle. Population (1981): 39 736.

invertebrate Any animal without a backbone, including insects, crustaceans, worms, molluscs, jellyfish, etc.

investment company (or investment trust) A company that buys and sells securities to make profits for its shareholders. In the USA it is called a closed-end investment company. Compare unit trust.

in vitro fertilization. See test-tube baby.

iodine (I) A purple solid *halogen that evaporates slowly at room temperature to give a purple gas. Discovered in 1811 by B. Courtois (1777–1838), it is insoluble in water but dissolves in organic solvents. Potassium iodide (KI) is widely used in photography. The radioactive isotope ^{131}I is used in *radiotherapy. Tincture of iodine is used as an antiseptic. At no 53; at wt 126.904; mp 113.5°C; bp 184.35°C.

ion An atom or group of atoms that has lost (cation, positively charged) or gained (anion, negatively charged) one or more electrons. The sign and magnitude of the charge is indicated by a superscript, as in the potassium cation, K^+. Electrovalent compounds are combinations of positive and negative ions; sodium chloride, for example is formed from sodium ions (Na^+) and chloride ions (Cl^-). See also chemical bond; ionization.

Iona 56 19N 6 25W A small sparsely populated island in NW Scotland, in the Inner Hebrides. St Columba landed here in 563 AD, establishing a monastery that became the centre of the Celtic Church. Area: 854 ha (2112 acres).

Ionesco, Eugène (1912–) French dramatist, born in Romania. He launched the *Theatre of the Absurd with The Bald Prima Donna (1950). Later plays include The Lesson (1951), Rhinoceros (1960), and Man With Bags (1977).

Ionia In antiquity, the central W coast of Asia Minor and the adjacent islands, settled by Greeks about 1000 BC. Between the 8th and 6th centuries BC *Miletus, Samos, *Ephesus, and other Ionian cities led Greece in trade and culture. After 550 BC Ionia was dominated by *Lydia and later Persia.

Ionian Islands A group of Greek islands in the Ionian Sea, including Páxos, Lévkas, Ithaca, and Cephalonia. They belonged to Britain from the Treaty of Paris (1815) until 1864, when they were handed over to Greece. Total area: 2307 sq km (891 sq mi). Population (1981): 182 651.

Ionic order. See orders of architecture.

ionization The process of producing *ions from neutral atoms or molecules, by solvation (surrounding of an ion by polar solvent molecules), heating (thermal ionization), or bombardment with particles or radiation. The minimum energy required to ionize an atom A (i.e. $A \rightarrow A^+ + e^-$) is called its **ionization potential**.

ionization chamber An instrument for measuring the intensity of *ionizing radiation. It consists of a gas-filled chamber containing two electrodes with a large potential difference between them. The *Geiger counter is an example.

ionizing radiation Any radiation that ionizes the atoms or molecules through which it passes. It may consist of particles (such as *electrons) or *electromagnetic radiation. Ionizing radiation occurs in *cosmic rays and is emitted by radioactive substances. It is also produced artificially in X-ray machines, particle accelerators, etc.

ionosphere A region of the upper atmosphere that reflects short radio waves, enabling transmissions to be made round the earth by sky waves. The gases in the ionosphere are ionized by absorption of radiation from the sun. Its existence was suggested in 1902 by A. E. Kennelly (1861–1939) and independently by O. Heaviside (1850–1925). Sir Edward Appleton (1892–1925) provided proof by bouncing radio waves off the different layers of the ionosphere, which vary in behaviour with the position of the sun. The ionization of the D region (50–90 kilometres altitude) disappears during the day. The E region (90–160 km) and the F region (160–400 km) enable radio transmissions to occur at night.

Iowa A state in the USA, in the Midwest. Major crops are cereals and soya beans. It is famed for its livestock and there is some mining for portland cement and gypsum. History: explored by the French in 1673, it formed part of the Louisiana Purchase (1803) by the USA. It became a territory (1838) and a state (1846). Area: 145 790 sq km (56 290 sq mi). Population (1986 est): 2 851 000. Capital: Des Moines.

ipecacuanha A South American plant, Uragoga ipecacuanha, of the madder family. It is cultivated in the tropics for its root, which yields a medicinal substance used in some cough mixtures.

Iphigenia In Greek legend, the eldest daughter of *Agamemnon and Clytemnestra. At the beginning of the *Trojan War, Artemis demanded the sacrifice of Agamemnon's daughter before his fleet could sail to Troy. He was about to comply when Artemis took pity on Iphigenia and transported her to Tauris, where she became a priestess of Artemis.

Ipoh 4 36N 101 02E A city in NW Peninsular Malaysia, the capital of Perak state. The tinmining centre of Malaysia, it has noted Chinese rock temples. Population (1980): 300 727.

Ipswich 52 04N 1 10E A town in SE England, the administrative centre of Suffolk at the head of the Orwell estuary. It is a port with several industries. Population (1982 est.): 120 908.

IRA. See Irish Republican Army.

Iráklion (or Herakleion; Italian name: Candia) 32 20N 25 08E The chief port of the Greek island of Crete, on the N coast. It has many Venetian fortifications and has become a tourist centre. Exports include raisins, grapes, and olive oil. Population (1981): 101 634.

Iran, Islamic Republic of (name until 1935: Persia) A country in the Middle East lying between the Caspian Sea and the Persian Gulf. Economy: agriculture supports 75% of the population. The main oilfields in the Zagros Mountains, first discovered in 1908, provide Iran's main source of revenue. Other minerals include coal, copper, iron ore, and lead. History: an early centre of civilization, Persia was ruled by two main dynasties, the Achaemenians and the Sasanians (see (*also* Greek-Persian Wars) before Arab domination, which established Islam in the area. They were followed by Turks and Mongols before the Persian Safavid dynasty (1502–1736) came to power. After 1629 Persia declined, encroached by Uzbeks, Arabs, Afghans, Turks, and Russians. The Kajar dynasty (1794–1925) was marked by rivalry for domination between Britain and Russia. In 1906 the Shah was forced to grant a constitution and National Assembly (the Majlis), which was disbanded by his successor. Further disorders brought Reza Khan to power (1921), from 1925 as *Reza Shah Pahlavi. Under his dictatorship order returned and the country was westernized; he was forced to abdicate in favour of his son *Mohammed Reza Pahlavi (1941). In 1951, the militant National Front nationalized the oil industry; the British responded with a blockade. After fleeing the country the Shah returned to implement a reform programme, which led to riots and many dissidents being executed or imprisoned. By 1978 opposition groups had united under the exiled Muslim leader Ayatollah *Khomeini. The Shah left the country in 1979, later dying in exile (1980), and Ayatollah Khomeini took over the government in the so-called Islamic Revolution. War with Iraq lasted from 1980 to 1988 (*see* Gulf War). Official language: Persian (Farsi). Official currency: Iranian rial of 100 dinars. Area: 1 648 000 sq km (636 160 sq mi). Population (1988 est): 53 920 000. Capital: Tehran.

Iranian languages A subgroup of the Indo-Iranian language family, spoken in Iran, Afghanistan, Turkey, and parts of the Caucasus. Related to *Sanskrit, modern Iranian languages include Persian, Kurdish, Pashto, and Ossetic.

Iraq, Republic of A country in the Middle East, bordering on the Persian Gulf. The population is 90% Muslim divided evenly between Shiite and Sunnite sects. *Economy*: the chief crops are cereals, dates, and cotton. Oil (discovered at Kirkuk in 1927) is the main industry. *History*: as *Mesopotamia, Iraq was the site of the world's first civilization. Conquered by Arabia, it became Muslim in the 7th century AD and was part of the Ottoman Empire from 1534 until UK troops expelled the Turks in World War I. Iraq became a kingdom in 1921; the monarchy was overthrown in 1958, since when there has been unrest between Kurds, Muslims, and communists. War with Iran lasted from 1980 to 1988 (*see* Gulf War). In 1990 Iraq invaded Kuwait, leading to its defeat in the second *Gulf War. President: Saddam *Hussein. Official language: Arabic. Official currency: Iraqi dinar of 1000 fils. Area: 438 446 sq km (169 248 sq mi). Population (1988 est): 17 064 000. Capital: Baghdad.

Ireland The second largest of the British Isles, separated from the rest of Britain by the Irish Sea. Since 1920 Ireland has been divided between Northern Ireland in the UK and the Republic of Ireland. *History*: invaded in the 4th century BC by the Celts, the country came to be divided into the five tribal kingdoms (the Five Fifths) of Ulster,

Meath, Leinster, Munster, and Connaught. In the 5th century the country was converted to Christianity, notably by St Patrick, and in the 9th and 10th centuries there were Viking invasions; the Norman conquerors of England also invaded Ireland and by the 13th century English law and administration had been introduced. In the 16th century revolts, inspired partly by Roman Catholic opposition to the Reformation, were suppressed and the settlement of Ireland by English and later by Scottish families began in Ulster. Irish resistance culminated in the rebellion of 1641. The rebels' land, redistributed among English colonists, gave the Protestant minority greater power. This was strengthened by the Restoration settlement extending Protestant landholdings and by William of Orange's defeat (1690) of the Irish supporters of the deposed Catholic James II. In 1782 the Irish parliament obtained legislative independence. However, the unsuccessful rebellion of 1798 by the Society of United Irishmen persuaded Pitt the Younger to unite Britain and Ireland (1800; *see* Union, Acts of), providing *Catholic emancipation, which was not fully obtained until 1829. The Irish (potato) famine (1846) created agitation by the *Fenians and later by the *Home Rule movement. Following the proclamation of an Irish republic by Sinn Fein (1919) and virtual civil war, Britain proposed dividing the country (1920) with separate parliaments in the Protestant NE and Catholic S and W. This was unacceptable to the Republicans and in 1921 the Irish Free State came into being. The NE (Northern Ireland) immediately withdrew, accepting self-government within the UK.

Northern Ireland The province comprises the six counties of Antrim, Armagh, Down, Fermanagh, Londonderry, and Tyrone. *Economy*: since the 1950s, the traditional industries of shipbuilding and linen manufacture as well as agriculture have declined. *History*: the Government of Ireland Act (1920) established a parliament, which met at Stormont Castle in Belfast. There are also 17 MPs in the UK parliament. Violent conflict between the Protestant majority (wishing to remain in the UK) and the Catholic minority (seeking union with the Republic) erupted in 1969, since when the British army has maintained a peacekeeping force in Northern Ireland. Terrorist activities both in Ireland and Great Britain led to the imposition (1972) of direct rule of Northern Ireland by the UK parliament. Meanwhile bombings and shootings, both by the Irish Republican Army and Protestant paramilitary groups, continue. The Anglo-Irish Agreement of 1985 allowed increased involvement by the Republic in Northern Irish affairs. Area: 14 121 sq km (5452 sq mi). Population (1987 est): 1 575 200. Capital: Belfast.

Republic of Ireland (Irish name: Éire) The country is administratively divided into 26 counties. *Economy*: predominantly agricultural. Tourism is a major source of revenue. Peat is widely used as a fuel for power stations and homes. In 1977 Europe's largest lead-zinc mines were opened at

Navan. *History*: Republican opposition to the division of Ireland was quelled by 1923. In 1932 De Valera, leader of Fianna Fáil, became prime minister and, in 1937, introduced a new constitution by which the Irish Free State was renamed Éire. In 1949 the country left the Commonwealth. In 1973 Ireland became a member of the EC. President: Mary Robinson (1944–). Prime minister: Charles *Haughey. Official languages: Irish and English. Chief religion: Roman Catholic. Official currency: punt. Area: 68 893 sq km (26 599 sq mi). Population (1988): 3 540 000. Capital and main port: Dublin.

Iridium (Ir) A brittle metal, discovered in 1803 by C. Tennant (1768–1838). Its salts are highly coloured, hence its name (Latin *iris*, rainbow). It is used in electrical contacts. At no 77; at wt 192.22; mp 2410°C; bp 4130°C.

Iris (anatomy) The muscular tissue in the eye that surrounds the pupil and is responsible for eye colour. Reflex contraction of the muscles in the iris in dim light causes the pupil to enlarge and more light to enter the eye.

Iris A widely cultivated flowering plant grown from bulbs or rhizomes (underground stems); their flowers can have three or more colours. *See also* flag.

Iris (mythology) The Greek goddess of the rainbow and messenger of the gods, especially of *Hera. She is portrayed carrying a herald's staff and bearing water to put perjurers to sleep.

Irish Republican Army (IRA) A militant organization established in 1919. It fought a successful war against British forces (1919–21) but the partition treaty was rejected by many IRA members, who wanted an all-Ireland republic. A bombing campaign against England in 1939 and against Northern Ireland (1956–62) both failed. The present troubles began in 1968. In 1969 both the IRA and *Sinn Féin, to which many IRA members belong, split into the Officials, wanting a socialist 32-county republic, and the Provisionals, concerned to expel the British from the North. Bombings, murders, and assassinations have continued, the mortar attack on the cabinet in Downing St (1991) being a recent outrage. The Irish National Liberation Army is a break-away terrorist group.

Irish Republican Brotherhood. *See* Fenians.

Irish Sea A section of the Atlantic, separating England, Scotland, and Wales from Ireland. Area: about 100 000 sq km (40 000 sq mi). Maximum width: 240 km (149 mi).

Irish wolfhound An ancient hunting dog originating in Ireland. It has a powerful body and narrow head with small eyes. The wiry coat can be grey, red, black, or fawn. Height: 78 cm minimum (dogs); 71 cm minimum (bitches).

Irkutsk 52 18N 104 15E A city in the S Soviet Union; the industrial and educational centre of E Siberia. Population (1987): 609 000.

iron (Fe) A metallic element that has been used since the *Iron Age. It occurs in the ores haematite (Fe_2O_3), magnetite (Fe_3O_4), and siderite ($FeCO_3$), from which it is obtained by smelting in a *blast furnace to give pig iron, which is then converted into cast iron or *steel.

Iron has two important valence states forming iron II (ferrous) and iron III (ferric) compounds. Common compounds include the sulphates ($FeSO_4$ and $Fe_2(SO_4)_3$), chlorides ($FeCl_2$, $FeCl_3$), and oxides (FeO, Fe_3O_4, Fe_2O_3). At no 26; at wt 55.847; mp 1535°C; bp 2750°C. *See also* ferromagnetism.

Iron Age The cultural period in which iron replaced bronze (*see* Bronze Age) in tools, weapons, etc. It was not until about 1500 BC that iron-working was perfected by the *Hittites. However the Chinese were both forging and casting iron about 500 BC, preceding Europe by about 1700 years in casting.

Iron Curtain A symbolic curtain separating the democratic and communist countries in Europe after World War II. The term was first used by Winston Churchill in 1946.

Iroquois North American Indian tribes of hunters and farmers, who spoke the Iroquois language. The *Mohawk, Oneida, Onondaga, Cayuga, and Seneca tribes formed the **Iroquois League** during the 16th century, which joined the British in wars against the French and, except for the Oneida and Tuscarora (members of the League from 1715), against the colonists in the American Revolution (1775–83).

Irrawaddy River The chief river in Burma. It flows across the country to the Andaman Sea through a swampy delta. Length: 2010 km (1250 mi).

Irving, Sir Henry (John Henry Brodribb; 1838–1905) British actor and manager who was London's leading actor (1870–1900) and manager (1878–1902) of the Lyceum Theatre, where, with Ellen *Terry he acted in a series of Shakespearean productions.

Isabella (I) the Catholic (1451–1504) Queen of Castile (1474–1504) whose marriage (1469) to Ferdinand of Aragon united the two Spanish kingdoms. The introduction of the Inquisition (1480) and the expulsion of the Jews (1492) were largely due to Isabella's influence. *See also* Ferdinand V and II.

Ischia, Island of 40 44N 13 57E A volcanic island in Italy in the Bay of Naples. Area: 47 sq km (18 sq mi). Population (1985): 26 000. Chief town: Ischia.

Isfahan (*or* Esfahan) 32 41N 51 41E A town in central Iran with some fine Persian architecture, including the 17th-century mosque. Population (1986): 1 001 248.

Isherwood, Christopher (1904–86) British novelist. His experiences in Berlin in the 1930s are described in *Mr Norris Changes Trains* (1935) and *Goodbye to Berlin* (1939), made into the film *Cabaret* (1968). He worked with his friend W. H. *Auden on several plays.

Ishtar The Babylonian and Assyrian goddess, the daughter of the sky god Anu or the moon god Sin. A mother goddess and a goddess of war, she descended to the underworld in search of her lover Tammuz.

Isidore of Seville, St (c. 560–636 AD) Spanish Archbishop of Seville from about 600. His encyclopedia of knowledge, the *Etymologiae*, was much used by medieval scholars. Feast day: 4 April.

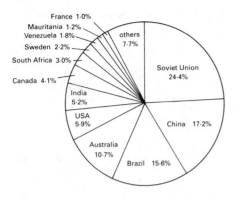

IRON *World production of iron ore (1989).*

Isis An Egyptian goddess, the sister and wife of *Osiris, whose dismembered body she magically restored to life, and mother of *Horus. She was portrayed holding Horus and wearing on her head the sun's disc and a cow's horns.

Islam (Arabic: submission to God) A world religion, started in Arabia in the 7th century AD, the main belief of which is that there is one God, Allah, and that *Mohammed is his prophet. The *Koran, the basis of Islamic belief, and its legal and social system (*see* Islamic law), records Mohammed's revelations. Followers of Islam, called Muslims, have five main duties: belief in Allah and Mohammed; observance at set times of five daily prayers; fasting during *Ramadan; payment of a tax for charity; and a pilgrimage to Mecca at least once. The main sects are the *Sunnites (*or* Sunni) and the *Shiites (*or* Shiah). There are an estimated 450 million Muslims.

Islamabad 33 40N 73 08E The capital of Pakistan, situated in the N of the country. The site was chosen in 1959 and construction began in 1961. Population (1981): 201 000.

Islamic law The law of *Islam, *shari'ah*, lays down a Muslim's religious duties and covers every aspect of his life, including marriage, divorce, and inheritance; it forbids the drinking of alcohol, the eating of pork, etc., and lays down punishments for crimes. In modern times most Muslim states use non-religious legal systems, especially for criminal, financial, and property law.

Islay An island in the Atlantic Ocean, off the W coast of Scotland. Area: 606 sq km (234 sq mi). Population (1981): 3792.

Ismaili A *Shiite Muslim sect, formed in the 8th century when some Shiites recognized Ismail the son of Jafar al-Sadiq as leader, while the rest of the Shiites supported his brother Musa. From 909 the Fatimid caliphs, who were Ismailis, ruled in Egypt and N Africa until 1171, competing for control of the Muslim world with the Abbasid dynasty of Baghdad. The best-known Ismaili sect now is headed by the Aga Khan.

Isocrates (436–338 BC) Athenian teacher, whose appeals to successive leaders to unite the feuding Greek states against Persia led to the

Philippus (346 BC), a treatise addressed to *Philip of Macedon.

isomers Chemical compounds with the same molecular formulae but different arrangements of atoms. For example, ethanol (C_2H_5OH) and dimethyl ether (CH_3OCH_3) have the molecular formula C_2H_6O, although they are different compounds. Another form occurs when functional groups appear at different positions in the molecule. These are examples of **structural isomerism**. Cis-trans isomerism, a form of **stereoisomerism**, occurs as a result of the positioning of groups in a planar molecule. Since rotation cannot occur about a double bond it is possible to have two isomers in organic compounds containing double bonds: one with groups on the same side of the bond (the cis isomer) and the other with groups on opposite sides of the bond (trans isomer). Another form of stereoisomerism is **optical isomerism**, in which the two forms of the molecule differ in that one molecule is a mirror image of the other; these are optically active, i.e. they rotate *polarized light passed through their solutions in different directions. Isomers of all types have different physical properties and different chemical properties. In some cases isomers can exist in equilibrium, a phenomenon known as **tautomerism**.

isoprene ($CH_2:C(CH_3)CH:CH_2$) A colourless volatile liquid made from oil, coal, or tar and used to make synthetic rubber. Natural rubber consists mainly of a polymer of isoprene.

isotherm A line on a map joining points of equal temperature. Corrections are usually made to compensate for the effect of altitude on temperature.

isotopes Atoms of the same element that contain equal numbers of *protons but different numbers of *neutrons in their nuclei. They have identical chemical properties but different physical properties. An isotope is indicated in various ways, for example uranium-235, U-235, ^{235}U. All naturally occurring elements are mixtures of isotopes.

Israel, State of A country in the Middle East, bordering on the Mediterranean Sea. The population consists largely of Jews who have immigrated since 1948. Many Palestinian Arabs left when Israel was created but some have returned. *Economy*: both industrial and agricultural. Mineral resources include copper ore, phosphates, and potash and bromine from the Dead Sea. Fishing and tourism are also important. *History*: Israel's history up to 1948 is that of *Palestine. According to a UN recommendation, Palestine was to be divided into a Jewish state, an Arab state, and an international zone around Jerusalem. When the state of Israel was proclaimed in 1948, however, Arab forces invaded; by early 1949 Israeli forces had gained control of 75% of Palestine, while Jordan annexed the *West Bank of the River Jordan, and Egypt annexed the *Gaza Strip. Jerusalem was divided between Jews and Arabs. In the Six Day War (1967) Israel occupied the Gaza Strip, the Sinai Peninsula, the *Golan Heights, the West Bank, and all Jerusalem. After the Yom Kippur War (1973; in which the Israelis were taken unawares by Egyptian forces) agreement was achieved in 1979 at the Camp David talks, following which Israel withdrew from Sinai (1980–82). In 1982 Israel invaded Lebanon and forced the Palestinian Liberation Organization to leave West Beirut, withdrawing in 1985. Since then Israel has been criticized for its treatment of the restive Palestinian population. Head of State: President Chaim Herzog (1918–). Prime minister: Yitzhak Shamir. Official languages: Hebrew and Arabic. Official currency: Israeli shekel of 100 new agorot. Area: 20 770 sq km (8018 sq mi). Population (1988 est): 4 480 000. Capital: Jerusalem. Main port: Haifa.

Issus, Battle of (333 BC) The battle in which Alexander the Great of Macedon defeated a Persian army under Darius III in a narrow pass.

Istanbul (or Stamboul) 41 02N 28 57E A city and port in W Turkey, on the Bosporus. Ancient buildings include the 6th-century Hagia Sophia (originally a church and now a museum), the Blue Mosque, and the Topkapi Palace (the former sultans' harem). History: ancient Byzantium, renamed Constantinople in 330 by *Constantine, became the capital of the Byzantine Empire until its capture (1453) by the Ottoman Turks; it was renamed Istanbul in 1926. Population (1985): 5 494 916.

Istria A peninsula in NW Yugoslavia. Passing to Italy at the end of World War I, it was handed over to Yugoslavia (1947) except for the Territory of Trieste, which was divided between Italy and Yugoslavia in 1954.

Italian A language of the *Romance family spoken in Italy. The standard literary and official form is based upon the Tuscan dialect of Florence.

Italian East Africa. See Somaliland.

Italic script A style of handwriting adopted in 15th-century Italy by papal scribes and later (c. 1500) adapted for printing. Italic cursive letters eliminate unnecessary lifts of the pen, permitting rapid legible handwriting. In print its sloped letters (as these) are used for emphasis, etc.

Italy, Republic of A country in S Europe, occupying a peninsula bordered by the Tyrrhenian Sea (W), the Ionian Sea (S), and the Adriatic Sea (E). The principal offshore islands are Sicily and Sardinia. Economy: agricultural with expanding industry. Wine and tourism are important. History: Italy was inhabited from the 7th century BC by the *Etruscans in the N, Italics and Latins in the centre, and Greek colonists in the south. By 275 BC most of the peninsula had come under the rule of Rome (see Roman Republic). As the *Roman Empire declined from the 4th century AD, Italy was invaded by the Visigoths and the Vandals. The last Roman emperor was deposed in 476 by the German king, Odoacer, who in 493 was overthrown by the Ostrogoths. They were expelled in the early 6th century by the Eastern

(Byzantine) Roman Empire. The Muslims invaded the S in the 9th century, Magyars, the N in the 10th century, and Normans, the S in the 11th century. In 962, Otto the Great of Germany was crowned Holy Roman Emperor in Rome. Conflict between successive popes and emperors from the 11th century led to the virtual self-government of the city states by single families, such as the *Medici in Florence. The French invasion (1494) was followed by conflict with the Spanish, who dominated Italy from the 16th century until the Austrian invasion in the 18th century. In 1746 the country was conquered by Napoleon. After the restoration of Austrian rule the movement for independence (the *Risorgimento) developed. By 1861 the kingdom of Italy had been proclaimed with Victor Emmanuel II of Sardinia-Piedmont as its first king. On the side of the Allies in World War I, Italy became fascist in 1922 when Mussolini came to power. In 1936 he conquered Ethiopia and in 1939, Albania. In World War II Italy joined Germany but the Allied conquest of Sicily (1943) brought Mussolini's fall and Umberto II's abdication (1946). The postwar Republic has seen over 40 governments. Italy was a founder member of the EC. President: Francesco Cossiga (1928–). Prime minister: Giulio Andreotti (1919–). Official language: Italian. Official religion: Roman Catholic. Official currency: lira of 100 centesimi. Area: 301 425 sq km (116 350 sq mi). Population (1988 est): 57 373 000. Capital: Rome. Main port: Genoa.

Ivan (IV) the Terrible (1530–84) Grand Prince of Muscovy (1533–84), crowned tsar in 1547. Ivan reformed the legal code (1555), conquered Kazan and Astrakhan, and established commercial relations with England. After 1560 his reign became brutal and tyrannical, made worse by the financial strains of the unsuccessful Livonian War (1558–82).

Ives, Charles (Edward) (1874–1954) US composer. He composed more than 500 works, including Central Park in the Dark (1898–1907), and Concord, Mass (1909–15).

ivory The white tissue forming the tusks of elephants, walruses, and narwhals and the teeth of hippos. Carved ivory objects from France date to Palaeolithic times and examples survive from Egyptian, Greek, and Roman civilizations. It continues in India and SE Asia.

Ivory Coast, Republic of See Côte d'Ivoire, Republic of.

ivy An evergreen climbing plant, Hedera helix, that has glossy leaves, greenish flowers, and small fruits. Small roots from the stem provide support.

Izmir (former name: Smyrna) 38 25N 27 10E A port in W Turkey, on the Aegean Sea. The modern town was largely rebuilt after a fire in 1922. Population (1985): 1 489 817.

J

Jabalpur (*or* Jubbulpore) 23 10N 79 59E A city in India, in Madhya Pradesh. It is an important railway junction and industrial centre. Population (1989): 649 085.

jacana A waterbird occurring in tropical regions, also called lily trotter. Jacanas have long legs with elongated toes, which enable them to run over floating vegetation. 25–32 cm long, they are usually reddish.

jacaranda A tree or shrub of South and Central America and the West Indies, often grown as an ornamental. *Jacaranda mimosifolia*, up to 15 m tall, has blue or violet tubular flowers.

jackal A carnivorous mammal found in Asia and Africa. Jackals are closely related to dogs and have bushy tails. The African black-backed jackal (*Canis mesomeles*) is up to 110 cm long and often hunts in packs, feeding on animal carcasses and hunting live animals.

jackdaw An intelligent crow of Europe and Asia, *Corvus monedula*. About 32 cm long, it has black plumage with a grey nape and a crest that can be erected for display. Often found in colonies, jackdaws feed on insects, grain, etc.

Jack Russell terrier A breed of dog developed in England from the fox terrier by the Rev John Russell (1795–1883) for flushing foxes from earth. It has a stocky body and a strong muscular head. The short coat is white, black, and tan. Height: up to 38 cm.

Jackson 32 20N 90 11W A city in the USA, the capital of Mississippi. Founded in 1821, it was virtually destroyed by Gen Sherman in 1863. Population (1986 est): 208 440.

Jackson, Glenda (1936–) British actress, who first achieved popular success as Elizabeth I in a television series (1971). Her films include *Women in Love* (1969), *A Touch of Class* (1972), *Hedda* (1976), *Stevie* (1978), and *Turtle Diary* (1985).

Jackson, Michael (1958–) US pop singer, who established himself as a solo star in the 1980s after appearing with his brothers as The Jackson Five in the 1970s. His albums include *Thriller* (1982) and *Bad* (1987).

Jackson, Stonewall (Thomas Jonathan J.; 1824–63) US Confederate general in the Civil War. In the first battle of Bull Run (1861), he and his brigade were described as standing "like a stone wall" blocking the Federal advance. His mastery of rapid tactical movement was particularly apparent in the Shenandoah valley campaign (1862). His accidental death at Chancellorsville left a gap in the Confederate command.

Jack the Ripper An unidentified murderer who killed at least six prostitutes in the East End of London in late 1888. One theory suggests that he was Vassily Konovalov, a Russian who committed similar murders in Paris and St Petersburg and who died in a Russian asylum.

Jacobites Supporters of the exiled *Stuart king, James II (Latin name: Jacobus), and his descendants. Between 1688, when the *Glorious Revolution overthrew James II, and 1745, the Jacobites (mainly Roman Catholics and Tories), opposed the Hanoverian monarchs. After two unsuccessful Jacobite rebellions, in 1715 (the "15 Rebellion" led by *James Edward Stuart, the Old Pretender) and 1745 (the "45 Rebellion" led by *Charles Edward Stuart, the Young Pretender) the movement broke up.

Jacob's ladder A plant, *Polemonium caeruleum*, native to Eurasia and widely cultivated. Growing to a height of 90 cm, it has bright-blue flowers.

jade A hard semiprecious stone, usually green, consisting of either the rare jadeite ($NaAlSi_2O_6$) or the more common nephrite ($Ca_2(Mg,Fe)_5$ $Si_8O_{22}(OH,F)_2$). It has been used for jewellery and carved ornaments since prehistoric times.

Jaffa. *See* Tel Aviv-Jaffa.

Jagannatha A Hindu god in some contexts identical to Krishna. Devotees have thrown themselves under the massive chariot on which his idol is annually wheeled during a festival at Puri, in Orissa, and from which the term "juggernaut" is derived.

Jagger, Mick *See* Rolling Stones.

jaguar The largest *cat, *Panthera onca*, found in the southern USA and South America. Up to 2.5 m long, it has dark spots on its yellow coat. Jaguars inhabit forest and scrub and attack domestic livestock.

jaguarundi A weasel-like *cat, *Felis yagouaroundi*, of Central and South America. Up to 110 cm long, it stands only 28 cm high at the shoulder. It has a red or grey coat and small ears. Jaguarundis feed on birds and fruits.

Jainism The religion of between two and three million Indians, founded by Mahavira in the 6th century BC. Right belief, knowledge, and conduct enable monks to obtain release from the endless round of rebirth caused by *karma; others aim for a better rebirth. Jainism has no god, although there are lesser spirits and demons.

Jaipur 26 53N 75 50E A city in India, the capital of Rajasthan. It is famous for its jewellery and stone, marble, and ivory carving. Population (1981 est): 1 004 669.

Jakarta (*or* Djakarta; name until 1949: Batavia) 6 09S 106 49E The capital of Indonesia, in NW Java. It became a major commercial centre as the headquarters of the Dutch East India Company. Population (1985): 7 829 000.

jalap A climbing plant, *Ipomoea purga*, of Mexico and South America, that has crimson flowers. The dried tubers yield a resin used as a laxative.

Jamaica, State of An island country in the Caribbean Sea, off the S coast of Cuba. *Economy*: sugar, bauxite, and tourism are important. Recent developments include the construction of an oil refinery with Mexican aid. A hurricane in 1988 caused considerable damage. *History*: discovered by Columbus in 1494, it was occupied by the Spanish, who exterminated the original Arawak inhabitants. Captured by the British in 1655, it became a colony and a centre of the slave trade. Self-government was introduced in 1944 and in 1962 Jamaica became independent within the Commonwealth. There has been considerable political unrest in recent years. Jamaica is a member of the OAS and CARICOM. Prime minister: Michael Manley. Official language: English. Official currency: Jamaican dollar of 100 cents. Area: 10 991 sq km (4244 sq mi). Population (1987 est): 2 300 000. Capital and main port: Kingston.

James I (1394–1437) King of the Scots (1406–37), whose rule began on his release (1424) from English imprisonment. He strengthened royal authority at the expense of the nobles and extended control over the administration of justice. He was assassinated by a group of nobles. He is believed to be the author of the poem "The Kingis Quair" ("The King's Book").

James I (1566–1625) The first Stuart King of England and Ireland (1603–25) and, as James VI, King of the Scots (1567–1625). He succeeded to the Scottish throne after the abdication of his mother Mary, Queen of Scots. He strengthened royal authority against the nobility and, less successfully, the Presbyterians. In 1589 he married Anne of Denmark. In England, James encountered opposition from his parliaments (1604–10, the 1614 "Addled" Parliament, 1621–22) and was unpopular for his choice of favourites and his attempts to obtain a Spanish marriage for his son. A great achievement was the publication (1611) of the *King James Version of the Bible.

James II (1430–60) King of the Scots (1437–60). He established his authority over rival factions and continued the extension of royal control and justice begun by his father James I. He was killed while besieging the English at Roxburgh Castle.

James II (1633–1701) King of England, Scotland, and Ireland (1685–88). The second son of Charles I, James (as Duke of York) escaped to Holland (1648) after his father's defeat in the Civil War and during the 1650s fought for the French and then the Spanish. In 1659 he married the daughter of the Earl of Clarendon, Anne Hyde (1637–71), by whom he had two daughters (later Queens Mary II and Anne). In 1669 he became a Roman Catholic: despite attempts to stop him, in 1685 he became king. The Protestant rebellion of the Duke of *Monmouth was suppressed, Roman Catholics were admitted to public office, and religious freedom was announced (1687). In 1688 James unsuccessfully prosecuted the Archbishop of Canterbury and six bishops who refused to proclaim religious toleration. This defeat and the threat of a Roman Catholic succession with the birth of a son (*see*

James Edward Stuart, the Old Pretender) to his second wife, Mary of Modena (1658–1718), led to the *Glorious Revolution. James fled and his subsequent attempt to regain the Crown from Ireland failed with his defeat by William III's forces at the *Boyne (1690) and *Aughrim (1691). He died in France.

James III (1452–88) King of the Scots (1460–88). Until 1469 Scotland was ruled by a regency and his personal rule was marked by baronial revolts. He was killed after defeat by rebel barons near Stirling.

James IV (1473–1513) King of the Scots (1488–1513). In 1503 he married *Margaret Tudor. He defeated the rebels who had killed his father James III, establishing internal stability. Continuing conflict with England led to the invasion of Northumberland (1513) and his defeat and death at *Flodden.

James V (1512–42) King of the Scots (1513–42). During his childhood Scotland was controlled by rival pro-French and pro-English factions. He died shortly after his unsuccessful invasion of England and was succeeded by his daughter Mary, Queen of Scots.

James VI (King of the Scots). *See* James I (King of England).

James, Henry (1843–1916) US novelist and critic, who spent much of his childhood in Europe, becoming a British citizen in 1915. His novel *Roderick Hudson* (1875) introduced the theme of Americans confronting European culture that reappeared in *The Portrait of a Lady* (1881) and other novels; he sometimes used American settings, as in *Washington Square* (1881) and *The Bostonians* (1886). He wrote more than a hundred shorter works of fiction, including *The Turn of the Screw* (1898). In *The Wings of the Dove* (1902), *The Ambassadors* (1903), and *The Golden Bowl* (1904), he adopted a highly elaborate style. He was also a critic and wrote several plays.

James, Jesse (Woodson) (1847–92) US outlaw, who fought with southern guerrilla groups during the Civil War; by 1867 he and his gang were robbing banks, stagecoaches, and trains in Missouri and surrounding states. He was shot and killed by Robert Ford, a gang member, for the $10 000 reward offered by Missouri.

James Edward Stuart, the Old Pretender (1688–1766) The son of James II, the dethroned Roman Catholic King of England. In exile, he was urged by his supporters (the *Jacobites) to claim the English throne. After their unsuccessful invasion of Scotland in 1715, James lived in Rome.

Jammu and Kashmir A state in N India, forming part of the disputed area of *Kashmir. Area: 100 569 sq km (38 820 sq mi). Population (1981): 5 981 600. Capital: Jammu (winter); Srinagar (summer).

Jamshedpur 22 47N 86 12E A city in India, in Bihar. Founded in 1907 by the industrialist Dorabji Jamsetji Tata, it is the site of India's principal iron and steel works. Population (1989): 457 061.

Janáček, Leoš (1854–1928) Czech composer. He was over 60 before he gained wide recognition as a composer. His works include the operas *Jenufa* (1894–1903), *The Excursions of Mr Broucek* (1908–17), and *The Makropulos Case* (1923–25), two string quartets, and the *Glagolitic Mass* (1926).

Jansenism A Roman Catholic movement of the 17th and 18th centuries based on the teaching of the Dutch theologian Cornelius Jansen (1585–1638). Their belief in predestination brought them into conflict with the Jesuits and was condemned by the Church. Jansenists also argued that the effectiveness of the sacraments depended on the moral character of the person receiving them. One of the most famous Jansenists was *Pascal.

Janus The Roman god of doors, thresholds, and beginnings, after whom the month January is named. He is usually portrayed as having two heads facing forwards and backwards.

Japan (Japanese name: Nippon *or* Nihon) A country in E Asia, consisting of a series of islands lying between the Pacific Ocean and the Sea of Japan. The four main islands are *Honshu, *Kyushu, *Hokkaido, and *Shikoku. *Economy*: Japan has developed into a highly industrialized country, manufacturing electronic goods, motor vehicles, and petrochemicals. Rice is the main crop, but cereals and soya beans are also grown; fishing is important. Japan is also one of the world's leading financial centres. *History*: about 200 BC the country was united under the Yamato dynasty, whose religion formed the basis of *Shinto. From 1186 AD real power was in the hands of the military *shoguns until the House of Yamato was restored to power in 1867 with the accession of Emperor Mutsuhito (1852–1912). Successful wars against China and Russia led to colonization in several Asian countries. It fought against the Allies in World War II, surrendering after the dropping of atomic bombs on Hiroshima and Nagasaki in 1945. By a new constitution of 1947 the emperor renounced his former claim to divinity and became a constitutional monarch. The Liberal Democratic Party has been in power since 1955. Head of state: Emperor Akihito. Prime minister: Toshiki Kaifu (1932–). Official language: Japanese. Official currency: yen of 100 sen and 1000 rin. Area: 372 480 sq km (143 777 sq mi). Population (1987 est): 122 053 000. Capital: Tokyo. Main port: Yokohama.

Japanese The language of the people of Japan. Its relationship to other languages is uncertain, but it is probably related to Korean. Of the many regional dialects, the most widely recognized is that of Tokyo. It usually stresses all syllables equally, although different pitches often distinguish adjacent syllables. In about the 5th century the Japanese adopted the Chinese writing system of characters (*kanji*), which have both Chinese-like pronunciations (*on*) and native Japanese pronunciations (*kun*). In modern Japanese about 2000 *kanji* are used. In about the 9th century the Japanese derived from the *kanji* two phonetic syllabaries, of 48 symbols each, called *hiragana* (used for modern texts) and *katakana*

(for foreign names, loanwords, and scientific words).

Japanese cedar A conifer, *Cryptomeria japonica*, native to China and Japan, where it is an important timber tree reaching a height of 55 m; elsewhere it is grown for ornament. Japanese cedar has round spiny cones, 2 cm across.

Japanese maple A *maple tree, *Acer palmatum*, native to Japan and up to 13 m tall. The lobed leaves turn scarlet in autumn making it a popular ornamental tree with many cultivated varieties.

japonica A shrub or tree of the rose family, native to Japan but widely cultivated. Flowering quince (*Chaenomeles japonica*) and Japanese quince (*C. speciosa*) are the most popular species. These have clusters of scarlet flowers, 5 cm across. The fruit is used in marmalade and jelly.

Jaruzelski, Wojciech (1923–) Polish general and statesman; defence minister (1968–81); prime minister and first secretary of the Polish Communist Party (1981–89); president 1989–90). To halt the liberal reforms obtained by the trade union *Solidarity, he introduced martial law (1981–83), detained Lech *Walesa and other union leaders (1981–82), and dissolved Solidarity (1982–89).

jasmine A widely cultivated shrub of the olive family. Many species yield an oil used in perfumery. Common jasmine (*Jasminum officinalis*) from S Asia, with fragrant white flowers, and Chinese winter jasmine (*J. nudiflorum*), the yellow flowers of which open in winter before the leaves, are suitable for temperate gardens.

Jason A legendary Greek hero, heir to the throne of Iolcos in Thessaly. Sent by his uncle, the usurper Pelias, to fetch the *Golden Fleece, he and the *Argonauts underwent many adventures before finally recovering the Fleece from Colchis with the help of *Medea. After many years of wandering he died at Corinth.

jaundice Yellowing of the skin and whites of the eyes due to the presence of *bile pigments. It may occur if there is excessive breakdown of red blood cells, as in haemolytic anaemia, or in disease of the liver, such as *hepatitis, or blockage of the bile duct by gallstones (*see* gall bladder).

Java An Indonesian island, the smallest of the Greater *Sunda Islands. Crops include rice, sugar cane, and kapok and forest products include teak. Indonesia's administrative and industrial centre, Java is heavily overpopulated. *History*: Indian colonies in the early centuries AD developed into Hindu and Buddhist kingdoms, with Hindu-Javanese culture reaching its height in the 14th century. The Dutch East India Company was centred here from 1619. Area: 132 174 sq km (51 032 sq mi). Population (1980): 91 269 528, with Madura. Capital: Jakarta.

javelin throw A field event in athletics. The men's javelin is 2.6–2.7 m (8.5–8.9 ft) long and weighs 800 g (1.8 lb). The women's measures 2.2–2.3 m (7.2–7.5 ft) and weighs a minimum of 600 g (1.3 lb). It is thrown with one hand, over the shoulder, after a run-up of approximately 36 m (120 ft), and the metal head must hit the ground first. Each competitor has six tries. World records: men: 87.66 m (1987) by Jan

Zelezny (Czechoslovakia); women: 80.00 m (1988) by Petra Felke (East Germany).

jay A crow, *Garrulus glandarius*, of Europe, Asia, and N Africa. It is about 34 cm long and brownish pink, with a black tail, and a black-and-white crest that can be erected for display. Jays are found mainly in woodland.

Jedda. *See* Jiddah.

Jefferson, Thomas (1743–1826) US statesman; the third president (1801–09) of the USA. A lawyer, Jefferson was elected to the second Continental Congress in 1775 and was the chief author of the *Declaration of Independence. Jefferson served as governor of Virginia (1779–81), minister to France (1785–89), secretary of state (1789–93), and vice president (1797–1801) under John Adams. During Jefferson's two terms as president, he approved the *Louisiana Purchase (1803) and encouraged US neutrality in the Napoleonic Wars.

Jefferson City 38 33N 92 10W A city in the USA, the capital of Missouri on the Missouri River. Population (1980): 33 619.

Jeffreys of Wem, George, 1st Baron (c. 1645–89) English judge. A firm supporter of the Crown, he became a leading prosecutor of suspected traitors following the *Popish Plot and, in 1685, James II's Lord Chancellor. Notorious for the death sentences he imposed during the Bloody Assizes following Monmouth's rebellion (1685), he was executed after the downfall of James II.

Jehovah. *See* Yahweh.

Jehovah's Witnesses A religious movement, first known as Bible Students, organized in the early 1870s by Charles Taze Russell (1852–1916) in Pittsburgh. Jehovah's Witnesses accept the Bible as their sole authority, worshipping Jehovah and acknowledging Jesus Christ as God's son and spokesman. They believe that 144 000, the Christian congregation, will rule with Christ in his heavenly kingdom over the rest of an obedient mankind, who will live on a paradise earth. They do not engage in politics and are pacifists.

jellyfish A marine invertebrate animal (*see* coelenterate). The gelatinous body, 1.5–2000 mm in diameter, is bell- or umbrella-shaped, with a central tube that hangs down and bears the mouth. They propel themselves by contracting muscles around the edge of the bell. Stinging tentacles capture and paralyse prey, ranging from plankton to small fish, and can seriously affect man. The free-swimming sexual form of any other coelenterate (*see* medusa) is also called a jellyfish.

Jenner, Edward (1749–1823) British physician, who developed the first vaccine—against smallpox. Jenner noticed that people who caught the mild disease cowpox never contracted smallpox. In 1796 he inoculated a boy with cowpox and, two months later, with smallpox. The boy did not get smallpox. Jenner published his findings in 1798 and vaccination—a word Jenner coined—became a widespread protective measure against smallpox and many other viral diseases.

jerboa A small hopping *rodent of Asian and N African deserts, also called desert rat. Jerboas

are 4–15 cm long and have kangaroo-like hind feet, a long balancing tail, and sandy-coloured fur. They spend the day in burrows and emerge at night to feed on seeds and tubers.

Jerez de la Frontera 36 41N 6 08W A city in SW Spain, in Andalusia. It is renowned for its wine industry and gave its name to sherry. Population (1990): 184 595.

Jericho 31 52N 35 27E A village in the Jordan Valley (Israel), N of the Dead Sea, now in the Israeli-occupied West Bank area. The site of the old city was excavated by the British archaeologist Kathleen Kenyon (1906–78), revealing one of the earliest towns (before 8000 BC); of the biblical city attacked by Joshua (Joshua 6) nothing remains. The ruins of the palace, Khirbat al-Mafjar, built (739–44 AD) by the Umayyad caliph Hisham (d. 743) can still be seen.

Jerome, St (c. 342–420 AD) Italian biblical scholar; author of the *Vulgate Bible, the first Latin translation from the Hebrew. After a period as a hermit, he was ordained by St Paulinus of Nola in Antioch. A secretary (382–385) to Pope Damasus I (reigned 366–94), he later settled in Bethlehem, where he established a monastery. Feast day: 30 Sept.

Jersey 49 13N 2 07W The largest of the Channel Islands, in the English Channel. Colonized from Normandy in the 11th century, it is mainly agricultural; dairy farming is important and Jersey cattle are bred for export. It is a financial centre and tourism is a major source of income. Area: 116 sq km (45 sq mi). Population (1986): 80 212. Capital: St Helier.

Jerusalem (Arabic name: El Quds) 31 47N 35 13E The capital of Israel, in the Judaea Heights between the Mediterranean and the Dead Seas. Jerusalem is a religious centre for Christianity, Judaism, and Islam. The modern city spreads to the W of the Old City, which is walled (1537–40) and contains the Western (Wailing) Wall (Jewish; consecrated 515 BC), the Dome of the Rock (691 AD; Islamic), and the Church of the Holy Sepulchre, (begun 335 AD on the traditional site of Christ's crucifixion). *History*: Jerusalem was conquered by King David in 1005 BC; it became the capital of Judah in 930 BC. Nebuchadnezzar, King of Babylon, destroyed the city in 586 BC, exiling the Jewish inhabitants to Babylon. In 538 BC, 40 000 Jews returned to the city. It was occupied by Alexander the Great (4th century BC), the Romans (63 BC), and later by the Turks. The Kingdom of Jerusalem was created in 1099 following conquest by the Crusaders. It was enlarged in the early 12th century by Baldwin I (c. 1058–1118) and his successors, but fell to Saladin in 1187. The Turks took the city again in 1517 and held it until 1917, when it was taken by the British. In 1948 Jerusalem was divided between the new state of Israel, of which it became the capital (1950), and Jordan. Israel occupied the whole city in June, 1967. Population (1986): 468 900.

Jerusalem artichoke A North American plant, *Helianthus tuberosus*, of the daisy family, that grows to a height of 2 m, and has edible tubers up to 10 cm long. They bloom only in hot summers, producing yellow flowers.

Jesuits Members of the Society of Jesus, founded by St *Ignatius Loyola in 1533 to spread the Roman Catholic faith. The order was organized along military lines; in addition to the traditional vows of chastity, poverty, and obedience, Jesuits swore to go wherever the pope sent them. They became a leading force in the *Counter-Reformation and in missions to America and the East. Their power eventually brought them into conflict with civil authorities throughout Europe, and in 1773 Pope Clement XIV suppressed the order; it was not reinstated until 1814. Jesuits are now active in most countries and are noted for their schools and universities.

Jesus (c. 6 BC–c. 30 AD) The founder of *Christianity; called by his followers the Messiah or Christ (Greek *khristos*, anointed one). According to the New Testament, Jesus was born at Bethlehem in the last years of the reign of *Herod the Great; he was the son of the Virgin *Mary, of Nazareth, who belonged to the tribe of Judah and the family of David. Mary's husband, Joseph, was a carpenter. Jesus was baptized in about 27 AD by John the Baptist and became a preacher in Galilee. His teaching, summarized in the Sermon on the Mount (Matthew 5–7), underlined the importance of charity, faith, and humility, the need for repentance, and the approaching kingdom of God. Miracles attributed to him included healing and feeding a crowd of 5000. Accompanied by his disciples (traditionally 12) he travelled to Jerusalem for Passover, apparently aware of the opposition that awaited him. There, after betrayal by Judas, he was condemned to death by the Sanhedrin (a Jewish tribunal) for claiming to be the Messiah and executed according to Roman law by crucifixion as a criminal by order of Pontius Pilate. In the New Testament his death is presented as fulfilling a divine purpose, made clear to the disciples at the resurrection (on the next day but one after the crucifixion) and by a number of other appearances. His ascension into heaven is said to have occurred 40 days after the resurrection.

jet engine A form of *gas turbine (*see also* internal-combustion engine) in which part of the energy released by burning the fuel drives a turbine, which in turn drives a compressor to increase the pressure of the air required for combustion, and part is used as a high-velocity jet to provide thrust to drive an aircraft. The jet engine was patented in 1930 by Sir Frank *Whittle, the first practical Whittle engine powering a Gloster aircraft in 1941. Early postwar commercial aircraft used a **turboprop** engine, in which a propeller is driven by the turbine shaft. For greater speed and economy the turboprop has now been replaced by the **turbojet** in which the turbine drives one or more compressors but most of the energy of combustion is used to provide **jet propulsion**. For bursts of extra energy, especially in military aircraft, extra fuel can be burnt in the exhaust gases (called **reheat** or **afterburning**). In the **turbofan** a large fan, driven by an inner shaft from the turbine, precedes the usual compressor and compresses the cool air, which bypasses the combustion chambers and mixes directly with

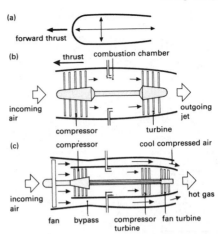

JET ENGINE *(a) The principle: equal pressure from the expanding gas inside the engine meets equal resistance except rearwards. The result is a forward thrust. The lower the outside pressure, the greater the thrust. (b) The turbojet, used for subsonic and supersonic flight (especially with reheat). (c) The turbofan, used for subsonic flight: cool air, compressed by the fan, bypasses the engine and mixes with the hot jet.*

the exhaust jet, giving greater fuel economy and quietness. These are used on modern subsonic jumbo jets.

At over twice the speed of sound (Mach 2), the forward pressure of the air is sufficient for the compressor, and therefore the turbine, to be dispensed with. The resulting engine is called a **ramjet** or, colloquially, a flying drainpipe. The main drawback of the ramjet is that it needs a rocket-assisted take-off. **Turboshaft** engines, similar to the turboprop, are used to drive helicopters, ships, trains, and power-station turbogenerators. *See also* rockets.

Jews A mainly Semitic people, claiming descent from the ancient Israelites and practising *Judaism. They inhabited Israel until the Babylonian exile (586 BC), returning in 1948. During the intervening 25 centuries they spread (*see* diaspora) throughout the world and despite frequent persecution, they have survived as minorities in many countries (*see* Ashkenazim; Sephardim). Since the late 18th century they have achieved acceptance in most countries, although the German slaughter of six million Jews in Europe (*see* holocaust) is one of the ugliest episodes in human history. It did, however, give force to *Zionism's claim for a national home for the Jews (*see* Israel, State of).

Jiang Jing Guo. *See* Chiang Kai-shek.

Jiang Qing (*or* Chiang Ch'ing; 1913–) Chinese communist politician; the third wife (from 1939) of Mao Tse-tung. A former actress, she attempted with three associates to seize power on Mao's death. Known as the **Gang of Four**, they were arrested within a month. She remained in prison after a public trial.

Jiddah (*or* Jedda) 21 30N 39 10E A town in Saudi Arabia, on the Red Sea coast. It is the chief port for Muslim pilgrims to Mecca. Population (1986 est): 1 000 000.

Jinan (Chi-nan *or* Tsinan) 36 41N 117 00E A city in E China, the capital of Shandong province. A city since the 8th century BC, it is a cultural centre. Population (1986): 1 430 000.

Jinnah, Mohammed Ali (1876–1948) Indian statesman, who was largely responsible for the creation of Pakistan. Born in Karachi, he studied law in England. As a member of both the Muslim League and the *Indian National Congress he championed Hindu-Muslim unity until his resignation (1930) from the Congress in opposition to Gandhi. He was president of the League (1916, 1920, 1934–48) supporting a separate state for Indian Muslims. This was achieved with the creation in 1947 of Pakistan, of which he was the first governor general.

Jiulong (*or* Kowloon) 22 20N 114 15E A port in SE China, on the Jiulong peninsula, opposite Hong Kong island and part of the British colony. Population (1981): 799 000.

Joan of Arc, St (French name: Jeanne d'Arc; c. 1412–31) French patriot, known as the Maid of Orléans. Of peasant origin, she claimed that Saints Michael, Catherine, and Margaret told her it was her divine mission to expel the English from France and enable Charles VII to be crowned. She persuaded Charles to allow her to lead an army to relieve the city of Orléans. Her success resulted in Charles' coronation at Rheims (July, 1429). Other victories followed but she failed to recapture Paris and was subsequently seized by the Burgundians and sold to their English allies, who burned her as a heretic. She was made a saint in 1920.

Jocasta. *See* Oedipus.

Jodhpur 26 18N 73 08E A city in India, noted for its handicrafts, such as ivory carvings and lacquerware. It gave its name to a style of riding breeches, introduced into Britain during the 19th century. Population (1981): 494 000.

Jodrell Bank The site, near Macclesfield, Cheshire (UK), of the Nuffield Radio Astronomy Laboratories of Manchester University. The principal instrument is the 76.2 m (250 ft) fully steerable radio-telescope dish.

Jogjakarta (*or* Yogyakarta) 7 48S 110 24E A city in Indonesia, in S Java. It was the capital of the 1945–49 Indonesian Republic and is rich in Buddhist monuments, notably the temple of Borobudur. Population (1980): 398 727.

Johannesburg 26 10S 28 02E The largest city in South Africa, in the Transvaal. It was founded in 1886 following the discovery of gold in the area. During the second Boer War it was taken by the British (1900). Today it is a major industrial, commercial, and banking centre containing the South African Stock Exchange (1887). Population (1983): 1 713 000.

John (1167–1216) King of England (1199–1216), nicknamed John Lackland; the youngest son of Henry II, he succeeded his brother Richard I. His reign saw the renewal of war with *Philip II Augustus of France, to whom he had lost several continental possessions, including Normandy, by 1205. Struggles with Pope Innocent III over John's objection to the election of Stephen Langton (c. 1150–1228) as Archbishop of Canterbury led to the king's excommunication (1212). He came into conflict with his barons and was forced to sign the *Magna Carta at Runnymede. His subsequent rejection of the Charter led to the first *Barons' War (1215–17).

John (II) the Good (1319–64) King of France (1350–64), who was taken prisoner by the English at the battle of Poitiers (1356) during the *Hundred Years' War. He was forced to sign the unfavourable Treaty of *Brétigny. Released in 1360, he was unable to raise the ransom demanded by the English and was forced to return to London, where he died.

John XXIII (Angelo Roncalli; 1881–1963) Pope (1958–1963). Elected at the age of 77, John summoned the second *Vatican Council in 1962. His best-known papal message, *Pacem in Terris* (*Peace on Earth*; 1963), argued for friendship between the western democracies and eastern communist countries.

John, Augustus (Edwin) (1878–1961) British painter, born in Wales. A lively unconventional character, he travelled widely, often in Gipsy style. His celebrated portraits of contemporaries included those of James Joyce and T. E. Lawrence. His sister **Gwen John** (1876–1939) was also a painter.

John, Elton (Reginald Kenneth Dwight; 1947–) British rock pianist and singer, who became popular with such songs as "Rocket Man" and "Daniel."

John, St In the New Testament, one of the 12 Apostles and traditionally the author of the fourth *Gospel and the three Epistles of John, written in the late 1st century AD, and the Book of Revelation. He escaped martyrdom and died at Ephesus. Feast day: 27 Dec.

John Dory (*or* dory) A sea fish with a round narrow body with deep sides, each having a black spot surrounded by a yellow ring, and spiny-rayed fins extended into filaments. The species *Zeus faber*, up to 90 cm long, is a food fish of the Atlantic and Mediterranean.

John of Gaunt (1340–99) The fourth son of Edward III of England; Duke of Lancaster from 1362. After a distinguished career in the *Hundred Years' War he assumed an increasingly important role in government at home. John supported *Wycliffe and the *Lollards and was opposed by *William of Wykeham. He unsuccessfully pressed his claim, through his second wife Constance, to Castile. In 1396 he married his mistress Catherine Swynford; their descendants included Margaret Beaufort (1443–1509), mother of Henry VII.

John O'Groats 58 39N 3 02W A village at the NE tip of Scotland, site of the house of John de Groot, a 16th-century Dutch immigrant. John O'Groats is 970 km (603 mi) in a straight line from Land's End, Cornwall.

John Paul II (Karol Wojtyła; 1920–) Pope (1978–). A Pole, he is the first non-Italian pope since 1522. He has outspokenly defended the Church in communist countries, especially in Poland. His strict position on contraception, abortion, homosexuality, and marriage of the clergy has led to considerable opposition. In 1981 he survived an assassination attempt. He succeeded **John Paul I** (Albino Luciani; 1912–78; reigned August–September, 1978), who took the names of his two predecessors, John XXIII and Paul VI.

Johnson, Amy (1903–41) British aviator. She established several long-distance records with her solo flights to Australia in 1930, to Tokyo in 1932, and to the Cape of Good Hope and back in 1936. In 1932 she married Jim Mollison (1905–59), another pilot, with whom she flew the Atlantic in 1936. She was killed in an air crash near London.

Johnson, Lyndon Baines (1908–73) US statesman; Democratic president (1963–69). A Texan, he succeeded to the presidency after Kennedy's assassination. His Great Society programme introduced broad social reform. He became unpopular for increasing US military involvement in the *Vietnam War.

Johnson, Samuel (1709–84) British poet, critic, and lexicographer. He left Oxford without taking a degree, married a wealthy widow in 1735, and went to London in 1737. His early publications include a biography of his friend the poet Richard Savage (1744) and a long poem, *The Vanity of Human Wishes* (1749). From 1750 to 1752 he produced the weekly *Rambler* almost single handed. His *Dictionary* appeared in 1755 after nine years' work and was well received, but he still relied on other writings for money, writing *Rasselas* (1759) in a week to pay for his mother's funeral. His last major works were an edition of Shakespeare (1765) and his *Lives of the Poets* (1779–81). From the early 1760s he enjoyed the security of a pension and the friendship of Reynolds, Goldsmith, Burke, and other men of letters, including his biographer *Boswell. His last years were clouded by the deaths of friends and conflict with his companion, Mrs Thrale.

John the Baptist, St In the New Testament, the son of a priest, Zacharias, and Elizabeth, a relative of the Virgin *Mary. He began in about 27 AD preaching on the banks of the River Jordan, urging repentance and baptism (Matthew 3.2). He baptized Christ, recognizing him as the Messiah. He was beheaded by *Herod Antipas, at the request of Salome, for criticizing his second marriage to Herodias. Feast days: 24 June (birth); 29 Aug (beheading).

Johore A swampy forested state in S Peninsular Malaysia. Chief products are rubber, copra, pineapples, palm oil, tin, and bauxite. Area: 18 958 sq km (7330 sq mi). Population (1980): 1 601 504. Capital: Johore Baharu.

joint The point at which two or more bones are connected to each other. There are three broad categories. Immovable joints include the sutures between the bones of the skull. Slightly movable joints include those connecting the individual bones of the spine. Freely movable joints include the hinge joints at the knee and elbow, the ball-and-socket joints at the hip and shoulder, and the gliding joints at the wrist and ankle. The bone ends at movable joints are covered by *cartilage and covered in a tough capsule thickened in parts to form *ligaments. The inside of the capsule is lined by synovial membrane, which secretes a lubricating fluid.

Joliot-Curie, Frédéric and Irène. *See* Curie, Marie.

Jolson, Al (Asa Yoelson; 1886–1950) US popular singer and songwriter, born in Russia. He became famous for his blacked-up face and the song "Mammy." In 1927 he appeared in the first full-length sound film *The Jazz Singer.*

Jones, Inigo (1573–1652) English classical architect. One of the first Englishmen to study architecture in Italy, Jones was particularly influenced by *Palladio in his two best-known buildings, the Queen's House, Greenwich (1616–35), and the Banqueting Hall, Whitehall (1619–22). His career effectively ended with the outbreak of the Civil War in 1642, and his style only became strongly influential in England in the 18th century. With Ben Jonson, he also designed numerous court masques.

jonquil. *See* Narcissus.

Jonson, Ben (1572–1637) English dramatist and poet. In *Every Man in His Humour* (1598) he introduced the "comedy of humours," each character being driven by a particular obsession. Other major satirical plays include *Volpone* (1606), *The Alchemist* (1610), and *Bartholomew Fair* (1614). Working with Inigo *Jones he produced many court masques. He also published two collections of poems and translations and influenced a number of younger poets known as "the Tribe of Ben."

Jordan, Hashemite Kingdom of A country in the Middle East. It is mainly desert but more fertile in the W and N, where the population is concentrated. *Economy*: industries include the extraction and processing of phosphates. Agriculture, concentrated in the irrigated Jordan Valley, produces cereals, vegetables, wool, and fruit. *History*: the area that is now Jordan appears to have flourished in the Bronze Age and was part of the Roman Empire by 64 BC. It was controlled by Arabs from the 7th century, Crusaders in the 11th and 12th centuries, and Turks from the 16th century until 1916, when the part E of the River Jordan was named Transjordan and came under British control. It became an independent kingdom in 1946. In the Arab-Israeli War of 1948–49, Jordan invaded the *West Bank, but it was occupied by Israel in the Six-Day War of 1967. Under Arab pressure, Jordan has recognized the *Palestine Liberation Organization as the body entitled to govern the West Bank. The present monarch, King Hussein II, succeeded to the throne in 1952. Prime minister: Mudar Badran (1934–). Official language: Arabic. Official currency: Jordanian dinar of 1000 fils. Area: about 97 740 sq km (37 738 sq mi), including the West Bank. Population (1988 est): 3 958 000, including the West Bank. Capital: Amman.

Jordan, River A river in the Middle East. It rises in Syria and Lebanon and flows due S through the Sea of Galilee, finally entering the Dead Sea. It forms for some of its course part of the border between Israel and Jordan. Length: 320 km (199 mi).

Joseph, St In the New Testament, the husband of the Virgin *Mary. He was a devout Jew belonging to the line of David but worked humbly as a carpenter. He was dead by the time of the crucifixion. Feast day: 19 March.

Joséphine (1763–1814) The wife (1796–1809) of Napoleon Bonaparte and Empress of the French in 1804. Her first husband was Alexandre, Vicomte de Beauharnais (1760–94), who was guillotined in the French Revolution. She presided over a brilliant court until divorced by Napoleon because of their childlessness.

Joseph of Arimathea, St In the New Testament, a man described as a councillor. He asked Pontius Pilate for the body of Christ after the crucifixion and arranged for its burial on the same day. According to medieval legend, he came to England after the crucifixion, bringing with him the *Holy Grail, and built the first English church, at Glastonbury. Feast day: 17 March.

joule (J) The *SI unit of work or energy equal to the work done when the point of application of a force of one newton moves through a distance of one metre. Named after James *Joule.

Joule, James Prescott (1818–89) British physicist, who performed a series of experiments during the 1840s to determine the mechanical equivalent of heat. His work greatly contributed towards *Helmholtz's development of the law of conservation of energy. He also investigated the heating effect of an electric current, stating in **Joule's law** that the heat produced is equal to the product of the resistance, the square of the current, and the time for which it flows. With Lord Kelvin he discovered the fall in temperature that occurs when a gas expands (the **Joule-Kelvin effect**). The unit of energy is named after him.

Joyce, James (1882–1941) Irish novelist and poet. Accompanied by Nora Barnacle (whom he did not marry until 1931), he left Ireland in 1904, living first in Trieste (until 1915) and later in Zurich during World War I and Paris (1920–40). *Dubliners* (1914), a volume of short stories, was followed by the semiautobiographical novel *Portrait of the Artist as a Young Man* (1916). In 1922 he published *Ulysses*, portraying a single day in the lives of several Dubliners. He carried linguistic experiment to further extremes in *Finnegans Wake* (1939), a dream mixed with puns and word play. Joyce died in Zurich.

Joyce, William (1906–46) Nazi broadcaster, known as Lord Haw-Haw. Born in the USA, he broadcast Nazi propaganda to Britain throughout World War II and was subsequently tried as a British subject for treason and executed.

JP. *See* justice of the peace.

Juan Carlos (1938–) King of Spain (1975–). The grandson of Alfonso XIII, he was named heir to the throne by Francisco *Franco and became king when he died, presiding over Spain's peaceful move to democracy. In 1962 he married Sophia (1938–), daughter of King Paul of Greece.

Juárez. *See* Ciudad Juárez.

Jubbulpore. *See* Jabalpur.

Judaea The southern division of ancient Palestine. The Old Testament kingdom of Judah survived Syrian, Assyrian, and Philistine attacks following Solomon's death but came to an end after conquest by *Nebuchadnezzar II of Babylon, when its capital, Jerusalem, was destroyed (586 BC) and the Jews were exiled. Judaea came next under Persian rule, when the Jews were allowed to return and rebuild Jerusalem. In 167 BC the *Maccabees' revolt against the *Seleucids brought Judaea a shortlived independence until the Roman conquest in 63 BC. After years of unrest the Roman province of Syria absorbed it in 135 AD.

Judaism The religion of the *Jews. Its central belief is in a single, eternal God, who created the world and desires its welfare. Judaism's most sacred text is the *Torah. There is no agreement as to its origin, but tradition attaches importance to the figures of Abraham and *Moses, but many of the main ideas and institutions were developed during the Babylonian exile (*see* Nebuchadnezzar II) and the period of the Second *Temple. After the destruction of the temple the *rabbis put the traditional teachings into a systematic form (*see* Midrash; Mishnah; Talmud), and in the middle ages philosophy and the *kabbalah greatly influenced Judaism. There are now several conflicting movements. Orthodox Judaism insists on the supernatural authority of Torah and right behaviour (halakhah). This is challenged by *Reform Judaism. Conservative Judaism and Reconstructionism stand between these extreme views.

Judas tree A shrub or small tree of the pea family, also called redbud, native to S Europe, Asia, and North America and cultivated in gardens. The pinkish-red flowers appear before the heart-shaped leaves have opened. The name is derived from the legend that Judas Iscariot hanged himself on one of these trees.

judge An officer who decides legal disputes and passes sentence on offenders. In England and Wales judges try cases in the House of Lords (the Lords of Appeal in Ordinary, or law lords), the Court of Appeal (the Lords Justices), the High Court of Justice (high-court judges), the Crown Court (high-court judges and circuit judges), and County Courts (circuit judges). A judge is appointed by the Crown on the recommendation of the Lord Chancellor (*see* Lord Chief Justice; Master of the Rolls) and must be a barrister (or a *solicitor) of at least ten years' standing. *See also* courts of law.

judo An international form of wrestling developed from *jujitsu in Japan by Jigoro Kano (1860–1938). Contestants wear kimonos and coloured belts to indicate their skill. The five *kyu* (pupil) grades wear white, orange, green, blue, or brown belts in order of increasing skill, the 12 *dan* (master) grades all wear black belts. Contests take place on a mat 9 m (30 ft) square and usually last two to ten minutes. The contestants score points by executing certain throws, ground holds, and locks. *See also* martial arts.

Juggernaut. *See* Jagannatha.

Jugoslavia. *See* Yugoslavia, Socialist Federal Republic of.

jujitsu (Japanese name: *yawara*) The form of self-defence, usually unarmed, used by the Japanese *samurai. The object was to disable, cripple, or kill an opponent by using his own momentum and strength against him. *Judo, *aikido, and *karate developed from it.

jujube A small thorny tree of the buckthorn family that produces sweet edible fruit. The Chinese species *Zizyphus jujuba* has been grown in other hot dry regions. It reaches a height of 9 m and has small yellow flowers.

Juliana (1909–) Queen of the Netherlands (1948–80) following the abdication of her mother Wilhelmina. In 1937 she married Prince Bernhard von Lippe-Biesterfeld (1911–). In 1980 Queen Juliana abdicated in favour of her eldest daughter *Beatrix.

Julian calendar. *See* calendar.

Jumna, River (R Jamuna *or* R Yamuna) A river in N India. Rising in Uttar Pradesh, it flows S and SE to the River Ganges near Allahabad. Length: 1385 km (860 mi).

Juneau 58 20N 134 20W A city in the USA, the capital of Alaska. A supply centre for a fur-trading and mining region, it is also an ice-free port. Population (1987 est): 25 369.

Jung, Carl Gustav (1875–1961) Swiss psychiatrist and pioneer psychoanalyst. Jung worked with Sigmund *Freud until, in 1912, their differences became irreconcilable. Jung developed the concept of introvert and extrovert personalities and made valuable studies of mental disorders, including schizophrenia. In his major work, *Psychology of the Unconscious* (1912), Jung regarded the unconscious part of the mind as containing both the personal experiences of the individual and common inherited cultural experiences. Jung later applied his theories to historical studies of religion and to dreams.

Jungfrau 46 33N 7 58E A mountain peak in S central Switzerland, in the Bernese Oberland. Height: 4158 m (13 632 ft).

jungle fowl An Asian forest bird. The males have a large fleshy comb and wattles at the sides of the bill and, in the breeding season, fight fiercely using their sharp leg spurs. The red jungle fowl (*Gallus gallus*) is the ancestor of the domestic *fowl.

juniper A coniferous tree or shrub of the cypress family, widely distributed in the N hemisphere. Male and female flowers grow on separate trees. The common juniper (*Juniperus communis*) is native to N Europe, North America, and SW Asia; it rarely exceeds 4 m in height and is often planted for ornament. The cones are used for flavouring gin and foods, as a source of oil, and in medicine.

Juno (mythology) A principal Roman goddess, the wife of Jupiter. She was concerned with all aspects of women's life and is usually portrayed as a matronly figure. She was identified with the Greek *Hera.

Jupiter (astronomy) The largest and most massive planet, orbiting the sun every 11.86 years at a mean distance of 778.3 million km. Its rapid axial rotation (in less than 10 hours) has produced a nonspherical shape: equatorial diameter 142 800 km, polar diameter 135 500 km. In a telescope light and dark bands of clouds are visible, together with spots and streaks. Jupiter is composed mainly (99%) of hydrogen and helium (in the ratio 82:17). Ammonia, methane, and other compounds are present in the cloud layers. The planetary interior is liquid hydrogen with possibly a small rocky core. Jupiter radiates heat and is also a source of radio waves. It has a magnetic field and radiation belts of great intensity. The planet has 16 known satellites, including the four large *Galilean satellites, and a satellite ring of rocks, discovered in 1979.

Jupiter (mythology) The principal Roman god, identified with the Greek *Zeus. Originally a sky god, he controlled the weather and used the thunderbolt as his weapon. His temple on the Capitoline hill was the principal Roman religious structure.

Jura Mountains A mountain range in E France and NW Switzerland. It extends along the border in a NE–SW arc, rising to 1723 m (5653 ft) at Crêt de la Neige.

Jurassic period A geological period of the Mesozoic era, between about 200 and 135 million years ago, following the Triassic and preceding the Cretaceous periods. The dinosaurs and other reptiles flourished and diversified in this period. Fossils of the earliest birds and mammals have also been found in Jurassic rocks.

jury A body of people, usually 12, who have taken an oath to decide questions of fact arising in a court case according to the evidence before them. To qualify for jury service a person must be a registered voter between 18 and 70 years old and resident in the UK for at least 5 years since the age of 13. Anyone involved in administering justice, the clergy, and the mentally ill cannot qualify for jury service. Others (MPs, medical personnel, etc.) have a right to be excused from jury service. Those who have received certain types of convictions are disqualified. Before taking the oath jurors may be "challenged" (rejected) for various reasons by either side in a court case. They may claim payment for loss of income while serving, as well as travel expenses and living costs. In 1967 a majority verdict (normally ten to two) was permitted in criminal law trials and in 1971 similar verdicts in civil proceedings in the High Court were permitted.

justice of the peace (JP) An unpaid *magistrate appointed by the Lord Chancellor to keep the peace within a county, with the power to try certain cases in a Magistrates' Court and to commit other more serious cases for trial by a higher court. JPs can also rule on certain matrimonial matters, including maintenance.

Justinian Code. *See* Roman law.

jute Either of two Indian plants, *Corchorus capsularis* or *C. olitorius*, cultivated in India, Pakistan, and Thailand for their fibres. Growing to a height of 3 m, they have small yellow flowers. The stems are cut, soaked in water, and beaten to remove the fibres, which are used for ropes, sacks, carpet backings, hessian, and tarpaulin.

Jutes A Germanic people, probably from Jutland, who invaded Britain together with the *Angles and *Saxons in the 5th century AD. Archaeological evidence supports *Bede's statement that the Jutes settled in what are now Kent, the Isle of Wight, and Hampshire.

Jutland (Danish name: Jylland) A peninsula in N Europe, between the North Sea, the Skagerrak, the Kattegat, and the Little Belt. It is occupied by mainland Denmark and part of Schleswig-Holstein, in Germany. The Battle of Jutland (1916) was a major naval engagement of World War I.

Jylland. *See* Jutland.

K

K2 (*or* Mt Godwin Austen) 35 53N 76 32E The second highest mountain in the world (after Mount Everest), in N Pakistan in the Karakoram Range. As it was the second peak to be measured in the range it was given the symbol, K2. The summit was first reached on 31 July, 1954, by an Italian team. Height: 8611 m (28 250 ft).

kabbalah (Hebrew: tradition) A mystical religious Jewish system. The classical kabbalistic text is the *Zohar* (*Book of Splendour*), written in Aramaic in 13th-century Spain, but the kabbalah has much older roots. It has strong connections with *Gnosticism and also with magical practices. An important 16th-century kabbalistic school flourished at Safed, in Galilee.

Kabul 34 30N 69 10E The capital of Afghanistan, situated in the NE of the country at an altitude of 1830 m (6000 ft). It was capital of the Mogul Empire (1504–1738), becoming capital of Afghanistan in 1773. Population (1984): 1 179 341.

Kaffirs The former name for the Pondo and *Xhosa peoples of the E Cape Province of South Africa, with whom the advancing White settlers fought a series of wars in the late 18th and 19th centuries.

Kafirs A people of the Hindu Kush mountains of Afghanistan and Pakistan, who speak a Dardic language. Their name (Arabic *kafir*: infidel) was acquired from their Muslim neighbours on account of their traditional religion.

Kafka, Franz (1883–1924) Czech writer. Born in Prague (then in Bohemia), the son of German Jewish parents, he wrote fantasies and parables that portray the individual isolated in a strange world. Most of his work was published after his death, against his instructions, by his friend Max Brod. Among his best-known writings are the stories *Metamorphosis* (1912) and *In the Penal Settlement* (1919) and the novels *The Trial* (1925) and *The Castle* (1926).

Kafue River A river in Zambia, rising on the Zaïre frontier and flowing S and E to the Zambezi River. Length: 966 km (600 mi). The **Kafue Dam** (1972) provides about two-thirds of Zambia's hydroelectric power.

Kaikoura Ranges Twin mountain ranges in New Zealand, comprising the Inland and the Seaward Kaikouras. They extend SW–NE in NE South Island, reaching 2885 m (9465 ft) at Tapuaenuku in the Inland Kaikouras.

Kalahari Desert An area of S Africa, chiefly in Botswana. It is sparsely inhabited by nomadic Bushmen, and although it has little rainfall and its few rivers are generally dry there is some vegetation. Area: about 250 000 sq km (96 505 sq mi).

kale A variety of *cabbage, also called borecole, grown for its large edible leaves, which are used as a winter vegetable and as livestock food.

Kalgan. *See* Zhangjiakou.

Kali In Hindu mythology, the goddess of death. The wife of *Shiva, she is represented as a hideous four-armed black woman.

Kalimantan The Indonesian part of *Borneo, comprising the SE two-thirds of the island. It is little developed, but its dense forests provide valuable timber. Small-scale agriculture includes the growing of rice, tobacco, sugar cane, coffee, and rubber. Area: 550 203 sq km (212 388 sq mi). Population (1980): 6 723 086. Chief towns: Banjarmasin and Pontianak.

Kama In Hindu mythology, the god of love. He is the son of *Shiva and was popularly known as Ananga (bodiless), having been reduced to ashes by a glance from his father's eye when Kama playfully shot his arrows at him.

Kama, River A river in the E Soviet Union, rising in the Ural Mountains and flowing mainly SW to the River Volga. Length: 2030 km (1260 mi).

Kamakura 35 19N 139 33E A city in Japan, in SE Honshu. A former Japanese capital (1192–1333), it is noted for its shrines and for its bronze Buddha, 13 m (43 ft) high. Population (1986 est): 175 975.

Kamchatka A peninsula in the extreme E Soviet Union. It is about 1200 km (746 mi) long and separates the Sea of Okhotsk from the Bering Sea. Area: about 270 000 sq km (104 225 sq mi).

Kamikaze A Japanese aircraft crashed deliberately by its pilot into its target. Such suicide missions were first flown at the battle of Leyte Gulf (1944) in World War II; at Okinawa (1945) 21 US ships were sunk in this way. The name refers to the typhoon that scattered Kublai Khan's fleet in 1281.

Kampala 0 20N 32 30E The capital of Uganda, N of Lake Victoria. Founded by the British in the late 19th century, it became the capital in 1962. Population (1989 est): 800 000.

Kampuchea, Democratic. *See* Cambodia.

Kananga (name until 1966: Luluabourg) 5 53S 22 26E A city in central Zaïre, on the River Lulua. It serves an agricultural and diamond-producing area. Population (1984): 290 898.

Kanchenjunga, Mount. *See* Kangchenjunga, Mount.

Kandahar (*or* Qandahar) 31 36N 65 47E A city in S Afghanistan. Situated on main routes to central Asia and India, it is built on the site of several ancient cities. Population (1984 est): 203 177.

Kandinsky, Wassily (1866–1944) Russian expressionist painter. He painted the first purely abstract pictures in European art (c. 1911). These featured freely applied paint and dazzling colours, which he likened to music in his book *Concerning the Spiritual in Art* (1911). He was a founder of the artistic groups Neue Künstlervereinigung (1909) and Der Blaue Reiter (1911) and taught at the *Bauhaus school.

Kandy 7 17N 80 40E A city in central Sri Lanka. Capital of the kingdom of Kandy from 1480 until 1815, when it was occupied by the British, it has a famous Buddhist temple, Dalada Malagawa. Population (1985): 140 000.

kangaroo The largest *marsupial mammal. There are two species, the red kangaroo (*Macropus rufus*) of Australia and the grey kangaroo (*M. kanguru*) of Australia and Tasmania. Red kangaroos can reach a height of 2 m and a weight of 90 kg. Kangaroos have short front legs and long hind legs and feet: they travel by a series of leaps. *See also* wallaby.

Kangchenjunga, Mount (*or* Mt Kanchenjunga) 27 44N 88 11E The third highest mountain in the world (after Mount Everest and K2), on the Sikkim (India)–Nepal border in the Himalayas. It was first climbed in 1955. Height: 8598 m (28 208 ft).

Kano 12 00N 8 31E A city in N Nigeria. It is an important trade centre. Population (1983): 487 100.

Kanpur (former name: Cawnpore) 26 27N 80 14E A city in India, in Uttar Pradesh. Handed over to the British East India Company (1801), it became an important British frontier station and during the Indian Mutiny was the scene (1857) of a massacre of British soldiers. Population (1981): 1 688 000.

Kansas A state in the centre of the USA. It consists mainly of undulating prairie. Its large mineral resources include oil, natural gas, coal, sand and gravel. Kansas is the USA's main wheat-growing area; other crops include sorghum grains and hay. *History:* first explored by the Spanish in the 16th century, it was claimed by the French (1682) and formed part of the Louisiana Purchase (1803). It became a state in 1861. Area: 213 063 sq km (82 264 sq mi). Population (1986 est): 2 461 000. Capital: Topeka.

Kansas City 39 05N 94 37W A city in the USA, in Missouri. Settled in 1821, it expanded rapidly with the arrival of the railways in the mid-18th century. Population (1986): 441 170.

Kant, Immanuel (1724–1804) German philosopher. His early works, notably *Theory of the Heavens* (1755), sought to examine metaphysics

in the light of the work of *Newton and *Leibniz. In the famous *Critique of Pure Reason* (1781) he explored the limitations of reason by which mankind interprets experience. Other important writings included the *Critique of Judgment* (1790). Kant also maintained that there was an absolute moral law and called the obligation to obey this moral law the "categorical imperative."

Kao-hsiung. *See* Gaoxiong.

Kapil Dev (Kapil Dev Ramlal Nikhanj; 1959–) Indian cricketer, who has played for Haryana, Northamptonshire, Worcestershire, and India (1978–). The second player to score 3000 runs and take 300 wickets in Test matches, he has also captained India (1983–84).

Kapitza, Peter Leonidovich (1894–1984) Soviet physicist, who worked with *Rutherford on magnetic fields. Returning to the Soviet Union in 1934 he transferred his attention to low-temperature physics, which led him to the discovery of superfluid helium (1941). For this work he was awarded the 1978 Nobel Prize.

kapok The fine silky hairs covering the seeds of the silk-cotton tree (*Ceiba pentandra*), which are used for stuffing mattresses, etc. The tree is native to tropical America and widely cultivated in the tropics. Growing to 35 m, it has white or red flowers.

Karachi 24 51N 67 02E The largest city and chief seaport in Pakistan, situated on the Arabian Sea just NW of the Indus delta. It became the capital of Pakistan in 1947; in 1959 the capital was removed to Islamabad. Population (1981): 5 103 000.

Karaganda 49 53N 73 07E A city in the SW Soviet Union. Founded in 1857, Karaganda grew rapidly as the Karaganda coal basin was exploited. Today it is one of the largest producers of bituminous coal in the Soviet Union. Population (1987): 633 000.

Karajan, Herbert von (1908–89) Austrian conductor. Musical director of the Vienna State Opera (1957–64), he founded the Salzburg Easter Festival in 1967 and conducted the Berlin Philharmonic Orchestra (1955–89).

Karakoram Range A mountain range mainly in SW China, NE Pakistan, and NW India. It extends about 450 km (280 mi) between the Pamirs and the Himalayas and includes *K2, the second highest mountain in the world. In 1978 the **Karakoram Highway** was opened connecting China with Pakistan over the Khunjerab Pass, 4933 m (16 188 ft) high.

Kara Kum A desert in the SW Soviet Union, between the Caspian Sea and the River Amu Darya. Area: about 300 000 sq km (115 806 sq mi).

karate An oriental form of unarmed combat that was developed in Okinawa in the 17th century and spread to Japan in the 1920s, where it absorbed elements of *jujitsu. Breath-control techniques as well as philosophical attitudes, such as the necessity of mental calm, were taken from Zen Buddhism. The aim is to focus the body's total muscular power in one instant. Hands, feet, elbows, etc., are toughened in set training sequences against padded or wooden blocks. In actual fights, however, which last two or three minutes, blows are stopped short before impact. As in *judo, grades are distinguished by coloured belts and points are awarded in combat. *See also* martial arts.

Karelian Isthmus A land bridge in the NW Soviet Union, connecting Finland with the Soviet Union. It is 40–113 km (25–70 mi) wide and 145 km (90 mi) long and its principal cities are Leningrad and Vyborg.

Kariba, Lake A reservoir in Zambia and Zimbabwe. It is formed by the Zambezi River above the **Kariba Dam** (completed 1959) and generates hydroelectric power. Length: 282 km (175 mi).

Karl-Marx-Stadt. *See* Chemnitz.

Karloff, Boris (William Pratt; 1887–1969) British film actor. Following his great success as the monster in *Frankenstein* (1931), he was cast in sinister roles in many subsequent horror films.

Karlsruhe 49 00N 8 24E A city in SW Germany, in Baden-Württemberg. The capital of the former *Land* of Baden, it is the site of the federal court of justice and has a harbour on the Rhine. It is a centre for nuclear research. Population (1987): 69 300.

karma (Sanskrit: action) The sum of all human actions, which according to *Hinduism and *Jainism are passed from one individual existence to the next and decide the nature of the individual's rebirth. In *Buddhism, karma is associated with mental and physical elements passed on in the cycle of rebirth until the personal self is reduced to nothing when *nirvana is reached.

Karnak 25 44N 32 39E A village near *Thebes (Upper Egypt), the site of the huge temple of Amon, built (c. 1320–1237 BC) mainly by the pharaohs Seti I (reigned 1313–1292) and *Ramses II. *See also* Luxor.

Karpov, Anatoly (1951–) Soviet chess player, who became an International Grandmaster at 19 and subsequently world champion (1975). He successfully defended his title against Victor Korchnoi (1931–) in 1978 and 1981 but was defeated by Gary Kasparov in 1985, 1986, 1987, and 1990.

Kasai, River A river in central Africa. Rising in Angola, it flows N into Zaïre to join the Zaïre River. It forms part of the Angola–Zaïre border. Length: 2100 km (1300 mi).

Kashmir The northernmost region of the Indian subcontinent, bordered by China to the NE and Afghanistan to the NW. The S Jammu lowlands rise into the Himalaya and Karakoram Mountains. Rice, other grains, silk, cotton, fruits, and sheep are farmed. Embroidery and other crafts help tourism to thrive. *History*: most Kashmiris became Muslims in the 14th century but in the 19th century Hindu princes won power under British control. Britain's withdrawal (1947) was followed by fighting between India and Pakistan and resulted in the division of the region. Pakistan rules 78 932 sq km (30 468 sq mi) of the W and barren N. China occupies 42 735 sq km (16 496 sq mi) in the E. The remainder forms the Indian state of *Jammu and Kashmir. Area (all Kashmir): 222 236 sq km (85 783 sq mi).

Kasparov, Gary (1963–) Soviet chess player, youngest-ever world champion. He won the world championship in 1985 at the age of 22 when he beat Karpov and successfully defended his title against Karpov in 1986, 1987, and 1990.

Kathmandu (*or* Katmandu) 27 42N 85 19E The capital of Nepal, near the meeting-point of the Rivers Baghmati and Vishnumati. Founded in the 8th century AD, it possesses numerous historical buildings and is the site of several religious festivals. Population (1982 est): 195 260.

Katmai, Mount An active volcano in the USA, in S Alaska. Following its violent eruption in 1912, the Valley of Ten Thousand Smokes was formed. Height: 2100 m (7000 ft). Depth of crater: 1130 m (3700 ft). Width of crater: about 4 km (2.5 mi).

Katowice (former name (1953–56): Stalinogrod) 50 15N 18 59E A city in S central Poland. It is an important industrial centre within the Upper Silesia coalfield. Population (1985): 363 000.

Kattegat A narrow channel between Denmark and Sweden linking the Skagerrak with the Baltic Sea. Length: about 240 km (149 mi).

Kauffmann, Angelica (1741–1807) Swiss painter. In England (1765–81) she painted portraits influenced by Reynolds and was employed on decorative work in country houses designed by Robert and James Adam.

Kaunas (Russian name: Kovno) 54 52N 23 55E A port in the Soviet Union, where the Rivers Neman and Viliya meet. It was held successively by Lithuania, Poland, and Russia before becoming (1918) the capital of independent Lithuania. Population (1987): 417 000.

Kaunda, Kenneth (David) (1924–) Zambian statesman; president (1964–). In 1958 he founded the militant Zambia African National Congress and was imprisoned. On his release in 1960 he became president of the United National Independence Party, which took Northern Rhodesia to independence as Zambia in 1964.

kauri pine A coniferous tree, *Agathis australis*, from New Zealand. Growing to a height of 46 m, it has round cones, 5–8 cm in diameter. It yields a resin (kauri copal or gum) used in making varnishes. Its timber is used for building.

kava A shrub, *Piper methysticum*, of the Pacific Islands and Australia, the ground and fermented roots of which are made into a narcotic drink. The roots are also chewed, and continued use produces inflammation and ulcers of the mouth. It has been used medicinally and as a local anaesthetic.

Kawasaki 35 32N 139 41E A city in Japan, in SE Honshu, part of the Tokyo-Yokohama industrial complex. Population (1987): 1 096 000.

Kazan (*or* Kasan) 53 45N 49 10E A city in the E Soviet Union on the River Volga, since 1920 the capital of the Tatar ASSR. *History*: founded in the 14th century by the *Tatars, it became the capital of an independent khanate and was captured (1552) by Ivan the Terrible. Its trade and industry developed during the 19th century. Population (1987): 1 068 000.

Kazan, Elia (E. Kazanjoglous; 1909–) US stage and film director and novelist, born in Turkey of Greek parentage. He helped to found the Actors' Studio in 1947. For the stage he directed *The Skin of Our Teeth* (1942), *A Streetcar Named Desire* (1947), *Death of a Salesman* (1949), and other outstanding plays. His films include *Viva Zapata* (1952), *On the Waterfront* (1954), *East of Eden* (1955), and *The Arrangement* (1969), which is based on his own novel.

KBE. See Order of the British Empire.

Kean, Edmund (c. 1787–1833) British actor. He was particularly successful as Shylock in *The Merchant of Venice*, his first London success in 1814, Richard III, Macbeth, Iago in *Othello*, and Barabas in Marlowe's *The Jew of Malta*, all roles suited to his passionate style of acting.

Keaton, Buster (Joseph Francis K.; 1895–1966) US comedian of silent films. He developed his character of the unsmiling but dogged clown in a series of classic silent comedies, including *The Navigator* (1924), *The General* (1926), and *The Cameraman* (1928).

Keats, John (1795–1821) British poet. Despite the failure of his first volume, *Poems* (1817), which contained the sonnet "On First Looking into Chapman's Homer," and the savage criticism directed at his second, *Endymion* (1818), Keats persisted and between 1819 and 1820 wrote most of his best-known poems. His short life was dogged by tragedies, especially the death of his brother from tuberculosis in 1818 and his unrequited love for Fanny Brawne. Such poems as *La Belle Dame Sans Merci*, *The Eve of Saint Agnes*, and the great odes ("To a Nightingale," "On a Grecian Urn," etc.), all published in 1820, eventually established his reputation. He died in Rome in search of a cure for his tuberculosis and was buried there.

Keeling Islands. See Cocos Islands.

Keflavík 64 01N 22 35W A town and fishing port in SW Iceland. It has a NATO air base. Population (1986): 6993.

Kekulé von Stradonitz, (Friedrich) August (1829–96) German chemist, whose main interest was in valence. He was the first chemist to establish the valence of the elements and to introduce the notion of single, double, and triple bonds. He went on to work out the structural formulae of many organic molecules, including that of benzene (**Kekulé formula**), which he claimed to have thought of in 1865 while dozing on a bus. See also aromatic compound.

Kelantan A state in central Peninsular Malaysia, bordering on Thailand. Rice is grown on the NE coastal plain, and rubber, copra, and minerals are produced. Area: 14 931 sq km (5765 sq mi). Population (1980): 877 575. Capital: Kota Baharu.

Kells (Irish name: Ceanannus Mór) 54 48N 6 14W A market town in the Republic of Ireland, in Co Meath. A monastery was founded here in the 6th century AD by St Columba in which *The Book of Kells*, an 8th-century illuminated manuscript of the Gospels, is reputed to have been written. Population (1981): 2623.

Kelly, Grace (1929–82) US film actress. Her films include *High Noon* (1952), *The Country Girl*

(1955), *To Catch a Thief* (1955), and *High Society* (1956). She retired from acting when she married Prince Rainier III of Monaco in 1956. She died following a road accident.

Kelly, Ned (1855–80) Australian outlaw. He and his brother Dan formed a gang in 1878 that became notorious for its daring robberies in Victoria and New South Wales. He was captured and hanged in 1880 after a gunfight with the police in which the other gang members were killed.

kelp A large brown *seaweed found in cold seas, usually below the level of low tide. The giant kelp, of the E Pacific coast, reaches a length of 65 m. The name kelp is also used for the ashes of seaweed, from which potassium and sodium salts and iodine were once obtained.

kelpie A breed of short-haired dog developed in Australia from the Border Collie and used for herding sheep and cattle. Named after a champion sheepdog of the 1870s, the kelpie has a long muzzle and pricked ears. The coat may be black or red (with or without tan), fawn, chocolate, or smoke-blue. Height: 43–50 cm.

kelvin (K) The *SI unit of *thermodynamic temperature equal to 1/273.16 of the thermodynamic temperature of the triple point of water. Named after Lord *Kelvin.

Kelvin, William Thomson, 1st Baron (1824–1907) Scottish physicist. Kelvin was the first physicist to take notice of *Joule's work. The two physicists then worked together, discovering the Joule-Kelvin effect; both also made great contributions to the new science of thermodynamics. In 1848 Kelvin suggested that there is a temperature at which the motions of particles cease and their energies become zero. He called this temperature *absolute zero and suggested a scale of temperature, now known as the Kelvin scale, in which the zero point is absolute zero. In 1852 he suggested that a heat pump could be made. During the 1860s he worked on the electrical properties of cables as well as with the laying of the first transatlantic cable in 1866. The unit of temperature (see kelvin) is named after him.

Kempis, Thomas à. See Thomas à Kempis.

Kendal 54 20N 2 45W A town in NW England, in Cumbria, called the Gateway to the Lakes. Catherine *Parr was born in the Norman castle. Population (1981): 23 411.

kendo A Japanese *martial art that developed from *samurai sword fighting. Combatants using bamboo staffs or wooden swords try to deliver blows on set target areas of each other's bodies. Two hits mean a win.

Kennedy, Cape. See Canaveral, Cape.

Kennedy, Joseph Patrick (1888–1969) US businessman and diplomat. He had five daughters and four sons, three of whom entered public life. **Joseph Patrick Kennedy, Jr** (1915–44), a naval pilot, was killed in World War II. **John Fitzgerald Kennedy** (1917–63), a Democrat, was the first Roman Catholic president of the USA (1961–63). His liberal domestic polices—the so-called New Frontier—involved tax and social reforms. He also established the Peace Corps. Abroad, he presided over the *Bay of Pigs invasion (1961) and confronted the *Soviet Union over its missile bases in Cuba (1962). In 1963 he agreed the *Nuclear Test-Ban Treaty. Kennedy's presidency also saw the beginning of US military involvement in Vietnam. He was assassinated in Dallas, apparently by Lee Harvey Oswald. In 1953 he married Jacqueline Bouvier (1929–), who became the wife of Aristotle *Onassis in 1968. **Robert Francis Kennedy** (1925–68), attorney general (1961–64) and then a senator (1965–68), campaigned for the Democratic presidential nomination in 1968, during which he too was assassinated. **Edward Moore Kennedy** (1932–) is a lawyer and Democratic senator.

Kennelly, Arthur Edwin. See ionosphere.

Kenneth I MacAlpine (died c. 858) King of the Scots of Dalriada (c. 844–c. 858). He formed the kingdom of Alba, the foundation of modern Scotland.

Kent A county of SE England, bordering on the English Channel and Greater London. It consists chiefly of undulating lowlands, crossed by the North Downs from W to E, and rising to the the Weald in the SW. Often called the Garden of England, it is the country's leading fruit-and hop-growing area. Area: 3730 sq km (1440 sq mi). Population (1988 est): 1 520 400. Administrative centre: Maidstone.

Kentucky A state in the central USA, lying to the E of the Mississippi River. It consists of the Appalachian Mountains in the E, the Bluegrass region in the centre, an undulating plain in the W, and the basins of the Tennessee and Ohio Rivers in the SW. It is an important coalmining state and also produces petroleum and natural gas. Local timber is used in the furniture and wood industries. Agricultural products include tobacco, corn, hay, and soya beans; cattle, sheep, and pigs are reared. It is also an important region for the breeding of thoroughbred horses. It became a state in 1792. Area: 104 623 sq km (40 395 sq mi). Population (1987 est): 3 727 000. Capital: Frankfort.

Kenya, Mount 0 10S 37 30E An extinct volcano in Kenya, the second highest mountain in Africa. Height: 5200 m (17 058 ft).

Kenya, Republic of A country in East Africa, on the Indian Ocean. *Economy:* the chief cash crops are coffee, tea, sisal, and pineapples; livestock rearing and dairy farming are also important. Forestry is being developed and mineral resources include soda ash, gold, limestone, and salt. Wildlife reserves include the huge Tsavo National Park. *History:* some of the earliest known fossil *hominid remains have been found in the region by the *Leakey family. The coastal area was settled by the Arabs from the 7th century AD and was controlled by the Portuguese during the 16th and 17th centuries. It became a British protectorate (East Africa Protectorate) in 1895 and a colony in 1920. In the 1950s independence movements led to the *Mau Mau revolt. Kenya gained independence in 1963 and in 1964 became a republic within the British Commonwealth, with Jomo *Kenyatta as its first president. President: Daniel Arap Moi (1924–). Official languages: Swahili and English. Official currency: Kenya shilling of 100 cents. Area: 582 600 sq km (224 960 sq mi). Population

(1988 est): 23 000 000. Capital: Nairobi. Main port: Mombasa.

Kenyatta, Jomo (c. 1891–1978) Kenyan statesman; president (1964–78). Son of a poor farmer, he became (1947) president of the Kenya African Union and in 1953 was imprisoned for seven years by the colonial government for his part in the *Mau Mau rebellion (involvement in which he always denied). While in gaol he was elected leader of the Kenya African National Union (1960), which achieved Kenya's independence in 1963. Kenyatta was prime minister before becoming president of a one-party state.

Kepler, Johannes (1571–1630) German astronomer, who was one of the first supporters of *Copernicus' heliocentric theory of the solar system. Kepler used Tycho Brahe's observations to work out the shape of planetary orbits, discovering that they were elliptical. He published this discovery, the first of **Kepler's laws**, together with his second law, stating that orbital velocity decreases with distance from the sun, in *Astronomia Nova* (1609). In 1619 he published his third law relating a planet's year to its distance from the sun. In 1610 he received a telescope built by *Galileo, which he used to observe Jupiter. In 1611 he constructed an improved version, now known as a Keplerian *telescope.

Kerala A state in SW India. It is India's most densely populated state. Rice, tea, coffee, pepper, rubber, nuts, and fruit are farmed. Fishing is also important. Area: 38 855 sq km (14 998 sq mi). Population (1981): 25 403 217. Capital: Trivandrum.

keratin An insoluble fibrous protein that is the major constituent of hair, nails, feathers, beaks, horns, and scales. Keratin is also found in the skin.

Kerguelen Islands 49 30S 69 30E A group of islands in the S Indian Ocean, in the French Southern and Antarctic Territories. Kerguelen Island, the largest, is the site of several scientific bases. Area: 7215 sq km (2786 sq mi).

Kérkira (or Kérkyra). See Corfu.

Kermanshah. See Bakhtaran.

kerosene. See paraffin.

Kerry (Irish name: Chiarraighe) A county in the SW Republic of Ireland. It rises in the *Macgillycuddy's Reeks and contains the famous Lakes of Killarney. The chief occupations are fishing, farming, and tourism. Area: 4701 sq km (1815 sq mi). Population (1986): 123 922. County town: Tralee.

Kesselring, Albert (1885–1960) German general, who commanded the Luftwaffe in the invasions of Poland (1939) and France (1940) and in the battle of Britain (1940). In 1943 he became commander of land and air forces in Italy and in 1945 on the Western Front. His death sentence as a war criminal was reduced to life imprisonment and he was released in 1952.

kestrel A small *falcon with a distinctive long tail and the ability to hover before diving on its prey. The common kestrel (*Falco tinnunculus*), 32 cm long, is widespread in Europe, Asia, and Africa and hunts small rodents, birds, and insects. The female has a brown streaked plumage; the male is blue-grey with black-streaked pale-brown underparts, a black-tipped tail, and a black eye stripe.

Ketch, Jack (d. 1686) English hangman, notorious for his cruelty. Appointed public hangman in 1663, he was responsible for the bungled execution of the Duke of Monmouth (1685).

ketone A group of organic chemicals having the general formula RCOR', where R and R' are *hydrocarbon groups. Acetone (dimethyl ketone) is a common example.

Kew Gardens Britain's most famous botanic garden, housing a collection of rare plants from all over the world. It is sited at Kew, near Richmond, Surrey, on land once owned by the royal family. The first botanic garden was created there in 1759, by Augusta (d. 1772), Princess of Wales, and in the late 18th and early 19th centuries Kew became internationally famous. Between 1848 and 1876 William Hooker (1785–1865) and his son Joseph (1817–1911) founded the Museum of Economic Botany, the Library, Herbarium, and Jodrell Laboratory. In Oct 1987 hurricane-force winds caused extensive damage, destroying many trees.

key. *See* tonality.

Keynes, John Maynard, 1st Baron (1883–1946) British economist. After attending the Versailles peace conference Keynes published *The Economic Consequences of the Peace* (1919), which attacked the amount of compensation demanded from Germany. In his greatest work, *General Theory of Employment, Interest and Money* (1936), he argued that unemployment can only be improved by increased public spending. He was the chief British representative at the *Bretton Woods Conference.

KGB (Committee of State Security) The Soviet secret police concerned with internal security and intelligence. It was founded in 1954 and replaced the more brutal MGB (Ministry of State Security; 1946–53).

Khachaturian, Aram Ilich (1903–78) Soviet composer. His music was deeply influenced by Caucasian folk music. His works include concertos for piano (1936) and violin (1940) and the famous ballets *Gayaneh* (1942) and *Spartacus* (1954).

Kharkov 50 00N 36 15E A city in the S Soviet Union. It was almost totally destroyed in World War II. Today, it is the third largest railway junction in the country. Population (1987): 1 587 000.

Khartoum (*or* al-Khurtum) 15 40N 32 52E The capital of the Sudan, at the meeting-point of the Blue and the White Nile Rivers. In 1885 *Gordon was besieged and killed here and the town destroyed by the forces of the Mahdi (*see* Mahdi, al-) but it was recaptured by Anglo-Egyptian forces in 1898 and rebuilt. It has several cathedrals and two mosques. Population (1983): 476 218.

Khazars A Turkic people who inhabited the lower Volga basin from the 7th to 13th centuries. Noted for their laws, tolerance, and cosmopolitanism, the Khazars embraced Judaism in the 8th century. Slavonic and nomadic Turkic invaders brought the downfall of the Khazars in

the 11th century. Itil, near modern Astrakhan, was their capital.

Khmer A people of Cambodia, Thailand, and Vietnam who speak the Khmer language, one of the Austro-Asiatic languages. They are rice cultivators and fishers, living in village communities headed by an elected chief. Their religion is Theravada Buddhism. The Khmer empire was founded in 616 AD, and its capital Angkor in about 880 AD. The name Khmer was later adopted by the communist Khmer Rouge movement (*see* Cambodia).

Khoisan The racial grouping consisting of the Hottentot and Bushmen people of S Africa. The Khoisan languages are noted for their click sounds. Formerly widespread S of the Zambezi River, the Khoisan tribes have been heavily reduced by Bantu and European intrusions into their territory since 1700. The Hottentots were wanderers, herding sheep and cattle, and were divided into clans. The Bushmen were traditionally hunters and gatherers, but most are now farm workers.

Khomeini, Ayatollah Ruholla (1902–89) Iranian Shiite Muslim leader (ayatollah) following the overthrow of the shah (1979). His rule was marked by the strict enforcement of Islamic principles and hostility to the West.

Khrushchev, Nikita S(ergeevich) (1894–1971) Soviet statesman; first secretary of the Soviet Communist Party (1953–64) and prime minister (1958–64). Khrushchev was a close associate of Stalin and emerged victorious from the power struggle that followed his death. In 1956 Khrushchev began to reverse Stalin's policies, giving rise to revolts in other communist countries. Owing to the failure of his economic policies and his unsuccessful foreign policy, notably his attempt to install missiles in Cuba (1962), he was overthrown by *Brezhnev and *Kosygin.

Khufu (*or* Cheops) King of Egypt (c. 2600 BC) of the 4th dynasty; the father of Khafre (reigned c. 2550 BC). He built the Great Pyramid at *Giza, which took 20 years to construct.

Khyber Pass (Khaybar Pass *or* Khaibar Pass) 34 06N 71 05E A mountain pass in the Hindu Kush, connecting Afghanistan with Pakistan and rising to 1072 m (3518 ft).

kibbutz An Israeli collective settlement in which land and property are owned or leased by all its members and work and meals are organized together. About 3% of the population live in *kibbutzim*. A **moshav** is a smallholders' cooperative in which machinery alone is shared. About 5% of the Israeli population live in *moshavim*.

Kidderminster 52 23N 2 14W A market town in W central England, in Hereford and Worcester. It is famous for carpet manufacture, begun in 1735. Population (1988 est): 54 194.

kidneys The two organs of excretion in vertebrate animals and man, which also regulate the amount of salt and water in the blood. The human kidneys are bean-shaped, each about 12 cm long and weighing about 150 g, and situated on either side of the spine below the diaphragm. They contain millions of tubules, which each have a specialized part for filtering water and dissolved substances from the blood. Most of the water and some substances are reabsorbed back into the blood further down the tubules: the remaining fluid (*see* urine) passes on to the *bladder. If one kidney ceases to function or is removed the other will enlarge and take over its function. Removal of both kidneys requires the use of an artificial kidney machine (*see* dialysis) unless a suitable donor kidney is available for *transplantation.

Kiel 54 20N 10 08E A city in N Germany, the capital of Schleswig-Holstein. A Baltic port, it was the chief naval port of Germany by the late 19th century. It has a 13th-century palace, restored after World War II. It is linked to the North Sea by the Kiel Canal. Population (1987): 243 600.

Kierkegaard, Søren (1813–55) Danish philosopher. Although critical of *Hegel, particularly in *The Concept of Irony* (1841), he remained under his influence. Much of his work is poetic and contradictory even in its titles, for example *Either-Or* (1843) and *Concluding Unscientific Postscript* (1846). Suspicious of both science and the established Church, he saw man as existing in isolation and relating only to God.

Kiev 50 28N 30 29E A city in the SW Soviet Union. It is the third largest city in the country and a major economic and cultural centre. Its opera and ballet companies have a worldwide reputation. Outstanding buildings include the 11th-century St Sophia cathedral and the Golden Gate of Kiev. *History*: Kiev was probably founded in the 6th or 7th century AD. Tatar attacks virtually destroyed the city, which subsequently passed to Lithuania. Russian rule was established in the 17th century. After the Russian Revolution Kiev became the capital of the short-lived Ukrainian republic and in 1934, the capital of the Ukrainian SSR. In World War II the city was occupied, after a long siege, by the Germans and thousands of its inhabitants were massacred. Population (1987): 2 554 000.

Kikuyu A *Bantu-speaking tribe of Kenya. Age grades are an important basis of social organization, boys being introduced into adulthood by *circumcision. Political power is held by a council of members of the senior age grade. The largest tribe in Kenya, the Kikuyu were deeply involved in the *Mau Mau movement and are now the most politically powerful tribe in Kenya.

Kildare (Irish name: Contae Chill Dara) A county in the E Republic of Ireland. It consists chiefly of a low-lying plain containing part of the Bog of Allen and the Curragh, an area noted for its racehorse breeding. Cattle rearing and arable farming are also important. Area: 1694 sq km (654 sq mi). Population (1986): 116 015. County town: Naas.

Kilimanjaro, Mount 3 02S 37 20E A volcanic mountain in Tanzania, the highest mountain in Africa. It has two peaks: Kibo at 5895 m (19 340 ft) and Mawenzi at 5273 m (17 300 ft).

Kilkenny (Irish name: Contae Chill Choinnigh) A county in the SE Republic of Ireland. Chiefly hilly, agriculture is the chief occupation. Area: 2062 sq km (796 sq mi). Population (1986): 73 094. County town: Kilkenny.

Killarney (Irish name: Cill Airne) 52 03N 9 30W A town in the Republic of Ireland in Co Kerry. A tourist centre near the three Lakes of Killarney, it is famous for its scenery. Population (1990): 7963.

killer whale A large toothed whale, *Orcinus orca*, common in Pacific and Antarctic waters but found in all other oceans. Up to 9 m long, killer whales are black above and pure white beneath. They are skilful hunters, and will even tackle other whales and dolphins. They are intelligent and trainable in captivity.

Killiecrankie, Pass of 56 43N 3 40W A pass in the Grampian Mountains, Scotland, in Tayside Region. It was the scene of a massacre of William III's troops by Jacobite Highlanders (1689).

killifish A small elongated fish, also called egg-laying top minnow. Killifish occur chiefly in tropical America, Africa, and Asia. Up to 15 cm long, many are brightly coloured and kept as aquarium fish.

Kilmarnock 55 37N 4 30W An industrial town in SW Scotland, in Strathclyde Region. The Burns museum contains many of Robert Burns's manuscripts. Population (1981): 52 080.

kilogram (kg) The *SI unit of mass equal to the mass of the platinum-iridium prototype kept at the International Bureau of Weights and Measures near Paris.

kiloton A measure of the explosive power of a nuclear weapon. It is equivalent to an explosion of 1000 tons of trinitrotoluene (TNT).

kilowatt-hour (kW-hr) A unit of energy used in charging for electricity. It is equal to the work done by a power of 1000 watts in 1 hour.

kilt. *See* Highland dress.

Kimberley 28 45S 24 46E A city in South Africa, in N Cape Province. It was founded (1871) following the discovery of diamonds and is today the world's largest diamond centre. Population (1980): 144 923.

Kimberleys. *See* Western Australia.

Kim Il Sung (Kim Song Ju; 1912–) North Korean statesman; prime minister (1948–72) and then president (1972–). He became leader of the Soviet-dominated N in 1945: in 1950 he ordered the invasion of South Korea in an unsuccessful attempt to reunite Korea (*see* Korean War).

kinetic energy Energy possessed by a body by virtue of its motion. If the body, mass m, is moving in a straight line with velocity v, its kinetic energy is $\frac{1}{2}mv^2$. If it is rotating its rotational kinetic energy is $\frac{1}{2}I\omega^2$, where I is its moment of inertia and ω its angular velocity.

kinetic theory A theory developed in the 19th century, largely by *Joule and *Maxwell, in which the behaviour of gases is explained by regarding them as consisting of tiny particles in constant random motion. Collisions, either between the particles or between the particles and the walls of the container, are assumed to be perfectly elastic. The theory explains the pressure of a gas as being due to collisions between the particles and the walls, its temperature as a measure of the *average* *kinetic energy of the particles.

King, Jr, Martin Luther (1929–68) US Black civil-rights leader. An outstanding speaker, he supported nonviolent resistance by organizing demonstrations against racial inequality and won the Nobel Peace Prize in 1964. He was assassinated in Memphis, Tennessee, by James Earl Ray.

King Charles spaniel A breed of *spaniel having a compact body, short legs, a short neck, and a large head with a short upturned nose. There are four colour varieties: Blenheim, ruby, tricolour, and black and tan, the last being associated with King Charles II. Weight: 3.5–6 kg; height: about 25 cm. The Cavalier King Charles spaniel is lighter bodied, with longer legs and a longer muzzle. Weight: 5–8 kg; height: about 30 cm.

king crab. *See* horseshoe crab.

kingcup. *See* marsh marigold.

kingfisher A bird that typically lives near water, feeding on small fish. Kingfishers are 12–45 cm long, with a bright plumage, and usually nest in burrows in banks. The European kingfisher, *Alcedo atthis*, is 14 cm long and has a greenish-blue and orange plumage.

King James Version The Authorized Version of the English *Bible that appeared in 1611 with the support of James I. It was based on the earlier Bishops' Bible (1568), but the translators also made use of the *Geneva Bible and the *Douai Bible.

Kingsley, Charles (1819–79) British clergyman and writer. In many works, such as *Alton Locke* (1850), he championed various social reforms. His works include the popular children's book *The Water Babies* (1863).

King's Lynn (Lynn *or* Lynn Regis) 52 45N 0 24E A historic market town in E England, in Norfolk. Its importance as a port has declined since the middle ages. Population (1990): 35 500.

Kingston 17 58N 76 48W The capital and main port of Jamaica, in the SE. Founded in 1692, it became the capital in 1872. In the 20th century it has suffered from hurricanes and an earthquake. Population (1983 est): 100 637.

Kingstown 13 12N 61 14W A port in SW St Vincent, in the West Indies. Exports include bananas, copra, arrowroot, and cotton. Population (1984 est): 32 600.

kinkajou A nocturnal tree-dwelling mammal, *Potos flavus*, of Central and South American forests. Up to 110 cm long including the tail (40–55 cm), it has a soft golden-brown coat, small ears, and a tail that can be used for clinging to branches. An agile climber, it feeds mainly on fruit and honey. It is related to the *racoon.

Kinneret, Lake. *See* Galilee, Sea of.

Kinnock, Neil (Gordon) (1942–) British Labour politician, born in Wales. He became a member of the National Executive Committee of the Labour Party in 1978 and Labour leader (1983–) following Michael Foot's resignation. He adopted a moderate stance in an attempt to regain popular support.

Kinshasa (name until 1966: Léopoldville) 4 18S 15 18E The capital of Zaïre, on the Zaïre River. It has a long history of human settlement and was occupied by the Humbu when *Stanley

discovered it in the late 19th century. Population (1985): 2 778 281.

Kipling, (Joseph) Rudyard (1865–1936) British writer and poet. Born in Bombay, he was educated in England, returning to India in 1882 to work as a journalist. After returning to England in 1888, he made his reputation with *Barrack Room Ballads and Other Verses* (1892). From 1892 to 1896 he lived in New England, where he wrote *The Jungle Books* (1894, 1895). *Kim* (1901) is the last novel he wrote with an Indian setting. Among his many other works are *Just So Stories* (1902) and *Puck of Pook's Hill* (1906), both for children. He won the Nobel Prize in 1907.

kipper. *See* herring.

Kirchhoff, Gustav Robert (1824–87) German physicist. Working with Robert *Bunsen, he invented the technique of spectroscopy and discovered caesium and rubidium in 1861. Kirchoff, working alone, also discovered several elements in the sun, by investigating the solar spectrum. He is also known for **Kirchhoff's laws**, relating to electrical networks.

Kiribati, Republic of (name until 1979: Gilbert Islands) A country in the S Pacific Ocean comprising the Gilbert Islands, the Phoenix Islands, and some of the Line Islands together with Ocean Island. The majority of the inhabitants are Micronesians. *Economy*: chiefly fishing and subsistence agriculture. Ocean Island is rich in phosphates, which, with copra, are the chief exports. *History*: part of the British protectorate of the Gilbert and Ellice Islands from 1892, they became a colony in 1915. Links with Ellice Islands (*see* Tuvalu, State of) were broken in 1975 and they became independent in 1979 as the Republic of Kiribati. Chief minister: Ieremia Tabai. Official languages: English and Gilbertese. Official currency: Australian dollar of 100 cents. Area: 861 sq km (332 sq mi). Population (1987): 66 250. Capital and main port: Tarawa.

Kirkwall 58 59N 2 58W A town in NE Scotland, the administrative centre of the island authority of Orkney, on the island of Mainland. Population (1985): 6000.

Kirov (name from 1780 until 1934: Vyatka) 58 38N 49 38E A port in the Soviet Union, on the River Vyatka. Founded in 1181, it was renamed in honour of the politician S. M. Kirov (1888–1934). Population (1987): 421 000.

Kirovabad (name until 1813 and from 1920 until 1935: Gandzha; name from 1813 until 1920: Yelisavetpol) 40 39N 46 20E A city in the S Soviet Union. A medieval commercial centre, it is now important for industry. Population (1987): 270 000.

Kirov Ballet A Soviet ballet company based at the Kirov State Theatre of Opera and Ballet in Leningrad. The theatre was renamed in honour of the politician S. M. Kirov (1888–1934) in 1935. Some of the Kirov's leading dancers, including Rudolf *Nureyev, Natalia Makarova (1940–), and Mikhail *Baryshnikov, have earned international reputations.

Kirovograd (name until 1924: Yelisavetgrad; name from 1924 until 1936: Zinoviyevsk) 48 31N 32 15E A city in the SW Soviet Union. It is a major agricultural centre. Population (1987): 269 000.

Kissinger, Henry (Alfred) (1923–) US diplomat and political scientist; secretary of state (1973–76). Appointed adviser to President Nixon (1969), Kissinger and Le Duc Tho (1911–) were jointly awarded the Nobel Peace Prize (1973) for helping to end the Vietnam War. Under President Ford he arranged a truce between Syria and Israel (1974).

Kitakyushu 33 52N 130 49E A city in Japan, on the Shimonoseki Strait. Formed in 1963 from the cities of Wakamatsu, Yawata, Tobata, Kokura, and Moji, it is one of Japan's leading trade and deepsea fishing ports. Population (1987): 1 042 000.

Kitchener of Khartoum, Horatio Herbert, 1st Earl (1850–1916) British field marshal. Appointed commander in chief of the Egyptian army in 1892, by 1898, with the battle of Omdurman, he had reconquered the Sudan, becoming its governor general (1899). In the second *Boer War he suppressed the guerrillas by a scorched-earth policy and the imprisonment of civilians in concentration camps. In 1914, as war secretary, his recruitment campaign was highly successful. He was drowned on his way to Archangel.

kite A *hawk occurring throughout the world, most commonly in warm regions. Typically reddish brown and 52–57 cm long, kites have long narrow wings, a long often forked tail, and a narrow bill and feed on insects, small mammals, and reptiles; some are scavengers.

kittiwake A North Atlantic *gull, *Rissa tridactyla*, that is adapted for nesting on narrow cliff ledges. It is 40 cm long and has a white plumage with black-tipped grey wings, short black legs, dark eyes, and a yellow bill. It feeds at sea on fish and animal scraps, going ashore only to breed.

Kitwe 12 48S 28 14E A town in N central Zambia. It is the chief commercial, industrial, and communications centre of the Copperbelt. Population (1980 est): 341 000.

kiwi (bird) A shy flightless bird occurring in forested regions of New Zealand. 25–40 cm long, kiwis have tiny wings hidden in coarse grey-brown plumage and strong legs with large claws. Kiwis are nocturnal and have weak eyes but well-developed hearing; the long bill is used to probe the soil for worms, insect larvae, etc.

kiwi (fruit) The fruit of a Chinese climbing shrub, *Actinidia chinensis*, also called Chinese gooseberry, with white or yellow flowers. The fruit, up to 5 cm long, has a rough skin and delicate-tasting flesh.

Klagenfurt 46 38N 14 20E A city in S Austria, the capital of Carinthia. It has a cathedral (1578–91) and is a tourist centre. Population (1981): 86 221.

Klee, Paul (1879–1940) Swiss painter and etcher. Working at first as an etcher, influenced by *Beardsley and *Goya, he became associated with the artistic group Der Blaue Reiter and taught at the *Bauhaus school of design (1920–33). Inspired by a visit to Tunisia (1914), he produced small watercolours in brilliant colours; af-

ter 1919 he used oils, creating a fantasy world influenced by children's art.

Klein bottle In *topology, a surface that has no edges and only one side. It is made by putting

KLEIN BOTTLE *A solid with no edges and only one side.*

the small end of a tapering tube through the side of the tube, stretching it, and joining it to the large end. It was discovered by the German mathematician Christian Felix Klein (1849–1925).

Klemperer, Otto (1885–1973) German conductor. He became conductor of the German Opera in Prague on the recommendation of Mahler in 1907. Expelled by the Nazis in 1933, he was principal conductor of the Philharmonia Orchestra from 1959 until his death and is particularly remembered for performances of Beethoven.

Klondike The valley of the Klondike River in NW Canada, in the central *Yukon, where gold was discovered in 1896. The subsequent gold rush opened up the Yukon, although the population dwindled when the gold started to run out (1900).

klystron An electronic device used to generate or amplify *microwaves.

Kneller, Sir Godfrey (1646–1723) Portrait painter of German birth. He worked successively for Charles II, William III, Queen Anne, and George I, and founded the first English academy of painting (1711). His portraits of the Whig Kit Cat Club (c. 1702–17; National Portrait Gallery), established a standard British portrait type.

Knock A village in the Republic of Ireland, in Co Mayo. Visions of the Virgin Mary were allegedly seen here, the first in 1879; it has become a place of pilgrimage with its own airport.

Knossos The principal city of Minoan Crete, near present-day Iráklion. Excavated and reconstructed (1899–1935) by Sir Arthur Evans, the Palace of Minos was luxurious and sophisticated. About 1450 BC the palace was burnt down. See Minoan civilization.

knot (unit) A unit of speed, used for ships and aircraft, equal to 1 nautical mile per hour (1.15 miles per hour or 1.85 km per hour).

knots Fastenings formed by looping and tying pieces of rope, cord, etc. The mathematical theory of knots, a branch of *topology, was developed mainly in the 20th century.

Knox, John (c. 1514–72) Scottish Protestant reformer. Influenced by the Protestant reformer George Wishart (c. 1513–46), in 1547 he joined the Protestants who had murdered Cardinal Beaton in revenge for Wishart's execution in St

297

KNOTS

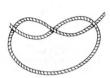

overhand knot *This is used either to make a knob in a rope or as the basis for another knot.*

reef knot *A non-slip knot for joining ropes of similar thickness.*

quick release knot *A tug on a will quickly unfasten this knot.*

surgeon's knot *The extra twist in the first part of the knot prevents it from slipping loose while the second part is tied.*

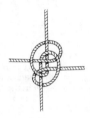

Hunter's bend *A strong, easily tied knot invented in 1978 by Dr Edward Hunter.*

bowline *A knot to form a non-slip loop.*

running bowline *A knot for making a running noose.*

sheepshank *A means of temporarily shortening a rope.*

sheet bend *A knot for securely joining two ropes of different thickness.*

double sheet bend *This follows the same principles as the sheet bend.*

fisherman's knot *Used especially for joining lengths of fishing gut.*

carrick bend *A knot well suited to tying heavy ropes together.*

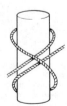

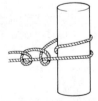

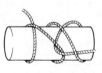

clove hitch *A simple knot for attaching a rope to a ring, rail, etc.*

round turn and two half hitches *Used for similar purposes as the clove hitch, this knot does not easily work loose.*

anchor bend *A secure means of attaching a cable to an anchor.*

rolling hitch *A quickly made and quickly unfastened knot for attaching a rope to a rail or another, standing rope.*

Andrew's Castle. The castle was stormed by the French, who imprisoned Knox as a galley slave. After his release (1549) he became a chaplain to Edward VI in England and contributed to the revision of the Second Book of Common Prayer. When Queen Mary was crowned he escaped to the Continent, where he met *Calvin in Geneva. Returning to Scotland in 1559, he became its leading reformer. In 1560 the Scottish parliament adopted Knox's *Confession of Faith*. His *First Book of Discipline* (1561) outlined a structure for the reformed Church of Scotland.

Knox-Johnston, Robin (William Robert Patrick K.-J.; 1939–) British yachtsman; the first person to sail alone around the world nonstop (1968–69). In 1981 he set the British transatlantic sailing record (11 days 7 hours 45 mins).

koala A tree-dwelling *marsupial mammal, *Phascolarctus cinereus*, of E Australia. About 60 cm high, koalas have thick greyish fur, tufted ears, a small tail, and long claws. Each adult eats more than 1 kg of eucalyptus leaves every day.

kob An antelope, *Kobus kob*, of African savanna regions, also called Buffon's kob. Males stand about 90 cm high at the shoulder; females are smaller. The coat ranges from orange-red to nearly black, with white markings on the face, legs, and belly and a black stripe down the foreleg.

Kobe 34 40N 135 12E A major port in Japan, on Osaka Bay. It forms the W end of the Osaka-Kobe industrial area. Population (1987): 1 413 000.

Koblenz (English name: Coblenz) 50 21N 7 36E A city in W Germany, where the Rivers Rhine and Moselle meet. The seat of Frankish kings during the 6th century AD, it was annexed by France in 1798, passing to Prussia in 1815. Notable buildings include the Ehrenbreitstein fortress (c. 1000) and the birthplace of Metternich. Population (1987): 110 300.

Kodály, Zoltan (1882–1967) Hungarian composer. Working with *Bartók he collected Hungarian peasant songs, which influenced his style of composition. He achieved international recognition with his *Psalmus Hungaricus* (1923); other works include the opera *Háry János* (1926) and *Dances of Galanta* (1933).

Kodiak bear. *See* brown bear.

Koestler, Arthur (1905–83) British writer, born in Hungary. His novel *Darkness at Noon* (1940) called on his experience as a prisoner in the Spanish Civil War; other novels include *Thieves in the Night* (1946). His nonfiction dealt with politics (*The Yogi and the Commissar*, 1945), scientific creativity (*The Sleepwalkers*, 1959; *The Act of Creation*, 1964; *The Ghost in the Machine*, 1967), and parapsychology (*The Roots of Coincidence*, 1972). He and his wife committed suicide after he became ill.

Koh-i-noor A famous diamond of 108 carats owned by the Mogul dynasty until the Shah of Iran looted it from Delhi (1739). It became Crown property in 1849, when Britain gained control of the Punjab. It was set in the coronation crown of George VI's consort, Queen Elizabeth (the Queen Mother).

Kohl, Helmut (1930–) German statesman; chancellor (1982–). A Christian Democrat, he presided over German reunification (1990), becoming leader of the united country.

kohlrabi A variety of *cabbage, sometimes called turnip-rooted cabbage. The green or purple stem base, which swells like a turnip, is used as a vegetable and as livestock food.

kola (*or* cola) Either of two trees, *Cola nitida* or *C. acuminata*, native to West Africa and widely grown in the tropics, that produce **kola nuts**. These are rich in caffeine and are chewed in Africa and the West Indies for their stimulating effects.

Kolyma, River A river in the NE Soviet Union. Rising in NE Siberia, it flows NE to the East Siberian Sea. Length: 2600 km (1615 mi).

Kommunizma, Pik. *See* Communism Peak.

Komodo dragon A rare *monitor lizard, *Varanus komodoensis*, which, at 3 m long and weighing 135 kg, is the largest living lizard. It has a long tail and short strong legs and is powerful enough to kill a man. Komodo dragons feed on animal carcasses and smaller monitors. They occur only on Komodo Island and some of the Lesser Sunda Islands of Indonesia.

KOMSOMOL (All-Union Leninist Communist League of Youth) A Soviet youth organization. Organized in 1918, its members fought in the civil war (1918–21). In 1922 it became a social organization to spread communist ideas.

Konakry. *See* Conakry.

Konoe Fumimaro, Prince (1891–1945) Japanese noble, who was prime minister three times. His first cabinet (1937–39) stepped up the conflict with China; his second (1940–41) took Japan into alliance in World War II with Germany and Italy; and his third (1941) made the decision to attack the USA. After Japan's surrender he committed suicide.

Kon-Tiki The name given by Thor *Heyerdahl to the balsawood raft on which, between 28 April and 7 August, 1947, he and five companions travelled the 5000 miles between Peru and the Tuamotu islands near Tahiti to show that ancient peoples of South America could have reached Polynesia. Kon-Tiki was an older name for the Inca creator god, Viracocha, said to have been known in Polynesia as Tiki.

Konya (ancient name: Iconium) 37 51N 32 30E A town in SW central Turkey. It is the centre of the Whirling Dervish sect and was the capital of the Seljuq kingdom of Rum. Population (1985): 438 859.

kookaburra A large grey-brown Australian kingfisher, *Dacelo novaeguineae*, also called laughing jackass because of its chuckling call. 43 cm long, it lives in trees and pounces on snakes, lizards, insects, and small rodents from a perch.

Koran (*or* Quran) The sacred scripture of *Islam. According to tradition, the divine revelations given to *Mohammed (d. 632 AD) were kept by his followers and collected as the Koran under the third caliph (spiritual leader), Uthman (d. 656). The Koran is one of the bases of *Islamic law. Muslims believe that the revelations exist complete in a heavenly book, which contains all that has happened and will happen.

Korda, Sir Alexander (Sandor Kellner; 1893–1956) British film producer and director, born in Hungary. He greatly boosted the British film industry during the 1930s and 1940s with a series of extravagant productions, including *The Private Life of Henry VIII* (1932), *The Scarlet Pimpernel* (1934), and *Anna Karenina* (1948).

Korea A country in NE Asia, occupying a peninsula between the Sea of Japan and the Yellow Sea, now divided (*see below*) into the Democratic Republic of Korea (North Korea) and the Republic of Korea (South Korea). The country became a Japanese protectorate in 1905, coming formally under Japanese rule in 1910. In 1945 the Allies divided Korea at the thirty-eighth parallel (the latitude of 38°N). The communist Democratic People's Republic of Korea under *Kim Il Sung was established in the Soviet-occupied N and the Republic of Korea, under Syngman Rhee, in the US-occupied S (1948). Soviet and US troops had withdrawn by 1949 and in 1950 the *Korean War broke out, ending in 1953 with the country still divided. Reunification talks began in 1990.

Korea, Democratic People's Republic of (Korean name: Chosŏn) The division of Korea left the North with almost all the country's mineral wealth and a large proportion of the industries, which had been developed by the Japanese. Mechanization has greatly increased agricultural production. President: Kim Il Sung. Official language: Korean. Official currency: won of 100 jun. Area: 122 370 sq km (47 225 sq mi). Population (1988 est): 21 890 000. Capital: P'yŏngyang.

Korea, Republic of (Korean name: Han Kook) The repressive government led by Syngman Rhee was ended by a military coup in 1961, followed by the rise to power of Gen Park Chung Hee (1917–79), who was assassinated in 1979. US aid has led to the development of a strong industrial sector. The 1988 Olympics took place at Seoul despite opposition from North Korea. President: Roh Tae Woo. Official language: Korean. Official currency: won of 100 chon. Area: 98 447 sq km (38 002 sq mi). Population (1987 est): 41 826 706. Capital: Seoul. Main port: Pusan.

Korean The language of the people of Korea. It is probably distantly related to *Japanese. The standard form is based on the dialect of Seoul. It is written in a script called onmun, invented in the mid-15th century to replace the Chinese characters in use before then.

Korean War (1950–53) A conflict, with no clear outcome, between communist North Korea and noncommunist South Korea. When North Korean troops crossed the thirty-eighth parallel in 1950 16 member nations of the UN sent troops, under the supreme command of the US general, Douglas *MacArthur, to support South Korea. The North Koreans were joined by Chinese Communist troops. A truce was eventually signed on 27 July, 1953, by which time some five million people had died.

Kosciusko, Mount 36 28S 148 17E The highest mountain in Australia, in SE New South Wales in the Snowy Mountains. Height: 2230 m (7316 ft).

Kosygin, Aleksei Nikolaevich (1904–80) Soviet statesman; prime minister (1964–80). He became prime minister after Khrushchev's fall, at first sharing power with *Brezhnev, but had less influence in the late 1960s.

Kovno. See Kaunas.

Kowloon. See Jiulong.

Kozhikode (former name: Calicut) 11 15N 75 45E A seaport on the W coast of India, in Kerala. Formerly famous as a cotton-manufacturing centre (Calicut gave its name to calico), it was visited by Vasco da Gama (1498) and in 1664 the British East India Company established a trading post here. Population (1981): 394 447.

Kra, Isthmus of The neck of the Malay Peninsula connecting it to the Asian mainland. It is occupied by Burma and Thailand and is 64 km (40 mi) across at its narrowest point.

krait A highly venomous snake occurring in S Asia. Kraits are usually patterned with blue-and-white or black-and-yellow bands; they prey chiefly on other snakes. The common blue krait (*Bungarus caeruleus*) of India and China is 1.5 m long and its venom can be fatal to humans.

Krakatoa (Indonesian name: Krakatau) 6 11S 105 26E A small volcanic Indonesian island in the Sunda Strait. Since its eruption in 1883, during which 36 000 people were killed, the island has been uninhabited.

Kraków (or Cracow) 50 03N 19 55E The third largest city in Poland, on the River Vistula. It was the capital of Poland from 1305 to 1609 and remains famous as a cultural centre. Notable buildings include the cathedral (14th century) and many churches. Population (1985): 716 000.

Krasnoyarsk 56 05N 92 46E A city in the E Soviet Union, on the River Yenisei. It developed greatly after the discovery of gold in the region in the 19th century. Population (1987): 899 000.

Krebs cycle (citric acid cycle *or* tricarboxylic acid cycle) A vital sequence of chemical reactions, taking place in the mitochondria of cells. It is named after its principal discoverer, Sir Hans Krebs (1900–81).The cycle is a crucial process in the conversion of food—carbohydrates, proteins, and fats—into usable energy in the form of *ATP. The cycle is also involved in the manufacture of carbohydrates, lipids, and proteins by cells.

Kremlin The citadel of any Russian city, now referring usually to that of Moscow. Built in 1156 but continually extended, it contains the Cathedral of the Assumption (1475–79), the Cathedral of the Annunciation (1484–89), the Great Kremlin Palace (1838–49), etc. Except for the period between 1712 and 1918 it has served continually as the seat of the Russian government and is now also a public museum of Russian architecture.

Krishna A popular Hindu god, the eighth incarnation of *Vishnu. In the *Bhagavadgita* he is revealed as the creator, sustainer, and destroyer of the universe (*see* Trimurti). Elsewhere he is worshipped as a fertility god. He is commonly represented as a beautiful youth with bluish skin wearing a crown of peacock feathers. *See also* Jagannatha.

Krishna Menon. *See* Menon, Krishna.

Krivoi Rog 47 55N 33 24E A city in the SW Soviet Union. Founded by the Cossacks in the 17th century, it is now an important ironmining centre. Population (1987): 698 000.

Kruger, (Stephanus Johannes) Paul(us) (1825–1904) Afrikaner statesman; president (1883–1902) of the South African Republic (Transvaal). A farmer of Dutch descent, Kruger settled with his parents in the Transvaal after taking part in the *Great Trek. He led the struggle to regain independence for the Transvaal from the British, achieved in 1881, after the first *Boer War. As president he resisted Uitlander (British immigrant) demands for political equality with the Afrikaner, a policy that led to the second Boer War (1899–1902).

Kruger National Park A game and plant reserve in NE South Africa, adjacent to the border with Mozambique. Area: about 21 000 sq km (8106 sq mi).

krugerrand A South African coin containing gold, minted since 1967. It has never been a true currency coin and was minted so that investors could escape restrictions on the private ownership of gold.

Krupp A German family of arms manufacturers. Under **Arndt Krupp** (d. 1624), the family settled in Essen, where in 1811 **Friedrich Krupp** (1787–1826) established a steel factory. His son **Alfred Krupp** (1812–87) expanded the family business into arms manufacture. Under Alfred's son-in-law **Gustav Krupp von Bohlen und Halbach** (1870–1950), the company developed Big Bertha, the World War I artillery piece named after Gustav's wife **Bertha Krupp** (1886–1957). Their son **Alfried Krupp** (1907–67) developed Gustav's ties with the Nazis, employed slave labour, and was imprisoned for war crimes.

krypton (Kr) A *noble gas discovered in 1898 by Sir William Ramsay and M. W. Travers (1872–1961). Compounds include the fluoride KrF_2. It is used for filling some fluorescent light bulbs; the *metre was (1960–83) defined in terms of the wavelength of a transition of one of its isotopes. At no 36; at wt 83.80; mp 156.6°C; bp –152.2°C.

Kuala Lumpur 3 10N 101 40E The capital of Malaysia, in central Peninsular Malaysia. It became capital of the Federated Malay States in 1895. Formerly also capital of the state of Selangor, it became a federal territory in 1974. Population (1985): 1 103 200.

Kuang-chou. *See* Canton.

Kublai Khan (1215–94) Emperor of China (1279–94), who founded the Yuan dynasty. Genghis Khan's grandson, Kublai established himself (1259) as chief of the Mongols after years of conflict with his brother Mangu (d. 1259). The acknowledged ruler of all China from 1279, he administered from Peking an empire extending from the River Danube to the East China Sea. More humane than his predecessors, he opened up communications with Europe, largely through Marco *Polo. However, his preoccupation with China and attempts to conquer SE Asia weakened the rest of the empire.

Kubrick, Stanley (1928–) US film writer, director, and producer. His films, mainly satirical and highly imaginative, include *Lolita* (1962), *Dr Strangelove* (1963), *2001: A Space Odyssey* (1968), and *The Shining* (1980).

kudu A large antelope, *Tragelaphus strepsiceros*, of African bush regions. About 130 cm high at the shoulder, kudus are red-brown with thin white vertical stripes on the flanks. Males have long corkscrew-shaped horns.

Kuei-yang. *See* Guiyang.

Kuibyshev (name until 1935: Samara) 53 10N 50 10E A port in the SW central Soviet Union, on the River Volga. Population (1987): 1 280 000.

Ku Klux Klan (KKK) A US secret society active against the Blacks. It started in Tennessee after the Civil War to prevent Blacks, who had newly been given the vote, from voting. Klansmen in white cloaks and hoods, burning fiery crosses, killed Blacks and destroyed their property. It was revived in 1915 and again in the 1950s in the South in response to the *civil-rights movement. It remains active against several minority groups.

Kumamoto 32 50N 130 42E A city in Japan, on the River Shira. One of the strongest centres in feudal Japan, it has a 17th-century castle. Population (1987): 550 000.

Kumasi 6 45N 1 35W The second largest city in Ghana. Formerly the capital of Ashanti, it was taken by the British in 1874. Population (1984): 348 880.

kumquat A shrubby plant of the rue family, of E and SE Asia, with fruits resembling small oranges. They are mainly used for pickling and preserves.

kung fu An ancient Chinese form of combat, mainly for self-defence. Among the other *martial arts it is most closely related to *karate, which possibly developed from it. In the second half of the 20th century the *wing chun* style has become particularly well known.

Kunlun Mountains A mountain system in W China, separating Tibet from the Tarim Basin. It extends 1600 km (1000 mi) E–W, reaching 7723 m (25 378 ft) at Ulugh Muztagh.

Kunming 25 04N 102 41E A city in S China, the capital of Yunnan province. It is noted for its Ming bronze temple. Population (1986): 1 490 000.

Kuomintang. *See* Guomindang.

Kura, River A river in W Asia. Rising in NE Turkey, it flows N into the Soviet Union, to the Caspian Sea. Length: 1515 km (941 mi).

Kurdistan An area in the Middle East inhabited by *Kurds, comprising parts of SE Turkey, N Syria, N Iraq, and NW Iran, including the Iranian province of Kordestan. The Turkish part includes a plateau that supports some agriculture, the remainder being mainly mountainous. The area was split between different countries at the end of World War I. Area: 192 000 sq km (74 600 sq mi).

Kurds The major population group in Kurdistan. Their language, Kurdish, is one of the *Iranian languages. The Kurds grow cereals and cotton and mostly no longer live in tribes but a few wandering groups still exist. They are Muslims but do not restrict women as much as other Islamic peoples. There have been nationalist revolts in the 19th and 20th centuries, especially in Turkey, Iran, and Iraq, where the most recent led to devastation of Kurdish villages (1988) by the Iraqis.

Kuria Muria Islands A group of five islands off the coast of Oman, in the Arabian Sea. Area: 72 sq km (28 sq mi).

Kuril Islands A Soviet chain of 56 islands extending 1200 km (746 mi) NE–SW between Kamchatka (Soviet Union) and Hokkaido (Japan). Discovered in 1634 by the Dutch, the islands were Japanese until seized by the Soviet Union in 1945. The largest are Paramushir, Urup, Iturup, and Kunashir. There are hot springs and 38 active volcanoes. Parallel to the chain, about 200 km (124 mi) to the E, is the **Kuril Trench**, which has a maximum depth of 10 542 m (34 587 ft). Total area: about 15 600 sq km (6022 sq mi).

Kurosawa, Akira (1910–   ) Japanese film director. His best-known films are action costume dramas such as *Rashomon* (1950) and *Seven Samurai* (1954). His literary adaptations include *Throne of Blood* (1957) and *Ran* (1985) (from Shakespeare's *Macbeth* and *King Lear*, respectively). Other films include *Dreams* (1990).

Kutch, Rann of An area of salt wasteland in central W India, near the border with S Pakistan. It consists of the Great Rann in the N and the Little Rann in the SE. Total area: about 23 000 sq km (8878 sq mi).

Kuwait 29 20N 48 00E The capital of the sheikdom of Kuwait, on the Persian Gulf. The traditional Islamic town has developed into a modern city with the development of the oil industry. Population (1985): 44 335.

Kuwait, State of A country in the Middle East, in Arabia situated at the head of the Persian Gulf. The country is sandy and barren and has a harsh climate. *Economy*: Kuwait is one of the largest oil producers in the world. It is a member of OPEC. *History*: Kuwait was originally settled in the early 18th century by nomads from the Ara-

bian interior, who established a sheikdom in 1756. In 1899 Kuwait gave Britain control over its foreign affairs and on the outbreak of World War I it became a British protectorate. Oil was discovered in 1938. Kuwait gained independence in 1961. In 1990 Iraq invaded Kuwait, which was liberated seven months later by a US-led multinational force after Iraq had devastated the country and its oil industry (*see* Gulf War). Head of state: Sheik Jabir al-Ahmad al-Jabir as-Sabah (1928–   ). Prime minister: Sheik Saad al-Abdullah as-Salim as-Sabah. Official language: Arabic. Official currency: Kuwait dinar of 1000 fils. Area: 24 286 sq km (9375 sq mi). Population (1988 est): 1 960 000. Capital: Kuwait.

kwashiorkor Severe protein deficiency in children under five years. Kwashiorkor develops in babies in poor countries where the diet does not contain sufficient protein (the name derives from a Ghanaian word). The children fail to grow and succumb to the slightest infection but recover rapidly with a good diet.

Kyoto 35 2N 135 45E A city in Japan, in S Honshu. It has been a leading cultural centre since early times, when it was the old Japanese capital (794–1192 AD), and the old imperial palace and ancient Buddhist temples still remain. Population (1987): 1 469 000.

Kyprianou, Spyros (1932–   ) Cypriot statesman; president (1977–88). He was previously minister of justice and then foreign minister (1960–72).

Kyushu The southernmost of the four main islands of Japan. Mountainous and volcanic, it has hot springs and a subtropical climate and is the most densely populated of the Japanese islands. There is a large rice-growing area in the NW, while heavy industry is centred on the N coalfield. Area: 35 659 sq km (13 768 sq mi). Population (1986): 13 295 000. Chief cities: Kitakyushu, Fukuoka, and Nagasaki.

Kyzyl Kum A desert in the W central S Soviet Union, lying between the Rivers Amu Darya and Syr Darya. Area: about 300 000 sq km (115 806 sq mi).

L

Labour Day The day on which the labour movement is celebrated. In 1889, the Second *International declared an international labour holiday on *May Day. In Britain, Labour Day was the first Sunday in May until 1977, when the first Monday of the month was declared a public holiday.

Labour Party The democratic socialist party in the UK. The party was formed in 1900 and named the Labour Party in 1906. Its origins lie in the trades-union movement of the 19th century, and the *trade unions still provide much of its funds. The *Fabian Society was also a

powerful influence on its formation and political beliefs. In 1922 the Labour Party became one of the two major UK parties (*compare* Conservative Party) and in 1924 and 1929–31 Labour formed a minority government under Ramsay *MacDonald. After World War II, in 1945, under Clement *Attlee, the party won a huge majority, enabling it to introduce far-reaching reforms, including widespread *nationalization and a comprehensive social security system. The party was in office again from 1964 to 1970 and from 1974 to 1979, under Harold *Wilson (1964–76) and then

James *Callaghan. The present leader, from 1983, is Neil *Kinnock.

Labrador (*or* Coast of Labrador) A district of NE Canada, on the Atlantic Ocean. Although the coast has belonged to Newfoundland for several centuries, the interior was finally awarded to Newfoundland in 1927. Labrador is mostly a rolling swampy plateau within the Canadian Shield. Generally barren except for forested river valleys, it has vast reserves of high-grade iron ore, which are being mined. Its hydroelectric potential is enormous. Area: 258 185 sq km (99 685 sq mi). Population (1976): 33 052.

Labrador retriever A breed of dog originating in Newfoundland and brought to Britain by fishermen in the early 19th century. It is about 56 cm high, with a tapering tail and a short dense water-resistant coat, usually black or yellow-brown.

laburnum A tree, *Laburnum anagyroides*, of the pea family, native to mountainous regions of central Europe and widely grown in parks and gardens. Up to 7 m high, it has bright-yellow flowers that grow in hanging clusters and produce slender brown pods. All parts of the plant are poisonous, especially the seeds.

labyrinth fish A small elongated fish with a deep narrow body, found in fresh waters of tropical Asia and Africa. It has a special breathing organ (labyrinth) to obtain oxygen from air gulped at the surface. Some species are popular aquarium fish.

lace An ornamental network of threads of silk, linen, etc., used mainly for dress collars, cuffs, altar cloths, etc. Needlepoint lace, originating in Italy in the early 16th century, is made with a needle on parchment or fabric. Pillow or bobbin lace, reputedly invented by Barbara Uttmann (b. 1514) in Saxony, is formed by twisting threads around pins stuck in a pillow. The best work was done in Italy, Flanders, France, and England in the 17th and 18th centuries, famous types of lace being Brussels, Valenciennes, Mechlin, and Honiton. Lace making as an art declined in the 19th century after machine manufacture was introduced.

lacewing A carnivorous insect having delicate net-veined wings. Green lacewings, also called golden-eyed lacewings, are about 10 mm long and occur worldwide near vegetation. The brown lacewings are smaller and often have spotted wings.

La Coruña (*or* Corunna) 43 22N 8 24W A port in NW Spain, in Galicia on the Atlantic Ocean. The Spanish Armada sailed from here on 26 July, 1588, and in 1589 the city was sacked by Sir Francis Drake. It is an important fishing centre. Population (1986): 239 505.

lacrosse A 10-a-side field game (12 for women) played with a ball and a long-handled stick (the crosse), which has a triangular head with a raw-hide strung pocket for catching, throwing, and picking up the ball. Of North American Indian origin, it is played mainly in the USA, Canada, Britain, and Australia. The object is to score goals by running with the ball and passing it. Each team consists of a goalkeeper, three defen-

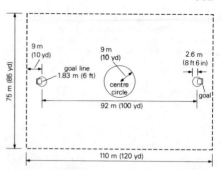

The optimum dimensions of the women's field, although the game is played with no boundaries.

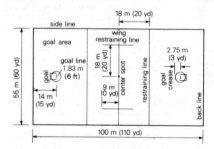

The dimensions of the men's field.

LACROSSE

sive players, three attackmen, and three midfielders.

lactation The secretion of milk from the breasts or mammary glands. In women lactation is controlled by hormones released from the ovary, placenta, and pituitary gland (*see* prolactin) and starts shortly after childbirth, in response to the sucking action of the baby at the nipple: it will continue for as long as the baby is breastfed. A protein-rich fluid called colostrum is secreted in the first few days of lactation, before the milk has been produced. It contains antibodies that give the baby temporary immunity to disease.

Ladoga, Lake A lake in the NW Soviet Union, the largest lake in Europe. It discharges via the River Neva into the Gulf of Finland. Area: about 17 700 sq km (6836 sq mi).

ladybird beetle A small round beetle, 8–10 mm long, widely distributed. Most species are red or yellow with black spots and are of great benefit to human beings. Both the larvae and adults feed on a variety of plant pests, including aphids, scale insects, mealybugs, and whiteflies.

Lady Day The Christian feast of the *Annunciation of the Virgin Mary. Celebrated on 25 March, it began the calendar year in England from 1155 to 1752 and is still a *quarter day.

Ladysmith 28 34S 29 47E A town in South Africa, in NW Natal. Founded in 1850, it was besieged for four months (1899–1900) by the Boers during the second Boer War. Population (1989): 56 599.

lady's slipper An orchid, *Cypripedium calceolus*, native to N Europe and Asia and up to 45 cm high. Each flower has small twisted red-brown petals and an inflated yellow slipper-like lip. The lady's slipper is nearly extinct in Britain. *See also* slipper orchid.

Lafayette, Marie Joseph Gilbert Motier, Marquis de (1757–1834) French general and politician, prominent at the beginning of the French Revolution. His early career was distinguished by his military successes (1777–79, 1780–82) against the British in the *American Revolution. In France as a representative in the *States General, he presented the Declaration of the *Rights of Man (1789) and after the storming of the Bastille he became commander of the new National Guard. In 1792 the rising power of the radicals threatened his life and he gave himself up to France's enemy, Austria. Lafayette was also prominent in the July Revolution (1830), which overthrew Charles X.

Lagos 6 27N 3 28E The main port and former capital (until replaced by Abuja in 1982) of Nigeria, on Lagos Island on the Bight of Benin. First settled by Yoruba fishermen in the 17th century, it became the centre of the Portuguese slave trade in West Africa and was handed over to Britain in 1861. It is an important commercial and industrial centre. Population (1983 est): 1 097 000.

Lahore 31 34N 74 22E The second largest city in Pakistan, near the River Ravi, founded about the 7th century AD. Traditionally the chief city of the Punjab, Lahore is situated close to the Indian border and has been the scene of much bloodshed and violence. It is a major railway, commercial, and political centre and the headquarters of the Muslim League. The famous Shalimar gardens lie to the E of the city. Population (1981): 2 922 000.

Laing, R(onald) D(avid) (1927–89) British psychiatrist, best known for regarding schizophrenia as a defence and madness as a journey of self-realization (*The Divided Self*, 1960). *The Politics of Experience* (1967) and his views on family life (*The Politics of the Family*, 1971) aroused controversy. His poetry includes *Knots* (1970).

laissez-faire The economic theory that governments should not interfere with market forces based on the profit motive. The concept, starting in France, was recommended by Adam *Smith and widely accepted until the beginning of the 19th century. By then capitalism had shown up its weaknesses: the rise of monopolies and the exploitation of labour. In western economies, laissez-faire policies have now been largely abandoned in favour of limited government control (mixed economies) and the introduction of welfare economics.

Lake District (*or* Lakeland) An area in NW England, in Cumbria, a national park since 1951. It consists of a high dome incised by glaciated valleys, many of which contain ribbon lakes including Derwentwater, Ullswater, and Windermere. High mountains rise between the valleys, the highest being *Scafell Pike and Helvellyn. It is a major tourist area; hill walking, rock climbing, and water sports are popular. Traditional occupations include hill farming, forestry, and quarrying. Area: about 1813 sq km (700 sq mi).

Lakshmi In *Hinduism, the goddess of wealth and happiness. As the wife of *Vishnu she appears in various forms according to his several incarnations. Many festivals are held in her honour (*see* Diwali). Lakshmi is also honoured by the Jains.

lamaism. *See* Tibetan Buddhism.

Lamarck, Jean-Baptiste de Monet, Chevalier de (1744–1829) French naturalist, noted for his work on evolution, particularly on the inheritance of acquired characteristics (*see* Lamarckism), published 1809. Lamarck also worked on a system of classification for invertebrate animals, published in his *Histoire naturelle des animaux sans vertèbres* (7 vols, 1815–22).

Lamarckism The first theory of *evolution as proposed by Jean-Baptiste *Lamarck in 1809 based on his ideas about the inheritance of acquired characteristics. He suggested that an organism develops changes to its body due to habits formed by the organism during its lifetime. Lamarck proposed that such changes (i.e. acquired characteristics) could be inherited by the individual's offspring. A favourite example of these acquired characteristics are the forelegs and neck of a giraffe, which he believed became longer through its habit of browsing on tall trees. This theory is now regarded as wrong, and is rejected in favour of Darwin's theory of evolution (*see* Darwinism).

Lamartine, Alphonse de (1790–1869) French poet, one of the major figures of the Romantic movement. He established his reputation with *Méditations poétiques* (1820). In the 1830s he became an active political champion of republican ideals and was briefly head of the government after the Revolution of 1848. His other major works include the poems *Jocelyn* (1836) and *La Chute d'un ange* (1836).

Lamb, Lady Caroline. *See* Byron, Lord; Melbourne, 2nd Viscount.

Lamb, Charles (1775–1834) British essayist and critic. He worked with his sister Mary on *Tales from Shakespeare* (1807), a children's book. He is best remembered for his *Essays of Elia* (1822).

Lamb, William. *See* Melbourne, 2nd Viscount.

Lambaréné 0 41S 10 13E A town in W Gabon, on an island in the River Ogooué. Its hospital (1913) was founded by the missionary Albert *Schweitzer. Population (1978 est): 26 257.

Lambeth Conferences Assemblies which normally gather every ten years under the chairmanship of the Archbishop of Canterbury at Lambeth Palace, London, to which all bishops of the Anglican Church are invited. The first was held in 1867. The conferences are important indications of the Anglican bishops' views and policies.

lammergeier A large *vulture, *Gypaetus barbatus*, also called bearded vulture because of the long bristles on its chin. It is over 1 m long with a wingspan of 3 m and occurs in mountainous regions of S Europe, central Asia, and E Africa. It is brown with tawny underparts and a black-and-white face.

Lamont, Norman (Stewart Hughson) (1942–) British Conservative politician, chancellor of the exchequer (1990–). He succeeded John Major as chancellor when the latter became prime minister.

lamprey A fishlike vertebrate with an eel-like body, one or two dorsal fins, and seven pairs of gill slits. They occur widely in fresh or salt water and many are parasitic on fish, attaching themselves with a circular sucking mouth and feeding on the blood and flesh.

Lanark 55 41N 3 48W A town in S central Scotland, in Strathclyde Region; now part of Clydesdale. Nearby New Lanark, founded as a cotton-spinning centre in 1784, is well known as the site of a model community established by the philanthropist Robert Owen (1771–1858). Population (1981 est): 9804.

Lancashire A county of NW England, bordering on the Irish Sea. The lowlands in the W are important agricultural regions. Industry is based chiefly on textiles, mining, and engineering. Tourism is important in the coastal towns of Blackpool, Southport, and Morecambe. Area: 3043 sq km (8191 sq mi). Population (1986 est): 1 380 700. Administrative centre: Preston.

Lancaster 54 03N 2 48W A town in NW England, in Lancashire on the River Lune, superseded by Preston as the administrative centre of Lancashire. The castle, partly 13th-century and enlarged by Elizabeth I, stands on the site of a Roman garrison. Population (1983 est): 126 400.

Lancaster A ruling dynasty of England descended from Edmund, the second son of Henry III, who was created Earl of Lancaster in 1267. In 1361 the title passed by marriage to the third son of Edward III, *John of Gaunt. His son seized the throne from Richard II and ruled (1399–1413) as Henry IV. He was succeeded by Henry V, whose son Henry VI led the Lancastrians against the Yorkists (*see* York) in the Wars of the Roses (1455–85), in which their emblem was a red rose. Following Henry VI's death (1471) the royal dynasty came to an end.

Lancaster, Duchy of A territory with its own courts and administration created in 1267 by Henry III for his son Edmund (1245–96). After the last Duke of Lancaster became Henry IV in 1399 the Duchy was attached to the Crown, but kept its own courts. The Crown continues to hold the Duchy's income and the chancellor of the Duchy of Lancaster is usually a member of the cabinet.

Lancelot In *Arthurian legend, a knight of the Round Table. While a child he was kidnapped by the Lady of the Lake, who educated him and later sent him to serve King Arthur. He was a celebrated warrior but failed in the quest of the *Holy Grail because of his love for Arthur's wife *Guinevere.

lancers Originally foot soldiers armed with a lance, they later became cavalrymen belonging to one of the regiments called lancers, both on the continent and in the UK. The name is kept in some armoured regiments.

Lanchow. *See* Lanzhou.

Land. *See* Germany, Federal Republic of.

land crab A large square-bodied tropical crab that is specialized for living on land. It feeds on plant and animal materials. The species *Cardiosoma guanhumi*, 11 cm across the back, is found in the West Indies and S North America.

Land Registry, HM An official record of ownership of land, established in 1862. This simplifies the sale of property: by searching in the Registry, outstanding leases, mortgages, etc., may be discovered. Not all land in the UK has to be registered yet.

Landseer, Sir Edwin Henry (1802–73) British artist. He achieved success, particularly with Queen Victoria, with his sentimental animal and Highland subjects, notably *Dignity and Impudence*. He sculptured the four bronze lions in Trafalgar Square.

Land's End 50 03N 5 44W A granite headland in Cornwall; the extreme western point of England. The southernmost point of England is the Lizard nearby.

Lang, Fritz (1890–1976) German film director. The best known of a number of influential silent films are *Dr Mabuse the Gambler* (1922), *Metropolis* (1926), and *M* (1931). He went to Hollywood in 1933, where he made commercially successful thrillers and westerns.

Langtry, Lillie (Emilie Charlotte le Breton; 1853–1929) British actress, known as the Jersey Lily. Having married a wealthy husband she pursued a successful acting career despite her high social position. She was noted for her beauty and was an intimate friend of the Prince of Wales, later Edward VII.

languages, classification of The division of languages into groups, by one of three methods. The first method groups languages together according to the continent or country in which they occur (e.g. the Indian languages). Such divisions do not always follow the genetic relationships that exist between languages. This relationship forms the second method of classification, which maps the development from one form of the language to another, as between Old English and modern English. The third method of classification depends on the three possible grammatical structures of the language, devised by W. von Humboldt (1767–1835): analytic (or isolating), agglutinative, and inflecting languages. English is an **analytic language**, relying on strict word order to express grammatical relations. In **agglutinative languages** (e.g. Turkish) words have the capacity to be split up into individual components with separate grammatical roles. In **inflecting languages** (e.g. Latin) words are built up of a root plus a component (morpheme) that represents several different grammatical categories.

Languedoc A former province in S France, on the Gulf of Lions. Its name derived from *langue d'oc*, the language of its inhabitants (*see* Provençal). It is chiefly part of the planning region of **Languedoc-Roussillon.** Area: 27 447 sq km (10 595 sq mi). Population (1986 est): 2 011 900.

langur A leaf-eating monkey of tropical Asia. The largest is the hanuman, or entellus langur (*Presbytis entellus*), 75 cm long with a 95-cm tail.

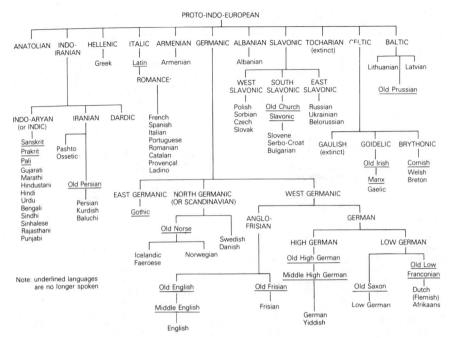

CLASSIFICATION OF LANGUAGES *A simplified family tree shows the relationships of the Indo-European languages, spoken by about half the world's population.*

The douc langur (*Pygathrix nemaeus*) of Vietnam is mainly grey with white forearms and is now an endangered species.

lanolin A purified *wax extracted from wool. Because it is easily absorbed by the skin, lanolin is used as a base for creams, soaps, and other skin preparations.

lantern fish A widely distributed deepsea bony *fish. Lantern fish have large mouths and eyes and numerous light-producing organs on the head, underside, and base of the tail.

lanthanides (*or* rare-earth metals) A group of 15 *transition elements, atomic numbers 57–71, which all have remarkably similar physical and chemical properties. They occur together in monazite and other minerals. They are used as catalysts in the petroleum industry, in iron alloys and permanent magnets, and in glass polishes. The **rare earths** are the oxides of these metals.

lanthanum (La) The first of the series of *lanthanides. At no 57; at wt 138.9055; mp 921°C; bp 3457°C.

Lanzhou (Lan-chou *or* Lanchow) 36 01N 103 45E A city in N China, the capital of Gansu province at the meeting-point of the Yellow and Wei Rivers. It is an ancient trade and communications centre and is now an industrial centre. Population (1986): 1 350 000.

Laois (*or* Laoighis *or* Leix; former name: Queen's County) A county in the E central Republic of Ireland, in Leinster. Predominantly low lying with bogs and drained chiefly by the Rivers Barrow and Nore, it rises to mountains in the

NW. Agriculture is the main occupation. Area: 1719 sq km (664 sq mi). Population (1986): 53 270. County town: Portlaoise.

Laos, People's Democratic Republic of A country in SE Asia, between Vietnam and Thailand. *Economy*: predominantly agricultural. The mineral resources (tin, iron ore, gold, and copper) have yet to be fully exploited. There is little industry. *History*: the origins of the area as a nation date from the 14th century. In 1893 Laos became a French protectorate. After Japanese occupation (1941–45), the French returned (1946) and a constitutional monarchy was formed in 1947. In 1949 Laos became independent within the French Union. In 1953 civil war, which was to last for 20 years, broke out between the government (supported by the USA and by Thai mercenaries) and the communist-led Pathet Lao movement (supported by the North Vietnamese). The Pathet Lao gained power (December, 1975) and the People's Democratic Republic of Laos was formed. President: Phoumi Vongvichit. Prime minister: Kaysone Phoumvihan (1920–). Official language: Laotian; French is widely spoken. Official currency: kip of 100 at. Area: 235 700 sq km (91 000 sq mi). Population (1987 est): 4 322 000. Capital: Vientiane.

Lao Zi (*or* Lao Tzu; ?6th century BC) The founder of *Taoism. A shadowy, possibly legendary, figure, he was eventually regarded as a god. His purpose, explained in books written about 300 years after his likely date of death, was to reach harmony with the *Tao* (way) by dwelling on the beauty of nature, by being self-sufficient, and by desiring nothing.

La Paz 16 30S 68 00W The administrative capital of Bolivia, situated in the W of the country. At an altitude of 3577 m (11 735 ft), it is the world's highest capital. Founded by the Spanish in 1548, it became the seat of government in 1898. Population (1985): 992 600. *See also* Sucre.

lapis lazuli A blue semiprecious stone composed mainly of the sulphur-rich mineral lazurite. It is formed from limestone. It often contains specks or threads of yellow iron pyrites. Lapis lazuli has been mined in Afghanistan for over 6000 years. The pigment ultramarine was formerly made by grinding up lapis lazuli.

Laplace, Pierre Simon, Marquis de (1749–1827) French mathematician and astronomer. Laplace worked with J. L. Lagrange (1736–1813) on the effects, known as perturbations, of the small gravitational forces that planets have on each other. They worked out that the perturbations have a minimal effect, thus proving the stability of the solar system. In the published account of their results, *Mécanique céleste* (1799–1825), Laplace suggested that the solar system was formed from a cloud of gas.

Lapland (*or* Lappland) A vast region in N Europe, inhabited by the *Lapps and extending across northern parts of Norway, Sweden, Finland, and into the extreme NW of the Soviet Union. Lying mainly within the Arctic Circle, it consists of tundra in the N, mountains in the W, and forests in the S; there are many lakes and rivers. Subsistence farming, fishing, trapping, and hunting are the principal occupations and reindeer are a particularly important source of income. There are rich deposits of iron ore in Swedish Lapland.

Lapps A people of N Scandinavia and the Kola peninsula of the Soviet Union. Reindeer herders, hunters, and fishers, they speak a *Finno-Ugric language, which differs from the related Finnish and *Estonian mainly in its sound system.

lapwing A Eurasian *plover, *Vanellus vanellus*, also called peewit and green plover. It occurs commonly on farmland, where it feeds on insects. 28 cm long, it has a greenish-black and white plumage and a long crest.

larch A deciduous conifer of the pine family, native to the cooler regions of the N hemisphere. Larches have needles growing in bunches on short spurs and produce small woody cones. The common European larch (*Larix decidua*), from the mountains of central Europe, is widely cultivated both for timber and ornament. It reaches a height of 40 m.

Lares and Penates Roman household gods. The Lares were originally gods of cultivated land who were worshipped at crossroads and boundaries. The Penates were gods of the storeroom. They were later worshipped in private homes as guardian spirits of the family, household, and state.

lark A slender long-winged songbird found mainly in mudflats, marshes, grasslands, and deserts of Europe, Asia, and Africa and noted for

its beautiful song. Larks commonly have a brown or buff streaked plumage that often matches the local soil colour. They have long slender bills and feed on seeds and insects. *See also* skylark.

Larkin, Philip (1922–85) British poet. His volumes include *The Whitsun Weddings* (1964) and *High Windows* (1974). He edited *The Oxford Book of Twentieth Century English Verse* (1973).

Larne 54 51N 5 49W A port in Northern Ireland, in Co Antrim at the entrance to Lough Larne. Larne is a tourist centre and has the shortest searoute between Ireland and Britain (Stranraer). Population (1981): 18 222.

La Rochefoucauld, François, Duc de (1613–80) French moralist. He was born into an ancient aristocratic family and played an active part in plots against *Richelieu. Thereafter he lived in retirement, writing his *Mémoires* (1664) and collecting his celebrated *Maximes* (1665), a series of observations on human conduct.

larva The immature form of insects and many other animals, which hatches from the egg and often differs in appearance from the adult form. Larvae usually avoid competing for food, etc., with the adults by occupying a different habitat or adopting a different lifestyle. For example, adult barnacles, which are permanently fixed in position, produce free-swimming larvae, whose role is to scatter widely and evenly. Other larvae, such as caterpillars and maggots, are responsible for gathering food reserves for the production of a fully formed adult, whose chief function is to breed. *See also* metamorphosis.

Larwood, Harold (1904–) British cricketer, who played for Nottinghamshire and England. Larwood was a fast bowler who was at the centre of the bodyline controversy during the 1932–33 tour of Australia.

larynx An organ in humans, situated at the front of the neck above the windpipe (*see* trachea), that contains the **vocal cords**. The larynx contains several cartilages (one of which —the thyroid cartilage—forms the Adam's apple) bound together by muscles and ligaments. Within are the two vocal cords: folds of tissue separated by a narrow slit (glottis). The vocal cords alter the flow of breathed out air through the glottis to produce the sounds of speech, song, etc. Similar organs occur in other mammals, amphibians, reptiles, and birds.

La Scala The principal Italian opera house, opened in Milan in 1776. It is noted for its varied repertoire and attained its highest reputation under Arturo *Toscanini, director 1898–1907 and 1921–31.

Lascaux Upper *Palaeolithic cave site in the Dordogne (France), discovered in 1940. Lascaux contains rock paintings and engravings of horses, oxen, red deer, and other animals, dating from about 18 000 BC. Deterioration of the paintings caused the cave to be closed again (1963).

laser (*l*ight *a*mplification by *s*timulated *e*mission of *r*adiation) A device that produces a beam of high-intensity radiation (light, infrared, or ultraviolet) that has a single wavelength (approximately) and is coherent (i.e. all the waves

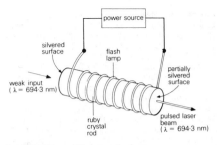

LASER *The solid-state ruby laser.*

are in phase). Stimulated emission is the emission of a photon when an atomic electron falls from a higher energy level to a lower level as a result of being stimulated by another photon of the same frequency. In the laser large numbers of electrons are "pumped" into a higher energy level, an effect called population inversion, and then stimulated to produce a high-intensity beam. Laser beams have been produced from solids, liquids, and gases. The simplest type is the ruby laser, consisting of a cylinder of ruby, silvered at one end and partially silvered at the other. A flash lamp is used to excite chromium ions in the ruby to a high energy level. When the ions fall back to their ground state photons are emitted. These photons collide with other excited ions producing radiation of the same wavelength (monochromatic) and the same phase (coherent), which is reflected up and down the ruby crystal and emerges as a narrow beam from the partially silvered end. Laser uses include surgery, *holography, compact-disc record players, computer printers, and scientific research.

Las Palmas 28 08N 15 27W The largest city in the Canary Islands, the capital of Las Palmas province in Gran Canaria. It is a popular resort. Population (1986): 372 270.

La Spezia 44 07N 9 48E A port and resort in Italy, in Liguria on the Gulf of Spezia. It is a major naval base, with the largest harbour in Italy. Population (1987): 107 435.

Las Vegas 36 10N 115 12W A city in the USA, in SE Nevada. Founded in 1855, it is famous for its nightclubs and the Strip (a row of luxury hotels and gambling casinos). Population (1987 est): 217 360.

latent heat The amount of heat absorbed or released by a substance when it changes from liquid to gas, liquid to solid, etc. For example, a liquid absorbs heat (**latent heat of vaporization**) from its surroundings on evaporation, as energy is needed to overcome the forces of attraction between the molecules as the liquid expands into a gas. Similarly a solid absorbs heat (**latent heat of fusion**) when it melts. The heat absorbed or released per unit mass of substance is called the **specific latent heat**.

Lateran Councils Five councils of the Roman Catholic Church which assembled in the Lateran Palace, Rome, in 1123, 1139, 1179, 1215, and 1512–17. The council of 1215, attended by most major European Church and non-Church powers, proclaimed the fifth *Crusade (1217–

21) and had great influence over Church organization and law.

Lateran Treaty (1929) An agreement between the Italian government of Mussolini and the Vatican. The *Vatican City state was created and the papacy gave up its claims to what had been the *papal states.

Latin language An Italic Indo-European language, the ancestor of modern *Romance languages. First spoken on the plain of Latium near Rome, Latin spread throughout the Mediterranean world as Roman power expanded. Written Latin developed at the same time as conversational Latin, which had a freer grammatical structure and vocabulary. Colloquial Vulgar Latin became the Latin of the provinces, contributing to the early development of the Romance languages. As the western Roman Empire's official language, Latin was used in W Europe for religious, literary, and scholarly works until the middle ages and was the Roman Catholic Church's official language until the mid-20th century.

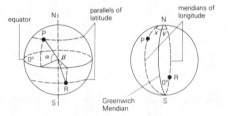

LATITUDE AND LONGITUDE *The latitude of P is given by the angle* α. *In this case it would be* α° *N. The latitude of R is* β° *S. The longitude of P is given by the angle* x. *In this case it would be* x° *W. R has a longitude* y° *E.*

latitude and longitude Imaginary lines on the earth's surface, enabling any point to be defined in terms of two angles. **Parallels of latitude** are circles drawn round the earth parallel to the equator; their diameters diminish as they approach the Poles. These parallels each lie at a particular angular distance (measured in degrees) north or south of the equator. All points on the equator therefore have a latitude of 0°, while the North Pole has a latitude of 90°N and the South Pole of 90°S. Parallels of latitude 1° apart are separated on the earth's surface by about 100 km (63 mi). **Meridians of longitude** are semicircles passing through both Poles; they cross parallels of latitude at right angles. In 1884 the meridian through Greenwich, near London, was selected as the prime meridian, longitude 0°. Other meridians are defined by the angle between the plane of the meridian and the plane of the prime meridian, specifying whether it is E or W of the prime meridian. At the equator meridians 1° apart are separated by about 112 km (70 mi).

latitudinarianism An attitude starting with certain 17th-century Anglican clergymen, who protested against squabbles over Church government and forms of ceremony and considered such matters unimportant in comparison with personal piety and practical morality. Between the 1690s and the rise of the *Oxford Movement in the 1830s latitudinarianism was the dominant tendency in the Church of England.

Latter-Day Saints, Church of Jesus Christ of. See Mormons.

Latvian A language belonging to the E division of the Baltic languages division of the Indo-European family, spoken by about two million Latvians. Most live in the Latvian SSR, where Latvian is the official language. Also known as Lettish, it is closely related to *Lithuanian. It is written in a Latin alphabet.

Latvian Soviet Socialist Republic (or Latvia) A constituent republic in the NW Soviet Union, on the Baltic Sea. Industries include shipbuilding, engineering, chemicals, and textiles. Fishing is important and Riga is an important seaport. *History*: the Latvians were conquered by the Livonian Knights (a German order of knighthood) in the 13th century, passing to Poland in the 16th century, to Sweden in the 17th century, and to Russia in the 18th century. Latvia gained independence in 1918; in 1940 it was incorporated into the Soviet Union as an SSR. In 1990 it voted to leave the Soviet Union. Area: 63 700 sq km (25 590 sq mi). Population (1987): 2 600 000. Capital: Riga.

Laud, William (1573–1645) Anglican churchman, with the Earl of Strafford (1593–1641) the chief adviser to Charles I immediately before the *Civil War. Appointed Archbishop of Canterbury (1633–45), he supported Charles I's personal rule. His pressure on the Scots to accept the Book of Common Prayer led to the Bishops' Wars and paved the way for the Civil War and his own downfall. He was accused of high treason by the Long Parliament in 1640 and executed.

laudanum. See opium.

Lauder, Sir Harry (Hugh MacLennan; 1870–1950) Scots singer and music-hall comedian. His most famous songs included "I Love a Lassie" and "Roamin' in the Gloamin'."

laughing jackass. See kookaburra.

Laughton, Charles (1899–1962) British actor. His international reputation was based on his numerous films, which included *The Private Life of Henry VIII* (1933), *Mutiny on the Bounty* (1935), and *Rembrandt* (1936).

Laurasia The supercontinent of the N hemisphere that is believed to have existed prior to 200 million years ago, when the drift of the continents to their present positions began. It probably consisted of Greenland, Europe, Asia (excluding India), and North America. See also Gondwanaland; continental drift.

laurel A shrub or small tree with attractive evergreen leaves. The so-called true laurels include the *bay tree. Other laurels include the ornamental Eurasian cherry laurel (*Prunus laurasocerasus*), the S Asian spotted laurel of the dogwood family, the North American mountain laurel (*Kalmia latifolia*), and the spurge laurel (*see* daphne).

Laurel and Hardy US film comedians. Stan Laurel (Arthur Stanley Jefferson; 1890–1965), the thin member of the team and writer of the gags, was born in Britain. He joined with Oliver Hardy (1892–1957), who played the fat partner, in 1926. They made numerous films in the 1920s and 1930s, including *The Music Box* (1932) and *Way Out West* (1937).

Laurentian Shield. See shield.

Lausanne 46 32N 6 39E A city and resort in W Switzerland, on the N shore of Lake Geneva. A cultural and intellectual centre, Lausanne is the seat of the Swiss Supreme Court and the headquarters of the International Olympic Committee. Population (1985): 125 000.

Lausanne, Conferences of 1. (1922–23) A conference between the Allied Powers and Turkey that altered the post-World War I Treaty of Sèvres (1920): Turkey regained territory from Greece and the Allies recognized Turkey's right to control its own affairs. 2. (1932) A conference between the UK, France, Belgium, and Italy, which ended the payments which Germany had had to make for damage caused in World War I.

lava *Magma that has reached the earth's surface through volcanic vents. Basic lavas tend to be liquid and flow over large areas, while acid lavas are thicker. On cooling, lava solidifies into a rock.

Laval, Pierre (1883–1945) French statesman. A socialist, Laval was prime minister in 1930, 1931, 1932, 1935, and 1936. After the collapse of France (1940) in World War II, he joined Marshal *Pétain's Vichy government, became increasingly powerful, and with the support of Germany gained the virtual leadership of the Vichy government in 1942. After the liberation of France (1944) he was tried and executed for working with Germany during the occupation.

lavender A small shrub, 30–80 cm high, with aromatic narrow grey-green leaves and small mauve or violet flowers growing on long stems. Native to the Mediterranean area, it is widely cultivated for its flowers, which retain their fragrance when dried, and for its oil, which is used in perfumes.

laver A widely distributed red *seaweed found growing at the high tide mark. It has wide irregular membranous fronds, which are edible: in the British Isles they are fried and known as laverbread (or sloke).

Lavoisier, Antoine Laurent (1743–94) French chemist. He became wealthy by investing in a private tax-collecting company. This enabled him to build a large laboratory where he discovered in 1778 that air consists of a mixture of two gases, which he called oxygen and nitrogen. He then went on to study the role of oxygen in combustion, finally disposing of the *phlogiston theory. Lavoisier also discovered the law of conservation of mass and introduced the modern method of naming compounds. Lavoisier was arrested and guillotined during the French Revolution for his involvement with the tax-collecting company.

law The body of rules that govern and regulate the relationship between one state and another (*see* international law), a state and its citizens (public law), and one person and another when the state is not directly involved (*see* civil law). Two great legal systems are dominant in the western world: *Roman law, as used in most countries of continental Europe and South America, and English law. The laws of England, which are enforceable by courts of law, can be divided into: (1) the *common law; (2) *equity; and (3) statute law, embodied in specific Acts of Parliament. *See also* courts of law; criminal law.

Law, (Andrew) Bonar (1858–1923) British statesman; Conservative prime minister (1922–23). He encouraged the revolt against *Asquith's government and in the subsequent coalition led by *Lloyd George became chancellor of the exchequer. He became prime minister after Lloyd George's resignation.

Lawrence, D(avid) H(erbert) (1885–1930) British novelist, poet, and painter. He published his first novel, *The White Peacock*, in 1911. The semiautobiographical *Sons and Lovers* (1913) established his reputation. In 1912 he eloped with Frieda Weekley. Their extensive travels provided material for the novels *Kangaroo* (1923), reflecting a stay in Australia, and *The Plumed Serpent* (1926), set in Mexico. Lawrence explored sexual relations in *The Rainbow* (1915) and *Women in Love* (1921); he treated this subject in more detail in *Lady Chatterley's Lover* (privately printed, Florence, 1928). The novel was not published in Britain in its complete form until 1961, after a long trial.

Lawrence, Gertrude (1898–1952) British actress. She performed in many revues and was especially successful in Noel *Coward's *Private Lives* (1930) and *Tonight at 8.30* (1935–36).

Lawrence, T(homas) E(dward) (1888–1935) British soldier and writer, known as Lawrence of Arabia. After the outbreak of World War I he worked for army intelligence in N Africa. In 1916 he joined the Arab revolt against the Turks, leading the Arab guerrillas triumphantly into Damascus in October, 1918. His exploits, which brought him almost legendary fame, were described in his book *The Seven Pillars of Wisdom* (1926).

lawrencium (Lr) A synthetic transuranic element discovered in 1961 and named after the US physicist E. O. Lawrence (1901–58). At no 103; at wt (257).

Lawson, Nigel (1932–) British Conservative politician; chancellor of the exchequer (1983–89). He became an MP in 1974 and was secretary of state for energy (1981–83).

laxatives (*or* purgatives) Drugs used to treat constipation. Such laxatives as magnesium sulphate (Epsom salts) mix with the faeces and cause them to hold water, which increases their bulk and makes them easier to pass. Irritant laxatives, such as castor oil, senna, and cascara, stimulate the bowel directly. Another group, which includes bran, both lubricates the faeces and increases their bulk.

lead (Pb) A dense soft bluish-grey metal, occurring in nature chiefly as the sulphide *galena (PbS). The metal is very resistant to damage by water, air, etc., and is used in plumbing (although it is now being replaced by plastics). It is

also used to shield X-rays, as ammunition, in crystal glass (as lead oxide), and as an antiknock in petrol (as *tetraethyl lead; $(C_2H_5)_4Pb$). Most lead salts are insoluble. At no 82; at wt 207.19; mp 327.50°C; bp 1740°C.

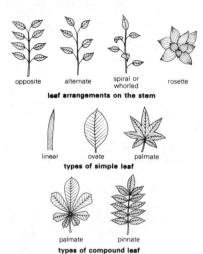

opposite   alternate   spiral or whorled   rosette

leaf arrangements on the stem

linear   ovate   palmate

types of simple leaf

palmate   pinnate

types of compound leaf

LEAF *The type and arrangement of the leaves are characteristic for a particular species of plant. For example, the pear has alternate ovate leaves; the horse chestnut has opposite palmate leaves.*

leaf An outgrowth from the stem of a plant in which most of the green pigment chlorophyll, used for photosynthesis, is concentrated. Foliage leaves have a large surface area for absorbing light, and they contain pores (stomata) through which gases and water vapour are exchanged with the atmosphere. Simple leaves consist of a single blade; compound leaves are composed of a number of leaflets. The veins form a branching system in *dicotyledons; parallel veins are a feature of *monocotyledons. The spines of cacti and the thorns of gorse are modified leaves.

League of Nations An international organization created (1920) after World War I with the purpose of achieving world peace. The USA's failure to approve the Treaty of *Versailles meant its exclusion from the League. The League failed to deal effectively with the aggression during the 1930s of Japan in China, Italy in Ethiopia, and Germany, which withdrew from the League in 1933. The UN replaced the League after World War II.

Leakey, Louis Seymour Bazett (1903–72) Kenyan palaeontologist. His work at *Olduvai Gorge uncovered crucial evidence of human evolution, notably an *Australopithecus* skull. In 1974 his wife **Mary Leakey** (1913–) unearthed hominid remains at Laetolil (N Tanzania) dating back 3.75 million years. Their son **Richard Leakey** (1944–) has made significant fossil finds around Lake Turkana (N Kenya).

Lean, Sir David (1908–) British film director. His early films with Noel Coward include *In Which we Serve* (1942), *Blithe Spirit* (1945), and *Brief Encounter* (1946). Adaptations of Charles Dickens' *Great Expectations* (1946) and *Oliver Twist* (1947) were followed by the classic *The Bridge on the River Kwai* (1957). Later films include *Lawrence of Arabia* (1962), *Dr Zhivago* (1965), and *A Passage to India* (1984).

Leander. *See* Hero and Leander.

leap year. *See* calendar.

Lear, Edward (1812–88) British artist and poet, noted for his four books of nonsense verse for children, beginning with *The Book of Nonsense* (1846). He also made a form of the *limerick highly popular.

leasehold. *See* estate.

leather Specially treated animal skin, chiefly that of domesticated animals, such as cows, sheep, goats, and pigs. The skin is first stripped of the fleshy inner and hairy outer layers and then tanned by soaking it in tannin, a preservative, or using chromium salts. Various finishing processes include rubbing to bring out the grain, as in Morocco leather (goatskin); dyeing; oiling; lacquering for patent leather; and sueding to raise a nap. Leather is strong, flexible, waterproof, and permeable to air. Uses range from industrial parts to bookbindings.

leatherback turtle The largest living turtle, *Dermochelys coriacea*, found worldwide. Up to 2.1 m long with a weight of 540 kg, it has no horny external shell and its bones are buried in a ridged leathery brown-black skin. It is a strong swimmer and feeds on marine invertebrates, especially large jellyfish.

Lebanon, Republic of A country in the Middle East, on the E coast of the Mediterranean Sea. *History:* Lebanon was an early convert to Christianity but in the 7th century broke away from the rest of the Church and was invaded by Muslims. Lebanon was held by the Mamelukes during the 14th and 15th centuries and by the Ottoman Turks from the early 16th century to 1918. France, having invaded Lebanon in 1861 to stop the massacres of Christians by Druses, was given control over Greater Lebanon after World War I. Lebanon became independent in 1941, although France retained control until 1945. In 1975, civil war broke out between Christians and Muslims, which after 19 months was brought to an end. In 1982 Israel invaded S Lebanon and, after besieging Beirut, forced the Palestine Liberation Organization to leave. Israel withdrew her forces in 1985 leaving the United Nations Interim Force in Lebanon (UNIFIL) and Syria to maintain peace between the Israeli-armed Christians, the Muslims, Druses, and Palestinian guerrillas. Elias Hrawi (1925–) became president in 1989. Prime minister: Selim Hoss (1929–). Official language: Arabic. Official currency: Lebanese pound of 100 piastres. Area: 10 452 sq km (4036 sq mi). Population (1987): 2 762 000. Capital: Beirut.

Le Carré, John (David Cornwell; 1931–) British novelist. He served in the foreign service in Germany (1961–64). His novels *The Spy Who Came in from the Cold* (1963), *Tinker, Tailor, Soldier, Spy* (1974), *Smiley's People* (1980), *A Perfect Spy* (1986), and *The Secret Pilgrim* (1991) are realistic studies of the world of espionage.

Le Corbusier (Charles-Édouard Jeanneret; 1887–1965) French architect, born in Switzerland, whose buildings and writings have been extremely influential. Until World War II he pioneered a simplified form of design called functionalism, especially with his villas at Garches (1927) and Poissy (1929). Afterwards he became more individual, for example at his extraordinary chapel at Ronchamp (1950) He was also concerned with town planning (e.g. *Chandigarh, 1950s) and large-scale housing projects (L'Unité, Marseilles, 1945).

Leda In Greek myth, the wife of Tyndareus, King of Sparta, and mother, either by her husband or by Zeus, of Clytemnestra, Helen, and Castor and Pollux. Helen was born from an egg after Zeus had visited Leda as a swan.

Lee, Robert E(dward) (1807–70) US Confederate commander in the Civil War. *See* Civil War, US.

leech A carnivorous aquatic *annelid worm. Leeches inhabit fresh and salt water throughout the world and also occur in wet soil. They have one sucker around the mouth and a second at the rear. Leeches can move by "looping," using their suckers. Most feed on animal and human blood; leeches are used to suck up excess blood after plastic surgery.

Leeds 53 50N 1 35W A city in N England, the largest city in West Yorkshire on the River Aire. Its main industries are clothing, textiles, printing, engineering, chemicals, and leather goods. Population (1981): 448 528.

leek A hardy plant, *Allium porrum*, related to the onion and native to SW Asia and E Mediterranean regions. It is widely grown in Europe as a vegetable. The stems and long broad leaves are eaten in the first year, before flowering. The leek is the national emblem of Wales.

Leeuwenhoek, Antonie van (1632–1723) Dutch scientist, noted for his microscopic studies of living organisms. He was the first to describe protozoa, bacteria, and spermatozoa and he also made observations of yeasts, red blood cells, and blood capillaries. Leeuwenhoek also traced the life histories of various animals, including the flea, ant, and weevil.

Leeward Islands 1. A West Indian group of islands in the Lesser Antilles, in the Caribbean Sea extending SE from Puerto Rico to the Windward Islands. 2. A former British colony in the West Indies (1871–1956), comprising Antigua, St Kitts-Nevis-Anguilla, Montserrat, and the British Virgin Islands. 3. A group of islands in French Polynesia, in the Society Islands in the S Pacific Ocean.

legionnaires' disease An acute severe pneumonia, caused by the bacterium *Legionella pneumophila*, first described in 1976 after an outbreak among US legionnaires in Philadelphia. Over 30 people died in Stafford, England, as a result of an outbreak in 1985. The treatment is with the antibiotic erythromycin. The disease is often caught from air-conditioning systems contaminated with the bacterium.

Legion of Honour   A French order of knight-hood, established by Napoleon in 1802. It has five ranks, to which foreigners are admitted. Its grand master is the president of France.

legume   Any plant of the pea family, which includes many important crop plants, such as beans, clovers, and alfalfa. Legumes produce pods containing a single row of seeds. Both pods and seeds are rich in protein. Most species possess root nodules that contain nitrogen-fixing bacteria and leguminous crops replenish nitrogen in the soil (*see* nitrogen cycle).

Lehár, Franz   (Ferencz L.; 1870–1948) Hungarian composer, noted for his operettas, of which *The Merry Widow* (1905) was his greatest success.

Le Havre   49 30N 0 06E A port in N France, in the Seine-Maritime department on the English Channel at the mouth of the River Seine. There is a transatlantic cargo service and a car-ferry service to England. Population (1982): 198 700.

Leibniz, Gottfried Wilhelm   (1646–1716) German philosopher and mathematician. His philosophy is summarized in his two books, *New Essays on the Human Understanding* (c. 1705) and *Theodicy* (1710), and numerous essays. Leibniz' best-known belief is that the universe consists of an infinite set of independent substances (monads) in each of which a life force is present. In creating the world, God took account of the wishes of monads and this led to the "best of all possible worlds." His claim to have invented the calculus was disputed by *Newton.

Leicester   52 38N 1 05W A city in central England, the administrative centre of Leicestershire. Lying on the Fosse Way, Leicester has many Roman remains. Parts of the Norman castle also remain. Industries include hosiery, knitwear, engineering, printing, and electronics. Population (1989): 279 791.

Leicester, Robert Dudley, Earl of   (c. 1532–88) English courtier; the fifth son of the Duke of *Northumberland. Elizabeth I made him Master of the Horse (1558) and then a privy councillor (1559). It was rumoured that he might marry the queen after the death of his wife Amy Robsart (c. 1532–60). His incompetent command (1585–87) of an English force in support of the Revolt of the Netherlands against Spain led to his recall but he kept Elizabeth's favour until his death.

Leicestershire   A county in the East Midlands of England. The River Soar, flowing N, separates Charnwood Forest from the uplands of the E. Its fertile soil makes it an important agricultural county. Hosiery is the staple industry. Area: 2553 sq km (986 sq mi). Population (1987 est): 879 400. Administrative centre: Leicester.

Leiden   (English name: Leyden)   52 10N 4 30E A city in the W Netherlands, in South Holland province. During the 17th and 18th centuries it was an artistic and educational centre. Population (1987): 106 808.

Leif Eriksson   (11th century) Icelandic explorer; the son of Eric the Red (late 10th century). He was converted to Christianity and on his way to promote the faith in Greenland, missed his course and became the first European to reach America (perhaps Newfoundland or Nova Scotia). His story is told in Icelandic sagas.

Leigh, Vivien   (Vivien Hartley; 1913–67) British actress. In the theatre, she played many leading Shakespearean roles, frequently appearing with Laurence *Olivier, her husband from 1937 to 1960. Her films include *Gone with the Wind* (1939) and *A Streetcar Named Desire* (1951).

Leinster   A province in the SE Republic of Ireland. It consists of the counties of Carlow, Dublin, Kildare, Kilkenny, Laois, Longford, Louth, Meath, Offaly, Westmeath, Wexford, and Wicklow. It incorporates the ancient kingdoms of Meath and Leinster. Area: 19 632 sq km (7580 sq mi). Population (1986): 1 851 134.

Leipzig   51 20N 12 21E A city in E Germany, near the meeting-point of the Rivers Elster, Pleisse, and Parthe. Leipzig is the country's second largest city and one of its chief industrial and commercial centres. Important international trade fairs have been held here since the middle ages. It is also a famous musical centre. Population (1990): 530 000.

Leitrim   A county in the NW Republic of Ireland, in Connacht bordering on Donegal Bay. Mainly hilly, descending to lowlands in the S, it contains several lakes, notably Lough Allen. Area: 1525 sq km (589 sq mi). Population (1986): 27 000. County town: Carrick-on-Shannon.

Leix.   *See* Laois.

Lely, Sir Peter   (Pieter van der Faes; 1618–80) Portrait painter, born in Germany of Dutch parents. He settled in London (1641), where he was patronized by Charles I and later Cromwell. As court painter to Charles II from 1661, he produced his best-known works, including his *Windsor Beauties*.

Le Mans   48 00N 0 12E A city in NW France, the capital of the Sarthe department. Its many historical buildings include the cathedral (11th–15th centuries). The Le Mans Grand Prix, a 24-hour motor race, is held here annually. Population (1982): 150 331.

lemming   A *rodent related to voles, found in northern regions of Asia, America, and Europe. They are 7.5–15 cm long and have long thick fur. When their food of grass, berries, and roots is abundant, they breed at a great rate. When food is scarce they migrate southwards, often in large swarms; although they can swim, they sometimes drown through exhaustion.

lemon   A small *citrus fruit produced by a tree, *Citrus limon*, widely cultivated in warm climates. It has yellow skin and acid-tasting pulp rich in vitamin C. The juice is used as a flavouring and as a drink.

lemon sole   A *flatfish, *Microstomus kitt*, found in the NE Atlantic and North Sea. Its upper side is red-brown or yellow-brown with light or dark marbling. It is an important food fish.

lemur   A small *primate found only in Madagascar and neighbouring islands. Most lemurs are nocturnal and live in trees, often in groups. The ring-tailed lemur (*Lemur catta*) is 70–95 cm long including the tail (40–50 cm) and lives mainly on the ground, sheltering among rocks and in caves. Dwarf lemurs are only 25–50 cm long including the tail (12–25 cm).

Lena, River The longest river in the Soviet Union. Rising in S Siberia, W of Lake Baikal, it flows mainly NE to the Laptev Sea. Its large delta is frozen for about nine months of the year. Length: 4271 km (2653 mi).

Lendl, Ivan (1960–) Czech tennis player. Despite becoming world champion and winning the US Open and other championships, he has never won at Wimbledon.

Lenin, Vladimir Ilich (V. I. Ulyanov; 1870–1924) Russian revolutionary and first leader of communist Russia. In 1893 Lenin, a Marxist, joined a revolutionary group in St Petersburg (subsequently renamed *Leningrad), where he worked as a lawyer. In 1895 he was imprisoned and in 1897 exiled to Siberia, where he married (1898) Nadezhda Krupskaya, a fellow Marxist. In 1902 he published *What Is to Be Done?*, in which he underlined the role of the party in bringing about revolution. This led to a split in the Russian Social Democratic Workers' Party between the *Bolsheviks under Lenin and the *Mensheviks. After the failure of the *Revolution of 1905, Lenin again went into exile, settling in Zurich in 1914. In April, 1917, after the outbreak of the *Russian Revolution, Lenin returned to Russia. Calling for the transfer of power from the Provisional Government to the soviets (workers' councils), he was forced to flee to Finland. Lenin returned in October to lead the Bolshevik revolution, which overthrew the Provisional Government and established the ruling Soviet of People's Commissars under Lenin's chairmanship. He made peace with Germany and then led the revolutionaries to victory against the Whites in the civil war (1918–20). He founded (1919) the Third *International and introduced far-reaching social reforms. In response to the disastrous economic effects of the war he introduced the New Economic Policy (1921).

Leningrad (name from 1703 until 1914: St Petersburg; name from 1914 until 1924: Petrograd) 59 55N 30 25E The second largest city in the Soviet Union and the capital of the Leningrad autonomous region (*oblast*), at the head of the Gulf of Finland on the River Neva. It is a major industrial and commercial centre and its port, although frozen between January and April, is one of the largest in the world. The most notable buildings include the Peter-Paul Fortress, the Winter Palace, and the Gostiny Dvor. *History:* the city was founded (1703) by Peter the Great and was the capital of Russia from 1712 until 1918. In 1905 a general strike took place and on Bloody Sunday (9 January, 1905) more than a thousand people were killed in a march on the Winter Palace. Leningrad was also prominent in the 1917 revolution (*see* Russian Revolution). During World War II the city withstood a siege by the Germans (8 September, 1941–27 January, 1944), in which nearly a million people perished. Population (1989): 5 023 500.

Leninism Developments in Marxist theory (*see* Marxism) by V. I. *Lenin. He gives an ac-count of the final stage of capitalism, in which the world is controlled by finance capital (banks) as opposed to industrial capital. Because capitalism is worldwide, socialist revolution becomes possible even in economically underdeveloped countries which are the "weak link". According to his theory of the revolutionary party, the most aware element of the working class provides the leadership in organizing the overthrow of the capitalist class.

lens A piece of transparent material, usually glass, quartz, or plastic, used for directing and focusing beams of light. The surfaces of a lens have a constant curvature; if both sides curve outwards at the middle the lens is called convex, if they curve inwards it is concave. The image formed by a lens may be real, in which case the rays converge to the image point (a converging lens), or virtual, in which the rays diverge from the image point (a diverging lens). The focal length of a lens is the distance from the lens at which a parallel beam of light is brought to a focus.

Lent The Christian period of fasting and penance before Easter. Beginning on *Ash Wednesday, the fast covers 40 days, imitating Christ's 40 days in the wilderness (Matthew 4.2). Since the Reformation the rules of fasting have been generally relaxed in both Roman Catholic and Protestant Churches.

lentil A plant, *Lens culinaris*, of the pea family, native to the Near East but widely cultivated. Each pod produces 1–2 flat round green or reddish seeds, which are rich in protein and can be dried and stored for use in soups, stews, etc.

Leonardo da Vinci (1452–1519) Italian artistic and scientific genius of the *Renaissance. He trained in Florence under Verrocchio and painted the *Adoration of the Magi* (1481). In 1482 he became painter, engineer, and designer to Duke Ludovico Sforza in Milan, where he painted the fresco of the *Last Supper* and the first version of the *Virgin of the Rocks*. After the French invasion of Milan (1499), he returned to Florence, becoming military engineer and architect (1502) to Cesare *Borgia. Paintings in this period include the *Battle of Anghiari*, *The Virgin and Child with St John the Baptist and St Anne*, and the *Mona Lisa*. After working again in Milan (1506–13) and in Rome (1513–15), he was invited by Francis I to France (1516), where he died. His notebooks reveal his wide range of interests, including anatomy, botany, geology, hydraulics, and mechanics.

leopard A large spotted *cat, *Panthera pardus*, found throughout Africa and most of Asia. Leopards are slender, up to 2.1 m long including the 90-cm tail, having a yellow coat spotted with black rosettes. The *panther is a variety of leopard. Leopards are solitary and nocturnal.

leopard lily A flowering plant, *Belamcanda chinensis*, of the iris family, native to E Asia and widely planted in gardens. Growing over 1 m tall, it has sword-shaped leaves, orange-spotted red flowers, and blackberry-like clusters of seeds.
The name is also given to several other garden flowers, including the snake's head *fritillary.

leopard seal A solitary Antarctic *seal, *Hydrurga leptonyx*, of the pack ice. Leopard seals are fast agile hunters, feeding mainly on penguins. Grey, with dark spots and blotches, females grow to 3.7 m and males to 3.2 m.

Leopold I (1790–1865) The first King of the Belgians (1831–65). He defended Belgium against William III of the Netherlands, who refused to recognize Belgian independence until 1838. A leading diplomat in Europe, at home he encouraged educational and economic reforms. He was briefly (1816–17) married to Charlotte (1796–1817), the daughter of George IV of Great Britain.

Leopold III (1901–83) King of the Belgians (1934–51). He surrendered to the Germans in *World War II, which led to opposition to his return to Belgium in 1945 and forced his abdication in favour of his son *Baudouin.

Léopoldville. See Kinshasa.

Lepanto, Battle of (7 October, 1571) A naval battle off Lepanto, Greece, in which the Holy League routed the Ottoman navy, which was threatening to dominate the Mediterranean. The Christian force was commanded by John of Austria (1545–78). About 10 000 Christian galley slaves were freed.

leprosy A chronic disease, occurring almost entirely in tropical countries, caused by the bacterium *Mycobacterium leprae* (which is related to the tuberculosis bacillus). Leprosy is caught only by close personal contact with an infected person. There are two forms of the disease. In one, lumps appear on the skin, which—together with the nerves—becomes thickened and progressively destroyed, resulting in deformity. The other form usually produces only discoloured patches on the skin associated with loss of sensation in the affected areas. There are now potent drugs —sulphones—available to cure the disease.

lepton. See particle physics.

lesbianism. See homosexuality.

Lesbos (Modern Greek name: Lésvos) A Greek island in the E Aegean Sea, situated close to the mainland of Turkey. Settled about 1000 BC, it is associated with the Greek lyric poet Sappho. Lesbos was a member of the Delian League. Area: 1630 sq km (629 sq mi). Population (1981): 104 620. Chief town: Mytilene.

Lesotho, Kingdom of (name until 1966: Basutoland) A small mountainous country in SE Africa, enclosed by South Africa. *History*: Basutoland came under British protection in 1868 and direct British administration in 1884. In 1966 it became an independent kingdom within the Commonwealth. Following a military coup in 1986 Gen Justin Lekhanya came to power. Head of state: King Letsie III. Official languages: Sesotho and English. Official currency: loti of 100 lisente. Area: 30 340 sq km (11 716 sq mi). Population (1988 est): 1 670 000. Capital: Maseru.

Lesseps, Ferdinand de (1805–94) French diplomat, who supervised the construction of the Suez Canal, which was completed in 1869. A subsequent project to construct the Panama Canal ended in disaster when Lesseps was prosecuted for pocketing funds.

Lesser Antilles (former name: Caribbees) A West Indian group of islands, comprising a chain extending from Puerto Rico to the N coast of Venezuela. They include the Leeward and Windward Islands, Barbados, Trinidad and Tobago, and the Netherlands Antilles.

Lessing, Doris (1919–) British novelist. Born in Iran and brought up in Rhodesia, she came to England in 1949. Political and social themes dominate her fiction, notably the sequence of five novels entitled *Children of Violence* (1952–69) and *The Golden Notebook* (1962). Later novels include *The Good Terrorist* (1985), and *The Fifth Child* (1988).

Lettish. See Latvian.

lettuce A plant, *Lactuca sativa*, of the daisy family, probably from the Near East and widely cultivated as a salad plant. It has juicy leaves, rich in vitamin A, and is usually eaten fresh. Cos lettuce has long crisp leaves and oval heads while cabbage lettuce has round or flattened heads and often curly leaves.

leucocyte (*or* white blood cell) A colourless cell found in large numbers in the blood. There are several kinds, all involved in the body's defence mechanisms. Granulocytes and monocytes destroy and feed on bacteria and other microorganisms that cause infection (*see also* phagocyte). The lymphocytes are involved with the production of *antibodies.

leukaemia A disease in which the blood contains an abnormally large number of white blood cells (*see* leucocyte) that do not function properly. Leukaemia is a type of cancer of the blood-forming tissues, and there are various different types, depending on the type of white cell affected. Certain leukaemias are fairly common in children and young adults; some can now often be controlled by means of radiotherapy or anticancer drugs. Leukaemias in old people are often not so severe and may not need any treatment.

Levellers An extremist English Puritan sect (*see* Puritanism), active 1647–49. They campaigned for a written constitution, extension of the right to vote, and abolition of the monarchy and of other social distinctions (hence their name).

Lewes 50 52N 0 01E A market town in SE England, the administrative centre of East Sussex, on the River Ouse. At the battle of Lewes (1264) Henry III was defeated by the rebel barons under Simon de Montfort. Population (1981): 77 507.

Lewis, C. Day. See Day Lewis, C(ecil).

Lewis, C(live) S(taples) (1898–1963) British scholar and writer. He wrote science-fiction including *Out of the Silent Planet* (1938), children's books set in the land of Narnia, and works on religious themes, notably *The Problem of Pain* (1940), *The Screwtape Letters* (1942), and *Mere Christianity* (1952).

Lewis, Carl (Frederick Carleton L.; 1961–) US athlete. He won the long jump, 100 metres, 200 metres, and 4 × 100 metres relay at the 1984 Olympic Games and the 100 metres at the 1988 Olympic Games.

Lewis, (Percy) Wyndham (1882–1957) British novelist and painter. In many theoretical works and brilliant satirical novels, which include *The Apes of God* (1930) and the trilogy *The Human Age* (1928–55), he attacked the liberal cultural establishment. He helped found the art movement vorticism.

Lewis with Harris The largest island of the Outer Hebrides, separated from the coast of NW Scotland by the Minch. Lewis in the N is linked with Harris by a narrow isthmus. It is famous for its Harris tweed. Area: 2134 sq km (824 sq mi). Population (1981): 23 390. Chief town: Stornoway.

lexicography The writing of dictionaries. Dictionaries can be monolingual (dealing with only one language) or bi- or multi-lingual (giving equivalents of words in other languages). Monolingual dictionaries vary in style: some list definitions in historical order, while others list them in order of current usage; some offer guidance on pronunciation, usage, *etymology, etc., while others do not. The most famous English dictionaries are Samuel *Johnson's *Dictionary* (1755) and the *Oxford English Dictionary on Historical Principles* (1884–1928; chief editor Sir James Murray). The best-known American dictionary is Noah Webster's *American Dictionary of the English Language* (1828).

Leyden. *See* Leiden.

Lhasa 29 41N 91 10E A city in W China, the capital of Tibet, surrounded by mountains. As the traditional centre of *Tibetan Buddhism, it is the site of many temples, monasteries, and of the Potala, the former palace of the Dalai Lama, the priest-ruler. Since the Chinese occupation (1951) many Tibetans have fled, including the Dalai Lama following the 1959 uprising; there were riots against the Chinese in the late 1980s. Population (1982 est): 110 000.

libel. *See* defamation.

Liberal Democrats. *See* Social and Liberal Democratic Party.

Liberal Party (UK) A political party that grew out of the *Whig party. The heyday of the party was from the mid-19th century to World War I, under the prime ministers *Gladstone, *Campbell-Bannerman, *Asquith, and *Lloyd George. Conflict between Asquith and Lloyd George led to a split in the party after World War I, and in 1922 the Labour Party replaced the Liberals as the official opposition. Under the leadership of David *Steel, the party made a political alliance with the newly-formed Social Democratic Party in 1981; in 1988 it merged with the SDP to form the *Social and Liberal Democratic Party under Paddy *Ashdown.

Liberia, Republic of A country in West Africa, on the Atlantic Ocean. *Economy*: the main food crops are rice and cassava. The main cash crop is rubber. Liberia's rich mineral resources form the basis of the country's economy, especially high-grade iron ore and diamonds. With many foreign vessels, Liberia's merchant fleet is the largest in the world. *History*: it was founded in 1822 by the American Colonization Society as a settlement for freed American slaves. In 1847 it became the Free and Independent Republic of Liberia. It has had considerable US aid. In 1980 the president Dr William R. Tolbert, Jr (1913–80) was as-

sassinated in a military coup led by Master Sergeant Samuel Doe, who was elected president in 1985. Doe died in civil war in 1990, when rival rebel forces, led by Charles Taylor and Prince Yormie Johnson, contested control of Liberia. Official language: English. Official currency: Liberian dollar of 100 cents. Area: 111 400 sq km (43 000 sq mi). Population (1988 est): 2 436 000. Capital and main port: Monrovia.

Library of Congress The national library of the USA founded in 1800. First housed in the Capitol, it was moved to its present site in Washington in 1897. It contains over 60 million items, and its system of classification is widely used in academic libraries.

libretto (Italian: little book) The words of an opera or operetta. *Wagner and *Berlioz wrote their own libretti. Notable partnerships between librettists and composers include da Ponte (1749–1838) and Mozart, Boito and Verdi, and Gilbert and Sullivan.

Libreville 0 25N 9 25E The capital of Gabon, a port in the NW on the Gabon Estuary. It was founded by the French in the 19th century, when freed slaves were sent there. Population (1985 est): 350 000.

Librium. *See* benzodiazepines.

Libya (official name: Great Socialist People's Libyan Arab Jamahiriya) A country in N Africa, on the Mediterranean Sea, divided into the three main areas (provinces until 1963) of Cyrenaica, Tripolitania, and Fezzan. *Economy*: between 1955 and 1970 oil was discovered, notably at Zelten (1959). Libya is now one of the world's major oil producers. Subsistence agriculture and livestock farming are important. *History*: during the 16th century the area came under Turkish domination and in 1912 was annexed by Italy. It was the scene of heavy fighting in World War II; the French occupied Fezzan and the British occupied Cyrenaica and Tripolitania. In 1951 the United Kingdom of Libya was formed and the Emir of Cyrenaica, Mohammed Idris Al-Senussi (1889–1983), became its first king. He was deposed in a coup led by Col Moammar al-*Gaddafi in 1969 and Libya was proclaimed a republic. In 1973 Gaddafi introduced a cultural revolution based on Islamic principles. In 1986 Libyan terrorist activity precipitated raids on Libyan cities by US jets. Official language: Arabic; English and Italian are also spoken. Official currency: Libyan dinar of 1000 millemes. Area: 1 759 540 sq km (679 216 sq mi). Population (1987 est): 3 883 000. Capital: Tripoli.

lichee. *See* litchi.

lichens A large group of plants consisting of two components, an alga and a fungus. Millions of algal cells are interwoven with fungal filaments to form the lichen body (a thallus), which may be crusty, scaly, leafy, or stalked and shrublike in appearance. Lichens occur in almost all areas of the world, mainly on tree trunks, rocks, and soil, and can survive in extremely harsh conditions. They normally reproduce asexually.

Liechtenstein, Principality of A small country in central Europe, between Switzerland and Austria. *Economy*: farming, and, since World War II, light industry. Tourism and postage stamps are also important. *History:* the principality was formed from the union of the counties of Vaduz and Schellenberg in 1719 and was part of the Holy Roman Empire until 1806. Head of state: Prince Hans Adam. Head of government: Hans Brunhart. Official language: German. Official religion: Roman Catholic. Official currency: Swiss franc of 100 centimes (*or* Rappen). Area: 160 sq km (62 sq mi). Population (1988 est): 28 181. Capital: Vaduz.

lie detector An instrument designed to detect whether a person is lying by measuring such factors as blood pressure, respiration rate, skin conductivity, and pulse rate. A sudden change in these factors in a person being questioned is taken to indicate that he is under stress and may be telling a lie. Lie detectors are not usually accepted in a court of law.

Liège (Flemish name: Luik) 50 38N 5 35E An industrial city in E Belgium, on the River Meuse. It has many old churches, including St Martin's (692 AD). Population (1988 est): 200 312.

life The process by which an organism takes nonliving materials from its surroundings and uses them in order to grow, repair itself, and reproduce itself (i.e. produce living offspring). *See also* animal; plant.
Life on earth is thought to have started between 4500 and 3000 million years ago. The atmosphere then consisted chiefly of the gases methane, hydrogen, and ammonia, and water vapour. From these materials simple organic molecules (such as amino acids, proteins, and fatty acids) were formed as a result of energy supplied by the sun's radiation, lightning, and volcanic activity. The first cells may have been formed by chance, as simple envelopes of protein and fat molecules. However, for it to have life such a cell would need enzyme molecules (necessary to perform primitive fermentations) and nucleic acid molecules, such as RNA and DNA, capable of directing the chemical processes of the cell and of passing on these directions to following generations. In the course of time the process of photosynthesis evolved in the first simple green plants. This led to the gradual build-up of oxygen in the atmosphere, which started about 2000 million years ago; by about 400 million years ago the *ozone layer in the upper atmosphere was sufficiently dense to shield the land from the sun's harmful ultraviolet radiation, enabling plants and animals to move from the seas and oceans onto the land. With increasing oxygen levels, aerobic respiration—the most efficient method of energy utilization—was adopted by most living organisms.

Liffey, River A river in the E Republic of Ireland, rising in the Wicklow Mountains and flowing mainly W and NE through Dublin to Dublin Bay. Length: 80 km (50 mi).

ligament A strong fibrous tissue that joins one bone to another at a *joint. Ligaments are flexible but do not stretch: they increase the stability of the joint and limit its movements to certain directions. Unusual stresses on a joint often damage ("pull") a ligament, as occurs in a "twisted" ankle.

light The form of *electromagnetic radiation to which the eye is sensitive. The wavelength of light varies from 740 nanometres (red light) to 400 nanometres (blue light), white light consisting of a mixture of all the colours of the visible spectrum. *Newton supported a corpuscular theory of light in which a luminous body was believed to emit particles of light. This theory adequately explained reflection but failed to explain other observed effects. The wave theory, supported in the 19th century by Augustin Fresnel (1788–1827) and Jean Foucault (1819–68), adequately explains *refraction, *diffraction, *interference, and *polarized light. It achieved a mathematical basis when *Maxwell showed that light is a form of electromagnetic radiation. The wave theory, however, does not explain the *photoelectric effect and *Einstein used the *quantum theory to postulate that in some cases light is best regarded as consisting of packets (quanta) of energy called photons. The present view is that both electromagnetic theory and quantum theory are needed to explain light. *See also* speed of light.

light-emitting diode. *See* semiconductor diode.

lighthouse A tall structure, built on a coastal promontory or cape or on an island at sea, equipped with a powerful beacon, visible at some distance, to mark an obstruction or other hazard. Modern lighthouses are also equipped with radio beacons. Both light and radio signals are emitted in a unique pattern to enable vessels to identify the lighthouse producing them.

lightning An electrical discharge in the atmosphere, accompanied by an intense flash of light, caused by the build up of electrical charges in a cloud. The potential difference causing the discharge may be as high as one thousand million volts. The electricity then discharges itself in a lightning flash, which may be between the cloud and the ground or, much more commonly, between two clouds or parts of a cloud. Thunder is the noise made by the rapid expansion of air heated by the discharge or its echoes.

lightning conductor A metal rod connected to the ground and placed at the top of buildings, etc., to protect them from damage by lightning. It acts by providing an easy low-resistance path to earth for the lightning current.

light year A unit of distance, used in astronomy, equal to the distance travelled by light in one year. 1 light year = 9.46×10^{15} metres or 5.88×10^{12} miles.

lignin A complex chemical deposited in plant cell walls to add extra strength and support. It is the main constituent of *wood cells, allowing the trunk to support the heavy crown of leaves and branches.

lignum vitae Wood from *Guaiacum officinale*, a tropical American evergreen tree. Lignum vitae is hard, dense, greenish-brown, and rich in fat (making it waterproof). It was formerly thought to have medicinal properties: its name (from the Latin) means "wood of life."

Liguria A region in NW Italy. It consists of a narrow strip of land between the Apennines and Maritime Alps in the N and the Gulf of Genoa in the S. Industry and tourism are both important. Area: 5415 sq km (2091 sq mi). Population (1987): 1 749 572. Capital: Genoa.

lilac A deciduous bush or small tree of the olive family. The species *Syringa vulgaris*, native to temperate Eurasia, is often grown in gardens. It has dense clusters of white, purple, or pink tubular fragrant flowers with four flaring lobes.

Lille 50 39N 3 05E A city in N France, the capital of the Nord department on the River Deûle. It is at the centre of a large industrial complex. Population (1983): 189 500.

Lillie, Beatrice (Constance Sylvia Munston, Lady Peel; 1898–1989) British actress, born in Canada, best known for her performances in revues and cabaret.

Lilongwe 13 58S 33 49E The capital of Malawi since 1975. Population (1985 est): 186 800.

lily A flowering plant native to N temperate regions and widely grown as garden and pot plants. Lilies grow from bulbs and produce clusters of showy flowers, usually with backward-curving petals. Some popular species are the tiger lily (*Lilium tigrinum*), from China and Japan, 60–120 cm high with purple-spotted golden flowers; the Eurasian Madonna lily (*L. candida*), 60–120 cm high with pure-white flowers; and the turk's-cap or martagon lily (*L. martagon*), also from Eurasia, 90–150 cm high, the purplish-pink flowers of which are marked with darker spots.
The name is also applied to numerous other unrelated plants, such as the *arum lily, and *leopard lily.

lily-of-the-valley A fragrant plant, *Convallaria majalis*, of the lily family, native to Eurasia and E North America and a popular garden plant. Growing from creeping underground stems (rhizomes), its stem bears a cluster of white bell-shaped flowers.

Lima 12 06S 77 03W The capital of Peru, situated in the E of the country near its Pacific port of Callao. Founded by Pizarro in 1535, it became the main base of Spanish power in Peru. Notable buildings include the 16th-century cathedral and university. Population (1988 est): 417 900.

Lima bean A plant, *Phaseolus lunatus*, of the pea family, also called butter bean or Madagascar bean, native to South America but widely cultivated in the tropics and subtropics as a source of protein. It is easily stored when dry.

Limassol 34 40N 33 03E A town in Cyprus, on the S coast. It is the island's second largest town and a major port. Population (1990): 121 300.

Limburg 1. A former duchy in W Europe, divided in 1839 between Belgium and the Netherlands. 2. (French name: Limbourg) A province in NE Belgium, bordering on the Netherlands. The N is an industrial region with rich coalfields. The S is chiefly agricultural. Area: 2422 sq km (935 sq mi). Population (1987 est): 736 981. Capital: Hasselt. 3. A province in the SE Netherlands. Coalmining has declined in recent years. Agriculture is varied. Area: 2208 sq km (852 sq mi). Population (1988 est): 1 095 424. Capital: Maastricht.

lime (botany) 1. A large deciduous tree, also called linden. Growing to a height of 30 m, it has toothed heart-shaped leaves and fragrant pale-yellow flowers that hang in small clusters on a long winged stalk. The small round fruits remain attached to the papery wing when shed. 2. A *citrus fruit produced by a tree, *Citrus aurantifolia*, growing to a height of about 4 m and cultivated in the tropics. Limes have a thick greenish-yellow skin and acid-tasting pulp; the juice is used to flavour food and drinks.

lime (chemistry) Calcium oxide (*or* quicklime; CaO), calcium hydroxide (*or* slaked lime; Ca(OH)$_2$), or, loosely, calcium salts in general. Ca(OH)$_2$ is prepared by reacting CaO with water and is used in *cement. CaO is used in making paper, in *steel manufacture, and in softening water.

limerick A short form of comic verse having five lines, the third and fourth being shorter than the other three, and usually rhyming aabba, as in:
There was a young lady of Lynn
Who was so uncommonly thin
That when she essayed
To drink lemonade,
She slipped through the straw and fell in.
The form, the origin of which is uncertain, was popularized by Edward *Lear in the 19th century.

Limerick A county in the SW Republic of Ireland, in Munster bordering on the River Shannon estuary. It consists chiefly of lowlands rising to hills in the S. Dairy farming is important. Area: 2686 sq km (1037 sq mi). Population (1986): 164 204. County town: Limerick.

limestone A common *sedimentary rock consisting largely of carbonates, especially calcium carbonate (calcite) or *dolomite. Most limestones were deposited in the sea in warm clear water, but some limestones were formed in fresh water. Organic limestones, including *chalk, consist of fossil skeletal material. Precipitated limestones include evaporites and oolites (spherically grained calcite). Clastic limestones consist of fragments of pre-existing limestones. Marble is metamorphosed limestone. Limestone is used as a building stone, in the manufacture of cement and glass, for agricultural lime, for road metal, and in smelting.

limitation, statutes of The Acts of Parliament that specify a time (period of limitation) within which legal proceedings must be started by any person seeking to enforce a right; failing this, the right of action is lost.

limited liability The restriction of a shareholder's obligation to meet company debts in the event of its going into liquidation (*see* bankruptcy). The liability of shareholders of incorporated companies is restricted either to the nominal amount of their shares ("company limited by shares") or to the amount that they have agreed to contribute if the company is wound up ("company limited by guarantee").

Limoges 45 50N 1 15E A city in W France, the capital of the Haute-Vienne department on the River Vienne. The centre of the French porcelain industry, it has Roman remains and a cathedral (13th–16th centuries). Population (1990): 175 646.

limpet A widely distributed sea snail with a flattened shell and powerful muscular foot for clinging to rocks and other surfaces. The true limpets are oval-shaped and up to 10 cm long whereas the keyhole limpets tend to be smaller and have an opening in the shell for the escape of waste products.

Limpopo River A river in SE Africa. Rising as the Crocodile River in the Witwatersrand, South Africa, it flows generally NE through Mozambique, to the Indian Ocean, forming part of the border between the Transvaal and Botswana. Length: 1770 km (1100 mi).

Lincoln 53 14N 0 33W A city in E central England, the administrative centre of Lincolnshire on the River Witham. The British settlement became Lindum Colonia under the Romans, at the intersection of Fosse Way and Ermine Street. The castle was begun in 1068 and the cathedral in 1075. Population (1988 est): 80 600.

Lincoln, Abraham (1809–65) US statesman; Republican president (1861–65). Lincoln became, in 1847, member of Congress for Illinois. He opposed the extension of slavery to the new western states and in 1856 joined the newly formed antislavery Republican Party. Elected president on the slavery issue just before the outbreak of the *Civil War, in 1863 Lincoln proclaimed the freedom of slaves in the South (the Emancipation Proclamation) and gave his famous *Gettysburg Address recalling the principles of equality established by America's founders. He oversaw the 13th amendment prohibiting slavery (1865) and supported the generous *Reconstruction measures but was assassinated a few days after the South surrendered.

Lincolnshire A county in E England, bordering on the North Sea. It is generally low lying, including part of the Fens, with the Lincolnshire Edge (a limestone ridge) in the W and the Lincolnshire Wolds in the E. It is mainly agricultural producing arable crops and livestock; horticulture is also important. Area: 5885 sq km (2272 sq mi). Population (1990 est): 602 155. Administrative centre: Lincoln.

Lincoln's Inn. *See* Inns of Court.

Lind, Jenny (1820–87) Swedish soprano, known as "the Swedish nightingale." She performed in opera and on the concert platform.

Lindbergh, Charles A(ugustus) (1902–74) US aviator who made the first solo nonstop flight across the Atlantic Ocean, from New York to Paris (1927), in the monoplane *Spirit of St Louis*. His two-year-old son was kidnapped and murdered in 1932.

Lindemann, Frederick Alexander, 1st Viscount Cherwell (1886–1957) German-born British physicist, who became Churchill's scientific adviser in World War II. Criticized for supporting mass bombing of civilians, Lindemann was highly praised by Churchill, who made him paymaster-general (1951–53).

linden. *See* lime.
Lindisfarne. *See* Holy Island.
linear accelerator. *See* accelerator.
linear motor A form of electric induction motor in which the stator and the rotor are linear instead of cylindrical and parallel instead of coaxial. The development of linear motors as a method of traction for monorail intercity trains has been proposed by E. R. Laithwaite (1921–89). In this arrangement one winding would be in the train and the other on the single rail, thus obviating the need for rotating parts.

linen A fabric manufactured from *flax (*Linum usitatissimum*), probably the first textile of plant origin. Flax growing was brought to Britain by the Romans and in the 16th century a flourishing trade grew up, especially in Scotland and Northern Ireland. Greatly reduced by the 18th-century expansion of the cotton trade, and even more so by the advent of man-made fibres, these strong absorbent fibres now constitute less than 2% of world fibre production.

line of force. *See* field.

linguistics The scientific study of language. Modern linguistics has three main branches: *semantics, grammar, and *phonetics. Various specialized interests exist within the field of linguistics. **Comparative linguistics** compares languages either to establish the history of and relationships among related languages (e.g. the Indo-European family) or to test theories about linguistics by comparing unrelated languages (*see also* etymology). The main contribution of **structural linguistics**, which developed in the early 20th century, was to free linguistics from the historical and comparative approach, viewing language in terms of structure. **Sociolinguistics** deals with social aspects of language, including such matters as how language affects and reflects the role and status of individuals within the community, attitudes to dialect and "correctness," linguistic taboos and preferences, bilingualism, etc. **Psycholinguistics** is the more recent branch of linguistics that deals with psychological aspects of language, including how children acquire language, how language is stored in and produced by the brain, the relationship between meaning and memory, etc.

Linnaeus, Carolus (Carl Linné; 1707–78) Swedish botanist, who established the principles for naming and classifying plants and animals. As a result of his botanical studies, Linnaeus proposed a system for classifying plants based on their flower parts (*see* binomial nomenclature). He published *Systema naturae* in 1735 followed by *Genera plantarum* (1737) and *Species plantarum* (1753). Linnaeus also applied his system to the animal kingdom.

linnet A small *finch, *Acanthis cannabina*, occurring in dry open regions of Europe and Asia. It feeds on the seeds of common weed plants. The female has a dull brown-streaked plumage; the male has a crimson crown and breast, a greyish head, and a red-brown back with darker wings and tail. Male linnets have a beautiful flutelike voice.

linseed The flat oval seed of cultivated *flax, which is a source of linseed oil, used in paints, inks, varnishes, oilcloth, and sailcloth. The crushed seed residues form linseed meal, an important protein feed for cattle, sheep, and pigs.

Linz 48 19N 14 18E The third largest city in Austria, the capital of Upper Austria on the River Danube. Its many historical buildings include two 13th-century baroque churches. Population (1983 est): 199 910.

lion A large carnivorous mammal, *Panthera leo*, one of the big *cats. Lions are found mainly in Africa (there are a few in India). They are heavily built with sandy-coloured coats: the shaggy-maned males grow to 2.8 m while females lack a mane and are more lightly built. Both sexes have a thin tail with a tuft at the end. Lions inhabit grasslands, living in groups (prides).

lipids A group of chemical compounds that includes *fats, *oils, *waxes, phospholipids, sphingolipids, and *steroids. Fats and oils function as energy reserves in plants and animals and form a major source of dietary energy in animals. Phospholipids form part of the structure of cell membranes, and sphingolipids are found mainly in nerve tissues. Steroids have many important derivatives, including cholesterol, bile salts, and certain hormones. Lipids often occur in association with proteins as lipoproteins.

Lipizzaner A breed of horse long associated with the Spanish Riding School in Vienna, where they are trained for spectacular displays. It is named after the breeding herd founded by Archduke Charles at Lipizza, near Trieste, in 1580. The Lipizzaner has a short back, strong hindquarters, a powerful neck, and a small head. Born black, they become grey as they age. Height: 1.47–1.52 m.

Lippershey, Hans (died c. 1619) Dutch lens grinder, who built the first *telescope. News of it eventually reached *Galileo, who built his own telescope.

Lippi, Fra Filippo (c. 1406–69) An early Renaissance Florentine painter, who was a Carmelite monk from 1421 to about 1432. He was frequently patronized by the Medici but his greatest works are his fresco decorations for the choir of Prato Cathedral (1452–64), showing scenes from the lives of St John the Baptist and St Stephen. He is also noted for his Madonnas. He kidnapped and later married a nun, Lucrezia Buti; their son, **Filippino Lippi** (1457–1504), was also a painter.

liquefaction of gases Gases are liquefied in several ways. If the temperature of the gas is below its critical temperature, it can be liquefied simply by compressing it. If the critical temperature is too low for this, the cascade process can be used. In this a gas with a high critical temperature is first liquefied by compression and then allowed to cool by evaporation under reduced pressure. This gas cools a second gas below its critical temperature, so that it in turn can be liquefied, evaporated, and cooled still further. Thus the temperature is reduced in stages. Other methods include cooling by adiabatic expansion.

Liquefied Petroleum Gas (LPG) One or more gases, such as propane or butane, stored under pressure as a liquid. LPG is a product of *oil refining and is also produced from *natural gas. Most of the LPG produced is sold in low-pressure cylinders for heating or used as a raw material for chemical manufacture.

liquid crystal A substance exhibiting some liquid properties, especially fluidity, and some crystalline properties. As liquid crystals change their reflectivity when an electric potential is applied to them, they are used to display numbers, letters, etc., on the **liquid crystal displays** (LCDs) of digital watches, electronic calculators, etc.

liquids A state of matter between that of *gases and the *solid state. Liquids assume the shape of a container in the same way as gases but being incompressible do not expand to fill the container. Intermolecular forces are considerably stronger than in gases but weaker than in solids.

liquorice A plant, *Glycyrrhiza glabra*, of the pea family, native to S Europe but cultivated throughout warm temperate regions. It bears clusters of blue flowers and long flat pods and its sweet roots, up to 1 m long, are a source of flavouring for confectionery, tobacco, and medicines.

Lisbon (Portuguese name: Lisboa) 38 44N 9 08W The capital of Portugal, in the SW on the River Tagus. The country's chief seaport. A major industrial and commercial centre, its historic buildings include the Tower of Belém and the Jerónimos Monastery; its university was founded in 1290. *History*: an organized community under the Roman Empire, it was captured by the Portuguese in the 12th century and became their capital in 1256. In 1755 it was almost totally destroyed by an earthquake. It has expanded considerably in the 20th century and in 1966 one of the world's longest suspension bridges was opened across the River Tagus. Population (1985 est): 827 800.

Lister, Joseph, 1st Baron (1827–1912) British surgeon, who pioneered antiseptic techniques in surgery. In 1865, while surgeon at Glasgow Royal Infirmary, Lister realized the significance of *Pasteur's germ theory of disease in trying to prevent the infection of wounds following surgical operations. Lister devised a means of eliminating contamination and introduced carbolic acid as an antiseptic to dress wounds. His antiseptic procedures eventually became standard practice in hospitals everywhere.

Liszt, Franz (Ferencz L.; 1811–86) Hungarian pianist and composer, considered the greatest performer of his time. As a composer he invented the symphonic poem and made use of advanced harmonies and original forms. His works include much piano music, the *Faust Symphony* (1854–57) and *Dante Symphony* (1855–56), and the symphonic poem *Les Préludes* (1854).

litchi (lychee *or* lichee) A Chinese tree, *Litchi chinensis*, cultivated in the tropics and subtropics for its fruits. The fruit is round with a warty deep-pink rind. The white translucent watery flesh has a sweet acid flavour and encloses a single large brown seed.

lithium (Li) The lightest metal (relative density 0.534), discovered by Arfvedson in 1817. It is an *alkali metal. It occurs in nature in various minerals as well as in brine, from which it is extracted commercially. The metal has the highest specific heat capacity of any solid element. It is corrosive, combustible, and reacts with water. Because of its efficiency in reflecting neutrons, lithium has important applications in both the hydrogen bomb and proposed *thermonuclear reactors. It forms salts, like the other alkali metals, and the hydride LiH. At no 3; at wt 6.941; mp 180.54°C; bp 1347°C.

lithography. *See* printing.

Lithuanian A language belonging to the E division of the Baltic languages division of the *Indo-European family, spoken mainly by the Lithuanians of the Lithuanian SSR, where it is the official language. Lithuanian is closely related to *Latvian. It is written in a Latin alphabet.

Lithuanian Soviet Socialist Republic (*or* **Lithuania**) A constituent republic in the NW Soviet Union, on the Baltic Sea. *History*: one of the largest states in medieval Europe, in the 14th century Lithuania united with Poland under the Jagiellon dynasty, passing in the 18th century to Russia. It became independent in 1918 but became an SSR of the Soviet Union in 1940. During World War II the large Jewish minority was virtually exterminated. In the late 1980s nationalists demanded Lithuanian independence. Area: 65 200 sq km (25 170 sq mi). Population (1986): 3 603 000. Capital: Vilnius.

litmus A soluble compound obtained from certain lichens. Litmus turns red in an acid solution and blue in an alkaline solution. It is therefore used as an *indicator, often as **litmus paper**, strips of paper impregnated with litmus.

litre A unit of volume in the *metric system formerly defined as the volume of one kilogram of pure water under specified conditions. In *SI units the litre is a special name for the cubic decimetre.

Little Bighorn, Battle of the (25 June, 1876) The battle fought on the S bank of the Little Bighorn River in which Gen *Custer and his men were massacred by Sioux Indians led by *Sitting Bull (Custer's Last Stand). It was one of the battles fought to seize the American West for White settlement.

liver A large glandular organ, weighing 1.2–1.6 kg, situated in the upper right region of the abdomen, just below the diaphragm. The liver has many important functions concerned with how the body uses absorbed foods. It converts excess glucose into glycogen, which it stores and reconverts into glucose when required; it breaks down excess amino acids (from proteins) into *urea; and it stores and converts fats. The liver forms and secretes *bile, which contains the breakdown products of worn-out red blood cells. It also manufactures the blood-clotting factors, proteins of blood plasma, and—in the fetus—red blood cells. It also breaks down (detoxifies) poisonous substances, including alcohol.

liver fluke A parasitic *flatworm that inhabits the bile duct of sheep, cattle, and man. The common liver fluke (*Fasciola hepatica*) produces larvae that enter marshland snails to develop further. The larvae then leave the snail to infect grazing animals (or, rarely, man). Larvae of the Chinese liver fluke (*Opisthorchus sinensis*) develop inside both a freshwater snail and a fish

before maturing in a human host; adults are 1–2 cm long.

Liverpool 53 25N 2 55W A major port and city in NW England, the administrative centre of Merseyside, on the estuary of the River Mersey. It is linked with Birkenhead and Wallasey on the Wirral Peninsula by two tunnels under the Mersey. Notable buildings include the Royal Liver Building (1910) at the Pier Head, St George's Hall (1854), and the Roman Catholic cathedral (1962–67). *History*: originally trading with Ireland, Liverpool grew rapidly in the 18th and 19th centuries as a result of trade with the Americas and the industrialization of S Lancashire. Liverpool developed also as a cultural centre, with the Walker Art Gallery (built 1876), the Royal Liverpool Philharmonic Orchestra, and the Tate Gallery (1988) in the restored Albert Dock area. Population (1984 est): 497 300.

liverwort A *bryophyte plant found growing on moist soil, rocks, trees, etc. There are two groups: leafy liverworts, in which the plant body has stems and leaves; and thallose liverworts, which have a flat lobed liverlike body (thallus).

livery companies Descendants of the medieval craft *guilds, so called because of the special dress (livery) worn by their members on ceremonial occasions. Some, such as the Mercers, Haberdashers, and Merchant Taylors, have educational interests. In 1878 the livery companies were involved in setting up the City and Guilds of London Institute to further technical education.

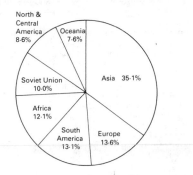

LIVESTOCK FARMING *Distribution of the world's livestock (1989; cattle, sheep, pigs, horses, asses, and mules).*

livestock farming The rearing of domesticated animals for the production of milk, meat, eggs, fibres, skins, etc.
Cattle produce milk and beef. Under European conditions, a cow may breed at any time of the year. The gestation (pregnancy) period is about 9 months, followed by about 10 months of lactation (milk production) and a 2-month dry period before calving again. A cow is known as a heifer until her second lactation. Heifers are reared either for beef or as dairy replacements and bull calves are generally castrated and reared for

beef, being known as bullocks or steers. Age at slaughter is generally about 18 months. Calves for veal are slaughtered at about 14 weeks. Sheep are farmed worldwide for meat and wool (and in some countries for milk). Under European conditions, one or two lambs per ewe are born in early spring. Males are castrated and reared for slaughter at weights of 20–45 kg. Selected females are reared as replacement ewes. Each sheep yields 2–5 kg of wool.

Pigs in modern intensive systems are housed under controlled conditions. Young females (gilts) are first mated at 7–8 months. Following the gestation period of 115 days, an average of 7–9 piglets are born per litter. Pork pigs are slaughtered at 40–50 kg, those reared for bacon at 80–100 kg.

Poultry are now usually kept indoors in an artificially controlled environment. Chicks are hatched artificially, the female birds starting to lay after about 20 weeks and producing about 250 eggs per year. Laying flocks are kept in "batteries" of cages with 3–5 birds per cage, feeding, cleaning, and egg collection being automatic. Table birds are fed freely and reach a weight of around 2 kg in 8–12 weeks. Turkeys are also reared for meat under intensive conditions.

Livingstone, David (1813–73) Scottish missionary and explorer of Africa, qualified as a doctor. He traced long stretches of the Zambezi, Shire, and Rovuma Rivers, and discovered Lake Ngami (1849), the Victoria Falls (1855), and Lake Nyasa (now Malawi). During an attempt to trace the source of the Nile (1866–73) his famous meeting with Sir Henry Morton *Stanley occurred.

Livy (Titus Livius; 59 BC–17 AD) Roman historian, noted for his massive history of Rome from its legendary foundation to the death of Drusus in 9 BC. Only 35 of the original 142 books survive.

lizard A *reptile occurring worldwide but most abundant in tropical regions. Lizards live mainly on land and have cylindrical or narrow scaly long-tailed bodies, some with limbs reduced or absent (*see* glass snake; skink), and often with crests, spines, and frills. They range in size from the smallest *geckos to the *Komodo dragon. Lizards lay leathery-shelled eggs although certain species of colder regions and many skinks bear live young.

Ljubljana (German name: Laibach) 46 04N 14 30E A city in NW Yugoslavia, the capital of Slovenia. It was largely destroyed by an earthquake in 1895. Population (1989): 335 798.

llama A hoofed mammal, *Lama glama*, of S and W South America. Up to 120 cm high at the shoulder, llamas are sure-footed, nimble, and hardy, with thick warm coats. They are now only found in the domesticated state, being used for meat, wool, and as pack animals.

Lloyd, Clive Hubert (1944–   ) West Indian cricketer. A batsman, he captained his country's team (1974–78; 1979–85) in 74 tests. He retired in 1985.

Lloyd, Harold (1893–1971) US film comedian. He appeared as a dogged little man in numerous early silent comedies, most of them featuring his use of dangerous stunts. His films include *Just Nuts* (1915), *Safety Last* (1923), and *The Freshman* (1925).

Lloyd, Marie (Matilda Wood; 1870–1922) British music-hall entertainer. Her songs, featuring cockney humour, include "Oh! Mr Porter" and "A Little of What You Fancy."

Lloyd George, David, 1st Earl (1863–1945) British statesman; Liberal prime minister (1916–22). Born in Manchester of Welsh parents, he entered parliament in 1890 and gained a reputation for radicalism as a Welsh nationalist and a supporter of the Afrikaners in the second Boer War (1899–1902). As chancellor of the exchequer (1908–15), he is best known for the so-called People's Budget (1909). This proposed higher death duties, a land value tax, and a supertax; the rejection of this budget by the House of Lords led ultimately to the 1911 Parliament Act, which reduced the Lords' power. Lloyd George also introduced old-age pensions (1908) and national insurance (1911). In World War I he served as minister of munitions (1915–16) and secretary for war (1916) before succeeding Asquith as prime minister. After the war he continued to lead a coalition government increasingly dominated by the Conservatives. He was criticized for dealing with Irish militants in the establishment of the Irish Free State (1921) and his government fell when Britain came close to war with the Turkish nationalists.

Lloyd's An association of *insurance underwriters named after the 17th-century London coffee house, owned by Edward Lloyd, where underwriters used to meet. Lloyd's was made into a corporation by Act of Parliament in 1871. The responsibility for loss is carried by groups of private underwriters, not by the corporation itself. There are over 6000 underwriters, none of whom are permitted to deal directly with the public, this being done by Lloyd's insurance brokers. The centre of business was transferred to a huge new building (by Richard Rogers) in Lime Street, London, in 1986. **Lloyd's Register of Shipping** is an organization formed by Lloyd's to inspect and list all oceangoing vessels over 100 tonnes. Lloyd's also publishes *Lloyd's List and Shipping Gazette*, giving shipping news for insurance purposes.

Lloyd Webber, Andrew (1948–   ) British composer. His musicals, some with lyrics by Tim Rice (1944–   ), include *Jesus Christ Superstar* (1970), *Evita* (1978), *Cats* (1981), *The Phantom of the Opera* (1986), and *Aspects of Love* (1989).

Llywelyn ap Gruffudd (d. 1282) The only native Prince of Wales (1258–82) to be recognized as such by England. He aided the English barons against Henry III (1263–67) and refused homage to Edward I (1276), who forced Llywelyn into submission. Llywelyn was killed in another revolt.

loach A small freshwater bony *fish found mainly in Asia, but also in Europe and N Africa. Loaches feed at night on bottom-dwelling invertebrates, which they detect by the three to six pairs of barbels around the mouth.

Lódź

lobelia A flowering plant that is found in most warm and temperate regions. The small flowers are tubular, with a two-lobed upper lip and a larger three-lobed lower lip. Ornamental species, called cardinal flowers, are usually blue or red.

lobster A large marine *crustacean that has a long abdomen ending in a tailfan. True lobsters have bodies made up of several segments, a pair of pincers, four pairs of walking legs, and several pairs of swimming legs (swimmerets). They live on the ocean bottom, feeding on seaweed and animals. Many species are commercially important as food.

local government The administration of an area. In the UK local government has developed from the Anglo-Saxon times. In 1835 178 municipal councils were established, elected by rate-payers. These gradually took over a wide range of responsibilities, including the police and public health. County councils were established in 1888. In 1894 borough and urban district councils were created in urban areas and parish councils in rural areas. The Local Government Act (1972) divided England and Wales into 53 *counties. These are divided into districts, and they in turn into parishes or, in Wales, communities. District councils are responsible for a number of important services, including education, housing, and refuse collection. A similar system was established in Scotland in 1973 but in Northern Ireland local government is in the hands of 26 district councils. Local-government spending is paid for by the community charge (*see* poll tax), business rates, rent, borrowing, and central-government grants.

Locarno Pact (1925) A series of treaties between Germany, France, Belgium, Poland, Czechoslovakia, the UK, and Italy, signed in the Swiss town of Locarno. The most important was an agreement between France, Germany, and Belgium, guaranteed by the UK and Italy, to maintain Germany's borders with France and Belgium and the demilitarized zone of the Rhineland (invaded by Hitler in 1936).

Loch Ness 57 15N 4 30W A lake in Glen More Valley, NW Scotland. Length: 36 km (22.5 mi). Depth: 229 m (754 ft). The existence of the **Loch Ness monster**, said to inhabit the lake, remains unconfirmed.

Locke, John (1632–1704) English philosopher. His greatest work, the *Essay concerning Human Understanding* (1690), reveals him as a pioneer of empiricism. Locke's two works *Of Government* (1690) were enormously influential in developing modern ideas of liberal democracy. He dismissed any divine right to kingship and supported liberal government.

lockjaw. *See* tetanus.

locomotive An engine that draws a train on a *railway. The first locomotives, designed by Trevithick and *Stephenson, were driven by steam engines and steam dominated the railways until the end of World War II. Thousands of steam locomotives are still in use throughout the world. However, the steam engine has a low efficiency, it takes a long time to become operational while steam is raised, it uses an awkward and dirty solid fuel (which it has to pull with it in a

LOCOMOTIVE *Stephenson's "Rocket" was the first locomotive to combine a multi-tubular boiler and a blast pipe. It was designed for the Liverpool-Manchester railway, which opened in 1830.*

tender immediately behind the engine), and it creates pollution. For these reasons steam locomotives have largely been replaced in the industrial countries by electric, Diesel-electric, or Diesel trains, all of which have greater efficiencies.

Where the traffic justifies the cost of installing overhead wires or a conductor rail, electric trains are usually preferred, as it is better to generate electricity in a power station than in the locomotive. When Diesel engines are used, these are either coupled hydraulically to the wheels, using a hydraulic torque converter (or fluid flywheel) and a gearbox, or to an electric generator or alternator, which produces current to power electric motors that drive the wheels. The first Diesel-electric train was used in Sweden in 1912 and the first Diesel-hydraulic in Germany a year later. Experiments in recent years have included locomotives running by magnetic levitation.

locust (botany) An evergreen Mediterranean tree, *Ceratonia siliqua*, of the pea family, also called carob tree. 12–15 m high, it produces leathery pods containing a sweet edible pulp and small flat beans. The black locust (*Robinia pseudoacacia*), also called robinia and false acacia, is a North American tree widely cultivated for ornament. Up to 24 m tall, it has deeply ridged dark-brown bark, hanging clusters of white flowers, and black pods.

locust (zoology) A *grasshopper that, when conditions are favourable, can reproduce very quickly to form huge swarms, which migrate long distances and devour all the crops and other vegetation on which they settle. Economically important species include the migratory locust (*Locusta migratoria*), about 55 mm long (all locusts are relatively large), found throughout Africa and S Europe and Asia and eastward to Australia and New Zealand; and the desert locust (*Schistocerca gregaria*), occurring from N Africa to the Punjab.

lodestone. *See* magnetite.

Lódź 51 49N 19 28E The second largest city in Poland. It developed rapidly during the 19th century and is now a leading industrial centre. Population (1985): 849 000.

loess A deposit consisting of wind-born dust from desert or vegetation-free areas at the margins of ice sheets. In Europe loess occurs in Germany, Belgium, and NE France. Deep well-drained soils develop from loess.

Logan, Mount 60 31N 140 22W The highest mountain in Canada, in SW Yukon in the St Elias Mountains. Height: 6050 m (19 850 ft).

loganberry A trailing bramble-like shrub of the rose family that is a cross between a raspberry and a blackberry. It bears heads of red fleshy berries, which are used for preserves, puddings, and wine. It is named after James H. Logan (1841–1928), who first grew it (in California) in 1881.

logarithms A mathematical function used to make multiplication and division easier. Based on the law that $a^x \times a^y = a^{x+y}$, two numbers p and q can be multiplied together by writing them in the form $p = a^x$ and $q = a^y$ and then adding together the values of x and y (the exponents). x is called the logarithm of p to the base a, i.e. $x = \log_a p$. Pocket calculators are now preferred to logarithms as a method of computation but they remain useful mathematical functions.

logic In the widest sense, the science of reasoned argument. As a mental discipline, it is concerned not so much with applying argument in specific cases as with the general rules covering the stages of argument. *Aristotle was the first to make a systematic study of these general rules (also called syllogism). His works were the sourcebooks for medieval logicians. After the *Renaissance, philosophers became increasingly aware of limitations in Aristotle's approach. Since the 19th century logic has become mainly the province of mathematicians. *Boole and Gottlob Frege (1848–1925) were important pioneers in what is now called "mathematical logic" to separate it from the wider still current sense. *Russell called "logic... the youth of mathematics, and mathematics... the manhood of logic."

logical positivism A philosophical movement that arose from the *Vienna Circle in the 1920s. It insisted that philosophy should be scientific. Any assertion claiming to be factual has meaning only if its truth (or falsity) can be verified. Propositions relating to *metaphysics, art, and religion cannot be verified, and are therefore meaningless.

Lohengrin In *Arthurian legend, the son of Percival (Parzival). He agrees to marry a young noblewoman, Elsa of Brabant, on condition that she does not enquire into his origins. When her curiosity overcomes her, he is taken back by his swan guide to the castle of the *Holy Grail, whence he came. The story was adapted by *Wagner in the opera *Lohengrin* (1850).

Loire, River The longest river in France. Rising in the Cévennes Mountains, it flows mainly W to the Bay of Biscay at St Nazaire, passing through Orléans, Tours, and Nantes. Its tributaries include the Allier, Vienne, and Maine. The Loire Valley is renowned for its vineyards and chateaux (Amboise, Blois, Chambord, Chaumont, Chenonceaux). It is linked by canal with the River Seine. Length: 1020 km (634 mi).

Loki In Norse mythology, a mischief-making giant with the ability to change his shape and sex, who lived among the gods until imprisoned in a cave for the murder of Balder. His offspring –Hel, the goddess of death, Jörmungandr, the evil serpent surrounding the earth, and Fenris, the wolf–are among the forces of evil, which he leads against the gods at doomsday.

Lollards The followers of the English reformer *Wycliffe. His teachings, at first confined to Oxford University, were taken up by nonacademics, including merchants, lesser clergy, and a few members of Richard II's court. Repressed during Henry IV's reign, the Lollards rebelled in 1414 led by Sir John Oldcastle (c. 1378–1417). They were defeated and the movement went underground and became increasingly working class. Many of its beliefs were adopted by the early Protestants.

Lombardo, Pietro (c. 1438–1515) Italian sculptor and architect. Lombardo worked mainly in Venice, where he was the leading sculptor of his generation. He was frequently assisted by his two sons **Antonio Lombardo** (c. 1458–c. 1516) and **Tullio Lombardo** (c. 1460–1532).

Lombardy A region in N Italy, consisting mainly of mountains in the N and lowlands in the S. It is Italy's most industrialized region. Area: 23 834 sq km (9191 sq mi). Population (1987): 8 886 402. Capital: Milan.

Lomond, Loch The largest lake in Scotland, in E Strathclyde Region. Length: about 38 km (24 mi). Width: 8 km (5 mi).

London (Latin name: Londinium) 51 30N 0 10W The capital of the UK, in SE England on the River Thames. It is one of the six largest cities in the world. London's financial centre is the **City of London**, roughly a square mile on the N bank of the Thames between Blackfriars Bridge and Tower Bridge. London's **East End**, centring on the borough of Tower Hamlets, has long provided a home for successive immigrant groups. The **West End** comprises the district around Oxford Street (constructed in the 19th century) and is the city's shopping and entertainment centre. London's cultural life is outstanding, with a large number of art galleries, museums, theatres, concert halls, and educational institutions.
Economy: the City of London is one of the world's greatest banking, commodity, shipping, and insurance centres: the *Bank of England is to be found in Threadneedle Street with the *Stock Exchange nearby, while *Lloyd's is in Lime Street. London's commercial development depended to a large extent on its port.
History: the Romans built London at the highest point at which the Thames could be forded and at the river's tidal limit–on what was later Cornhill and Ludgate Hill. London prospered in the middle ages and both the Church and the *guilds sponsored exceptional building programmes. Westminster Abbey dates from the 11th century, being largely rebuilt in the 13th century, when Southwark Cathedral was begun. To the 15th century belong the Guildhall and Lambeth Palace and to the 16th century, when London began to extend westwards, *St James'

Palace. London's population was decimated by the Plague (1665) and many of its buildings were destroyed in the Fire of the following year. Sir Christopher *Wren was responsible for much of the work of reconstruction, including 49 new parish churches in the City. Many of London's finest squares were built in the late 17th and early 18th centuries; the 19th century produced Regent's Park, the *Palace of Westminster, the Law Courts, and such railway stations as St Pancras. London was seriously damaged by fire and bomb attacks during World War II and subsequent rebuilding has consisted largely of high-rise offices and flats, including the Barbican (1973) and the National Westminster building (1977), which at 183 m (600 ft) is the tallest building in London. A new London City Airport opened in the former docklands in 1987. Area: 1580 sq km (610 sq mi). Population (1987 est): 6 770 400.

London, Jack (1876–1916) US novelist, best known for *The Call of the Wild* (1903). His other novels include *White Fang* (1906) and the autobiographical *Martin Eden* (1909).

London Bridge A bridge spanning the River Thames from the SE region of the City of London to the borough of Southwark. Bridges on this site date back to Roman times. The stone bridge built between 1176 and 1209 had a drawbridge, shops, and houses. It was replaced by a new bridge in the 1820s, designed by John Rennie (1761–1821). The present bridge was completed in 1973.

Londonderry (Derry) 55 00N 7 19W A city and port in Northern Ireland, the county town of Co Londonderry on the River Foyle. The City of London Corporation was granted Londonderry and the Irish Society established (1610) to administer it. In a famous siege (1688–89) it held out for 105 days against the forces of James II. Population (1981): 62 697.

longbow A bow of straight-grained yew used from about 1400 to about 1600. Originally Welsh, longbows were up to 1.8 m (6 ft) long and could fire a 110 cm (37 in) arrow capable of piercing chainmail and some plate armour at 183 m (200 yd) every 10 seconds.

Longfellow, Henry Wadsworth (1807–82) US poet. He achieved enormous popularity with such long poems as *Evangeline* (1847) and *The Song of Hiawatha* (1855).

Longford (Irish name: Longphort) A county in the N central Republic of Ireland, in Leinster, chiefly low lying with areas of bog. Area: 1043 sq km (403 sq mi). Population (1986): 31 491. County town: Longford.

Long Island An island in the USA, in New York state separated from the mainland by Long Island Sound. Chiefly residential with many resorts, it contains the New York City boroughs of Brooklyn and Queens and the international John F. Kennedy Airport. Area: 4462 sq km (1723 sq mi).

longitude. *See* latitude and longitude.

long jump A field event in athletics. Competitors sprint up a runway and leap as far as possible into a sandpit from a take-off board. The competitor who makes the longest jump in three or six tries is the winner. World records: men: 8.90 m (1968) by Robert Beamon (USA); women: 7.52 m (1988) by Galina Chistyakova (USSR).

Longleat An English country house near Warminster, in Wiltshire, owned by the Marquess of Bath. Dating from 1572, Longleat is typical of the Elizabethan style of architecture. The house and its grounds, originally laid out by Capability *Brown and now containing a lion safari park, are open to the public.

Long March (1934–35) The flight of the Chinese communists from the province of Jiangxi, which they were forced by the *Guomindang to leave, to Yan'an, a distance of 10 000 km (6000 mi). Over 100 000 people, led by Mao Tse-tung, took part in the heroic march but only about 30 000 reached Yan'an. The Long March established Mao as the leader of the Chinese Communist Party.

Long Parliament (1640–60) The parliament that was first summoned by Charles I of England in 1640. The deteriorating relationship between Charles and the members of the parliament led to the outbreak of the Civil War. The parliament's power declined as that of the *New Model Army increased and in 1648 its moderate members were expelled. The remaining Rump Parliament was dismissed in 1653 by Oliver Cromwell, who established the *Protectorate. The Rump was recalled in 1659 and the full membership of the Long Parliament was restored in 1660. Shortly afterwards it dissolved itself, being replaced by the Convention Parliament, which organized the *Restoration.

longship A large sailing vessel equipped with a bank of oars on each side. Longships were used by Scandinavian maritime peoples until the mid-18th century. They had square sails and very high prows and were steered by a long tiller attached to a large rudder.

longsightedness (*or* hypermetropia) Inability to see close objects clearly, because the lens of the eye focuses light to a point behind the retina (light-sensitive layer). This is less common than shortsightedness among young people, but, owing to changes in the lens with age, many people need glasses for reading by the time they are 50. This type of longsightedness is known as **presbyopia.**

loofah The fibrous skeleton of the fruit of the tropical dishcloth gourd, or vegetable sponge (*Luffa cylindrica*). The cucumber-like fruits are about 30 cm long. When mature, the pulp and seeds are removed leaving a dense network of fibres, which is used as a bath sponge, dish washer, and industrial filter.

loom. *See* weaving.

loquat A small evergreen tree, *Eriobotrya japonica*, of the rose family, native to China and Japan but cultivated in Mediterranean countries for its edible fruit.

Lorca, Federico García. *See* García Lorca, Federico.

Lord Chief Justice The presiding judge of the Queen's Bench Division of the High Court of Justice and the Criminal Division of the Court of Appeal; he is second in rank to the

Lord Chancellor. The present holder of the office (since 1980) is Geoffrey Dawson, Baron Lane (1918–).

Lord Lyon King of Arms The highest authority in the deciding of heraldic matters in Scotland. Originally a herald in the 14th century, the Lord Lyon now heads four heralds and two pursuivants at the Lyon Office where, since 1677, all claims to arms must be registered. Also a judge, the Lord Lyon decides issues of clan chieftainship and pedigrees.

Lords, House of. See parliament.

Lord's cricket ground The world's most famous cricket ground, owned by the Marylebone Cricket Club (MCC) and situated in St John's Wood, London. It was founded by Thomas Lord (1757–1832) in Dorset Square and was moved to its present site in 1814. It has been the home of the Middlesex County Cricket Club since 1877.

Loren, Sophia (S. Scicoloni; 1934–) Italian film actress. Her films include Two Women (1961), The Millionairess (1961), Marriage Italian Style (1964), and The Cassandra Crossing (1977).

Lorenz, Konrad (1903–89) Austrian zoologist, who was one of the founders of modern ethology (the study of animal behaviour). In the 1930s Lorenz identified the phenomenon of *imprinting in young chicks. Lorenz wrote several popular books about his work, including King Solomon's Ring (1949) and Man Meets Dog (1950). He applied his theories to the human species, with controversial implications (On Aggression, 1963). He shared a Nobel Prize (1973).

loris A nocturnal Asian *primate. Lorises are 20–35 cm long with almost no tail and very large dark eyes. They are generally slow-moving and live in trees. See also potto.

Lorraine A planning region and former province in NE France, bordering on Belgium, Luxembourg, and Germany. It has valuable iron-ore deposits. It became a province of France in 1766. Following the Franco-Prussian War (1871) part of Lorraine (now Moselle department) was lost to Germany and united with *Alsace to form the imperial territory of Alsace-Lorraine. Area: 23 540 sq km (9087 sq mi). Population (1986 est): 2 313 200.

Los Alamos 28 54N 103 00W A town in the USA, in New Mexico. The first atom bombs were made here during World War II. The H-bomb was later developed here by the scientific laboratory of the University of California. Population (1980): 11 039.

Los Angeles 34 00N 118 15W A city and seaport in the USA, in S California on the Pacific coast, founded in 1781 by Franciscan missionaries. It comprises a large industrial and urban complex, with the second largest population in the USA. It is the centre of the US film industry. Industrial pollution is a serious problem. Population (1986 est): 3 259 300.

Los Angeles, Victoria de (1923–) Spanish soprano. She established herself as a popular prima donna, particularly in the title roles of Massenet's Manon Lescaut and Puccini's Madame Butterfly.

Lothian Region An administrative region in SE Scotland, created in 1975 from the counties of East Lothian, Midlothian, and West Lothian. It consists of lowlands bordering on the Firth of Forth in the N and rising gently to the S. The fertile lowlands are important agriculturally. Area: 1756 sq km (677 sq mi). Population (1989 est): 741 179. Administrative centre: Edinburgh.

Lotto, Lorenzo (c. 1480–1556) Venetian painter. He travelled widely but, unable to compete with Titian's success, worked chiefly in Bergamo. He is noted for his altarpieces, e.g. the Crucifixion (Monte San Giusto, Bergamo), and such portraits as A Young Man (Kunsthistorisches Museum, Vienna), and Andrea Odoni (Hampton Court).

lotus A water plant. The sacred lotus of ancient Egypt was probably Nymphaea lotus, a sweet-scented white night-flowering *water lily with broad petals, or N. caerulea, a blue-flowered species (both native to tropical Africa and Asia). The sacred Indian lotus, Nelumbo nucifera, has roselike pink flowers and edible seeds, called lotus nuts.

loudspeaker A device for converting electrical signals into sound. It usually consists of a small coil of wire fixed to the centre of a movable cone. The coil lies between the poles of a strong *magnet. An audio-frequency electrical signal fed to the coil creates a varying magnetic field, which interacts with the steady field in the gap. This causes the coil, and the attached cone, to vibrate and produce sound waves of the same frequencies as the electrical signal. Generally, larger cones give a better response at low frequencies and the smaller cones are best at high frequencies; for the best results two or more different-sized cones are therefore used, either in the same or in separate cabinets.

Louis (VII) le Jeune (c. 1120–80) King of France (1137–80). He was engaged in a bitter struggle with Henry II of England between 1152, when Henry acquired Aquitaine through his marriage to Louis' former wife *Eleanor of Aquitaine, until 1174.

Louis VIII (1187–1226) King of France (1223–26), known as the Lionheart. He was offered the English throne by King John's barons but his invasion of England was defeated in 1217.

Louis IX, St (1214–70) King of France (1226–70), regarded as the model medieval Christian king. After defeating Henry III of England (1242) he set out as leader of the sixth *Crusade (1248), during which he was captured by the Egyptians. On his return to France he introduced administrative reforms and encouraged learning and the arts. He died on a Crusade in Tunisia and was made a saint in 1297.

Louis XI (1423–83) King of France (1461–83), who united most of France under his rule and in 1477 finally defeated Charles the Bold of Burgundy. He extended royal authority over the church and encouraged commerce, gaining the support of the middle classes.

Louis XII (1462–1515) King of France (1498–1515). His reign was dominated by the wars that his father Charles VIII had begun in Italy.

Louis XIII (1601–43) King of France (1610–43), whose reign was dominated by his chief minister Cardinal de *Richelieu. He was the son of the assassinated Henry IV and of Marie de' Medici (1573–1642), who was regent during his childhood. In 1617 he exiled Marie from court but mother and son were later reunited by Richelieu, her adviser, who in 1624 became Louis' chief minister. The king defeated two *Huguenot uprisings (1622, 1628).

Louis XIV (1638–1715) King of France (1643–1715), known as the Sun King because of the splendour of his reign. His youth was dominated by Cardinal Mazarin (1602–61), after whose death Louis allowed no single minister to dominate. He was a firm supporter of the *divine right of kings and is remembered for his claim *L'état c'est moi* (I am the state). His patronage of artists, including the writers Molière and Racine, added to the magnificence of his court. In 1660 he married Maria Theresa (1638–83), the daughter of Philip IV of Spain. His mistresses included Mme de Montespan (1641–1707) and then Mme de Maintenon (c. 1635–1719), whom he secretly married after Maria Theresa's death. Abroad, France became the dominant power in Europe during Louis' reign, although the many wars in which he involved France left it economically weak. France was further weakened by Louis' rejection (1685) of the Edict of Nantes, ending toleration of Protestants and driving many of France's most useful citizens into exile. The **Louis Quartorze style** of late 17th-century interior design was developed to establish a French national style. The formal baroque furniture was richly gilded or veneered for such regal settings as *Versailles.

Louis XV (1710–74) King of France (1715–74), whose weak rule contributed to the French Revolution of 1789. His early reign was dominated by Cardinal Fleury (1653–1743), after whose death Louis' weakness and the influence of his mistresses, especially Mme de *Pompadour and, later, Mme *Du Barry, led to plotting and unrest. The loss of almost all France's colonies in the *Seven Years' War (1756–63) increased his unpopularity, which hasty reforms at the end of his reign did nothing to lessen. The **Louis Quinze style** of French interior decoration and furnishing lasted from about 1723 until Louis' death. A complex and informal style, it was a reaction to the formal baroque pomp of Louis XIV's court. *See also* rococo.

Louis XVI (1754–93) King of France (1774–93), who was guillotined during the *French Revolution. The opposition of Louis' wife *Marie Antoinette and the aristocracy thwarted the attempted reforms of his ministers Turgot (1727–81) and Necker (1732–1804). The resulting economic crisis forced the king to summon (1789) the States General and revolution soon followed. The royal family was confined to the Tuileries Palace from which they attempted to flee in 1791, reaching Varennes. Brought back to the Tuileries, Louis was dethroned after it had

been stormed by the Paris mob. In 1793 he and his wife were guillotined. The **Louis Seize style**, a neoclassical French style of furnishing, came into fashion after Louis XVI's coronation. It featured straight lines rather than the curves of the rococo style. After the French Revolution (1789–99) this style remained popular for some time.

Louis XVII (1785–95) King of France in name (1793–95) following the execution of his father Louis XVI during the French Revolution. He died in prison.

Louis XVIII (1755–1824) King of France, in name from 1795, following the death in prison of his nephew *Louis XVII, and in fact from 1814, following the overthrow of Napoleon. He fled Paris when Napoleon returned from Elba, being restored after Waterloo (1815). His attempts to be a moderate constitutional monarch were thwarted by the ultraroyalists.

Louis, Joe (Joseph Louis Barrow; 1914–81) US boxer, called the Brown Bomber, who was world heavyweight champion from 1937 to 1948, when he retired.

Louisiana A state in the S USA, on the Gulf of Mexico. Chiefly low lying, it is crossed by the Mississippi River, the delta of which dominates the coastal lowlands in the S. The state produces chemicals and petrochemicals, paper and food products. Oil is exploited throughout the state and there are major deposits of natural gas, sulphur, and salt. New Orleans and Baton Rouge are important ports and tourism is a growing industry. Its favourable climate and fertile soils make it an important agricultural state. *History*: although discovered by the Spanish, it was claimed for France and named after Louis XIV in 1682. It was acquired by the USA as part of the Louisiana Purchase (1803), becoming a state in 1812. Area: 125 675 sq km (48 523 sq mi). Population (1987 est): 4 460 578. Capital: Baton Rouge.

Louisiana Purchase (1803) About 2 144 250 sq km (828 000 sq mi) of land between the Mississippi River and the Rocky Mountains, purchased by the USA from France for $27,267,622. The purchase doubled the size of the USA and established US dominance in North America.

Louis Philippe (1773–1850) King of the French (1830–48), the son of the Duke of *Orléans. He supported the *French Revolution until 1793, when he deserted to the Austrians. He joined the liberal opposition to the restored Louis XVIII and came to the throne after the July Revolution had overthrown Louis' successor Charles X. Styled King of the French rather than of France, Louis Philippe relied on the support of the middle class. His moderation turned to repression in the face of the many rebellions against his rule and he abdicated in the Revolution of 1848.

Lourdes 43 06N 0 02W A town in SW France, in the Hautes-Pyrénées department situated at the foot of the Pyrenees. It is a major pilgrimage centre for Roman Catholics (*see* Bernadette of Lourdes). Population (1982): 17 619.

Lourenço Marques. See Maputo.

louse A wingless insect that is a parasite of warm-blooded animals. The sucking lice suck the blood of mammals. They have hairy flattened bodies, 0.5–6 mm long, and claws for attaching themselves to the host. One of the most important species is the human louse (*Pediculus humanus*), of which there are two varieties–the head louse (*P. humanus capitis*) and the body louse (*P. humanus humanus*). Both are transmitted by contact with an infested person and lay their eggs ("nits") on hair or clothing. Body lice are carriers of typhus and related diseases. Biting lice feed on the skin, feathers, etc., of birds–their principal hosts.

Louth (Irish name: Contae Lughbhaidh) The smallest county in the Republic of Ireland, in Leinster bordering on the Irish Sea. It is chiefly low lying. Agriculture is important. Area: 821 sq km (317 sq mi). Population (1986): 91 698. County town: Dundalk.

Louvre The national museum of France containing the art collection of the French kings and housed in the former royal palace and Tuileries palace in Paris. It was opened to the public in 1793.

lovage A herb, *Ligusticum scoticum*, of the carrot family, that has large leaves with pairs of divided toothed leaflets and clusters of greenish-white flowers. It is native to Europe and used in cookery and as a salad plant.

lovebird A small brightly coloured *parrot occurring in Africa and Madagascar. Lovebirds typically have a short tail, a red bill, and a prominent eye ring. They often feed in large flocks and may damage crops. They are popular cagebirds.

Lovelace, Richard (1618–57) English Cavalier poet. One of his best-known poems is "To Althea, from Prison." *Lucasta* (1649) contains most of his best lyrics.

Lowry, L(awrence) S(tephen) (1887–1976) British painter, born in Manchester. His most famous works have bleak industrial landscapes and towns dotted with matchstick figures.

Lozi A *Bantu-speaking people of Zambia, also known as Barotse. They are cereal cultivators on the fertile flood plain of the upper Zambezi, but hunting and animal rearing are also important. Political power is held by a divine king and lower-ranking queen who rule from separate northern and southern capitals.

LPG. See Liquefied Petroleum Gas.

LSD (lysergic acid diethylamide) A drug that –in very small doses–produces hallucinations, altered sensory perception, and a sense of happiness and relaxation or, in some people, fear and anxiety. Long-term use of LSD can cause a schizophrenia-like illness.

Lualaba, River A river in SE Zaïre. Rising in the Shaba region, it flows N to join the River Luvua and becomes the Zaïre River at the Boyoma Falls. Length: 1800 km (1100 mi).

Luanda 8 58S 13 09E The capital of Angola, a port in the NW on the Atlantic Ocean. Founded by the Portuguese in 1575, it became a centre of the slave trade to Brazil. Oil was discovered nearby in 1955 and a refinery was established. Population (1988): 960 000.

Lübeck 53 52N 10 40E A city in N Germany, in Schleswig-Holstein on the Trave estuary. A leading city of the Hanseatic League, it has a cathedral (1173) and city hall (13th–15th centuries). It is a major Baltic port. Population (1987): 209 200.

Lubitsch, Ernst (1892–1947) US film director, born in Germany. Following the success of *Madame Dubarry* (1919), a historical romance, he went to Hollywood, where he made a series of clever comedies during the 1920s and 1930s. These include *Forbidden Paradise* (1924), *Bluebeard's Eighth Wife* (1938), *Ninotchka* (1939), and *Heaven Can Wait* (1943).

Lubumbashi (name until 1966: Elizabethville) 11 30S 27 31E A city in SE Zaire. Founded in 1910 as a coppermining settlement, it is the industrial centre of an important mining area. Population (1984): 543 268.

lucerne. See alfalfa.

Lucifer In Christian tradition, the leader of the angels expelled from heaven for rebelling against God. Known thereafter as Satan (Hebrew: adversary) or the Devil, he presides over the souls condemned to torment in *hell. He is identified with the serpent that tempted Eve (Genesis 3.1–6) and the great red dragon cast out of heaven by Michael (Revelation 12.3–9). The exact nature of Lucifer's sin was much debated; the commonest view is that his sin was pride.

Lucknow 26 50N 80 54E A city in India, the capital of Uttar Pradesh. The British Residency was besieged in 1857 during the Indian Mutiny. Population (1989): 916 954.

Lucretius (Titus Lucretius Carus; c. 95–c. 55 BC) Roman philosopher and poet. His single work, *De rerum natura*, explains the philosophy of *Epicurus, including his theory about atoms and beliefs about the soul.

Lucullus, Lucius Licinius (died c. 57 BC) Roman general. After service with *Sulla, he successfully led the third war against Mithridates (120–63 BC) until his troops mutinied. Lucullus retired to private life and luxury.

Lüda (or Lü-ta) 38 53N 121 37E A port complex in NE China, at the end of the Liaodong Peninsula. It comprises the two cities **Lüshun** (English name: Port Arthur) and **Dalian** (or Talien; English name: Dairen). Lüshun, a major naval base from 1878, was the base of the Russian Pacific fleet during the Russian occupation (1898–1905). The Russians began the construction of the commercial port at Dalian, completed under Japanese occupation (1905–45). Population (1983 est): 4 500 000.

Luddites A group of Nottingham frameworkers, named after their probably mythical leader, Ned Ludd, who destroyed labour-saving machinery in 1811. Luddism, which spread to other parts of industrial England, showed the hostility to the new machines that were taking the men's livelihood from them. It was severely repressed.

Luftwaffe The German air force. The Luftwaffe, which fought in *World War I, was further developed by *Göring in the 1930s. In

*World War II it was involved in the Blitzkrieg but was defeated in the battle of Britain.

Lugansk. *See* Voroshilovgrad.

lugworm A burrowing *annelid worm, *Arenicola marina*, of Atlantic shores. Up to 40 cm long, lugworms have about 20 segments, with tufts of red gills on all but the last few. They feed on organic material in the mud and pass the indigestible mud as faeces, which form casts on the mud surface.

Luik. *See* Liège.

Luke, St A New Testament evangelist, traditionally the author of the third Gospel and of the Acts of the Apostles. He seems to have been a Gentile doctor and to have accompanied *Paul on numerous missions, notably to Greece, Macedonia, and Jerusalem. He is the patron saint of doctors and artists. Feast day: 18 Oct.

Luluabourg. *See* Kananga.

lumen (lm) The *SI unit of luminous flux equal to the light emitted per second in a cone of one steradian solid angle by a point source of one candela.

luminescence The emission of light by a substance for any reason except high temperature. It occurs when an atom of the substance changes from an excited state to its ground state. The atom may be excited by absorbing a photon (photoluminescence), colliding with an electron (electroluminescence), etc. If the luminescence stops as soon as the exciting source is removed, it is known as fluorescence; if it persists for longer than 10^{-8} seconds it is called phosphorescence.

luminosity The brightness of an object, such as a star, equal to the total energy radiated per second from the object. A star's luminosity increases both with surface temperature and with surface area: the hotter and larger a star, the greater its luminosity. Stellar luminosity is related (logarithmically) to absolute *magnitude.

luminous flux The rate of flow of light energy, taking into account the sensitivity of the observer or detector to the different wavelengths. For example, the human eye is most sensitive to the colour green. Luminous flux is measured in *lumens.

luminous intensity The amount of light emitted per second by a point source per unit solid angle in a specified direction. It is measured in *candela.

lumpsucker A slow-moving carnivorous bony *fish, also called lumpfish, found in cold northern seas. They have a thickset body, sometimes studded with bony tubercles, and a sucking disc formed from fused pelvic fins. *Cyclopterus lumpus* is the largest species, reaching 60 cm long. The roe is used as a substitute for caviar.

lungfish A freshwater bony *fish occurring in South America, Africa, or Australia. Lungfish have slender bodies, narrow paired fins, and tapering tails. Their swim bladders are modified for breathing air; this enables them to survive droughts, when some burrow in the mud and breathe air through vents above the mouth. They re-emerge in the rainy season to feed and spawn.

lungs The organs with which many animals and man breathe air. The human lungs are situ-

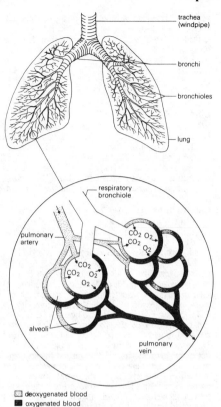

LUNGS *The air passages in the lungs terminate in millions of tiny air sacs (alveoli), into which blood from the pulmonary artery releases its carbon dioxide. Inhaled oxygen in the alveoli is absorbed by the blood, which is carried back to the heart by the pulmonary vein.*

ated within the rib cage on either side of the heart. Each lung is enclosed by a smooth moist membrane (the pleura), which permits it to expand without friction, and contains many tiny thin-walled air sacs (alveoli), through which oxygen and carbon dioxide are exchanged between the blood and air during breathing (*see* respiration). Air to the lungs passes through the *trachea (windpipe) to the two main airways (bronchi), which divide into smaller and smaller branches that end in the alveoli.

Lupercalia An ancient Roman festival of purification and fertility held annually on 15 Feb. After performing sacrifices, priests carrying whips of goat hide walked around the Palatine. Women struck by their whips were ensured fertility. The ceremony was suppressed in 494 AD by Pope Gelasius.

lupin A flowering plant of the pea family, native to the N hemisphere and widely cultivated in gardens. The leaves have radiating leaflets and the pastel-coloured flowers grow in tall heads.

Lusaka 15 03S 28 30E The capital of Zambia, lying on the Tanzam Railway. It became the capital of Northern Rhodesia in 1935 and of Zambia on independence in 1964. The centre of an important agricultural region, it has expanded rapidly. Population (1987): 818 994.

Lüshun. *See* Lüda.

Lü-ta. *See* Lüda.

lute A plucked stringed instrument of Moorish origin. The European lute, popular during the 15th, 16th, and 17th centuries, had a body in the shape of a half pear, six or more pairs of strings and a fretted fingerboard. The lute was used chiefly as a solo instrument and to accompany singers; it has been revived in the 20th century.

luteinizing hormone. *See* gonadotrophin.

lutetium (Lu) The heaviest *lanthanide element named by its discoverer, G. Urbain (1872–1938) after his native Paris (Latin: *Lutetia*). It was formerly known as **cassiopeium**. At no 71; at wt 174.97; mp 1663°C; bp 3395°C.

Luther, Martin (1483–1546) German Protestant reformer, founder of *Lutheranism. An Augustinian monk and from 1507 a priest, he became a professor at Wittenberg University in 1511. Several visits to Rome convinced him of the corruption of the papacy, the Dominican monk Johann Tetzel (c.1465–1519), who sold *indulgences for money, being a particular target of his attacks. In 1517 he nailed his 95 arguments against this practice to the church door at Wittenberg. He disobeyed the papal summons to Rome (1518) and further attacked the papal system in his writings. His public burning of a papal order condemning his writings resulted in his excommunication in 1521. He appeared before Charles V's court at Worms and was declared an outlaw. While in hiding at Wartburg, under the protection of the Elector of Saxony, he completed a German translation of the New Testament. In 1522 he returned openly to Wittenberg, where he led the reform of its church. With the *Augsburg Confession (1530) a separate Protestant church emerged.

Lutheranism The belief and practice of the Protestant Churches based on the teaching of Martin Luther, especially as set out in the *Augsburg Confession (1530). There are wide differences in matters of belief among Lutherans. Essentially Scripture is taken to be the only rule of faith and conservative Lutherans accept Luther's basic teaching that salvation can be gained through faith alone. Lutheranism is the national faith in all Scandinavian countries, is the main Protestant Church in Germany, and is also strong in North America. There are some 80 million Lutherans world wide, which makes it the largest Protestant body.

Lutine bell The ship's bell taken from the *Lutine* (sank 1799) and that now hangs at *Lloyd's and is rung when news arrives of a ship previously posted "missing, fate unknown."

Luton 51 53N 0 25W A town in SE England, in Bedfordshire. It has an important motor-vehi-

cle industry. Nearby is Luton Airport. Population (1988): 167 600.

Lutuli, Albert (John Mvumbi) (1898–1967) South African Black leader, whose support of nonviolent opposition to racial discrimination won him the Nobel Peace Prize in 1960. A Zulu chief, in 1952 he became president of the African National Congress, formed in 1912 to further the Black cause in South Africa.

Lutyens, Sir Edwin Landseer (1869–1944) British architect. Known as the last English designer of country houses, he also designed the central square of Hampstead Garden Suburb (1908–10) and the Cenotaph (1919–20) but his most spectacular work was the layout and viceregal palace of New Delhi (1912–30).

lux (lx) The *SI unit of intensity of illumination equal to the illumination resulting from a flux of one lumen falling on an area of one square metre.

Luxembourg A province in SE Belgium, bordering on the Grand Duchy of Luxembourg and France. The *Ardennes is an important tourist area. Area: 4416 sq km (1705 sq mi). Population (1987 est): 226 462. Capital: Arlon.

Luxembourg, Grand Duchy of A small country in central Europe, between France and Germany. *Economy*: predominantly industrial, especially the manufacture of iron and steel. Agriculture remains important. The city of Luxembourg is an important international centre with the headquarters of the European Parliament and the European Coal and Steel Community. *History*: with the Netherlands and Belgium it formed part of the so-called Low Countries. It became a grand duchy in 1815 under the Dutch Crown. In 1830 it joined the Belgian revolt against the Netherlands, W Luxembourg joining independent Belgium and the E forming part of the Netherlands until obtaining independence in 1867. In 1921 it formed an economic union with Belgium and in 1948 both joined with the Netherlands to form the *Benelux Economic Union. Luxembourg is now a member of the EC. Head of state: Grand Duke Jean (1921–   ). Head of Government: Jacques Santer. Official languages: Luxembourgish, French, and German. Official currency: Luxembourg franc of 100 centimes. Area: 2586 sq km (999 sq mi). Population (1989): 377 100. Capital: Luxembourg.

Luxor (*or* El Aksur) 25 40N 32 38E A town in central Egypt, on the River Nile. It occupies the S part of the ancient city of *Thebes and has numerous ruins and tombs. Population (1986 est): 147 900.

Luzon A volcanic island in the N Philippines, the largest and most important. Largely mountainous, its central fertile plain is a major grain growing area with rice terraces to the N. Most industry is concentrated around Manila. Area: 108 378 sq km (41 845 sq mi). Population (1980): 23 900 796. Chief town: Manila.

Lvov 49 50N 24 00E A city in the Soviet Union, in the W Ukrainian SSR. It is a major industrial and cultural centre. Under Austrian rule from 1772, it became the capital of Galicia. It was handed over to Poland after World War I and to the Soviet Union in 1939. Population (1987): 767 000.

Lyceum The gardens and gymnasium in ancient Athens in which *Aristotle lectured and which gave their name to the school and research foundation that he established there in about 335 BC. The name is now applied particularly to Aristotle's philosophical principles.

Lydia In antiquity, a region of W Asia Minor with its capital at Sardis. Its last native king, *Croesus (ruled 560–546 BC), enriched by Lydia's gold, controlled Anatolia eastwards to the River Halys, until his defeat by Cyrus the Great (d. 529 BC). The Lydians invented coined money (c. 700 BC).

Lyle, Sandy (1958–) British golfer who became the first British golfer to win the US Masters event (1988). His other successes have included the British Open Championship in 1985.

lymph A clear colourless fluid, consisting of water and dissolved substances, that is contained in a network of vessels running throughout the body and called the **lymphatic system**. It is derived from blood and bathes the cells, supplying them with nutrients and absorbing their waste products, before passing into the lymphatic vessels. Here the lymph passes through a series of small swellings called **lymph nodes**, which filter out bacteria and other foreign particles, before draining into the main lymphatic vessels in the neck. These two vessels are connected to veins in the neck and so drain the lymph back into the bloodstream.

lymphocyte. *See* leucocyte.

lynx A short-tailed *cat, *Felis lynx*, that inhabits forests of Europe, Asia, and North America.

Lynxes are about 1 m long with faintly spotted yellow-brown thick fur; their ears are tipped with black tufts. They hunt at night, usually for small mammals.

Lyon 45 46N 4 50E The third largest city in France, the capital of the Rhône department where the Rivers Rhône and Saône meet. Notable buildings include the cathedral (12th–15th centuries). Lyon is an important financial centre and has been a leading textile centre since the 15th century. Population (1982): 418 476.

lyre An ancient plucked string instrument. It consists of a sound box with two symmetrical arms supporting a cross piece from which strings are stretched to a bridge on the belly.

lyrebird A primitive ground-dwelling bird living in forests of E Australia. The male superb lyrebird (*Menura superba*) is brown with grey underparts. Its magnificent tail is spread out into a lyre shape during the courtship display, which is performed on a mound of mud and debris. All lyrebirds sing loudly and are excellent mimics.

Lysander (d. 395 BC) Spartan general and politician. He commanded the fleets that defeated the Athenians at Notium (407) and Aegospotami (405) towards the end of the *Peloponnesian War.

lysergic acid diethylamide. *See* LSD.

lysosome A saclike structure occurring in large numbers in nearly all animal cells and containing enzymes that break down materials both within and outside the cell. For example, the lysosomes in white blood cells destroy harmful bacteria engulfed by the cell.

M

Mabuse. *See* Gossaert, Jan.

Macao (Portuguese name: Macáu; Chinese name: Aomen) 22 13N 113 36E A Portuguese-administered free port in S China, across the Zhu estuary from Hong Kong. Chief industries are textiles and fishing. Sovereignty is to be given to China in 1999. Area: 16 sq km (6 sq mi). Population (1986 est): 426 400.

macaque A *monkey found mainly in the forests of S Asia. 35–78 cm long, macaques have short legs and areas of bare skin on the rump. They feed on plants and animals. *See also* Barbary ape; rhesus monkey.

MacArthur, Douglas (1880–1964) US general. He was Allied commander in the SW Pacific in World War II and commanded the occupation of Japan (1945–51). As commander of the UN forces in the Korean War, his support of active operations against China went against US policy and President Harry S. Truman dismissed him (1951).

Macassar. *See* Ujung Pandang.

Macaulay, Thomas Babington, 1st Baron (1800–59) British essayist and historian. He was

a leading contributor to the *Edinburgh Review* and had a long career in parliament. His Whig sympathies are revealed in his *History of England* (5 vols, 1849–61).

macaw A large brightly coloured *parrot ranging from Mexico to Paraguay. Up to 100 cm long, macaws have a long tail and a huge hooked bill.

Macbeth (d. 1058) King of Scots (1040–58), after killing Duncan I in battle at Bothnagowan. He was killed by Duncan's son Malcolm.

Maccabees The Hasmonean dynasty, founded in Jerusalem by Judas Maccabee (d. 161 BC) after a revolt against Syrian (*Seleucid) rule. It continued until the capture of Jerusalem by the Romans in 63 BC. In Christian usage it is applied to seven young brothers martyred during the revolt.

The **Books of Maccabees** are four books of the *Apocrypha.

McCarthy, Joseph R(aymond) (1908–57) US Republican senator, who led Senate investigations of supposed communists during the Cold War. In 1954 his anticommunist witchhunt

—commonly known as McCarthyism—came to an end.

McCullers, Carson (1917–67) US novelist and playwright. Her novels, which include *The Heart Is a Lonely Hunter* (1940) and *A Member of the Wedding* (1946), are set in her native South.

MacDonald, (James) Ramsay (1866–1937) British statesman; the first Labour prime minister (1924, 1929–31, 1931–35). He joined the Independent Labour Party in 1894. Elected an MP (1906) he became leader of the parliamentary *Labour Party (1911) but resigned in opposition to World War I (1914). Re-elected to parliament in 1922 he again led the Labour Party, becoming prime minister in 1924. His government was defeated after a vote of no confidence. His 1929–31 government became a coalition (1931–35), increasingly dominated by the Conservatives.

mace. *See* nutmeg.

Macedonia The central region of the *Balkans. Inhabited from *Neolithic times, Macedonia was settled by many migrating northern tribes. About 640 BC Perdiccas I became the first ruler of the kingdom of Macedon. *Philip II founded Macedon's military power, which under his son *Alexander the Great was extended to the East. Macedonia became a Roman province in 146. The region is now divided between Yugoslavia, Greece, and Bulgaria.

McEnroe, John (Patrick, Jr) (1959–) US tennis player. He won the US singles title in 1979, 1980, 1981, and 1984. An intense competitor noted for his unruly court behaviour, he became Wimbledon singles champion in 1981, 1983, and 1984.

Macgillicuddy's Reeks A mountain range in the Republic of Ireland, in Co Kerry. It extends W of the Lakes of Killarney, reaching 1041 m (3414 ft) at Carrantuohill.

Machiavelli, Niccolò (1469–1527) Italian political theorist. He served the Florentine republic as statesman and diplomat from 1498 to 1512, when the restoration of the Medici family forced him into exile. In *The Prince* (1532), written in 1513, he argued that any means could be used to achieve a stable state.

Mach number The ratio of the speed of a body in a fluid to the speed of sound in that fluid. The speed is supersonic if the Mach number is greater than one. If it exceeds five it is hypersonic. Named after the Austrian physicist Ernst Mach (1838–1916).

Machu Picchu A well-preserved *Inca town in the Urubamba valley (Peru), standing on a steep ridge with agricultural terraces on each side. Discovered in 1911, it contains a central plaza, royal palace, and sun temple, built of polygonal stone blocks.

Macias Nguema. *See* Equatorial Guinea, Republic of.

McIndoe, Sir Archibald Hector (1900–60) New Zealand surgeon, who pioneered plastic surgery, especially with badly burnt airmen during World War II in Britain.

Mackenzie, Sir (Edward Montague) Compton (1883–1972) British novelist. His early novels include the semiautobiographical *Sinister Street* (1913). His later work includes several volumes of memoirs and many humorous novels, notably *Whisky Galore* (1947).

Mackenzie River The longest river in Canada, flowing from Great Slave Lake in the North West Territories W and NNW to an extensive delta on the Beaufort Sea. It carries oil and minerals from the Arctic Ocean to S Canada. Length: 1705 km (1065 mi).

mackerel An important food and game fish belonging to the genus *Scomber*, related to tuna. Mackerels live in shoals, feeding on fish and invertebrates. They have a streamlined body, two dorsal fins, and a forked tail. The common Atlantic mackerel (*S. scombrus*), about 30 cm long, is marked with black and green bands above.

McKinley, Mount A mountain in the USA, in the Alaska Range. The highest peak in North America, it was first climbed in 1913 by the US explorer Hudson Stuck (1863–1920). Height: 6194 m (20 320 ft).

Maclean, Donald (1913–83) British Foreign Office official and Soviet secret agent. He fled to Russia in company with Guy Burgess (1911–63) in 1951. Kim Philby (1912–88) and Anthony Blunt (1907–83), a distinguished art historian, were also involved in the affair.

Macmillan, Daniel (1813–57) Scottish bookseller and publisher, who with his brother **Alexander Macmillan** (1818–96) founded (1843) Macmillan and Company, which became one of the world's largest publishing houses. Apprenticed to a bookseller in Irvine, Scotland, in 1824, Daniel moved (1833) to Cambridge, where he opened his own shop in 1843.

Macmillan, (Maurice) Harold, 1st Earl of Stockton (1894–1986) British statesman; Conservative prime minister (1957–63). The grandson of Daniel *Macmillan, he was MP for Stockton (1924–29; 1931–45) and for Bromley (1945–64). During World War II he was resident minister in North Africa. In 1951 he became minister of housing and local government and then minister of defence (1954) and foreign secretary (1955). As chancellor of the exchequer (1955–57) he introduced Premium Bonds (1957). He succeeded Sir Anthony Eden as prime minister. His "wind of change" speech in 1958 marked his government's support of independence for African states. His second ministry suffered a major blow when de Gaulle frustrated Britain's attempt to join the EEC (1963). However, he improved relations with the USA and helped to achieve the *Nuclear Test-Ban Treaty (1963). He became chancellor of Oxford University in 1960.

MacMillan, Sir Kenneth (1929–) British ballet dancer and choreographer. He choreographed many ballets, notably *Romeo and Juliet* (1965), *Anastasia* (1967), *Sleeping Beauty* (1973), and *Prince of the Pagodas* (1989). He was director of the Royal Ballet from 1970 to 1977.

MacNeice, Louis (1907–63) Irish-born British poet. He published his first volume of poetry, *Blind Fireworks*, in 1929. Among his other volumes are *Autumn Journal* (1939), *The Burning Perch* (1963), and a distinguished collection of plays for radio, *The Dark Tower* (1947).

Madagascar, Democratic Republic of (name until 1975: Malagasy Republic) An island country in the Indian Ocean, off the SE coast of Africa. *Economy*: rice, manioc, coffee, sugar, and spices are the main crops. Minerals include graphite, chrome, and ilmenite. Industry, previously based on food processing, now includes metals, plastics, and oil refining. *History*: settled by Indonesians from the 1st century AD and by African Muslim traders from the 8th century, it remained a native kingdom until the French established a protectorate (1896). It became a French overseas territory in 1946 and a republic within the French Community in 1958, gaining independence in 1960. In 1975 Madagascar became a democratic republic, with Admiral Didier Ratsiraka (1936–   ) as its first president. Official languages: Malagasy and French. Official currency: Malagasy franc of 100 centimes. Area: 587 041 sq km (229 233 sq mi). Population (1988 est): 10 919 000. Capital: Antananarivo. Main port: Taomasina.

madder A plant, *Rubia tinctorum*, native to Eurasia. It has trailing stems with narrow leaves, small yellow flowers, and blackish berry-like fruits. A red dye is extracted from the roots.

Madeira Islands (*or* Funchal Islands) A group of Portuguese islands in the Atlantic Ocean, about 640 km (398 mi) off the coast of Morocco, comprising Madeira and Porto Santo and two uninhabited groups. Madeira, the most important island, is a major tourist centre and produces fruit, sugar, and the famous Madeira wine. Area: 777 sq km (300 sq mi). Population (1988): 280 000. Capital: Funchal.

Madras 13 05N 80 18E A city and major seaport in India, the capital of Tamil Nadu on the Coromandel Coast. Founded (1639) by the British East India Company, the city developed around Fort St George, the site of the first English church built in India (1678–80). Madras manufactures cars, bicycles, and cement and its chief exports are leather, iron ore, and cotton textiles. Population (1981 est): 4 276 635.

Madrid 40 27N 3 42W The capital of Spain, situated on a high plateau in the centre of the country on the River Manzanares. Its industries include the manufacture of leather goods, textiles, chemicals, engineering, glassware, and porcelain and food processing. A cultural centre, Madrid possesses a university, art galleries, and the national library (founded in 1712). Buildings include the former royal palace and the 17th-century cathedral. *History*: Madrid was captured from the Moors in 1083 by Alfonso VI. Philip II established it as the capital in 1561. Population (1986): 3 123 713.

madrigal An unaccompanied part song, often a setting of a love poem. In 14th-century Florence, Landini wrote madrigals for voices and instruments. The Italian madrigal of the 16th and 17th centuries developed in the compositions of Marenzio, Monteverdi, and Gesualdo. The English school (Byrd, Morley, etc.) wrote in a simpler style.

Maeander, River. *See* Menderes, River.

Maes, Nicolas (*or* N. Maas; 1634–93) Dutch painter of domestic scenes and portraits, born in Dordrecht. Influenced at first by his teacher *Rembrandt, in such paintings as *Girl at the Window* (c. 1655; Rijksmuseum, Amsterdam), he later adopted the style of Flemish portraiture.

Maeterlinck, Maurice (1862–1949) Belgian poet and dramatist. Having established his reputation as a poet he became the leading dramatist of the Symbolist movement with such plays as *Pelléas et Mélisande* (1892). He won the Nobel Prize in 1911.

Mafeking (*or* Mafikeng) 25 53S 25 39E A town in South Africa, in Bophutha Tswana. It was besieged for 217 days by Boers during the second *Boer War (1899–1902) but was held by Col *Baden-Powell until relieved. It was the capital of the protectorate of Bechuanaland (now Botswana) until 1965. Population (1980): 6775.

Mafia A criminal organization that started as a secret society in 13th-century Sicily. The word (meaning "swank") came into use in the 19th century, when the Mafia was employed by the great landowners of Sicily to manage their estates. By extortion, "protection," ransom, and blackmail, the Mafia formed an organization that virtually ruled Sicily. Emigrants took the Mafia to the USA in the early 20th century, where as Cosa Nostra (Our Affair), it has flourished.

Magdalenian A culture of the Upper *Palaeolithic, succeeding the Solutrean in W Europe. Named after La Madeleine cave in the Dordogne (SW France), the Magdalenian is marked by an abundance of bone and antler tools. Dating from about 15 000 to 10 000 BC, it was the heyday of prehistoric art with magnificent cave paintings (e.g. at *Altamira).

Magdeburg 52 8N 11 35E A city and port in E Germany, the capital of Saxony-Anhalt on the River *Elbe. It was a leading member of the Hanseatic League. Its industries include iron, oil and sugar refining, chemicals, and textiles. Population (1986): 288 798.

Magellan, Ferdinand (c. 1480–1521) Portuguese explorer who led several expeditions to India and Africa (1505–16). In 1519, he headed a Spanish expedition seeking a passage W to the Moluccas. In 1521 they reached the East Indies, where Magellan was killed. Only one ship returned to Spain, thus completing the first circumnavigation of the world. The **Strait of Magellan**, separating South America from Tierra del Fuego, is named after him, and he was the first to record (1519) the **Magellanic Clouds**, two small *galaxies that can be seen by eye from the S hemisphere.

Maggiore, Lake (Latin name: Lacus Verbanus) A long lake in Italy and Switzerland. Sheltered from the N by the Alps, it enjoys a mild climate: its resorts include Locarno, in Switzerland. Area: 212 sq km (82 sq mi).

Magi 1. In ancient times, the priests of Zoroaster, famous for their knowledge of astronomy (*see* Zoroastrianism). 2. The wise men from the East, who followed a star, to worship the infant Christ at Bethlehem (Matthew 2.1–12). Kings in early Christian tradition, they were named Caspar, Melchior, and Balthazar. A symbolic meaning was given to their gifts: gold (kingship), frankincense (divinity), and myrrh (death).

magic A system of practices believed to enable humans to control the forces that affect life. Generally regarded as superstition in industrial societies, magic plays an important role in preindustrial societies. Those who practise it are believed to communicate with good and evil spirits to ensure success in war, hunting, and in fertility.

Maginot line Fortifications built (1929–38) to protect the E frontier of France. Their construction was authorized by André Maginot (1877–1932), French minister of war (1929–32), but they were never tested, being outflanked by the invading Germans in World War II.

magistrate An officer who administers the law. In England magistrates are either *justices of the peace or stipendiary (paid) magistrates, who try cases in some metropolitan Magistrates' Courts and have wider powers than justices.

magma Hot liquefied rock lying beneath the earth's surface, either in the crust or upper mantle. It may rise to the surface through volcanic fissures and be forced out as lava; if it solidifies under ground it forms intrusive *igneous rock.

Magna Carta (1215) The Great Charter sealed at Runnymede by King *John of England in response to the barons' unrest. It set out the barons' feudal duties to the monarch and confirmed the liberties of the English Church. Annulled by the pope, it was reissued, with some changes, in 1216, 1217, and 1225 and later upheld as a statement of civil rights. Of the four originals still in existence, two are in the British Library, one in Salisbury Cathedral, and one in Lincoln Cathedral.

magnesium (Mg) A light silvery-white reactive metal, first obtained pure by Sir Humphry Davy in 1808. The eighth most common element in the earth's crust, it is a major constituent of the earth's mantle as the minerals olivine (Mg_2SiO_4) and enstatite ($MgSiO_3$). It is extracted by *electrolysis of magnesium chloride ($MgCl_2$) from sea water. Magnesium forms many other ionic salts, such as the sulphate ($MgSO_4$; Epsom salts), the oxide (MgO), the carbonate ($MgCO_3$; magnesite), the nitrate ($Mg(NO_3)_2$), and the hydroxide ($Mg(OH)_2$; milk of magnesia). It plays a role in plant life, occurring in *chlorophyll. When alloyed with aluminium it is used in aircraft construction. At no 12; at wt 24.312; mp 648.8°C; bp 1090°C.

magnet A body that has a *magnetic field (see also magnetism). Every magnet has two distinct areas around which the field is greatest—called the north and south poles. If two magnets are brought together, the like poles repel each other and the opposite poles attract each other. Iron, steel, and other ferromagnetic materials (see ferromagnetism) are attracted to magnets; the magnet causes a magnetic field to arise in the material in line with its own field. **Permanent magnets** are made of ferromagnetic materials and retain their magnetism unless they are heated above a certain temperature or are demagnetized by a strong opposing field. **Electromagnets** only func-

tion when an electric current flows through their coils.

magnetic declination The angle between geographical north and the horizontal component of the *geomagnetic field at the same point. It is also known as the magnetic variation.

magnetic dip The angle formed between the horizon and a compass allowed to swing freely in the vertical plane. It thus indicates the direction of the vertical component of the *geomagnetic field.

magnetic field The concept, devised by *Faraday, to explain the action-at-a-distance forces produced by a *magnet. The magnet is thought of as being surrounded by a field of force, the strength and direction of which is indicated by the lines of force that join the magnet's north and south poles. These lines of force can be seen if a card is laid over a magnet and iron filings sprinkled onto the card; when the card is tapped, the filings congregate along the lines of force. A wire carrying an electric current is also surrounded by a magnetic field, with concentric lines of force. See also electromagnetic field.

magnetic tape. See tape recorder.

magnetism A phenomenon in which one body can exert a force on another body with which it is not in contact (action at a distance). The space in which such a force exists is called a *magnetic field. Stationary charged particles are surrounded by an *electric field; when these charged particles move or spin, an associated effect, the magnetic field, is created. The behaviour of materials when placed in such a field depends on how the spinning electrons inside its atoms align themselves to reinforce or oppose the external field. See also ferromagnetism.

magnetite (or lodestone) A black magnetic mineral, a form of iron oxide (Fe_3O_4). It often has distinct north and south magnetic poles and was known around 500 BC for its use as a compass. It is one of the ores from which iron is extracted.

magneto An alternating-current *electric generator that uses a permanent *magnet, rather than an electromagnet, to create the magnetic field. It usually consists of one or more conducting coils rotating between a number of pairs of magnetic poles. It is used in some small internal-combustion engines to produce the ignition spark.

magnetomotive force (mmf) A measure of the magnetic effect of an electric current in a coil. It is analogous to *electromotive force and is measured in ampere-turns, being dependent on the number of turns in the coil.

magnetosphere A region surrounding a planet in which the magnetic field of the planet has a noticeable effect, for example on charged particles. Its shape arises from the interaction between *solar wind and planetary magnetic field. The earth's magnetosphere, which includes the *Van Allen radiation belts, extends 60 000 km from the sunward side of the planet but is drawn out to a much greater extent on the opposite side.

magnification In optical systems, the ratio of the width of an object to the width of its image, both being measured perpendicular to the axis of the system. For a single lens this reduces to the ratio of the distances of the image and the object from the lens when the image is in focus. For optical instruments the magnification is defined as the ratio of the size of the image at the eye produced with and without the instrument.

magnitude A measure of the brightness of stars and other astronomical objects. An object's **apparent magnitude** is its brightness as observed from earth and depends primarily on its *luminosity and its distance. An object's **absolute magnitude** is its apparent magnitude if it lay at a distance of 10 parsecs (32.616 light years).

magnolia An evergreen or deciduous tree native to North America and Asia and widely grown as an ornamental. Up to 45 m high, they have large leaves and big white, or pink flowers, producing conelike structures containing winged fruits.

magpie A widely occurring black-and-white crow, *Pica pica*. 44 cm long, it has a long tail. Magpies eat a wide range of plant and animal material. The name is also given to the group of Australian songbirds that includes the *currawongs.

Magritte, René (1898–1967) Belgian surrealist painter. Initially a wallpaper designer and commercial artist, he became associated with the Paris surrealists (*see* surrealism) in the late 1920s.

Magyars The largest ethnic group in Hungary. They came from mixed Ugric and Turkic stock, who migrated from Siberia during the 5th century and reached their present location during the late 9th century. *See also* Hungarian.

Maharashtra A state in W central India, on the Arabian Sea. Cotton, millet, wheat, and rice are farmed. The second most industrialized state, it produces cotton textiles, chemicals, machinery, and oil products. Bauxite, manganese, and iron ore are mined. Area: 307 690 sq km (118 774 sq mi). Population (1981): 62 693 898. Capital: Bombay.

Mahdi, al- (Arabic: the guided one) In Islamic tradition, a religious leader who will appear shortly before the end of the world and, for a few years, restore justice and religion. The best-known claimant to the title was the Sudanese leader **Muhammad Ahmad** (1844–85), who proclaimed himself the Mahdi and led an uprising against the Egyptian Government. In 1885, after a ten-month siege, he captured Khartoum, which was defended by General *Gordon.

mahjong An ancient Chinese game. It is usually played by 4 people using 2 dice and 136 tiles of bone, ivory, or plastic. 108 of the tiles are arranged in 3 suits: circles, bamboos, and characters. There are also four each of red, white, and green dragons and four each of east, south, west, and north winds. The tiles are built into a square of four walls, symbolizing a walled city.

Mahler, Gustav (1860–1911) Austrian composer and conductor. He directed the Viennese Court Opera from 1897–1907. In 1909 he became conductor of the New York Philharmonic Society. His nine large-scale symphonies (and uncompleted tenth) were written during brief holidays. The second (*Resurrection Symphony*), third, fourth, and eighth (*Symphony of a Thousand*) use vocal soloists. He also wrote song cycles.

mahogany Any of various tropical evergreen trees widely cultivated for timber. The most important species are *Swietenia macrophylla* and *S. mahagoni* of Central America and the West Indies: their hard red-brown wood is highly valued for furniture.

mahonia An evergreen shrub related to *berberis, native to N temperate regions and often grown in gardens. It has leaves with paired, sometimes spiky, leaflets, and bunches of yellow or orange flowers that produce berries.

maidenhair fern An ornamental *fern, *Adiantum capillus-veneris*, found worldwide in warm places. From a creeping rhizome (underground stem) arise delicate stalks, about 2.5–30 cm high, bearing fan-shaped leaflets with clusters of spore capsules (sori) situated on the edges.

maidenhair tree. *See* ginkgo.

Mailer, Norman (1923–) US novelist and journalist. He established his reputation with the World War II novel *The Naked and the Dead* (1948). His concern with American society, which provided the themes for novels such as *An American Dream* (1965), is more directly expressed in later works, such as *The Armies of the Night* (1968) and *The Executioner's Song* (1979), both of which were awarded a Pulitzer Prize. More recent works include *Ancient Evenings* (1983).

Maine A coastal New England state in the extreme NE USA. Major products are paper and pulp, leather goods, food, timber, and textiles. An area of considerable mineral wealth, limestone, building stone, sand, and gravel are exploited. The state's agricultural products include potatoes, poultry, apples, and beef. *History*: it became a British possession (1763). It entered the Union as part of Massachusetts (1788) and later became a separate state (1820). Area: 86 027 sq km (33 215 sq mi). Population (1986 est): 1 174 000. Capital: Augusta.

Mainland 1. (*or* Pomona) The largest of the Orkney Islands, divided into two main parts by Kirkwall Bay and *Scapa Flow. Area: 492 sq km (190 sq mi). Population (1981): 14 279. Chief town: Kirkwall. 2. The largest of the Shetland Islands. Area: about 583 sq km (225 sq mi). Population (1986): 19 236. Chief town: Lerwick.

maize A *cereal grass, *Zea mays*, also called Indian corn, sweet corn, or corn, native to America and widely cultivated. 1–4.5 m high, it bears a tassel of male flowers at the top of the stem and spikes of female flowers that develop into cobs bearing rows of grains. Maize is used as a vegetable, in breakfast cereals, flour, livestock feed, and for corn oil. It is the third most important cereal crop (after wheat and rice), the USA being the chief producing country.

Major, John (1943–) British Conservative politician; prime minister (1990–). He entered parliament in 1979 and served as foreign secretary (1989) and chancellor of the exchequer (1989–90).

Majorca (Spanish name: Mallorca) A Spanish island in the Mediterranean Sea, the largest of the Balearic Islands. The chief occupations are agriculture and tourism; cereals, legumes, oranges, olives, and figs are produced and marble is quarried. Area: 3639 sq km (1465 sq mi). Population (1981): 561 215. Capital: Palma.

Makarios III (Mikhail Khristodolou Mouskos; 1913–77) Cypriot churchman and statesman; archbishop of the Orthodox Church of Cyprus (1950–77) and president of Cyprus (1960–74, 1974–77). In 1956 he was deported to the Seychelles by the British for supporting Greek-Cypriot union, which he subsequently abandoned, contributing to the achievement of Cypriot independence.

Makassar. *See* Ujung Pandang.

Malabar Coast (*or* Malabar) The W coast of India from Goa in the N to Cape Comorin in the S. The shore is fringed by sand dunes and coconut palms.

Malabo (name until 1973: Santa Isabel) 3 45N 8 48E The capital of Equatorial Guinea, a port in the N of the island of Bioko (formerly Macias Nguema), founded by the British in 1827. Population (1986): 10 000.

Malacca A state in W Peninsular Malaysia, on the Strait of Malacca. It produces rice, rubber, copra, tin, and bauxite. Area: 1650 sq km (637 sq mi). Population (1980): 453 153. Capital: Malacca.

malachite An ore of copper consisting of hydrated copper carbonate, $Cu_2(OH)_2CO_3$. It is bright green and is found in deposits of copper minerals.

Málaga 36 43N 4 25W A city in S Spain, in Andalusia on the Mediterranean Sea. Founded by the Phoenicians (12th century BC), it passed successively to the Romans, the Visigoths, and the Moors, before falling to Ferdinand and Isabella in 1487. A major tourist centre and port, it exports olives, almonds, and dried fruits. Population (1986 est): 566 480.

Malagasy Republic. *See* Madagascar, Democratic Republic of.

malaria An infectious disease caused by protozoa of the genus *Plasmodium*. Malaria is spread by the female *Anopheles* mosquito, which lives only in the tropics. Different species of *Plasmodium* cause different types of malaria. Malignant tertian malaria (caused by *P. falciparum*) is the most severe; benign tertian malaria (caused by *P. vivax*) is less often fatal but there are repeated attacks. The parasites invade the red blood cells making them burst, causing fever, fits, diarrhoea, shock, and jaundice. Drugs can treat and prevent the disease, but malaria remains a major cause of death and ill health in the tropics.

Malawi, Republic of (name until 1963: Nyasaland) A country in SE Africa, between Tanzania, Zambia, and Mozambique. Lake Malawi lies at its E border. *Economy*: the main subsistence crop is maize; cash crops include tobacco, tea, sugar, and groundnuts. Mineral resources are sparse. *History*: the area became a British protectorate in 1891. In 1953 it was joined with Northern and Southern Rhodesia to form the Federation of *Rhodesia and Nyasaland. Nyasaland became independent in 1964.

In 1966 it became a republic within the British Commonwealth with Dr Hastings Banda (c.1906–) as its first president. Official language: English. Official currency, since 1971: kwacha of 199 tambala. Area: 94 079 sq km (36 324 sq mi). Population (1985 est): 7 058 800. Capital: Lilongwe.

Malay A language spoken in SE Asia and Indonesia. The dialect of the S Malay peninsula is the basis of standard Malay. It can be written in Roman or Arabic script. The Malay people probably migrated to this area from China between 2500 and 1500 BC. Since the 15th century Islam has been the accepted religion.

Malay Archipelago (former name: East Indies) An island group in SE Asia. It lies between the Pacific and Indian Oceans and between the Asian and Australian continents. It comprises the Indonesian, Malaysian, and Philippine islands; New Guinea is sometimes included.

Malaysia, Federation of A country in SE Asia, consisting of the 11 states of Peninsular Malaysia (formerly the Federation of Malaya) and the states of *Sabah and *Sarawak in N Borneo. *Economy*: Malaysia is a major exporter of rubber, tin, and palm oil. Besides the cash crops of rubber and palms, rice (the chief food crop) and timber are extensively produced; fishing is also important. Minerals exploited include tin, iron ore, bauxite, ilmenite, and gold. *History*: from the 9th to the 14th centuries the Srivijaya empire dominated the area. In the 14th century it was overrun by Hindu Javanese and in about 1400 Malacca was established as an Islamic centre. British interest in Malaysia began in the 18th century and increased with the opening of the Suez Canal. The Federation of Malaya was established in 1948. Malaya became independent in 1957 and in 1963 part of the federal state of Malaysia. Supreme head of state: Sultan Azlan Muhibuddin Shah. Prime minister: Datuk Seri Mahathir Muhammed. Official language: Bahasa Malaysia. Official religion: Islam. Official currency: ringgit of 100 cents. Area: 329 749 sq km (127 289 sq mi). Population (1989 est): 17 400 000. Capital: Kuala Lumpur. Main port: Georgetown.

Malcolm III (c. 1031–93) King of the Scots (1057–93). He became king after killing *Macbeth, the murderer of his father Duncan I (d. 1040; reigned 1034–40). He became a vassal of William the Conqueror (1072) and was murdered during the last of frequent raids into N England.

Malcolm X (1925–65) US militant Black leader. Formerly a member of the Black Muslims, he founded the rival Organization of Afro-American Unity (1964), which supported violent means of achieving racial equality. He was assassinated while addressing a rally.

Maldives, Republic of (Divehi name: Divehi Raajje; name until 1969: Maldive Islands) A small country in the Indian Ocean, to the SW of Sri Lanka. It consists of a large number of small coral islands, grouped in atolls, of which over 200 are inhabited. *Economy*: coconuts and fish are the main exports. Other sources of revenue include shipping and tourism. *History*: formerly a dependency of Ceylon, the islands were officially under British protection from 1887 to 1965. They were ruled by an elected sultan until 1968, when they became a republic. The Republic of Maldives became a special member of the Commonwealth of Nations in 1982. Head of state: President Maumoon Abdul Gayoom (1937–   ). Official language: Divehi. Official religion: Islam. Official currency: rufiyaa of 100 laari. Area: 298 sq km (115 sq mi). Population (1988 est): 200 000. Capital and main port: Malé.

Mali, Republic of (name until 1959: French Sudan)   A large country in West Africa. *Economy*: subsistence agriculture includes livestock (sheep, cattle, camels), rice millet, cassava, cotton, and groundnuts. River fishing is important and dried and smoked fish, together with cattle and groundnuts, are the main exports. Industry is based on hides and food processing. Bauxite, uranium, and oil are present but only salt and small quantities of gold are exploited. *History*: occupied by successive empires, the area was conquered in the 19th century by the French and, as French Sudan, it became part of French West Africa. It achieved internal self-government as part of the French Community in 1958 and became a fully independent republic in 1960. In 1968 the government was overthrown in a military coup led by Lt Moussa Traoré (1936–   ), who became president in 1969. Official language: French. Official currency: Mali franc of 100 centimes. Area: 1 204 021 sq km (464 752 sq mi). Population (1988 est): 7 784 000. Capital: Bamako.

mallard   A *duck, *Anas platyrhynchos*, common on ponds and lakes in the N hemisphere. About 55 cm long, females are mottled brown and males greyish with a green head, white collar, reddish breast, black rump, and yellow bill. Both sexes have a purple wing patch.

Mallarmé, Stéphane (1842–98) French poet. He became a major figure of the Symbolist movement, believing that the function of poetry should expose the truth behind the world of actual appearances. His best-known works include *Hérodiade* (1864) and *L'Après-midi d'un faune* (1865).

Mallorca. *See* Majorca.

mallow   A plant that is native to N temperate regions. Mallows may grow along the ground or up to 90 cm tall. They have hairy lobed leaves and five-petalled flowers, which are usually purple, pink, or white. The tree mallow (*Lavatera arborea*) is up to 3 m high, with rose-purple flowers. *See also* marsh mallow.

Malmö   55 38N 12 57E A city and port in S Sweden, on the Sound opposite Copenhagen. It was a prominent trade and shipping centre in the middle ages. Malmö's varied industries include shipbuilding, textiles, and food processing. Population (1987): 230 838.

Malory, Sir Thomas (?1400–1471) English writer. He was the author of *Morte d'Arthur* (c. 1469), a history in 21 books of the legendary court of King Arthur, drawn mostly from French sources. The work was printed by Caxton in 1485. Malory's identity remains uncertain, but

he was probably a Warwickshire knight who had fought in France, became an MP in 1445, and was several times imprisoned.

Malraux, André (1901–76) French novelist and essayist. He served with communist revolutionaries in China in the 1920s, with the Republicans in the Spanish Civil War, and with the French Resistance in World War II. His novels, which deal with the issues involved in these conflicts, include *Man's Estate* (1933) and *Days of Hope* (1938). He also wrote on art and produced a volume of memoirs, *Antimémoires* (1967).

Malta, Republic of   A small country in the Mediterranean Sea, to the S of Sicily comprising the two main islands of Malta and Gozo and several islets. *Economy*: Malta was previously heavily dependent on foreign military bases. There is some agriculture, both crops and livestock, and fishing. Tourism is important. Exports include clothing, textiles, machinery, and food. *History*: occupied successively by the Phoenicians, Greeks, Carthaginians, and Romans, the island was conquered by the Arabs in 870 AD. In 1090 it was united with Sicily and in 1530 was granted to the Knights Hospitallers. The island was formally handed over to the British in 1814. As a crown colony it became an important naval and air base. Independence was granted in 1964; in 1974 it became a republic within the Commonwealth. President: Paul Xuereb. Prime minister: Dr Eddie Fenech Adami. Official languages: Maltese and English; Italian is widely spoken. Official religion: Roman Catholic. Official currency: Maltese pound of 100 cents and 1000 mils. Area: 316 sq km (122 sq mi). Population (1988 est): 349 014. Capital and main port: Valletta.

Malthus, Thomas Robert (1766–1834) British clergyman and economist. In his *Essay on the Principle of Population* (*First Essay*, 1798; *Second Essay*, 1803) Malthus argued that mankind is doomed to remain at near-starvation level as arithmetical growth in food production is matched by the geometrical increase in population. He advocated sexual restraint and birth control.

Maluku. *See* Moluccas.

Malvinas, Islas. *See* Falkland Islands.

mamba   A large agile highly venomous egg-laying snake belonging to the African genus *Dendroaspis* (4–5 species). The aggressive black mamba (*D. polylepis*) is 4.3 m long, lives in rocky regions, and preys on birds and small mammals. The smaller green mamba (*D. angusticeps*) lives in trees and reaches a length of 2.7 m.

mammal   A warm-blooded animal of which there are about 4250 species. Mammals evolved from reptiles, and the most primitive mammals (such as the *duck-billed platypus) lay eggs like reptiles. *Marsupial mammals carry their young, which are born in an under-developed state, in a pouch, but the advanced mammals have a special membrane (the *placenta) in the uterus through which the young are nourished, so that they are born in a well-developed state. All mammals feed their young with milk from *mammary glands. Their skin typically bears fur and sweat glands, to control body temperature. Most mammals live on land, ranging in size from tiny shrews to the elephant. However, bats are flying mammals and whales are aquatic mammals.

mammary gland The gland in female mammals that secretes milk; it is the breast in women. Believed to have evolved from sweat glands, there are one or more pairs on the under side of the body; the more young produced at one birth, the greater the number of glands Each gland consists of branching ducts leading from milk-secreting cells and opening to the exterior through a nipple. In primitive mammals (*Monotremata*) there are no nipples and the milk is secreted directly onto the body. *See also* lactation.

mammoth An extinct elephant whose remains have been found in India, Europe, and North America. Of the four types known, the imperial mammoth was the largest, 4.5 m at the shoulder. The woolly mammoth had thick body hair and tusks up to 2.5 m long.

Man, Isle of An island in the Irish Sea, between England and Ireland. It has been a British Crown possession since 1828 but is virtually self-governing with its own parliament, the Court of Tynwald. Tourism is the main source of revenue; attractions include the famous annual Tourist Trophy (TT) motorcycle races. Sheep and cattle are raised and produce includes cereals, turnips, and potatoes. *History*: originally inhabited by Celts, the island became a dependency of Norway in the 9th century AD and was handed over to Scotland (1266), coming under English control after 1406. Area: 588 sq km (227 sq mi). Population (1986): 55 482. Capital: Douglas.

Managua 12 06N 86 18W The capital of Nicaragua, on the S shore of Lake Managua. Formerly an Indian settlement, it became capital in 1857. It suffered severe damage from earthquakes in 1931 and 1972 and from the civil war (1979). Population (1985): 682 111.

manatee An aquatic mammal of warm Atlantic waters and coastal rivers of Africa and America. Up to 4.5 m long, manatees have a rounded body with tail fin and flippers and a squarish snout. They feed on vegetation. *See also* dugong.

Manaus (*or* Manáos) 3 06S 60 00W A city in NW Brazil, the capital of Amazonas state on the Rio Negro. Founded in 1660, it became the centre of the rubber boom (1890–1920). It remains the chief inland port of the Amazon basin. Exports include rubber, brazil nuts, timber, and other forest products. Population (1980): 613 098.

Manchester 53 30N 2 15W A city in NW England, the administrative centre of Greater Manchester, situated on the River Irwell. Linked with the Mersey estuary by the Manchester Ship Canal (opened 1894), it is an important port as well as England's second largest commercial centre. Industries include chemicals, engineering, clothing, printing, paper, food products, and electrical goods. It has art galleries and the Hallé Orchestra, and the national newspaper the *Guardian* was founded here as the *Manchester Guardian* in 1821. The 15th-century parish church became Manchester Cathedral in 1847. *History*: the Roman fort of Mancunium developed as a regional market for wool and flax. From the mid-18th century onwards it became the world's main cotton-manufacturing town. Its rapid growth led to industrial discontent and political agitation (*see* Peterloo Massacre). Population (1987 est): 450 100.

Manchuria A region in NE China bordering on the Soviet Union, roughly comprising the provinces of Heilongjiang, Jilin, and Liaoning. Products include timber, minerals, such as coal and iron, and fish. *History*: the area was for centuries inhabited and fought over by the Manchu, Mongols, and Chinese. In the late 19th century it was dominated by Russia (1898–1904) and then by Japan (1905–45). After 1945 the area received aid from the Soviet Union until the 1960s, when the break between China and the Soviet Union took place. Area: about 1 300 000 sq km (502 000 sq mi).

Mandalay 21 57N 96 04E A city in Burma, on the Irrawaddy River. The last capital of the Burmese kingdom, it fell to the British in 1885. It has numerous monasteries, temples, and pagodas, and a university (1964). Mandalay is the principal commercial centre of Upper Burma. Population (1983): 417 266.

mandarin (fruit). *See* tangerine.

mandarin (official) Before 1911, a Chinese government official whose appointment to salaried posts in the civil service was by examination. Mandarins occupied an important position in society and spoke the Mandarin dialect of *Chinese, which is its standard, Peking, form is now spoken by 70% of the population.

Mandela, Nelson (Rolihlahla) (1918–) Black South African politician and lawyer, vice-president of the African National Congress. He was found not guilty of treason in 1961 but retried (1963–64) and sentenced to life imprisonment. His release was finally achieved, after international pressure, in 1990; since then he has been involved in talks with the South African government about ending apartheid. His wife, **Winnie Mandela** (1934–), is also active in South African politics.

mandolin A plucked musical instrument, generally having four pairs of wire strings tuned as the violin. It is played with a plectrum vibrated between pairs of strings (tremolo) to sustain longer notes. It is used for informal music.

mandrake A plant, *Mandragora officinarum*, of the nightshade family, native to Europe. It has large simple leaves, white flowers, and a thick forked root, which was formerly believed to have healing and aphrodisiac properties.

mandrill A large *monkey, *Mandrillus sphinx*, of West African coastal forests. They are 66–84 cm long including the tail (5–7.5 cm), with red and blue muzzle and buttocks and shaggy yellow-brown hair. They live in small family groups and feed on plants and insects.

Manet, Edouard (1832–83) French painter. By 1860 he was painting contemporary scenes influenced by Velázquez and Hals. He exhibited mainly at the Paris Salon, where such paintings as *Olympia* and *Déjeuner sur l'herbe* (both Louvre) became targets for derision. In the 1870s he adopted the technique of the impressionists.

Such paintings as *The Balcony* (Louvre) and *The Luncheon* (Neue Staatsgaleries, Munich) foreshadowed 20th-century painting by making brushwork, colour, and design more important than the subject.

manganese (Mn) A hard grey brittle *transition element that resembles iron, first obtained in pure form in 1774 by J. G. Gahn (1745–1818). It occurs in many minerals, especially pyrolusite (MnO_2) and rhodochrosite ($MnCO_3$), in addition to the deposits of manganese nodules discovered on ocean floors. It is obtained from the oxide, with magnesium or aluminium, or by *electrolysis. The metal is used in many alloys, particularly in steel to improve the strength and hardness. Manganese forms compounds in a number of different *valence states: for example MnO, Mn_3O_4, MnO_2. The permanganate, or manganate(VII), ion (MnO_4^-) is a well-known oxidizing agent. At no 25; at wt 54.9380; mp 1244°C; bp 1962°C.

mange A skin disease, caused by mites, that can affect domestic livestock, pets, and man. The parasites burrow into the skin causing hair loss, scaly skin, pimples, blisters, and itching. The disease is spread by bodily contact. Treatment is with an insecticide.

mangel-wurzel. *See* beet.

mango A large evergreen tropical tree, *Mangifera indica*, native to SE Asia but cultivated throughout the tropics for its fruit. Growing 15–18 m high, it has long narrow leaves and pinkish flowers. The oblong fruit, up to 2.3 kg in weight, has a green, yellow, or reddish skin and contains a stony seed, surrounded by juicy spicy edible flesh.

mangrove A tropical shrub or tree forming dense thickets and low forests on coastal mudflats, salt marshes, and estuaries. There are several species, many of which are evergreen. Mangroves have roots above ground that either support the plant or assist in breathing.

Manhattan. *See* New York.

Manichaeism A religion influenced by both *Gnosticism and Christianity. It started in Persia (c. 230 AD), spread throughout Asia and the Roman Empire, and survived in Chinese Turkistan until the 13th century. Its founder, Mani (c. 216–c. 276), was martyred by the followers of *Zoroastrianism. He believed that matter is entirely evil, but within each individual is imprisoned a soul, which is a spark of the divine light.

Manila 14 30N 121 12E The capital and main port of the Philippines, on Manila Bay in Luzon. Founded by the Spanish in 1571, it suffered several foreign occupations over the centuries and the old town was destroyed in World War II. An educational centre, it has over 20 universities. It has one of the finest harbours in the world; its industries include textiles, pharmaceuticals, and food processing. Population (1984 est): 1 728 441.

manioc. *See* cassava.

Manitoba A province of central Canada. Although it is one of the Prairie Provinces, only the SW is true prairie. Further to the NE lies the *Red River Valley and three large lakes (Winnipeg, Winnipegosis, and Manitoba). Large mech-

anized farms produce grains and livestock; forests, fisheries, and hydroelectricity are also important. Copper, gold, zinc, silver, nickel, and oil are mined. *History*: originally exploited for furs, Manitoba was first settled by Scots Highlanders (1812). Acquisition of the area by Canada (1869) provoked the Riel Rebellion (1869–70), an uprising of French-speaking halfbreeds (Métis). Manitoba became a province in 1870. Area: 548 495 sq km (211 774 sq mi). Population (1986): 1 063 016. Capital: Winnipeg.

Manley, Michael (1924–) Jamaican statesman, who, as leader of the People's National Party, was prime minister of Jamaica (1972–80; 1989–). His socialist policies have included nationalizing 51% of the bauxite industry, developing close ties with Cuba, and speaking out for the Third World.

Mann, Thomas (1875–1955) German novelist. *Buddenbrooks* (1901), *Death in Venice* (1912), *The Magic Mountain* (1924), and *Doctor Faustus* (1947) are his best-known works. Other works include *Joseph and His Brothers* (1933–44), a series of four novels based on the biblical story of Joseph, and *Felix Krull* (1954). Mann opposed Nazism and was forced to emigrate to the USA in the 1930s. He was awarded a Nobel Prize in 1929.

mannerism An art movement dominant in Italy from about 1520 to 1600. Mannerism developed out of the *Renaissance style, aiming for greater brilliance and impact. In painting this led to a distortion of scale, an elongation of form, and dissonance of colour. Leading mannerist painters were Pontormo, Parmigianino, *Vasari, and *Bronzino. Some characteristics appear in the late work of *Raphael and *Michelangelo.

Mannheim 49 30N 8 28E A city in SW Germany, in Baden-Württemberg where the Rivers Rhine and Neckar meet. It was the seat of the Electors Palatine (1720–98) and has a notable baroque castle. It is a major port with an oil refinery and its manufactures include motor vehicles and agricultural machinery. Population (1987): 294 600.

manometer An instrument for measuring pressure differences. The simplest form consists of a U-shaped tube containing mercury, one arm of which is connected to a source of pressure and the other is open. The difference in height of the liquid in the arms is a measure of the pressure difference.

manor The most common unit of land organization in medieval Europe, introduced into England by the Normans. The manor was essentially the lord's landed estate, usually consisting of the lord's own farm (the demesne), and land let out to peasant tenants, chiefly *villeins, who worked for the demesne and were legally dependent upon their lord.

Manpower Services Commission (MSC). *See* Training Agency.

Mansell, Nigel (1954–) British racing driver. Since winning the European Grand Prix in 1985 he has been Britain's top Formula One driver.

Mansfield, Katherine (Kathleen Mansfield Beauchamp; 1888–1923) New Zealand short-story writer. She came to Europe in 1908 and published her first collection of stories in 1911. *Bliss* (1920) and *The Garden Party* (1922) contain her best-known stories.

manslaughter The crime of killing a person either (1) accidentally by an unlawful act or by neglect of duty or (2) in the heat of passion, after being provoked. The second case is related to murder but there must be no evidence of advance planning.

manta ray A *ray fish, also called devil ray or devil fish. 60–660 cm long, mantas swim near the surface of warm-temperate and tropical waters, feeding on plankton and small animals swept into the mouth by hornlike feeding fins projecting from the front of the head.

Mantegna, Andrea (c. 1431–1506) Italian Renaissance painter, born near Vicenza. His marriage (1453) to the daughter of Jacopo *Bellini connected him with the Venetian school. As court painter to the Duke of Mantua from 1459, he painted nine panels depicting *The Triumph of Caesar* Hampton Court, London. His frescos for the bridal chamber of the ducal palace include members of the Mantuan court.

mantis An insect found in tropical and warm-temperate regions. Up to 125 mm long, mantids blend with the surrounding vegetation, using their forelegs to capture insects and other small animals. The "praying" position held by the forelegs at rest accounts for the name praying mantis.

Mantua (Italian name: Mantova) 45 10N 10 47E A city in N Italy, in Lombardy on the River Mincio. It has a cathedral (10th–18th centuries) and a 14th-century castle. An important tourist centre, Mantua's industries also include tanning, printing, and sugar refining. Population (1983 est): 60 468.

Manx An extinct language of the *Celtic family. An offshoot of Irish Gaelic, it was spoken on the Isle of Man until the 19th century.

Manx cat A breed of short-haired tailless cat from the Isle of Man. The Manx has a short body with deep flanks and a large head.

Maoism The theories developed by *Mao Tse-tung. Mao's plan for revolution in China gave central importance to peasant armies rather than to the action of the industrial working class in the cities. Similarly, on a world scale, he believed that the socialist revolutions would develop first in the underdeveloped countries rather than in advanced capitalist countries (*compare* Marxism).

Maori A *Polynesian people of New Zealand, who make up about 10% of the population. Originally migrants, probably from the Cook Islands, they came in canoes around 1350, settling mainly in the North Island. The traditional arts of wood carving and dancing still survive but the Maori culture has largely been destroyed.

Mao Tse-tung (*or* Mao Ze Dong; 1893–1976) Chinese communist statesman. Born into a peasant family, he was a Marxist by 1920 and helped to form the Chinese Communist Party (CCP) in 1921. In 1931 he became chairman of the Jiangxi Soviet. Forced to evacuate Jiangxi in 1934, Mao led the communist forces on the *Long March. Following the defeat of Japan in the *Sino-Japanese War of 1937–45, civil war was renewed, ending in communist victory. In 1949 Mao, as chairman of the Communist Party, declared the establishment of the People's Republic of China. Mao's political writings (*see* Maoism) formed the basis of the government and led to the Great Leap Forward. He stepped down as chairman in 1958, but reappeared with greater standing during the *Cultural Revolution.

maple A shrub or tree widespread in N temperate regions, often grown for timber and ornament. 6–35 m high, maples usually bear lobed leaves, which turn orange or red in autumn, and small greenish flowers, which give rise to paired winged fruits (samaras). The sap of the North American sugar maple (*Acer saccharum*) is the source of maple sugar.

map projection The representation of the curved surface of the earth on a plane surface. The parallels of latitude and meridians of longitude (*see* latitude and longitude) are represented as a network of intersecting lines. It is not possible to produce a projection of the earth's surface without some distortion of area, shape, or direction.

Maputo (name until 1975: Lourenço Marques) 25 58S 32 35E The capital and chief port of Mozambique, on Delagoe Bay. It became the capital of Portuguese East Africa in 1907. A major East African port, its exports include minerals from South Africa, Swaziland, and Zimbabwe. Population (1986): 882 800.

Maracaibo 10 44N 71 37W The second largest city in Venezuela, a port on the NW shore of Lake Maracaibo. Its economic importance is based on oil production; industries include petrochemicals. Population (1987 est): 1 124 432.

Maradona, Diego (1960–) Argentinian footballer, who captained the team that won the World Cup in 1986; he has also played for Barcelona and Naples.

marasmus. *See* kwashiorkor.

Marat, Jean Paul (1743–93) French politician. A radical journalist during the French Revolution, he became editor of *L'Ami du peuple*. He was elected to the National Convention in 1792, but was murdered by Charlotte Corday (1768–93), a member of the Girondins, whom Marat had helped to overthrow (1793).

marathon A long-distance running race over 42 195 m (26 mi 385 yd) that derives its name from a soldier who ran from the battlefield of Marathon to Athens with news of the Greek victory. As different courses vary, there is no official world record; the fastest time for men is 2 hours 6 minutes 50 seconds (1988) by Belanyeh Dinsamo (Ethiopia), for women 2 hours 21 minutes 6 seconds (1985) by Ingrid Kristiansen (Norway).

Marathon, Battle of (490 BC) The battle during the *Greek-Persian Wars in which the Athenians under Miltiades defeated the Persians. *Phidippides was sent to summon Spartan help but the Spartans arrived too late.

marble **1.** A rock consisting of *limestone altered by the effects of pressure and heat (metamorphosed). Pure marble is white recrystallized calcite, but impurities, such as dolomite, silica, or clay minerals result in variations of colour. Certain quarries in Greece and Italy have been producing large quantities of marble since pre-Christian times. **2.** Any rock that can be polished for ornamental use.

Marceau, Marcel (1923–) French mime. He began to study mime in 1946, gradually developing the original character Bip, a white-faced clown. As well as giving solo performances, he formed his own mime company.

Marcellus, Marcus Claudius (d. 208 BC) Roman general in the second *Punic War. Chosen to check Hannibal's advance through Italy, he captured Syracuse and wore down the Carthaginian armies in S Italy.

Marches The border areas of England and Wales, conquered between 1067 and 1238 by vassals of the English kings. The so-called **marcher lords** enjoyed enormous powers until the union of Wales and England in the 1530s.

Marciano, Rocky (Rocco Francis Marchegiano; 1923–69) US boxer. He took the world heavyweight championship from Joe Walcott in 1952 and retired undefeated in 1956, after 6 defences. Unbeaten in his 49 professional fights, he was killed in an aircrash.

Marconi, Guglielmo (1874–1937) Italian electrical engineer, who invented, independently of Aleksandr Popov (1859–1905), communication by radio. On reading about radio waves, Marconi built a device that would convert them into electrical signals, experimenting with transmitting and receiving them over increasing distances until, in 1901, he succeeded in transmitting a signal across the Atlantic. For this work he shared the Nobel Prize for Physics in 1909.

Marcos, Ferdinand E(dralin) (1917–89) Philippine statesman; president (1965–86). Threatened by civil unrest, in 1972 he assumed dictatorial powers. The murder in 1983 of opposition leader Begnino Aquino Jr, with alleged government support, caused a popular uprising in 1986 when Marcos was forced into exile. In 1988 he and his wife Imelda were charged in the USA with embezzlement and fraud. He died before he could be tried: Imelda was cleared in 1990.

Marcus Aurelius (121–180 AD) Roman emperor (161–180), in association with Lucius Verus (130–169) from 161 and alone from 169. Although he is known as the philosopher emperor on account of his *Meditations* (12 books of sayings), he was an active ruler.

Marduk The supreme god in Babylonian mythology. He created order out of the universe after defeating the sea dragon Tiamat and the forces of chaos. This victory was celebrated in a festival at the start of each year.

Margaret (Rose) (1930–) Princess of the United Kingdom; the younger daughter of George VI and sister of Elizabeth II, she is eleventh in succession to the throne. In 1960 she married Antony Armstrong-Jones (later Lord *Snowdon); they were divorced in 1978. Their children are David, Viscount Linley (1961–), and Lady Sarah Armstrong-Jones (1964–).

Margaret of Anjou (1430–82) The wife (1445–71) of Henry VI of England; their marriage was an attempt to make peace between England and France during the Wars of the *Roses, in which she was one of the most formidable Lancastrian leaders. She was captured and imprisoned after the Lancastrian defeat in the battle of Tewkesbury (1471). After her husband's death she returned to France (1476).

Margaret Tudor (1489–1541) Regent of Scotland (1513–14) for her son James V. The elder daughter of Henry VII of England and the wife of James IV of the Scots (d. 1513), she was ousted from the regency by the English but continued to play an active role in politics until 1534.

margarine A butter substitute consisting of pasteurized fat-free milk powder, mixed with water and certain refined vegetable oils. Vitamins A and D are also added. Soft margarines contain only lightly hydrogenated oils.

margay A spotted *cat, *Felis wiedi*, of Central and South America. It is 90 cm long including the tail (30 cm) and is found in forests hunting small mammals.

Margrethe II (1940–) Queen of Denmark (1972–), who succeeded her father Frederick IX after the Danish constitution had been altered to permit the accession of a woman. In 1967 she married a French diplomat Henri de Laborde de Monpezat (Prince Henrik; 1934–); they have two sons, Prince Frederick (1968–) and Prince Joachim (1969–).

marguerite See oxeye daisy.

Mariana Islands (or Ladrone Islands) A group of mountainous islands in the W Pacific Ocean, comprising *Guam and the US commonwealth territory of the Northern Marianas. They include the islands of Tinian and Saipan. Discovered in 1521, the islands were colonized by Spanish Jesuits after 1668. Sugar cane, coffee, and coconuts are produced. Area: 958 sq km (370 sq mi). Population (1984 est): 135 391. Administrative centre: Garapan, on Saipan.

MARIANAS TRENCH

Marianas Trench A deep trench in the earth's crust in the W Pacific; it is the greatest known ocean depth (11 033 m), marking the site of a plate margin (see plate tectonics).

Maria Theresa (1717–80) Archduchess of Austria (1740–80). Her father Emperor Charles VI issued the Pragmatic Sanction (1713) to enable her to succeed to his Austrian territories, which nevertheless caused the War of the *Austrian Succession (1740–48). Under the influence of Count von Kaunitz (1711–94), Maria Theresa exchanged her English alliance for a French coalition but in the subsequent *Seven Years' War (1756–63) Austria suffered defeat. At home she achieved a measure of reform.

Marie Antoinette (1755–93) The wife of Louis XVI of France, whose uncompromising attitude to the *French Revolution contributed to the overthrow of the monarchy. The daughter of Emperor Francis I and Maria Theresa, she married the dauphin Louis in 1770. Her extravagance and rumoured immorality contributed to the unpopularity of the Crown. After the overthrow of the monarchy and Louis' execution, she was herself guillotined.

marigold A flowering plant of the daisy family, widely grown in gardens. The pot marigold (*Calendula officinalis*), native to S Europe, bears orange or yellow flowers, whose petals can be eaten in salads. The African and French marigolds, native to Mexico, have single or double flowers. See also marsh marigold.

marihuana. See cannabis.

Mariner probes A series of successful US spacecraft that sent back information about the planets. Mariners 2 and 5 approached Venus in 1962 and 1967, while Mariner 10 flew past Venus in 1974 and then three times past Mercury in 1974–75. Mariners 4 (1965), 6 and 7 (1969), and 9 (1971–72) investigated Mars, with Mariner 9 going into Martian orbit. Mariners 11 and 12 were renamed the *Voyager probes. Mariners 1, 3, and 8 did not achieve their missions.

maritime law The branch of law relating to shipping. The Romans imposed an international uniform code in the Mediterranean, which was preserved until the 17th-century when various individual codes developed. The English **Admiralty Court**, established in the 14th century, developed broad powers in deciding questions of commercial law, but in the 17th century was restricted to matters "done upon the sea." Today the Admiralty Court is mainly concerned with cases involving salvage and collisions at sea. International uniformity has recently been achieved by the member states of the Comité maritime international (CMI).

Maritime Provinces (Maritimes or Atlantic Provinces) The easternmost provinces of Canada, on the Atlantic coast and the Gulf of St Lawrence. They consist of *New Brunswick, *Nova Scotia, *Prince Edward Island, and usually *Newfoundland and lie in the Appalachian Highlands.

marjoram An aromatic herb native to Eurasia. Wild marjoram (*Origanum vulgaris*), is a hairy plant, 30–80 cm tall, bearing clusters of small tubular pinkish-purple flowers. Sweet marjoram (*Majorana hortensis*), is cultivated for its aromatic leaves and flowers, used in cookery.

Mark, St The author of the second Gospel of the New Testament. A cousin of *Barnabas, he

went with him and Paul on their first mission. Subsequently he seems to have assisted Paul in Rome, where he also acted as interpreter for Peter. He was believed to have founded the Church in Alexandria and is also associated with Venice, of which he is patron saint. Feast day: 25 April.

Mark Antony (Marcus Antonius; c. 83–31 BC) Roman general and statesman. Following Julius Caesar's assassination, Antony came into conflict with Octavian (see Augustus) but later they formed the second *Triumvirate with Lepidus (43). In 42 Antony defeated his opponents, Brutus and Cassius, at *Philippi. In 37 Antony abandoned his wife Octavia (Octavian's sister) to live with Cleopatra in Egypt. In 32 the Senate declared war on Egypt and Antony was defeated at *Actium. Both he and Cleopatra committed suicide.

Markova, Dame Alicia (Lilian Alicia Marks; 1910–) British ballet dancer. She joined Diaghilev's Ballets Russes in 1925 and the Vic-Wells Ballet in 1931. With Anton Dolin she formed a company in 1935 and joined the Ballet Theatre, USA, in 1941.

marl A *clay that consists mainly of calcium carbonate and is plastic when wet; marl can be transformed into a hard rock, called marlstone. Marls are deposited in water, either fresh or marine, and are used in the manufacture of cement.

Marlborough, John Churchill, 1st Duke of (1650–1722) British general. He put down *Monmouth's rebellion against James II (1685) but subsequently supported the *Glorious Revolution (1688) against James. As commander in chief in the War of the *Spanish Succession, he won the great victories of *Blenheim (1704), Ramillies (1706), Oudenaarde (1708), and Malplaquet (1709). A *Whig, his political importance owed much to his wife **Sarah Churchill** (*born* Jennings; 1660–1744), a friend of Queen Anne. Following Sarah's fall from favour, he was charged with embezzlement and dismissed (1711). See also Blenheim Palace.

marlin A large widespread fast-swimming game fish, also called spearfish. It has an elongated body, up to 2.5 m long, a cylindrical snout, and a rigid dorsal fin.

Marlowe, Christopher (1564–93) English dramatist and poet. His political activity while a student at Cambridge may have had some bearing on his death in a tavern fight in Deptford. His plays, which include *Tamburlaine the Great* (about 1587) and *Faustus* (probably 1592), show his mastery of blank verse and dramatic characterization.

Marmara, Sea of A sea lying between European and Asian Turkey and between the Bosporus and the Dardanelles. The island of Marmara has long been a source of marble and granite. Area: 11 474 sq km (4429 sq mi).

marmoset A small South American monkey with claws instead of fingernails. Marmosets are 20–90 cm long including the tail (10–38 cm) and have silky fur, often strikingly marked, and long tails for balancing. They feed on fruit, insects, eggs, and small birds.

marmot   A large squirrel, also called ground-hog, of Europe, Asia, and North America. Marmots are 30–60 cm long and inhabit burrows in mountainous country. The woodchuck (*Marmota monax*) is a North American species.

Marquesas Islands   A group of 12 volcanic islands in the S Pacific Ocean, in French Polynesia (annexed 1842). Nuku Hiva is the largest. The islands export copra, cotton, and vanilla. Area: 1287 sq km (497 sq mi). Population (1984): 6548. Capital: Atuona on Hiva Oa.

Marrakech (*or* Marrakesh)   31 49N 8 00W The second largest city in Morocco. Founded in 1062, it was the capital of the Moorish kingdom of Morocco. It produces carpets and leather goods. Population (1982): 439 728.

marram grass   A coarse *grass, also called beach grass or sand reed, which grows on sandy coasts of Europe, North America, and N Africa. About 1 m high, it has spikelike leaves and scaly spreading underground stems, which help to prevent sand dunes from shifting.

marrow (botany)   A climbing American plant, *Cucurbita pepo*, of the gourd family, several varieties of which are cultivated as vegetables. Marrows bear yellow or orange cup-shaped flowers and elongated fleshy fruits, which have green or yellow skins. *See also* courgette.

marrow (zoology)   The soft tissue in the central cavities of bones. In early life the red marrow of all bones manufactures blood cells. In adult life the marrow of the limb bones becomes filled with fat cells and ceases to function: this is yellow marrow.

Mars (astronomy)   The fourth planet from the sun, orbiting the sun every 687 days at a mean distance of 227.9 million km. Its diameter is 6794 km and its period of axial rotation 24 hours 37 minutes 23 seconds. It has two small *satellites. The Martian atmosphere is 95% carbon dioxide and is very thin (surface pressure 7 millibars). The dry reddish dust-covered surface is heavily cratered in the S hemisphere while N regions show signs of earlier volcanic activity. *See* Mariner probes; Viking probes.

Mars (mythology)   The Roman war god, the son of Juno. He was identified with the Greek *Ares and is usually portrayed as an armed warrior. Originally a god of agriculture, he was later worshipped at Rome as a protector of the city.

Marsala (ancient name: Lilybaeum)   37 48N 12 27E A port in Italy, in W Sicily. Founded in 397 BC as a Carthaginian stronghold, it has ancient remains and a baroque cathedral. Marsala wine, grain, and salt are exported. Population (1981 est): 79 093.

Marseillaise, La   The French national anthem, written in 1792, by Claude Rouget de l'Isle (1760–1836). It was originally a patriotic song entitled "Le Chant de guerre de l'armée du Rhin." It was taken up by republican soldiers from Marseille, who were prominent in the storming of the Tuileries, and became the revolutionary anthem.

Marseille (English name: Marseilles)   43 18N 5 22E The principal seaport in France, the capital of the Bouches-du-Rhône department. Founded about 600 BC, it was destroyed by the

Arabs in the 9th century AD, redeveloped during the Crusades, and came under the French Crown in 1481. Industry includes oil refining at Fos. Population (1982): 878 689.

Marshall, George C(atlett) (1880–1959) US general and statesman. As army chief of staff (1939–45) he organized the build-up of US forces. As secretary of state (1947–49) he developed the **Marshall Plan**, in which the USA undertook to provide economic aid to Europe after World War II. For this he won a Nobel Peace Prize (1953).

marsh gas.   *See* methane.

marsh mallow   A stout plant, *Althaea officinalis*, of marshy coastal areas of Eurasia. 60–90 cm high, it has lobed leaves and flesh-coloured flowers. The roots yield a sticky substance, formerly used to make marshmallows (spongy sweets).

marsh marigold   A stout plant, *Caltha palustris*, of the buttercup family, also called kingcup, growing in marshes and wet woods throughout arctic and temperate Eurasia and North America. It grows upright or along the ground; up to 80 cm long, its stems bear round leaves and bright golden flowers.

Marston Moor, Battle of (2 July, 1644) The battle in the English *Civil War in which the parliamentarians and the Scots defeated the royalists at Marston Moor, W of York, destroying the king's hold on N England.

marsupial   A primitive *mammal (176 species), found mostly in Australia and New Guinea and including the *kangaroos, *bandicoots, and *phalangers. The only American marsupials are the *opossums.
Marsupials have relatively small brains and lacking a placenta their young are born at a very early stage and complete their development in a pouch of skin on the mother's belly surrounding the teat, from which they are fed until fully formed.

Martello towers   Fortifications containing cannon built in S Britain, Ireland, and Guernsey from 1804 to 1812. The towers were intended to check the possible invasion of Britain by Napoleon–which never happened. They were named after the single tower mounting cannon at Mortella Point, Corsica.

marten   A carnivorous mammal related to weasels and badgers and found in forests of Europe, Asia, and North America. Up to 90 cm long including the tail (15–30 cm), martens are skilful climbers and hunters with dark fur. The two European species are the *pine marten and the smaller stone marten (*Martes foina*).

martial arts   Armed and unarmed combat developed in the East. The Japanese forms, such as *karate, *judo, and sumo, developed from the fighting skills of the *samurai. Since the 19th century they have become sports, as has the Chinese form, *kung fu.

martin   A bird related to the *swallows. The widely distributed brown sand martin (*Riparia riparia*) is about 12 cm long. It nests in colonies in tunnels excavated in sand banks. The black-and-white house martin (*Delichon urbica*), about 13 cm long, nests beneath the eaves of houses.

Martin, Pierre-Émile (1824–1915) French engineer, who invented the Siemens-Martin process of producing steel. In this process Martin adapted the open-hearth furnace developed in 1856 by Sir William Siemens (1823–83) utilizing pig iron and scrap steel.

Martin, St (c. 316–97 AD) A patron saint of France; Bishop of Tours (372–97). A soldier in the imperial army, he later settled at Poitiers and founded the first monastery in Gaul. His military cloak, traditionally given to a naked beggar, has become a symbol of charity. Feast day: 11 Nov.

Martinique A French overseas region in the West Indies, in the Windward Islands of the Lesser Antilles. It consists of a mountainous island of volcanic origin. The chief exports are sugar, bananas, and rum. Area: 1090 sq km (420 sq mi). Population (1988 est): 336 000. Capital: Fort-de-France.

Martinmas The feast of St *Martin (11 Nov), traditionally the date for slaughtering livestock to be salted as winter food. In Scotland it is a *quarter day recognized in common law.

Marvell, Andrew (1621–78) English *metaphysical poet. He was employed as tutor by Cromwell and Fairfax and as secretary by Milton. From 1659 until his death he served as MP for Hull. He published several satires and pamphlets attacking religious intolerance and government corruption. His poems include "To his Coy Mistress" and "The Garden."

Marx, Karl (Heinrich) (1818–83) German philosopher, economist, and revolutionary. In 1842 Marx became the editor of a radical paper; after its suppression he spent the rest of his life in exile. In Paris he met Friedrich *Engels, who contributed to many of Marx's writings and provided him with financial support. While in Brussels, Marx's association with a group of German handicraftsmen led to *The Communist Manifesto* (1848). In 1849 Marx moved to London, where he remained for the rest of his life. Following the establishment of the International Working Men's Association in 1864, Marx devoted many years to the affairs of the First *International. The first volume of *Das Kapital* was published in 1867. See also Marxism.

Marx brothers A US family of comic film actors: **Chico** (Leonard M.; 1886–1961), **Harpo** (Adolph M.; 1888–1964), **Groucho** (Julius M.; 1890–1977), and, until 1933, **Zeppo** (Herbert M.; 1901–79). Their film comedies included *Horse Feathers* (1932), *Duck Soup* (1933), and *A Night at the Opera* (1935). The team disbanded in 1949.

Marxism The theory of scientific socialism introduced by *Marx and *Engels, which explains the beginnings, development, and death of the capitalist system. In the working-class revolution, a socialist and eventually a classless society would be achieved by the violent overthrow of the state power (army, police, etc.) of the bourgeois class. The working class would establish its own more democratic state power. As classes gradually disappeared, however, state power would wither away. Since World War I there have been many different interpretations of Marxism (*see also* communism).

Mary I (1516–58) Queen of England and Ireland (1553–58), succeeding her younger half-brother *Edward VI. The daughter of Henry VIII and Catherine of Aragon, Mary became queen after the failure of a plot to place Lady Jane *Grey on the throne. Known as Bloody Mary, she repealed Edward's Protestant laws in an attempt to restore Catholicism; in 1554 heresy laws were reintroduced, resulting in almost 300 deaths at the stake. Her marriage (1554) to Philip II of Spain involved England in Philip's foreign policy and the loss in 1558 of Calais.

Mary II (1662–94) Queen of England, Scotland, and Ireland (1689–94), joint monarch with her husband William III. Daughter of James II, she was brought up as a Protestant and came to the throne after the flight of her Roman Catholic father during the *Glorious Revolution.

Mary, Queen of Scots (1542–87) The daughter of James V and the French noblewoman Mary of Guise (1515–60); she succeeded to the throne shortly after her birth. From 1547 Mary, a Roman Catholic, lived at the French court, where in 1558 she married the dauphin (later Francis II). After Francis' death (1561) Mary returned to Scotland and in 1565 married, unpopularly, her cousin Lord *Darnley. In 1566 she gave birth to the future James VI (James I of England). In 1567 Darnley was murdered by *Bothwell, who subsequently married Mary. A rebellion of Scottish nobles defeated Mary and Bothwell at Carberry Hill (1567) and Mary abdicated in favour of her son. Fleeing to England, where her claim to the English throne was an embarrassment to Elizabeth I, she was imprisoned for the rest of her life. The focus of several plots against Elizabeth, she was finally executed for involvement in the conspiracy of Anthony Babington (1561–86).

Mary, the Virgin In the New Testament, the mother of *Jesus Christ. The fullest accounts of Mary are contained in the *Gospels of Luke and Matthew. John (19.25) reports her presence at the crucifixion while Luke records the Annunciation and her betrothal to *Joseph. The Gospels also state that she was a virgin. See also Immaculate Conception.

Mary Magdalene, St In the New Testament, the first person to see Jesus after the resurrection. Said to have been cured of possession by evil spirits by Jesus, she aided his work in Galilee and was present at the crucifixion and burial. Medieval scholars associated her with the repentant prostitute who annointed Jesus' feet, mentioned in Luke's Gospel. Feast day: 22 July. Emblem: an ointment jar.

Maryland A state on the E coast of the USA. Industries include metal working, food processing, transportation and electrical equipment, printing and publishing, and textiles. Agricultural products include livestock, dairy products, corn, tobacco, soya beans, and vegetables. *History*: one of the 13 original colonies, it was first settled by the English. It was named after Henrietta Maria, wife of Charles I. Area: 27 394 sq km (10 577 sq mi). Population (1986 est): 4 463 000. Capital: Annapolis. Chief port: Baltimore.

Mary Rose A Tudor warship (Henry VIII's flagship), which sank in 1545 in Portsmouth Harbour while sailing into battle. The wreck was positively identified in 1971. The ship's contents, most of which were remarkably preserved, were raised during the following ten years and the hull itself was lifted in 1982 and placed in dry-dock in Portsmouth. The Mary Rose Trust, of which the Prince of Wales is president, was formed in 1979.

Masaccio (Tommaso di Giovanni di Simone Guidi; 1401–28) Florentine painter of the early Renaissance. He worked with Masolino (1383–?1447) on the *Madonna and Child with St Anne* (Uffizi) and other works. His independent paintings include the *Trinity* (Sta Maria Novella, Florence). Masaccio introduced the use of linear perspective and a single light source in painting.

Masada 31 19N 35 21E A rocky hilltop near the W shore of the Dead Sea, in Israel. The site of one of *Herod the Great's fortified palaces, it was later an *Essene centre and a stronghold of the Jews in their revolt against Rome (66 AD). In 73 AD the defenders committed suicide rather than surrender. The site is an Israeli national monument.

Masai A wandering people of Kenya and Tanzania who speak a Sudanic language. Milk and blood from cattle form an important part of their diet, the blood being drawn from a vein in the animal's neck without killing it. Tall and active, the Masai highly value courage in their warriors.

Masefield, John (1878–1967) British poet. Having served briefly in the merchant navy, he captured the fascination of the sea in his first volume, *Salt-Water Ballads* (1902). He also wrote long poems, such as *Reynard the Fox* (1919), and several adventure novels, including *Sard Harker* (1924) and *Odtaa* (1926). He became poet laureate in 1930.

maser (*m*icrowave *a*mplification by *s*timulated *e*mission of *r*adiation) A device that works on the same principle as the *laser, the radiation produced being in the *microwave region. Masers are used in electronics as microwave oscillators and amplifiers.

Maseru 29 19S 27 29E The capital of Lesotho, near the South African border. It was founded in 1869. Population (1986 est): 109 382.

Mason-Dixon line A line drawn in 1767 by two surveyors, Charles Mason and Jeremiah Dixon, to settle the conflict over borders between Pennsylvania and Maryland. Until the Civil War it divided the southern states, in favour of slavery, from the northern free states.

masque A court entertainment popular in England during the late 16th and early 17th centuries. Perfected by Ben *Jonson and Inigo *Jones, it consisted of a combination of verse, dance, and music, usually with a slight dramatic plot based on a mythological theme.

mass (physics). *See* mass and weight.

Mass (religion). *See* Eucharist.

Massachusetts A state on the NE coast of the USA, in New England. Its industries produce electrical and communications equipment, instruments, chemicals, textiles, and metal and food products. Boston is an important financial and educational centre. Agricultural products include eggs, poultry, cranberries, and horticultural goods. *History*: one of the 13 original colonies, it was a centre for opposition to British colonial policy leading to the American Revolution. Area: 21 386 sq km (8257 sq mi). Population (1985 est): 5 819 087. Capital: Boston.

mass action, law of The rate of a chemical reaction for a uniform system at constant temperature is proportional to the concentration of each reacting substance, raised to the power equal to the number of molecules of the substance appearing in the balanced equation. Thus, for the reaction $2H_2 + O_2 = 2H_2O$ the speed of the forward reaction is proportional to the concentration of O_2 (written $[O_2]$) and to $[H_2]^2$; the reverse reaction depends on $[H_2O]^2$.

mass and weight Two physical quantities measuring how much of a substance is present; they are sometimes confused. The mass of a body was defined by *Newton as the ratio of a force applied to the body to the acceleration it produces. This is now called the **inertial mass**. **Gravitational mass** is proportional to the gravitational force between two bodies according to Newton's law of gravitation. Lóránt Eotvos (1848–1919) showed experimentally that inertial mass and gravitational mass are equal.
Weight is the force by which an object is attracted to the earth. It is therefore equal to the product of the mass and the *acceleration of free fall (i.e. $W = mg$). Thus, the weight of a body may vary according to its position; the mass is a constant.

mass-energy equation. *See* relativity.

Massenet, Jules (1842–1912) French composer. He studied at the Paris conservatoire and won the Prix de Rome in 1863. Massenet wrote 27 operas, of which *Manon* (1884) and *Werther* (1892) are still performed today.

Massif Central A plateau in S central France, rising to 1885 m (6188 ft) at Puy de Sancy. The central N area is known as the Auvergne and the SE rim as the Cévennes. Area: about 90 000 sq km (34 742 sq mi).

Massine, Léonide (Leonid Miassin; 1896–1979) Russian ballet dancer and choreographer. He worked for many companies, notably the Ballet Russe de Monte Carlo. Most controversial were his experimental symphonic ballets *Les Présages* (1933) and *Symphonie Fantastique* (1936).

mass number (*or* nucleon number) The total number of protons and neutrons in the *nucleus of an atom.

mastectomy An operation to remove a breast, usually for the treatment of breast cancer. In a partial mastectomy (or lumpectomy) only the tumour is removed, while in a total mastectomy the entire breast is removed. More extensive is a radical mastectomy—removal of the breast with the lymph nodes in the armpit and the chest muscles associated with it.

Master of the Rolls The presiding judge of the Civil Division of the Court of Appeal. The office, which started as the guardian of all charters, patents, etc., entered upon parchment rolls, has existed in its present form since 1881.

mastic An evergreen Mediterranean shrub, *Pistacia lentiscus*, up to 1.8 m high. An aromatic yellowish resin obtained from the bark is used in varnishes and adhesives.

mastiff An ancient breed of dog, originally from Europe and Asia, used as a guard dog and (formerly) for bull- and bear-baiting. It is powerfully built with a large head and a short muzzle. The smooth coat may be brown, silver, or fawn; the muzzle, ears, and nose are black. Height: 76 cm (dogs); 69 cm (bitches). *See also* bull mastiff.

mastodon An extinct elephant that originated in Africa 34 million years ago and spread throughout Europe, Asia, and America. Early mastodons had two pairs of tusks; later forms were larger and more elephant-like. The American mastodons survived until 8000 years ago.

Matabeleland An area in W Zimbabwe, between the Limpopo and Zambezi Rivers. Consisting chiefly of extensive plains, the area has important gold deposits. Area: 181 605 sq km (70 118 sq mi).

Mata Hari (Margaretha Geertruida Zelle; 1876–1917) Dutch secret agent. She became a professional dancer in Paris in 1905 and in World War I worked for both French and German intelligence; she was executed by the French in 1917.

maté The dried leaves of a *holly shrub or tree, *Ilex paraguariensis*, native to Paraguay and Brazil. Roasted, powdered, and infused with water, they make a stimulating tealike beverage.

materialism In classical *metaphysics, the doctrine developed by *Democritus that everything in the universe consists of matter. *Marx's economic materialism was developed by *Lenin in *dialectical materialism. More popularly, the term has also been used to mean worldly outlooks and behaviour.

mathematics The study of numerical and spatial relationships. **Pure mathematics** studies theoretical principles. Its branches are *arithmetic, *algebra, *calculus, *geometry, and *trigonometry. The Egyptians, Sumerians, and Chinese were all using a form of *abacus to carry out calculations for thousands of years BC. It was not until the 9th century AD that the Arab mathematician al-Khwarizmi began writing down calculations. The Venetian mathematicians of the 11th and 12th centuries were responsible for the introduction of these methods to the West. The application of mathematics to the physical sciences, a development inspired by *Galileo, led to **applied mathematics**, which is now largely concerned with *mechanics and *statistics.

Matilda (*or* Maud; 1102–67) The daughter of Henry I of England, who named her his heir. On his death (1135), his nephew Stephen seized the throne and Matilda invaded England (1139) opening a period of inconclusive civil war. She captured Normandy and in 1152 the Treaty of Wallingford recognized her son Henry as Stephen's heir.

Matisse, Henri (1869–1954) French painter and sculptor. Matisse created *fauvism in the early 1900s with his strongly coloured still lifes, portraits, and nudes, notably the controversial *Woman with the Hat* (1905). He was also inspired by Islamic art. A stained glass design for the Dominican chapel at Vence (S France) was among his last works.

Ma-tsu. *See* Mazu.

Matterhorn (French name: Mont Cervin; Italian name: Monte Cervino) 45 59N 7 39E A mountain on the Swiss-Italian border in the Alps near Zermatt. First climbed in 1865 by the British mountaineer, Edward Whymper, it has a striking pyramidal shape. Height: 4478 m (14 692 ft).

Matthew, St In the New Testament, one of the 12 *Apostles. He was a tax collector until he became a follower of Jesus. According to tradition, he preached in Judaea, Ethiopia, and Persia and suffered martyrdom. Feast day: 21 Sept. Emblem: a man with wings. **The Gospel according to St Matthew** is believed to have been written after St Mark's Gospel, upon which it drew.

Maud. *See* Matilda.

Maugham, W(illiam) Somerset (1874–1965) British novelist and dramatist. Born in Paris, he qualified in medicine but abandoned it after the success of his first novel, *Liza of Lambeth* (1896). His later fiction includes *Of Human Bondage* (1915), *The Moon and Sixpence* (1919), *Cakes and Ale* (1930), and *The Razor's Edge* (1944). He wrote popular comedies, such as *The Circle* (1921), and many short stories with Far Eastern settings.

Mau Mau A secret organization among the *Kikuyu people of Kenya, which led a revolt (1952–57) against the British colonial government. Appalling atrocities were committed against Whites and uncooperating Blacks. Jomo *Kenyatta was thought to be a Mau Mau leader.

Maundy Thursday The Thursday before *Good Friday. Its name comes from Latin *mandatum*, commandment, and its traditional ceremonies of foot-washing and giving to the poor originated at the Last Supper (John 13). The British sovereign's annual distribution of special Maundy money commemorates these ceremonies.

Maupassant, Guy de (1850–93) French writer. Introduced into literary circles by Flaubert, he joined Zola's group of naturalist writers (*see* Naturalism). Following the success of "Boule de Suif" (1880), he wrote about 300 short stories and 6 novels, including *Bel-Ami* (1885). He suffered from syphilis and died in an asylum.

Mauriac, François (1885–1970) French novelist. His novels, which include *Thérèse Desqueyroux* (1927) and *Le Noeud de vipères* (1933), portray the conflict between passions and religion in provincial families. He wrote several plays and much criticism. He won the Nobel Prize in 1952.

Mauritania, Islamic Republic of (French name: Mauritanie; Arabic name: Muritaniyah)

A country in West Africa, on the Atlantic Ocean. *Economy*: livestock, especially cattle, are important and the main crops are millet, sorghum, beans, and rice. Fishing and fish processing are the main industries. Iron ore and copper are exploited. *History*: dominated by Muslim Berber tribes from about 100 AD, the area became a French protectorate in 1903 and a colony in 1920 achieving self-government within the French Community in 1958. It subsequently joined the Arab League and the Arab Common Market. In 1976, with Morocco, it took over Western Sahara, withdrawing from all but the southern tip in 1979. Its third president, Lt Col Khouna Ould Kaydalla (1940–), was ousted in a coup in 1984. President: Moauya Ould Sidi-Ahmad Taya. Official language: French; Arabic, known as Hassaniya, is widely spoken. Official religion: Islam. Official currency: ougiya of 5 khoums. Area: 1 030 700 sq km (397 850 sq mi). Population (1988 est): 1 894 000. Capital and main port: Nouakchott.

Mauritius An island country in the Indian Ocean, about 800 km (500 mi) E of Madagascar. *Economy*: sugar formerly accounted for 90% of its total exports. Fishing is being developed and industry is being encouraged. *History*: the island was settled by the Dutch in 1598. In 1715 it came under French rule as Île de France and in 1814 it was handed over to Britain. After riots in 1968 it became independent within the Commonwealth. Official languages: English and French; Creole is widely spoken. Official currency: Mauritius rupee of 100 cents. Area: 1843 sq km (720 sq mi). Population (1988 est): 1 077 087. Capital and main port: Port Louis.

Maxwell, James Clerk (1831–79) Scottish physicist, who achieved the unification of electricity, magnetism, and light into one set of equations (known as **Maxwell's equations**), first published in their final form in 1873. Maxwell observed that the electromagnetic field spread at the speed of light, which led him to identify light as a form of electromagnetic radiation. Maxwell also made important advances in the kinetic theory of gases by introducing Maxwell-Boltzmann statistics, developed independently by the Austrian physicist Ludwig Boltzmann (1844–1906).

may. *See* hawthorn.

Maya An American Indian people of Yucatán (Mexico) Guatemala, and Belize, now living mainly in farming villages. Between 300 and 900 AD they established an advanced civilization, using picture writing and displaying considerable knowledge of astronomy and mathematics. Their ceremonial life was centred on large pyramid temples, constructed for the worship of the sun, moon, and rain gods.

Mayer, Louis B. (1885–1957) US film producer, born in Russia. With Samuel *Goldwyn in 1924 he founded the Metro-Goldwyn-Mayer (MGM) production company, whose films were largely determined by his taste for lavish entertainment.

Mayflower The ship that carried the *Pilgrim Fathers to America. The *Mayflower* reached Plymouth (Massachusetts) in December, 1620. There, the Pilgrims drew up the **Mayflower Com-**

pact, which based their government on the will of the colonists, not the English Crown.

mayfly A slender insect found near fresh water. Up to 40 mm long, mayflies are usually brown or yellow with two pairs of membranous wings; the hind pair are much smaller than the fore pair. The adults only live long enough to mate and lay eggs. The eggs hatch into aquatic young, which feed on plant debris and algae.

Mayo (Irish name: Contae Mhuigheo) A county in the W Republic of Ireland, in Connacht bordering on the Atlantic Ocean. Cattle, sheep, and pigs are raised and potatoes and oats are grown. Area: 5397 sq km (2084 sq mi). Population (1986): 115 016. County town: Castlebar.

mayor The chief officer of a municipal council. In the UK a mayor or mayoress is the chairperson of a district council having *borough status. The mayor's counterpart in Scotland is called a provost. The mayor of the City of London and certain other cities is called a **Lord Mayor** (Lord Provost in Scotland).

Mbabane 26 30S 31 30E The capital of Swaziland, in the Mdimba Mountains. Tourism is important and nearby is a large iron mine. Population (1986): 38 290.

MBE. *See* Order of the British Empire.

Mc–. Names beginning Mc are listed under Mac.

meadowsweet A plant, *Filipendula* (or *Spiraea*) *ulmaria*, of the rose family, common in damp places throughout Eurasia. 60–120 cm high, it has small creamy fragrant flowers. An oil distilled from the buds is used in perfumes.

mealworm. The larva of a flightless beetle (*Tenebrio molitor*) that is a common pest of flour mills, etc. Mealworms are also reared commercially as food for birds and fish.

mean life (*or* lifetime) The average time for which a radioactive isotope, elementary particle, or other unstable state exists before decaying. *See* radioactivity.

measles An infectious disease caused by a virus, which usually affects children. After an incubation period of about two weeks the child becomes fevered and has a running nose and inflamed eyes. Two or three days later a rash appears on the head and face and spreads over the body. Usually the child recovers after a week. *Compare* German measles.

Meath (Irish name: Contae na Midhe) A county in the E Republic of Ireland, in Leinster bordering on the Irish Sea. It is important for agriculture; cattle are fattened and oats and potatoes grown. Area: 2338 sq km (903 sq mi). Population (1986): 103 762. County town: Trim.

Mecca (Arabic name: Makkah) 21 26N 39 49E A city in W Saudi Arabia. As the birthplace of Mohammed, every Muslim is expected to visit Mecca once in his lifetime; nonbelievers are not allowed to enter the city. The chief shrines are in the court of the al-Haram Mosque. Population (1980 est.): 550 000.

mechanics The study of the motion of bodies and the forces acting on them. It is divided into statics, the study of bodies in equilibrium, and dynamics, the study of forces that affect the motion of bodies. Dynamics is further divided into kinetics, the effects of forces on motion, and kinematics, the study of velocity, acceleration, etc., without regard to the forces causing them. Aristotelian (see Aristotle) mechanics relied on the erroneous concept that a force is required to maintain motion. Newtonian mechanics recognizes that once a body is moving a force is required to stop it but no force is needed to keep it moving. *Fluid mechanics is the application of mechanical principles to fluids, both stationary (hydrostatics) and flowing (hydrodynamics).

Medawar, Sir Peter Brian (1915–87) British immunologist, noted for his investigation of the development of the immune system in embryonic and young animals, including the phenomenon of acquired immunological tolerance to foreign tissue grafts. Medawar shared the 1960 Nobel Prize with Sir Macfarlane Burnet.

Medea In Greek legend, a sorceress, the daughter of King Aeetes of Colchis and niece of *Circe. She helped *Jason steal the *Golden Fleece. When Jason deserted her for Glauce, daughter of the Corinthian King Creon, she killed Glauce, Creon, and her own two children.

Media A region SW of the Caspian Sea settled by tribes of Medes. Between the 8th and 6th centuries BC they united against Assyria, destroying *Nineveh in 612 and overthrew the Assyrian empire.

media Any means (such as radio, TV, and newspapers) for communicating or spreading news, information, opinions, etc. among people. See pages 348–349.

median 1. The line joining the vertex of a triangle to the midpoint of the opposite side. 2. The middle value of a set of numbers arranged in order of magnitude. For example, the median of 2, 3, 3, 4, 5 is 3.

Medici A family of merchants and bankers that dominated Florence from 1434 to 1737 (as grand dukes from 1532). The family's power, gained by influencing the elections of magistrates, was established by **Cosimo de' Medici** (1389–1464), who was the first Medici patron of the arts. His son **Piero de' Medici** (1416–69) succeeded him, but it was **Lorenzo the Magnificent** (1449–92) who patronized Renaissance artists and scholars at the expense of the family business, which he allowed to decline. He was succeeded by his son **Piero de' Medici** (1472–1503), who was forced to flee Florence in a revolt stirred up by *Savonarola. Piero's brother **Giovanni de' Medici** (1475–1521) was restored to Florence in 1512, a year before he became Pope Leo X (1513–21). **Alessandro de' Medici** (1511–37) became the first Duke of Florence; later grand dukes included **Cosimo I** (1519–74), **Francesco I** (1541–87), and **Ferdinando I** (1549–1609).

Medina (Arabic name: Al Madinah) 24 30N 39 35E A city in W Saudi Arabia, N of Mecca. The tomb of Mohammed is in the mosque of this holy Muslim city. Date-packing supplements the city's income from pilgrims. Population (1980 est): 290 000.

Mediterranean Sea A sea extending between Africa and Europe to Asia. It connects with the Atlantic Ocean at Gibraltar, the Black Sea via the Sea of Marmara, and the Red Sea via the Suez Canal. It is saltier and warmer than the oceans; pollution is a serious problem.

medlar A thorny shrub or tree, Mespilus germanica, of the rose family, native to SE Europe and central Asia and cultivated for its fruit. Growing to a height of 6 m, it bears white five-petalled flowers. The brownish fruit has an opening at the top through which the five seed chambers can be seen. Medlars are eaten when partly decayed and are also made into jelly.

medulla oblongata. See brain.

medusa The free-swimming sexual form that occurs during the life cycle of many *coelenterates. Medusae resemble small *jellyfish and release eggs or sperm into the water. Fertilization of the eggs produces larvae, which settle and develop into asexual forms (see polyp); these remain fixed to a surface.

Medusa In Greek mythology, the only mortal *Gorgon. Athena, angered by her love affair with Poseidon, made her hair into serpents and her face so ugly that all who saw it were turned to stone. She later sent *Perseus to behead her. From her blood sprang *Pegasus and Chrysaor, her children by Poseidon.

Medway, River A river in SE England. Rising in Sussex, it flows N and E through Kent to join the River Thames by a long estuary. It passes through Tonbridge, Maidstone, Rochester, Chatham, and Gillingham. Length: 113 km (70 mi).

Meegeren, Hans van (1889–1947) Dutch painter, notorious for his *Vermeer forgeries. He misled the art world, with such works as Christ at Emmaus, bought by the Boymans Museum, Rotterdam, as an early Vermeer. In 1945 he was arrested as a friend of the Nazis, confessed his deceptions, was imprisoned, and died in poverty.

meerkat A small carnivorous mammal, Suricata suricata, also called suricate, of South African grasslands. It is about 60 cm long including the tail (17–25 cm), and lives in burrows, feeding on insects, reptiles, and small mammals.

Meerut 29 00N 77 42E A city in India, in Uttar Pradesh. The scene of the first uprising (1857) of the Indian Mutiny, Meerut is an important army headquarters and has diverse industries. Population (1981): 538 000.

megalith (Greek: large stone) A large stone used for building monuments in the *Neolithic and *Bronze Age. These were placed singly, in lines, or in circles as at *Stonehenge.

megapode A brownish bird ranging from Australia to Malaysia. 48–68 cm long, megapodes build a nest mound in which the eggs are incubated by the heat of fermenting plants, the sun's rays, or volcanic heat. See also brush turkey.

megaton A measure of the explosive power of a nuclear weapon, equivalent to one million tons of trinitrotoluene (TNT).

meiosis The process by which the nucleus of a germ cell divides to produce the sex cells, or gametes (such as sperm, pollen, or eggs). Meiosis consists of two divisions during which one cell with the normal (diploid) set of chromosomes (ie. with a matching pair of each type) gives rise

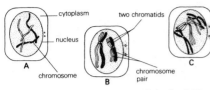

prophase I *The four chromosomes appear as thin threads (A), which form pairs (B). Each chromosome divides into two chromatids and exchange of genetic material occurs between the chromatids of each pair (C).*

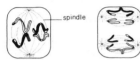

metaphase I *The chromosomes of each pair separate from each other and move to opposite poles of the spindle.*

metaphase II *Two new spindles form and the chromatids of each group separate from each other.*

telophase II *Four new nuclei form, each containing two chromosomes.*

MEIOSIS *The formation of four egg or sperm cells from one parent cell takes place in two divisions, each of which is divided into several phases. Only four phases are shown here.*

to four cells each with only one chromosome of each type (haploid). Meiosis differs from *mitosis in that genetic material is exchanged between the chromosomes of each pair. There is no duplication of chromosomes between the two divisions of meiosis.

Meir, Golda (1898–1978) Israeli stateswoman, born in Russia; prime minister (1969–74). A founder member of the Israeli Workers' Party (Mapai) she was its secretary general (1966–68). She was minister of labour (1949–56) and minister of foreign affairs (1956–66) before becoming prime minister.

Meissen porcelain The first hard-paste porcelain made in Europe following the discovery (1709) in Dresden of the technique by the alchemist J. F. Böttger (1682–1719). The manufacture moved to Meissen in 1710, where an extensive range of domestic ware, figures, chinoiseries, etc., have been produced.

Meitner, Lise (1878–1968) Austrian physicist. She worked with Otto Hahn in Berlin (1907–38); together they discovered protactinium (1918) and caused the first splitting of a uranium atom by neutron bombardment (1934). Expelled by the Nazis, she moved to Stockholm, becoming a Swedish citizen in 1949.

Mekong, River A major SE Asian river, rising in Tibet and flowing generally SE through China, Laos, Kampuchea, and Vietnam to the South China Sea. The extensive delta is one of the greatest Asian rice-growing areas. Length: about 4025 km (2500 mi).

Melanesia A division of Oceania in the SW Pacific Ocean, consisting of an arc of volcanic and coral islands NE of Australia. It includes the Bismarck Archipelago, the Solomon, Admiralty, and D'Entrecasteaux Islands, Vanuatu Republic, New Caledonia, and Fiji. *See also* Micronesia; Polynesia.

Melanesians The people of the Melanesian islands and similar peoples of New Guinea (often known as Papuans). They are of Oceanic Negroid race and speak languages of the Austronesian family. The Melanesians cultivate yams, taro, and sweet potatoes and live in small scattered homesteads. In coastal areas fishing is important.

melanin A pigment, varying from brown to yellow, that occurs in hair, skin, feathers, and scales. In the skin it helps to protect underlying tissues from damage by sunlight; dark-skinned races have more melanin than pale-skinned ones. Melanin is also responsible for colouring the iris of the eye.

melanoma A form of cancer, mainly affecting the skin, that arises in the cells producing the pigment *melanin. Most melanomas develop from an existing mole, and lengthy exposure to sunlight is a contributory factor.

Melba, Dame Nellie (Helen Porter Armstrong; 1861–1931) Australian soprano. She made her debut in 1887 as Gilda in Verdi's opera *Rigoletto*. Her worldwide career ended with a number of farewell performances in 1926.

Melbourne 37 45S 144 58E The second largest city of Australia, the capital of Victoria on Port Phillip Bay. Port Melbourne is sited 4 km (2.5 mi) away, on the mouth of the Yarra River; exports include wool, scrap metal, and dairy products. The chief industries are heavy engineering, food processing, and the manufacture of textiles and clothes. *History*: founded in 1835, it developed rapidly following the 1851 gold rush. It was the capital of the Commonwealth of Australia from 1901 until 1927. Population (1986 est): 2 832 893.

Melbourne, William Lamb, 2nd Viscount (1779–1848) British statesman; Whig prime minister (1834, 1835–41). He was chief secretary for Ireland (1827–28) and then home secretary (1830–34), when he dealt harshly with the *Tolpuddle Martyrs. His attempted resignation (1839) led to Victoria's *Bedchamber Crisis. His wife, Lady Caroline Lamb, had a love affair (1812–13) with Lord Byron; in 1825 they formally separated.

melon A widely cultivated trailing vine, *Cucumis melo*, of the gourd family, native to tropical Africa. The plants bear separate male and female yellow flowers, the female flowers developing into fruits with tough skins and sweet juicy flesh surrounding a core of seeds. There are many varieties. *See also* water melon.

Melos (*or* Milos) A Greek island in the Aegean Sea, one of the Cyclades. The famous statue, the *Venus de Milo*, was discovered here in 1820. Area: 150 sq km (58 sq mi). Population (1981): 4554.

Without using speech, animals communicate by sounds and body language to help them live together in social groups. Honeybees 'tell' other members of the hive that a food source is nearby by a 'dance' consisting of a series of clockwise and anticlockwise circles.

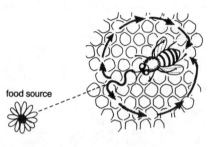

food source

Primitive humans invented a whole range of languages for communicating. Apart from face-to-face, they could only communicate over short distances by flame torches, smoke signals, and drum tapping.

The art of writing meant that humans need not rely on memory for knowledge. The earliest writing systems were pictographic using pictures; gradually syllabaries evolved based on word sounds. From these the alphabets developed.

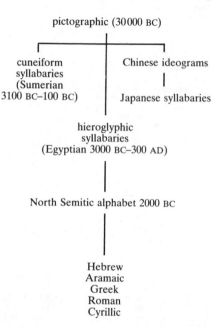

Writing Systems

pictographic (30000 BC)

cuneiform syllabaries (Sumerian 3100 BC–100 BC)

Chinese ideograms

Japanese syllabaries

hieroglyphic syllabaries (Egyptian 3000 BC–300 AD)

North Semitic alphabet 2000 BC

Hebrew
Aramaic
Greek
Roman
Cyrillic

The invention of printing in 808 AD and movable type in the 15th century enabled books to spread knowledge. This is a 16th century printing shop.

With the invention of the telephone and then the radio, instant worldwide communication became possible. Satellites have made this reliable, instantaneous, and relatively cheap. Telex and fax have added a new dimension, enabling instant written communications to be exchanged.

The radio also brought entertainment and information into the home. TV and (later) home videos have revolutionized both the entertainment industry and home entertainment. In the UK the average person watches TV for 4 hours per day. Media personalities, including politicians, now enter the home and are known to millions.

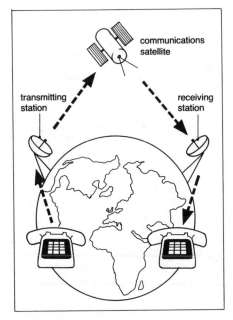

communications satellite

transmitting station

receiving station

Daily newspapers, originating in the 17th century, brought the latest news to ordinary people. Mass-market tabloids first appeared in 1903. *TODAY* is the last daily tabloid to appear – and the first to use colour.

Melville, Herman (1819–91) US novelist. In 1841 he joined the crew of a whaler; his experiences in the South Seas provide the background for *Moby Dick* (1851). *Billy Budd*, published in 1924 after his death, became an opera by Benjamin Britten.

Memel. See Klaipeda.

memory The process of remembering experiences from the past. It has three parts: registration, in which an experience is received into the mind; retention, in which a record is preserved in the brain; and recall, in which a particular memory is brought to mind. Short-term memories are soon forgotten unless they are registered in the long-term memory. *See also* amnesia; Alzheimer's disease.

memory, computer The part of a computer that stores information. It usually refers to the computer's internal store, in which the programs and data are held; this is under the direct control of the central processing unit.

Solid-state electronic memory devices operate at very high speeds and are used for the internal memory. Magnetic tapes and disks form the external memory.

Memphis 35 10N 90 00W A city and port in the USA, in Tennessee situated above the Mississippi River. It is a major cotton, timber, and livestock market and its manufactures include textiles and chemicals. Population (1986 est): 652 640.

Memphis An ancient city of Lower Egypt, S of modern Cairo, founded as the capital of all Egypt after its unification by Menes (c. 3100 BC). It remained the capital until supplanted by *Thebes (c. 1570 BC). The necropolis of Saqqarah and the *pyramids and sphinx at Giza formed part of its complex of monuments.

Menai Strait A channel separating the island of Anglesey from the mainland of NW Wales. It is crossed by Thomas Telford's suspension bridge (1819–26).

Menander (c. 341–c. 290 BC) Greek dramatist. The most celebrated dramatist of the New Comedy, his only surviving complete play is the *Dyscolus*.

Mendel, Gregor Johann (1822–84) Austrian monk and botanist, who discovered the basic principles governing the inheritance of characteristics in living things (*see* genetics). In 1856 he began a series of breeding experiments using pea plants. Mendel concluded that such characteristics as tallness and dwarfness in the plants were determined by factors of inheritance (now called alleles of the gene) carried in the sex cells of the parent plants. Mendel reported his findings in 1865 but his achievement was not appreciated until 1900.

mendelevium (Md) A synthetic element, first produced in 1955 by Ghiorso and others; it is named after the chemist Mendeleyev. At no 101; at wt (256).

Mendeleyev, Dimitrii Ivanovich (1834–1907) Russian chemist, who was professor at St Petersburg (now Leningrad) from 1866 to 1890. In 1869 he succeeded in arranging the elements in order of increasing atomic weights so that those with similar properties were grouped together (*see* periodic table).

Mendelssohn, Felix (Jacob Ludwig Felix Mendelssohn-Bartholdy; 1809–47) German composer. His overture to *A Midsummer Night's Dream* (1826) demonstrated his brilliance while still a child. In 1836 he became conductor of the Leipzig Gewandhaus orchestra and subsequently founded the Leipzig conservatoire. His works include five symphonies, overtures, the oratorios *St Paul* (1836) and *Elijah* (1846), chamber music, and piano music.

Mendip Hills (*or* Mendips) A range of limestone hills in Somerset. It extends between Axbridge and the Frome Valley, reaching 325 m (1068 ft) at Blackdown. Its many features include Cheddar Gorge and the caves of Cheddar and Wookey Hole.

Mengele, Josef (1894–?1979) German medical scientist notorious for atrocities committed in the Nazi concentration camp at Auschwitz. Known as "the Angel of Death," he was camp doctor (1943–45) at Auschwitz. Held responsible for the deaths of 400 000 people, mostly Jews, in medical experiments, he was widely sought after the war. In 1985 a body in Brazil was identified as his.

meningitis Inflammation of the meninges –the membranes that surround the brain. This is usually caused by bacteria or viruses and occurs most commonly in children. Symptoms include headache, vomiting, stiff neck, irritability, and fits. Treatment for bacterial meningitis is with antibiotics and the patient usually recovers rapidly. Viral meningitis is often mild but may have serious effects.

menopause The change of life: the time in a woman's life when the menstrual periods become irregular and finally cease because egg cells are no longer produced by the ovaries. The menopause can occur at any age between the late 30s and late 50s. Some women experience symptoms, including "hot flushes", palpitations, and irritability, due to reduced secretion of oestrogen.

Menorca. See Minorca.

Mensheviks One of the two groups into which the Russian Social Democratic Workers' Party split in 1903 in London. Unlike the rival *Bolsheviks, the Mensheviks (meaning those in the minority) believed in a loosely organized party. They supported Russia's participation in World War I and were a force in the *Russian Revolution until the Bolsheviks seized power in October, 1917. They were finally suppressed in 1922.

menstruation The monthly discharge of blood and fragments of womb lining from the vagina. This is part of the **menstrual cycle**, occurring in women from puberty to the *menopause, during which an egg cell is released from the ovary (ovulation). Menstruation is the stage at which the egg cell (with blood, etc.) is expelled from the womb if conception has not occurred. Ovulation occurs at around the middle of the cycle.

menthol ($C_{10}H_{20}O$) A white crystalline solid. It is a constituent of peppermint oil and is responsible for the characteristic smell of the mint plant, but can also be prepared synthetically. Menthol is used to relieve pain and in sweets and cigarettes.

Menuhin, Sir Yehudi (1916–) British violinist, of Russo-Jewish parentage. A pupil of Georges Enesco, he became famous in boyhood. From 1959 to 1968 Menuhin was director of the Bath Festival, where he also worked as a conductor. He founded the Yehudi Menuhin School for musically gifted children in 1963.

Menzies, Sir Robert Gordon (1894–1978) Australian statesman; prime minister as leader of the United Australia Party (1939–41) and then of the Liberal Party (1949–66). He increased US influence in Australian affairs and encouraged immigration from Europe. Loyal to the British Commonwealth, he became Lord Warden of the Cinque Ports in 1965.

Mercator, Gerardus (Gerhard Kremer; 1512–94) Flemish geographer, best known for the **Mercator projection**, a cylindrical map projection first used in 1569. Prosecuted for heresy in 1544, he emigrated to Protestant Germany in 1552, where he was appointed cartographer to the Duke of Cleves.

merchant banks Financial institutions many of which became banks as a result of their foreign trading as merchants. Their business now includes the issue of shares for firms; long-term loans to governments and institutions abroad; advising on investments; managing takeover bids; and dealings in foreign exchange.

Mercia A kingdom of Anglo-Saxon England. The Mercians were *Angles, whose territory included most of England south of the Humber under *Offa (757–96), their most powerful king. Mercia later declined and was merged in the 9th century into a united England under Wessex.

Mercouri, Melina (1925–) Greek actress and politician; minister of culture (1981–89). Her best-known films include *Never on Sunday* (1960) and *Topkapi* (1964). She campaigned in exile against the military junta (1967–74) and returned to Greece when civilian government was restored.

mercury (Hg) The only liquid metal at room temperature (relative density of 13.546). It occurs chiefly as the sulphide, cinnabar (HgS), from which it is obtained by heating in air. It is used in thermometers, barometers, and batteries and as an amalgam in dentistry. Compounds include the oxide (HgO), mercury(I) and mercury(II) chlorides (Hg_2Cl_2, $HgCl_2$), and the explosive mercury fulminate ($Hg(ONC)_2$), used as a detonator. Mercury and its compounds are poisonous and are only slowly excreted by the human body. At no 80; at wt 200.59; mp –38.87°C; bp 356.58°C.

Mercury (astronomy) The innermost planet (4880 km diameter), orbiting the sun every 88 days at a mean distance of 57.9 million km. Its long period of axial rotation, 58.6 days, is two-thirds of its orbital period. Like the moon, Mercury exhibits *phases. Its surface is heavily cratered, with intervening lava-flooded plains. It has only a very tenuous atmosphere, mainly helium and argon. See Mariner probes.

Mercury (mythology) The Roman god of commerce and patron of astronomy. He is usually portrayed as holding a purse, and also with a cap, winged sandals, and staff, like the Greek *Hermes, with whom he was identified.

Meredith, George (1828–1909) British poet and novelist. His long poem *Modern Love* (1862) was partly based on his unhappy marriage to Mary Ellen Nicholls, daughter of Thomas Love *Peacock. His novels include *The Egoist* (1879) and *The Tragic Comedians* (1880).

merganser A duck of the N hemisphere, also called sawbill. 40–57 cm long, mergansers have a long bill with sawtooth edges for feeding on worms, fish, etc. Males have a green double-crested head, a chestnut breast, and a grey-and-white back; females are brown with a white wing bar.

Mérida 20 59N 89 39W A city in E Mexico, the commercial centre for an agricultural area specializing in henequen (a fibre) production. It has a 16th-century cathedral and the University of Yucatán (refounded 1922). Population (1984 est): 285 000.

meridian. See latitude and longitude.

Merino A breed of sheep from Spain, noted for its thick white fleece. Merinos have been widely exported, especially to Australia.

meristem An area of actively dividing plant cells responsible for growth in the plant. The main regions of meristem in dicotyledon plants are the shoot tip and root tip (apical meristems) and the *cambium (lateral meristem).

merlin A small *falcon, *Falco columbarius*, occurring in moorland regions of the N hemisphere. The female, 32 cm long, is brown with streaked underparts; the male, 26 cm long, has a grey back and tail.

Merlin In *Arthurian legend, the wizard who advised Arthur and his father, Uther Pendragon. There are accounts of Merlin's life in the work of *Geoffrey of Monmouth and later writers. He helped Uther win Igraine, Arthur's mother, made the Round Table, cared for Arthur, and armed him with the sword Excalibur.

mermaid A legendary creature (perhaps based on the *dugongs) whose form is that of a beautiful woman above the waist and a fish below. A mermaid's male counterpart is called a **merman**.

Mersey, River A river in NW England. Formed by the Rivers Goyt and Tame at Stockport, it flows W to enter the Irish Sea by way of a 26 km (16 mi) long estuary, with the ocean ports of *Liverpool and Birkenhead on its banks. Length: 113 km (70 mi).

Merseyside A metropolitan county of NW England, created in 1974 from SW Lancashire and NW Cheshire. It comprises the districts of Sefton, Liverpool, St Helens, Knowsley, and Wirral. Area: 648 sq km (250 sq mi). Population (1987 est): 1 456 800. Administrative centre: Liverpool.

Merthyr Tydfil (Welsh name: Merthyr Tudful) 51 46N 3 23W A town in South Wales, in Mid Glamorgan on the River Taff. Formerly a world iron and steel centre based on the surrounding coalfields, the main industries are now light and electrical engineering. Population (1982 est): 60 000.

mesembryanthemum. *See* fig marigold.

Mesmer, Franz Anton (1734–1815) German physician, who claimed to cure diseases by correcting the flow of "animal magnetism" in his patients. Investigation of "mesmerism" concluded that any cures were due to suggestion, but Mesmer's claims stimulated study of hypnosis.

Mesolithic The middle division of the *Stone Age, especially in N Europe, where a distinct cultural stage, the Maglemosian, came between the last ice age and the evolution of farming communities. The Mesolithic is characterized by microliths (minute stone tools) with wooden or bone handles.

mesons. *See* particle physics.

Mesopotamia The region between the Rivers Tigris and Euphrates. The Sumerians settled in S Mesopotamia about 4000 BC: they established the world's first civilization and founded city states, such as *Ur, Kish, and Uruk. *Babylon became Mesopotamia's capital under Hammurabi (d. 1750 BC). After his death Mesopotamia was overrun successively by Kassites, Assyrians, and Persians.

Mesozoic era The geological era (*see* geological time scale) following the Palaeozoic and preceding the Cenozoic. It contains the Triassic, Jurassic, and Cretaceous periods, and lasted from about 240 to 65 million years ago. The reptiles were most active during the Mesozoic but became extinct before it ended.

Messerschmitt, Willy (1898–1978) German aircraft designer, best known for his World War II planes, particularly the Me-109 fighter (1935) and the Me-262, the first jet fighter.

Messiaen, Olivier (1908–) French composer and organist. His works, influenced by Catholicism and eastern rhythms, include *La Nativité du Seigneur* (for organ; 1935), the symphony *Turangalîla* (1948), *La Transfiguration* (for chorus and orchestra; 1965–69), and the opera *St Francis d'Assise* (1986).

Messina 38 13N 15 33E A port in Italy, in NE Sicily on the Strait of Messina. Successively occupied by Greeks, Carthaginians, Mamertines, Romans, Saracens, Normans, and Spaniards, in 1860 it became the last city in Sicily to be united with Italy. Its products include macaroni, chemicals, and soap. Population (1987): 270 546.

metabolism The processes and chemical reactions that occur in living organisms. **Anabolism** involves building up tissues and organs from simple substances, such as amino acids, sugars, etc., to construct the proteins, carbohydrates, and fats of which they are made. The required energy is obtained from food or the body's reserves. Energy production and the chemical breakdown of substances (with the production of waste products) are known as **catabolism**.

metal An *element that is usually a hard crystalline solid, a good conductor of heat and electricity, and forms a salt and hydrogen with an acid. Exceptions include mercury, which is a liquid at normal temperatures, and sodium, which is soft. The heavy metals (iron, copper, lead, and zinc) used in engineering and the rarer heavy metals (nickel, chromium, tungsten, etc.) are used in *alloys. The noble metals (gold, silver, and platinum), and the light metals (aluminium and magnesium) also have important uses. The *alkali metals (sodium, potassium, and lithium), the *alkaline-earth metals (calcium, barium, etc.), and the rare-earth metals (*see* lanthanides) have great chemical significance. Uranium is important in the nuclear industry (*see* nuclear energy). Most metals occur in the earth's crust and have to be mined before being extracted from their ores (*see* metallurgy).

metallography The study of the crystalline structure of metals. It includes various techniques and is used to test the quality of steel after *heat treatment. Usually a small sample is taken from a batch and polished before being examined under a microscope for cracks, impurities, or holes. The technique of *X-ray diffraction developed by Max von Laue (1879–1960) is used to examine metallic crystals.

metalloids Elements, such as arsenic and germanium displaying the physical and chemical properties both of *metals and nonmetals. They may form positive ions as well as covalently bonded compounds (*see* chemical bond). The metalloid elements are often *semiconductors.

metallurgy The science and technology of producing metals. It includes the extraction of metals from their ores, the production of *alloys to obtain specific properties, and *heat treatment to improve their properties.

metamorphic rock One of the three major rock categories (*compare* igneous rock; sedimentary rock) consisting of rocks produced by the alteration of existing rocks by heat, pressure, and chemically active fluids. Contact (*or* thermal) metamorphism occurs around igneous intrusions and results from heat alone. Regional metamorphism occurs over large areas and results from heat and pressure created within the earth's crust. Dislocation metamorphism results from localized mechanical deformation, as along fault planes. Metamorphic rocks often form areas of high ground. Marble is a metamorphic rock formed from recrystallized limestone.

metamorphosis The process in animals by which the immature stage, or *larva, changes into an adult. Certain insects, such as dragonflies, undergo incomplete metamorphosis, during which several stages (known as nymphs) in turn become increasingly like the adult through a series of moults. In complete metamorphosis, seen in such insects as butterflies and houseflies, the larva passes into an inactive pupal stage, during which the adult tissues are developed. Metamorphosis also occurs in amphibians (*see* frog). The process in insects and amphibians is controlled by hormones.

metaphysical poets A group of 17th-century English poets whose work was characterized by wit, ingenuity, and elaborate figures of speech. The leading poet was John *Donne, and his successors included George Herbert (1593–1633), Henry Vaughan (c. 1622–95), Andrew *Marvell, and Abraham Cowley (1618–67).

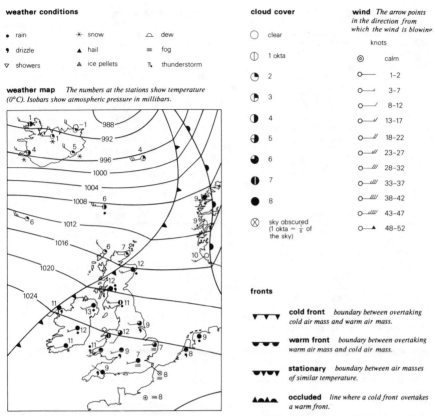

weather conditions

• rain	✳ snow	◿ dew		
❪ drizzle	▲ hail	≡ fog		
▽ showers	▲ ice pellets	⊼ thunderstorm		

weather map   *The numbers at the stations show temperature (0°C). Isobars show atmospheric pressure in millibars.*

cloud cover

○	clear
◍	1 okta
◖	2
◗	3
◑	4
◒	5
◕	6
◕	7
●	8
⊗	sky obscured (1 okta = $\frac{1}{8}$ of the sky)

wind *The arrow points in the direction from which the wind is blowing.*

knots

◉	calm
○—	1–2
○—̸	3–7
○—̷	8–12
○—̸̸	13–17
○—̸̸	18–22
○—̸̸̸	23–27
○—̸̸̸	28–32
○—̸̸̸̸	33–37
○—̸̸̸̸	38–42
○—̸̸̸̸̸	43–47
○—▲	48–52

fronts

▼▼▼   **cold front** *boundary between overtaking cold air mass and warm air mass.*

◡◡◡   **warm front** *boundary between overtaking warm air mass and cold air mass.*

▼◡▼◡   **stationary** *boundary between air masses of similar temperature.*

▲◡▲◡   **occluded** *line where a cold front overtakes a warm front.*

METEOROLOGY *Internationally agreed symbols are used throughout the world by meteorological stations to represent current weather conditions. These are plotted on weather maps from which forecasts can be made.*

metaphysics The study of existence or being in general. The term comes from the title given to a group of Aristotle's writings. *Kant thought this kind of investigation impossible because our minds can only cope with the world of appearances and the British philosopher Sir Alfred Ayer (1910–) used the word to indicate the meaninglessness of much traditional philosophy. However, metaphysics is still held to be one of the main divisions of philosophy.

metempsychosis. *See* reincarnation.

meteor A streak of light seen in the night sky when a **meteoroid**–an interplanetary rock or dust particle–enters and burns up in the earth's atmosphere. A decaying *comet gradually produces a **meteor stream** of meteoroids around its orbit. When the earth passes through a meteor stream, an often spectacular **meteor shower** is observed. A **meteorite** is a large piece of interplanetary debris (iron or stone; mass usually over 100 kg) that falls to the earth's surface.

meteorology The study of the physics, chemistry, and movements of the *atmosphere and its interactions with the ground. Meteorology is concerned mainly with the troposphere and

stratosphere, the lower layers of the atmosphere in which most weather phenomena occur. A **weather forecast** is a prediction of what weather conditions will be over a stated future period; it is made by studying weather maps, especially those obtained from satellites. Weather forecasts are essential to shipping and aviation and are of great use to farmers and others. *See also* climate.

methane (CH_4) A colourless odourless flammable gas that is the main constituent of *natural gas. It is the simplest *alkane and is used as a fuel and a source of other chemicals. Coal gas and marsh gas also contain methane. Recently the generation of methane from sewage has been investigated as an *alternative energy source.

methanol (methyl alcohol *or* wood alcohol; CH_3OH) A colourless poisonous flammable liquid. Originally obtained from wood, it is now usually made from hydrogen and carbon monoxide. It is used as a solvent, antifreeze, and a raw material for making other chemicals. *See also* methylated spirits.

Methodism The Christian body that developed out of the religious practices of the *Wesley brothers. Methodism developed its own church organization during the 1790s. The higher decision-making body is the Conference; local societies (congregations) are highly organized. 80% of all Methodists live in the USA.

methyl alcohol. *See* methanol.

methylated spirits A form of *ethanol (ethyl alcohol) that has been made unsuitable for drinking by the addition of about 9.5% of methanol (methyl alcohol), about 0.5% of pyridine, and a methyl violet dye. In this form it is used as a fuel for spirit burners. Industrial methylated spirits (IMS) consists of ethanol with about 5% of methanol and no pyridine; it is used as a solvent.

metre (m) The unit of length in the *metric system. Originally defined in 1791 as one ten-millionth of the length of the quadrant of the earth's meridian through Paris, it was redefined in 1927 as the distance between two marks on a platinum-iridium bar. It is now defined (General Conference on Weights and Measures, 1983) as the length of the path travelled by light in a vacuum in 1/299 792 458 second, which replaces the 1960 definition based on the emission of a krypton lamp.

metre (poetry) The rhythmic pattern of a line of verse measured in terms of basic metrical units or feet. In rhythmical verse, as in English, a foot consists of various arrangements of stressed (') and unstressed (˘) syllables. In classical Greek and Latin verse, the quantity or length rather than the stress of syllables determines the foot. In English the most common feet are the iamb (˘ '), the trochee (' ˘), the anapaest (˘ ˘ '), the dactyl (' ˘ ˘), and the spondee (' '). Most traditional poetic forms, such as the *sonnet, are written according to strict metrical patterns.

metric system A system of measurement based on the decimal system. Units of length, mass, etc., form smaller units by dividing them by 10, 100, 1000, etc., and into larger units by multiplying them by 10, 100, 1000, etc. First suggested in 1585, it was not given formal acceptance until 1795, when a French law provided definitions for the *metre and other metric units. However, the metric system was not widely used, even in France, until the third decade of the 19th century; during this period it was also adopted by most European countries. Although the metric system was authorized in the UK in 1864, reluctance to abandon "Imperial units" did not weaken until 1963, when the yard and pound were given legal definitions in terms of metric units. The **Metrication Board**, set up in 1969, was disbanded in April 1980, metrication proceeding thereafter on a voluntary basis.

For scientific purposes, former metric systems (such as the *c.g.s. system) have been replaced by *SI units.

metronome A small device consisting of a pendulum with a small sliding weight on it enabling the number of pendulum beats to be regulated. The most common type is the clockwork metronome invented by J. N. Maelzel (1770–1838); electric metronomes also exist. Metronome markings are often given in musical scores to indicate the exact speed.

Metropolitan Museum of Art The principal museum in New York City and one of the most important in the world. Founded in 1870, it was opened in its present premises in Central Park in 1880.

Metternich, Klemens Wenzel Nepomuk Lothar, Fürst von (1773–1859) Austrian statesman, the leading figure in European diplomacy from the fall of Napoleon (1815) until the Revolutions of 1848. As foreign minister (1809–48) he sought to maintain the balance of power in Europe, supporting dynastic monarchies and suppressing liberalism. His policies dominated the great Congresses of *Vienna (1814–15), Aix-la-Chapelle (1818), Troppau (1820), Laibach (1821), and Verona (1822).

Meuse, River (Dutch and Flemish name: Maas) A river in W Europe. Rising in NE France and flowing mainly N past Liège in Belgium and Maastricht in the S Netherlands, it enters the North Sea at the Rhine Delta. It was the scene of heavy fighting in World War I (1914) and World War II (1940). Length: 926 km (575 mi).

Mexican War (1846–48) The war between Mexico and the USA over disputed border territory. Military operations began when Gen Zachary *Taylor invaded New Mexico and ended with the fall of Mexico City (1847). Peace was concluded with the Treaty of *Guadalupe-Hidalgo.

Mexico, United States of A country in Central America between the Gulf of Mexico and the Pacific Ocean. *Economy*: Mexico is among the main oil-producing countries. It also has large reserves of natural gas and substantial deposits of uranium. Other minerals extracted include iron ore, zinc, sulphur, silver, and copper, and Mexico is the world's largest producer of fluorite and graphite. Maize is the main crop; cash crops include cotton, sugar, coffee, and fruit and vegetables, as well as sisal. Fishing has been developed, including sardines, shrimps, and oysters. Tourism is also important. *History*: Mexico was the site of the Mayan civilization from the 2nd to the 13th centuries AD, and between the 8th and the 12th centuries AD, the *Toltecs flourished. The 14th century saw the rise of the *Aztecs, who were conquered by the Spanish under Cortés in 1521, when Mexico became part of the viceroyalty of New Spain. The struggle for independence from Spain was achieved in 1821. A turbulent period dominated by *Santa Anna (1794–1876) was followed by the *Mexican War (1846–48), in which territory was lost to the USA. The Mexican Revolution culminated in the constitution of 1917. Mexico is now dominated by the Party of Institutionalized Revolution (PRI). In the 1980s there has been high inflation and devaluation of the peso. Mexico is a member of the OAS. President: Carlos Salinas de Gortari. Official language: Spanish; Indian languages, especially Nahuatl, are widely spoken. Official currency: Mexican peso of 100 centavos. Area: 1 967 183 sq km (761 530 sq mi). Population (1989 est): 84 278 992. Capital: Mexico City. Main port: Veracruz.

Mexico City (Spanish name: Ciudad de México) 19 25N 99 10W The capital of Mexico, in the S of the high central plateau at a height of 2380 m (7800 ft), surrounded by mountains. The 14th-century Aztec city of Tenochtitlán was destroyed by Cortés in 1521. A new Spanish city was built on the site and it rapidly became the most important in the New World. It was captured by the USA and then by France in the 19th century and in the 20th century was the centre of several revolutions. It is the site of the national library, the museum, and the Palace of Fine Arts Theatre. In 1985 the city and surrounding areas were devastated by an earthquake. Population (1985): 15 667 000.

Miami 25 45N 80 15W A city and port in the USA, in Florida on Biscayne Bay. A major tourist resort and retirement centre, it is famous for its citrus fruit and winter vegetables. Industries include aircraft repairing, sponge fisheries, clothing, and concrete. Population (1987 est.): 417 714.

micas A group of common rock-forming silicate minerals with a layered structure and complex composition. Muscovite, $K_2Al_4(Si_6Al_2)O_{20}(OH,F)_4$, is a white mica and economically the most important. The other principal micas are phlogopite (amber), biotite (dark), and lepidolite (a source of lithium). Since it is a good insulator and can withstand high temperatures, mica has many electrical uses and is used for furnace windows.

Michaelmas daisy. See aster.

Michelangelo Buonarroti (1475–1564) Italian sculptor, painter, architect, and poet. Working in Rome from 1496 until 1501, he produced his first major sculptures, notably the *Pietà* (St Peter's, Rome). This was followed (1501–05) by his work in Florence, including *David* (Accademia, Florence) and the painting of the *Holy Family* (Uffizi). The Sistine Chapel ceiling (1508–12), in the Vatican, established his reputation as the greatest painter of his day. Returning to Florence (1516), Michelangelo became the architect and sculptor of the Medici funerary chapel (1520–34) in S Lorenzo. This project and the fresco of the *Last Judgment* (1534–41) for the Sistine Chapel were his first works in the mannerist style (*see* mannerism). In 1547 he became chief architect of St Peter's, Rome.

Michelin, André (1853–1931) French tyre manufacturer, who founded, with his brother Édouard Michelin (1859–1940), the Michelin Tyre Company (1888). In 1895 they became the first to demonstrate the feasibility of using pneumatic tyres on motor cars. The company is now also famous for its maps and guidebooks.

Michelson, Albert Abraham (1852–1931) US physicist, born in Germany. He designed the Michelson interferometer and used it to measure precisely the speed of light. He also used it in the **Michelson-Morley experiment**, performed with the US chemist E. W. Morley (1838–1923) in 1881, which failed to demonstrate the existence of the ether and was explained by Einstein's theory of *relativity in 1905.

Michigan A state in the N central USA, bordered largely by water (Lakes Superior, Huron, Michigan, Erie, and St Clair). Manufacturing is important, especially of cars in Detroit; other industries include machinery, iron and steel, and chemicals. Reserves of gypsum, calcium, magnesium compounds, natural gas, and oil are exploited. *History*: first explored by the French in the 17th century, it remained under French control until acquired by the British (1763) as part of Canada. It came under American control (1783), becoming a state in 1837. Area: 150 779 sq km (58 216 sq mi). Population (1986 est): 9 145 000. Capital: Lansing.

Michigan, Lake The third largest of the Great Lakes in North America, the only one wholly in the USA. It is linked with Lake Huron via the Straits of Mackinac; the city of Chicago is on its S bank. Area: 58 000 sq km (22 400 sq mi).

microbiology The study of microorganisms that are invisible to the naked eye, including bacteria, small fungi (e.g. yeasts and moulds), algae, protozoa, and viruses. They are vital to numerous industries, including brewing, baking, dairying, and food processing, and they have revolutionized medical treatment with the discovery of antibiotics. Some microorganisms, however, are parasites that cause disease (*see* infection).

microchip. See integrated circuit.

microcomputers Small sophisticated *computers designed for a single user and often for a specific application. The tiny central processing unit is a *microprocessor. Microcomputers were introduced in the 1970s for industrial, commercial, and domestic applications.

microcopy A greatly reduced photographic copy of a printed page or other image. **Microfilm** is a strip of standard-width film containing microcopies. It was introduced in the 1920s for use in banks and is now widely used for compact storage. Special enlarging viewers can rapidly wind the film to the correct page. **Microfiche** is a similar system on cards holding a single film negative, with even greater reduction of the pictures. The viewers often have a printer attached to reproduce paper copies.

micrometer An instrument for measuring small lengths with great accuracy. The object to be measured is held between the jaws of a C-shaped metal piece, one jaw of which can be adjusted by a screw. The screw is turned by rotating a drum with a *Vernier scale marked on it, from which the required dimension can be read.

Micronesia, Federated States of An island country in the W Pacific Ocean, consisting of 607 islands E of the Philippines. A former Trust Territory, it was founded in 1986 and is divided into the states of Kosrae, Pohnpei, Truk, and Yap. Land area: 702 sq km (271 sq mi). Population (1988): 86 094.

microphone A device that converts sound into electrical signals. A telephone mouthpiece usually consists of a carbon microphone in which the sound waves exert a varying pressure on carbon granules, so varying their electrical resistance. In capacitor microphones, the most commonly used type in music recording, a diaphragm forms one plate of a capacitor, across which the sound waves produce a fluctuating potential difference. Crystal microphones rely on the *piezoelectric effect.

microprocessor The compact central processing unit of a *microcomputer. Its development was made possible in the 1970s by advances in solid-state electronics, in particular the design of integrated circuits of such complexity that all the main calculating functions of the microcomputer can be carried out by a single silicon chip (see integrated circuit).

microscope An optical instrument used for producing a magnified image of a small object. The most common type is the compound microscope, which contains an objective lens and an eyepiece. It was invented in 1609 by a Dutch spectacle maker Zacharias Janssen (1580–c. 1638) and his father, but Robert *Hooke gave the first extensive description of its use in biology in his *Micrographia* (1665). In a compound microscope the objective produces a real magnified image, which is further magnified by the eyepiece. The magnification (which may be up to a thousand, is limited by the *resolving power of the lenses; the smallest detail capable of resolution by an optical microscope is about 0.2 micrometre. Still higher magnifications are obtained by using shorter wavelength radiations as in the *electron microscope.

microwave background radiation. See big-bang theory.

microwaves Electromagnetic radiation with wavelengths between 1 and 300 millimetres, lying between infrared rays and radio waves in the electromagnetic spectrum. They are used in *radar and **microwave heating**. A microwave oven is used in the rapid cooking of food as the radiation penetrates to the interior of the food.

Midas In Greek legend, a king of Phrygia whose wish that everything he touched be turned to gold was granted by Dionysus in gratitude for his hospitality to the satyr *Silenus. In another legend, Midas was asked to judge between the music of Pan and Apollo and chose the former. Apollo punished his tactlessness by changing his ears into those of an ass.

middle ages The period of European history commencing in the 5th century with the fall of the western *Roman Empire and ending with the *Renaissance. This period begins with the creation of the barbarian kingdoms, which developed into the nation states of W Europe, includes the rise of the Roman Catholic Church, saw the creation of a feudal society, and culminated in the flourishing of cities and trade.

Middle Temple. See Inns of Court.

midge A small harmless *fly, that resembles a mosquito. Midges are found near fresh water, often in large swarms. The wormlike aquatic larvae are often red.

Mid Glamorgan A county of SE Wales created in 1974 from central Glamorgan and a small part of Breconshire and Monmouthshire. It consists of uplands dissected by the deep parallel valleys of the Rivers Taff, Rhymney, and Ogmore. There is sheep farming on the uplands. The traditional coalmining and iron industries have been replaced by light industry. Area: 1019

sq km (393 sq mi). Population (1986 est): 534 500. Administrative centre: Cardiff.

Midrash (Hebrew: enquiry, exposition) Jewish explanation of the Old Testament or a book of such explanation. There are many Midrashim, mostly dating from the early middle ages. The *Talmuds also contain a great deal of Midrash.

Mies van der Rohe, Ludwig (1886–1969) German architect. His most influential building was the glass, steel, and marble German pavilion at the Barcelona international exhibition (1929). In 1937 he moved to the USA, where he designed such buildings as the Illinois Institute of Technology (1939) and the Seagram building, New York (1958).

migraine Recurrent headaches, usually affecting one side of the head and thought to be caused by narrowing and then widening of the arteries in the brain. The attacks are often preceded by blurring of vision and flickering lights (called an aura). During the headache itself vomiting commonly occurs.

migration, animal The periodic movement of animal populations between one region and another, usually associated with seasonal climatic changes or breeding cycles. Migration is best known among birds, but occurs in many other animals, including fish (notably salmon), butterflies, bats, lemmings, and whales. The mechanism of navigation and homing is not completely understood. In birds it seems to involve sighting of landmarks, as well as a compass sense, using the sun or stars as bearings.

Mikonos (or Mykonos) A Greek island in the S Aegean Sea, one of the Cyclades. It is popular with tourists. Area: 90 sq km (35 sq mi). Population (1981): 5503.

Milan (Italian name: Milano; Latin name: Mediolanum) 45 28N 9 12E A city in N Italy, the capital of Lombardy on the River Olona. Milan is the chief commercial and industrial centre of Italy. Its manufactures include motor vehicles, machinery, silk and other textiles, and chemicals. Milan has a gothic cathedral (duomo), the Brera Palace (containing the city's art collection), and *La Scala opera house. *History*: founded by the Gauls about 600 BC, it was captured by the Romans in 222. Having fallen to Spain in 1535, it was under Austrian rule (1713–96) and in 1797 Napoleon made it capital of the Cisalpine Republic (1797) and capital of the kingdom of Italy (1805–14). Population (1987): 1 478 505.

mildew Any fungus that grows as dense threads forming visible white patches. Many fungal diseases of plants are called mildews: these can be classed as powdery mildews or downy mildews.

mile A unit of length traditionally used in the UK and USA. A statute mile is equal to 1760 yards. A nautical mile (UK) is equal to 6080 feet; a nautical mile (international) is equal to 1852 metres (6076.12 ft). The unit is based on the Roman mile of 1000 paces.

Miletus An ancient Greek city in *Ionia, founded about 1000 BC. Milesians were prominent among the 6th-century Ionian thinkers. An important trading centre, even after destruction by Persia (494 BC) Miletus remained commercially active until its harbours silted up.

Milhaud, Darius (1892–1974) French composer, a member of Les Six. With Jean Cocteau he wrote the ballets *Le Boeuf sur le toit* (1919) and *Le Train bleu* (1924); with Paul Claudel he wrote the opera *Christophe Colomb* (1928). His other works include 12 symphonies, 15 string quartets, concertos, and Jewish religious music.

milk A fluid secreted by the *mammary glands of mammals to feed their young. Cows' milk consists mainly of water, plus fat, protein, and lactose (milk sugar), small quantities of minerals (mainly calcium and phosphorus), and vitamins (mainly A and B). Human milk is similar but contains less protein and more lactose. Milk is a highly nutritious food; sterilized and UHT (ultraheat-treated) milk both have a longer shelf-life than pasteurized milk. *See also* dairy products; pasteurization.

Milky Way The diffuse band of light seen on a clear night stretching across the sky. It is composed of innumerable stars that are too faint to be seen individually. They lie around the sun in the flattened disc of our *Galaxy.

Mill, John Stuart (1806–73) British economist and philosopher. His *Principles of Political Economy* (1848) restates the ideas of Adam *Smith and Ricardo. Other works include *On Liberty* (1859) and the *Subjection of Women* (1869). Also a journalist, he edited (1835–40) the *London Review*.

Millais, Sir John Everett (1829–96) British painter and one of the founders of the *Pre-Raphaelite Brotherhood. His paintings include the controversial *Christ in the House of His Parents* (1850) and *Ophelia* (1852; both Tate Gallery). After abandoning Pre-Raphaelitism in the 1860s, he painted more sentimental works, such as *Bubbles* (1886), a portrait of his grandson.

Miller, Arthur (1915–) US dramatist. His plays include *All My Sons* (1947), *Death of a Salesman* (1947), which won a Pulitzer Prize, *The Crucible* (1953), *After the Fall* (1964), which is in part a portrait of his late wife Marilyn Monroe, and *Two-Way Mirror* (1983).

Miller, Glenn (1904–44) US trombonist, band leader, who composed "Moonlight Serenade" and "In the Mood." He entertained the troops during World War II and died when his plane disappeared on a flight between England and France.

millet A *grass that is cultivated in Asia and Africa as a cereal crop and in parts of Europe and North America chiefly as a pasture grass and fodder crop. It grows 30–130 cm high. Common or broomcorn millet (*Panicum miliaceum*) is used for poultry feed or for flour milling. Pearl millet (*Pennisetum glaucum*) is grown for food, Italian millet (*Setaria italica*) as a grain crop, and Japanese millet (*Echinochloa crus-galli*) mainly for fodder. A variety of sorghum (durra) is also known as millet.

Millet, Jean François (1814–75) French painter of peasant origin. He studied in Cherbourg and in Paris under Paul Delaroche (1797–1859), achieving acclaim in 1844. After settling in Barbizon (1849), he became linked with the

Barbizon school and painted melancholy and sometimes sentimental agricultural scenes, notably *The Gleaners* (1857) and *The Angelus* (1859; both Louvre).

millibar. *See* bar.

millipede A slow-moving wormlike *arthropod, 2–280 mm long. Its body is covered by a protective cuticle and consists of 20–100 segments, most of which bear two pairs of legs (*compare* centipede). Millipedes live in dark damp places, scavenging for dead plant and animal materials. When attacked they secrete a toxic fluid containing cyanide and iodine.

Milne, A(lan) A(lexander) (1882–1956) British novelist and dramatist. He is best known for his books for and about his son Christopher Robin. These include two collections of verse and two books about toy animals, *Winnie-the-Pooh* (1926) and *The House at Pooh Corner* (1928).

Milton, John (1608–74) English poet. His early works include the poems *L'Allegro* and *Il Penseroso* (1632), the masque *Comus* (1633), and the elegy *Lycidas* (1637). He actively supported the Puritan revolution (1640–50) and wrote many pamphlets, notably *Areopagitica* (1644), a defence of free speech. In 1649 he was appointed Latin Secretary to the Council of State, but by 1652 he had become blind. After the Restoration he retired to write *Paradise Lost* (1667), its sequel *Paradise Regained* (1677), and *Samson Agonistes* (1671).

Milton Keynes 52 02N 0 42W A city in S England, in Buckinghamshire. Developed since 1967 as a new city around the old village of Milton Keynes, it is the headquarters of the Open University (1969) and has varied light industries. Population (1983 est): 146 000.

Milwaukee 43 03N 87 56W A city and port in the USA, in Wisconsin on Lake Michigan. It is a leading producer of heavy machinery, electrical equipment, and diesel and petrol engines. Population (1986 est): 605 200.

mime Acting without words by physical gestures alone. It was practised in ancient Greek and Roman drama and was an important constituent of the *commedia dell'arte in the 16th century. Modern mime artists include Jean-Louis Barrault (1910–) and Marcel *Marceau.

mimicry The phenomenon of two or more organisms (commonly different species) resembling each other closely, which gives one or both of them an advantage, usually protection. In **Batesian mimicry**, named after H. W. *Bates (1825–92), a poisonous or inedible species (the model) has a striking coloration, which acts as a warning to predators. This coloration is copied by a harmless edible species (the mimic), causing predators to avoid it. In **Müllerian mimicry**, first described by the German naturalist Fritz Müller (1821–97), two or more species–all inedible –have the same warning coloration. After a predator has associated this pattern with an inedible species it learns to avoid all similarly coloured species.

mimosa A type of *acacia plant whose yellow flowers are sold by florists as cut flowers (*see* wattle).

Mindanao An island in the S Philippines, the second largest. Hemp, maize, pineapples, timber, nickel, and gold are the chief products. Area: 101 919 sq km (39 351 sq mi). Population (1987 est): 13 093 000. Chief towns: Davao and Zamboanga.

minerals Naturally occurring substances of definite chemical composition. Some consist of a single element but most are compounds of at least two. Minerals are solid (except native mercury) and are inorganically formed, although the constituents of organic limestones are usually considered minerals. Minerals are identified by crystal system (e.g. cubic) and habit or form (e.g. fibrous), hardness (see Mohs' scale), relative density, lustre (e.g. metallic), and colour. *Rocks are composed of mixtures of minerals.

Minerva A Roman goddess originally of the arts and crafts and of wisdom, later identified with the Greek *Athena. As goddess of war her importance almost equalled that of Mars.

minesweeper A powerful fast vessel equipped to neutralize mines. Traditional minesweepers have partially submerged cables that are towed through a minefield so that the cable, passing under the mines, cuts their anchor chains, allowing the mines to float so that they can be detonated by gunfire. Some mines are now laid on the sea bed; these can be detected by a submersible acoustic or magnetic mine-finder that places an explosive next to the mine and thus destroys it. To avoid detonating such mines minesweepers have plastic or wooden hulls.

Ming (1368–1644) A native Chinese dynasty that followed the Mongol Yuan dynasty. It was founded by Hong-wu (1328–98), the first of 17 Ming emperors. The Ming provided a period of stable government controlled by the emperor. Pottery, especially blue and white porcelain, flourished under the Ming.

miniature painting The art of painting on a very small scale, using watercolour on a vellum, card, or ivory base. The medieval Persian and Indian miniatures are the first examples. In Europe it flourished in the form of oval, circular, and occasionally rectangular portraits from the 16th to mid-19th centuries. There it developed from the medieval art of manuscript illumination and *Renaissance portrait medals. Nicholas *Hilliard was the first specialist in England. Other famous British miniaturists were Isaac Oliver (?1556–1617), Samuel Cooper (1609–72), and Richard Cosway (1742–1821).

minicomputer A small *computer, especially one that fits into a single cabinet. Compared with a large mainframe computer it is slower, has a smaller memory, and is considerably cheaper. The term *microcomputer is now more usual for a small personal device.

minimal art An abstract style of painting and sculpture developed in New York in the late 1960s. In reaction against action painting, it aims to eliminate artistic self-expression by reducing creativity to a minimum. This has been achieved by using simple hard-edged geometrical shapes and unmodulated vibrant colours. Leading minimalists include the painters Kenneth Noland (1924–) and Frank Stella (1936–) and the sculptor Carl André (1935–).

mink A small carnivorous mammal related to weasels and stoats, prized for its fur. The American mink (Mustela vison) is the largest species (about 70 cm long) and has the most valuable fur. Mink are nocturnal and live near water, preying on fish, rodents, and waterfowl; escaped captive mink have become a dangerous pest in the UK.

Minneapolis 45 00N 93 15W A city in the USA, in Minnesota on the Mississippi River. Adjacent to St Paul, the Twin Cities comprise the commercial, industrial, and financial centre of a large grain and cattle area; flour milling is the main industry. Population (1986 est): 356 840.

Minnelli, Liza. See Garland, Judy.

Minnesota A state in the USA, bordering on Canada in the N and Lake Superior in the NE. Manufacturing industries (especially food processing) are the most important sector of the economy, but mining remains important. Agriculture produces maize and soya beans. History: part of the Louisiana Purchase in 1803, it became a state in 1858. During the 1880s many Scandinavians settled in Minnesota. Area: 217 736 sq km (84 068 sq mi). Population (1987 est): 4 245 870. Capital: St Paul.

minnow A small fish, Phoxinus phoxinus, found in clear fresh waters of Europe and N Asia. Related to the carp, it is about 7.5 cm long and ranges in colour from gold to green. The name is also applied to various other small fish.

Minoan civilization The civilization of Bronze Age Crete, named by the British archaeologist Sir Arthur Evans (1851–1941) after the legendary King *Minos. Arising about 2500 BC, it is divided into three phases: Early (2500–2000), Middle (2000–1700), and Late (1700–1400). Crete's wealth during the Middle Minoan period led to palace building at *Knossos, Mallia, and Phaistos. Around 1700 these structures were replaced by grander ones, the centres of power in a marine empire covering the S Aegean. A catastrophic eruption on Thera (between 1645 and 1450) ended Minoan prosperity. Frescoes and artefacts show that Minoan culture was highly sophisticated. Three scripts were used: hieroglyphics (c. 1900–1700), Linear A (c. 1700–1450), and Linear B (c. 1450–1400).

Minorca (Spanish name: Menorca) A Spanish island in the Mediterranean Sea, the second largest of the Balearic Islands. Shoe manufacture is important and it has a thriving tourist industry. Area: 702 sq km (271 sq mi). Population (1985): 55 500. Chief town: Mahón.

minor planet (or asteroid) A small nonluminous rocky body that orbits a star. Over 100 000 orbit the sun, about 95% in a belt between the orbits of Mars and Jupiter. The smallest minor planets are less than 1 km across with only about 200 exceeding 100 km: the largest is *Ceres (1003 km). They are probably debris from collisions of bodies that formed between Mars and Jupiter.

Minos A legendary king of Crete, son of Zeus and Europa. Although usually regarded as a good ruler, the Athenians portrayed him as a tyrant, who had seven youths and seven maidens fed to the *Minotaur each year.

Minotaur In Greek legend, a Cretan monster with a bull's head and a man's body. It was the offspring of Pasiphae, wife of *Minos, and a bull with which Poseidon had caused her to fall in love. *Theseus killed it with the help of Ariadne.

Minsk 53 51N 27 30E A city in the W Soviet Union, the capital of the Belorussian SSR. Dating from at least the 11th century, it came under Lithuanian and then Polish rule; it was restored to Russia in 1793. Industries include machine and vehicle manufacturing, textiles, and food processing. Population (1987): 1 543 000.

mint A widely distributed aromatic herb, with creeping roots, toothed leaves, and clusters of purple, pink, or white flowers. Many species, especially *peppermint and *spearmint, are used in cooking, etc. An oil extracted from mint stems and leaves is used in perfumes and medicines.

Mint. See Royal Mint.

Miocene epoch. See Tertiary period.

miracle plays Medieval European dramas based on religious themes. In England, they flourished particularly in the 14th and early 15th centuries. A distinction between mystery plays (based on episodes in the Bible) and miracle plays (based on the lives of saints) is often made with regard to French examples. Originally performed in churches, they became less and less religious and were eventually performed on mobile stages in public marketplaces.

Miró, Joan (1893–1983) Surrealist painter, born in Barcelona. He moved to Paris (1919) and began painting in a childlike style. His "savage" paintings expressed the horrors of the Spanish Civil War; his *Constellations* were painted (during World War II) with his characteristic blobs intertwined with threadlike lines.

mirrors Devices for reflecting light, usually consisting of a sheet of glass with one surface silvered. A plane mirror, in which the sheet is flat, forms a laterally inverted image in which the righthand side of something appears as the lefthand side. Spherical mirrors, concave or convex, magnify or reduce the image. Parabolic mirrors are used in reflecting *telescopes.

miscarriage. See abortion.

Mishnah (Hebrew: instruction) An early code of Jewish law. Written in Hebrew, it is thought to have been edited in Palestine in the early 3rd century AD. It consists of halakhah on a wide range of subjects, coming partly from the Bible as interpreted by the early rabbis (called *Tannaim*) and partly from customs over a long period. See also Talmud.

Mississippi A state in the S central USA, on the Gulf of Mexico. There is a large Black community. Its main products are cotton, soya beans, poultry, eggs, and livestock. Ship construction and repair, timber and paper products, textiles, chemicals, and food processing are important industries. Petroleum is the main mineral but natural gas, clay, and sand are also exploited. Mississippi remains, however, one of the country's poorest states. *History*: explored by the Spanish, it was later claimed for France and

was handed over to Britain (1763). Colonization followed and the area came under US control (1783). Made a state in 1817, it became a leading cotton producer and slave state until the US Civil War. Area: 123 584 sq km (47 716 sq mi). Population (1985 est): 2 656 600. Capital: Jackson.

Mississippian period. See Carboniferous period.

Mississippi River A river in the central USA, the second longest in North America. Rising in N Minnesota, it flows generally S into the Gulf of Mexico. Famous for its steamboats, it is one of the world's busiest commercial waterways, with major ports at St Louis and New Orleans. Length: 3780 km (2348 mi).

Missouri A state in the central USA, lying immediately W of the Mississippi River. Manufacturing includes transport and aerospace equipment, food processing, chemicals, and printing. The leading lead producer in the USA, it also exploits barytes, iron ore, and zinc deposits. Agriculture produces livestock and dairy products, soya beans, corn, wheat, cotton, and sorghum. *History*: explored by the French from Canada and claimed for France (1682), it formed part of the Louisiana Purchase (1803) by the USA, becoming a state in 1821. Area: 180 486 sq km (69 686 sq mi). Population (1986 est): 5 066 000. Capital: Jefferson City.

Missouri River A river in the central USA, the longest river in North America and chief tributary of the Mississippi River. Rising in the Rocky Mountains, it flows N and E through Montana, then SE across North and South Dakota before joining the Mississippi at St Louis. Length: 4367 km (2714 mi).

mistletoe An evergreen shrub of temperate and tropical regions, growing on the branches of many trees. The Eurasian mistletoe (*Viscum album*) occurs mainly on apple trees, poplars, willows, and hawthorns. It has rootlike suckers that penetrate the host's tissues, yellow flowers, and white berries. Mistletoe was believed by the Druids to have medicinal properties and is a traditional Christmas decoration.

mistral A strong cold dry northerly wind that is funnelled down the Rhône Valley in S France to the Mediterranean Sea.

Mitchell, R(eginald) J(oseph) (1895–1937) British aeronautical engineer. He joined Vickers in 1916 and was a leading designer of seaplanes entered for the Schneider Trophy in the 1920s. He designed the first Spitfire (1936), although he did not live to see its supremacy as a fighter in World War II.

mite A tiny *arachnid, up to 6 mm long, with eight bristly legs. Mites occur in a wide range of habitats throughout the world; some are parasitic on animals, such as the itch mite (*Sarcoptes scabei*), which causes skin disease in man and animals (*see* mange). They may transmit diseases (including *typhus). Mites are closely related to *ticks. See also harvest mite.

Mithraism A mystery religion that worshipped Mithra, the Persian god of the sun who represented justice and goodness. It spread through Asia Minor, finally reaching Rome in about 68 BC. Here Mithra was known as Mithras and was worshipped widely among Roman soldiers. Mithraism rivalled Christianity until its decline in the 3rd century AD.

mitochondria Oval or sausage-shaped structures found in the cytoplasm of nearly all cells. They contain various enzymes that provide energy for the cell. In active cells, such as heart muscle, mitochondria are large and numerous.

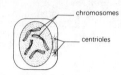

prophase *The genetic material becomes visible in the form of chromosomes and the nuclear membrane disappears.*

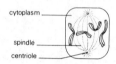

metaphase *The chromosomes become attached to the equator of a fibrous spindle.*

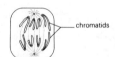

anaphase *The two chromatids of each chromosome move to opposite poles of the spindle.*

telophase *Nuclear membranes form around the two groups of chromatids, which become less distinct.*

MITOSIS *Division of the nucleus of an animal cell takes place in four phases, which grade into each other.*

mitosis The process by which the nucleus of a body cell (i.e. any cell that is not a germ cell) duplicates itself, producing two nuclei with chromosomes that are identical to those of the parent nucleus. By the start of mitosis, each chromo-

some has duplicated itself and consists of two identical chromatids. These separate and form two groups at opposite ends of the cell. In the final phase each group becomes enclosed in a new membrane. After this the cytoplasm divides to form two new cells. Mitosis occurs in most animals and plants to form new cells for normal growth and repair of tissues. *Compare* meiosis.

Mitterrand, François (Maurice) (1916–) French statesman; president (1981–). He was president of a democratic-socialist union (1965–68) and in 1971 assumed leadership of the newly unified Socialist Party. In 1981 he became the first socialist president in 35 years.

m.k.s. system A system of *metric units based on the metre, kilogram, and second. It has now been replaced for scientific purposes by *SI units, which are derived from it.

M'Naghten's Rules. *See* insanity.

moa An extinct flightless bird of New Zealand. Moas were 60–300 cm tall and had a small head, a long neck, and long stout legs. They were fast runners but were hunted by early Polynesian settlers for food.

Moabites A highly civilized Semitic tribe living E of the Dead Sea from the late 14th century BC. They successfully rebelled against Israelite occupation in the 9th century BC. In 582 BC, according to Josephus, they were conquered by the Babylonians.

Mobutu, Sese Seko (Joseph Désiré M.; 1930–) Zaïrese statesman; president (1970–). He came to power in 1965 in a coup. In 1967 he founded the country's only political party—the Popular Movement of the Revolution—and the stability of his strict government is fostered by his personal cult.

Moçambique. *See* Mozambique, People's Republic of.

mockingbird An American songbird noted for its ability to mimic sounds. Mockingbirds live on or near the ground, feeding on insects and fruit. About 25 cm long, they have grey plumage.

mock orange A shrub, also called syringa and philadelphus, native to N temperate regions and commonly grown in gardens. The fragrant white flowers resemble orange blossom. *Philadelphus coronarius* is the only native European species.

Modena (ancient name: Mutina) 44 39N 10 55E A city in N Italy, in Emilia-Romagna. It has an 11th-century romanesque cathedral, several palaces, and an ancient university (1175). The centre of a rich agricultural area, its industries include agricultural engineering, textiles, and motor vehicles. Population (1986): 176 880.

modes Musical scales derived from ancient Greek music, on which European music was based up to the 16th century. Each mode consists of a different pattern of the five tones and two semitones of the octave; the patterns can be demonstrated using the white notes of the piano keyboard. Two of the most common modes were the Ionian (C-C) and the Aeolian (A-A), which became the basis of the major and minor scales.

Modigliani, Amedeo (1884–1920) Italian painter and sculptor. His mature work, executed in Paris (1906–20), was influenced by *Cézanne and *Brancusi. From 1909 to 1915 he worked chiefly on sculptures; from 1915 he painted many nudes and portraits.

modulation A method of carrying information (the signal) on an electromagnetic wave or an oscillating electric current (the carrier). In **amplitude modulation** (AM) the amplitude of a carrier is changed according to the magnitude of the signal. This is used in medium-wave sound broadcasting in which audio-frequencies (50–20 000 hertz) are carried on radio waves with a frequency of about one megahertz. In **frequency modulation** (FM) the frequency of the carrier is changed. FM is used in VHF *radio (about 100 megahertz). Its main advantage over AM is its better signal-to-noise ratio.
In **pulse modulation** the carrier is a series of pulses whose height, width, or some other factor is altered by the signal. It is used in digital equipment, such as computers, and in telegraphy.

Mogadishu (or Mogadiscio) 2 01N 45 25E The capital and main port of Somalia, on the Indian Ocean. It was founded as an Arab settlement in the 10th century and sold to Italy in 1905 becoming the capital of Italian Somaliland. It is the chief commercial centre of the republic. Population (1987 est): 1 000 000.

Moguls An Indian Muslim dynasty, descended from the Mongol leader *Genghis Khan, that ruled from 1526 until 1858. Its founder, Babur, and the first 5 of his 18 successors are known as the Great Moguls. During the late 17th and the 18th centuries Mogul power declined; the last emperor, Bahadur Shah II (reigned 1837–58), was removed from power after the *Indian Mutiny.

mohair A wool-like fabric manufactured from the hair of *Angora goats. Warm, light, and durable and frequently blended with wool, silk, or cotton, for use in for lightweight suiting and knitwear.

Mohammed (or Muhammad; c. 570–632 AD) The founder of *Islam, said to have been born in Mecca. In 610 he received messages from God and called upon his pagan fellow townsmen to repent and prepare for the Last Day. The Meccans rejected him and in 622 he fled from Mecca to Yathrib (now called Medina), where he established the first Muslim community. By 629 the Muslims in Yathrib were strong enough to defeat the Meccans and obtained control of Mecca. By the time of Mohammed's death, Islam had begun to spread throughout Arabia. Mohammed's sayings were collected after his death to form the *Koran.

Mohammed Reza Pahlavi (1918–80) Shah of Iran (1941–79) after the Allies forced his father *Reza Shah Pahlavi, to abdicate in World War II. In 1979 civil war forced him into exile and an Islamic republic was established under the leadership of Ayatollah *Khomeini.

Mohawk An Iroquoian-speaking American Indian tribe of New York state. They were one of the five tribes that formed the league of the *Iroquois, said to have been founded by the Mohawk chief *Hiawatha.

Mohican An Algonkian-speaking American Indian tribe of New England. Primarily cultivators, they lived in fortified communities or in enclosed villages, but were displaced by wars with the Mohawks.

Mohorovičić discontinuity The boundary between the earth's crust and upper mantle, marked by a sudden increase in velocity in seismic waves as the denser mantle is reached. It lies at a depth of 33–35 km (20–22 mi) beneath the continents and 5–10 km (3–6 mi) beneath the oceans. It is named after the Croatian scientist, Andrija Mohorovičić (1857–1936), who discovered it in 1909.

Mohs' scale A scale of hardness of minerals named after the mineralogist Friedrich Mohs (1773–1839). In ascending order of hardness they are: 1. talc, 2. gypsum, 3. calcite, 4. fluorite, 5. apatite, 6. orthoclase feldspar, 7. quartz, 8. topaz, 9. corundum, and 10. diamond. Each can be scratched by any mineral higher up the scale; other minerals can be assigned numbers according to which materials will scratch them.

Moji. See Kitakyushu.

Moldavia A former principality in SE Europe. It was occupied by the Mongols in the 13th century, becoming independent in the 14th century. In 1859 Moldavia and Walachia formed Romania. Russian Moldavia became the Moldavian Soviet Socialist Republic in 1940.

mole (metrology; symbol mol) The *SI unit of amount of substance equal to the amount of substance that contains the same number of entities as there are atoms in 0.012 kg of carbon-12. One mol of any substance contains $6.022\,52 \times 10^{23}$ entities (see Avogadro). The entities may be atoms, molecules, ions, electrons, etc.

mole (zoology) A widespread burrowing mammal. The common Eurasian mole (*Talpa europaea*) is about 14 cm long. It is thickest, with black fur, and has long-clawed digging forefeet. Moles make an extensive system of underground tunnels, feeding on earthworms. They are practically blind above ground. See also desman.

molecular biology The branch of science that deals with the molecular basis of living processes. Molecular biology involves both *biochemistry and biophysics: its growth since the 1930s has been made possible by the development of such techniques as chromatography, *electron microscopy, and *X-ray diffraction, which have revealed the structures of biologically important molecules, such as DNA, RNA, and enzymes.

molecule The smallest portion of a compound that can exist independently and retain its properties. The atoms that make up a molecule are linked by *chemical bonds either covalently, e.g. CO_2, or electrovalently, e.g. NaCl. However, in crystalline substances (see crystals) the bonds extend throughout the whole crystal structure and the molecule has only a notional existence. **Relative molecular mass** (or molecular weight) is the ratio of the average mass per molecule to one-twelfth of the mass of a carbon-12 atom.

Molière (Jean-Baptiste Poquelin; 1622–73) French dramatist, the father of modern French comedy. His plays include *Tartuffe* (1664), *Le

Misanthrope (1666), *L'Avare* (1668), and *Le Malade imaginaire* (1673). His ridicule of hypocrisy and his satire brought him into conflict with the religious authorities. He frequently acted in his own productions.

mollusc An invertebrate animal of which there are about 100 000 species occurring on land, sea, and fresh water. Molluscs are common on rocky coasts. They have a soft body with a muscular foot, used for crawling, burrowing, or swimming. Some have a protective shell, as in *snails and *limpets. However, in some (e.g. *cuttlefish) the shell is concealed within the body, while others (e.g. *slugs) have no shell. Most molluscs graze on plant material, although some are carnivorous. *See also* bivalve.

moloch A desert-dwelling ant-eating Australian lizard, *Moloch horridus*, also called thorny devil. Its yellow-and-brown body is covered in thorny spines, which provide camouflage.

Moloch A Semitic god whose worship was characterized by the sacrificial burning of children. There are several biblical references to his worship by the Israelites during the period of the Kings (c. 961–c. 562 BC).

Molotov. *See* Perm.

Molotov, Vyacheslav Mikhailovich (V. M. Scriabin; 1890–1986) Soviet statesman. As prime minister (1930–41) and foreign minister (1939–49, 1953–56), Molotov signed the Soviet-German nonaggression treaty in 1939; after the German invasion in 1941, he made alliances with the Allies. The **Molotov cocktail**, named after him, is a type of hand grenade.

Moluccas (*or* Maluku) An Indonesian group of islands between Sulawesi and West Irian. It includes the islands of Ambon, Halmahera, and Ceram. The indigenous population fishes, hunts, and collects sago; spices, fish, and copra are exported. *History*: before the Portuguese arrival (1512), the islands were ruled by Muslims and known as the Spice Islands. Dutch control was established in the 19th century. Indonesia was granted independence in 1949. Area: about 74 504 sq km (28 766 sq mi). Population (1980): 1 411 006. Chief town: Ambon.

molybdenum (Mo) A hard silvery metal of high melting point, first prepared in 1782 by P. J. Hjelm (1746–1813). It occurs as molybdenite (MoS_2) and as wulfenite (lead molybdenate; $PbMoO_4$). Molybdenum is used in high-temperature filaments and as an alloying agent in the production of high-strength steels. At no 42; at wt 95.94; mp 2617°C; bp 4612°C.

Mombasa 4 04S 39 40E A port in Kenya, on an island in an inlet of the Indian Ocean. It was an important port for Arab traders and was taken in the 16th and 17th centuries by the Portuguese. The modern deepwater port at Kinlindini handles most of Kenya's trade; industries include oil refining. Population (1984 est): 481 000.

moment The product of a force and its perpendicular distance from the axis about which it acts. A moment produces a turning effect and is sometimes called a torque. The inertia of a body to a torque is called its **moment of inertia**. This quantity is equal to mr^2 for a single mass (m) ro-

tating about an axis at a distance r from the axis. The moment of inertia of a system of masses is equal to the sum of these products.

momentum The linear momentum of a body is the product of its mass and its linear velocity. The angular momentum of a body is the product of its *moment of inertia and its angular velocity. During any process the total momentum of the system always remains constant (the law of conservation of momentum).

Mona. *See* Anglesey.

Monaco, Principality of A small country on the Mediterranean Sea, an enclave within France. It consists of the business district around the ports, *Monte Carlo, and the capital Monaco. *Economy*: the main sources of revenue are tourism and the sale of postage stamps. *History*: ruled by the house of Grimaldi since 1297, it has been under French protection since 1641. Head of state: Prince Rainier III. Official language: French; Monégasque, a mixture of French and Italian, is also spoken. Official currency: French franc of 100 centimes. Area: 189 hectares (467 acres). Population (1985): 28 000.

Monaghan (Irish name: Contae Mhuineachain) A county in the NE Republic of Ireland, in Ulster bordering on Northern Ireland. Agricultural produce includes oats and potatoes; dairy farming is also important. Area: 1551 sq km (499 sq mi). Population (1986): 52 332. County town: Monaghan.

mona monkey. *See* guenon.

monarch A widespread American butterfly, *Danaus plexippus*. Light brown with black borders and white dots, the adults migrate southwards for the winter. In spring they move north, breeding on the way. The caterpillars are green with black and yellow bands and feed on milkweed.

Mönchengladbach (*or* München Gladbach) 51 12N 6 25E A city in W Germany, in North Rhine-Westphalia. It is the centre of the German textile industry and headquarters of the NATO forces in N central Europe. Population (1990 est): 252 000.

Mond, Ludwig (1839–1909) German industrial chemist, who lived in Britain from 1862. He discovered nickel carbonyl and used it to extract platinum from its ores, a method now known as the **Mond process**.

Mondrian, Piet (Pieter Cornelis Mondriaan; 1872–1944) Dutch painter. While in Paris (1912–14) he came under the influence of *cubism. His first abstract paintings (1917) used only horizontal and vertical lines, primary colours, and black and white. During this period he helped to launch the art movement of de Stijl. After 1919 his style, known as neoplasticism, influenced the *Bauhaus school.

Monet, Claude (1840–1926) French impressionist painter. In the late 1860s and 1870s he developed the impressionist technique in views of Paris and boating scenes at Argenteuil. He excelled in his series of the same scenes painted at different times of day, e.g. *Gare St Lazare*, *Haystacks*, *Rouen Cathedral*, and the *Poplars*, the last of which anticipates *abstract art.

monetarism A revision of old-established economic theories supported by Milton *Friedman. Monetarists believe in government control of the economy, favouring a gentle increase of the money supply at roughly the rate of growth of the economy. They blame *inflation on overexpansion of the money supply.

money A medium of exchange that has to be divisible, have a high value-to-weight ratio, and not be easily forged. Money also functions as means of credit and a store of wealth. Said to have been invented by the Lydians in the 7th century BC, it originally took the form of something valuable in itself, but most money is now in the form of paper.
The total stock of money in the economy is known as the **money supply**. In the UK two definitions of the money supply are used: the narrow M1 (essentially, the total amount of cash and current accounts) and the broad M3 (essentially, the total amount of cash plus both current and deposit accounts).

money spider A tiny *spider with a reddish or black body. Money spiders build sheetlike webs on vegetation to which they cling upside down, waiting to catch insects that drop onto the web.

mongolism. *See* Down's syndrome.

Mongoloid The racial grouping of populations of E Asia and the Arctic region of North America. They usually have medium skin colouring, a fold of skin on the upper eyelid, straight coarse black hair, a rather flat face with high cheekbones, and little facial and body hair.

Mongols An Asiatic people united in the early 13th century by *Genghis Khan, who built up an empire that included much of central Asia. The Mongols ruled China as the Yuan dynasty until 1368. They were later confined to the area corresponding to the present Mongolian People's Republic.

mongoose A carnivorous mammal found in warm regions of the Mediterranean, Africa, and Asia. They range in size from 50 to 100 cm including the long tail (25–50 cm); they have short legs and long grey-brown fur. Mongooses are skilled at catching snakes and rats; they also eat eggs and small mammals.

monitor lizard A lizard occurring in tropical and subtropical regions. 0.2–3 m long, monitors have a long body and well-developed legs. They feed on mammals, snakes, and animal remains. *See also* Komodo dragon.

monkey A tree-dwelling *primate native to Africa, Asia, and Central and South America. Monkeys are 20–110 cm long and most have a long tail used in climbing, although some are tailless. Agile and intelligent, they have fingernails and an arrangement of thumb and fingers similar to the human hand, giving them skill in handling objects. Most monkeys eat a varied diet but prefer fruit and vegetation.

monkey puzzle A coniferous tree, *Araucaria araucana*, also called Chile pine, native to Chile and Argentina and widely grown as an ornamental. Up to 30 m high, it has horizontal branches covered with leathery prickly overlapping leaves,

3–4 cm long. The round spiny cones break up to release large edible seeds.

monkfish A *shark with a broad flattened head, a long tapering body, and winglike pectoral fins. Monkfish occur in tropical and temperate seas and feed on bottom-dwelling fish, molluscs, and crustaceans.

Monmouth, James Scott, Duke of (1649–85) The illegitimate son of Charles II of England and Lucy Walter (d. 1658). A leader of the Protestant opposition, he was banished (1684) after being implicated in the Rye House Plot. After the accession of James II (1685), Monmouth landed at Lyme Regis to raise a rebellion and was defeated at *Sedgemoor and beheaded.

monoclonal antibody A type of pure antibody that can be produced artificially in large quantities and used, for example, to distinguish the major blood groups. Mouse lymphocytes producing the required antibody are fused with mouse cancer cells; the resulting hybrid cells multiply rapidly and all produce the same type of antibody as their parent lymphocytes.

monocotyledons The smaller of the two main groups of flowering plants, which includes the palms, bananas, orchids, grasses, lilies, and many garden bulbs (*compare* dicotyledons). Monocots have a single seed leaf (cotyledon) in the embryo, the flower parts are in threes (or multiples of three), and the leaves have parallel veins.

monomer A simple molecule or group of atoms forming a repeated unit in a dimer (two molecules), trimer (three molecules), or polymer (*see* polymerization).

monopoly An industry in which the market has only one supplier, enabling the monopolist to restrict supply, demand excessive prices, and make large profits. In the *public sector monopolies on services are commonplace. In the private sector they are usually restricted by laws. In the UK the **Monopolies Commission** investigates monopolies and mergers.

monosaccharide (*or* simple sugar) A *carbohydrate consisting of a single sugar unit. The most widely occurring monosaccharides are *glucose and fructose.

Monroe, James (1758–1831) US statesman; president (1817–25). He was minister to France (1794–96) and Britain (1803–07) before becoming secretary of state (1811). His presidency saw the opening of the West and the acquisition of Spanish Florida. The **Monroe Doctrine** (1823) warned European powers not to intervene in the Americas and declared that the USA would likewise keep out of Europe.

Monroe, Marilyn (Norma Jean Baker *or* Mortenson; 1926–62) US film actress. Promoted as a sex symbol in such films as *Gentlemen Prefer Blondes* (1953), she later developed as a talented comedienne. Her third husband, Arthur *Miller, wrote her last film *The Misfits* (1961). She died from an overdose of sleeping pills.

Monrovia 6 20N 10 46W The capital and main port of Liberia, on the Atlantic Ocean. Founded in 1822 as a settlement for freed North American slaves, it was named after President Monroe of the USA. Population (1985): 500 000.

monsoon A seasonal large-scale reversal of winds in the tropics, resulting chiefly from the different heating properties of the land and oceans. The period of heavy rainfall in S Asia extending from April to September that accompanies the wind reversals is also called a monsoon.

Montaigne, Michel de (1533–92) French essayist. In 1568 he resigned his position as magistrate in Bordeaux and began writing his *Essais*. In 1580 he travelled widely in Europe and was mayor of Bordeaux from 1581 to 1585. His *Essais*, which launched a new literary form, expressed his mature humanistic philosophy and constitute a moving self-portrait. They were published in two editions in 1580 and 1588, and an edition after his death included his final alterations.

Montana The fourth largest state in the USA, bordering on Canada. Predominantly agricultural, it relies largely on cattle ranching and wheat production. Other crops include barley and sugar beet. Its mineral resources include copper (at Butte) and coal. There are several Indian reservations. *History*: it formed part of the Louisiana Purchase in 1803. During the mid-19th century a gold rush caused an influx of immigrants to the state. Area: 377 070 sq km (145 587 sq mi). Population (1986 est): 819 000. Capital: Helena.

Mont Blanc (Italian name: Monte Bianco) 45 50N 6 52E The highest mountain in the Alps, on the French–Italian border. It was first climbed in 1786. A road tunnel (1958–62) beneath it, 12 km (7.5 mi) long, connects the two countries. Height: 4807 m (15 771 ft).

Monte Carlo 43 44N 7 25E A resort in the principality of *Monaco. It is famous for its casinos, motor rally, and other cultural events. Population (1985): 12 000.

Monterrey 25 40N 100 20W The third largest city in Mexico. Founded in 1579, it is a major industrial centre specializing in metallurgy. Population (1980): 1 916 472.

Monteverdi, Claudio (1567–1643) Italian composer. From 1613 until his death he was maestro di cappella at St Mark's Cathedral, Venice. Monteverdi was the first great composer of *opera. His works include the operas *Orfeo* (1607) and *The Coronation of Poppea* (1642), a set of *Vespers* (1610), and many madrigals.

Montevideo 34 55S 56 10W The capital (since 1828) and main port of Uruguay, on the Río de la Plata. Founded in 1726 by the Spanish, in the 20th century it developed rapidly, as an industrial centre. Population (1985 est): 1 246 000.

Montezuma II (1466–c. 1520) The last Aztec Emperor of Mexico (1502–20). During his reign his empire was weakened by tribal warfare, which enabled the Spaniards, led by Hernán *Cortés, to establish themselves in Mexico.

Montfort, Simon de, Earl of Leicester (c. 1208–65) English statesman, born in Normandy. After serving Henry III of England in Gascony, he joined the antiroyalist faction, becoming the leader in the subsequent *Barons' War. At first successful, he became virtual ruler of England, summoning a parliament in 1265. In the same year, however, he was defeated and killed at Evesham.

Montgolfier, Jacques-Étienne (1745–99) French balloonist, who with his brother **Joseph-Michel Montgolfier** (1740–1810) invented the hot-air balloon, which was publicly launched in 1782. A much larger balloon, which rose 2000 m, was demonstrated in June 1783 and in October a series of passenger-carrying ascents were made.

Montgomery of Alamein, Bernard Law, 1st Viscount (1887–1976) British field marshal. In World War II he commanded the Eighth Army (1942) and after the battle of Alamein drove *Rommel back to Tunis and surrender (1943). He became chief of land forces in the 1944 Normandy invasion and helped plan the Arnhem disaster (September, 1944), but pushed back the subsequent German offensive, receiving Germany's surrender. After the war he was chief of the imperial general staff (1946–48) and deputy commander of NATO forces (1951–58).

month The time taken by the moon to complete one revolution around the earth. The length of the month depends on the choice of reference points. The **sidereal month**, of 27.32 days, is measured with reference to the background stars. The **synodic month**, of 29.53 days, is measured between two identical phases of the moon.

Montpellier 43 36N 3 53E A city in S France, the capital of the Hérault department. A Huguenot stronghold, it was besieged and captured by Louis XIII in 1622. Montpellier trades in wine and brandy and has numerous manufacturing industries. Population (1990 est): 220 000.

Montreal 45 30N 73 36W A city and port in E Canada, in Quebec on Montreal Island at the junction of the Ottawa and St Lawrence Rivers. Canada's largest city, its many industries include oil refining, meat packing, brewing and distilling, food processing, textiles, and aircraft. With four universities, it is a major cultural centre. Two-thirds of the population is French-speaking. *History*: founded as Ville-Marie (1642), Montreal quickly became a commercial centre. Captured by Britain (1760), it acquired an English-speaking merchant community. Population (1986): 1 015 420.

Montserrat A British crown colony comprising one of the Leeward Islands, in the Caribbean Sea to the SE of Puerto Rico. *Economy*: the main crops are cotton, coconuts, and fruit and vegetables. *History*: discovered by Columbus in 1493, it was colonized by the Irish in the 17th century. Formerly administratively joined to the Leeward Islands, it became a separate colony in 1960. Official language: English. Official currency: East Caribbean dollar of 100 cents. Area: 106 sq km (40 sq mi). Population (1985): 11 852. Capital and main port: Plymouth.

Mont St Michel 48 38N 1 30W A granite islet in NW France, in the Manche department in the Bay of St Michel. The islet is connected to the mainland by a causeway. It is about 78 m (256 ft) high and is crowned by a Benedictine monastery (founded 966 AD).

Monument. *See* Fire of London.

moon The natural satellite of the earth. The moon orbits the earth every 27.32 days at a mean distance of 384 400 km, keeping more or less the same face (the nearside) towards the earth. As it revolves, different *phases can be seen from earth, together with up to two or three lunar *eclipses per year. The moon is only 81 times less massive than the earth and has a diameter of 3476 km.
The major surface features are the light-coloured highlands and the much darker lava plains—the maria. The surface is heavily cratered with roughly circular walled depressions produced by impacting bodies from space. The first landing on the moon was made by Neil *Armstrong and Edwin *Aldrin on 20 July, 1969. *See* Apollo moon programme.

Moonies. *See* Unification Church.

Moore, Henry (1898–1986) British sculptor. Influenced by primitive African and Mexican art, he produced many characteristic mother and child sculptures and reclining figures. After his abstract work in the 1930s, he returned to the humanist tradition in the early 1940s with his *Shelter Sketch Book.*

moorhen A blackish waterbird, *Gallinula chloropus*, also called common gallinule and waterhen, occurring worldwide except for Australia. It is 32 cm long and has a red bill and forehead and a white patch beneath the tail. It breeds in thick vegetation near ponds and marshes.

Moors The conventional European name for the *Arabs and *Berbers of NW Africa, and for the 8th-century Muslim conquerors of the Iberian peninsula. The Moors, who were the leading power in Spain until the 11th century, were a highly civilized people.

moose. *See* elk.

moped. *See* motorcycles.

Moral Rearmament (MRA) A controversial movement founded by a US evangelist Frank Nathan Daniel Buchman (1878–1961), in the 1920s. At first it received most support at Oxford University and was called the Oxford Group until 1938. It seeks the renewal of spirituality through conversion.

Moravia (Czech name: Morava; German name: Mähren) An area and former province (1918–49) of central Czechoslovakia, lying chiefly in the basin of the River Morava. Mineral deposits include coal and iron ore. *History*: settled by Slavic tribes in the late 8th century AD, it formed the centre of an important medieval kingdom (Great Moravia). It became part of Czechoslovakia in 1918. Chief town: Brno.

Moravia, Alberto (Alberto Pincherle; 1907–) Italian novelist. Early novels attacked fascism and the corrupt society that produced it. His later works, which include *The Woman of Rome* (1947), *The Lie* (1966), and *Erotic Tales* (1985) concern social themes. His literary and political essays are collected in *Man As an End* (1963).

moray eel A brightly coloured thick-bodied *eel, up to 1.5 m long. Moray eels live in rock crevices and reefs of warm and tropical seas.

Moray Firth An inlet of the North Sea in NE Scotland, extending SW from a line between Tarbat Ness in the Highland Region and Burghead in Grampian Region. Length: about 56 km (35 mi).

More, Sir Thomas (1477–1535) English lawyer, scholar, and saint. He joined Henry VIII's Privy Council in 1518 and succeeded Wolsey as chancellor in 1529. He resigned in 1532, opposing Henry as the supreme head of the English Church. Imprisoned (1534) after refusing to swear to the new Act of Succession, he was tried (1535) for treason, convicted on false evidence, and beheaded. His best-known scholarly work is *Utopia* (1516).

morel A club-shaped fungus with a cap that is pitted like a honeycomb. The edible common morel (*Morchella esculenta*) has a yellowish-brown cap, 4–8 cm high, and a stout whitish stalk.

Morgan, John Pierpont (1837–1913) US financier, who founded (1895) J. P. Morgan and Co, one of the most powerful banking corporations in the USA. During the 1880s he reorganized many railway companies and later financed the US Steel Corporation and General Electric organizations. His son **John Pierpont Morgan, Jr** (1867–1943) succeeded him and helped to organize the credit requirements of the Allies in World War I.

Morgan le Fay In *Arthurian legend, an evil sorceress who plotted the overthrow of her brother King Arthur. According to Malory's *Morte d'Arthur* (1485) she revealed *Guinevere's adultery to Arthur. However, in the earlier *Vita Merlini* (c. 1150) by *Geoffrey of Monmouth she is a benevolent figure.

Moriscos Muslims forced to become Christians in Spain. Many Muslims continued to live in Spain after the former Muslim areas came under Christian rule; by the 15th century they were forced to become Christians or go into exile. Many chose to remain, privately practising Islam. Between 1609 and 1614, about 500 000 Moriscos were forced into exile, settling mainly in Africa.

Mormons Members of the Christian group formally called the Church of Jesus Christ of Latter-Day Saints, founded in 1830 by Joseph Smith in New York state. Smith claimed to have discovered tablets that contained the sacred Book of Mormon. After Smith's murder by a mob, the persecuted Mormons moved, under Brigham *Young, to Salt Lake, Utah, in 1847. Mormons have no professional clergy, reject infant baptism, do not take alcohol, and run educational and missionary programmes.

morning glory A trailing or twining plant, native to tropical America and Australia and cultivated for its beautiful flowers. The leaves are often heart-shaped and the trumpet-shaped flowers, up to 12 cm across, are deep blue, purple, pink, or white.

Morocco, Kingdom of A country in NW Africa, bordering on the Atlantic Ocean and Mediterranean Sea. *Economy*: cereals and citrus fruits are the main crops. Morocco is a leading exporter of phosphates; other mineral resources are iron ore, coal, lead, zinc, cobalt, and manganese. Industries include food processing, textiles, and traditional handicrafts. Fishing, especially sardines and tuna, and tourism are important. *History*: part of the Roman province of Mauretania, it fell to the Vandals in the 5th century AD. In the early 20th century Morocco was divided into French and Spanish protectorates (1912) and the international zone of Tangier (1923). In 1956 Morocco became a sultanate, later a kingdom (1957) under King Mohammed V; his son, Hassan II, came to the throne in 1961. Prime minister: Azeddine Laraki (1919–). Official religion: Islam. Official language: Arabic. Official currency: dirham of 100 centimes. Area: 458 730 sq km (144 078 sq mi). Population (1987 est): 23 000 000. Capital: Rabat.

morphine A drug obtained from *opium and used in medicine for the relief of severe pain. Its depressant effect on the brain accounts for the pain-killing properties; in high doses it also affects breathing and coughing. Morphine is an addictive drug and readily leads to severe physical dependence. *See* narcotic.

Morris, Desmond John (1928–) British zoologist, noted for his popularization of biology, especially in *The Naked Ape* (1967), *The Human Zoo* (1969), and *Manwatching* (1977), all treating humans as subject to the laws of animal behaviour.

Morris, William (1834–96) British designer and poet. Associated with the *Pre-Raphaelite Brotherhood, he later started a firm of decorators and designers (1861). He produced stained glass, carpets, and furniture, and his wallpaper designs are still used. His Kelmscott Press, founded in 1890, influenced book design and printing. He was also a founder of British socialism.

Morris dance An English folk dance performed by groups of men dressed in white, wearing bells, and often carrying sticks or handkerchiefs. A common theme is fertility through death and rebirth. Similar dances are found elsewhere, often featuring the black-faced Morisco (Moor), whence the name Morris is thought to derive.

Morse, Samuel Finley Breese (1791–1872) US inventor, who erected the first telegraph line, between Washington and Baltimore (1844). Messages were sent by **Morse code**, a system in which each letter of the alphabet is represented by a sequence of dots and dashes.

mortar (building material) A mixture of sand, hydrated lime, and Portland cement, used to bind together building bricks, etc. It is applied wet as a paste, which sets solid.

mortar (weapon) A short-barrelled muzzle-loading *artillery piece with a high-angled trajectory. In World War II the largest Allied mortar had a calibre of 4.2 inches (107 mm), the German version being 8.3 inches (210 mm) with six barrels. Mortars are used to fire explosive and smoke bombs.

mortgage Rights in property (usually land, buildings, etc.) given by a borrower (mortgagor) to a lender (mortgagee) as security for a loan. In the UK, building societies and banks lend money for house purchase. They have the right to sell the property to recover their debt if the borrower fails to pay his regular instalments of interest and capital repayment until the debt is cleared.

letters			
A · —		N — ·
B — · · ·		O — — —
C — · — ·		P · — — ·
D — · ·		Q — — · —
E ·		R · — ·
F · · — ·		S · · ·
G — — ·		T —
H · · · ·		U · · —
I · ·		V · · · —
J · — — —		W · — —
K — · —		X — · · —
L · — · ·		Y — · — —
M — —		Z — — · ·

numbers		punctuation marks	
1 · — — — —		. · — · — · —
2 · · — — —		, — — · · — —
3 · · · — —		: — — — · · ·
4 · · · · —		? · · — — · ·
5 · · · · ·		' · — — — — ·
6 — · · · ·		- — · · · · —
7 — — · · ·		/ — · · — ·
8 — — — · ·		(or) — · — · — ·
9 — — — — ·		" · — · · — ·
0 — — — — —			

MORSE CODE

Mortimer, John Clifford (1923–) British barrister, novelist, and playwright. He was called to the bar in 1948 and is best known for the novels and televised tales featuring Horace Rumpole. His many plays include *The Dock Brief* (1958) and *A Voyage Round My Father* (1970). His novels include *Paradise Postponed* (1985) and *Summer's Lease* (1988).

Morton, Jelly Roll (Ferdinand Joseph La Menthe; 1885–1941) US Black jazz pianist and composer, who made recordings in the 1920s with the group Morton's Red Hot Peppers. He claimed to have "invented jazz in 1902."

mosaic A picture or ornamental design made from small coloured cubes of glass, stone, tile, etc. Mosaics were common in ancient Greece, where they were principally used for floors and made from coloured pebbles. During the Roman Empire mosaics of glass became popular for wall and vault decoration. The 6th-century decorations in S Vitale, in Ravenna, are among the most famous mosaics of the middle ages.

Moscow (Russian name: Moskva) 55 45N 37 42E The capital of the Soviet Union (since 1922) and of the Moscow autonomous region (*oblast*), in the RSFSR on the River Moskva. It is the cultural, economic, and political centre of the Soviet Union. Industries include heavy engineering, cars, textiles, electronics, chemicals, publishing, and food processing. The Kremlin encloses a number of notable ecclesiastical buildings. Red Square is the traditional setting for military parades. Its famous institutions include the Bolshoi Theatre of Opera and Ballet (1780), the Moscow Art Theatre, and the Moscow State Circus. *History*: settlement dates back to prehistoric times. By the beginning of the 13th century it was the centre of the Muscovy principality and the seat of the Russian Church. Invaded by Napoleon (1812), the city was largely destroyed by the ensuing fire. Since World War II Moscow has developed an important tourist industry. Population (1987): 8 815 000.

Moselle, River (German name: R. Mosel) A river in W Europe, flowing N from NE France to join the River Rhine at Koblenz. It forms part of the border between Germany and Luxembourg. Its valley is one of the most important wine-growing areas of Germany. Length: 547 km (340 mi).

Moses According to the Old Testament, the leader of Israel who took the people from slavery in Egypt (Exodus) and brought them close to the Promised Land. As a child in Egypt, Moses was saved from the slaughter ordered by Pharaoh by being hidden in bulrushes on the Nile. On Mt Sinai he was given the Ten Commandments by Jehovah.

Moses, Grandma (Anna Mary Robertson M.; 1860–1961) US primitive painter, born in Greenwich, New York (*see* primitivism). Entirely self-taught, she turned to painting at the age of 67, specializing in scenes of farm life.

Mosley, Sir Oswald Ernald (1896–1980) British fascist. He was a Conservative MP (1918–22), an Independent MP (1922–24), and then a Labour MP (1924, 1926–31), serving as chancellor of the Duchy of Lancaster (1929–30). In 1932 he established the British Union of Fascists, which stirred up violence against Jews, especially in the East End of London. In World War II he was imprisoned (1940–43) and in 1948 founded the Union Movement.

mosque A Muslim place of worship. The first mosque was built by Mohammed at Medina in 622 AD. Prayers are said in a covered area on the side facing *Mecca, the direction being shown by a niche (*mihrab*) in the wall. Mosques are often domed and have minarets (tall slender towers). The mosque is traditionally the centre of Muslim social, intellectual, and religious life.

mosquito A small *fly occurring worldwide, especially in the tropics. It has long legs and a slender abdomen. In most species the males feed on plant juices, while the females suck the blood of mammals, often transmitting serious diseases (including malaria and yellow fever).

moss A *bryophyte plant of which there are about 15 000 species, growing worldwide on moist soil, trees, rocks, etc. The moss plant has stems and leaves and produces sex cells (gametes), which give rise to a spore capsule that grows from the plant on a long stalk. *See also* sphagnum.
The name is also applied to several unrelated plants, for example Spanish moss.

moss pink. *See* phlox.

motet A polyphonic composition for voices, generally unaccompanied. In the medieval motet the fundamental tenor (holding) part was based on a plainchant or popular song while the upper triplex (treble) and motetus (worded) parts had a different text and a quicker rhythm. In the 16th-century, motets with Latin text were used during church services but not as

part of the liturgy. Since the 17th century the word has been used to describe a serious but not necessarily religious choral work.

mother-of-pearl. *See* pearl.

moths. *See* butterflies and moths.

motorcycle racing Racing single-seater motorcycles or sidecar combinations, in classes according to engine size. In road racing, run usually on special circuits, the main classes are 125, 250, 350, and 500 cc. World championships are awarded according to points won in Grand Prix and other races, such as the Tourist Trophy (TT) races on the Isle of Man (first held 1907). Motorcycle trials are events in which a cross-country course has to be completed within a certain time, with points lost for stopping, touching the ground, etc. Moto-cross (or scrambling) takes place on a circuit marked out across rough country. *See also* drag racing.

motorcycles Two-wheeled engine-powered vehicles. The concept of a steam-powered bicycle was first realized by S. H. Roper in the USA in the 1860s. However, the true forerunner of the modern motorcycle was Gottlieb *Daimler's 1885 bicycle powered by an *Otto four-stroke engine. The first production model was Hildebrand and Wolfmüller's 1894 *Pétrolette*. By 1900 there were some 11 000 motorcycles in France and by the start of World War I over 100 000 were registered in the UK. During the war, motorcycles were extensively used by both sides. The interwar period produced many classic designs: the Harley-Davidson in the USA; the Brough Superior and Triumph Speed Twin in the UK; and the German BMW four-stroke. All these were in military use in World War II. In the 1950s and 1960s interest in motorcycles in Europe and the USA declined; the motor scooter, a low-powered Italian-originated version, and the moped, an engine-assisted bicycle, acquired some popularity. In the 1970s, the Japanese developed a whole new range of motorcycles, which now dominate world markets. See p. 368.

motor racing Racing in cars, from family saloons at club level to highly specialized Grand Prix vehicles. Early races were held on roads, but since 1903 they have usually been held on closed-circuit courses, the first of which in England was Brooklands (1907) in Surrey. The most prestigious form of racing is Grand Prix (Formula One) racing, using special vehicles raced by professional drivers for manufacturers or private owners. The Drivers' World Championship (begun in 1950) is awarded according to points won in certain Formula One races. Sports-car racing is for production or modified sports cars; the most famous being the Le Mans 24 Hours. Autocross races are amateur races over grass, while rallycross is a similar but more professional form on circuits that are half grass and half tarmac. *See also* drag racing.

mould Any fungus that forms a fine woolly mass growing on food, clothing, etc. The fungus from which *penicillin is obtained is a type of mould.

mountain. *See* orogeny.

mountain ash A widely cultivated tree, *Sorbus aucuparia*, of the rose family, also called

MOTORCYCLES

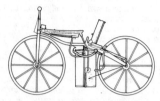

1860s S.H. Roper Velocipede *One of the earliest steam-powered cycles, this machine survives in the Smithsonian Institute, Washington, USA.*

1885 Daimler *The forerunner of the modern motorcycle, it had a wooden frame, iron tyres, and a 264 cc four-stroke engine.*

1894 Hildebrand and Wolfmüller "Pétrolette" *The first production motor cycle, it had direct rearwheel drive, pneumatic tyres, and a 1488 cc engine. Production was ten machines a day.*

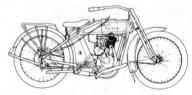

1917 Harley-Davidson *This 989 cc Vee-twin chaindrive machine had the first twist-grip throttle control.*

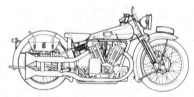

1930 Brough Superior *Built from 1919 to 1940 this Rolls Royce of motorcycles had a 980 cc Vee-twin JAP engine. Only 3000 were ever made.*

1938 Triumph 500 cc Speed Twin *Capable of over 100 mph, it was widely used by the police.*

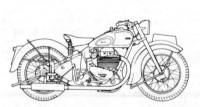

1949 Ariel Square Four *The compact arrangement of the four cylinders gave the machine its name. It had telescopic front forks and a sprung rear wheel.*

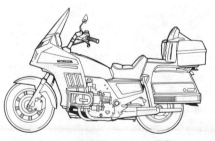

1988 Honda Goldwing Aspencade *A Japanese tourer with a flat four 1182 cc engine, 5-speed gearbox, drive shaft, and transistorized ignition.*

rowan, native to temperate Eurasia. Up to 15 m high, it has paired leaflets and clusters of small cream flowers, which give rise to scarlet berries with a bitter taste, used to make wine and jelly.

mountain lion. *See* cougar.

Mountbatten of Burma, Louis, 1st Earl (1900–79) British admiral and colonial administrator; son of Prince Louis of Battenberg (1854–1921) and Princess Victoria of Hesse-Darmstadt, granddaughter of Queen Victoria. In World War II he was supreme Allied commander in SE Asia (1943–45), retaking Burma. As viceroy of India (1947) he presided over the transfer of power to India and Pakistan and was then governor general of India (1947–48). He was subsequently commander in chief of the Mediterranean fleet (1952–54) and first sea lord (1955–59). He died in Ireland, the victim of an IRA bomb.

Mounties. *See* Royal Canadian Mounted Police.

Mount of Olives The highest point in a range of summits E of Jerusalem. Its W slope was the site of the Garden of Gethsemane. According to the Acts of the Apostles (1.2–12), Christ ascended to heaven from the Mount of Olives.

Mount Rushmore National Memorial The gigantic sculpture of the heads of four US presidents—Washington, Jefferson, Lincoln, and Theodore Roosevelt—carved (1927–41) to the design of the sculptor Gutzon Borglum (1871–1941) on the NE cliffs of Mount Rushmore, South Dakota. Each head is about 18 m (60 ft) high.

mouse A worldwide *rodent belonging to a group that includes African tree mice, jumping mice, and dormice, as well as *rats. The house mouse (*Mus musculus*) is common in buildings. Greyish, it is 14–16 cm long including its tail (7–8 cm) and feeds on a variety of foods.

mouse deer. *See* chevrotain.

mouth organ. *See* harmonica.

Mozambique, Republic of (Portuguese name: Moçambique) A country in S Africa, bordering on the Indian Ocean. The chief rivers, notably the Zambezi and Limpopo, flow E and provide both irrigation and hydroelectric power. *Economy*: the staple food crops are rice and maize. The main cash crops are cashew nuts, cotton, and sugar. Industry is based on food processing and textiles. *History*: the N coast was settled by Arabs from the 10th century and became a Portuguese colony in the early 16th century. In 1951 it became an overseas province of Portugal. From 1963 FRELIMO (Frente de Libertação de Moçambique) waged a guerrilla campaign that achieved the establishment (1975) of an independent socialist republic under Samora Machel (1933–86). The South African-backed Mozambique National Resistance (MNR) has applied military pressure in Mozambique with raids on guerrillas in Maputo. President: Joaquim Chissano. Official language: Portuguese; the main African language is Makua Lomwe. Official currency: Mozambique escudo of 100 centavos. Area: 784 961 sq km (303 070 sq mi). Population (1988 est): 14 907 000. Capital and main port: Maputo.

Mozart, Wolfgang Amadeus (1756–91) Austrian composer, born in Salzburg, the son of the violinist and composer Leopold Mozart (1719–87). Mozart showed extraordinary musical talent at the age of four; in 1762 his father took him on a tour of Germany and to Paris and London. After a period of unhappy service with the Archbishop of Salzburg (1779–81) he settled in Vienna, composing such operas as *The Marriage of Figaro* (1786) and *Don Giovanni* (1787). He composed 49 symphonies, over 40 concertos, 6 string quintets, 26 string quartets, piano sonatas, violin sonatas, and much other music. Some of his finest works, such as the operas *Così fan tutte* (1790) and *The Magic Flute* (1791) and the *Jupiter* symphony (1788), were written in the last years of his life.

Mubarak, (Mohammed) Hosni (Said) (1928–   ) Egyptian statesman; president (1981–   ). A general, he commanded (1972–75) the Egyptian air force in the *Yom Kippur War (1973). He became vice president to Anwar *Sadat in 1975 and succeeded him on his assassination. He has contained inflation and improved relations with the USA and Arab countries.

mucous membrane A moist membrane that lines the digestive and respiratory tracts and the nasal sinuses. It is a type of epithelium containing cells that secrete **mucus**, a slimy substance that protects its surface and—in the digestive tract—also lubricates the passage of food and faeces. In the air passages (bronchi) the mucus traps particles that are breathed in with air.

mudskipper A fish found in swamps, estuaries, and mud flats of Africa, Polynesia, and Australia. Up to 30 cm long, mudskippers have a blunt head and upwardly protruding eyes. They climb and walk over land using their limblike pectoral fins.

Mugabe, Robert (Gabriel) (1925–   ) Zimbabwe statesman; prime minister (1980–87); president (1987–   ). He helped found the Zimbabwe African National Union (ZANU) in 1963 and, after ten years' (1964–74) detention in Rhodesia, formed the Patriotic Front (PF) with Joshua Nkomo, leader of the Zimbabwe African People's Union (ZAPU). They waged guerrilla warfare against the governments of Ian Smith and then Bishop Muzorewa until agreeing to disarm (*see* Zimbabwe). His party's election victory (1980) brought Mugabe the leadership of newly independent Zimbabwe.

Muhammad. *See* Mohammed.

Muhammad Ahmad. *See* Mahdi, al-.

Muir, Edwin (1887–1959) Scottish poet. Born in Orkney, he moved to Glasgow in 1901 and to London in 1919. During the 1930s he and his wife Willa lived in Prague, where they translated the novels of Franz *Kafka and other German writers. His poetry includes *The Voyage* (1946) and *The Labyrinth* (1949). His *Autobiography* (1954) contains much of his best prose.

Mukden. *See* Shenyang.

mulberry A tree that is native to N temperate and subtropical regions. The black mulberry (*Morus nigra*) is commonly cultivated for its fruit. About 12 m high, it has toothed leaves and round green catkins. The blackberry-like fruit is used in jellies, desserts, etc. The leaves of the white mulberry (*M. alba*) are the staple food of silkworms.

mule The sterile offspring of a female horse and a male ass. Mules are hardy, sure-footed, and strong but smaller than a horse. They are used for carrying and pulling loads.

Mull An island off the W coast of Scotland, in the Inner Hebrides. It is chiefly mountainous; some sheep and cattle are raised. Other occupations include fishing, forestry, and tourism. Area: 909 sq km (351 sq mi). Population (1981): 2605. Chief town: Tobermory.

mullein A plant that is native to Eurasia. The common mullein (*Verbascum thapsus*), also called Aaron's rod, occurs in dry limy regions. 0.6–2 m tall, it bears woolly leaves and pale-yellow flowers.

mullet A food fish, also called grey mullet, found in temperate and tropical coastal waters and estuaries. It has a slender silvery body, 30–90 cm long, with two dorsal fins. *See also* red mullet.

Mulroney, (Martin) Brian (1939–) Canadian statesman and lawyer; prime minister 1984–). He became leader of the Progressive Conservative Party in 1983 and prime minister a year later, promising to strengthen Canada's economy, extend social services, and improve relations with the USA.

multiple sclerosis (MS) A chronic disease of the nervous system in which the fatty sheaths that surround the nerves in the brain or spinal cord are destroyed. It usually begins in young adults; the commonest first symptoms are blurring of the vision or weakness in one limb. Later, in most cases, it returns causing permanent handicap.

mummers' play An English folk drama based on the legend of St George and the Seven Champions of Christendom; it was a dumb show (*mummer*, from Middle English *mum*, silent), traditionally enacted on Christmas Day by masked performers.

mummy A human or animal body prepared and embalmed for burial according to ancient Egyptian religious practice. The internal organs were extracted and sealed in Canopic jars and the body was dried out by packing in dry natron, anointed, and wrapped in linen bandages.

mumps An acute virus infection that usually occurs in children. After an incubation period of 12 to 20 days the child develops headache and fever; later, the parotid salivary glands (situated under the ear) become tender and swollen. The disease is usually mild and clears up rapidly. In adult male patients the infection may spread to the testicles, which may occasionally lead to sterility.

Munch, Edvard (1863–1944) Norwegian painter and printmaker, who was a major influence on 20th-century German *expressionism. His symbolic paintings of love, death, and despair include the famous *Cry* (1893; Nasjonalgalleriet, Oslo).

München. *See* Munich.

München Gladbach. *See* Mönchengladbach.

Münchhausen, Karl Friedrich, Freiherr von (1720–97) German soldier famous for the exaggerated accounts of his feats. They were the basis of *The Adventures of Baron Münchhausen* (1793), written by R. E. Raspe (1737–94).

mung bean A *bean plant, *Phaseolus aureus*, also known as green gram, native to India and cultivated in tropical and subtropical regions chiefly as a vegetable crop. The slender pods contain up to 15 small edible seeds, which can be dried and stored or germinated in the dark to produce bean sprouts.

Munich (German name: München) 48 08N 11 35E A city in S Germany, the capital of Bavaria on the River Isar. It has a 15th-century cathedral and many baroque and rococo buildings. It is also noted for its annual Oktoberfest (beer festival). A commercial and industrial centre, its manufactures include precision instruments, electrical goods, chemicals, and beer. Population (1987): 1 274 700.

Munich Agreement (1938) The settlement, resulting from the conference between Neville Chamberlain (UK), Daladier (France), Hitler (Germany), and Mussolini (Italy), that recognized Hitler's territorial claims to the *Sudetenland. Described by Chamberlain as achieving "peace in our time," it was followed in March, 1939, by Hitler's invasion of Czechoslovakia and in Sept by World War II.

Munro, Hector Hugh. *See* Saki.

Münster 51 58N 7 37E A city and port in NW Germany, in North Rhine-Westphalia on the Dortmund-Ems Canal. It was an important member of the Hanseatic League and the capital of the former province of Westphalia. It has a 13th-century cathedral and service industries. Population (1986): 268 900.

Munster A province and ancient kingdom of the SW Republic of Ireland. It consists of the counties of Clare, Cork, Kerry, Limerick, Tipperary, and Waterford. Area: 24 125 sq km (9315 sq mi). Population (1986): 1 019 694.

Munthe, Axel (1857–1949) Swedish doctor and author. Munthe practised in Paris and Rome before retiring to Capri, where he built the Villa San Michele, described in *The Story of San Michele* (1929), which has been translated into 44 languages.

muntjac A small deer belonging to the subfamily *Muntiacinae* (6 species), occurring in forests of Asia, Sumatra, Java, and Borneo. The Indian muntjac (*Muntiacus muntjak*), also called barking deer or rib-faced deer, is 55 cm high at the shoulder with short unbranched antlers and short sharp fangs. Muntjacs are mainly solitary and nocturnal.

muon A negatively charged unstable elementary particle (lifetime 2×10^{-6} second; mass 207 times that of the electron) that decays into an electron and two *neutrinos. *See* particle physics.

mural painting The decoration of walls and ceilings by a variety of techniques, such as *fresco painting. *Renaissance painters often used perspective and architecture in their murals to create the illusion that they were real extensions of buildings. Murals were revived during the

20th century, principally by the Mexican painters *Rivera, Orozco, and Siqueiros.

Murdoch, Dame Iris (1919–) British novelist. Born in Dublin, she studied and taught philosophy at Oxford. Her novels include *The Bell* (1958), *A Severed Head* (1961), *The Sea, the Sea* (1978), for which she won the Booker Prize, *The Good Apprentice* (1985), and *The Book and the Brotherhood* (1987).

Murdoch, (Keith) Rupert (1931–) US publisher and entrepreneur, born in Australia. His company, News International, runs several British national papers and the only national Australian newspaper. He also owns US newspapers, 20th Century Fox, and US TV networks; in 1989 he introduced four satellite TV channels in the UK.

Murillo, Bartolomé Esteban (1617–82) Spanish painter. He spent most of his life in Seville, working for the religious orders and helping to found the Spanish Academy (1660), of which he became first president. After abandoning his early realism, he painted urchins and religious scenes in style influenced by Rubens.

Murmansk 68 59N 33 08E A port in the NW Soviet Union, in the RSFSR on the Kola inlet of the Barents Sea. Its ice-free harbour is an important fishing base. Population (1987): 432 000.

Murray River The chief river in Australia. Rising near Mount Kosciusko, in New South Wales, it flows W and S forming the boundary with Victoria. It enters Encounter Bay on the Indian Ocean through Lake Alexandrina. The main tributaries are the Darling and Murrumbidgee Rivers. Length: 2590 km (1609 mi).

Muscat 23 37N 58 38E The capital of Oman, on the Gulf of Oman. Most port traffic is now handled at Matrah to the NW. There is an oil terminal to the W. Population (1982): 80 000.

Muscat and Oman. See Oman, Sultanate of.

muscle Tissue specialized to contract, producing movement or tension in the body. It contains spindle-shaped cells (muscle fibres) that convert chemical energy (*see* ATP) into mechanical energy. Voluntary muscles are consciously controlled via the central nervous system. Such muscles are also called skeletal muscles (because they are attached to the bones) and striated (or striped) muscles (because they appear banded under the microscope). Individual muscles are made up of bundles of fibres enclosed in a strong fibrous sheath and attached to bones by tendons. Involuntary muscles occur in the walls of hollow organs, such as blood vessels, intestines, and the bladder. They are not under conscious control, being regulated by the autonomic nervous system. Heart muscle is a special type of muscle: its rhythmic contractions produce the heartbeat.

muscovite. See micas.

muscular dystrophy A group of chronic disorders involving wasting and weakening of the muscle fibres, which gradually worsens. The disease is inherited and the commonest type, Duchenne muscular dystrophy, affects mainly boys. There is no specific treatment but physiotherapy and orthopaedic measures can help.

Muses In Greek mythology, the nine patrons of the arts and sciences, daughters of Zeus and Mnemosyne. Calliope was the muse of epic poetry; Clio, history; Euterpe, flute playing and music; Erato, love poetry and hymns; Terpsichore, dancing; Melpomene, tragedy; Thalia, comedy; Polyhymnia, song and mime; and Urania, astronomy.

mushroom The umbrella-shaped spore-forming body produced by many fungi. (Sometimes the word toadstool is used for species that are inedible.) It consists of a stem (stipe) and a cap, which may be flat, conical, spherical, or cylindrical and has numerous radiating gills underneath in which the spores are produced. The well-known mushrooms have a smooth white or scaly brown cap with brown gills. Toadstools can be highly poisonous.

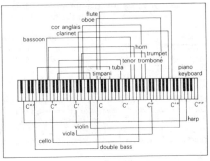

range of some musical instruments

MUSICAL INSTRUMENTS

musical instruments Devices used to produce music. In the orchestra musical instruments are grouped into families. The *stringed instruments (or strings)* include the violin, viola, cello, double bass, and harp (*see also* piano). The wind instruments are divided into the woodwind (flute, clarinet, oboe, and bassoon) and brass (horn, trumpet, trombone, and tuba). The percussion instruments include the triangle, cymbals, xylophone, timpani, and other instruments. Many instruments are used chiefly in jazz or pop (e.g. guitar, vibraphone, and maracas) while others, such as the Indian sitar, feature predominantly in the music of particular countries.

music hall A type of popular entertainment featuring a variety of performers including singers, dancers, comedians, and conjurors. It attained its greatest popularity in 19th-century England, and declined in the 1920s and 1930s with the rise of the cinema and the radio. Notable music-hall performers were Marie *Lloyd, Harry *Lauder, and Gracie *Fields. The US equivalent is known as vaudeville. Celebrated vaudeville performers include W. C. *Fields and Will Rodgers (1879–1935).

musk 1. A substance included in perfumes because of its persistence and strong odour. It is obtained from a gland of the male **musk deer**, of central Asia, which is about 60 cm high, lacks antlers, but has long fangs. 2. A North American plant, *Mimulus moschatus*, grown in gardens for its musky fragrance. 20–60 cm tall, it has tubular yellow flowers. The musk mallow (*Malva moschata*) and musk rose (*Rosa moschata*) also have a musky odour.

musket A smoothbore firearm fired from the shoulder. The earliest form, known as a harquebus (*or* arquebus) evolved in the 15th century as a hand-held form of the *cannon. In the second half of the 16th century a Spanish general invented a heavy shoulder weapon with a sufficiently large charge to penetrate armour. This musket still relied on the matchlock, which ignited the powder using a slow match. In the mid-17th century wheellocks and flintlocks were adopted, using sparks to ignite the powder. The percussion cap, invented at the beginning of the 19th century, led to the breech-loading musket with cartridge and percussion-cap ammunition. Muskets were superseded by *rifles in the mid-19th century.

musk ox A large hoofed mammal, *Ovibos moschatus*, inhabiting the Arctic tundra of North America. About 150 cm high at the shoulder, musk oxen have long dark shaggy hair and prominent curved horns. Bulls have a strong musky scent in the rutting season.

muskrat A large North American water *vole, *Ondatra zibethica*, also called musquash. It grows up to 35 cm long, excluding its black tail, and its soft coat is used for fur. Muskrats inhabit marshland and feed on water plants, mussels, etc.

Muslim. See Islam.

musquash. See muskrat.

mussel A *bivalve mollusc that lives in the sea or fresh water. Marine mussels have wedge-shaped shells measuring 5–15 cm. The edible mussel (*Mytilus edulis*) is an important seafood. Freshwater mussels inhabit ponds, lakes, and streams.

Musset, Alfred de (1810–57) French poet and dramatist, one of the major figures of the Romantic movement. He published his first volume of poetry, *Contes d'Espagne et d'Italie*, at the age of 20. His autobiographical *La Confession d'un enfant du siècle* (1836) includes an account of his love affair with George *Sand.

Mussolini, Benito (Amilcare Andrea) (1883–1945) Italian fascist dictator. At first a socialist, his support of Italian participation in World War I led to his expulsion from the Socialist Party (1915). In 1919 he formed the Fasci di combattimento (Blackshirts) in Milan and came to power following the March on Rome (1922). He was prime minister until the murder of Giacomo Matteotti persuaded him to establish (1924–29) a dictatorship. As *duce* ("leader"), he invaded Ethiopia (1935) and formed an alliance with Hitler. In 1939 he took over Albania and after the outbreak of World War II he declared war on France and Britain (June, 1940). Following the Allied invasion of Sicily, Mussolini was forced to resign (July, 1943). Rescued by the Germans to head a new fascist republic, he was subsequently captured and shot by Italian partisans.

Mussorgski, Modest Petrovich (1839–81) Russian composer. An army officer and civil servant, he had little formal training. His works include the opera *Boris Godunov* (1868–72), the piano work *Pictures at an Exhibition* (1874), and the orchestral tone poem *A Night on the Bare Mountain* (1860–66).

mustang The wild horse of North America. Mustangs are descended from the domesticated European stock of Spanish settlers and have become tough and small in the harsh conditions. Many were caught and tamed by cowboys and Indians, including the Mustang tribe.

mustard A plant native to Europe and W Asia, cultivated chiefly for its seeds—source of the spice mustard. Related to the cabbage, it has lobed leaves and yellow flowers. The leaves are used as fodder, fertilizer, or herbs.

mutation A change in the hereditary material (*see* DNA) of an organism, which results in some physical change in the organism or its offspring. Only a mutation in a germ cell is inherited by the offspring; a change in any other cell (somatic cell) affects only those cells produced by division of the mutated cell. Mutations may occur quite by chance (spontaneous mutations) or they may be caused by certain chemicals, ionizing radiation (such as X-rays), and by ultraviolet light. Mutations provide an important source of genetic variation in the population on which natural selection can act, which eventually results in the *evolution of new species.

mute swan A *swan, *Cygnus olor*, found in marshy areas and estuaries and on rivers and lakes. It is 160 cm long and has a white plumage, black legs, and an orange bill with a black base. It is less vocal than other swans, hence the name.

mutualism. See symbiosis.

Muzorewa, Bishop Abel (Tendekayi) (1925–   ) Zimbabwe statesman and bishop of the Methodist Church. One-time president of the African National Congress and the All Africa Conference of Churches, Muzorewa agreed a new constitution with Ian *Smith's government in 1978 and headed a nominally Black government in *Zimbabwe until 1980.

MX missile A US nuclear strategic missile with a range of 9650 km (6000 mi). Carrying 10 warheads, the MX missile was developed in response to the vulnerability of the concrete underground silos in which other ICBMs are housed. The MX missile can be launched from ships, aircraft, submarines, mobile land launchers, or from specially reinforced silos.

Myanmar, Union of. See Burma, Socialist Republic of the Union of.

Mycenae An ancient citadel in the Peloponnese (S Greece). Famed in legend as the home of *Agamemnon, Mycenae reached its peak between 1600 and 1200 BC. Massive fortifications indicate Mycenae's readiness for battle; exquisite bronze, gold, and silver articles have been found in its royal graves.

Mycenaean civilization The civilization of Bronze Age Greece. It developed after about 1650 BC in mainland centres, such as *Mycenae and Pylos, and after 1450 BC its influence extended to Crete. The Mycenaeans spoke a form of Greek, used Linear B script, and lived in luxurious palaces decorated with frescoes. About

1200 BC the palaces were destroyed, but Mycenaean culture survived until about 1100 BC.

mynah A songbird related to starlings and native to SE Asia. Mynahs usually have a dark plumage with bright wattles on the face. They feed chiefly on insects found on cattle. The cagebird that mimics human speech is the hill mynah (*Graculus religiosa*).

myocardial infarction Death of part of the heart muscle: this causes "heart attack", and usually results from *atherosclerosis. The patient experiences sudden severe chest pain, which may spread to the neck and arms and is usually accompanied by sweating and nausea.

myopia. *See* shortsightedness.

Myron (5th century BC) Athenian sculptor. His *Discus-Thrower* and *Marsyas*, described by ancient critics, are known through Roman copies.

myrrh An aromatic yellow to red gum resin from several small tropical thorny trees; Somalia is now the only producing country. A traditional embalming material, it is used in incense, perfumes, cosmetics, dentistry, and medicine.

myrtle An evergreen shrub, *Myrtus communis*, native to the Mediterranean area and W Asia. Up to 5 m tall, it has aromatic leaves, fragrant five-petalled white flowers, and blue berries. An oil obtained from the leaves, flowers, and fruit is used in perfumery.

Mysore 12 18N 76 37E A city in India, in Karnataka. Industries include textiles, chemicals, and food processing and it has a university (1916). Population (1981): 476 000.

mystery plays. *See* miracle plays.

mysticism A religious experience in which the individual claims to achieve knowledge of or union with God. Mystics occur in all religions; St *Francis of Assisi, St *Teresa of Avila, and Julian of Norwich (c. 1342–c. 1413) are among the many Christian mystics.

mythology Imaginative stories, traditions, etc., concerning gods and supernatural as well as heroic human beings. Mythology often involves an explanation of the origin of the universe, of mankind, or of a particular race or culture. The mythologies of particular cultures have provided some of the world's great literature and art.

myxomatosis An infectious disease of rabbits that is caused by a virus. Symptoms include swollen eyes, nose, and muzzle, closed eyelids, and fever. The disease, which is usually fatal, was introduced to the UK and Australia during the 1950s as a pest-control measure.

N

Nabokov, Vladimir (1899–1977) US novelist. He achieved popular success with *Lolita* (1955), whose academic antihero lusts after young girls. His other novels include *The Defence* (1930), one of several originally written in Russian, *Pale Fire* (1962), and *Ada* (1969).

nacre. *See* pearl.

Na-Dené languages An American Indian language group covering the northern USA, NW Canada, and Alaska. It includes the Athabascan, Tlingit, Haida, and Eyak subgroups.

nadir. *See* zenith.

naga In Hindu mythology, one of a race of minor serpent deities. Vishnu is often portrayed sleeping on the naga Sesha, and there is a Buddhist legend of a naga raising the Buddha on its coils above a flood sent to prevent his attaining enlightenment. Nagas are variously depicted as half-snake and half-human, as many-headed cobras, or in human form posed beneath a canopy of cobras.

Nagasaki 32 45N 129 52E A port in Japan, in W Kyushu. On 9 August, 1945, an atomic bomb was dropped on Nagasaki, killing or wounding about 75 000 people and precipitating Japanese surrender in World War II. Population (1987): 447 000.

Nagorno-Karabakh An autonomous region (*oblast*) in the W Soviet Union, in the Azerbaidzhan SSR. It was formed in 1923 and its population comprises chiefly Azerbaidzhani and a majority of Armenians. It is chiefly agricultural, producing cotton, grapes, and wheat. In 1988 Armenian claims to the region led to riots. Area:

4400 sq km (1700 sq mi). Population (1986 est): 177 000. Capital: Stepanakert.

Nagoya 35 8N 136 53E A port in Japan, in SE Honshu. The fourth largest city in the country, it was largely rebuilt following heavy bombing in 1945. Population (1987): 2 138 000.

Nagpur 21 10N 79 12E A city in India, in Maharashtra. Founded in the early 18th century, it came under British control in 1853. Population (1981 est): 1 297 977.

Nahuatl The most widely used American Indian language of the Uto-Aztecan family, spoken in Mexico. It was the language of the *Aztecs and *Toltecs. The Nahua people grow maize, beans, tomatoes, and chilis.

Naipaul, Sir V(idiadhur) S(urajprasad) (1932–) British novelist, born in the West Indies. A witty ironic tone characterizes his early novels, such as *A House for Mr Biswas* (1961). His later novels include *A Bend in the River* (1979) and *The Enigma of Arrival* (1987).

Nairobi 1 17S 36 50E The capital of Kenya. It is the trading centre of a fertile agricultural region and has a university (1970). Population (1991): 1 500 000.

Namibia (name until 1968: South West Africa) A country in SW Africa. *Economy*: chiefly subsistence agriculture. Fishing is important, especially for pilchards. Rich mineral resources include diamonds (the main export), copper, lead, zinc, tin, vanadium, and uranium. *History*: a German protectorate from 1884, during World War I it surrendered (1915) to South Africa, which administered South West Africa under a League of Nations mandate and refused to acknowledge that the mandate was at an end in 1966. South Africa granted independence in 1990; Namibia joined the Commonwealth the same year. President: Sam Nujoma. Official languages: Afrikaans and English. Official currency: South African rand of 100 cents. Area: 824 269 sq km (318 261 sq mi). Population (1988 est): 1 288 000. Capital: Windhoek. Main port: Walvis Bay.

Nanak (1469–1539) Indian founder of *Sikhism. Born near Lahore, he settled finally in Kartarpur, where he attracted a large community of disciples. His teachings are contained in a number of hymns.

Nancy 48 42N 6 12E A town in NE France, on the River Meurthe. The former capital of the Dukes of Lorraine, it passed to France in 1766. Population (1982): 99 307.

Nanjing (Nan-ching *or* Nanking) 32 05N 118 55E A port in E China, on the Yangtze River. An ancient cultural centre, it was the centre of the Taiping Rebellion (1851–64). Population (1986): 2 250 000.

Nansen, Fridtjof (1861–1930) Norwegian explorer, zoologist, and statesman. In 1888 he led an expedition across the Greenland icefield and in 1893, in the *Fram*, set sail across the Arctic. In 1895, with F. J. Johansen (1867–1923), he left the ship and reached 18 14N, the nearest point to the North Pole then attained. He subsequently contributed greatly to the League of Nations and pioneered the **Nansen passport**, an identification card for displaced persons (1922). He won the Nobel Peace Prize (1923).

Nantes 47 14N 1 35W A major port in W France, on the Loire estuary. Its commercial importance dates back to Roman times and it was here that the **Edict of Nantes**, guaranteeing religious toleration for the Huguenots, was signed in 1598. Population (1982): 247 227.

Nantucket An island in the USA, off SE Massachusetts. A former whaling centre, it is now chiefly a resort. Length: 24 km (15 mi). Width: 5 km (3 mi). Population (1988 est): 7000.

napalm An inexpensive jelly consisting of a mixture of the aluminium salts of *na*pathenic acid and *palm*itic acid used to thicken petrol so that it can be used in incendiary bombs and flamethrowers. It was used in World War II, the Korean War, and in Vietnam.

naphthalene ($C_{10}H_8$) A white crystalline aromatic *hydrocarbon that occurs in coal tar. **Naphthol** ($C_{10}H_7OH$) is the hydroxy derivative. It consists of two forms; the most important, betanaphthol, is used in antioxidants for rubbers and dyes and in drugs.

Napier 39 29S 176 58E A port in New Zealand, in E North Island. It is the most important centre of New Zealand's wool trade. Population (1985): 50 100.

Napier, John (1550–1617) Scottish mathematician, who invented *logarithms. In 1614 he published a table of logarithms, now known as Napierian logarithms. Napier also produced an elementary calculating machine, known as **Napier's bones**.

Naples (Italian name: Napoli; ancient name: Neapolis) 40 50N 14 15E A city in S Italy, overlooking the Bay of Naples. It is an important port and a centre of tourism. Its many historic buildings include medieval castles, a gothic cathedral (13th–14th centuries), the 17th-century Royal Palace, and the university (1224). *History*: founded by Greek colonists about 600 BC, it fell to Rome in 326. It was under Byzantine rule (6th–8th centuries AD) and in 1139 it became part of the Norman kingdom of Sicily. Following the revolt known as the Sicilian Vespers (1282), the Italian peninsula S of the Papal States became known as the kingdom of Naples (with Naples as its capital) until it fell to Garibaldi (1860) and was united with the rest of Italy (*see also* Sicily). In 1980 it was badly damaged by an earthquake. Population (1987): 1 200 958.

Napoleon I (1769–1821) Emperor of the French (1804–15). Born Napoleon Bonaparte in Corsica, he became an artillery officer and rose to prominence in 1795, when he turned the guns of the Paris garrison on a mob. Shortly afterwards he married *Josephine de Beauharnais and was appointed to command the French army in Italy (*see* Revolutionary and Napoleonic Wars). Napoleon then obtained the Directory's support for his plan to break British imperial power by conquering Egypt and India. In Egypt his great victory of the Pyramids was undermined by Nelson's destruction of a French fleet at the Battle of the Nile (1798) and in 1799 he returned to France. In the coup d'état of 18 Brumaire (9–10 November, 1799) he became first consul; in 1802 he became consul for life and in 1804 had himself proclaimed emperor.

The *Code Napoléon* at home and victories in Europe gave him lasting fame. In 1802 he agreed both the Treaty of Lunéville, which marked his defeat of the Austrians at Marengo, and the Treaty of Amiens with the British. Despite the disaster at *Trafalgar (1805), which forced him to abandon his invasion of Britain, his victories, especially at *Austerlitz (1805), Jena (1806), and Friedland (1806), drew most continental powers within the French orbit.

However, an attempt to break the British by blockade (the Continental System) failed and the lengthy *Peninsular War (1808–14) drained French resources. In 1812 Napoleon invaded Russia with half a million men, of whom nearly 400 000 died in the Russian winter. In 1813 Europe rose against Napoleon, inflicting a defeat at Leipzig that forced his abdication and subsequent exile to Elba. In 1815, however, he returned to France and attempted to regain his former power. He suffered a decisive defeat at *Waterloo and spent the remainder of his life on the island of St Helena. Napoleon's claim to the French Crown was pursued after his death by the son of his second marriage, to Marie Louise of Austria (*see* Napoleon II), and then by his nephew, Emperor *Napoleon III.

Napoleon II (1811–32) The title accorded by supporters of the Bonapartist claim to the French throne to the son of Napoleon I and Empress Marie Louise. At birth entitled King of Rome, he was brought up, after his father's fall (1814), in Austria, with the title Duke of Reichstadt.

Napoleon III (1808–73) Emperor of the French (1852–70); nephew of Napoleon I. He used the prestige of his name to win the presidential election after the Revolution of 1848. By a coup d'état at the end of 1851, he dissolved the legislative assembly and, a year later, declared himself emperor. His domestic policies encouraged industry and transformed Paris. Abroad, his diplomacy involved France in the Crimean War (1854–56), in war against the Austrians in Italy (1859), and in conflict in Mexico (1861–67). Finally, his aggressive stance towards Bismarck helped to cause the *Franco-Prussian War, in which the Second Empire was destroyed and Napoleon was driven into exile.

Napoleonic Code. *See* Code Napoléon.

Napoleonic Wars. *See* Revolutionary and Napoleonic Wars.

Narayan, R(asipuram) K(rishnaswamy) (1906–) Indian novelist and short-story writer. Writing in English and setting his stories in imaginary Malgudi, Narayan drew upon his experiences as a teacher for his first novel, *Swami and Friends* (1935). Later works include *The Man-Eater of Malgudi* (1961) and *Under the Banyan Tree* (1985).

narcissus (botany) A flowering plant native to Eurasia and N Africa and widely planted as bulbs in gardens. The poet's narcissus (*Narcissus poeticus*) has flowers with white petals surrounding an orange-tipped crown. Closely related are the *daffodils and the sweet-scented jonquils (*N. jonquilla*), which have small yellow flowers with small cuplike crowns.

Narcissus (Greek mythology) A beautiful youth who was punished for rejecting the love of the nymph Echo by being made to fall in love with his own reflection in a pool. He died and was transformed into a flower.

narcotics Drugs that cause drowsiness or sleep and relieve pain by depressing activity of the brain. The term is used particularly for *opium and its derivatives (opiates), including morphine and codeine. Synthetic narcotics include heroin, methadone, and pethidine.

Narraganset An Algonkian-speaking North American Indian people of Rhode Island. In 1675, after wars with White settlers, they were broken up.

narwhal An Arctic toothed *whale, *Monodon monoceros*. Up to 5 m long, narwhals feed on fish and squid. Males have a long straight spirally twisted tusk that grows to a length of 3 m.

NASA (National Aeronautics and Space Administration) The US civilian agency, formed in 1958, that is responsible for all nonmilitary aspects of the US space programme. Its major projects have included the manned *Apollo moon programme, Skylab, reusable *space shuttles, and the *Mariner and *Voyager probes.

Naseby, Battle of (14 June, 1645) The battle in the English Civil War that decided Charles I's defeat. The *New Model Army under Fairfax and Oliver Cromwell defeated Prince *Rupert's royalist forces at Naseby, near Market Harborough, Leicestershire.

Nash, John (1752–1835) British architect of the Regency period. Under the patronage of the Prince of Wales (later George IV), Nash redeveloped parts of London, laying out Marylebone Park (later called Regent's Park) as a formal park surrounded by curved terraces of houses. Regent's Street (1825) was designed to link the park with Westminster. Nash's colonnades were removed later but his All Souls, Langham Place, remains. In London Nash also built Carlton House Terrace (1833), laid out Trafalgar Square and St James's Park (1829), and redesigned *Buckingham Palace with the triumphal Marble Arch (1828) as its gateway (it was moved to its present position in 1851). In *Brighton he redesigned the Royal Pavilion as an oriental fantasy.

Nash, Paul (1889–1946) British painter. He became known for his symbolic war landscapes during World Wars I and II, the finest example being *Totes Meer* (1940–41; Tate Gallery). Nash was also a leading member of Unit One (1933), a group of artists dedicated to promoting modern art. His brother **John Nash** (1893–1977) produced fine watercolour landscapes and botanical illustrations.

Nashville 36 10N 86 50W A city in the USA, the capital of Tennessee. Founded in 1779, it is a centre of country and western music. Population (1986 est): 473 670.

Nassau 25 2N 77 25W The capital of the Bahamas, a port on New Providence Island. Built in 1729, it is an important tourist centre. Population (1982 est): 135 000.

Nasser, Gamal Abdel (1918–70) Egyptian statesman; prime minister (1954–56) and president (1956–70). An army officer, he helped to found the nationalist Free Officers group, which overthrew the monarchy in 1952. He became prime minister and then president of the Republic of Egypt (United Arab Republic from 1958). His nationalization of the Suez Canal led to an unsuccessful Israeli and Anglo-French attack on Egypt (1956), after which he was established as a leader of the Arab world.

nasturtium An annual garden plant, also called Indian cress, native to Central and South America. It has orange, yellow, pink, or red flowers. *Tropaeolum majus* is the most popular ornamental species and its seeds may be used in salads.

Natal 5 46S 35 15W A port in NE Brazil, near the mouth of the Rio Potengi. The chief exports are sugar, cotton, and carnauba wax. Population (1985): 512 241.

Natal The smallest province in South Africa. The land rises sharply from the Indian Ocean in the E to the Drakensberg Mountains in the W. Sugar cane is the major crop and pine, eucalyptus, and wattle plantations supply the timber and paper industries. Durban is the main industrial centre and port. Coal is the chief mineral. Natal was annexed by Britain in 1843 and with additions became a province of the Union of South Africa (1910). Area: 86 967 sq km (33 578 sq mi). Population (1985): 2 145 018. Capital: Pietermaritzburg.

Natchez A Muskogean-speaking North American Indian tribe of the Lower Mississippi. They were cultivators who, like the *Creeks, built mound temples and worshipped the sun.

National Aeronautics and Space Administration. See NASA.

National Curriculum The curriculum of subjects taught in state schools in England and Wales. Established by the Education Reform Act 1988, it comprises ten foundation subjects, three of which (the core subjects–English, maths, science) must be studied by all children from the age of five and taken at GCSE. Of the remaining subjects, design and technology, history or geography, and a modern language are a compulsory part of secondary education.

national debt The money that a government borrows; together with the income from taxation it makes up the government's income. In the UK it consists of two parts: the funded debt, which is money that the government does not have to repay on a fixed date; and the unfunded debt, the floating debt (e.g. treasury bills), *gilt-edged securities, and such small savings as Savings Bonds. Money borrowed as unfunded debt has to be repaid on a fixed date.

National Gallery An art gallery in Trafalgar Square (London), containing the largest collection of paintings in the UK. Founded for the nation in 1824, it was housed in Pall Mall until William Wilkins (1778–1839) built the present premises (1832–38). The National Gallery collects paintings of every leading school and period (except the modern) in Europe.

National Health Service (NHS) A medical service in the UK, paid for mainly by taxation. The National Health Service Act (1946) covered all aspects of health care except that of the school child and the worker. Contrary to the expectations of its first minister, Aneurin Bevan, the success of the Service in keeping people alive into old age and advances in medical science have made costs rise fast. Complaints about the structure and policies of the NHS led to substantial reorganization of the Service in 1974, 1982, and 1988. In England and Wales responsibility lies with the secretary of state for health. Administration is based on a system of Regional Health Authorities (RHAs) and District Health Authorities (DHAs).

National Insurance A UK insurance scheme providing funds to pay for the National Health Service and social security benefits. Contributions are paid into the National Insurance Fund, from which the benefits (including unemployment, sickness, maternity, and child benefits as well as retirement pensions) are paid. Under the State-Earnings-Related Pension Scheme (SERPS) of 1978, pensions are earnings-related and index-linked. Those wishing to contract out may pay contributions into an approved occupational or personal pension scheme.

nationalization The policy of taking into public ownership industries that were formerly privately owned. In the UK after World War II, *Attlee's Labour government (1945–51) nationalized such industries as coal and railways. After 30 years of mixed results, several industries were returned to the private sector in the 1980s by the Conservatives. See also privatization.

National Portrait Gallery An art gallery in London founded in 1856 to house portraits of famous personalities in British history. The main gallery is close to the National Gallery, and there are annexes in Carlton House Terrace and at Montacute House, Somerset.

National Socialist German Workers' Party. See Nazi Party.

National Society for the Prevention of Cruelty to Children (NSPCC) A British charity, made into a corporation in 1884, that investigates reports of cruelty to or neglect of children. Every year it deals with some 30 000 children.

National Trust An independent charity in the UK, founded in 1895, that acquires and protects country houses, castles, gardens, and places of interest or natural beauty.

NATO. See North Atlantic Treaty Organization.

natterjack A European *toad, Bufo calamita: a protected species in the UK. About 7 cm long, it has a yellow stripe down its back. If alarmed, it raises its inflated body on its hind legs.

natural gas A naturally occurring gas consisting mainly of *methane with smaller amounts of heavier hydrocarbons. It is widely used as a fuel and is obtained from underground reservoirs, often associated with *oil deposits. It originates in the decomposition of animal matter.

Natural History Museum. See British Museum.

Naturalism A literary and artistic movement of the late 19th century characterized by the use of realistic techniques to express the philosophical belief that everything can be explained by natural or material causes. Its literary manifesto was Le Roman expérimentale (1880) by *Zola.

natural selection. See Darwinism.

Nauru, Republic of (or Naoero; former name: Pleasant Island) A small country in the central Pacific Ocean, NE of Australia comprising a coral island. Economy: based entirely on the mining of phosphates, the only export. History: discovered by the British in 1798, it was under British control from 1920 to 1947. In 1968 it became an independent republic and a special member of the British Commonwealth. President: Bernard Dowigogo (1946–). Official language: English. Official currency: Australian dollar. Area: 21 sq km (8 sq mi). Population (1987): 8100. Capital and main port: Yaren.

nautical mile. See mile.

nautilus A mollusc related to squids and octopuses but having an external shell. The **pearly nautilus** lives in the Pacific and Indian Oceans. Up to 20 cm across, it lives in the outermost chamber of its flat coiled shell. The **paper nautilus** is found in the Atlantic and Pacific Oceans. The female, 20 cm long, secretes a papery boat-shaped shell in which the eggs develop.

Navajo A North American Indian Athabascan-speaking people of New Mexico, Arizona, and Utah. Like their relatives, the Apache, they migrated from the far north, probably during the

17th century. They are farmers and herders and now the most numerous North American Indian tribe.

Navarre A former kingdom in N Spain, corresponding to the present-day Spanish province of Navarre and part of the French department of Basses-Pyrénées. S Navarre was conquered by Ferdinand the Catholic of Aragon in 1512 and united with Castile in 1515. French Navarre passed to the French Crown in 1589.

Navratilova, Martina (1956–) Czech-born tennis player who defected to the USA in 1975. She was Wimbledon singles champion 1978–79, 1982–87, and 1990, and doubles champion 1976, 1979, 1981–86. She also holds a record of 74 consecutive wins.

Náxos A Greek island in the S Aegean Sea, the largest in the Cyclades. Area: 438 sq km (169 sq mi). Population (1981): 14 037. Chief town: Náxos.

Nazareth 32 41N 35 16E A town in N Israel, between Haifa and the Sea of Galilee. The city's many churches commemorate its associations with the early life of Jesus Christ. Population (1982 est): 44 900.

Nazi Party (*N*ationalsozialistische Deutsche Arbeiterpartei) The National Socialist German Workers' Party, founded in 1919 as the German Workers' Party and led from 1921 until 1945 by Adolf *Hitler. See also fascism.

N'djamena (name until 1973: Fort Lamy) The capital of Chad, a port in the SW. It was founded by the French in 1900. Population (1985): 511 700.

Neagh, Lough A lake in Northern Ireland, divided between Co Antrim, Co Armagh, and Co Tyrone. It is the largest lake in the British Isles. Area: 388 sq km (150 sq mi).

Neanderthal man An extinct *hominid race that inhabited Europe and the nearest areas of Africa and Asia between about 115 000 and 40 000 years ago. With heavy brow ridges, receding forehead, heavy protruding jaw, and robust bone structure, Neanderthal man nonetheless had a large brain and walked upright. They were cave-dwelling hunters. *See also* Homo.

Nebraska A state in the N central USA, lying W of the Missouri River. Part of the Central Lowlands cover the eastern third of the state, with the higher Great Plains in the W. Traditionally an agricultural state, it is still a leading producer of cattle, corn, and wheat. Most of the population is situated in the industrial E. *History*: explored by the French and Spanish, it formed part of the Louisiana Purchase (1803). It became a state in 1867. Area: 200 018 sq km (77 227 sq mi). Population (1987 est): 1 594 000. Capital: Lincoln.

Nebuchadnezzar II (*or* Nebuchadrezzar; c. 630–562 BC) King of *Babylon (605–562). Nebuchadnezzar extended Babylonian power in Elam, N Syria, and S Asia Minor. He captured Jerusalem in 597 and again in 586, when he destroyed the city and forced the Jews into exile.

nebula A cloud of interstellar gas and dust that becomes visible for one of three reasons. In an **emission nebula** the gas is ionized by ultraviolet radiation and light (predominantly red

and green) is emitted. In a **reflection nebula** light from a nearby star is reflected in all directions by dust in the cloud, thus illuminating the cloud. The dust in a **dark nebula** reduces the amount of light passing through it (by absorption and scattering) and a dark region is seen against a brighter background.

nectar A sugary solution produced by glandular structures (nectaries) in animal-pollinated flowers. Nectar attracts insects, birds, or bats to the flower and encourages pollination as the animal collects nectar from different sources.

nectarine. *See* peach.

needlefish A carnivorous fish, also called garfish, that occurs in tropical and warm-temperate seas. Needlefishes have a slender silvery-blue or green body, up to 1.2 m long, with elongated jaws and numerous sharp teeth.

Nefertiti (died c. 1346 BC) The cousin and chief wife of Akhenaton (1379–1362 BC) of Egypt. Her portrait bust is perhaps the best-known work of Egyptian art.

Negev A desert in S Israel. In recent years large areas have been irrigated by pipeline from the River Jordan. Area: about 12 000 sq km (4632 sq mi).

Negro, Río **1.** (Portuguese name: Rio Negro) A river in NE South America. Rising in E Colombia as the Guainía, it joins the River Amazon about 16 km (10 mi) below Manaus. Length: about 2250 km (1400 mi). **2.** A river in S Argentina, rising in the Andes and flowing generally SE to the Atlantic Ocean. Length: 1014 km (630 mi).

Negros A volcanic island in the central Philippines. The chief industry is sugar production. Area: 13 670 sq km (5278 sq mi). Population (1980): 2 749 700. Chief town: Bacolod.

Nehru, Jawaharlal (1889–1964) Indian statesman; the first prime minister of independent India (1947–64). He was elected president of the *Indian National Congress in 1929 in succession to his father Motilal Nehru (1861–1931). Between 1921 and 1945 he served nine prison sentences for participating in the movement of noncooperation against the British. After World War II he helped negotiate independent India. As premier, he carried through many social reforms and adopted a policy of neutrality in foreign affairs. His daughter was Indira *Gandhi.

Nelson 41 18S 173 17E A port and resort in New Zealand, in N South Island. Population (1988): 45 200.

Nelson, Horatio, Viscount (1758–1805) British admiral. At the outbreak of the French Revolutionary Wars he was given command of the *Agamemnon* in the Mediterranean. In 1794, at Calvi, he lost the sight in his right eye but went on to play an important part in the victory off Cape St Vincent (1797), for which he was knighted. Shortly afterwards he lost his right arm in action but in 1798 he destroyed France's naval power in the Mediterranean by his great victory in the battle of the *Nile. Nelson spent the following year in Naples, where, although married, he fell in love with Emma, Lady *Hamilton. Returning to England in 1800, Nelson, now Baron Nelson of the Nile, was given command in the Baltic and was responsible for the victory at Copenhagen (1801); he was created a viscount on his return. In 1803 he became commander in the Mediterranean. He blockaded Toulon for 18 months but in 1805 the French escaped; the ensuing chase ended in the battle of *Trafalgar (1805). Nelson directed this British triumph from aboard the *Victory* but was himself mortally wounded.

Neman, River (*or* R. Nyeman) A river in the W Soviet Union. It flows mainly NW to the Baltic Sea. Length: 937 km (582 mi).

nematode A colourless worm, also called roundworm, of which there are over 10 000 species. Nematodes live in soil, fresh water, and the sea. Some are parasites of plants or animals; others feed on dead organic matter. *See also* eelworm; guinea worm; hookworm; pinworm.

Nemesis In Greek mythology, a goddess personifying the gods' anger at and punishment of human arrogance (hubris).

neoclassicism 1. In art and architecture, a style dominant in Europe from the late 18th to mid-19th centuries. Although essentially a revival of classical art and architecture, it was distinguished from similar revivals by its new scientific approach, largely stimulated by archaeological discoveries at *Pompeii, *Herculaneum, and elsewhere. Key figures of neoclassicism were the German art historian Johann Winckelmann (1717–68), the painter *Ingres, the Italian sculptor Antonio Canova (1757–1822), and the architect Robert *Adam. *See also* Empire style. 2. A style of musical composition originating in the 1920s.

neodymium (Nd) A *lanthanide element, occurring in the mineral monazite. It is used with lanthanum in misch metal and, as the oxide (Nd_2O_3), together with praseodymium, to produce special dark glasses used in welding goggles. At no 60; at wt 144.24; mp 1021°C; bp 3068°C.

Neolithic The final division of the *Stone Age. It is characterized by the development of the earliest settled agricultural communities and increasing domestication of animals (*see* Jericho). Although man still used only stone tools and weapons, he evolved improved techniques of grinding stone. With the invention of pottery, food could be better prepared and stored.

neon (Ne) A *noble gas present in very small amounts in the earth's atmosphere, discovered in 1898 by Ramsay and M. W. Travers (1872–1961) by fractional *distillation of liquid air. It is commonly used in advertising signs and voltage indicator lamps. At no 10; at wt 20.179; mp −248.67°C; bp −246.048°C.

Neoplatonism The philosophy influenced by *Plato and formulated principally by *Plotinus that emphasizes an eternal world of order, goodness, and beauty, of which material existence is a weak and unsatisfactory copy.

Nepal, Kingdom of A country in the Himalayas, between China (Tibet) and India. *Economy*: chiefly agricultural, the main crops are rice, maize, millet, and wheat. Mineral resources are sparse. Tourism is an important source of revenue. *History*: the independent principalities

that comprised the region in the middle ages were conquered by the Gurkhas in the 18th century and Nepal was subsequently ruled by the Shah family and then by the Rana, who continue to reign. Head of state: King Birendra Bir Bikram Shah Dev. Prime minister: Krishna Prasad Bhattarai. Official language: Nepali. Official currency: Nepalese rupee of 100 paisa. Area: 141 400 sq km (54 600 sq mi). Population (1987): 17 567 000. Capital: Kathmandu.

Neptune (astronomy) The most distant giant planet, orbiting the sun every 165 years at a mean distance of 4497 million km. It is somewhat smaller (48 600 km in diameter) and more massive (17.2 earth masses) than *Uranus, but is thought to be almost identical to Uranus in atmospheric and internal structure. It has eight *satellites. It was discovered in 1846 by J. G. Galle.

Neptune (mythology) The principal Roman sea god, identified with the Greek *Poseidon. He is usually portrayed holding a trident and riding a dolphin.

neptunium (Np) The first synthetic *transuranic element, produced in 1940 at Berkeley, USA, by bombarding uranium with neutrons. It is available in small quantities in nuclear reactors and forms halides (for example NpF_3, $NpCl_4$) and oxides (for example NpO_2). At no 93; at wt 237.0482; mp 640°C; bp 3902°C.

Neri, St Philip (1515–95) Italian mystic, who founded the Congregation of the Oratory. Over the nave of the Church of San Girolamo he built an oratory to hold religious meetings and concerts of sacred music, from which both the name of Neri's order and the word *oratorio* derive. Feast day: 26 May.

Nero (Claudius Caesar) (37–68 AD) Roman emperor (54–68), notorious for his cruelty. His early reign was dominated by his mother Agrippina the Younger, *Seneca, and Sextus Afranius Burrus but by 62 Nero had thrown off these influences: Agrippina was murdered (59), Burrus died, perhaps by poison (62), and Seneca retired (62). Also in 62, he murdered his wife Octavia in order to marry Poppaea, who herself died in 65 after being kicked by her husband. A plot to assassinate him, after which Seneca was forced to kill himself, failed in 65. In 68, however, revolts in Gaul, Spain, and Africa and the mutiny of his palace guard caused his suicide.

nerve. *See* neurone.

nerve gases War gases that inhibit the transmission of impulses from nerve to nerve or muscle. Death results from paralysis of the diaphragm leading to suffocation. Most nerve gases are derivatives of phosphoric acid. *See* chemical warfare.

nervous system The network of nervous tissue in the body. The central nervous system (CNS) consists of the *brain and *spinal cord. This gives rise to the peripheral nervous system, which includes the cranial and spinal nerves and the autonomic nervous system (ANS). The ANS controls unconscious body functions, such as digestion and heartbeat, and is coordinated by the *hypothalamus. The nervous system conveys messages in the form of nerve impulses. Incoming information passes along sensory nerve cells (*neurones) to the brain, where it is analysed and compared with *memory; nerve impulses then leave the central nervous system along motor nerves.

Ness, Loch. *See* Loch Ness.

netball A seven-a-side court game adapted from *basketball. The court is 100 × 50 ft (30.5 × 15.25 m), divided into three equal zones. The goal is a net mounted 10 ft (3.05 m) above the ground. The game is played by throwing the ball; players may not run with it.

Netherlandic A subgroup of the Western Germanic languages. It is spoken in Holland and Belgium, where it is called Dutch and Flemish respectively. It is the parent language of Afrikaans.

Netherlands, Kingdom of A country in NW Europe, on the North Sea. It is almost entirely flat and considerable areas have been reclaimed from the sea. *Economy*: highly developed industries include oil and gas, chemicals, electronics, printing, metals, and food processing. Agriculture is highly mechanized and market gardening is important. *History*: under Roman occupation from the 1st century BC to the 4th century AD, it was overrun by German tribes. The region ultimately came under the influence of Burgundy and Spain. In 1581, during the *Revolt of the Netherlands, the seven northern provinces —Holland, Zeeland, Utrecht, Overijssel, Gröningen, Drenthe, and Friesland—proclaimed their independence as the United Provinces of the Netherlands under the leadership of William the Silent. War with Spain continued intermittently until, at the conclusion of the Thirty Years' War, Spain recognized the independence of the Dutch Republic in the Peace of Westphalia (1648). In the 17th century the Netherlands reached a peak of prosperity. In 1795, however, it fell to Revolutionary France and in 1806 Napoleon made his brother Louis Bonaparte King of Holland. Following Napoleon's defeat the former Dutch Republic was reunited with the southern provinces to form the Kingdom of the Netherlands (1814). In 1830 the S revolted against the union, forming Belgium (1831), and in 1867 Luxembourg became an independent state. In 1948 the Netherlands joined with Belgium and Luxembourg to form the *Benelux economic union; it was a founder member of the EEC. In 1980 Queen Juliana abdicated and was succeeded as head of state by her daughter Princess Beatrix (1939–). Prime minister: Ruud Lubbers (1939–). Official language: Dutch. Official currency: guilder of 100 cents. Area: 41 160 sq km (15 892 sq mi). Population (1988): 14 714 948. Capitals: Amsterdam (legal and administrative); The Hague (seat of government). Main port: Rotterdam.

Netherlands Antilles (Dutch name: Nederlandse Antillen) Two groups of West Indian islands in the Lesser Antilles, in the Caribbean Sea some 800 km (497 mi) apart. The S group lies off N Venezuela and consists of *Curaçao, Aruba, and Bonaire; the N group (geographically part of the Leeward Islands) consists of St Eustatius, Saba, and the S part of St Martin. Under Dutch

control since the 17th century, the islands became self-governing in 1954. The economy is based chiefly on oil refining. Area: 996 sq km (390 sq mi). Population (1987): 176 000. Capital: Willemstad.

nettle A plant, also called stinging nettle, found in temperate regions worldwide. Up to 1.5 m in height, it has toothed leaves with stinging hairs and small green flowers. Dead nettles are unrelated; their leaves resemble those of stinging nettles but lack stinging hairs.

neurohormone A chemical (*see* hormone) that is secreted by nerve cells and modifies the function of other organs in the body. The *hypothalamus, for example, releases several hormones that cause the *pituitary gland to secrete its own hormones, the kidney to retain water in the body, and the breast to produce milk.

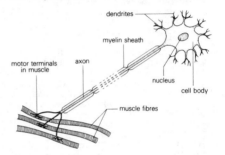

NEURONE *When a nerve impulse transmitted down the axon of a neurone reaches the motor terminals in muscle fibres, the muscle is stimulated to contract.*

neurone (*or* nerve cell) The basic unit of the *nervous system. A neurone consists of a cell body, containing the nucleus; small irregular branching extensions called dendrites; and a single long nerve fibre, or axon. Some axons are ensheathed by layers of fatty material (myelin). The neurones either make contact with other neurones at *synapses, or with muscle fibres or gland cells. When a neurone is stimulated from outside or by another neurone, a nerve impulse is transmitted down the axon. Bundles of nerve fibres are bound together to form **nerves**. These transmit impulses from sense organs to the brain or spinal cord (sensory nerves), or outwards from the central nervous system to a muscle or gland (motor nerves).

Neuroptera An order of slender carnivorous insects (4500 species) with long antennae and two similar pairs of net-veined wings. The order includes the alderflies, snakeflies, and dobsonflies (suborder *Megaloptera*) and the *lacewings and *antlions (suborder *Plannipennia*).

neurosis A mental illness in which there is a disordered way of behaving or thinking that causes suffering to the patient. However, the neurotic patient does understand the root of his problems. The symptoms may include anxiety or *depression; distressing behaviour and thoughts, as in *phobias or obsessions; and physical complaints, as in hysteria. Treatment can include *tranquillizers and *psychotherapy.

neutrinos A group of three elementary particles and their antiparticles. They have no charge and are probably massless. One type of neutrino is associated with the *electron, one with the *muon, and one with the tau particle. *See also* particle physics.

neutron An elementary particle that is a constituent of all atomic nuclei except hydrogen–1. It has no electric charge and its mass is slightly greater than that of the *proton. Inside the nucleus the neutron is stable but when free it decays, with a mean life of 12 minutes, to a proton, an electron, and an antineutrino (*see* beta decay). The neutron was discovered by *Chadwick in 1932. *See also* particle physics.

neutron bomb. *See* nuclear weapons.

neutron star A star that has undergone *gravitational collapse to the extent that most of the protons and electrons making up its constituent atoms have been forced together to form *neutrons. It has a diameter of only 20–30 km. The density is extremely high (about 10^{17} kg m^{-3}) and the pressure exerted by the densely packed neutrons can support the star against further contraction. Neutron stars are thought to form when the mass of the stellar core remaining after a *supernova exceeds about 1.4 times the sun's mass. *See also* pulsar.

Nevada One of the mountain states in the W USA. Most of its population and manufacturing industry is located in the two main cities of Las Vegas and Reno. Tourism is by far the most important industry. *History*: it became a state (1864) during a mining boom (1860–80). Area: 286 297 sq km (110 540 sq mi). Population (1986 est): 1 053 230. Capital: Carson City.

Nevis. *See* St Kitts-Nevis.

Newark 40 44N 74 11W A city in the USA, in New Jersey on Newark Bay. Founded in 1666, it attracted several inventors, whose developments included patent leather (1818), malleable cast iron (1826), the first photographic film (1888), and electrical measuring instruments (1888). Population (1986): 316 300.

New Britain A volcanic island in the SW Pacific Ocean, in Papua New Guinea, the largest of the Bismarck Archipelago. Copra and some minerals are exported. Area: 36 520 sq km (14 100 sq mi). Population (1987 est): 268 400. Chief town: Rabaul.

New Brunswick A province of E Canada, on the Gulf of St Lawrence. There is some mixed farming and fishing is important along the Bay of Fundy. Lead, zinc, and some copper are mined at Bathurst. *History*: settlement by French peasants was followed by colonization from Britain and New England, and New Brunswick became a separate colony (1784). It was a founding member of the Dominion of Canada (1867). Area: 72 092 sq km (27 835 sq mi). Population (1986): 709 442; approximately 30% are French speaking. Capital: Fredericton.

New Caledonia (French name: Nouvelle Calédonie) A French island in the SW Pacific Ocean. Together with its dependencies (the Isle of Pines, the Loyalty Islands, and others) it forms a French overseas territory. The main industries are nickel mining and processing and meat preserving. Violence in the 1980s led to a referendum (1988) on the issue of independence; the result favoured reconsideration of New Caledonia's status in 1998. Area: 19 103 sq km (7374 sq mi), including dependencies. Population (1988 est): 153 700. Capital: Nouméa.

Newcastle, Thomas Pelham-Holles, 1st Duke of (1693–1768) British statesman; Whig prime minister (1754–56, 1757–62). He resigned as prime minister in 1756 because of early reverses in the *Seven Years' War but returned in 1757 with foreign affairs in the hands of Pitt the Elder. His brother **Henry Pelham** (1696–1754) was prime minister (1743–54) in the Broad-Bottom administration, which included members of opposing political factions.

Newcastle upon Tyne 54 59N 1 35W A city in NE England, on the River Tyne. Founded as a Roman settlement (Pons Aelius), it is the principal port and commercial and cultural centre of NE England. Population (1981): 192 454.

Newcomen, Thomas (1663–1729) English blacksmith, who in 1712 constructed an early steam engine. It was based on Thomas Savery's engine and was widely used for pumping water out of mines.

New Deal (1933–41) Laws introduced by the US president, F. D. Roosevelt, to improve the effects of the Depression and to bring about social and economic reforms. Sound banks were able to reopen and credit, currency, and foreign exchange were controlled; the *gold standard was abandoned and the dollar devalued. Loans were made to support farmers, and help given to the unemployed.

New England An area in the extreme NE USA, bordering on the Atlantic Ocean. It consists of the states of Maine, New Hampshire, Vermont, Massachusetts, Rhode Island, and Connecticut. It was first settled by the Puritans (1620). Area: about 164 000 sq km (63 300 sq mi).

New Forest An area of woodland and heath in S England, in Hampshire. Originally an ancient hunting forest, it is a popular tourist area, noted for its breed of small ponies. Area: 336 sq km (130 sq mi).

Newfoundland A province of E Canada, consisting of the sparsely populated Coast of *Labrador on the Atlantic Ocean and the triangular island of Newfoundland. Pulp and paper has replaced the declining fisheries as the major industry. *History*: discovered by John Cabot (1497), Newfoundland developed steadily until World War I, when it became a dominion. In 1949 it became the newest Canadian province. Area: 370 485 sq km (143 044 sq mi). Population (1986): 568 349. Capital: St John's.

Newfoundland dog A breed of working dog originating in Newfoundland. The heavy dense black, brown, or black-and-white coat enables them to withstand icy water. Height: 71 cm (dogs); 66 cm (bitches).

New France The French colonies in E Canada. From about 1600 French trading posts extended along the St Lawrence River to the Great

Lakes. France lost these colonies to Britain in the *Seven Years' War (1756–63).

Newgate A prison that formerly stood on the present site of the Old Bailey. Originally a gatehouse at the wall of the City of London, it was established as a prison under Henry I. Last used as a prison in 1881, it was pulled down in 1902.

New Guinea An island in the SW Pacific Ocean, separated from Australia by the Torres Strait. It consists of the Indonesian province of West Irian in the W and *Papua New Guinea in the E. History: known to Europeans from 1511, the island was colonized by the Dutch in the 18th century. The W part became part of Indonesia in 1963. The SE was colonized by Britain and the NE by Germany in the late 19th century. Area: 775 213 sq km (299 310 sq mi).

New Hampshire A state in the NE USA, in New England. Manufacturing is the principal source of employment. Tourism is the other major industry. History: one of the 13 original colonies, it was first settled by English colonists about 1627, becoming a royal province in 1679. It became a state in 1788. Area: 24 097 sq km (9304 sq mi). Population (1987 est): 1 057 000. Capital: Concord.

New Hebrides. See Vanuatu Republic.

New Jersey A state in the NE USA, on the mid-Atlantic coast. It is a major industrial centre; agriculture is also well developed. Its beaches, forests, and mountain regions form the basis of a thriving tourist industry. History: one of the original 13 colonies, it was first settled by the Dutch in the 1620s, coming under British control in 1664. It became a state in 1787. Area: 20 295 sq km (7836 sq mi). Population (1985 est): 7 562 000. Capital: Trenton.

Newman, John Henry, Cardinal (1801–90) British churchman and a leader of the *Oxford Movement, until his conversion to Roman Catholicism (1845). He wrote many essays including the controversial Tract 90. In Rome (1846) he joined the Oratorians and later established his own Oratorian congregation at Edgbaston. He was made a cardinal in 1879.

Newman, Paul (1925–) US film actor. He has frequently played the roles of cynical and witty heroes, notably in Hud (1963), Butch Cassidy and the Sundance Kid (1969), and The Sting (1973); among his other films are The Verdict (1982), The Color of Money (1986), for which he won an Oscar, and Blaze (1990).

New Mexico One of the mountain states in the SW USA. Its oil and natural-gas deposits are important. Tourism is an important source of revenue. History: a Spanish possession from the 16th century, it was under Mexican rule when it was annexed by the USA in 1848. It became a state in 1912. Area: 315 113 sq km (121 666 sq mi). Population (1987 est): 1 500 000. Capital: Santa Fe.

New Model Army The parliamentary army formed in 1645 during the English *Civil War. Organized by Sir Thomas Fairfax (1612–71), its main forces were led by Oliver *Cromwell. It had increasing political power after its success at *Naseby (1645). In 1650 Cromwell became its commander in chief.

New Orleans 30 00N 90 03W A city and major port in the USA, in Louisiana. It is one of the leading commercial and industrial centres of the South. The Vieux Carré (French Quarter) has many historic buildings. The famous Mardi Gras festival is held here annually. History: founded in 1718, New Orleans became the capital of the French colonial region of Louisiana before passing to Spain in 1763 and to the USA in 1803. Jazz had its origins among the Black musicians of New Orleans during the late 19th century. Population (1990 est): 600 000.

Newport (Welsh name: Casnewydd ar Wysg) 51 35N 3 00W A port in South Wales, the administrative centre of Gwent. Its parish church became the cathedral for the Monmouth diocese in 1921. Population (1983): 130 200.

New South Wales A state of SE Australia, bordering on the Pacific Ocean. Agricultural products include beef cattle, cereals, fruit and vegetables, wool, and dairy produce. Fishing and forestry are also important. Minerals extracted include coal, silver, lead, zinc, and copper. Over half the population live in Sydney, where most of the industries are located. Area: 801 428 sq km (309 433 sq mi). Population (1986): 5 401 881. Capital: Sydney.

newt A type of *salamander occurring in Europe, Asia, and North America. The European smooth newt (Triturus vulgaris) is greenish brown with dark-brown spots and has a blackspotted orange belly. It grows to a length of 10 cm (including a 5 cm tail). Newts live mainly on land, hibernating under stones in winter and returning to water to breed in spring.

New Testament The 27 books that constitute the second major division of the Christian *Bible. Originally written in Greek, the New Testament has four divisions: the four *Gospels (Matthew, Mark, Luke, and John); the Acts of the Apostles; the *Epistles, mainly written by St Paul; and the Book of *Revelation. It was written between about 50 and 100 AD.

newton (N) The *SI unit of force defined as the force required to give a mass of one kilogram an acceleration of one metre per second per second. Named after Sir Isaac *Newton.

Newton, Sir Isaac (1642–1727) British physicist and mathematician. His first discovery was the law of gravitation, supposedly inspired by the realization that an apple falling from a tree is attracted by the same force that holds the moon in orbit. Gravitation required a precise definition of force, this Newton also supplied in his laws of motion (see Newtonian mechanics). Newton's second major work was the invention of the calculus; *Leibniz and Newton bickered unbecomingly for some years as to who had the idea first. His third contribution was in optics: he recognized that white light is a mixture of coloured lights, which can be separated by refraction. His incorrect belief that this effect could not be corrected in certain circumstances inspired him to invent the reflecting telescope. Newton's principal publications were Philosophiae naturalis principia mathematica (1686–87) and Optics (1704). He also reformed the coinage when he was Master of the Mint

(1699–1727) and was president of the Royal Society from 1703 until his death.

Newtonian mechanics The branch of *mechanics concerned with systems in which *Newton's three laws of motion are obeyed. The first law states that a body remains at rest or moves with constant velocity in a straight line unless acted upon by a *force. The second law states that the *acceleration (*a*) of a body is proportional to the force (*f*) causing it. The constant of proportionality is the mass (*m*) of the body: *f* = *ma*. The third law states that the action of a force always produces a reaction in the body. The reaction is of equal magnitude but opposite in direction to the action.

New World A name for the American continent, used especially by early emigrants from Europe in describing the geographical distribution of plants and animals. *Compare* Old World.

New York The chief manufacturing state in the USA. The presence of New York City also makes it the commercial, financial, and cultural centre of the nation. The most important agricultural activity is dairying. *History*: one of the 13 original colonies, it was first settled by the Dutch in the early 17th century. It became an English colony in 1664. Area: 128 402 sq km (49 576 sq mi). Population (1985 est): 17 783 000. Capital: Albany.

New York 40 45N 74 00W The largest city in the USA, situated in New York state at the mouth of the Hudson River. Divided into five boroughs—Manhattan, Brooklyn, the Bronx, Queens, and Richmond (on Staten Island), it is the nation's leading seaport. As one of the world's financial centres (*see* Wall Street), it is the site of many large corporations and the New York and American Stock Exchanges. Its most notable features include Central Park, the fashionable shops of Fifth Avenue, the *Statue of Liberty, Times Square, *Greenwich Village, the Brooklyn Bridge (1883), Rockefeller Center, St Patrick's Cathedral (1858–79), and a large number of skyscrapers, such as the Empire State Building (1931; 381 m) and the World Trade Center (1973; 412 m). As well as the famous Broadway theatre district, there are numerous museums, art galleries, and libraries. *History*: on 3 September, 1609, Henry Hudson sailed into New York Bay; its founding Dutch colonists arrived in 1620. In 1625 New Amsterdam, situated at the S tip of Manhattan, became the capital of the newly established colony of New Netherland and the following year the whole island of Manhattan was bought from the Indians for the equivalent of $24. In 1664 the city was captured by the English for the Duke of York and promptly renamed. From 1789 until 1790 it was the first capital of the USA. The Erie Canal was opened in 1825. Early in the 20th century the arrival of millions of European immigrants supplied New York with limitless cheap labour. Population (1986): 7 262 700.

New Zealand, Dominion of A country in the Pacific Ocean, to the SE of Australia. It consists of *North Island and *South Island, together with several smaller islands. *Economy*: the main basis of the economy is livestock rearing, especially sheep farming. Mineral resources include coal, gold, limestone and silica sand. *History*: from about the 14th century the islands were inhabited by the Maoris, a Polynesian people. The first European to discover New Zealand was Tasman in 1642, who called it Staten Land, later changed to Nieuw Zealand. During the early part of the 19th century it was used as a whaling and trading base. By the Treaty of *Waitangi in 1840 the Maori chiefs handed over sovereignty to Britain and a colony was established. New Zealand was made a dominion in 1907 and became fully independent by the Statute of Westminster in 1931. Since World War II New Zealand has played an increasing role in international affairs, especially in the Far East. Prime Minister: James Bolger. Official language: English. Official currency: New Zealand dollar of 100 cents. Area: 268 704 sq km (103 719 sq mi). Population (1989 est): 3 400 000. Capital: Wellington. Main port: Auckland.

Nguni A division of the *Bantu-speaking peoples of S Africa. It includes the *Swazi, *Xhosa, and *Zulu.

Niagara Falls Two waterfalls on the US–Canadian border, on the Niagara River. The American Falls, 51 m (167 ft) high and 300 m (1000 ft) wide, are straight while the Horseshoe Falls (Canada), 49 m (162 ft) high and 790 m (2600 ft) wide, are curved.

Niamey 13 32N 2 05E The capital (since 1926) of Niger, on the River Niger. It has grown rapidly as the country's administrative and commercial centre. Population (1983): 399 100.

Nicaea, Councils of Two councils of the Christian Church held at Nicaea, now Iznik (Turkey). **1.** (325) The council that was summoned by the Byzantine emperor Constantine to establish Church unity. The *Nicene Creed was adopted by the council. **2.** (787) The council that approved a formula for restoring the veneration of *icons.

Nicaragua, Republic of A country in Central America between the Caribbean Sea and the Pacific Ocean. *Economy*: chiefly agricultural, the main crops are maize, rice, cotton, coffee, and sugar. Minerals include gold, silver, and copper. *History*: it was colonized by Spain from 1522, becoming part of the captaincy general of Guatemala. It broke away from Spain in 1821 and formed part of the Central American Federation until 1838, when Nicaragua became a republic. From 1933 the government was dominated by the Somoza family until civil war forced (1979) the resignation of the president, Gen Anastasio Somoza (1925–80). The victorious Sandinista National Liberation Front (FSLN) instituted socialist policies. Accusing the Sandinistas of supplying arms to the rebels in El Salvador, the USA supported an army of 'Contras' until 1989; in 1990 Violeta Chamorro, heading a coalition, won free elections. Nicaragua is a member of the OAS and the Central American Common Market. Official language: Spanish. Official currency: córdoba of 100 centavos. Area: 148 000 sq km (57 143 sq mi). Population (1987 est): 3 500 000. Capital: Managua. Main ports: Corinto and Bluefields.

Nice 43 42N 7 16E A city in SE France, the capital of the Alpes-Maritimes department. Transferred from Sardinia to France in 1860, it is one of the leading resorts of the French Riviera. Population (1982): 338 486.

Nicene Creed The statement of Christian belief accepted as orthodox by the first Council of *Nicaea (325). The Nicene Creed used in the *Eucharist service of Orthodox, Roman Catholic, and Protestant Churches is a version of this creed.

Nicholas I (1796–1855) Emperor of Russia (1825–55), noted for his strict rule. Nicholas' accession was followed by the *Dekabrist revolt, which hardened his conservatism. His ambitions in the Balkans led to the *Crimean War.

Nicholas II (1868–1918) The last Emperor of Russia (1894–1917). Nicholas' ambition in Asia led to the unpopular *Russo-Japanese War, which in turn led to the *Revolution of 1905. Forced to accept the establishment of a representative assembly, Nicholas nevertheless continued attempts to rule personally. In 1915 he took supreme command of Russian forces in World War I, leaving Russia to the mismanagement of the Empress *Alexandra and *Rasputin. Following the Russian Revolution in 1917, Nicholas was forced to abdicate (March). He and his family were imprisoned by the Bolsheviks and executed at Ekaterinburg (now Sverdlovsk).

Nicholas, St (4th century AD) The patron saint of Russia, sailors, and children. He is thought to have been Bishop of Myra in Asia Minor. Legends telling of his gifts of gold to three poor girls for their wedding dowries gave rise to the practice of exchanging gifts on his feast day, 6 Dec. As he is also identified with the legendary Santa Claus this now happens on 25 Dec in most countries.

Nicholson, Ben (1894–1982) British artist. Some of his best abstract works were produced in the 1930s, while a member of the British art group Unit One (see Nash, Paul). These include white-painted plaster rectangles combined with circles.

Nicholson, Jack (1937–) US film actor. After success in Easy Rider (1969), he became a leading star. His films include One Flew Over the Cuckoo's Nest (1976), Prizzi's Honour (1985), Ironweed (1988), and Batman (1989). He won an Oscar for Terms of Endearment (1983).

nickel (Ni) A hard silvery metal similar to iron, discovered in 1751 by A. F. Cronstedt (1722–65). It occurs in nature chiefly as pentlandite, NiS, and pyrrhotite, (Fe,Ni)S. It is chemically similar to cobalt and copper, and forms a green oxide (NiO), the chloride ($NiCl_2$), the sulphate ($NiSO_4$), and other compounds. It is used widely in alloys, such as stainless steel, and in coinage. At no 28; at wt 58.71; mp 1453°C; bp 2732°C.

Nicklaus, Jack William (1940–) US golfer, who has won more major championships than any other. His titles since 1959 include five Masters championships.

Nicobar Islands. See Andaman and Nicobar Islands.

Nicosia (Greek name: Leukosia; Turkish name: Lefkosa) The capital of Cyprus, on the River Pedieas. Originally known as Ledra it has been successively under Byzantine, Venetian, Turkish, and British control. It possesses many old buildings, including the Cathedral of St Sophia (completed 1325). Population (1987 est): 201 900.

nicotine ($C_{10}H_{14}N_2$) A toxic colourless oily liquid alkaloid that rapidly turns brown on exposure to air. It is obtained from the dried leaves of the tobacco plant and is also present in small quantities in cigarettes. It is also used as an insecticide.

nicotinic acid. See vitamin B complex.

Niemeyer, Oscar (1907–) Brazilian architect. A disciple of Le Corbusier, Niemeyer has made a major contribution to the development of modern architecture in Brazil. His designs for Brasília include the president's palace (1959) and the cathedral (1964).

Niemöller, Martin (1892–1984) German Lutheran pastor and Protestant leader. A U-boat commander in World War I, he became head of the Pastors' Emergency League, which became the Confessing Church, and opposed the Nazis in Germany. In 1937 he was sent to a concentration camp, where he remained until the end of the war.

Nietzsche, Friedrich (1844–1900) German philosopher. His first book, The Birth of Tragedy (1872), argued that Wagnerian opera was the successor to Greek drama. Nietzsche rejected Christianity in favour of the "will to power". In Thus Spake Zarathustra (1883–92), he praises the man who is free, titanic, and powerful, an ideal adopted by the Nazis. After 1889 he was permanently insane.

Niger, Republic of A large country in West Africa, lying mainly in the Sahara. Economy: agriculture, particularly livestock raising, is important. Mineral resources include salt, natron, tin, and uranium. The main exports are uranium and groundnuts, followed by livestock. History: occupied by France (1883–99), it became a territory of French West Africa in 1904. It won independence in 1960. President: Col Ali Seybou. Population (1988 est): 7 190 000. Capital: Niamey.

Niger, River The third longest river in Africa. Rising in the S highlands of Guinea, it flows NE and then SE through Mali, Niger, and Nigeria to the Gulf of Guinea. Length: 4183 km (2600 mi).

Niger-Congo languages An African language family spoken in central and S Africa. It is subdivided into six groups: the *West Atlantic languages; the Mande languages; the Voltaic languages; the Kwa languages; the Benue-Congo group, which includes the *Bantu languages; and the Adamawa-Eastern group.

Nigeria, Federal Republic of A large country in West Africa, on the Gulf of Guinea. Economy: oil production accounts for about 90% of exports; Nigeria is a member of OPEC and the world's eighth largest producer. There are also important reserves of natural gas, tin, coal, iron ore, and columbite. Agriculture is still important; the main cash crops are groundnuts and cotton in the N and palms, coconut, and rubber in the S. *History*: in the middle ages there were highly developed kingdoms in the area, such as those of the Hausa in the N and the Yoruba (e.g. Oyo, Benin) in the SW; the Ibo occupied the SE. The coast was explored in the 15th century by the Portuguese, who developed the slave trade. In 1861 Lagos was annexed by Britain; by 1906, the British were in control of Nigeria, which was divided into the protectorate of Northern Nigeria and the colony (of Lagos) and protectorate of Southern Nigeria. These were united in 1914. Nigeria became a federation in 1954, gained independence in 1960, and became a republic within the Commonwealth in 1963. In 1967 the eastern region withdrew to form the Republic of *Biafra. Civil war followed, lasting until Biafra's surrender in 1970. In 1985, in the most recent of a series of coups, Maj Gen Ibrahim Babangida came to power. Official currency: naira of 100 kobo. Area: 923 773 sq km (356 669 sq mi). Population (1988 est): 105 000 000. Capital: Abuja. Main port: Lagos.

nightingale A woodland bird, *Luscinia megarhynchos*, that winters in tropical Africa and breeds in S Europe and Asia Minor during the summer. It is about 16 cm long with reddish-brown plumage and pale underparts and feeds on insects and spiders. Nightingales are noted for their beautiful song.

Nightingale, Florence (1820–1910) British hospital reformer and founder of the nursing profession. On the outbreak of the Crimean War, in 1854, she volunteered to lead a party of nurses to work in the military hospitals. She set about transforming the appalling conditions, earning herself the title Lady with the Lamp from her patients. In 1860, she established the Nightingale School for Nurses at St Thomas's Hospital –the first of its kind.

nightjar A nocturnal bird occurring in most temperate and tropical regions. About 30 cm long, nightjars have a soft mottled grey, brown, and reddish-brown plumage and a long tail. The short bill opens wide and is surrounded by long sensitive bristles, enabling the bird to catch insects in flight.

nightshade One of several plants, the most notorious being *deadly nightshade. The Eurasian **woody nightshade**, or bittersweet (*Solanum dulcamara*), is a scrambling shrubby plant, up to 2 m tall, with poisonous red berries. The widely distributed **black nightshade** (*S. nigrum*) grows up to 50 cm high and has poisonous black berries. The unrelated **enchanter's nightshade** (*Circaea lutetiana*), of the willowherb family, native to Eurasia, grows in shady places. Up to 60 cm tall, it has tiny white flowers.

nihilism A view that rejects all traditional values and institutions. *Turgenev invented the label in *Fathers and Sons* (1861) for the philosophy of the character of Basarov. The political expression of nihilism is *anarchism.

Niigata 37 58N 139 2E A city in Japan, in NW Honshu. It is the main port for the Sea of Japan. Population (1987): 467 000.

Nijinsky, Vaslav (1890–1950) Russian ballet dancer. In 1909 he joined Diaghilev's company in Paris, and quickly achieved an international reputation. Michel *Fokine created *Petrushka*, *Scheherazade*, and other ballets for him, and from 1913 he also began to choreograph. He retired in 1919 suffering from schizophrenia.

Nikolaev 46 57N 32 00E A port in the Soviet Union, where the Rivers Bug and Ingul meet. Long a naval base, it has important shipbuilding industries. Population (1987): 501 000.

Nile, Battle of the (1 August, 1798) A naval battle in which the British, under *Nelson, defeated the French during *Napoleon's invasion of Egypt (*see* Revolutionary and Napoleonic Wars). This engagement gave Britain control of the Mediterranean.

Nile, River A river in N Africa, the longest river in the world. The longest of its three main tributaries, the White Nile, rises in Burundi and flows N through Lake Victoria and Lake Mobutu. At Khartoum it is joined by the Blue Nile (which rises in the Ethiopian highlands) and later by the River Atbara before flowing through a broad delta into the Mediterranean Sea. The Nile's annual floodwaters are controlled by the *Aswan Dams. Length: 6741 km (4187 mi).

nimbostratus A form of *cloud common in temperate latitudes. Dark grey and solid in appearance it has a low base but may show extensive vertical development. Snowfall or rainfall is often prolonged although not usually heavy.

Nîmes 43 50N 4 21E A city in S France, the capital of the Gard department. An important Roman settlement, it was a Protestant stronghold (16th–17th centuries). Population (1982): 129 924.

Nimrod A legendary biblical figure described in Genesis as a mighty hunter. He founded a Mesopotamian kingdom that included the cities of Babel, Erech, and Akkad and is credited with building the cities of Nineveh and Kalhu (modern Nimrud).

Nimrud An Assyrian capital (ancient Kalhu) near Mosul (Iraq). Founded about 1250 BC it was destroyed by the Medes in 612 BC. Excavations (1845–51) by Sir Austen Layard (1817–94) of the 9th-century city yielded gigantic sculptures and *cuneiform tablets. *See also* Nineveh.

Nineveh An Assyrian capital (modern Kuyunjik) near Mosul (Iraq). Nineveh was made joint capital with Nimrud by Sennacherib (c. 700 BC). The Medes sacked it in 612 BC. Sir Austen Layard's great find here was the library of Ashurbanipal.

Ningbo (*or* Ning-po) 29 54N 121 33E A river port in E China, in Zhejiang province. Important for overseas trade (5th–9th centuries), it was also a religious centre. Population (1986): 1 020 000.

niobium (Nb) A soft ductile white metal, discovered in 1801. It was formerly known as columbium in the USA. Niobium is used in specialist alloys in spacecraft, and at low temperatures it has superconducting properties. Its compounds include the white oxide (Nb_2O_5) and the volatile fluoride and chloride (NbF_5,

NbCl$_5$). At no 41; at wt 92.9064; mp 2468 ±
10°C; bp 4742°C.

nirvana The supreme goal of *Buddhism, in
which release from the limitations of existence
and rebirth are attained through the wiping out
of desire. In Hinduism nirvana also means spiritual release in the sense of freedom from reincarnation, or union with God or the Absolute.

Niš 43 20N 21 54E A city in E Yugoslavia, in
Serbia. For five centuries to 1877 it was a centre
for Serbian resistance to Turkish control. Population (1981): 230 711.

Niterói 22 54S 43 06W A city in SE Brazil, opposite the city of Rio de Janeiro. It is a popular
resort. Population (1985): 442 706.

nitric acid (HNO$_3$) A fuming corrosive liquid
made by the oxidation of ammonia by air in the
presence of a platinum catalyst or the action of
sulphuric acid on sodium or potassium nitrate. It
is used in the manufacture of fertilizers and explosives.

nitrocellulose. See cellulose nitrate.

nitrogen (N) A colourless odourless gas, discovered by D. Rutherford (1749–1819) in 1772.
It makes up 78% of the earth's atmosphere by
volume. The element exists as diatomic molecules (N$_2$) bonded very strongly together. It
forms a range of chemical compounds including
ammonia (NH$_3$), the oxides (N$_2$O, NO, N$_2$O$_3$,
NO$_2$, N$_2$O$_5$), nitric acid (HNO$_3$), and many nitrates (for example NaNO$_3$). Liquid nitrogen has
a wide range of applications at low temperatures.
Ammonia and nitrates are of great importance
as fertilizers. At no 7; at wt 14.0067; mp
−290.86°C; bp −195.8°C.

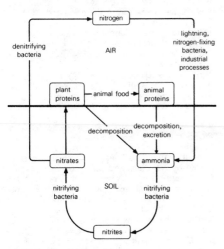

NITROGEN CYCLE

nitrogen cycle The sequence of processes by
which nitrogen and its compounds are utilized in
nature. Nitrogen gas in the air is converted
(fixed) to ammonia by certain soil bacteria and
fertilizer manufacturers (see nitrogen fixation).
Nitrifying bacteria in the roots of leguminous
plants convert ammonia to nitrites and then to
nitrates, which are used by plants to manufacture amino acids. When animals eat plants some
of this nitrogenous plant material is incorporated into animal tissues. Nitrogen in urine and faeces, as well as dead organic matter, decompose to
produce ammonia, so completing the cycle.

nitrogen fixation The conversion of atmospheric nitrogen gas into nitrogen compounds.
The process occurs naturally by the action of
bacteria in the roots of peas, beans, clover, and
other leguminous plants (see nitrogen cycle). Industrial methods of fixing nitrogen are of immense importance in the manufacture of nitrogen fertilizers.

nitroglycerin (C$_3$H$_5$(NO$_3$)$_3$) A yellow oily
highly *explosive liquid. It is used as an explosive either alone or as *dynamite or *gelignite.

Niven, David (1909–83) British film actor.
His films include The Prisoner of Zenda (1937),
Wuthering Heights (1939), and Separate Tables
(1958), for which he won an Oscar. He published
two highly successful volumes of autobiography,
The Moon's a Balloon (1972) and Bring on the
Empty Horses (1975).

Nixon, Richard Milhous (1913–) US
statesman; Republican president (1969–74). A
Californian-born lawyer, he contributed to Mc-
Carthy's anticommunist investigations and was
Eisenhower's vice president from 1953 until
1960, when he became the Republican presidential candidate. As president he reduced US troop
commitments abroad and in 1973 ended US military involvement in Vietnam. In 1972 he paid a
successful visit to the People's Republic of China. His role in illegal efforts to ensure re-election
in 1972 and the subsequent cover-up attempt led
to the *Watergate scandal, when he became the
first president to resign office. President *Ford
granted him a free pardon after succeeding him
as president.

Nizhnii Novgorod. See Gorkii.

Nkomo, Joshua (1917–) Zimbabwean
politician. Nkomo became president of the
Zimbabwe African People's Union (ZAPU) in
1961. With headquarters in Zambia, it allied
with Robert Mugabe's Zimbabwe African National Union (ZANU) in 1976 to form the Patriotic Front (PF) against the government of Ian
Smith in Rhodesia (see also Zimbabwe). Nkomo
became vice-president of Zimbabwe under
Mugabe in 1990.

No A form of Japanese drama. It is performed
with a minimum of scenery and properties and is
characterized by the use of dance, mime, and
masks. The acting is highly stylized.

Noah In the Old Testament, the only man
judged by God as worthy of being saved from the
coming flood. Noah was instructed to build an
ark for his family and representatives of each
animal species. Noah and his sons Ham, Shem,
and Japheth and their wives became the ancestors of the present human race.

Nobel, Alfred Bernhard (1833–96) Swedish
chemist and businessman. From his invention of
dynamite (1866) and a smokeless gunpowder
(1889) and his involvement in the Baku oilfields
he amassed a considerable fortune, leaving £1.75
million as a foundation for the **Nobel Prizes.**

	1987	1988	1989	1990
Physics	Alex Muller Georg Bednorz	Leon Lederman Melvin Schwartz Jack Steinberger	Hans Dehmelt Wolfgang Paulm Norman Ramsey	Jerome Friedman Henry Kendall Richard Taylor
Chemistry	Donald Cram Jean-Marie Lehn Charles Pedersen	Johann Deisenhofer Robert Huber Hartmut Michel	Sidney Altman Thomas Cech	Elias Cory
Medicine	Susumu Tonegawa	James Black	Michael Bishop Harold Varmus	Joseph Murray E. Donnall Thomas
Literature	Joseph Brodsky	Naguib Mahfouz	Camilo José Cela	Octavio Paz
Peace	Oscar Arias Sánchez	United Nations peace-keeping forces	Dalai Lama	Mikhail Gorbachov
Economics	Robert M. Solow	Maurice Allais	T. Haavelmo	Harry M. Markowitz William F. Sharpe Merton Miller

NOBEL *Recent prizewinners.*

nobelium (No) A synthetic *transuranic element discovered in 1957. Five isotopes with short half-lives are known. Named after Alfred Nobel. At no 102; at wt (255).

noble gases (*or* inert gases) The elements forming group O of the *periodic table: helium, neon, argon, krypton, xenon, and radon. All are colourless odourless tasteless gases, which are slightly soluble in water. They are inert chemically owing to their filled outer electron shells.

noctule An insect-eating *bat, *Nyctalus noctula*, of Europe and Asia. About 12 cm long, it has bright-chestnut fur and long narrow wings. Noctules hibernate only from Dec to Jan.

Nolan, Sir Sidney (1917–) Australian painter. He is internationally known for his paintings of Australian historical figures, such as Ned *Kelly, and landscapes of the outback.

Nonconformists In its original early-17th-century sense, the term referred to members of the Church of England who did not conform with its rituals. Later it came to include members of separate Protestant groups, such as the Quakers and Methodists.

Nootka A North American Indian people of the NW Pacific coast region who speak a *Wakashan language. They were traditionally hunters, fishers, and expert whale catchers, using large canoes and harpoons.

noradrenaline (*or* norepinephrine) A hormone that is secreted by the central core (medulla) of the adrenal glands. It is similar to *adrenaline but produces different effects in certain organs; for example it decreases heart rate (adrenaline increases it). Noradrenaline is used by certain nerve cells to transmit nerve impulses to the next nerve cell: when released at a nerve ending it triggers an impulse in nearby nerve cells. However, in the hypothalamus it is thought to inhibit transmission of impulses.

Norfolk A county of E England, in *East Anglia. It is mainly low lying, with fens in the W and the *Broads in the E. It is mainly agricultural with arable farming and intensive turkey rearing. Tourism is important. Area: 2763 sq km (1067 sq mi). Population (1988 est): 744 300. Administrative centre: Norwich.

Norfolk, Thomas Howard, 3rd Duke of (1473–1554) English statesman. He became president of the privy council in 1529 and in 1536 put down the *Pilgrimage of Grace. He lost power after Catherine Howard's execution (1542) and was imprisoned under Edward VI for involvement in the treason (1546) of his son Henry Howard, Earl of *Surrey (1517–47). Surrey's son **Thomas Howard, 4th Duke of Norfolk** (1538–72) was imprisoned (1559–60) by Elizabeth I for planning to marry Mary, Queen of Scots. He subsequently plotted with Roberto Ridolfi (1531–1612) against Elizabeth and was executed.

Norfolk Island 29 05S 167 59E A mountainous Australian island in the SW Pacific Ocean. Formerly a British penal colony, some of the descendants of the *Bounty* mutineers were moved here from *Pitcairn Island (1856). Area: 36 sq km (14 sq mi). Population (1986): 1977. Chief town: Kingston.

Norman conquest (1066–72) The conquest of England by William, Duke of Normandy (*see* William the Conqueror). After defeating Harold II at the battle of Hastings (1066), William captured London and was crowned. English risings were suppressed by 1070 and with the defeat of the Scots in 1072 the conquest was complete. Although structures of government continued almost unchanged, the English aristocracy was replaced by Normans and other continentals and *feudalism was introduced. Latin became the language of government and Norman French, the literary language; the Norman influence was also felt in church organization and architecture.

Normandy (French name: Normandie) A former province in N France, on the English Channel. *History*: during the medieval period Normandy flourished as a major state. William II, Duke of Normandy, conquered England in 1066. Disputed between England and France during the following centuries, it finally reverted to France in 1449. During World War II it suffered severe damage, the Normandy invasion taking place in 1944.

Normans Viking settlers in N France (later Normandy) whose rule, under their leader Rollo, was formally recognized (911) by Charles the Simple (879–929; reigned 898–923). By the end of the 11th century they had also conquered England (*see* Norman conquest) and much of S Italy and Sicily and had established crusading states in Palestine, besides gaining a foothold in Wales and Scotland. They were noted for their military inventiveness (they introduced the castle into England).

Norrköping 58 35N 16 10E A port in SE Sweden, on an inlet of the Baltic Sea. Population (1989): 119 926.

North, Frederick, Lord (1732–92) British statesman; prime minister (1770–82). As prime minister, he was criticized for failing to prevent the *American Revolution (1775–83), and for British defeats in the conflict, and eventually resigned.

North American Indian languages A geographical classification of the languages of the native peoples of North America. It is estimated that these languages originally numbered about 300. They have been grouped into: Eskimo-Aleut; Algonkian-Wakashan; Na-Dené; Penutian; Hokan-Siouan; and Aztec-Tanoan.

Northampton 52 14N 0 54W A town in central England, the administrative centre of Northamptonshire. It is a centre of the footwear industry. Population (1989): 183 167.

Northamptonshire (*or* Northants) A county in the East Midlands of England. It is predominantly agricultural producing livestock, cereals, potatoes, and sugar beet. Area: 2367 sq km (915 sq mi). Population (1988 est): 570 300. Administrative centre: Northampton.

North Atlantic Treaty Organization (NATO) An alliance formed in 1949 by Belgium, Canada, Denmark, France, Iceland, Italy, Luxembourg, the Netherlands, Norway, Portugal, the UK, and the USA; Greece and Turkey joined in 1952, West Germany in 1955, Spain in 1982, and the united Germany in 1990. All member states are bound to protect any member against attack. Its secretariat headquarters is in Brussels and its military headquarters near Mons.

North Borneo. *See* Sabah.

North Carolina A state in the USA, on the S Atlantic coast. It is heavily populated and the leading industrial state in the South. *History*: one of the 13 original colonies, it shares its early history with South Carolina. It was made a separate colony in 1713 and it became a state in 1789. Area: 136 197 sq km (52 586 sq mi). Population (1986 est): 6 331 000. Capital: Raleigh.

North Dakota A state in the N central USA. Agriculture and mining are the two principal economic activities. *History*: early attempts to settle were made by Scottish and Irish families at Pembina in 1812. It formed part of the territory of Dakota from 1861 until 1889 when it was made a separate state. Area: 183 022 sq km (70 665 sq mi). Population (1986 est): 679 000. Capital: Bismarck.

Northeast Passage (Russian name: Severny Morskoy Put) The sea route along the N Eurasian coast, kept open in summer by Soviet icebreakers. The Swedish explorer, Niels Nordenskjöld was the first to pass along it (1878–79). *See also* Northwest Passage.

Northern Ireland. *See* Ireland.

Northern Territory An administrative division of N central Australia. The main agricultural activity is the rearing of beef cattle. Minerals are important, especially uranium, iron ore, manganese, copper, gold, and bauxite. In 1978 the Northern Territory became an independent state. Area: 1 346 200 sq km (519 770 sq mi). Population (1986): 154 000. Capital: Darwin.

Northern War, Great (1700–21) The war fought for Baltic supremacy between Russia, Denmark, and Poland, on one side, and Sweden, on the other. The war between Denmark, Poland, and Sweden was ended by the Treaties of Stockholm (1719–20). With the Treaty of Nystad (1721) between Russia and Sweden, Russia emerged as the major Baltic power.

North Island The more northerly of the two principal islands of New Zealand, separated from South Island by Cook Strait. Area: 114 729 sq km (44 281 sq mi). Population (1986): 2 438 249.

North Pole. *See* Poles.

North Sea A section of the Atlantic Ocean in NW Europe, between the British Isles and the continent N of the Strait of Dover. The entire floor is part of the continental shelf, with an average depth of about 300 m (914 ft). Recent exploitation of North Sea oil and natural-gas finds have increased its economic importance.

Northumberland The northernmost county of England. There are outstanding Roman remains, notably Hadrian's Wall. The main agricultural activity is sheep farming. Area: 5033 sq km (1944 sq mi). Population (1989): 303 500. Administrative centre: Morpeth.

Northumberland, John Dudley, Duke of (1502–53) English statesman, who was virtual ruler of England (1549–53) under Edward VI. He replaced the Duke of Somerset as head of the regency council in 1549, securing his execution in 1552. In 1553 he married his son Guildford Dudley to Lady Jane *Grey, whom he persuaded the king to name as his heir. On Edward's death Jane was proclaimed queen but lack of support forced Northumberland's surrender to Mary (I) and he was executed.

Northumbria A kingdom of Anglo-Saxon England north of the Humber. Northumbria became politically important in England in the 7th century under *Edwin, Saint *Oswald, and Oswiu (d. 670). By 829, however, Northumbria had recognized the overlordship of Wessex and in the late 9th century its unity was destroyed by the Danes.

North-West Frontier Province A province in NW Pakistan, SE of Afghanistan. Its Pathan inhabitants mostly herd livestock or cultivate grains, fruit, sugar cane, and tobacco. Over the centuries several great powers have sought to control the province. Area: 74 522 sq km (28 773 sq mi). Population (1985 est): 12 287 000. Capital: Peshawar.

Northwest Passage The sea route along the coast of North America, between the Atlantic and Pacific Oceans. Roald *Amundsen was the first to pass along it (1903–06). *See also* Northeast Passage.

Northwest Territories A territory of N Canada, stretching from 60°N to the North Pole. One of the most sparsely populated areas in the world. Rich in mineral resources, the economy is dominated by the mining industry. At present, the territory's vast oil reserves are being explored. Plans to divide the territory on ethnic grounds were agreed in 1987. Area: 3 246 389 sq km (1 253 432 sq mi). Population (1986): 51 384. Capital: Yellowknife.

North Yorkshire A county in N England. It is chiefly agricultural. There is some industrial activity in the larger towns, such as York. Coal is mined from a new field centred on Selby (opened 1983). Tourism is centred on Harrogate and Scarborough. Area: 8321 sq km (3213 sq mi). Population (1986 est): 699 800. Administrative centre: Northallerton.

Norway, Kingdom of (Norwegian name: Norge) A country in N Europe occupying the W part of the Scandinavian Peninsula. The islands of Svalbard and Jan Meyen Island are also part of Norway together with the dependencies of Bouvet Island, Peter I Island, and Queen Maud Land. *Economy*: abundant hydroelectric power has enabled Norway to develop as an industrial nation. Norway is also one of the world's great fishing nations. Revenues from tourism are important. Minerals include iron ore, limestone, coal, copper, zinc, and lead. *History*: its early history was dominated by the Vikings. During the reign (1204–63) of Haakon IV Haakonsson Norway acquired Iceland and Greenland and in the 14th century, under Margaret, was united with Sweden and Denmark. Sweden broke free in 1523 but Norway remained under Danish domination until 1814, when it was united with Sweden, while maintaining internal self-government. Only in 1907 was full independence achieved. Norway declared its neutrality in both World Wars but from 1940 to 1944 was occupied by the Germans. After World War II Norway joined the UN and NATO. In 1972 Norwegians rejected membership of the EEC in a referendum. Head of state: Olav V. Prime minister: Gro Harlem Brundtland (1938–　). Official language: Norwegian. Official religion: Evangelical Lutheran. Official currency: Krone of 100 o/re. Area: 323 886 sq km (125 053 sq mi). Population (1987): 4 174 005. Capital and main port: Oslo.

Norwegian A North Germanic language of the West Scandinavian division, spoken in Norway. There are two distinct forms known as Dano-Norwegian (Bokmål or Riksmål) and New Norwegian (Nynorsk or Landsmål).

Norwegian Antarctic Territory The area in Antarctica claimed by Norway, lying S of latitude 60°S and between longitudes 20°W and 45°E. It consists of the end of Coats Land, Queen Maud Land, and islands.

Norwich 52 38N 1 18E A city in E England, the administrative centre of Norfolk. Towards the end of the 16th century Dutch weavers settled in the city and it became a major textile centre. It has a Norman cathedral (1096) and the University of East Anglia (1963). Industries include shoe manufacture, machinery, chemicals, and printing. Population (1981): 122 270.

nose The organ of smell, which is also an entrance to the air passages. It leads to the nasal cavity, which is lined by *mucous membrane, extends back to the pharynx and windpipe, and is connected to the air *sinuses of the skull. Hairs in the nostrils filter particles from inhaled air, which is further cleaned, warmed, and moistened in the nasal cavity. The membrane at the top of the nasal cavity contains olfactory cells, which are sensitive to different smells and are connected to the brain via the olfactory nerve.

Nostradamus (Michel de Notredame; 1503–66) French physician and astrologer, who became famous with his publication of *Centuries* (1555–58), in which he made a number of prophecies in verse form. His prophecies are obscure and open to various interpretations.

notochord A flexible supportive rod that runs along the length of the body in the embryos of all animals of the phylum Chordata (including vertebrates). In primitive chordates, such as the lancelets and lampreys, the notochord remains the main support along the length of the body in the adults.

Notre-Dame de Paris The gothic cathedral built (1163–1345) on the Île de la Cité, Paris, to replace two earlier churches. The nave, choir, and west front were completed by 1204; the flying buttresses and the great rose windows are notable features. Damaged during the French Revolution, Notre-Dame was fully restored (1845–64) by Eugène Viollet-le-Duc (1814–79).

Nottingham 52 58N 1 10W A city in N central England, the administrative centre of Nottinghamshire. Once famous for its lace, its industries now include textiles, pharmaceuticals, cigarettes, and electronics. Population (1981): 271 080.

Nottinghamshire A county in the East Midlands of England. Agriculture is important with arable and dairy farming, orchards, and market gardening. It contains important coalfields. Area: 2164 sq km (835 sq mi). Population (1986 est): 1 006 400. Administrative centre: Nottingham.

Nouakchott 18 09N 15 58W The capital of Mauritania, in the W near the Atlantic coast. A small village until the 1950s, it was developed as the capital after independence in 1960. Population (1985 est): 500 000.

Nouméa 22 16S 166 26E The capital of New Caledonia. A port, it exports nickel, chrome, manganese, and iron. Population (1983): 60 112.

nova A *binary star that suddenly increases in brightness by perhaps 10 000 times or more and then fades over months or years, usually to its original brightness. Nova eruptions occur in close binary systems comprising a *white dwarf with a nearby companion star that is expanding and is losing matter to the white dwarf.

Nova Scotia A province of E Canada. It consists of a peninsula protruding into the Atlantic Ocean and Cape Breton Island. Agriculture includes dairying, mixed farming, livestock, and fruit. Coal output is down significantly, but Nova Scotia also mines gypsum, salt, and copper.

History: from the first colonization (1605), Britain and France contested the area, Britain eventually gaining possession (confirmed by the Treaty of Paris in 1763). It joined Canada in 1867. Area: 52 841 sq km (20 402 sq mi). Population (1986): 873 199. Capital: Halifax.

Novello, Ivor (David Ivor Davies; 1893–1951) British composer, dramatist, and actor. He composed the World War I song "Keep the Home Fires Burning," and is best known for his series of romantic musicals including *Careless Rapture* (1936) and *The Dancing Years* (1939).

Novgorod 58 30N 31 20E A city in the Soviet Union, on the River Volkhov. It has varied manufacturing industries and is a famous tourist centre, its buildings including the St Sofia Cathedral (1045–50). *History*: dating at least to the 9th century, it was a trading centre in the middle ages. Self-governing from 1019, it was forced to acknowledge Tatar overrule in the 13th century and that of Moscow in the 15th century. Population (1987): 228 000.

Novosibirsk 55 04N 83 05E A city in the central Soviet Union, on the River Ob and the Trans-Siberian Railway. It is the most important economic centre in Siberia. Population (1987): 1 423 000.

NSPCC. *See* National Society for the Prevention of Cruelty to Children.

Nu, U (*or* Thakin Nu; 1907–) Burmese statesman; prime minister (1948–56, 1957–58, 1960–62). A leading nationalist from the 1930s, he became prime minister on the achievement of independence. In 1988 he became a leader of the opposition in unrest against the current regime.

Nubia A region of NE Africa, between Aswan (Egypt) and Khartoum (Sudan). Much of Nubia is now drowned by Lake Nasser. From about 2000 BC the Egyptians gradually occupied Nubia, which they called Cush. As Egyptian power weakened, Nubian kings became influential, even dominating Egypt itself (c. 730–670). Their independent culture lasted until the 4th century AD.

Nubian Desert A desert in the NE Sudan, between the River Nile and the Red Sea. It consists of a sandstone plateau with peaks of up to 2259 m (7411 ft). Area: about 400 000 sq km (154 408 sq mi).

nuclear energy The energy produced by nuclear fission or nuclear fusion. The energy is liberated in fission when a heavy atomic nucleus, such as uranium, splits into two or more parts, the total mass of the parts being less than the mass of the original nucleus. This difference in mass is equivalent to the *binding energy of the nucleus and most of it is converted into the kinetic energy of the components formed in the reaction. In a fusion reaction, two light nuclei, such as hydrogen, combine to form a stable nucleus, such as helium; with light nuclei the nucleus formed has a lower mass than the sum of the component nuclei, and again energy is released. In the case of fission, when a nucleus of uranium-235 is struck by a neutron, a U-236 nucleus is formed, which immediately splits into two roughly equal parts. Two or three neutrons are produced at the same time. As these neutrons

can cause further fissions, a chain reaction builds up and a lump of U-235 will disintegrate almost instantaneously with enormous explosive power, provided its mass is greater than a certain value, called the critical mass (*see* nuclear weapons).

In nuclear power stations the fission reaction is harnessed to produce heat at a controlled rate (to raise steam to drive a turbine). They use natural uranium, which contains only 0.7% of the fissionable U-235 isotope, nearly all of the rest being the isotope U-238. The U-238 isotope absorbs the fast-moving neutrons emitted by the fission of U-235 and prevents a chain reaction from occurring in natural uranium. There are, however, two ways of producing a chain reaction. One is to use a moderator to slow down the fast neutrons so that they are not absorbed by U-238 nuclei. This occurs in a **thermal reactor**. The other is to enrich the natural uranium with extra quantities of U-235 (or plutonium-239) so that there are sufficient neutrons to sustain the chain reaction in spite of absorption by U-238. This occurs in a **fast reactor**. Most present commercial reactors are thermal, although fast reactors are operating in the UK, France, and the Soviet Union. See p. 390.

The fusion process is the basis of the hydrogen bomb (*see* nuclear weapons) and the so far unsuccessful thermonuclear reactor.

nuclear fission. *See* nuclear energy; nuclear weapons.

nuclear fusion. *See* nuclear energy; nuclear weapons; thermonuclear reactor.

nuclear power The generation of electricity from nuclear energy. The nuclear power industry has expanded rapidly over the last 30 years. Some 30% of Europe's electricity is now produced by nuclear energy; in 1988 it provided 70% of electricity in France, 19% in the UK, 19.5% in the USA, and 25% in Japan. The Soviet disaster in 1986 (*see* Chernobyl) caused considerable public concern over nuclear safety, however, leading several countries to postpone plans for nuclear expansion. The Chernobyl graphite-moderated light-water reactor, a unique Soviet design, is now regarded as unsafe, especially as it is contained in a single-shell building, unlike the US water-cooled reactors (*see* thermal reactor), which are contained in double-walled buildings. This prevented disaster in the Three Mile Island incident in the USA in 1979. *See also* nuclear energy; thermonuclear reactor.

nuclear reactor. *See* nuclear energy.

Nuclear Test-Ban Treaty (1963) A treaty banning nuclear testing by the countries who signed it on the ground, in the atmosphere, in space, and under water. Those countries were the Soviet Union, the UK, and the USA; many other countries agreed to the treaty.

nuclear waste. *See* radioactive waste.

nuclear weapons Missiles, bombs, shells, or land mines that use fission or fusion of nuclear material (*see* nuclear energy) yielding enormous quantities of heat, light, blast, and radiation. The first **atomic bomb** (*or* fission bomb), manufactured by the USA in World War II, was dropped on Hiroshima in 1945. It consisted of two small masses of uranium-235 forced together by a

NUCLEAR ENERGY

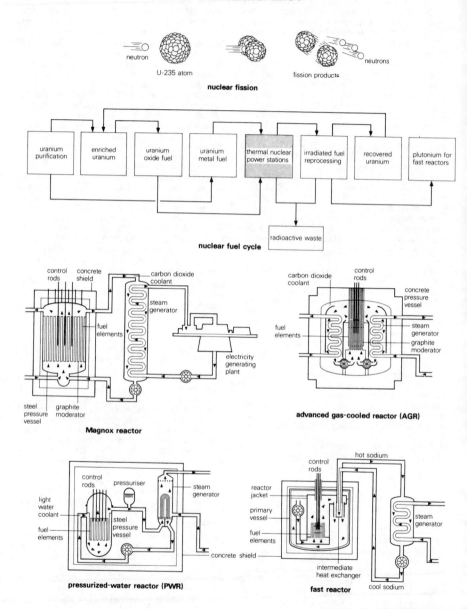

nuclear fission

nuclear fuel cycle

Magnox reactor

advanced gas-cooled reactor (AGR)

pressurized-water reactor (PWR)

fast reactor

NUCLEAR ENERGY *Natural uranium metal fuel clad in Magnox (magnesium alloy) is used in Magnox thermal reactors. Enriched uranium dioxide pellets clad in steel are used in AGR and PWR fuel elements. Plutonium for fast reactors and recycled enriched uranium is obtained by reprocessing spent fuel from thermal reactors. The electricity generating plant is similar with all reactor types.*

chemical explosion to form a supercritical mass, in which an uncontrolled chain reaction occurred. The bomb had an explosive power equivalent to 20 000 tons of TNT. Later models used plutonium-239 to even greater effect.
The **hydrogen bomb** (fusion bomb *or* thermonuclear bomb) consists of an atom bomb surrounded by a layer of hydrogenous material, such as lithium deuteride. The atom bomb creates the temperature (about 100 000 000°C) needed to ignite the fusion reaction (*see* thermonuclear reactor). Hydrogen bombs have an explosive power measured in tens of millions of tons of TNT. The first hydrogen bomb was exploded by US scientists on Eniwetok Atoll in 1952.

nucleic acids A group of organic compounds that include *DNA and *RNA—molecules that store genetic information in living cells and are the key to life itself.

nucleon A collective name for a proton or neutron. *See also* mass number; nucleus.

nucleus (biology) A large spherical or egg-shaped structure found in most cells. It is surrounded by a nuclear membrane, which is perforated with pores to allow materials to pass between the nucleus and the cytoplasm which surrounds it. The nucleus contains the *chromosomes, made up of the hereditary material (DNA), and is therefore essential for the control and regulation of the cell's activities. During cell division the nuclear membrane breaks down to allow the chromosomes to separate (*see* meiosis; mitosis).

nucleus (physics) The central core of the atom (*see* atomic theory) discovered by Lord Rutherford in 1911. All nuclei consist of protons and neutrons (jointly called nucleons), except for hydrogen, which consists of a single proton. The number of protons in the nucleus determines its charge and atomic number; the number of neutrons (in addition to the number of protons) determines the mass number and the isotope. **Nuclear physics** is the study of the structure and reactions of the nucleus. *See also* particle physics.

Nuffield, William Richard Morris, 1st Viscount (1877–1963) British car manufacturer and philanthropist. He established a car factory in Cowley, near Oxford, which in 1913 produced the first Morris Oxford, soon followed by the Morris Cowley. He founded Nuffield College, Oxford, the Nuffield Trust, and the Nuffield Foundation.

Nuku'alofa 21 09S 175 14W The capital of Tonga in the S Pacific, in N Tongatabu. It is the site of the Royal Palace (1865–67) and Royal Tombs. Population (1986): 28 899.

Nullarbor Plain A plain of SW South Australia and SE Western Australia, bordering on the Great Australian Bight. It consists of a treeless arid plateau. Area: 260 000 sq km (100 000 sq mi).

numbat A rat-sized *marsupial, *Myrmecobius fasciatus*, of SW Australia, also called marsupial (*or* banded) anteater. It is rust-coloured, with white stripes across the back and a long tail, and it feeds on ants and termites with its long sticky tongue. Numbats have no pouch.

numbers Mathematical symbols used to denote quantity. The natural numbers, 1, 2, 3, 4, 5 . . . , etc., were developed first by the Hindus and Arabs for simple counting. Subtraction led to negative numbers and to zero, which together with natural numbers make up the set of integers . . . -3, -2, -1, 0, 1, ... Division of whole numbers results in fractions or rational numbers. Some numbers, such as $\sqrt{2}$, cannot be expressed as the ratio of two integers. These are called irrational numbers and they occur as the solutions to simple algebraic equations. They can be calculated to any required accuracy but cannot be written as exact values. Other numbers, called transcendental numbers, do not come from algebraic relationships. Some of these occur as basic properties of space, for example π, the ratio of a circumference of a circle to its diameter. Real numbers include all rational and irrational numbers. The equation $x^2 = -1$ can have no real solution for x, since the square of any number is positive. The imaginary number, $i = \sqrt{-1}$, was introduced to overcome this problem. *See* complex numbers; number theory.

number theory The study of the properties of numbers. It includes various theorems about *prime numbers, many of which are unproved but apparently true, and the study of Diophantine equations (named after the 3rd-century Greek mathematician Diophantus of Alexandria), i.e. equations that have integer solutions.

Numidia An ancient kingdom of N Africa, W of *Carthage. Its *Berber population was nomadic until Masinissa (c. 240–149 BC) promoted agriculture and urbanization. After supporting Pompey against Julius Caesar (46 BC), Numidia lost its monarchy and became part of the Roman province of Africa.

numismatics (*or* coin collecting) Collecting and studying coins, medals, or banknotes as a hobby or as a form of historical research. Coins in good condition are a form of investment, the best being "proof" coins, struck especially for sale to collectors.

Nuremberg (German name: Nürnberg) 49 27N 11 05E A city in S Germany, in Bavaria. It became the centre of the German Renaissance, when the mastersingers' contests were held here. It was the site of the Nazi Party congresses (1933–38) and the war-crime trials following World War II. Population (1990): 473 910.

Nureyev, Rudolf (1938–) Russian ballet dancer. He danced with the Leningrad Kirov Ballet from 1958 until 1961, when he defected from Russia. In 1962 he joined the Royal Ballet, where he frequently partnered Margot *Fonteyn in such ballets as *Giselle* and *Swan Lake*. His own productions have included *The Nutcracker* (1967) and *Romeo and Juliet* (1977); his films include *Valentino* (1977) and *Exposed* (1982).

Nusa Tenggara (former name: Lesser *Sunda Islands) A volcanic Indonesian island group E of Java, the chief islands being Bali, Lombok, Sumbawa, Sumba, Flores, and Timor. Area: 73 144 sq km (28 241 sq mi). Population (1986 est): 6 156 600.

nut Loosely, any edible nonfleshy fruit, including the peanut and brazil nut. In strict botanical terms, a nut is a large dry fruit containing a single seed that is not released from the fruit at maturity. An example is the chestnut.

nutcracker A songbird found in coniferous forests of E Europe and Asia. The common nutcracker (*Nucifraga caryocatactes*) is dark brown speckled with white, about 32 cm long, and cracks open pine cones with its sharp bill to extract the seeds.

nuthatch A small stocky bird occurring everywhere except South America and New Zealand. Nuthatches have long straight bills, for hammering open nuts, and long-clawed toes, for running up and down tree trunks in search of insects. The European nuthatch (*Sitta europaea*), about 14 cm long, has a blue-grey upper plumage with paler underparts and a black eyestripe.

nutmeg A fragrant tropical evergreen tree, *Myristica fragrans*, native to Indonesia but widely cultivated in SE Asia and the West Indies. It grows up to 20 m high. The yellow fleshy fruit, about 3 cm across, splits when ripe to expose the seed, which has a red fleshy covering (aril). The dried aril (mace) and whole or ground seeds (nutmeg) are used as spices.

nutria. *See* coypu.

Nuuk (name until 1979: Godthåb) 64 10N 51 40W The capital of Greenland, founded in 1721. Population (1986): 11 209.

nyala An antelope, *Tragelaphus angasi*, of SW Africa. About 100 cm high at the shoulder, nyalas are shy and nocturnal and have spiral-shaped horns and a greyish-brown coat with vertical white stripes on the flanks.

Nyasaland. *See* Malawi, Republic of.

Nyerere, Julius (Kambarage) (1922–) Tanzanian statesman; president (1962–85). In 1954 Nyerere formed the Tanganyika African National Union, which led the fight for independence (achieved in 1960). He became chief minister (1960), prime minister (1961), and then president of Tanganyika, which was renamed Tanzania in 1964 after union with Zanzibar.

nylon A synthetic material with a translucent creamy white appearance, widely used both in fibre form and in solid blocks because of its lightness, toughness, and elasticity. It is made by *polymerization to form a polyamide. Nylon is used to make small engineering components and is also spun and woven into fabrics for clothing, etc., and can be coloured with pigments. Introduced commercially in 1938, nylon was the first truly synthetic fibre.

nymph A stage in the life cycle of insects that show incomplete *metamorphosis, including dragonflies, grasshoppers, and bugs. The egg hatches into a nymph, which undergoes a series of moults to form a line of nymphs that show increasing similarity to the adult.

nymphs In Greek mythology, female spirits of nature, often portrayed as youthful and amorous dancers or musicians. The several classes of nymphs associated with particular natural phenomena include the dryads (trees), the naiads (rivers and lakes), and the nereids (the sea).

Nyoro A *Bantu-speaking people of the western lakes region of Uganda. They live in small scattered settlements.

O

Oahu A US island in Hawaii, the administrative centre. *Pearl Harbor is on Oahu. Area: 1584 sq km (608 sq mi). Population (1987 est): 830 600. Chief town: Honolulu.

oak A tree of N temperate and subtropical regions. The leaves usually have lobed or toothed edges and the tree bears yellow male catkins and tiny green female flowers. The fruit—an acorn—is partly enclosed by a round cup. Often 30–40 m high, many species are important timber trees, especially the common or pedunculate oak (*Quercus robur*) and the *durmast oak (both Eurasian).

Oaks A flat race for three-year-old fillies only, run over the *Derby course (2.4 km; 1.5 mi) at Epsom, three days after the Derby in early June. One of the English *Classics, it was first run in 1779 and was named after the 12th Earl of Derby's hunting lodge.

oarfish A fish, *Regalecus glesne*, found in all seas. It has a long silvery ribbon-like body, up to 9 m long, a long red dorsal fin that extends forwards to form a crest, and long red oarlike pelvic fins situated near the pectoral fins.

OAS. *See* Organisation de l'Armée secrète; Organization of American States.

oasis An area within a desert where water is available for vegetation and human use. It may consist of a single small spring around which palms grow or be an extensive area where the water table is at or near the ground surface.

Oates, Lawrence Edward Grace (1880–1912) British explorer and a member of R. F. *Scott's expedition to the Antarctic (1910–12). After reaching the Pole Oates, fearing that his lameness (resulting from frostbite) might hinder the already struggling expedition on the return journey, walked out into the blizzard to die. His gallant act, related in Scott's diaries, failed to save his companions.

Oates, Titus. *See* Popish Plot.

oats *Cereal grasses native to temperate regions. The common oat (*Avena sativa*) was first cultivated in Europe and is grown widely in cool temperate regions. The grain is used as a livestock feed, especially for horses, and for oatmeal, breakfast cereals, etc. Wild oats can be a serious weed in cereal crops.

OAU. *See* Organization of African Unity.

Ob, River A river in the N central Soviet Union, flowing N from the Altai Mountains to the **Gulf of Ob** on the Kara Sea. One of the world's largest rivers, its drainage basin covers an area of about 2 930 000 sq km (1 131 000 sq mi). Length: 3682 km (2287 mi).

OBE. *See* Order of the British Empire.

Oberammergau 47 35N 11 07E A town in S Germany, in the Bavarian Alps. It is noted for its *Passion play, performed every ten years following a vow made by the villagers (1633) when they were saved from the plague. Population (1980 est): 4900.

oboe A woodwind instrument with a double reed, made in three jointed sections and having a conical bore and small bell-shaped end. It derives from the ancient shawm. It has a range of about three octaves above the B flat below middle C and because of its constant pitch usually gives the A to which other orchestral instruments tune.

obsidian A black glassy volcanic rock formed by the rapid cooling of acid lava.

obstetrics. *See* gynaecology.

O'Casey, Sean (1880–1964) Irish dramatist and nationalist. His early realistic tragicomedies include *The Shadow of a Gunman* (1923) and *Juno and the Paycock* (1924). His later work includes *The Silver Tassie* (1929), *Red Roses for Me* (1943), *The Bishop's Bonfire* (1955), and *The Drums of Father Ned* (1958).

Occitan. *See* Provençal.

occupational therapy The branch of medicine concerned with restoring the physical and mental health of the sick and disabled. The occupational therapist plays an important role in keeping long-stay hospital patients interested and usefully occupied, in helping them gain confidence to return to work, and in training disabled persons for new employment.

Oceania The islands of the Pacific Ocean, usually taken to exclude Japan, Indonesia, Taiwan, the Philippines, and the Aleutian Islands, but often including Australasia.

oceans The large areas of water (excluding lakes and seas) covering about 70% of the earth's surface. The oceans are the Pacific (covering about one-third of the world), Atlantic, Indian, and Arctic; the Southern Ocean (waters south of 40°S) is sometimes distinguished. Major structural features are the continental margins (continental shelf and slope), mid-ocean ridges, ocean basins, and trenches. The study of the oceans is called **oceanography**. See p. 394.

ocelot A *cat, *Felis (Panthera) pardalis*, of Central and South American forests. 100–150 cm long including the tail (30–50 cm), it has a black-spotted yellowish-brown coat with stripes on the legs. It preys on small mammals and reptiles.

Ockham's Razor The metaphysical principle, associated with the English medieval philosopher William of Ockham (c. 1285–1349), that in analysing a problem one should always choose the theory that makes the least number of assumptions.

OCR (Optical Character Recognition). *See* computer.

Octavia (d. 11 BC) The sister of Emperor Augustus, who married her to Mark Antony (40) to seal their reconciliation. Antony divorced her in 32, when he returned to Egypt and Cleopatra.

Octavian. *See* Augustus.

octopus A mollusc with eight arms found in most oceans. The common octopus (*Octopus vulgaris*) has a pair of well-developed eyes, a ring of tentacles around its horny beak, and a saclike body. Octopuses feed mainly on crabs and lobsters and may eject a cloud of ink when alarmed.

Oder, River A river in E Europe. Rising in the Oder Mountains of Czechoslovakia, it flows N and W through Poland and enters the Baltic Sea at Szczecin. Linked by canals to both E and W Europe, it is of great commercial importance. Length: 886 km (551 mi).

Oder-Neisse Line The boundary between Germany and Poland, following the River Oder and Neisse. It was confirmed by the Allies at the end of World War II, recognized by East Germany and Poland in 1950 but not by West Germany until 1970.

Odessa 46 30N 30 46E A port and industrial centre in the Soviet Union, in the S Ukrainian SSR on the Black Sea. Founded in the 14th century as a Tatar fortress, it passed to Russia in 1791 and became a naval base. Population (1987 est): 1 141 000.

Odin The principal god of the ancient Teutonic peoples, the husband of Frigga and, according to some legends, the father of *Thor. Also known as Woden and Wotan, he was the god of war, learning, and poetry and possessed great magical powers. He was the protector of slain heroes, who were brought to *Valhalla by his servants the *Valkyries.

Odysseus (or Ulysses) A legendary Greek king of Ithaca and hero of Homer's *Odyssey*, notable for his cunning. His many adventures during his voyage home from the *Trojan War included encounters with the Cyclops Polyphemus, the enchantress *Circe, and the goddess Calypso, with whom he lived for eight years. Having reached Ithaca, he was reunited with his faithful wife *Penelope after killing her suitors with the help of his son Telemachus.

Oedipus In Greek legend, a king of Thebes who unwittingly fulfilled the prophecy of the oracle at Delphi that he would kill his father and marry his mother. He was brought up by Polybus, King of Corinth. He killed his true father, Laius, in a roadside quarrel, and after winning the throne of Thebes by solving the riddle of the *sphinx he married his mother, the widowed Jocasta. When they discovered the truth, Jocasta committed suicide and Oedipus blinded himself and went into exile.

Oedipus complex The sexual feelings of a boy for his mother, of which the boy is unaware. They are accompanied by aggressive feelings for his father. According to psychoanalysis this is a normal desire, but one which we grow up to consider as undesirable (*see* repression). The female

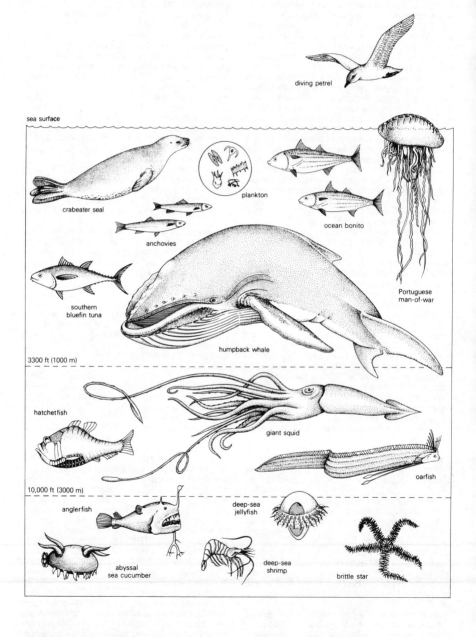

diving petrel

sea surface

crabeater seal

plankton

ocean bonito

anchovies

southern
bluefin tuna

Portuguese
man-of-war

humpback whale

3300 ft (1000 m)

hatchetfish

giant squid

oarfish

10,000 ft (3000 m)

anglerfish

deep-sea
jellyfish

abyssal
sea cucumber

deep-sea
shrimp

brittle star

OCEANS *A selection of animals and plants found at different depths of the ocean.*

equivalent (in which a girl desires her father) is called the **Electra complex**.

Oersted, Hans Christian (1777–1851) Danish physicist. He discovered the magnetic effect of an electric current and thus established the relationship between electricity and magnetism.

oesophagus The gullet: a muscular tube, about 25 cm long, running from the pharynx at the back of the mouth to the stomach. Contractions of the oesophagus propel swallowed food towards the stomach: the food is lubricated with mucus secreted by the walls of the oesophagus.

oestrogens A group of steroid hormones that function chiefly as female sex hormones. The most important oestrogens in mammals are oestradiol and oestrone. Oestrogens are produced by the ovaries. They promote the development of the reproductive organs and secondary sexual characteristics (such as enlargement of breasts) at puberty and regulate the changes of the menstrual cycle. Oestrogens are also produced by the placenta, adrenal glands, and testes. Man-made oestrogens are used to treat disorders associated with the menstrual cycle and with the *menopause in older women. They are also constituents of *oral contraceptives.

oestrus The period of "heat" in the sexual cycle of nonhuman female mammals, when the female will attract males and permit copulation. It corresponds to the time of ovulation (i.e. release of the egg from the ovary), so that mating is most likely to result in pregnancy.

Offa (d. 796) King of Mercia (757–96) and overlord of all England S of the Humber. He accepted greater papal control of the Church, introduced a new currency, and devised a code of laws. **Offa's Dyke**, an earthwork dividing England from Wales, built c. 784–c. 796, marks the frontier established by his wars with the Welsh.

Offaly (Irish name: Uabh Failghe) A county in the central Republic of Ireland, in Leinster bordered in the W by the River Shannon. Area: 2000 sq km (770 sq mi). Population (1986): 59 806. County town: Tullamore.

Offenbach, Jacques (J. Eberst; 1819–80) German composer of French adoption. He wrote a series of popular operettas, including *Orpheus in the Underworld* (1858), *La Belle Hélène* (1864), and *La Vie Parisienne* (1866). He also composed one grand opera, *The Tales of Hoffman* (produced after his death, 1881).

Ogaden, the A semidesert area in E Ethiopia, enclosed by Somalia except to the W. The nomadic inhabitants are chiefly Muslim Somalis and in the 1960s a claim to the area by Somalia provoked fighting. Somalia invaded the Ogaden in 1977 but withdrew in 1978.

Ohio A state in the USA, in the Midwest situated to the S of Lake Erie. A major industrial state, it lies at the centre of the most industrialized area of the USA. Agriculture is important, especially livestock. Handed over to Britain in 1763 and to the USA in 1783, it became a state in 1802. Area: 106 764 sq km (41 222 sq mi). Population (1986 est): 10 752 000. Capital: Columbus.

Ohio River A river in the USA flowing mainly SW from Pittsburgh in W Pennsylvania to join

the Mississippi (in Illinois) as its main E tributary. Length: 1577 km (980 mi).

ohm (Ω) The *SI unit of electrical resistance equal to the resistance between two points on a conductor when a potential difference of one volt between the points produces a current of one ampere. Named after Georg *Ohm.

Ohm, Georg Simon (1787–1854) German physicist, who discovered in 1827 that the current flowing through a wire (or circuit element) is directly related to the potential difference between its ends (**Ohm's law**). The unit of resistance is named after him.

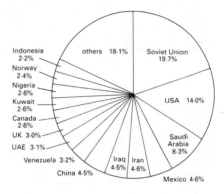

OIL *World crude petroleum production (1989).*

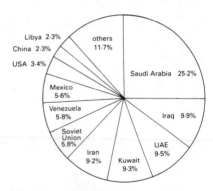

OIL *World crude petroleum reserves (1989).*

oil There are three types of oil: lipids (*see* fats and oils), *essential oils, and mineral oil. Petroleum (*or* rock oil) is the thick greenish mineral oil that occurs in certain types of underground rock. It consists mainly of *hydrocarbons derived from the remains of living organisms deposited many millions of years ago and occurs in large underground reservoirs, often floating on a layer of water and held under pressure beneath a layer of *natural gas (mostly methane). The modern oil industry began when oil was discovered in Pennsylvania in 1859 and has grown with the development of the *internal-combustion engine. Once the presence of oil has been detected and its extent determined, the oil well is made by drilling through the rock; a specially prepared mud is pumped through the hollow bit to collect the debris, which is forced back up the shaft around the drilling bit. The mud controls the pressure of the oil so that none is wasted by gushing out; when the mud has been removed, the oil pressure is controlled by valves. Drilling for oil below the sea is achieved in a similar manner, except that the drilling rig has to be supported on a base, which has legs sunk into the sea bed. Petroleum must be refined by fractional distillation (i.e. separating the components according to their boiling points) before it is of commercial value. Natural gas is widely used as a fuel, having largely replaced coal gas. Products made by blending the distillation fractions include aviation spirit, petrol, kerosene, Diesel oil, lubricating oil, paraffin wax, and petroleum jelly. Catalytic reforming is used to make a number of valuable chemicals (petrochemicals), which are required to manufacture detergents, plastics, fibres, fertilizers, drugs, etc.

oil palm An African *palm tree, *Elaeis guineensis*, cultivated in Africa, Indonesia, Malaysia, and tropical America as the source of palm oil. The small fleshy fruits contain a white kernel inside a hard black shell. Palm oil is extracted from the pulp and kernel and used in making soaps, margarine, lubricants, etc. The residue from the kernels is a valuable livestock feed.

oilseeds Oil-bearing seeds of plants from which the edible oil is extracted for making margarine, soaps, etc. Examples include rapeseed, cottonseed, groundnuts, and soya beans. The oil is obtained from the seeds by expelling it under pressure or by extracting it using a solvent; the **oilcake** remaining after most of the oil has been removed is widely used as animal feed.

Ojibwa A North American Indian people of the Great Lakes region, who speak a language of the Algonkian family. They are also known as Chippewa.

okapi A hoofed mammal, *Okapia johnstoni*, of central African rain forests. Okapis have a dark-brown coat with horizontal black and white stripes on the legs and rump. The smaller male has short bony backward-pointing horns.

Okeechobee, Lake A large freshwater lake in the USA, in S Florida. It drains into the Atlantic Ocean through the Everglades. Area: 1813 sq km (700 sq mi).

Okinawa A mountainous Japanese island, the main one of the *Ryukyu group. Captured by the USA in World War II, it was returned to Japan in 1972, the USA retaining military bases there. Area: 1176 sq km (454 sq mi). Population (1987): 1 190 000. Capital: Naha.

Oklahoma A state in the S central USA. An oil-rich state, agriculture (especially cattle) remains a major source of revenue. Most industry is located around Oklahoma City and Tulsa (one of the world's leading oil centres). Oklahoma formed part of the Louisiana Purchase in 1803. It was reserved as Indian territory (1828) but after

the US Civil War White settlement began and it became a state in 1907. Area: 181 089 sq km (69 919 sq mi). Population (1986 est): 3 305 000. Capital: Oklahoma City.

Oklahoma City 35 28N 97 33W A city in the USA, the capital of Oklahoma on the North Canadian River. Founded in 1889, it expanded rapidly following the discovery of oil (1920s). Today it is a commercial, industrial, and distribution centre for an oil-producing and agricultural area. Population (1986 est): 445 300.

okra An African plant, *Hibiscus esculentus*, of the mallow family, widely cultivated in the tropics and subtropics. The edible pods are picked before they are ripe and eaten fresh, canned, or pickled.

Olaf V (1903–91) King of Norway (1957–91). A talented sportsman, he took part as a yachtsman in the 1928 Olympic Games. In 1929 he married Princess Märtha of Sweden (1901–54); he was succeeded by his son Prince Harald (1937–).

Old Catholics Christian Churches from several European countries that separated from the Roman Catholic Church at various times and in 1932 entered into communion with the Church of England. They consist of the Church of Utrecht (1724), the Old Catholic Churches of Germany, Switzerland, and Austria (1870), the National Polish Church (established 1897), and the Yugoslav Old Catholic Church (1924).

Old English sheepdog A breed of working dog originating in England. It has a long dense shaggy coat that may be grey or blue-grey with white markings. Height: 55–66 cm.

Old Norse A North Germanic language which used to be spoken in Iceland and Norway (c. 1150–c. 1350). It is the language of the Norse *sagas and was closely related to the speech of Denmark and Sweden of that time. The modern Scandinavian languages come from this group.

Old Sarum. *See* Salisbury.

Old Testament The collection of 39 books which make up the sacred scriptures of *Judaism. Together with the *New Testament they also form the first of the two major divisions of the Christian *Bible. The title comes from the Latin word for *covenant and refers to the pact between God and Israel. The books claim to cover the period from the creation of the universe and man (Adam) to about 400 BC. They are traditionally divided into three parts: the Law or *Torah, the first five books, said to be by Moses and often called the Pentateuch; the Prophets, containing much historical information; and the Writings or Hagiographa, the latest books admitted to the Hebrew Old Testament (c. 100 AD).

Olduvai Gorge A site in N Tanzania yielding important Lower *Palaeolithic fossils and tools and remains of *Homo and *Australopithecus, many found by the *Leakey family.

Old Vic A London theatre built in 1818 and named the Royal Victoria in 1833. It became famous for its music-hall entertainments and, after Lilian Baylis (1874–1937) became manager in 1912, its productions of Shakespeare. It was the temporary home of the National Theatre Company (1963–76). It is now owned by the Canadian entrepreneur Ed Mirvish (1914–   ).

Old World A name for Europe, Africa, and Asia, used especially by early emigrants from Europe. Compare New World.

oleander A poisonous evergreen ornamental shrub, *Nerium oleander*, native to the Mediterranean region and widely cultivated in warm regions. Up to 7 m high, it has clusters of white, pink, or purplish five-petalled flowers (up to 7.5 cm across) and dangling pods.

olefines. See alkenes.

Oligocene epoch. See Tertiary period.

olive An evergreen Asian tree, *Olea europaea*, cultivated throughout Mediterranean and subtropical regions for its fruits. It has a gnarled grey trunk, lance-shaped leathery grey-green leaves, and fruits (drupes) containing a hard stone. Unripe green olives and ripe black olives are usually pickled for use in hors d'oeuvres and other dishes. **Olive oil**, pressed from the fruit, is one of the finest edible oils.

Olives, Mount of (*or* Olivet) 31 47N 35 15E A hill to the E of the old city of Jerusalem. Near its foot is the Garden of Gethsemane, the scene of the betrayal of Christ (Mark 14.26–50) and it is the traditional site of Christ's Ascension into Heaven (Acts 1.2–12).

Olivier, Laurence (Kerr), Baron (1907–89) British actor. He played many Shakespearean roles while with the Old Vic Theatre Company, 1937–1949, and a number of outstanding modern roles, including Archie Rice in *The Entertainer* (1957). His films include the Shakespeare adaptations *Henry V* (1944), *Hamlet* (1948), and *Richard III* (1956). While director of the National Theatre Company (1961–73), he played many leading roles. His second marriage to Vivien *Leigh ended in divorce; in 1961 he married Joan Plowright (1929–   ).

Olympia A sanctuary of *Zeus, established about 1000 BC in the NW *Peloponnese, in W Greece. From 776 BC until 261 AD it was the venue of the *Olympic Games. The temple of Zeus in the Altis (sacred grove), which later held *Phidias' famous statue, was completed in 457 BC.

Olympic Games An international amateur sports contest that takes place every four years. The modern games are based on the ancient Greek athletic festival held at *Olympia. They were revived at Athens in 1896. The Winter Olympics were first held in 1924. The Games are governed by the International Olympic Committee, a self-elected international body. Although officially a contest between individuals, hosted by a particular city, the Games have recently been disrupted by international political tensions, with a US boycott of the Moscow games in 1980, and an East bloc boycott of the Los Angeles games in 1984. In 1988 both blocs attended Seoul (South Korea); the 1992 Games will be held in Barcelona.

Olympus, Mount 40 05N 22 21E A small group of mountains in NE central Greece, held in ancient times to be the home of the gods. Highest point: 2917 m (9570 ft).

OM. *See* Order of Merit.

Oman, Sultanate of (name until 1970: Muscat and Oman) A country in the Middle East, in E *Arabia. It is mainly flat with coastal mountains in the N. The majority of the population is nomadic Arab, Ibadhi Muslim by religion. Oil, which has been extracted since 1967, accounts for about 90% of the country's revenue. Oman was settled by the Portuguese, Dutch, and English in the 16th century. Since the 19th century Britain has been influential. Head of State: Sultan Qaboos ibn Sa'id. Official language: Arabic. Official currency: Rial Omani of 1000 baiza. Area: 300 000 sq km (120 000 sq mi). Population (1987 est): 1 200 000. Capital: Muscat.

Omar (*or* Umar) (d. 644 AD) The second caliph (634–44), regarded by Islam as the founder of the Muslim state. Omar continued the Muslim conquests and in 638 visited Jerusalem after its capture. He was murdered by a discontented slave.

'Omar Khayyam (?1048–?1122) Persian poet, mathematician, and astronomer. His philosophical poems were written in the form of *ruba'is* (quatrains). The free translation of 75 of them by Edward *Fitzgerald in 1859 became widely popular; more recent translations have also been made.

Omayyads. See Umayyads.

ombudsman A person appointed to investigate complaints about administration. In the UK an ombudsman (the parliamentary commissioner for administration) was first appointed in 1967 to investigate complaints against central government departments; complaints against health authorities are investigated by Health Service Commissioners, appointed since 1973; there have been ombudsmen for local government since 1974.

Omdurman 15 37N 32 29E A city in the Sudan, on the River Nile. The Mahdi made it his capital in 1885 but his successor, the Khalifa, was defeated by Anglo-Egyptian forces under Lord Kitchener in the battle of Omdurman (1898). Population (1983): 526 287.

Omsk 55 00N 73 22E A port in the Soviet Union, in the W central RSFSR where the Rivers Irtysh and Om meet. It is also on the Trans-Siberian Railway. Population (1987): 1 134 000.

Onassis, Aristotle Socrates (1906–75) Greek businessman, who owned one of the largest independent shipping lines in the world and during the 1950s became one of the first to construct supertankers. In 1968 he married Jacqueline *Kennedy, his second wife, after a long relationship with Maria *Callas.

O'Neill, Eugene (1888–1953) US dramatist. His plays include *Beyond the Horizon* (1920), *Emperor Jones* (1920), *Anna Christie* (1921), *Mourning Becomes Electra* (1931), *The Iceman Cometh* (1946), and *Long Day's Journey into Night* (1956). He won the Nobel Prize in 1936.

One Thousand Guineas A flat race for three-year-old fillies only, run each spring at Newmarket over the Rowley Mile course. It was the last of the English *Classics to be established (1814).

onion A hardy plant, *Allium cepa*, of the lily family, cultivated worldwide, mainly in temperate regions, for its edible bulb. Immature bulbs, together with their leaves, are eaten raw in salads, etc.: these are spring onions.

Ontario The second largest province of Canada, stretching from the Great Lakes N to Hudson Bay. Most of the population live in the fertile lowlands near the S Great Lakes, dominated by the highly industrialized belt stretching from Toronto to Windsor. Manufacturing and mining are both important. Penetrated by French explorers and fur traders in the 17th century, Ontario became British (1763) and was settled by expatriate Americans loyal to Britain after the American Revolution. Area: 891 194 sq km (344 090 sq mi). Population (1985 est): 9 100 000. Capital: Toronto.

Ontario, Lake A lake in E North America, the smallest and easternmost of the Great Lakes. It is fed by the Niagara River and empties into the St Lawrence River. Area: 18 941 sq km (7313 sq mi).

ontogeny. *See* phylogeny.

ontology The branch of philosophy that deals with the theory of being. Ontological theories may assert that only minds exist (extreme *idealism), or that only physical objects do (*see* materialism).

onyx A semiprecious stone consisting of a variety of *chalcedony characterized by straight parallel bands, often distinctly coloured. Onyx occurs in the lower part of steam cavities in igneous rocks.

opal A semiprecious stone consisting of a water-containing variety of *silica. The precious variety, used as a gem, shows a characteristic internal play of colours (opalescence) resulting from internal reflection and refraction of light passing through adjacent thin layers of different water content. It occurs in cavities in many rocks.

Op art A form of abstract art, developed in the 1950s and 1960s, that exploits optical techniques to produce dramatic effects, such as the illusion of movement. Violent colour contrasts and subtly distorted patterns are commonly used. Exponents include Victor Vasarely in the USA and Bridget Riley in the UK.

OPEC. *See* Organization of Petroleum Exporting Countries.

open-hearth process A technique for making *steel from *pig iron, scrap steel, and iron ore, developed in the 1850s. The process uses gaseous fuel, which is preheated by the exhaust gases from the furnace. The molten metal lies in a shallow pool at the bottom or hearth of the furnace.

Open University (OU) A nonresidential university in the UK, established in Milton Keynes in 1969 to provide further education on a part-time basis for adults by means of correspondence courses and radio and television programmes, supported by a tutor-counselling service at regional centres throughout the country. It is open to anyone regardless of previous qualifications, age, or school attended. The first courses started in 1971.

opera A dramatic work in which all or most of the text is set to music. Opera originated in Florence in the early 17th century as the result of attempts to revive Greek tragedy and to reproduce its musical elements. These became the aria, recitative, and chorus of operatic convention. The earliest opera still in the modern repertory is Monteverdi's *Orfeo* (1607). Opera seria is the Italian style of opera developed by such composers as Scarlatti and Handel and characterized by a heroic or mythological plot. Opera buffa is a form of comic opera containing some spoken dialogue. It developed in the early 18th century and was originally performed between the acts of opera seria. At the end of the 18th century Mozart perfected opera buffa. In the early 19th century the influence of Romanticism gave rise to the works of Weber and Meyerbeer, while the Italian bel canto tradition was maintained by Bellini, Rossini, and Donizetti. In the mid-19th century the musical and dramatic elements of opera were combined by Wagner in his opera cycle *Der Ring des Nibelungen* (1869–76) and his subsequent operas. Verdi extended the emotional and dramatic range of Italian opera. The realism of Bizet's *Carmen* (1875) influenced Leoncavallo, Mascagni, and Puccini. In the 20th century a wide variety of operatic styles have flourished, including the dramatic realism of Janáček and the neoclassicism of Stravinsky.

ophthalmology The branch of medicine concerned with the study, diagnosis, and treatment of diseases of the eye. Ophthalmologists are doctors specializing in this. **Optometry** is the assessment and correction of sight defects, usually performed by opticians, who are not doctors: ophthalmic opticians both test eyesight and prescribe suitable lenses; dispensing opticians make and fit glasses.

opium The dried juice obtained from the seed capsule of the opium poppy, *Papaver somniferum*, which grows best in warm and subtropical regions. Opium is extracted from the latex of the plant, which oozes from notches made in the half-ripened capsule. Opium has been used for centuries in medicine as a drug for the relief of pain. Although still sometimes given in the form of laudanum (tincture of opium), its main legal uses today include the extraction of its active ingredients—*morphine (first isolated in 1803), codeine, papaverine, etc.—and preparation of their derivatives (e.g. heroin). Because opium causes *drug dependence and overdosage can be fatal, its preparation and use are strictly controlled. (Illegal trading continues however.) India and Turkey are the main opium-producing countries.

Opium Wars 1. (1839–42) The war between Britain and China brought on by the confiscation by the Chinese Government of British opium stores in Canton and the murder of a Chinese by British sailors. The British victory led to five Chinese ports being opened to British trade and residence. 2. (1856–60) The war between Britain and France, on one side, and China. The allied victory opened further ports to western trade.

Oporto 41 09N 8 37W The second largest city in Portugal, on the River Douro near the Atlantic coast. It is famous for the export (chiefly to Britain) of its port wine. Population (1987): 350 000.

opossum An American *marsupial, the only type found outside Australasia. The common, or Virginian, opossum (*Didelphys marsupialis*) is cat-sized, with a large pouch containing up to 16 teats.

Oppenheimer, J. Robert (1904–67) US physicist, who contributed to quantum mechanics and particle physics. In 1943 he was put in charge of the development of the atom bomb at Los Alamos, New Mexico. After the war he opposed the development of the hydrogen bomb and was labelled a security risk by Senator Joseph *McCarthy's committee.

opposition An alignment of two celestial bodies in the solar system, usually the sun and a planet, that occurs when they lie directly opposite each other in the sky. The angle planet-earth-sun is then 180°.

optical activity The rotation of the plane of polarization of plane *polarized light as it passes through certain solutions and crystals. The angle through which the plane is rotated is directly proportional to the path length of the light in the substance and, in the case of a solution, to its concentration. If the plane is rotated clockwise (looking at the oncoming light) the substance is said to be dextrorotatory. Laevorotatory substances rotate the plane anticlockwise.

optics The branch of physics concerned with *light and vision. Optics is divided into two major branches: geometrical optics studies the geometry of light rays as they pass through an optical system; physical optics concerns light's properties (e.g. *diffraction, *interference, and polarization) and its interaction with matter (e.g. in *refraction, scattering, and absorption).

Opuntia. *See* prickly pear.

oracle A response given by a deity, usually through a priest or priestess, to an individual's inquiry; also, the sacred place at which such responses were sought. Although occurring in Egyptian and other ancient civilizations, the best-known oracles were those of classical Greece, especially the oracle of Apollo at Delphi.

Oracle. *See* teletext.

oral contraceptive A drug containing hormones—usually a mixture of an *oestrogen and a synthetic *progesterone—taken in the form of tablets ("the Pill") by women to prevent conception and pregnancy. Oral contraceptives act by preventing the monthly release of an egg cell from the ovary. They may cause depression, high blood pressure, weight gain, and in rare cases thrombosis.

orange A *citrus fruit with a dimpled orange or yellow rind and a juicy pulp, rich in sugars, acids, and vitamin C. The orange tree is a small evergreen, cultivated throughout the tropics and subtropics, with fragrant white flowers. The sweet orange is eaten fresh while the Seville orange is used to make marmalade. Oranges are also used in soft drinks and confectionery. *See also* tangerine.

Orange The ruling dynasty of the Netherlands since 1815. In the 16th century *William

the Silent Prince of Orange-Nassau, led the *Revolt of the Netherlands against Spain. He and his descendants (one of whom became *William III of England) were stadholders (chief magistrates) of the *United Provinces of the Netherlands until its collapse in 1795. In 1815 the family were restored as monarchs of the newly established kingdom of the Netherlands.

Orange Free State An inland province in South Africa, consisting mainly of the undulating plain of the Highveld. Agriculture is the leading economic activity. Mining has developed recently; diamonds, gold, uranium, and coal are produced. First settled by Voortrekkers in the early 19th century, the area was under British rule from 1848 until an independent Orange Free State was recognized in 1854. It joined the Union of South Africa in 1910. Area: 129 152 sq km (49 886 sq mi). Population (1987): 1 863 327. Capital: Bloemfontein.

Orange Order An Irish society, named after William III of England (previously William of Orange), pledged to maintain the Protestant succession. Formed in 1795, following William's defeat of the Roman Catholic former king James II, it organized Ulster resistance to the *Home Rule movement and is now the backbone of the pro-British party in Northern Ireland.

Orange River A river in SW Africa. Rising in NE Lesotho, it flows mainly W across the South African plateau to the Atlantic Ocean. The largest river in South Africa, it forms part of the border between South Africa and Namibia. In 1963 the Orange River Project was begun to provide, through a series of dams, irrigation and hydroelectric power. Length: 2093 km (1300 mi).

orang-utan A long-armed great *ape, *Pongo pygmaeus*, of Borneo and Sumatra. Orang-utans grow up to 120 cm tall, have long coarse reddish-brown hair, and are mainly vegetarian. They are the only great apes outside Africa.

oratorio A musical composition, usually on a religious subject, for soloists, chorus, and orchestra. The name derives from the Oratory of St Philip Neri in 16th-century Rome where semidramatized versions of biblical stories were performed with musical accompaniment. Among notable oratorios are the *St Matthew* and *St John Passions* of J. S. Bach, Handel's *Messiah*, Haydn's *The Creation*, Mendelssohn's *Elijah*, Elgar's *Dream of Gerontius*, and Tippett's *A Child of Our Time*.

orbital An atomic orbital is the region around the nucleus in which it is likely that an electron will be found. Each orbital has a fixed energy and a shape determined by three quantum numbers, one (n) indicating the most probable distance of the electron from the nucleus, one (l) giving its angular momentum, and one (m) giving the orientation of the orbital if it is not spherical. In the formation of a covalent bond between two atoms, a molecular orbital containing two electrons is formed. *See also* wave mechanics.

orchid A flowering plant of which there are about 20 000 species found worldwide, especially in damp tropical regions. Most temperate orchids grow normally in the soil; while tropical orchids tend to grow on trees. Each flower consists of three petal-like sepals and three petals – the lowest being very distinctive. The stamens and stigma form a central column that bears pollen grains grouped into masses, which are transferred to other flowers by insects. The flowers of many species can be pollinated only by a particular species of insect; examples are the bee, fly, and spider orchids. Many orchids are cultivated as garden and pot plants. *See also* slipper orchid; vanilla.

Order in Council A command or direction issued by the queen with the advice of the *Privy Council, although in fact it is issued only with the advice of the cabinet.

Order of Merit (OM) A British order of chivalry, instituted in 1902. It consists of the sovereign and not more than 24 men and women of great distinction.

Order of the British Empire, The Most Excellent A British order of knighthood, instituted in 1917 and having five classes: Knights or Dames Grand Cross (GBE); Knights or Dames Commanders (KBE or DBE); Commanders (CBE); Officers (OBE); and Members (MBE).

orders of architecture The fundamental elements of classical architecture (*see illustration at* architecture), comprising five main types of supportive column – Doric, Tuscan, Ionic, Corinthian, and Composite. The column was developed by the Greeks and Romans to such an extent that the proportions between its constituent parts determined the proportions of the entire building. Each order usually consists of four main parts, the base, shaft, *capital, and entablature (the part of the building above the column), these having individual shapes and types of decoration.

Ordnance Survey The official map-making body of the UK. Established in 1791, following the mapping of Scotland (1726–90), it published its first map in 1801. Maps ranging from the large-scale 1:1250 (used for major urban areas) to the small-scale 1:1 000 000 (covering the entire UK in two parts) have since been produced. The original scale to be used was the 1:63 360, indicating that 1 inch on the map represented one 1 mile, or 63 360 inches. This was converted to the metric scale of 1:50 000 in the 1970s and remains the most widely used scale. The First Series of the 1:50 000 was completed in 1976 and is gradually being replaced by a Second Series with redrawn maps. *See also* digital mapping.

Ordovician period A geological period of the Lower Palaeozoic era, between the Cambrian and Silurian periods. It lasted from about 515 to 445 million years ago. It is divided into the Upper and Lower Ordovician.

ore A rock body or mineral deposit from which one or more useful materials, usually metals, can be economically extracted. The gangue is the waste material left when the desired mineral has been extracted.

oregano An aromatic herb, *Origanum vulgare*, native to the Mediterranean and W Asia. The dried leaves and flowers are used as a flavouring in cookery and the plant is a source of oils used in perfumery.

Oregon A state in the USA, on the NW Pacific coast. Oregon is the nation's leading timber state and approximately half its area is forested. Oregon became a state in 1859, following considerable migration of White settlers from the Midwest. Area: 251 180 sq km (96 981 sq mi). Population (1987 est): 2 690 000. Capital: Salem.

Orestes In Greek legend, the son of *Agamemnon, King of Mycenae, and Clytemnestra. Encouraged by his sister *Electra, he avenged his father's murder by killing his mother and her lover Aegisthus.

orfe A carnivorous fish, *Idus idus*, also called ide, caught for food and sport and found in rivers and lakes of Europe and NW Asia. Its stout elongated body, 30–50 cm long, is blue-grey or blackish with a silvery belly. The golden orfe is a reddish-gold variety.

Orff, Carl (1895–1982) German composer, teacher, conductor, and editor. He developed his own style of composition using lively rhythms; his best-known work is the oratorio *Carmina Burana* (1935–36).

organ A musical wind instrument originating in the 3rd century BC. The modern organ consists of a large number of pipes of increasing size, some of which contain reeds, fitted over a wind chest and blown by manual or electric bellows. The pipes are made to sound by pressing keys or pedals. Each pipe sounds one note, but groups of duplicate pipes, called stops, can be made to sound together or successively. Different stops produce different sounds, many of which resemble orchestral instruments. An organ console may have as many as five or more keyboards, as well as pedals. Each keyboard has a separate range of stops and different characteristics. The modern **electronic organ** consists of a series of electronic oscillators to produce notes, which are then amplified.

organic chemistry. *See* chemistry.

Organisation de l'Armée secrète (OAS) An organization established in 1961 by French settlers in Algeria opposed to Algerian independence from France. Its campaign of terrorism in Algeria and France included the attempted assassination of the French president, de Gaulle. In 1962, de Gaulle agreed to Algerian independence and the OAS collapsed.

Organization of African Unity (OAU) An intergovernmental organization of independent African countries. It was founded in 1963 to discuss political and economic problems affecting African states and to agree policies towards such problems.

Organization of American States (OAS) A body founded in 1948 to strengthen mutual understanding and cooperation between American republics, and security. It is based on the principle of the *Monroe Doctrine. Cuba was expelled in 1962.

Organization of Central American States An international organization founded in 1951. Its members include Costa Rica, El Salvador, Guatemala, Honduras, and Nicaragua, and its headquarters are in Guatemala City. Its aim is to encourage social, cultural, and economic development through joint action.

Organization of Petroleum Exporting Countries (OPEC) An organization founded in 1960 to represent the interests of the 11 chief oil-exporting nations (Abu Dhabi, Algeria, Indonesia, Iran, Iraq, Kuwait, Libya, Nigeria, Qatar, Saudi Arabia, and Venezuela) in dealings with the major oil companies. In recent years it has been split by internal dissension.

organ-pipe cactus A tall branching *cactus, *Lemacrocereus thurberi*, which resembles a candelabra and is found in deserts of the S USA and Mexico.

orienteering A navigational sport, held over rugged country, that began in Sweden in 1918 and is designed to test both intellectual and athletic ability. Using a map and compass, competitors run round a series of control points that must be visited in a set order.

origin of life. *See* life.

Orinoco, River The third largest river system in South America. Rising in S Venezuela, it flows in an arc forming part of the Venezuela–Colombia border before entering the Atlantic Ocean via an extensive delta region. Drainage basin area: 940 000 sq km (365 000 sq mi). Length: about 2575 km (1600 mi).

oriole A songbird occurring mainly in African and Asian tropical forests. Orioles generally have a black-and-yellow plumage, measure 18–30 cm, and feed on fruit and insects. The golden oriole (*Oriolus oriolus*) is the only species reaching Europe, visiting Britain in the summer. American orioles belong to a different family. They usually have a black plumage with red, yellow, or brown markings.

Orion A very conspicuous constellation that can be seen from most parts of the world. The brightest stars, Rigel and the slightly fainter *Betelgeuse, lie at opposite corners of a quadrilateral of stars with Bellatrix and Saiph at the other corners. Inside the quadrilateral three 2nd-magnitude stars form **Orion's Belt**, S of which lies the **Orion nebula.**

Orkney Islands (*or* Orkneys) A group of about 70 islands off the N coast of Scotland, separated from the mainland by the Pentland Firth. The chief ones are Mainland (Pomona), South Ronaldsay, Westray, Sanday, and Hoy. The population is of Scandinavian descent, reflecting the Islands' long connections with Norway and Denmark. It became an island authority in 1975. Agriculture, producing chiefly beef cattle and poultry, is of major importance. It serves as a base for the exploitation of North Sea oil. Area: 974 sq km (376 sq mi). Population (1987 est): 19 388. Administrative centre: Kirkwall.

Orléans 47 54N 1 54E A city in N France, the capital of the Loiret department on the River Loire. In 1429 the city was delivered from the English by Joan of Arc. Its cathedral, which was destroyed by the Huguenots in 1568, was rebuilt in the 17th century. The focal point of road and rail routes, Orléans has an extensive trade in wine, brandy, and agricultural produce. Population (1982): 105 589.

Orléans, Louis Philippe Joseph, Duc d' (1747–93) French revolutionary. A cousin of Louis XVI of France, he nevertheless supported the rebellious Third Estate at the beginning of the *French Revolution, joining the radical Jacobins in 1791. He was executed after his son (later King Louis Philippe) had joined the Austrian alliance against France.

ornithology The scientific study of birds. Ornithologists undertake serious studies into bird behaviour, distribution, ecology, and other aspects of bird biology. Numbered rings (called "bands" in North America) are used to mark birds to trace their migrations, determine mortality rates, and undertake other studies. Some conservation organizations (e.g. the *Royal Society for the Protection of Birds) are devoted to the protection and conservation of birds and their habitats.

orogeny A period of mountain building. Several major orogenies have occurred in the earth's geological history, major ones since the Precambrian including the Caledonian (in the Lower Palaeozoic) and the Alpine (in the Tertiary). **Orogenesis** is the process of mountain building, including folding, faulting, and thrusting, resulting from the collision of two continents, which compresses the sediment between them into mountain chains (*see* plate tectonics).

Orpheus A legendary Greek poet and musician, the son of the muse Calliope by either Apollo or Oeagrus, King of Thrace. After sailing with the *Argonauts he married *Eurydice. After her death, he descended to Hades to recover her. *Persephone, charmed by his playing on the lyre, released Eurydice but Orpheus lost her when he disobeyed the gods' command not to look back at her. He was murdered by the Maenads, followers of *Dionysus.

orrisroot The fragrant rhizome (underground stem) of several European iris plants. It is dried and ground for use in perfumes and medicines.

orthodontics. *See* dentistry.

Orthodox Church The group of self-governing Churches historically associated with the eastern part of the Roman Empire and separated from the Latin Church since 1054; also called the Eastern Orthodox Church. The four ancient patriarchs (leading bishops) of Orthodoxy are in Constantinople, Alexandria, Antioch, and Jerusalem; in addition there are patriarchs of Moscow, Georgia, Serbia, Bulgaria, and Romania. Independent Orthodox Churches exist in Greece, Cyprus, Albania, Czechoslovakia, and Poland. There are numerous congregations in other countries. Government is by bishops, priests, and deacons. The Orthodox Church claims the authority of *apostolic succession and regards itself as the one true Church, accepting as doctrine only the *Nicene Creed. Its worship is centred on the *Eucharist. Easter is the main feast of the Church year. *See also* Greek Orthodox Church; Russian Orthodox Church.

orthopaedics The branch of medicine concerned with treating deformities caused by disease of and injury to the bones and joints. This includes the use of surgery (especially for artificial hip joints), manipulation, traction, etc., in correcting deformities and fractures, together with teaching patients to cope with their disabilities.

ortolan A *bunting, *Emberiza hortulana*, of Europe and Asia. It is about 16 cm long, having a brown-streaked plumage with a yellow throat and pinkish belly. Large numbers are slaughtered on their autumn migration to N Africa and the Middle East because they are considered a delicacy in some countries.

Orwell, George (Eric Blair; 1903–50) British novelist and essayist, born in India. His works include *Down and Out in Paris and London* (1933), *The Road to Wigan Pier* (1937), *Homage to Catalonia* (1936), *Animal Farm* (1945), and *Nineteen Eighty Four* (1949).

oryx A desert antelope, *Oryx gazella*, of S and E Africa. Oryxes have long slender straight horns and are greyish brown with black markings on the face and legs. The white Arabian oryx (*O. leucoryx*) and the greyish-white N African scimitar-horned oryx (*O. tao*) are both endangered species.

Osaka 34 40N 135 30E A port in Japan, in SW Honshu on the Yodo delta. The third largest city in Japan, it was a leading commercial centre by the 17th century. Together with Kobe, Kyoto, and several small cities it forms the **Osaka-Kobe** industrial area, of major importance. Population (1989 est): 2 633 008.

Osborne, John (1929–) British dramatist, one of the original *Angry Young Men, best known for his play *Look Back in Anger* (1956). His criticism of modern Britain continued in such plays as *The Entertainer* (1957), *A Patriot for Me* (1965), and *West of Suez* (1971). Other plays include *Luther* (1960) and *Inadmissible Evidence* (1964).

Oscar An award given annually by the Academy of Motion Picture Arts and Sciences, founded in Hollywood in 1927, for excellence in acting, writing, directing, or other aspects of film production.

oscilloscope. *See* cathode-ray oscilloscope.

osier A small *willow tree, *Salix viminalis*, with flexible hairy branches used in basket making. Osiers are found in marshy areas throughout central and S Eurasia and often cultivated.

Osiris The Egyptian god of the dead, the brother and husband of *Isis; as the father of *Horus (the sun), he was also the god of renewal and rebirth. He was killed by his evil brother *Set. After Isis had magically reconstructed his body, he became ruler of the underworld. Dead pharaohs became identified with Osiris.

Oslo (former name (1877–1925): Kristiania) 59 56N 10 54E The capital and main port of Norway, situated in the SE at the head of Oslo Fjord. It is the financial and industrial centre of Norway. Founded in the 11th century, Oslo became capital in 1299 and developed into an important trading post under the influence of the Hanseatic League. Population (1988): 453 730.

osmium (Os) An extremely hard bluish-silver metal of the platinum group. It is one of the densest elements known (relative density 22.6). Its major use is in the production of hard alloys with other noble metals (gold, silver, platinum, etc.) for pen nibs and electrical contacts. At no 76; at wt 190.2; mp 3045 ± 20°C; bp 5027 ± 100°C.

osmosis The passage of a solvent from a less concentrated into a more concentrated solution through a semipermeable membrane (one allowing the passage of solvent, but not solute, molecules). Osmosis stops if the pressure of the more concentrated solution exceeds that of the less concentrated solution by an amount known as the **osmotic pressure** between them. In living organisms the solvent is water and osmosis plays an important role in bringing about the distribution of water in plants and animals, causing water to pass into and out of cells.

osprey A large *hawk, *Pandion haliaetus*, also called fish hawk, occurring worldwide (except in South America). It is 65 cm long and its plumage is brown above and white below. It feeds almost entirely on fish caught in its talons, which are covered in rough spikes to help grasp prey.

Ostend 1 13N 2 55E A seaport in NW Belgium, on the North Sea. Ostend is the headquarters of the country's fishing fleet and maintains a cross-Channel ferry service to Dover, England. Population (1989): 68 366.

osteoarthritis A disease of the joints, mainly back, hips, and knees, in which their internal surfaces are rubbed away and they become swollen and painful. This becomes increasingly common as people grow old. Treatment is with drugs, and with replacement of joints by artificial hips and knees. *See also* arthritis.

osteopathy A system of healing by manipulation and massage, based on the theory that nearly all diseases are due to the displacement of bones, especially the bones of the spine. Osteopathy is of benefit in treating dislocations, fractures, and disorders of the joint, but it is not legally recognized as a branch of mainstream medicine.

Ostia A town of ancient Rome, at the mouth of the River Tiber. A major naval base under the Republic, its prosperity was greatest in the 2nd century AD, when it was an important commercial centre.

ostrich A fast-running flightless African bird, *Struthio camelus*, occurring in open grassland and semidesert regions. It is the largest living bird. Males may reach 2.5 m tall and are black with white wing and tail plumes; females are smaller and mainly brown. Ostriches have a long almost naked neck, a small head, and a ducklike bill used to feed on plant material.

Ostrogoths A branch of the *Goths, forced W of the River Dniester by the *Huns (375 AD). In the 6th century they frequently invaded N Italy and captured much of the Balkans. Between 493 and 526 Theodoric (c. 445–526), their leader, ruled Italy. The Roman Empire later destroyed the Ostrogoths (562).

Oswald, Saint (c. 605–41) King of Northumbria (634–41) after defeating and killing the Welsh king, Cadwallader. He restored Christianity in Northumbria with the help of St *Aidan. Oswald was killed in battle by Penda. Feast day: 5 Aug.

Oświęcim (German name: Auschwitz) 50 02N 19 11E A town in S Poland, site of a notorious Nazi concentration camp during World War II. Population (1982 est): 45 200.

Ottawa 45 25N 75 43W The capital of Canada, in SE Ontario on the Ottawa River. It is two-thirds English speaking and one-third French speaking. Founded in the early 19th century as a lumbering centre, it became national capital in 1867. Population (1986): 300 763.

otter A carnivorous mammal found worldwide except in Polar regions, Australasia, and Madagascar. Otters spend a lot of time in water; they have waterproof fur, short legs, partially webbed feet, and a thick tapering tail. The Eurasian otter (*Lutra lutra*) is about 1.2 m long. The sea otter (*Enhydra lutris*) lives in the N Pacific.

otterhound A breed of dog once used to hunt otters. It is a strongly built powerful swimmer with large webbed feet and a large head with long drooping ears. Otterhounds have a dense water-resistant undercoat and a long shaggy outer coat.

Otto (I) the Great (912–73 AD) Holy Roman Emperor (936–73; crowned 962). He subdued his rebellious vassals, defeated a Hungarian invasion at the great victory of Lechfeld (955), and extended his influence into Italy.

Otto, Nikolaus August (1832–91) German engineer, who in 1876 devised the four-stroke cycle, known as the Otto cycle, for the *internal-combustion engine. His engine made the development of the motor car possible.

Ottoman Empire A Turkish Muslim empire ruling large parts of the Middle East as well as territories in Europe from the 14th to the 20th centuries. Its capital was *Istanbul (formerly Constantinople) and its rulers descendants of its founder Osman I (c. 1258–c. 1326). Originating around 1300 as a small Turkish state in Asia Minor, in 1453 the Ottomans captured Constantinople and destroyed the Eastern Roman (Byzantine) Empire. Ottoman power reached its peak in the 16th century with the conquest of Egypt and Syria (1517) and, under *Suleiman the Magnificent, Hungary (1529) and territories in the Middle East and N Africa. From the 17th century the Empire declined. In World War I the Ottomans supported Germany and defeat brought the loss of territories outside Asia Minor. The nationalist revolution of Kemal *Atatürk replaced the Ottoman Empire with the state of Turkey (1922).

Ouagadougou 12 25N 1 30W The capital of Burkina Faso, founded in the 11th century as the centre of a Mossi empire. Population (1985): 442 223.

Oudry, Jean-Baptiste (1686–1755) French *rococo painter and tapestry designer, head of the *Beauvais (1734) and *Gobelin (1736) tapestry works. His illustrations to La Fontaine's *Fables* are particularly well known.

ounce. *See* snow leopard.

Ouse, River The name of several rivers in England, including: **1.** A river in NE England, flowing mainly NE through Yorkshire to join the River Trent, forming the Humber estuary. Length: 92 km (57 mi). **2.** A river in S England, flowing E and S across the South Downs to the English Channel at Newhaven. Length: 48 km (30 mi). *See also* Great Ouse River.

ouzel. *See* ring ouzel.

ovary **1.** The organ of female animals in which the *egg cells (ova) are produced. In mammals (including women) there are two ovaries close to the openings of the Fallopian tubes, which lead to the uterus (womb). They produce both eggs and steroid hormones (*see* oestrogens; progesterone) in a regular cycle (*see* menstruation). **2.** The part of a flower that contains the *ovules. It is situated at the base of the carpel(s) and becomes the fruit wall after fertilization.

Ovett, Steve (1955–) British middle-distance runner. He was a gold medallist in the 800 m event at the 1980 Olympic Games and in the 5000 m event in the 1986 Commonwealth games.

Ovid (Publius Ovidius Naso; 43 BC–17 AD) Roman poet. His poems include the *Amores* and the *Ars amatoria*, on the theme of love. His greatest work, the *Metamorphoses*, is a poem in 15 books including mythological and historical tales. In 8 AD he was exiled by the emperor Augustus to the Black Sea.

ovule The structure within the ovary of a *flower that contains an egg cell and nutritive tissue. After fertilization it develops into the *seed containing the embryo.

ovum. *See* egg.

Owen, Dr David (Anthony Llewellyn) (1938–) British politician. As a Labour MP, he was foreign secretary (1977–79). A cofounder of the Social Democratic Party, he became leader in 1983 but refused to participate in the formation of the Social and Liberal Democratic Party in 1988, remaining leader of a reduced SDP. He wound up the SDP in 1990 and sat as an independent social democrat.

Owen, Wilfred (1893–1918) British poet. His poetry written during World War I includes "Strange Meeting" and "Anthem for Doomed Youth." He was killed in action. His friend Siegfried *Sassoon edited his *Poems* (1920).

Owens, Jesse (John Cleveland O.; 1913–80) US athlete. In 1935 he set six world records in 45 minutes (in the long jump, 100 yards, 220 yards, 220 metres, 220 yards hurdles, and 220 metres hurdles). At the Berlin Olympics (1936) he won four gold medals; this success of a Black athlete went against the racist theories of Hitler.

owl A nocturnal bird of prey occurring worldwide. Owls have a large head with large forward facing eyes, soft plumage, usually brown and patterned, and a short sharp hooked bill. They hunt mammals, birds, and insects and range in size from 16 cm (pygmy owls) to 70 cm (eagle owls). *See* barn owl; tawny owl.

ox. *See* cattle.

oxalic acid (*or* ethanedioic acid; (COOH)$_2$) A colourless poisonous soluble crystalline solid. Potassium and sodium salts are found in plants. Oxalic acid is used as a metal cleaner and for bleaching textiles and leather.

oxeye daisy A plant, *Chrysanthemum leucanthemum*, also called moon daisy or marguerite, found in grassland and wasteland throughout Europe. Its flower heads resemble large daisies.

OXFAM A British charity founded in 1942, and registered in 1948 as the Oxford Committee for Famine Relief. Its purpose is to relieve suffering, throughout the world, caused by natural disaster or lack of resources. Its long-term projects include medical, social, and economic research and training schemes.

Oxford 51 46N 1 15W A city in S central England, the administrative centre of Oxfordshire on the Rivers Thames and Cherwell. Oxford is famous as a centre of learning (*see* Oxford, University of). The college buildings dominate the centre of the city but there is considerable industrial development, particularly the huge motor-car works at Cowley. It has one of the world's greatest libraries (the *Bodleian Library, 1602). Population (1983 est): 116 000.

Oxford, Provisions of (1258) The scheme of government reform imposed upon Henry III by his barons at Oxford following their opposition to excessive taxation. His rejection of the Provisions (1261) led to the *Barons' War.

Oxford, University of One of the oldest universities in Europe, dating from the 12th century. It is organized as an association of colleges, which are governed by their own teaching staff ("Fellows"). The University organizes a lecture programme, maintains the large libraries (such as the *Bodleian Library), and conducts examinations. The first college, University College, was founded in 1249. Other notable colleges include All Souls (founded 1438), Christ Church (founded in 1546 by Cardinal Wolsey), and Lady Margaret Hall (founded 1878), the first women's college. Modern colleges include Nuffield (1937), Wolfson (1966), and Green (1979), all for postgraduates.

Oxford Group. *See* Moral Rearmament.

Oxford Movement A movement within the Church of England in the 19th century aimed at emphasizing the Catholic principles on which it rested. Led by *Newman, John Keble (1792–1866), Edward Pusey (1800–82), and James Froude (1818–94) of Oxford University, it was started in 1833 and gave new strength to Anglicanism. *See also* Anglo-Catholicism.

Oxfordshire A county in the South Midlands of England. It consists mainly of a broad vale, crossed by the River Thames, with the *Chiltern Hills in the SE and the *Cotswold Hills in the NW. It is chiefly agricultural. Area: 2611 sq km (1008 sq mi). Population (1987 est): 578 000. Administrative centre: Oxford.

oxidation and reduction Oxidation is the chemical combination of a substance with oxygen. An example is the combustion of carbon to carbon dioxide: $C + O_2 \rightarrow CO_2$. The opposite process, removal of oxygen, is known as reduction; an example is the reduction of iron oxide to iron: $Fe_2O_3 + 3C \rightarrow 2Fe + 3CO$. Reduction also refers to reaction with hydrogen and oxidation to removal of hydrogen. More generally, an oxidation reaction is one involving loss of electrons and a reduction reaction is one in which electrons are gained. Usually oxidation and reduction reactions occur together. Thus, in the reaction of iron(III) ions (Fe^{3+}) with tin(II) ions (Sn^{2+}), the iron(III) ions are reduced to iron(II) ions (Fe^{2+}) and the tin(II) ions oxidized to tin

(IV) ions (Sn^{4+}). Reactions of this type are called **redox reactions**.

oxidation number (*or* oxidation state) The number of electrons that would have to be added to an atom to neutralize it. Thus Na^+, Cl^-, and He have oxidation numbers of 1, −1, and 0, respectively. Rules have been developed for assigning oxidation numbers to covalently bound atoms depending on the electric charge that the atom would have if the molecule ionized.

oxpecker An African songbird, related to starlings, that feeds on ticks and maggots pecked from the hides of cattle and game animals.

oxygen (O) A colourless odourless gas discovered by J. *Priestley. The element exists in two forms—the diatomic molecule (O_2), which constitutes 21% of the earth's atmosphere, and trace amounts of the highly reactive triatomic molecule, *ozone. Oxygen is very reactive and forms oxides with most elements. In addition to its vital importance for plants and animals, its major use is in the production of steel in blast furnaces. It is obtained by the *distillation of liquid air. At no 8; at wt 15.9994; mp −218.4°C; bp −182.96°C.

oxygen cycle The process by which oxygen —present in the atmosphere or dissolved in water —is taken in by plants and animals for use in *respiration (i.e. the combustion of food to provide energy) and released into the environment as a waste product, mostly in the form of free oxygen (by plants in *photosynthesis). Oxygen is often combined in organic and inorganic compounds, which may also be considered as part of the cycle. *See also* carbon cycle; nitrogen cycle.

oyster A *bivalve mollusc found in temperate and warm seas. The lower shell valve is larger and flatter than the upper valve; they are held together by an elastic ligament and powerful muscles. Edible oysters are cultivated for their white flesh; pearl oysters are cultivated for their pearls, which they make by coating a grain of sand lodged inside their shell with chalky material.

oystercatcher A black or black-and-white wading bird, occurring in temperate and tropical coastal regions. 40–50 cm long, oystercatchers have a long or flattened orange-red bill used for opening oysters and similar molluscs and probing in mud for worms and crustaceans.

ozone (O_3) A pale blue gaseous form of *oxygen, formed by passing an electrical discharge through oxygen (O_2). Ozone is a poisonous unstable gas. It is used as an oxidizing agent, for example in water purification. It is present in small amounts in the atmosphere, mostly in the **ozone layer**, which forms 10–50 km (6–30 mi) above the earth's surface as a result of solar ultraviolet radiation on molecular oxygen. The ozone layer absorbs in the 230–320 nm waveband, protecting the earth from dangerous excessive ultraviolet radiation. There is concern that the amount of ozone is being reduced by its reaction with man-made chemicals, especially CFCs (chlorofluorocarbons) used in refrigeration air-cooling systems, in the production of foamed plastic, and as propellants in aerosol cans (*see* pollution).

P

pacemaker A specialized heart muscle situated in the right upper chamber (atrium) that contracts spontaneously: the impulse to contract is transmitted from the pacemaker to both atria and then to the ventricles, creating the heartbeat. If the pacemaker ceases to function (heart block) it may be replaced by an artificial battery-operated device that stimulates the heart to contract.

Pacific Ocean The world's largest and deepest ocean, covering a third of its surface. It extends between Asia, Australia, Antarctica, and America. It reaches its maximum depth in the *Marianas Trench.

Padang 1 00S 100 21E A port in Indonesia, in W Sumatra. An early Dutch settlement, it flourished when railways were built in the 19th century. It exports coal, cement, coffee, copra, and rubber. Population (1980): 480 922.

Paderewski, Ignacy (Jan) (1860–1941) Polish musician and statesman. He achieved an international reputation as a pianist and composed a piano concerto and many solo pieces. He was the first prime minister (1919) of Poland but resigned after ten months to return to music.

Padua (Italian name: Padova) 45 24N 11 53E A city in NE Italy, near Venice. An important city in Roman and Renaissance times, it has several notable buildings, including the Basilica of St Anthony. Machinery and textiles are produced. Population (1987): 223 907.

paediatrics The branch of medicine concerned with illnesses of infants and children, including the management of handicaps at home and in school as well as the treatment and prevention of childhood diseases.

Pagalu. *See* Equatorial Guinea, Republic of.

Paganini, Niccolò (1782–1840) Italian virtuoso violinist. He astonished European audiences with his technique and composed six violin concertos, a set of variations on the G string, and other works.

pagoda A tower for housing relics of the Buddha. Pagodas originated in India, whence they spread to Sri Lanka, SE Asia, China, and Japan. The pagoda is usually a vertical arrangement of units of the same shape but decreasing size.

paint A finely powdered insoluble pigment suspended in a binding medium; on application to a surface the volatile components evaporate, the drying oils oxidize, and the resins polymerize, leaving a decorative or protective skin. The binding medium consists of a drying oil (e.g. linseed oil or tung oil), a resin (rosin or a synthetic alkyd), a thinner (turpentine, benzene, etc.), and a drier (e.g. lead linoleate) to accelerate film formation. Water-based emulsion paints consist of emulsions of a synthetic resin in water.

painted lady An orange, black, and white butterfly, *Vanessa cardui*, of worldwide distribution. It cannot survive cold winters but migrates

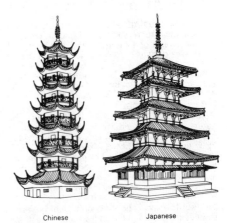

Chinese   Japanese

PAGODA *The exuberantly curving roofs of the typical multi-storeyed Chinese pagoda contrast with the more restrained Japanese form.*

from warmer regions each year. The caterpillars feed mainly on thistles and nettles.

Paisley, Ian (1926–) Northern Irish politician. A minister of the Free Presbyterian Church from 1946, he was a Protestant Unionist MP in the Northern Irish parliament (1970–72) before becoming (1974) a Democratic Unionist MP in the House of Commons.

Pakistan, Islamic Republic of A country in S Asia, bordering on Iran, Afghanistan, China, and India. 97% of the population is Muslim. *Economy*: mainly agricultural, producing rice, wheat, sugar cane, and cotton. Pakistan is a major exporter of cotton and cotton goods; steel, fertilizers, cement, sugar, and handicrafts are also produced. Fishing is increasingly important. Resources include coal, iron ore, copper, limestone, oil, and large quantities of natural gas. *History*: Pakistan was created (1947) from part of India to satisfy the Muslim League's demand for a separate state for the Muslim minority. It consisted of two areas; West Pakistan (Baluchistan, the Northwest Frontier, West Punjab, and Sind) and East Pakistan (East Bengal). The electoral victory in East Pakistan of the Awami League (1970), which demanded regional autonomy, led to its withdrawal as *Bangladesh (1971). In 1972, Pakistan withdrew from the British Commonwealth. Unrest following the 1977 elections led to a military coup in which Gen Mohammed Zia ul-Haq replaced and later executed the former prime minister, Zulfikar Ali *Bhutto (1979). Gen Zia became president of a strict Islamic regime in 1978 and was killed in an air crash in 1988. In the ensuing election Benazir Bhutto, daughter of

Zulfikar Bhutto, became the first woman prime minister of Pakistan. She was replaced in 1990 by Nawaz Sharif. Pakistan rejoined the Commonwealth in 1989. President: Ghulam Ishaq Khan. Official language: Urdu. Official currency: Pakistan rupee of 100 paise. Area (excluding Jammu and Kashmir): 803 943 sq km (310 322 sq mi). Population (1989 est): 105 400 000. Capital: Islamabad.

Palace of Westminster The British Houses of Parliament in Westminster, London, containing the House of Commons and the House of Lords (*see* parliament). A medieval royal palace until the 16th century, when it assumed its present function, it was largely burnt down in 1834, only the Great Hall surviving. It was rebuilt in the *gothic revival style by *Barry and *Pugin.

Palaeocene epoch. *See* Tertiary period.

Palaeolithic The earliest division of the *Stone Age. It extends from the emergence of man to the end of the last ice age and is divided into three phases: Lower, beginning 3 500 000 years ago and characterized by pebble-tool manufacture; Middle, beginning about 70 000 years ago and associated with *Neanderthal man; and Upper, beginning about 40 000 years ago and associated with *Cro-Magnon man.

palaeontology The study of ancient lifeforms from their *fossil remains in the rocks. Fossils are used to determine the geological history of rock strata.

Palaeozoic era The era of geological time between the Precambrian and the Mesozoic, lasting from about 590 to 240 million years ago. It is divided into the Lower Palaeozoic, which contains the Cambrian, Ordovician, and Silurian periods, and the Upper Palaeozoic, containing the Devonian, Carboniferous, and Permian.

palate The roof of the mouth. The soft palate at the back of the mouth is composed of *mucous membrane and prevents food passing into the nose during swallowing. The hard palate, further forward, is composed of two fused halves made up of the palatine bone and part of the maxillary (upper jaw) bones.

Palatinate Two regions of W Germany: the Lower (*or* Rhenish) Palatinate is now in Rheinland-Pfalz, Baden-Württemberg, and Hessen and the Upper Palatinate in Bavaria. From 1356 the counts palatine were electors of Holy Roman Emperors. In the early 19th century the Lower Palatinate was divided between France and various German states and the Upper Palatinate passed to Bavaria.

Palau. *See* Belau.

Palermo 38 08N 13 23E A port in Italy, the capital of Sicily. Founded by the Phoenicians in the 8th century BC, it became capital under the Arabs (9th–11th centuries). Its notable buildings include the gothic cathedral and the Norman palace. Population (1987): 728 843.

Palestine (*or* Holy Land) A historic and much disputed area in the Middle East that now comprises *Israel and territories belonging to Jordan and Egypt. In about 1000 BC a Hebrew kingdom was founded by Saul. Following the reign of Solomon it was split into Israel, later conquered by the Assyrians, and Judah (*see* Judaea), later conquered by the Babylonians. From the late 4th century AD many Jews left Palestine, which became a centre for Christian and Muslim pilgrimage (following Arab conquest in 636 AD). The Crusaders brought Christianity back to the area (1099 until the 13th century). After a period of Egyptian rule it fell to the Ottoman Turks (1516), who ruled it until World War I. The late 19th century saw the beginning of *Zionism and the return of Jews from the *Diaspora. In 1918 Palestine was captured by the British, who supported the demand for a Jewish nation in Palestine. This provoked unrest among the Arab population. In 1947 the UN divided Palestine into two separate states, Jewish and Arab. Britain renounced control in 1948. The state of Israel was then proclaimed, the rest of Palestine being divided between Jordan and Egypt. See also West Bank.

Palestine Liberation Organization (PLO) An organization of Palestinian groups opposed to Israel, led by Yassir Arafat's al-*Fatah. Terrorist actions carried out by the PLO include the murder of 11 Israeli athletes at the Munich Olympics (1972). In 1982 PLO forces were expelled from Lebanon, which they had been using as a base, when Israel invaded. PLO groups that remained later became involved in conflict with other groups within the country and in establishing a Palestinian state in the West Bank (declared in 1988).

Palladio, Andrea (1508–80) Italian architect, born in Padua, who developed the architectural style known as Palladianism, based on classical Roman public architecture. This was introduced into England in the early 17th century by Inigo Jones. Trained as a stonemason, he produced villas, palaces, and churches, the most famous being S Giorgio Maggiore in Venice (begun 1566).

palladium (Pd) A silvery-white metal that does not rust or tarnish, discovered by W. H. Wollaston (1766–1828) in 1803. Palladium readily absorbs hydrogen and is used as a catalyst for hydrogenation reactions; it is alloyed with gold to form white gold. At no 46; at wt 106.4; mp 1552°C; bp 3140°C.

Pallas Athena. *See* Athena.

palm A treelike plant occurring in tropical and subtropical regions. Ranging from 1 to 60 m in height, the trunk of the palm has no branches and is crowned with a cluster of very large leaves, which are fan-shaped or feather-like. Palms are commercially important as a source of food (*see* coconut; date; sago), oil (*see* oil palm), wax, and various fibres.

Palma (*or* Palma de Mallorca) 39 35N 2 39E The capital of the Spanish Balearic Islands, in Majorca. Its buildings include the gothic cathedral (1230–1601) and the 14th-century Bellver Castle. Noted as a tourist resort, it is also a port and commercial centre; industries include textiles, footwear, and pottery. Population (1986 est): 295 351.

Palmer, Samuel (1805–81) British landscape painter and etcher. His best landscapes, often moonlit and either in sepia or watercolour, were painted during his association (1826–35) with a group of painters in Shoreham.

Palmerston, Henry John Temple, 3rd Viscount (1784–1865) British statesman; foreign secretary (1830–34, 1835–41, 1846–51) and Liberal prime minister (1855–58, 1859–65). He entered parliament in 1807 as a Tory, serving as secretary for war from 1809 to 1828, but by 1830 he had joined the Whigs (later Liberals). As prime minister Palmerston supported the Confederacy in the US Civil War but was dissuaded by his colleagues from actively involving Britain.

Palmyra (or Tadmor) 34 36N 38 15E An ancient Syrian desert city on the route of the E–W caravan trade in the 2nd and 3rd centuries AD. The ruins of the ancient city include the remains of the Temple of Bel (Palmyra's chief god).

Pamirs (or Pamir) A mountainous area of central Asia, situated mainly in the Tadzhik SSR of the Soviet Union. Its highest point in the Soviet Union is Mount Communism, at 7495 m (24 590 ft). In China it reaches 7719 m (25 326 ft) at Kungur.

Pampas The flat treeless plains of Argentina. They are of major agricultural importance in the E, producing wheat, corn, and beef in particular.

pampas grass A South American *grass widely cultivated in gardens. The species *Cortaderia argentea* grows in clumps, with leaves up to 2 m long and flowering stems, over 3 m long, bearing silvery plumelike flowers.

Pamplona 42 49N 1 39W A city in NE Spain, in the Basque Provinces. It has a cathedral and holds a fiesta (during which bulls are driven through the streets). It is an agricultural centre and its industries include traditional crafts and chemicals. Population (1989 est): 183 423.

Pan The Greek god of shepherds and their flocks, the son of Hermes. He is usually portrayed with the legs, ears, and horns of a goat. He lived in the mountains and was associated especially with Arcadia, where he played his pipes (see panpipes).

Panama, Republic of A country in Central America, occupying the Isthmus of Panama. *Economy*: considerable revenue comes from the Panama Canal. The main agricultural products are bananas, rice, sugar, and maize; fishing (especially for shrimps) is also important. Industries include oil refining, cement production, and paper and food processing. *History*: discovered by Columbus in 1502 and colonized by the Spanish, Panama later became part of the viceroyalty of Peru and then of New Granada. In 1821 it became part of newly independent Colombia, from which it broke free in 1903 after a revolution supported by the USA. A military coup in 1968 brought Gen Omar Torrijos (1929–81) to power; after his death Gen Manuel Antonio Noriega (1938–) emerged as effective ruler. He was deposed by a US military task force and taken to the USA to face drug charges. President: Guillermo Endara Gallimany. Official language: Spanish. Official currency: balboa of 100 centésimos. Area: 78 046 sq km (30 134 sq mi). Population (1990 est): 2 420 000. Capital and main port: Panama City.

Panama Canal A canal across the Isthmus of Panama connecting the Atlantic and Pacific Oceans. Some 82 km (51 mi) long, it was begun in 1880 by the French Panama Canal Company under Ferdinand de *Lesseps. In 1903 the USA acquired the construction rights from Panama and the canal was opened in 1914. The USA also acquired sovereignty over the **Panama Canal Zone**, a region extending 8 km (5 mi) on either side of the canal. In 1978 two treaties provided for Panamanian sovereignty over the canal and the Zone by 2000. Area: 1676 sq km (647 sq mi).

Panama City 5 58N 79 31W The capital of Panama. Founded by the Spanish in 1519 on the site of an Indian fishing village, it was destroyed in 1671 and rebuilt two years later 8 km (5 mi) to the SW. It became capital of the newly independent Panama in 1904. Population (1987): 439 996.

pancreas A gland, about 15 cm long, in the abdomen behind the stomach. Food in the intestine causes the pancreas to secrete several digestive enzymes, which enter the intestine through the pancreatic duct. In addition, small clusters of cells (called islets of Langerhans) scattered throughout the pancreas secrete the hormones *insulin and glucagon.

panda A bearlike mammal related to raccoons. The rare giant panda (*Ailuropoda melanoleuca*) lives in the bamboo forests of central China, feeding on young bamboo shoots. Up to 1.6 m long, it has black and white markings. The red (or lesser) panda (*Ailurus fulgens*), lives in the forests of the Himalayas and W China. 80–110 cm long, it is reddish with black markings on its white face.

Pandora In Greek mythology, the first woman, fashioned by Hephaestus and invented by Zeus. She married Epimetheus, brother of Prometheus. Her dowry was a box, which, when opened, released all the varieties of evil and retained only hope.

pangolin A mammal of Africa and S Asia, also called scaly anteater. 30–80 cm long, its back is covered with horny scales. It feeds at night on ants and termites using its long sticky tongue.

Pankhurst, Emmeline (1858–1928) British suffragette, who founded the Women's Social and Political Union (1903). Imprisoned several times, she underwent hunger strikes and forcible feeding. During World War I, she encouraged the industrial recruitment of women. Her daughters **Dame Christabel Pankhurst** (1880–1958) and **Sylvia Pankhurst** (1882–1960) were also suffragettes.

panpipes (or syrinx) An ancient musical instrument consisting of a row of small pipes of increasing size bound together. According to Greek legend, when the nymph Syrinx was changed into a reed by Apollo, Pan made the instrument from the reed stem.

pansy A garden plant developed as a hybrid of the wild pansy (*Viola tricolor*) in the 19th century. The many varieties, up to 20 cm high, have coloured flowers. The wild pansy, or heartsease, found throughout Eurasia, has small purple, yellow, or white flowers. See also violet.

pantheism Any belief or doctrine presenting the natural world, including man, as part of the divine. Pantheism is a strong tendency in Hinduism but is frowned on by orthodox Christianity.

Pantheon 1. A temple dedicated to the worship of many gods. The Pantheon in Rome, begun in 27 BC but rebuilt about 118 AD, was circular and topped by a huge concrete dome; it became the Church of Sta Maria Rotonda in 609 AD. 2. A building honouring the famous, such as the Pantheon in Paris, designed by Jacques Soufflot (1713–80) in 1759.

panther A black variety of leopard. Panthers can occur among a litter of normally spotted leopards.

pantomime A British entertainment for children, traditionally performed at Christmas, developed during the 19th century from the harlequinade (see Harlequin). Based on fairy tales, the principal boy is traditionally played by a girl, and the dame, a comic old woman, by a man.

papal states The central Italian states under papal rule between 756 and 1870. They included parts of Emilia-Romagna, Marche, Umbria, and Lazio. They were taken over in the movement for Italian unification (see Risorgimento) in 1870. The popes refused to give up their claims until the *Lateran Treaty (1929) established the Vatican City as an independent papal state.

papaw (or papaya) A small tropical American tree, Carica papaya. About 7.5 m tall, it has yellowish fruits resembling long melons: the juicy pinkish flesh encloses a mass of seeds. The fruits are eaten fresh, boiled, and in preserves or in pickles.

Papeete 17 32S 149 34W The capital of French Polynesia, in NW Tahiti. A tourist centre, it is a stop on many Pacific routes. Population (1983): 62 735.

paper A substance made from a moist mixture (pulp) of the *cellulose fibres of wood, grass, cotton, etc. The Chinese invented paper (c. 2nd century BC), but the first successful mill in England was not set up until 1589. All early paper was handmade; a machine for making a continuous roll was invented in 1798, in France. Brought to England in 1803 by Henry Fourdrinier (1766–1854), this machine picked up the pulp on a travelling wire mesh and shook it until the fibres interlaced and the water drained off, before passing it through pressing and drying rollers. The pulp for papermaking is obtained chiefly from wood, but also from esparto grass and rags (for high-quality paper), and increasingly from recycled wastepaper.

papilloma A non-malignant tumour that grows from the surface of the skin or from the lining of a hollow organ, for example the bladder, womb, or lungs. *Warts and *polyps are types of papilloma.

paprika. See Capsicum.

Papua New Guinea, State of A country in the Pacific Ocean, E of Indonesia. It consists of the E part of *New Guinea and several islands, including the Bismarck Archipelago, the N part of the Solomon Islands, and the Admiralty Islands. Economy: subsistence agriculture with cash crops, such as coconuts, cocoa, coffee, and rubber. The chief mineral and export is copper. History: the SE part of the island of New Guinea was annexed by Queensland in 1883, becoming a British colony (Territory of Papua) in 1888. The NE part came under Australian rule in 1914 (Trust Territory of New Guinea). In 1921 the two territories were merged. Renamed Papua New Guinea in 1971, it achieved self-government in 1973, and became fully independent in 1975. Prime minister: Rabbie Namaliu. Official language: English; Pidgin is widely spoken. Official currency: kina of 100 toea. Area: 462 840 sq km (178 656 sq mi). Population (1987 est): 3 480 000. Capital and main port: Port Moresby.

papyrus An aquatic reedlike plant, Cyperus papyrus, up to 3 m tall, originally cultivated in the Nile delta of Egypt to make paper and now growing wild in parts of Africa and in Syria. The pith was a common food.

parabola The curve, formed by a *conic section, in which the distance from a fixed point (focus) and a fixed line (directrix) are equal. In *Cartesian coordinates a standard form of its equation is $y^2 = 4ax$, for a parabola that is symmetrical about the x-axis and cuts it at the origin (vertex).

Paracelsus (Theophrastus Bombastus von Hohenheim; 1493–1541) Swiss physician, who influenced the development of medicine during the Renaissance. He stressed the importance of chemical compounds in treating disease, rejected the notion that mental illness was caused by demons, and linked goitre with minerals in drinking water.

paraffin 1. (or kerosene) A mixture of *hydrocarbons that boil in the range 150–300°C and have a relative density of 0.78–0.83. It is obtained from crude *oil by distillation and is used as a fuel for domestic heating and for aircraft. 2. See alkanes.

paraffin wax A wax obtained during the refining of crude *oil. Fully refined, it is a white tasteless solid (mp 50–60°C) consisting of higher *alkanes; it is extensively used in the manufacture of waxed papers, candles, and polishes.

Paraguay, Republic of A country in the centre of South America. Economy: chiefly agricultural, livestock rearing and meat packing are the main occupations. Crops include cotton, soya beans, cassava, and sugar cane. Meat, cotton, and timber are the chief exports. History: colonized by the Spanish in the 16th century, it became independent of Spain in 1811, and in 1814 José Gaspar Rodríguez de Francia (1766–1840) was elected dictator. The population suffered great losses in the War of the *Triple Alliance and again in the Chaco War (1932–35) with Bolivia (see Gran Chaco). In 1954 Gen Alfredo Stroessner (1912–) seized power and became president; he was overthrown in a coup (1989) and after free elections Gen Andrés Rodríguez (1924–) was sworn in as president. Paraguay is a member of the OAS and LAFTA. Official language: Spanish; the majority speak Guaraní. Official currency: guaraní of 100 céntimos. Area: 406 752 sq km (157 042 sq mi). Population (1988 est): 4 040 000. Capital and main (river) port: Asunción.

Paraguayan War. See Triple Alliance, War of the.

parakeet A small seed-eating *parrot with a long tapering tail and a predominantly green plumage. It is found especially in SE Asia and Australia. Brightly coloured species are popular as cagebirds. *See also* budgerigar.

paralysis Failure of a muscle or group of muscles to work, usually as a result of damage to the nerve supplying the muscle, caused by injury or infection (*see* poliomyelitis). It may also be due to failure of the nerve impulse to be transmitted to the muscle (as in myasthenia gravis) or by wasting of the muscle (as in *muscular dystrophy). A *stroke causes damage to the part of the brain that controls movement and commonly results in **hemiplegia**, i.e. one half of the body and face becomes paralysed. **Paraplegia** (paralysed legs) results from injury to the spinal cord. **Quadriplegia** (paralysed legs and arms) results when the spinal cord is damaged close to the brain.

paramagnetism A form of *magnetism caused by the presence in atoms or molecules of electrons with unpaired spins. The atom or molecule therefore acts like a tiny magnet (*see* ferromagnetism). In the presence of an external magnetic field these microscopic magnets tend to align with the field, reinforcing it. The effect is destroyed by random thermal motion and in general the *permeability (a measure of the extent of alignment) is inversely proportional to the temperature.

Paramaribo 5 52N 55 14W The capital and main port of Suriname, near the N coast on the River Suriname. Founded by the French (1540), it was later under English and then Dutch rule. Population (1986 est): 77 558.

paranoia A mental disorder in which the patient is governed by irrational beliefs; he may believe that he is being persecuted, or that he is overwhelmingly important. The condition can result from *schizophrenia, *alcoholism, or manic-depressive psychosis.

paraplegia. *See* paralysis.

Paraquat ($C_9H_{20}N_2(SO_4)_2$) The trade name for a yellow water-soluble solid used as a weedkiller. Highly toxic, it concentrates in the lungs and also causes kidney damage.

parasite An organism living in or on another organism of a different species (called the host), from which it obtains food and protection. Many parasites have complex life cycles, with one or more intermediate hosts (of different species) supporting them during their development. The study of parasites—**parasitology**—is of importance in medicine since many parasites, such as bacteria and fleas, either cause or transmit disease. Many plants are either partly or completely parasitic.

parathyroid glands Two pairs of endocrine glands lying behind the thyroid gland in the neck, which secrete **parathyroid hormone** when the level of calcium in the blood falls. This hormone causes the release of calcium from the bones and its transfer to the blood. Deficiency of parathyroid hormone results in muscle spasms and cramps (tetany).

parchment Skin, usually of the goat, sheep, or calf, treated for writing on. Its name comes from Pergamum, where in the 2nd century BC methods of treating skins were developed. It was used for manuscripts and early bound books. Delicate skin from young animals is called vellum. *See also* leather.

Paris 48 52N 2 18E The capital of France and a department of the Paris Region, situated in the N of the country on the River Seine. The administrative, commercial, and cultural centre of France, Paris houses many international organizations, including UNESCO. In the middle of the Seine, the Île de la Cité contains the cathedral of *Notre-Dame. On the Left Bank lie the Eiffel Tower, Montparnasse, and the Latin Quarter. On the Right Bank stands the Louvre art gallery. The Champs Élysées runs from the Arc de Triomphe to the Place de la Concorde. Further N lies Montmartre, dominated by the Basilica of Sacré Coeur (1919). *History*: the Île de la Cité was settled in Roman times. In the 6th century Clovis made it the capital of his Frankish kingdom but it later suffered attacks from Vikings. It regained importance as the capital under the Capetians. The storming of the Bastille (1789), heralding the beginning of the French Revolution, occurred here. Population (1982): 2 176 243.

Paris In Greek legend, a son of *Priam and Hecuba. His abduction of *Helen with the help of Aphrodite caused the *Trojan War, during which he killed Achilles and was himself killed by Philoctetes. *See also* Eris.

Park, Mungo (1771–c. 1806) Scottish explorer. In 1795–96 he ascended the Niger from the mouth of the Gambia, crossed the Sénégal Basin, and was imprisoned by Arabs. His *Travels in the Interior Districts of Africa* (1797) related his adventures. In 1805, with 40 companions, he resumed his exploration. The expedition was attacked by Africans and Park died.

Parker, Charlie (Christopher) (1920–55) US Black jazz saxophonist and composer, known as "Bird" or "Yardbird." With Dizzy Gillespie he created the bop style of jazz and appeared with a number of bands.

parkinsonism (*or* Parkinson's disease) A disease affecting the part of the brain controlling voluntary movement, first described in 1817 by a British physician, James Parkinson (1755–1824). Sometimes the disease may result from infection or injury, but usually no cause is apparent. The symptoms are tremor of the hands and difficulty in starting movements. It is treated with drugs or surgery.

parliament The law-making assembly of a country. In the UK it consists of the sovereign, the House of Lords, and the House of Commons; its seat is the *Palace of Westminster. Parliament developed in the 13th century from the *Curia Regis (King's Court), in which the monarch consulted with his barons. Representatives of the shires, and later, boroughs were also summoned to attend parliament. The *Glorious Revolution (1688) achieved the beginning of parliamentary dominance over the Crown. The 18th century saw the emergence of party politics and the *prime minister. The House of Commons has (1989) 650 members of parliament

(MPs), each representing a geographical constituency, and is regulated by the *Speaker. The House of Lords has over 1000 members (see peerage). Its speaker is the Lord Chancellor. Laws are introduced as private or public bills. After a first reading a bill is printed and debated in a second reading. It is then referred to a committee, whose amendments are considered by the whole house; it then receives a third reading after which it is sent to the Lords, where it goes through a similar procedure. After passing both houses the bill receives the royal assent and becomes an Act of Parliament.

parliamentary commissioner for administration. See ombudsman.

Parma 44 48N 10 19E A city in N Italy, in Emilia-Romagna. Dating from Roman times, it became an important cultural centre in the middle ages. It has a university (1222), a romanesque cathedral, and a 16th-century palace. The centre of an agricultural district, its industries include the manufacture of Parmesan cheese, Parma ham, perfume, and glass. Population (1989): 172 313.

Parnassus, Mount (Modern Greek name: Parnassós) 38 32N 22 41E A mountain in S central Greece, held in ancient times as sacred to the god Apollo and the Muses. Height: 2457 m (8061 ft).

Parnell, Charles Stewart (1846–91) Irish politician, who in 1880 became the leader of the *Home Rule party in the House of Commons. An MP from 1875, he enjoyed widespread support in Ireland. He allied his party with the Liberals in 1886, when Gladstone introduced the Home Rule bill.

Parr, Catherine (1512–48) The sixth wife (1543–47) of Henry VIII of England. After Henry's death, she married (1547) Thomas, Baron Seymour of Sudeley (d. 1549).

parrot A bird (300 species) found worldwide in warm regions. 10–100 cm long, parrots have a short neck and strong wings. The plumage is brightly coloured and the short hooked bill is used to open nuts and to feed on fruits. Most live in trees and are excellent climbers, having clawed feet. See also cockatoo; lovebird; macaw; parakeet.

Parry, Sir (Charles) Hubert (Hastings) (1848–1918) British composer. He was the director of the Royal College of Music (1894–1918) and professor of music at Oxford University (1900–08). He wrote the song *Jerusalem* (1916).

parsec A unit of distance, used in astronomy. 1 parsec = 3.26 light-years or 3.084 × 10^{16} metres.

Parseeism The religion of the descendants of Persians who fled their country in the 8th century AD to avoid persecution following the Arab conquest. Mostly located in Bombay, Madras, Calcutta, and Karachi, they practise *Zoroastrianism.

parsley A widely cultivated herb, *Petroselinum crispum*, of the carrot family, native to the Mediterranean region. The leaves are used in cooking. The flowers are yellowish.

parsnip A widely cultivated plant, *Pastinaca sativa*, of the carrot family, native to Eurasia. Its starchy white root is eaten as a vegetable or used as cattle feed. The plant bears yellow flowers on stems up to 150 cm high.

parthenogenesis A method of reproduction in which the egg develops without *fertilization to produce an individual usually identical to the parent. It occurs among lower plants and animals, particularly aphids, ants, and wasps.

Parthenon A temple on the Acropolis in Athens dedicated to the goddess Athena. Built between 447 and 432 BC by Ictinus and Callicrates at the instigation of Pericles, its rectangular exterior of Doric columns originally contained a walled chamber with *Phidias' statue of Athena. In the 5th century AD it became a Christian church and in the 15th century a mosque. It was badly damaged during the Venetian siege of Athens in 1687. See also Elgin Marbles.

Parthia The region S of the Caspian Sea approximately equivalent to present-day Khorasan (NE Iran). It controlled a great empire from about 250 BC to 224 AD when it was conquered by the Sasanians of Persia.

particle physics The study of elementary particles. The discovery of the *electron (J. J. Thomson; 1897) and the *proton (Rutherford; 1911) made it clear that the atom had an internal structure (see atomic theory). When the *neutron was discovered (Chadwick; 1932), it appeared that the whole universe was constructed of these three particles. The outstanding problem was the nature of the force that held neutrons and protons together in the atomic nucleus. The only two fundamental forces known at that time were *gravitation and the electromagnetic (em) force: the gravitational force was too weak to account for the stability of the nucleus and the em force had no effect on the electrically uncharged neutron.

In 1935 *Yukawa suggested that there might be a short-lived particle that jumped between protons and neutrons and held them together. The discovery of these short-lived particles and the exchange forces associated with them led to intensive worldwide research (see accelerators). By the 1960s some 200 particles and four fundamental forces had been identified; in addition to gravitational and em forces there were strong interactions (100 times more powerful than em forces) and weak interactions (10^{10} weaker than em forces). There are now believed to be two classes of particles: leptons (the electron, *muon, tau particle, and *neutrinos), which interact by the em or the weak forces and have no internal structure; and hadrons (including the proton, neutron, pion, etc.), which interact by the strong interaction and do have an internal structure.

The current model of the hadron is based on Murray Gell-Mann's concept of the quark, introduced in 1963, hadrons being divided into two classes: baryons and mesons. Baryons consist of three quarks and mesons consist of a quark-antiquark pair. Thus all the matter in the universe is now seen as being made of leptons and quarks. See also antimatter.

partridge A small gamebird native to Europe, Africa, and Asia but widely introduced elsewhere. Partridges are 25–40 cm long and have rounded bodies with short wings. The European partridge (*Perdix perdix*) has a greyish plumage with a red face and tail. Family: *Phasianidae* (pheasants, quail, partridges).

pascal (Pa)   The *SI unit of pressure equal to one newton per square metre. Named after Blaise *Pascal.

Pascal, Blaise (1623–62) French mathematician, physicist, and theologian. He invented **Pascal's triangle** for calculating the coefficients of a binomial expansion. In fluid mechanics he discovered that the pressure in a fluid is everywhere equal (**Pascal's principle**). In 1641 he invented the first calculating machine. At the age of 31 he had a mystical experience and became a Jansenist; his *Lettres provinciales* (1656–57) defended *Jansenism against the *Jesuits. His greatest work was *Pensées sur la religion* (1669), a poetical essay on human nature.

Passchendaele.   *See* World War I.

passionflower   A widely cultivated climbing plant native to America. The distinctive flowers have five coloured sepals and petals topped by a coloured fringe. The fruit of some species (e.g. *Passiflora quadrangularis*) is edible (passionfruits *or* granadillas).

Passion plays   Religious dramas concerning the crucifixion and resurrection of Christ. They were performed on Good Friday throughout medieval Europe. The Passion play at *Oberammergau in W Germany has been performed every ten years since 1634.

Passover (Hebrew word: *Pesah*)   One of the three biblical pilgrimage festivals (the others are Weeks and Tabernacles). It commemorates the Exodus from Egypt and includes a spring harvest festival. In *Judaism, it is celebrated for seven or eight days. In Christianity it has been replaced by *Easter.

Pasternak, Boris (1890–1960) Russian poet and novelist. His Symbolist poetry was published between 1917 and 1923, but his novel *Dr Zhivago* was banned in Russia; it became internationally successful after its publication in Italy in 1957. Under political pressure, he declined the Nobel Prize in 1958.

Pasteur, Louis (1822–95) French chemist and microbiologist. In 1854, working at Lille University, he found that fermentation was caused by microorganisms and that by excluding these, souring or decay could be prevented (*see* pasteurization). Although partially paralysed in 1868, by 1881 he had devised a means of safely causing immunity to anthrax by injecting a vaccine of heat-treated (attenuated) live anthrax bacilli. Pasteur also produced a vaccine for chicken cholera and an effective rabies vaccine. The Pasteur Institute was founded in 1888 to treat rabies and has since developed into a world centre for biological research.

pasteurization   A form of heat treatment used to destroy the microorganisms in milk and so make it safe to drink. The method involves heating milk for 30 minutes at 60°C, which kills the bacteria without affecting the quality of the milk. This process is named after Louis *Pasteur.

Patagonia   A geographic area of S South America in Argentina and Chile, extending S of the River Colorado to the Strait of Magellan. It consists chiefly of an arid plateau rising to the Andes. Sheep raising is the principal economic activity. It contains the major oilfield of Comodoro Rivadavia and the Río Turbio coalfield. Area: about 777 000 sq km (300 000 sq mi).

pathology   The branch of medicine concerned with the study of diseases and their causes. Virchow, Pasteur, and Koch, in the 19th century, helped found pathology by identifying bacteria as a major cause of disease. But it was not until the beginning of the 20th century that this knowledge was applied to the treatment and prevention of disease. The role of the body's own chemicals was discovered, for example with the work of Banting and Best on the importance of insulin in diabetes, and that of Landsteiner in the discovery of the blood groups. Pathology now includes studies of the chemistry of blood, urine, faeces, and diseased tissue, together with the use of X-rays and many other investigative techniques.

Patna   25 37N 85 12E A city in India, the capital of Bihar on the River Ganges. It was founded in 1541 on the former site of Pataliputra, ancient capital of the Maurya and Gupta empires. Population (1981): 916 000.

patricians   The hereditary aristocracy of ancient Rome, who held all political and religious offices. During the *Roman Republic they were forced to admit *plebeians to political offices.

Patrick, St (c. 390–c. 460 AD)   The patron saint of Ireland. Abducted from England at the age of 16 by Irish marauders, he was sold into slavery but escaped to Gaul, later returning to Ireland as a missionary. By the time of his death he had established Christianity in Ireland. His only certain works are an autobiography, the *Confession*, and the *Epistle to Coroticus*. Feast day: 17 March. Emblems: snakes and shamrock.

Patton, George S(mith) (1885–1945) US general. In World War II he commanded the Seventh Army in Sicily (1943) and then the Third Army in France. He breached the German defences in Normandy and advanced to the Moselle. In the Ardennes he crossed the Rhine and encircled the Ruhr.

Paul VI (Giovanni Battista Montini; 1897–1978) Pope (1963–78). Succeeding *John XXIII, Paul recalled the second *Vatican Council after his election.

Paul, St (c. 3–c. 64 AD) Christian Apostle, born Saul of Tarsus, who spread Christianity among the Gentiles; the 13 Epistles attributed to him form part of the New Testament. The son of a Pharisee and a Roman citizen, he was at first anti-Christian, having taken part in the martyrdom of St *Stephen. While travelling to Damascus, he had a vision that led to his conversion. He began his activity as an Apostle in Damascus, later joining the other Apostles in Jerusalem. His missionary work consisted of journeys to Cyprus, Asia Minor, Macedonia, Greece, Ephesus, and elsewhere. Arrested by Roman soldiers on his return to Jerusalem, he was tried in Rome and imprisoned for two years; he may then have been released before his final arrest and beheading under Nero. Feast day: 29 June.

Pauli, Wolfgang (1900–58) US physicist, born in Austria, who in 1925 discovered the Pauli exclusion principle (that no two fermions can exist in the same state), for which he received the 1945 Nobel Prize. In 1931 he suggested that some of the energy of a *beta decay was carried away by massless particles, which *Fermi named neutrinos.

Pauling, Linus Carl (1901–) US chemist, who studied the nature of chemical bonding in molecules, publishing *The Nature of the Chemical Bond* in 1939. He received the Nobel Prize for Chemistry (1954) for his research and the Nobel Peace Prize (1962) for his pacifist stance against nuclear weapons.

Pavarotti, Luciano (1935–) Italian operatic tenor. He made his debut at La Scala, Milan, in 1966. He specializes in the works of Bellini, Verdi, and Puccini. His rendering of 'Nessum Dorma' became a bestseller in 1990.

Pavlov, Ivan Petrovich (1849–1936) Russian physiologist who showed how heartbeat is regulated by the vagus nerve and how eating stimulates secretion of digestive juices by the stomach. This led to work on the *conditioned reflex, which he extended to human behaviour, such as learning. He was awarded the 1907 Nobel Prize.

Pavlova, Anna (1885–1931) Russian ballet dancer. She joined Diaghilev's company in Paris in 1909, and from 1914 she devoted her career to touring with her own company. She created the chief role in *Les Sylphides* and was associated with *Le Cygne*, choreographed for her by *Fokine in 1907.

pea A widely cultivated plant, *Pisum sativum*, native to the Mediterranean and W Asia. The leaves have curling tendrils for climbing. The edible round seeds are contained in an elongated pod and are an important source of protein.

peach A widely cultivated tree, *Prunus persica*, of the rose family, probably native to China. Up to 6 m high, it has pink flowers. The round fruit has thin yellowish velvety skin. The sweet flesh encloses a wrinkled stone. Peaches are eaten fresh, canned, or in preserves. Nectarines are varieties with smooth-skinned fruits.

peacock. *See* peafowl.

Peacock, Thomas Love (1785–1866) British satirical novelist. He worked (1819–56) for the East India Company and was a close friend of Shelley. His seven novels, which include *Nightmare Abbey* (1818) and *Gryll Grange* (1860), satirize contemporary ideas.

peacock butterfly A common butterfly, *Inachis io*, of Europe and Asia. The adults are brownish with an eyespot on each wing. They fly from early spring into summer. The black spiny caterpillars feed on stinging nettles.

peafowl A gamebird native to forests of India and SE Asia. Peafowl are 75 cm long and the female (**peahen**) has a greenish plumage; males (**peacocks**) have elaborate lacy tails, 150 cm long, the feathers of which are tipped by blue-and-bronze markings and are raised during display.

Peak District A hilly area in N central England, in Derbyshire, at the S end of the Pennines. It reaches 727 m (2385 ft) at Kinder Scout and contains many limestone caves.

peanut. *See* groundnut.

pear A widely cultivated tree, *Pyrus communis*, of the rose family, native to temperate Eurasia. Up to 13 m high, it has oval leaves and white flowers. The fruit is eaten fresh or canned. The wood is used for furniture making.

pearl A hard glossy growth formed around a foreign body in certain bivalve *molluscs, known as pearl oysters or pearl mussels. Used for jewellery since earliest times, pearls consist of concentric films of nacre (mostly calcium carbonate), which also forms the smooth lustrous lining (mother-of-pearl) in the shells of the molluscs. **Cultured pearls** are beads of mother-of-pearl artificially inserted into the mollusc for three to five years.

Pearl Harbor An inlet of the Pacific Ocean in the USA, in Hawaii on Oahu Island. On 7 December, 1941, the Japanese launched an air attack on US military installations in Hawaii, bringing the USA into World War II. It is now a naval shipyard and submarine base.

Pears, Sir Peter (1910–86) British tenor. He was well known for his performances of Bach and Schubert and was closely associated with the music of his friend *Britten.

Peasants' Revolt (1381) A major revolt in England during the middle ages, caused by heavy poll taxes and a general discontent with government policies. The peasants, led by Wat *Tyler and John Ball (d. 1381), marched on London, achieving some initial success, but the revolt soon collapsed and its supporters ruthlessly suppressed.

peat Partially decomposed plant debris laid down in waterlogged conditions in temperate or cold climates. The remains of *Sphagnum (peat or bog moss) are important constituents. Peat is the starting point for coal formation and is itself used as a fuel.

pecan. *See* hickory.

peccary A small pig-like hoofed mammal of South and Central American forests. The collared peccary (*Tayassu tajacu*) is dark grey with a light chest stripe and grows to a length of 90 cm. It has two pairs of short tusks. The white-lipped peccary (*T. albirostris*) is larger and has a white patch on the snout. Both eat plant and animal material.

pectin A carbohydrate found combined with cellulose in the cell walls of plants. Ripening fruits change any other pectic compounds present into jelly-like pectin–an essential ingredient for the gelling of jam.

Peel, Sir Robert (1788–1850) British statesman; Conservative prime minister (1834–35, 1841–46). As home secretary (1822–27, 1828–30), he introduced prison and criminal-law reforms and founded the Metropolitan Police (1829). He is best remembered for the repeal of the *Corn Laws (1846).

peepul. *See* bo tree.

peerage In the UK and Ireland, the hereditary nobility (those with inherited titles) and the life peers, consisting of (since 1876) the Lords of Appeal in Ordinary and (since 1958) those created in recognition of public service. The five ranks of the hereditary peerage are, in descending order, duke, marquess, earl, viscount, and baron. A life peer has the rank of baron. All peers are permitted to sit in the House of Lords.

peewit. See lapwing.

Pegasus (Greek mythology) A winged horse that sprang from the blood of *Medusa. It carried the legendary hero Bellerophon in his battles. It became a constellation and the bearer of thunderbolts for Zeus.

Peking (Chinese name: Beijing or Pei-ching) 39 55N 116 25E The capital of the People's Republic of China, situated in the NE of the country in Hobei province. The city has expanded considerably since 1949. History: as Ta-tu, it first became the capital (of N China) under the Yuan dynasty in 1272. The capital was later moved to Nanjing, returning to Peking (1420) under the third Ming emperor. In 1928 the Nationalist (Guomindang) government moved the capital to Nanjing. Peking became the capital of the People's Republic of China in 1949. In 1989 thousands of students demanding reform were massacred in Peking's Tiananmen Square. Population (1986): 5 860 000.

Pekingese A breed of dog originating in China and brought to the West by British forces who captured the Imperial Palace, Peking, in 1860. It has a long coat and a black short-muzzled face. Height: 15–23 cm.

Peking man A fossil *hominid of the species Homo erectus; its skeletal remains were found near Peking. Formerly known as Sinanthropus, Peking man lived during the middle Pleistocene period (c. 500 000 years ago).

pelargonium. See geranium.

Pelé (Edson Arantes do Nascimento; 1940–) Brazilian Association footballer. A renowned inside forward, he became a world star at 17 when Brazil first won the World Cup (1958). He scored over 1300 goals.

Pelham, Henry. See Newcastle, Thomas Pelham-Holles, 1st Duke of.

pelican A waterbird found on rivers and coasts of temperate and tropical regions. 125–180 cm long, pelicans have short legs and tail and very large wings. Their long bills have a pouch, which expands to hold fish before swallowing.

pellagra A disease causing skin inflammation, diarrhoea, and mental disorder. It occurs in poor countries where the diet consists chiefly of maize, due to lack of nicotinic acid (see vitamin B complex).

Peloponnese The S peninsula of Greece, joined to central Greece by the Isthmus of Corinth. It includes the towns Corinth, Patrás (the chief port), and *Sparta. Area: 21 637 sq km (8354 sq mi). Population (1981): 1 012 528.

Peloponnesian War (431–404 BC) The conflict between Athens and Sparta and their allies, in which Sparta was finally victorious. Sparta's superior infantry invaded Athens in 431 while Athens, under Pericles, attacked at sea. The war ended when besieged Athens surrendered to Sparta under *Lysander.

Peltier effect. See thermoelectric effects.

pelvis A basin-like structure composed of the hip bones and lower part of the spine. It protects the soft organs of the lower abdomen and provides attachment for the bones and muscles of the legs.

Penal Laws (1571, 1581, 1593) A series of Acts passed during the reign of Elizabeth I to punish those (recusants), especially Roman Catholics, who refused to attend Church of England services. Recusants were fined, imprisoned, banished, or executed. The Laws were withdrawn in 1829 (see Catholic emancipation). See also Test Acts.

Penang A state in NW Peninsular Malaysia, on the Strait of Malacca, consisting of Penang island and Province Wellesley on the mainland. The main products are rice, rubber, and tin. Area: 1031 sq km (398 sq mi). Population (1985 est): 1 049 282. Capital: Georgetown.

Penates. See Lares and Penates.

pendulum A device used in clocks in which a mass (the bob) swings freely about a fixed point with a constant period. In the simple pendulum the bob is connected to the fixed point by a length (l) of string. Its period is $2\pi(l/g)^{1/2}$, where g is the *acceleration of free fall.

Penelope In Homer's Odyssey, the wife of *Odysseus. During her husband's absence she put off her suitors by saying that she must first make a shroud for her father-in-law Laertes, unravelling each night what she had woven by day.

penguin A flightless black-and-white seabird occurring on cold coasts of the S hemisphere. Adapted for life in the water, their wings (reduced to flippers) provide fast propulsion. 40–120 cm long, their dense plumage enables them to tolerate extreme cold. See also emperor penguin; fairy penguin.

penicillins A group of *antibiotics. The first was discovered in the mould Penicillium notatum, in 1929, by Sir Alexander *Fleming but was not used to treat infections until 1941. Penicillins can cause allergic reactions in certain patients.

Peninsular War (1808–14) The part of the Napoleonic Wars fought in Spain and Portugal. The French took Portugal in 1807 and in 1808 Napoleon's brother, Joseph Bonaparte (1768–1844), replaced Ferdinand VII as King of Spain. Revolts turned into a vicious guerrilla war, until British troops under the Duke of *Wellington eventually liberated the Peninsula.

penis The male organ of copulation, found in mammals, some reptiles, and a few birds. In men (and other mammals) it contains a tube (urethra) through which semen and urine are discharged. Erectile tissue making up the bulk of the penis fills with blood and enlarges during sexual excitement, allowing the penis to be inserted in the female genital tract. The corresponding part in women is the clitoris, a small erectile mass of tissue situated in front of the urinary opening.

Pen-ki. See Benxi.

Penn, William (1644–1718) English Quaker and founder of Pennsylvania, son of Admiral Sir William Penn (1621–70). He joined the Quakers in 1664, being imprisoned (1668) in the Tower, where he wrote *No Cross, No Crown* (1669), a classic of Quaker practice. From 1682 he established Quaker settlements in America, including Pennsylvania.

Pennines (*or* Pennine Chain) An upland range in N England. It extends from the Cheviot Hills in the N to the valley of the River Trent in the S. Sometimes known as the "backbone of England" it rises to 893 m (2930 ft) at Cross Fell.

Pennsylvania A state in the E USA. It produces iron and steel and nearly all the country's hard coal. The world's first oil well was drilled near Titusville in 1859. Dairy farming predominates in the NE, while the SE yields cereals, fruit, and vegetables. *History*: one of the 13 original colonies, the first settlers, the Swedes, were soon driven out by the Dutch (1655). In 1681 the area was given to William *Penn by Charles II of England as a haven for Quakers. It became a state in 1787. Area: 117 412 sq km (45 333 sq mi). Population (1986 est): 11 889 000. Capital: Harrisburg.

Pennsylvanian period. *See* Carboniferous period.

Pentagon The five-sided headquarters of the US Defense Department in Virginia, built (1941–43) during World War II. It is the largest office building in the world.

pentathlon An athletic competition comprising five events, first introduced in an Olympic contest in 708 BC. The **modern pentathlon** comprises a 5000 m cross-country horseback ride, fencing, pistol shooting, a 300 m swim, and a 4000 m cross-country run. It was first included in the Olympic Games in 1912.

Pentecost. *See* Whit Sunday.

Pentecostal Churches A Christian movement starting in the USA in 1906. Its members seek spiritual renewal through baptism by the Holy Spirit, as on the first Pentecost (Acts 2.1–4).

pentlandite A mineral that is the principal ore of nickel, (Ni,Fe)S, found in igneous rocks. It is mined in Canada, Australia, and the Soviet Union.

peony A large perennial plant of N temperate regions, cultivated for its showy white or red flowers. The fruit is a large leathery pod containing black seeds.

Pepin the Short (d. 768 AD) King of the Franks (751–68) after overthrowing the Merovingians. Founder of the Carolingian dynasty, Pepin checked Lombard expansion and in 756 presented Pope Stephen II with the first of the *papal states.

pepper A spice derived from a climbing vine, *Piper nigrum*, native to India. Up to 10 m high, it bears chains of up to 50 flowers that form berrylike fruits (peppercorns), about 5 mm in diameter. *See also* capsicum.

peppered moth A European moth, *Biston betularia*, which has similar coloration to the lichen-encrusted tree bark on which it rests. During the past century a dark variety has become common in sooty industrial areas.

peppermint A herb, *Mentha* × *piperata*: a hybrid between water mint (*M. aquatica*) and *spearmint. It has reddish-lilac flowers and is

the source of oil of peppermint, used as a flavouring.

pepsin A protein-digesting enzyme found in gastric juice. The inactive form, pepsinogen, is secreted by glands in the stomach wall and converted to pepsin by the hydrochloric acid in the stomach. Pepsin strongly coagulates milk.

peptic ulcer An inflamed and damaged area in the wall of the stomach (**gastric ulcer**) or, more commonly, the small intestine (or duodenum), hence **duodenal ulcer**. They may cause abdominal pain and vomiting but are easily treated with drugs. Serious complications occur when untreated ulcers bleed or perforate (burst).

peptide A chemical compound consisting of a chain of two or more *amino acids. **Polypeptides** contain between three and several hundred amino acids. They are the constituents of *proteins. Some peptides are important as hormones and as antibiotics.

Pepys, Samuel (1633–1703) English diarist. He was secretary to the Admiralty (1669–88), an MP, and president of the Royal Society. His *Diary*, which extends from 1660 to 1669 and includes descriptions of the Restoration, the Plague, and the Fire of London, was written in code.

perch A freshwater fish, *Perca fluviatilis* of Europe and Asia. Usually about 25 cm long, it is greenish, with dark vertical bars on its sides and a spiny dorsal fin. Perch usually live in shoals. *See also* sea bass.

Percy, Sir Henry (1364–1403) English rebel, called Hotspur. Together with his father, Henry, 1st Earl of Northumberland (1342–1408), he led the most serious revolt against Henry IV, whom they had helped to the throne in 1399. He was defeated and killed at Shrewsbury.

peregrine falcon A large powerful *falcon, *Falco peregrinus*, occurring in rocky coastal regions worldwide. It is 33–48 cm long and has long pointed wings and a long tail. The male is blue-grey with black-barred white underparts; females are brownish. It feeds mainly on ducks, shorebirds, and mammals.

perennials Plants that live for many years. In herbaceous perennials the parts above ground die each winter and the plants survive in underground organs (rhizomes, bulbs, corms, etc.). Woody perennials have woody stems, which survive above ground.

Peres, Shimon (1923–) Israeli statesman, prime minister (1984–86), foreign minister (1986–88), and finance minister (1988–90). Born in Poland, Peres emigrated to Palestine in 1934. When a coalition government was formed in 1984, he became Labour prime minister under a special power-sharing agreement with Yitzhak *Shamir.

perestroika. *See* glasnost.

Pérez de Cuéllar, Javier (1920–) Peruvian diplomat; UN secretary-general (1982–). A respected negotiator, he sought peaceful solutions to the Falklands conflict, the Gulf War, and other conflicts.

Pericles (c. 495–429 BC) Athenian statesman, who became leader of the democratic party in 461 and dominated Athens until 430 by virtue

1A	2A	3B	4B	5B	6B	7B	8			1B	2B	3A	4A	5A	6A	7A	0
1 H																	2 He
3 Li	4 Be											5 B	6 C	7 N	8 O	9 F	10 Ne
11 Na	12 Mg				← TRANSITION ELEMENTS →							13 Al	14 Si	15 P	16 S	17 Cl	18 Ar
19 K	20 Ca	21 Sc	22 Ti	23 V	24 Cr	25 Mn	26 Fe	27 Co	28 Ni	29 Cu	30 Zn	31 Ga	32 Ge	33 As	34 Se	35 Br	36 Kr
37 Rb	38 Sr	39 Y	40 Zr	41 Nb	42 Mo	43 Tc	44 Ru	45 Rh	46 Pd	47 Ag	48 Cd	49 In	50 Sn	51 Sb	52 Te	53 I	54 Xe
55 Cs	56 Ba	57† La	72 Hf	73 Ta	74 W	75 Re	76 Os	77 Ir	78 Pt	79 Au	80 Hg	81 Tl	82 Pb	83 Bi	84 Po	85 At	86 Rn
87 Fr	88 Ra	89‡ Ac															

† Lanthanides	57 La	58 Ce	59 Pr	60 Nd	61 Pm	62 Sm	63 Eu	64 Gd	65 Tb	66 Dy	67 Ho	68 Er	69 Tm	70 Yb	71 Lu
‡ Actinides	89 Ac	90 Th	91 Pa	92 U	93 Np	94 Pu	95 Am	96 Cm	97 Bk	98 Cf	99 Es	100 Fm	101 Md	102 No	103 Lr

PERIODIC TABLE

of his outstanding leadership and reputation for honesty. Under Pericles, Athens achieved its golden age and leadership of the *Delian League. By 431, rivalry between Athens and Sparta led to the outbreak of the *Peloponnesian War. Pericles' strategy was undermined by the plague of 430 and he briefly lost office. He died shortly after his reinstatement.

period. See geological time scale; periodic table; simple harmonic motion.

periodic table An arrangement of the chemical *elements in order of increasing atomic number. The earliest version was devised in 1869 by D. *Mendeleyev, who predicted the existence of several elements from gaps in the table. The rows across the table are known as periods and the columns as groups. The elements in a group all show similar chemical behaviour. Across each period, atoms are electropositive (form positive ions) to the left and electronegative to the right. *Atomic theory explains this behaviour on the basis of electron shells. Electrons within an atom are grouped in a series of shells according to their energy; the electrons in a group all have the same number of outer electrons, on which chemical reactions depend.

periodontal disease Disease of the gums and other structures surrounding the teeth caused by the action of bacteria on food debris, which forms a hard deposit (tartar) in the spaces between the gums and teeth. The resulting swelling and bleeding of the gums can cause the teeth to loosen and eventually fall out.

periscope An optical device consisting of a tube in which mirrors or prisms are arranged so that light entering at right angles to the tube is reflected through the tube to emerge at the other end also at right angles to the tube. Periscopes are used by submarines to see above the surface of the water.

peritonitis An illness involving inflammation of the peritoneum (the membrane that lines the abdominal cavity), resulting from the bursting of an abdominal organ (such as the appendix) or of a peptic ulcer or from bacterial infection. An operation is essential to repair the perforated organ and cleanse the abdomen; antibiotics are also given.

periwinkle (botany) An evergreen creeping shrub or plant, native to Europe and W Asia with blue or white flowers. *Vinca major* is an important species.

periwinkle (zoology) A sea snail, also called winkle. The common edible winkle (*Littorina littorea*) of European seashores is about 2 cm high and has a green rounded shell with a pointed spire.

permafrost The permanent freezing of the ground, sometimes to great depths, in areas bordering ice sheets. During the summer the top soil may thaw, while the ground below remains a frozen impermeable barrier.

permeability, magnetic (μ) A measure of the response of a material to a *magnetic field equal to the ratio of the magnetic *flux brought about in the material to the magnetic field strength producing it. The relative permeability, μ_r, is the ratio of μ in the medium to that in free space, μ_0; μ_0 has a constant value, $4\pi \times 10^{-7}$ henry per metre, and is called the magnetic constant. Ferromagnetic materials can have a μ_r as high as 100 000.

Permian period The last geological period of the Palaeozoic era, between the Carboniferous and Triassic periods, lasting from about 280 to 240 million years ago. It was first identified in the Soviet port Perm. The period was marked by an increasingly dry climate that continued into the Triassic.

permittivity (ε) The absolute permittivity of a medium is a measure of how well it can resist a flow of electric charge. The absolute permittivity of free space (ε_0) is called the electric constant, and has the value 8.854×10^{-12} farad per metre. The relative permittivity *or* dielectric constant (ε_r) of a capacitor is the ratio of its capacitance with a specified dielectric between the plates to its capacitance with free space between the plates.

Pernambuco. *See* Recife.

Perón, Juan (Domingo) (1895–1974) Argentine statesman; president (1946–55, 1973–74). Elected in 1946, his position was strengthened by the popularity of his second wife, **Evita Perón** (María Eva Duarte de P.; 1919–52), who was idolized by the poor for her charitable work. After her death, support for Perón waned and he was overthrown. He was re-elected president in 1973.

Perpendicular The style of gothic architecture predominant in England between about 1370 and the mid-16th century. The name derives from the window design, with its vertical divisions (mullions) broken regularly by horizontal divisions. King's College chapel, Cambridge (1446–1515) is a fine example.

Perpignan 42 42N 2 54E A city in S France, the capital of the Pyrénées-Orientales department. The capital of the former province of Roussillon in the 17th century, it has a gothic cathedral and a 13th-century castle. It trades in wine, fruit, and vegetables and is a tourist centre. Population (1982): 113 646.

Persephone (Roman name: Proserpine) Greek goddess of the underworld, daughter of Zeus and *Demeter. She was abducted by *Hades, who made her queen of the underworld. Zeus allowed her to spend part of each year on earth, symbolizing the regeneration of natural life in the spring.

Perseus Mythological Greek hero. The son of Zeus and Danae, he beheaded the *Medusa with the help of Athena, who gave him a mirror to avoid looking at the Gorgon and being turned to stone. He married Andromeda, daughter of the Ethiopian king.

Pershing missile A US army two-stage solid-fuelled nuclear surface-to-surface missile launched from mobile vehicles and having a range of 740 km (460 mi). Several versions have been produced; Pershing II missiles were deployed in Europe in 1984. It is named after Gen J. J. Pershing (1860–1948).

Persia. *See* Iran.

Persian cat A domesticated cat, also called a Longhair, having a long coat, which may be of any colour, although the Blue Persian is most popular.

Persian Gulf An arm of the Arabian Sea, extending some 950 km (590 mi) NW beyond the Gulf of Oman. The large offshore oil deposits are exploited by the surrounding *Gulf States. Area: 233 000 sq km (89 942 sq mi).

Persian Wars. *See* Greek–Persian Wars.

persimmon The edible fruit of the Japanese persimmon (*Diospyros kaki*), the American persimmon (*D. virginiana*), or the Asian date plum

(*D. lotus*). Persimmons are round orange or red fruits, 5–8 cm across, eaten fresh, cooked, or candied.

Perspex (polymethyl methacrylate) A colourless transparent plastic material made by *polymerization of methyl methacrylate. It can be moulded into different shapes and coloured for use as an unbreakable substitute for glass.

perspiration. *See* sweat.

Perth 31 58S 115 49E The capital of Western Australia, on the Swan River. Founded in 1829, it expanded following the discovery of gold (1893) at Kalgoorlie. The University of Western Australia was founded in 1913 and there are two cathedrals. Its port is *Fremantle. Population (1986): 1 025 340.

Perth 56 24N 3 28W A city in E Scotland, in Tayside Region on the River Tay. It was an early capital of Scotland. There are dyeing, textiles, whisky distilling, and carpet industries and it is a popular tourist centre. Population (1989 est): 44 000.

Peru, Republic of A country in the NW of South America, on the Pacific Ocean. *Economy*: a fishing country producing fishmeal; agriculture is also important, crops include maize, rice, sugar cane, cotton, and coffee, while livestock breeding centres on the production of wool. Mineral resources include copper, silver, lead, zinc, and iron. Peru also has a valuable tourist trade. *History*: the civilization of the Chimú was replaced by that of the *Incas, who were conquered by the Spanish under Pizarro in 1533. Peru was the last of Spain's American colonies to declare its independence (1821), the Spanish being finally defeated in 1824. Gen Ramón Castilla (1797–1867) developed Peru's economy, but prosperity was undermined by the War of the *Pacific (1879–83). Since World War II Peru has witnessed a series of coups. In 1980 Fernando Belaúnde Terry was elected president; in 1985 he was replaced by Alan García Pérez (1949–   ). In 1990 Alberto Fujimori became president. Peru is a member of the OAS and LAIA. Official languages: Spanish and Quechua; Aymará is also widely spoken. Official currency: inti of 1000 soles. Area: 1 285 215 sq km (496 093 sq mi). Population (1988 est): 21 300 000. Capital: Lima. Main port: Callao.

Perugia 43 07N 12 23E A city in Italy, the capital of Umbria. Originally an Etruscan city, it has 13th-century city walls, a 14th-century cathedral, and a university (1200). An agricultural trading centre, its manufactures include furniture and textiles. Population (1987): 147 602.

Peshawar 34 01N 71 40E A city in N Pakistan, situated at the E end of the Khyber Pass. Industries include textiles, shoes, and pottery. Population (1981): 555 000.

Pestalozzi, Johann Heinrich (1746–1827) Swiss educationalist. His book *Wie Gertrud ihre Kinder lehrt* (1801) reflected his ideas on education. Pestalozzi's work is commemorated in the **Pestalozzi International Children's Villages**, the first was established in 1946 for war orphans at Trogen (Switzerland), the second in 1958 at Sedlescombe, East Sussex, in the UK.

Pétain, (Henri) Philippe (1856–1951) French general and statesman. In World War I he organized the defence of Verdun (1916), becoming marshal of France (1918). In World War II, when France was on the verge of defeat, Pétain became prime minister. In June, 1940, he signed an armistice with Hitler allowing for a third of France to remain unoccupied by Germany. Pétain was sentenced to death in August, 1945, for collaboration but was reprieved.

Peter (I) the Great (1672–1725) Tsar (1682–1721) and then Emperor (1721–25) of Russia, who established Russia as a major power. Having travelled in W Europe in the late 1690s he introduced many reforms in government, industry, and in the army. In the Great Northern War (1700–21), he acquired Livonia, Estonia, and Ingria, where in 1703 he founded St Petersburg (now *Leningrad). He campaigned less successfully against the Turks (1710–13) but gained territory in the Caspian region from war with Persia (1722–23).

Peter, St In the New Testament, one of the 12 Apostles. He was a fisherman until called by Jesus. Although his faith often wavered, notably at the crucifixion, when he denied Christ three times, Peter was named as the rock upon which the Church was to be built. He was also entrusted with the "keys of the Kingdom of Heaven" (Matthew 16.19)—hence his symbol of two crossed keys. After Christ's death, he dominated the Christian community for 15 years. Feast day: 29 June.

Peterborough 52 35N 0 15W A city in E central England, in Cambridgeshire on the River Nene. The cathedral (begun 12th century) contains the tomb of Catherine of Aragon. Designated a new town in 1967, it is an agricultural marketing centre. Population (1985 est): 138 500.

Peterloo Massacre (1819) The name, recalling the battle of Waterloo, given to the violence used to break up a meeting in St Peter's Fields, Manchester. A crowd had gathered to hear a speech on parliamentary reform. The magistrates called in local troops, the cavalry were ordered to charge, and 11 people were killed.

Petition of Right (1628) A parliamentary declaration accepted by Charles I. It made illegal imprisonment without trial, taxation without parliamentary approval, and the billeting of soldiers on private individuals.

petit mal. *See* epilepsy.

Petrarch (Francesco Petrarca; 1304–74) Italian poet. His works of scholarship anticipated the Renaissance. Other works include *Secretum meum*, and *Africa*, but he is remembered chiefly for the *Canzoniere*, a series of love poems addressed to Laura.

petrel A sea bird with a musky smell, webbed feet, and a hooked bill with long nostrils. 27–90 cm long, petrels feed on fish and molluscs. Diving petrels belong to a different family. Occurring in the S hemisphere, they are 16–25 cm long and feed mostly on crustaceans. *See also* fulmar; shearwater; storm petrel.

petrochemicals. *See* oil.
Petrograd. *See* Leningrad.
petroleum. *See* oil.
petrology The study of *rocks, including their formation, structure, texture, and mineral and chemical composition.

petunia A tropical American plant of the nightshade family, cultivated for its funnel-shaped flowers. Ornamental species include *Petunia integrifolia*, with pink or purple flowers, the white-flowered *P. axillaris*, and many hybrids.

pewter An *alloy of tin with lead or copper, antimony, and bismuth. Formerly used for plates and other utensils, it is now confined to beer mugs.

peyote A blue-green *cactus, *Lophophora williamsii*, also called mescal, native to Mexico and the SW USA. Its dried flower heads, known as "mescal buttons," contain the alkaloid mescaline and produce hallucinations when chewed.

pH A measure of the acidity or alkalinity of a solution, equal to the logarithm to the base 10 of the reciprocal of the number of moles per litre of hydrogen ions it contains. In neutral solutions, therefore, the hydrogen ion concentration is 10^{-7} and the pH is consequently 7. In acid solutions the pH is less than 7; alkaline solutions have pH values greater than 7. The pH scale is logarithmic; for example, a solution with a pH of 2 is ten times more acidic than one with a pH of 1. *See also* acids and bases.

Phaedra In Greek mythology, the daughter of *Minos and Pasiphaë and the wife of Theseus. She fell in love with her stepson Hippolytus. When he rejected her, she hanged herself.

phagocyte A cell that engulfs and then digests particles from its surroundings: this process is called phagocytosis. In vertebrate animals, phagocytes are a type of white blood cell that protect the body by engulfing bacteria and other foreign particles.

phalanger A small plant-eating *marsupial, occurring in woodlands of Australia and New Guinea. They are adapted for climbing trees, having strong claws and grasping tails. Species include the *cuscus, flying phalanger, honey mouse, *koala, and *possum.

PHARAOH *The pharaoh's double crown, combining the red crown of Lower Egypt with the white crown of Upper Egypt, symbolized the unification of the two lands (c. 3100 BC).*

pharaoh The title of ancient Egyptian rulers. The word derives from the Egyptian for great house. The first dynasty, or line of pharaohs, was founded about 3200 BC; the last pharaoh died in 343 BC.

Pharisees An ancient Jewish religious and political party. The party started in the 2nd century BC and competed with the *Sadducees for political influence. In the *Gospels they are frequently criticized by Jesus.

pharmacology The study of the action of drugs on living organisms. Pharmacologists examine how drugs are absorbed, their effects, the interaction between different drugs, etc. **Pharmacy** is the science concerned with the preparation, manufacture, packaging, quality, and supply of medicinal drugs. The official **pharmacopoeia** is a government-approved list giving details of drugs.

Pharos of Alexandria An ancient lighthouse, one of the *Seven Wonders of the World. Built in about 280 BC by Sostratus of Cnidos for Ptolemy II of Egypt, it was over 135 m (440 ft) high. It was demolished in the 13th century AD.

Pharsalus, Battle of (48 BC) The decisive battle near present-day Fársala (Greece) in the Roman civil war, in which Julius *Caesar defeated *Pompey. Pompey's defeat opened the way to Caesar's dictatorship.

pharynx A muscular tube in vertebrate animals between the back of the mouth and the oesophagus (gullet). It acts as a passageway for food and conducts air from the nasal cavity to the larynx and windpipe. Inflammation of the pharynx (pharyngitis) is a common cause of a sore throat.

phase (astronomy) The fraction of the face of the moon or a planet that is illuminated at a particular time in its orbit. Lunar phases include new moon (unilluminated), first quarter (half illuminated), full moon, and last quarter (other half illuminated).

phase (physics) **1.** The fraction of its whole cycle that a periodically varying system has completed. For example, two *alternating currents of the same frequency are **in phase** if they reach their maximum values at the same instant. In an electricity-supply system there are usually three phases. **2.** Any portion of a system that is physically distinct, is homogeneous throughout, and can be mechanically separated from other phases. For example, a salt solution is a one-phase system, whereas a mixture of ice and water is a two-phase system.

pheasant A gamebird occurring in open or woodland regions of Europe, Asia, and Africa. Pheasants have short rounded wings, a short bill, and strong claws for scratching up grain, roots, and grubs. Males are brightly coloured, with bright fleshy wattles, large leg spurs, and long tail feathers. See also tragopan.

phenols Organic compounds with the general formula ROH, in which the – OH group is linked directly to a carbon atom in a benzene ring (see aromatic compound). The simplest example, phenol itself (or **carbolic acid**), C_6H_5OH, is used as a disinfectant and in the production of drugs, weedkillers, and synthetic *resins.

pheromone A chemical substance produced by animals in order to communicate with others of the same species. The best-known pheromones are the sex attractants secreted by moths to attract mates.

Phidias (c. 490–c. 417 BC) Athenian sculptor, one of the most influential artists of his time.

Phidias designed and supervised the sculptures of the *Parthenon (see Elgin Marbles). His works included gold-and-ivory statues of Athena in the Parthenon and *Zeus at Olympia.

Phidippides (5th century BC) Greek runner who ran 241 km (150 mi) from Athens to Sparta in two days to ask for help against the Persians before the Battle of *Marathon in 490 BC.

Philadelphia 40 00N 75 10W A city in the USA, situated on the Delaware River in Pennsylvania. Founded in 1681 by the Quaker, William Penn, it has many historic buildings, including Independence Hall (1732–59), where the Declaration of Independence was adopted. It has the world's largest freshwater port. Industries include oil refining, textiles, and shipbuilding. Population (1986): 1 642 900.

philadelphus. See mock orange.

Philip II (1527–98) King of Spain (1556–98). He married Mary I of England in 1554. Philip faced the *Revolt of the Netherlands, suppressed the *Moriscos, launched the Spanish *Armada against Protestant England (1588), and intervened in the French *Wars of Religion against the Huguenots.

Philip II Augustus (1165–1223) King of France (1179–1223), who waged war with the English kings Henry II (1187–89), Richard I (1194–99), and John. He took Normandy in 1204, followed by Maine, Touraine, and Anjou (1204–05).

Philip (II) of Macedon (382–336 BC) King of Macedon (359–336) and father of Alexander the Great. Philip unified Macedonia, expanded the economy, and trained a professional army. After defeating the Greeks at the Battle of Chaeronea (338) he planned to lead a combined force against Persia but was assassinated.

Philip V (1683–1746) The first Bourbon King of Spain (1700–24, 1724–46). The grandson of Louis XIV of France, his accession caused the War of the *Spanish Succession. He abdicated in 1724 in favour of his son Luis (1707–24) but returned to the throne when Luis died.

Philip, Prince, Duke of Edinburgh (1921–) The husband (from 1947) of Elizabeth II of the United Kingdom. The son of Prince Andrew of Greece, he served in the Royal Navy in World War II and took British citizenship in 1947. In 1956 he introduced the **Duke of Edinburgh's Award Scheme** to encourage the leisure activities of young people.

Philip, St In the New Testament, one of the 12 Apostles. In medieval art he is symbolized by loaves because of his participation in the miracle of the loaves and fishes. Feast day: 11 May.

Philippi, Battle of (42 BC) The battle in which Mark Antony and Octavian (later Emperor *Augustus) defeated *Brutus and *Cassius Longinus in the Roman civil war.

Philippines, Republic of the A country in SE Asia, consisting of over 7000 islands between the Pacific Ocean and the South China Sea. *Economy:* based principally on agriculture, forestry, and fishing, the main cash crops being sugar, coconuts, bananas, and pineapples. The country's metallic minerals include copper, gold, iron ore, manganese, molybdenum, zinc, lead, and silver. The main industries are food processing, textiles, wood processing, and oil refining. *History*: colonized by Spain in 1565, the islands were handed over to the USA in 1898 following the Spanish-American War. They became an independent republic in 1946. Following the election of President *Marcos in 1965 rapid economic development brought increased prosperity, but communist guerrilla activity in the N and a Muslim separatist movement in the S led to the declaration of martial law (1972). Unrest increased when the exiled opposition leader Benigno S. Aquino was assassinated on his return to Manila in 1983. After elections in early 1986, Marcos went into exile and Corazon Aquino, widow of Benigno, became president. Official languages: Pilipino (a new language based on Tagalog) and English. Official currency: Philippine peso of 100 centavos. Area: 300 000 sq km (115 830 sq mi). Population (1987 est): 57 360 000. Capital and main port: Manila.

Philistines A non-Semitic people who were driven from Egypt about 1200 BC and settled in *Canaan; the region took the name Palestine from its new settlers. A warlike seafaring people, without cultural pretensions (hence the derogatory word philistine), they were largely absorbed into the kingdom of Israel under King David about 1000 BC.

Philodendron A woody, usually climbing, plant native to tropical America. It clings to trees or other supports by means of roots growing from its stems. Some species are cultivated as house plants for their foliage.

philosopher's stone A substance sought by alchemists for its ability to turn less valuable minerals into gold. It was sometimes thought to have the power of curing all diseases and of making its possessors immortal. *See* alchemy.

philosophy (Greek: love of wisdom) The study of reality and the first principles of thinking, knowledge, and truth. The main branches are *epistemology, *ethics, and *metaphysics. Philosophy arose in Greece in the 6th century BC; the most important ancient philosophers were *Socrates, *Plato, and *Aristotle. Aristotelianism influenced medieval *scholasticism (*see* Anselm; Aquinas) and led to the work of *Descartes, *Spinoza, and *Leibniz. Their rationalism contrasted with the empiricism of the English philosophers *Locke, *Berkeley, and *Hume. *Kant, the most significant thinker of the 18th century, stimulated German idealism in the works of *Hegel, *Schopenhauer, and *Nietzsche in the 19th century. Philosophy in the 20th century has included the existentialism of *Heidegger and *Sartre as well as the logical analysis and the study of the role of language by Bertrand *Russell, G. E. *Moore, and *Wittgenstein, logical positivism (*see* Vienna circle), and the current school of "ordinary language" philosophy centred at Oxford.

phloem Plant tissue specialized to transport foods, mainly sugars, around the plant. It consists chiefly of tubelike cells linked to each other by porous walls (sieve plates). The cells are controlled by small neighbouring cells, known as companion cells.

phlogiston theory An 18th-century theory of combustion based on the belief that all combustible substances contain phlogiston, which is liberated when the substance is heated, leaving calx or ash. The theory was overthrown in the late 18th century by *Lavoisier.

phlox A garden plant native to North America. The flowers have five white, pink, red, or purple spreading petals. The creeping phlox, or moss pink (*Phlox subulata*), forms carpets of flowers in rock gardens.

Phnom Penh (*or* Pnom Penh; Cambodian name: Phnum Pénh) 11 35N 104 55E The capital of Cambodia, a port at the head of the Mekong delta. It is the site of the royal palace, many museums and pagodas, and several universities. Its industries include textiles and food processing. Population (1983 est): 500 000.

phobia An unhealthily strong fear of a particular situation or thing. The main kinds are agoraphobia (fear of open spaces), claustrophobia (fear of enclosed places), social phobias of meeting people, and animal phobias (as of spiders, rats, or snakes). Phobias can be treated by *behaviour therapy or *psychotherapy.

Phoenicia A group of city states on the coastal plain of Syria N of ancient *Canaan. The Semitic peoples who settled here became outstanding navigators and merchants after about 1000 BC. Their major cities were *Tyre, Sidon, and Byblos. The Phoenician alphabet was the ancestor of all western alphabets. Phoenicia was attacked by *Alexander the Great (332 BC), becoming part of the Hellenistic and later the Roman Empires. See p. 420.

phoenix A legendary bird associated with sun worship, especially in Egypt, and representing resurrection and immortality. It resembled an eagle with red and golden plumage and lived for 500 years. The dying phoenix was burnt in a nest of aromatic materials and a new bird arose from its ashes.

Phoenix 33 30N 112 03W A city in the USA, the capital of Arizona on the Salt River. The commercial centre for a cotton and farming region, its industries include the manufacture of aircraft and textiles. Population (1986 est): 881 640.

phonetics The study of sounds in languages. Sounds are classified in terms of the way in which they are produced by the speech organs. The study of the sounds within any given language is called **phonology** and the selected individual sounds are called phonemes.

phosphorescence. *See* luminescence.

phosphorus (P) A nonmetallic solid element discovered by H. Brand (died c. 1692) in 1669. It exists in at least four forms: white (α and β), red, and black. White phosphorus is a waxy solid, which ignites spontaneously in air to form the pentoxide (P_2O_5). Red phosphorus is formed when white phosphorus is heated to 400°C; it is used in matches. Black phosphorus forms when white phosphorus is heated to 200–300°C. Phosphorus occurs chiefly as the mineral *apatite ($Ca_3(PO_4)_2$), from which it is extracted. Phosphates are used extensively as *fertilizers (mainly as "superphosphate"—calcium hydro-

PHOENICIA *From their homeland along the E Mediterranean shore (modern Lebanon and Syria) the Phoenicians traded throughout the Mediterranean and beyond and established many settlements.*

gen phosphate) and also in detergents, water softeners, and specialist glasses. At no 15; at wt 30.9738; mp (white) 44.1°C; bp (white) 280°C.

photoemissive cell *Illumination releases electrons from the cathode.*

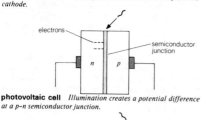

photovoltaic cell *Illumination creates a potential difference at a p–n semiconductor junction.*

photoconductivity cell *Illumination increases the conductivity of a semiconductor, such as selenium.*

PHOTOCELL

photocell (*or* photoelectric cell) A device that makes use of a *photoelectric effect to measure or detect light or other electromagnetic radiation. Photocells are used in light-operated controls (such as fire alarms), solar cells (*see* solar power), and photographic light meters.

photoelectric effects A number of effects in which *electromagnetic radiation interacts with matter, frequently with the emission of electrons. The frequency of the radiation has to be sufficient to liberate the electron. For most substances, an ultraviolet frequency is needed to eject an electron, but for some metals, such as caesium, visible light is sufficient. *See* photocell.

photography The recording of images on specially prepared material. The first photograph

was taken in 1826 by Joseph Nicéphore Niépce (d. 1833). In 1839, *Daguerre introduced the daguerrotype, a positive image of milky white on a silver background, produced directly from silver iodide emulsion on plates exposed inside a simple *camera. Modern photography involves a negative made by developing *film coated with silver salts. The positive picture is obtained by shining light through the negative onto light-sensitive paper with a coating similar to that on the original film. Lenses can be used to enlarge the final image on the print. Transparencies, for use with a slide projector, may also be made. Film is usually developed and printed in a darkroom by dipping it in baths of chemicals. Polaroid photography, however, produces positive pictures directly from the camera in one stage. This system was invented by Edwin Land in 1947 and is used for instant pictures. In **colour photography**, the film has three layers of emulsion, one for each *primary colour; in the subtractive process light from different areas of the scene forms negatives for each primary colour. These are dyed to form filters that subtract colours from white light to construct the image.

photoluminescence. *See* luminescence.

photolysis The breaking of a chemical bond by absorbed *electromagnetic radiation, which can be light, ultraviolet radiation, or X-rays. Examples occur in *photosynthesis, suntan, and photography.

photon The quantum of *electromagnetic radiation, having an energy hf, where h is the Planck constant and f is the frequency of the radiation. It may also be regarded as a massless elementary particle that travels at the speed of *light. *See also* quantum theory.

photosphere The boundary between the atmosphere of a star and its much denser interior. The sun's photosphere is seen as its visible surface but is actually several hundred kilometres thick. Almost all the energy emitted by the sun is radiated from the photosphere. Its temperature is about 4000°C where it merges with the sun's atmosphere. *See also* sunspots.

photosynthesis The means by which plants and certain bacteria produce food (in the form of carbohydrates) from carbon dioxide and hydrogen. The energy for the process is provided by light absorbed by the green pigment chlorophyll, which is contained in the *chloroplasts. Plants use water (H_2O) as the hydrogen source and release oxygen as a by-product. The reaction can be summarized by the equation:

$$6CO_2 + 6H_2O \rightarrow C_6H_{12}O_6 + 6O_2.$$

Phrygia The central and W areas of Asia Minor inhabited after the Hittite empire collapsed (12th century BC) by Thracian migrants. The shortlived Phrygian kingdom reached its peak in the late 8th century. The legendary *Midas was King of Phrygia.

phylloxera A plant-eating insect closely related to the *aphids. The grape, or vine, phylloxera (*Phylloxera vitifoliae* or *Viteus vitifolii*) is a notorious pest of grapevines. The grape phylloxera almost destroyed the wine industry in France in the 19th century.

phylogeny The history of the *evolution of a species or other group of organisms. By studying both fossil remains and the present-day organisms, it is possible to work out how the various groups of plants or animals are related. This can be used to produce a phylogenetic tree, rather like an ancestral tree. Phylogeny forms the basis for most classification systems (*see* taxonomy). It should be distinguished from **ontogeny**, which is the series of developmental stages through which an individual organism passes during its lifetime.

phylum. *See* taxonomy.

physics The study of the relationship between matter and energy, without reference to chemical change. Traditionally the subject was divided into the study of mechanics, electricity and magnetism, heat and thermodynamics, optics, and acoustics. More modern aspects of the subject include quantum mechanics, relativity, nuclear physics, particle physics, solid-state physics, and astrophysics.

physiology The study of how living organisms and their constituent parts function. Physiology is closely linked with both *anatomy and *biochemistry.

pi In mathematics, the ratio of the circumference of a circle to its diameter, denoted by the Greek letter π. It was proved to be an irrational *number by J. H. Lambert (1728–77) and a transcendental number by F. Lindemann (1852–1939). Its value is 3.14159 . . . .

Piaf, Edith (Edith Giovanna Gassion; 1915–63) French cabaret and music-hall singer. Originally a street singer, her small size earned her the nickname "piaf" (French slang: sparrow). Her songs include "Je ne regrette rien" and "La Vie en rose."

piano A musical instrument consisting of a number of wire strings stretched over a metal frame, which are hit by felt-covered wooden hammers operated by a keyboard. The piano was invented by Bartolommeo Cristofori (1655–1731) in the early 18th century; the name derives from the Italian *pianoforte*, soft-loud, referring to the variation in volume obtainable on the piano in contrast to the earlier *clavichord and *harpsichord. In the modern instrument the frame is either horizontal, as in the **grand piano**, or vertical, as in the **upright piano**. The piano has a range of seven and a quarter octaves.

Picardy (French name: Picardie) A planning region and former province in N France. It was made part of France in 1477 by Louis XI of France. Area: 19 411 sq km (7493 sq mi). Population (1986 est): 1 774 000.

Picasso, Pablo (1881–1973) Spanish artist, who trained in Barcelona but worked chiefly in Paris after 1900. Although his most popular paintings are those of his blue (1901–04) and rose (1905–08) periods, his most original work began with Les Demoiselles d'Avignon (1907), influenced by Cézanne and African sculpture, and resulted in his development of *cubism with *Braque. One of his major works, *Guernica* (1937) is a horrific depiction of the destruction of the Basque capital during the Spanish Civil War.

Piccard A family of Swiss scientists and explorers. **Auguste Piccard** (1884–1962) and his twin **Jean-Félix Piccard** (1884–1963) pioneered the scientific study of the stratosphere in balloons, reaching a height of 16 940 metres in 1932. In 1948 Auguste designed a bathyscaphe, using it to explore the sea depths. His son **Jacques Piccard** (1927–   ) worked with his father designing bathyscaphes; he reached a depth of 10 917 metres in 1960.

piccolo A woodwind instrument, the smallest and shrillest member of the *flute family. It is pitched an octave higher than the flute and its music is written an octave lower than it sounds.

picketing The act of employees in guarding their place of work to persuade others not to work, to help their case in a trade dispute. **Primary picketing** (in which the employer is directly involved in the dispute) is not wrongful if carried out peacefully. **Secondary picketing** (in which the employer is not directly involved) is usually illegal, but employees may, for example, picket an employer who is a supplier of the employer in the dispute. **Flying pickets** are ready to move at a moment's notice to a plant at which they are not employed. Flying picketing is against the law in the UK.

pick-up A device that converts information stored in a gramophone record or compact disc into an electrical signal. In a record player, the pick-up cartridge, usually removable, consists of a stylus and a transducer. The stylus is forced to vibrate by the rippled surface in the record groove. The transducer responds electrically to these vibrations. *See also* recording of sound.

Picts (painted people) The Roman name (referring to their tattoos) for all Scottish tribes living N of the *Antonine Wall. The Picts had forced the Romans to withdraw behind *Hadrian's Wall by 200 AD, and remained independent until Kenneth I MacAlpine unified S Scotland in the 9th century.

piddock A burrowing *bivalve mollusc of cold and temperate seas. Piddocks have shells with serrated cutting edges for boring into rock. They can damage concrete breakwaters, sea walls, and wharves.

Piedmont (Italian name: Piemonte) A region in NW Italy. It was the nucleus of Italian unification in the mid-19th century. Manufacturing is important, with engineering and steel centred on Turin; other industries include textiles, chemicals, rubber, and food products. Agriculture is also important. Area: 25 400 sq km (9807 sq mi). Population (1987): 4 377 229. Capital: Turin.

Piero della Francesca (c. 1420–92) Italian Renaissance painter. *The Baptism of Christ* (National Gallery, London) shows his monumental figure style. At the court of Urbino he painted the double portrait of the duke and his wife in profile (Uffizi). His lifelong interest in perspective is reflected in his fresco series *The Legend of the True Cross*, painted for the church of S Francesco, Arezzo.

Pietermaritzburg 29 36S 30 24E A city in South Africa, the capital of Natal. It was founded by Boers (1838) and named after their leaders, Piet Retief and Gert Maritz, massacred by the Zulus. Population (1986): 133 809.

piezoelectric effect The production of electric charges on the opposite faces of certain crystals, such as quartz and Rochelle salt, when they are compressed or expanded. The charges on the two faces are of equal magnitude but opposite in sign and depend on whether the crystal is expanded or compressed. In the opposite effect a voltage applied across a piezoelectric crystal causes it to expand or contract. The effect is used in the piezoelectric oscillator, the crystal microphone, and the piezoelectric loudspeaker.

pig A hoofed mammal native to Europe, Asia, and Africa, also called hog or swine, having a large head with a long cylindrical snout used for digging up food from the soil. Descended from the wild *boar, modern breeds of domestic pig (*Sus scrofa*) are reared for pork and bacon (*see* livestock farming). Other members of the pig family include the *warthog. *See also* peccary.

pigeon A bird occurring worldwide except in the coldest regions; the smaller long-tailed forms are called doves. 17–75 cm long, pigeons have soft plumage, short bill and legs, and a characteristic cooing call. They are often fast fliers and some migrate long distances. Domesticated breeds are used as messengers and for racing. *See also* wood pigeon.

Piggott, Lester Keith (1935–) British jockey, who rode his first winner at the age of 12 (1948). Champion jockey eleven times and Derby winner a record nine times. He retired to become a trainer in 1985, having won a record 29 *Classics. He was imprisoned (1987–88) for tax evasion. He returned as a jockey in 1990.

pig iron The type of iron produced by *blast furnaces and used as the first stage in *steel making. It has a high carbon content (about 4% by weight) and contains impurities, including some slag, which make it brittle. *See also* cast iron.

pika A small mammal of Asia and North America, related to rabbits and also called mouse hare, cony, and rock rabbit. 12.5–30 cm long and resembling large short-tailed mice, pikas live in cold rocky areas at high altitudes.

pike A freshwater fish found in temperate regions of Europe, Asia, and America. It has a broad flat snout and strong teeth, feeding on fish and other animals. The common pike (*Esox lucius*) is olive-grey above with silvery underparts and pale spots.

Pilate, Pontius (1st century AD) Roman governor. As procurator of Judaea and Samaria (26–36) he condemned Christ to death but, according to the New Testament Gospels, did so reluctantly. He came into frequent conflict with the Jews and was finally dismissed for his cruel suppression of a Samaritan rebellion.

pilchard A food fish, *Sardina pilchardus*, related to the herring and sprat, that occurs in the Mediterranean, E Atlantic, and English Channel. 25–35 cm long, it is bluish green above and whitish below and swims in large shoals. Pilchards up to one year old are called sardines.

piles. *See* haemorrhoids.

Pilgrimage of Grace (1536) A revolt in N England against the government of Henry VIII. The rebels opposed the recent *Reformation laws and the dissolution of the monasteries. Some 230 men, including their leader Robert Ashe, were executed.

Pilgrim Fathers The 102 English colonists who established the first settlement in New England in 1620. They included 35 Puritans, escaping persecution in England, and sailed in the *Mayflower* to New Plymouth, Massachusetts.

Pill, the. *See* oral contraceptive.

Piltdown man Skeletal remains once thought to be those of a fossil *hominid, found on Piltdown Common, near Lewes (England), in 1912. In 1953–54 the "find" was shown to be a hoax.

pimento. *See* allspice.

pimpernel A slender plant of the primrose family, found in Eurasia, Africa, and America. Growing 5–30 cm tall, pimpernels have small red, pink, blue, or white bell-shaped flowers. The most common species is the scarlet pimpernel (*Anagallis arvensis*).

pine A coniferous tree widely distributed in the N hemisphere. Pines have long slender needles and hanging cones. Pines are important softwoods: the timber is easily worked and yields turpentine, tar, pitch, and other resinous products. A widely planted species is the Scots pine (*Pinus sylvestris*), of N and W Europe and Asia, up to 40 m high. *See also* stone pine.

pineal gland A small gland within the brain. In certain lizards it can sense light and is visible externally as a third eye (pineal eye); in humans its function is unknown, although it may help to regulate the onset of puberty.

pineapple A plant, *Ananas comosus*, native to tropical and subtropical America and cultivated in many warm and tropical regions for its fruit. This ripens 5–6 months after flowering begins and can weigh up to 10 kg. The major producing countries are the Hawaiian Islands, Brazil, Mexico, Cuba, and the Philippines.

pine marten A European carnivorous mammal, *Martes martes*. About 70 cm long, it inhabits dense evergreen forests, preying on squirrels, birds, insects, and eggs. The female has a litter (2–5 cubs) only every second year.

Pinero, Sir Arthur Wing (1855–1934) British dramatist. His early plays, which included *The Magistrate* (1885) and *Dandy Dick* (1887), were successful farces. His later plays, notably *The Second Mrs Tanqueray* (1893), were more serious treatments of contemporary social problems.

pink A garden plant related to the *carnation. Pinks have long slender leaves and showy white, pink, or red fragrant flowers, often with fringed petals.

Pinochet, Augusto (1915–) Chilean general and head of state (1973–). He led a military coup that overthrew the government of Salvador Allende and became the head of a repressive military junta. After electoral defeat in 1988 he relinquished office in 1990 but retained control of the army.

pintail A duck, *Anas acuta*, that breeds on inland waters in the N hemisphere and winters in coastal areas. The male has a dark-brown head and neck with a white band down the neck, grey flanks, and long black central tail feathers. Females have mottled brown plumage.

Pinter, Harold (1930–) British dramatist. In his plays, which include *The Birthday Party* (1958), *The Caretaker* (1960), *The Homecoming* (1965), and *Mountain Language* (1988), he evokes an atmosphere of tension and mystery. He has also written film scripts and directed plays.

pinworm A slender parasitic *nematode worm, *Enterobius vermicularius*, also called seatworm or threadworm. Up to 1 cm long, pinworms inhabit the human intestine; female worms migrate to the anus to lay thousands of eggs, causing itching, especially at night.

Pinyin. *See* Chinese.

pion Any of three elementary particles (*see* particle physics) classified as mesons (symbol: π). The charged pions (π^+ and π^-) have a mass slightly greater than that of the neutral pion (π°).

pipal. *See* bo tree.

Piper, John (1903–) British painter and writer. He painted abstract works in the 1930s and was an official war artist in World War II. He is best known for his watercolours and aquatints of architecture. He has also designed stained glass, notably for Coventry Cathedral.

pipistrelle A small widely distributed insect-eating *bat. The Eurasian pipistrelle (*Pipistrellus pipistrellus*) is about 3.5 cm long with a 20-cm wingspan. Pipistrelles have a grasping tail, used when crawling into crevices to roost.

pipit A small insect-eating songbird, 14–16 cm long, with a brown-streaked plumage and paler speckled underparts. The meadow pipit (*Anthus pratensis*) occurs on moors and downs in Britain. The water pipit (*A. spinoletta*) inhabits the high mountains of Europe, Asia, and North America.

Piraeus (Modern Greek name: Piraiévs) 37 57N 23 42E The chief port of Greece, SW of Athens on the Saronic Gulf. It was founded during the 5th century BC as the port of Athens. Industries include shipbuilding, oil refining, and chemicals. Its exports include wine and olive oil. Population (1981): 196 389.

Pirandello, Luigi (1867–1936) Italian dramatist and novelist. His writing was greatly influenced by life with his insane wife. He gained international success with his plays exploring the nature of reality and illusion, notably *Six Char-*

acters in Search of an Author (1921) and *Henry IV* (1922). He won the Nobel Prize in 1934.

piranha A South American freshwater fish, also called caribe and piraya. It has a deep body, ranging from silver to black in colour, strong jaws, and razor-sharp teeth. Piranhas swim in groups and eagerly devour other fish; they will also attack larger animals and humans.

Pisa 43 43N 10 24E A city in Italy, in Tuscany on the River Arno. Dating from Etruscan times, it is a popular tourist centre, the most famous of its buildings being the Leaning Tower of Pisa, 59 m (194 ft) high and about 5 m (17 ft) out of perpendicular. Machinery, textiles, bicycles, and glass are manufactured. Population (1987): 103 527.

Pisano, Nicola (c. 1220–c. 1278) Italian sculptor. He launched the revival of antique Roman forms that led eventually to Renaissance sculpture, beginning with his pulpit in the Baptistry, Pisa. Later works reveal the cooperation of his son **Giovanni Pisano** (c. 1250–1314). Giovanni introduced French gothic elements into his sculptures for the façade of Siena Cathedral.

Pissarro, Camille (1830–1903) French impressionist painter, born in the West Indies. Chiefly influenced by *Corot, he was more interested in landscape structure than the other impressionists. In the 1880s he experimented with *pointillism.

pistachio A small Eurasian tree, *Pistacia vera*, 7–10 m high, widely cultivated in Mediterranean regions for its edible green kernels ("nuts"). These are used as dessert nuts and for decorating and flavouring confectionery, cakes, etc.

pistil The part of a flower consisting of the female reproductive organs. It consists of one or more *carpels, which may be united into a single structure. Some plants, such as the cucumber, have separate male and female flowers: the latter are described as pistillate.

pistol A short-range low-weight firearm that can be used with one hand. Pistols are divided into two classes: the *revolver and the automatic. The first automatics (1893) combined a box magazine in the butt with a recoil loading action.

Pitcairn Islands A small island group in the central S Pacific Ocean, a British dependent territory, consisting of Pitcairn Island and three uninhabited islands. Subsistence agriculture is the chief occupation. Pitcairn Island was occupied in 1790 by mutineers from the *Bounty* and women from Tahiti. Area: 4.6 sq km (1.75 sq mi). Population (1990): 49. Chief town: Adamstown.

pitchblende The chief ore of uranium. It is a form of uraninite, UO_2, a black radioactive mineral found in hydrothermal veins and certain igneous rocks.

pitcher plant A *carnivorous plant with pitcher-shaped leaves. The pitcher is often brightly coloured and secretes nectar to attract insects, which often fall inside and drown in the digestive juices at the bottom of the pitcher.

Pitman, Sir Isaac. *See* shorthand.

pitot tube An instrument for measuring the velocity of liquids, aircraft airspeeds, and other fluids, invented by Henri Pitot (1695–1771). It consists of an L-shaped tube placed in the moving fluid; the vertical limb of the tube has an opening facing into the flow. The difference in pressure between the interior of the tube and the surroundings enables the velocity of the fluid to be calculated.

Pittsburgh 40 26N 80 00W A city in the USA, in Pennsylvania where the Allegheny and Monongahela Rivers form the Ohio River. It is a major steel centre and the country's largest inland port. Other manufactures include machinery, petroleum, coal, glass, and chemicals. Population (1986): 387 490.

Pitt the Elder, William, 1st Earl of Chatham (1708–78) British statesman, known as the Great Commoner. Entering parliament in 1735, he established a reputation as an outstanding speaker. In 1756 he became secretary of state and leader of the House of Commons but was dismissed in 1757 and then recalled to form a ministry with *Newcastle. In charge of foreign affairs, he was largely responsible for British victory in the *Seven Years' War, reorganizing the militia and navy.

His second son **William Pitt the Younger** (1759–1806) was twice prime minister (1783–1801, 1804–06), the youngest in British history. He reduced the public debt by adopting the ideas of Adam *Smith. He also reformed the Indian administration. Pitt agreed the first (1793) and second (1798) alliances against France (see Revolutionary and Napoleonic Wars) and resolved the Irish crisis by the Act of *Union (1800). His second ministry was marked by an alliance with Russia, Sweden, and Austria against Napoleon.

pituitary gland The major *endocrine gland, about 12 mm by 8 mm, lying within the skull close to the centre of the head. It controls all other parts of the endocrine system. The anterior (front) lobe produces *growth hormone, *prolactin, and hormones that regulate the function of other glands. The posterior (back) lobe is attached to the *hypothalamus and stores various *neurohormones that are manufactured in this part of the brain.

Pius V, St (Michele Ghislieri; 1504–72) Pope (1566–72). A Dominican friar, he enforced the decrees of the Council of *Trent and expanded the activities of the *Inquisition. He excommunicated the Protestant Elizabeth I of England in 1570. He was made a saint in 1712. Feast day: 30 April.

Pius IX (Giovanni Maria Mastai-Ferretti; 1792–1878) Pope (1846–78). At first sympathetic to liberal and nationalist movements, he abandoned radicalism after the Revolution of 1848, in which he fled Rome. He refused to acknowledge the newly established kingdom of Italy, in which Rome was included in 1870.

Pizarro, Francisco (c. 1475–1541) Spanish conquistador, who explored the NW coast of South America in the 1520s. In 1531 he treacherously murdered the Inca king, Atahuallpa. Over the next nine years he completed the Spanish conquest of the Inca empire, founding Lima in 1535.

placenta 1. An organ formed within the womb of mammals and certain other animals during pregnancy. Composed of tissues from both mother and fetus, it enables the fetus to receive nutrients and oxygen from the mother's blood via the umbilical cord and its waste products to be absorbed into the mother's circulation. **2.** A tissue in plants that connects the ovules (later the seeds) to the ovary (later the fruit wall).

plague An infectious disease caused by the bacterium *Yersinia pestis*, which is transmitted to man by rat fleas. The most common, bubonic plague, causes fever, vomiting, and inflamed lymph nodes (buboes). Epidemics afflicted Europe throughout the middle ages, the *Black Death (1348) being the most devastating. The **Great Plague of London** (1665–66) claimed 70 000 lives. Plague is now restricted to areas of poor sanitation in tropical countries.

plaice A *flatfish, *Pleuronectes platessa*, extensively fished in the North Atlantic and British coastal waters. Usually 25–40 cm long, it is brown with orange spots above and white beneath.

Plaid Cymru A political party, founded in 1925, dedicated to Welsh independence from the UK. Support for the party declined after Welsh voters rejected *devolution (1979).

Planck, Max Karl Ernst Ludwig (1858–1947) German physicist, who discovered the *quantum theory. *See also* Planck's radiation law. For this work he received the Nobel Prize in 1918. His eldest son, **Erwin Planck** (1914–44) was executed for his involvement in the plot to assassinate Hitler.

Planck's radiation law The basic law of *quantum theory, that electromagnetic radiation (frequency f) is emitted from and absorbed by matter in discrete amounts (quanta) known as *photons. The energy (E) of a photon is given by $E = hf$, where h is the **Planck constant** (which has the value $6.626\ 196 \times 10^{-34}$ J s). Max *Planck discovered the law (1900) while investigating the distribution of wavelengths of the radiation emitted by a *black body.

planet A celestial body that moves around a star and shines by light reflected from its surface. The only known planets are those orbiting the sun (solar system): there are nine major planets and numerous *minor planets. The major planets in order from the sun are *Mercury, *Venus, *earth, and *Mars (the **terrestrial planets**), *Jupiter, *Saturn, *Uranus, and *Neptune (the **giant planets**) and *Pluto.

plane tree A large tree native to the N hemisphere. Up to 50 m tall, the trees have patchy bark, lobed leaves, and clusters (catkins) of male and female flowers: the female flowers give rise to bristly fruits. The hybrid London plane (*P. × acerifolia*) is a valuable hardwood.

plankton Minute or microscopic animals (zooplankton) and plants (phytoplankton) that float in open waters. The phytoplankton carry out *photosynthesis in the surface waters. The zooplankton include protozoa, small crustaceans, and larvae. Plankton are of great importance as a food for fish and whales.

plant Any of a vast group of living organisms classified in the kingdom *Plantae*; there are some 400 000 species. Plants are typically immobile

PLANT

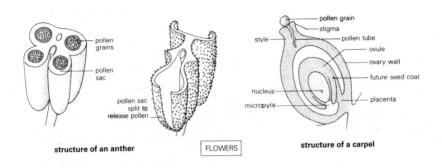

structure of an anther

FLOWERS

structure of a carpel

pollen grains
pollen sac

pollen sac split to release pollen

pollen grain
stigma
style
pollen tube
ovule
ovary wall
future seed coat
nucleus
placenta
micropyle

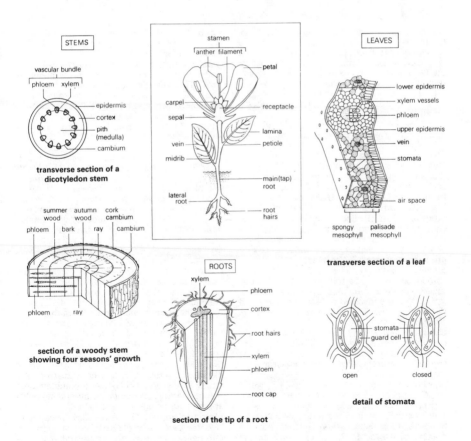

STEMS

vascular bundle
phloem xylem

epidermis
cortex
pith (medulla)
cambium

transverse section of a dicotyledon stem

summer wood autumn wood cork cambium
phloem bark ray cambium
phloem ray

section of a woody stem showing four seasons' growth

stamen
anther filament
petal
carpel
sepal
receptacle
lamina
vein
petiole
midrib
main(tap) root
lateral root
root hairs

ROOTS

xylem
phloem
cortex
root hairs
xylem
phloem
root cap

section of the tip of a root

LEAVES

lower epidermis
xylem vessels
phloem
upper epidermis
vein
stomata
air space
spongy mesophyll palisade mesophyll

transverse section of a leaf

stomata
guard cell
open closed

detail of stomata

broad category	major groups (usually divisions)	important classes	representative members
ALGAE	Chlorophyta Chrysophyta Phaeophyta Rhodophyta		green algae (*Spirogyra*, sea lettuce, etc.) yellow-green algae, diatoms brown algae (wracks, kelps, etc.) red algae
FUNGI	Myxomycophyta Eumycophyta	Phycomycetes Ascomycetes Basidiomycetes	slime fungi (clubroot, etc.) pin mold *Penicillium, Aspergillus* mushrooms, puffballs, bracket fungi
MOSSES and LIVERWORTS	Bryophyta	Hepaticae Musci	liverworts (e.g. *Pellia*) mosses (e.g. *Sphagnum*)
VASCULAR PLANTS (TRACHEOPHYTES)	Pteridophyta	Lycopsida Sphenopsida Pteropsida	clubmosses horsetails ferns
	Spermatophyta (seed plants)	Gymnospermae Angiospermae	cycads, *Ginkgo*, conifers (pines, larches, spruces, etc.) monocotyledons (grasses, palms, orchids, lilies, etc.), dicotyledons (most trees and flowering plants)

PLANT *A simplified classification of the plant kingdom.*

and most manufacture their own food by *photosynthesis. Plant cells have rigid walls and grow to give support, from specialized zones of tissue (*see* meristem), continuously or periodically. Plants lack sense organs and a nervous system; response to external stimuli is usually slow and often irreversible. Green plants are the primary source of food and oxygen (from photosynthesis) for all animals.

Plantagenet The surname (formally adopted in the 15th century) of the Angevin, Lancastrian, and Yorkist Kings of England (1154–1485). They were descended from Queen Matilda and Geoffrey Martel, Count of Anjou (d. 1151), who was nicknamed Plantagenet because he wore a sprig of broom (*plante genêt*) in his cap.

Plantagenet, Richard, Duke of York. *See* York, Richard Plantagenet, 3rd Duke of.

plantain 1. A plant occurring in temperate regions and on mountains in the tropics, often as a troublesome weed. The stalk bears a dense head of green, white, yellow, or brown flowers with protruding stamens. 2. *See* banana.

plasma (anatomy) The fluid constituent of *blood, consisting of a solution of various salts, sugars, etc., and containing numerous proteins, including those involved in *blood clotting and the immunological response (i.e. antibodies). *Compare* serum.

plasma (physics) A gas in which the atoms are completely ionized. Sometimes called the fourth state of matter, plasmas occur at enormously high temperatures (*see also* thermonuclear reactors).

plaster A paste used to coat ceilings, walls, etc. A number of forms are in use, the traditional one being a mixture of lime, sand, and water, which hardens in air owing to drying and reaction with atmospheric carbon dioxide.

plaster of Paris Hydrated calcium sulphate ($CaSO_4.\frac{1}{2}H_2O$) made by partial dehydration of *gypsum by heating. When mixed with water it

sets into a hard mass, consisting of the dihydrate ($CaSO_4.2H_2O$). It is used for casts for broken limbs and for modelling.

plastics Synthetic materials consisting of polymers, which are moulded during manufacture. **Thermosetting plastics**, such as *polyurethanes, *polyesters, and *epoxy resins, harden on heating to give a rigid product that cannot then be softened. **Thermoplastic materials**, including *polythene and *cellulose derivatives, soften when heated and harden again when cooled.

The first synthetic material was Celluloid, made in 1870 from cotton and camphor. This highly inflammable substance was replaced during World War I by cellulose acetate and casein products. These materials were all based on naturally occurring large molecules. The first polymers to be made by joining together smaller molecules were the phenol-formaldehyde resins (trade name Bakelite) invented in 1908 by Leo Baekeland (1863–1944). Since then a vast number of resins have been synthesized.

Plata, Río de la (English name: River Plate) The estuary of the Río Paraná and the River Uruguay, on the Atlantic coast of SE South America. Montevideo, the capital of Uruguay, lies on the N shore and Buenos Aires, the capital of Argentina, is situated on the S shore. A naval battle was fought off its mouth in 1939 (*see* World War II). Length: 275 km (171 mi). Width (at mouth): 225 km (140 mi).

platelet A small particle, 0.001–0.002 mm in diameter, produced by the bone marrow and found in the blood. Platelets are essential for *blood clotting, accumulating in large numbers at the site of an injured blood vessel.

plate tectonics The theory, developed mainly in the 1960s, that the earth's crust is divided into rigid plates (oceanic, continental, or a combination of both), which move about the earth's surface at rates of 1–9 cm per annum. At constructive plate margins new oceanic crust is created where two plates move apart and magma rises to fill the gap; this occurs at midocean ridges. At destructive plate margins two plates collide and one dips beneath the other, producing deep-sea trenches. Where two continental plates collide, mountain chains are formed.

platinum (Pt) A high-melting precious silvery metal that does not rust or tarnish. Found in nature in nickel ore, it can absorb large quantities of hydrogen and is used as a catalyst, particularly in making sulphuric acid. It is also used in thermocouple wires and jewellery. Its compounds include the hexafluoride (PtF_6), a powerful oxidizing agent. At no 78; at wt 195.09; mp 1772°C; bp 3827 ± 100°C.

Plato (429–347 BC) Greek philosopher. An Athenian nobleman and follower of *Socrates. In 387 he founded his *Academy, to which he devoted the rest of his life. Some of Plato's poetry and all his prose survive. Apart from 13 letters possibly by him and the *Apology*, which is supposedly Socrates' defence of himself before his judges, they are dramatic dialogues of outstanding literary merit, illustrating Socrates' philosophy. The *Phaedo*, *Symposium*, and *Republic* of Plato's middle period develop Plato's views on metaphysics, love, and government.

platypus. See duck-billed platypus.

plebeians Romans other than the privileged *patricians. At first without civil rights, they forced the Senate in 493 BC to appoint their own tribunes and an assembly. During the following two centuries the plebeians gained admission to all Roman offices.

Pléiade, La A group of seven French 16th-century writers who sought to free French poetry from medieval tradition. Their principles, deriving from the study of Greek, Latin, and Italian literature, were laid down in *Défense et illustration de la langue française* (1549) by Joachim du Bellay (1522–60); their innovations included the sonnet, the ode, and the alexandrine. Led by Pierre de Ronsard (1524–85), the group included du Bellay, J.-A. de Baïf (1532–89), Etienne Jodelle (c. 1532–73), Rémy Belleau (c. 1528–77), Pontus de Tyard (c. 1522–1605), and Jacques Peletier (1517–82) or Jean Dorat (1508–88).

Pleistocene epoch The epoch of geological time between the Pliocene and the Holocene, at the beginning of the Quaternary period. It lasted from about 1.8 million to 10 000 years ago. It is often called the *Ice Age because during this time the earth experienced great fluctuations in temperature. Fossils from the Pleistocene include horses, pigs, and elephants.

plesiosaur A widely distributed marine reptile of the Jurassic and Cretaceous periods (200–65 million years ago). Up to about 12 m long, plesiosaurs had broad turtle-like bodies with paddle limbs and jaws with sharp teeth used to catch fish.

pleurisy An illness involving inflammation of the pleura—the membrane that covers the lungs and lines the chest cavity. The commonest cause of pleurisy is bacterial or viral infection. The pa-

tient will often have a fever, cough, and a pain in the chest.

Plimsoll line A series of lines on the outside of a cargo ship's hull showing the safe levels to

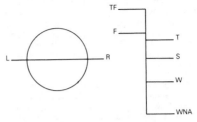

PLIMSOLL LINE *The lines and letters mark the waterline under various conditions. TF = fresh water in the tropics; F = fresh water; T = salt in the tropics; S = salt water in the summer; W = salt water in the winter; WNA = winter in the N Atlantic. LR represents Lloyd's Register.*

which the ship can be loaded. The measure was introduced in the UK as a result of the Merchant Shipping Act (1876) at the instigation of the MP Samuel Plimsoll (1824–98).

Pliny the Elder (Gaius Plinius Secundus; 23–79 AD) Roman scholar, whose encyclopedia, *Natural History*, was a source of knowledge until the 17th century. During his military career, Pliny assembled material from numerous sources on many subjects, including astrology, geography, agriculture, medicine, zoology, and botany. His nephew and adopted son **Pliny the Younger** (Gaius Plinius Caecilius Secundus; c. 61–c. 113 AD) held various administrative posts and was a prominent legal speaker. His ten volumes of letters provide an unofficial history of his time.

Pliocene epoch. See Tertiary period.

PLO. See Palestine Liberation Organization.

Plotinus (205–70 AD) Greek philosopher and founder of *Neoplatonism. Born in Egypt, he finally settled in Rome. Developing *Plato's ideas, he taught that the impersonal "One" is the ground of all existence. From it come the mind, soul, and nature. By rejecting material nature and improving the intellect, man may briefly unite with the One.

plover A widespread bird having brown or grey plumage, often mottled, with white underparts. They feed on insects and other small invertebrates and nest on the ground. See also lapwing.

plum A widely cultivated small tree, *Prunus domestica*, of the rose family, native to SW Asia. It has white flowers and the fruit is eaten fresh, cooked, canned, or dried as prunes. See also blackthorn; damson.

Plutarch (c. 46–c. 120 AD) Greek biographer, essayist, and a priest of Delphi. His *Parallel Lives* consists of biographies of 23 pairs of Greek and Roman statesmen and soldiers. The *Moralia* contain 83 essays.

Pluto (astronomy) The smallest and usually outermost planet, orbiting the sun every 248 years at a mean distance of 5900 million km. Pluto was discovered in 1930 but little was known about it until its satellite was discovered in 1978. It is a very cold low-density body about 3000 km in diameter.

Pluto (mythology). *See* Hades.

plutonium (Pu) An important *transuranic element discovered in 1940. Trace quantities exist in ores. It is produced in large quantities in nuclear reactors by beta-decay from uranium-239 (*see* nuclear energy). Plutonium was used in the atomic bomb dropped on Nagasaki in 1945 (*see* nuclear weapons). It forms oxides (PuO, PuO_2), halides (for example PuF_3), and other compounds. It is used in fast reactors and small power units for spacecraft. At no 94; at wt (244); mp 641°C; bp 3235°C.

Plymouth 50 23N 4 10W A port in SW England, in Devon between the Tamar and Plym estuaries. On Plymouth Hoe Drake is reputed to have finished his game of bowls while the Spanish Armada approached. Plymouth is an important naval base with associated marine industries. More recent industries include clothing, radio equipment, and processed foods. Population (1981): 243 895.

Plymouth Brethren A strict Protestant sect founded at Plymouth in 1830 by a former Anglican priest, J. N. Darby (1800–82). The Brethren have strict standards of behaviour and avoid many trades and professions. Small groups exist throughout the world.

pneumoconiosis Chronic lung disease caused by breathing in dust, most commonly coal dust (causing coalworkers' pneumoconiosis) and silica (causing *silicosis). Usually, the signs (breathlessness, shadows on the lungs) do not appear until long after initial exposure. *See also* asbestosis.

pneumonia Inflammation of the lungs, most commonly caused by infection. The most common form is **bronchopneumonia**, which also affects the bronchi. The patient has a fever, cough, and pain in the chest.

Po, River (Latin name: Padus) The longest river in Italy rising in the Cottian Alps and flowing mainly ENE through Turin to enter the Adriatic Sea. The Po Valley is the most fertile and economically important region in Italy. Length: 652 km (405 mi).

pochard A large-headed *duck, *Aythya ferina*, occurring in temperate inland waters of Europe and Asia. It has grey legs and a grey-blue bill; males have a reddish head, black breast, and grey body; females are brown.

pocket gopher A *rodent found in North and Central America. They inhabit open dry country, where they dig extensive burrows. Their large cheek pouches have an outside opening like a pocket.

Poe, Edgar Allan (1809–49) US poet, short-story writer, and critic. Among his many prose tales and horror stories are "The Fall of the House of Usher" (1839), "The Black Cat" (1843), and the first ever detective story, "The Murders in the Rue Morgue" (1841). His best-known poems are "The Raven" (1845) and *The Bells* (1849).

poet laureate A title given by the British monarch to a contemporary poet, whose traditional duties include the writing of commemorative odes on important public occasions. The first official poet laureate was John Dryden (from 1668 to 1688); the most recent include C. Day Lewis (1968–72), John Betjeman (1972–84), and Ted Hughes (1984–).

poinsettia An ornamental shrub, *Euphorbia pulcherrima*, native to Mexico and tropical America and a popular pot plant at Christmas in Europe and North America. It has clusters of tiny greenish-yellow flowers surrounded by large scarlet or cream-coloured petal-like bracts.

pointer A breed of sporting dog originating in England and named after its habit of pointing its nose towards game. It has a long tapering tail, a long muzzle, and drooping ears. The short smooth coat is white combined with yellow, orange, liver, or black. Height: 63–68 cm (dogs); 61–66 cm (bitches).

pointillism A style of painting using dots of pure colour. The pointillists applied primary colours to the canvas in dots and allowed the colours to be mixed by the eye. It was developed by *Seurat in France in the 1880s.

point-to-point. *See* steeplechase.

Poisson, Siméon Dénis (1781–1840) French mathematician. He made important contributions to the mathematical theory of electricity, magnetism, and mechanics. His work on electricity led him in 1837 to discover **Poisson's equation** concerning electric fields. **Poisson's distribution** is widely used in probability calculations and **Poisson's ratio** is used by engineers in studying stress.

Poland, People's Republic of A country in N Europe, on the Baltic Sea. The Carpathian Mountains in the S reach heights of over 2500 m (8000 ft). *Economy*: agriculture is important, the chief crops being rye, wheat, oats, sugar beet, and potatoes. Minerals include copper and sulphur. Poland's industries include shipbuilding, textiles, engineering, steel, cement, chemicals, and food products. *History*: Poland first appeared as a separate state in the 10th century and became a leading power under the Jagiellon dynasty (1386–1572). Foreign intervention in the 18th century culminated in division by Russia, Austria, and Prussia (in 1772, 1793, and 1795). After World War I independence was declared (1918). Germany's invasion of Poland (1939) precipitated *World War II, at the end of which Poland was occupied by the Russians. The first postwar elections (1948) brought a communist-controlled government to power under Wladyslaw Gomulka. In December, 1981, the independent trade union *Solidarity, led by Lech *Walesa, was accused of attempting to overthrow the government, and a state of martial law was declared. Martial law was lifted in 1983 but unrest continued. In 1989 Solidarity was relegalized and won elections; Walesa became president in 1990. Official language: Polish. Official currency: zloty of 100 groszy. Area: 312 677 sq km (120 624 sq mi). Population (1989 est): 38 000 000. Capital: Warsaw. Main port: Gdańsk.

Polanski, Roman (1933–) Polish film director, born in Paris. After 1961 he worked in Britain and the USA. His films include *Repulsion* (1965), *Rosemary's Baby* (1968), and *The Tenant* (1976), marked by an atmosphere of tension and menace, *Tess* (1979), and *Frantic* (1988).

polar bear A white bear, *Thalarctos maritimus*, living on the shores of the Arctic Ocean. Up to 2.5 m long and weighing 500–700 kg, polar bears hunt seals, fish, and birds.

Polaris missile A US navy two-stage solid-fuelled nuclear missile launched from a submarine and having a range of 4500 km (2800 m). Travelling at speeds of over mach 10 (*see* Mach number), some versions (Poseidon) are capable of delivering 10 separately guided 15-*kiloton warheads.

polarized light Light in which the direction of vibration is restricted. In ordinary light the transverse vibrations of the electric and magnetic fields are at right angles to each other in all possible planes. In **plane-polarized light** the vibrations of the electric field are confined to one plane and the magnetic field to one at right angles to it. Plane-polarized light can be produced by reflection at a certain angle or by passing light through certain materials, such as Polaroid.

polder An area of low-lying land reclaimed from the sea or other water, often for agricultural purposes. Polders are usually formed by constructing dykes around the area, which is then drained. The most notable polders are those of Holland, next to the IJsselmeer.

polecat A carnivorous mammal, *Mustela putorius*, of Europe, Asia, and N Africa. About 50 cm long, it has a dark-brown coat with yellowish patches on the face and ears. Polecats are active at night; they eject a vile-smelling fluid when alarmed. *See also* ferret.

Poles, North and South The most northerly and southerly points of the earth's surface and the ends of the earth's axis, about which it rotates. The magnetic north and south poles are the points to which a magnetic compass needle points. They do not coincide with the geographical poles and their positions slowly change. *See also* Arctic Circle; Antarctica.

pole star Either of two bright stars that are nearest the N or S celestial pole (*see* celestial sphere). The poles are not fixed in position but trace out two circles in the sky over a period of 25 800 years. There is thus a sequence of stars that slowly, in turn, become the N or S pole star. The present N pole star is Polaris, the brightest star in the constellation Ursa Minor. There is no bright star near the S celestial pole.

pole vault A field event for men in athletics, in which competitors use a fibreglass pole to lever themselves over a horizontal bar. A competitor is allowed three tries at each height and is eliminated if he fails to clear it. The height is increased until only one competitor is left. World record: 6.06 m (1988) by Sergei Bubka (Soviet Union).

poliomyelitis A virus infection of the central nervous system. In most cases the infection is mild, but sometimes a more severe illness develops, which may lead to weakness and paralysis of the muscles. Polio is now uncommon in devel-oped countries and vaccines are available that give complete protection (the Sabin and Salk vaccines).

Polish (*or* Lekhitic) A West Slavonic language spoken in Poland and closely related to *Czech, *Slovak, and Sorbian. It is written in a Latin alphabet and the standard form is based on the dialect of Poznań.

polka A Bohemian folk dance in 2/4 time, which became a ballroom dance in 19th-century Europe and rivalled the waltz in popularity. It is characterized by three steps and a hop.

pollen The male gametes of seed plants; they are produced in the *stamens of flowering plants and in the male *cones of conifers. In the process of **pollination**, the pollen is transferred to the stigma (in flowering plants) or the female cone (in conifers). Many flowers are cross-pollinated, i.e. the pollen from one plant is deposited on the stigma of another of the same species by means of animal carriers (usually insects), wind, or water. Some flowers are self-pollinated, the pollen being transferred from the anthers to the stigma of the same plant. After pollination, a pollen tube grows down from the pollen grain into the pistil of the pollinated flower until it reaches the ovule. A pollen nucleus travels down this tube and fertilizes the egg cell.

Pollock, Jackson (1912–56) US painter. By 1947 he had developed an abstract style (*see* abstract art), pouring and dripping paints onto very large canvases to form patterns of interweaving lines.

poll tax A tax on every individual (*poll*, head), regardless of means. First levied regularly in England in 1377, it was a direct cause of the *Peasants' Revolt in 1381 and was abolished in 1698. As the **community charge** it replaced domestic rates in Scotland in 1989 and in the rest of the UK in 1990.

pollution The addition to the environment of substances that cannot be broken down naturally to harmless substances. Modern industries and farming have led to the pollution of land, rivers, seas, and the atmosphere by either man-made toxic substances (such as pesticides and fertilizers) or by the overproduction of naturally occurring substances (such as carbon dioxide gas). Current problems include the disposal of radioactive wastes; increasing amounts of heavy metals (such as lead) in the atmosphere; atmospheric pollution by carbon dioxide, carbon monoxide, etc.; and unacceptable noise levels. *See also* acid rain; greenhouse effect. See p. 430–431.

polo A four-a-side stick-and-ball game, in which the players are mounted on specially bred ponies. It was played in Persia by 600 BC and was popular with British officers in India in the 19th century. The riders use long sticks with mallet heads to hit a solid wooden ball, with the object of scoring goals. A game consists of up to eight seven-minute periods, or "chukkas," after each of which mounts are changed. After every goal the teams change ends. See p. 432.

Polo, Marco (c. 1254–1324) Venetian traveller. He accompanied his father and uncle to Peking in 1271, entering the service of the Mongol emperor, Kublai Khan. Leaving China in 1292, he subsequently fought for the Venetians against

Lakes and other enclosed bodies of water can be artificially enriched by minerals and organic matter from agricultural fertilizers and sewage. This process is called eutrophication. The enriched water causes enormous growth of algae, which use up the oxygen in the water. Bacteria, which decompose the algae when they die, deplete the oxygen even more, so that the fish and other animals are unable to survive.

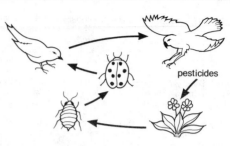

pesticides

There are more individuals found at the base of a food chain than at the top. In this example there are more plants than hawks. This means that the pesticides polluting the plants reach dangerously high levels in the hawk.

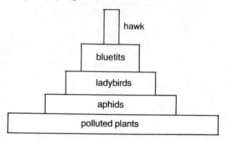

hawk

bluetits

ladybirds

aphids

polluted plants

The enormous growth in the use of oil in the 20th century – as the main fuel for transport – has meant that vast quantities are shipped from mines to refineries and from refineries to users. Modern supertankers carry up to 75 000 tonnes of oil. An accident can discharge crude oil into the sea; the resulting oil slicks, the consequences of which on beaches can be seen here, are a pollution menace of the 20th century.

GREENHOUSE EFFECT

HEAT

CO

CO_2

Factory waste
RIVER POLLUTION

Waste disposal is an important cause of land
and water pollution. Industrial and domestic
solid waste that is dumped in open tips (as the
one seen here) despoils the landscape and can
provide a breeding ground for pests.
The problem could be alleviated by using
more biodegradable materials and by
increased recycling of paper, glass, metal, etc.

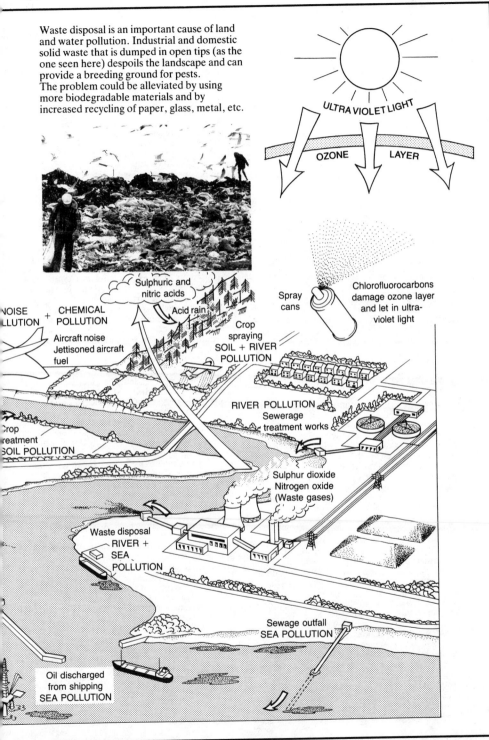

ULTRA VIOLET LIGHT

OZONE   LAYER

Sulphuric and
nitric acids

Acid rain

NOISE   CHEMICAL
LLUTION + POLLUTION

Spray
cans

Chlorofluorocarbons
damage ozone layer
and let in ultra-
violet light

Aircraft noise
Jettisoned aircraft
fuel

Crop
spraying
SOIL + RIVER
POLLUTION

RIVER POLLUTION
Sewerage
treatment works

Crop
reatment
SOIL POLLUTION

Sulphur dioxide
Nitrogen oxide
(Waste gases)

Waste disposal
RIVER +
SEA
POLLUTION

Sewage outfall
SEA POLLUTION

Oil discharged
from shipping
SEA POLLUTION

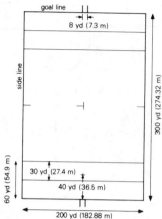

POLO *The dimensions of the ground. If the side lines are boarded, the width is 160 yd (146.4 m) and there is a safety area extending 10 yd (9 m) beyond each side line and 30 yd (27 m) beyond each goal line.*

the Genoese and was captured. In prison (1296-98) he dictated an account of his travels.

polonium (Po) A highly radioactive element discovered in 1898 by Marie Curie in minute amounts in pitchblende. It is 5000 times as radioactive as *radium and liberates considerable amounts of heat. Polonium has 27 isotopes, more than any other element. It is used in compact power sources. At no 84; at wt (209); mp 254°C; bp 962°C.

poltergeist A noisy, mischievous, and frequently destructive invisible agent said to persecute the occupants of a house, most commonly by throwing or moving objects. Famous poltergeist hauntings were the 17th-century "demon drummer of Tedworth" and the 20th-century Borley Rectory haunting.

polyanthus A hardy perennial derived from a cross between the common primrose and the cowslip. There are many varieties, with yellow, brown, blue, or red flowers, grown as garden plants. *See also* primula.

polyesters Synthetic resins or *plastics that are polymers of *esters. Saturated polyesters (those with no double bonds), made by a condensation reaction, are widely used in such synthetic fibres as Dacron and Terylene. Unsaturated polyesters are used as resins to make thermosetting plastics.

polymerization The chemical combination of simpler molecules (monomers) to form long chain molecules (**polymers**) of repeating units. In **addition polymerization**, the monomers simply add together: polythene is made in this way. In **condensation polymerization**, water, alcohol, or some other small molecule is formed in the reaction, as in the production of *nylon.

Polynesia A division of Oceania in the S and central Pacific Ocean. The volcanic and coral islands include those of French Polynesia, Hawaii, Samoa, Tonga, Tuvalu, Kiribati, and the Line and Cook Islands. *See also* Melanesia; Micronesia.

Polynesian The people of the Pacific islands contained within the roughly triangular area between and including Hawaii, New Zealand, and Easter Island. The Polynesian languages include Samoan, *Maori, Tongan, Tahitian, and Hawaiian.

polyp (biology) A form that occurs during the life cycle of many *coelenterate animals. It has a stalklike body attached to a surface, with the mouth at the free end surrounded by tentacles bearing stinging cells (nematocysts). Polyps occur singly or in colonies.

polyp (*or* polypus) (medicine) A growth that has a narrow base or stalk. Polyps may occur in the bowel, the nose, the womb, the larynx, and other sites. They often cause obstruction or infection and some may become cancerous.

polypeptide. *See* peptide.

polypropylene A thermoplastic material (*see* plastics) made by *polymerization of propylene (CH_2:$CHCH_3$). Similar to high-density *polythene but stronger, lighter, and more rigid, it is used for such products as beer crates, luggage, and hinges. Polypropylene fibres are used to make sacks and carpet backings.

polysaccharide A carbohydrate consisting of chains of sugar units. Polysaccharides, such as *starch, *glycogen, and *cellulose, are important as energy reserves and structural components of plants and animals.

polytechnics Institutes of higher education concentrating on courses relevant to jobs while maintaining high academic standards. The first polytechnic was established in Paris in 1794. The polytechnic movement in the UK began with the establishment of the Regent Street Polytechnic in 1880. In 1987 UK polytechnics began to award their own independent degrees.

polytetrafluoroethene (PTFE) A synthetic material produced by the *polymerization of tetrafluoroethylene (F_2C:CF_2). It can withstand temperatures of up to 400°C and has a very slippery surface. PTFE is used to coat nonstick cooking utensils and in gaskets, bearings, and electrical insulation. It is sold under the tradenames Teflon and Fluon.

polythene (polyethylene) A white semitransparent *plastic material (a thermoplastic) made by *polymerization of ethylene. **Low-density polythene** is made at high pressure and is a soft material used for flexible pipes, sheets, and bags. **High-density polythene** is made at lower pressures, is more rigid, and softens at a higher temperature. It is used for moulded articles.

polyurethane A synthetic material produced by *polymerization, the molecules of which contain the $-NH.CO.O-$ group. Some polyurethanes form thermosetting *resins and others, thermoplastic resins. They are used in paints, adhesives, moulded articles, rubbers, lacquers, and foams.

polyvinyl chloride (PVC) A vinyl *resin or plastic produced by *polymerization of vinyl chloride (chloroethene; CH_2:$CHCl$), a toxic gas. Rigid PVC products are made by moulding. The addition of a plasticizer produces flexible PVC.

PVC is tough, nonflammable, resistant to moisture, and a good electrical insulator.

pomegranate A small tree, *Punica granatum*, native to W Asia and widely cultivated in the tropics and subtropics. 5–7 m tall, it has orange-red flowers. The fruit has a leathery yellowish-reddish skin and contains many seeds coated with a pinkish acid-sweet pulp. Pomegranates are eaten fresh or used in drinks.

Pomeranian A breed of dog developed in Pomerania, a region of NE Europe now divided between Poland and E Germany. The Pomeranian has a compact body and foxlike head with small erect ears. The short undercoat is covered by a long straight outercoat and the fluffy tail is held over the back. The coat may be white, black, brown, or reddish. Height: 14–18 cm.

Pomona (Orkneys). *See* Mainland.

Pompadour, Mme de (Jeanne Antoinette Poisson, Marquise de P.; 1721–64) The mistress of Louis XV. She influenced the Austrian alliance against Prussia and was blamed for French defeats in the subsequent *Seven Years' War. She was a notable patron of artists and scholars.

Pompeii An ancient city near Naples, in Italy. It was buried four to six metres deep under volcanic ash by the eruption of Mount *Vesuvius (79 AD) and rediscovered in 1748. Pompeii provides unparalleled evidence for daily life in Roman times, including wall paintings, food, wooden furniture, and personal possessions abandoned by the fleeing inhabitants.

Pompey (Gnaeus Pompeius; 106–48 BC) Roman general and statesman, called Pompeius Magnus (Pompey the Great). In 60 he joined Julius Caesar and Crassus in the first *Triumvirate, marrying Caesar's daughter Julia (d. 54) in 59, but in 50 he supported the Senate's demand for Caesar to resign his armies. In the civil war that followed Pompey was defeated by Caesar at Pharsalus (48) and fled to Egypt, where he was murdered.

Pompidou, Georges (Jean Raymond) (1911–74) French statesman; prime minister (1962–68) and president (1969–74). He agreed a settlement with the Algerians (1961) and with the students in the revolt of May, 1968.

Pondicherry A Union Territory in SE India, on the Coromandel Coast. Founded by the French in 1674, it was their chief settlement in India until transferred to Indian administration in 1954. Rice and millet are the chief products. Area: 479 sq km (185 sq mi). Population (1989): 604 471. Capital: Pondicherry.

pondweed An aquatic plant found worldwide in fresh water. It has submerged or floating stems. The Canadian pondweed (*Elodea canadensis*) has long submerged stems, with narrow backward-curving dark-green leaves. Native to North America, it is also found in Europe.

Ponte Vecchio A bridge over the River Arno in Florence. Topped by buildings, it was designed by Taddeo Gaddi and finished in 1345.

pontoon (*or* vingt-et-un) A card game in which the aim is to score 21. One card is dealt to each player, who puts up a stake accordingly; a second card is then dealt. Players may then buy another card face down or accept another card face up at no cost. The winner is the player with the score nearest to 21. Players scoring exactly 21 win double their stakes.

pony A *horse that does not exceed 1.47 m (14½ hands) in height at maturity. Traditionally used as pack animals, ponies are now popular as children's mounts and for pony trekking.

poodle A breed of dog of uncertain origins but long associated with France and Germany. The dense coat was originally clipped to enable them to swim and retrieve in water. The miniature poodle and toy poodle have been developed from the standard poodle. Height: 38 cm minimum (standard); 28–38 cm (miniature); under 28 cm (toy).

Poona (*or* Pune) 18 34N 73 58E A city in India, in Maharashtra. Capital of the Marathas in the late 18th century, it was taken by the British in 1817. A commercial, manufacturing, and military centre, it has cotton textiles, rubber, paper, and munitions industries. Population (1981 est): 1 685 266.

Poor Laws The laws that governed assistance to the poor in Britain. From the 16th century parishes were responsible for providing for their poor and from 1572 imposed a tax for poor relief. The Poor Law Amendment Act of 1834 abolished such relief and those seeking assistance had to enter a *workhouse. The Poor Law system was not abolished until 1947.

Pope, Alexander (1688–1744) British poet, crippled from childhood. His biting wit is apparent in *An Essay on Criticism* (1711) and the mock epic *The Rape of the Lock* (1712–14). His other works include the mock epic *The Dunciad* (1728; revised 1742–43), the philosophical poem *An Essay on Man* (1733–34), and poems modelled on the satires of Horace.

Popish Plot (1678) A conspiracy invented by Titus Oates (1649–1705) and Israel Tonge, who claimed that there was a plot to assassinate Charles II and place his Roman Catholic brother, James, on the throne. The anti-Catholic passions aroused by this claim led to the execution of 35 suspects and the exclusion of Catholics from parliament (*see* Test Acts).

poplar A shrub or tree of the willow family, native to N temperate regions and grown for wood pulp and ornament. Up to 40 m tall, the trees may have a broad spreading crown, as in the European black poplar (*Populus nigra*), or a tall slender one, as in the Lombardy poplar (a variety of black poplar). *See also* aspen.

poppy A plant native mainly to the N hemisphere and often grown in gardens. It yields a milky sap (latex) and bears showy white, pink, or red flowers; the fruit is a *capsule. Species include the red-flowered corn, or field, poppy (*Papaver rhoeas*) and the *opium poppy.

porcelain White ceramic developed by Chinese potters about 900 AD. Hard-paste porcelain consists of china clay (kaolin) and the mineral petuntse finely mixed and fired to about 1400°C; it is usually glazed with pure petuntse during firing. For soft-paste porcelain the clay or kaolin is mixed with an artificial flux, such as sand with lime, flint, soda, etc. The mixture is fired at about 1100°C and the glaze, usually of glass, is applied in a second firing at about 1000°C. Bone china is an 18th-century English invention using bone ash as a flux.

porcupine A large plant-eating spiny *rodent. American porcupines tend to be tree dwellers and have grasping tails. The North American porcupine (*Erethizion dorsatum*) is about 75 cm long and grows a soft winter coat. African and Asian porcupines are mainly ground-dwelling. The Indian crested porcupine (*Hystrix indica*), up to 1 m long, may have spines 35 cm long. Porcupines respond to a threat by turning their backs and raising their spines.

porgy. *See* sea bream.

porpoise A small toothed *whale of coastal waters. The common, or harbour, porpoise (*Phocoena phocoena*), of the N Atlantic and Pacific, is blue-grey above and pale grey beneath. It feeds on fish, squid, and crustaceans.

port A fortified *wine from Oporto (N Portugal). The grapes grown on the Douro hillsides are trodden in stone presses. Fermentation is halted by adding brandy. Subsequently the wine is taken to the lodges near Oporto, where it is matured and blended.

Port-au-Prince 18 40N 72 20W The capital of Haiti, a port in the SW on the Gulf of Gonaïves. Its main exports are coffee and sugar. The University of Haiti was founded here in 1944. Population (1987 est): 472 895.

Porter, Cole (Albert) (1893–1964) US composer of musical comedies and popular songs. He wrote a series of musicals, including *Anything Goes* (1934), *Kiss Me Kate* (1948), and *Can Can* (1953). His songs included "Night and Day" and "Begin the Beguine."

Port Louis 20 10S 57 30E The capital of Mauritius, in the NW of the island. Founded in about 1736, it is the site of two cathedrals. Sugar is exported. Population (1987): 139 038.

Pôrto Alegre 30 03S 51 10W A city in S Brazil, the capital of Rio Grande do Sul state. It is a major commercial and industrial centre; industries include meat processing, tanning, and the manufacture of textiles. It is the seat of two universities. Population (1985): 1 275 483.

Port-of-Spain 10 38N 61 31W The capital and main port of Trinidad and Tobago since 1783, on the W coast of Trinidad. Notable buildings include the Anglican and Roman Catholic cathedrals. Petroleum products, sugar, and rum are among the main exports. Population (1989): 59 200.

Porto Novo 6 30N 2 47E The capital of Benin, on the Gulf of Guinea. A former centre of the slave trade with the Portuguese, it came under French rule in the late 19th century. Trade includes palm oil and cotton. Population (1982): 208 258.

Port Said (*or* Bur Said) 31 17N 32 18E A major port in Egypt, situated at the Mediterranean entrance to the Suez Canal. Founded in 1859, it suffered from the closure of the Suez Canal (1967–75) and Israeli occupation of the E bank. Population (1986 est): 382 000.

Portsmouth 50 48N 1 05W A port in S England, in Hampshire at the entrance to Portsmouth Harbour. It is the chief naval base in the

UK; notable landmarks include Nelson's flagship HMS *Victory* and the *Mary Rose*. Population (1987 est): 179 400.

Portugal, Republic of A country in SW Europe, occupying the W section of the Iberian Peninsula and bordering on the Atlantic Ocean. *Economy*: traditionally agricultural; Portugal's principal exports are textiles, clothing, cork, wood products, sardines, and fortified wines. Minerals include coal, copper pyrites, kaolin, and haematite. *History*: Portugal as a distinct Christian territory dates from 868. It became a kingdom in 1139 under Alfonso I (1112–85) and its long alliance with England began in the 14th century. From the 15th century Portuguese explorers opened up new trade routes and an extensive overseas empire was established. A revolution in 1910 overthrew the monarchy and established a republic. A long period of political instability culminated in a military coup in 1926; António Salazar (1889–1970) became prime minister in 1932 and his repressive dictatorship lasted until 1968. Mario *Soares restored constitutional government in 1976 and became president in 1986. In 1986 Portugal joined the EC. Official language: Portuguese. Official religion: Roman Catholic. Official currency: escudo of 100 centavos. Area: 91 631 sq km (34 861 sq mi). Population (1987): 10 312 000. Capital and main port: Lisbon.

Portuguese A *Romance language spoken in Portugal, Galicia (Spain), Brazil, Madeira, and the Azores. Brazilian Portuguese differs slightly in grammar and sound system.

Portuguese Guinea. *See* Guinea-Bissau, Republic of.

Portuguese man-of-war A *coelenterate animal found mainly in warm seas. It has a translucent bladder-like float that acts like a sail in the wind. Attached underneath are clusters of *polyps bearing stinging tentacles, up to 50 m long, used to paralyse fish and other prey.

Poseidon The Greek god of the sea and earthquakes, brother of Zeus and Hades. His many offspring included Theseus, Polyphemus, and the winged horse Pegasus. He was identified with the Roman *Neptune.

positron The antiparticle of the *electron, having the same mass and *spin as the electron but opposite electric charge. A positron and an electron annihilate each other on collision, producing two gamma-ray photons.

possum The most common Australian *marsupial, *Trichosurus vulpecula*, also called brush-tailed phalanger. It lives in trees and is active at night. About the size of a cat, the possum has a soft greyish coat and bushy tail and feeds mainly on vegetation.

postimpressionism The art of the late 19th-century French painters *Cézanne, *Seurat, *Van Gogh, *Gauguin, *Toulouse-Lautrec, and their followers, whose work developed out of and, to some extent, in reaction to *impressionism.

postmortem. *See* autopsy.

potassium (K) A reactive *alkali metal discovered by Sir Humphry Davy in 1807. It is a common constituent of the earth's crust, forming *feldspars ($KAlSi_3O_8$), clays, and minerals. The metal is prepared by *electrolysis of the molten hydroxide. It is soft, reacts readily with water, and oxidizes rapidly in air; it must therefore be stored under oil. Its largest use is in *fertilizers, potassium being essential for plant growth. One of the three isotopes (potassium-40) is used in *potassium-argon dating. At no 19; at wt 39.102; mp 63.65°C; bp 774°C.

potassium-argon dating A method of dating geological specimens based on the decay of the radioactive isotope potassium-40, which is present in all naturally occurring potassium. Its half-life is 1.3×10^9 years and it decays to argon-40; thus an estimate of the ratio of the two isotopes in a specimen of rock gives an indication of its age.

potato A plant, *Solanum tuberosum*, of the nightshade family, native to the Andes but cultivated throughout the world. Potatoes were first introduced to England in the late 16th century by Sir Walter Raleigh. The plants grow to a height of 50–100 cm, with clusters of white and purple flowers. The tubers, which are rich in starch, are eaten cooked or ground into flour. *See also* sweet potato.

potential, electric A measure of electrical work. The potential at a point in an *electric field is one volt when one joule of energy is needed to bring a positive charge of one coulomb to that point from infinity. Usually the potential difference between two points, rather than the absolute potential, is used. *See also* electromotive force.

potential energy *Energy stored in a body by virtue of its position or configuration. Thus a body, mass m, at a height h above the ground has a potential energy equal to mgh, where g is the *acceleration of free fall, relative to the ground. A compressed spring and an electrically charged body also store potential energy.

potentilla A plant of the rose family, found mainly in N temperate and arctic regions. Several species and hybrids are grown in gardens. They have yellow, white, or red flowers.

potholing. *See* speleology.

pot marigold. *See* marigold.

Potsdam 52 19N 13 15E A city in E Germany, capital of Brandenburg, on the River Havel adjoining Berlin. Notable buildings include the Brandenburg Gate (1770) and the Sanssouci Palace (1745–47). An industrial city, Potsdam has many scientific institutes. After World War II, Truman, Stalin, and Churchill (later Attlee) met here to confirm the conclusions of the Yalta Conference. Population (1986): 140 198.

Potter, Beatrix (1866–1943) British children's writer and illustrator. *The Tale of Peter Rabbit* (1900) was the first of a series of famous children's books concerning the domestic lives of such animals as Jemima Puddle-Duck and Mrs Tittlemouse.

potter wasp A solitary *wasp common in North America and Europe. It constructs juglike nests of mud or clay attached to plant stems. A single egg is laid in each nest.

potto A *loris, *Perodictus potto*, of African forests. It is about 40 cm long with a short tail, a catlike face, and strong grasping hands. Pottos have a row of spines on the neck and shoulders, used for self-defence.

Poulenc, Francis (1899–1963) French composer. He produced a wide variety of works, including the song series *Le Bestiaire* (1919), the operas *Les Mamelles de Tirésias* (1944) and *Les Dialogues des Carmélites* (1953–56), and the ballet *Les Biches* (1923).

Pound, Ezra (1885–1972) US poet and critic. He went to Europe in 1908 and became associated with modernist literary and artistic movements in London (e.g. Vorticism). His early poetry included *Aliume Spento* (1908), and the long poems *Homage to Sextus Propertius* (1917) and *Hugh Selwyn Mauberly* (1920). He moved to Paris and, in 1924, to Italy, where he worked on the *Cantos* (1925–69).

Poussin, Nicolas (1594–1665) French painter, one of the greatest exponents of *classicism, who lived mainly in Rome from 1624. His works include *The Martyrdom of St Erasmus* (1628; Vatican), *The Worship of the Golden Calf* (c. 1635; National Gallery, London), and *Landscape with Diogenes* (1648; Louvre).

Powell, Anthony (1905–   ) British novelist. His novel sequence *A Dance to the Music of Time* comprises 12 social satires beginning with *A Question of Upbringing* (1951) and ending with *Hearing Secret Harmonies* (1975). He has also written four volumes of memoirs.

Powell, (John) Enoch (1912–   ) British politician. He became a Conservative MP in 1950 and from 1960 to 1963 was minister of health. In 1968 he was dismissed from Edward Heath's shadow cabinet following a controversial speech against immigration. From 1974 to 1987 he was the United Ulster Unionist Council MP for South Down.

power The rate at which a body or system does work. It is measured in watts or horsepower.

power station An electricity generating plant that forms part of the *electricity supply system. In **thermal power stations**, heat from the burning of fossil fuels (oil, coal, and gas) or from *thermal reactors is used to generate steam. The steam drives *turbines connected to alternating-current generators (turbo-alternators), thus converting heat into electricity. Gas turbines are also used, missing out the steam-generation stage. Usually in a steam-turbine thermal station about 30 to 40% of the heat is converted to electricity, most of the rest being lost when steam is condensed to water before it is returned to the boilers. *Hydroelectric power stations are more efficient (up to 90%) and provide a significant proportion of UK electricity supplies. *See also* energy.

Powys A county of E Central Wales, bordering on England. It was formed in 1974 from Montgomeryshire, Radnorshire, and most of Breconshire. It is generally mountainous, rising to 886 m (2907 ft) in the Brecon Beacons. Agriculture and forestry are important. Area: 5077 sq km (1960 sq mi). Population (1989): 115 000. Administrative centre: Llandrindod Wells.

Pozsony

436

Pozsony. *See* Bratislava.

Prado An art gallery in the Prado Avenue, Madrid. Designed originally as a natural-history museum by the neoclassical architect Juan de Villanueva (1739–1811), the art gallery was founded in 1818 by Ferdinand VII. Its works by *Velázquez, *Goya, *El Greco, *Titian, and *Bosch are among the finest in the world.

Praetorian Guard The official bodyguard of the Roman emperors created by Augustus in 27 BC. Composed of up to 16 long-serving cohorts (infantry divisions) each of 500–1000 men, the Guard developed great political influence as senatorial power diminished.

Prague (Czech name: Praha) 50 8N 14 25E The capital of Czechoslovakia, in the centre of the country on the River Vltava. Its various manufactures include machinery, cars, aircraft, food processing, clothing, and chemicals. Notable buildings include Hradčany Castle and the mainly gothic Cathedral of St Vitus. Under Habsburg rule from the 16th century, it was made the capital of newly independent Czechoslovakia in 1918. Population (1989): 1 213 792.

prairie dog A large North American ground *squirrel, *Cynomys ludovicanis*, also called black-tailed prairie marmot. About 30 cm long, prairie dogs feed on grass and have been treated as pests by cattle ranchers.

prairies The extensive grasslands of the interior of North America. They extend S from Alberta and Saskatchewan through the Midwest into Texas. Little of the original true prairie now remains, having been extensively ploughed for wheat production. *See also* steppes.

prairie wolf. *See* coyote.

praseodymium (Pr) A *lanthanide element that was separated from its mixture with neodyminium by von Welsbach in 1885. It forms trihalides (for example $PrCl_3$) and an oxide (Pr_2O_3), which is used to give a strong yellow colour to glass. At no 59; at wt 140.9077; mp 931°C; bp 3512°C.

prawn A large shrimplike *crustacean, up to 20 cm long. The antennae are longer than the body and the second pair of appendages form pincers (*compare* shrimp). The common edible prawn (*Leander serratus*) occurs in temperate coastal waters and is 5–8 cm long.

Precambrian Geological time from the formation of the earth's crust, about 4500 million years ago, to about 590 million years ago when the *Cambrian period began. Precambrian rocks contain few fossils and most have been greatly altered from their original state by heat and pressure. The largest areas of exposed Precambrian rocks are the *shield areas.

premium bond A UK government bond, held in numbered units of one pound, the interest on which is put into a fund and shared out to bond holders by a monthly lottery, as tax-free prizes. The numbers of winning bonds are selected by Electronic Random Number Indicator Equipment (ERNIE). Premium bonds were introduced in 1956 by Harold Macmillan.

Pre-Raphaelite Brotherhood A group formed in 1848 by the British painters Dante Gabriel *Rossetti, John Everett *Millais, and

William Holman *Hunt. Rejecting British painting of the time and its enthusiasm for *Raphael, they sought to imitate earlier Italian painters and favoured subjects of a moral or religious character. The group had a strong influence on such artists as William *Morris and Edward *Burne-Jones.

presbyopia. *See* longsightedness.

Presbyterianism A Protestant church organization based on government by elders, who decide policy through church courts of different ranks: presbyteries, synods, and general assemblies. Presbyterianism started with the 16th-century followers of *Calvin. In Scotland the principles of Presbyterianism were formulated (1560) by *Knox and it became the established church in 1696.

Presley, Elvis (Aaron) (1935–77) US popular singer, whose first big hit, "Heartbreak Hotel" (1956), was followed by "Hound Dog" and "Don't Be Cruel." Presley also appeared in numerous films. His death was probably due to drug dependence.

Pressburg. *See* Bratislava.

press gang A band of men employed to force paupers, vagabonds, or criminals into the army or navy. This was common throughout the world in the 18th century until improved pay and conditions in the army and navy led people to join by choice.

pressure Force per unit area. For a liquid, density d, the pressure at a depth h is hdg, where g is the *acceleration of free fall. Pressure is usually measured in pascals or millibars.

pressure gauge An instrument for measuring the pressure of a gas or liquid. Atmospheric pressure is measured with a *barometer. Pressures above atmospheric pressure are usually measured with a Bourdon gauge, which consists of a flattened curved tube that tends to straighten under pressure. Low pressures are measured with such vacuum gauges as the McLeod gauge or Pirani gauge.

Preston 53 46N 2 42W A town and port in NW England, the administrative centre of Lancashire on the River Ribble. It has plastics, chemical, motor-vehicle, aircraft, and electronics industries as well as the traditional cotton and engineering works. Population (1983 est): 125 000.

Pretender, Old. *See* James Edward Stuart, the Old Pretender.

Pretender, Young. *See* Charles Edward Stuart, the Young Pretender.

Pretoria 25 36S 28 12E The administrative capital of South Africa and the capital of the Transvaal. Founded in 1855, it became the capital of the Union of South Africa in 1910. Its industries include iron and steel processing, engineering, and food processing. Population (1985): 741 300.

Priam In Greek legend, the last king of Troy, husband of Hecuba. As an old man he witnessed the deaths of many of his 50 sons in the *Trojan War.

price index A single figure used to measure the average percentage change in the price of a set of goods over a period of time, taking a base figure of 100 for a specified year. The best-known indexes are the Wholesale Price Index and the Retail Price Index, the latter providing a reliable guide to the cost of living. **Indexation** is the system in which wages, salaries, and costs are index-linked (i.e. increased in proportion to a specified price index) to cover the devaluation of money as a result of *inflation.

prickly pear A *cactus of the Americas that is also found in Australia and South Africa. It has flat spiny stems bearing large orange or yellow flowers, which give rise to edible pear-shaped fruits. The seeds yield an oil and the shoots are eaten as vegetables or used as animal feed.

Priestley, J(ohn) B(oynton) (1894–1984) British novelist and dramatist. He first won popular success with his novel *The Good Companions* (1929). His plays on social issues include *Laburnum Grove* (1933) and *An Inspector Calls* (1946) and several experimental dramas, including *The Glass Cage* (1957).

Priestley, Joseph (1733–1804) British chemist and one of the discoverers of oxygen, the other being Carl Scheele (1742–86). A firm believer in the *phlogiston theory, Priestley named his gas dephlogisticated air and prepared it in 1774 by heating mercuric oxide. In 1778–79 *Lavoisier demolished the phlogiston theory and named the gas oxygen. Priestley also produced and studied several other gases, including ammonia. He collected them over mercury, since some of these gases dissolved in water.

primary colours The minimum number of *colours that, when mixed in the correct proportions, are capable of giving all the other colours in the visible spectrum. When light of three **primary additive colours** (usually red, green, and blue) is mixed in equal intensities, white light results. This principle is used in colour *television and colour *photography. Any particular colour can also be obtained by subtracting from white light a mixture of three **primary subtractive colours**, usually cyan (blue-green), magenta (purplish red), and yellow, which are complementary to red, green, and blue. Adding pigments of these in equal proportions gives black pigment.

primate A mammal belonging to a group that contains *lemurs, *monkeys, *apes, and humans. Primates probably evolved from animals similar to *tree shrews. They have five fingers and five toes with the first finger or toe able to meet the other digits in a grasping action (except in the hind feet of man). They have well-developed brains.

prime minister A head of government. In the UK the post developed in the 18th century with the growth of the *cabinet. Sir Robert *Walpole is generally regarded as the first prime minister (1721–42) but the post was not formally recognized until 1905. The prime minister is the leader of the dominant political party in the House of Commons.

prime number An integer greater than one that has no factors except itself and one; for example 2, 3, 5, 7, 11, 13, 17. Every natural number can be expressed uniquely as a product of prime numbers; for example $1260 = 2^2 \times 3^2 \times 5 \times 7$.

primitivism In art, the style of untrained artists, characterized by meticulous detail, brilliant colours, childlike representation, and faulty perspective. The best known primitive is the French painter Henri *Rousseau. Recent primitives include the Yugoslav peasant Ivan Generalič (1914–) and the American Grandma *Moses.

primrose A flowering plant, *Primula vulgaris*, growing in woodlands and hedge banks in Europe and N Africa. It has spoon-shaped leaves and pale-yellow flowers. *See also* evening primrose.

primula A plant native mainly to N temperate regions and often grown in gardens. They have five-petalled flowers, red, pink, purple, blue, white, or yellow in colour and usually with a different coloured centre. Species include the *cowslip and *primrose.

Prince Edward Island An island province of E Canada, in the S Gulf of St Lawrence. Farming, tourism, and fishing are important. *History*: discovered (1534) and colonized (1720) by France, the island was captured (1758) and resettled by Britain. In 1873 it joined Canada. Area: 5657 sq km (2184 sq mi). Population (1986): 126 646. Capital: Charlottetown.

Prince of Wales A title customarily given to the eldest son of the British sovereign. It was a native Welsh title until 1301, when Edward I, having subdued Wales, gave it to his son, the future Edward II. The present holder of the title is Prince *Charles.

Príncipe Island. *See* São Tomé and Príncipe.

printed circuit An electronic circuit in which the connections between components are formed by a pattern of conducting film on a board, instead of by wires. The method greatly assists mass-production. An insulating board is coated with a conducting material, such as copper, and a protective pattern is deposited on it using photographic techniques. The unprotected metal is then etched away and components are soldered in place.

printing The production of multiple copies of text or pictures, usually on paper. The oldest method, in use in China and Japan before 800 AD, is **letterpress**, in which the raised surfaces of etched, engraved, or cast material are inked and pressed onto the paper. This method was revolutionized by the invention of movable type in the 15th century. Early printing presses were hand-operated. Faster production became possible on the power-driven presses of the 19th century: first the cylinder press, and later the rotary press. In **lithography**, invented by the German engraver Aloys Senefelder (1771–1834) in 1798, the printing surface is smooth, the printing and nonprinting areas being made grease-receptive and grease-repellent respectively. Greasy ink rolled over the entire area is taken up only by the grease-receptive areas; the ink is then transferred by rolling onto the paper. In **offset printing** a rubber-covered cylinder transfers the ink from plate to paper. In **gravure printing**, the small square etched holes (cells) in the copper printing plate are filled with ink, the rest of the plate is wiped clean, and the plate is rolled against the paper, which absorbs the ink out of the cells. Letterpress and off-

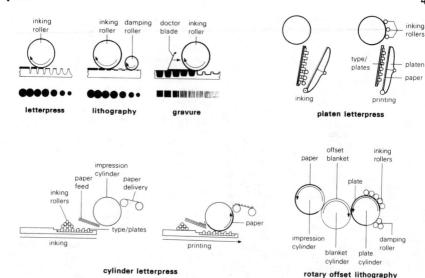

inking roller | inking roller | damping roller | doctor blade | inking roller

letterpress **lithography** **gravure**

inking rollers | type/plates | platen | paper

inking | printing

platen letterpress

impression cylinder | paper feed | paper delivery | inking rollers | type/plates

inking | printing | paper

cylinder letterpress

paper | offset blanket | inking rollers | plate | impression cylinder | blanket cylinder | plate cylinder | damping roller

rotary offset lithography

PRINTING *Principles of three major printing processes and the three major designs of printing press.*

set lithography are used for all types of printing job; gravure is limited to long runs. Direct lithography has been used almost exclusively by artists.

In **silk-screen printing** (screen-process printing *or* serigraphy), a piece of taut open-weave silk, metal, or synthetic fabric carries the negative of the desired image in an impervious substance, such as glue; ink is forced through the clear (printing) areas by a squeegee onto the paper, glass, fabric, or other material, behind. It is used for printing posters, electronic circuit boards, labelling on bottles, etc.

prism A piece of glass or other transparent material having parallel polygonal (usually triangular) ends, with a number of rectangular surfaces meeting them at right angles. They are used in optical instruments, such as cameras and binoculars, for changing the direction of light, either by refraction or by reflection from their walls.

prisons Institutions for confining convicted criminals (*see* criminal law). Throughout much of history, prisons were mainly places in which people were held until other punishments could be carried out. In the 18th century their role in the UK changed and the reform movements of John *Howard and Elizabeth Fry (1780–1845) led to improved conditions. During the 19th century many prisons were built in the UK, modelled on Pentonville (1842) and based on the principle of solitary confinement. Since the 19th century the emphasis in prisons has changed from punishment to correction and rehabilitation. The first "open prison," in which prisoners are permitted some personal freedom, was opened in 1936. *See also* community service.

privatization The sale of a public corporation to the private sector. Margaret *Thatcher's Conservative government in the 1980s sold its inter-

ests in British Aerospace, Britoil, British Telecom, British Gas, British Airways, the water and the electricity companies, etc., to private investors in order to increase the efficiency of these organizations and to increase the number of shareholders in the community. *See* nationalization.

privet A shrub or small tree of the olive family, native to Eurasia and Australia and widely used for ornamental hedges. The European common privet (*Ligustrum vulgare*), up to about 5 m high, has oval leaves and small creamy flowers.

Privy Council A body advising the British monarch, now having chiefly formal functions. It consists of all cabinet ministers, the Archbishops of Canterbury and York, the speaker of the House of Commons, and a number of senior British and Commonwealth statesmen, who are all addressed as the Right Honourable.

probability The mathematical concept concerned with the effects of chance on an event, experiment, or observation. It originated in 1654, when the mathematicians *Pascal and *Fermat worked on problems sent to them by a gambler. If an event can occur in n ways and r is the number of ways it can occur in a specified way, then the **mathematical probability** of it occurring in the specified way is r/n. For example, the probability of the number 5 coming up on a six-faced dice in one throw is $1/6$.

probation In English law, a court order, given instead of a sentence, requiring an offender to be under the supervision of a probation officer for between 1 and 3 years. Failure to comply with the order makes the offender liable to be sentenced for the original offence.

proboscis monkey A large leaf-eating monkey, *Nasalis larvatus*, of Borneo. Up to 1.5 m tall, proboscis monkeys have a protruding nose and live in groups in forests.

productivity The output of goods and services in a factory, country, etc., in relation to inputs (men, machines, land) used to produce them. Output per manhour can be used as a rough measure of productivity. Increases in productivity are probably largely due to increased investment in new machines. Low productivity may be due to overmanning or underproduction. **Productivity bargaining** is a form of collective bargaining in which wage increases are agreed depending on a corresponding increase in productivity.

progesterone A steroid hormone secreted mainly by the mammalian ovary following ovulation. It prepares the womb to receive the embryo and maintains this state during pregnancy. Progestogens—man-made steroids with progesterone-like actions—are used in *oral contraceptives and to treat menstrual disorders.

program, computer A series of instructions that controls the operation of a *computer. The programs executed by the computer are in a machine code, a series of numbers that the device interprets as either instructions or data. These instructions perform very simple tasks and many thousands are required for all but the most rudimentary programs. Programming languages simplify the programmer's task. Low-level languages resemble closely the logic of the machine; high-level languages, such as *Basic, *Fortran, *Cobol, Algol, and *Pascal, are more suited to human thought and are independent of any particular machine. *See also* software.

Prohibition (1919–33) A period during which the manufacture, sale, and transportation of alcoholic drinks were prohibited in the USA. It arose from the temperance movement against alcohol and the need to divert grain from distilleries to food manufacture. It proved impossible to enforce, and in 1933 prohibition was withdrawn.

Prokofiev, Sergei (1891–1953) Soviet composer and pianist. He lived abroad from 1918 to 1933 and in 1948 was officially condemned for "undemocratic tendencies" in his music. His work includes seven symphonies, five piano concertos, two violin concertos, the opera *Love for Three Oranges* (1919), the ballet *Romeo and Juliet* (1935–36), and *Peter and the Wolf* (1936) for speaker and orchestra.

prolactin A protein hormone, produced by the pituitary gland, that starts and maintains *lactation in mammals. In other animals it is involved in growth and the balance of water and salts, as well as reproduction. *See also* gonadotrophin.

promenade concerts Originally, concerts in which some of the audience can stand while listening to the music. The most famous series of such concerts is the BBC Promenade Concerts (the Proms), which were begun by Henry *Wood in 1895. They have been held in the Royal Albert Hall since World War II.

Prometheus (Greek: forethought) In Greek mythology, a Titan's son who created man and gave him reason. He also stole fire from heaven to give to man. Zeus chained him to a rock in the Caucasus and sent an eagle each day to devour his liver, which grew again by night.

promethium (Pm) A radioactive element obtained from nuclear reactors (it does not occur naturally on earth). The most stable isotope has a half-life of 17.7 years. Promethium salts exhibit bluish-green *luminescence and can be used in photoelectric cells. At no 61; at wt (145); mp about 1080°C.

pronghorn A hoofed mammal, *Antilocapra americana*, resembling an antelope and found in rocky deserts of the W USA. Up to 100 cm high at the shoulder, pronghorns are brown above and white beneath with white V-shaped marks under the neck.

proof spirit. *See* alcohol strength.

propellant 1. A solid or liquid substance, usually explosive, used to provide the forward-driving force (thrust) in a rocket engine or gun. Propellants utilize very fast heat-releasing chemical reactions to produce large quantities of expanding gas quickly. 2. The pressurized inert liquids used to drive an *aerosol from its container.

propeller A device for converting the rotation of a shaft into a forward-driving force acting in the direction of its axis. A **marine propeller** has between two and six specially shaped blades. It acts as a screw, accelerating a column of water rearwards. An **air propeller** (*or* airscrew) has longer thinner blades (usually two or four) and a higher rotational speed. It, too, accelerates a mass of air rearwards.

proportional representation (PR) A voting system that aims to reflect accurately the wishes of the voters and to ensure that votes for candidates standing for minority parties are not wasted. In the system known as the **single transferable vote** voters number the candidates in order of preference on their ballot paper. First-choice candidates who obtain the required quota are elected. First-choice votes for an unsuccessful candidate are then redistributed to second-choice votes for that candidate, and so on. In the **party-list system** voters vote for a party, which is then given seats in proportion to its total vote.

Proserpine. *See* Persephone.

Prost, Alain (1955–) French motor racing driver. In 1987 he became the most successful Formula One driver ever, having won 28 Grand Prix races and the World Championship in 1985, 1986, and 1989.

prostaglandins A group of compounds found in the body tissues of mammals. Their effects include contraction of the womb during birth and widening of blood vessels.

prostate gland A gland found in certain male mammals. In men it is just beneath the bladder and secretes a fluid that forms part of the semen. Enlargement of the prostate commonly occurs in elderly men, obstructing the bladder and preventing urination. It is treated by surgical removal (prostatectomy) or laser treatment of the gland.

protactinium (Pa) A radioactive *actinide element, first identified in 1913. It is present in pitchblende as a member of the uranium decay series. At no 91; at wt (231); mp <1600°C.

Protectorate (1653–59) The period during which England was governed by Oliver *Cromwell. The Instrument of Government (1653) gave

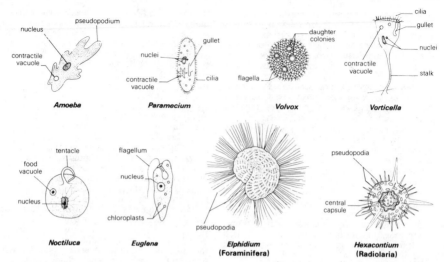

nucleus
pseudopodium
contractile vacuole
Amoeba

nuclei
gullet
contractile vacuole
cilia
Paramecium

daughter colonies
flagella
Volvox

cilia
gullet
nuclei
contractile vacuole
stalk
Vorticella

tentacle
food vacuole
nucleus
Noctiluca

flagellum
nucleus
chloroplasts
Euglena

pseudopodia
Elphidium (Foraminifera)

pseudopodia
central capsule
Hexacontium (Radiolaria)

PROTOZOA *Although consisting only of single cells, these primitive animals show a surprising complexity of structure. Many have organs of locomotion (pseudopodia, flagella, or cilia) and some have gullets.*

the Lord Protector (Cromwell) and a state council the authority to carry out the law, and the Protector and parliament the authority to make laws. The Instrument was altered by the Humble Petition and Advice (1657), which gave more power to parliament. Cromwell's relations with parliament later grew worse and he dismissed it in 1658.

protein A complex organic compound that consists of one or more linked chains of *amino acids (i.e. polypeptides; *see* peptide). Proteins are manufactured within cells according to the genetic information carried in the chromosomes and the specific function of the cell (*see* DNA; RNA). Proteins perform many important biological roles: some, including *collagen and *keratin, are important structural materials of body tissues, while the proteins of *muscle—actin and myosin —are responsible for muscle contraction. Other vital proteins include *enzymes, *antibodies, and many *hormones.

Protestantism The movement for Church reform that arose in the Western Church in the 16th century and led to the establishment of the Reformed Churches. The early leaders of the *Reformation—*Luther, *Calvin, and the Swiss reformer Ulrich Zwingli (1484–1531)—each encouraged his own brand of Protestantism. Under Elizabeth I Protestantism became the established religion in England. All Protestants reject a number of principles and practices of Catholicism. In general they rely less upon Church tradition, believing the Bible to be the sole source of truth. They deny the authority of the Pope and allow a variety of forms of Church government. *Transubstantiation, *purgatory, special veneration of the Virgin Mary, and praying to saints are all rejected. Among the sacraments only baptism and the *Eucharist are widely accepted.

Proteus A Greek sea god who served Poseidon as a shepherd of seals. He had prophetic powers but changed his form to avoid communicating his knowledge.

proton A positively charged elementary particle (*see* particle physics). It forms part of all atomic nuclei, a single proton being the nucleus of the hydrogen atom. It is a stable particle, 1836 times heavier than the electron.

protozoa Microscopic single-celled organisms of which there are about 30 000 species. Usually classified as simple animals, they are widely distributed in moist and watery places. Protozoans range in size from 0.1 mm to several centimetres. Most forms take in dissolved nutrients or solid food particles. Asexual reproduction is by simple division of the parent cell (binary fission) or by budding to form new cells; various forms of sexual reproduction may occur. Protozoans can survive dry or adverse conditions by forming resistant cysts or spores. Some are important parasites of man and animals, including species of *Plasmodium*, which cause malaria, and trypanosomes, which cause sleeping sickness.

Proust, Marcel (1871–1922) French novelist. After the deaths of his parents (1903, 1905), he dedicated his life to writing. In 1912 he financed the publication of the first volume (*Swann's Way*) of what was to become his masterpiece, *Remembrance of Things Past*, a detailed portrait of fashionable aristocratic society. The second volume, *Within a Budding Grove* (1919), won the Prix Goncourt; it was followed by *The Guermantes Way* (1920–21) and *Cities of the Plain* (1921–22).

Provençal A *Romance language, spoken by about nine million people in France. It includes the dialects of both *Provence and of various other regions of S France. These dialects are also collectively described as the *langue d'oc*, in contrast to the *langue d'oïl* spoken in northern and central areas of France (*oc* and *oïl* being the medieval forms for *yes* in these two dialect areas).

Provence A former province in SE France, bordering on Italy and the Mediterranean Sea. A kingdom during the 9th century AD, it became part of France in 1481 and now forms the modern planning region of **Provence-Côte-d'Azur**. Its fertile river valleys produce grapes, olives, and mulberries. It contains the French *Riviera along the S coast. Area: 31 435 sq km (12 134 sq mi). Population (1986 est): 4 058 800.

Prussia A former state in N Germany on the NE Baltic coast. Established in the 13th century, Prussia became a duchy in 1525. United with *Brandenburg in 1618, it became the most powerful N German state. In the 18th century, under *Frederick the Great, Prussia acquired Silesia and parts of Poland and became a major European power. Under *Bismarck's leadership, Prussia defeated Austria and Austria's German allies (1866), acquiring *Schleswig-Holstein. Following victory in the *Franco-Prussian War (1870–71) the German Empire was proclaimed under Prussian leadership. Prussia was abolished by the Allies after World War II.

Przewalski's horse The single surviving species of wild horse, *Equus przewalskii*, discovered in Mongolia in about 1880 by the Russian explorer Nicolai Mikhailovich Przewalski (1839–88). It is reddish-brown with a short erect dark-brown mane and a dark stripe along the back. Height: 1.22–1.42 m (12–14 hands).

pseudopodium A temporary extension of the cytoplasm found in some *protozoa (including *Amoeba*) and used for moving about and for engulfing food particles.

psoriasis A chronic skin disease in which there is excessive flaking of the skin. It begins with small red scaly patches and may spread extensively. The knees, elbows, lower back, scalp, and nails are most commonly affected. A sufferer may have repeated bouts of the disease.

psychiatry The study and treatment of mental disorders. A psychiatrist is a medically qualified physician specializing in mental illness. The range of mental disorders includes psychosis, *neurosis, psychosomatic disorders, drug dependence, and mental retardation.

psychoanalysis A method of treating mental disorders based upon the teachings of Sigmund *Freud (*see also* Adler, Alfred; Jung, Carl). Psychoanalysts regard unconscious mental forces as the key to many disorders. These forces may be the result of emotions and conflicts that have long been ignored or of which the patient is unaware. The object of psychoanalysis is to make the patients aware of their hidden conflicts so that they can be resolved. The main technique is free association, in which the patient speaks his thoughts prompted by key words from the analyst. *See also* repression.

psychology The scientific study of the behaviour of man and animals. Different schools of psychology use differing methods and theories. Clinical psychology applies the observations of psychologists to the understanding and treatment of mental illness (*see* psychiatry; psychoanalysis). Educational psychology studies the ways in which children learn, in order to improve teaching methods. *See also* ethology.

psychotherapy Methods of treatment for mental disorders that are based on *psychology. Approaches to psychotherapy include *psychoanalysis and *group therapy. Psychotherapy aims to help self-understanding and personal development through the relationship between the client (or patient) and the therapist.

ptarmigan A grouse, *Lagopus lagopus*, found in Arctic tundra and mountain regions. 35 cm long, it has white wings and a mottled blackish-brown body that changes to white in winter. Its feet are covered with feathers.

pteridophyte A flowerless perennial plant that shows a distinct *alternation of generations. The dominant form is the asexual spore-bearing sporophyte, which consists typically of leaves, stems, and roots and bears spores in special capsules (sporangia). Pteridophytes include *ferns, *clubmosses, and horsetails.

pterodactyl. *See* pterosaur.

pterosaur An extinct flying reptile, also called pterodactyl, that lived during the Jurassic and Cretaceous periods (200–65 million years ago). A thin wing membrane stretched from the long fourth finger of the fore limb to the knee. It had long slender hind limbs, probably used to cling, batlike, to rocks and trees. Its toothless beaked jaw resembled that of modern birds.

PTFE. *See* polytetrafluoroethene.

Ptolemaic system A theory of astronomy originally advanced in Greece in the 3rd century BC and completed by *Ptolemy in the 2nd century AD. It proposed that the moon, Mercury, Venus, Sun, Mars, Jupiter, and Saturn moved around the earth. Ptolemy suggested that each orbiting body moved in a small circle (an epicycle) the centre of which moved in a larger circle (a deferent) around the earth. The Ptolemaic system was abandoned when the system of *Copernicus was accepted.

Ptolemy (*or* Claudius Ptolemaeus; 2nd century AD) Egyptian mathematician, astronomer, and geographer. The foremost of his works outlines the *Ptolemaic system of astronomy and was known to Arab astronomers as the *Almagest*, the name by which it is still known.

Ptolemy I Soter (?367–?283 BC) The first Macedonian King of Egypt and founder of the Ptolemaic dynasty. He was a general of Alexander the Great, after whose death he became governor of Egypt. He conquered Palestine, Cyprus, and much of Asia Minor, taking the title of king in 304. He made *Alexandria his capital.

public school In the USA the term means a school that is not under private ownership, whereas in the UK it means a fee-paying school, usually a boarding school. Although traditionally for boys, most public schools now admit girls, especially at sixth-form level, and a number of well-known independent girls' schools were established in the 19th century. Public schools include many of the former direct-grant schools (state-assisted schools that have been either incorporated into the state system or have become totally independent).

public sector Those parts of the productive and nonproductive sectors of the economy that are paid for out of taxation, are under state control, or both. It includes central and local government, public institutions and utilities, and nationalized industries (*see* nationalization). The amount by which the receipts of the public sector, including taxation, fall short of public expenditure constitutes the Public Sector Borrowing Requirement.

Puccini, Giacomo (1858–1924) Italian opera composer. His first major success was *Manon Lescaut* (1893). The operas that followed established Puccini as the master of the Italian stage and of the *verismo* (Italian: realism) style: *La Bohème* (1896), *Tosca* (1900), and *Madame Butterfly* (1904). His final masterpiece, *Turandot*, was produced in 1926 after his death.

Pueblo Indians North American Indian tribes of the SW region including the Tewa, Keres, Hopi, and Zuni. The name comes from the Spanish term for their villages—*pueblos*. They began to abandon their hunting existence and adopt their present farming economy about 1600 years ago. They were always extremely peaceful peoples, much given to ritual and ceremonial pursuits.

Puerto Rico, Commonwealth of (name from 1898 until 1932: Porto Rico) An island and self-governing commonwealth in association with the USA. It is in the West Indies, the smallest and most easterly island in the Greater Antilles. *Economy*: manufacture (chemicals, textiles, plastics, food processing) is the main source of income, while income from dairy and livestock farming has overtaken that of sugar, the principal crop. *History*: discovered by Columbus in 1508, it was under Spanish rule for nearly 400 years until handed over to the USA in 1898. Full US citizenship was granted in 1917 and it attained its present status in 1952. In 1976 the New Progressive Party regained control, led by Carlos Romero Barceló (1932–), who is in favour of Puerto Rico becoming a state of the USA. Since 1974, however, there has been growing militant pressure for the independence of Puerto Rico. Official language: Spanish; English is also widely spoken. Official currency: US dollar of 100 cents. Area: 8674 sq km (3349 sq mi). Population (1987): 3 300 000. Capital: San Juan.

puff adder A large highly venomous *adder occurring in semiarid areas of Africa. The name derives from its habit of hissing loudly and inflating its body in a threatening posture. Puff adders are brown or grey marked with yellow V-shapes.

puffball A fungus with a round or pear-shaped fruiting body (spore-producing structure). As it matures, the outer layer cracks and falls off; the spongy interior produces powdery spores. The greyish-white giant puffball (*Calvatia giganteum*) occurs in pastures, woodlands, and road verges and may reach over 1 m across.

puffer A fish, also called globefish, that inflates its body with air or water when disturbed. The tough spiny skin contains a highly toxic chemical, which can be fatal. Puffers live mainly in tropical and subtropical seas.

puffin A N Atlantic seabird, *Fratercula arctica*. 29 cm long, it is black with a white face and underparts, red legs, and a blue ring around the eye. Its large triangular bill is striped red, yellow, and blue in the breeding season.

pug A breed of dog originating in China and introduced to Britain from Holland in the 17th century. It is stockily built, with wrinkled skin, a large head, a short square muzzle, and black face. The short smooth coat can be silver, black, or apricot-fawn. Height: 25–28 cm.

Pugin, Augustus Welby Northmore (1812–52) British architect. Pugin was a leader in the English *gothic revival, which he defended in his most influential book, *Contrasts* (1836). He was most accomplished at designing churches, such as Nottingham Cathedral (1842). However, he is best known for his work on the *Palace of Westminster, for which he designed the interior.

Pulitzer Prizes Annual awards provided by the US editor and publisher Joseph Pulitzer (1847–1911) for achievements in journalism and literature. The $1,000 prizes for journalism, and the $500 prizes for literature were first awarded in 1917. Since 1943 a prize for musical composition has also been awarded.

pulsar A celestial object that emits regular pulses of radiation and is almost certainly a rapidly rotating *neutron star. Pulsars were originally discovered, in 1967, at radio wavelengths. The Crab and Vela pulsars also emit pulses at optical and gamma-ray wavelengths. Pulsars are thought to originate in *supernovae.

pulsating stars. *See* variable stars.

puma. *See* cougar.

pumice A light volcanic rock derived from acidic lava. It resembles sponge in having many cavities produced by bubbles of gas trapped on rapid solidification. Pumice is used for scouring and polishing.

pumpkin The fruit of certain plants of the gourd family, cultivated in North America and Europe. It is round, up to 30 kg in weight with a lightly furrowed yellow rind surrounding an edible fleshy pulp and numerous seeds. It is cooked and eaten as a vegetable or used as animal feed.

Punic Wars Three wars between Rome and Carthage, which gave Rome control of the Mediterranean. The first Punic (from the Latin *Punicus*, Carthaginian) War (264–241 BC) was provoked when Rome intervened in Sicily, its new naval power leading to victory off the Aegates Insulae (241). The second Punic War (218–201) was brought about by *Hannibal's capture (219) of Saguntum, a Roman ally in Spain. His advance into Italy was eventually checked by *Fabius Maximus and Scipio Africanus, who defeated Hannibal at Zama (202). Roman fears of a revival of Carthaginian power caused the third Punic War (149–146), in which Carthage was destroyed and its territory became the Roman province of Africa.

Punjab A region of the NW Indian subcontinent, in India and Pakistan on the flat alluvial plain of five Indus tributaries. Its population is 60% Sikh in India's Punjab state, and almost entirely Muslim in Pakistan's Punjab province. *History*: the Punjab was conquered by Muslims (11th century) but eventually became a Sikh stronghold until Britain established control (19th century). On the division of India and Pakistan (1947), the Punjab was divided on a religious basis. The W section became the Pakistan province of West Punjab (renamed Punjab in 1949), with an area of 205 346 sq km (79 284 sq mi) and its capital at Lahore; its population in 1985 was 53 840 000. The Indian section was reorganized in 1966 when the Punjabi-speaking state of Punjab was created, 50 376 sq km (19 445 sq mi), with its capital at Chandigarh; its population in 1981 was 16 669 755.

pupa A stage in the life cycle of certain insects, including flies, butterflies, ants, bees, and beetles, during which complete *metamorphosis from larva to adult takes place. The adult emerges after a period of a few days to several months.

pupil. *See* eye; iris.

Purcell, Henry (1659–95) English composer and organist. In 1677 he was appointed composer to the orchestra of the Chapel Royal and, in 1682, organist there. He wrote keyboard pieces, sonatas, anthems, songs, cantatas, and much music for the stage, including incidental music for *King Arthur* (1691) and *The Fairy Queen* (1692) and one opera, *Dido and Aeneas* (1689).

purgatory In Roman Catholic doctrine, the state in which souls are purified after death to make them fit for heaven. Masses or prayers for the dead are believed to shorten a soul's purgatorial sufferings. The doctrine of purgatory was officially adopted by the Church in the late 6th century.

Purim A Jewish festival, commemorating the frustration of an attempt to exterminate the Jews of the Persian Empire (473 BC), as told in the book of Esther. It is celebrated on the 14th Adar (Feb–March).

Puritanism A movement among Protestants in 16th-and 17th-century England. In Elizabeth I's reign the Puritans wished to get rid of Roman Catholic elements in the Church's form of service and organization. In the 17th century the Puritans, many of them now forming extremist sects (*see* Levellers), became associated with the parliamentarian side in the Civil War. After the Act of *Uniformity (1662) Puritans became known as *Nonconformists.

Purple Heart The oldest US military decoration, established as the Badge of Military Merit by George Washington in 1782 and awarded during the American Revolution. Reintroduced in 1932, it is awarded to those wounded in battle. It is a purple heart of cloth, bordered by bronze.

Pusan 35 05N 129 02E A port in SE South Korea, on the Korea Strait, capital of South Kyongsang province and South Korea's second largest city. Its varied industries include shipbuilding. Population (1985): 3 516 768.

Pushkin, Aleksandr (1799–1837) Russian poet, novelist, and dramatist. In 1820 he was exiled to the southern provinces for his revolutionary political verse. In exile he began the epic verse novel *Eugene Onegin* (1833), on which

Tchaikovsky based his opera (1877–78). In 1824 he was transferred to NW Russia, where he wrote the historical drama *Boris Godunov* (1831), which became the basis of Mussorgsky's opera (1874). He returned to Moscow in 1826 and was killed in a duel.

puss moth A moth, *Cerura vinula*, of Europe, Asia, and N Africa. The adult has a fat white hairy body with black spots. The caterpillar is green with black markings and when alarmed it presents a grotesque appearance with the head and tail appendages raised up.

PVC. *See* polyvinyl chloride.

Pygmalion In Greek mythology, a legendary king of Cyprus who made an ivory statue and fell in love with it. When he prayed for a wife who would be as beautiful as the statue, Aphrodite gave the statue life.

Pygmies Peoples of the tropical forest region of Africa, who are much smaller than their Bantu neighbours. The males are less than 150 cm (4 ft 11 in) in height. They are hunters and gatherers, wandering in small bands of around 30 members. They speak various *Bantu languages.

pygmy hippopotamus A small *hippopotamus, *Choeropsis liberiensis*, of West African forests. Up to 100 cm high at the shoulder and weighing about 200 kg, pygmy hippos sleep during the day.

P'yŏngyang 39 00N 125 47E The capital of North Korea, in the NW on the River Taedong. Reputedly the oldest city in Korea, it is a major industrial as well as administrative centre. Population (1984 est): 2 639 448.

pyracantha A thorny evergreen shrub of the rose family, also known as firethorn, native to SE Eurasia and widely cultivated in gardens. A commonly grown species is *Pyracantha coccinea*. It has white or pinkish-yellow flowers and scarlet berries, which may last all winter.

pyramids Royal burial monuments in ancient Egypt. The greatest are the pyramids of *Khufu, Khafre, and Menkaura at Giza (built c. 2600–2500 BC), the only survivors of the *Seven Wonders of the World. Pyramids were also built in ancient Mexico.

Pyramus and Thisbe Legendary lovers in a Babylonian story retold by *Ovid. The couple were forbidden to marry by their parents but exchanged vows through a chink in the wall between their houses. Arriving first for a secret meeting, Thisbe was frightened by a lion and fled, dropping her veil. Pyramus, finding her veil and thinking her dead, stabbed himself, and when Thisbe returned she killed herself also.

Pyrenean mountain dog (*or* Great Pyrenees) A breed of large dog, possibly of Asian origin, used in Europe for over 3000 years to guard shepherds and their flocks. They have drooping ears and the long thick slightly wavy coat is white, with or without grey or brown patches. Height: 71 cm (dogs); 66 cm (bitches).

Pyrenees (French name: Pyrénées; Spanish name: Pirineos) A mountain range in SW Europe. It extends between the Bay of Biscay in the W and the Mediterranean Sea in the E, forming a barrier between France and Spain. The entire republic of Andorra lies within the range, which rises to 3404 m (11 168 ft) at Pico de Aneto.

pyrethrum A plant, *Chrysanthemum coccineum* (or *Pyrethrum roseum*), of the daisy family, with red, pink, lilac, or white flowers. It is native to Persia and the Caucasus and widely cultivated in gardens in temperate regions. An insecticide is prepared from its dried flowers.

Pyrex The trade name for a heat-resistant glass containing borosilicate. It is also resistant to many chemicals and is an electrical insulator. Pyrex is used in laboratory glassware, ovenware, and large telescopes.

pyridoxine. *See* vitamin B complex.

pyrite (*or* iron pyrites) A pale brassy yellow mineral, FeS_2, the most common sulphide mineral. Occurring widely, it is usually mined for its sulphur, used for the manufacture of sulphuric acid, or for the gold and copper found in association with it. Because of its colour it has been called fool's gold.

pyroelectricity The development of opposite electric charges on opposite faces of asymmetric crystals when they are heated. The charges occur on those faces that are responsible for the crystal's asymmetry. Quartz and tourmaline have pyroelectric properties. *See also* piezoelectric effect.

Pythagoras (6th century BC) Greek philosopher and religious leader. Born at Samos, he migrated in about 530 BC to Crotone (S Italy), where he founded an ascetic religious society that governed Crotone for many years until its suppression (460–440 BC). Pythagoras probably discovered the geometrical theorem named after him and certainly discovered the arithmetical ratios governing musical intervals, which led him to interpret the universe in terms of mathematics alone. Pythagoreans were pioneers in several branches of science.

python A large *constrictor snake occurring in tropical and temperate regions of Africa and Asia. Pythons usually live near water and ambush their prey (goats, pigs, deer, etc.). The reticulated python (*Python reticulatus*) is the largest of all constrictors, reaching 10 m in length.

Q

Qaboos ibn Sa'id (1940–) Sultan of Oman (1970–). He became sultan after deposing, with British support, his reactionary father Sa'id ibn Taymur. With Omani oil revenues Qaboos has introduced modernization programmes.

Qatar, State of A country in the Middle East, in *Arabia. *Economy*: oil extraction accounts for over 90% of the national income. Qatar is a member of OPEC. *History*: Qatar relied on Britain for most of the 19th and 20th centuries, becoming a protectorate in 1916; it became independent in 1971. Head of state: Emir Sheik Khalifa bin Hamad Al-Thani (1937–). Official language: Arabic. Official currency: Qatar riyal of 100 dirhams. Area: 11 000 sq km (4246 sq mi). Population (1987): 371 863. Capital: Doha.

Qin (*or* Ch'in; 221–206 BC) The dynasty under which China became a unified empire. The first Qin emperor, Shi Huangdi (*or* Shih Huang Ti; c. 259–210 BC), unified weights, measures, coinage, and the writing system. During the Qin reign much of the *Great Wall of China was built. Excavations near his tomb in the late 1970s revealed several thousand life-size terracotta men and horses. The remains of the Qin capital were discovered in 1985.

Qing (*or* Ch'ing; 1644–1911) A Manchu dynasty, founded by Nurhachi (1559–1626), that ruled China from the fall of the Ming dynasty until 1911. At its height in the 18th century the Qing ruled a vast empire that included Outer Mongolia, Tibet, and Turkistan. However, corruption became rife and China suffered a series of defeats by foreign powers (*see* Opium Wars) as well as internal rebellions (*see* Taiping Rebellion) that led to the overthrow of the Qing in 1911.

Qingdao (Ch'ing-tao *or* Tsingtao) 36 04N 120 22E A port in E China, in Shandong province on the Yellow Sea. From 1898 to 1922 it was under German and then Japanese control. Population (1986): 1 250 000.

quadratic equation An algebraic equation in which the greatest power of the unknown quantity, x, is two. It is usually written in the form $ax^2 + bx + c = 0$, in which the two solutions (called roots) are given by $x = [-b \pm \sqrt{(b^2 - 4ac)}]/2a$.

quadriplegia. *See* paralysis.

Quadruple Alliances 1. (1718) The alliance formed by Britain, France, the Holy Roman Emperor, and the Netherlands to maintain the Treaties of Utrecht (1713–14), which ended the War of the Spanish Succession, and had been rejected by Spain. 2. (1814) The alliance formed by Britain, Austria, Prussia, and Russia against Napoleon. 3. (1834) The alliance between Britain, France, Spain, and Portugal that sought to maintain constitutional monarchy in Spain and Portugal.

quail A round-bodied short-tailed gamebird of open grassland and farmland. Quail in Europe and Asia are 13–20 cm long and have a smooth-edged bill and leg spurs; they are stocky and usually sandy coloured. Quail from America are up to 30 cm long and have a strong serrated bill, no leg spurs, and are brightly coloured.

Quakers The Christian religious group formally known as the Religious Society of Friends, founded in England by George *Fox in the late 1640s. They suffered violent persecution for many years and in 1682 William *Penn led a colony of Friends to *Pennsylvania. In the USA they were leaders in the fight against *slavery.

The early Quakers adopted a simple dress and way of life. They were (and remain) pacifists, refused to take oaths, and rejected the use of titles.

quaking grass A *grass, *Briza media*, that is native to temperate Eurasia and grows 20–50 cm high. Its long slender flower stalks quiver in the wind. Similar species grow in South America.

quango (*quasi-autonomous national government organization*) An organization, such as the Monopolies Commission and the Equal Opportunities Commission, set up by the government as an independent body but remaining dependent on the government for their existence. In the USA quango stands for "quasi-autonomous non-governmental organization."

quantity theory of money A theory that seeks to explain how the money supply (*see* money) affects the economy. Developed in its modern form by the US economist Milton *Friedman, it states that if there is a change in the money supply, either the price level will change or the supply of goods in the economy will alter.

quantum theory The theory first developed by Max *Planck in 1900 to explain the distribution of wavelengths of electromagnetic radiation emitted by a *black body. The experimental observations could only be explained when Planck assumed that the radiation was emitted and absorbed in discrete amounts, which he called quanta. The energy of each quantum has the value hf, where h is a universal constant (now known as the Planck constant) and f is the frequency of the radiation. Planck's theory was used by *Einstein to explain the *photoelectric effect and in 1913 by Niels *Bohr to explain the spectrum of hydrogen. **Quantum mechanics** is the application of quantum theory to the mechanics of atomic systems.

quarantine The period during which a person or animal suspected of carrying an infectious disease is kept in isolation. The term was originally applied to the 40-day period (French: *quarantaine*) during which ships suspected of carrying infected people were prevented from communicating with the shore. The quarantine period is now slightly longer than the incubation period of the disease.

quarks. *See* particle physics.

quarter days In law, days in each quarter of the year on which rent and other dues on land were traditionally paid. In England they are 25 March (Lady Day), 24 June (Midsummer Day), 29 Sept (Michaelmas Day), and 25 Dec (Christmas Day).

quartz The commonest of all minerals, consisting of crystalline *silica. It occurs in many rocks, particularly igneous rocks (such as granite), many metamorphic rocks (such as gneisses), and in sands and sandstones. Pure quartz is colourless and as rock crystal is used in glassmaking, in jewellery, and (because of its piezoelectric properties) in making electrical oscillators. Some coloured varieties, such as amethyst (violet), rose quartz (pink), and citrine (yellow), are used as gemstones.

quasar (*quasi-stellar object; or* QSO) A class of celestial objects discovered in 1964–65, lying far beyond our galaxy. They appear as points of light but are each emitting more energy than several hundred giant galaxies. Quasar *redshifts are extremely large, indicating that they are the most distant and hence the youngest objects known outside our galaxy. The vast energy could result from matter spiralling into a supermassive *black hole lying at the centre of a galaxy.

Quaternary period The most recent period of geological time, from the end of the *Tertiary (about 1.8 million years ago) to the present day. It includes the *Pleistocene (Ice Age) and *Holocene epochs.

Quathlamba. *See* Drakensberg Mountains.

Quebec The largest province of Canada, stretching from the *St Lawrence River N to Hudson Bay and Strait. Asbestos, iron-ore, copper, zinc, gold, and other minerals are mined. Fishing, farming, and tourism are also important. *History*: claimed by France (1534), Quebec or New France was a French colony (1608–1763) until handed over to Britain. French-Canadian culture was preserved after the formation of Canada (1867). Area: 1 356 791 sq km (523 858 sq mi). Population (1986): 6 532 461; over 80% are French speaking. Capital: Quebec. *See also* Montreal.

Quebec 46 50N 71 15W A city and port in E Canada, the capital of Quebec. First settled in 1608, it is strategically located above a sudden narrowing of the St Lawrence River. Most of the workforce is employed by government and service industries. Population (1986): 164 580.

Quechua The language of the *Incas and of the present-day American Indian peoples of the central Andean highlands.

Queen Anne style An English architectural and decorative style with some baroque elements, dating from about 1700 to 1715. Beautiful walnut veneered furniture was made, while chairs became lighter, more comfortable, and invariably had cabriole legs. Wall mirrors in gilt frames were used to decorate panelled rooms.

Queen Charlotte Islands A group of islands of W Canada, in British Columbia 160 km (100 mi) off the Pacific coast. Mountainous with lush vegetation, the islands are mostly inhabited by Haida Indians engaged in fishing and forestry. Area: 9596 sq km (3705 sq mi). Population (1981): 5884.

Queen Maud Land. *See* Norwegian Antarctic Territory.

Queen's Award An award to industry in the UK, instituted in 1965 and made on the birthday (21 April) of Queen Elizabeth II. Awarded to firms, rather than individuals, it entitles holders to make use of a special emblem for five years.

Queensberry Rules. *See* boxing.

Queen's Counsel (QC) A barrister appointed to senior rank as counsel to the English queen (or king) on the recommendation of the Lord Chancellor. QCs have no special duties to the Crown; they wear a silk gown, sit within the Bar of the court, and are senior to the "utter barristers" (i.e. the outer barristers, who sit outside the Bar).

Queen's County. *See* Laois.

Queensland The second largest state of Australia, situated in the NE. The *Great Barrier

Reef runs parallel to the Pacific coast. Coal is the most important mineral. Other minerals include copper, bauxite, lead, silver, and zinc; oil is mined and natural gas is piped to Brisbane. Beef, sugar, and wool are major industries. Another growing industry is tourism. Area: 1 728 000 sq km (667 000 sq mi). Population (1986): 2 587 315. Capital: Brisbane.

quetzal A Central American bird, *Pharomachus mocinno*, that lives in forests. The male reaches 1.3 m including its curved ornamental tail feathers; its plumage is green, red, and white.

Quezon City 14 39N 121 01E A city in the N Philippines, in S Luzon near to Manila. It was the nation's former capital (1948–76). Population (1984): 1 326 000.

quince A small tree, *Cydonia vulgaris*, of the rose family, probably native to W Asia but widely cultivated for its fruit. 4.5–6 m high, it has white or pink flowers. The pear-shaped fruit is 7.5–10 cm long with a golden skin.

quinine A drug obtained from the bark of *Cinchona* trees. Originally used to treat malaria, it has now been largely replaced by other drugs having fewer side effects. Related compounds (e.g. quinidine) are used to treat abnormal heart rhythms.

Quisling, Vidkun (Abraham Lauritz Jonsson) (1887–1945) Norwegian army officer and Nazi collaborator, whose name now signifies a traitor. After serving as a diplomat, Quisling formed (1933) the fascist National Union Party in Norway. He encouraged the Nazi occupation of Norway (1940), and as "minister president" sent a thousand Jews to concentration camps. Arrested in 1945, he was found guilty of war crimes and executed.

Quito 0 20S 78 45W The capital of Ecuador, on the slopes of the volcano Pichincha at an altitude of 2850 m (9350 ft). It was the capital of the Inca kingdom of Quito until 1534, when it was captured by the Spanish. It contains many Spanish-colonial churches. Population (1982): 1 110 248.

Qumran The site on the NW shore of the Dead Sea in Israel, where a Jewish sect called the *Essenes lived from about 125 BC to 68 AD. The community produced the *Dead Sea Scrolls. Excavations from 1951 revealed a complex of buildings.

R

Ra (*or* Re) The Egyptian sun god and lord of creation, usually portrayed with a falcon's head bearing the disc of the sun. During the 18th dynasty (1567–1320 BC) he became identified with the Theban god Amon as Amon-Ra.

Rabat (Arabic name: Ribat) 34 00N 6 42W The capital of Morocco, near the Atlantic coast. Founded in the 12th century, it became the capital under the French protectorate in the early 20th century. Population (1984): 556 000.

rabbi A Jewish scholar and religious authority, since the 1st century AD. In modern Jewish communities rabbis are communal leaders, preachers, and pastoral workers.

rabbit A burrowing mammal related to the *hare. The European rabbit (*Oryctolagus cuniculus*) grows to about 45 cm; it has long ears, a short tail, and soft grey-brown fur. Rabbits live in groups in large warrens and feed on vegetation.

Rabelais, François (1483–1553) French satirist. He became a Franciscan and then a Benedictine monk, left the monastery to practise medicine, and visited Italy. His humanist philosophy is expressed in his works of comic satire, *Pantagruel* (1532) and *Gargantua* (1534). The classic English translation of his works is by Sir Thomas Urquhart (1653).

rabies A virus infection of the brain that can affect all warm-blooded animals and may be transmitted to man through the bite of an infected animal (usually a dog). Symptoms, which appear after a period of from ten days to two years, include painful spasms of the throat. Later, the sight of water can induce convulsions (hence the alternative name–hydrophobia, "fear of water") and the patient eventually dies. Antirabies vaccine and antiserum given immediately after being bitten may prevent the infection from developing. The UK has strict quarantine regulations for imported domestic animals to prevent the disease from reaching Britain.

raccoon An omnivorous mammal of the Americas, related to the panda. About 1 m long, raccoons have long hind legs and short forelegs. A black patch across the eyes and a striped tail contrast with the thick grey coat.

Rachmaninov, Sergei (1873–1943) Russian composer, pianist, and conductor, who lived in the USA from 1917. His works include four piano concertos, three symphonies, four piano concertos (which he also recorded), the *Rhapsody on a Theme of Paganini* (1934), and *The Bells* (1910).

racial discrimination The practice of making unfavourable distinctions between the members of different races. In South Africa (*see* apartheid) race relations are charaterized by an inflexible tradition, which has led to the separation of peoples on the basis of their ethnic backgrounds. A similar tradition characterizes southern states of the USA. In the UK the Race Relations Acts (1965, 1968, 1976) aimed to secure the integration of Commonwealth and other immigrants into the community and to prevent racial prejudice.

Racine, Jean (1639–99) French dramatist. His major classical verse tragedies include *Andromaque* (1667), *Bérénice* (1670), and *Phèdre*

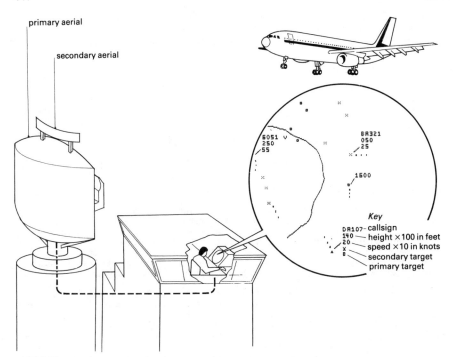

primary aerial

secondary aerial

6051 V
250
55

BR321
050
25

1600

Key
DR107 — callsign
140 — height ×100 in feet
20 — speed ×10 in knots
  — secondary target
  — primary target

RADAR *The high-frequency pulses sent out by the transmitting aerial are reflected back by the target and displayed on a screen. The typical air-traffic control picture seen here shows East Anglia (only a few of the targets are labelled, for clarity).*

(1677). In 1677 he retired from the theatre and accepted a post at the court of Louis XIV. His final works were two religious dramas *Esther* (1689) and *Athalie* (1691).

rad A unit of absorbed dose of ionizing radiation, now replaced by the *gray (100 rad = 1 gray).

radar (*ra*dio *d*etection *a*nd *r*anging) A method of locating distant objects developed before World War II by a British team led by Sir Robert *Watson-Watt. High-frequency (300 to 30 000 megahertz) radio waves are sent out in pulses from a rotating transmitter and are reflected back by any object they encounter to a receiving antenna. The signal from this antenna deflects the electron beam in a *cathode-ray tube. The beam scans the screen of the tube by rotating at the same speed as the antenna, so that its angular position indicates the direction of the located object. The distance from the centre of the screen shows the distance of the object. Radar is widely used in aircraft and nautical navigation.

radian (rad) The *SI unit of plane angle equal to the angle subtended at the centre of a circle by an arc equal in length to the radius of the circle.

radiation The emission or transfer of energy by a beam of particles or waves. It includes all electromagnetic waves, beams of elementary particles, ions, etc., and sound waves.

radiation sickness Illness caused by *ionizing radiation. Short-term effects include nausea and diarrhoea; long-term effects include sterility, haemorrhage, and cancer.

radical A group of atoms in a chemical compound that behaves as a unit in reactions. For example, methanol (CH_3OH) can be considered as a methyl radical (CH_3.) and a hydroxyl radical (.OH) which is the functional group of alcohols. **Free radicals** are able to exist independently for a short time and are very reactive.

radio The transmission of information by radio-frequency (3 kilohertz to 300 gigahertz) electromagnetic waves. The use of radio waves for communication was pioneered by *Marconi in 1895, although their existence had been proposed by *Maxwell in 1873 and demonstrated by *Hertz in 1888.

A **radio transmitter** generates a radio-frequency electrical signal (carrier wave) in an oscillator and 'adds' a sound signal by a *modulation process. The composite signal is then fed to an *aerial, which transmits electromagnetic waves. Long-wave (30 to 300 kilohertz) and medium-wave (300 to 3000 kilohertz) radio is used for direct (ground-wave) transmission in amplitude-modulated (AM) sound broadcasting. Short-wave radio is used for AM sound broadcasting over longer distances using a layer of the upper

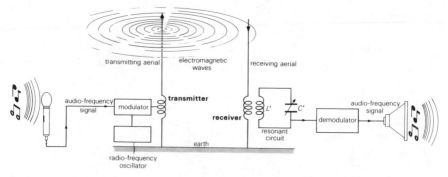

RADIO *The transmission and reception of sound broadcasts.*

atmosphere (the ionosphere) to reflect the waves (sky waves) back to earth. VHF (very high frequency; 30 to 300 megahertz) is used for *stereophonic sound broadcasting in frequency modulated (FM) transmissions. Television uses mostly UHF (ultrahigh frequency). Neither VHF nor UHF are reflected by the ionosphere, but can be relayed by *communications satellites. All **radio receivers** convert the incoming radio signals into audible signals using electronic devices that include an *aerial, an amplification system, and one or more *loudspeakers.

radioactive tracer A radioactive *isotope used for following the course of a substance during a physical, biological, or chemical process. A nonradioactive isotope in the substance is replaced by a radioactive isotope of the same element, which can then be detected by its emitted radiation with a *Geiger counter.

radioactive waste Waste products from nuclear reactors, uranium-processing plants, etc., that have become radioactive. Solid waste is either stored underground or placed in drums weighted with concrete and sunk in deep sea water (banned at present).

radioactivity The emission of a particle by an atomic nucleus without any external cause; first discovered (1898) by *Becquerel in uranium. The particle may be an alpha particle (a helium nucleus consisting of two protons and two neutrons), a process known as alpha decay; or it may be a beta particle (an *electron), known as *beta decay. Highly energetic *gamma radiation may also be emitted at the same time. In both alpha and beta decay the nucleus changes into that of another element. Radioactive decay is a random process; for a single nucleus it can be neither predicted nor controlled. However, for a large number of nuclei the time taken for a certain fraction of nuclei to decay can be accurately predicted as either its *mean life or *half-life. These quantities vary from about 10^{-8} second to 10^{10} years depending on the isotope.

radio astronomy The study of celestial objects by means of the radio waves they emit. This radio emission was first noticed by K. G. Jansky in 1932. It now forms an important branch of *astronomy.

radiocarbon dating A method of estimating the age of a material, such as wood, that was once living. All living things absorb a small proportion of radioactive carbon-14 from atmospheric carbon dioxide; however, once dead, the level of carbon-14 falls due to *beta decay. By measuring the radioactivity of a material, the concentration of carbon-14 and hence its age can be estimated.

radiography The examination of the internal structure of a body by passing *X-rays or *gamma radiation through it to produce a photographic image. Radiography is used in medicine (*see* radiology), and in industry to find structural defects.

radio interferometer. *See* radio telescope.

radioisotope (*or* radioactive isotope) An *isotope that is radioactive. Radioisotopes are used in *nuclear reactors, in *radiotherapy, as *radioactive tracers, and in *radiocarbon dating and other dating techniques. Some are naturally occurring (those with mass numbers in excess of 208) while others can be made by neutron bombardment.

radiolarian A single-celled animal (*see* protozoa) found in the sea as part of the plankton. Radiolarians are typically spherical, 0.1 mm to several millimetres in diameter, with a hard skeleton of radiating spines from which long food-catching structures extend.

radiology The branch of medicine involving radiation in the diagnosis and treatment of disease. Recent advances in radiology include the use of computer-aided tomography scanners (CT scanners), in which X-ray "slices" of the body are scanned by X-rays and processed by a computer to produce a complete image. *See also* radiotherapy.

radio sources Celestial objects, such as the sun and Jupiter, that emit radio waves. Other radio sources within our Galaxy are pulsars, supernova remnants, and the galactic centre. Extragalactic sources include spiral galaxies, and some quasars.

radio telescope An instrument for detecting the radio emissions from *radio sources. It consists of an antenna from which radio-frequency signals are carried by wires or waveguides to a receiver. The antenna may be a metal dish, usually steerable, that focuses radio waves from a source onto a secondary antenna. A **radio interferometer**, using dipole antennas, has a greater resolving power than a single antenna.

radiotherapy   The use of X-rays and other radiation to treat disease. The radiation may be directed at the target organ from outside. Alternatively, radioactive needles, pellets, etc., may be placed inside the body. Radiation is used in treating various forms of *cancer and overactivity of the thyroid gland.

radish   A plant, *Raphanus sativus*, of the mustard family, grown for its red or white edible root eaten in salads, etc.

radium (Ra)   A radioactive alkaline-earth element, discovered (1898) in pitchblende by Pierre and Marie Curie. It forms a number of simple salts, such as the chloride ($RaCl_2$). It decays to form *radon and is used in radiotherapy. At no 88; at wt (226); mp 700°C; bp 1140°C.

radon (Rn)   The heaviest *noble gas, produced by the decay of radium, thorium, and actinium. It is radioactive, the longest-lived isotope (^{222}Rn) having a half-life of 3.825 days. At no 86; at wt (222); mp −71°C; bp −61.8°C.

RAF.   *See* Royal Air Force.

raffia (*or* raphia)   A Madagascan *palm tree, *Raphia pedunculata* (or *R. ruffia*). Its leaves, up to 20 m long, are composed of 80–100 leaflets from which the fibre is torn in thin strips and dried in the sun. Raffia is woven into mats, baskets, etc.

Raglan, FitzRoy James Henry Somerset, 1st Baron   (1788–1855) British field marshal. In 1854 he became commander in the *Crimean War and, in spite of success at *Inkerman, his strategy was much criticized (*see also* Balaclava, Battle of). The Raglan sleeve is named after him.

Ragnarök   In Norse mythology, doomsday, when a catastrophic battle between the gods and the forces of evil will occur. After the defeat of the gods everyone will be destroyed except for Lif and Lifthrasir, a man and woman who will eventually found a new race.

ragtime   A style of piano music characterized by syncopation in the melody against a marchlike accompaniment. Popular from the 1890s, it influenced New Orleans jazz. Scott Joplin was the first ragtime composer to write down his music.

ragworm   A marine *annelid worm, *Nereis cultrifera*, also called chainworm, of European coastal waters. 5–10 cm long, ragworms swim by means of paddle-like structures occurring in pairs on each body segment. Most live in burrows.

rail   A slender ground-dwelling bird usually occurring in swamps and fresh waters. 11–45 cm long, rails have short rounded wings, a short tail, and typically a dull greyish barred plumage. *See also* coot; gallinule.

railway   A permanent track on which *locomotives draw trucks transporting goods or passengers. Flanged wheels on horse-drawn trucks running on cast-iron rails were introduced in 1789 but the first effective railway opened in England in 1825, between Stockton and Darlington, using *Stephenson's *Locomotion* as the locomotive. By 1885 some 26 900 km (16 700 mi) of track had been laid in the UK. The Railways Act

(1921) consolidated the 250 railway companies then operating into four companies: London Midland and Scottish Railway (LMS), London and North Eastern Railway (LNER), Great Western Railway (GWR), and Southern Railway (SR). In 1947 these were amalgamated in the state-owned British Railways (becoming British Rail in 1965).
Until the 1860s railways were an exclusively British expertise. After the Civil War, however, US railways developed independently and by 1887 had 140 000 km (87 000 mi) of rail. The USA now has more than any other nation, with 338 000 km (209 000 mi).
Since World War II the growth of air services, road-haulage, and private motoring have led to the decline of the railways in industrial countries, causing services to be reduced. However the high-speed trains and road congestion have enabled them to survive.

rainbow   An arc of light across the sky composed of the *colours of the spectrum. It is caused by the *refraction of sunlight through falling water drops; the larger the drops the stronger the colours.

rain forest.   *See* forest.

Rainier III   (1923–) Prince of Monaco (1949–). He dropped the principle of the *divine right of kings in a new constitution (1962). In 1956 he married Grace *Kelly. Their three children are Prince Albert (1958–), Princess Caroline (1957–), and Princess Stephanie (1965–).

Rajput   A group of clans in N and central India, now numbering about 11 million people, descended from invading tribes from Central Asia. The Rajput states resisted the Muslim invaders, maintaining their independence in Rajasthan. They came under the overlordship of the *Moguls in the 16th century, the Marathas in the 18th century, and the British in 1808.

Raleigh, Sir Walter   (1554–1618) British explorer and writer. Unsuccessful in founding (1584–89) a colony in Virginia, he brought back the potato and tobacco plants from America. In 1595 he led an expedition to South America and in 1596 took part in the sack of Cádiz. A favourite of Elizabeth I, on James I's accession (1603) he stood trial for treason, but the death sentence was reduced to imprisonment; while in the Tower of London he wrote *The History of the World* (1614). He was released in 1616 to search for gold along the Orinoco but his mission was a failure and after his return he was executed.

Ramadan   The ninth month of the Muslim year. Muslims observe a strict fast daily from dawn to dusk until the new moon of the next month is visible, to make amends for their sins.

Ramapithecus   A genus of fossil *hominids that lived during the late Miocene and early Pliocene (*see* Tertiary period). About the size of a gibbon, they may have walked erect and been ancestors of man.

Ramayana   (Sanskrit: romance of Rama) Hindu epic poem in seven books, relating how Rama regained his wife, Sita, with the aid of *Hanuman, after she was abducted by the demon king Ravana.

Rambert, Dame Marie (Cyvia Rabbam, later Miriam Rambach; 1888–1982) British ballet dancer and choreographer, born in Poland. As director of the Carmargo Society, which in 1935 became the Ballet Rambert, she trained and encouraged many young British dancers.

Ramillies, Battle of (23 May, 1706) The battle in the War of the *Spanish Succession in which Marlborough defeated the French 21 km (13 mi) N of Namur. The victory gave much of the Spanish Netherlands to the allies.

Ramsay, Sir William (1852–1916) Scottish chemist. Working with Rayleigh, he discovered (1894) argon, from which he isolated neon, xenon, and krypton in 1898. In 1895 he also discovered helium. For this work he was awarded the 1904 Nobel prize.

Ramses (II) the Great King of Egypt (1304–1237 BC) of the 19th dynasty. His warfare against the Hittites ended in lasting peace (1284). Ramses built the temple of *Abu Simbel and is probably the pharaoh who oppressed the Israelites.

Rand, the. See Witwatersrand.

Rangoon 16 47N 96 10E The capital of Burma, a port in the S on the River Rangoon. Industry has increased greatly since independence in 1948. *History*: a settlement grew around the Shwe Dagon Pagoda, the focal point of Burmese religious life. Twice captured by the British in the 19th century, it became the capital of all Burma in 1886. Population (1983): 2 458 712.

Rapanui. See Easter Island.

rape (botany) A plant, *Brassica napus*, of the mustard family, also called oilseed rape or coleseed, that grows to 1 m and has yellow flowers. It is widely cultivated for the edible oil extracted from its seeds.

Raphael (Raffaello Sanzio; 1483–1520) Italian Renaissance painter and architect. He trained in Perugia, where he painted *The Marriage of the Virgin* (Brera, Milan) before moving to Florence in 1504. There, influenced by *Leonardo and *Michelangelo, he painted numerous Madonnas and portraits of Angelo and Maddalena Doni (Palazzo Pitti, Florence). Settling in Rome in 1508, he decorated the papal apartments with frescoes. In 1514 he succeeded Bramante as architect of St Peter's, designing (1515) tapestries for the Sistine Chapel.

Rarotonga 21 15S 159 45W A mountainous island in the SW Pacific Ocean, the administrative centre of the *Cook Islands. Copra and citrus fruit are exported. Area: 67 sq km (26 sq mi). Population (1986): 9281. Chief town: Avarua.

Rashid. See Rosetta Stone.

raspberry A prickly plant, *Rubus idaeus*, of the rose family, native to Eurasia and North America. Up to 1.5 m high, it is cultivated for its fruits. The plants bear fruit in their first autumn or second summer.

Rasputin, Grigori Yefimovich (c. 1872–1916) Russian mystic, who was a favourite of Emperor *Nicholas II and *Alexandra. A Siberian peasant, Rasputin's apparent ability to ease the bleeding of the haemophiliac crown prince brought him considerable power. His unpopularity, made worse by his wild behaviour, led to his murder by a group of nobles: when poison

failed he was shot and thrown into the River Neva.

Rastafarians Members of a West Indian religious sect, who believe that Ras Tafari Makonnen (Haile Selassie) will secure for the black races a homeland in Ethiopia. Rastafarian men wear their hair in long matted curls (dreadlocks).

rat A *rodent found all over the world. The black rat (*Rattus rattus*), originally Asian, lives in human habitations and sewers. The brown rat (*R. norvegicus*) is larger, measuring 30–45 cm including its tail (15–20 cm), and lives outdoors in burrows. Both species can transmit disease.

rationalism A philosophical movement developing from 17th-century attempts to study the universe using reason rather than the experience of the senses.

rat kangaroo An Australian *marsupial. Measuring 23–44 cm excluding the tail (15–38 cm), rat kangaroos are related to kangaroos and have a ratlike face. They forage for grubs, tubers, etc.

rattan The stems of certain tropical climbing *palms. Up to 130 m long, they are used in furniture, matting, etc.

Rattigan, Sir Terence (1911–77) British dramatist. His successful plays include comedies (*French without Tears*, 1936), more ambitious studies (*The Deep Blue Sea*, 1952), and historical studies (*Ross*, 1960).

rattlesnake An American *viper having loosely connected horny tail segments, which it vibrates to produce a warning rattle. Rattlesnakes are 0.3–2.5 m long with dark diamond or spotted markings on a pale background. See also sidewinder.

Ravel, Maurice (1875–1937) French composer of the impressionist school. His works include, for piano, Le Tombeau de Couperin (1914–17), the suite Gaspard de la nuit (1908), and two piano concertos; for orchestra, La Valse (1920), Boléro (1927), the ballet Daphnis and Chloe (1909–12), and the opera L'Enfant et les sortilèges (1920–25).

raven A large black crow, *Corvus corax*, about 63 cm long with a massive bill. Ravens occur in mountains and moorlands of the N hemisphere, often in large colonies.

Ravenna 44 25N 12 12E A city and port in N Italy, connected to the Adriatic Sea by canal. Ravenna was the capital of the western Roman Empire (402–76 AD), of the Ostrogothic kings (476–526), and of the Byzantine military governorship (584–751). It is noted for its mosaics. Population (1986): 136 016.

Rawalpindi 33 40N 73 08E A city in N Pakistan. It was the temporary capital (1959–69) while the new capital at Islamabad was being built. Population (1981): 982 000.

ray A marine cartilaginous *fish occurring worldwide. Rays have a flattened head and body with greatly enlarged winglike pectoral fins; the tail often bears sharp poison spines. Rays usually live on the sea bed and feed on fish and invertebrates.

Rayleigh, John William Strutt, 3rd Baron (1842–1919) British physicist. His work on black-body radiation was superseded by

*Planck's discovery of quantum theory but he contributed to optics, hydrodynamics, and the theory of electrical units. He was awarded the 1904 Nobel Prize with Sir William *Ramsay for their discovery of argon.

rayon A textile fibre made from *cellulose. **Viscose rayon** is made by dissolving wood pulp in sodium hydroxide and carbon disulphide. The fibres are formed in an acid bath. **Acetate rayon** is made by mixing wood pulp with acetic acid and sulphuric acid to form cellulose acetate, which is then dissolved in a solvent and forced through holes to form fibres.

razorbill A black-and-white *auk, *Alca torda*, that breeds around N Atlantic coasts and winters in the Mediterranean. 40 cm long, it has a slender sharp bill. It dives to catch fish, shellfish, etc.

razor shell A burrowing *bivalve mollusc, of which there are about 40 species, also called jack-knife clam, of Atlantic and Pacific coasts. The common razor (*Ensis siliqua*), about 15 cm long, has a narrow shell with squared ends; its curved foot is used to burrow.

reactance A property (X) of a circuit containing inductance and *capacitance that, with its resistance (R), makes its *impedance (Z), i.e. $Z^2 = R^2 + X^2$.

Reading 51 28N 0 59W A town in S England, the administrative centre of Berkshire. It is the headquarters of several international industries. Population (1985): 138 000.

Reagan, Ronald (1911–) US statesman; Republican president (1981–89). He achieved fame as a film actor before entering politics. In 1981 he survived an assassination attempt. As president he approved the US invasion of Grenada (1983) and CIA operations in Nicaragua, despite Congress opposition. In 1984 he unveiled his Strategic Defence Initiative. In 1987 he agreed with Gorbachov the reduction of US and Soviet nuclear arsenals.

realism **1.** The medieval philosophical theory that general terms (called universals), such as blueness, have a real existence independent of particulars, such as blue objects. *Aquinas and *Duns Scotus were leading realists. **2.** In modern philosophy, a theory opposed to *idealism, asserting that objects exist independently of being perceived.

real tennis (royal tennis) A racket-and-ball indoor court game, which developed in France in the 12th–13th centuries. It was originally played with the bare hand, the strung racket being developed in about 1500. The stone floor area is approximately 29 × 10 m (96 × 32 ft). The cloth ball is hit over a central net, as in *tennis, but it also bounces off the side walls, as in *squash rackets and *fives.

Réaumur, René-Antoine Ferchault de (1683–1757) French physicist, whose work on thermometers led him to devise the temperature scale that bears his name. On this scale water freezes at 0° and boils at 80°.

received pronunciation (RP) The pronunciation of English most generally accepted as standard or correct. The term was originally used to describe the characteristic accent of the public schools.

Recife (*or* Pernambuco) 8 06S 34 53W A major port in NE Brazil, on the Atlantic Ocean. Population (1985): 1 289 627.

recombinant DNA. *See* genetic engineering.

Reconstruction (1865–77) The period after the US *Civil War in which the defeated Confederate states were brought back into the Union.

recorder (law). *See* judge.

recorder (music) A woodwind instrument of medieval origin. The recorder is end-blown, through a whistle mouthpiece mounted in a block (*or* fipple). The holes are covered with the fingers; the tone is quieter than that of the flute.

recording of sound The most common methods of recording music are by means of *tape recorders (usually in the form of cassettes) or gramophone records. A gramophone record is made by converting the sound into an electrical signal, which is amplified and used to control a cutter that produces a spiral undulating groove in a master disc. The magnitude of the signal determines the size of the undulations in the groove. Plastic (vinyl) copies of the master disc are mass-produced for sale. In a record-player, the stylus travels along the groove and reproduces the mechanical vibrations of the cutter. The *pick-up then converts these to an electrical signal, which is amplified and fed to a loudspeaker. Many electronic devices ensure that sounds in the frequency range 80–12 000 hertz are reproduced without distortion. Recent innovations include **digital recording** on a *compact disc, in which the characteristics of the signal are represented by digits, which are then transmitted or recorded and reconstituted in the receiver or player. In this way the actual signal suffers no interference or distortion during transmission or recording.

rectifier A device that allows electric current to flow in one direction only; it is generally used to convert alternating current to direct current. *Semiconductor diodes have now replaced thermionic valves (diodes) for lower voltage applications. For power supplies of several megawatts, mercury-arc rectifiers are used.

rectum. *See* intestine.

red admiral A butterfly, *Vanessa atalanta*, found throughout Europe, Asia, and North America. The wings are black with red and white markings. The caterpillars feed mainly on stinging nettles.

red algae *Algae that are usually red or blue due to the presence of the pigments phycoerythrin (red) or phycocyanin (blue). They range from small cells or filaments to large *seaweeds.

Red Cross, International An organization founded by the Geneva Convention of 1864 to provide care for the casualties of war. Its headquarters are in Geneva and its emblem, the red cross, represents the Swiss flag with its colours reversed. The International Red Cross has twice won the Nobel Peace Prize, in 1917 and 1944.

redcurrant A shrub of the gooseberry family that is cultivated for its small round red berries, which may be made into jellies, jams, etc.

red deer A large reddish-brown deer, *Cervus elaphus*, of European and Asian woodlands. Over 120 cm high at the shoulder, males (stags) have spreading branched antlers up to 125 cm long; females (hinds) are more lightly built.

Redford, Robert (1936–) US film actor. He costarred with Paul *Newman in *Butch Cassidy and the Sundance Kid* (1969) and *The Sting* (1973). His other films include *The Candidate* (1972), *All the President's Men* (1976), and *Out of Africa* (1986).

red giant A greatly expanded cool but very luminous *giant star. It is one of the final evolutionary stages of a normal *star, attained when its central hydrogen has been converted to helium.

Redgrave, Sir Michael (1908–85) British Shakespearian actor, who also performed in and directed modern plays. His films included *The Browning Version* (1951) and *The Go-Between* (1971). His children, also actors, are **Vanessa Redgrave** (1937–), whose films include *Blow-Up* (1967) and *Julia* (1977) and is well known for her left-wing political activities; **Corin Redgrave** (1939–), also a political activist; and **Lynn Redgrave** (1944–).

Red Guards Chinese high-school and university students during the *Cultural Revolution who destroyed property, humiliated foreign diplomats, and attacked those officials who opposed Mao's policies.

red-hot poker An African plant, *Kniphofia uvaria* or *K. rufa* of the lily family, widely grown in gardens. 45–120 cm tall, it has tubular flowers, usually scarlet and yellow.

red mullet A food fish usually found in shallow warm seas. It has an elongated body, up to 25 cm long, with two long chin barbels.

redox reactions. *See* oxidation and reduction.

redpoll A tiny finch, *Acanthis flammea*, about 12 cm long with a brown streaked plumage, a red crown, and a black chin. The male has a red breast in summer. It breeds in the Arctic tundra and high mountains of Europe, migrating to central Europe and the N USA in winter.

Red River (Vietnamese name: Song Hong) The chief river of N Vietnam, rising in S China and flowing SE to the Gulf of Tonkin. Length: 500 km (310 mi).

Red River of the North (*or* Red River) A river in central North America, rising in W Minnesota and flowing N into Canada. Length: 1000 km (621 mi).

red salmon. *See* sockeye salmon.

Red Sea A long narrow arm of the Indian Ocean between Africa and Asia, extending some 2400 km (1491 mi) NNW beyond the Gulf of Aden and the Bab el-Mandeb. In the N, it is connected to the Mediterranean Sea by the Suez Canal. Area: 438 000 sq km (169 076 sq mi).

redshank A *sandpiper, *Tringa totanus*, that breeds in cool marshy regions of Europe and Asia. 30 cm long, it has long reddish legs, a black-tipped red bill, and a brown-grey plumage with a white rump. It winters on mudflats of Africa and Asia.

redshift An overall displacement towards larger wavelengths of the spectral lines of a celestial object. Its astronomical importance was suggested by Edwin Hubble (1889–1953) in 1929, when the observed redshift of *galaxies was used as the basis of the theory that the universe is expanding (*see* expanding universe). A redshift usually arises from the *Doppler effect.

red squirrel A tree squirrel, *Sciurus vulgaris*, of Europe and Asia. About 20 cm long with a 20-cm tail, red squirrels have dark red fur and tufted ears. They feed mainly on seeds and nuts and have been replaced in many areas by the grey *squirrel.

redstart A Eurasian thrush, about 14 cm long. The male European redstart (*Phoenicurus phoenicurus*) is grey with a russet breast, black throat and face with a white stripe, and a red tail, which it fans out in its courtship display to the yellow and brown female.

reduction. *See* oxidation and reduction.

redwood A coniferous tree, *Sequoia sempervirens*, thought to be the tallest tree in the world: a specimen in California is over 111 m tall. It is native to the Pacific coast between Oregon and California and is an important timber tree. It has brown-red fibrous bark and red-brown round cones, about 2 cm long. *See also* sequoia.

reed A tall aquatic grass. The common reed (*Phragmites communis*) grows worldwide along the edges of marshes, lakes, streams, etc.

Reed, Sir Carol (1906–76) British film director. His best-known films include *The Fallen Idol* (1948) and *The Third Man* (1949), both with screenplays by Graham *Greene. His later films include *The Agony and the Ecstasy* (1965) and *Oliver!* (1968).

reedbuck An African antelope. The common reedbuck (*Redunca arundinium*), 90 cm high at the shoulder, has a stiff grey coat and slender ridged horns.

reedling A Eurasian bird, *Panurus biarmicus*, also called bearded tit. About 16 cm long, it lives in reedbeds, feeding on insects and seeds. The plumage is brown with pale underparts: the male has a grey head with a black moustache of feathers.

reedmace A widely distributed plant, *Typha latifolia*, also called bulrush or cat's-tail, growing in reed swamps. Its stem, 1.5–2.5 m high, bears cylindrical fruit.

reed warbler An acrobatic *warbler, *Acrocephalus scirpaeus*, about 12 cm long with a reddish-brown plumage, pale underparts, and a pale eyestripe. It winters in SE Africa and breeds in European reedswamps.

referendum A vote on a specific law by all the voters of a country. In the UK referendums have been held concerning membership of the EEC (1975) and *devolution for Scotland and Wales (1979).

reflection The rebounding of a wave of light or other radiation when it strikes a surface. Reflected light obeys two laws: first, the normal (an imaginary line vertical to the surface at the point of impact), the incident ray, and the reflected rays all lie in the same plane; second, the angle between the incident ray and the normal is equal to the angle of reflection. *See also* mirrors.

reflex An automatic and involuntary response by an organism to a change in its surroundings, which occurs before the brain has had time to convey the necessary information to the muscles involved. *See also* conditioned reflex.

Reform Acts The laws that reformed the British parliamentary system. The Reform Act of 1832 gave many more people the right to vote and gave parliamentary representation to new industrial towns. The 1867 Reform Act gave the vote to many working-class householders for the first time. The 1884 Reform Act made the right to vote the same in the counties as in the towns, thus increasing the voters to about five million.

Reformation A religious movement in 16th-century Europe that began as an attempt to reform the *Roman Catholic Church and ended with the establishment of independent Protestant Churches (*see* Protestantism).
The Reformation began at Wittenburg on 31 October, 1517, when Martin *Luther attacked the sale of *indulgences and, later, papal power and the *sacraments (except baptism and the Eucharist). He was supported by several German princes and the resulting conflict (*see* Charles V) was not resolved until the Peace of *Augsburg (1555). In Switzerland, the Reformation was started by Ulrich Zwingli (1484–1531) in Zurich in 1520. In Geneva, it was led by John *Calvin. In France, where Protestants were called Huguenots, the Reformation gave rise to the *Wars of Religion, and in the Low Countries it led to the *Revolt of the Netherlands.
In England, the Reformation began when *Henry VIII was proclaimed supreme head of the English Church by the Act of Supremacy (1534). Under Edward VI Protestantism was established by the 1552 Book of *Common Prayer, the accompanying Acts of *Uniformity, and the 42 Articles (1553). Protestantism finally became the established *Church of England under Elizabeth I. In Scotland, the Reformation was influenced by John *Knox and *Presbyterianism was established in 1592. *See also* Counter-Reformation.

Reformed Churches. *See* Protestantism.

Reform Judaism A religious movement attempting to adapt traditional Judaism to modern circumstances. It began in Germany in the early 19th century. The first Reform synagogue in England was established in 1840; the Liberal movement (founded 1903) brought more radical reforms typical of US Reform Judaism. The World Union for Progressive Judaism was founded in London in 1926 (it is now based in Jerusalem).

refraction The bending of a beam of radiation as it passes from one medium into another. For a light ray the amount by which it is bent depends on the angle of the incident ray and on the refractive indices of the two media (*see* Snell's law). Refraction is caused by the difference in the velocity of the radiation in the two media. The ratio of the velocity of light in the two media is known as the **refractive index**.

refrigeration The process of lowering the temperature inside a closed insulated container.

In the domestic refrigerator the method most commonly used is the vapour-compression cycle in which a liquid refrigerant, such as Freon (a compound of chlorine, fluorine, and carbon), is pumped through cooling coils formed into the ice-making compartment. In these coils the refrigerant evaporates, taking the latent heat required to make it into a gas from the surroundings. It is then passed to an electrically driven compressor; after compression it condenses back to liquid, when the absorbed heat is given out (usually at the back of the refrigerator). This cycle is repeated until the required temperature (about $1-2°C$ in the food chamber and $-15°C$ in the deep-freeze compartment) is achieved.

Regency style An English decorative style fashionable from about 1800 to 1830 and influenced by the French *Empire style. Dark woods and veneers were popular and were set off by ormolu mounts. There was a vogue for oriental motifs (*see* chinoiserie) and some magnificent lacquer was produced, for example for the Prince Regent's Pavilion at Brighton.

regeneration In biology, the regrowth and development of tissues or organs lost through injury, as a normal process (e.g. during moulting), or by any other means. It is particularly well developed in plants and simple animals (such as sponges), in which whole organisms can regenerate from small fragments. More complex animals, such as crustaceans, replace lost appendages, while lizards can grow new tails. In mammals regeneration is limited to wound healing and regrowth of nerve fibres.

Regina 50 30N 104 38W A city in W Canada, the capital of Saskatchewan. Founded in 1882, it is now a centre of agricultural industries and oil refining. Population (1986): 186 521.

Reichstag (Imperial Diet) The law-making assembly of the German Empire (1871–1918) and the Weimar Republic (1919–33). Originally the assembly of the Holy Roman Empire, it was revived by Bismarck in 1867. In 1933 the Reichstag building was burnt out; Nazi claims of communist responsibility provided an excuse to ban opposition parties.

Reign of Terror (1793–94) The most violent period of the *French Revolution, conducted by the governing Committee of Public Safety under *Robespierre. About 1400 were summarily guillotined. Public reaction caused Robespierre's downfall and execution in July, 1794.

Reims (*or* Rheims) 49 15N 4 02E A city in NE France, in the Marne department. An important Roman town, it has a magnificent gothic cathedral. It has manufacturing industries and is a centre for marketing Champagne wines. Population (1983): 178 000.

reincarnation (*or* metempsychosis) The passing of the soul from one body at death into another (human or animal) body. The cycle of reincarnation (*samsara*) is fundamental to Hindu, Buddhist, and Jain conceptions of the world, all spiritual effort being directed towards release (*moksa*) from the cycle. Orthodox Christianity rejected it as contrary to belief in the resurrection of the body.

reindeer A large deer, *Rangifer tarandus*, of European and North American tundra (in America it is called a caribou). About 125 cm high at the shoulder, reindeer have a grey-brown coat and spreading branched antlers. Reindeer feed mainly on lichens.

Reinhardt, Django (Jean Baptiste R.; 1910–53) Belgian jazz guitarist of gipsy origin. He injured his hand in a fire at the age of 18 but developed an original guitar technique. From 1934 to 1939 he led the quintet of the Hot Club de France with the French violinist Stephane Grappelli.

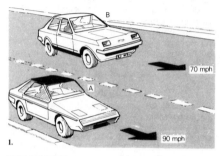

RELATIVITY 1. *Two cars, A and B, travelling along a motorway. The speed of car A relative to the earth is 90 mph. The speed of car B relative to the earth is 70 mph. The speed of car A relative to car B is 90 − 70 = 20 mph.* 2. *Car B is now stationary; its headlight beams are turned on as supercar A passes, travelling at 5000 miles per second. The speed of car B's headlight beam relative to car A is 186 000 miles per second (not 186 000 − 5000 miles per second). The velocity of light is absolute.*

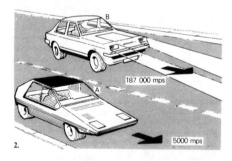

relativity A scientific theory proposed by Albert *Einstein. The special theory (published 1905) applies only to motion in which there is no *acceleration. Up to this time it was thought that light travelled through a stationary medium, called the ether, and that its speed relative to an observer could be calculated in the same way as the relative speed of any two moving objects. For example, if one car (A) is travelling at 90 mph on a motorway and overtakes another (B) travelling at 70 mph, A's speed relative to car B is 20 mph, but relative to the earth it is 90 mph. Relative to

the sun it is about 24 million mph. Because two American scientists, Michelson and Morley, had shown that light travelled at the same speed whether measured in the direction of the earth's rotation or at right angles to it, Einstein suggested that light always has the same speed of 2.998×10^8 metres per second (186 000 miles per second), irrespective of the motion of the observer.

In the general theory of 1916, Einstein considered the speed of a body increases to a speed approaching that of light it becomes shorter and heavier. An electron travelling at 99% of the speed of light becomes seven times heavier than its mass at rest.

The increase in mass and decrease in length that a body undergoes when moving at high speeds led Einstein to the conclusion that an energy (E) has a mass (m); they are related by the simple equation $E = mc^2$, where c is the speed of light. The atom bomb and *nuclear energy both depend on this equation.

In the general theory of 1915, Einstein considered accelerated relative motion, especially as it is concerned with gravitation. The gravitational force experienced by a body is treated as a property of space and time, which Einstein suggested was "curved" by the presence of the mass. The observed bending of light rays as they pass close to the sun and the shift of certain lines in the solar *spectrum have provided experimental verification of the theory.

Rembrandt (Harmenszoon) van Rijn (1606–69) Dutch painter and etcher. Settling permanently in Amsterdam (1631), he made his name as a portrait painter with the group portraits *The Anatomy Lesson of Dr Tulp* (1632; The Hague) and *The Nightwatch* (1642; Rijksmuseum, Amsterdam). He also painted mythological and biblical subjects and fine landscapes. Some of his greatest works were painted in the last 20 years of his life, after he became bankrupt and his work was no longer popular.

Remembrance Sunday The day on which the British remember the dead of both World Wars. Since 1956 it has been observed on the second Sunday of November. A two-minute silence marks the time, 11 am, of the signing of the Armistice and wreaths of Flanders poppies are laid at the Cenotaph in Whitehall, London, and at other war memorials.

Remus. *See* Romulus and Remus.

Renaissance (French: rebirth) A movement in art, literature, science, and thought that began in Italy in the 14th century, spread to N Europe, and flourished until the mid-16th century. The Renaissance was based on the revival of classical learning, art, and architecture and the concept of the dignity of man, which characterized *humanism. Great writers of the Italian Renaissance included *Dante, *Boccaccio, *Machiavelli, and Ludovico Ariosto (1474–1533). The first painter to adopt these new ideals was *Giotto. He was followed in the 15th century by *Masaccio, *Uccello, *Piero della Francesca, *Mantegna, and, during the High Renaissance (1500–20), by *Leonardo da Vinci, *Raphael, and *Michelangelo. In sculpture the major figures were Nicola *Pisano, *Donatello, *Ghiberti, Verrocchio, and Michelangelo. In building *Brunelleschi was the first to revive the classical use of the *orders of architecture.

In the 16th century the Renaissance spread to N Europe, where it was seen in the art of *Dürer, the scholarship of *Erasmus, the plays of *Shakespeare, and particularly in the courts of such rulers as Elizabeth I of England.

Rennes 48 06N 1 40W A city in NW France, in the Ille-et-Vilaine department. The capital of of Brittany, it was badly damaged by fire in 1720. It is now the main commercial centre of W France. Population (1983): 195 785.

rennet An extract, prepared from cows' stomachs, that contains the milk-coagulating enzyme rennin. It is used in the manufacture of cheese and junket.

Renoir, Pierre Auguste (1841–1919) French painter. A leading impressionist, he abandoned this genre after studying Renaissance art in Italy (1881–82) and spent his last years in the south of France, painting nudes. His best-known works include *Les Parapluies* (National Gallery, London) and *Le Moulin de la Galette* (Louvre). His son **Jean Renoir** (1894–1979) was a film director whose films include *La Grande Illusion* (1937) and *La Règle du jeu* (1939).

Representatives, House of. *See* Congress.

repression In *psychoanalysis, the process of excluding unacceptable ideas from the conscious mind. Repressed wishes and thoughts continue to exist in the unconscious mind and may give rise to symptoms of mental disorder. One of the goals of psychoanalytic treatment is to bring repressed material back into conscious awareness so that it can be coped with rationally.

reptile A vertebrate animal of which there are about 6000 species, including *crocodiles, *turtles, *lizards, *snakes, and the *tuatara. Reptiles, which evolved from amphibians, occur on land, in fresh water, and the sea, chiefly in tropical regions. They have horny scales and are cold-blooded. The egg is fertilized within the female, unlike fish and most amphibians, and when it is laid it has a leathery shell. In some lizards and snakes the eggs hatch inside the female and live young are born. See p. 456.

Republican Party One of the two major political parties of the USA (*compare* Democratic Party). The modern Republican Party originated in 1854. After the election of the first Republican president, Lincoln, in 1860, the Republicans were usually the dominant party until the 1930s. Recent Republican presidents include *Eisenhower, *Nixon, *Reagan, and *Bush.

resale price maintenance (rpm) A *restrictive trade practice operated by a manufacturer, who prohibits retailers from selling a product below a certain price. It prevents price competition between retailers and keeps inefficient retailers in business.

resins Adhesive nonflammable organic polymers (*see* polymerization), usually insoluble in water but soluble in organic solvents. **Natural resins**, such as rosin (*or* colophony) and *shellac, are exuded by plants and insects. **Synthetic**

resins are made by modifying natural polymers or by *polymerization of petrochemicals. **Thermosetting resins**, which harden on heating, include *epoxy and some *polyurethane resins. **Thermoplastic resins**, which soften on heating, include *polythene, *polyvinyl chloride, and *polypropylene.

resistance The property of all materials, except superconductors (*see* superconductivity), that reduces the flow of electricity through them. It is defined by *Ohm's law as the ratio of the potential difference between the ends of a conductor to the current flowing through it (*see also* impedance).

resolving power 1. The ability of a *microscope to produce separate images of two neighbouring points; the closer the points, the greater the resolving power of the microscope. The resolving power may be increased by using shorter wavelength radiation (e.g. ultraviolet radiation) or a beam of electrons (as in the *electron microscope). 2. A measure of the ability of a *telescope to distinguish detail, usually the smallest angle between two point objects that produces distinct images.

Respighi, Ottorino (1879–1936) Italian composer. He wrote several operas, the symphonic poems *The Fountains of Rome* (1917) and *The Pines of Rome* (1924), the orchestral suite *The Birds* (1927), and ballets, including *La Boutique fantasque* (1919).

respiration The process by which an organism takes up oxygen from its surroundings and discharges carbon dioxide. In humans and most air-breathing animals the organs through which this takes place are the *lungs (aquatic animals use *gills; insects use *tracheae). Blood is pumped from the *heart to the air sacs (alveoli) of the lungs, where it receives oxygen (from inhaled air) and releases carbon dioxide (which is exhaled). Oxygen in the blood is carried to the tissues and cells, where it is used in the chemical breakdown (i.e. oxidation) of foodstuffs to produce energy.

Restoration (1660) The re-establishment of the monarchy in England following the fall of the *Protectorate. The Restoration of Charles II, whose father Charles I had been executed (1649) during the Civil War, was engineered by General Monck (1608–70). Charles promised religious toleration and an amnesty to all but 57 of those who had fought the Crown.

restrictive trade practices Agreements between traders that limit competition in an industry. In the UK, under the Fair Trading Act (1973) restrictive practices are held to be against the public interest unless proved otherwise in the Restrictive Practices Court.

resurrection plant. *See* rose of Jericho.

retina The light-sensitive layer that forms the inner surface of the eye. Light is focused by the lens onto the retina, which contains numerous interconnecting light-sensitive cells (rods and cones) that send signals to the brain via the optic nerve. The rods are responsible for the ability to see in dim light and the cones are sensitive to colour and fine detail. *See also* detached retina.

REPTILE

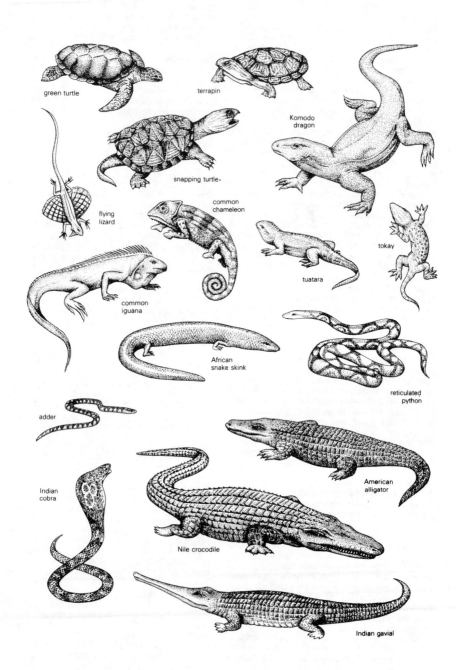

green turtle

terrapin

Komodo
dragon

snapping turtle

flying
lizard

common
chameleon

tokay

common
iguana

tuatara

African
snake skink

reticulated
python

adder

American
alligator

Indian
cobra

Nile crocodile

Indian gavial

REPTILE *Some representative reptiles.*

retriever A large strongly built sporting dog descended from the *Labrador retriever. It is a good swimmer. The flat-coated retriever has a dense coat while the curly-coated retriever has a coat of small tight curls. Height: 56–68 cm. *See also* golden retriever.

Réunion A volcanic island and French overseas department in the W Indian Ocean, in the Mascarene Islands. It was settled in about 1642 by the French with their African and Indian slaves. Sugar, rum, and molasses are exported. Area: 2512 sq km (970 sq mi). Population (1988 est): 574 800. Capital: Saint-Denis.

Reval. *See* Tallinn.

Revelation, Book of A prophetic book, the last in the New Testament, written perhaps about 90–95 AD by "John the Divine," who is often identified with the apostle John. It consists of seven highly symbolic visions that trace the fortunes of the Christian Church from its beginning to the end of the world.

Revere, Paul (1735–1818) American silversmith and revolutionary. On 18 April, 1775, he rode out to warn the people of Massachusetts that the British troops were on the march. On the following morning the first shots of the American Revolution were fired on the British at Lexington.

Revolt of the Netherlands The rebellion against Spanish rule in the Netherlands, inspired by political and economic complaints and anger at the suppression of Protestantism. The revolt broke out in 1568 but the independence of the United Provinces of the Netherlands was not acknowledged until 1648, when the Peace of Westphalia was signed.

Revolutionary and Napoleonic Wars (1792–1815) A series of European wars brought on by the *French Revolution and *Napoleon's ambitions for the conquest of Europe. War broke out as a result of the hostile reaction of Austria and Prussia to the arrest of *Louis XVI. Britain, the Netherlands, and Spain closed ranks with Austria and Prussia in the first coalition (1793). After a series of French victories, Prussia, the Netherlands, and Spain sued for peace in 1795 and Austria followed suit in 1797. Britain defeated France in the Battle of the *Nile (1798), but the second coalition of Britain, the Ottoman Empire, Naples, Portugal, and Austria collapsed (1801) in the face of Napoleon's victories. The Revolutionary Wars ended with the uneasy Treaty of Amiens (1802) between Britain and France.
Naval war resumed between Britain and France, and in 1805 Napoleon was defeated by Nelson at *Trafalgar. Napoleon then defeated Austria and Russia at *Ulm and Austerlitz (1805), Prussia at Jena and Auerstadt (1806), and Russia again at Friedland (1807). With Wellington's victories in the *Peninsular War, Napoleon's power weakened and he was finally defeated at *Waterloo (1815). The post-Napoleonic settlement of Europe was decided at the Congress of *Vienna.

Revolution of 1905 A rebellion in Russia, an expression of the widespread discontent that led to the *Russian Revolution of 1917. It began on 22 January, 1905 (Bloody Sunday), when a group of workers marched peacefully on the Winter Palace in St Petersburg and were fired on by troops. The massacre led to nationwide uprisings, which were crushed by the end of December.

Revolutions of 1848 A series of revolutions in continental Europe caused by economic distress and liberal unrest. In France rebels overthrew *Louis Philippe, but a split in their ranks led to the election of Louis Napoleon (later *Napoleon III) as president. In the Italian states the revolution formed part of the *Risorgimento. In the Austrian Empire revolts in Vienna secured the resignation of *Metternich. In Prussia, Frederick William IV was forced to summon a constituent assembly. The revolutions were all quelled, but liberal and nationalist movements made some gains.

revolver A type of *pistol having a revolving cylinder containing the rounds of ammunition behind the barrel. Calibres range from .21 inches to .455 inches. The first successful revolver was the *Colt, designed in 1835.

Reykjavik 64 10N 21 53W The capital of Iceland, an important fishing port, on Faxa Fjord in the SW. Founded by the Vikings in 874 AD, it became the seat of parliament (the *Althing) in 1843 and capital of Iceland in 1918. Population (1987): 93 245.

Reynolds, Sir Joshua (1723–92) British portrait painter. He used the techniques of the Old Masters in such paintings as *Sarah Siddons as the Tragic Muse* (San Marino, California). In 1768 he became the first president of the *Royal Academy, where he delivered the *Discourses*, which contain his artistic theories. His friends included Dr *Johnson and *Garrick, both of whom he painted.

Reza Shah Pahlavi (1878–1944) Shah of Iran (1925–41). After leading an army coup in 1921, he overthrew Ahmad Shah Qajar (1898–1930) in 1925. As shah himself, Reza aimed at the modernization of Iran. In 1941 Britain and the Soviet Union, fearing German influence in Iran, forced Reza Shah to abdicate in favour of his son *Mohammed Reza Pahlavi.

rhea A large flightless South American bird. 120 cm tall, rheas have a brownish plumage and long legs with three toes. They live in flocks, feeding on leaves, roots, seeds, insects, and small vertebrates.

Rhea In Greek mythology, a Titan, daughter of Uranus and Gaea. Her consort *Cronus swallowed her children, fearing that they would overthrow him. Rhea substituted a stone for one child, *Zeus, who eventually overthrew Cronus.

Rheims. *See* Reims.

rhenium (Re) A dense (relative density 21.02) silvery-white transition metal with a very high melting point. The metal is very ductile and is used to alloy with tungsten. Alloys with molybdenum are superconducting. The metal is obtained as a by-product of molybdenum refining. At no 75; at wt 186.2; mp 3180°C; bp 5620°C.

rhesus factor (Rh factor) A protein present on the red blood cells in 83% of the human population: the presence or absence of the Rh factor is the basis of the Rh *blood group system. If a

Rh-negative woman has a Rh-positive baby she may produce anti-Rh antibodies that will react against any Rh-positive pregnancies she may have in the future. The affected baby's blood cells may be destroyed by these antibodies, leading to severe anaemia. The incidence of this disease has been reduced by taking steps to prevent the mother producing anti-Rh antibodies soon after delivery of the first baby.

rhesus monkey A *macaque monkey, *Macaca mulatta*, of S Asia, widely used in medical research. In the wild, rhesus monkeys live in large colonies in forests or on hillsides.

rheumatic fever A disease of children that occurs (rarely) after infection with a streptococcus bacterium. The symptoms develop 10–14 days after the original infection (which is usually of the throat) and include fever, aching joints, chorea (involuntary movements), and inflammation of the heart, which—in a few cases—may lead to chronic heart disease. Treatment is with bed rest, penicillin, aspirin, and sometimes steroids.

rheumatism Any condition involving pain in the joints. This may be caused by a simple strain or by rheumatoid *arthritis, *osteoarthritis, *gout, or *rheumatic fever.

Rhine, River (German name: Rhein; Dutch name; Rijn) A river in central and W Europe. Rising in SE Switzerland, it flows W along the Swiss-German border, then N along the Franco-German border and into Germany and the Netherlands before entering the North Sea. It is W Europe's main navigable waterway. Length: 1320 km (820 mi).

rhinoceros A large hoofed mammal of Asia and Africa. The Indian rhinoceros (*Rhinoceros unicornis*) has a single horn; all other rhinos have two horns. Rhinos range in size from the large rare African white rhinoceros (*Diceros simus*), up to 2 m high and weighing 3.5 tonnes, to the Sumatran rhinoceros (*Didermocerus sumatrensis*), which is up to 150 cm high and weighs 500–1000 kg. All are now endangered species.

rhinoceros beetle A horned *scarab beetle, up to 150 mm long (including the horn). The species *Oryctes rhinoceros* is sometimes a serious pest in oriental coconut groves. See also hercules beetle.

rhizome An underground plant stem that produces leaves and shoots above ground. It may be fleshy (as in the iris) or wiry (as in couch grass). Rhizomes can give rise to new plants and enable the plant to survive the winter.

Rhode Island The smallest state in the USA, indented by Narragansett Bay. One of the New England states, it is highly industrialized and has important naval installations. History: it was first settled in 1636 and was the first colony to declare its independence from Britain. Area: 3144 sq km (1214 sq mi). Population (1987 est): 986 000. Capital: Providence.

Rhode Island Red A breed of domestic fowl developed on Rhode Island farms in the 19th century. It has red plumage, a nearly horizontal back, and a slightly curved beak. Weight: 3.8 kg (cocks); 3.0 kg (hens).

Rhodes (Modern Greek name: Ródhos) A Greek island in the SE Aegean Sea, the largest of the Dodecanese group. It produces cereals, fruit, and wine; tourism is important. History: colonized by Dorians before 1000 BC, Rhodes suffered several earthquakes, one of which destroyed the *Colossus of Rhodes in 244 BC. It was occupied by the Knights *Hospitallers from 1282 until 1528, when it became part of the Ottoman Empire. Conquered by Italy in 1912, it was handed over to Greece in 1947. Area: 1400 sq km (540 sq mi). Population (1981); 40 392. Capital: Rhodes.

Rhodes, Cecil (John) (1853–1902) South African financier and statesman. Born in Britain, he went to South Africa in 1870 and entered the Cape Colony parliament in 1881. In 1889 he gained a charter for the British South Africa Company to develop the territory that in 1895 was named Rhodesia in his honour. He became prime minister of Cape Colony in 1890 but was forced to resign in 1896 over the unsuccessful Jameson raid into the Transvaal. He established 170 Rhodes scholarships at Oxford University for students from the British Empire, the USA, and Germany.

Rhodesia. See Zimbabwe.

Rhodesia and Nyasaland, Federation of (or Central African Federation) A former (1953–63) federation of the British colony of Southern Rhodesia (now Zimbabwe) and the British protectorates of Northern Rhodesia (now Zambia) and Nyasaland (now Malawi).

Rhodesian ridgeback A breed of hunting dog originating in South Africa and having a ridge of hair along the back. Height: 63–68 cm (dogs); 61–66 cm (bitches).

rhodium (Rh) A metal similar to platinum, discovered in 1803 by W. H. Wollaston (1766–1828). It is a very hard highly reflective metal used to plate jewellery and optical instruments. At no 45; at wt 102.905; mp 1966 ± 3°C; bp 3727 ± 100°C.

rhododendron A small tree or shrub, mainly of N temperate regions. It has leathery often evergreen leaves and colourful fragrant bell- or funnel-shaped flowers. See also azalea.

Rhône, River A major river in W Europe. Rising in the Rhône Glacier in Switzerland, it flows through Lake Geneva to enter France, flowing generally SW. It is canalized from Lyon to the Mediterranean Sea. Length 812 km (505 mi).

rhubarb A plant, *Rheum rhaponticum*, possibly of Asian origin, widely cultivated for its juicy red or green leafstalks, up to 1 m high, which are cooked in sugar. The leaves are poisonous.

rib A curved bone, 12 pairs of which make up the rib cage, enclosing and protecting the heart and lungs. One end of each rib forms a movable joint with the spine, permitting movement of the rib cage during breathing. The other ends of the upper seven ribs are fixed directly to the breastbone by a cartilage. Each of the next three pairs is connected to the rib above it, and the two lowest ribs end in the muscles of the body wall.

Ribbentrop, Joachim von (1893–1946) German Nazi politician and diplomat. He was ambassador to the UK (1936–38), then became

Hitler's foreign minister. Arrested in 1945, he was hanged for war crimes.

Ribera, José de (or Jusepe R.; 1591–1652) Spanish-born painter and etcher. He settled in Naples (1616), where he was known as Lo Spagnoletto (Little Spaniard). The best examples of his work are The Martyrdom of St Bartholomew (Prado) and Clubfooted Boy (Louvre).

riboflavin. See vitamin B complex.

ribonucleic acid. See RNA.

ribosome A particle present in enormous numbers in the cytoplasm of nearly all *cells of living organisms. Ribosomes are composed of *RNA and protein and are the site of protein synthesis.

rice A *cereal grass, Oryza sativa, or its edible grain, probably native to India but widely cultivated throughout warm regions. Seedlings are planted in flooded paddy fields, which are drained to enable mechanical harvesting. Milling the grain removes either the outer husk alone, resulting in brown rice, or both the husk and the bran layer, resulting in vitamin-B-deficient white rice. Rice is a major staple food.

Richard (I) the Lionheart (1157–99) King of England (1189–99), who spent all but six months of his reign abroad. Succeeding his father Henry II, he joined the third Crusade in 1189 and conquered Messina and Cyprus before arriving in the Holy Land. His victory at Arsuf gained Joppa (1191). On his way home he was captured in Austria and was only released after payment of an enormous ransom (1194). He died campaigning in France.

Richard II (1367–1400) King of England (1377–99). Succeeding his grandfather Edward III as a child, government was in the hands of his uncle *John of Gaunt. Power struggles led to the banishment in 1398 of Gaunt's son Henry Bolingbroke. He returned in 1399 and seized the throne as Henry IV. Richard died at Pontefract Castle in mysterious circumstances.

Richard III (1452–85) King of England (1483–85). He was the youngest brother of Edward IV, on whose death in 1483 he became protector for his son Edward V, a child. Richard imprisoned Edward and his brother and seized the throne. It is suggested that Richard murdered the boys, who disappeared in August, 1483. As king, he made important administrative and financial reforms but faced considerable opposition, finally being defeated and killed by Henry Tudor (subsequently *Henry VII) at Bosworth.

Richards, Sir Gordon (1904–86) British jockey, who was champion jockey a record 26 times (1925–53). He rode 4870 winners out of a total of 21 843 mounts (1920–54).

Richardson, Sir Ralph (1902–83) British actor. He established his reputation in Shakespearian roles with the Old Vic Company during the 1930s and 1940s. He also acted in modern plays, such as David Storey's Home (1970) and Harold Pinter's No Man's Land (1976), and made many films.

Richardson, Samuel (1689–1761) British novelist. His pioneering novel Pamela (1740) was planned as a book of model letters for inexperienced writers. His brilliant characterization was further developed in Clarissa (1748).

Richelieu, Armand Jean du Plessis, Cardinal de (1585–1642) French statesman, who greatly increased the absolute authority of the Crown and France's power in Europe. He rose to prominence as adviser to Louis XIII's mother Marie de' Medici (1573–1642), becoming Louis' chief minister in 1629. He ruthlessly suppressed the *Huguenots, directed France with brilliance in the Thirty Years' War, and founded the French Academy.

Richmond 37 34N 77 27W A city and port in the USA, the capital of Virginia. It has a university (1882) and the chief manufacture is tobacco. Population (1986): 217 700.

Richter scale A scale of *earthquake magnitude devised in 1935 by C. F. Richter (1900–85). It is a logarithmic scale from 0–9, the largest earthquakes having the highest numbers.

Richthofen, Manfred, Freiherr von (1892–1918) German air ace of World War I, who shot down 80 Allied aircraft before being killed himself in action. His nickname, the Red Baron, referred to the colour of his plane.

rickets A disease of children affecting the bones and caused by *vitamin D deficiency. With a poor diet and/or inadequate sunshine the bones become soft and do not grow properly.

rickettsia A microorganism belonging to a group of parasites that cannot reproduce outside the bodies of their hosts. They infect arthropods (especially ticks and mites) and can be transmitted to man, in whom they cause such diseases as *typhus and Rocky Mountain spotted fever. They were named after the US pathologist H. T. Ricketts (1871–1910).

Ridgeway A prehistoric trackway in S England. It runs along the edge of the Berkshire Downs, linking the *Avebury region with the Thames.

rifle A shoulder firearm with a spiral groove inside its long barrel to make the bullet spin during its flight. Invented in the 15th century, the rifle took over from the *musket during the 18th and 19th centuries. During the 1880s breech-loading rifles became capable of firing more than one cartridge without reloading. These developed into the modern repeating rifle. See also Browning Automatic Rifle.

riflebird A large *bird of paradise having a black plumage with iridescent throat patches and small ornamental plumes. The magnificent riflebird (Craspedophora magnifica) is about 30 cm long; the male performs its courtship display on fiercely defended perches.

rift valley A steep-sided valley with a flat floor formed as a result of the valley floor subsiding between two roughly parallel *faults. The most notable example is the vast *Great Rift Valley in Africa.

Riga 56 53N 24 08E A port in the W Soviet Union, on the Baltic Sea. It is an industrial and cultural centre. History: in 1282 Riga became a member of the *Hanseatic League. It then passed to Poland (1581), to Sweden (1621), and to Russia (1710). It was the capital of indepen-

Rituals play a prominent role in animal behaviour, especially in attracting mates and defending territory. The display of the male sage grouse both attracts females and deters rival males.

Aggressive behaviour often involves apparently irrelevant ritualized postures and actions, which convey the intentions of the participants without inflicting serious injuries. Red deer act out a series of rituals before coming to blows; either participant may withdraw at any stage before the fight begins.

Ritual ceremonies are not restricted to primitive peoples – they have a major role in secret societies. The Ancient Order of the Druids holds annual ceremonies at Stonehenge to celebrate the summer solstice. These have little connection with the rites of the ancient druids, many of which were performed in sacred oak groves – the oak and mistletoe were important symbols.

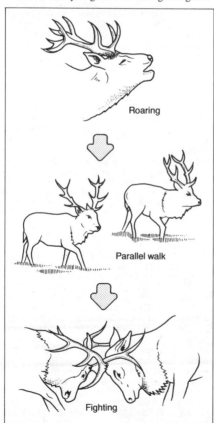

Roaring

Parallel walk

Fighting

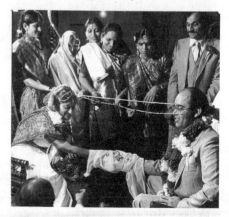

Religion is based on the ritual celebration of some sacramental act. Those of birth, death, and marriage occur in most religions. Here a Hindu couple are being married, the binding together of their hands symbolizing the union of their bodies.

Rites of passage are rituals performed when a person moves from one social status to another. Here young Aborigines from Arnhem Land in Australia are about to submit to circumcision in a ritual that symbolizes their transition to adult status.

The crowning of a new monarch is a state ceremony that often involves rituals going back to very early times. Here James II is being crowned in 1685 in Westminster Abbey. A British coronation incorporates both pagan rituals, such as the offering of symbolic objects, and Christian ceremonies, such as the anointing. For the latter, the sovereign wears a plain white robe, symbolizing humility. After the anointing, the sovereign is offered a variety of objects symbolizing different aspects of the monarchy, including: gold spurs (for chivalry); the orb surmounted by a cross (symbolizing worldwide dominion of the Christian Church); a sceptre with a cross (royal power); and a sceptre with dove (spiritual authority).

dent Latvia (1918–40). Population (1987): 900 000.

Rights of Man and of the Citizen, Declaration of the (1789) The formal expression of the ideals of the *French Revolution, drawn up to preface the constitution of 1791. The Declaration asserted that "all men are born free and equal in rights."

Rijeka (Italian name: Fiume) 45 20N 14 27E The chief seaport in Yugoslavia, in Croatia on the Adriatic Sea. Annexed by Italy in 1924, it passed to Yugoslavia in 1947. Industries include oil refining. Population (1983): 193 044.

Rijksmuseum A museum and art gallery in Amsterdam, housing the national collection of the Netherlands. It originated in 1808 as the Royal Museum and became the Rijksmuseum in 1817. Its paintings of the Dutch school include *Rembrandt's Night Watch.*

Rimbaud, Arthur (1854–91) French poet. He formed a tempestuous relationship with *Verlaine that eventually ended in a violent quarrel. His theories about poetry were expressed in *Une Saison en enfer* (1873) and *Les Illuminations* (1886). At the age of 20 he renounced poetry and wandered in Europe and the Near East, eventually becoming a gun-runner in Ethiopia.

Rimini (Latin name: Ariminium) 44 03N 12 24E A town and resort in Italy, on the N Adriatic coast, with Roman and medieval remains. It produces textiles and pasta. Population (1987): 130 787.

Rimsky-Korsakov, Nikolai (1844–1908) Russian composer, a member of the nationalist composers known as the Mighty Five. He wrote 15 operas, including *The Snow Maiden* (1880–81) and *The Golden Cockerel* (1906–07), such orchestral works as *Scheherazade* (1888), chamber music, and songs.

ring ouzel A shy songbird, *Turdus torquatus*, of mountainous regions. The male is black with a broad white crescent around the throat; the female is dark brown with less distinct markings.

ringworm A highly infectious disease of the skin, hair, and nails that is caused by various fungi. Ringworm is usually caught by direct contact with an infected person or animal. The affected area is typically ring-shaped (especially on the scalp). It is treated with the antibiotic griseofulvin.

Río Bravo. *See* Río Grande.

Rio de Janeiro 22 53S 43 17W The chief port in Brazil, the capital of Rio de Janeiro state. Discovered by the Portuguese in 1502, it was the capital of Brazil from 1763 until 1960. It is backed by mountains, a giant figure of Christ standing on the highest peak overlooking the conical Sugar Loaf Mountain. The chief industries are shipbuilding, sugar refining, and railway engineering. Population (1985): 5 615 149.

Rio Grande (Spanish names: Río Bravo; Río Bravo del Norte) The fifth longest river of North America. Rising in the Rocky Mountains, it forms the entire border between Texas (USA) and Mexico. Length: 2040 km (1885 mi).

Río Muni. *See* Equatorial Guinea, Republic of.

Risorgimento (Italian: resurgence) The nationalist movement in 19th-century Italy that achieved the country's independence and unification. Beginning with secret societies and abortive uprisings, it achieved success in 1859, when the Piedmontese prime minister *Cavour freed Lombardy from Austrian rule. In 1860 *Garibaldi surrendered to Piedmont his conquests made in the S. Tuscany, Modena, Parma, Bologna, and Romagna then accepted entry into the kingdom of Italy under the House of Piedmont, proclaimed in 1861. Unification was completed when Italy took Venetia in 1866 and the papal states in 1870.

ritual Any formal repeated behaviour, procedure, rite, or ceremony. Primitive societies have used a great variety of ritual ceremonies, both to unite its individual members (as in war dances, etc.) and to impress upon an individual any newly acquired obligations or privileges (as in initiation, marriage, etc.). Some of these rituals have been retained by more sophisticated human cultures, usually, but not always, in a religious context. See pages 460–461.

Rivera, Diego (1886–1957) Mexican mural painter. In Mexico in the 1920s, he revived the old techniques of *fresco painting. His communist-inspired subject matter made him notorious in the USA.

Riviera (French name: Rivière) The narrow Mediterranean coastal belt of France and Italy, extending roughly between Toulon and La Spezia. Its climate, scenery, and beaches have made it a popular resort.

Riyadh 24 39N 46 46E A city in Saudi Arabia, in the centre of the Arabian Peninsula. Riyadh and Mecca are joint capitals of the kingdom. Population (1986 est): 1 500 000.

RNA (*or* ribonucleic acid) A substance that is important in the manufacture of proteins by living organisms. In some viruses RNA is the genetic material. Structurally, it is a nucleic acid, similar to *DNA but consisting of only one strand of molecules. One type of RNA (messenger RNA) relays the genetic instructions in the DNA from the chromosomes to the *ribosomes, where proteins are assembled. Another type of RNA (transfer RNA) brings the component parts of the protein – the amino acids – to the ribosomes.

roach A freshwater fish related to the carp. The European species *Rutilus rutilus* has an elongated body, 15–45 cm long, olive-green to grey-green above and silvery white below with reddish fins and red eyes.

robber crab (*or* coconut crab) A *crab, *Birgus latro*, found on the shores of the SW Pacific and Indian Oceans. It has an extremely large body (about 1 m from head to tail), ranging from violet to brown in colour. It emerges from its burrow at night to feed on coconuts.

robber fly A predatory insect-eating fly, also called assassin fly. Some species (e.g. *Asilus crabroniformis*) resemble bees and wasps. Most larvae are plant eaters and live in the soil.

Robert (I) the Bruce (1274–1329) King of the Scots (1306–29). Robert seized the Scottish throne in 1306. Although immediately forced into exile by Edward I of England, on the accession of Edward II he slowly recovered the kingdom, decisively defeating the English forces at Bannockburn (1314).

Robert II (1316–90) The first *Stuart King of the Scots (1371–90). He was three times regent of Scotland (jointly 1334–35; alone 1338–41 and 1346–57) while his uncle David II (1324–71) was imprisoned or in exile. His own rule was of little consequence.

Robeson, Paul (1898–1976) US Black actor and singer of Negro spirituals. His stage performances include the title role of Othello, and he actively campaigned for Black civil rights.

Robespierre, Maximilien François Marie Isidore de (1758–94) French revolutionary. A lawyer, Robespierre was elected to the States General in 1789 and became one of the leaders of the radical Jacobins. After the execution of Louis XVI he helped to overthrow the Girondins (1793). He subsequently enjoyed supreme power and instigated the *Reign of Terror. In 1794 he was guillotined.

robin A small Eurasian songbird, *Erithacus rubecula*, of the thrush family. About 13 cm long it has an olive-brown plumage with an orange-red breast, throat, and forehead. It feeds on insects, earthworms, and seeds and defends its territory fiercely.

Robin Hood An English outlaw, probably legendary. According to the *Lytell Geste of Robyn Hoode* (c. 1495) he killed the evil sheriff of Nottingham, was visited in his forest home by the king, and was subsequently employed in the royal household.

robinia. *See* locust.

Robinson, Sugar Ray (Walker Smith; 1920–) US boxer, world welterweight champion (1946–51) and five times middleweight champion (twice in 1951, 1955, 1957, 1958–60). He fought 202 professional bouts, of which he lost only 19.

robotics The study of automatic machines that are capable of imitating and replacing human activities. Most robots in current industrial use carry out a fixed sequence of computer-controlled operations to perform simple jobs many times.

Rob Roy (Robert Macgregor; 1671–1734) Scottish outlaw, whose violent life was romanticized in Sir Walter Scott's novel *Rob Roy* (1818). He embarked on his career of banditry after losing his family fortunes in 1712.

Robson, Dame Flora (1902–84) British actress. She was successful in both comedy, as in *Captain Brassbound's Conversion* (1948), and serious drama, such as Ibsen's *Ghosts* (1958). In her many films she usually played character parts.

rock A solid mixture of *minerals forming part of the earth's crust. Rocks are classified according to their formation, age, and composition (*see* igneous rock; metamorphic rock; sedimentary rock). The principal minerals in rocks are the silicates (including silica), carbonates, and oxides. The study of rocks is called **petrology**.

rock crystal. *See* quartz.

Rockefeller, John D(avison) (1839–1937) US industrialist, who founded the oil-refining company, Standard Oil (1870). He founded the University of Chicago in 1891 and, with his son **John D(avison) Rockefeller, Jr** (1874–1960), established the Rockefeller Institute for Medical Research (now Rockefeller University) in 1901. The latter's nephew **Nelson A(ldrich) Rockefeller** (1908–79) was Gerald Ford's vice-president (1974–77).

rockets Vehicles or missiles powered by jet propulsion that carry their own fuel and oxidizer and thus do not rely on air for their combustion reactions. They can therefore travel both in space and in the atmosphere. Rockets obtain both lift and thrust from their propulsive jets. Solid-fuel firework rockets were known to the Chinese in the 13th century; the first liquid-fuelled rocket to fly was designed by the American R. H. Goddard (1882–1945) in 1926. During World War II, at the Peenemünde rocket research station in Germany, Werner *von Braun produced the *V-2 rocket. Intercontinental *ballistic missiles (with nuclear warheads) developed from this model. Space rockets are built in stages, a high-thrust vehicle providing lift-off and acceleration into the thinner atmosphere, where this first stage is jettisoned and the second stage takes over. The world's biggest rocket, the US Saturn V, is a three-stage rocket weighing 3000 tonnes fully laden. The first stage burns kerosene and the second and third stages burn liquid hydrogen. Liquid oxygen (lox) is the oxidizer for all stages.

Rocky Mountains (*or* Rockies) The chief mountain system in North America. It extends roughly N–S for about 4800 km (3000 mi) between New Mexico (USA) and the Yukon (Canada). It rises to 4399 m (14 431 ft) at Mount Elbert.

rococo An artistic style dominant in France between about 1700 and 1750. Developing in reaction to the *baroque, it was characterized by curved slender forms, asymmetry, and pastel colours. Famous rococo artists include the painters *Fragonard, *Boucher, and *Watteau and the sculptor Clodion (1738–1814). The style spread to Austria and Germany, where the leading exponent was the architect Balthazar Neumann (1687–1753). England remained largely untouched by it.

rodent A mammal of which there are over 1700 species occurring worldwide. They range in size from about 7.5 cm (the smallest mice) to 130 cm (the *capybara). The chisel-like incisor teeth of rodents continue to grow throughout life, as they are worn away by gnawing. Rodents include the porcupines, cavies, squirrels, beavers, marmots, chipmunks, rats, mice, lemmings, and voles.

Rodgers, Richard Charles (1902–79) US composer of musical comedies. With the lyricist Lorenz Hart (1895–1943) he wrote such works as *The Girl Friend* (1926) and *Pal Joey* (1940). After Hart's death he worked with Oscar *Hammerstein II on *Oklahoma* (1943), *The King and I* (1951), and other musicals.

Rodin, Auguste (1840–1917) French sculptor. His first major work, *The Age of Bronze* (1877), was influenced by the work of *Michelangelo and *Donatello. *The Burghers of Calais* (1884–86), his nude monument of Victor Hugo, and his dressing-gowned Balzac were all at first rejected. Nevertheless, by 1900 Rodin had established an international reputation, his bronze portrait busts and his marble *The Kiss* (1886; Tate Gallery), being particularly admired.

Rodney, George Brydges, 1st Baron (1719–92) British admiral. He wrecked (1759–60) a French invasion fleet during the Seven Years' War and won victories (1780–82) against the powers that supported the American Revolution.

Rodrigo, Joaquín (1902–   ) Spanish composer, blind from the age of three. His works include the *Concierto de Aranjuez* (for guitar and orchestra; 1940) and *Concierto Pastorale* (for flute and orchestra; 1978).

roe deer A small deer, *Capreolus capreolus*, found in temperate forests of Europe and Asia. About 70 cm high, roe deer have a dark-brown winter coat, a red-brown summer coat, and a large white rump patch; males have small three-pointed antlers.

roentgen A unit of dose of ionizing radiation equal to the dose that produces ions of one sign carrying a charge of 2.58×10^{-4} coulomb in one kg of air. The SI unit coulomb per kilogram is replacing the roentgen.

Roentgen, Wilhelm Konrad (1845–1923) German physicist. In 1895 Roentgen discovered that cathode rays remained luminous even when they were blocked by cardboard. He correctly concluded that some unknown type of radiation was coming from the cathode-ray tube. He named the radiation *X-rays.

Rogation Days Four days in the Christian calendar devoted to prayer and fasting. The Major Rogation is on 25 April and the Minor Rogations are on the three days before *Ascension Day.

Rogers, Ginger (Virginia McMath; 1911–   ) US actress and singer. During the 1930s she partnered Fred *Astaire in many popular film musicals, including *Top Hat* (1935), *Swing Time* (1936), and *Follow the Fleet* (1936).

Rolland, Romain (1866–1944) French novelist, dramatist, and essayist. His best-known novel, *Jean Christophe* (1904–12), concerns a German composer. He won the Nobel Prize in 1915.

Rolling Stones, the A British rock group, formed in 1962. Their early hits included "The Last Time" and "Satisfaction". The original members of the group were Mick Jagger (1944–   ), Keith Richard (1943–   ), Bill Wyman (1941–   ), Charlie Watts (1941–   ), and Brian Jones (1944–69).

Romains, Jules (Louis Farigoule; 1885–1972) French poet, novelist, and dramatist associated with the philosophical theory of *unanimisme*. His best-known works are the satirical play *Knock* (1923) and the novel series *Les Hommes de bonne volonté* (1932–46).

Roman Catholic Church The Christian Church of which the pope is the earthly leader. After the split with the Eastern *Orthodox Churches (1054), Roman Catholicism was the unchallenged spiritual power in W Europe until

the *Reformation. In the early 16th century *Protestantism showed the need for urgent reforms within the Church; these were discussed at the Council of Trent (1545–63), which largely decided the present character of Roman Catholicism (*see also* Counter-Reformation; Vatican Councils). The Church's doctrines include *infallibility of the pope, *transubstantiation, and *purgatory. The number of the *sacraments has been fixed at seven since the 12th century. Until the mid-20th century Latin was the sole language of the Mass. Roman Catholicism has spread worldwide and is the largest Christian group.

Romance languages Descendants of the Italic language group, in particular of the spoken form of *Latin, called Vulgar Latin. The group consists of *French, *Italian, *Spanish, *Portuguese, *Romanian, *Catalan, *Romansch, Sardinian, and the now extinct Dalmatian.

Roman Curia (Latin: *Curia Romana*) The papal court, made up of the chief legal and administrative bodies of the *Roman Catholic Church. It was reformed in 1967 by Pope Paul VI.

Roman Empire The imperial period of ancient Roman history from 27 BC, when Octavian became emperor as *Augustus, until 476 AD. Many of the political institutions of the *Roman Republic continued to function under Augustus, who fostered peace and prosperity; this continued under the rule of the Flavian (69–96 AD) and Antonine (96–180) emperors. The 3rd century saw a rapid succession of army-nominated emperors. *Diocletian reorganized the Empire between East (*see* Eastern Roman Empire) and West (293). It was reunited (324) under *Constantine the Great, who founded a new imperial capital at Constantinople (*see* Istanbul). Civil war and economic decline followed his death. In 476 the last Roman emperor of the West, Romulus Augustulus (b. ?461), was deposed by the German king Odoacer. The Eastern Roman, or Byzantine, Empire survived until 1453.

Romania, Republic of A country in SE Europe, with an E coastline on the Black Sea. *Economy*: the main crops are maize, wheat, potatoes, sugar beet, and fruit. Livestock and the wine industry are also important. Minerals include oil and gas, salt, lignite, iron, and copper; there is a considerable timber industry. *History*: formed in 1861, it became independent in 1878 and a kingdom in 1881. After World War II it became a communist state and King Michael abdicated (1947). In 1989 there were mass demonstrations, leading to a revolution against the repressive regime of Nicolae Ceaucescu (1918–89); he was executed and a reformist administration installed. President: Ion Iliescu. Official language: Romanian. Official currency: leu of 100 bani. Area: 237 500 sq km (91 699 sq mi). Population (1987 est): 22 800 000. Capital: Bucharest. Main port: Constanţa.

Romanian A *Romance language, the main form of which is spoken in Romania and is known as Daco-Romanian. Other forms are spoken in parts of Greece, Yugoslavia, Albania, and Bulgaria.

Roman law The body of laws drawn up by the Romans, which forms the basis of the *civil law

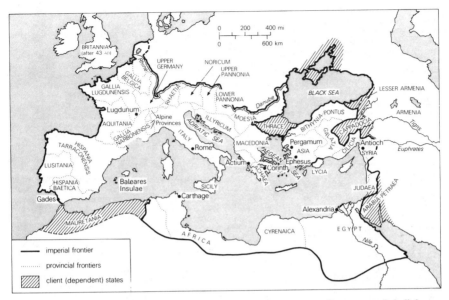

ROMAN EMPIRE *In 14 AD, at the death of Augustus, Roman rule or influence extended all the way round the Mediterranean.*

of many countries. Before about 150 BC the *jus civile* (civil law) applied only to Roman citizens. With increasing interests abroad, another system, the *jus gentium* (law of nations), was also applied by Roman courts. The Byzantine emperor Justinian I (482–565 AD) sponsored the *Corpus Juris Civilis* (Body of Civil Law) or Justinian Code. This consisted of four parts: (1) the *Codex Constitutionum*, ordinances of the emperors; (2) the *Digest*, statements by jurists on points of law; (3) the *Institutes*, a textbook explaining legal institutions; and (4) the *Novellae* or *Novels*, the new ordinances issued by Justinian after the publication of the *Codex*. The *Code Napoléon* was based on the Justinian code.

Roman numerals The system of numbers used by the Romans, based on letters of the alphabet: I = 1, V = 5, X = 10, L = 50, C = 100, D = 500, and M = 1000. Intermediate numbers are given by the sum of a larger number and the smaller number that follows it (e.g. VI = 6) or the difference between a larger number and the smaller number that precedes it (IV = 4).

Roman Republic (510–27 BC) The period of ancient Roman history between the time when *Tarquin the Proud was expelled and *Augustus became the first Roman emperor. Republican government consisted of two chief magistrates (later *consuls), subordinate magistrates, the *Senate, and popular assemblies. By the early 3rd century Rome dominated the whole of Italy. By the mid-2nd century Cisalpine *Gaul, Greece, and much of Asia Minor had been subdued, and the *Punic Wars with Carthage brought control of the Mediterranean (146). In

the mid-1st century *Caesar completed the conquest of Transalpine Gaul.

However, provincial unrest and the military weakness of the Senate in the late 2nd century brought a series of ambitious army commanders to the fore. These included *Sulla, under whose dictatorship (83–79) the powers of the Senate were strengthened. In 60, *Pompey and *Crassus formed the first *Triumvirate with Caesar. The death of Crassus (53) and Pompey's intrigues brought civil war; Caesar's victory led to a short-lived dictatorship. The Roman Republic was finally destroyed when Octavian defeated *Mark Antony and took absolute power as Augustus. *See also* Roman Empire.

Romansch A *Romance language spoken in N Italy and in the Rhine Valley in Switzerland.

Romanticism A fundamental development in western art, literature, and music in the late 18th and early 19th centuries. Romanticism was a reaction against classicism, with an emphasis on the relationship between human beings and their natural environment. Romantic writers include Wordsworth, Coleridge, Keats, Byron, Goethe, Schiller, and Victor Hugo. Composers include Beethoven and painters, Turner.

Romany The language spoken by *gipsies. It is related to *Sanskrit and the Indo-Aryan languages of N India but has been greatly influenced by the languages spoken in regions the gipsies have passed through.

Rome (Italian name: Roma)   41 53N 12 33E The capital of Italy, on the River Tiber. It is mainly an administrative and cultural centre and the focal point of the Roman Catholic Church (*see* Vatican City). Relics of classical times include the Forum, the *Pantheon, and the *Colosseum and the city contains many outstanding Renaissance buildings, such as St Peter's Basilica. *History*: according to legend Rome was founded on the Palatine Hill in 753 BC by Romulus, its first king. The *Roman Republic was replaced by the *Roman Empire in the 1st century BC. In the 5th century AD Rome was sacked by Germanic tribes. From the 6th century it was an important ecclesiastical centre, remaining under papal control until 1871, when it became capital of the newly unified Italy. Population (1987): 2 817 227.

Rome, Treaties of (1957) Two treaties signed in Rome, which led to the establishment of the *European Economic Community and the *European Atomic Energy Community.

Rommel, Erwin (1891–1944) German general, known as the Desert Fox. In 1940 he became commander of the Seventh Panzer Division and, in 1941, of the Afrika Corps. In N Africa he gained the respect of the Allies but in 1943, after his defeat at El Alamein (1942), he was recalled and became commander of the Channel defence. His involvement in the attempt to assassinate Hitler in 1944, organized by Claus von Stauffenberg, led to his suicide, under pressure from Hitler.

Romney, George (1734–1802) British portrait painter. He attracted a fashionable clientele and rivalled Reynolds when he moved to London in 1762. He is best known for his numerous portraits of Emma, Lady *Hamilton.

Romulus and Remus The legendary founders of Rome, the sons of Mars and Rhea Silvia, daughter of Numitor, King of Alba Longa. Amulius, who had deposed Numitor, threw the twin babies into the Tiber. Washed ashore and suckled by a she-wolf, they eventually founded Rome at the place where they had been rescued.

rook A large blue-black crow, *Corvus frugilegus*, of Europe and Asia. About 45 cm long, rooks nest in colonies (rookeries) and may form large flocks, feeding on earthworms, larvae, carrion, and grain.

Roosevelt, Franklin D(elano) (1882–1945) US statesman; Democratic president (1933–45). Despite being paralysed from the waist down by poliomyelitis in 1921, he became the only US president to be re-elected three times. He helped US recovery from the Depression with the *New Deal relief programmes. After the Japanese bombing of Pearl Harbor (1941), he took the USA into World War II. He attended the *Tehran and *Yalta Conferences but died in office before the end of the war.

Roosevelt, Theodore (1858–1919) US statesman; Republican president (1901–09). His social reforms included the *Square Deal programme, and his foreign policy was to "speak softly and carry a big stick." Roosevelt established US control over the building of the Panama Canal and made the USA a policing power in the Americas.

root (algebra) **1.** One of the equal factors of a number. The square root is one of two equal factors; for example $9 = 3 \times 3$ so the square root of 9, written $\sqrt{9}$, is 3 (or -3). The cube root is one

of three equal factors; for example the cube root of 8 is 2. **2.** The solution of an equation, i.e. the values of the variable that will satisfy the equation. *See* quadratic equation.

root (botany) The part of a plant that provides anchorage and enables the uptake of water and nutrients from the soil. Some plants, such as the dandelion, have one main root with smaller branches—a tap root system; others, such as grasses, have a mass of similar-sized roots—a fibrous root system. Roots can act as food-storage organs, as in the carrot and turnip (tap roots).

root-mean-square value (*or* rms value) The square *root of the arithmetic average of the squares of a set of numbers; for example the rms of 2, 4, 5, 6 is $\sqrt{[(2^2 + 4^2 + 5^2 + 6^2)/4]} = 4\frac{1}{2}$. The rms value is useful in continuous quantities, such as alternating electric current, in which the heating effect is proportional to the current squared.

rorqual A small-headed fast-moving whalebone *whale. The common rorqual (*Balaenoptera physalus*), also called fin whale or razorback, occurs in all oceans. Up to 25 m long, it has a dark back, shading to white underneath.

Rosario 33 00S 60 40W The second largest city in Argentina, on the Río Paraná. It is an industrial and commercial centre and the terminus of the pampas railways. Population (1980): 935 471.

Roscommon (Irish name: Ros Comáin) A county in the N Republic of Ireland, in Connacht. It has many lakes and extensive bogs. Agriculture is the chief occupation. Area: 2463 sq km (951 sq mi). Population (1986): 54 551. County town: Roscommon.

rose A prickly shrub or climbing plant native to N temperate regions and widely cultivated. The flowers are usually white, yellow, pink, or red and the fruits (hips) are rich in vitamin C. Modern hybrid roses—usually with double flowers—include the hybrid teas, derived from the tea rose (*Rosa odorata*), and the floribundas. Wild species include *dog rose and sweet briar.

rosemary An evergreen shrub, *Rosmarinus officinalis*, native to the Mediterranean region and W Asia and widely cultivated. Up to 2 m high, it has bluish flowers and its leaves are used as a herb in cookery.

rose of Jericho A W Asian plant, *Anastatica hierochuntica*, of the mustard family, also called resurrection plant. During the dry season the whole plant forms a wickerwork-like ball that is blown by the wind. When moistened, the plant regains its shape and produces tiny white flowers.

rose of Sharon. *See* hibiscus; St John's wort.

Roses, Wars of the (1455–85) The civil wars between the Houses of *Lancaster (the red rose) and *York (the white rose) for possession of the English Crown. The Lancastrian *Henry VI's inability to govern resulted in opposition from Richard Plantagenet, Duke of *York, and the Earl of *Warwick (the Kingmaker), which led to open warfare. York was killed in 1460 but his son seized the Crown in 1461, becoming Edward IV, and crushed the Lancastrians. In 1470–71 Henry VI was briefly restored but Edward returned

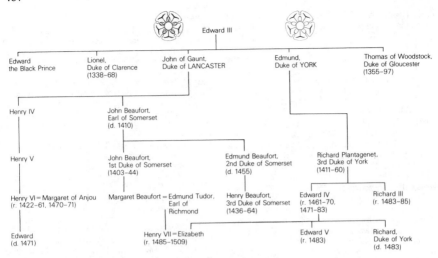

WARS OF THE ROSES *The rival Houses of Lancaster and York.*

to the throne after his victory at Tewkesbury. He was succeeded by his brother Richard III, who was defeated by Henry VII at Bosworth (1485). The remaining Yorkists were finally overcome at Stoke in 1487.

Rosetta Stone An inscribed stone slab discovered (1799) at Rosetta (Arabic name: Rashid), near Alexandria (Egypt). It carries a decree (196 BC) of Ptolemy V Epiphanes (reigned 205–180) in Egyptian *hieroglyphic and *demotic, and Greek. The repetition of Ptolemy's name in the different scripts enabled Thomas *Young to decipher hieroglyphs.

rosewood An attractive hardwood, usually dark reddish and often rose-scented, derived from several tropical evergreen trees. These include Brazilian rosewood (or blackwood), Honduras rosewood, and East Indian rosewood.

Rosh Hashana (Hebrew: head of the year) The Jewish New Year festival, celebrated in Sept or Oct. It is regarded as a time of penitence and preparation for *Yom Kippur.

Rosicrucianism A movement for spiritual renewal that started in Protestant Germany in the early 17th century. It has links with freemasonry.

Ross Dependency An area in Antarctica claimed by New Zealand (since 1923), lying between longitudes 160°E and 150°W and including the Ross Sea and islands S of latitude 60°S. Area: about 414 400 sq km (160 000 sq mi).

Rossetti, Dante Gabriel (Gabriel Charles Dante R.; 1828–82) British painter and poet. In 1848 Rossetti joined with John Everett *Millais, William Holman *Hunt, and other artists to found the *Pre-Raphaelite Brotherhood. He founded the Pre-Raphaelite journal *The Germ* (1850–51) and his works include *Poems* (1870) and *Ballads and Sonnets* (1881). His sister was the poet **Christina Georgina Rossetti** (1830–74).

Her *Goblin Market and Other Poems* (1862) gave literary expression to Pre-Raphaelite ideals.

Rossini, Gioacchino Antonio (1792–1868) Italian composer. He wrote 36 highly successful operas, including *Tancredi* (1813), *The Barber of Seville* (1816), *The Thieving Magpie* (1817), and *William Tell* (1829). He also invented a number of recipes, including Tournedos Rossini.

Ross Sea A large inlet of the S Pacific Ocean, in the Antarctic continent between Victoria Land and Byrd Land.

Rostock 54 03N 12 07E A city and Baltic port in NE Germany. It has fine medieval buildings and a university (1419); industries include shipbuilding and fisheries. Population (1986): 245 606.

Rostov-na-Donu 47 15N 39 45E A port in the S Soviet Union, on the River Don. It has ship-repairing, food-processing, and textile industries. Population (1987): 1 004 000.

Rostropovich, Mstislav (1927–) US cellist, born in the Soviet Union, which he left in 1975. Prokofiev, Britten, and Shostakovich all wrote cello works for him.

Rothschild, Mayer Amschel (1744–1812) German merchant and banker, whose business in Frankfurt prospered during the Napoleonic Wars, making loans and trading in arms, wheat, and cotton. His sons later established branches of the firm in Vienna, London, Naples, and Paris.

rotifer A tiny invertebrate animal, also called wheel animalcule, found mainly in fresh water. 0.1 and 0.5 mm long, rotifers have a ring of hairlike cilia for wafting food particles into the mouth and providing a means of locomotion.

Rotorua 38 07S 176 17E A spa city in New Zealand, in N North Island. A Maori centre, situated within a volcanic area with hot springs, it has been developed as a health resort. Population (1990): 63 000.

Rotterdam 51 55N 4 29E The chief port and second largest city in the Netherlands, on the New Meuse River. Its importance dates from the opening (1872) of the 35 km (12 mi) long Nieuwe Waterweg (New Waterway) linking it to the North Sea. Its extensive dockyards, handling much export trade from Germany, include the vast Europoort. Industries include oil refining, shipbuilding, brewing, and engineering. Population (1989): 576 218.

Rottweiler A breed of working dog developed in Rottweil, Germany, with a reputation for aggression. It has a broad body, a strong neck, and a large head with a deep muzzle. The coat is black with tan markings. Height: 63–68 cm (dogs); 58–63 cm (bitches).

Rouault, Georges (Henri) (1871–1958) French artist. A major 20th-century religious artist, he executed many paintings of clowns and prostitutes. As a graphic artist his main achievement was his series of etchings (1916–27), entitled *Miserere* and *Guerre*.

Rouen (Latin name: Rotomagus) 49 26N 1 05E A city and port in NW France, on the River Seine. The ancient capital of Normandy, it has a cathedral (13th–16th centuries) and university (1966). Industries include textiles, petrochemicals, engineering, and electronics. Population (1988): 101 945.

rounders A nine-a-side bat-and-ball field game, from which *baseball probably developed. The two teams take turns at batting and fielding and a match consists of two innings per team. The batsmen try to score rounders by hitting the ball and running round the four bases without being caught or run out.

Roundheads The parliamentary party during the English *Civil War. The name referred originally to the short haircuts of the apprentices who demonstrated against the king at Westminster in 1640.

Round Table Conference (1930–32) Three meetings held in London to discuss a form of government acceptable to India. The meetings were attended by representatives of the British Government and of India's major political parties and all its states. They resulted in the Government of India Act of 1935.

roundworm. *See* nematode.

Rousseau, Henri (1844–1910) French painter. Initially his work, which resembled folk art in technique (*see* primitivism), was ridiculed. But after exhibiting *War* (1894; Louvre) and *Sleeping Gypsy* (1897; New York), he received more serious attention. The childlike quality of his jungle landscapes influenced many 20th-century painters.

Rousseau, Jean Jacques (1712–78) French philosopher and writer, one of the *Encyclopedists. In the *Discourse on the Origin and Foundations of Inequality amongst Men* (1754) he argued that man's perfect nature is spoiled by corrupt society. *Emile* (1762), a novel on education, expanded these views. Such political works as *Du contrat social* (1762) found favour with revolutionaries.

rowan. *See* mountain ash.

Rowlandson, Thomas (1756–1827) British caricaturist. Using a reed pen and delicate washes of colour, he produced the satirical *Dr Syntax* series (1812–21) and the *English Dance of Death* (1815–16).

Royal Academy An art society in Burlington House, London, that holds annual summer exhibitions of contemporary British art, as well as loan exhibitions of modern artists and the old masters. Founded in 1768, it moved to its present premises in 1867.

Royal Academy of Dramatic Art (RADA) The leading British school of acting, founded in London in 1904 by Sir Herbert Beerbohm *Tree. It has received a government subsidy since 1924.

Royal Air Force (RAF) A British armed service formed in 1918 by the amalgamation of the Royal Flying Corps (1912) with the Royal Naval Air Service (1914). It played a decisive role in *World War II. It is now divided into Strike Command (the operational command), Maintenance Command, and Training Command and is administered by the Air Force Department of the Ministry of Defence. The **Women's Royal Air Force** was formed in 1949 in succession to the Women's Auxiliary Air Force (WAAF) of World War II. *See also* aircraft.

royal antelope The world's smallest antelope, *Neotragus pygmaeus*, of West African forests. 25–30 cm high, it is red-brown with white underparts; males have short spiky horns.

Royal Ballet The leading British ballet company and school. Based at the Royal Opera House, Covent Garden, since 1946, it was founded by Dame Ninette de Valois in 1931 and known as the Sadler's Wells Ballet until 1956.

Royal British Legion An organization for ex-servicemen and women, founded in 1921 largely through the efforts of Douglas *Haig. It provides housing and employment assistance and runs homes for the sick and aged.

Royal Canadian Mounted Police (*or* Mounties) Canadian police force. Founded in 1873 as the North West Mounted Police, it has become famous for the efficiency of its members, dressed in scarlet tunics, blue breeches, and wide-brimmed hats.

Royal Geographical Society A British learned society, established in 1830 and made into a corporation in 1859, for the advancement of geographical knowledge. Two Royal Medals are awarded annually by the Queen to geographers recommended by the Society.

Royal Greenwich Observatory An observatory founded in 1675 by Charles II at Greenwich, London, in a building designed by Sir Christopher Wren. The meridian through Greenwich (0°) was internationally adopted as the prime meridian in 1884. The observatory has been based at Herstmonceux, Sussex since 1948; in 1990 it will move to Cambridge.

Royal Institution One of the first scientific research centres, founded by Count *Rumford in 1799. Scientists who worked at its premises in Albermarle Street, London, include *Davy, *Faraday, and *Bragg.

royal jelly A thick white mixture of proteins, carbohydrates, minerals, and vitamins that is secreted by worker bees and fed to the larvae. Larvae destined to become queens are fed entirely on royal jelly. *See also* honeybee.

Royal Marines A corps of troops, founded in England in 1664, which serves on land, at sea, or in the air. Their ranks correspond to those of the army but they are administered by the Navy Board.

Royal Mint The factory in which the UK's coins are made. It was formerly in the Tower of London, moving to Tower Hill in 1811 and to Llantrisant, South Wales, in 1968.

Royal National Lifeboat Institution A voluntary organization, founded in 1824, that operates a 24-hour lifeboat service around British coasts. Each lifeboat has a full-time mechanic but the other crew members are volunteers.

Royal National Theatre Company A British theatre company established in 1963. Sir Laurence *Olivier, its first director, was succeeded by Peter Hall in 1973 and Richard Eyre in 1988. The company's new building on the South Bank of the Thames was designed by Sir Denys Lasdun and opened in 1976. The prefix Royal was added in 1988.

Royal Navy (RN) The senior of Britain's three armed services. Founded in the 9th century by Alfred the Great, the RN emerged as "the wooden walls of England" in the 16th century with such victories as that over the Spanish *Armada (1588). In the 18th century, the conditions for sailors led to mutinies even as the RN entered its greatest era with a series of victories under *Nelson against Napoleonic France. It fought its last set-piece battle at Jutland (1916) during World War I, after which it was limited in size. The modern RN's duties include fishery protection, mine sweeping, and NATO roles.

Royal Opera House. *See* Covent Garden.

Royal Society The oldest and most important scientific society in the UK. It originated in 1645 and was incorporated by royal charter in 1662. Under the presidency (1703–27) of Isaac *Newton, the Royal Society achieved great standing and financial security. It publishes scientific papers in the *Proceedings* and the *Philosophical Transactions*, maintains a large library, pays out grants, and awards medals for scientific achievement.

Royal Society for the Prevention of Cruelty to Animals (RSPCA) A British charity founded in 1824 to investigate reports of cruelty to animals. Funded by voluntary contributions, it has branches in the Commonwealth.

Royal Society for the Protection of Birds (RSPB) A British charity founded in 1889 to protest against the killing of birds for their plumage. Since then it has encouraged the conservation of wild birds throughout Britain.

Royce, Sir (Frederick) Henry (1863–1933) British car manufacturer, who founded, with Charles Rolls (1877–1910), Rolls-Royce Ltd (1906). In 1884 Royce opened an engineering business in Manchester and in 1904 began to build cars, which impressed Rolls and led to the merger of their businesses. Royce and his team

designed the aeroengine that became the Merlin (used in Spitfires and Hurricanes in World War II).

RSPB. *See* Royal Society for the Protection of Birds.

RSPCA. *See* Royal Society for the Prevention of Cruelty to Animals.

Ruapehu, Mount 39 18S 175 36E An active volcano in New Zealand, the highest peak in North Island. Height: 2797 m (9175 ft).

rubber A tough elastic organic polymer (*see* polymerization). Natural rubber, which consists mainly of polyisoprene $(CH_2CH:C.CH_3:CH_2)_n$, is obtained from the *rubber tree. The rubber is coagulated from latex (using acids) and pressed into sheets. *Vulcanization makes it more longlasting. Synthetic rubbers are made from petrochemicals (*see* oil). Styrene-butadiene rubber (SBR), now the commonest synthetic rubber, was introduced during World War II.

rubber plant A tree, *Ficus elastica*, of the mulberry family, native to India and Malaysia. Its latex is the source of Assam or India rubber. Rubber plants are also widely grown as house plants.

rubber tree A Brazilian tree, *Hevea brasiliensis*, also called Pará rubber, up to 20 m high. It is widely cultivated in humid tropical regions for its milky latex, the chief source of natural *rubber. Trees yield latex from about the sixth year.

rubella. *See* German measles.

Rubens, Peter Paul (1577–1640) Flemish painter, the greatest of the *baroque artists. His first major works were *The Raising of the Cross* and *Descent from the Cross* (both Antwerp Cathedral). Many commissions followed, including a series for Marie de' Medici (Louvre) and the ceiling of the Banqueting House, Whitehall, for Charles I. He also painted portraits of his family, notably *Helena Fourment with a Fur Cloak* (Kunsthistorisches Museum, Vienna), and such landscapes as *The Château de Steen* (National Gallery, London).

Rubicon A stream in N central Italy, which formed the boundary between Italy and Cisalpine *Gaul in the time of the Roman Republic. In 49 BC Julius Caesar brought on civil war by leading his army across the Rubicon into Italy, an illegal act. Hence "crossing the Rubicon" has come to mean taking an irrevocable step.

rubidium (Rb) An *alkali metal, discovered spectroscopically by R. W. Bunsen and G. R. Kirchhoff in 1861. The element is soft and silvery-white. It ignites spontaneously in air and reacts violently with water. The radioactive isotope ^{87}Rb is used in *rubidium-strontium dating. Rubidium forms ionic salts and four oxides (Rb_2O, Rb_2O_2, Rb_2O_3, RbO_2). At no 37; at wt 85.47; mp 38.89°C; bp 688°C.

rubidium-strontium dating A method of dating, used mainly for rocks, fossils, etc. Naturally occurring rubidium contains about 28% of the radioactive isotope rubidium-87, which undergoes *beta decay to strontium-87 with a half-life of 5×10^{11} years. Thus by measuring the ratio of rubidium-87 to strontium-87 in the sample, its age may be estimated.

Rubinstein, Artur (1888–1982) Polish-born US pianist. He acquired a worldwide reputation, particularly as a performer of Chopin.

ruby A red transparent variety of *corundum, the colour being due to traces of chromium. It is used as a gemstone and in lasers, watches, and other precision instruments.

rudd A game fish, *Scardinius erythrophthalmus*, found in fresh waters of Europe and W Asia. 35–40 cm long, it is golden- or olive-brown above and silvery white below, with deep-red fins.

rue An evergreen shrub, *Ruta graveolens*, also known as herb of grace, native to S Europe. Growing up to 90 cm high, it has yellow flowers. The leaves yield a bitter oil, once used as a spice and in medicines.

ruff A *sandpiper, *Philomachus pugnax*, that breeds in coastal wetlands of N Europe and Asia and winters on mudflats of South Africa and S Asia. The grey-brown female (called a reeve) is 25 cm long; the larger male has a double crest and a colourful collar in the breeding season.

Rugby 52 23N 1 15W A town in the English Midlands, in Warwickshire. According to tradition the game of rugby football originated here in 1823 at the famous public school (1567). Rugby's industries include engineering and cement. Population (1981): 59 564.

rugby football. *See* football.

Ruhr, River A river in W Germany, rising in the Sauerland and flowing NW and W to the River Rhine. The Ruhr Valley is the centre of the German iron and steel industry. Length: 235 km (146 mi).

Ruisdael, Jacob van (?1628–82) The greatest of Dutch landscape painters. His baroque compositions are noted for their dramatic contrasts of light and shade. *The Jewish Cemetery* (c. 1660) is a striking depiction of human mortality.

rum A spirit distilled from molasses derived from sugar cane. Better-quality rums are aged in oak casks for several years.

Rumania. *See* Romania, Socialist Republic of.

Rumford, Benjamin Thompson, Count (1753–1814) American-born scientist, who spied for the British in the American Revolution. In England he carried out scientific research in ballistics and the theory of heat. Suspected of spying for the French, he left England in 1785 and worked for the elector of Bavaria, becoming a count of the Holy Roman Empire in 1791. In 1795 he returned to England, where he founded the *Royal Institution (1799).

ruminant A hoofed mammal with a four-chambered stomach and the ability to regurgitate food (vegetation) to "chew the cud," which helps digestion. Ruminants include deer, cattle, antelopes, sheep, and goats.

Rump Parliament. *See* Long Parliament.

Runcie, Robert Alexander Kennedy, Baron (1921–) British churchman; Archbishop of Canterbury (1980–91). He was formerly bishop of St Albans (1970–80).

Rundstedt, (Karl Rudolf) Gerd von (1875–1953) German field marshal, who was recalled from retirement at the outbreak of World War II, becoming (1942) commander in chief in France. He was captured in 1945 but his ill health secured his release.

runic alphabet A writing system used for Norse and certain other Germanic languages. It originated in the 2nd or 3rd century AD and went out of use gradually after the 14th century. The runes were always associated with magical powers.

runner bean A climbing plant, *Phaseolus coccineus*, also known as scarlet runner, native to South America and widely cultivated as a vegetable crop. Growing up to 3 m high, it bears usually red flowers, which give rise to long pods. *See also* bean.

Runnymede (*or* Runnimede) 51 26N 0 33W A meadow in SE England, on the S bank of the River Thames. The Magna Carta was granted here by King John (1215).

Runyon, Damon (1884–1946) US humorous writer. His stories about New York characters were first collected in *Guys and Dolls* (1932).

Rupert, Prince (1619–82) Cavalry officer, who fought for the Royalists in the Civil War; he was the son of Frederick the Winter King of the Palatinate and Elizabeth, daughter of James I of England. Defeated at *Marston Moor (1644) and *Naseby (1645), he was banished from England after Charles' surrender. He returned at the Restoration (1660) and served as an admiral in the Dutch Wars.

Rupert's Land (*or* Prince Rupert's Land) A region in N and W Canada around Hudson Bay. In 1670 it was granted by Charles II to the *Hudson's Bay Company, the first governor of which was Prince *Rupert.

rupture. *See* hernia.

rush A grasslike plant found in damp temperate and cold regions. Rushes have slender rigid stalks, up to about 1 m high, bearing long flat leaves. The name is also applied to similar plants, including the *bulrush, *flowering rush, and woodrush.

Rushdie, Salman (1947–) British novelist, born in India. His first novel *Grimus* (1975) was followed by the Booker prizewinner *Midnight's Children* (1981) and *Shame* (1983). *The Satanic Verses* (1988) provoked death threats from Islamic extremists led by the Ayatollah *Khomeini and Rushdie went into hiding.

Ruskin, John (1819–1900) British art and social critic. He wrote *Modern Painters* (1843–60) to defend the paintings of Turner. In *The Stones of Venice* (1851–53) he promoted the gothic style in architecture. His books on social criticism include *Unto This Last* (1862). During his last years he suffered attacks of insanity.

Russell, Bertrand Arthur William, 3rd Earl (1872–1970) British philosopher, grandson of the Liberal statesman Lord John Russell (1792–1878). His first major philosophical work, *Principia Mathematica* (1910–13), written with A. N. *Whitehead, presented pure mathematics as a development of *logic. *Our Knowledge of the External World* (1914) discussed knowledge itself. He was imprisoned (1918) for his outspoken pacifism and again in 1961 for civil disobedience during the Campaign for Nuclear Disarmament. He was awarded the Nobel Prize for Literature in 1950.

Russell, Ken (1927–) British film director. His films include *Women in Love* (1969), *The Rainbow* (1989), and controversial biographical films, such as *The Music Lovers* (1970), about Tchaikovsky, *Mahler* (1974), and *Valentino* (1977).

Russia. *See* Soviet Union.

Russian The main language of the Soviet Union, belonging to the East *Slavonic family. It is written in the *Cyrillic alphabet. The standard form is based on the dialect of Moscow.

Russian Orthodox Church An offshoot of the *Greek Orthodox Church, dating from the baptism of the emperor Vladimir (later St Vladimir) in 988.

Russian Revolution (1917) The revolution between March and November (Old Style February and October), 1917, that established the world's first communist state. It began with the February Revolution, when riots in Petrograd led to the establishment of a provisional government that forced *Nicholas II to abdicate. The failure of this government, under Aleksandr Kerenski, to end Russia's participation in World War I and to deal with food shortages led to the October (*or* *Bolshevik) Revolution, in which *Lenin seized power and established the Soviet of People's Commissars. In the civil war that followed (1918–21), the Red Army was victorious against the anticommunist White Russians.

Russo-Finnish War (*or* Winter War; 1939–40) The war between the Soviet Union and Finland at the beginning of World War II. It was won by the Soviet Union, the aggressor, which gained part of the Karelian Isthmus.

Russo-Japanese War (1904–05) A confrontation arising from conflicting Japanese and Russian interests in Manchuria. In 1904 Japan attacked Port Arthur (now Lüda), which fell in January, 1905. In May a Japanese fleet destroyed Russia's Baltic Fleet in the Tsushima Straits, forcing Russia's surrender.

rust A reddish-brown solid consisting of hydrated iron oxide. Rusting is a type of corrosion in which both water and oxygen must be present; it can cause great damage to iron and steel.

rust fungi Fungi that are parasites of plants, forming spots, blotches, and pustules on the stems and leaves. Several are important pests of cereal crops, including black rust (*Puccinia graminis*) of wheat.

Ruth, Babe (George Herman R.; 1895–1948) US baseball player. Known as the "Sultan of Swat", he became the top player of the 1920s and revitalized the sport.

ruthenium (Ru) A hard metal, similar to platinum, first separated in 1844 by K. K. Klaus (1796–1864). It is used to harden platinum and palladium for use in electrical contacts and is a useful catalyst. The element shows a wide range of *valence states. At no 44; at wt 101.07; mp 2310°C; bp 3900°C.

Rutherford, Ernest, 1st Baron (1871–1937) British physicist, born in New Zealand. He made important discoveries concerning the nature of *radioactivity, distinguishing between alpha, beta, and gamma rays. Working with Hans Geiger, he discovered that alpha radiation consisted of positively charged helium atoms. In 1906 he suggested the existence of the atomic *nucleus. In 1908, Rutherford received the Nobel Prize for Chemistry.

rutherfordium. *See* kurchatovium.

Rutland A former county in the East Midlands of England. In 1974 it became part of *Leicestershire. It was the smallest county in England.

Rwanda, Republic of A small country in E central Africa. *Economy*: chiefly subsistence agriculture. The principal cash crop is coffee. *History*: a Tutsi kingdom from the 16th century, the area came under German East Africa in 1890. From 1919, it was administered by Belgium. In 1959 the Tutsi kingdom was overthrown by the Hutu, who in 1961 declared Rwanda a republic; independence was recognized by Belgium in 1962. In 1973 Maj Gen Juvénal Habyalimana (1937–) came to power. Ugandan-based rebels invaded in 1990 but were contained by troops from France, Belgium, and Zaïre. Official languages: Kinyarwanda and French. Official currency: Rwanda franc of 100 centimes. Area: 26 330 sq km (10 166 sq mi). Population (1986 est): 6 324 000. Capital: Kigali.

Ryazan 54 37N 39 43E A city in the W central Soviet Union. Founded in 1095, it was the capital of a principality until annexed by Russia in 1521. Population (1987): 508 000.

Rybinsk (name from 1946 until 1958: Shcherbakov; name from 1984: Andropov) 58 01N 38 52E A port in the W central Soviet Union, on the River Volga. It is situated below the **Rybinsk Reservoir**, 5200 sq km (2000 sq mi) created in 1941. There are shipbuilding, engineering, and food-processing industries. Population (1987): 254 000.

Ryder, Sue. *See* Cheshire, (Geoffrey) Leonard, Group Capt.

rye A cereal *grass, *Secale cereale*, native to W Asia but widely cultivated in cool temperate and upland regions. The grain is milled to produce a dark flour, used in making black bread or for livestock feed.

Ryle, Sir Martin (1918–84) British astronomer; astronomer royal (1972–84). A pioneer of radio telescopy, he developed a technique for studying distant radio sources. In 1974 he shared the Nobel Prize for Physics.

Ryukyu Islands A group of volcanic and coral islands in the W Pacific Ocean, extending almost 650 km (400 mi) from Kyushu to N Taiwan. An independent kingdom until the 14th century, the islands were dominated by the Chinese before becoming a part of Japan (1879). They were under US control (1945–72). Area: 2196 sq km (849 sq mi). Population (1985): 1 179 000. Chief city: Naha (on Okinawa).

S

Saarbrücken 49 15N 6 58E An industrial city in SW Germany, near the French border. It was under French administration 1801–15, 1919–35, 1945–57. Population (1987): 184 400.

Sabah (former name: North Borneo) A state in Malaysia, in NE *Borneo on the South China and Sulu Seas. Forested and mountainous, it has copper and oil resources. North Borneo was first colonized by the British in 1877, becoming a protectorate in 1882. In 1963 it joined Malaysia under its present name. Area: 76 115 sq km (29 388 sq mi). Population (1985 est): 1 222 718. Capital: Kota Kinabalu.

Sabines The peoples of the scattered hilltop communities NE of ancient Rome. Sabine influence on Roman religion was especially strong. They became Roman citizens in 268 BC.

sable A carnivorous mammal, *Martes zibellina*, native to N Europe and Asia. It is less than 50 cm long and has thicker legs and longer ears than other *martens. Its coat is valued as fur (Siberian sable).

sabre-toothed tiger An extinct *cat that lived 30 million years ago and became extinct in the Pleistocene epoch (1 million years ago). It was about the size of a tiger, with very long upper canine teeth.

saccharin An organic compound (C_7H_5-NO_3S) used as a sweetening agent in the food industry and as a sugar substitute. It has about five hundred times the sweetening power of table sugar.

sackbut. *See* trombone.

sacrament In Christian theology, a ritual conferring inner grace in its participants. The Roman Catholic Church and Orthodox Churches accept seven sacraments: baptism, confirmation, penance, the *Eucharist, marriage, holy orders, and anointing of the sick (formerly called extreme unction). Baptism and the Eucharist are the only commonly accepted sacraments among the Protestant Churches.

Sacramento 38 32N 121 30W A city in the USA, the capital of California on the Sacramento River. Founded in 1839, it grew after the discovery of gold nearby in 1848. Linked by canal (1963) to San Francisco Bay, it is a deepwater port and serves an extensive agricultural area. Population (1986 est): 323 550.

Sadat, Anwar (1918–81) Egyptian statesman; president (1970–81). He negotiated a peace agreement with Israel in 1979 and shared the 1978 Nobel Peace Prize with Israel's President Begin. He was assassinated (1981) by Islamic extremists.

Sadducees An ancient Jewish religious and political party. They formed a conservative and aristocratic group centring on the priesthood in Jerusalem. With the destruction of the temple (70 AD) the party ceased to exist. *See also* Pharisees.

Sade, Donatien Alphonse François, Marquis de (1740–1814) French novelist. Most of his works of sexual fantasy and perversion, which include *Justine, La Philosophie dans le boudoir*, and *Les 120 Journées de Sodome*, were written in the 1780s and 1790s, during his imprisonment for sexual offences. Sadism, in which sexual pleasure is derived from causing or observing pain, is named after him.

Sadler's Wells Theatre A theatre in London where Lilian Baylis (1874–1937) established an opera and ballet company in 1931. From the 1680s the medicinal wells on the site were exploited and its owner, Mr Sadler, later erected a music hall. In 1753 this became a theatre. Since the removal of the Sadler's Wells Opera Company to the London Coliseum in 1969, the theatre has been used by touring companies. *See also* Royal Ballet.

safflower A plant, *Carthamus tinctorius*, of the daisy family, native to Asia and Africa. It is cultivated for its seeds, which yield safflower oil, used in paints, varnishes, cooking oils, and margarines.

saffron The dried orange-yellow stigmas of the saffron crocus (*Crocus sativa*), used for flavouring and colouring foods and liqueurs and formerly as a fabric dye. The crocus, which has purple flowers, is cultivated mainly in France, Spain, and Italy.

sagas Stories about heroes in Old Norse, the best of which were written in Iceland in the 12th and 13th centuries. Subject matter was drawn from ancient Scandinavian legends and included fictionalized accounts of the deeds of Norwegian kings, for example *Heimskringla* by Snorri Sturluson (1178–1241).

sage A herb or shrub, *Salvia officinalis*, native to the Mediterranean region and widely cultivated for its leaves, which are used for flavouring foods. It has blue, pink, or white flowers. *See also* salvia.

sago A starchy food obtained mainly from the pithy stems of the Indonesian sago palms (*Metoxylon sagu* and *M. rumphii*), cultivated in Malaysia.

Sahara The largest desert in the world, covering most of N Africa. The terrain consists chiefly of a plateau with central mountains rising to 3415 m (11 204 ft) and some areas of sand dunes. There are large deposits of oil and gas in Algeria and Libya and phosphates in Morocco and Western Sahara. Area: about 9 000 000 sq km (3 474 171 sq mi).

saiga A small antelope, *Saiga tatarica*, of Asian deserts and steppes. Saigas have a swollen snout with highly twisted nasal passages, thought to be used for warming inhaled air or to be related to their keen sense of smell. Males have straight ridged horns.

Saigon. *See* Ho Chi Minh City.

saint In Christian belief, a person having special holiness. In the Roman Catholic Church, persons admitted to the calendar of saints by *canonization can be addressed in prayer. Protestantism rejects this, although the Church of England's calendar recognizes a number of saints' days.

St Albans 51 46N 0 21W A city in SE England, in Hertfordshire. It was an important Romano-British town, Verulamium, where the martyrdom of St *Alban took place. The Benedictine abbey, founded in 793 AD, was made a cathedral in 1877. Industries include printing and electrical equipment. Population (1981): 50 888.

St Andrews 56 20N 2 48W A resort in E Scotland, in Fife Region on St Andrews Bay. An ancient ecclesiastical centre, its university (1412) is the oldest in Scotland. The famous Royal and Ancient Golf Club was founded here in 1754. Population (1985 est): 16 000.

St Bartholomew's Day Massacre The slaughter of *Huguenots that began on 24 August, 1572, in Paris. The massacre was ordered by Charles IX of France under the influence of his mother, Catherine de' Medici. Some 3000 Huguenots died in Paris and many more were murdered in the provinces.

St Bernard A breed of large working dog developed in Europe from Asian ancestors and employed as a rescue dog by the hospice of St Bernard in the Swiss Alps since the 17th century. It has a large head with drooping ears. The coat is white marked with red-brown or brindle (tawny with dark flecks). Height: 65 cm minimum.

St Croix (*or* Santa Cruz) A West Indian island, the largest of the US Virgin Islands. The economy is based on tourism and agriculture. Area: 207 sq km (80 sq mi). Population (1985) 55 300. Chief town: Christiansted.

St David's 51 54N 5 16W A village in SW Wales in Dyfed, the smallest cathedral city in Britain. The 12th-century cathedral, the largest in Wales, was an important medieval pilgrimage centre for the shrine of St David. Population (1984): 1595.

St Dunstan's (for Men and Women Blinded on War Service) A British organization for the training, settlement, and lifelong care of those blinded in war. It was founded in 1915 by a blind newspaper proprietor, Sir Arthur Pearson (1866–1921).

St George's 12 04N 61 44W The capital of Grenada, on the SW coast, both a port and tourist resort. Founded by the French in the 17th century, it was capital of the British Windward Islands from 1885 to 1958. Population (1981): 4788.

St George's Channel A channel between SE Ireland and Wales, linking the Irish Sea with the Atlantic Ocean. Length: about 160 km (100 mi). Maximum width: 145 km (90 mi).

St Helena 15 58S 5 43W A mountainous island in the S Atlantic Ocean, a British dependent territory. Napoleon I was exiled here (1815–21).

Area: 122 sq km (47 sq mi). Population (1988): 5564. Capital: Jamestown.

St Helens, Mount 46 12N 122 11W A volcano in the USA, in SW Washington state in the S Cascade Range. Dormant since 1857, the mountain erupted in May, 1980, causing widespread destruction. Height: 2950 m (9677 ft).

St Helier 49 12N 2 07W A market town and resort in the Channel Islands, on the S coast of Jersey. There is a substantial trade in early vegetables and Jersey cattle. Population (1981): 25 698.

St James's Palace A royal palace in Pall Mall, in London, built for Henry VIII on the site of an 11th-century hospital. It was the principal London residence of the monarch from 1697, when Whitehall was burnt down, until superseded by Buckingham Palace in 1837.

St John's 47 34N 52 41W A city in E Canada, the capital and commercial centre of Newfoundland. Settled in the 16th century, it is located beside a huge protected harbour. Population (1986): 96 216.

St John's wort A perennial plant found in temperate regions. It has yellow five-petalled flowers with many stamens and some species are cultivated in gardens, including *Hypericum calycinum* (also known as rose of Sharon).

St Kilda 57 49N 8 34W A group of three small mountainous islands off the Scottish mainland, the most westerly of the Outer Hebrides. Evacuated in 1930, they are now a nature reserve. Area: about 16 sq km (6 sq mi).

St Kitts-Nevis, Federation of (*or* St Christopher-Nevis) A country in the West Indies, in the Leeward Islands in the E Caribbean Sea. From 1967 it was a UK associated state consisting of three islands: St Kitts, Nevis, and Anguilla. Anguilla became a separate British dependency in 1980. St Kitts-Nevis became fully independent within the British Commonwealth in 1983. The economy is primarily agricultural, with tourism increasing. Prime minister: Dr Kennedy Simmonds. Area: 262 sq km (101 sq mi). Population (1987 est): 47 000. Capital: Basseterre, on St Kitts.

Saint-Laurent, Yves (1936–) French fashion designer, who trained with Dior and took over his fashion house (1957), opening his own in 1962. He was the first to introduce ready-to-wear designer clothes on a mass basis.

St Lawrence River A river in North America that drains the *Great Lakes into the Atlantic Ocean at the Gulf of St Lawrence. From Lake Ontario it flows NE along the Canadian-US border to Quebec, where it broadens into a long estuary. Length: Lake Ontario to Quebec 480 km (298 mi); St Louis River headwaters to Anticosti Island 3395 km (2110 mi). *See also* St Lawrence Seaway.

St Lawrence Seaway A navigable waterway in North America through the St Lawrence River and the Great Lakes, completed in 1959. It admits ships of up to 9000 tons.

St Leger A flat race for three-year-old horses, run in September at Doncaster over 2.9 km (1 mi 6½ furlongs). It was the earliest of the English *Classics to be established (1776).

St Louis 38 40N 90 15W A city and port in the USA, in Missouri on the Mississippi River. A major centre in the colonization of the West, it is now a large industrial and university city and an important agricultural market. Population (1986 est): 429 300.

St Lucia An island country in the West Indies, in the Windward Islands in the E Caribbean Sea. The economy is mainly agricultural, with a growing tourist industry. St Lucia became internally self-governing in 1967 and attained full independence within the British Commonwealth in February, 1979. Prime minister: John Compton. Official language: English. Official currency: East Caribbean dollar of 100 cents. Area: 616 sq km (238 sq mi). Population (1988 est): 146 600. Capital: Castries.

St Mark's Cathedral The cathedral church of Venice since 1807. It was built in the 9th century to house the relics of St Mark and rebuilt in the 11th century after a fire. Designed as a Greek cross with five domes, it is strongly influenced by *Byzantine art.

St Moritz 46 30N 9 51E A resort in SE Switzerland, on St Moritz Lake. A renowned wintersports centre, its Cresta Run (for bobsleds) dates from 1885. Population (1980): 5900. Altitude: 1822 m (5978 ft).

St Paul 45 00N 93 10W A city in the USA, the capital of Minnesota on the Mississippi River. Adjacent to Minneapolis, the Twin Cities comprise the commercial and industrial centre of an extensive grain and cattle area. Population (1986 est): 263 680.

St Paul's Cathedral The cathedral of the diocese of London; there have been five cathedrals on this site, the first three of which were Saxon. The present building was designed (1672–1717) by Sir Christopher Wren and replaced the Norman structure burnt down in the Great Fire (1666). Built in the traditional shape of a cross, it has a classical two-tiered portico, a great dome, and flanking towers.

St Peter Port 49 27N 2 32W A resort in the Channel Islands, the only town in Guernsey. It has a large protected harbour. Population (1986): 16 085.

St Peter's Basilica The largest church in the world, in the Vatican City, Rome. Dating from the 16th century, it was designed by Michelangelo to replace the original gothic building. Giacomo da Vignola (1507–73) continued the work and the nave and façade were added by Carlo Maderna (1556–1629). *Bernini completed the building in the 17th century.

St Petersburg. *See* Leningrad.

Saint-Saëns, Camille (1835–1921) French composer, conductor, pianist, and organist. His compositions include 12 operas, five symphonies, *The Carnival of the Animals* (published posthumously; 1922), and five piano concertos.

St Vincent, Cape 37 01N 8 59W A promontory in the extreme SW of Portugal, in the Algarve on the Atlantic Ocean. In 1797 the Spanish fleet was defeated by the British during the Napoleonic Wars.

St Vincent and the Grenadines A country in the E Caribbean Sea, in the Windward Islands of the Lesser Antilles. It consists of the principal island of St Vincent together with its dependencies of the Grenadine islets. A British possession since 1763 it became fully independent in 1979. It is predominantly agricultural. Prime minister: James Mitchell. Area: 390 sq km (150 sq mi). Population (1987): 112 000. Capital: Kingstown.

saké (*or* rice wine) An alcoholic drink made in Japan from fermented steamed rice and yeast. It resembles sherry in taste and is served warm.

Sakharov, Andrei Dimitrievich (1921–89) Soviet physicist. After helping to develop the Soviet hydrogen bomb during the 1940s and 1950s he spoke out against nuclear weapons in the 1960s and argued for freedom of speech in the Soviet Union. He was awarded the Nobel Peace Prize in 1975. His exile to Gorkii in 1980 aroused international protest; released in 1986, he became a member of the new Congress of People's Deputies in 1989.

Saki (H(ector) H(ugh) Munro; 1870–1916) British writer. Born in Burma, he settled in London in 1908. He published several volumes of humorous short stories many of which featured his snobbish heroes Clovis and Reginald. He was killed in action in World War I.

Saladin (?1137–93) The leader of the Muslims against the Crusaders in Syria. He obtained control over the Muslim lands in Egypt, of which he became sultan in 1175, and Syria. After defeating the Crusaders at the battle of Hattin (1187) he captured the Kingdom of Jerusalem. During the third *Crusade he won his legendary reputation as a chivalrous warrior.

Salam, Abdus (1926–) Pakistani physicist, who became professor of physics at Imperial College, London, in 1957. In 1979 he shared the Nobel Prize with the US physicists Sheldon Glashow (1932–) and Steven Weinberg (1933–) for their work on weak interactions. *See* particle physics.

Salamanca 40 58N 5 40W A city in central Spain, in Salamanca province. In 1812, during the Peninsular War, Wellington defeated the French here. Salamanca is an important cultural centre with a university (founded 1218). Its many notable old buildings include two cathedrals. Population (1986): 166 615.

salamander A widely distributed tailed *amphibian with short legs and a long body. Salamanders usually hide in damp places when not hunting worms and insects. Some live entirely in water while others spend all their time on land.

Salerno 40 40N 14 46E A port in Italy, in Campania on the Gulf of Salerno. Founded by the Romans in 197 BC, its medical school flourished in the middle ages. Population (1987): 153 807.

Salic Law The law of the Salian *Franks issued under Clovis in the early 6th century. Its prohibition against women inheriting land was used in France in 1316 and 1321 to prevent a woman from succeeding to the throne. In 1328 Edward III's claim to the French Crown was rejected on the grounds that his claim was by female descent.

Salisbury. *See* Harare.
Salisbury 51 05N 1 48W A city in S England, in Wiltshire. Its 13th-century cathedral has the highest spire (123 m) in the country. Industries include light engineering and brewing. Population (1983 est): 40 000.
Salisbury, Robert Cecil, 1st Earl of. *See* Burghley, William Cecil, Lord.
Salisbury, Robert Arthur Talbot Gascoyne-Cecil, 3rd Marquess of (1830–1903) British statesman; Conservative prime minister (1885–86, 1886–92, 1895–1902). Elected an MP in 1853, he became Disraeli's foreign secretary in 1878. Under Salisbury, Britain made no formal alliances until that with Japan in 1902.
saliva The fluid that binds food in the mouth and lubricates the gullet to aid swallowing. It also contains a starch-digesting enzyme. In humans, saliva is secreted by three pairs of **salivary glands.**
Sallust (Gaius Sallustius Crispus; c. 86–c. 34 BC) Roman politican and historian. Expelled from the Senate for alleged immorality, he supported Julius Caesar in the war against Pompey and became governor of Numidia. He was accused of corruption and extortion and retired from politics in about 44 BC.
salmon One of several fish valued as food, especially the Atlantic salmon (*Salmo salar*), up to 150 cm long. Salmon live mainly in the sea, feeding on other fish, but migrate into fresh water to lay their eggs (spawn). After spawning the adult fish either die or return to the sea and spawn in following years. At about two years, the young salmon migrate to the sea. After about two to three years they return to their native spawning waters, guided upstream by their sense of smell.
Salmonella Rod-shaped bacteria that are parasites of animals and humans and cause several diseases, including *typhoid fever and *food poisoning.
Salonika. *See* Thessaloníki.
salp. *See* tunicate.
salsify A plant, *Tragopogon porrifolius*, of the daisy family, native to the Mediterranean region. It is cultivated in temperate regions for its fleshy white root, supposed to taste like oysters when cooked. The plant has long narrow leaves, used in salads, and purple flowers.
salt **1.** (sodium chloride; NaCl) The crystalline solid that is used for seasoning and preserving food and is present in sea water and the mineral halite, its chief sources. It has an important function in the human body and is used in the manufacture of many chemicals, such as soap, fertilizer, and ceramics. **2.** Any similar compound formed, together with water, when an acid reacts with a base.
Salt Lake City 40 45N 111 55W A city in the USA, the capital of Utah near Great Salt Lake. Founded in 1847 by the Mormons under the leadership of Brigham Young, it is the world headquarters of the Mormon Church. Population (1986 est): 158 440.
saltpetre (potassium nitrate *or* nitre; KNO_3) A white crystalline solid used as a *fertilizer, a food preservative, and in *gunpowder and fireworks.

Salvador (*or* Bahia) 12 58S 38 29W A port in NE Brazil, the capital of Bahia state on the Atlantic Ocean. It has a fine natural harbour. Population (1985): 1 811 367.
Salvador. *See* El Salvador, Republic of.
Salvation Army The international Christian organization founded in 1865 in London by William *Booth and run on strictly military lines. It is famous for its social and evangelistic work.
salvia A plant or shrub widely distributed in temperate and tropical regions. Many species are cultivated in gardens, including the Brazilian scarlet sage (*Salvia splendens*). *See also* sage.
Salyut A series of manned Soviet space stations first launched into earth orbit in 1971. Crews were conveyed to and from the orbiting laboratory by Soyuz spacecraft. They lived in weightless conditions, conducting a variety of experiments and observations. The series was superseded by the Mir stations.
Salzburg 47 54N 13 03E A city in central Austria. Mozart was born here and a famous musical event, the Salzburg Festival, is held annually. Population (1981): 138 317.
Samar The third largest island in the Philippines, in the Visayan Islands linked by bridge to Leyte. The chief products are rice, coconuts, and hemp. Copper and iron ore are mined. Area: 13 415 sq km (5181 sq mi). Population (1980): 1 200 592. Chief town: Catbalogan.
Samara. *See* Kuibyshev.
Samaria **1.** The central region of ancient Palestine, which became part of the northern kingdom of Israel in the 10th century BC. *See also* Samaritans. **2.** 32 17N 35 12E The capital city of Israel from the 9th century until its destruction in about 721 BC by the Assyrians. It was rebuilt in the 1st century AD and renamed Sebaste.
Samaritans **1.** A people of ancient *Samaria with a religion close to Judaism but much disliked by the Jews. **2.** A British telephone service for the suicidal and despairing, started in 1953 by the Rev Chad Varah (1911–) in a London church (St Stephen Walbrook). A nonreligious charity, it has over 183 branches in the UK, manned by 22 000 volunteers.
samarium (Sm) A *lanthanide element, discovered 1879, that occurs naturally, with other lanthanides, in monazite ($CePO_4$). At no 62; at wt 150.4; mp 1077 ± 5°C; bp 1791°C.
Samarkand 39 40N 66 57E A city in the S central Soviet Union. It was the chief junction of the ancient *Silk Road between China and the Mediterranean and became (9th–10th centuries) a great Islamic centre. In the 14th century it was the capital of *Timur's empire, then came under the rule of the Muslim *Uzbek people (16th–19th centuries). The city's historic buildings include Timur's mausoleum. Population (1987): 388 000.
Samoa A chain of volcanic islands in the S central Pacific Ocean. Discovered by the Dutch in the 18th century, the islands were politically divided in 1900 between the USA and Germany. **American Samoa** comprises the E islands of the chain; the chief island is Tutuila. Area: 197 sq km (76 sq mi). Population (1981 est): 33 000. Capital: Pago Pago. **Western Samoa** was a Ger-

man protectorate until World War I and then under New Zealand control, becoming an independent state in 1962; the main islands are Savai'i and Upolu. Head of state: HH Malietoa Tanumafili II (1913–). Official languages: Samoan and English. Official currency: Western Samoa dollar. Area: 2842 sq km (1097 sq mi). Population (1986 est): 163 000. Capital: Apia.

Samoyed A group of Siberian peoples of the tundra and N forest region of the central Soviet Union. They are now mainly reindeer breeders. *Shamanism dominates their religious life. They developed the Samoyed breed of dog for pulling sledges; it resembles the husky.

samurai The provincial warriors who rose to power in Japan in the 11th century. Most became the vassals of *daimyo* (feudal lords) and were regarded as a superior class. After the Meiji restoration (1868) the samurai became leaders in various areas of modern Japanese life.

Sana'a 15 23N 44 14E The capital of Yemen. Notable buildings include the Great Mosque, where there is a sacred Muslim shrine. Population (1986): 427 185.

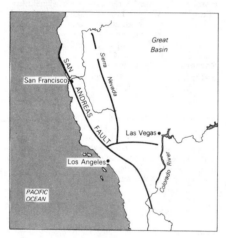

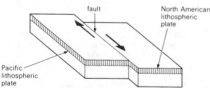

SAN ANDREAS FAULT *An example of a tear fault in which the rocks are being displaced horizontally.*

San Andreas Fault A fracture in the earth's crust, 1200 km (750 mi) in length, running through California. In 1906 a horizontal displacement of about six metres and a lateral displacement (widening) of only one metre caused an earthquake that devastated San Francisco. In 1989 another earthquake damaged the city.

San Antonio 29 25N 98 30W A city in the USA, in Texas. Founded in 1718, it was the scene of the Mexican attack on the *Alamo (1836) during the Texan revolution. San Antonio is a commercial and industrial centre for a large agricultural region. Population (1986 est): 914 350.

sanctions Penalties imposed for breaking a law, especially international law, first imposed by the *League of Nations on Italy following its invasion of Ethiopia. Recent sanctions include those imposed by UN countries against Rhodesia (now *Zimbabwe), following its unilateral declaration of independence in 1965, against South Africa (1985), and against Iraq (1990).

sand Loose grains of rock, varying in size from 0.06 to 2 mm in diameter. Consolidated sands form *sandstones. Most sands consist principally of *quartz, derived from the weathering of quartz-bearing rocks. Sand is used in glass and cement producticon, and as an abrasive.

Sand, George (Aurore Dupin, Baronne Dudevant; 1804–76) French novelist. *Indiana* (1832) was the first of an enormous number of successful novels. Among her many lovers were Alfred de Musset and Frédéric Chopin.

sandalwood An evergreen tree, *Santalum album*, native to SE Asia and the Pacific Islands. Its white wood is used to make boxes and furniture and, when distilled, yields sweet-scented sandalwood oil.

sanderling A bird, *Calidris alba*, that nests on Arctic coasts and winters on shores worldwide. 20 cm long, it has a rust-coloured upper plumage, changing to pale-brown in winter, and a long white wing stripe. It feeds on shrimps and other small animals.

sand flea. *See* sand hopper.

sandfly A small fly that is one of the worst pests of the tropics: the bloodsucking females can give a painful bite and several species are carriers of serious human diseases. The name has also been used for many bloodsucking gnats and midges of sandy places.

sand hopper A small jumping *crustacean, also called sand flea. Its deep narrow body lacks a carapace. During the day it is buried in sand but at night it emerges to feed on organic debris.

Sandhurst 51 02N 0 34E A village in SE England, in Berkshire. The Royal Military Academy (1799) for training officers and the National Army Museum are situated here. Population (1985 est): 17 832.

San Diego 32 45N 117 10W A city in the USA, in California on San Diego Bay. It has a US naval base and is also an important centre of scientific research. Population (1989 est): 1 086 600.

sandpiper A wading bird occurring chiefly in the N hemisphere. Sandpipers breed in northerly latitudes and migrate south to winter. They typically have long legs, long wings, a mottled brown or grey plumage, which commonly changes colour seasonally, and a long slender bill. They nest in marshy regions or on mud flats.

Sandringham 52 49N 0 30E A village in E England, in Norfolk. The Sandringham estate was bought by Queen Victoria for the Prince of Wales (later Edward VII) in 1861. Sandringham

House remains a royal residence. Population (1981): 440.

sandstone A *sedimentary rock formed from deposits of *sand grains in deserts, shallow seas, estuaries and deltas, and along low-lying coasts by water. Sandstones vary in colour from red to yellow to white.

Sandwich, John Montagu, 4th Earl of (1718–92) British politician; first lord of the admiralty (1748–51, 1771–82). The failure of the navy during the American Revolution was blamed on his corrupt practices. He gave his name to the sandwich, a snack to keep up his strength during a 24-hour gambling session.

San Francisco 37 40N 122 25W A city in the USA, in California situated on a peninsula between San Francisco Bay and the Pacific Ocean. It is a major seaport, the financial and insurance centre of the West Coast, and a major cultural and educational centre. Its many famous landmarks include the Golden Gate Bridge (1937). Founded by the Spanish in 1776, it was captured by the USA (1846) during the Mexican War. It expanded rapidly following the discovery of gold in California (1848). In 1906 San Francisco was almost completely destroyed by an earthquake and three-day fire. In 1989 another earthquake caused some 70 deaths. Population (1986 est): 749 000.

San José 37 20N 121 55W A city in the USA, in California on the S arm of San Francisco Bay. Founded in 1777, it was the first city in California and state capital (1849–51). It has food-processing plants and wineries as well as aerospace and electronics industries. Population (1986 est): 712 080.

San José 9 50N 84 02W The capital of Costa Rica, situated in the centre of the country. Founded in 1736, it is the centre of the tobacco trade and coffee production. Population (1984): 241 464.

San Juan 18 29N 66 08W The capital and main port of Puerto Rico, in the N. Founded by the Spanish in 1508, it was captured by the US navy in 1898. It is an industrial and tourist centre. Population (1984 est): 431 227.

San Marino, Republic of A small independent republic, an enclave in Italian territory, situated on the slopes of the Apennines mountain range, SW of Rimini. Farming, tourism, and the sale of postage stamps are the main sources of income. Official language: Italian. Official currency: both Italian and Vatican City currencies are in use. Area: 61 sq km (24 sq mi). Population (1988): 22 746. Capital: San Marino.

San Martín, José de (1778–1850) South American soldier and statesman; the national hero of Argentina. He raised and trained an army in Argentina (1814–16) and, with Bernardo O'Higgins, defeated the Spanish at Chacubuco (1817) and Maipo (1818), liberating Chile. In 1821 he entered Lima, proclaimed the independence of Peru, and became its "protector." He resigned in 1822, after arguments with Bolivar, and retired to France.

San Salvador 13 59N 89 18W The capital of El Salvador since 1839. Founded by the Spanish in 1525, it has suffered several severe earthquakes,

most recently in 1986. Industries include textiles and food processing. Population (1985 est): 459 902.

Sanskrit The classical literary language of the Hindu scriptures, belonging to the Indo-Aryan family. From it modern N Indian languages developed. It was spoken in NW India from 1500 BC, becoming a scholarly language in the 5th century BC, and is still used as a sacred language.

Santa Anna, Antonio López de (1794–1876) Mexican soldier and statesman; president (1833–36) and dictator (1839, 1841–45). Santa Anna dominated Mexican politics from 1823 until driven into exile in 1845. He is best known for his defeat of Texan forces at the *Alamo (1836).

Santa Cruz 17 45S 63 14W A city in SE Bolivia. It is the commercial centre for an area producing chiefly sugar cane, rice, and coffee. Industries include the manufacture of cigarettes and sugar refining. Population (1985 est): 441 717.

Santa Isabel. *See* Malabo.

Santayana, George (1863–1952) Spanish-born US philosopher and poet. His philosophy was set out in *Realms of Being* (1927–40). His works include *The Sense of Beauty* (1896), *The Life of Reason* (1905–06), *Scepticism and Animal Faith* (1923), and *The Last Puritan* (1935).

Santiago (or Santiago de Chile) 33 35S 70 40W The capital of Chile, situated in the centre of the country at the foot of the Andes. It was founded by the Spanish in 1541 and is now a major industrial centre. Population (1987 est): 4 858 342.

Santo Domingo 18 32N 69 50W The capital of the Dominican Republic, a port on the S coast. Founded by Columbus in 1496, it became the capital of the first Spanish colony in the Americas and is the site of the first cathedral (1521) and the first university (1538) in the New World. It became the capital of the new Dominican Republic in 1844. Population (1983 est): 1 410 000.

Saône, River A river in E France, rising in Lorraine and flowing mainly S to join the River Rhône at Lyons. It is linked by canal to the Rivers Moselle, Rhine, Loire, Seine, and Meuse. Length: 480 km (298 mi).

São Paulo 23 33S 46 39W The largest city in Brazil. Founded in 1554, it grew rapidly after 1880 with the development of coffee plantations. There has been considerable diversification of industry and it is now the fastest-growing city in Brazil. Population (1985): 10 099 086.

São Tomé and Príncipe, Democratic Republic of A small island country off the coast of West Africa, in the Gulf of Guinea, comprising two main islands and two islets. The main crops are cocoa, copra, palm oil and kernels, and coffee. Discovered by the Portuguese in 1471, the islands came under Portuguese rule in 1522. They became an overseas province in 1951 and gained independence in 1975. President: Dr Manuel Pinto da Costa. Official language: Portuguese. Official currency: dobra of 100 centavos. Area: 964 sq km (372 sq mi). Population (1988 est): 115 600. Capital and main port: São Tomé.

sap The fluid found in the vascular (conducting) system of plants. It consists of water and minerals in the *xylem vessels and sugars in the *phloem.

sapodilla An evergreen tree, *Achras sapota*, native to Central America but cultivated elsewhere in the tropics. It produces large edible brown rounded fruits, with a juicy pulp surrounding black seeds. Its milky latex is a source of chicle gum, used in chewing gum.

sapphire A transparent variety of *corundum that is usually blue but may be any colour except red. It is used as a gemstone and in record-player styluses. Sapphires are obtained from igneous and metamorphic gravels.

Sappho (c. 612–c. 580 BC) Greek lyric poet. Her passionate poetry was written for her group of female admirers on the island of Lesbos (from which the term "lesbianism" is derived).

Sapporo 43 5N 141 21E A city in Japan, in SW Hokkaido. It is the island's main administrative and educational centre and a ski resort. Industries include brewing. Population (1989): 1 642 011.

saprophyte An organism that obtains its energy by feeding on dead or decaying tissue. Bacteria and fungi are important saprophytes, using enzymes to break down organic material and release nutrients into the soil, which can be used by plants.

Saragossa. *See* Zaragoza.

Sarajevo 43 52N 18 26E A city and industrial centre in W central Yugoslavia, the capital of Bosnia and Hercegovina. It was here that *Francis Ferdinand was assassinated (28 June, 1914). Population (1982): 448 500.

Saratoga, Battles of (19 September and 7 October, 1777) Two battles fought near Saratoga, New York, in which the British were defeated during the *American Revolution. The outcome of the battles helped persuade the French to recognize and support the USA.

Sarawak A state in Malaysia, in NW *Borneo on the South China Sea. Rubber, pepper, sago, and rice are grown on the swampy coastal plain, and oil production is of prime importance. Given in 1841 by the sultan of Brunei to the Englishman James Brooke, it became a British protectorate in 1888 and joined Malaysia in 1963. Area: 124 970 sq km (48 250 sq mi). Population (1985 est): 1 477 428. Capital: Kuching.

sardine. *See* pilchard.

Sardinia The second largest island in the Mediterranean Sea, comprising an autonomous region of Italy. It is largely mountainous. Agriculture is important. Its major industry is mineral production, especially lead, zinc, coal, fluorspar, and sea salt. First settled by the Phoenicians, it was given to Savoy by Austria (1720) in exchange for Sicily and formed the kingdom of Sardinia with Piedmont. Area: 23 813 sq km (9194 sq mi). Population (1987 est): 1 651 218. Capital: Cagliari.

Sargasso Sea An oval section of the N Atlantic Ocean between latitudes 20°N and 35°N and longitudes 30°W and 70°W. Still and warm, it takes its name from the floating brown seaweed (*Sargassum*), found in it.

Sargent, Sir Malcolm (1895–1967) British conductor and organist. He was chief conductor at the London Promenade Concerts (1957–67) and conductor of the BBC Symphony Orchestra (1950–57).

Sark 49 26N 2 22W The smallest of the four main Channel Islands. It consists of Great Sark and Little Sark, connected by a narrow isthmus. Cars are prohibited here. Area: 5 sq km (2 sq mi). Population (1981): 560.

sarsaparilla An extract of the roots of a climbing or trailing vine, *Smilax aristolochiaefolia*, cultivated in Central and South America. The dried roots are used as a tonic and as flavouring for medicines and drinks.

Sartre, Jean-Paul (1905–80) French philosopher, novelist, dramatist, and critic. A leading existentialist (*see* existentialism), his major works of philosophy include *Being and Nothingness* (1943). His novels include *Nausea* (1938) and the trilogy *The Roads to Freedom* (1945–49). Among his plays are *In Camera* (1944) and *Lucifer and the Lord* (1951).

SAS. *See* Special Air Service.

Saskatchewan A province of W Canada, on the Great Plains. The open prairie of the S is one of the world's most important wheatlands. The province is rich in minerals, including uranium, oil, natural gas, potash, zinc, and copper; associated industries are important. Explored in the 17th and 18th centuries, Saskatchewan became a province in 1905. Area: 570 269 sq km (220 181 sq mi). Population (1986): 1 009 613. Capital: Regina.

sassafras A North American tree, *Sassafras albidum*, of the laurel family. It bears clusters of yellow flowers and dark-blue berries. The aromatic roots are dried for use in medicines and yield oil of sassafras, used in perfumes and flavourings.

Sassoon, Siegfried (1886–1967) British poet and writer. In 1917 his disgust with the progress of World War I led him to make a public refusal to serve, for which he was sent to a military hospital. His antiwar poetry appeared in *The Old Huntsman* (1917) and *Counterattack* (1918), and he wrote several volumes of autobiographical war memoirs.

satellite 1. A celestial body orbiting a *planet. There are at least 50 known satellites, including the rings of Saturn, Uranus, and Jupiter; Mercury and Venus have no satellites. Spacecraft have sent back information on various satellites, including the earth's moon, the *Galilean satellites, Saturn's rings and its largest satellite Titan, and the satellites of Uranus. Many small satellites have been discovered by these spacecraft, notably several of Uranus (1986).
2. A spacecraft that orbits the earth or some other solar-system body. It may be a *communications satellite or it may gather information from earth or from other celestial objects and transmit it, by radio signals, to ground-based receiving stations. This information is used, for example, in weather forecasting, navigation, scientific and astronomical research, and for military purposes.

Planet & Satellite	diameter (km)	distance from primary (km)	year of discovery	Planet & Satellite	diameter (km)	distance from primary (km)	year of discovery
EARTH				SATURN			
Moon	3476	384 400	—	Janus	200	159 000	1966
MARS				Mimas	400	186 000	1789
Phobos	27	9380	1877	Enceladus	600	238 000	1789
Deimos	15	23 500	1877	Tethys	1000	295 000	1684
JUPITER				Dione	800	377 000	1684
Adrastea	40?	128 000	1979	Rhea	1500	527 000	1672
Metis	40?	128 000	1979	Titan	5800	1 222 000	1655
Amalthea	150	181 000	1892	Hyperion	400	1 483 000	1848
Thebe	80?	221 000	1979	Iapetus	1500	3 560 000	1671
Io	3630	422 000	1610	Phoebe	200	12 950 000	1898
Europa	3140	671 000	1610	URANUS			
Ganymede	5260	1 070 000	1610	Miranda	400	130 000	1948
Callisto	4800	1 880 000	1610	Ariel	1400	192 000	1851
Leda	10?	11 110 000	1974	Umbriel	1000	267 000	1851
Himalia	180?	11 470 000	1904	Titania	1800	438 000	1787
Lysithea	20?	11 710 000	1938	Oberon	1600	586 000	1787
Elara	80?	11 740 000	1905	NEPTUNE			
Ananke	20?	20 700 000	1951	Triton	3800	355 000	1846
Carme	30?	22 350 000	1938	Nereid	300	5 562 000	1949
Pasiphae	40?	23 300 000	1908	PLUTO			
Sinope	30?	23 700 000	1914	I	800?	20 000?	1978

Satie, Erik (1866–1925) French composer, whose clarity of style influenced many 20th-century composers. His works include the ballet *Parade* (1916), piano pieces, including *Trois Gymnopédies* (1888), and many songs.

satinwood A tree, *Chloroxylon swietenia*, native to S India and Sri Lanka. Its wood is valued in furniture making for its fine golden-yellow finish. The wood of certain West Indian trees is also known as satinwood.

satsuma. *See* tangerine.

Saturn (astronomy) The second largest planet, orbiting the sun every 29.5 years at a mean distance of 1427 million km. Its equatorial diameter is 120 000 km and it is made up primarily of hydrogen and helium. The dominant feature is **Saturn's rings**, lying in the equatorial plane and tilted at 27° to the orbital plane. There are six rings, differing in brightness and width but are all composed of small icy chunks. The overall diameter is almost 600 000 km but the thickness is only a few hundred metres. Saturn also has at least 20 *satellites.

Saturn (mythology) The Roman god of agriculture and father of the gods, identified with the Greek *Cronus. Various aspects of the Saturnalia, his annual festival held in December, were taken over by the Christian festival of Christmas.

Satyrs and Sileni In Greek mythology, male fertility spirits of the woods and fields, usually portrayed with goats' legs and pointed ears or horns. Associated with *Dionysus, they were typically drunk and lustful. *See also* Silenus.

Saudi Arabia, Kingdom of A country in the Middle East comprising most of *Arabia, bordering on the Red Sea and the Persian Gulf. In the N and SE are large areas of desert. The population is mainly Arab Muslim. *Economy*: based on oil in the Persian Gulf, exploited since 1938. The country, a member of OPEC, is the world's greatest exporter of oil. *History*: the establishment of Saudi Arabia (1932) under *Ibn Saud followed the 19th-century struggle by the Saud family to dominate the warring tribes of the peninsula and take overall control from Turkey. Saudi Arabia became a founding member of the Arab League (1945). Under Ibn Saud's son, *Faisal Ibn Abdul Aziz, there was economic development. The present king, since 1982, is a brother of Faisal, Fahd Ibn Abdul Aziz. In 1991 Saudi Arabia became a member of the alliance against Iraq in the second Gulf War. Official language: Arabic. Official currency: rial of 100 nilalas. Area: 2 400 000 sq km (927 000 sq mi). Population (1988 est): 12 000 000. Capital: Riyadh. Chief port: Jidda.

Saul In the Old Testament, the first King of Israel, who reigned in the 11th century BC. Son of Kish, he was anointed king by Samuel. He won a great victory over the Ammonites and fought many battles against the Philistines. His last years saw a growing enmity with *David.

Saunders, Dame Cicely Mary Strode (1918–) British philanthropist. After training as a nurse, in 1967 she founded St Christopher's Hospice in London for the care of the terminally ill. *See also* hospice movement.

savanna (*or* savannah) The tropical grasslands bordering on the equatorial rain forests in both the N and S hemispheres. They cover extensive areas in N Australia, Africa, and South America. The vegetation of savannas is dominated by tall grasses, such as elephant grass, which provide ideal grazing for cattle.

Savonarola, Girolamo (1452–98) Italian religious reformer. A Dominican prior in Florence from 1491, he began a crusade against religious and political corruption, attacking the papacy and the Medici. He became the virtual ruler of Florence when the Medici were expelled in 1494.

Excommunicated in 1497, he was hanged and burned for heresy.

savory A herb of warm and temperate regions. Summer savory (*Satureja hortensis*) is native to central Europe and Asia. Both the dried leaves and the oil extract are used for flavouring foods. Winter savory (*S. montana*) is also used in cookery.

Savoy An Alpine frontier region of SE France corresponding to the present-day departments of Savoie and Haute-Savoie. The county of Savoy was founded in 1034. Piedmont was acquired in the 14th century and Sardinia in 1720; Savoyard dukes then took the title King of Sardinia. In 1748 the kingdom became Piedmont-Sardinia and was prominent in the movement for Italian unification (*see* Risorgimento). Savoy became part of France in 1860, but the House of Savoy ruled the newly formed kingdom of Italy (1861–1946).

sawfly An insect, related to bees and wasps, the females of which possess a sawlike tubular organ used for inserting eggs into foliage and timber. The larvae, resembling caterpillars, damage trees.

Saxe-Coburg-Gotha The ruling dynasty of a German duchy. The children of Duke Francis Frederick (1750–1806) included Victoria Mary Louisa (1786–1861), who married (1818) Edward, Duke of Kent (their daughter was Queen Victoria), and Ernest I (1806–44), father of Prince Albert, who married Queen Victoria in 1840. The UK royal house was called Saxe-Coburg-Gotha until 1917, when the name *Windsor was adopted.

saxifrage A plant found in cold and temperate regions. The leaves may form a rosette at the base or grow in pairs along the stem and the flowers are white, yellow, purple, or red.

Saxons A Germanic people who, during the 5th century AD, expanded from their Baltic coastal homelands to other areas of N Germany, the coast of Gaul (France), and (with the *Angles and *Jutes) to Britain. *Charlemagne eventually defeated the continental Saxons in the 8th century and converted them to Christianity. *See also* Anglo-Saxons.

Saxony (German name: Sachsen) An ancient NW German duchy. Named after its original inhabitants, the *Saxons, it became part of Charlemagne's empire. In the 16th and 17th centuries Saxony became a leading German Protestant state. In 1697 Elector Frederick Augustus I (1670–1733) became King of Poland. Conquered by Napoleon in 1806, N Saxony was acquired by Prussia in 1815 and the remainder of Saxony joined the German Empire in 1871.

saxophone A woodwind instrument with a brass body, keys, and a single reed mouthpiece similar to that of a *clarinet. It was invented by the Belgian Adolphe Sax (1814–94) and patented in France in the 1840s. Saxophones are most commonly used as solo instruments in jazz.

scabious A plant that is native to the Mediterranean region and temperate parts of Eurasia and Africa. The small scabious (*Scabiosa columbaria*) has a cluster of small bluish-lilac flowers on a long stalk.

Scafell Pike 54 28N 3 12W The highest peak in England, in Cumbria, in the Lake District. Height: 978 m (3210 ft).

scale (music) An ascending or descending series of notes, characterized by a fixed pattern of intervals between the notes. In western music there are three **diatonic scales**: the major scale, the harmonic minor scale, and the melodic minor scale. The octave is divided into 12 notes and any of these scales may be constructed on these notes. The version of the scale produced is associated with a particular *tonality (key). The **chromatic scale** includes all 12 semitones of the octave.

scale insect An insect abundant in warm and tropical regions. Scale insects are usually small and the females are often legless, wingless, and eyeless and covered by a waxy scale. They become encrusted on plants and suck the juices, often becoming serious pests. Other species are of value by producing *shellac, *cochineal, and various waxes.

scallop An edible *bivalve mollusc of warm and temperate seas. The two plates, or valves, of the shell are broad, flattened, and deeply fluted, and the animal swims by flapping them with a single powerful muscle.

Scandinavian languages A subgroup of the Germanic group of languages consisting of *Swedish, *Norwegian, *Danish, *Icelandic, and Faeroese. The first three are similar enough to be mutually intelligible. They all developed from a common Scandinavian ancestor, which originally used the *runic alphabet (*see also* Old Norse). This language spread with the Vikings to Iceland and the Faeroes.

scandium (Sc) The first *transition metal, predicted by Mendeleyev and discovered in 1879. It is light (relative density 2.989) and has a high melting point. At no 21; at wt 44.956; mp 1541°C; bp 2831°C.

Scapa Flow A section of the Atlantic Ocean off the N coast of Scotland, in the Orkney Islands. It was the main base of the British Grand Fleet in World War I. Following its surrender, the German fleet scuttled itself here (1919). Length: about 24 km (15 mi). Width: 13 km (8 mi).

scarab beetle A beetle occurring worldwide. Scarabs include the largest beetles (the *goliath and *hercules beetles) and the *rhinoceros beetle. *Dung beetles are types of scarabs: the sacred scarabs of the ancient Egyptians were of this type.

Scarborough 54 17N 0 24W A resort in NE England, on the North Yorkshire coast. The promontory separating the North and South Bays is the site of a prehistoric settlement, a Roman signal station, and a 12th-century castle. There is fishing and tourism. Population (1989): 50 908.

Scarlatti, Domenico (1685–1757) Italian composer, harpsichordist, and organist, working in Lisbon from 1720 and in Madrid from 1729. Besides some operas and church music, he wrote over 600 harpsichord sonatas. His father **Alessandro Scarlatti** (1660–1725) was also a composer. His works include over a hundred operas, 600 chamber cantatas, 200 masses, 12 chamber symphonies, and 14 oratorios.

scarlet fever A highly infectious disease of children caused by streptococcus bacteria and characterized by a red rash over the whole body. Before antibiotics, scarlet fever killed many children or left them disabled with *rheumatic fever, kidney disease, or ear infections; it can now be rapidly cured with penicillin.

Schiller, (Johann Christoph) Friedrich (von) (1759–1805) German dramatist, poet, and writer. With Goethe's encouragement from 1794, Schiller produced brilliant dramas: the trilogy *Wallenstein* (1798–99), *Maria Stuart* (1800), *Die Jungfrau von Orleans* (1801), and *Wilhelm Tell* (1804). His other works include poems and an important essay on aesthetics.

schipperke A breed of dog originating in Flanders and used as a guard dog on barges. It has a stocky tailless body with short legs and a foxlike head with erect ears. The dense coat is usually black and thick around the neck, forming a mane. Height: 30.5–33 cm.

schistosomiasis (*or* bilharziasis) A widespread disease of the tropics caused by blood parasites (called flukes) of the genus *Schistosoma* (or *Bilharzia*). The disease is caught by bathing in water contaminated by snails, which harbour the larvae of the parasite. The symptoms include anaemia and dysentery or cystitis and blood in the urine. The disease is treated by drugs that destroy the parasite.

schizophrenia A severe mental disorder in which the normal thinking processes break down and the sufferer tends to lose contact with reality. Delusions and *hallucinations are common. Treatment consists of tranquillizing drugs and therapy to enable a return to normal life.

Schleswig-Holstein An administrative region of N Germany bordering on the North Sea, the Baltic Sea, and Denmark. During the 19th century Denmark and the Austrian-led German confederacy both laid claim to the two duchies of Schleswig and Holstein. The duchies were annexed to Prussia in 1866. Area: 15 696 sq km (6059 sq mi). Population (1987): 2 612 000. Capital: Kiel.

Schliemann, Heinrich (1822–90) German archaeologist. After a successful business career, Schliemann retired (1863) to search for *Troy. He excavated Hissarlik on the Asia Minor coast of Turkey, finding ruins of nine consecutive cities. His spectacular finds at *Mycenae (1874–76) and elsewhere established him as the discoverer of *Mycenaean civilization.

Schmidt telescope A *telescope that uses a thin "correcting" lens in front of the spherical primary mirror. It was developed by the Estonian instrument maker Bernard Voldemar Schmidt (1879–1935). It produces very sharp photographic images of celestial objects over a very wide angle of sky.

schnauzer A breed of dog originating in Germany and used as a guard dog. Strongly built with a docked tail, it has a square muzzle with long sidewhiskers. The wiry coat is black or light grey and brown. Height: 33–35 cm (miniature); 45–48 cm (standard); 54–65 cm (giant).

Schoenberg, Arnold (1874–1951) Austrian-born composer. Forced as a Jew to leave Berlin (1933), he became a US citizen in 1941. His early compositions, in a late Romantic style, include two string quartets and the symphonic poem *Pelleas und Melisande* (1902–03). In 1924 Schoenberg developed the theory and technique of *serialism, which he used in most of his subsequent works, including a violin concerto (1936), a piano concerto (1942), and the unfinished opera *Moses und Aaron* (1932–51).

scholasticism The philosophical and theological activities pursued in the medieval universities (schools) of Christian countries. For scholastics, such as Abelard and Aquinas, religion was predominant and governed the scope of philosophical and scientific enquiry.

Schopenhauer, Arthur (1788–1860) German philosopher. He placed emphasis upon the human will as a means to understanding. *The World as Will and Idea* (1818) sets out his principal ideas. He distrusted rationalism and the scientific method, believing that contemplative freedom could be achieved through art.

Schrödinger, Erwin (1887–1961) Austrian physicist, who worked in Dublin (1940–56). He shared the 1933 Nobel Prize with *Dirac for his development of the form of the *quantum theory known as *wave mechanics.

Schubert, Franz (Peter) (1797–1828) Austrian composer. Schubert's melodic genius is evident in his 600 *Lieder* (songs), which include "Death and the Maiden", "The Trout", and the song-cycles *Die Schöne Müllerin* (1823) and *Die Winterreise* (1827). His large-scale compositions include nine symphonies, string quartets, piano trios, an octet, two quintets, and piano sonatas.

Schumann, Robert (Alexander) (1810–56) German composer. Known particularly for his piano compositions, including *Kreisleriana* (1838), and songs, his works also include four symphonies and chamber music. Gradual insanity developed in later life and he died in an asylum.

His wife **Clara Schumann** (1819–96), whom he married in 1840, was a famous pianist and teacher; she became a great interpreter and editor of her husband's works.

Schwarzkopf, Elisabeth (1915–) German soprano, especially noted for her interpretation of Mozart and Richard Strauss.

Schweitzer, Albert (1875–1965) Alsatian-born theologian, medical missionary, and organist. From 1913 until his death, Schweitzer practised as a doctor in the hospital he founded in Gabon at the jungle village of Lambaréné. In 1952 he received the Nobel Peace Prize.

Science Museum A museum in South Kensington, London, devoted to the history and development of science, engineering, and industry. Originally part of the *Victoria and Albert Museum, it became a separate museum in 1909.

scientology A tradename for a religious doctrine followed by the Church of Scientology, founded in 1954 in California by L(afayette) Ron(ald) Hubbard (1911–86). Originally a method of psychotherapy, this doctrine aims to develop a member's spiritual potential. The Church's methods have been widely criticized.

Scilly, Isles of (*or* Scillies) A group of about 140 islands and islets in the Atlantic Ocean, off the extreme SW coast of England. Only five are inhabited, namely St Mary's (the largest), Tresco, St Martin's, St Agnes, and Bryher. Their mild climate has been exploited to produce early spring flowers for the UK market. Area: 16 sq km (6 sq mi). Population (1981): 2628. Chief town: Hugh Town.

scops owl A small mainly tropical *owl, also called screech owl because of its call. Scops owls are mostly tree dwellers, with camouflaging plumage resembling bark.

scorpion An *arachnid found in warm dry regions. The head carries a pair of large pincers and the elongated abdomen curls upwards and bears a poisonous sting, which can be fatal to humans. Scorpions prey at night, mainly on insects and spiders.

scorpion fish A carnivorous fish, often called rockfish or zebra fish, found mainly on rocky beds of tropical and temperate coastal waters. Up to 1 m long, it has a large spiny head and strong fin spines, which may be venomous.

scorpion fly An insect of the N hemisphere, so called because the males of many species curl the abdomen over the body, like a scorpion. Scorpion flies have long legs and antennae. Larvae and adults feed on dead animals and plants.

Scotland A country occupying the N part of Great Britain and comprising a political division of the *United Kingdom. There are many islands off the N and W coasts, including the Hebrides to the W and the Orkneys and Shetlands to the N. The principal rivers are the Clyde, Forth, Tay, and Spey. Administratively, Scotland is divided into nine regions and three island areas. *Economy*: the central lowland belt of the country is highly industrialized, with shipbuilding, coalmining, and steelmaking; North Sea oil is important on the E coast. Whisky is produced in Highland and Grampian Regions. Agriculture includes sheep and cattle farming and market gardening. Forestry is important in the Highlands. Fishing is another source of revenue. *History*: Scotland was never completely subdued by the Romans. The Picts, Scots, Britons, and Angles of Scotland gradually united, and Kenneth I MacAlpine (died c. 858) is regarded as their first king. During the middle ages there was recurrent war between England and Scotland. The 14th century saw the establishment of a long-standing alliance between France and Scotland and the succession of the *Stuart dynasty. The Scottish Church became Presbyterian (*see* Church of Scotland) during the reign of Mary, Queen of Scots. In 1603 her son James VI succeeded as James I to the throne of England but political union was not established until 1707 (*see* Union, Acts of). After the Hanoverian succession the *Jacobites, staged two unsuccessful rebellions (1715, 1745) against George I and George II. Rapid industrialization in the 19th century encouraged considerable Irish immigration. *Devolution plans were rejected in a referendum in 1979. Area: 78 769 sq km (30 405 sq mi). Population (1986 est): 5 121 000. Capital: Edinburgh.

Scots law Originally Scots law differed little from English law, but from the beginning of the 16th century the introduction of elements of *Roman law resulted in marked differences from English law. Modern statutes have, however, introduced many new laws that are the same for both countries.

Scott, Sir George Gilbert (1811–78) British architect. An advocate of the *gothic revival style, Scott renovated many churches and cathedrals, including Westminster Abbey. His original buildings include the Albert Memorial (1864) and St Pancras station (1865). His grandson, the architect **Sir Giles Gilbert Scott** (1880–1960), designed the Anglican Cathedral in Liverpool (begun 1904), the new Bodleian Library, Oxford (1936–46), and the new Waterloo Bridge (1939–45).

Scott, Robert Falcon (1868–1912) British explorer and naval officer. He led two expeditions to the Antarctic (1900–04 and 1910–12). With a party of four he reached the South Pole on 17 January, 1912, only to find that *Amundsen had beaten them. Delayed by illness and blizzards, they died on the return journey only a few miles from safety. His son **Sir Peter Markham Scott** (1909–) is a noted ornithologist and wildlife painter. In 1946 he founded the Wildfowl Trust based at Slimbridge, Gloucestershire, for the study and conservation of birds.

Scott, Sir Walter (1771–1832) Scottish novelist. His early works include the popular narrative poem *The Lay of the Last Minstrel* (1805). *Waverley* (1814) was the first of a series of hugely successful historical novels that included *Rob Roy* (1817) and *Ivanhoe* (1819).

Scottish National Party (SNP) A political party, founded in 1928, with the aim of achieving Scottish independence from the UK. The party secured 11 seats and 30.4% of the Scottish vote in the 1974 parliamentary election, but declined after the *devolution referendum in 1979.

Scottish terrier A breed of dog, originally called Aberdeen terrier, used to chase foxes from earth. It is thickset with short legs, a short erect tail, and pricked ears. The long muzzle has long whiskers and the wiry coat is usually black. Height: 25–28 cm.

Scout Association An association founded by Robert *Baden Powell in 1908 to encourage boys to become adventurous members of society. It classifies its members into Cub Scouts (aged 8–11), Scouts (11–16), and Venture Scouts (16–29). The first British Girl Scouts were admitted in 1990. *See also* Girl Guides Association.

screech owl *See* scops owl.

screw pine A treelike plant of the African and Asian tropics. The name derives from the spiral arrangement of the leaves, which are used for matting and weaving. Stout roots grow down from the stem into the ground: the part of the stem below these roots decays, so that the plant is supported entirely by the roots. The fruits of some species are edible.

Scriabin, Alexander (1872–1915) Russian composer and pianist. His works include three symphonies, a piano concerto (1894), ten piano sonatas, and *Prometheus* or *The Poem of Fire* (1909–10).

scurvy A disease caused by deficiency of *vitamin C (which is present in most fresh fruits and vegetables). In the past scurvy was common among sailors on long voyages, but it is now rarely seen.

Scylla and Charybdis In Greek mythology, two sea monsters on opposite sides of the Strait of Messina who menaced *Odysseus, the *Argonauts, and other legendary heroes. Scylla was a monster with six heads and a pack of baying hounds, while Charybdis was a raging whirlpool.

Scythians An Indo-European people who settled in what is now S Russia in the 6th century BC. The true Scythians, called Royal Scyths, established a kingdom N of the Black Sea. They disappeared from history during the 3rd century AD.

sea anemone A widely distributed marine invertebrate animal (a *coelenterate). It has a soft cylindrical body (*see* polyp) with a mouth at the top surrounded by rings of tentacles, which –when expanded–give the animal a flower-like appearance. Sea anemones are attached to rocks and weeds and feed mainly on fish and other animals.

sea bass A carnivorous fish, also called sea perch, found mainly in coastal waters of tropical and temperate seas. It is up to 3.75 m long. Many species are valued food and game fish. *See also* bass.

sea bream A fish, also called porgy, found mainly in shallow waters of tropical and subtropical seas. It has a deep slender body, a single long dorsal fin, and well-developed teeth. It lives in shoals and feeds by scraping algae and small animals off rocks.

sea cow. *See* dugong.

sea cucumber A widely distributed invertebrate animal (an *echinoderm) living on the sea bed. At one end of its leathery cucumber-shaped body is a mouth surrounded by a ring of tentacles. It feeds on plankton and detritus.

sea-floor spreading A concept developed in the 1960s to explain *continental drift. Magma rises from the earth's mantle to the surface along midocean ridges (constructive plate margins; *see* plate tectonics), cools to form new oceanic crust, and displaces the older material sideways at an average rate of 4 cm per year.

seagull. *See* gull.

sea horse A small marine fish that lives in shallow warm waters. The horselike head is set at an angle to the body and the fish swims in a vertical position by wavelike movements of the dorsal fin. The male has a brood pouch in which the eggs are hatched.

sea kale A bushy plant, *Crambe maritima*, of the mustard family, found on Atlantic coasts of Europe. It is cultivated for its young edible cabbage-like leaves.

seal A widely distributed carnivorous marine mammal. Seals have a streamlined body with a smooth rounded head and an insulating layer of blubber under the skin. Both pairs of limbs are flattened into flippers. They feed mainly on fish

and breed on land or ice. The **eared seals**, including fur seals and *sealions, have external ears and can use their hind flippers for walking on land; the **true seals** lack external ears and have trailing hind flippers.

sea lettuce A green *seaweed found mainly between high and low tide levels on most rocky shores. Its broad flat translucent fronds are rich in iodine and vitamins and sometimes used in salads and soups.

sealion One of several large *seals. Californian sealions (*Zalophus californianus*), used in circuses, grow to 2 m. Steller's sealion (*Eumetopias jubatus*) is the largest species, growing to over 3 m.

Sealyham terrier A breed of dog developed (1850–91) on the Sealyham estate, Haverfordwest, Wales, for hunting foxes and badgers. It is sturdily built with short legs, drooping ears, and a short thin tail. White with darker markings, Sealyhams have a soft undercoat and a wiry outer coat. Height: 27–30 cm.

Sea Peoples The seafaring tribes, not clearly identified, who colonized Asia Minor, the Aegean, and N Africa in the 13th and 12th centuries BC, destroying the *Hittite empire. About 1170 they were almost wiped out by Rameses III of Egypt and those that survived scattered.

sea perch. *See* sea bass.

sea robin. *See* gurnard.

sea slug A widely distributed marine mollusc with feathery gills, two pairs of tentacles, and no shell. They browse on sponges, sea anemones, and corals and are often brightly coloured.

sea snake A venomous fish-eating snake occurring mainly in coastal waters of Australasia and SE Asia. Sea snakes are adapted to an underwater life by having a flattened body with an oarlike tail and valvelike closures in the nostrils to prevent the entry of water. Most produce live young (rather than eggs).

sea squirt. *See* tunicate.

SEATO. *See* South East Asia Treaty Organization.

Seattle 47 35N 122 20W A city and port in the USA, in Washington state. A port of entry to the Klondike, it became a boom town with the 1897 Alaska Gold Rush. There are large timber mills and various forest-based industries. Population (1987 est): 491 300.

sea urchin A widely distributed marine invertebrate animal (*see* echinoderm) having a spherical rigid body covered by long movable spines. Sea urchins live on shores and ocean floors and eat algae and other organic material scraped off rocks.

seaweed Large red, brown, or green marine *algae that are generally found attached to the sea bed, rocks, or other solid structures by rootlike structures called holdfasts. The plants have flat, threadlike, or branched fronds. Many are of commercial importance as food (e.g. *laver and *sea lettuce), as fertilizers, in chemical and medicinal products, etc. *See also* kelp; wrack.

sebaceous glands. *See* skin.

Sebastian, St (3rd century AD) Roman martyr, killed by archers. According to tradition, he was an officer of the Praetorian Guards until his

Christianity was discovered by Diocletian. Feast day: 20 Jan.

Sebastiano del Piombo (S. Luciano; c. 1485–1547) Venetian painter. His early works, notably *St John Chrysostom* (c. 1509; S Giovanni Crisostomo, Venice), were influenced by Giorgione. Moving to Rome in 1511, he painted decorations in the Farnesina with *Raphael, whose *Transfiguration* he directly challenged with his *Raising of Lazarus* (1517–19; National Gallery, London).

Sebastopol. *See* Sevastopol.

second 1. (s) The *SI unit of time equal to the duration of 9 192 631 770 periods of the radiation corresponding to a specified transition of the caesium-133 atom. 2. A unit of angle equal to one-sixtieth of a minute.

secondary education Education for children aged approximately from 11 to 18. In the UK the Education Act (1944) introduced secondary education for all (compulsory to the age of 15, extended to 16 in 1972). At first there was a three-part system (*grammar, secondary modern, and technical schools), selection being by examination (the eleven-plus). This exam has now been largely phased out and a widespread system of *comprehensive schools introduced.

secretary bird A large long-legged ground-dwelling bird of prey, *Sagittarius serpentarius*, that lives in dry uplands of Africa. It has a hawk-like face and a grey plumage with a long pair of central tail feathers and a black crest of quills behind its head. The quills were formerly used for quill pens, hence its name.

Sedan, Battle of (1 September, 1870) The battle in the *Franco-Prussian War in which German forces, invading NE France, defeated the army of Napoleon III. This brought revolution in Paris and marked the end of the Second Empire.

sedatives Drugs that relieve restlessness, anxiety, and tension. The most widely used sedatives are the minor tranquillizers, for example *benzodiazepines.

sedge A grasslike plant growing throughout the world, mainly in swampy places. Sedges have solid triangular stems, long narrow leaves, and small male and female flowers usually grouped into separate clusters (spikes).

Sedgemoor, Battle of (6 July, 1685) The battle, SE of Bridgwater, Somerset, in which the forces of James II of England defeated the rebellion of his nephew, the Duke of *Monmouth.

sedimentary rock One of the three major categories into which rocks are divided (*compare* igneous rock; metamorphic rock). Sedimentary rocks are deposited mainly under water, usually in approximately horizontal layers (beds). **Clastic sedimentary rocks** are formed from the erosion and deposition of pre-existing rocks and include sandstones, siltstones, breccias, conglomerates, etc. Organically formed sedimentary rocks are derived from the remains of plants and animals, for example limestone and coal.

sedum. *See* stonecrop.

Seebeck effect. *See* thermoelectric effects.

seed The reproductive structure formed after pollination (*see* pollen) and fertilization in higher plants. All seeds contain an embryo and usually a food store, which supplies the nutrients needed for germination. The seeds of flowering plants (angiosperms) are surrounded by a seed coat and contained within a *fruit. The seeds of gymnosperms (conifers and related plants) are naked (*see* cone).

Segovia, Andrés (1893–1987) Spanish guitarist, who revived the popularity of the guitar as a concert instrument.

Seine, River A river in N France. Rising on the Plateau de Langres, it flows mainly NW through Paris to the English Channel, S of Le Havre. It is the second longest river in France (the longest is the Loire). Length: 776 km (482 mi).

seismic belts (*or* seismic zones) The narrow belts on the earth's surface that are subject to frequent earthquakes. They usually follow the line of plate boundaries (*see* plate tectonics), especially along midocean ridges, island arc systems, and major *faults.

seismic wave A wave produced at the centre of an *earthquake or explosion and travelling away from it. Several types of wave can be recorded. The preliminary tremor consists of small rapid longitudinal P (*primae*) waves and transverse S (*secundae*) waves coming directly through the earth's interior. The main earthquake consists of large slow L (*longae*) waves travelling along the surface.

seismology The branch of geophysics concerned with the study of *earthquakes: their origin, the waves they produce (*see* seismic wave), their effects, their distribution, and their prediction and modification. A **seismograph** is an instrument that records the magnitude of the oscillations during an earthquake.

Selene The Greek moon-goddess, daughter of the Titan Hyperion and sister of Helios (the sun) and Eos (dawn). She became identified with the later Greek goddess *Artemis and with the Roman *Diana.

selenium (Se) A chemical element that is a member of the sulphur family and exists in several forms; the commonest form is grey. The element is used in photocells, light meters, and in photocopying machines. It is a semiconductor and is widely used in rectifiers. At no 34; at wt 78.96; mp 217°C; bp 685°C.

Seleucids A Middle Eastern dynasty of the *Hellenistic age founded by Seleucus I Nicator (c. 356–280 BC), who became governor and then ruler (312) of *Babylonia. He extended his kingdom to the frontiers of India in the east and into Syria in the west. Rome's Mediterranean expansion weakened the empire, and the Parthians brought about its final disintegration. In 64 BC Pompey acquired what was left of it to form the Roman province of Syria.

Sellafield (former name: Windscale) An atomic power station in W Cumbria, NW England. Several accidents, together with a high incidence of cancer among local inhabitants, have made Sellafield a controversial focus for the nuclear power debate.

Sellers, Peter (1925–80) British comic actor. He made his name in the 1950s with the BBC radio comedy series *The Goon Show*. His many films include *I'm All Right, Jack* (1959), *The Millionairess* (1961), *Dr Strangelove* (1963), *The Pink Panther* series (1963–77), and *Being There* (1980).

semantics The study of the relationship between words and meanings. Semantics can be part of both *linguistics and philosophy.

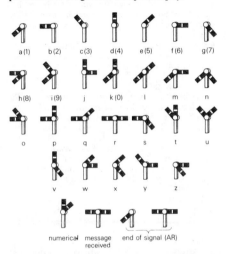

a (1)   b (2)   c (3)   d (4)   e (5)   f (6)   g (7)

h (8)   i (9)   j   k (0)   l   m   n

o   p   q   r   s   t   u

v   w   x   y   z

numerical   message   end of signal (AR)
received

SEMAPHORE

semaphore **1.** A visual method of communication between ships at sea, used mainly by warships wishing to maintain radio silence. It uses flags held in different positions to indicate alphabetical or numerical characters. **2.** A mechanical railway signalling device, consisting of a movable steel arm.

Semarang 6 58S 110 29E A port in Indonesia, in central Java on the Java Sea. A commercial centre with textile and shipbuilding industries, it exports sugar, rubber, coffee, kapok, and copra. Population (1984): 1 077 000.

semen *See* sperm.

semiconductor A crystalline material in which the conductivity is between that of a conductor and an insulator. The conductivity increases with temperature and the presence of impurities in the crystal lattice. Some (donor) impurities increase the number of negative charge carriers (electrons), creating an n-type semiconductor. Other (acceptor) impurities increase the number of positive charge carriers (holes), creating a p-type semiconductor. The region at which a p-type and an n-type semiconductor meet is called a p-n junction. *Solid-state electronic components, such as *semiconductor diodes, *transistors, and *integrated circuits depend on the properties of p-n junctions. Metal oxide semiconductor (MOS) devices also use a thin layer of insulating oxide on the semiconductor surface.

semiconductor diode A *solid-state electronic device with two electrodes. It consists of a single p-n junction (*see* semiconductor). When the p-region is more positive than the n-region (forward bias), the current flow increases as the voltage rises. In reverse bias, very little current flows. The diode is, therefore, a rectifier, allowing current to flow in one direction. Semiconductor diodes are also used to generate *microwaves, to detect light in *photocells, and to emit light in **light-emitting diodes** (LEDs).

Semites A group of peoples, including the *Jews and *Arabs, said in the Bible to be descended from Shem, Noah's eldest son. The Babylonians, Assyrians, and Phoenicians were ancient Semitic peoples.

Semitic alphabets The earliest known truly alphabetic writing systems, developed among the Semitic peoples of the E Mediterranean around 2000 BC. From them come all the major alphabets of today.

Semitic languages A group of languages spoken in N Africa through Palestine to the SW corner of Asia. The Semitic languages originated in Mesopotamia in the 3rd millennium BC. Examples of living Semitic languages are *Hebrew, modern *Arabic, and Maltese.

Senate In ancient Rome, the state council. During Republican times the Senate was largely composed of ex-magistrates and it carried much weight, especially in foreign policy, finance, and religion. Under the Empire, membership of the Senate was usually inherited and its chief function was to approve imperial decisions. *See also* Roman Curia.

Senate, US. *See* Congress.

Sendai 38 16N 140 52E A city in Japan, in NE Honshu. It is the largest city of N Japan and an important commercial centre. Population (1987): 686 000.

Seneca the Elder (Marcus Annaeus Seneca; c. 55 BC–c. 41 AD) Roman rhetorician, born at Córdoba (Spain). Parts of his work on oratory, addressed to his sons, have survived. One of his sons, **Seneca the Younger** (Lucius Annaeus Seneca; c. 4 BC–65 AD), was an author and politician. He was tutor and later chief minister to *Nero. Retiring in 64 AD, he was accused of treason and forced to commit suicide. His works include philosophical writings on *Stoicism and nine tragedies.

Senegal, Republic of A country in West Africa, on the Atlantic Ocean. The Gambia forms an enclave within Senegalese territory. *Economy*: chiefly agricultural, the production of groundnuts being dominant. Phosphates, iron ore, and offshore oil and natural gas are mined. *History*: by the mid-19th century the French controlled most of the region. The country achieved self-government in 1958 as a member of the French Community and became a separate independent republic in 1960. In 1982 it formed the Senegambia Confederation with The Gambia, each country retaining its independence but having joint defence, foreign, and monetary policies. President: Abdou Diouf (1935–   ). Official language: French. Official currency: CFA (Communauté financière africaine) franc of 100 centimes. Area: 197 722 sq km (76 320 sq mi). Population (1988 est): 6 982 000. Capital and main port: Dakar.

Seoul 37 30N 127 00E The capital of South Korea, in the NW on the River Han near the coast. It was the capital of Korea from 1394. The industrial and commercial centre of the country, it has 16 universities. Population (1985): 9 645 824.

Sephardim (Hebrew *Sepharad*: Spain) Jews who went to Spain and Portugal in the *diaspora. When the Jews were expelled from Spain in 1492 they spread to many parts of the world. Among the first Jewish settlers in England in the 17th century were Sephardim from Holland. The term is now sometimes applied to all non-*Ashkenazim.

sequoia Either of two Californian coniferous trees, the *redwood (*Sequoia sempervirens*) or the giant sequoia (*Sequoiadendron giganteum*), also called wellingtonia. The giant sequoia forms natural forests in California's Sierra Nevada, where some trees are over 3000 years old, with a height of over 80 m and a girth of over 24 m. The red-brown bark is soft and fibrous.

seraphim. *See* cherubim and seraphim.

Serbia A constituent republic of Yugoslavia. Agriculture and mining, especially for copper, antimony, coal, and chrome, are important. *History*: first settled by the Serbs in the 7th century AD, it later came under Turkish control (1389–1804), finally regaining its independence in 1878. In 1918 Serbia became part of the kingdom of Serbs, Croats, and Slovenes, later renamed Yugoslavia. There has been recent unrest in the autonomous region of Kosovo between the Serbs, who are demanding less autonomy, and the ethnic Albanian population. Area: 128 278 sq km (49 528 sq mi). Population (1986): 9 660 000. Capital: Belgrade.

Serbo-Croat The language of the Serbs and Croats of Yugoslavia, where it is the most widely spoken language. Serbian and Croatian differ very little but Serbian is written in *Cyrillic and Croatian in Latin script.

serf An unfree peasant of the middle ages. A serf was bound to the land he worked, paying the lord of the *manor a fee and providing service in return for protection and the use of his land. While serfdom declined in W Europe in the late middle ages, it was not abolished in E Europe until the 19th century.

serialism (*or* twelve-tone music) A method of composing music using all 12 notes of the chromatic *scale equally. It was invented in the 1920s by Schoenberg, who used a fixed sequence of 12 notes (called a **series** or tone row) as a source of melody and harmony. In strict serialism no single note of the row could be repeated until the other 11 had occurred in melody or harmony; Schoenberg himself did not always follow this rule.

series The sum of the terms in an ordered collection of numbers (a sequence), written as $a_1 + a_2 + a_3 + \ldots a_r + \ldots$. The partial sum to the nth term is denoted by S_n. A series is convergent if S_n approaches a particular value as n increases

and divergent if it increases without limit. A geometric series has the general form $a + an + an^2 + \ldots$, where a and n are constant. A power series has the general form $a_0 + a_1x + a_2x^2 + a_3x^3 + \ldots$, where x is a variable.

serpentine A group of minerals consisting mainly of hydrous magnesium silicates, with a layered structure. They are usually green or white, and often streaked or mottled like a snake's skin. They occur in igneous rocks. Rock consisting mainly of serpentine is sometimes quarried for ornamental stone.

serum The fluid that remains after blood has been allowed to clot. It is similar in composition to blood plasma, except that it lacks blood-clotting factors.

serval A slender long-legged *cat, *Felis serval*, of the African bush. It is about 1.25 m long including the tail and has large ears and a spotted coat. Servals hunt birds and small mammals, mainly at night.

service tree A tree, *Sorbus domestica*, of the rose family, about 15 m high, native to S Europe, W Asia, and N Africa and commonly grown for ornament. Related to the *mountain ash, it has small green fruits that are used for making wine.

sesame A plant, *Sesamum indicum*, cultivated in Central and South America, the Middle East, and SE Asia for its seeds, which are used in confectionery, food flavouring, and as the source of an edible oil.

Set An Egyptian deity. Originally a sun and sky god, he murdered his brother *Osiris and so came to represent all evil. He was killed by *Horus, son of Osiris.

setter One of three breeds of sporting dog with drooping ears. Setters are named after their habit of squatting flat ("setting") after finding game. The English setter has a long white silky coat flecked with darker markings. The Irish, or red, setter has a flat silky chestnut coat. Height: 61–69 cm.

$a \in A$ $\quad A \subset B$ $\quad A \cup B$

$A \cap B$ $\quad A^c$ or A' $\quad a \in (A \cap B)$

SET THEORY *Venn diagrams.*

set theory The study, founded by Georg *Cantor, of the logical and mathematical laws of sets. A set is a defined collection of objects or elements; for example the set of odd integers between 0 and 10 is 1, 3, 5, 7, 9. All sets are contained in the universal set E. The relationships between sets can be illustrated in a **Venn diagram**, named after the British logician John Venn (1834–1923), or shown by symbols. $a \in A$ means the element a is a member of the set A.

$A \subset B$ means set A is contained in set B. $A \cup B$ means the union of A and B. $A \cap B$ means the intersection of A and B. A^c or A' is the complement of A.

Settlement, Act of (1701) The Act that established the Hanoverian succession to the English throne. In the absence of heirs to William III or Anne, the Crown was to pass to James I's granddaughter Sophia (1657–1714), Electress of Hanover, or to her Protestant descendants. Anne was succeeded by the first Hanoverian king, George I, in 1714.

Seurat, Georges (1859–91) French painter, famous for developing neoimpressionism, popularly called *pointillism. He finished only seven paintings in this demanding style, including the famous *Sunday Afternoon on the Island of the Grande Jatte* (1884–86).

Sevastopol (English name: Sebastopol) 44 36N 33 31E A port in the Soviet Union, in the Crimea on the Black Sea. It is a popular seaside resort. Founded in 1783 it became an important naval base and, later, a commercial port. It was besieged by the British and French during the Crimean War, falling after 11 months. Population (1987): 350 000.

Seven Deadly Sins Pride, covetousness, lust, envy, gluttony, anger, and sloth. The traditional Christian list was already established by the 6th century.

Seventh Day Adventists. See adventists.

Seven Weeks' War. See Austro-Prussian War.

Seven Wonders of the World The supreme man-made structures of the ancient world. They were the *Pyramids of Egypt, the *Colossus of Rhodes, the *Hanging Gardens of Babylon, the Mausoleum of Halicarnassus, the statue of *Zeus at Olympia, the temple of *Artemis at Ephesus, and the *Pharos of Alexandria. Only the Pyramids have survived.

Seven Years' War (1756–63) The war between Prussia, Britain, and Hanover on one side and France, Austria, Russia, and Spain on the other. The war had two main aspects: the rivalry between Austria and Prussia for domination of Germany and the struggle between France and Britain for overseas supremacy. Prussian dominance was confirmed by the Peace of Hubertusberg. The British won a series of spectacular victories in India (by *Clive) and Canada (by *Wolfe). By the Treaty of Paris (1763) Britain was confirmed as the supreme world power.

Severn, River The longest river in the UK, rising in central Wales and flowing NE and E into England, then S to the Bristol Channel. It is spanned near its estuary by the **Severn Bridge**, a suspension bridge 988 m (3240 ft) long, built in the 1960s. Length: 354 km (220 mi).

Seville 37 24N 5 59W A city and port in SW Spain, in Andalusia on the River Guadalquivir. Now a major industrial centre, it thrived under the Moors (711–1248) as a cultural centre and became a major port with a monopoly of trade with the West Indies in the 16th century. There is a university (founded 1502) and one of the world's largest cathedrals (1401–1591). Population (1986): 668 356.

sex chromosome A *chromosome that carries the genes for determining the sex of an individual. In humans there are two types of sex chromosomes, called X and Y. The body cells of normal males possess one X and one Y chromosome while those of normal females have two X chromosomes. Human sperm is therefore either "male" or "female" depending on whether it carries an X or a Y chromosome. The egg cell always carries an X chromosome. If a "male" sperm fertilizes the egg, the embryo (and hence the baby) will be male. A "female" sperm will produce a female embryo.

sex hormones Hormones that regulate the growth, development, and functioning of the reproductive organs and determine external sexual characteristics. The major female sex hormones are the *oestrogens, *progesterone, and *prolactin; the male sex hormones are the *androgens.

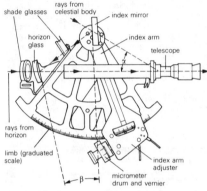

SEXTANT *Angle α measures the angle between horizon and reference arm; β is the angle between index mirror and horizon glass, marked by the angular movement of the index arm along the limb. $\alpha = 2\beta$, therefore the graduations on the scale are marked twice the actual angular movement to give the correct altitude.*

sextant An instrument used primarily in navigation for determining latitudes by measuring the angle subtended by some celestial body to the horizon. Thomas Godfrey of Philadelphia and John Hadley of London, working independently, discovered the sextant's principle in 1730. The graduated metal strip, shaped in an arc of the sixth part of a circle, gave the instrument its name.

sexton beetle. See burying beetle.

sexually transmitted disease (STD) Any disease transmitted by sexual intercourse, also known as venereal disease. STDs include genital herpes, nonspecific urethritis, hepatitis B, AIDS, syphilis, and gonorrhoea.

Seychelles, Republic of A country consisting of 87 widely scattered islands in the W Indian Ocean, NE of Madagascar. The main island is Mahé. *Economy*: the chief products and exports are copra and cinnamon bark. *History*: the uninhabited islands became a French colony in the mid-18th century as a spice plantation. Captured by the British in 1794, they became a dependency of Mauritius in 1814, a British crown colony in 1903, and an independent republic within the Commonwealth in 1976. President: Albert René (1935–). Official languages: English and French; the majority speak Creole. Official currency: Seychelles rupee of 100 cents. Area: 444 sq km (171 sq mi). Population (1988 est): 67 305. Capital and main port: Victoria.

Seymour, Jane (c. 1509–37) The third wife (1536–37) of Henry VIII of England. A lady in waiting to both his former wives, Catherine of Aragon and Anne Boleyn, she married Henry 11 days after Anne's execution. Jane was the mother of Edward VI, dying shortly after his birth.

's Gravenhage. *See* Hague, The.

Shackleton, Sir Ernest Henry (1874–1922) British Antarctic explorer. On his expedition of 1908–09 he nearly reached the South Pole. In an expedition of 1914–16 his ship, the *Endurance*, was marooned but he and his men reached Elephant Island by sledge and boats. He died on his fourth expedition.

shad A food fish, related to herrings, that occurs in the N Atlantic, Mediterranean, and North Sea. It has black spots along each side. Shad migrate in large shoals to spawn in fresh waters.

Shaffer, Peter (1926–) British dramatist. His plays include *Five-Finger Exercise* (1958), *Equus* (1973), *Amadeus* (1979), *Yonadab* (1985), and *Lettice and Lovage* (1987). His twin brother **Anthony Shaffer** (1926–) is also a playwright, best known for the thriller *Sleuth* (1970).

Shah Jahan (1592–1666) Emperor of India (1628–58) of the Mogul dynasty; the son of Jahangir (1569–1627). A ruthless ruler, he came to power by putting his nearest relatives to death in 1628. His passion for fine architecture produced such monuments as the *Taj Mahal and the Delhi Red Fort. He was deposed by his son Aurangzeb (1618–1707).

Shah of Iran. *See* Mohammed Reza Pahlavi; Reza Shah Pahlavi.

Shakespeare, William (1564–1616) English dramatist, universally recognized as the greatest English writer. Born in Stratford-upon-Avon, he married Anne Hathaway in 1582. Soon afterwards he went to London, where he became an actor in the Lord Chamberlain's Men (called the King's Men after 1603). The three parts of *Henry VI* and *Richard III* were his first plays (1589–92). His early comedies (1593–95) were *Love's Labour's Lost*, *The Two Gentlemen of Verona*, and *The Taming of the Shrew*. These were followed (1595–1600) by *A Midsummer Night's Dream*, *The Merchant of Venice*, *Much Ado About Nothing*, *Twelfth Night*, and *As You Like It*. During this period he also wrote his first significant tragedy, *Romeo and Juliet*, as well as *Richard II* and *Julius Caesar*. The two parts of *Henry IV* were completed before *Hamlet*, *Othello*, *King Lear*, and *Macbeth*, his major tragedies (1600–06). His final experimental plays included *The Winter's Tale* (c. 1610) and *The Tempest* (c. 1611). His poems include *Venus and Adonis* (1593), *The Rape of Lucrece* (1594), and the *Son-*

nets (1609). In about 1611 he retired to Stratford, where he died. The first collected edition of his works, known as the First Folio, was published in 1623.

shale A fine-grained *sedimentary rock that consists of layers of clay mineral particles and splits easily. Shales may disintegrate in water. They are softer and lighter than slate, which is a fine-grained *metamorphic rock.

shallot A plant, *Allium ascalonium*, related to the onion and probably of Asiatic origin. Its small hollow cylindrical leaves are often used in garnishes and salads. Its small bulbs are used for flavouring and pickling.

shamanism The religious beliefs and practices common in certain tribal societies of Asia, such as the *Samoyed. The term is also applied to North American Indian practices. The shaman is a tribal priest generally felt to have supernatural powers.

Shamir, Yitzhak (1915–) Israeli statesman, born in Poland; prime minister (1983–84; 1986–). He led the Israeli Freedom Fighters (1940–41), served in Israel's secret service (1955–65), and was foreign minister (1980–83; 1984–86). From 1984 to 1988 he was deputy prime minister under a special power-sharing agreement with Shimon *Peres. He formed new coalitions in 1988 and 1990.

shamrock A plant bearing leaves with three leaflets, such as *clover, black medick (*Medicago lupulina*), or wood sorrel (*Oxalis acetosella*). The shamrock is worn on St Patrick's Day.

Shanghai 31 13N 121 25E A port in E China, on the Yangtze estuary. The largest city in China, it is its chief port and industrial city. It grew rapidly after it was opened to foreign trade in 1842, coming under British, US, and French rule until World War II. Population (1987 est): 7 330 000.

Shannon, River The longest river in the Republic of Ireland. Rising in NW Co Cavan, it flows S to Limerick and then W into a long estuary before entering the Atlantic Ocean. Length: 386 km (240 mi).

Shari, River. *See* Chari, River.

shari'ah. *See* Islamic law.

Sharjah. *See* United Arab Emirates.

shark A marine cartilaginous *fish occurring worldwide. Ranging in size from the smallest *dogfish to the enormous whale shark, they have a torpedo-shaped body with a muscular tail used in swimming, five to seven pairs of gill slits on the sides of the head, and numerous sharp teeth. They are carnivorous.

Sharpeville A Black African town in South Africa, in the S Transvaal near Vereeniging. It was the scene of a riot on 21 March, 1960, in which a crowd of African demonstrators were fired on by the police. A riot in 1984 led to the controversial sentencing to death of six demonstrators, the "Sharpeville Six"; they were reprieved in 1988.

Shaw, George Bernard (1856–1950) Irish dramatist, critic, and man of letters. He went to London in 1876, becoming a music and drama critic, an active socialist, and a founding member of the Fabian Society. He wrote more than 40 plays. *Plays Pleasant and Unpleasant* (1898) included *Mrs Warren's Profession* (on prostitution), *Arms and the Man*, and *Candida*. His *Three Plays for Puritans* (published 1901) comprised *The Devil's Disciple*, *Caesar and Cleopatra*, and *Captain Brassbound's Conversion*. The epic comedy of ideas, *Man and Superman* (1903), was followed by *Major Barbara* (1905), *The Doctor's Dilemma* (1906), and *Androcles and the Lion* (1913). *Pygmalion* (1913), an outstanding commercial success, was followed by *Heartbreak House* (1917) and the series of plays entitled *Back to Methuselah* (1921). The historical drama *St Joan* (1924) is generally regarded as his greatest work. He also wrote many important prose works. In 1925 he was awarded the Nobel Prize.

Shcherbakov. *See* Rybinsk.

shear stress. *See* stress.

shearwater A marine bird having dark plumage (some species have white underparts), long narrow wings, and a slender bill; it feeds on fish from the sea surface. The great shearwater (*Puffinus gravis*) breeds in the South Atlantic, migrating to spend summer and autumn in the North Atlantic. The Manx shearwater (*P. puffinus*) breeds off British and Mediterranean coasts and winters in E South America and Australia. *See also* petrel.

Sheba In the Bible, a land corresponding to Sabaea in present-day Yemen (SW Arabia). It was known for its trade in spices and gold. Its most famous monarch was the Queen of Sheba who visited King Solomon in Jerusalem (I Kings 10.1–13).

sheep A hoofed *ruminant mammal native to mountainous regions of Europe, Asia, and North America. Related to goats, sheep are generally 75–100 cm tall. The coat ranges from white to brown in colour. Males (rams) have large spiralled horns; females (ewes) have smaller less curved horns. There are over 200 breeds of domestic sheep (*Ovis aries*), which are reared worldwide for meat, wool, and milk (*see* livestock farming).

sheepdog A dog used for handling sheep, such as the *collie, *German shepherd dog, *Old English sheepdog, and *Shetland sheepdog.

Sheffield 52 23N 1 30W A city in N England, the largest in South Yorkshire on the River Don at the edge of the Pennines. It is world famous for steel, produced here since the mid-18th century. Population (1986): 538 700.

shelduck A large *duck, *Tadorna tadorna*, found around coasts of W and central Europe and Asia. It is 65 cm long and has black-and-white plumage with a green head, chestnut shoulders, and a red bill, which in the male has a red knob at the base.

shellac A natural thermoplastic *resin made from the secretions of the lac insect, *Laccifer lacca*, which is parasitic on certain trees in India and Thailand. Its solution in alcohol is used as a varnish and in lacquers.

Shelley, Percy Bysshe (1792–1822) British poet. He wrote the revolutionary poem *Queen Mab* in 1813 and soon after left for the Continent, where he met Byron. From 1818 until his death he lived in Italy, where he wrote the verse dramas *The Cenci* (1819) and *Prometheus Unbound* (1818–19), the elegy *Adonais* (1821) prompted by the death of Keats, and much lyrical poetry. He was drowned in a sailing accident. His second wife, the novelist **Mary Wollstonecraft Shelley** (1797–1851), was best-known for her book *Frankenstein: the Modern Prometheus* (1818).

shells The hard casings secreted by some animals to protect themselves or their eggs. The term usually refers to the shells of molluscs, which consist largely of calcium carbonate. They may consist of a single structure (in snails) or two halves, or valves (as in mussels). The pearly nautilus has a many-chambered shell, which provides buoyancy. See p. 490.

Shelter (National Campaign for the Homeless) A British organization, founded in 1966, to raise funds for housing projects and housing aid centres for the homeless and to campaign for more and better housing.

Shenyang (former name: Mukden) 41 50N 123 26E A city in NE China, on the River Hun, the capital of Liaoning province. China's fourth largest city, it is a major industrial centre. Population (1986): 4 200 000.

Sheraton, Thomas (1751–1806) British furniture designer, who made his name with the designs in his *Cabinet-Maker and Upholsterer's Drawing Book* (1791–94). Influenced by *Adam and contemporary French styles, these designs were characterized by elegance, delicacy, and inlaid decoration.

Sheridan, Richard Brinsley (1751–1816) Anglo-Irish dramatist, who lived in England from childhood. He wrote witty comedies of manners, of which the best known are *The Rivals* (1775) and *School for Scandal* (1777). A Whig MP (1780–1812), he was a great parliamentary orator.

sheriff An official with administrative and legal responsibilities in England, Scotland, and the USA. The post began in the 10th century as the king's representative in the shire and at the shire court. The sheriffs' powers were later reduced and became little more than ceremonial in the 16th century. Sheriffs in England and Scotland are normally appointed by the Crown to each county. In Scotland sheriffs are also the chief county judges. In the USA they are elected and are the principal law enforcement officers in a county.

Sherpa A people of Nepal who speak a dialect of Tibetan. They often act as porters for Himalayan expeditions. With Edmund Hillary, the Sherpa *Tenzing Norgay reached the summit of Everest in 1953.

sherry A fortified *wine, originally made around Jerez de la Frontera (whence its name) in S Spain. There are two basic types of sherry: fino is a pale dry wine on which the *flor (flower or yeast) has developed fully; oloroso is a rich full-bodied wine on which the *flor is little developed. Amontillado is a strong dark derivative of a fino and cream sherry is a heavily sweetened oloroso.

Shetland Islands (*or* Shetland; official name until 1974: Zetland) An island authority of about 100 islands in the North Sea, off the N

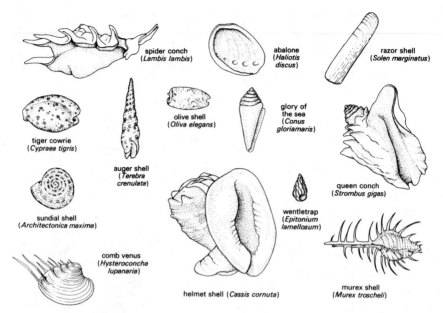

spider conch
(*Lambis lambis*)

abalone
(*Haliotis
discus*)

razor shell
(*Solen marginatus*)

tiger cowrie
(*Cypraea tigris*)

olive shell
(*Oliva elegans*)

glory of
the sea
(*Conus
gloriamaris*)

auger shell
(*Terebra
crenulata*)

queen conch
(*Strombus gigas*)

sundial shell
(*Architectonica maxima*)

wentletrap
(*Epitonium
lamellosum*)

comb venus
(*Hysteroconcha
lupanaria*)

helmet shell (*Cassis cornuta*)

murex shell
(*Murex troscheli*)

SHELLS *A selection of mollusc shells, drawn to scale (the largest, the helmet shell, is 35 cm long). All these species are marine and several, including the glory of the sea, are collectors' items.*

coast of Scotland. The largest islands include Mainland, Yell, and Unst. Shetland is famous for its ponies and knitted goods (especially in the Shetland and Fair Isle patterns). The islands are a base for North Sea oil exploitation. Area: 1427 sq km (551 sq mi). Population (1987 est): 22 429. Administrative centre: Lerwick.

Shetland pony The smallest British pony breed, native to the Shetland Islands. It has a sturdy compact body with short legs and a relatively large head. The mane and tail are profuse and the coat becomes thick in winter. Height: up to 1.05 m (10½ hands).

Shetland sheepdog (*or* Sheltie) A breed of dog developed in the Shetland Islands for working sheep. Related to and resembling the *collie, it has a soft undercoat and a long outer coat and may be black, brown, or blue-grey, with white and tan markings. Height: about 35 cm.

shield An extensive rigid block of *Precambrian rocks. Shields are the oldest continental regions and were once the site of Precambrian mountain belts, although the mountains have been completely eroded. The **Canadian** (*or* **Laurentian**) **Shield** is the largest, covering several million square kilometres of NE North America.

Shih Huang Ti. *See* Qin.

Shiites (*or* Shiah) The general term applied to a number of different Muslim groups, the main body of which is dominant in Iran. The Shiites, unlike the other major Muslim group, the *Sunnites, believe that *Ali, the fourth caliph, is the only legitimate successor of Mohammed. The leader of Islam, the imam, must be a descendant of Ali.

Shikoku The smallest of the four main islands of Japan, separated from Honshu and Kyushu by the Inland Sea. Its population is concentrated on the coastal plains, with industry mainly in the N. Area: 17 759 sq km (6857 sq mi). Population (1986): 4 226 000. Chief cities: Matsuyama and Takamatsu.

shingles An infection caused by the *herpes zoster virus, which lodges in nerve cells in the spinal cord. It usually starts with pain along the course of a sensory nerve, followed by a band of blisters round half of the body or face. The rash usually eventually disappears but the patient may be left with severe pain associated with the affected nerve.

Shinto The native religion of Japan. Shinto is primarily an attitude of reverence towards familiar places and traditions. The central themes are the belief in numerous *kamis* or nature spirits, together with ancestor worship and an ideal of military chivalry. After World War II, Shinto was no longer recognized as the state religion.

ships Early mariners included the Egyptians, Chinese and Phoenicians. The short broad Phoenician merchant ships of the 13th century BC were propelled by oars and a single square sail to catch the prevailing wind. The Greeks developed biremes (with two banks of oars) and triremes (with three banks) as warships, especially strengthened for ramming enemy vessels. The Romans also relied on oars, but their larger grain ships had a number of square sails. The double-ended longships of the Vikings were designed to cope with the rough and windy North Sea. Developed in the 8th century AD and propelled by

SHIPS

Roman merchantman (c. 100 AD) *The Romans' need to transport grain from N Africa to Europe encouraged the building of imposing ships up to 180 ft (55 m) long.*

Portuguese caravel (c. 1450) *Although it was only a little longer than a large rowing boat, the caravel took part in most of the 15th-century voyages of discovery. The lateen sail, derived from Arab examples, enabled it to sail against the prevailing winds.*

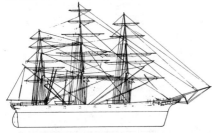

Cutty Sark (1869) *The 19th-century clippers were renowned for their speed and grace. The Cutty Sark, built to bring tea from China, was one of the fastest and most consistent sailing ships of its time. It is now permanently moored at Greenwich, England.*

Great Britain (1843) *The second steam ship designed by I. K. Brunel, the Great Britain was the first all-iron propeller-driven ship to cross the Atlantic, taking 15 days between Liverpool and New York. Wrecked off the Falkland Islands in 1937, it was restored in the 1970s in Bristol, where it is kept in dry dock.*

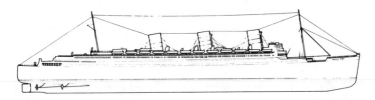

Queen Mary (1934) *In 1938 this British passenger liner captured the Blue Riband for the fastest Atlantic crossing with a time of 3 days 20 hours 42 minutes. In 1967 it was anchored off Long Beach, California, as a tourist attraction.*

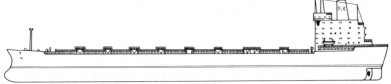

oil tanker (1968) *The largest vessels afloat today, some of these giant ships have a deadweight capacity of over 300 000 tons.*

WARSHIPS

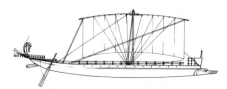

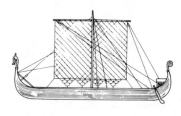

Greek bireme (c. 500 BC) *Propelled during an attack by its two ranks of oars, the bireme was strongly built around a keel to support the strain of the ram attached to its bows.*

Viking longship (c. 1000 AD) *The clinker-built, double-ended longship, propelled by oars and sail, was used mainly to transport fighting men.*

medieval nef (c. 1400) *This single-masted vessel had platforms (castles) for fighting men at either end and one on the mast (topcastle) from which missiles could be hurled.*

Victory (1778) *Nelson's flagship at the battle of Trafalgar (1805), the* Victory *carried 100 guns and a crew of 850. It is now preserved at Portsmouth, England.*

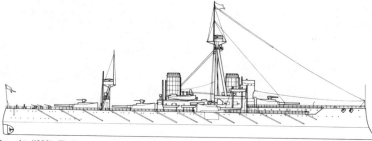

Dreadnought (1906) *The design of the British* Dreadnought *became the model for battleships in a period in which a country's naval strength was calculated in terms of how many battleships it possessed. The* Dreadnought *carried ten 12-inch guns, 27 smaller guns, and five underwater torpedo tubes.*

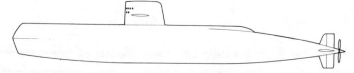

Nautilus (1954) *The first nuclear-powered warship, the US* Nautilus *heralded an era in which naval strength is calculated in terms of nuclear submarines. They are armed with torpedoes and long- and short-range missiles carrying nuclear warheads, all of which can be fired while the vessel is submerged.*

sail and oars, ships of this kind brought William the Conqueror to England. It was not until the 12th century that sails were sufficiently developed for oars to be dispensed with. By the 14th century sailing ships were commonplace. The warships of the period had "castles" built at each end to house fighting men, and guns were usually carried on the forecastle. By the end of the 15th century the heavy muzzle-loading cannons were carried in gun ports low in the hull. The single-master with one large heavy sail gave way to the three-master with more manageable small sails and full rigging.

During the next 300 years sailing ships developed in many ways, reaching their peak in the 19th-century *clippers, which remained supreme until the *steam engine revolutionized seafaring. The first steamer to cross the Atlantic (in April, 1827) was the Dutch *Curaçao* (built 1826), the first British ship to do so (in April, 1838) being Brunel's *Great Western*, a wooden paddle steamer. In the 20th century the propeller completely replaced the paddle and Parson's steam *turbine largely replaced the steam engine.

Warships in the age of steam were largely modelled on the turbine-driven battleship *Dreadnought* (1906), which together with the *cruiser, *destroyer, frigate, and *submarine dominated naval warfare in World War I. In World War II the *aircraft carrier was the supreme weapon of the war at sea. Today, the strength of navies is reckoned in terms of their missile- and aircraft-carrying capabilities and in their numbers of nuclear-powered submarines.

Shire horse A breed of horse descended from the English warhorse. It is massively built, being used for pulling loads, and has long white hair (called feathering) covering the lower parts of the legs. The coat is grey, bay, or black. Height: about 1.73 m (17 hands).

Shiva The third member of the Hindu trinity, the *Trimurti. He is known as the Destroyer, but also represents the principle of generation symbolized by the lingam or phallus. His female counterpart is Parvati. He is often portrayed in human form with four arms and a third eye in the centre of the forehead. His most famous portrayal is as *Nataraja* (king of dancing).

shock **1.** A severe disorder resulting from failure of the circulatory system to supply adequate blood to the tissues. Shock may occur after a heart attack, through bleeding (haemorrhage) or burns, or after injury or during a very severe infection. **2.** Injury resulting from electrocution. The extent of the injury depends on the current passing through the body, which is related to the voltage and the skin resistance. As skin resistance is greatly reduced when it is wet, mains voltage (240 V) can cause a lethal current (about 15 milliamps) to flow through the body if live terminals are touched with wet hands.

Shockley, William Bradfield (1910–89) US physicist, born in England, who shared the 1956 Nobel Prize with John *Bardeen and Walter *Brattain for their discovery of the *transistor while working at the Bell Telephone laboratories in 1948.

shock wave A narrow region of a high pressure in a fluid, created when a fast-moving body passes through the fluid. The waves spread outwards from the body and occur, for example, when an aircraft passes through the *sound barrier.

shogun A hereditary military title, the holders of which were the actual rulers of Japan, although the emperors retained formal sovereignty. In 1192 Minamoto Yoritomo became the first shogun. From 1338 to 1573 the Ashikaga family held the title and in 1603 Tokugawa Ieyasu (1542–1616) revived it. The last shogun was Tokugawa Keiki (1827–1913; ruled 1867–68).

shooting Discharging a weapon at a target or at game. The two main types of **target shooting** for rifles are small bore (.22 calibre) at ranges of 25–200 m (27–219 yd), and full bore (7.62 calibre) at ranges of 200–1200 yd (183–1097 m). Weapons for pistol shooting range from the .177 air pistol to the .45 pistol, with ranges between 10 and 50 yd (9–45 m). In **clay-pigeon shooting** (or trapshooting) clay discs are mechanically flung into the air and fired at with shotguns. In **grouse shooting** (in the UK permitted only from 12 Aug to 10 Dec), **pheasant shooting** (1 Oct to 1 Feb), and **partridge shooting** (1 Sept to 1 Feb) the birds are driven from cover towards the shooters by hunting dogs and beaters.

Shorthorn A breed of cattle originating in NE England and formerly popular for both beef and dairy purposes. Stocky, with short legs, Shorthorns range from red to white with various mottled mixtures.

shortsightedness (or myopia) Inability to focus on distant objects. The commonest visual defect, it often runs in families: it is due to a slightly misshapen eyeball, in which the light rays are focused in front of the retina (light-sensitive layer). It is corrected by wearing glasses with concave lenses or contact lenses.

Shoshoni A group of North American Indian tribes of the Great Basin region who speak a language of the Uto-Aztecan family. Some acquired horses and moved onto the Plains, including the *Comanche.

Shostakovich, Dmitri (1906–75) Soviet composer. His 15 symphonies include the very successful first symphony (1924) and the wartime seventh symphony (*The Leningrad*; 1941). He also composed two concertos each for piano, violin, and cello, 15 string quartets, operas, and much other music.

shot put (or putting the shot) A field event in athletics, in which an iron or brass sphere is thrown (put) one-handed as far as possible. It weighs 7.26 kg (16 lb) for men and 4 kg (8.8 lb) for women. The putter must stay within a circle 2.1 m (7 ft) in diameter. World records: men: 23.12 m (1990) by Eric Randolph Barnes (USA); women: 22.63 m (1987) by Natalya Lisovskaya (USSR).

shoveler duck A *duck, Spatula clypeata, of the N hemisphere, having a large bill for feeding on water plants and invertebrates on the surface of fresh water. 50 cm long, it has a pale-blue wing flash; the male has a dark-green head, white breast, and chestnut underparts and the female is speckled brown.

shrew A small insect-eating mammal found all over the world except Australasia and the Polar regions. The dwarf shrew (*Suncus etruscus*) is the smallest mammal in the world, weighing only 2 g and measuring 7–8 cm. Shrews are very active: the common shrew (*Sorex araneus*) eats its own weight in food every 24 hours in order to meet its energy requirements.

Shrewsbury 52 43N 2 45W A town in W central England, the administrative centre of Shropshire on the River Severn and a market town for the surrounding agricultural area. It has a castle (built 1070) and the famous boys' public school was founded here in 1552. Population (1987): 91 900.

shrike A fierce songbird occurring in Europe, Asia, Africa, and North America and also called butcherbird. Shrikes dive on insects and small vertebrates from the air, killing them with their hooked bills; they often impale prey on thorns.

shrimp A *crustacean, usually 4–8 cm long, occurring in fresh and salt water. Shrimps have a semitransparent body with long slender legs (the first pair pincer-like), a fanlike tail, and whiplike antennae, nearly as long as the body. They feed on small animals or plants. Many species, including the European shrimp (*Crangon vulgaris*), are commercially important as food.

Shropshire A county in the West Midlands of England, bordering on Wales. During the 18th century it became the main iron-producing county in England; the world's first cast-iron bridge was built at Ironbridge in 1779. It is now chiefly agricultural. Area: 3490 sq km (1348 sq mi). Population (1988 est): 400 800. Administrative centre: Shrewsbury.

Shroud of Turin A relic traditionally believed to be the linen cloth used to wrap Christ's body for burial. It bears impressions of a human body marked with wounds consistent with Christ's at the crucifixion. It has been kept in Turin since 1578. In 1988 carbon-dating tests established that it was woven from flax gathered between 1260 and 1390.

Shrove Tuesday The day before the beginning of Lent (*see* Ash Wednesday), so called from the "shriving" (i.e. confession and absolution) of the faithful that was customary before Lent. In many countries carnivals are held and in England pancakes are traditionally eaten—hence the popular name Pancake Day.

Siam. *See* Thailand.

Siamese cat A breed of slender short-haired cat, originating from SE Asia. The Siamese has blue eyes and large pointed ears. The fur is cream-coloured or off-white, shading into one of several colours (most popularly seal-brown or blue-grey) on the ears, face, paws, and tail (the "points").

Siamese twins Identical twins who are fused together, usually at the head or along the trunk. They can sometimes be surgically separated, providing that vital organs are not involved in the point of union. The original Siamese twins, Chang and Eng (1811–74), were born in Siam; they were joined at the hip and remained fused.

Sian. *See* Xi An.

Sibelius, Jean (Johan Julius Christian S.; 1865–1957) Finnish composer. Many of his works have Finnish associations. They include seven symphonies, symphonic poems such as *The Swan of Tuonela* (1893) and *Finlandia* (1899–1900), a violin concerto, and many songs.

Siberia A region comprising most of the Soviet Union E of the Ural Mountains. It is notorious for its long harsh winters. Its outstandingly rich mineral resources include coal and petroleum. Forestry is also important and Siberia's many rivers (notably the Ob, Yenisei, and Lena) are used for hydroelectric power. Russian settlement was intermittent until the building (1891–1905) of the Trans-Siberian Railway. Siberia has long been a place of exile for Russian criminals and political prisoners. Area: about 13 807 037 sq km (5 330 896 sq mi).

Sicily The largest island in the Mediterranean Sea, which together with adjacent islands comprises an autonomous region of Italy. It is separated from the mainland by the Strait of Messina. Sicily is largely mountainous and underdeveloped. The mining industry is important, especially oil. *History*: occupied successively by the Greeks, Carthaginians, Romans, and Arabs, it came under Norman rule in 1060. In 1266 Charles I became the first Angevin King of Sicily. The island was conquered by Aragon in 1284 following the revolt (called the Sicilian Vespers) in 1282 against Charles' oppressive regime. Naples and Sicily formally became the Kingdom of the Two Sicilies in 1815 under Ferdinand I. After conquest by Garibaldi (1860), Sicily was united with the rest of Italy. Area: 25 710 sq km (9927 sq mi), with adjacent islands. Population (1987 est): 5 141 343. Capital: Palermo. *See also* Mafia.

Sickert, Walter Richard (1860–1942) British impressionist painter and etcher, born in Munich of Danish and Irish parentage. His paintings of Venice and Dieppe (1895–1905) and scenes from the music hall and domestic life make use of sombre colours.

sickle-cell disease A disorder due to the body's red blood cells containing an abnormal form of the pigment haemoglobin. The disease is hereditary and affects only Blacks. When the blood is deprived of oxygen the abnormal haemoglobin distorts the red cells into a sickle shape: these sickle cells are removed from the blood by the spleen, which leads to *anaemia.

Siddons, Sarah (*born* Kemble; 1755–1831) British actress, acclaimed at her London debut in 1782 as the leading tragic actress of her time.

sidereal period The time taken by a planet or satellite to return to the same point in its orbit, i.e. to complete one revolution, with reference to the background stars.

sidewinder A small nocturnal *rattlesnake, *Crotalus cerastes*, occurring in deserts of the S USA and Mexico. It has a sideways looping method of locomotion enabling it to move quickly over loose sand.

Sidney, Sir Philip (1554–86) English poet and courtier. His works include *Arcadia* (1580), *Astrophel and Stella* (1591), and an important work of critical theory, *The Defence of Poesy* (1595).

Siegfried A hero of Germanic legend, who also appears in early Scandinavian legend as Sigurd. In the Germanic *Nibelungenlied*, Siegfried wins Brunhild for his brother-in-law Gunther, but a quarrel between Brunhild and Siegfried's wife Kriemhild leads to Siegfried's death by treachery. In the Old Norse *Volsungasaga*, Sigurd is betrothed to Brynhild but is tricked (by a magic potion) into forgetting her and marries Gudrun. He then wins Brynhild for his brother-in-law Gunnar; later Brynhild incites Gunnar to kill him.

siemens (S) The *SI unit of conductance equal to the conductance between two points on a conductor when a potential difference of one volt between the points causes a current of one ampere to flow. Named after the German electrical engineeer Ernst Werner von Siemens (1816–92).

Siena 43 19N 11 19E A city in central Italy, in Tuscany. Founded by the Etruscans, it was an important commercial and artistic centre in the middle ages. Its many fine buildings include a 13th-century cathedral and a university (1240). Population (1989): 58 534.

Sierra Leone, Republic of A country in West Africa, on the Gulf of Guinea. *Economy*: chiefly agricultural, with recent development in fishing, forestry, and mining industries. *History*: in 1787 local chiefs gave Britain a piece of land along the coast for the settlement of slaves freed in the colonies. In 1896 the region became a British protectorate, gaining independence within the Commonwealth in 1961. In 1971 Sierra Leone became a republic. In 1977 one-party government (by the All-People's Congress) was introduced. President: Joseph Saidu Momoh. Official language: English; Krio is widely spoken. Official currency, since 1964: leone of 100 cents. Area: 73 326 sq km (27 925 sq mi). Population (1988 est): 3 875 000. Capital and main port: Freetown.

Sierra Madre The chief mountain system of Mexico. It extends for about 2500 km (1500 mi) SE from the US border, reaching 5699 m (18 697 ft) at Citlaltépetl.

Sierra Nevada A mountain range in the USA. It extends generally NW–SE through California, reaching 4418 m (14 495 ft) at Mount Whitney. It contains the famous Yosemite National Park.

Sierra Nevada A mountain range in S Spain. It rises to 3481 m (11 421 ft) at Mulhacén, the highest point in Spain.

Sihanouk, Norodim, Prince (1923–) King (1941–55) of Cambodia. When the Japanese occupation ended in 1945, Sihanouk achieved Cambodia's independence from France (1953). Abdicating in 1955, he was prime minister until 1970, when he was deposed. Briefly head of state (1975–76), he returned into exile and headed a coalition of opposition parties.

sika A deer, *Cervus nippon*, also called Japanese deer, native to S Asia, Japan, and Taiwan and introduced to New Zealand and Europe.

70–100 cm high, it is grey-brown in winter and chestnut with white spots in summer. Stags have slender eight-pointed antlers about 80 cm long.

Sikhism The religion of some nine million Indians, mostly inhabiting the Punjab. Founded in the 15th century by *Nanak, Sikhism combines Hindu and Islamic ideas. Sikhs accept the Hindu concept of *karma; the guidance of the *guru is essential. The concept of Khalsa, a chosen race of warrior-saints, is central, as are the so-called five Ks: *kangha* (comb); *kacch* (shorts); *kirpan* (sword); *kara* (steel bracelet); and *kes* (uncut hair and beard).

Sikorski, Władysław (1881–1943) Polish general and statesman. Sikorski was prime minister (1922–23) and then minister of military affairs (1924–25). After Poland's collapse in 1939, he became prime minister of the Polish government-in-exile in London. He died in an aeroplane crash near Gibraltar.

Sikorsky, Igor Ivan (1889–1972) US aeronautical engineer, born in Russia, who invented the helicopter. He produced the S-1 biplane in 1910. After moving to the USA (1919) he completed the first successful helicopter, the VS-300, in 1939.

Silbury Hill A prehistoric mound in S England, near *Avebury, Wiltshire. Begun about 2150 BC, it is the largest man-made hill in Europe, standing 40 m (130 ft) high.

Silenus In Greek mythology, an elderly *Satyr, companion of the god *Dionysus. He was famed for his wisdom and prophetic powers as well as his drunkenness. The Sileni were his fellow nature spirits.

Silesia A region of E central Europe now in Czechoslovakia and Poland. Because of its geographical position and mineral wealth, Silesia has been disputed territory since the 17th century, when it was claimed by both Austria and Prussia. Prussia acquired most of it in 1763, after the *Seven Years' War. After World War I it was divided between Czechoslovakia, Germany, and Poland and after World War II, between Czechoslovakia and Poland.

silica The mineral silicon dioxide, SiO_2, the most abundant of all minerals. There are three main forms of silica: *quartz, tridymite, and cristobalite. Silica is the main constituent of igneous rocks.

silicon (Si) The second most abundant element in the earth's crust, after oxygen. It is a major constituent of almost all rock-forming minerals. Pure silicon is of great importance in the electronics industry as a semiconductor. Silicates are the main constituents of pottery, glasses, and many building materials. Organic silicon compounds are known as *silicones. At no 14; at wt 28.086; mp 1410°C; bp 2355°C.

silicon chip. *See* integrated circuit.

silicones Synthetic substances produced by *polymerization and consisting of chains of alternating silicon and oxygen atoms, with organic groups attached to the former. Silicones are stable to heat, oxidation, many chemicals, and oils. They are used in adhesives, paints, elastomers, and waterproofing agents.

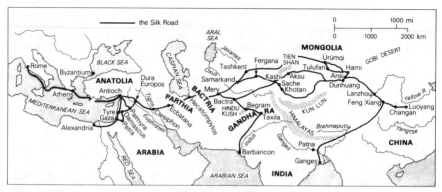

SILK ROAD *Between the 1st century* BC *and the 3rd century* AD *Chinese silks travelled westwards to the Mediterranean in exchange for precious metals.*

silicosis   A lung disease caused by breathing in silica dust over long periods: it is an occupational disease of stone cutters, quarry workers, etc. The air sacs of the lungs become thickened and scarred, causing breathlessness and coughing. There is no specific treatment so prevention is essential. *See also* pneumoconiosis.

silk   The thread produced by the caterpillar of the Chinese *silkworm moth and the luxury fabric woven from it. The cocoons are unravelled and the filaments from several twisted together; processing this raw silk includes combining these strands and washing away the sticky secretion. China, where silk production was first practised, and Japan are the leading producers of pure silk; wild silk, produced by other species of silkworms, includes a coarser brown Indian silk.

silk-cotton tree.   *See* kapok.

Silk Road   A trade route, 6400 km (4000 mi) long, that connected China with the Mediterranean. It was most used in ancient times, when silk was taken westwards and wool and precious metals eastwards, but was again travelled in the later middle ages, notably by Marco Polo.

silkworm   A caterpillar that spins a cocoon of silk that is suitable for commercial *silk production. The commonest is the Chinese silkworm (*Bombyx mori*), which feeds on mulberry leaves.

silky oak   Either of two Australian trees. The species *Grevillea robusta* has fernlike leaves and is widely cultivated in the tropics for ornament or shade. The northern silky oak (*Cardwellia sublimis*) has pinkish soft wood and is an important timber tree.

silt   A fine-grained sedimentary deposit, the particles of which range from 0.002 to 0.06 mm in diameter. Silts consist mainly of clay minerals, with iron oxides and hydroxides and silica. They collect in sheltered marine environments, such as estuaries, making dredging necessary.

Silurian period   A geological period of the Lower Palaeozoic era between the Ordovician and Devonian periods, lasting from about 445 to 415 million years ago. Conditions were mainly marine and the first true fish appeared. The first evidence of land plants also comes from Silurian rocks.

silver   (Ag)   A metallic element that occurs as the metal, as argentite (Ag_2S), and in lead, zinc, and copper ores. Pure silver has the highest electrical and thermal conductivity known. In air, silver tarnishes forming a coating of the black sulphide (Ag_2S). Sterling silver (92.5% pure) is used for jewellery. Silver salts are of great importance in photography as they are light sensitive. At no 47; at wt 107.868; mp 961.93; bp 2212°C.

silverfish   A widely distributed primitive wingless insect, *Lepisma saccharina*. A species of *bristletail, it is covered with silvery scales and is common in buildings, feeding on starchy materials, including books and fabrics.

silverplate   Any object that is plated with silver rather than being solid silver. The original Sheffield plate (silver-coated copper) was first produced in 1742. In 1840 *electroplating brought silverplated domestic articles to a much wider public. Many silverplated articles are marked EPNS (electroplated nickel silver)—a layer of silver is electroplated onto a base of nickel silver, an alloy of copper, nickel, and zinc.

Simenon, Georges   (1903–89) Belgian novelist. The best known of his several hundred novels are the detective stories featuring the Parisian *commissaire de police*, Maigret, who first appeared in 1931.

simple harmonic motion   Any regular (periodic) motion performed by a body about some reference point so that the restraining force is directly proportional to its displacement from that point. Examples of simple harmonic motion include a *pendulum swinging through a small angle and a vibrating string.

Simplon Pass   An alpine pass linking Brig in Switzerland with Iselle in Italy. Built 1800–07 on Napoleon's orders, it reaches a height of 2009 m (6590 ft). The **Simplon Tunnel** to the NE is, at 20 km (12 mi), formerly the longest rail tunnel in the world. It was opened in 1906.

Simpson, Wallis.   *See* Edward VIII.

Simpson Desert   (*or* Arunta Desert) A desert of central Australia, mainly in Northern Territory. It is an arid region covered by parallel sand dunes. Area: about 77 000 sq km (29 723 sq mi).

Sinai A desert peninsula in Egypt, bounded by Israel and the Gulf of Aqaba to the E and the Gulf of Suez and mainland Egypt to the W. Mount Sinai, 2285 m (7497 ft) high, is in the mountain range in the S. The chief resources are manganese and the oil deposits in the W, based on Sudr. Sinai was occupied by Israel in the 1956 and 1967 Arab-Israeli Wars; following the 1973 war, Egyptian and Israeli lines were established on either side of a UN buffer zone. Under the 1979 Egyptian-Israeli agreement a large proportion of the area was returned to Egypt with Israeli withdrawal completed in 1982.

Sinatra, Frank (Francis Albert S.; 1915–) US singer and film actor, who recorded his first hit, "All or Nothing at All," in 1943. His nonsinging role in the film *From Here to Eternity* (1953) earned him an Oscar. He has remained a popular singer and recorded such hits as "Strangers in the Night" (1966).

Singapore, Republic of A republic in SE Asia, off the S tip of Peninsular Malaysia, consisting of the island of Singapore and over 50 islets. The city of Singapore is in the S. *Economy*: Singapore is the world's busiest port. It is a major commercial centre and in recent years industry has been expanded and diversified, oil refining being important. *History*: although a prosperous commercial centre in the middle ages, the island was largely uninhabited in 1819 when Sir Stamford Raffles (1781–1826) established a station of the British East India Company here. In 1824 it was handed over to Britain. During World War II it was occupied by the Japanese (1942–45). It became a separate British colony in 1946 and gained its independence in 1959. It joined the Federation of Malaysia (1963) but broke away in 1965 and formed an independent republic. President: Wee Kim Wee. Prime minister: Goh Chok Tung (1941–). Official languages: Chinese, English, Malay, and Tamil. Official currency: Singapore dollar of 100 cents. Area: 602 sq km (232 sq mi). Population (1988 est): 2 650 000.

Singer, Isaac Bashevis (1904–) Polish-born US writer. His novels and collections of stories, written in Yiddish and frequently dramatizing traditional themes from Jewish life in Poland, include *Gimpel the Fool* (1957), *The Slave* (1960), *Shosha* (1978), and *The King of the Fields* (1989). He won the Nobel Prize in 1978.

Sinhalese The major ethnic group in Sri Lanka. They speak an Indo-Aryan language and are descended from migrants from Bengal who colonized Sri Lanka during the 5th century BC.

Sinn Féin (Irish: Ourselves) An Irish nationalist party organized by Arthur Griffith in 1905. In 1918, under Eamon *De Valera, it won a majority of the Irish seats in the British parliament and achieved the creation of the Irish Free State in 1922. Sinn Féin exists today as the political wing of the republican movement. *See also* Irish Republican Army.

Sino-Japanese Wars 1. (1894–95) The war between China and Japan resulting from rivalry in Korea. China, heavily defeated, was forced to give up Taiwan, the Pescadores, and the Liaodong peninsula. 2. (1937–45) The war be-tween China and Japan brought about by Japanese expansion into China in the 1930s. The Japanese position remained strong until the USA entered World War II (1941) and gave China assistance. After Japan's surrender (1945) China regained Manchuria, Taiwan, and the Pescadores.

Sino-Tibetan languages A group of languages spoken in E Asia. It includes all the *Chinese dialects, the Tibeto-Burman languages (Tibetan, Burmese, and many related languages of the Himalayas), and probably the Tai languages, such as Siamese, Laotian, and Shan.

sinus A hollow cavity, especially one in a bone. The term usually refers to the air sinuses in the facial bones; all are connected to the nasal cavity and may become infected and inflamed (**sinusitis**).

Siouan languages A family of North American Indian languages including Dakota Sioux, Crow, and several others. Most are spoken by Plains tribes.

Sioux A confederation of North American Plains Indian tribes, also known as the Dakota. They defeated Gen Custer at the battle of the *Little Bighorn (1876) under their leaders Sitting Bull and Crazy Horse. They were eventually subdued, one group making a last stand at *Wounded Knee (1890).

Sirens In Greek mythology, female creatures who lured sailors to their island by their singing and then destroyed them. *Odysseus was protected by tying himself to the mast of his ship and filling the ears of his crew with wax.

sirocco (*or* scirocco) A southerly wind occurring in N Africa, Sicily, and S Italy. Hot and dry on the N African coast, it picks up moisture as it crosses the Mediterranean Sea bringing extensive cloud to S Italy.

sisal An *agave plant, *Agave sisalana*, native to central America and cultivated throughout the tropics for its fibre, which is extracted from the leaves. It is used in shipping, general industry, and agriculture.

siskin A Eurasian *finch, *Carduelis spinus*, of Europe and Asia. It is about 12 cm long with a dark yellow-green plumage, paler streaked underparts, bright-yellow wingbars, and in the male a black chin and crown.

Sisley, Alfred (1839–99) Impressionist painter, born in Paris of British parents. In the 1870s he produced some of his best landscapes, for example *Misty Morning*, and three pictures of the *Floods at Port-Marly*.

Sistine Chapel The principal chapel of the Vatican, built for Pope Sixtus V (1473) by Giovanni dei Dolci. It is famous for its murals by Perugino (c. 1450–1523), Botticelli, and Ghirlandaio and roof and ceiling by Michelangelo.

Sisyphus A legendary Greek king of Corinth. For various offences he was condemned in the underworld to spend eternity rolling a boulder to the top of a hill, whence it always rolled down again.

sitar An Indian long-necked *lute with a resonating body made from a large gourd, seven metal strings stopped against movable arched frets, and a series of sympathetic strings that vibrate when the other strings are plucked.

Sitting Bull (c. 1834–93) American Sioux Indian chief. Resisting US expansion into the Plains, Sitting Bull led the massacre of Gen Custer and his men at the *Little Bighorn (1876).

Sitwell, Edith (1887–1964) British poet and writer. Her poetry includes *Façade* (1923), for which Sir William Walton wrote a musical accompaniment. Her brother **Sir Osbert Sitwell** (1892–1969) wrote poems, short stories, and novels, but his best-known works are his nostalgic autobiographical memoirs. Both he and his sister encouraged writers, artists, and musicians.

SI units (Système International d'Unités) An international system of units, based on the *m.k.s. system, used for all scientific purposes. It has seven base units (metre, kilogram, second, ampere, kelvin, candela, and mole) and two supplementary units (radian and steradian). All physical quantities are expressed in these units or in derived units consisting of combinations of these units. Decimal multiples of all units are expressed by a set of prefixes, such as kilo-, milli-, and mega-.

Six Day War. *See* Israel.

Skagerrak A channel in N Europe, lying between Denmark and Norway and connecting the Kattegat to the North Sea.

skate A large widely distributed *ray fish. 50–200 cm long, skates have a diamond-shaped flattened body with spiny or thorny structures on the upper surface and often an extremely long snout.

skimmer A black-and-white bird occurring chiefly around western Atlantic coasts and African and Asian rivers. The skimmer fishes by flying close to the water, shaving the surface with the lower mandible and snapping the bill shut as soon as a fish is caught.

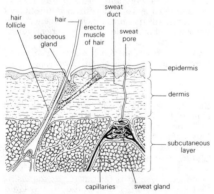

SKIN *A vertical section through the human skin shows its microscopical structure. The subcutaneous layer of fat cells provides insulation.*

skin The tissue that covers the body of a vertebrate. The outermost layer of the epidermis contains dead cells made of keratin, which are constantly shed and replaced by the deeper layers of continuously dividing cells. The skin protects the body from external injury, prevents tissues from drying out, assists in regulating body temperature (e.g. by sweating), and is sensitive to touch, temperature, and pain. The branch of medicine concerned with skin disorders is called **dermatology**. **Skin grafting** is one of the most important and successful *transplantation operations.

skink A lizard occurring throughout the tropics and in temperate North America. Skinks are well adapted for burrowing: they have cylindrical streamlined bodies with smooth scales, a transparent covering over the eye, and often small and simple limbs.

Skinner, Burrhus Frederic (1904–90) US psychologist and advocate of behaviourism. Many of Skinner's experiments involved teaching animals (such as rats and pigeons) by reinforcing the desired action with rewards of food. He also applied his principles to human educational aids.

Skopje 42 00N 21 28E A city in S Yugoslavia, the capital of Macedonia, on the River Vardar. It was almost completely destroyed by an earthquake in 1963. Industries include cement, brick, glass, and steel. Population (1981): 506 547.

skua A large hook-billed seabird that breeds in Arctic and Antarctic regions and winters in warmer latitudes. Skuas have a dark plumage with two long central tail feathers. They scavenge around seabird colonies, feeding on eggs, chicks, and food scraps.

skull The skeleton of the head, made up of 22 bones of varying shapes and sizes. The cranium consists of eight flat platelike bones that surround and protect the brain. The remaining 14 bones, including the mandible, form the face: the mandible is the only movable bone in the skull; the rest are connected by immovable joints called sutures.

skunk A black and white carnivorous mammal, related to weasels and badgers, that is known for its habit of ejecting a foul-smelling fluid when threatened. Skunks are found in North, South, and Central America.

Skye The largest and most northerly island of the Inner Hebrides group, off the W coast of Scotland. Crofting and tourism are important. Area: 1735 sq km (670 sq mi). Population (1985 est): 7500. Chief town: Portree.

skylark A *lark, *Alauda arvensis*, occurring in Europe, Asia, and N Africa and noted for its sustained warbling song. It is about 17 cm long, with brown plumage, a small crest and a white stripe above the eye.

slander. *See* defamation.

slate A fine-grained *metamorphic rock produced from deposits of silts and clays. It is easily split into thin layers. Slate is used as a building material, for example as roofing tiles.

slavery The condition in which human beings are owned by others. In ancient Greece and early Rome captives from conquered lands were the chief source of slaves, who were well treated and might be freed (manumission). Slaving became a profitable business in the 16th century, when European traders began to transport thousands of Africans to the Americas. By the early 19th century William *Wilberforce and others had begun to attack slavery and it was abolished in all British territories by 1834. In the USA, slavery in the South became one of the causes of the Civil War; in 1865 slavery was abolished in the USA.

Slavonic languages A subgroup of the *Indo-European language family, spoken by the Slav peoples of E Europe and NW Asia. They are often classified into three groups: South Slavonic (including *Serbo-Croat, Slovene, *Bulgarian, and Macedonian); West Slavonic (including Czech, *Slovak, and Polish); and East Slavonic (Russian, Belorussian, and Ukrainian).

sleep A naturally occurring state of unconsciousness. In orthodox sleep the electrical activity of the brain reacts less to outside stimuli. At intervals it is interrupted by paradoxical sleep, associated with dreams, in which the eyes move rapidly and the brain is more active. Sleep is necessary for health, and probably helps to control physical growth; individuals' needs vary widely between three and ten hours a night.

sleeping sickness A disease caused by infection with a parasitic protozoan (*Trypanosoma*), which is transmitted by the tsetse fly and occurs only in East, central, and West Africa. Symptoms include lethargy, weakness, and depression: without treatment (by drugs) the patient dies.

Sligo (Irish name: Contae Shligigh) A county in the NW Republic of Ireland, in Connacht bordering on the Atlantic Ocean. Cattle rearing and dairy farming are important. Area: 1795 sq km (693 sq mi). Population (1986): 55 979. County town: Sligo.

Slim, William Joseph, 1st Viscount (1891–1970) British field marshal. In World War II he became commander of the 14th Army (the "forgotten army") in Burma (1943). After successful operations against the Japanese he became commander in chief of Allied land forces in SE Asia. In 1948 he became chief of the imperial general staff and was then governor general of Australia (1953–60).

slipper orchid A tropical Asian *orchid the flowers of which have a pouched slipper-shaped lip. It is a popular greenhouse pot plant.

Sloane, Sir Hans (1660–1753) British physician and naturalist, whose collection of books, manuscripts, pictures, etc., formed the nucleus of the *British Museum.

sloe. *See* blackthorn.

sloth A primitive tree-dwelling *mammal of Central and South America, also called ai or unau. 50–65 cm long, sloths are slow-moving and hang upside down from branches, feeding on leaves and fruit.

Slough 51 31N 0 36W A town in SE England, in Berkshire. It grew rapidly after a large trading estate was built here in the 1920s and now has a great variety of light industries. Population (1981): 87 005.

Slovak A Western Slavonic language, closely related to *Czech, spoken in E Czechoslovakia, where it is an official language. It is written in the Latin alphabet.

Slovakia A mountainous area and former province of E Czechoslovakia. Conquered by the Magyars in the 10th century, Slovakia was part

of Hungary until 1918, when it became a province of the Czechoslovak Republic, remaining as such until 1949. Chief town: Bratislava.

Slovenia A constituent republic of N Yugoslavia. It possesses important deposits of coal, mercury, and zinc. Slovenia was chiefly under Habsburg rule from the 14th century until 1918, when it became part of the kingdom of Serbs, Croats, and Slovenes, later renamed Yugoslavia. In 1990 it declared itself a sovereign state. Area: 20 251 sq km (7819 sq mi). Population (1986): 1 930 000. Capital: Ljubljana.

slowworm A legless lizard, *Anguis fragilis*, also called blindworm, occurring in heaths and open woodlands of Europe. It is about 30 cm long, usually brown, grey, or reddish, and feeds on snails, slugs, and worms.

slug A mollusc, related to snails, widely distributed in moist habitats on land. Slugs have slimy soft bodies and range in colour from yellow through red-brown to black. Some eat live or dead animal material while others feed on soft plant tissues. *Compare* sea slug.

smallage. *See* celery.

smallpox A highly infectious virus disease marked by a skin rash that leaves permanent pitted scars. Smallpox is caught by direct contact with an infected person. The disease may allow staphylococci bacteria to set up their own infection, which is often fatal. After a worldwide vaccination programme sponsored by the World Health Organization, smallpox was officially declared to have been totally wiped out in 1979.

smell, sense of. *See* nose.

smelt A slender food fish occurring in coastal and estuarine waters of Europe and North America. It migrates to fresh water to spawn. The European smelt (*Osmerus eperlanus*), up to about 30 cm long, is greenish grey above and silvery below.

smelting The extraction of a metal from its ore by heating. The smelting takes place either in a *blast furnace (e.g. to extract iron) or a reverberatory furnace (e.g. to extract copper); in the latter the ore is heated indirectly.

Smetana, Bedřich (1824–84) Bohemian composer. In 1859 he joined a group of composers in Prague who were establishing a national opera. *The Brandenburgers in Bohemia* (1862–63) and *The Bartered Bride* (1863–66) were composed for it. In 1874 he became totally deaf but continued to compose, writing the four symphonic poems *Má Vlast* (1874–79) and a string quartet (1876).

Smith, Adam (1723–90) Scottish moral philosopher and political economist. In 1776, he published *An Enquiry into the Nature and Causes of the Wealth of Nations*. He held that employment, trade, production, and distribution are as much a part of a nation's wealth as its money.

Smith, Ian (Douglas) (1919–) Prime minister (1964–79) of Rhodesia (now *Zimbabwe). An advocate of White supremacy, in 1965 he made a unilateral declaration of independence (UDI), maintained until 1976 when he agreed to the principle of Black majority rule.

Smith, Joseph (1805–44) US founder of the *Mormons. Smith announced in 1827 his discovery of the sacred *Book of Mormon*, which he claimed he had translated from two gold tablets written by a prophet named Mormon. His new church, founded in Fayette, New York (1830), attracted considerable opposition. While in jail on charges of conspiracy, Smith was killed by an angry mob.

Smith, Dame Maggie (1934–) British actress. She appeared in such films as *The Prime of Miss Jean Brodie* (1969), *A Private Function* (1984), and *A Room with a View* (1986).

Smith, Stevie (Florence Margaret S.; 1902–71) British poet, whose deceptively simple poetry blended tenderness, toughness, and humour. The best known of her novels is *Novel on Yellow Paper* (1936). Her *Collected Poems* (1975) were published after her death.

Smithsonian Institution A research institution in Washington, DC, founded in 1846 with a bequest from the Englishman James Smithson (1765–1829). It administers several important museums, including the National Air and Space Museum and the National Collection of Fine Arts.

smoke tree (*or* smoke bush) A tree or shrub that has a whitish cloudy appearance at some stage of the season. The American smoke tree (*Cotinus obovatus*) grows to a height of 9 m and has a smokelike mass of whitish flower heads. *Rhus cotinus* is the common smoke bush native to the Mediterranean area and parts of Asia.

Smollett, Tobias (George) (1721–71) Scottish writer. His lively novels include *Roderick Random* (1748), *Peregrine Pickle* (1751), and *Humphry Clinker* (1771).

smooth snake A nonvenomous snake, *Coronella austriaca*, of Europe and Asia. Up to 65 cm long, it has smooth glossy scales and is brown or reddish with a pale belly and dark spots along its back and tail.

Smuts, Jan (Christiaan) (1870–1950) South African statesman and general; prime minister (1919–24, 1939–48). He played an important part in the achievement of responsible government for the Transvaal (1906) and the Union of South Africa (1910). A member of Lloyd George's imperial war cabinet in World War I, he helped establish the League of Nations. He supported South Africa's entry into World War II. His desire to maintain South Africa's links with the British Commonwealth made him unpopular among Afrikaners.

Smyrna. *See* Izmir.

snail A mollusc with a spirally coiled shell. Snails live on land, in fresh water, or in the sea. They have two pairs of sensory head tentacles which can be withdrawn when threatened; one pair bears simple eyes. A rasping tongue (radula) is used for scraping animal or plant material as food. Snails may be hermaphrodite or may have separate sexes.

snake A legless *reptile of which there are about 3000 species, occurring worldwide, especially in the tropics. Snakes range from 0.12–10 m in length and grow throughout their lives, periodically shedding the skin in one piece. They swallow their prey whole, having jaws that move apart during swallowing. Prey may be killed by constriction (crushing), by engulfing it alive, or by injecting a venom through hollow or grooved fangs.

Snake River A river in the NW USA. Rising in the Yellowstone National Park in Wyoming, it flows W through Idaho to join the Columbia River in Washington State. Length: 1670 km (1038 mi).

snapdragon. *See* antirrhinum.

snapper A carnivorous fish found in shoals in tropical seas. It has an elongated body, a large mouth, and sharp teeth. Some species are valuable food fish, especially the red snapper (*Lutjanus blackford*); others are poisonous.

Snell's law When a ray of light passes from one medium to another the angle (*r*) between the refracted ray and a line normal to the interface between the media is related to the angle (*i*) of the incident ray, also taken to the normal, by the equation $\sin i/\sin r = n$, where *n* is the relative refractive index of the media (*see* refraction). It is named after the Dutch astronomer Willebrord Snell (1591–1626).

snipe A *sandpiper occurring in wet areas of warm and temperate regions. Snipe have a long flexible bill used to probe for worms, and a barred and striped brown, black, and white plumage.

snooker A game, developed from *billiards, that arose among British officers in India (1875). It is played on a billiards table using 22 balls: 1 white cue ball, 15 red balls (value 1 point each), and 6 coloured balls—yellow (2 points), green (3), brown (4), blue (5), pink (6), black (7). The object is to pocket a red ball and a coloured ball alternately, each time returning the coloured ball to its own spot on the table. When all the red balls have been potted the colours are potted in order of points.

Snow, C(harles) P(ercy), Baron (1905–80) British novelist and scientist. The moral problems of politics and power are a recurrent theme of his series of novels beginning with *Strangers and Brothers* (1940) and ending with *Last Things* (1970).

snowball tree. *See* guelder rose.

Snowdon 53 04N 4 05W The highest mountain in Wales, in Gwynedd. The surrounding area, **Snowdonia**, was designated a National Park in 1951. Height: 1085 m (3560 ft).

Snowdon, Antony Armstrong-Jones, Earl of (1930–) British photographer. His work includes several television documentaries, photographic books, and the design of the Snowdon Aviary, London Zoo (1965). His marriage (1960–78) to Princess Margaret ended in divorce.

snowdrop A small early spring-blooming plant that is native to Europe and W Asia. Snowdrops grow from bulbs to produce grasslike leaves and slender stems bearing nodding white flowers. *Galanthus nivalis* is the common European snowdrop.

snow goose An Arctic *goose, *Anser caerulescens*. It is either pure white with black wingtips, or blue-grey with a white head. Snow geese winter in the southern USA, Japan, and China.

snow leopard   A big *cat, *Panthera* (or *Uncia*) *uncia*, also called ounce, found in the mountains of central Asia. It is 1.9 m long, with a thick ash-grey coat marked with dark rosettes.

Snowy Mountains   A mountain range in Australia. It lies within the *Australian Alps, in New South Wales, and contains Australia's highest mountain, Mount *Kosciusko.

snuff   A tobacco preparation that is sniffed rather than smoked. Ingredients such as lavender and menthol add flavour and scent to the mixture.

soaps   Salts of *fatty acids. Normal household soap (**hard soap**) is a mixture of sodium stearate, oleate, and palmitate. It is made by the hydrolysis of *fats with caustic soda (sodium hydroxide), thus converting the glycerides of stearic, oleic, and palmitic acids into sodium salts and glycerol. **Soft soap** is made with potassium hydroxide instead of sodium hydroxide. Soaps have a cleansing action because they are chemically attracted to grease and oil. Particles of grease or oil therefore form an emulsion in soapy water. *See also* detergents.

soapstone.   *See* talc.

Soares, Mario   (1924–   ) Portuguese statesman; prime minister (1976–79; 1983–85); president (1986–   ). He was a critic of Salazar and lived in exile from 1970 to 1974. He became prime minister as leader of the Portuguese Socialist Party.

Sobers, Gary   (Sir Garfield Saint Aubrun S.; 1936–   ) West Indian cricketer, who captained the West Indies and Nottinghamshire. One of the greatest all-rounders, he played in 93 Test matches, scoring 8032 runs, including 26 centuries, and taking 235 wickets and 110 catches.

Social and Liberal Democratic Party (SLD) A British political party of the centre, established in 1988 when a majority of the *Social Democratic Party merged with the Liberal Party. Paddy *Ashdown was elected as the first leader.

Social Democratic Party (SDP)   A British political party of the centre, formed in 1981 by four ex-members of the Labour Party: Roy Jenkins (1920–   ), Shirley Williams (1930–   ), Dr David *Owen (elected leader in 1983), and William Rodgers. The SDP formed a political alliance with the Liberal Party in 1981. After poor results in the 1987 general election, the party voted to merge with the Liberals to form the *Social and Liberal Democratic Party. Owen resisted this move and launched a reduced SDP in 1988, winding it up in 1990.

socialism   A concept and political movement that stresses the need for cooperation rather than competition. In the early 19th century the emphasis was on reform of the social system to develop liberal values, with the aim of producing a society based on social ownership and control. In the second half of the 19th century, *Marxism became the basis for most socialist thought. The *Fabian Society's interpretation of socialism later found political expression in the *Labour Party. In Russia, the split between the *Bolsheviks and the *Mensheviks emphasized the distinction between *communism and socialism: socialists

seek change by peaceful reform, while communists are dedicated to change by revolution.

Society Islands   A group of islands in French Polynesia, discovered in 1767. It consists of the **Windward Islands** (including Tahiti and Moorea) and the **Leeward Islands** (including Raiatea and Huahine). The capital of French Polynesia, Papeete, is on Tahiti. Area: 1595 sq km (616 sq mi). Population (1983): 142 129.

Society of Friends.   *See* Quakers.

Society of Jesus.   *See* Jesuits.

sociology   The systematic study of the development, organization, functioning, and classification of human societies. It uses such techniques as the systematic comparison of different societies, and surveys of social conditions, attitudes, and behaviour. Specialized areas include demography (the study of populations) and political, educational, and urban sociology.

sockeye salmon   A *salmon, *Oncorhynchus nerka*, also called red salmon or blueback, that lives in the N Pacific and spawns in Canadian fresh waters.

Socrates   (c. 469–399 BC) Athenian philosopher, whose ideas are known through his disciples *Plato and *Xenophon. Socrates steered philosophy towards *ethics and the beginning of *logic. His opposition to tyranny led to his trial on charges of atheism and "corrupting the youth;" he was condemned to die by drinking hemlock.

Soddy, Frederick   (1877–1956) British chemist, who worked under *Rutherford and *Ramsay and went on to win the 1921 Nobel Prize for his discovery of *isotopes.

sodium (Na)   A highly reactive *alkali metal, first isolated as the element by Sir Humphry Davy in 1807. It is obtained commercially by *electrolysis of common salt (NaCl). It occurs in some silicate minerals (such as *feldspars), salt deposits, and in the oceans. The metal is soft, bright, and less dense (relative density 0.97) than water, with which it reacts violently, liberating hydrogen. It forms many ionic salts of great importance, such as the chloride (common salt; NaCl), the carbonate (soda ash; Na_2CO_3) and the bicarbonate (baking soda; $NaHCO_3$). At no 11; at wt 22.9898; mp 97.8°C; bp 882.9°C.

sodium bicarbonate (sodium hydrogencarbonate *or* bicarbonate of soda; $NaHCO_3$) The white soluble powder that is a constituent of baking powder and is used to make fizzy drinks and to treat indigestion.

sodium carbonate (Na_2CO_3)   A white soluble salt. The commercial form (**soda ash**) is an anhydrous (water-lacking) powder used in making glass, soap, paper, and chemicals. **Washing soda**, its hydrated form, is a crystalline solid used as a domestic cleanser and water softener.

sodium hydroxide (*or* caustic soda; NaOH) A white solid that is strongly alkaline when dissolved in water and is very corrosive to organic tissue. It is used in making rayon, paper, detergents, and other chemicals.

Sodom and Gomorrah   In the Old Testament, two cities of Palestine, known as the "cities of the plain," S of the Dead Sea in the area in which Lot, the nephew of Abraham, settled. Ac-

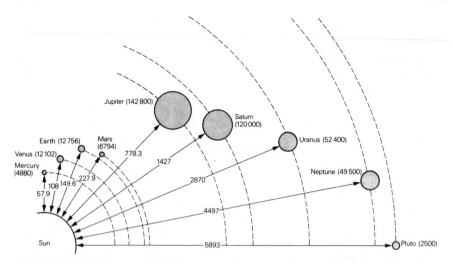

SOLAR SYSTEM *The planets with their equatorial diameters in kilometres (in brackets after the planet's name) and their distance from the sun in millions of kilometres (not to scale).*

cording to Genesis (18, 19), they were destroyed by fire and brimstone from heaven because of the utter wickedness of their inhabitants.

Sofia 42 40N 23 18E The capital of Bulgaria, in the W. Under Turkish rule from 1382, it was liberated by the Russians in 1878 and became the national capital (1879). Its ancient churches include St Sofia (6th–7th centuries). Industries include engineering, textiles, and food processing. Population (1987): 1 128 859.

software The suite of *programs that sets up a *computer system for operation, as distinct from the physical equipment (hardware). Software supplied by the computer manufacturer controls various parts of the system and provides facilities for further programming. Additional programs are purchased separately or written by the user.

soil The loose material that covers much of the earth's land surface and provides a medium for plant growth. It consists of mineral particles, derived from weathered rock, and organic matter (humus), derived from the breakdown of plant tissue by living organisms.

sol. *See* colloid.

solar cell. *See* solar power.

solar flare A sudden brightening, within minutes, of areas in the sun's atmosphere, resulting from an explosive release of energetic particles and radiation. Flares often occur above *sunspot groups. Large flares affect radio transmission on earth and produce *auroras.

solar power The use of the sun's energy to provide heating or to generate electricity. Solar energy is used for the direct heating of water flowing through special panels on the roof of a building. The small temperature rise reduces the energy required from other sources for hot water and space heating. Higher temperatures, sufficient to form steam for electricity generation, are

possible using large mirrors to collect and focus the sun's rays. Direct conversion of solar radiation into electrical energy is possible with **solar cells**. These are semiconductor devices in which the sun's radiation produces an *electromotive force. The method is used mainly in small-scale applications, for example powering marine beacons.

solar system A system comprising the *sun, the nine major *planets and their *satellites, and the *minor planets, *comets, and other smaller rocky bodies. Almost all the mass of the solar system (99.86%) resides in the sun. The planets orbit the sun in the same direction and, with the exception of Pluto, move in paths close to the earth's orbital plane. The solar system formed some 4600 million years ago, following the contraction and subsequent flattening of a rotating cloud of interstellar gas and dust.

solar wind An almost radial outflow of charged particles from the sun's outer atmosphere into interplanetary space. The particles, mainly protons and electrons, are moving at speeds between 200 and 900 km per second in the vicinity of the earth's orbit. They interact with the earth's *magnetosphere.

solder An *alloy that is melted to form a joint between other metals or, occasionally, nonmetals. **Soft solder** is usually made of lead and tin and melts in the range 200–250°C. It is used for making secure electrical connections. **Brazing**, also called **hard soldering**, uses a harder alloy with a higher melting temperature (850–900°C), usually a *brass with 60% zinc and 40% copper. **Silver solder**, which melts at 630–830°C, often contains antimony or other metals but no longer contains silver. Like brazing, its strength makes it useful in engineering applications.

sole An elongated *flatfish found in temperate and tropical seas. The common European sole (*Solea solea*), also called Dover sole, is a valuable food fish.

solenoid A coil of wire usually forming a long cylinder. When electric current flows through it a *magnetic field is created. This field can be used to move an iron rod placed on its axis. Solenoids are often used to operate mechanical valves attached to the iron rod.

Solent, the A channel between the coast of Hampshire in S England and the Isle of Wight. It is an important shipping route between Southampton and the English Channel.

solicitor In the UK, a member of the legal profession qualified to give legal advice to clients, to present cases in Magistrates' Courts, County Courts, and (since 1971) to present certain cases in the Crown Court, and to undertake other legal work, such as the transfer of property (conveyancing). A barrister must always be instructed through a solicitor.

Solidarity A Polish trade union. Formed in Gdansk (1980) and led by Lech *Walesa, Solidarity became a focus of resistance to *Jarulzelski's Soviet-dominated government. Proclaimed illegal in 1981, Solidarity continued underground and was legalized in 1989. In the same year it formed the first noncommunist government in the Communist world.

solid state One of the four states of matter and that to which all substances, except helium, revert at sufficiently low temperatures. It is distinguished from the other states (*gases, *liquids, *plasma) by being the only one in which matter retains its shape, as a result of the stronger intermolecular forces.

Solo. *See* Surakarta.

Solomon In the Old Testament, the third King of Israel, son of *David and Bathsheba, who reigned in the 10th century BC. During his reign foreign alliances were formed with Phoenicia and Egypt, trade and commerce were expanded and the *Temple at Jerusalem was built. He was famous for his wisdom.

Solomon Islands A country in the Pacific Ocean, E of New Guinea. The largest islands are *Guadalcanal, Malaita, San Cristobal and New Georgia. Copra and timber are the chief exports. The islands were discovered by the Spanish in 1568. The four main islands became a British protectorate in 1893 and others were added in 1898–99. They became independent within the British Commonwealth in 1978. Chief minister: Solomon Mamaloni. Official language: English. Official currency: Australian dollar of 100 cents. Area: 29 785 sq km (11 500 sq mi). Population (1987): 291 800. Capital and main port: Honiara.

Solon (6th century BC) Athenian statesman, who laid the foundations of Athenian democracy. As archon (magistrate) (c. 594–593), Solon introduced a new coinage and weights and measures. He also instituted a new constitution and a more lenient legal code.

solstice Either of two points on the ecliptic, midway between the *equinoxes, at which the sun reaches its greatest angular distance above or below the celestial equator (*see* celestial sphere). In the N hemisphere the sun's northernmost position occurs at the **summer solstice**, usually on 21 June,

when daylight hours are at a maximum. Its southernmost position occurs at the **winter solstice**, usually on 22 December, when daylight hours are minimal.

Solti, Sir Georg (1912–) Hungarian-born naturalized British conductor. He was conductor of the Royal Opera, Covent Garden (1961–71), the Orchestre de Paris (1972–75), the London Philharmonic Orchestra (1979–83), and the Chicago Symphony Orchestra (1969–89).

solution A homogenous liquid mixture of two or more substances. Solutions, unlike *colloids, contain no identifiable particles. When a solid or gas is dissolved in a liquid, the liquid is known as the solvent and the dissolved material the solute. If all the components are liquid, the one in excess is the solvent.

Solvay process An industrial process for the production of sodium carbonate. Limestone is heated to produce calcium oxide and carbon dioxide, which is passed through brine saturated with ammonia, precipitating sodium hydrogen-carbonate ($NaHCO_3$). This, on mild heating, yields sodium carbonate and some carbon dioxide, which is recycled. The ammonia is also recovered. Named after E. Solvay (1833–1922).

Solzhenitsyn, Aleksandr (1918–) Russian-born novelist. After World War II he was held in prison camps until 1956. In 1974 he left the Soviet Union and now lives in the USA. His major works include *Cancer Ward* (1968), *The First Circle* (1968), and *The Gulag Archipelago* (1974–78). He won the Nobel Prize in 1970.

Somali An E African people occupying Somalia, Djibouti (where they are called Issas), Ethiopia, and NW Kenya. Their language belongs to the Cushitic branch of the Hamito-Semitic family.

Somalia (official name: Somali Democratic Republic) A country in East Africa, occupying most of the Horn of Africa between the Gulf of Aden and the Indian Ocean. The economy is chiefly agricultural, livestock raising being especially important. The region was occupied in the 19th century by the French, British, and Italians (*see* Somaliland). British Somaliland became independent as Somalia in 1960. In 1969, after a military coup, a Supreme Revolutionary Council was established under Gen Mohammed Siad Barré (1919–). The country has had serious territorial disputes with Ethiopia (*see* Ogaden) and has been torn by civil war: in 1991 Barré was overthrown and Ali Mahdi Mohammed became president. Official language: Somali; Arabic, Italian, and English are used extensively. Official religion: Islam. Official currency: Somali shilling of 100 centesemi. Area: 700 000 sq km (270 000 sq mi). Population (1987 est): 6 110 000. Capital and main port: Mogadishu.

Somaliland A region corresponding to present-day Somalia and Djibouti. Between the 7th and 12th centuries AD the coastal region was occupied by Muslim traders while the N was settled by travelling Somalis. During the 19th century the region was divided between France, Britain, and Italy. Italian Somaliland was united with Ethiopia by Mussolini (1935) and was acquired by Britain in World War II. British Somaliland became independent as Somalia in 1960 and the French territory, Afars and Issas, as Djibouti in 1977.

somatotrophin. *See* growth hormone.

Somerset A county of SW England, bordering on the Bristol Channel. Exmoor is in the W and the Mendip Hills (containing Cheddar Gorge) in the NE. It is predominantly agricultural; dairy farming is especially important and there is the traditional cider making. Area: 3458 sq km (1335 sq mi). Population (1986 est): 448 900. Administrative centre: Taunton.

Somme, River A river in N France, rising in the Aisne department and flowing mainly W through Amiens and Abbeville to the English Channel. It was the scene of extensive fighting in *World War I (1916). Length: 245 km (152 mi).

sonar. *See* echo sounding.

sonata (Italian: sounded, as opposed to *cantata*, sung) A piece of music for one or more instruments. **Sonata form,** the normal structure of the first movement of the classical sonata, was based on two contrasting themes. It was applied to the first movement of the *symphony and of *chamber music compositions as well as the sonata itself.

Sondheim, Stephen (Joshua) (1930–) US composer. He wrote the lyrics for the musicals *West Side Story* (1957), *A Little Night Music* (1973), *Sweeney Todd* (1979), and *Assassins* (1991). The revue *Side by Side by Sondheim* (1976) contains many of his songs.

sonic boom. *See* sound barrier.

sonnet A poem of 14 lines originating in Italy in the 13th century and introduced into England in the 16th century by Sir Thomas Wyatt. The Shakespearean sonnet usually rhymes *abab cdcd efef gg*.

Soochow. *See* Suzhou.

Sophists The Greek sages of the 5th and early 4th centuries BC who travelled from place to place teaching public speaking, grammar, ethics, literature, mathematics, and elementary physics. They believed that virtue could be taught. From their opponent *Plato, they acquired a bad name as philosophical tricksters.

Sophocles (c. 496–406 BC) Greek dramatist; with Aeschylus and Euripides, one of the three great Athenian tragic dramatists. Of his 123 plays, 7 survive, including *Electra, Oedipus Rex,* and *Antigone.* He held several important civil and military administrative posts.

Sopwith, Sir Thomas Octave Murdoch (1888–1989) British aircraft designer, best known for the World War I biplane, the Sopwith Camel, which he designed and built. He learned to fly in 1910 and founded the Sopwith Aviation Company Ltd in 1912. He was chairman of the Hawker Siddeley Group (1935–63).

sorghum An African *grass, *Sorghum vulgare,* several varieties of which are widely cultivated as cereal crops. They have flower clusters bearing 800–3000 starch-rich seeds, which are used as grain for making bread, etc., and as a source of edible oil, starch, and sugar. The stalks, which sometimes contain sweet sap, are used as fodder or for syrup manufacture.

sorrel A tall plant, *Rumex acetosa,* common throughout temperate Eurasia and North America. It bears numerous small red flowers. The tangy-tasting leaves are used as a flavouring in cookery and in salads. *See also* wood sorrel.

Sotho A large group of *Bantu-speaking peoples of S Africa. The term applies in a general sense to the peoples of Botswana, Lesotho, and the Transvaal (South Africa), but, more specifically, to one of the four main divisions of these peoples, the Sotho of Lesotho.

sound A disturbance that is carried (propagated) through a medium by longitudinal waves. Strictly the term applies only to those waves that are audible to the human ear, i.e. with frequencies between about 20 and 20 000 hertz. Sound is propagated by vibrations of molecules in the medium. Sound waves are longitudinal as the molecules vibrate in the direction of propagation; the speed of sound in air at 0°C is about 332 metres per second (760 mph). The three principal characteristics of a sound are its pitch (the frequency of the wave), loudness (the amplitude of the wave), and timbre (the extent to which it contains harmonics of the fundamental frequency). *See also* acoustics; sound intensity.

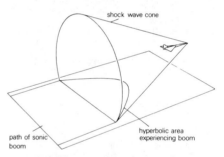

SOUND BARRIER *As an aircraft passes through the sound barrier the sonic boom is heard along a hyperbolic area on the ground.*

sound barrier An obstacle experienced by subsonic *aircraft attempting to fly at or above the speed of sound. At supersonic speeds the pressure waves created by the aircraft as it flies through the air cannot escape in a forward direction as the aircraft is moving faster than the waves. Thus *shock waves build up on the wings and fuselage of the aircraft, which becomes difficult to control. Many aircraft are now capable of supersonic flight (including Concorde) by greater streamlining, sweptback wings, and more powerful engines. As these aircraft cross the sound barrier a **sonic boom** is heard. This is created by a shock-wave cone with the nose of the aircraft at its vertex.

sound intensity The rate at which *sound energy is propagated through a unit area perpendicular to the direction of propagation. It is measured in watts per square metre. The intensities of two sound levels are compared by a unit called the *decibel.

Sousa, John Philip (1854–1933) US composer and bandmaster. He wrote military marches, including "The Stars and Stripes Forever," "The Washington Post," and "Liberty Bell," and invented the **sousaphone**, a tuba-like band instrument with a forward-facing bell.

souslik (*or* suslik)   A nocturnal squirrel, that lives in underground burrows in E Europe, Asia, and North America (where it is sometimes called a gopher). The European souslik (*Citellus citellus*) is yellowish brown with large eyes and small ears.

South Africa, Republic of   A country occupying the S tip of Africa. The Limpopo, Molopo, and Orange Rivers mark the N boundary. The majority of the inhabitants are Africans (71%) with White, Coloured, and Asian (mostly Indian) minorities. *Economy*: rich mineral resources include gold, diamonds, chrome, platinum, uranium, coal, manganese, phosphates, and iron. Well-developed industry includes metals, machinery, chemicals, food processing, and textiles. Exports include gold, fruit, and wine. *History*: Bantu tribes arrived from the north between 1000 and 1500. The Dutch East India Company settlement (1652) at Table Bay (Cape Town) expanded and spread into the interior. During the Napoleonic Wars Britain acquired the Cape Colony. In the 1830s Dutch farmers (or Boers, forebears of the modern Afrikaners) moved E and N to escape British rule, clashing with the Bantu peoples who were then migrating southwards (*see* Great Trek). The Boers founded two independent republics, the Orange Free State and the Transvaal, but their republic in Natal was soon annexed by the British (1843). In 1880 war broke out between the Boers and the British (*see* Boer Wars). The two former Boer republics and the two British colonies combined in the Union of South Africa in 1910. In both World Wars South Africa, under *Smuts, supported Britain, but in 1948 Smuts was ousted by the anti-British Afrikaner National Party and in 1961 South Africa became a republic outside the British Commonwealth. Since 1910 the treatment of the non-White majority has been the crucial political issue (*see* apartheid). In the face of increasing internal unrest, some non-Whites received limited parliamentary power under a new constitution instituted in 1984. Race riots resulted in the declaration of a state of emergency (1985–90). In 1989 P. W. *Botha was replaced as president by F. W. de Klerk, who legalized the *African National Congress, released *Mandela, and began to dismantle apartheid. Official languages: Afrikaans and English. Official currency, since 1959: rand of 100 cents. Area: 1 221 042 sq km (472 359 sq mi). Population (1989): 30 190 000. Capitals: Pretoria (administrative), Bloemfontein (judicial), Cape Town (legislative).

South America   The fourth largest continent, lying chiefly in the S of the W hemisphere between the Pacific and Atlantic Oceans. It is linked to North America by the Isthmus of Panama. The Brazilian and Guiana Highlands in the NE are separated by the vast basins of the Orinoco, Amazon, and Paraná–Paraguay river systems. In the extreme W are the *Andes. Much of South America is tropical with vast areas of tropical rainforest (selva). *History*: the flourishing kingdoms of South America (such as those of the

*Incas), were vanquished by the Spanish conquistadors. The entire continent was divided –Portugal taking the NE portion (now Brazil) and Spain the remainder–during the 16th century. With the collapse of the Spanish Empire during the early 19th century, there followed struggles for independence under national leaders, who included *Bolívar and *San Martin. Large-scale European immigration occurred in the 19th century. The 20th century has seen increasing industrialization and rapid population rises. Area: 17 767 331 sq km (6 858 527 sq mi). Population (1985): 263 300 000.

Southampton   50 55N 1 25W A city in S England, in Hampshire on Southampton Water (an inlet of the English Channel). It is the UK's principal passenger port and an industrial centre with a large oil refinery at Fawley, on Southampton Water. Population (1981): 204 406.

South Australia   A state of S central Australia, bordering on the Indian Ocean and Great Australian Bight. It consists chiefly of plains; the only major river is the Murray. Intensive agriculture is restricted to the S. The vineyards of the fertile Barossa Valley produce almost half of Australia's wine. Mineral resources include iron ore, coal, natural gas in the N, and opals. Industry is concentrated in Adelaide. Area: 984 377 sq km (380 070 sq mi). Population (1986): 1 345 945. Capital: Adelaide.

South Carolina   A state in the SE USA, on the Atlantic coast. The large areas of woodland supply the furniture industries and the large textile and clothing industries are based on the region's cotton crop. One of the 13 original colonies, it separated from North Carolina in 1713 and was the first state to withdraw from the Union (1860). Area: 80 432 sq km (31 055 sq mi). Population (1988 est): 3 493 000. Capital: Columbia. *See also* Charleston.

South Caucasian languages   A group of languages, also known as the Kartvelian languages, spoken by the people of W Transcaucasia and nearby regions. It includes *Georgian, Svan, Mingrelian, and Laz.

South Dakota   One of the Plains states in N central USA. The flat fertile prairie in the E forms the basis of South Dakota's predominantly agricultural economy. Livestock and livestock products are the chief source of revenue. Part of the *Louisiana Purchase (1803), the gold rush and land boom of the 1880s brought many settlers and South Dakota became a state in 1889. Area: 199 551 sq km (77 047 sq mi). Population (1986 est): 708 000. Capital: Pierre.

South East Asia Treaty Organization (SEATO) An organization formed to protect SE Asia from possible communist aggression. The treaty was signed in Manila in 1954 by Australia, France, New Zealand, Pakistan, the Philippines, Thailand, the UK, and the USA. Pakistan withdrew in 1973 and the organization was formally ended in 1977.

Southend-on-Sea   51 33N 0 43E A resort in SE England, in Essex on the lower Thames estuary. It is the nearest seaside resort to London and has the world's longest pleasure pier. Population (1988): 165 400.

South Georgia An island in the S Atlantic Ocean, a dependency of the Falkland Islands. King Edward Point is a British Antarctic Survey base. With the Falkland Islands, it was invaded by Argentina (April, 1982) but was soon recaptured. Area: 3755 sq km (1450 sq mi).

South Glamorgan A county of SE Wales, bordering on the Bristol Channel. It was created in 1974 from S Glamorgan and SW Monmouthshire. Agriculture is important with industry centred on Barry and Cardiff. Area: 416 sq km (161 sq mi). Population (1987 est): 399 500. Administrative centre: Cardiff.

South Island The larger of the two principal islands of New Zealand, separated from North Island by Cook Strait. It is generally mountainous, including the Southern Alps in the W, with coastal plains.

Southport 53 39N 3 01W A town and resort in NW England, in N Merseyside on the Irish Sea. There is a well-known golf course at nearby Birkdale. Population (1981): 89 745.

South Sea Bubble The collapse of the British market in South Sea stocks in 1720. The South Sea Company was founded in 1711 to trade with Spanish America and in 1718 George I became its governor. A boom in the stock was followed by a collapse; the subsequent inquiry revealed corruption among ministers and even the king. Sir Robert *Walpole saved the situation by transferring the South Sea stocks to the Bank of England and the East India Company.

South Shields 55 00N 1 25W A port in NE England, in Tyne and Wear on the Tyne estuary opposite North Shields. Industries include petrochemicals and paint manufacture. The first lifeboat was built here (1790). Population (1981): 87 203.

South West Africa. *See* Namibia.

South Yorkshire A metropolitan county of N England, created in 1974 from the S part of the West Riding of Yorkshire and a small part of NE Derbyshire. It comprises the districts of Sheffield, Rotherham, Doncaster, and Barnsley. Agriculture is important and the main industries are iron and steel, engineering, and coalmining. Area: 1562 sq km (603 sq mi). Population (1987 est): 1 295 600. Administrative centre: Barnsley.

Soutine, Chaim (1893–1943) Lithuanian-born painter, who emigrated to Paris in 1913. Using thick paint and distorted forms, he was, with *Chagall, a leader of French expressionism.

soviet A government council in the Soviet Union. Starting as committees of workers' deputies in the *Revolution of 1905, they were again established in the *Russian Revolution of 1917. The Supreme Soviet is the government in the Soviet Union.

Soviet Union (official name: Union of Soviet Socialist Republics) The world's largest country with the third largest population, covering N Eurasia. It consists of 15 constituent republics: the Armenian, Azerbaidzhan, Belorussian, Estonian, Georgian, Kazakh, Kirghiz, Latvian, Lithuanian, Moldavian, Russian Soviet Federal, Tadzhik, Turkmen, Ukrainian, and Uzbek Soviet Socialist Republics. Administrative subdivisions include 20 Autonomous Soviet Socialist Republics and,

within some of these, 8 autonomous regions (Russian *oblast*, region). *Economy*: formerly based on state ownership, and controlled through Gosplan (the State Planning Commission) and Gosbank (the State Bank), it began to introduce free-market policies in the late 1980s. The Soviet Union is the world's leading producer of oil, coal, iron ore, cement, and steel; manganese, gold, natural gas, and other minerals are also of major importance. Industry has concentrated on the production of capital goods. Agriculture is highly mechanized; fishing, forestry, and dependent industries are also important. Largely self-sufficient, it has a relatively small international trade, which is increasing. *History*: in the 8th century AD, European and Middle Eastern traders began to explore the region. By 1000 control of the area between the Baltic and Black Seas was established by Scandinavian adventurers. After 1223 the area submitted to the Golden Horde (the western part of the Mongol Empire). By the 14th century, Moscow had emerged as a powerful principality, becoming the capital of a united Russia under Ivan the Great in the 15th century. Contact with W Europe was established in the late 17th century by Peter the Great, who built a new capital, St Petersburg (now Leningrad). By the 19th century Russia had greatly expanded but was industrially far behind the UK and Germany. Its Romanov emperors (tsars) abolished serfdom in 1861 on terms unfavourable to the peasants; this encouraged the revolutionaries, a group of whom assassinated Alexander II in 1881. Following the Revolution of 1905, a parliament, the Duma, was established in 1906, but political unrest continued. The February and October Revolutions (*see* Russian Revolution) were followed by civil war (1918–22), after which communist control was complete. After Lenin's death (1924) Stalin emerged as leader in 1928, having ousted Trotsky. Under Stalin, the Soviet Union (established 1922) became a totalitarian state. World War II established the Soviet Union as one of the two major superpowers. Relations with the USA improved after the *Cold War although the Soviet occupation of Afghanistan (1979–89) provoked condemnation. Since Mikhail *Gorbachov came to power in 1985 there has been considerable reform, with the introduction of *glasnost and perestroika, and relations with the West have improved greatly. In 1989 a new parliament was established and in 1990 the Communist Party renounced its monopoly of power. Unrest in constituent republics now threatens the unity of the Soviet Union and has led to fears of a crackdown. The Soviet Union is a member of *COMECON. Official language: Russian. Official currency: rouble of 100 kopeks. Area: 22 402 200 sq km (8 647 675 sq mi). Population (1988): 284 500 000. Capital: Moscow.

Soweto 26 10S 28 02E A large suburb of Johannesburg in South Africa. It is inhabited by Black Africans and comprises 36 townships, divided into tribal areas. In June, 1976, it was the scene of serious rioting by African students. Population (1983): 915 872.

soya bean (*or* soybean) A plant, *Glycine max*, of the pea family, widely cultivated for its seeds (35% protein), which are eaten whole and ground into flour. Soya-bean oil is extracted for making margarines, cooking oils, etc. The residue is an important protein food for livestock and meat substitute for man.

Soyinka, Wole (1934–) Nigerian writer. His works include the play *The Lion and the Jewel* (1963) and the novels *The Interpreters* (1965), *The Man Died* (1973), *Aké* (1982), and *Isara* (1990). He won the 1986 Nobel Prize.

Soyuz. *See* Salyut.

spacecraft A vehicle designed to be launched into space. Unmanned craft include several thousand *satellites of diverse functions and numerous planetary probes, including the *Mariner and *Voyager craft. *Space stations and *space shuttles carry crews.

space shuttle One of a series of manned reusable US space transportation systems developed by *NASA. First launched in April 1981 it was operational by 1982. It consists of a delta-wing Orbiter that has three rocket engines, a large cargo bay, and living space. See pages 502–503.

space station A large orbiting spacecraft on which people can live and work in weightless conditions. Crews are ferried to and from the station, remaining on board for up to several months. The first space station was the Soviet *Salyut–1, launched in 1971; America's Skylab was orbited in 1973.

space travel Travel outside the earth's atmosphere. The space age began with the Soviet Sputnik I satellite, launched on 4 October, 1957 and the subsequent manned flight by the Soviet cosmonaut Yuri Gagarin on 12 April, 1961. The US astronaut, Neil Armstrong, was the first man to set foot on the moon (20 July, 1969). Both Americans and Russians have sent unmanned probes to most planets and have sent *space stations into orbit. See pages 502–503.

Spain, Kingdom of A country in SW Europe, occupying over four-fifths of the Iberian Peninsula. The Balearic and Canary Islands are also part of Spain. *Economy*: traditionally agricultural, industry had begun to predominate by the early 1970s. Tourism is a major source of currency. Forestry, fishing, and wine are important and there are rich mineral resources. *History*: following settlements by Iberians, Celts, Phoenicians, and Greeks, the Carthaginians conquered most of Iberia in the 3rd century BC but were expelled by the Romans in the second *Punic War (218–201 BC). By the 5th century the Romans had given way to the Vandals and then the Visigoths. The Visigothic kingdom collapsed (711) in the face of Muslim invaders, who dominated most of the peninsula under a series of powerful dynasties. The Reconquest of Muslim Spain by the Christian kingdoms was completed in 1492 with the conquest of Granada by Ferdinand of Aragon and Isabella of Castile. 1492 also saw the expulsion of the Jews, who were followed (1609) by the Muslims. Overseas exploration in the 16th century led to an empire in the Americas, which brought great wealth to Spain. The country's power was furthered by the Habsburg kings Charles I (who as *Charles V was also Holy Roman Emperor) and his son Philip II. However, during the latter's reign, decline began with the

*Revolt of the Netherlands against Spanish rule and the defeat of the Spanish Armada by the English (1588). The death (1700) of the last Habsburg king (Charles II) without an heir, led to the War of the *Spanish Succession (1701–14). In the second half of the 18th century Spain's decline was halted by the Bourbon Charles III, but in 1808 Napoleon established his brother Joseph Bonaparte on the throne. The Spanish resistance to their French conquerors contributed to the defeat of Napoleon (*see* Peninsular War) and in 1814 the Bourbon Ferdinand III (1716–88) was restored. Conflict between monarchists and republicans dominated the 19th century, during which Spain also lost its last American possessions. It was neutral in World War I, following which Miguel Primo de Rivera (1870–1930) established a military dictatorship. In 1931 Alfonso XIII abdicated and the Second Republic was established. The electoral victory of the Popular Front under Azaña in 1936 precipitated a military revolt led by Gen *Franco that became the *Spanish Civil War (1936–39), followed by over 30 years of Nationalist dictatorship. After Franco's death (1975) Juan Carlos de Borbón became king and head of state. In 1978 provisional regional self-government was granted to Catalonia, Valencia, the Canary Islands, Aragon, Galicia, and the Basque provinces, but terrorist activities by Basque separatists have continued. A Socialist government was elected in 1982 under Felipe González (1942–). Spain joined NATO in 1982 and the EC in 1986. Official language: Spanish. Official religion: Roman Catholic. Official currency: peseta of 100 céntimos. Area: 504 879 sq km (194 883 sq mi). Population (1988 est): 39 200 000. Capital: Madrid. Main port: Barcelona.

spaniel Several breeds of sporting dogs developed in Britain and thought to have originated in Spain. The English springer spaniel has a lean body and long drooping ears. It is longer in the leg than the similar *cocker spaniel but has the same wavy coat. It is generally black and white, while the smaller Welsh springer spaniel is red and white. *See also* King Charles spaniel.

Spanish A *Romance language spoken in Spain, Latin America, the Philippines, and elsewhere by about 308 million people. The standard form is based on the Castilian dialect.

Spanish Civil War (1936–39) The civil war in Spain started by a military revolt on 18 July, 1936, led by the Nationalist Gen *Franco, against the Republican Government of Manuel Azaña (1880–1940). By the end of 1936 the Nationalists controlled most of W and S Spain. During 1937, with Italian and German help, they captured Bilbao. In 1938–39, in spite of the assistance of the *International Brigade and the Soviet Union, the Republicans lost Barcelona, Valencia, and then Madrid, and Franco set up a pro-fascist dictatorship that lasted for over 30 years.

Spanish Riding School A centre for classical horsemanship in Vienna, originally in the Habsburg palace (probably founded late 16th century). *Haute école* *dressage of the 16th and

Man needed two inventions to get him into space. First, the telescope, to enable him to map the heavens accurately, and then the rocket to enable him to escape the earth's gravitational field.

Telescope The first refracting telescope was invented in 1608 by Lippershey and adapted for astronomical investigation a year later by Galileo. Newton invented the first reflecting telescope in 1668. All modern optical astronomical telescopes use this principle.

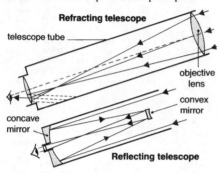

Refracting telescope

telescope tube

objective lens

convex mirror

concave mirror

Reflecting telescope

A 13th-century Chinese military rocket using gunpowder as propellant.

Wernher von Braun's V2 rocket was launched against London in 1944-45. It became the basis for US space rockets.

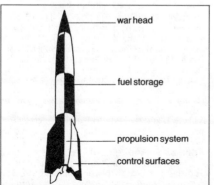

war head

fuel storage

propulsion system

control surfaces

Satellite The first satellites proved that flight in space was possible and were used to study such phenomena as cosmic rays and radiation belts. Later they were developed for meteorology, communications, photography of the earth's surface, and various military roles, notably under the star wars programme. They can also house powerful space telescopes.

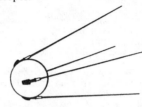

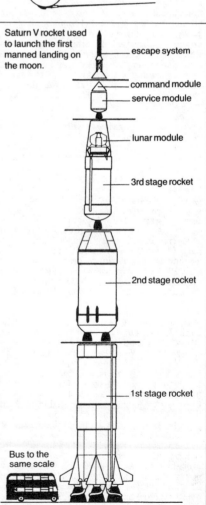

Saturn V rocket used to launch the first manned landing on the moon.

escape system

command module

service module

lunar module

3rd stage rocket

2nd stage rocket

1st stage rocket

Bus to the same scale

The greatest human achievement in space has been to land a man on the moon - a feat dreamed of in science fiction only a decade before World War II. Neil Armstrong's first steps on the moon were in July 1969.

Shuttle Use of reusable shuttle aircraft reduces the cost of space travel. Its versatility makes it useful for numerous purposes, including satellite launching and repair.

Salyut 1 docking with Soyuz spacecraft.

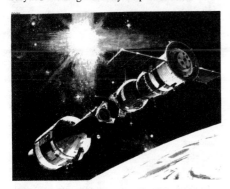

Probe The US probe Pioneer 10 carries a plaque and other records to provide alien life forms with information about the spacecraft's origin and its creators.

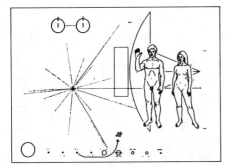

Chronology

1926	First liquid fuel rocket launched.
1937-45	V2 rocket developed by Wernher von Braun.
1957	First satellite, Sputnik 1, launched.
1958	First US satellite, Explorer 1, launched.
1961	Yuri Gagarin became first man in space.
1965	First commercial communications satellite, Intelsat 1, launched.
1966	Soviet space probe, Venera 3, landed on Venus.
1969	Apollo 11 landed on Moon, commanded by Neil Armstrong.
1970	Soviet Lunokhod vehicle landed on Moon.
1971	First space station, Salyut 1, launched.
1971-72	Mariner 9 orbited Mars.
1972	Pioneer 10 launched.
1973	Pioneer 10 reached Jupiter; US space station, Skylab, launched.
1975	Apollo 18 and Soyuz 19 linked up in space.
1976	Viking 1 and 2 landed on Mars.
1977	Voyager 1 and 2 launched.
1979	Voyager 1 and 2 reached Jupiter; first Ariane rocket launched.
1981	First US space shuttle launched.
1982	Venera 13 and 14 landed on Venus.
1983	Pioneer 10 reached Neptune.
1986	Voyager 1 and 2 reached Uranus.
1989	Voyager 1 and 2 reached Neptune.

17th centuries is practised. The white *Lipizzaner stallions used have been bred from horses imported from Spain in the 16th century.

Spanish Sahara. *See* Western Sahara.

Spanish Succession, War of the (1701–14) The third European war caused by Louis XIV's attempts to increase French power. He proclaimed his grandson king of Spain (as Philip V), after the death of Charles II. England felt threatened, and with the Dutch Republic and the Holy Roman Emperor formed an alliance (1701) against France; they were joined by most German states (1702). Spain, Bavaria, Portugal, and Savoy supported France. The English won a series of victories under *Marlborough but pressed for peace in 1712, when a Spanish-Austrian union threatened. The Treaties of *Utrecht (1713–14) ended the war.

Spark, Muriel (1918–) British novelist. Her works include *Memento Mori* (1959), *The Prime of Miss Jean Brodie* (1961), *Territorial Rights* (1979), *The Only Problem* (1984), *A Far Cry from Kensington* (1988), and *Symposium* (1990).

sparrow A small member of the *weaverbird family. Generally brown and grey, they are mostly tropical but also occur in Europe and Asia. The house sparrow (*Passer domesticus*) has been introduced from Europe and Asia to North America.

sparrowhawk A small woodland *hawk, *Accipiter nisus*, occurring in Europe, Asia, and NW Africa. It has a long tail and the male (27 cm long) is grey with brown-barred white underparts; females (38 cm long) are brown above. It hunts small birds.

Sparta 37 05N 22 25E In ancient Greece, the capital of Laconia in the S Peloponnese. Developing during the 10th century BC, Sparta controlled much of Laconia and Messenia by 700 BC. It became a militaristic state, where boys from the age of seven underwent military training. Its defeated (404) Athens in the *Peloponnesian War: but defeat by the Thebans at Leuctra (371) marked the beginning of Spartan decline. The ancient city was destroyed by the Visigoths in 396 AD.

Spartacus Thracian gladiator, who led a slave revolt against Rome in 73 BC. After defeating the Romans, he moved to N Italy. When his followers refused to disperse, Spartacus marched S again and was defeated by Marcus Licinius *Crassus (71). He and his followers were crucified.

spastic. *See* cerebral palsy.

Speaker of the House of Commons The presiding officer of the lower chamber of the British parliament. Elected by each new parliament, he (or his deputy) regulates all proceedings of the House, except in committee.

spearmint An aromatic herb, *Mentha spicata*, native to central and S Europe and widely used in cookery. The oil from the leaves is used to flavour sweets, etc.

Special Air Service (SAS) A division of the British army, formed in 1942. The unit is trained for action behind enemy lines and other clandestine operations. Its motto is "Who dares wins."

species A unit of classification of animals and plants. Individuals of the same species can breed among themselves, producing fertile offspring that resemble the parents. Some species are divided into subspecies and varieties. Breeds of domestic animals and cultivated varieties of plants have been developed by man and are derived from wild species. All breeds of domestic dog, for instance, belong to the same species –*Canis familiaris*–and can breed together.

specific gravity. *See* density.

specific heat capacity (*c*) The quantity of heat (joules) needed to raise 1 kilogram of substance by 1 K. For gases, the specific heat capacity at constant pressure (c_p) exceeds that at constant volume (c_v) as heat is required to do work against the surroundings during the expansion.

spectacles Lenses worn in frames in front of the eyes to correct defective vision. Convex lenses bend parallel light rays inward; they are used by those unable to focus on close objects (*see* longsightedness). Concave lenses have the opposite effect (*see* shortsightedness). *Astigmatism is also treated by lenses. Bifocal spectacles have convex lenses consisting of upper and lower parts of different curvatures, for focusing on distant and near objects, respectively: they are worn for presbyopia. *See also* contact lenses.

spectral type. *See* Harvard classification system.

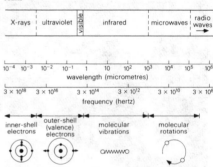

SPECTRUM *Photons in the X-ray region of the spectrum alter the excitation of atomic inner-shell electrons. The ultraviolet and visible photons interact with the outer-shell electrons that participate in chemical reactions. Infrared photons alter the vibrational states of molecules and microwave photons affect molecular rotation.*

spectrum The way in which a property of a system is distributed over its components. The visible spectrum, for example, is observed in a *rainbow, which shows the distribution of frequencies (colours) when sunlight is split up into its components by raindrops. The visible spectrum, however, is only a small part of the electromagnetic spectrum, which ranges from gamma rays to radio waves (*see* electromagnetic radiation). **Spectroscopy** is concerned with analysing the emission and absorption of electromagnetic energy by atoms and molecules. Atoms emit and absorb radiation at characteristic frequencies, which show up as lines in their spectrum and can be used to identify particular elements.

speed of light (*c*)   The speed with which all *electromagnetic radiation travels through a vacuum, equal to $2.997\,925 \times 10^8$ metres per second. It is one of the *fundamental constants; according to the special theory of *relativity it is independent of the speed of the observer.

speedwell   A flowering plant, also called veronica, occurring throughout temperate regions. The flowers are usually blue.

Speedwriting.   *See* shorthand.

Speke, John Hanning   (1827–64) British explorer. He accompanied Richard Burton (1821–90) on the expeditions (1855, 1857–58) to the source of the Nile. They discovered Lake Tanganyika and then Speke went on alone to discover Lake Victoria; on a second visit (1860) he established this as the source of the Nile. Burton disputed Speke's claim.

speleology (*or* spelaeology)   The exploration and mapping of *caves and underground water channels, including the study of their formation, plant and animal life (past and present), and geology.

Spence, Sir Basil   (1907–76) British architect, who became known for the new Coventry Cathedral (consecrated 1962). More recent buildings include Sussex University.

Spencer, Herbert   (1820–1903) British philosopher. His *The Man versus the State* (1884) set out his support for laissez-faire economics. *First Principles* (1862) was the first of a series of books on philosophy.

Spencer, Sir Stanley   (1891–1959) British painter. He is known for his religious subjects, often depicted in the everyday setting of his native village of Cookham, Berkshire.

Spender, Sir Stephen   (1909–) British poet. A friend of W. H. Auden, he published left-wing poetry during the 1930s. Later poetry included *Collected Poems* (1955) and *The Generous Days* (1971).

Spenser, Edmund   (c. 1552–99) English poet. His major work, *The Faerie Queene* (1590–96), was dedicated to Elizabeth I. Other works include *The Shepheardes Calendar* (1579), the sonnet sequence *Amoretti* (1595) and the *Epithalamion* (1595), celebrating his second marriage.

sperm (*or* spermatozoon)   The reproductive cell of male animals, which is formed in the *testis and fertilizes an egg cell during *reproduction. A sperm usually has a head, containing the genetic material, and a tail, enabling it to swim to the egg. In man, they are mixed with secretions from various glands (including the *prostate gland) at ejaculation to form semen.

sperm whale   A large toothed *whale, *Physeter cathodon*, also called cachalot. It is 18 m long, grey-blue with tiny flippers and large tail lobes (flukes). The blowhole is near the tip of the snout.

sphagnum   A widely distributed moss, also called bog or peat moss. Green to dark red in colour, the stems bear clusters of branches, covered with tiny leaves, and round spore capsules. Its ability to retain water enables it to drain wet ground and form bogs. The remains of the plants accumulate to form peat.

spherical polar coordinates.   *See* coordinate systems.

sphinx   A mythological creature with a lion's body and a human head, occurring in the art of Near and Middle Eastern civilizations. The most famous is the Great Sphinx at Giza, Egypt, dating from the 3rd millennium BC. In Greek legend, the Sphinx was a female monster that preyed on travellers to Thebes. She killed those unable to answer her riddle, which was solved by *Oedipus.

sphygmomanometer   A device for measuring *blood pressure in the arteries. It consists of an inflatable arm cuff connected via a rubber tube to a column of mercury with a graduated scale, or aneroid pressure-measuring device. The cuff is inflated until the pulse cannot be detected (using a stethoscope) and then slowly deflated until the systolic and then the diastolic pressure can be recorded as the pulse returns.

Spice Islands.   *See* Moluccas.

spices.   *See* herbs and spices.

spider   An *arachnid of which there are over 30 000 species. The body consists of a fused head and thorax (cephalothorax) and a rear abdomen separated by a narrow "waist." There are eight legs, up to eight eyes, and several pairs of spinnerets, which produce silk for making webs, cocoons, etc. Spiders prey mainly on insects, trapping them in their webs and killing them with poison-bearing fangs; in a few species the poison is harmful to man. The female is usually larger than the male, which she sometimes eats after mating. *See also* black widow; tarantula; water spider; wolf spider.

spider monkey   A monkey of Central and South American forests, with long legs and a long grasping tail, capable of supporting its weight. They live in groups, feeding on seeds, leaves, etc.

spider plant   A plant, *Chlorophytum elatum*, of the lily family, native to South Africa and widely grown. It has long green and white striped leaves and produces a stem bearing small white flowers or young plantlets.

spiderwort.   *See* tradescantia.

Spielberg, Steven   (1946–) US film director, whose films include *Jaws* (1975), *Close Encounters of the Third Kind* (1977), *ET* (1982), and *Empire of the Sun* (1988).

spin   A property of elementary particles such as the electron, as a result of which they possess a constant angular momentum independent of their motion. The spin is quantized, i.e. it is restricted to certain values.

spina bifida   A human defect, present at birth, in which the backbone fails to fuse, leaving the spinal cord and its coverings exposed. Commonly the child has paralysed legs and disordered bladder and bowel function. Handicap varies but intelligence is often normal. Frequently associated with hydrocephalus, the condition can be diagnosed during pregnancy (*see* amniocentesis).

spinach A plant, *Spinacia oleracea*, native to Asia and widely cultivated as a vegetable. Its edible leaves are rich in iron and vitamins A and C.

spinal cord The part of the central *nervous system that runs through the spine from the brain. It consists of a core of grey matter (nerve cell bodies) surrounded by white matter (nerve fibres). Protected by the spine, it is enclosed in membranes (meninges). Through it run the nerve fibres between the brain and the body; injury can therefore cause paralysis and loss of sensation.

spine The backbone, or vertebral column: a series of small bones (26 vertebrae in humans) that runs up the centre of the back. The spine encloses the *spinal cord, forms joints with the skull, ribs, and pelvis, and provides attachment for back muscles. The vertebrae are connected by tough discs of cartilage (intervertebral discs), which absorb the shock produced by movements.

spinet A plucked keyboard instrument of the *harpsichord family that superseded the *virginals in the 17th century. It is wing shaped, the single strings being at an angle of 45° to the keyboard.

spinning The process of converting fibres into yarn by twisting overlapping fibres together. Yarn was made originally by drawing out a length of fibre and attaching it to a hanging stick (spindle) that was weighted to help it spin. This process was mechanized first by the spinning wheel (in Europe in the 14th century). The inventions of *Hargreaves, *Arkwright, and *Crompton in the 18th century industrialized the process. As applied to synthetic fibres, spinning is the extrusion of viscous solutions to form continuous filaments.

Spinoza, Benedict (*or* Baruch de S.; 1632–77) Dutch philosopher of Jewish parentage. Influenced by the writings of *Descartes, *Hobbes, and Giordano Bruno (1548–1600), Spinoza rejected the concepts of a personal God and immortality. His *Tractatus Theologico-Politicus* (1670) was attacked by Christian scholars. The idea of God was, however, central to his philosophy. His major work, the *Ethics*, was published after his death.

spirochaete A spiral-shaped bacterium of the order *Spirochaetales*: they swim by bending and looping motions, achieved by contraction of fibrils within the cell. Some spirochaetes cause diseases, including syphilis and yaws in man.

spirogyra A *green alga, also called mermaid's tresses or pond scum, in the form of strands of cells up to about 30 cm long. Large masses may float near the surface of quiet fresh waters. Reproduction is asexual (by fragmentation) or sexual (*see* conjugation).

Spitsbergen. *See* Svalbard.

spittlebug. *See* froghopper.

spitz A group of dog breeds originating in N Europe and Asia and having a thick coat, small ears, and a tail carried over the back. The Finnish spitz, a hunting and guard dog, has a reddish-brown coat.

spleen A rubbery organ, about 14 cm long, in the abdomen beneath the left side of the rib cage.

It produces antibodies in newborn babies and digests bacteria in the bloodstream. It also removes worn-out and abnormal red blood cells and other particles from the circulation. The spleen becomes enlarged in some diseases, including liver disease and severe infections.

Split (Italian name: Spalato) 43 31N 16 28N A port in W Yugoslavia, in Croatia on the Adriatic Sea. The vast 3rd-century AD Palace of Diocletian contains the city centre and cathedral. Population (1981): 235 922.

sponge An aquatic invertebrate animal found in the sea attached to rocks or the sea bed. Up to several metres across, they may be treelike, cylindrical, or flat masses. Sponges possess an intricate framework (skeleton) of lime, silica, or a fibrous protein (spongin). Bath sponges are spongin skeletons without the living animals. The simplest type has a vase-shaped body with a hole at the top and smaller holes in the sides. Water flows in through the side holes and out at the top, food particles being extracted in the body.

spoonbill A long-legged white wading bird, most species of which occur around estuaries and lakes in tropical and subtropical regions. 60–80 cm long, they feed on fish and crustaceans picked up by sweeping the large spoon-shaped bill from side to side. The common spoonbill (*Platalea leucorodia*) breeds in parts of Europe and is a regular summer visitor to E England.

Spooner, William Archibald (1844–1930) British clergyman and somewhat eccentric Oxford don. He became famous for his tendency to exchange the first letters of words (**Spooner-isms**), for example "a well-oiled bicycle" became "a well-boiled icicle."

spore The small, often single-celled, reproductive structure of plants, protozoa, and bacteria, which may produce new individuals or be a dormant stage in the life cycle. Spores may be produced sexually or asexually.

sprat A small food fish, *Clupea* (*Sprattus*) *sprattus*, similar and related to the herring. It lives in shoals in the E Atlantic, N Mediterranean, and British coastal waters. The young are known as *whitebait.

springbok A rare antelope, *Antidorcas marsupialis*, inhabiting dry regions of S Africa. It has a white face with a black line along each side of the muzzle and a patch of white hairs on the rump, which can be flashed as an alarm signal.

springtail An eyeless wingless insect found worldwide. It has a forked organ on the abdomen, which is used for jumping.

spruce A coniferous tree of the pine family, widely distributed in the N hemisphere. Its needles grow in spirals and leave peglike projections on the shoots when they fall. The woody cones hang down from the branches. An important timber tree is the Norway spruce (*Picea abies*), from N and central Europe. Young specimens are used as Christmas trees.

Sputnik A series of Soviet unmanned satellites, the first of which was the first spacecraft to be launched (4 October, 1957). It burnt up in the atmosphere after 92 days.

Square Deal A programme of reform intended by Theodore *Roosevelt (president 1901–09) to benefit the "plain man" in the USA. It sought improved labour conditions, food regulations, and laws against *monopolies.

square root. *See* root.

squash The fruit of the plant *Cucurbita maxima*, of the gourd family. Native to America, they are widely cultivated, producing edible fruits, usually served as a vegetable. *Compare* gourd; pumpkin.

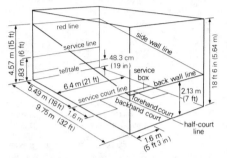

SQUASH RACKETS *The dimensions of the court.*

squash rackets A racket-and-ball game played in a four-walled court. Players hit a small rubber ball so that it hits the front wall of the court and may hit any other wall. The service each time goes to the winner of the previous point. The British competitive singles game goes to nine or sometimes more points and only the server scores.

squid A *mollusc related to the *octopuses. Surrounding the mouth, squids have ten arms bearing suckers; two arms are long and used for capturing prey, which includes fish and other molluscs. Their tapering bodies have fins on either side. Squids have a siphon producing a jet of water to push them forwards. The giant squid (genus *Architeuthis*) can reach 20 m.

squint (*or* strabismus) A condition in which the eyes cannot both focus on the same object at the same time. This may be caused by paralysis of one of the nerves moving the eye, in which case the squint is often temporary. Nonparalytic squints are often seen in children and may be corrected.

squirrel A *rodent with a bushy tail that nests in trees. The grey squirrel (*Sciurus carolinensis*), native to North America but now found worldwide, is an agile climber and garden pest. Other types of squirrel (called ground squirrels) live in underground burrows (*see* chipmunk; marmot; prairie dog). *See also* flying squirrel; red squirrel.

Sri Lanka, Democratic Socialist Republic of (name until 1972: Ceylon) An island country in the Indian Ocean, to the E of the S tip of the Indian subcontinent. *Economy*: predominantly agricultural, with tea, rubber, and coconuts exported. Industry has recently expanded. *History*: in 1505 the Portuguese established settlements in the W and S, which passed to the Dutch in the mid-17th century and to the British in 1796. In 1802 the whole of the island was made a separate crown colony. Following World War II Ceylon became a dominion (1948) within the Commonwealth and in 1972 a republic as Sri Lanka. Conflict between the Sinhalese (Buddhist) and Tamil (Hindu) communities has been a continuing problem. The presence (1987–90) of an Indian peacekeeping force led to fears of war between the two states. Head of state: President Ranasinghe Premadasa. Prime minister: Dingiri Banda Wijetunge. Official language: Sinhala. Official currency: Sri Lanka rupee of 100 cents. Area: 65 610 sq km (25 332 sq mi). Population (1987): 16 353 000. Capital: Colombo.

SS (German: *Schutzstaffel*, Defence Squad) The Nazi corps, created in 1925 as Hitler's bodyguard, commanded by Heinrich Himmler from 1929. The SS, or Blackshirts, by the mid-1930s controlled the Nazis' security system, including the *Gestapo, concentration camp guards, and the Waffen SS, a corps of combat troops in World War II. The activities of the SS were condemned at the Nuremburg trials of Nazi criminals (1946).

St. Names beginning St are listed under Saint.

Staffordshire A county in the Midlands of England. Agriculture is important, especially dairy farming. Industries are based on the coalfields in the N and include the pottery industry, famous since the 18th century. Area: 2716 sq km (1049 sq mi). Population (1986 est): 1 021 000. Administrative centre: Stafford.

Staffordshire bull terrier A breed of dog developed from a cross between a bulldog and a terrier for use in coal mines, etc. It has a broad deep head and a short smooth coat that may be of various colours. Height: 35–40 cm (English).

stag beetle A beetle occurring mainly in tropical regions. The males have well-developed jaws (mandibles) that in many species resemble antlers, used during combat with other males. Most stag beetles are black.

stainless steel An alloy *steel containing up to 20% chromium and 10% nickel. It is corrosion resistant as the oxide that forms on the surface remains intact and protects the metal, unlike other steels in which it flakes off. Stainless steel is used in a wide variety of applications where this property is important.

stalactites and stalagmites Deposits of calcium carbonate in limestone caves; stalactites are conical projections from the cave roof, while stalagmites grow upwards from the floor. They sometimes meet to form a continuous column. They are gradually formed from water containing calcium bicarbonate dripping from the roof. When the water evaporates a residue of calcium carbonate is left.

Stalin, Joseph (J. Dzhugashvili; 1879–1953) Soviet statesman. Born in Georgia, Stalin (whose adopted name means "man of steel") became a Marxist in the 1890s. In 1903 he joined the *Bolsheviks under Lenin and was repeatedly imprisoned and exiled. In 1922 he became general secretary of the Communist Party. After Lenin's death (1924) he eliminated his rivals, including *Trotsky, emerging as dictator in 1929. His five-year plans to collectivize industry and agriculture were brutally enforced. The 1930s reign of terror, culminating in the great purge, enabled Stalin to increase his power. In World War II, Stalin became chairman of the Council of People's Commissars; after Hitler's invasion of the Soviet Union (1941), he reversed his alliance with Germany of 1939. In the postwar years he pursued an imperialist foreign policy towards the communist countries with unremitting hostility towards the noncommunist world.

Stalingrad. *See* Volgograd.

Stalingrad, Battle of (1942–43) A battle in World War II, in which the German 6th Army under Friedrich Paulus (1890–1957), having entered Stalingrad (now Volgograd), surrendered to the Russians under *Zhukov.

Stalinsk. *See* Novokuznetsk.

Stamboul. *See* Istanbul.

stamen The male organ of a flower; it produces the *pollen (male gametes). It comprises an anther, a lobed structure consisting of four pollen sacs, borne on a stalk (filament). The pollen develops within the sacs, which split open to release it. In self-pollinated flowers, the stamens open inwards to release pollen onto the female part (pistil); in cross-pollinated flowers the stamens open outwards. *See also* flower.

Stamford Bridge 53 59N 0 55W A village in N England, in Humberside. Here King Harold defeated his brother Tostig and King Harald of Norway in 1066, three weeks before his defeat at Hastings by William the Conqueror.

Stamp Act (1765) The first British Act that imposed taxes on documents, newspapers, and stamps in the American colonies. Parliament was forced by colonial hostility to withdraw the Act but insisted upon its right to impose laws on the colonies (Declaratory Act, 1766); this led to the *American Revolution.

standard deviation. *See* variance.

Stanislavsky, Konstantin (K. Alekseyev; 1863–1938) Russian actor and director. He was a founder (1898) and director of the Moscow Art Theatre. His theories later developed in the USA as "method" acting at the Actors' Studio, emphasized the actor's identification with the character.

Stanley 51 45S 57 56W The capital of the Falkland Islands, in NE East Falkland Island on the Atlantic Ocean. Population (1986 est): 1200.

Stanley, Sir Henry Morton (1841–1904) British explorer and journalist. He went to the USA in 1859, joined the *New York Herald*, and in 1871 was sent to search for David Livingstone in Africa. Having found him at Ujiji, they explored Lake Tanganyika together. On a second expedition (1874–77) Stanley followed the Congo River (now Zaïre River) to its mouth.

Stanley Falls. *See* Boyoma Falls.

Stannaries The tinmining district of Cornwall and Devon. Until 1897 the Stannaries held its own courts, with legal authority over tinminers except in cases of murder or land disputes.

Staphylococcus Spherical bacteria that include species responsible for various disorders,

such as boils, wound infections, and food poisoning.

star A luminous celestial body composed of gas, deriving its energy from *thermonuclear reactions in its core. The sun is a typical star: star masses range from about 0.05 to 60 times the sun's mass. The higher the mass, the brighter and larger the star and the shorter its life. Thermonuclear reactions continue for some 10^{10}years for stars of solar mass but for only a few million years for the most massive stars. When the hydrogen is exhausted, stars evolve into *giant stars, those of near solar mass becoming *red giants, and further thermonuclear reactions occur. A low-mass star finally evolves to a *white dwarf. More massive stars explode as *supernovae. Stars are grouped into enormous assemblies, called *galaxies, as a result of gravitational forces. The nearest star to the sun is 4.3 light years away.

starch A carbohydrate that is an important storage product of plants. Chemically it consists of linked glucose units. Starch occurs as white powdery granules that are insoluble in cold water but form a gelatinous solution in hot water. Plants manufacture starch by photosynthesis; it is a constituent of seeds, fruits, and roots and a source of energy for animals (including man).

Star Chamber, Court of A court, developing from the king's council of medieval England, that met in the Star Chamber at Westminster Palace. It was concerned chiefly with breaches of the peace. Its misuse by Charles I to enforce his unpopular policies led to its abolition (1641) by the *Long Parliament on the eve of the Civil War.

starfish A marine invertebrate animal (*see* echinoderm). Its star-shaped body is covered with a spiny skin. Starfish occur on shores and ocean floors and move slowly, using saclike tube feet on the underside of the arms. They feed mainly on molluscs, crustaceans, and other invertebrates.

starling A songbird, *Sturnus vulgaris*, having a speckled black plumage. It probes the soil for insects, and also occurs as a scavenger in cities.

star-of-Bethlehem A widespread spring plant, *Ornithogalum umbellatum*, of the lily family, native to the Mediterranean. Growing from a bulb, it has star-shaped white flowers striped with green.

star of David (Hebrew *magen David*; shield of David) A six-pointed star, composed of two equilateral triangles. It has been regarded since the 17th century as a Jewish symbol, and was imposed on the Jews as a "badge of shame" by the Nazis. Officially adopted (1897) as an emblem of *Zionism, it appears on the flag of Israel.

States General In France, the assembly of representatives of the three estates—clergy, nobility, and the Third Estate or commons. It did not meet after 1614 until summoned by Louis XVI in 1789 on the eve of the *French Revolution. The Third Estate declared itself a National Assembly, which replaced the States General.

static electricity The effects created by electrical charges at rest. In static electricity electrons from one object are pulled onto another object, usually by rubbing them together, but they do not flow, as in current electricity. Many nonconducting materials become charged, for example a comb passing through dry hair. A force exists between two charged bodies (*see* electric field), attractive if they have opposite charges, repulsive if the charges are similar. *See* electric charge.

statics. *See* mechanics.

Stationery Office, Her Majesty's (HMSO) The UK government office that supplies all the stationery, office supplies, and printing and binding needed by the civil service. HMSO also publishes and sells government publications.

Stations of the Cross A series of 14 pictures depicting the final events in the life of Christ, beginning at *Pilate's house and ending at the sepulchre. They are usually arranged on the walls of a church and form the basis of a devotion in which prayers are recited as each station is visited.

statistics The study of methods for collecting and analysing numerical data. The data measure certain characteristics of a group of people or objects, called the population; usually the population is large, so data are collected from a representative sample and conclusions are drawn about the whole population, using *probability theory.

Statue of Liberty A statue of a woman 46 m (152 ft) high holding a torch in her raised right hand, on Liberty Island in New York harbour. Designed by the French architect Frédéric Bartholdi, it was given to the Americans by the French in 1884 (unveiled 1886) to commemorate the French and American Revolutions.

steam engine A heat engine in a furnace is used to raise steam, the expansion of which forces a piston to move in a cylinder to provide mechanical energy. A steam engine was invented in 1698 by a Capt Savery to pump water from mines. In 1711 *Newcomen improved this design but still relied on cooling the cylinder with water after each piston stroke. *Watt's single-acting steam engine, patented in 1769, was the first to use a condenser. Watt subsequently invented the double-acting engine, the crosshead mechanism, and the governor. It was largely this engine that created the *industrial revolution. The steam engine was the source of power for the *railways from 1829 (*see* locomotive) until electric and Diesel-electric trains were introduced (1950s). Steam engines were also used in place of sails in *ships. Moreover, it was the steam engine that drove the first municipal electricity generators, although the more efficient steam *turbine has now replaced it.

steatite. *See* talc.

steel An *alloy of iron containing usually less than 1% of carbon. Steel products form the basis of modern technology and are a key factor in world economy. The starting material is often **mild steel**, with between 0.2% and 0.8% carbon and sometimes a little manganese or silicon. It can be further improved by *heat treatment. **Alloy steels**, such as *stainless steel, are usually

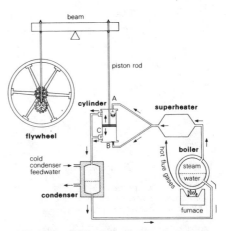

STEAM ENGINE *The principle of a double-action beam engine of the kind patented by James Watt. During the first half of the cycle, valve A opens, steam flows in and pushes the cylinder down, and steam flows out to the condenser through valve C. During the second half of the cycle, B opens and the steam pushes the piston the other way.*

more expensive, being used where special strength or corrosion resistance are needed. Steel is made by *smelting iron ore in a blast furnace to produce pig iron, which is added to melted down scrap iron before being further purified by the basic-oxygen process, *Bessemer converter, or electric-arc furnace.

Steel, Sir David (Martin Scott) (1938–) British politician; leader of the Liberal Party (1976–88). He entered parliament in 1964, heading the SDP-Liberal Alliance (1981–87) with the SDP leader, David Owen, before stepping down on the party's merger with the SDP.

steeplechase 1. A horse race that grew out of *foxhunting, in which horses jump artificial hedges and ditches. Hurdling is a less taxing version over lower lighter fences and shorter distances. Point-to-points are steeplechases for amateur riders, run by the local hunts. *See also* Grand National Steeplechase. 2. A track event for men in athletics over a 3000 m course that includes 28 hurdles 91 cm (3 ft) high and seven water jumps 3.66 m (12 ft) across. World record: 8 minutes 5.4 seconds (1978) by Henry Rono (Kenya).

Stegosaurus A dinosaur of the late Jurassic period (about 150–135 million years ago). 7 m long and weighing 1.75 tonnes, it had large triangular plates arranged in pairs along its back. It fed on soft plants. See p. 516.

Steinbeck, John (1902–68) US novelist. *Of Mice and Men* (1937) and *The Grapes of Wrath* (1939), both filmed, deal with social conditions in California. Other works include *East of Eden* (1952). He won the Nobel Prize in 1962.

Steiner, Rudolf (1861–1925) Austrian-born philosopher. His anthroposophy seeks to reinte-

STEGOSAURUS *It was originally thought that the plates on the back of this dinosaur were erect and probably functioned as weapons. Recent theories, however, postulate a horizontal arrangement of plates, which acted as heat exchangers.*

grate man with the world of the spirit. He founded his first school in 1919; there are now over 70 Rudolf Steiner schools.

Stendhal (Henri Beyle; 1783–1842) French novelist. His two major novels, *Le Rouge et le noir* (1830) and *La Chartreuse de Parme* (1839) blend romantic vigour with psychological analysis. He also wrote many critical works.

stephanotis An evergreen climbing shrub native to Madagascar. *Stephanotis floribunda* is a greenhouse plant with fragrant white flowers.

Stephen (c. 1097–1154) King of England (1135–54); grandson of William the Conqueror. Stephen seized the throne from Henry I's daughter Matilda, who invaded England in 1139. Civil war followed. In 1152 Stephen recognized Matilda's son Henry (later Henry II) as heir.

Stephenson, George (1781–1848) British engineer, who greatly improved steam *locomotives. His *Blucher* (1815) could draw 30 tons of coal at 4 mph. He assisted his son **Robert Stephenson** (1803–59) on the famous locomotive, the *Rocket* (1829). This carried passengers at 36 mph on the new Liverpool–Manchester line and stimulated railway development.

steppes The grasslands of Eurasia extending in a belt from the Ukraine to SW Siberia. They correspond to the prairies of North America and consist chiefly of level, treeless, plains.

steradian (sr) The *SI unit of solid angle equal to a solid angle that encloses a surface on a sphere equal to the square of its radius.

stereophonic sound Sound reproduction in which two signals and two loudspeakers are used to give a directional quality. It gives more realistic reproduction than a single signal system (monophonic sound) because the brain distinguishes between the sound in each ear. For recording, either two directional *microphones at right angles in one place or two separated microphones are needed.

sterility Inability to produce offspring by sexual reproduction. Sterility in men may result from too few sperms being produced or in the sperms having some defect. It may also result from psychological problems causing impotence. In women sterility may be due to disease

of the womb, blockage of the Fallopian tubes from the ovaries to the womb, or failure of the ovaries to produce eggs. *See also* sterilization.

sterilization Any procedure that produces *sterility. Surgical sterilization may be performed to prevent pregnancy, e.g. as a form of contraception or when pregnancy would damage the mother's health. For men, the operation—vasectomy—involves cutting and tying the duct (vas deferens) that carries sperm from the testicle. In women the Fallopian tubes are clipped or tied, preventing egg cells reaching the womb. Neither operation affects sexual desire. *See also* castration.

sterling 1. The currency of the UK. The pound sterling is named after the Norman *steorling*, a coin with a star (*steorra*) on one face. 2. Sterling silver is silver containing at least 92.5% silver.

Sterne, Laurence (1713–68) Irish-born British novelist and clergyman, known for his comic novel *Tristram Shandy* (1759).

steroids A class of organic chemical compounds that with the related compounds (**sterols**) fulfil many biological roles; they include the *sex hormones, *corticosteroids, *bile acids, *vitamin D, and *cholesterol.

stethoscope An instrument used by doctors to listen to sounds within the body. Modern instruments consist of two earpieces joined by two tubes to a head, which usually has a diaphragm (for high-pitched sounds) and a bell (for low-pitched sounds). More sophisticated stethoscopes are fitted with electronic amplification devices.

Stettin. *See* Szczecin.

Stevenage 51 55N 0 14W A town in SE England, in Hertfordshire. The first of the new towns (1946) to be developed after World War II. It manufactures aircraft, electrical, and plastic goods. Population (1985 est): 75 700.

Stevenson, Robert Louis (1850–94) Scottish novelist. His best-known books are *Treasure Island* (1883), *Kidnapped* (1886), *The Strange Case of Dr Jekyll and Mr Hyde* (1886), and *The Master of Ballantrae* (1889). Constantly troubled by respiratory disease, he travelled widely and died in Samoa.

Stewart, James (Maitland) (1908–) US film actor. An incorruptible hero with a distinctive drawl, his films include *Mr Smith Goes to Washington* (1939), *Destry Rides Again* (1939), *The Philadelphia Story* (1940), *The Glenn Miller Story* (1953), *Shenandoah* (1965), and *Airport 77* (1977).

Stewarts. *See* Stuarts.

stick insect An insect with a twiglike body and long legs; the wings are reduced or absent. Males are rare; the females live in trees, producing eggs that drop to the ground and develop without fertilization (*see* parthenogenesis).

stickleback A fish found in fresh and salt water in the N hemisphere. Sticklebacks have a row of spines along the back. The male builds a nest for the eggs and guards the young.

stigma The part of the female organ (pistil) of a flower that receives *pollen. In insect-pollinated flowers the stigma is sticky, whereas wind-pollinated flowers have feathery stigmas.

stimulants A large group of drugs that stimulate activity of the nervous system. Caffeine (in tea and coffee) and nicotine (in cigarettes) are stimulants used to reduce tiredness and to improve concentration. *Amphetamine and *cocaine are also stimulants. Stimulants may affect other parts of the body, particularly the heart.

stingray A round or diamond-shaped *ray fish found in warm shallow ocean waters. Most species have a tail armed with saw-edged venomous spines, which can inflict a painful wound causing paralysis and occasionally death.

stinkhorn A fungus that has a whitish stalk arising from an egg-shaped structure at the base and bears a thimble-shaped cap containing spores. The cap produces a strong-smelling secretion that attracts flies, which disperse the ripe spores.

Stirling 56 07N 3 57W A market town in Scotland, the administrative centre of the Central Region. The first Scottish parliament was held here in 1326. The castle occupies a prominent position. Population (1985 est): 29 238.

stoat A widespread small carnivorous mammal, *Mustela erminea*. About 35 cm long, with a long body and short legs, it can be distinguished from a *weasel by its black-tipped tail. Stoats prey mainly on rabbits.

stock A flowering plant of the mustard family, cultivated in gardens. Many varieties are derived from the European species *Matthiola incana*, which has purple flowers. The night-scented stock (*M. bicornis*) has small lilac flowers that are fragrant at night.

stock exchange A market in which securities are bought and sold. The three largest are in London, New York, and Tokyo. A stock exchange provides capital for industry and income for investors. Members of the London Stock Exchange, founded in 1773, were formerly either stockbrokers or stockjobbers, but this distinction ceased with the change known as the "Big Bang" (October, 1986). Thereafter the market became computerized, with negotiable commissions, and some brokers acting as market makers (replacing the stockjobbers).

Stockhausen, Karlheinz (1928–) German composer. Rejecting traditional forms, he developed the concept of music as a sequence of sound "events" in such works as *Gruppen* (for three orchestras; 1955–57) and *Kontra-Punkte* (for ten instruments; 1962). Such works as *Mantra* (for two pianos and percussion; 1970) were influenced by Indian mysticism. Later works include the opera *Donnerstag aus Licht* (1978–80).

Stockholm 59 20N 18 95E The capital of Sweden and its second largest port, built on several islands between Lake Mälar and the Baltic Sea. A settlement from very early times, Stockholm became the capital in 1436. Population (1987): 666 810.

Stockport 53 25N 2 10W A town in Greater Manchester on the River Mersey. Traditionally a textile town (particularly for cotton), Stockport also makes textile and electrical machinery, pa-

per, plastics, and chemicals. Population (1981): 136 496.

stocks and shares Documents representing investments in industrial and commercial corporations or loans to a government. In the UK, stocks are fixed-interest loans to the government (*see* gilt-edged security), foreign governments, local authorities, or companies (*see* debenture stock). Shares represent capital subscribed to a company in return for a share of the profit. Shares in public companies can be bought and sold on a *stock exchange. In the USA ordinary shares are called common stock.

Stockton, 1st Earl of. *See* Macmillan (Maurice) Harold.

Stockton-on-Tees 53 34N 1 19W A town in NE England, in Cleveland on the River Tees. The first passenger railway was built from here to Darlington in 1825. Population (1981): 154 585.

Stoicism The philosophical school founded about 300 BC in Athens by *Zeno of Citium. Stoics believed that God (identified with reason) was the basis of the universe, that human souls were sparks of the divine fire, and that the wise man lived "in harmony with nature." Stoicism influenced many later thinkers.

Stoke-on-Trent 53 00N 2 10W A city in England, in the N Midlands in Staffordshire, on the River Trent. Formed in 1910 by the amalgamation of five towns, the area is known as the Potteries and is the centre of the ceramic industry. Population (1981): 252 351.

stomach A muscular sac forming part of the digestive system and lying just beneath the diaphragm. It opens from the oesophagus (gullet) and leads to the duodenum (part of the small intestine). The stomach secretes gastric juice, containing hydrochloric acid and the enzyme *pepsin, and has a churning action to mix the food and its secretions to enable the food to be digested.

Stone Age The cultural phase during which man used stone, supplemented by wood, bone, or antler, for weapons and tools. It is the earliest phase in a system devised (1816) for classifying human progress (*compare* Bronze Age; Iron Age). The Stone Age is subdivided into: Old (*see* Palaeolithic), Middle (*see* Mesolithic), and New (*see* Neolithic).

stone bass. *See* wreckfish.

stonechat A small widespread chat, *Saxicola torquata*, that feeds on insects. The male has a brown head and back, chestnut underparts, and white rump; the female is a drabber brown.

stonecrop A plant, also called sedum, found in temperate regions and in Central and South America. Stonecrops have white, pink, or yellow flowers. Some species, such as autumn glory (*Sedum spectabile*), are garden plants.

stone curlew A widely distributed ground-nesting bird. The legs have thickened tarsal joints, or "knees," hence the other name of thickknee. Stone curlews are active at night, feeding on worms, etc.

Stonehenge A megalithic structure on Salisbury Plain in Wiltshire (England), probably built between 2500 BC and 1550 BC. Sarsens and

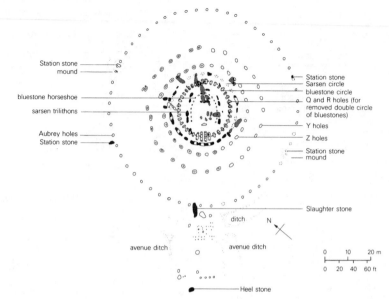

Station stone
mound

bluestone horseshoe

sarsen trilithons

Aubrey holes
Station stone

Station stone
Sarsen circle
bluestone circle
Q and R holes (for
removed double circle
of bluestones)
Y holes
Z holes
Station stone
mound

Slaughter stone

ditch   N

avenue ditch   avenue ditch

0   10   20 m
0 20 40 60 ft

Heel stone

STONEHENGE *The plan reveals features of consecutive building phases that may no longer be visible.*

bluestones (types of sandstone), the latter probably brought from S Wales, are set in concentric circles and horseshoes, possibly to enable observation of the sun and moon. The "Druid" connection dates from the 18th century AD. *See also* megalith.

stone pine   A *pine tree, *Pinus pinea*, native to SW Europe and Asia but planted throughout Mediterranean regions since Roman times for its edible seeds. Up to 30 m high, it has cones about 12.5 cm long.

Stoppard, Tom   (1937–   ) British dramatist, born in Czechoslovakia. He achieved success with *Rosencrantz and Guildenstern Are Dead* (1967). Other works include *Jumpers* (1972), *Travesties* (1975), *Night and Day* (1978), *The Real Thing* (1982), and *Hapgood* (1988).

stork   A large bird occurring in warm and temperate regions. 60–150 cm tall, storks have long necks, legs, and are white with black markings. They feed chiefly on fish, frogs, etc., and build a flat nest of twigs. *See also* adjutant stork.

storksbill   A widely occurring plant of the geranium family. The common storksbill (*Erodium cicutarium*) grows to a height of 60 cm and has purplish flowers.

Stormont   A castle in Belfast that housed the parliament of Northern Ireland (1921–72), before the reintroduction of direct rule from London.

storm petrel   A small seabird, 13–25 cm long, with brown plumage, often with paler underparts. Species found in southern oceans feed by "walking" on the water with wings outstretched, picking up plankton. Northern species feed by swooping on fish.

Stornoway   58 12N 6 23W A port in NW Scotland, on the Isle of Lewis. It is the administrative centre of the Western Isles Islands Area. Population (1989): 8400.

stout.   *See* beer and brewing.

Stowe, Harriet Beecher   (1811–96) US novelist. *Uncle Tom's Cabin* (1852) greatly stimulated antislavery feeling.

strabismus.   *See* squint.

Stradivari, Antonio   (?1644–1737) Italian violin maker. A pupil of Niccolò Amati, he and two sons made outstanding violins, violas, and cellos at their workshop in Cremona from 1666.

strain   In physics, the change in shape of a body when it is subjected to a *stress. **Longitudinal strain** is the extension per unit length when a body is stretched; **bulk strain** is the volume change per unit volume when a body is compressed; and **shear strain** is an angular measure of the change in shape.

Strasbourg   (German   name: Strassburg) 48 35N 7 45E A city in NE France, on the River Ill. An important inland port, it is famous for its *pâté de foie gras*. Population (1983): 252 300.

Strategic Defence Initiative (SDI)   A US research project, also known as "star wars," announced by President Reagan in 1983, which aims to destroy incoming nuclear missiles in space using ground-based or satellite-mounted lasers.

Stratford-on-Avon   52 12N 1 41W A town in central England, in Warwickshire on the River Avon. It was the birthplace of William Shakespeare. The Royal Shakespeare Theatre opened in 1932. Population (1986): 20 860.

Strathclyde Region   An administrative region in W Scotland created under local government reorganization in 1975. It includes the islands of Mull, Arran, and Jura. Agriculture is important, and traditional industries include shipbuilding and coal-mining. Area: 13 856 sq km (5348 sq mi). Population (1989 est): 2 311 110. Administrative centre: Glasgow.

stratocumulus cloud (Sc) A low type of *cloud composed of dark grey globular masses, often forming extensive sheets.

stratosphere. *See* atmosphere.

stratus cloud A low type of grey *cloud forming below 2400 m (7874 ft); it may occur as hill fog.

Strauss, Richard (1864–1949) German composer. His tone poems include *Death and Transfiguration* (1889), *Till Eulenspiegel* (1894–95), *Also sprach Zarathustra* (1895–96), *Don Quixote* (1897), and *Ein Heldenleben* (1898). His 15 operas include *Salome* (1905), *Elektra* (1906–08), *Der Rosenkavalier* (1909–10), and *Ariadne auf Naxos* (1912).

Strauss the Younger, Johann (1825–99) Austrian composer of such waltzes as "The Blue Danube" and "Tales from the Vienna Woods", as well as polkas and marches. He also wrote 16 operettas, including *Die Fledermaus* (1874) and *The Gipsy Baron* (1885). His father **Johann Strauss the Elder** (1804–49) composed 152 waltzes as well as quadrilles, marches (including the "Radetzky March"), etc.

Stravinsky, Igor (1882–1971) Russian-born US composer. His ballet scores commissioned by Diaghilev including *The Firebird* (1910), *Petrushka* (1911), and *The Rite of Spring* (1913), which strongly influenced 20th-century music. Stravinsky's subsequent neoclassical style attempted to revive classical composition in a modern form.

strawberry A plant of the rose family, native to N temperate regions, widely cultivated for its fruit. Most commercial varieties are hybrids derived from the European hautbois strawberry (*Fragaria moschata*), the Chilean strawberry (*F. chiloensis*), and the North American scarlet strawberry (*F. virginiana*). The plants have white flowers.

Streep, Meryl (Mary Louise S.; 1949–) US actress. After *The Deerhunter* (1978), she became a leading US actress; other films include *Kramer vs. Kramer* (1980), *The French Lieutenant's Woman* (1981), *Sophie's Choice* (1982), *Out of Africa* (1986), and *She-Devil* (1990).

Streisand, Barbra (1942–) US actress. Her stage and film musicals include *Funny Girl* (1968), *Hello Dolly* (1969), *A Star is Born* (1976), and *Yentl* (1983).

Streptococcus Spherical anaerobic bacteria many of which are parasites in the respiratory and digestive systems of man. *S. pyogenes* causes scarlet fever.

streptomycin An *antibiotic, obtained from the bacterium *Streptomyces griseus*, that dramatically cures tuberculosis. It is usually administered (by injection) with other antibiotics.

stress (physics) The force per unit area that causes a deformation (or *strain) in a body. **Tensile stress** tends to stretch a body; **bulk stress** to compress it; and **shear stress** to twist it.

strike Industrial action in which employees refuse to work unless their demands are met by their employers. An official strike is one recognized by a *trade union, whereas an unofficial (or wildcat) strike is a walkout without official backing. *See also* picketing.

Strindberg, August (1849–1912) Swedish dramatist. His unhappy childhood and three unsuccessful marriages led to mental illness and a hatred of women, reflected in the plays *The Father* (1887) and *Miss Julie* (1888), *Confessions of a Fool* (1912), and a study of mental illness *Inferno* (1897). Other works include the trilogy *To Damascus* (1904), *The Dance of Death* (1900), and *A Dream Play* (1901) and such chamber plays as *The Ghost Sonata* (1907).

stringed instruments Musical instruments in which notes are produced by the vibration of stretched strings. The strings may be plucked (e.g. guitar), bowed (the violin family), struck or plucked mechanically (piano, harpsichord), or played with hammers (dulcimer).

stroke (*or* apoplexy) Sudden loss of consciousness with weakness or paralysis of one side of the body, caused by a blood clot in one of the arteries of the brain (*see* embolism; thrombosis) or rupture of a blood vessel in the brain (cerebral haemorrhage). With physiotherapy many patients recover completely.

Stromboli An Italian island in the Tyrrhenian Sea, in the Lipari Islands with an active volcano.

strong interaction. *See* particle physics.

strontium (Sr) A reactive *alkaline-earth metal, discovered by Sir Humphry Davy in 1808 and named after Strontian, a town in Scotland where the carbonate ($SrCO_3$) is found. It also occurs as the sulphate, celestine ($SrSO_4$). The isotope ^{90}Sr is produced in nuclear fallout. At no 38; at wt 87.62; mp 769°C; bp 1384°C.

Stuarts (*or* Stewarts) The ruling dynasty of Scotland from 1371 to 1714 and of England from 1603 to 1714. The first Stuart king was Robert II (crowned 1371) of Scotland. The direct male line ended with the death of James V in 1542, when the throne passed to his daughter Mary, Queen of Scots, and following her abdication (1567) to her son James VI, who inherited the English Crown (1603) as James I. He was succeeded by Charles I, Charles II, James II, Mary II (and her husband William III), and Anne (d. 1714). The Crown then passed to the Hanoverians (*see* Settlement, Act of) but the Stuart claim was kept alive by *James Edward Stuart the Old Pretender, and his son, *Charles Edward Stuart the Young Pretender. The last royal Stuart was Henry Stuart, Cardinal York (d. 1807).

Stubbs, George (1724–1806) British animal painter. He is best known for his horse paintings, such as *Mares and Foals in a Landscape* (Tate Gallery), but he also painted portraits and farming scenes.

sturgeon A *fish found in N temperate waters. The sharklike body, up to 8.4 m long, has five rows of bony plates arranged lengthwise, a small mouth on the under surface, and four sensory barbels. Eggs are eaten as caviar.

Stuttgart 48 47N 9 12E A city in SW West Germany, on the River Neckar. It became the capital of Württemberg in 1482. Population (1987): 565 200.

Styx In Greek mythology, the main river of Hades across which the souls of the dead were ferried by *Charon. It was sometimes personified as the daughter of Oceanus.

sublimation The evaporation of a solid without melting. Liquids of many substances only occur within limits of temperature and pressure – if the pressure is low enough, heating a solid results in sublimation. Substances that sublime at atmospheric pressure include carbon dioxide (dry ice) and iodine.

submarine A warship that operates under water for long periods. The earliest submarine was developed by Cornelis Drebbel (1572–1634) of Holland in 1620. A more practical model, the "Turtle," invented by David Bushnell (1742–1824) of Connecticut in 1776, saw limited use in the American Revolution. Submarines, called **U-boats** (German name: *Unterseeboot*, undersea boat), were first used by the Germans in World War I. They became an important armament in World War II. Submarines powered by nuclear reactors can remain submerged for months. These vessels carry one or more guns mounted on deck, as well as torpedoes and missiles fired under water.

substitution reaction A type of chemical reaction in which one atom or group of atoms is displaced by another. An example is the reaction of chlormethane (CH_3Cl) with hydroxide ions (OH^-), the substituent, to give methanol (CH_3OH) and chloride ions (Cl^-).

succession In ecology, the process of change in a *community of organisms occupying a particular habitat from the time it is first colonized to the establishment of a stable climax community.

Sucre 19 00S 65 15W The capital of Bolivia, at an altitude of 2790 m (9153 ft). It was founded by the Spanish in 1538 on the site of an Indian settlement. The seat of government was moved to La Paz in 1898. Population (1985 est): 86 609.

sucrose (cane sugar *or* beet sugar *or* saccharose) A carbohydrate consisting of one molecule each of *glucose and fructose linked together. It is commercially the most important *sugar.

Sudan, Republic of the A large country in NE Africa, bordering on the Red Sea. *Economy*: chiefly agricultural, the main cash crop and export is cotton. Livestock rearing is important. Forest products include gum arabic and iron ore, gold, and manganese are mined. *History*: the NE was part of ancient *Nubia. Christianized in the 6th century, the region was converted to Islam after the 13th century. In 1821 it was conquered by the Egyptians, against whom a revolt under the *Mahdi took place in 1881. In 1898 an Anglo-Egyptian force under Kitchener subdued his followers and in 1899 an Anglo-Egyptian condominium was established. In 1956 the Sudan became an independent republic. A coup in 1969 brought Col Jaafar al Nemeiry (1929–) to power. In the midst of widespread famine and virtual civil war in 1985, Nemeiry was overthrown and civilian rule re-established. Sudan suffered widespread flooding of the Nile in Sep-

tember 1988. Military rule returned in 1989 with a coup led by Brig Omar Hassan Ahmed el-Bashir. Official language: Arabic; English is widely spoken. Official currency: Sudanese pound of 100 piastres and 1000 millièmes. Area: 2 500 000 sq km (967 500 sq mi). Population (1987 est): 25 550 000. Capital: Khartoum. Main port: Port Sudan.

Sudetenland A mountainous region on the W borders of Czechoslovakia. The Sudetenland, incorporated in Czechoslovakia in 1919, was reoccupied by Germany in 1938. After World War II Czechoslovakia regained the Sudetenland and expelled the Sudeten Germans.

Suez (Arabic name: As-Suways) 29 59N 32 33E A port in Egypt, near the mouth of the Suez Canal. An important refuelling station, it was rebuilt after the Arab-Israeli War of 1967. Population (1986 est): 265 000.

Suez Canal A canal in Egypt connecting the Mediterranean and Red Seas. Running between Port Said in the N and Suez in the S, it is 165 km (103 mi) long. It was designed by the French engineer Ferdinand de Lesseps and opened in 1869. In 1888 it became a neutral zone. In 1956, President Nasser nationalized the canal, provoking an Anglo-French attack on Egypt.

Suffolk A county in E England, on the North Sea. It is mainly agricultural, producing cereals and sugar beet. Area: 3800 sq km (1467 sq mi). Population (1988 est): 636 580. Administrative centre: Ipswich.

Suffolk Punch A breed of chestnut draught horse originating in Suffolk, England. It has a powerful body and thick neck and legs. Height: about 1.63 m (16 hands).

Sufism (Arabic *sufi*: wearer of a woollen cloak, mystic) A mystical movement within *Islam that dates to the 8th and 9th centuries AD. Their goal is mystical union with God, achieved by fervent worship.

sugar beet A plant derived from the European *beet plant. Sugar beet is cultivated for its large roots, which contain *sucrose.

sugar cane A tropical grass, *Saccharum officinarum*, cultivated for the sugar in its stalks (canes), 3–8 m high. The sugary liquid from the crushed canes is concentrated and refined to produce table sugar, etc. The remaining liquid (molasses) is used for feedstuffs, etc. The fibrous residue (bagasse) is used as fuel, etc.

sugars Sweet-tasting *carbohydrates, classified as *monosaccharides or disaccharides. The sugar used to sweeten food, confectionery, etc., is the disaccharide *sucrose, from sugar cane (11–15% sucrose) and from sugar beet (17% sucrose). Sugar manufacture is believed to have originated in India (Sanskrit *sarkara*, sand) around 3000 BC; it was taken to America by Christopher Columbus in 1493. Sucrose is extracted from cane by pressure, the extract being crystallized by evaporation. It is extracted from beet by hot water. By-products include molasses and sugar-beet pulp, both used in animal feedstuffs.

Sukarno (1901–70) Indonesian statesman, the first president of Indonesia (1945–65). He helped to found the Indonesian Nationalist Party in 1927 and was Indonesia's leader during the

Japanese occupation (1942–45), becoming president on independence. A military coup deposed him in 1965–66.

Sulawesi (former name: Celebes) An island in Indonesia, off E Borneo. It has rich mineral deposits. Area, including adjacent islands: 189 033 sq km (72 986 sq mi). Population (1986 est): 11 803 100. Chief towns: Ujung Pandang and Menado.

Suleiman (I) the Magnificent (?1494–1566) Ottoman sultan (1520–66), a notable lawgiver under whom the Ottoman Empire reached its peak. Suleiman captured Belgrade in 1521, Rhodes in 1522, and annexed large parts of Hungary in 1526. He made many conquests in Persia and the Ottoman navy controlled the E Mediterranean.

Sulla, Lucius Cornelius (c. 138–78 BC) Roman dictator. He stormed Rome in 87, forcing Gaius Marius and *Cinna to flee. Although outlawed when his rivals returned, in 83 he invaded Italy. Elected dictator, Sulla butchered his opponents. After restoring the Senate's constitutional powers, he retired (79).

Sullivan, Sir Arthur (1842–1900) British composer, best known for his comic operas with words by W. S. *Gilbert. They include *The Pirates of Penzance* (1879), *The Mikado* (1885), and *The Yeomen of the Guard* (1888).

sulphur (S) A yellow element, occurring in various crystalline and noncrystalline forms, and known in ancient times as brimstone. It is found near volcanoes and in large deposits associated with oil. Extraction is by the Frasch process, in which the sulphur is melted and pumped to the surface. Sulphur reacts with many elements to form sulphides, sulphates, and oxides. The gaseous oxides SO_2 and SO_3 dissolve in water to form sulphurous acid (H_2SO_3) and *sulphuric acid (H_2SO_4). At no 16; at wt 32.06; mp 113°C; bp 444.6°C.

sulphuric acid (H_2SO_4) A colourless oily liquid that has many industrial uses; it is made by the contact process, in which heated sulphur dioxide is passed through columns of platinized asbestos catalyst to produce sulphur trioxide (SO_3). The SO_3 is then dissolved in water to form H_2SO_4. Adding further SO_3 to H_2SO_4 produces fuming sulphuric acid (oleum; $H_2S_2O_7$), which forms a solid on cooling.

sumach (*or* sumac) A tree native to warm temperate regions. The leaves of the Sicilian sumach (*Rhus coraria*) yield a substance used in tanning; the stag's-horn sumach (*R. typhina*) of North America grows to a height of 7–12 m and has a crimson autumn foliage.

Sumatra (*or* Sumatera) The second largest Indonesian island, separated from Peninsular Malaysia by the Strait of Malacca. It is Indonesia's chief rubber and oil producer. Crops include coffee, tea, and pepper. *History*: the Buddhist kingdom of Sri Vijaya (7th–13th centuries) was based in Palembang. During the 15th century Islam became dominant, resisting Dutch colonization in the N until 1908. Area: 524 097 sq km (202 311 sq mi). Population (1986 est): 19 105 900. Chief towns: Palembang and Medan.

Sumer The area in S Mesopotamia in which civilization evolved during the 4th millennium BC. The fertile environment encouraged settlements that grew into such independent cities as *Ur and Eridu. The Sumerians probably invented the *cuneiform writing system. After 2000 BC Sumer was gradually absorbed into *Babylonia.

sun The nearest star, lying at an average distance of 149.6 million km from earth at the centre of the *solar system. It has a diameter of 1 392 000 km, a mass of 1.99×10^{30} kg, and rotates on its axis in a mean period of 25.38 days. It is composed (99%) of hydrogen and helium in the approximate ratio 3:1 by mass, energy being generated in its central core, about 400 000 km in diameter, by nuclear fusion. The surface, called the *photosphere, is the boundary between the sun's interior and its transparent atmosphere. The atmosphere comprises the chromosphere and the inner and outer *corona. There are regions of intense localized magnetic fields, where *sunspots and *solar flares occur. *See also* solar wind.

sun bear A *bear, *Helarctos malayanus*, of tropical forests of Asia, Sumatra, and Borneo. It is the smallest bear (110–140 cm long) and hunts small vertebrates, fruit, etc.

sunbird A tropical tree-dwelling bird ranging from Africa to Australasia. 9–15 cm long, they have brilliant plumage, slender bills, and extensible tongues for feeding on nectar.

Sunda Islands An Indonesian group of islands, between the Indian Ocean and South China Sea. It consists of the **Greater Sunda Islands** including Sumatra, Java, Borneo, and Sulawesi and *Nusa Tenggara.

Sunderland 54 55N 1 23W A port in NE England, in Tyne and Wear at the mouth of the River Wear. It has exported coal from the Durham coalfield since the 14th century. Population (1981): 196 152.

sundew A *carnivorous plant of temperate and tropical regions. The leaves are covered in sticky hairs used to trap insects.

sunfish A widely occurring sea fish, *Mola mola*. It has a disc-shaped body, up to 3 m long, with the tail fin reduced to a frill attached to the triangular dorsal and anal fins. Several North American carnivorous freshwater food and game fish are also called sunfish. They are similar to the marine sunfish but smaller (2.5–80 cm long).

sunflower A flowering plant of the daisy family, native to North and South America. The species *Helianthus annuus* is about 3 m high with yellow flowers, up to 35 cm in diameter. It is cultivated for ornament and its seeds, from which oil is obtained.

Sunnites (*or* Sunni; Arabic *sunna*: custom) The larger of the two main Muslim groups. In contrast to the *Shiites, the Sunnites accept the first three caliphs as Mohammed's legitimate successors. They form the majority in most Islamic countries except Iran.

sunspots Dark markings on the sun's *photosphere, typically a few thousand kilometres across. They are centres of intense magnetic fields. The number of sunspots seen in a year, and their mean solar latitude, varies in a cycle of about 11 years, known as the **sunspot cycle**.

superconductivity The disappearance of the electrical resistance of a substance at a very low temperature, called the transition temperature; it is different for different substances. A loop of superconductor cooled below its transition temperature, will allow a current to flow through it indefinitely. This phenomenon was originally confined to substances at temperatures close to absolute zero. Ceramic superconductors have now been found that operate at higher temperatures, which may be useful for power transmission and generating high magnetic fields.

supercooling The reduction in the temperature of a liquid below its freezing point without solidification. The effect can be achieved by slow cooling with pure liquids. Any disturbance will cause solidification.

superfluid A fluid that exhibits a very high thermal conductivity and virtually no friction at temperatures close to absolute zero. Such a fluid will flow up the sides of a container.

supergiant The largest and most luminous type of star. They evolve from very massive but more compact stars. Rigel, Betelgeuse, and Antares are examples. *See also* giant star.

Superior, Lake The largest of the Great Lakes, situated between the USA and Canada. The lake is important for shipping. Area: 82 362 sq km (31 800 sq mi).

supernova A stellar explosion, seen as a sudden increase in a *star's brightness. Most of the star's substance is blown into an expanding gas shell—the **supernova remnant**. If the star's core survives, it probably becomes a *neutron star or *black hole.

superphosphates Highly active phosphorus-containing fertilizers. Single superphosphate is made by reacting sulphuric acid with insoluble calcium phosphate rock to form calcium sulphate and soluble calcium hydrogen phosphate $Ca(H_2PO_4)_2$. Triple superphosphate is more concentrated.

Supreme Court of the United States The highest law court in the USA, consisting of the chief justice and eight associate justices appointed for life by the president. Its functions include interpreting the *constitution.

Sur. *See* Tyre.

Surabaja 7 14S 112 45E A port in Indonesia, in E Java. It is Indonesia's second largest city and chief naval base. Population (1985): 2 345 000.

Surakarta (*or* Solo) 7 32S 110 50E A city in Indonesia, in central Java. A cultural centre, it is the site of a sultan's palace (1745). Population (1980): 469 888.

Surat 21 10N 72 54E A city in India, in Gujarat on the River Tapti. It was the Mogul Empire's chief port (16th–17th centuries). Population (1981): 913 000.

surface tension A force on the surface of a liquid making it behave as if the surface has an elastic skin. It is caused by forces between the molecules of the liquid: only those at the surface experience forces from below, whereas those in the interior are acted on by intermolecular forces

from all sides. Surface tension causes a meniscus to form, liquids to rise up capillary tubes, paper to absorb water, and bubbles to form.

surfactant A substance that lowers the surface tension of a liquid, allowing easier spreading. Also known as **wetting agents**, they are used in *detergents, paints, inks, etc.

Suriname, Republic of (name until 1948: Dutch Guiana) A country on the N coast of South America. *Economy*: based primarily on bauxite, the chief industry is aluminium processing. Fishing is important. *History*: the first permanent settlement was established by the English in 1650. It was handed over to the Netherlands in 1667. During the Revolutionary and Napoleonic Wars it was again (1799–1802, 1804–16) under British rule. In 1949 it gained a measure of self-government, becoming an independent republic in 1975. Military rule (1984–88) was followed by the restoration of democracy and a further coup (1990). Suriname is a member of the OAS. President: Johan Kraag. Official language: Dutch; English, Hindustani, and Javanese are widely spoken and Surinamese, is also used. Official currency: Suriname guilder of 100 cents. Area: 163 265 sq km (63 020 sq mi). Population (1987): 415 000. Capital and main port: Paramaribo.

surrealism A movement in art and literature of the 1920s and 1930s. It began when the poet André Breton (1896–1966), published the surrealist manifesto in Paris (1924). It aimed, under the influence of *Freud, to express in art and poetry the irrational forces of the subconscious mind. The leading surrealists were the poets Louis *Aragon (1897–1982) and Paul Eluard (1895–1952) and the painters *Ernst, *Miró, *Dali, *Magritte, Paul Delvaux (1897–), and Yves Tanguy (1900–55).

Surrey A county in SE England, bordering on Greater London. Primarily a residential area, agriculture is important in the S. Area: 1655 sq km (639 sq mi). Population (1988 est): 999 752. Administrative centre: Kingston-upon-Thames.

surrogate motherhood. *See* artificial insemination.

Surya In Hindu mythology, the sun-god who appears in the *Vedas and is prominent as patron of numerous Hindu dynasties.

Susa (*or* Shushan) An ancient city in SW Iran. Occupied since the 4th millennium BC, it was a capital of Elam and subsequently capital of the Achaemenian kings of Persia (521–331).

Sussex. *See* West Sussex; East Sussex.

Sutherland, Graham (Vivian) (1903–80) British artist. He specialized in scenes of war; and portraits, e.g. of Somerset Maugham (Tate Gallery). His *Crucifixion* (1946; St Matthew's, Northampton) and tapestry for Coventry Cathedral are also well known.

Sutherland, Dame Joan (1926–) Australian soprano, who established her reputation at Covent Garden in 1959 in Donizetti's *Lucia di Lammermoor*. She retired in 1990.

suttee An ancient Hindu custom in which widows threw themselves onto their husbands' funeral pyres. It was officially abolished in India by the British in 1829.

Sutton Hoo   The site of a Saxon ship burial near Woodbridge, in Suffolk (England). Excavations in 1939 revealed the remnants of a 38-oar boat containing a treasure hoard. The mound is thought to be a cenotaph to King Raedwald (died c. 625 AD).

Suva   18 08S 178 25E The capital of Fiji, on the S coast of Viti Levu. Its industries include tourism and the production of coconut oil and soap. Population (1986): 69 481.

Suwanee River (*or* Swannee R.)   A river in the USA, flowing from Okefenokee Swamp in SE Georgia across Florida to the Gulf of Mexico. Length: 400 km (200 mi).

Suzhou   (Su-chou   *or*   Soochow)   31 21N 120 40E A city in E China, on the Yangtze delta. Known for its canals and gardens, it is a centre of the silk industry. Population (1985 est): 611 500.

Svalbard (*or* Spitsbergen)   A group of Norwegian islands in the Arctic Ocean. Covered largely by icefields, they are a source of coal. Area: 62 050 sq km (23 958 sq mi). Population (1982): 4000. Chief town: Longyearbyen.

Sverdlovsk (name until 1924: Ekaterinburg) 56 52N 60 35E A city in the central Soviet Union. Nicholas II and his family were executed here in 1918. Population (1987): 1 331 000.

Swabia (German name: Schwaben)   A former region in SW Germany now divided between Germany, Switzerland, and France. One of the leading German duchies in the middle ages, it was divided among neighbouring states in 1807 by Napoleon.

Swahili (*or* Kiswahili)   A *Bantu language of East Africa, used as the common language in Tanzania, Kenya, Zaïre, and Uganda. There are three main dialects.

swallow   A widely distributed songbird, 10–22 cm long, with a short neck, pointed wings, and a forked tail. All temperate swallows migrate to hot climates for the winter. *See also* martin.

swallowtail butterfly   A butterfly having long swallow-like tails on the hindwings. Many species are tropical. The caterpillars give off a strong odour if disturbed.

swamp cypress   A deciduous conifer, *Taxodium distichum*, also called bald cypress, native to swampy regions of the USA and grown for its timber. Up to 45 m high, it has globular cones, 2.5 cm across.

swan   A waterbird occurring worldwide on rivers or sheltered estuaries. 100–160 cm long, they are white with black legs, and have a long neck and a powerful broad-tipped bill to feed on underwater plants. Immature swans (cygnets) have a brown plumage. *See also* mute swan.

Swansea (Welsh name: Abertawe)   51 38N 3 57W A city and port in South Wales, the administrative centre of West Glamorgan. The second largest city in Wales, it is an industrial centre. Population (1981): 167 796.

swastika   An ancient cross of uncertain origin, generally held to signify prosperity and creativity. Revered by Buddhists, Hindus, Celts, and North American Indians, it was adopted by the Nazis, who believed it to be of pure Aryan origins.

Swazi   A *Bantu-speaking people who occupy Swaziland and nearby areas of South Africa. They are an agricultural people. Traditionally ancestor worship and witchcraft were part of their religious life.

Swaziland, Kingdom of   A small country in SE Africa between South Africa and Mozambique. *Economy:* chiefly agricultural, the main food crop being maize. The chief cash crop is sugar. Mineral resources include iron ore, asbestos, and coal. *History:* the *Swazi occupied the area in the late 18th century. It became a South African protectorate in 1894 and, in 1902, it came under British rule. Independence within the British Commonwealth was granted in 1968. Head of state: King Mswati III. Official languages: Siswati and English. Official currency: emalangeni of 100 lilangeni; South African currency is also legal tender. Area: 17 400 sq km (6705 sq mi). Population (1987): 716 000. Capital: Mbabane.

sweat (*or* perspiration)   A fluid, consisting mainly of sodium chloride (common salt) and urea in solution, secreted by the sweat glands. It is a means of excreting nitrogenous waste and of cooling the body (by evaporation).

swede   A plant, *Brassica napus napobrassica*, related to the cabbage. Growing to a height of 1 m, it is cultivated for its edible root, used as a vegetable and cattle food.

Sweden, Kingdom of (Swedish name: Sverige) A country in N Europe occupying the E part of the Scandinavian peninsula. *Economy:* mineral resources include iron ore, which forms the basis of the country's heavy industry and is a major export. The forests support pulp and paper industries and there is a thriving fishing industry. *History:* the area was inhabited from early times by German tribes, the Swedes in the N and the Goths in the S, and its people took part in the exploits of the Vikings. Finland was acquired in the 13th century and the 14th century witnessed the Kalmar Union of Sweden with Denmark and Norway. Independence was achieved in 1523 under Gustavus I Vasa, and in the 17th century, under Gustavus Adolphus, Sweden emerged from the *Thirty Years' War as a major European power, a position undermined by the Great *Northern War (1700–21). In 1809, during the Napoleonic Wars, Finland was surrendered to Russia. In 1814 Norway was handed over to Sweden, the two countries remaining united until 1905. When Carl XVI Gustaf came to the throne in 1975 a new constitution reduced the power of the monarchy. After the Social Democrat prime minister Olaf Palme was assassinated in 1986, Ingvar Carlsson (1934–   ) took over. Official language: Swedish. Official currency: krona of 100 oere. Area: 411 479 sq km (158 830 sq mi). Population (1988): 8 500 000. Capital and main port: Stockholm.

Swedish   A language belonging to the *Scandinavian branch of the North Germanic group. It is the official language of Sweden and is spoken by a minority in Finland. The literary form is based on the dialect of Stockholm.

sweet corn. *See* maize.

sweet pea A climbing plant, *Lathyrus odoratus*, of the pea family, native to Sicily and widely cultivated for its coloured flowers.

sweet potato A plant, *Ipomoea batatas*, native to tropical America and widely cultivated for its starchy tubers (swollen roots), which are brown with white or orange flesh.

sweetsop A small tree, *Annona squamosa*, also called sugar apple, native to tropical America and cultivated for its yellowish sweet fruits.

sweet william A flowering plant, *Dianthus barbatus*, native to S Europe and widely cultivated. Growing to 30–70 cm, sweet williams produce coloured flowers.

swift A widely distributed bird, 9–23 cm long, with brownish plumage with white markings and a forked tail. With sickle-shaped wings and a high-speed flight, they capture insects and mate and sleep on the wing.

Swift, Jonathan (1667–1745) Anglo-Irish clergyman and satirist. Born in Dublin, he recounted his life in London in *Journal to Stella* (1710–13). While in England, he wrote *A Tale of a Tub* (1704). He wrote his satirical masterpiece, *Gulliver's Travels* (1726) after his return to Dublin.

swiftlet A small *swift of SE Asia and Australia. 9–15 cm long, swiftlets nest in caves and navigate by listening to the reflection of the sounds they emit from the cave walls.

Swinburne, Algernon Charles (1837–1909) British poet. He is remembered for *Poems and Ballads* (1866). He supported republican movements in Europe and rebelled against conventional British morality.

Swindon 51 34N 1 47W A town in S England, in Wiltshire. It developed around the workshops of the former Great Western Railway and has a railway museum. Population (1985 est): 129 300.

swine fever An infectious virus disease of pigs. In young pigs the disease is usually acute, resulting in death. In the UK infected animals are slaughtered.

Swithin, St (d. 862) English churchman, who became Bishop of Winchester in 852. According to legend the weather on his feast day, 15 July, continues for 40 days.

Switzerland, Confederation of (French name: Suisse; German name: Schweiz; Italian name: Svizzera) A small country in central Europe. *Economy*: a centre for trade, banking, and insurance, it has magnificent scenery, which has long been a tourist attraction. The principal exports are machinery, watches, chemicals, and textiles. *History*: its Celtic inhabitants (the Helvetii) were conquered by the Romans in the 1st century BC and the region was overrun by German tribes in the 5th century AD, becoming part of the Holy Roman Empire in the 10th century. In 1291 Uri, Schwyz, and Nidwalden formed the Everlasting League, traditionally the origin of the Swiss Federation. By 1499 the Federation had achieved virtual independence and in 1648 this was recognized by the European powers. The French conquered Switzerland in 1798, but after Napoleon's fall (1815) the Congress of Vienna guaranteed Swiss neutrality. It maintained its neutrality through both World Wars, becoming the headquarters of many international organizations. Official languages: French, German, Italian, and Romansch. Official currency: Swiss franc of 100 centimes (*or* Rappen). Area: 41 288 sq km (15 941 sq mi). Population (1988): 6 600 000. Capital: Bern.

swordfish A food and game fish, *Xiphias gladius*, related to tuna and found in all tropical and temperate seas. Up to 4.6 m long, it has an elongated swordlike snout used to slash at shoals of fish on which it feeds.

swordtail A tropical freshwater fish, *Xiphophorus helleri*. Up to 13 cm long, males have a long swordlike extension of the tail fin. Swordtails are naturally green with a red strip on each side.

Sybaris 39 39N 16 20E A Greek settlement founded about 700 BC in S Italy. Sybarites were famous for their luxurious lives (hence "sybaritic", meaning pleasure seeking). In 510 and again in 457 Sybaris was destroyed by its neighbour Croton.

sycamore A large *maple tree, *Acer pseudoplatanus*, native to Europe and widely grown elsewhere. Up to 30 m tall, it produces winged fruits. The wood is used for violins and furniture.

Sydney 33 55S 151 10E The oldest and largest city in Australia, the capital of New South Wales, situated on Port Jackson inlet. A commercial and cultural centre, it is predominantly residential to the N of Port Jackson. The two shores are connected by Sydney Harbour Bridge (1932). Cultural centres include the Sydney Opera House (opened 1973). Area: 1735 sq km (670 sq mi). Population (1986 est): 3 430 600.

syllabaries Writing systems in which each symbol represents a syllable in the language rather than a concept (*compare* ideographic writing systems). The only major language using a syllabary today is Japanese.

symbiosis Any close relationship between individuals of different species of organisms, including parasitism (*see* parasite), *commensalism, and inquilinism. However, it often refers to an association in which both partners (symbionts) benefit from the association; this is also called **mutualism**. An example is the sea anemone (*Adamsia paliata*), which lives attached to the snail shell inhabited by the hermit crab (*Eupagurus prideauxii*). The anemone protects the crab, from which it receives food and transport.

symphony An orchestral composition, usually in four movements. The classical symphony evolved in the mid-18th century and was perfected by Haydn and Mozart: the fast first movement was generally in *sonata form, the second was slow, the third a minuet and trio, and the fourth fast. Beethoven extended the symphony, introducing a chorus and soloists in the last movement of his ninth symphony. Such composers as Bruckner and Mahler further enlarged the symphony: Mahler's eighth symphony (1907), for example, requires a thousand performers.

synagogue A Jewish place of worship. In ancient times it was a meeting place, devoted to explanation of the *Torah. It is now mainly a house of prayer, in which the focus is the cupboard (Ark) containing the Torah scrolls.

synapse The connection between one nerve cell and another (*see* neurone). The nerve impulse arriving at one nerve ending, causes a chemical neurotransmitter, e.g. acetylcholine or noradrenaline, to be released. This triggers a new nerve impulse in the adjacent nerve cell.

synchrocyclotron. *See* accelerator.

synchrotron. *See* accelerator.

syncline. *See* fold.

syndicalism A type of *socialism in which the workers, rather than the state, take over the productive resources of industry. Syndicalists were influential in Europe from the late 19th century until World War I.

Synge, John Millington (1871–1909) Anglo-Irish dramatist. His plays include *The Aran Islands* (1907) and *The Playboy of the Western World* (1907), which caused a riot at its first performance.

synodic period The average time taken by a planet or satellite to return to the same point in its orbit, relative to the sun, as seen from earth or from the satellite's primary (i.e. the body it orbits). It is therefore the interval between *oppositions or between identical *phases.

synthesizer A device that reproduces the sounds of conventional musical instruments and also produces a variety of artificial tones by means of electronic oscillators, whose signals are converted to sound waves. Individual circuits can be switched in and out by the player, enabling a wide range of sounds to be produced.

syphilis A sexually transmitted disease caused by the *spirochaete bacterium *Treponema pallidum*. In primary syphilis chancres (hard ulcers) appear after about 25 days, usually around the genitals. Weeks or months later the rash of secondary syphilis occurs. *Arthritis, *meningitis, and *hepatitis may also occur at this stage. Without treatment the third (tertiary) stage of syphilis may appear up to 30 years later, causing blindness, madness, and paralysis. Syphilis is now treated with penicillin. The *Wasserman test is one of many for diagnosing the disease.

Syracuse (Italian name: Siracusa) 37 04N 15 18E A seaport in Italy, in SE Sicily. Founded by Greeks in 734 BC, it became a cultural centre in the 5th century. In 212 BC Syracuse fell to the Romans after a three-year siege. Ancient remains include a Greek temple, a Roman amphitheatre, and a fortress. Population (1987): 123 706.

Syria (official name: Syrian Arab Republic) A country in the Middle East, bordering on the Mediterranean Sea. *Economy*: largely agricultural. Natural resources include oil, natural gas, phosphates, and salt. *History*: before the 20th century Syria, with Palestine, extended over much of the Middle East. In ancient times the Amorites settled here and later *Phoenicia flourished. Islam was introduced by conquering Arabs (c. 640 AD). Under Turkish control from the 11th century, it was the site of battles with the Crusaders. From 1517 until World War I it was part of the Ottoman Empire. In 1920 it came under French control. Demands for independence were finally satisfied in 1946. It united with Egypt in the United Arab Republic (1958–61). In 1971 Syria, Libya, and Egypt united loosely in the Federation of Arab Republics. Syria is a member of the Arab League. President: Lieut Gen Hafiz al-Assad (1928–). Prime minister: Mahmoud Zubi. Official language: Arabic. Official currency: Syrian pound of 100 piastres. Area: 185 680 sq km (71 772 sq mi). Population (1988 est): 11 400 000. Capital: Damascus.

syringa. *See* lilac; mock orange.

syrinx The vocal organ of birds, located at the base of the windpipe. Air from the lungs vibrates membranes within a resonating chamber, the pitch being controlled by muscles; and the two halves of the syrinx can produce different notes simultaneously.

Syros (Modern Greek name: Siros) A Greek island in the S Aegean Sea. The chief town, Hermopolis, is the capital of the Cyclades. Area: 85 sq km (33 sq mi). Population (1981): 19 668.

systole. *See* blood pressure; heart.

Szczecin (German name: Stettin) 53 25N 14 32E A city in the extreme NW of Poland, on the River Oder. It is a major port, the chief export being coal. *History*: it became a member of the Hanseatic League in 1360. Seized by the Swedes (1648) it passed to Prussia in 1720, remaining under German control until 1945. Population (1985): 391 000.

Szilard, Leo (1898–1964) US physicist, born in Hungary, who, while working in England (1934), developed the idea of a nuclear chain reaction. He joined *Teller in persuading Einstein to write to Roosevelt warning him that Germany might make an atom bomb first. During World War II he worked on the atom bomb, but later argued against nuclear weapons.

T

tabasco A hot red pepper or sauce made from the fruits of a South American *capsicum plant. It is used as a flavour.

table tennis (*or* Ping-Pong) An indoor game for two or four players that developed in England in the late 19th century from *real tennis. It is played on a table 2.74 m (9 ft) long and 1.52 m (5 ft) wide, divided across its width by a net 15.25 cm (6 in) high. The players hit a small hollow plastic ball with a rubber-faced wooden bat.

Tabriz 38 05N 46 18E A city in NW Iran. The most notable buildings are the Blue Mosque

(15th century) and the citadel; Tabriz is famous for carpets. Population (1986): 994 377.

tachometer An instrument for measuring the speed of rotation of a shaft, such as a revolution counter in a car.

Tacitus, Cornelius (c. 55–c. 120 AD) Roman historian and public orator. He became consul in 97 AD; in 112–13 he was governor of Asia. In 98 he wrote *Germania* and *Agricola*, the latter an account of his father-in-law's career. His major works, the *Histories* and the *Annals*, survey Roman history during 69–96 AD and 14–68 AD.

tadpole The larva of frogs and toads, which lives entirely in water. The newly hatched tadpole feeds on vegetation but later becomes carnivorous. The external gills of the young tadpole are gradually replaced by internal gills, and after about ten weeks the limbs start to appear, the tail degenerates, the lungs develop, and the circulatory system changes to enable the adult to live out of water.

Tadzhiks An Iranian agricultural people of Afghanistan and Soviet Turkistan. Speaking a form of Persian they are Muslims; most grow cereal crops and fruit trees.

Taegu 35 52N 128 36E A city in SE South Korea, the capital of North Kyongsang province. An old cultural centre, it has an important textile industry. Population (1985): 2 030 649.

Taft, William Howard (1857–1930) US statesman; Republican president (1909–13). His antitrust legislation and high protective tariffs split the Republican vote and lost the 1912 election to the Democrats.

Tagore, Rabindranath (1861–1941) Indian poet and philosopher. Knighted in 1915, he resigned the honour in 1919 as a protest against the Amritsar massacre. An advocate of cultural links between the East and the West, he won the Nobel Prize for Literature in 1913 after the publication in English of *Gitanjali* (1912), a volume of spiritual poetry. His father **Debendranath Tagore** (1817–1905) established the "Abode of Peace," a retreat in Bengal made famous by his son as an educational centre.

Tagus, River (Portuguese name: Tejo; Spanish name: Tajo) A river in SW Europe. Rising in E central Spain, it flows NW and then SW to the Atlantic Ocean at Lisbon. Length: 1007 km (626 mi).

Tahiti The largest of the Society Islands in the S central Pacific Ocean, in French Polynesia. Settled by Polynesians in the 14th century, it was first visited by Europeans in 1767. It became French in 1842. Tourism is important, and copra, sugar cane, vanilla, and coffee are exported. Area: 1005 sq km (388 sq mi). Population (1983 est): 116 000. Chief town: Papeete.

Tai Peoples of SE Asia and China who speak a group of related languages probably belonging to the *Sino-Tibetan family. They are traditionally rice cultivators and conservative Buddhists.

Taibei. *See* Taipei.

taiga The coniferous forests of spruces, pines, and firs, in the N hemisphere in subpolar latitudes. They extend from Norway across Sweden,

Finland, the Soviet Union (including Siberia), and America.

Tainan 23 01N 120 14E A city in SW Taiwan. It is the island's former capital (1683–1891). Population (1985): 633 607.

taipan A small-headed *cobra, *Oxyuranus scutellatus*, that occurs in NE Australia and New Guinea. Up to 3.3 m long, it has a ridged brown back and a yellow belly. Its venom causes its victim's blood to clot and proves fatal within a few minutes.

Taipei (*or* Taibei) 25 00N 121 32E The capital of Taiwan, in the N of the island. Founded in the 18th century, it was under Japanese occupation (1895–1945) and became the seat of the Nationalist Government (*see* Guomindang) in 1949. Population (1987): 2 640 000.

Taiping Rebellion (1851–64) A peasant rebellion in China that weakened the Qing dynasty. In 1851 a Hakka peasant, Hong Xiu Quan, raised an army of rebels and marched N, capturing Nanjing in 1853. They marched on Peking but imperial forces, and cold weather, drove them back. When Nanjing fell, Hong and his followers committed mass suicide.

Taiwan (Republic of China) An island off the SE coast of mainland China. Together with several nearby islands, including the Penghu Islands and the islands of Jinmen and Mazu, it comprises the Republic of China. *Economy*: in recent years the economy has shifted from agriculture to industry. Iron and steel are important and exports include electronic equipment, plastic goods, chemicals, textiles, sugar, and vegetables. Coal, gold, minerals, oil, and natural gas have been found, although timber remains the main natural resource. The chief crops are sugar cane, rice, and sweet potatoes. *History*: the island, named Formosa ("beautiful") by the Portuguese, who discovered it in 1590, passed from China to Japan in 1897. It surrendered to Gen *Chiang Kai-shek in 1945. Following threats by the People's Republic of China, the USA undertook in 1955 to protect Taiwan from outside attacks. Relations with China have recently improved. President: Lee Teng-hui. Official language: Mandarin Chinese. Official currency: new Taiwan dollar of 100 cents. Area: 35 981 sq km (13 892 sq mi). Population (1987): 19 630 000. Capital: Taibei. Main port: Kaohsiung.

Taiyuan 37 50N 112 30E A city in NE China, the capital of Shanxi province. An ancient fortified city, it is a centre of technology, coalmining, and heavy industry. Population (1986): 1 880 000.

Taj Mahal The mausoleum in Agra (N India) built (1631–53) for Mumtaz-i-Mahal, wife of the Mogul emperor, *Shah Jahan, who is also buried here. Set in formal gardens, it is built of white marble, carved and inlaid with precious stones.

Tajo, River. *See* Tagus, River.

Takao. *See* Gaoxiong.

talc A white or green mineral of hydrated magnesium silicate, $Mg_3(Si_4O_{10})(OH)_2$, with a layered structure. It is soft (hardness 1 on *Mohs' scale) and greasy. Soapstone (steatite) consists almost wholly of talc. It is used as talcum powder, a lubricant, and soft abrasive.

Ta-lien. See Lüda.

talipot palm A *palm tree, Corypha umbraculifera, cultivated in India and Burma. It has fan-shaped leaves up to 5 m in diameter. The pyramid-shaped flower cluster, more than 7 m tall, is the largest in the plant kingdom. The seeds are used for buttons and the leaves for matting, thatching, etc.

Talleyrand (Charles Maurice de Talleyrand-Périgord; 1754–1838) French politician and diplomat. He was foreign minister from 1797 until 1807, and again under Louis XVIII. He represented France at the Congress of *Vienna and was ambassador to Great Britain (1830–34).

Tallinn (German name: Reval) 59 22N 24 48E A port in the NW Soviet Union, the capital of the Estonian SSR in the Gulf of Finland. Its industries include shipbuilding and it possesses many historic buildings. It was independent Estonia's capital (1918–40). Population (1987): 478 000.

Tallis, Thomas (c. 1505–85) English composer. He was joint organist of the Chapel Royal with his pupil Byrd. In 1575 he and Byrd produced Cantiones Sacrae, a collection of their motets. Tallis' most famous works are The Lamentations of Jeremiah and the 40-part motet Spem in Alium.

Talmud Two of the most important works of Jewish religious literature: the Babylonian and the Palestinian (or Jerusalem) Talmud. Both are written in a mixture of Hebrew and Aramaic and are a commentary (gemara) on the *Mishnah. They contain records of rabbinic discussions on Jewish laws.

tamandua A mammal, Tamandua tetradactyla, of Central and South American forests, also called lesser anteater. Almost 1 m long including the grasping tail, it is pale in colour and feeds on termites using its long sticky tongue.

tamarin A South American monkey found in open woodland and forests, closely related to *marmosets. Tamarins have tusklike lower canine teeth and feed on fruit, insects, eggs, etc.

tamarind An evergreen tree, Tamarindus indica, of the pea family, cultivated in tropical regions for its pods. These contain seeds and a bitter-sweet pulp and are used in chutneys, curries, and medicines.

tamarisk A tree or shrub native to W and S Europe, central Asia, and India. Tamarisks have small scalelike leaves and feathery clusters of small pink flowers. They have been widely planted to prevent sand dunes from shifting.

Tamerlane. See Timur.

Tamil A *Dravidian language of S India and Sri Lanka. It is the official language of the state of Tamil Nadu. There are a number of regional dialects and marked differences between the written and spoken forms. Tamils are mainly Hindu.

Tampere (Swedish name: Tammerfors) 61 32N 23 45E The second largest city in Finland and its industrial centre. Products include rolling stock, textiles, wood pulp, paper, and footwear. Population (1987): 170 533.

tanager A brightly coloured songbird occurring in tropical and subtropical America. Tanagers are 10–20 cm long, plumpish, with a short neck and a conical bill. They live mainly in forests and feed on fruit, nectar, and insects.

Tang (or T'ang; 618–906 AD) A Chinese dynasty that established an empire extending over much of central Asia and Korea. In Tang times many Chinese scientific inventions, such as gunpowder, spread to the West. Arts flourished, printing was invented, and paper money was used for the first time. In 751 Arab forces recaptured Turkestan and the Tang empire began to break up. Two rebellions finally led to the collapse of the dynasty.

Tanganyika. See Tanzania, United Republic of.

Tanganyika, Lake A lake in E central Africa, in Zaïre, Burundi, Tanzania, and Zambia. Area: about 33 000 sq km (12 738 sq mi).

tangerine An orange *citrus fruit, also called mandarin, of a tree (Citrus reticulata) native to SE Asia and cultivated in the S USA and the Mediterranean region. Varieties include the satsuma and clementine.

Tangier (or Tangiers) 35 48N 5 45W A port and tourist centre in N Morocco, on the Strait of Gibraltar. An important Roman town, it was an international zone (1923–56). Its industries include textile manufacture and fishing. Population (1982): 266 346.

tank An armour-plated military vehicle, self-propelled on caterpillar tracks and typically armed with a gun (usually turret-mounted) and machine guns. Tanks are classified as main battle tanks (MBTs), for independent operation, and light tanks, for reconnaissance and other specialized uses. Based on a design of Sir Ernest Swinton (1868–1951), they were first used during the Somme offensive in September, 1916. In World War II tank battles across Europe and N Africa replaced the static trench warfare of World War I. Modern tank development has concentrated on improving weapons, armour, and computer-aided navigation and fire control.

tanker A seagoing vessel equipped with a large cargo tank for transporting liquids, especially oil. Modern **supertankers** with a carrying capacity of 75 000 tonnes were developed after World War II. Ultra-Large Crude Carriers (ULCCs) have a carrying capacity of up to nearly half a million tonnes.

tannin (or tannic acid) One of a group of chemicals present in the bark, leaves, fruits, and galls of many plants. Tannins are used as mordants for many dyes, in tanning leather, and in making ink.

tansy A perennial herb, Tanacetum (or Chrysanthemum) vulgare, of the daisy family, native to temperate Eurasia. It has clusters of yellow flowers and was formerly cultivated for its aromatic leaves.

tantalum (Ta) A very hard grey dense metallic element, discovered in 1802 by A. K. Ekeberg (1767–1813). Tantalum occurs naturally in the ore columbite ($Fe(Nb,Ta)_2O_6$). It is resistant to chemical attack and is used in alloys, for example in surgical materials and in incandescent filaments. The oxide (Ta_2O_5) is used in special glass for camera lenses. At no 73; at wt 180.948; mp 2996°C; bp 5425 ±100°C.

Tantalus A legendary Greek king of Lydia, son of Zeus and Pluto and father of Niobe and Pelops. In Hades he was punished for certain offences against the gods by being made to stand within reach of water and fruits that moved away whenever he tried to drink or eat.

Tantras A group of Sanskrit religious texts written in India in the 5th century AD. They form the basis of systems of meditation in Hinduism and Buddhism. In the **Tantric yoga** of Hinduism, there are two principles: Shiva and Shakti, male and female, mind and creative energy. **Tantric Buddhism** involves mudras (gestures), mantras (symbolic sounds), and mandalas (diagrams). The imagery of sexual union is the distinctive feature of both systems.

Tanzania, United Republic of A country in East Africa, on the Indian Ocean. It consists of a mainland area (formerly the republic of Tanganyika) and the islands of *Zanzibar and Pemba, as well as some smaller islands. *Economy*: chiefly subsistence farming. In mainland Tanzania the chief crops are cotton, maize, and cassava. Zanzibar (with Pemba) is the world's largest producer of cloves, with coconuts as the second cash crop. Food crops include rice, bananas, and cassava. Minerals include diamonds, gold, tin, and salt, and coal and iron have been found, as well as offshore gas. The main exports are coffee, cloves, cotton, and diamonds. *History*: important prehistoric remains have been found by the *Leakey family. Tanganyika was occupied by the Germans in the 1880s, becoming a German protectorate in 1891. After World War I it was under British rule. It gained independence in 1961 and in 1962 became a republic within the British Commonwealth with Dr Julius K. Nyerere as its first president. In 1964 Tanganyika and Zanzibar joined to form the United Republic of Tanganyika and Zanzibar, now known as Tanzania. President: Ndugu Ali Hassan Mwinyi. Official languages: Swahili and English. Official currency, since 1966: Tanzanian shilling of 100 cents. Area: 945 087 sq km (364 900 sq mi). Population (1987 est): 23 200 000. Capital: Dodoma. Main port: Dar es Salaam.

Taoism One of the two great Chinese religious systems (the other is Confucianism) and a major influence on Chinese culture. The goal of Taoism is a joyful and mystical harmony with the universe. Since the Chinese Cultural Revolution (1966–68) Taoism survives mainly in Taiwan. Western interest has been aroused by philosophical Taoism, especially by the *I Ching* (12th century) a book on divination.

tape recorder A device for recording and playing back sound stored on magnetic tape, which is usually wound into cassettes. In recording, the sound is converted to an electrical signal by a *microphone, amplified, then fed to an electromagnet in the recording head. The varying field of the magnet leaves a pattern of magnetization in the iron (or sometimes chromium) oxide coating of the tape. To play back, the magnetized

tape produces a current in a coil as it passes the reproducing head. The coil current is amplified and fed to loudspeakers. Tapes (cassettes) are now widely used for recording music (*see also* recording of sound).

tapeworm A parasitic *flatworm ranging from 20 mm to 15 m. Tapeworms anchor themselves inside the intestine of their host by means of hooks and suckers on the head. The body consists of a chain of ribbon-like segments through which food is absorbed. The segments at the rear are full of eggs and are shed from the host's body to infect a different host. Species infecting man include the beef tapeworm (*Taenia saginata*) and the pork tapeworm (*T. solium*).

tapioca. *See* cassava.

tapir A shy nocturnal hoofed mammal. The largest species is the black and white Malayan tapir (*Tapirus indicus*), about 1 m high and weighing up to 350 kg. All tapirs have a large head with a short snout. Young tapirs are marked with white spots and stripes.

tar A black semisolid substance, especially coaltar obtained when *coal is heated to over 1000°C in the absence of air (1 kg of coal yielding about 50 g of tar). Tar can be used as it is, or distilled to produce a range of organic chemicals including benzene and its derivatives. The substance remaining is called pitch.

Tara 53 34N 6 35W A village in the Republic of Ireland, in Co Meath. The Hill of Tara was the ancient religious and political centre of Ireland and here the early Irish Kings lived and were crowned.

tarantula A large hairy spider (up to 75 mm long) of tropical America. Tarantulas feed mainly at night on insects, etc. Their poisonous bite is painful but not fatal. The name was originally given to a *wolf spider (*Lycosa tarentula*) of Taranto (Italy).

taro A plant, *Colocasia esculenta*, also known as eddo, dasheen, and elephant's ear, native to tropical Asia and widely cultivated for its large edible tubers. These contain more protein than potatoes and are eaten cooked or made into puddings.

tarot A pack of 78 cards used mainly in fortune telling, although they are the forerunners of playing cards. They were first introduced in 14th-century Italy. The original pack, known as the Greater Arcana, consists of 22 cards (believed to follow the letters of the Hebrew alphabet), 21 numbered cards representing natural elements, vices, and virtues and a "Fool" (the joker). During the 14th century these were combined with 56 number cards, known as the Lesser Arcana, in 4 suits: cups, swords, money, and clubs or rods, representing clergy, nobility, merchants, and peasants. Each suit consists of number cards from one to ten and four court cards: king, queen, knave, and knight.

Tarquin the Proud (Tarquinius Superbus) The last King of Rome, who ruled, according to Roman tradition, from 534 to 510 BC. Tarquin is probably a historical figure but there are many myths explaining the nickname Superbus.

tarragon A herb, *Artemisia dracunculus*, of the daisy family, native to central Asia. It has slender leaves and flowers, which are often dried and used in salads, etc. It also yields an oil used in cooking and perfumery.

tarsier A small nocturnal *primate of Sumatra, Borneo, Celebes, and the Philippines. 22–43 cm long including the tail (13–27 cm), tarsiers have enormous eyes and gripping pads at the end of their digits. They live mainly in trees.

tartan. See Highland dress.

Tashkent 41 16N 69 13E A city in the S central Soviet Union, the capital of the Uzbek SSR. It is the oldest and largest city of central Asia, being a major communications, industrial, and cultural centre. *History*: dating from at least the 1st century BC, it fell successively to the Arabs (7th century), the Turks (12th century), and Russia (1865). Population (1987): 2 124 000.

Tasmania An island and the smallest state of Australia, separated from the mainland by Bass Strait. Discovered by the Dutch navigator Abel Tasman (c. 1603–c. 1659) in 1642, it was called Van Dieman's Land, after Tasman's patron, until 1856. Agriculture includes dairy farming, sheep rearing, and the cultivation of apples and hops. Mineral deposits include tin, iron ore, zinc, lead, and copper. Area: 68 332 sq km (26 383 sq mi). Population (1985): 442 111. Capital: Hobart.

Tasmanian devil A carnivorous marsupial, *Sarcophilus harrisi*, now restricted to Tasmania. About 1 m long, it is black with a large head and wide jaws. Strong and heavily built, it feeds on wallabies, etc.

Tasmanian wolf. See thylacine.

Tasman Sea A section of the SW Pacific Ocean, lying between SE Australia and Tasmania on the W and New Zealand on the E. Area: about 2 300 000 sq km (900 000 sq mi).

taste. See tongue.

Tatars A mainly Muslim people living in the Tatar ASSR of the Soviet Union, who belong to the NW division of the Turkic-speaking peoples. There are many Tatar dialects. The Tatars are descended from all the wandering Turkic and Mongol peoples of the *steppes.

Tate Gallery An art gallery on Millbank, London, housing paintings of the British school (notably by Turner and the Pre-Raphaelites in the Clore Gallery) and modern foreign paintings and sculpture. It was built in 1897 with the financial support of the sugar merchant and philanthropist Sir Henry Tate (1819–99). There is a Liverpool branch in the Albert Dock, opened 1988.

Taunton 51 01N 3 06W A market town in SW England, the administrative centre of Somerset. Textiles, computer software, precast concrete, aeronautical instruments, and cider are manufactured. Population (1987 est): 53 285.

tautomerism. See isomers.

Taverner, John (c. 1495–1545) English composer of 28 motets, a *Te Deum*, 8 masses, etc. A choirmaster at Oxford, he was imprisoned (1528) for heresy.

tawny owl A common *owl, *Strix aluco*, occurring in Europe and SE Asia. It has short rounded wings, dark-brown eyes, a mottled brown plumage, and lacks ear tufts.

taxidermy The art of making lifelike zoological models of creatures by preserving their skins and mounting them on suitable dummies. Taxidermy dates from the 17th century; improved technology and the use of plastic body forms have produced more realistic results.

taxis The movement of a living organism or cell in response to an external stimulus: the movement is either towards or away from the stimulus, i.e. a positive or negative taxis. **Chemotaxis** is the response to a change in the concentration of a chemical. Many insects, for example, respond chemotactically to the scents emitted by the opposite sex. **Phototaxis** is the response to light: for example cockroaches move away from light. *Compare* tropism.

taxonomy The study of how organisms are scientifically named and classified. The principles of taxonomy were established in the 18th century by the work of *Linnaeus (*see also* binomial nomenclature). As far as possible, organisms are arranged into a hierarchy of groups based on degrees of relationship (*see* phylogeny), rather like a family tree. The basic unit of classification is the *species. Related species are grouped into genera, which are arranged into orders and then classes, and finally phyla.

Tay, River The longest river in Scotland, rising in the Grampian Mountains and flowing through Loch Tay. It enters the North Sea through the Firth of Tay. Length: 193 km (120 mi).

Taylor, Elizabeth (1932–) US film actress, born in England. She began as a child star, notably in *National Velvet* (1944). Other films include *Cleopatra* (1962) and *Who's Afraid of Virginia Woolf?* (1966), in both of which she costarred with Richard *Burton, to whom she was twice married.

Taylor, Zachary (1784–1850) US statesman and general; president (1849–50). In the *Mexican War (1846–48), he won the victory of Buena Vista although his forces were outnumbered by four to one.

Tayside Region An administrative region in SE Scotland, bordering on the North Sea. It was created under local government reorganization in 1975 from the counties of Angus, most of Perth, and Kinross. Produce includes arable crops and soft fruit; dairy and beef cattle are important. Area: 7668 sq km (2959 sq mi). Population (1987 est): 393 762. Administrative centre: Dundee.

Tbilisi (former name: Tiflis) 41 43N 44 48E A city in the SW Soviet Union, the capital of the Georgian SSR on the River Kura. Engineering and the manufacture of textiles, wine, and food are the principal industries. *History*: founded in the mid-5th century, it fell successively to the Persians, Byzantines, Arabs, Mongols, Turks, and Russians (1801). It witnessed nationalist riots in 1989. Population (1987): 1 194 000.

Tchaikovsky, Peter Ilich (1840–93) Russian composer. He became professor at the Moscow conservatoire in 1866. Among his compositions are six symphonies, including the *Pathétique* (1893), three piano concertos (one unfinished), a violin concerto, string quartets, the opera *Eugene Onegin* (1877–78), and the ballets *Swan Lake* (1876–77) and the *Nutcracker* (1891–92).

tea The dried leaves and shoots of an evergreen shrub, *Camellia sinensis*, used to make a drink. Native to India and China, the plant has three varieties: China, Assam, and Cambodia. The shoots and young leaves are picked by hand and left to wilt before being rolled and dried. The major tea exporters are India and Sri Lanka; China consumes most of its own production. Tea contains caffeine (about 3.5%), which gives it a stimulating effect, and tannins, which are responsible for its colour.

teak A tropical tree, *Tectonia grandis*, native to SE Asia and cultivated for its timber. The golden wood (brown when seasoned) is hard and durable, being used for doors, window frames, etc. Burma is the major exporter.

teal A small duck, *Anas crecca*, of the N hemisphere, nesting on marshes and wintering on mudflats. It feeds on water plants and aquatic invertebrates. Drakes are grey and have a chestnut head; females are brown and both sexes have a green-and-black wing patch.

tear gas (*or* lachrymator) A substance, generally a fine spray, used to control crowds by causing temporary blindness and a copious flow of tears. Chloroacetophenone (Mace) is the best-known example. *See also* chemical warfare.

teasel A widespread plant, *Dipsacus fullonum*. The prickly stems grow to 2 m and bear heads of blue or white flowers with stiff hooks. The flower heads of fuller's teasel (*D. fullonum sativus*) were formerly used to (tease) give fabrics a fluffy surface.

technetium (Tc) A grey radioactive element, the first to be produced artificially. It does not occur naturally. It is chemically similar to rhenium and the compound $KTcO_4$ is a corrosion inhibitor. At no 43; at wt (99); mp 2227°C; bp 4627°C.

Tees, River A river in N England. Rising in the Pennines in Cumbria, it join the North Sea in the Teesmouth estuary at Middlesbrough. **Teesside** is an industrial district on the estuary. Length: 113 km (70 mi).

teeth Hard structures embedded in the jaws, used for biting and chewing food. The human adult's dentition consists of 32 teeth, including incisors (8), canines (4), premolars (8), and molars (12), which replaces the milk teeth of young children. The third molars (wisdom teeth) do not normally appear until the age of about 20. The crown of a tooth consists of hard enamel (largely *apatite) overlying the yellow dentine, which is slightly spongy and very sensitive to touch. The pulp at the centre contains blood vessels and nerve fibres. *See also* dentistry.

Tegucigalpa 14 20N 87 12W The capital of Honduras, situated in the centre of the country in a high valley. Founded in 1579, it was an important centre of gold and silver mining. It became the capital in 1824. Population (1986): 604 600.

Tehran (*or* Teheran) 35 40N 51 26E The capital of Iran, at the foot of the Elburz Mountains. Tehran is the commercial, industrial, and admin-

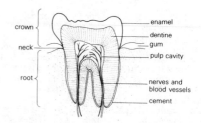

molar tooth *The root of the tooth is anchored into the socket by a bonelike substance, cement.*

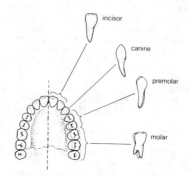

teeth in the adult upper jaw *The incisors and canines are used principally for biting; the premolars and molars are for grinding and chewing. The lower jaw contains the same number and type of teeth.*

TEETH

istrative centre of the country, with six universities (oldest 1934). It became the capital in 1788. Population (1986): 6 022 078.

Tehran Conference (1943) The conference in World War II attended by F. D. Roosevelt (USA), Stalin (Soviet Union), and Churchill (UK). Its chief purpose was to coordinate Allied strategy in W and E Europe.

Tejo, River. *See* Tagus, River.

Te Kanawa, Dame Kiri (1944–) New Zealand soprano. She made her major debut in *The Marriage of Figaro* at Covent Garden in 1971. She became a DBE in 1982.

Tel Aviv-Jaffa 32 05N 34 46E A city in central Israel, on the Mediterranean coast. It is the largest city in Israel, and the country's commercial, industrial, and cultural centre. The city's port is at Ashdod. *History*: Tel Aviv was originally a suburb of Jaffa, founded in 1909 to relieve the overpopulation of the Jewish quarter. Following tension between Arabs and Jews, the towns were separated in 1921. The Arab population fled Jaffa on its capture by Jewish forces in 1948 and the cities were reunited in 1950. Population (1988 est): 319 500.

Telemann, Georg Philipp (1681–1767) German composer. While studying law at Leipzig University he taught himself to compose. His large output included operas, oratorios, church music, and chamber music.

refractors

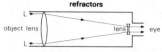

Galilean *The simplest practical form of refracting telescope was developed by Galileo in about 1609 from Lippershey's invention.*

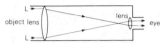

Keplerian *Kepler's arrangement produces an inverted image but was much used for astronomical observations in which the inversion did not matter.*

reflectors

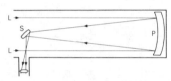

Gregorian *James Gregory proposed this design in 1663 but it has had little general application.*

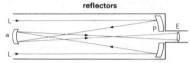

Newtonian *In Newton's 1671 design the secondary mirror is placed at an angle of 45° to the axis of the beam.*

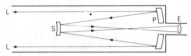

Cassegrain *Widely used, this form was invented by the obscure French astronomer N. Cassegrain in 1672.*

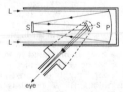

coudé (French: angled) *This arrangement is valuable in larger telescopes as it increases their focal length.*

L = *light rays*   P = *primary mirror*
E = *eyepiece*   S = *secondary mirror*

TELESCOPE

telepathy. *See* extrasensory perception.

telescope An optical instrument that produces a magnified image of distant objects.

The **refracting telescope**, invented (1608) by *Lippershey in Holland and developed (1609) by *Galileo as an astronomical instrument has a converging long-focus objective lens. The resulting image is magnified by the short-focus eyepiece to produce the final image. An example is the **Keplerian telescope**. Refractors are also used as terrestrial telescopes, usually containing an additional lens or prism to form an upright image. The first **reflecting telescope**, produced by *Newton (1668), uses a concave, usually paraboloid, mirror of long focal length to collect the light. This primary mirror reflects the light into a secondary optical system, which in turn reflects it into a short-focus eyepiece. The eyepiece lenses produce an image that can be viewed, photographed, or studied using electronic equipment. Depending on the secondary optics, reflectors are called **Gregorian**, **Newtonian**, **Cassegrain**, or **coudé telescopes**. *See also* Schmidt telescope; radio telescope.

teletext An information service in which pages of text are transmitted together with normal television broadcasts for display on a modified domestic television set. The information, weather reports, news flashes, sports results, etc., is sent out continuously in a cycle. The required pages are selected for display by keyboard. The two systems in use in the UK are **Ceefax** (BBC) and **Oracle** (Independent Broadcasting Authority).

television (TV) The broadcasting of pictures and sound by *radio waves or cable. Television was invented by John Logie *Baird in 1926. A television camera converts the picture into an electrical signal. In most of Europe the picture consists of 625 lines made by an electron beam scanning the screen of a *cathode-ray tube, 25 such pictures being formed every second. A brightness signal and a synchronization signal (to form the lines and frames of the picture) make up the picture signal, which is used to modulate (*see* modulation) a VHF or UHF carrier wave and is broadcast with the modulated sound carrier wave (which has a slightly different frequency). In colour TV, a colour signal has to be added to the picture signal.

An aerial or dish (for satellite broadcasts) of the TV receiver detects the broadcast radio waves. The picture and sound signals are separated within the receiver. The picture signal is demodulated, and the resulting current controls the electron beam in a cathode-ray tube to reconstruct the picture. See p. 532.

In a **colour television** camera light from the scene to be televised is filtered into three primary colour components: red, green, and blue. Light of each colour goes to a separate image tube. There are three systems in use for encoding colour picture information for transmission, all of which combine colour and intensity information with sound and synchronization in a similar way to black-and-white television. The colour receiver splits the signal into red, green, and blue components and applies these to three separate electron guns. The beam from each gun activates a set of phosphor dots of that colour on the screen, thus reconstructing the red, green, and blue components.

Telex A system using telephone lines to transmit printed messages. The message is typed onto

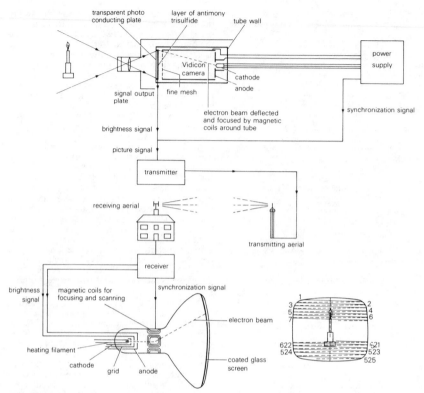

TELEVISION

a keyboard transmitter (teleprinter), which converts the characters into a coded electrical signal for transmission. A printing receiver carries out the reverse process, typing out messages as they arrive. The system is extensively used by many organizations. *See also* fax.

Telford, Thomas (1757–1834) British civil engineer. His suspension bridge over the Menai Strait, completed in 1825, is 177 metres long. Telford also designed some 1500 kilometres of roads, many bridges, and canals, as well as St Katherine's Dock in London.

Tell, William A Swiss national hero, first mentioned in a 15th-century chronicle, who, in Schiller's play *Wilhelm Tell* (1804), is a symbol of the Swiss struggle for independence from the Austrian Habsburgs. Refusing to pay homage to Gessler, the Austrian governor, he was ordered to shoot an apple from his son's head with a crossbow at 80 paces. He passed this test and later killed Gessler.

Teller, Edward (1908–) US physicist, born in Hungary. He worked on the fission bomb during World War II and subsequently on the fusion bomb, making a significant contribution to its development.

tellurium (Te) A silvery element, chemically similar to sulphur, discovered by Müller von Reichenstein in 1782. The metal is used in some special alloys and semiconducting devices. At no 52; at wt 127.60; mp 449.5 ± 0.3°C; bp 989 ± 3°C.

Telstar. *See* communications satellite.

temperature A physical quantity that is a measure of the average *kinetic energy of the constituent particles of a body. It determines the direction in which *heat flows when two bodies are in contact, the body with the higher temperature losing heat to that with the lower. The temperature of a body is measured in kelvins, degrees Celsius, or degrees Fahrenheit.

Templars (Poor Knights of Christ and of the Temple of Solomon) A religious order of knighthood founded (c. 1120) in Jerusalem by a group of French knights. The Templars were, with the *Hospitallers, the most important military order of the *Crusades. The Templars were suppressed by the papacy in 1312.

Temple, Shirley (1928–) US film actress and diplomat. She featured as a child star in many films during the 1930s, including *Little Miss Marker* (1934) and *Heidi* (1937). In 1974 she became US ambassador to Ghana under her married name, Shirley Temple Black; in 1989 she became US ambassador to Czechoslovakia.

Temple of Jerusalem The first Temple, built by King *Solomon (c. 950 BC) and destroyed by *Nebuchadnezzar in 586 BC, was the religious centre of Judaism. The second Temple, built later in the 6th century BC, restored by the *Maccabees and later by Herod the Great, was destroyed by the Romans in 70 AD. Both temples were built on the same platform, known as the Temple Mount; part of this structure is the **Western (Wailing) Wall**, still a holy site for Jews. Since 691 AD the Muslim Dome of the Rock has stood on the Temple Mount.

tench An elongated fish, *Tinca tinca*, related to *carp, that occurs in European fresh waters. Its body is greenish above with lighter undersides. It feeds on small animals and plants.

tendon A strong fibrous cord that joins a muscle to a bone. The tendon fibres merge with the muscle fibres and extend to the fibrous tissue lining the bone. They concentrate the pull of the muscle on a small part of the bone.

Tenerife 28 15N 16 35W A Spanish island in the Atlantic Ocean, the largest of the Canary Islands. A tourist resort, it produces early fruit and vegetables. Area: 2020 sq km (780 sq mi). Population (1981): 688 273. Chief town: Santa Cruz de Tenerife.

Teniers the Younger, David (1610–90) Flemish painter. Known chiefly for his peasant scenes, he also made copies of the paintings in the collection of Archduke Leopold Wilhelm, whose court painter he became in Brussels in 1651. His father **David Teniers the Elder** (1582–1649) was a painter of religious subjects.

Ten Lost Tribes of Israel *See* tribes of Israel.

Tennessee A state in the S central USA. Its major crops are tobacco, soya beans, and cotton. Beef and dairy products are also important. Industries produce chemicals, food products, machinery, and textiles. It is the USA's largest producer of zinc. *History*: disputed by the English and French in the 17th century, it was under British rule during the American Revolution. It became a state in 1796. Area: 109 411 sq km (42 244 sq mi). Population (1987 est): 4 855 000. Capital: Nashville.

Tennessee River A river in SE USA. It flows from E Tennessee, through NE Alabama before returning across Tennessee to join the Ohio River at Paducah, Kentucky. **The Tennessee Valley Authority**, created in 1933, built dams along the river to control floods and generate electricity. Length: 1049 km (652 mi).

Tenniel, Sir John (1820–1914) British cartoonist and book illustrator. He worked (1851–1901) for *Punch*, specializing in political cartoons. He is best-known for his illustrations for *Alice in Wonderland*.

tennis (*or* lawn tennis) A game for two or four players using rackets to hit a cloth-covered rubber ball on a grass or composition (hard) court. It developed in England in the mid-19th century. The scoring system was taken from *real tennis and a minimum of four points is needed for a game: 15, 30, 40, and game; a lead of two points is also needed to win a game. Players take turns to serve for a game. A player is allowed two attempts to serve into the service court diagonally opposite, alternating courts between points. To win points players must return the ball over the net either before it bounces (volley) or after the

TENNIS *The dimensions of the court. For singles the posts holding the net are moved inside the doubles sidelines. The net is 3 ft (91.4 cm) high at the centre.*

first bounce, positioning it so that their opponents cannot return it. The game is immensely popular, from the local club level to the All England Championships at Wimbledon, in which professionals have competed since 1968. Other highly prized trophies are the Davis Cup and the Wightman cup.

Tennyson, Alfred, Lord (1809–92) British poet. He gained recognition with his third volume (1842), which included "Morte d'Arthur." In 1850 he became poet laureate, and published *In Memoriam*, mourning the death of his friend Arthur Hallam (1811–33). He reinforced his popularity with *Idylls of the King* (1859). He accepted a peerage in 1884.

tenrec A mammal found only in Madagascar and the Comoro Islands. Measuring 5–40 cm, some with long tails and some tailless, they generally have a brownish coat of bristly hairs. Most are nocturnal, feeding on small invertebrates with plant material.

Tenzing Norgay (c. 1914–86) Sherpa mountaineer, who, with Sir Edmund *Hillary, was the first man to reach the summit of Mount Everest (1953). He later became a director at the Himalayan Mountaineering Institute, Darjeeling.

tequila A Mexican alcoholic drink from the town of Tequila, made of the fermented juice of an *agave plant, water, and, sometimes, sulphuric acid and yeast.

terbium (Tb) A soft *lanthanide metallic element, discovered in 1843 by C. G. Mosander (1797–1858) and named after the village Ytterby in Sweden. It is obtained from monazite ($CePO_4$); the brown oxide (Tb_2O_3) is used as a phosphor in colour-television tubes. At no 65; at wt 158.92; mp 1356°C; bp 3041.

Teresa, Mother (Agnes Gonxha Bejaxhui; 1910–   ) Yugoslav nun, who founded the Order of the Missionaries of Charity in Calcutta in 1948 to help lepers, cripples, and the aged. In 1979 she received the Nobel Peace Prize.

Teresa of Avila, St (1515–82) Spanish Carmelite nun, who joined the Carmelites at Avila in 1533 and in 1555 experienced a spiritual awakening. She founded the Convent of St Joseph in Avila in 1562 and later other religious houses with the help of St John of the Cross (1542–91). Her mystical experiences are described in her books, *Life* (1562–65), *The Way of Perfection* (after 1565), and *The Interior Castle* (1577).

Teresina 5 09S 42 46W A city in NE Brazil, the capital of Piauí state on the Río Parnaíba. It is a commercial centre; exports include cattle, hides, cotton, rice, and manioc. Population (1980 est): 348 900.

termite A tropical social insect, also called white ant (although unrelated to the ants). Termite colonies nest in tunnels in wood or earth mounds (termitaria). In each colony there are winged reproductives, workers, and soldiers. The reproductives found new colonies; the workers construct tunnels, feed the colony, and care for the young; while the soldiers are concerned with defence. Termites eat cellulose and are very destructive when they invade houses.

tern A seabird found around coasts and inland waters. Terns have long wings, usually a forked tail, and their plumage is white, black-and-white, or almost black. They feed on fish and crustaceans and often migrate long distances.

terracotta (Italian: baked earth) A fired reddish clay, used to make sculpture, tiles, bricks, etc. Terracotta figurines, often painted, were very common in ancient Greece and Rome and later during the *Renaissance.

terrapin A small edible turtle occurring in America. The diamondback terrapin (*Malaclemys terrapin*), found in coastal waters and salt marshes of North America, has diamond-shaped patterns on its shell and is yellow with black speckles. It is regarded as a table delicacy.

terrier One of about 20 breeds of sturdy dogs used for hunting. The Scottish breeds, such as the *cairn terrier, tend to be smaller and longer haired than others. *See also* Airedale terrier; bull terrier; fox terrier.

Territorial Army A British force of volunteers, created as the Territorial Force in 1907 and renamed in 1922. Between 1967 and 1979 it was known as the Territorial Army Volunteer Reserve. Its 84 000 men make up a pool of trained reinforcements for the army.

Terry, Dame Ellen (Alice) (1847–1928) British actress. A member of a large family of actors, from 1878 to 1898 she acted with Sir Henry *Irving at the Lyceum Theatre. Her correspondence with G. B. *Shaw was published in 1931. She was the mother of the actor Gordon Craig (1872–1966).

Tertiary period The first geological period of the Cenozoic era, following the Cretaceous period and preceding the Quaternary. It lasted from about 65 to 1.8 million years ago and contains the Palaeocene, Eocene, Oligocene, Miocene, and Pliocene epochs. Invertebrates and mammals evolved and became increasingly abundant; angiosperms became the dominant plants. The Alpine period of mountain formation reached its peak in the Miocene. The climate deteriorated in the Oligocene, leading to the Ice Age of the Pleistocene.

tesla (T) The *SI unit of magnetic flux density equal to one weber per square metre. Named after Nikola *Tesla (1856–1943), US engineer.

Test Acts 1. In England, the Acts requiring public office holders to take Holy Communion in the Church of England (1673) and excluding all Roman Catholics, except the Duke of York (later James II) from parliament (1678). They were not formally withdrawn until the mid-19th century. 2. In Scotland, the Act (1681) requiring public office holders to declare their belief in Protestantism; it was withdrawn in 1889.

testis The organ of male animals in which *sperm is produced. In men there is a pair of testes, or testicles, which produce both sperm and sex hormones (*see* androgens). The sperms complete their development in a highly coiled tube (epididymis) outside the testis.

testosterone A steroid hormone—the most important of the male sex hormones (*androgens). First isolated from bull testes in 1935, testosterone is now manufactured for medical uses, including the treatment of sterility.

test-tube baby A baby produced by fertilizing the mother's egg with sperm from the father in a test tube (*in vitro* fertilization): the fertilized egg is then placed into the mother's womb and allowed to develop normally. It is a means of overcoming sterility due to blocked Fallopian tubes, etc. The first test-tube baby was born in 1978; the first born from a frozen embryo was born in 1988. *See also* artificial insemination.

tetanus A serious disease caused by the bacterium *Clostridium tetani* entering wounds and producing a toxin (poison) that, after an incubation period of seven–ten days, causes rigidity of the jaw muscles (hence the popular name—lockjaw) and spreads to other muscles. The disease can be prevented by antitetanus immunization.

tetra A small coloured freshwater fish found in South America and Africa. Well-known species include the black tetra (*Gymnocorymbus ternetzi*), neon tetra (*Hyphessobrycon innesi*), and silver tetra (*Ctenobrycon spilurus*).

tetracyclines A group of *antibiotics, derived from *Streptomyces* bacteria, that are active against many bacteria. They may cause the side effects of diarrhoea, nausea, and discoloration of teeth.

tetraethyl lead ($Pb(C_2H_5)_4$) A colourless oily liquid made by treating lead-sodium alloys with chloroethane. It is added to petrol to prevent knocking in internal-combustion engines and hence improve engine efficiency. The lead content causes atmospheric pollution and the sale of lead-free petrol is now being encouraged.

Texas The second largest state in the USA, situated in the SW of the country. It leads the nation in the production of oil and natural gas and is also a major producer of sulphur. There is also an important space centre at Houston and

Dallas is a major commercial centre. Crops include cotton, sorghum, rice, and peanuts and it is a leading livestock producer. *History*: colonized by the Spanish in 1682, the first permanent Anglo-American settlement was established in 1821. In 1836 the Texans set up a provisional government in opposition to the Mexican dictatorship of Antonio López de Santa Anna; following the defence of the *Alamo, the revolutionary army defeated Mexican forces. A republic was established and Texas remained independent for almost a decade until it became a state. Area: 692 402 sq km (267 338 sq mi). Population (1985 est): 16 370 000. Capital: Austin.

Thackeray, William Makepeace (1811–63) British novelist. After publishing several novels in magazines under pseudonyms, he won recognition with *Vanity Fair* (1847–48), which he followed with the semiautobiographical *The History of Pendennis* (1848–50) and the historical novel *Henry Esmond* (1852). In his last years he edited the *Cornhill Magazine* (1860–62).

Thailand, Kingdom of (name until 1939: Siam) A country in SE Asia, on the Gulf of Thailand. *Economy*: the chief food crop and main export is rice. Forests cover 60% of the land, producing teak and rubber in the N and yang in the S. Mineral resources include tin, manganese, antimony, and zinc. Industry is based on textiles and cement. *History*: by the 6th century AD the Thais had reached the area from the N. They conquered the Mons to the S and in succeeding centuries were involved in frequent struggles with the Burmese and Khmers. In 1932 the long-standing absolute monarchy was replaced by a constitutional monarchy, since when civil and military governments have alternated. Head of state: King Bhumibol Adulyadej (1927–). Official language: Thai. Official religion: Hinayana Buddhism. Official currency: baht of 100 satang. Area: 514 000 sq km (198 250 sq mi). Population (1988): 54 500 000. Capital and main port: Bangkok.

Thales (c. 624–547 BC) Greek scientist, born at *Miletus. He predicted the solar eclipse of 28 May, 585 BC, advised on navigation by the stars, and introduced Egyptian methods of land measurement into Greece.

thalidomide A sedative drug that caused severe defects in the fetus when taken by pregnant women, commonly a condition in which the hands and feet developed normally but the arms and legs were very short. Between 1959 and 1962 some 500 deformed babies were born in the UK and over 2000 in West Germany.

thallium (Tl) A soft metallic element, discovered spectroscopically by Sir William Crookes in 1861 and named after the Greek *thallos*, a green shoot, because of its green spectral line. It occurs naturally in sulphide ores of lead and zinc and in iron pyrites (FeS_2). At no 81; at wt 204.37; mp 303.5°C; bp 1457 ± 10°C.

Thames, River The longest river in England. Rising in the Cotswold Hills near Cirencester, it flows mainly ESE through Oxford and London to enter the North Sea at the Nore. A tidal barrier was constructed (1973–83) below London to prevent flooding. Length: 346 km (215 mi).

Thanet, Isle of 51 22N 1 15E An island in SE England, separated from the Kent mainland by two channels of the River Stour. It contains the resorts of Ramsgate and Margate. Area: 109 sq km (42 sq mi).

Thanksgiving Day A national holiday in the USA, celebrated on the fourth Thursday in November. First observed by the *Pilgrim Fathers in 1621 to celebrate their harvest, it became a national holiday in 1863. It is celebrated in Canada on the second Monday in October.

Thant, U (1909–74) Burmese diplomat; secretary general of the UN (1962–72). U Thant helped to resolve the Cuba missile crisis.

Thatcher, Margaret (Hilda) (1925–) British stateswoman; Conservative prime minister (1979–90). She entered parliament in 1959. In 1969 she became opposition spokesman on education and was secretary of state for education and science from 1970 to 1974. In 1975 she succeeded Edward Heath as Conservative leader and in 1979 became the first woman prime minister of the UK. In office she increased privatization, cut government spending, and used military force to retain control of the Falkland Islands (1982). In 1988 she became the longest serving peacetime prime minister of the UK in the 20th century. She resigned in 1990 after controversy over her attitude to the EC, the introduction of the poll tax, and her personal style of leadership.

Theatre of the Absurd Plays, popular in the 1960s, in which the human condition is presented as absurd. It includes the plays of *Ionesco, *Beckett, and others, which are characterized by lack of logical form, pessimism, and comic effects.

Thebes An ancient city in Upper Egypt and capital of all Egypt (c. 1570–c. 1085 BC).

Thebes 88 19N 23 19E A town in Boeotia, in central Greece. Founded in *Mycenaean times, it was a favourite theme in Greek drama. Thebes lost influence by supporting the Persians in 480 BC, but briefly became the leading Greek state after defeating the Spartans at Leuctra (371). Population (1981 est): 18 712.

thegn A person in Anglo-Saxon England who held land from his lord in return for service. The status of thegn (meaning one who serves) was inherited. The king's thegns had military and administrative duties and also attended the *witan (king's council). The thegns died out after the Norman conquest.

theism The belief in a personal God as creator and preserver of the universe, who reveals himself by supernatural means to his creatures. The word theism, apparently invented as an opposite to atheism, now excludes both *pantheism and *deism.

Themistocles (c. 528–462 BC) Athenian statesman. Themistocles persuaded Athens to expand its navy (483) and to transfer its port from Phaleron to the more defensible Piraeus. These policies, and his leadership at the battle of Salamis (480), saved Greece from Persia (*see* Greek-Persian Wars).

Theodosius (I) the Great (347–95 AD) Roman emperor in the East (379–94) and sole emperor (394–95). A devout Christian, he imposed Christianity on the Empire in 391, closing pagan temples and forbidding sacrifices.

theology The study of God. Christian theology includes the nature of God, his relationship with the universe, his providence regarding man, and the teachings of the Church. Different traditions exist within the various Christian communions.

Thérèse, St (Marie Françoise Thérèse Martin; 1873–97) French *Carmelite nun, known as the Little Flower of Jesus. She entered the Carmelite convent at Lisieux when only 15 and died there 9 years later of tuberculosis. Her fame rests on her spiritual autobiography, *Histoire d'une âme* (1898). She was canonized in 1925. Feast day: 3 Oct.

thermal reactor A nuclear reactor (*see* nuclear energy) in which natural or enriched uranium is used with a moderator so that the velocities of the emitted neutrons are comparable to the velocities of gas molecules ("thermal" velocities). The reactor core consists of fuel rods made of uranium surrounded by a moderator, the heat of the reaction being removed by a coolant. The coolant then passes to a heat exchanger in which steam is raised. The rate of reaction is controlled by control rods, which can move in and out of the core: the rods contain a neutron-absorbing element, such as boron. *See* nuclear power.

thermionic valve A device consisting of an evacuated tube containing two or more electrodes. One heated electrode, the cathode, emits electrons, which are attracted to the positively charged anode, forming an electric current. This current flows in one direction only and can be controlled by a voltage applied at one or more other electrodes (called grids). The **diode valve** was invented in 1904 by Sir John Ambrose Fleming. The **triode valve** with one grid was invented in 1910 by the US electrical engineer Lee De Forest; it was the first to function as an amplifier. The weak signal fed to the grid produces a stronger signal in the anode circuit. Diodes and triodes enabled radio transmitters and receivers to develop, although now *semiconductor diodes and *transistors have replaced them.

thermocouple A type of thermometer consisting of an electric circuit formed by two dissimilar metals joined at each end. One junction is exposed to the temperature to be measured, a voltage being generated between it and the other (reference) junction as a result of the *thermoelectric effect. The output is usually displayed on a *galvanometer. Copper-constantan junctions are used up to 500°C and platinum-rhodium alloy up to 1500°C. A **thermopile** consists of several thermocouples connected in series.

thermodynamics The study of *heat and energy. Thermodynamic quantities include *temperature and *entropy. There are three fundamental laws of thermodynamics. The first law states that the energy of a closed system remains constant during any process. The second states that heat cannot flow from a cold body to a hot body without the expenditure of external work; or, that the entropy of a closed system can never decrease. The third law states that as the thermo-

dynamic temperature of a system aproaches *absolute zero, its entropy approaches zero.

thermoelectric effects The effects of changes of temperature on electric circuits. The **Seebeck effect**, named after Johann Seebeck (1770–1831), provides the basis for the *thermocouple; when a circuit has two junctions between dissimilar metals, maintained at different temperatures, a voltage is generated between them. The **Peltier effect**, named after Jean Peltier (1785–1845), is the converse. One junction heats up and the other cools down when a steady current flows through such a circuit. In the **Thomson** (*or* Kelvin) **effect**, named after Lord *Kelvin, a temperature gradient along a single metal conductor causes a current to flow through it.

thermometer An instrument for measuring temperature. Thermometers make use of some property of a substance that varies uniformly with temperature, most commonly the expansion of a liquid, such as mercury. A clinical thermometer is a typical mercury-in-glass thermometer; other thermometers include the more accurate gas thermometer; the resistance thermometer, which depends on the variation in resistance of a wire (usually platinum); the bimetallic strip, which makes use of the unequal expansion of two metals welded together; and the thermistor, in which the conductivity of a semiconductor changes with temperature.

thermonuclear reactor A reactor in which a fusion reaction (*see* nuclear energy) takes place with the controlled release of energy.
A typical fusion reaction is the combination of deuterium and tritium to form helium ($^2_1$H + $^3_1$H = $^4_2$He + n + 17.6 MeV). To achieve fusion a temperature of about 40 million °C is needed. Containing the resulting *plasma (high-temperature ionized gas) is the subject of current research.

thermopile. *See* thermocouple.

Thermopylae, Battle of (480 BC) The battle during the *Greek-Persian Wars in which the Greeks under the Spartan king, Leonidas (reigned ?490–480), attempted for three days to hold the pass of Thermopylae in E central Greece against the Persians. After the main Greek force had retreated the Spartans and Thespians, surrounded and outnumbered, fought to the death.

Theseus A legendary Greek hero, who freed the Athenians from their annual tribute to *Minos by killing the *Minotaur of Crete. He extended the rule of Athens and was the subject of many legends.

Thessaloniki (English name: Salonika) 40 38N 22 58E The second largest port in Greece, on the Gulf of Salonika. Founded in 315 BC as Thessalonica, it became the capital of Macedonia. It was captured by the Turks (1430) and remained in the Ottoman Empire until 1913. Industries include the manufacture of textiles and food processing. Population (1981): 402 443.

Thessaly (Modern Greek name: Thessalía) A region of central Greece, bordering on the Aegean Sea. In the 4th century BC it fell to Philip of Macedon. Freed from Macedonian rule by Rome in 196 BC, it became part of the Roman

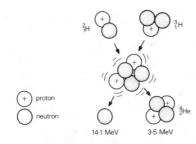

deuterium-tritium fusion reaction

| proton |
| neutron |

14·1 MeV   3·5 MeV

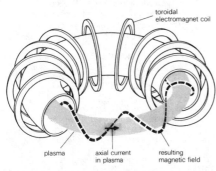

fusion reactor experiment

THERMONUCLEAR REACTOR *The combination of deuterium ($^2_1$H) and tritium ($^3_1$H) in a fusion reaction that forms helium. This is being attempted using a toroidal electromagnet to contain plasma consisting of deuterium and tritium nuclei.*

province of Macedonia in 148 BC. It subsequently formed part of the Byzantine Empire, falling to Turkey in the late 14th century AD. It was annexed by Greece in 1881.

thiamine. *See* vitamin B complex.

Third Reich (1933–45) The Nazi administration in Germany that ended with Germany's defeat in World War II. The name refers to the Nazi ambition to revive the Holy Roman Empire (the first Reich) and the German Empire (the second Reich; 1871–1918).

Thirty-Nine Articles (1563) The doctrine, together with the Book of *Common Prayer, of the *Church of England. They were developed from Thomas Cranmer's 42 Articles (1553), withdrawn by Mary I in re-establishing Roman Catholicism in England. The Articles deal with controversial points, giving the Anglican position. The clergy of the Church of England no longer have to approve them formally but promise not to teach beliefs that contradict them.

Thirty Years' War (1618–48) The conflict in the *Holy Roman Empire that turned into a European war. It was caused by the revolt of Protestants in Bohemia against the *Counter-Reformation policies of the imperial government at Prague. In 1635 France, hoping to contain the power of Spain and the Empire, entered the conflict. The war ended with the Peace of *Westpha-

lia (1648), although the Franco-Spanish conflict continued until 1659.

Thisbe. *See* Pyramus and Thisbe.

thistle A prickly plant of the daisy family, found throughout the N hemisphere, having small purple flowers and spiny stems. The perennial creeping thistle (*Cirsium arvense*) grows 1 m tall and is a persistent weed.

Thistle, Order of the A Scottish order of knighthood, probably founded by James III (1451–88); it was revived by James VII (II of England) in 1687. It consists of the sovereign and 16 knights and its motto is *Nemo me impune lacessit* (Wha daur meddle wi' me?).

Thomas, Dylan (1914–53) Welsh poet. Born in Swansea, he moved to London after the publication of *18 Poems* in 1934 and worked for the BBC. *Deaths and Entrances* (1946) contains many of his best-known poems. In 1949 he returned to Wales, where he wrote his radio play *Under Milk Wood* (1954). Alcoholism led to his death.

Thomas, St In the New Testament, one of the 12 Apostles. He is known as "Doubting Thomas" because he refused to believe in the resurrection until he had seen and touched Christ. Feast day: 21 Dec.

Thomas à Kempis (Thomas Hemmerken; c. 1380–1471) German monk, who spent most of his life writing and teaching at the Augustinian convent of Agnietenberg (Netherlands). His fame rests on his religious treatise, *The Imitation of Christ.*

Thompson, Daley (Francis Morgan T.; 1958–) British decathlete. Originally a sprinter, in 1975 he switched to the *decathlon, which he won in the Commonwealth Games in 1978. He won all the decathlons he entered until 1987 and two Olympic gold medals (1980 and 1984).

Thomson, Sir Joseph John (1856–1940) British physicist, who discovered the *electron. In 1897 he succeeded in deflecting cathode rays by an electric field, showing that they consisted of negatively charged particles. He also worked out that electrons were about 2000 times lighter than the hydrogen atom. Thomson's atomic theories were largely displaced by *Rutherford's model. He was awarded the Nobel Prize in 1906.

Thomson, William. *See* Kelvin, William Thomson, 1st Baron.

Thomson effect (*or* Kelvin effect). *See* thermoelectric effects.

Thor The Teutonic god of thunder, in some legends the son of *Odin. He presided over the home and controlled the weather and crops; he was also worshipped as a god of war. His name survives in *Thursday.*

thorax In mammals (including man), the region between the *diaphragm and the neck, which contains the lungs and heart and their associated vessels. The skeleton of the thorax is formed by the breastbone at the front, the spine at the back, and the ribs at the sides. In arthropods (e.g. insects) the thorax is between the head and abdomen.

thorium (Th) A naturally occurring radioactive metallic element. Thorium oxide (ThO_2) has one of the highest known melting points

(3300°C). The thorium series of radioactive decay is headed by thorium-232, which undergoes a series of decays ending with the stable isotope lead-208. At no 90; at wt 232.038; mp 1750°C; bp 3800°C.

Thoroughbred A breed of horse descended from three Arab stallions brought to England between 1689 and 1728. Streamlined and sensitive, Thoroughbreds are noted for speed and stamina, being used worldwide for racing and as bloodstock to improve other breeds. They may be any colour. Height: 1.52–1.73 m (15–17 hands).

Thrace The Balkan region bordered by the Black Sea, the Aegean, Macedonia, and the River Danube, divided between Turkey, Greece, and Bulgaria. From the 8th century BC Greek cities colonized the coasts, while the inland tribes were an easy target for invaders—the Persians in about 516 BC and then Philip II of Macedon in the mid-4th century. Thrace became a Roman province in 46 AD. It was famous for its horses and ecstatic religious rituals.

threadworm. See pinworm.

thrift A plant, *Armeria maritima*, also called sea pink, native to mountains, salt marshes, and sandy coastal regions of N Europe. It has narrow grasslike leaves and pink or white flowers.

thrips A minute insect, also called thunder fly, with a dark body, 0.5–5 mm long, and two pairs of fringed wings. Many species suck the juices of plants, often causing damage and spreading diseases.

thrombosis The formation of a blood clot inside a blood vessel, obstructing the flow of blood. Thrombosis is more likely if the vessel is damaged or if the blood flow is slow. The commonest site is in the veins of the legs, particularly if a person is bedridden. The clot may be carried to the lungs, causing pulmonary *embolism (blockage of an artery).

Thrombosis can also occur in the arteries supplying the heart (coronary thrombosis), causing a heart attack (*see* myocardial infarction), or the brain, causing *stroke.

thrush (bird) A widely distributed songbird with brown plumage, often with speckling of red, yellow, or blue. Thrushes feed on insects and fruit and often have melodious songs, as in the song thrush (*Turdus philomelus*). The mistle thrush (*T. viscivorus*) feeds on berries (including mistletoe), snails, and worms. Northern species are migratory. See also blackbird; ring ouzel.

thrush (disease). See candidiasis.

Thucydides (c. 460–c. 400 BC) Greek historian. His eight-volume *History of the Peloponnesian War* is notable for its analysis of the issues.

thulium (Tm) The least abundant of the *lanthanide elements, discovered in 1879 by P. T. Cleve (1840–1905). Radioactive ^{169}Tm is used in portable X-ray generators. At no 69; at wt 168.934; mp 1545°C; bp 1947°C.

Thurber, James (1894–1961) US humorous writer and cartoonist. A contributor to the *New Yorker*, he satirized intellectual fashions. His essays are collected in *The Thurber Carnival* (1945) and other volumes.

Thutmose III (d. 1450 BC) King of Egypt (c. 1504–1450) of the 18th dynasty, who ruled Egypt at its most powerful. In 1468 he defeated Syrian rebels at Megiddo and later advanced beyond the River Euphrates. He was an athlete and hunter and a patron of art.

thylacine The largest carnivorous *marsupial, *Thylacinus cynocephalus*, also called Tasmanian wolf or tiger and now probably extinct. About 1.5 m long, it resembles a dog with dark stripes across its grey-brown back.

thyme A small shrub native to Eurasia. Garden thyme (*Thymus vulgaris*) is cultivated for its fragrant leaves, which are used in cookery. An oil extract is used in perfumes. The common wild thyme (*T. drucei*) has clusters of rose flowers.

thymus An organ situated at the base of the neck, above the heart. The thymus grows until puberty, after which it shrinks and ceases to function. During infancy the thymus produces lymphocytes that form the *antibodies associated with allergic responses and the rejection of transplanted tissues and organs. See also immunity.

thyroid gland An *endocrine gland situated at the base of the neck. It secretes the hormone thyroxine, which controls the chemical processes involved in the growth and maintenance of tissues. Secretion is regulated by thyroid-stimulating hormone, released from the *pituitary gland. Because thyroxine production requires iodine, deficiency of iodine causes the thyroid to enlarge in an attempt to produce adequate amounts of the hormone (*see* goitre). See also cretinism.

Tiananmen Square. See Peking.

Tiber, River (Italian name: Tevere; Latin name: Tiberis) A river in central Italy, rising in the Apennines of Tuscany and flowing mainly S through Rome to the Tyrrhenian Sea near Ostia. Length: 405 km (252 mi).

Tiberias, Sea of. See Galilee, Sea of.

Tiberius (42 BC–37 AD) Roman emperor (14–37 AD); stepson of Emperor Augustus. As emperor his policies were unambitious but he faced the Senate's hostility, family intrigue, and military rebellion. He retired to Capri in 26 AD, with a reputation for depravity.

Tibet (Chinese name: Xizang Autonomous Region) An administrative region in W China, bordering on India, Nepal, Bhutan, and Burma. It is surrounded by mountains, including the Himalayas. The area is rich in minerals. *History*: Buddhism was introduced in the 7th century AD. The lamas (priests) of *Tibetan Buddhism attained political power in the 13th century. In 1642, the fifth *Dalai Lama became ruler of all Tibet. In 1720 the Chinese Qing dynasty established a control over Tibet that lasted until 1911. Independence was declared, but in 1950 Tibet again fell to the Chinese. Recent years have seen an upsurge in resistance to Chinese occupation. Area: 1 221 601 sq km (471 660 sq mi). Population (1986): 2 030 000. Capital: Lhasa.

Tibetan Buddhism (*or* lamaism) A form of Buddhism as practised in Tibet and Mongolia. Introduced to Tibet in the 7th century AD, it has a complex literature and severe discipline. See also Dalai Lama.

tick A widely distributed parasitic *arachnid that sucks the blood of birds and mammals and may transmit such diseases as *typhus and relapsing fever. Its round body, up to 30 mm long, bears eight bristly legs. After feeding, the adults drop off the host and lay eggs on the ground. The larvae attach themselves to a suitable victim, feed, then drop off and moult into *nymphs, which repeat the procedure. *Compare* mite.

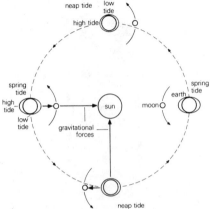

TIDES *The force of gravity between the earth and the moon pulls the waters of the seas towards the moon, creating high tides once a day. The second daily high tide occurs because the moon pulls the earth itself away from the water on the far side from the moon. Exceptionally high spring tides occur twice monthly when the gravitational force of the moon is in line with that of the sun. The lower neap tides occur when these two forces are at right angles.*

tides The regular rising and falling of seawater resulting from the gravitational attraction between the earth, sun, and moon. Most parts of the world experience semidiurnal tides (occurring twice per tidal day—24 hours 50 minutes). Tidal currents are periodic horizontal flows of water resulting from the rise and fall of the tide. Near the coast they are usually perpendicular to it and reversing, but in the ocean they are rotary flowing around a series of nodal points.

Tierra del Fuego A group of islands separated from South America by the Strait of Magellan. The W and S belong to Chile, the E to Argentina. Sheep farming and oil production are the principal activities. Chief towns: Punta Arenas (Chile); Ushuaia (Argentina).

Tiflis. *See* Tbilisi.

tiger A large *cat, *Panthera tigris*. Tigers are usually about 3 m long, but Siberian tigers can reach 4 m. Tigers evolved in Siberia and have spread to most of Asia. They shed their coat seasonally and shelter from hot sun during the day, hunting (mainly antelope) at night.

tiger moth A widely distributed moth. The adults have a stout body and are often orange and black. The hairy caterpillars, commonly called woolly bears, are seldom destructive.

Tigris, River A river in SW Asia, rising in SE Turkey and flowing SE through Diyarbakir, along the Turkish-Syrian border, and into Iraq. It joins the River Euphrates to form the Shatt al-Arab. Length: 1850 km (1150 mi).

Tijuana 39 29N 117 10W A city in NW Mexico, on the US border. The main entry point to Mexico from California, it is a popular resort. Population (1980): 461 257.

timber wolf A large shaggy-coated *wolf of North America, also called the grey wolf. A Texan variety with a reddish-brown coat is called the red wolf.

Timbuktu (French name: Tombouctou) 16 49N 2 59W A town in E central Mali, on the River Niger. It was an important centre on the trans-Saharan caravan route and an Islamic cultural centre (1400–1600). Population (latest est): 19 165.

time A concept that measures the duration of events and the periods that separate them; it provides a scale of measurement enabling events that have occurred to be distinguished from those that are occurring and those that will occur. It appears, intuitively, to be flowing at a constant rate in one direction only, for all observers. However, according to Einstein's theory of *relativity this is not the case. The rate at which time passes (as measured by a clock) is not the same for observers in different frames of reference that are moving at a constant velocity with respect to each other (see illustration on page 541). Historically, the measurement of time on earth has been based on astronomical observations –the time taken for the earth to revolve on its axis (the day) or for it to complete its orbit round the sun (the year). However, in modern science the basis of time measurement is the *second, which is defined in terms of the frequency of the radiation emitted in a specified transition of an isotope of caesium (see illustration on page 540).

Timor An Indonesian island, the largest of the *Nusa Tenggara group. Crops include coffee, coconut, and sandalwood. Area: 39 775 sq km (11 883 sq mi). Chief towns: Kupang and Dili.

Timothy, St In the New Testament, a disciple of *Paul, whom he accompanied on many missions. According to tradition he was martyred in Ephesus. Feast day: 6 Feb.

Timur (*or* Tamerlane; c. 1336–1405) Mongol conqueror, a descendant of Genghis Khan. After winning control of Turkestan in central Asia, Timur swept ruthlessly through Mongolia, Persia, Turkey, Russia, and India, leaving death and destruction behind him.

tin (Sn) A silvery metal known to the ancients. Its principal ore is the oxide cassiterite (SnO_2). The element exists in two forms—the grey alpha-tin, and beta-tin, which is the common form above 13.2°C. At low temperature beta-tin slowly changes into alpha-tin causing **tin plague**. The major use of tin is in tinplate, used mainly for food cans (tins). Tin alloys with copper to form *bronzes and with niobium to give a superconducting composition, used in electromagnets. At no 50; at wt 118.69; mp 231.89°C; bp 2270°C.

tinamou A solitary ground-dwelling bird occurring in Central and South America. Well

Man's first attempt to measure the passage of time was based on the sun. Sundials are known to have existed in Greece in 1450 BC, but probably were used in China before this. This copy of a Saxon sundial can be seen in Kent.

Sundials measure the rotation of the earth on its axis, giving a measure of the solar day. To measure longer periods, taking into account the cycle of the seasons (essential for agriculture), it is necessary to measure the time taken for the earth to orbit the sun - the tropical (or solar) year. The other easily observed event humans used to measure time is the regular reappearance of the new moon, giving the lunar month. Unfortunately there are no simple relationships between these three events. This has given religious and political calendar makers a hard time. The Gregorian calendar (introduced in 1582 by Pope Gregory XIII) is now almost universally used, although Hebrew and Islamic calendars are still based on lunar months.

Sundials only work in sunshine. Water clocks (water leaking out of or into a container at a controlled rate) and sand clocks (like the modern egg timer) appeared in the first few centuries before Christ.

In the 9th century the candle clock was invented - as the candle burns it reaches marks made in its body. Another flame clock was the oil-burning clock, in which oil burnt at a steady rate, the level in the glass reservoir indicating the passage of time. This was a 16th century device.

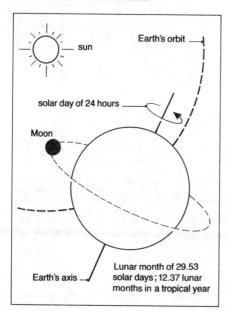

sun

Earth's orbit

solar day of 24 hours

Moon

Lunar month of 29.53 solar days; 12.37 lunar months in a tropical year

Earth's axis

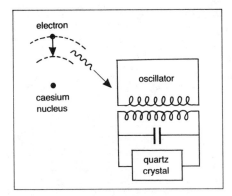

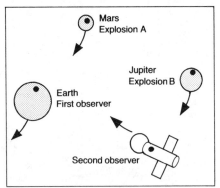

Scientific research requires an accurately measured unit of time. The convenient unit is the second, which before 1956 was defined as a fraction of the solar day. Between 1956 and 1967 it was a fraction of the tropical year. Since 1967 it has relied, not on astronomical events, but on the atomic clock. In the caesium clock, caesium atoms emit electromagnetic radiation of exact period, as an outer electron falls from one energy level to another. This oscillation is used to control the frequency of a quartz-crystal clock.

Until the beginning of this century, there appeared to be no ambiguity in saying that two events were simultaneous. However, Einstein's theory of relativity recognized that because the speed of light is constant, the measurement of time depends on the observer's motion. If two explosions, A and B, on Mars and Jupiter appear simultaneous to an observer on earth, they might not appear so to another observer in a spacecraft in motion relative to the earth. Thus, according to relativity, time is not absolute but relative to the motion of the person or thing measuring it. Time, in fact, is one aspect of a four-dimensional space-time continuum.

The first mechanical clocks appeared in the 13th century using a falling weight and a verge and foliot escapement. A greater accuracy came with Huygens' use of the pendulum in clockwork in 1657. With the development of the coiled spring to store energy (in the 15th century) replacing falling weights, clocks became smaller and more widely available. A 17th century clock workshop is shown here.

camouflaged with a mottled grey plumage, tinamous have small wings and a short tail and are poor fliers. They feed on seeds, insects, etc.

Tintagel 50 40N 4 45W A village and resort on the N coast of Cornwall. The ruined Tintagel Castle was reputedly the site of King Arthur's court.

Tintoretto (Jacopo Robusti; 1518–94) Venetian painter, whose nickname, meaning "little dyer," derived from his father's profession of silk dyeing. His three paintings of the *Miracles of St Mark* (1562–66) for the Confraternity of S Marco were followed by his series of the life of Christ (1564–87; Scuola di S Rocco) and his paintings for the Doge's Palace, including the enormous *Paradise*.

Tipperary (Irish name: Contae Tiobraid Árann) A county in the S Republic of Ireland, in Munster. It contains part of the Golden Vale (one of the most fertile areas in Ireland) in the SW. Dairy farming is especially important. Area: 4255 sq km (1643 sq mi). Population (1986): 136 504. County town: Clonmel.

Tippett, Sir Michael (1905–) British composer. He has written five operas, including *The Midsummer Marriage* (1947–52), *The Knot Garden* (1966–70), and *New Year* (1989). Other works include four symphonies, four string quartets, three piano sonatas, and the oratorios *A Child of Our Time* (1940) and *The Mask of Time* (1982). In 1983 he was appointed to the OM.

Tirana (Albanian name: Tiranë) 41 20N 19 49E The capital of Albania. Founded in the 17th century, it became the capital in 1920. Population (1983): 206 000.

Tirol (*or* Tyrol) A mountainous federal state in W Austria, bordering on Germany and Italy. Tourism is important, especially winter sports. The chief occupations are agriculture and forestry, with some mining and manufacturing industries. Area: 12 648 sq km (4883 sq mi). Population (1986): 605 774. Capital: Innsbruck.

Tissot, James Joseph Jacques (1836– 1902) French painter. After settling in England in the 1870s he became known for his scenes of Victorian life, notably *The Ball on Shipboard* (Tate Gallery).

tit A widely occurring small songbird (also called titmouse) that frequents woodlands and gardens, feeding on insects. Usually grey or black, it often has blue and yellow markings. *See also* bluetit.

Titanic A luxury passenger ship that on 14– 15 April, 1912, struck an iceberg near Newfoundland on its maiden voyage and sank with the loss of 1513 lives. As a result of the disaster safety rules for ships at sea were drawn up. The wreck of the Titanic was located on the sea bed and photographed in 1985.

titanium (Ti) A light strong transition metal discovered in 1791 by W. Gregor (1761–1817). It occurs in the minerals rutile (TiO_2), ilmenite ($FeTiO_3$), sphene ($CaTiO_3$), and in some iron ores. The dioxide (TiO_2) is used in white paint. The metal is as strong as steel but 45% lighter (relative density 4.54). It is used in alloys for missiles and aircraft. At no 22; at wt 47.90; mp 1660°C; bp 3287°C.

Titans In Greek mythology, 12 gods and goddesses, the children of *Uranus and *Gaea. They were Oceanus, Coeus, Crius, Hyperion, Iapetus, Cronus, Thea, Rhea, Themis, Mnemosyne, Phoebe, and Tethys. They were overthrown by Zeus and the Olympian deities.

tithes The tenth part of an income donated for religious purposes. Tithes were required by Mosaic law, which demanded payment in kind from all agricultural produce. Church law also required tithes to maintain churches and clergy. They were abolished in Britain in 1936.

Titian (Tiziano Vecellio; c. 1488–1576) Venetian painter of the High Renaissance. He collaborated with Giorgione on frescoes for the façade of the German Exchange (1508). His *Assumption of the Virgin* (Sta Maria dei Frari) is reminiscent of such Florentine painters as Raphael. His equestrian portraits of the Habsburgs, his patrons from 1530, can be seen in the Prado. Mythological works include *Bacchus and Ariadne* (National Gallery, London).

Titicaca, Lake A lake in South America, between Peru and Bolivia, in the Andes. At an altitude of 3809 m (12 497 ft) it is the world's highest lake navigable to large vessels. Area: 8135 sq km (3141 sq mi). Depth: 370 m (1214 ft).

titmouse. *See* tit.

Tito (Josip Broz; 1892–1980) Yugoslav statesman; president 1953–80. Captured by the Russians in World War I, he subsequently fought with the Red Army in the Russian civil war. He returned to Yugoslavia in 1920 and joined the Communist Party, becoming secretary general in 1937. In World War II he led partisan resistance to the German occupation, becoming Yugoslavia's leader after the war. Tito maintained Yugoslavia independent from Soviet interference.

Titus (Flavius Vespasianus) (39–81 AD) Roman emperor (79–81). He fought with his father Vespasian in Judaea and ended the Jewish revolt (70) by capturing Jerusalem. A popular emperor, he was deified after his death.

Tivoli 41 58N 12 48E A town in central Italy, in Lazio. A summer resort in Roman times, it possesses the remains of Hadrian's villa and the Renaissance Villa d'Este, with its terraced water gardens. Population (1981 est): 51 528.

Tiw. *See* Tyr.

TNT (trinitrotoluene; $C_6H_2(NO_2)_3CH_3$) A highly explosive pale yellow crystalline solid. It is prepared from toluene treated with concentrated sulphuric and nitric acids and is used in shells, bombs, etc., and blasting explosives.

toad A widely distributed tail-less amphibian related to frogs. Toads have long hind legs and short forelegs; they swim by means of partially webbed feet. Their long sticky tongue that can extend rapidly to capture insects. *See also* natterjack; tree frog.

toadfish A carnivorous bony *fish found mainly in tropical and subtropical seas, living on the seabed. It has a brownish body and makes croaking sounds resembling a toad.

toadstool. *See* mushroom.

tobacco A plant of the nightshade family. The species *Nicotiana tabacum* and *N. rustica* are cultivated for their large leaves, which are slowly dried and then fermented to make cigarettes, etc. The main growing regions are the USA, China, India, and the Soviet Union. Tobacco contains about 2–4% nicotine, which gives it a stimulating effect but its tar content is damaging to health.

Tobago Island. *See* Trinidad and Tobago, Republic of.

Tobata. *See* Kitakyushu.

Toc H A fellowship for Christians, open to anyone over the age of 16 and devoted to social service. Founded in 1915 in Belgium by the Rev P. B. Clayton (1885–1972), a Church of England chaplain, as a military chapel and club, it was named Talbot House in memory of Gilbert Talbot (1891–1915), an Anglican British lieutenant, killed in action. Its name comes from the army signals for the initials *T H*.

Togo, Republic of (French name: République Togolaise) A small country in West Africa, on the Gulf of Guinea between Ghana and Benin. *Economy*: chiefly agricultural, food crops consist of cassava, maize, and rice; cash crops include cocoa, coffee, and cotton. Forests produce timber, oil palms, and dyewoods. There are rich deposits of phosphates, which, with cocoa and coffee, are the main export. Bauxite, limestone, and iron ore are found. Industry concentrates on food processing, but there is a large cement plant and a refinery. *History*: settled by the Ewe in the 12th and 13th centuries, the area was raided for slaves from the 17th to 19th centuries. From 1884 to 1914 Togoland was a German protectorate and after World War I it was divided between France and the UK. The French territory gained full independence in 1960. (The British part joined Ghana in 1957.) A coup in 1967 brought Lt Col (later Gen) Etienne Gnassingbe Eyadéma (1937–   ) to power. Official language: French. Official currency: CFA (Communauté financière africaine) franc of 100 centimes. Area: 56 000 sq km (21 616 sq mi). Population (1988 est): 3 246 000. Capital and main port: Lomé.

tokay. *See* gecko.

Tokyo 35 40N 139 45E The capital of Japan, in E central *Honshu on Tokyo Bay. Administratively joined to its port Yokohama and to the industrial centre of Kawasaki, Greater Tokyo is the world's largest city. It has over 100 universities. *History*: the village of Edo was founded in the 12th century, growing in importance as a city by the 17th century. As Tokyo, it replaced Kyoto as imperial capital in 1868. Population (1987): 8 209 000.

Toledo 41 40N 83 35W A city in the USA, in Ohio on Lake Erie at the mouth of the River Maumee. It is a major Great Lakes port, shipping oil, coal, and farm products. Industrial activities include oil refining. Population (1986 est): 340 680.

Toledo 39 52N 4 02W A city in central Spain, in New Castile on the River Tagus. It was formerly the capital of Spain. It is known for its metalwork engraved in the Moorish tradition. Population (1982 est): 61 813.

Tolkien, J(ohn) R(onald) R(euel) (1892–1973) British scholar and writer. His novel *The Lord of the Rings* (1954–55), created a detailed fantasy world. Related works include *The Hobbit* (1937) and *The Silmarillion* (1977).

Tolpuddle Martyrs Six members of the Friendly Society of Agricultural Labourers of Tolpuddle, Dorset, founded in 1833 to secure fair wages for its members. Unfairly charged with administering unlawful oaths, they were transported to Australia but pardoned in 1836.

Tolstoy, Leo (Nikolaevich), Count (1828–1910) Russian writer. Following his marriage in 1862 he wrote two widely acclaimed novels, *War and Peace* (1865–69) and *Anna Karenina* (1875–77). His other literary work filled 45 volumes. A spiritual crisis (1879) led to a faith in a form of Christian anarchism. He dressed as a peasant, became a vegetarian and a pacifist, repudiated his former works, and divided his property among his family.

Toltecs An Indian people who dominated much of central Mexico between the 10th and 12th centuries AD. Their language, *Nahuatl, was also spoken by the Aztecs. They fused the many small states of the area into an empire. The *Aztecs destroyed their capital of Tula in the mid-12th century.

tomato A South American plant, *Lycopersicon esculentum*, of the nightshade family, widely cultivated for its red fruit. Tomatoes are grown in fields in warm regions and in greenhouses in cooler regions. The yellow flowers produce the fruits which are eaten fresh or canned.

Tombouctou. *See* Timbuktu.

Tomsk 56 30N 85 05E A port in the central Soviet Union, in the RSFSR on the River Tom. Industries include engineering and it has a university (1888). Population (1987): 489 000.

ton An Imperial unit of weight equal to 2240 lb (long ton) or 1016 kilograms. In the USA a unit equal to 2000 lb (short ton) is also used. The metric ton (or **tonne**) is equal to 1000 kilograms.

tonality The presence of a key in a musical composition. Musical compositions from the early 17th century to about 1900 are in distinct keys, based on individual scales, in which certain notes (the first and fifth) form tonal centres to which the music periodically returns. *See also* serialism.

Tonga, Kingdom of (*or* Friendly Islands) A country in the SW Pacific Ocean, E of Fiji. It consists of 169 small islands. *Economy*: chiefly agricultural, the main products and exports are copra and bananas. Oil has been discovered. *History*: under King Taufa'ahau Tupou (George I; 1797–1893) the civil war between rival dynasties ended and the islands converted to Christianity. The country became a British protectorate in 1900, and in 1970 an independent state within the British Commonwealth. Head of State: King Taufa'ahau Tupou IV (1918–   ). Official languages: Tongan and English. Official currency: pa'anga of 100 seniti. Area: 700 sq km (270 sq mi). Population: (1988 est) 95 200. Capital and main port: Nuku'alofa.

tongue A muscular organ in the floor of the mouth. Its root is attached by muscles to the U-shaped hyoid bone in the neck. The tongue is the main organ of taste: its surface is covered by taste buds. It also manipulates food in the mouth and plays an important role in speech.

tonsils Patches of tissue situated on each side at the back of the mouth. They produce lymphocytes, which protect the body against infection. Inflammation of the tonsils (tonsillitis) may be caused by a variety of infections.

topaz A mineral, $Al_2SiO_4(OH,F)_2$, that occurs in igneous rocks. It is usually colourless or yellow, and is used as a gemstone. The finest specimens come from the Urals, Brazil, and Ceylon.

top minnow. See killifish.

topology The branch of *geometry concerned with the properties of an object that do not change when the object is bent, stretched, or shrunk but not torn or deformed so that several points on it are fused. Topology is often called rubber-sheet geometry.

Torah (Hebrew: instruction) The five books of Moses (Genesis, Exodus, Leviticus, Numbers, and Deuteronomy), which make up the first of the three divisions of the *Bible. In *Judaism, the term is also applied to the whole body of religious teachings.

Torino. See Turin.

tornado A violently rotating column of air, small in diameter, characterized by a funnel-shaped cloud, which may reach ground surface. Wind speeds of up to 200 knots (100 m per second) have been experienced. Occurring over land, tornadoes cause destruction and are a problem in central USA and Australia.

Toronto 43 42N 79 25W A city and port in E Canada, the capital of Ontario on Lake Ontario. Canada's third largest city, it has a stock exchange and many business headquarters. Industries include engineering, electrical, chemical, and wood products, foods, and clothing. Population (1986): 612 289.

torpedo (armament) A self-propelled guided underwater missile carrying a high explosive. They can be launched by ships, aircraft, or submarines. Designed in 1866 by a British engineer, Robert Whitehead (1823–1905), they sunk 25 million tons of Allied shipping in World Wars I and II. Modern torpedos are driven by steam turbines or by battery-powered electric motors and have sophisticated acoustic homing systems.

torpedo (fish). See electric ray.

Torquemada, Tomás de (1420–98) Spanish Dominican friar and Grand Inquisitor. Head of the Spanish *Inquisition (from 1483), his sentences were extremely harsh and he was responsible for the expulsion of the Jews from Spain in 1492.

Torricelli, Evangelista (1608–47) Italian physicist. He demonstrated that the atmosphere exerts a pressure by showing that it could support a column of mercury in a tube, thus inventing the mercury barometer (1643), which also created the first man-made vacuum; the space above the mercury is still called a Torricellian vacuum.

tort In law, a civil wrong that is a breach of a duty established by law rather than by *contract. It differs from a crime in that it affects the interests of the injured person rather than of the state.

tortoise A slow-moving plant-eating reptile with a protective shell and tough scaly legs. Tortoises are widely distributed, especially in Africa, and range in size from about 10 cm to 1.5 m. They lay eggs and have long lifespans (up to 150 years). Compare turtle; terrapin.

tortoiseshell butterfly A widely distributed butterfly whose wings are mainly orange with black markings. The caterpillars feed mainly on nettles and willows.

Toscanini, Arturo (1867–1957) Italian conductor. He made his debut in 1886 and subsequently conducted at La Scala, Milan, and at the Metropolitan Opera in New York. From 1937 until his death he conducted the NBC (National Broadcasting Company) Symphony Orchestra.

toucan A noisy forest-dwelling bird occurring in tropical America. Toucans have huge coloured bills and black plumage with a coloured breast. They feed on fruit.

Toulon 43 07N 5 55E A port in SE France, in the Var department on the Mediterranean Sea. Toulon is one of France's principal naval bases and has marine engineering, chemical, oil, and textile industries. Population (1989): 185 000.

Toulouse 43 33N 1 24E A city in S France, the capital of the Haute-Garonne department on the River Garonne. A major commercial centre, it has aircraft, armaments, chemical, and textile industries. Notable buildings include the basilica (11th–13th centuries), the gothic cathedral, and the university (1230). Population (1982): 354 289.

Toulouse-Lautrec, Henri (Marie Raymond) de (1864–1901) French artist. Stunted in growth by a childhood accident, he settled in Paris, where he led an unconventional life among the music halls and cafés of Montmartre. He produced studies of entertainers, circus life, and prostitutes in posters, lithographs, and paintings, including At the Moulin Rouge (Art Institute of Chicago).

touraco. See turaco.

Tour de France The main Continental professional cycling race. Founded in 1903, the road race lasts three weeks or more and has a maximum length of approximately 4000 km (2480 mi). The race starts in a different town each year but always ends in Paris.

tourmaline A group of minerals found in granite, composed of complex silicates containing boron. Some are used as gemstones and some for their piezoelectric and polarizing properties.

Tours 47 23N 0 42E A city in central France, the capital of the Indre-et-Loire department and a tourist centre. Notable buildings include the gothic cathedral, the archiepiscopal palace (17th–18th centuries), and the university (1970). Population (1982): 136 483.

Tower Bridge A bridge over the River Thames, next to the *Tower of London. Built in 1894 in the gothic style, its central portion lifts to allow large ships to pass through.

Tower of London A royal fortress on the N bank of the River Thames, to the E of the City. It was begun by William I in the 11th century and added to in subsequent centuries. It was a royal palace until the 17th century and a state prison.

It is now a museum, containing the British crown jewels and regalia.

toxaemia The presence in the blood of poisons (toxins) produced by bacteria; this occurs, for example, in diphtheria and tetanus. The term also describes a condition affecting pregnant women, formerly thought to be due to toxins but is now known to be caused by *hypertension (raised blood pressure).

toxin A poison produced by a living organism, including bacteria and fungi. In diphtheria and tetanus the toxin is produced by the bacteria within the body; in botulism the toxin occurs in contaminated food eaten by the patient. Some toxins are useful: penicillin is a toxin that kills bacteria and is used as a drug (see antibiotic).

Trabzon (former name: Trebizond) 41 00N 39 43E A port in NE Turkey, on the Black Sea. It was the capital of the Comnenian empire (1204–1461) and has a university (1963). Population (1985): 155 960.

trachea 1. The windpipe: a tube that conducts air from the larynx to the bronchi, which form the air passages to the *lungs. The trachea is lined by *mucous membrane and supported by hoops of cartilage in its wall. **2.** One of the air passages in insects, which lead directly to the tissues. Each trachea has an external opening (spiracle) that can be opened and closed.

trachoma An eye disease that occurs in poor parts of the world and is caused by microorganisms called chlamydias. It is a severe form of *conjunctivitis in which the membrane lining the eyelids and covering the cornea becomes scarred and shrunken and the eyelids become deformed. It is a common cause of blindness.

Tracy, Spencer (1900–67) US film actor. In the 1930s he played gangsters, but later costarred with Katharine *Hepburn in *Adam's Rib* (1949) and *Guess Who's Coming to Dinner* (1967). Other notable films include *The Old Man and the Sea* (1958) and *Judgement at Nuremberg* (1961).

trade cycle The repeated economic cycle of boom, recession, *depression, recovery, and boom. The *Depression of the 1930s was followed, after World War II, by a boom, interrupted by only minor recessions, until another depression in the 1970s. The cycle may result from shocks to the economy, such as wars, political rises in the prices of commodities (such as oil), etc. Many government policies attempt to avoid the excesses of the cycle.

trademarks Distinctive signs owned by a manufacturer or trader and applied to his goods to identify them. The owner of a trademark has the sole right to its use; this can be protected by legal action.

tradescantia A flowering plant native to North and Central America. Varieties of the wandering Jew (*Tradescantia fluminensis*) are popular house plants, having oval leaves, tinged with pink or silver stripes. Spiderworts, derived from *T. virginiana*, have three-petalled flowers and grasslike leaves.

trade union An organization of employees enabling them to negotiate jointly with an employer and to provide security for its members. Trade unions began with local clubs of skilled craftsmen in 18th-century Britain. Robert Owen's Grand National Consolidated Trades Union (1834), the first attempt to unite skilled and unskilled workers, collapsed following the transportation of the *Tolpuddle Martyrs. In 1851 the first successful national trade union, the Amalgamated Society of Engineers, was formed and in 1868 the first Trades Union Congress (TUC) met. Granted legal status in 1871, UK trade unions became secure when the Trade Disputes Act (1906) prevented employers from suing unions for damages after a *strike. The failure of the *General Strike (1926) and the Trade Disputes Act (1927), which made general strikes illegal, was a blow to unionists. This measure was withdrawn after the war, although the law regarding strikes and *picketing is still a subject of debate. National union organizations (such as the TUC) have become important political forces in negotiations with governments. The first international trade union was the first *International (1864); the international trades union movement is now represented by the World Federation of Trade Unions and the International Confederation of Free Trade Unions.

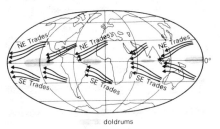

doldrums

TRADE WINDS

trade winds (or tropical easterlies) The tropical winds that blow generally from a NE direction in the N hemisphere and from a SE direction in the S hemisphere, converging towards the equator.

Trafalgar, Battle of (21 October, 1805) The naval battle in the Napoleonic Wars in which the British under Nelson (in the *Victory*) defeated the French W of Cape Trafalgar, between Cádiz and Gibraltar (SW Spain). Despite Nelson's death, his success ended the threat of a French invasion of Britain and established British naval dominance.

tragacanth. *See* gums.

tragedy A form of drama recounting the fall (usually death) of a hero. It evolved in ancient Greece from the dithyramb, a choral song, and was fully developed in the plays of Aeschylus, Sophocles, and Euripides. Little tragedy of worth was written until the tragedies of Shakespeare and his followers. In 17th-century France the neoclassical tragedies of Racine and Corneille were based on principles derived from Aristotle's *Poetics*. Ibsen and Strindberg in Europe and Eugene O'Neill in the USA contributed to the development of tragic drama in the 19th and 20th centuries.

tragopan A short-tailed *pheasant occurring in forests of the Himalayas. Male tragopans have vivid plumage and two erectile blue "horns" on the head; a fold of skin beneath the bill forms a bib during display.

tranquillizers A group of drugs used to quieten restless or anxious patients. The major tranquillizers are powerful and addictive drugs used in the treatment of schizophrenia and other mental disorders. Minor tranquillizers, which include the *benzodiazepines, are used for neuroses and anxiety.

transcendentalism A philosophy that stresses the ways of thinking and understanding beyond the world of experience. In the philosophy of *Kant, everything beyond man's limited experience is transcendental and unknowable. Intuition about time and space and understanding of quality and quantity are vital for experience, but are transcendent in that they do not come from that experience.

transformer A device for converting alternating current from one voltage to another. The input is fed to a coil of wire (primary) wound round a soft iron core, creating an oscillating magnetic field in the core. This field induces a secondary current of the same frequency in a second winding (secondary) on the same core (see electromagnetic induction). The ratio of primary to secondary voltage is equal to the ratio of the number of turns in the secondary to that in the primary. The device is used both in electronic circuits and in the distribution of electricity (see electricity supply).

transistor A *semiconductor device with three or more electrodes. Transistors form the basic elements of electronic *amplifiers and logic circuits, often combined with other components in *integrated circuits. They were first developed in 1948 by William *Shockley and his coworkers at the Bell Telephone Co and now replace *thermionic valves. A **bipolar junction transistor** consists of two junctions between p-type and n-type semiconductors forming either a p-n-p or n-p-n structure. (The two semiconductor types differ in the impurities, called dopants, added to them.) Current is carried across these junctions by negative and positive charge carriers (electrons and holes). Depending on how it is connected into a circuit, the junction transistor can act as a voltage or current amplifier.
The **field effect transistor** (FET) is a device in which current is carried by only one type of charge. There are two sorts: the junction FET (JFET) has a region of semiconductor of one dopant type flanked by two highly doped layers of the opposite type. Current flows parallel to the junctions, between the so-called source and drain electrodes, through a narrow channel between the highly doped regions (the gate); it is controlled by the electric field arising from the gate input voltage, which alters the width of the conducting channel. The JFET is used as a separate component in amplifiers and switches. In the insulated-gate FET (IGFET) the source and drain electrodes are highly doped regions in a substrate of the opposite type. The gate electrode is a conductor separated from the substrate by a thin insulating layer across the surface. The electric field caused by the gate voltage controls the source-drain current on the other side of the insulator. The IGFET is used mainly in metal-oxide semiconductor (MOS) integrated circuits.

transition elements A group of metallic elements, including most of the common metals, the inner electron shells of which are incomplete. The *lanthanides and the *actinides are sometimes included. The elements show considerable similarities to their horizontal neighbours in the *periodic table. In general, they are hard, high-melting, conductors of heat and electricity. They have multiple *valences and form coloured compounds.

Transjordan. See Jordan, Hashemite kingdom of.

Transkei, Republic of A homeland in South Africa. *Economy*: subsistence agriculture, especially livestock, with tea, coffee, and flax as cash crops. *History*: created in 1963, when South Africa granted self-government to the *Xhosa nation, as the first of the Bantu Homelands, it became "independent" in 1976, although this independence is recognized only by South Africa. In the second of two coups in 1987 Maj-Gen Bantu Holomisa came to power. President: Tutor Nyangelizwe Vulinolela Nolamase. Official currency: South African rand. Area: 43 188 sq km (16 675 sq mi). Population (1985 est): 3 000 000. Capital: Umtata.

transmigration of souls. See reincarnation.

transmutation The conversion of one element into another. An early (unfulfilled) aim of *alchemy was the transmutation of base metals into gold. Transmutations were achieved in the 20th century by bombarding elements with *alpha particles or *neutrons.

transpiration The loss of water vapour from the surface of a plant, which occurs primarily through small pores (stomata) in the leaves but also (slowly) through the outer layer (cuticle) of the leaves and stem (see epidermis). The rate of water loss is controlled by the opening and closing of the stomata, greater loss occurring during the day than at night.

transplantation An operation in which a patient receives a tissue or organ derived from his own body or from another individual (the donor). Skin grafting uses tissue derived from the patient himself: it is used to repair burns and other injuries. Transplanting organs from another person requires matching of the donor's and recipient's tissues and drugs to prevent the recipient's immune system from rejecting the organ. The first successful heart transplant was performed by the South African surgeon Christiaan Barnard in 1967; other organs that have been transplanted include the kidneys, lung, and liver. The first successful implanting of an artificial heart, made of titanium and plastic, took place in 1988.

transportation In law, the practice of sending a convicted criminal to some place outside his native country, usually to a colony. In Britain, transportation, which dates back to Elizabeth I, ceased in 1868.

TRANSISTOR

Germanium is a typical semiconductor. The four outer electrons in each of its atoms form covalent bonds with adjacent atoms. In the pure state it acts as an insulator as no electrons are available to carry current.

Arsenic atoms have five outer electrons. Germanium containing arsenic atoms as an impurity can carry current because the fifth electron is available as a carrier. This is an n-type semiconductor because current is carried by negative electrons.

Indium atoms have three outer electrons. Germanium doped with indium therefore has holes in its electronic structure. These can be filled by electrons from neighbouring atoms, creating new holes; this has the effect of positive charge moving through the crystal in the opposite direction to electrons. This is p-type germanium.

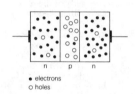

● electrons
○ holes

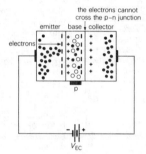

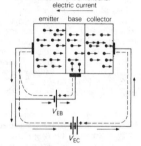

In the bipolar junction transistor a piece of p-type material is sandwiched between two n-type pieces, making an n-p-n structure (p-n-p transistors are also used).

In an n-p-n transistor, a negative voltage is applied to one end (the emitter) and a positive to the other (the collector). No current flows, however, because a potential barrier forms at the junction between the emitter and the central region (the base).

If the base region is positively biased, the free electrons in the emitter are attracted to the p-type base and current flows through the thin base to the collector. As the collector current depends on the amount of bias to the base, the device can be used as an amplifier.

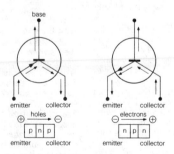

In the symbolic representation of a transistor, the direction of the arrow on the emitter indicates current direction and the type of transistor (n-p-n or p-n-p).

TRANSISTOR *The operation of the bipolar junction transistor.*

transputer *See* computer.

Trans-Siberian Railway The world's longest railway, running 9335 km (5800 mi) from Moscow to Vladivostok. Built between 1891 and 1905, it has nearly a hundred stops and takes nine days on the modern double-track electrified line.

transubstantiation In Roman Catholic theology, the doctrine that the substance of the elements of bread and wine in the *Eucharist is changed into the substance of the body and blood of Christ. Only the accidents (i.e. the qualities apparent to the senses) of the bread and wine remain.

transuranic elements Elements with higher atomic numbers than uranium. Apart from traces of neptunium and plutonium, none exist in nature, since there are no isotopes of sufficient *half-life; they have been created in nuclear reactions. *See also* actinides.

Transvaal The most northerly province in South Africa, containing the country's main industrial area, centred on the Witwatersrand; iron, steel, and chemicals are produced. Mineral deposits include gold, diamonds, uranium, coal, tin, and platinum. Agriculture produces maize, wheat, peanuts, fruit, cotton, and tobacco; sheep and cattle are raised. *History*: originally an Afrikaner republic, it joined the Union of South Africa in 1910. Area: 283 917 sq km (109 621 sq mi). Population (1985): 7 532 179. Capital: Pretoria.

Transylvania A region of SE Europe, bounded by the Carpathian Mountains and the Transylvanian Alps. During the 16th and 17th centuries, it was a self-governing princedom within the Ottoman Empire. Restored to Hungary in 1687, Transylvania became part of Romania after World War I.

trap-door spider A *spider that constructs a silk-lined burrow in the ground covered by a tight-fitting silk-hinged door. They are brown, with short legs, and occur in tropical and subtropical regions.

Trappists A Roman Catholic order of monks, officially known as the *Cistercians of the Strict Observance. It was founded in 1664 at the abbey of La Trappe in Normandy. The order is notable for its severity, which includes the observance of strict silence.

treason A citizen's betrayal of the sovereign or the state. In England, the Statute of Treasons (1352) defined high treason, which is punishable by death, as (1) to plot to kill or maim the sovereign; (2) to wage war against him or to join his enemies; (3) to kill his eldest son or heir; (4) to violate his wife, eldest daughter, or heir's wife; (5) to kill the chancellor, or any judge. Treason was redefined in the Treason Act (1795), which no longer includes (4) and (5) above.

treasure trove In law, coin, gold, silver plate, or bullion of unknown ownership found hidden. In England it belongs to the Crown provided its owner is unknown; if it has been abandoned or lost the finder has the first claim after the true owner. The finder of treasure trove is rewarded the value of the property found, unless he con-

ceals it, in which case he is liable to imprisonment.

Treasury The UK government department, established in 1653, responsible, with the *Bank of England, for the management of the economy and the sharing of government money between the spending departments. The prime minister is the first lord of the treasury, but it is run by the chancellor of the exchequer.

Trebizond. *See* Trabzon.

tree A tall perennial woody plant, usually with a main stem (the trunk) and secondary stems (the branches) arising some distance above ground level. Most tree species are either *dicotyledons (angiosperms) the broad-leaved trees —or *conifers (gymnosperms). These are of importance as timber, yielding hardwoods and softwoods, respectively. Other groups containing trees are the cycads (gymnosperms), monocotyledons (notably the *palms), and ferns. The conifers and tropical trees are mostly *evergreen plants, while broad-leaved trees in regions with changes in climate between summer and winter are typically deciduous. The study of the ecology and classification of trees is called **dendrology**. *See also* forest.

Tree, Sir Herbert (Draper) Beerbohm (1853–1917) British actor and theatre manager, half-brother of the writer Max Beerbohm (1872–1956). He was manager of the Haymarket Theatre from 1887 to 1899 and then of Her Majesty's Theatre. In 1904 he founded the *Royal Academy of Dramatic Art.

treecreeper A widely occurring small songbird. It has a streaked plumage with silvery underparts, long claws, and a slender bill. The European treecreeper (*Certhia familiaris*) creeps up tree trunks to probe for insects, etc.

tree frog A small widely distributed toad that lives in trees. It has adhesive pads on its toes, enabling it to leap to capture insects.

tree of heaven A tree, *Ailanthus altissima*, native to central Asia. Growing to a height of 30 m, it has large leaves, up to 1 m long, composed of paired leaflets. Its flowers form greenish clusters; the female flowers produce winged fruits.

tree-ring dating. *See* dendrochronology.

tree shrew A primitive *primate found in Java, Borneo, Sumatra, the Philippines, and S Asia. The common tree shrew (*Tupaia glis*) is 30–45 cm long including the tail (15–23 cm) and has a pointed face. It feeds on insects, fruit, and seeds.

Trent, Council of (1545–63) The 19th general council of the Roman Catholic Church, an expression of the *Counter-Reformation, which was summoned by Pope Paul III to strengthen the Church in confronting Protestantism. It was held in Trento (N Italy).

Trent, River A river in central England. Flowing mainly NE from Staffordshire through Nottingham, it joins the River Ouse to form the Humber estuary. It is linked to the Mersey by the Trent, Mersey, and Grand Union Canals. Length: 270 km (170 mi).

Trento (German name: Trent) 46 04N 11 08E A city in N Italy, the capital of Trentino-Alto Adige on the River Adige. Dating from pre-Ro-

TREE

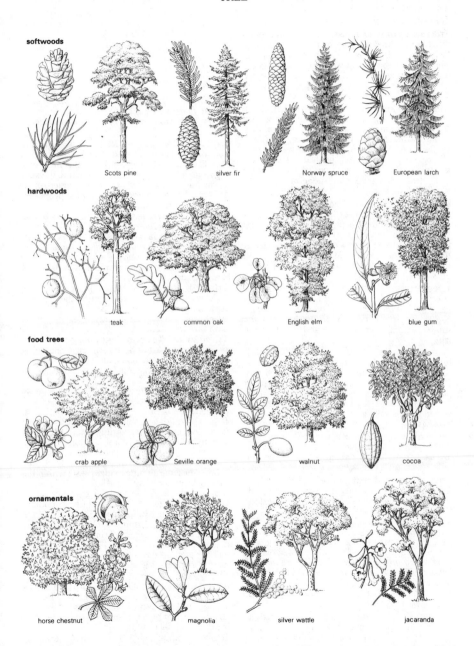

softwoods

Scots pine silver fir Norway spruce European larch

hardwoods

teak common oak English elm blue gum

food trees

crab apple Seville orange walnut cocoa

ornamentals

horse chestnut magnolia silver wattle jacaranda

man times, it has a romanesque cathedral (12th-century) and the 16th-century Church of Sta Maria Maggiore, where the Council of *Trent met. Population (1987): 100 202.

Trèves. *See* Trier.

Triassic period (*or* Trias) A period of geological time at the beginning of the Mesozoic era, lasting from about 240 to 200 million years ago. The rocks of the period were laid down mainly under continental conditions. The dinosaurs, ichthyosaurs, and plesiosaurs appeared in the Triassic.

tribes of Israel The 12 biblical tribes, descended from the sons and grandsons of Jacob, were Reuben, Simeon, Judah, Issachar, Zebulun, Benjamin, *Dan, Naphtali, Gad, Asher, Levi, and Ephraim and Manasseh. These last two were usually counted as one. After the death of Solomon, ten tribes (the Ten Lost Tribes of Israel) broke away from Benjamin and Judah to form the northern kingdom of Israel.

tribune In ancient Rome, a plebeian magistrate appointed to protect *plebeians' rights. Instituted during the 5th-century political struggles between *patricians and plebeians, the tribunes could reject law-making proposals of the Senate or popular assemblies and could themselves propose laws without senatorial approval.

Triceratops A plant-eating dinosaur of the late Cretaceous period (about 100–65 million years ago). 8 m long and weighing 8.5 tonnes, it had an enormous head with one horn on the snout and one over each eye and a bony neck frill.

Trident missile A US navy three-stage solid-fuelled nuclear missile launched from a submarine and having a range of 7800 km (4800 mi). Designed as a replacement for the *Poseidon missile, Trident missiles are capable of great accuracy. The first UK tridents will come into service in the mid-1990s.

Trier (French name: Trèves) 49 45N 6 39E A city in SW Germany, in Rhineland-Palatinate on the River Moselle. Founded by the Emperor Augustus, it has Roman remains. It is a wine and industrial centre. Population (1989): 94 119.

Trieste (Serbo-Croat name: Trst) 45 39N 13 47E A seaport in Italy, the capital of Friuli-Venezia Giulia, situated on the Gulf of Trieste at the head of the Adriatic Sea. It has shipyards, oil refineries, and a steel industry. *History*: an important Roman port in the 1st century AD, it passed to Austria in 1382. It expanded rapidly in the 19th century and in 1920 was handed over to Italy. Following World War II it became the capital of the Free Territory of Trieste. In 1954 most of the N of the Territory (including Trieste) passed to Italy and the remainder to Yugoslavia. Population (1987): 237 191.

triggerfish A shallow-water fish, related to *puffers, that occurs in tropical seas. It has a narrow body. The strong spine of the first dorsal fin is erected and locked by the second dorsal fin, forming a "trigger" that wedges the fish into crevices.

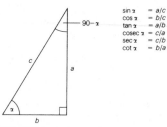

$$\begin{aligned}
\sin \alpha &= a/c \\
\cos \alpha &= b/c \\
\tan \alpha &= a/b \\
\operatorname{cosec} \alpha &= c/a \\
\sec \alpha &= c/b \\
\cot \alpha &= b/a
\end{aligned}$$

TRIGONOMETRY *Definitions of the trigonometric functions sine, cosine, and tangent and of their reciprocals cosecant, secant, and cotangent.*

trigonometry A branch of mathematics founded by Hipparchus in the mid-2nd century BC. The ratios of the lengths of the sides of a right-angled triangle are used to define the sine, cosine, and tangent of one of the angles of the triangle. Trigonometry deals with the properties of these and related functions.

trilobite An extinct marine *arthropod that flourished 500–200 million years ago. Trilobite fossils are abundant in rocks of this period. Its oval body, 10–675 mm long, was divided by two furrows into three lobes. Each segment of the thorax and tail region carried a pair of forked appendages.

Trimurti The three Hindu gods, *Brahma, *Vishnu, and *Shiva, representing the creative, sustaining, and destructive aspects of reality respectively, sometimes portrayed as one body with three heads.

Trinidad and Tobago, Republic of A country off the N coast of South America, consisting of the islands of Trinidad and Tobago. *Economy*: oil and asphalt have replaced cocoa and sugar as the main exports; offshore gas has also been discovered. Other industries include aluminium smelting, plastics, electronics, iron and steel, and petrochemicals. It is a member of CARICOM. *History*: Trinidad was inhabited by Arawak and Carib Indians when it was discovered by Columbus in 1498. It was a Spanish colony from the 16th century until 1802, when it was handed over to Britain; it joined with Tobago in 1809. The country became an independent state within the British Commonwealth in 1962. In 1976 it became a republic with the former governor general, Ellis Clarke (1917–), as its first president. President: Noor Mohammed Hassanali. Prime minister: A. N. R. Robinson. Official language: English. Official currency: Trinidad and Tobago dollar of 100 cents. Area: 5128 sq km (1980 sq mi). Population (1988 est): 1 198 000. Capital and main port: Port-of-Spain.

Trinity, the A central doctrine of Christian theology, stating that God is one substance with three distinct and eternal "persons," the Father, the Son, and the *Holy Spirit. The belief is based on a number of passages in the New Testament.

triode. *See* thermionic valve.

Triple Alliance (1882) An alliance between Germany, Austria-Hungary, and Italy, which with the opposing *Triple Entente shaped European diplomacy in the decades before World

War I. At the outbreak of war (1914) Italy declared its neutrality, thus breaking the alliance.

Triple Alliance, War of the (or Paraguayan War; 1865–70) The war between Paraguay and an alliance of Argentina, Brazil, and Uruguay. Conflict was precipitated by the aggression of Paraguay's dictator, F. S. López (1826–70), towards Argentina, which with Brazil and Uruguay invaded Paraguay. López refused to surrender and following the capture of Asunción in 1868 waged a guerrilla war in the N until taken prisoner in 1870.

Triple Entente An informal combination of France, Russia, and Britain, formed in opposition to the *Triple Alliance.

triple jump (former name: hop, step, and jump) A field event for men in athletics, similar to the *long jump but executed as a series of three jumps. The jumper lands first on the takeoff foot and then on the other, which becomes the takeoff foot for the final jump. World record: 17.97 m (1985) Willie Banks (USA).

Tripoli (Arabic name: Tarabulus) 32 58N 13 12E The capital and main port of Libya, on the Mediterranean Sea. Originally founded as Oea by the Phoenicians, it became the capital of Libya on independence in 1951. Exports include fruit and olive oil. Population (1982): 980 000.

Tripoli (Arabic name: Tarabalus) 34 27N 35 50E A port in NW Lebanon, on the Mediterranean Sea. It was the capital of a Phoenician federation of three other cities. Iraqi oil is brought by pipeline to the refinery here. Population (1985 est): 500 000.

trireme. See ships.

Tristan The tragic hero of a Celtic legend that appeared in a French poem of 1150. After accidentally drinking a love potion, he becomes the lover of Iseult (Isolde), who is engaged to his uncle, King Mark of Cornwall. He later renounces Iseult and goes to Brittany, where he marries the duke's daughter. Dying from a wound, he sends for Iseult; she arrives too late and dies of grief at his side. Other versions include Gottfried von Strassburg's *Tristan und Isolde*, the source of Wagner's opera. In a 13th-century version it was part of the *Arthurian legend.

Tristan da Cunha 37 15S 12 30W A group of four small islands in the S Atlantic Ocean, a dependency of St Helena. The only settlement, Edinburgh, is on Tristan (the largest island). In 1961 the inhabitants were evacuated to the UK to escape a volcanic eruption but most returned in 1963. Area: about 100 sq km (40 sq mi). Population (1982): 325.

tritium (T or ³H) A radioactive isotope of hydrogen, the nucleus of which contains one *proton and two *neutrons. It does not occur naturally but is produced in nuclear reactors and is used as a radioactive tracer. Tritium decays with a half-life of 12.3 years, emitting beta-rays.

triumvirate A board of three Romans appointed for special administrative duties. The so-called first Triumvirate (60 BC) of Caesar, Pompey, and Crassus was a private arrangement. The triumvirate, or triple dictatorship, of Mark Antony, Lepidus, and Octavian, appointed in 43

BC to maintain public order, held office with absolute powers until Lepidus was ousted in 36.

trogon A bird occurring in forested regions of Africa, Asia, and America, having iridescent plumage, which in males is usually dark with a red or yellow belly. They have rounded wings, a curved bill, and a long tail; they feed on insects. See also quetzal.

Troilus In Greek mythology, a son of King Priam of Troy who was killed by Achilles. The story of his love for Cressida, who deserted him for the Greek Diomedes, first appeared in the *Roman de Troie* by the 12th-century French poet Benoît de Sainte-Maure.

Trojan Horse In Greek legend, a gigantic hollow wooden horse used in the *Trojan War. The Trojans hauled it inside their city, believing it to be a gift to Athena, and Greek warriors then emerged from it to open the gates to their army.

Trojan War In Greek legend, a ten years' war fought by the Greeks against *Troy after the abduction of *Helen by Paris. Probably based on a war fought in the 12th century BC, it is described in Homer's *Iliad*. The Greeks were led by *Agamemnon and their champions included *Achilles and *Odysseus. The chief Trojan warriors were *Hector and *Paris, sons of Priam. The war ended in the capture of Troy using the *Trojan Horse.

troll In Scandinavian folklore, a gigantic ogre believed to guard treasure, inhabit a castle, and stalk through the forest at night. In later folklore, they were craftsmen dwarfs who lived in caves.

Trollope, Anthony (1815–82) British novelist. He worked for the General Post Office (1834–67), establishing his reputation with a series of novels, including *Barchester Towers* (1857), set in the imaginary county of Barsetshire. A second series of novels, set against a political background, includes *Phineas Finn* (1869) and *The Eustace Diamonds* (1873).

trombone A brass musical instrument, consisting of a cylindrical tube, about 3 m (9 ft) long, turned back upon itself, a cup-shaped mouthpiece, and a flaring bell. By means of a slide and lip pressure, a range of almost three octaves can be produced. The trombone has been part of the symphony orchestra since the late 18th century and is frequently used in jazz. The old English name was the **sackbut**.

Trondheim 63 36N 10 23E A city and seaport in W Norway on Trondheim Fjord. It has a cathedral (12th–14th centuries) where sovereigns have been crowned since early times. Industries include shipbuilding and fishing; the main exports are timber, wood pulp, fish, and metal goods. Population (1988): 135 524.

trooping the Colour Traditionally, the parade of the British sovereign's flag (Colour), displayed in battle so that foreign hired soldiers would recognize it. It is now a military revue held on the Horse Guards parade in Whitehall, London, on the sovereign's official birthday.

tropic bird A white seabird occurring in tropical and subtropical waters. Tropic birds have black eye and wing markings and are up to 50 cm long excluding the tail feathers.

tropics The area of the earth's surface lying roughly between the Tropic of Cancer on the 23°30′N parallel of latitude and the Tropic of Capricorn on the 23°30′S parallel.

tropism The growth of a plant or permanently fixed animal either away from or towards an external stimulus: growth movement towards the stimulus is a positive tropism; the opposite response is a negative tropism. For example, positive **hydrotropism** is growth towards water; negative **geotropism** is growth away from the pull of gravity.

troposphere. *See* atmosphere.

Trotsky, Leon (Lev Bronstein; 1879–1940) Russian revolutionary, who became a Marxist in the 1890s and was imprisoned and exiled twice for taking part in revolutionary activities. On the outbreak of the *Russian Revolution, he returned to Russia and became a *Bolshevik. He played a major role in the October Revolution and as war commissar during the civil war (1918–20) directed the Red Army to victory. Trotsky lost to Stalin the power struggle that followed Lenin's death and was banished from the Soviet Union. He was later murdered in Mexico. *See also* Trotskyism.

Trotskyism The form of *Marxism developed by Leon *Trotsky, who advocated world revolution, believing that capitalism could only be defeated by the solidarity of the working class throughout the world. To this end Trotsky and his supporters founded the Fourth *International in 1937.

troubadours Provençal poets of the 12th to 14th centuries whose poetry had a profound influence on European verse. Both poets and composers, the troubadours' songs introducing a new idea of love, later called courtly love. They developed several types of verse forms. The earliest troubadour was Guillaume, 9th Duc d'Aquitaine (1071–1127); others were Vicomte de Hautefort (c. 1140–c. 1207), Arnaut Daniel (c. 1180), and Bernard de Ventadour (late 12th century).

trout A predatory fish, related to salmon, that is native to the N hemisphere. Its blackish to olive body has black or red markings. Trout occur mainly in fresh water. Species include the common European brown trout (*S. trutta*) and the North American rainbow trout (*S. gairdneri*).

Troy An ancient city in Asia Minor, near the Dardanelles. According to legend, when *Paris abducted *Helen, *Agamemnon led a Greek force to recover her and captured Troy (*see* Trojan War). Schliemann's excavations (1870) discovered Troy at Hissarlik. Excavations revealed nine cities, each built on the ruins of the previous one, the seventh existed at the time of the legendary siege. *See also* Homer.

Trudeau, Pierre Elliott (1919–) Canadian statesman; Liberal prime minister (1968–79, 1980–84). A French Canadian, he nevertheless opposed French separatism and in 1970 briefly introduced martial law to deal with separatist agitation in Quebec. Defeated in 1979 by Joseph Clark (1939–), he was re-elected in 1980. He retired from office in 1984.

Trueman, Fred (Frederick Sewards T.; 1931–) British cricketer, who played for Yorkshire and England. A fast bowler, he was the first to take 300 Test wickets.

Truffaut, François (1932–84) French film director. His films, noted for their visual charm and elegance, include *Jules et Jim* (1961), *L'Enfant sauvage* (1970), *La Nuit Américaine* (1973), and *Le Dernier Métro* (1980).

truffle A round fungus, up to 10 cm across, that occurs in chalky soils, usually around tree roots. Several species are eaten, including the black Périgord truffle (*Tuber melanosporum*) and the white Piedmont truffle (*T. magnatum*), both of France. They are collected in oak woods using trained pigs or dogs.

Trujillo 8 06S 79 00W A city in Peru, situated 13 km (8 mi) from its port, Salaverry, on the Pacific coast. Founded in 1535, Trujillo is the commercial centre for an area producing sugar cane and rice. Population (1988 est): 491 100.

Truman, Harry S. (1884–1972) US statesman; Democratic president (1945–53). In 1945 he ordered the atomic bombing of Hiroshima and Nagasaki to end the war with Japan. In the **Truman Doctrine** he announced aid to countries threatened by interference from other states. His administration established of the *North Atlantic Treaty Organization (1949). In domestic politics his Fair Deal programme promised social reform.

trumpet A brass musical instrument consisting of a cylindrical tube, 1.5 m (5 ft) long, turned back on itself, a cup-shaped mouthpiece, and a flaring bell. Three valves alter the effective length of the tube; with varying lip pressure the B flat trumpet has a chromatic range of two and a half octaves.

Truro 50 16N 5 03W A cathedral city in SW England, the administrative centre of Cornwall. It is a small port and market town, with pottery and biscuit manufacturing. Population (1982): 16 040.

trypsin A digestive enzyme, secreted by the pancreas, that breaks down food proteins in the small intestine. It is secreted in an inactive form, which is converted to trypsin by the enzyme enterokinase in the intestine.

tsar The title (coming from the Latin, Caesar) of the rulers of Russia from 1547 to 1721. It was first adopted by *Ivan the Terrible and, though commonly used until 1917, was officially replaced with the title Emperor by Peter the Great.

Tsaritsyn. *See* Volgograd.

tsetse fly A tropical African fly, 6–16 mm long. Both sexes bite and suck the blood of mammals; the species *Glossina palpalis* transmits sleeping sickness to man.

Tsinan. *See* Jinan.

Tsingtao. *See* Qingdao.

tuatara A lizard-like reptile, *Sphenodon punctatus*, whose closest relatives lived 200 million years ago. It is found on islands off the North Island of New Zealand and has a brown to greenish body with spines running from head to tail; up to 70 cm long, it may live 100 years. Tuataras live in burrows during the day and emerge at night to feed on insects, etc.

tuba A valved brass musical instrument with a conical tube and low pitch, derived originally from the saxhorn. It is used in the symphony orchestra as well as the military band.

tuber A swollen underground plant stem in which carbohydrates (often starch) are stored. Some, e.g. potatoes and yams, are important human foods. Tuber-bearing plants may reproduce vegetatively from buds on the tuber.

tuberculosis An infectious disease caused by the bacterium (bacillus) *Mycobacterium tuberculosis* (which was first recognized by the bacteriologist Robert Koch (1843–1910) in 1882). In pulmonary tuberculosis, bacteria in the lungs form a primary tubercle that usually heals without trouble. Alternatively the disease may smoulder for months without showing any symptoms. However, the infection may flare up and lead to active tuberculosis ("consumption"), with cough, fever, and breathlessness. The TB bacterium can also enter the body through drinking infected cows' milk. Improved living conditions, pasteurization of milk, X-ray screening, and *BCG vaccinations have all reduced the incidence of TB in developed countries.

TUC. *See* trade union.

Tucson 32 15N 110 57W A city and health resort in the USA, in Arizona. Tucson is an industrial centre for the surrounding agricultural and mining district. Population (1990 est): 431 195.

Tudors The ruling dynasty of England from 1485 to 1603. Owen Tudor (c. 1400–61), a Welshman, entered the service of Henry V and married (1422) his widow Catherine of Valois (1401–37). Their eldest son Edmund, Earl of Richmond (c. 1430–56), married Margaret Beaufort (1443–1509), the great-great-granddaughter of Edward III, and their son became the first Tudor monarch, Henry VII. Later Tudor monarchs were Henry VIII, Edward VI, Mary I, and Elizabeth I.

tulip A widely occurring flowering plant of the lily family. Growing from bulbs, most tulips have a single bell-shaped flower, with leaves clustered at the base of the plant. There are nearly 4000 varieties.

tulip tree A tree, *Liriodendron tulipifera*, native to E North America and widely planted. Reaching a height of 58 m, it has three-lobed leaves and large tulip-like flowers, which produce papery cones containing winged fruits. The wood, known as white wood, is used for furniture, paper, etc.

Tull, Jethro (1674–1741) English agriculturist, best known for his invention in 1701 of the seed drill. He made many other improvements in agricultural methods.

Tulsa 36 07N 95 58W A city in the USA, in Oklahoma on the Arkansas River. Oil was discovered in 1901 and today over 800 oil companies have established plants here. Population (1986 est): 373 000.

tumour Any swelling in the body caused by an abnormal increase in cells. Benign tumours that do not spread to other parts of the body (i.e. are noncancerous) are usually harmless. Malignant tumours destroy the tissue in which they arise and spread to other parts of the body (*see* cancer).

tuna A carnivorous fish, sometimes called tunny, found in warm seas. Its elongated body is generally dark above and silvery below. The large bluefin tuna (*Thunnus thynnus*) reaches 4.3 m in length. Large quantities are consumed throughout the world.

tundra The level areas in the N hemisphere lying between the northerly region in which trees grow and the polar regions of perpetual ice. Winters are severe with brief summers in which temperatures remain below 10°C (50°F); *permafrost is a feature. Vegetation includes mosses, lichens, shrubs, perennials, and a few stunted trees.

tungsten (*or* wolfram; W) A grey metal with the highest melting point of any element. Discovered in 1779, it is obtained from wolframite ($FeWO_4$) and scheelite ($CaWO_4$). It oxidizes readily when heated, forming the oxide WO_3. The metal is used as filaments in light bulbs, in television and X-ray tubes, and in alloys for cutting tools. Tungsten carbide (WC) is very hard and used for tipping drills. At no 74; at wt 183.85; mp 3410 ± 20°C; bp 5660°C.

tunicate A small marine animal belonging to the phylum *Chordata*. Tunicates range from several millimetres to over 30 cm in size. They have a cellulose tunic covering the body; food particles are filtered from water through a siphon at the top and expelled through a second siphon. The tadpole-like larvae resemble other chordates but the adults lose their chordate features. Tunicates include the sea squirts, which live attached to rocks, etc., and the salps, which float in the sea.

Tunis (Arabic name: Tunus) 36 48N 10 13E The capital of Tunisia, on the Gulf of Tunis. It was developed by the Arabs in the 7th century AD. It came under French rule in the late 19th century, and became the capital on independence in 1956. Industries include chemicals, lead smelting, and textiles. Population (1984): 556 654.

Tunisia, Republic of (Arabic name: al-Jumhuriyah at-Tunisiyah) A small country in N Africa, bordering on the Mediterranean Sea. *Economy*: predominantly agricultural, the chief products include wheat, olive oil, citrus fruits, dates, and wine; livestock is also important. Tunisia is one of the world's largest producers of phosphates. Oil, iron ore, and lead are also mined. Industry includes oil refining, cement, and steel processing. *History*: first settled by the Phoenicians, it developed into the empire of Carthage and was later absorbed into the Roman Empire. Under the dynasty of the Berber Hafsids (1207–1574) it became powerful. In 1883 it became a French protectorate, gaining independence from France in 1956. Habib Bourguiba was elected president in 1957 and re-elected as life president in 1974. He was deposed in 1987 and replaced as president by Gen Zine el-Abidine Ben Ali. Official religion: Islam. Official language: Arabic; French is widely spoken. Official currency: Tunisian dinar of 1000 mil-

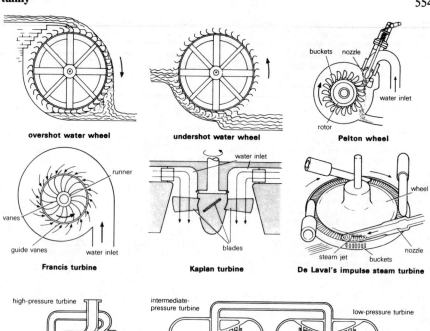

overshot water wheel   undershot water wheel   Pelton wheel

Francis turbine   Kaplan turbine   De Laval's impulse steam turbine

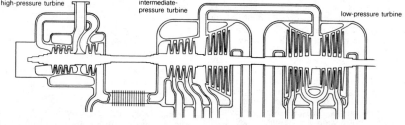

TURBINE

multistage steam turbine

limes. Area: 164 150 sq km (63 362 sq mi). Population (1988): 7 750 000. Capital: Tunis.

tunny. *See* tuna.

Tupi A group of South American Indian peoples and languages including the *Guarani. They mainly inhabit tropical rainforest and also fish in the rivers and off the coast. Cannibalism was formerly common.

turaco (*or* touraco) A greenish tree-dwelling African bird. Turacos have short wings, a downcurved bill, and are often crested.

turbine A device in which a moving fluid (gas or liquid) drives a wheel or motor, converting the kinetic energy of the fluid into mechanical energy. Its simplest form it is known as a **water wheel**, in use since ancient times to drive mills, pumps, etc. The water wheel forms the basis of the hydraulic turbine, used in the generation of *hydroelectricity. The Pelton wheel (patented in 1889 by L.A. Pelton) consists of a ring of buckets or bucket-shaped vanes arranged around the periphery of a wheel. The Francis turbine (designed in 1849 by J.B. Francis) has an outer ring of stationary guide vanes and an inner ring of curved vanes on the surface of one side of the wheel.

The steam-driven turbine was invented in the 1st century AD by the Greek engineer and mathematician Hero of Alexandria. However, the first practical turbine driven by steam had several rows of turbine wheels (enabling the energy of the expanding steam to be utilized in stages) invented in 1884 by the British engineer, Sir Charles Parsons (1854–1931). An impulse turbine using several steam nozzles was invented by Carl de Laval (1845–1913) in the 1890s. Since the beginning of the 20th century steam turbines have replaced the *steam engine in *power stations. *See also* gas turbine.

turbot A food *flatfish, *Scophthalmus maximus*, that occurs off European shores. It has a circular body, up to 1 m long, which is usually grey-brown on the upper (left) side and whitish underneath.

Turgenev, Ivan (1818–83) Russian novelist. His *Sportsman's Sketches* (1852) criticized the Russian social system; later works, such as the novel *Fathers and Sons* (1862) and the story *The Torrents of Spring* (1872) analyse social trends. He also wrote poetry and plays, notably *A Month in the Country* (1870).

Turin (Italian name: Torino) 45 04N 7 40E A city in NW Italy, the capital of Piedmont on the River Po. Dating from Roman times, it was the first capital (1861–65) of united Italy. Notable buildings include a 15th-century cathedral and a 17th-century palace. Industries include car manufacture, engineering, publishing, textiles, paper, and leather goods. Population (1987): 1 025 390.

turkey A large bird native to American woodlands. Wild turkeys have green plumage, a warty red neck, and a fleshy bill ornament and throat wattle. The common turkey (*Meleagra gallopavo*) was brought to Europe in the 16th century and is now farmed for its flesh.

Turkey, Republic of A country in the Middle East. The large Asian area, Anatolia, lies between the Mediterranean Sea and the Black Sea. The small European area, Thrace, is bordered by Greece and Bulgaria. *Economy*: mainly agricultural. Wheat, barley, sugar beet, potatoes, and rice are grown in the interior, and cotton, tobacco, and citrus fruit are grown for export. Cattle, sheep, and goats are kept for skins, wool, and mohair, which are exported. Copper, chromium, borax, coal, bauxite, and oil are produced. The main industries are steel, cement, textiles, and fertilizers. Turkey is an associate member of the EEC. *History*: Anatolia, formerly known as *Asia Minor, was dominated by the Seljuqs (1055–1243) and later became the core of the *Ottoman Empire (c. 1300–1922). Under Kemal *Atatürk, the Republic of Turkey (declared 1923) was rapidly westernized. The Democratic Party came to power in 1950 but unrest increased until a military coup took place in 1960. The army again intervened in 1971, when martial law was imposed (until 1973). Rivalry with Greece over Cyprus almost resulted in war in 1974, when the island was invaded by Turkish troops. In 1980 a military coup overthrew the government of Suleiman Demeril (1924–   ). In 1987 Turkey applied to join the EC. President: Turgut Özal. Official language: Turkish; Kurdish and Arabic are also spoken. Official currency: Turkish lira of 100 kurus. Area: 779 452 sq km (330 883 sq mi). Population (1987): 52 845 000. Capital: Ankara.

Turkic languages A group of languages related to Mongolian. Spoken by more than 66 million people from Turkey to Siberia. The languages are now written in the *Cyrillic alphabet in the Soviet Union and in Latin script in Turkey.

Turkish A *Turkic language, spoken mainly in Turkey. Since 1929 it has been written in an adapted Latin alphabet, replacing Arabic script.

Turkistan (*or* Turkestan) A region of central Asia, now consisting of the Xinjiang Uygur AR of the People's Republic of China and the Kazakh, Turkmen, Tadzhik, Kirghiz, and Uzbek SSRs of the Soviet Union. Turkistan has come under many different rulers. The W has been ruled by the Persians from the 6th century BC, Islam from the 7th century AD, and the Russians from the 18th century; the E was long disputed between Chinese dynasties and wandering tribes.

Turkmen (*or* Turkoman) A people of SW Asia speaking a language of the *Turkic language group. The majority live as farmers in the Turkmen SSR, but groups in Iran, Afghanistan, E Turkey, N Syria, and N Iraq retain their traditional wandering existence. They are Sunni Muslims.

Turks and Caicos Islands A British crown colony consisting of over 30 islands in the Atlantic Ocean, to the SE of the Bahamas. The most important are Grand Turk, Grand Caicos, and Salt Cay. *Economy*: mainly based on fishing, with exports of conch shells, crawfish, salt, and fishmeal. *History*: the islands were discovered by the Spanish in 1512. A dependency of Jamaica (1874–1959), they became a crown colony in 1962 and gained internal self-government in 1976. In 1986 they were put under the direct control of the governor following allegations of widespread corruption; they returned to constitutional rule in 1988. Official language: English. Official currency: US dollar of 100 cents. Area: 430 sq km (192 sq mi). Population (1989 est): 13 000. Capital: Grand Turk.

turmeric A plant, *Curcuma longa*, native to S India and Indonesia and cultivated for its underground stems (rhizomes). These are boiled and dried in the sun for 5–7 days, then polished and ground. Turmeric is used in curries, etc., and as a yellow dye.

Turner, Joseph Mallord William (1775–1851) British painter. After painting many watercolours, he achieved success in the late 1790s with his landscapes in oil. In 1809 he made the first of several continental tours, which provided him with such subjects as the Alps, Venice, and Rome. While supervising the publication of his *Liber Studiorum* (1807–19), a series of engravings based on his works, his style evolved into a romantic vision of colour in such paintings as *Rain, Steam, and Speed* (National Gallery, London) and *Interior at Petworth* (Tate Gallery).

turnip A plant, *Brassica rapa*, related to the cabbage, probably native to Asia and widely cultivated for its fleshy root, which is used as a vegetable.

turnstone A small *plover, *Arenaria interpres*, that breeds around Arctic coasts and migrates to the S hemisphere to winter. It has a brown plumage, becoming tortoiseshell in summer, and white underparts. Turnstones have black bills used to turn over pebbles in search of molluscs, fish, etc.

turpentine An oily liquid extracted from pine resin. Its main constituent is pinene ($C_{10}H_{16}$); it is used as a solvent for paints.

Turpin, Dick (1706–39) British highwayman. He was hanged at York for murder and horse stealing. The story of his ride from London to York on his horse Black Bess, popularized in Harrison Ainsworth's novel *Rookwood* (1834), is probably based on a much older legend.

turquoise An opaque greenish-blue mineral used as a gem. It consists of an aluminium phosphate, traces of copper providing the colour.

turtle An aquatic reptile related to the *tortoises and *terrapins. 10–200 cm long, turtles have paddle-like flippers and a streamlined shell and occur in most seas. They eat worms, crustaceans, and fish. Some live in fresh water. *See also* green turtle; leatherback turtle.

turtle dove A small slender dove, *Streptopelia turtur*, occurring in S Europe and N Africa, visiting N Europe in the summer. It has a chequered reddish back, grey wings, a black-and-white striped neck patch, and a white-tipped tail.

Tuscan order. *See* orders of architecture.

Tuscany (Italian name: Toscana) A region in N central Italy. It is predominantly agricultural, producing cereals, wines (Chianti), olives, and fruit. The major industries are iron, steel, and shipbuilding. Lignite, iron, mercury, salt, borax, and marble are mined. Area: 22 989 sq km (8876 sq mi). Population (1987 est): 3 568 308. Capital: Florence.

Tussaud, Marie (Marie Grosholtz; 1761–1850) French wax modeller, who went to London in 1802, where she founded the waxworks museum known as Madame Tussaud's.

Tutankhamen King of Egypt (c. 1361–1352 BC) of the 18th dynasty. Tutankhamen became king at the age of 11. He replaced Akhenaton's worship of the sun-god Aton with that of Amon and returned the capital to Thebes. His splendid and elaborate tomb was discovered by Howard Carter (1874–1939) in 1922.

Tutu, Desmond (1931–) South African clergyman, noted for his opposition to *apartheid. Ordained in 1960, he became the first black general secretary of the South African Council of Churches in 1978, Anglican Bishop of Johannesburg in 1984, and Archbishop of Cape Town in 1986. He won the Nobel Peace Prize in 1984.

Tuvalu (name until 1976: Ellice Islands) A small country in the SW Pacific Ocean. It consists of a group of nine islands, the main one being Funafuti. *Economy*: subsistence agriculture and fishing are the chief occupations. The main export is copra. *History*: formerly part of the Gilbert and Ellice Islands colony, it became a separate colony in 1974 and gained independence in 1978. Tuvalu is a member of the Commonwealth of Nations. Prime minister: Dr Tomasi Puapua. Official language: Tuvalu. Official currency: Australian dollar of 100 cents. Area: 24 sq km (9.5 sq mi). Population (1987): 8200. Capital: Funafuti.

Twain, Mark (Samuel Langhorne Clemens; 1835–1910) US novelist. He worked as a steamboat pilot on the Mississippi before gaining a national reputation for his humorous journalism. He wrote several works based on his early life, notably *Life on the Mississippi* (1883) and *The Adventures of Huckleberry Finn* (1884).

Tweed, River A river in SE Scotland and NE England. Flowing E from the Tweedsmuir Hills to the North Sea at Berwick, it forms part of the border between England and Scotland. Length: 156 km (97 mi).

Twelfth Day. *See* Epiphany.

twelve-tone music. *See* serialism.

twins Two individuals born from the same pregnancy. Identical twins are produced when a fertilized egg splits in two and develops as two fetuses of the same sex. More commonly, non-identical (or fraternal) twins are produced when two eggs are fertilized at the same time; they may be of different sexes. *See also* Siamese twins.

Two Thousand Guineas A flat race for three-year-old horses, run each spring at Newmarket over the Rowley Mile course. One of the English *Classics, it was established in 1809.

Tyler, Wat (d. 1381) English rebel, who led the Kentish peasants during the *Peasants' Revolt (1381). He was murdered during negotiations with Richard II at Smithfield.

Tyne, River A river in N England. Flowing E from the SW Cheviot Hills to the North Sea at Tynemouth, it passes through Newcastle, Gateshead, and Jarrow. Length: 48 km (30 mi).

Tyne and Wear A metropolitan county of NE England, created in 1974 from SE Northumberland and NE Durham. It comprises the districts of Newcastle upon Tyne, North Tyneside, Gateshead, South Tyneside, and Sunderland. In the 19th century the shipyards were important. Area: 540 sq km (208 sq mi). Population (1987 est): 1 135 800. Administrative centre: Newcastle upon Tyne.

typewriter A machine for producing printed symbols. The first machine was invented in the USA in 1867 but the commercial success of the typewriter began in 1874 with the machines produced by Remington and Sons. This design, with the paper held in a moving platen (roller), remained the basis of the typewriter until the advent of electric golf-ball machines, with a stationary platen, in the early 1960s. *Word processors are gradually replacing them.

typhoid fever A disease of the digestive tract caused by the bacterium *Salmonella typhi*. This disease (and paratyphoid fever) are usually caught from infected water. The symptoms include fever, loss of appetite, and constipation; a characteristic red rash may appear. If untreated, the patient may develop damage to the bowel.

typhoon A tropical cyclone or *hurricane with winds above force 12 on the *Beaufort scale occurring in the China Sea and the W Pacific Ocean. The name is derived from a Chinese word meaning great wind.

typhus An infection caused by certain bacteria-like microorganisms (*see* rickettsia), which are carried and passed to man by lice, fleas, mites, or ticks. The many forms of typhus have the symptoms of fever, pains in muscles and joints, delirium, and a rash. Treatment is with antibiotics.

Tyr (or, in Old English, Tiw) In Teutonic mythology, the god of war; with *Odin and *Thor, he is one of the three main Germanic gods. His name is linguistically related to *Zeus* and survives in *Tuesday*.

Tyrannosaurus A huge dinosaur that lived in North America during the late Cretaceous period (about 100–65 million years ago). This animal was 15 m long, stood 6.5 m tall, and weighed up to 10 tonnes. It had a massive body with a thick neck supporting a large head, large muscular hind limbs with clawed feet, and tiny fore legs. It was a meat eater with long teeth.

Tyre (modern name: Sur) 33 12N 35 11E A port in SW Lebanon, on the Mediterranean Sea.

It was important to the Phoenicians for several centuries and was taken by Alexander the Great in 322 BC and by the Romans in 68 BC. The city was long held by the Crusaders but fell to Muslim forces in 1291. Population (1980 est): 14 000.

Tyrol. *See* Tirol.

U

Ubangi-Shari. *See* Central African Republic.

Uccello, Paolo (P. di Dono; 1397–1475) Florentine painter. His frescoes for Sta Maria Novella, Florence, include the famous *Flood.*

Ufa 54 45N 55 58E A city in the W central Soviet Union. Situated in the Ural Mountains, it has oil refineries. Population (1987): 1 092 000.

Uffizi An art gallery in Florence, containing the art treasures of the Medici. Built by *Vasari, the Uffizi was opened as a museum in 1765. The major part of its collection comprises Italian Renaissance paintings.

Uganda, Republic of A country in East Africa. *Economy*: chiefly agricultural, cash crops include coffee tea, tobacco, and cotton; livestock is also important. The chief mineral resource is copper. *History*: the area was dominated by the kingdom of *Buganda before becoming a British protectorate in 1894. It became an independent state within the British Commonwealth in 1962 and the following year a republic was established with Obote as prime minister. In 1971 a military coup brought Gen Idi *Amin to power. His repressive regime was overthrown in 1979. In 1986 Yoweri Museveni came to power. Official language: English; Swahili is widely spoken. Official currency, since 1967: Ugandan shilling of 100 cents. Area: 236 860 sq km (91 343 sq mi). Population (1989 est): 17 000 000. Capital: Kampala.

ugli A hybrid fruit produced in the West Indies by crossing a *grapefruit with a *tangerine. It resembles a grapefruit with brownish warty skin and orange flesh.

Ujung Pandang (Makassar *or* Macassar) 5 09S 119 08E A port in central Indonesia, in SW Sulawesi. Its exports include coffee, copra, and vegetable oils. Population (1980): 709 038.

UKAEA. *See* Atomic Energy Authority.

ukulele A small guitar, patented in Hawaii in 1917. The four gut or nylon strings are strummed with fingers or a small plectrum.

Ulan Bator (*or* Ulaanbaatar; former name: Urga) 47 54N 106 52E The capital of the Mongolian People's Republic. Built around a monastery, in the 17th century it developed as a centre of trade between China and Japan. It became the capital when Outer Mongolia declared its independence in 1911. Population (1988): 500 000.

Ulbricht, Walter (1893–1973) East German statesman. A fervent Stalinist, Ulbricht played a leading role in the creation of the German Democratic Republic. He was general secretary of the Socialist Unity Party (from 1950) becoming (1960) chairman of the council of state. In 1961 he erected the Berlin Wall.

ulcer An inflamed eroded area of skin or mucous membrane. There are many forms of ulcer, one of the most common being *peptic ulcers, which affect the stomach and duodenum (first part of the small intestine). Ulcers may also occur in the mouth and in the intestine (*see* colitis).

Ulm, Battle of (25 September–20 October, 1805) A battle in which Napoleon with 210 000 men defeated 72 000 Austrians in Bavaria. Napoleon thus prevented a union between Austrian and Russian forces.

Ulster A province and former kingdom of N Ireland. The earldom of Ulster passed to the English Crown in 1461. It was divided in 1921, six counties forming Northern Ireland and the counties of Cavan, Donegal, and Monaghan becoming part of the Republic of Ireland. Area: 8013 sq km (3094 sq mi). Population (1981): 230 159.

ultrasonics The study of *sound waves the frequencies of which are too high to be audible to the human ear, i.e. above 20 000 hertz. Ultrasound waves may be produced, for example, by applying an alternating voltage across a *piezoelectric crystal. Ultrasonic scanning is used in medical diagnosis in place of X-rays.

ultraviolet radiation *Electromagnetic radiation the wavelength of which lies between that of the violet end of the visible spectrum and *X-rays, i.e. between about 380 and 5 nanometres. Ultraviolet radiation is produced during arc discharges and by gas-discharge tubes. It is also produced by the sun, although below 200 nm it is absorbed by the *ozone layer.

Ulyanovsk (name until 1924: Simbirsk) 54 19N 48 22E A port in the W central Soviet Union, on the River Volga. It was renamed in honour of Lenin (originally V. I. Ulyanov), who was born here. Population (1987): 589 000.

Ulysses. *See* Odysseus.

Umar. *See* Omar.

Umayyads (*or* Omayyads) The ruling dynasty of Islam from 661 to 750 AD. The Umayyads were overthrown by a rebellion of discontented Arabs and pious Muslims. In Muslim Spain, an Umayyad, 'Abd ar-Rahman, seized power in 756 and established a dynasty that ruled until 1030.

Umberto I (1844–1900) King of Italy (1878–1900). He led Italy into the *Triple Alliance (1882) and encouraged Italian colonialism in Africa. He was assassinated at Monza.

umbilical cord The structure in mammals that connects an embryo to the *placenta in the womb. In humans it is about 50 cm long and contains three blood vessels (two arteries and one vein) that convey blood to and from the placenta. At birth the cord is tied off and cut.

Un-American Activities Committee US House of Representatives committee established in 1935 to investigate various organizations suspected of communist leanings in the USA. Spurred on by Senator *McCarthy, it blacklisted several Hollywood writers and directors and investigated government officials. Public protest resulted in the committee being disbanded (1975).

uncertainty principle. *See* Heisenberg uncertainty principle.

undulant fever. *See* brucellosis.

UNESCO. *See* United Nations Educational, Scientific and Cultural Organization.

uniat churches Various churches of Eastern Orthodox Christianity that are in full communion with the Roman Catholic Church. They retain their own traditional forms of service and Church law.

UNICEF. *See* United Nations International Children's Emergency Fund.

unicorn A mythical animal resembling a white horse, but with one horn on its forehead. In the middle ages it was associated with chastity (and thus could be captured only by a virgin) and also with Christ's love of mankind.

Unification Church A religious group founded in South Korea in 1954 by a millionaire Korean businessman, Sun Myung Moon (1920–), whose ideas appear in his book, *Divine Principle*, which he claims was revealed to him by Christ in 1936. Absolute obedience is demanded of members ('Moonies'). Moon was imprisoned for tax evasion in 1984 and released in 1985.

Uniformity, Acts of A series of Acts (1549, 1552, 1559, 1562) that enforced the use of the Book of *Common Prayer in England during the *Reformation.

Union, Acts of **1.** The Acts (1536–43) uniting England and Wales. They imposed English law on Wales, made English the official language, and provided for Welsh representation in parliament. **2.** The Act (1707) uniting England and Scotland to form Great Britain. Scotland retained its legal system and Presbyterian Church and was to be represented in parliament by 16 peers and 45 MPs. **3.** The Act (1800) that united Great Britain and Ireland to form (1801) the United Kingdom. It provided for Irish representation in parliament (4 spiritual peers, 28 life peers, 100 MPs). *See* Home Rule.

Union of Soviet Socialist Republics. *See* Soviet Union.

Unitarians A group of Christians who reject the doctrine of the Trinity and the divinity of Christ, believing instead in the single personality of God. Modern Unitarian thought dates from the Reformation, but congregations were first formed in Britain and the USA in the 18th century.

United Arab Emirates (UAE; former name: Trucial States) A federation of seven sheikdoms in the Middle East, in *Arabia, comprising Abu Dhabi, Ajman, Dubai, Fujairah, Ras al-Khaimah, Sharjah, and Umm al-Qaiwain. *Economy*: the oil of Abu Dhabi and Dubai is the chief export. *History*: in 1892 the sheikdoms became British protectorates–the Trucial States. The

federation was formed in 1971 and is a member of OPEC. President: Sheik Zayed bin Sultan al-Nahayan of Abu Dhabi (1918–). Prime minister: Sheik Maktoum bin Rashid al-Maktoum. Official language: Arabic. Official currency: UAE dirham of 10 dinars and 1000 fils. Area: 83 650 sq km (32 290 sq mi). Population (1988): 1 600 000. Provisional capital: Abu Dhabi. Chief port: Dubai.

United Arab Republic (UAR) The state created by the union of Egypt and Syria in 1958. Joined by North Yemen in the same year, it collapsed in 1961 but Egypt retained the name until 1971.

United Kingdom (UK) A country in N Europe consisting of *England, *Scotland, *Wales, and Northern Ireland (*see* Ireland). The UK does not include the Channel Isles and the Isle of Man, which are direct dependencies of the Crown. The United Kingdom of Great Britain and Ireland, formed in 1801, became the United Kingdom of Great Britain and Northern Ireland in 1922, following the creation of the Irish Free State. Head of state: Queen Elizabeth II. Prime minister: John Major. Area: 244 014 sq km (94 214 sq mi). Population (1987): 56 878 000. Capital: London.

United Nations (UN) An organization founded on 24 October, 1945 to maintain international peace and to foster international cooperation in resolving economic, social, cultural, and humanitarian problems. There were 51 founder members; most countries are now members of the UN, whose headquarters are in New York. The organization's main forum is the **General Assembly**. Each member state has one equal vote in the Assembly. The **Security Council** bears the chief responsibility for maintaining peace. Its permanent members are China, France, the Soviet Union, the UK, and the USA. The **Economic and Social Council** (ECOSOC) coordinates the economic and social work of the UN. The principal judicial organ of the UN is the *International Court of Justice. The **Secretariat**, headed by the secretary general (currently Javier Pérez de Cuellar), is responsible for administration.

United Nations Educational, Scientific and Cultural Organization (UNESCO) A specialized agency of the *United Nations established in 1945 to encourage international cooperation in education, science, and culture. Its headquarters are in Paris. The USA withdrew from UNESCO in 1984, and the United Kingdom in 1985.

United Nations High Commissioner for Refugees, Office of the (UNHCR) A *United Nations body established in 1950 to provide international protection for refugees. Its headquarters are in Geneva. It won the Nobel Peace Prize in 1981.

United Nations International Children's Emergency Fund (UNICEF) A *United Nations body established in 1946, concerned with providing health care, education, and improved nutrition to developing countries. Its headquarters are in Geneva. It won the Nobel Peace Prize in 1965.

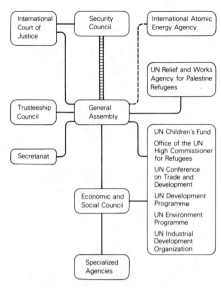

UNITED NATIONS *The structure of the organization.*

United Provinces of the Netherlands The northern provinces of the Netherlands, which united (1579) during the *Revolt of the Netherlands against Spain and formed (1581) a self-governing independent federation.

United States of America (USA) A country in North America, the fourth largest in the world. It is a federal republic comprising 50 states, including Alaska and Hawaii. *Economy*: the greatest industrial nation, it produces natural gas, lead, copper, aluminium, and sulphur. Cereals, cotton, and tobacco are the main crops. Main exports include motor vehicles, aircraft, machinery, grain, and chemicals. *History*: extensively explored following its discovery by Columbus in 1492, America was settled from 1565, most successfully by the British. However, during the 18th century conflict developed between local colonial assemblies and their British governors, particularly over taxation. The 13 colonies finally won independence in the *American Revolution (1775–83). Through the *Mexican War (1846–48) the USA acquired California where the discovery of gold (1848) encouraged settlement. By 1820 conflict was developing between the cotton-growing states of the South (where African slaves had worked since the late 17th century) and the commercial North (where slavery was opposed). This led to the *Civil War (1861–65), which ended in victory for the North and the abolition of slavery. Expansion continued with the purchase of Alaska (1867), the annexation of Hawaii (1898), and the Spanish-American War (1898), in which the USA acquired the Philippines, Puerto Rico, Guam, and a measure of control over Cuba. The USA entered World War I in 1917. The 1920s saw another economic boom, which ended in the *Depression that followed the Crash of 1929. The USA was forced to enter World War II by the Japanese bombing of Pearl Harbor in Hawaii (December, 1941). Postwar fear of Soviet expansion resulted in the *Cold War and the intervention in Korea (1950–53), Cuba (1961–62), and Vietnam (1961–75). After 1963 relations with the Soviet Union improved and diplomatic relations were established with China in 1979. Relations with the USSR were strained by the deployment of US nuclear missiles in W Europe, and Reagan's *Strategic Defence Initiative but improved in the mid-1980s with the advent of the Soviet policy of *glasnost. US forces have intervened most recently in Lebanon (1982), Grenada (1983), Libya (1986), Panama (1989), and Iraq (1991). President: George *Bush. Official language: English. Official currency: US dollar of 100 cents. Area: 9 363 123 sq km (3 614 343 sq mi). Population (1990 est): 250 000 000. Capital: Washington, DC.

unit trust An organization that uses funds raised by selling "units" to the public to buy and sell securities in order to make profits for distribution to unit holders. The small investor buying unit trusts has the advantages of a wide spread of professionally managed investments. *Compare* investment company.

Upanishads About 200 prose and verse metaphysical writings, produced as commentaries on the *Vedas* and dating from 400 BC.

Upper Volta, Republic of. See Burkina Faso.

Uppsala 59 55N 17 38E A city in E central Sweden. It is a historic and cultural centre, with Sweden's oldest university (1477). Population (1988): 161 828.

Ur An ancient city of *Sumer (S Iraq). Sir Leonard Woolley unearthed (1922–34) rich royal burials of about 2500 BC, providing evidence for *Noah's flood. The leading city in Sumer when it was sacked by barbarians about 2000 BC, Ur was superseded by *Babylon.

Ural, River A river in the central Soviet Union, rising in the S Urals, and flowing S to the Caspian Sea. Length: 2534 km (1575 mi).

Uralic languages A major language family consisting of two related groups of languages, the *Finno-Ugric and the Samoyedic (*see* Samoyed). They have developed into many forms covering an extensive area.

Ural Mountains A mountain range in the NW central Soviet Union. It extends 2000 km (1243 mi) N–S from the Kara Sea to the steppes NE of the Caspian Sea. The highest point is Mount Narodnaya, in the N, at 1894 m (6214 ft).

uranium (U) A radioactive element (*see* nuclear energy). Uranium is a silvery metal, almost as hard as steel and very dense (relative density 18.95), with the highest atomic number of the naturally occurring elements. It was first obtained in pure form in 1841 by E. Péligot (1811–90), although it had been identified before this in pitchblende. Natural uranium contains three isotopes: ^{238}U (99.283%), ^{235}U (0.711%), and ^{234}U (0.006%). ^{238}U has a half-life of 4.51×10^9 years and is useful in dating rocks, as well as in fuel for fast reactors. ^{235}U is used in *thermal reactors. At no 92; at wt 238.029; mp 1132°C; bp 3818°C.

uranium series One of three naturally occurring series of radioactive decays. The uranium series is headed by uranium-238, which undergoes a series of alpha and beta decays ending with the stable isotope lead-206. *See also* actinium; thorium.

Uranus (astronomy) A giant planet, orbiting the sun every 84 years (between Saturn and Neptune) at a mean distance of 2870 million km. Somewhat larger (50 800 km in diameter) than Neptune, it exhibits a similar greenish disc in a telescope. In its equatorial plane lie fifteen *satellites (only five of major size) and about twenty inconspicuous rings. Its atmosphere and structure are thought to resemble those of Neptune. Uranus was discovered telescopically in 1781 by Sir William Herschel.

Uranus (Greek mythology) The personification of Heaven. He was the son of Gaea (Earth), and his children by her included the *Titans and the Cyclops. He was castrated by his son Cronus and his genitals were thrown into the sea, which gave birth to *Aphrodite.

Urdu A language of N India and Pakistan. Like *Hindi it arose from *Hindustani. It is written in an adapted Arabic script.

urea (*or* carbamide) A white crystalline compound ($CO(NH_2)_2$) derived from ammonia and carbon dioxide. It is widely used as a nitrogen fertilizer, a feed supplement for cattle, and in industry. Urea is also present in *urine.

urea-formaldehyde resins Synthetic thermosetting *resins that are made by *polymerization of urea and formaldehyde. Cellulose filler is added to produce a moulding powder. This powder is used to make cups, bathroom fittings, etc.

urethane A white crystalline solid, $CO(NH_2)(OC_2H_5)$, made by heating ethanol with urea nitrate. It is used to manufacture *polyurethane foam.

Urga. *See* Ulan Bator.

urine The fluid that is formed by the kidneys and contains the waste products of the body's chemical processes, as well as surplus water and salts. In man the kidneys normally produce 0.9–1.5 l of urine per day.

Ursa Major (Latin: Great Bear) A large constellation in the N sky. The seven brightest stars form the Plough.

Ursa Minor (Latin: Little Bear) A constellation in the N sky that contains the N celestial pole. The brightest star is *Polaris.

Ursula, St A legendary British martyr. According to tradition, she and 11 000 virgins were murdered by the Huns at Cologne while returning from a pilgrimage to Rome in the 3rd or 5th century. Feast day: 21 Oct.

Uruguay, Oriental Republic of A country in SE South America. *Economy*: the traditional livestock industry was badly affected by the 1974 EC ban on meat imports. The cultivation of wheat, maize, and sorghum has been intensified and fishing has been expanded. Industries include food processing, hides and leather, textiles, metallurgy, and rubber. *History*: explored by the Spanish in the 16th century, it became part of the Spanish viceroyalty of the Río de la Plata in 1776. In 1828, with British help, Uruguay achieved independence. The late 19th century saw considerable immigration from Europe. In 1973 the army took over; military rule officially ended in early 1985. Uruguay is a member of the OAS and LAIA. President: Luis Alberto Lacalle. Official language: Spanish. Official currency: new Uruguayan peso of 100 centésimos. Area: 186 926 sq km (72 172 sq mi). Population (1988 est): 3 080 000. Capital and main port: Montevideo.

Uruguay, River A river in South America. Rising in S Brazil, it flows SW forming the Argentina–Brazil and Argentina–Uruguay borders before joining the Rio Paraná. Length: about 1600 km (1000 mi).

USSR. *See* Soviet Union.

Ustinov, Sir Peter (Alexander) (1921–) British actor, director, and dramatist of Russian descent. His own plays include *Romanoff and Juliet* (1956) and *Beethoven's Tenth* (1983); his many films include *Death on the Nile* (1978). He has written novels and an autobiography; he is a well-known television personality.

Utah One of the mountain states in the SW USA. Livestock is the principal agricultural activity. There are significant deposits of copper, oil, natural gas, and uranium. *History*: the persecuted Mormons began major settlements here in 1847 and continue to dominate the state. Handed over to the USA by Mexico in 1848, Utah was finally admitted to the Union in 1896. Area: 219 931 sq km (84 916 sq mi). Population (1985 est): 1 645 000. Capital: Salt Lake City.

uterus. *See* womb.

utilitarianism The doctrine that the best action is the one bringing the most happiness and least pain to the greatest number of people. Utilitarianism flourished in Britain from the mid-18th century to the mid-19th century. *Hume and *Bentham put forward the doctrine and John Stuart *Mill defended it.

utopianism A programme of social and political reform with the object of establishing a perfect society, on the basis of the imaginary state depicted in Thomas *More's *Utopia* (1516). Utopian experiments have included the New Lanark community established by Robert Owen (1771–1858). However, no way has been found of reconciling individual freedom and happiness with social justice.

Utrecht 52 06N 5 07E A city in the central Netherlands. The Treaties of *Utrecht (1713–14), ending the War of the Spanish Succession, were concluded here. Its notable buildings include the gothic cathedral (14th century). Population (1987): 229 326.

Utrillo, Maurice (1883–1955) French painter. For almost his entire life, he suffered from alcoholism and drug addiction. He specialized in painting street scenes, notably of Montmartre.

V

V-1 A German World War II unguided missile, also called a flying bomb. Powered by an air-breathing ramjet (*see* jet engine), it carried about 2000 pounds (900 kg) of high explosive. Some 8000 were launched against London between June 1944 and March 1945, killing over 5500 civilians.

V-2 A German World War II *ballistic missile powered by a rocket using alcohol and liquid oxygen as fuel. It carried about 2000 pounds (900 kg) of high explosive and had a preset guidance system. Some 4000 were used against Britain and the Low Countries in 1944 and 1945. It became the basis for both US and Soviet postwar rocket design.

Vaal River A river in South Africa, rising in the SE Transvaal. It flows generally W and SW, to join the Orange River and forms part of the Orange Free State–Transvaal border. Length: 1210 km (750 mi).

vaccination (*or* inoculation) The introduction of inactivated or dead disease-causing microorganisms (vaccine) into the body to stimulate the formation of *antibodies and so prevent the disease they cause (*see also* immunity). The first vaccination (against smallpox) was performed by Edward *Jenner in 1798.

vacuum A region of space that contains no matter. Impossible to obtain, it is approached in technical work by a soft (*or* low) vacuum with a pressure of about 10^{-2} pascal, a hard (*or* high) vacuum of between 10^{-2} and 10^{-7} pascal, and an ultrahigh vacuum below 10^{-7} pascal. Vacuum technology is used in cathode-ray tubes, light bulbs, and food preservation.

vacuum flask. *See* Dewar flask.

Vaduz 47 08N 9 32E The capital of Liechtenstein. Its castle (restored 1905–16) is the official residence of the ruling prince. Population (1989): 4891.

vagina The part of the reproductive tract of women and other female mammals into which the *penis is inserted during sexual intercourse. It connects the womb to the exterior and can enlarge greatly to allow for childbirth.

valence (*or* valency) The combining power of an atom, ion, or radical, equal to the number of hydrogen atoms that the atom, ion, or radical can combine with or replace in forming compounds. Many elements have more than one valence. A **valence electron** is an electron in the outer shell of an atom that participates in forming chemical bonds.

Valencia 39 29N 0 24W The third largest city in Spain, on the Guadalaviar estuary. In 1021 it became the capital of the Moorish kingdom of Valencia. El Cid took the city from the Moors in 1094. Its many notable buildings include the cathedral (1262–1482). Population (1987): 856 455.

Valentine, St (died c. 269) Roman priest and martyr, known as the patron of lovers. The sending of cards on his feast day (14 Feb) has no connection with his life.

Valentino, Rudolf (Rodolpho Gugliemi di Valentina d'Antonguolla; 1895–1926) US film actor, born in Italy. *The Sheik* (1921), *Blood and Sand* (1922), *Son of the Sheik* (1926), and other silent dramas established him as the cinema idol of the 1920s.

Valera, Eamon De. *See* De Valera, Eamon.

Valhalla In Teutonic mythology, one of the three homes of *Odin. Half of the warriors who die in battle are brought by the *Valkyries to Valhalla, where they spend their days in battle and their nights in feasting and listening to songs of their heroic exploits.

Valium. *See* benzodiazepines.

Valkyries In Teutonic mythology, maidens, who attend *Odin. They wear armour and, led by *Freyja, ride on horseback over battlefields to carry away the slain warriors whom Odin has chosen to live with him in *Valhalla.

Valladolid 41 39N 4 45W A city in central Spain, in Old Castile. It was formerly the capital of Castile and León (14th–15th centuries). It has a fine 16th-century cathedral. Population (1986): 341 194.

Valletta 35 54N 14 32E The capital of Malta. Founded in 1566 by the Knights of St John, it was formerly an important British naval base. Population (1988): 9210.

valley An elongated depression in the earth's surface. Valleys have various origins but the common **V-shaped valley** is formed as the result of erosion by a river. Those that originated through glacial erosion are **U-shaped valleys**, often occupied by deep lakes (*see* fjord). *See also* rift valley.

Valley of the Kings The cemetery of the Egyptian pharaohs from about 1580 to about 1085 BC, near *Thebes. All the tombs were robbed, except that of *Tutankhamen.

Valois The royal dynasty of France from 1328 to 1589. The *Hundred Years' War (1337–1453) nearly destroyed Valois power, which was saved by *Charles VII (reigned 1422–61). Succeeding rulers, Charles VIII (reigned 1483–98) and *Louis XII, waged disastrous wars in Italy, where they opposed the *Habsburgs. The last Valois were the victims of rival religious groups at court (*see* Wars of Religion).

Valois, Dame Ninette de. *See* de Valois, Dame Ninette.

Valparaíso 33 05S 71 40W The second largest city in Chile, on the Pacific Ocean. Founded by the Spanish (1536), Valparaíso is a major port. Population (1987 est): 278 762.

value-added tax (VAT) A tax on goods calculated by adding a percentage to the value of a product as it increases at each stage of production; the whole cost of the tax is eventually passed on to the consumer. The tax was introduced in the UK in 1973.

vampire bat A bat of Central and South America. The most common species is *Desmodus rotundus*, 7.5–9 cm long. They feed on blood and can transmit dangerous diseases.

vanadium (V) A transition metal, named after the Norse goddess Vanadis. At no 23; at wt 50.942; mp 1890 ± 10°C; bp 3380°C.

Van Allen radiation belts Two regions of charged particles in the earth's *magnetosphere. The inner belt lies 1000–5000 km above the equator; the outer belt lies 15 000–25 000 km above the equator, curving down towards the earth's magnetic poles. The belts were discovered in 1958 by the US physicist James Van Allen (1914–).

Vanbrugh, Sir John (1664–1726) English architect, soldier, and playwright. His plays included *The Relapse* (1697) and *The Provok'd Wife* (1697). England's most successful *baroque architect, his most impressive buildings were Castle Howard (1699–1726) and *Blenheim Palace (begun 1705), on which he collaborated with *Hawksmoor.

Vancouver 49 13N 123 06W A city and port in W Canada, in British Columbia. Established in 1862, Vancouver is the commercial and industrial centre of British Columbia. Population (1986): 431 147.

Vancouver Island A Canadian island off the Pacific coast of British Columbia. The economy depends on timber, mining, fishing, and tourism. Area: 32 137 sq km (12 408 sq mi). Population (1981): 461 573. Chief town: Victoria.

Vandals A Germanic tribe that during the first four centuries AD migrated southwards from Scandinavia and the S Baltic coast. In 455 they sacked Rome. The devastation they caused gave rise to the word vandalism.

Van de Graaff generator An electrostatic generator that creates an electric potential by building up electric charge. It was invented by the US physicist Robert Jemison Van de Graaff (1901–67), and produces potentials of millions of volts. Charge from an external source is fed onto a continuously moving belt, which transfers it to the inside of a large hollow conducting sphere. The charge moves to the outer surface of the sphere, leaving the inside neutral and able to collect more charge.

Van der Post, Sir Laurens (1906–) South African novelist. His travel books include *The Lost World of the Kalahari* (1958). His novels include *The Hunter and the Whale* (1967) and *A Story Like the Wind* (1972).

Van der Waals' equation A modification of the ideal gas equation, $pV = nRT$, where p is the pressure exerted by a gas with volume V and thermodynamic temperature T and n is the number of moles present; R is the gas constant (*see* gas laws). The Dutch physicist Van der Waals (1837–1923) adjusted V to $(V - b)$ to take account of the volume occupied by the gas molecules. He also assumed that some attraction exists between molecules, adjusting the pressure

term to $(p - a/V^2)$. Both a and b are constant for a particular gas. The intermolecular forces are known as **Van der Waals' forces.**

van de Velde A family of 17th-century Dutch painters. **Willem van de Velde the Elder** (1611–93) and his eldest son **Willem van de Velde the Younger** (1633–1707) were both marine artists, living in England after 1672. His younger son **Adriaen van de Velde** (1636–72) was a landscape painter. **Esaias van de Velde** (c. 1591–1630) was probably the brother of Willem van de Velde the Elder. He is best known for such works as *Winter Scene* (National Gallery, London).

Van Dieman's Land. *See* Tasmania.

Van Dyck, Sir Anthony (*or* Vandyke; 1599–1641) Flemish *baroque painter. Working chiefly in England, he painted many religious and mythological subjects. *Charles I on Horseback* (National Gallery, London) and *Thomas Killigrew and Lord Croft* (Windsor Castle) are examples of his court portraits.

Vänern, Lake The largest lake in Sweden. It drains into the Kattegat via the River Göta. Area: 5546 sq km (2141 sq mi).

van Eyck, Jan (c. 1390–1441) Flemish painter. He is noted for his realistic portraits, particularly *The Arnolfini Marriage* and *Man in a Red Turban* (both National Gallery, London). He possibly invented the Flemish technique of mixing pigment with oil and turpentine and applying it in thin glazes.

Van Gogh, Vincent (1853–90) Dutch post-impressionist painter. On moving to Paris (1886) he briefly adopted the style of *impressionism and later of *pointillism. In Arles in 1888 he painted his best-known works —orchards, sunflowers, etc. In a quarrel with his friend *Gauguin Van Gogh cut off part of his ear and in 1889 he entered a mental asylum. The *Wheatfield with Crows* (Stedelijk Museum, Amsterdam) was painted shortly before his suicide, in Auvers. *See* expressionism.

vanilla A flavouring extracted from the pods of a climbing *orchid native to tropical Asia and America. The plants have long stems attached to trees and produce large flowers.

Van't Hoff, Jacobus Henricus (1852–1911) Dutch chemist, who pioneered stereoisomerism, showing how the bonds of a carbon atom are arranged. This enabled him to explain *optical activity in terms of molecular structure. He also contributed to thermodynamics and to the theory of solutions, for which he won the 1901 Nobel Prize.

Vanuatu, Republic of (formerly: New Hebrides) A chain of about 80 forested volcanic islands in the SW Pacific Ocean. Espíritu Santo is the largest island. Discovered by the Portuguese (1606), they were jointly administered by France and the UK (1906–80). In 1980 they became independent as the Vanuatu Republic. Copra, cocoa, coffee, and beef are exported. President: Fred Timakata (1937–). Area: about 14 760 sq km (5700 sq mi). Population (1989 est): 142 630. Capital: Vila, on Efate.

Varanasi (*or* Benares) 25 20N 82 00E A city in India, on the River Ganges. A place of pilgrimage for Hindus, Jains, Sikhs, and Buddhists, it has 5 km (3 mi) of ghats (steps), from which Hindus bathe in the river. Population (1989): 720 755.

variable stars Stars the brightness of which varies with time. In regular variables the brightness changes cyclically in a period ranging from minutes to years. The three major groups are: eclipsing *binaries, cataclysmic variables, including *novae, and pulsating stars, in which the continuous expansion and contraction of the star often causes the brightness variation.

variance In a set of numbers, usually measurements, the quantity obtained by summing the squares of the differences between each number and the average value of the set and then dividing by the number of members of the set. Variance and its square root, called the **standard deviation**, are used to estimate random error in experimental results.

varicose veins Swollen and twisted veins in the legs caused by faulty valves in the veins, which obstruct blood flow. Varicose veins tend to run in families and are commoner in those who are constantly standing.

Varna 43 12N 27 57E A city and port in E Bulgaria, on the Black Sea. Founded in the 6th century BC, it finally passed to Bulgaria in 1878. Population (1987): 305 891.

varnish A resinous solution in oil or alcohol that dries to form a transparent coating on wood, metal, etc. Natural resins used include *shellac and copal. *Polyurethane is a durable and chemical-resistant synthetic resin. Polyesters and alkyds are also used.

varnish tree. See lacquer tree.

Vasa The ruling dynasty of Sweden (1523–1818) and of Poland (1587–1668) founded by Gustavus I Vasa (1496–1560). The best-known Vasa monarchs in Sweden were Gustavus II Adolphus (1594–1632) and Christina (1626–89).

Vasari, Giorgio (1511–74) Italian painter and architect. In Florence he painted fresco cycles and built the *Uffizi. His *Lives of the Most Eminent Italian Architects, Painters, and Sculptors*, traces the history of Renaissance art.

vasectomy. See sterilization.

VAT. See value-added tax.

Vatican City, State of the An independent state within the city of Rome, the seat of government of the Roman Catholic Church. It was created in 1929, when Pius XI signed the *Lateran Treaty with Mussolini, and is governed by a commission appointed by the pope. Official language: Italian. Area: 44 hectares (109 acres). Population (1985 est): 1000.

Vatican Councils 1. (1869–70) The council summoned by *Pius IX, proclaiming the doctrine of papal *infallibility. 2. (1962–65) The council that was summoned by *John XXIII and continued by *Paul VI, in which critics freely expressed their views.

Vaughan Williams, Ralph (1872–1958) British composer. Influenced by English folksong, his works include *Fantasia on a Theme by Tallis* (for string orchestra; 1910), nine symphonies, the ballet *Job* (1931), the opera *The Pil-*

grim's Progress (1951), and much orchestral, chamber, and choral music.

vector (mathematics) A quantity that has both magnitude and direction. Examples include velocity, force, and magnetic flux density. A vector is defined by three numbers (called components), representing its magnitude in three mutually perpendicular directions.

vector (medicine) An organism capable of transmitting a disease-causing organism (pathogen) from one organism to another. Transmission may be accidental or the vector may play a significant role in the life cycle of the pathogen; for example the malarial parasite spends part of its life cycle in the mosquito, which transmits it to man.

Vedanta The various philosophical schools of *Hinduism, which come from the commentaries on the *Vedas, especially the *Upanishads, the *Brahmasutras*, and the *Bhagavadgita*. They all believe in *reincarnation, the truth of the *Vedas*, the law of *karma, and the need for spiritual release.

Vedas (Sanskrit: divine knowledge) The Hindu scriptures, written in archaic Sanskrit (Vedic) around 1500 BC. It consists of hymns, mantras, and rituals, mostly concerning the worship of gods representing natural forces.

vegetarianism The practice of not eating animal flesh for ethical, religious, or nutritional reasons. **Vegans** will not eat any animal products, including milk, cheese, eggs, etc., and usually require dietary supplements.

vein (physiology) A thin-walled blood vessel that carries deoxygenated blood from the tissues to the *heart. The veins opening directly into the heart are the superior and inferior vena cavae and the pulmonary veins from the lungs; the latter are the only veins to carry oxygenated blood.

Velázquez, Diego Rodríguez de Silva (1599–1660) Spanish painter. He originally painted religious subjects and still-lifes; later work included royal portraits, *Pope Innocent X* (Rome), and the *Rokeby Venus* (National Gallery, London).

veld (or veldt) A tract of open grassland on the plateau of S Africa. It includes the Highveld (over 1500 m), Middleveld (1500–900 m), and Lowveld (below 900 m).

velocity The rate of change of a body's position in a given direction. The speed of a body is not in a specified direction. Velocity is thus a *vector quantity and speed is a scalar quantity. **Angular velocity** is the rate of change of a body's motion about an axis. It is measured in radians per second.

Venda, Republic of The smallest homeland in South Africa, only recognized by South Africa. *Economy*: chiefly agricultural. *History*: it was the third *Bantu Homeland to be granted full independence from South Africa (1979). There was a coup in 1990, led by supporters of reintegration with South Africa. Official currency: South African rand. Area: 7410 sq km (2861 sq mi). Population (1985 est): 424 000. Capital: Thokoyandou.

venereal disease See sexually transmitted disease.

Venezuela, Republic of A country on the N coast of South America. *Economy*: based chiefly on oil. Venezuela is also rich in diamonds, gold, zinc, copper, lead, silver, phosphates, manganese, and titanium. Crops include coffee, cocoa, sugar, maize, and rice. *History*: it was visited in 1499 by Vespucci, who named it Venezuela ("Little Venice") on seeing Indian villages built on stilts over Lake Maracaibo. Spanish settlement began in 1520 and Spanish rule continued until it was liberated by Bolívar in 1821. It then formed part of Colombia until 1830. Independent Venezuela was ruled by a succession of dictators until World War II. Venezuela is a member of the OAS, LAIA, and OPEC. President: Carlos Andrés Pérez Rodriguez. Official language: Spanish. Official currency: bolívar of 100 céntimos. Area: 912 050 sq km (352 143 sq mi). Population (1988): 18 770 000. Capital: Caracas. Main port: Maracaibo.

Venice (Italian name: Venezia) 45 26N 12 20E A city and port in NE Italy built on over 100 islands in the Lagoon of Venice. A centre of commerce and tourism, its manufactures include glassware, textiles, and lace. The Grand Canal and about 170 smaller canals provide waterways for transport. Famous bridges include the Rialto Bridge and the Bridge of Sighs. St Mark's Square (Piazza San Marco) is overlooked by *St Mark's Cathedral, the 15th-century Clock Tower, the Campanile, and the Doge's Palace. The Lido, a seaside resort, is 3 km (2 mi) to the SE. *History*: united under the first *doge in 697, Venice became an independent republic in 1380. A great commercial and maritime power for the next two centuries, it came under Austrian rule in 1797 and was absorbed into the Kingdom of Italy in 1866. Population (1989): 328 249.

Venn diagram. *See* set theory.

ventricle. *See* brain; heart.

Venturi tube A device consisting of an open-ended tube with a central constriction, used to measure the rate of flow of a fluid or an aircraft's airspeed, which can be calculated from the pressure difference between the centre and the ends. Invented by G. B. Venturi (1746–1822).

Venus (goddess) A Roman goddess originally of gardens and fertility who became identified with the Greek *Aphrodite as goddess of love.

Venus (planet) The second planet in order from the sun, which it orbits every 225 days at an average distance of 108 million km. It is 12 102 km in diameter and has an extremely long period of rotation (243 days). Its surface is totally obscured by dense swirling yellowish clouds of sulphuric acid droplets and sulphur particles. The atmosphere is 98% carbon dioxide. Spacecraft have shown that the surface temperature is a hostile 470°C and the surface atmospheric pressure is about 90 times that of earth.

Venus flytrap A *carnivorous plant, *Dionaea muscipula*, native to the eastern USA. The upper part of each leaf is hinged in the middle. When an insect lands on the leaf it snaps shut, trapping the prey.

Veracruz (*or* Veracruz Llave) 19 11N 96 10W A major port in E Mexico, on the Gulf of Mexico. Population (1980): 305 456.

Verde, Cape (French name: Cap Vert) 14 43N 17 33W The westernmost point of Africa, in Senegal, consisting of a promontory extending into the Atlantic Ocean.

Verdi, Giuseppe (1813–1901) Italian composer of operas. His first mature work was *Rigoletto* (1851), followed in 1853 with *La Traviata* and *Il Trovatore*. In 1869 he wrote *Aida* (1871). His last works were the *Requiem* (1874) and the operas *Otello* (1887) and *Falstaff* (1893).

verdigris 1. A green copper acetate used as a paint pigment. 2. The green coating, consisting of copper sulphate or carbonate, that forms on copper roofs, etc.

Verdun 49 10N 5 24E A town in NE France, on the River Meuse. It was the scene of a major battle in 1916 (*see* World War I). Population (1982): 24 120.

Verlaine, Paul (1844–96) French poet. His tempestuous relationship with *Rimbaud resulted in the break-up of his marriage and imprisonment (1873) for shooting Rimbaud. His works include the experimental *Romances sans paroles* (1874) and *Les Poètes maudits* (1884).

Vermeer, Jan (1632–75) Dutch painter. His best-known paintings include *The Milkmaid* (Rijksmuseum, Amsterdam), *The Lacemaker* (Louvre), and *Allegory of Painting* (Kunsthistorisches Museum, Vienna), showing himself at work.

vermiculite A *clay mineral with the property of expanding up to 22 times its original thickness on heating.

vermilion Red mercury(II) sulphide (HgS). It sublimes readily on heating and occurs naturally as the mineral cinnabar. It is used as a pigment.

Vermont A state in the NE USA, in New England. Small manufacturing industries, mining, and tourism are important. Agriculture produces dairy products, hay, potatoes, corn, and maple syrup. *History*: settled by the British in 1724, it declared its independence in 1777 and joined the Union in 1791. Area: 24 887 sq km (9609 sq mi). Population (1986 est): 541 000. Capital: Montpelier.

Verne, Jules (1828–1905) French writer. His many books, including *Journey to the Centre of the Earth* (1864) and *Twenty Thousand Leagues Under the Sea* (1873) introduced submarines and space travel. Other stories included *Around the World in Eighty Days* (1873).

Vernier scale A device for measuring subdivisions of a scale, such as those on a pair of calipers. The auxiliary Vernier scale is divided so that ten of its subdivisions correspond to nine of those on the main scale. Named after Pierre Vernier (1580–1637).

Verona 45 26N 11 00E A city in N Italy, on the River Adige. A tourist centre, it possesses a Roman amphitheatre, a 12th-century cathedral, and the medieval Castelvecchio. Population (1987): 258 523.

Veronese, Paolo (P. Caliari; 1528–88) Italian painter of the Venetian school. In the Villa Barbaro at Maser he painted landscapes, mythological scenes, and portraits. His religious works, for example *Marriage at Cana* (Louvre), often

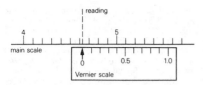

VERNIER SCALE *An auxiliary scale used to measure accurately to two places of decimals.*

depicted banquets in impressive architectural settings.

veronica.   *See* speedwell.

verruca.   *See* wart.

Versailles   48 48N 2 08E A town in N central France. Its baroque palace was the residence of the French kings from 1678 to 1769. The **Treaty of Versailles** (1919), signed in the palace, demanded compensation from Germany after World War I and established the League of Nations. Population (1982): 95 240.

vertebra.   *See* spine.

vertebrate (*or* craniate)   Any animal that has a backbone consisting of interlocking vertebrae, which forms the main support for the body and protects the nerve cord (spinal cord). The brain of vertebrates is contained in and protected by a skull. Vetebrates include fish, amphibians, reptiles, birds, and mammals.

Verwoerd, Hendrik Frensch (1901–66) South African statesman; prime minister (1958–66). He took South Africa out of the Commonwealth in 1960. He was assassinated in parliament in Cape Town.

Vespasian (9–79 AD) Roman emperor (69–79). Vespasian's decisive policies brought an end to civil war. He was deified after his death.

Vespucci, Amerigo (1454–1512) Italian navigator, after whom America is named. In 1499 he explored the NE coast of South America.

Vesta (goddess)   The Roman goddess of the hearth, identified with her Greek counterpart Hestia. She was worshipped in private households, and her annual festival, the Vestalia, was held in June. The **Vestal Virgins**, her priestesses, tended the eternal fire at her shrine in Rome.

Vesuvius   40 49N 14 26E A volcano in S central Italy, near Naples. In 79 AD it engulfed *Herculaneum and *Pompeii; the last eruption was in 1944. Average height: 1220 m (4003 ft).

vetch   A climbing or trailing plant of the pea family, native to temperate regions and South America. The leaves comprise pairs of leaflets. Some species are grown as fodder.

viburnum   A shrub or small tree native to N temperate regions. They have white or pink flowers and many species are grown in gardens.

Vichy   46 07N 3 25E A spa in central France, on the River Allier. It was the seat of the French government (1940–44) of Marshal Pétain. Its bottled waters, which were known to the Romans, are exported worldwide. Population (1982): 30 554.

Victor Emmanuel II (1820–78) King of Italy (1861–78). He fought the Austrians and coordinated with *Garibaldi in the campaign that freed S Italy. As King of Italy he acquired Venetia (1866) and Rome (1870), which he made the capital.

Victor Emmanuel III (1869–1947) King of Italy (1900–46) following the assassination of his father Umberto I. He acquiesced in Mussolini's seizure of power (1922) and after Mussolini's fall (1943) relinquished his powers to his son Umberto II.

Victoria   A state of SE Australia. Cattle production is concentrated in S Victoria. Brown coal is mined in Central Gippsland and gas and oil are piped from the Bass Strait. Industry is concentrated on Melbourne. Area: 227 600 sq km (87 884 sq mi). Population (1987 est): 4 188 300. Capital: Melbourne.

Victoria   22 16N 114 13E The capital of Hong Kong, situated on the N of the island. Population (1981): 590 771.

Victoria (1819–1901) Queen of the United Kingdom (1837–1901). The granddaughter of George III, Victoria succeeded her uncle William IV. In 1840 she married her cousin Prince *Albert of Saxe-Coburg-Gotha; they had nine children. Her refusal to dismiss her Whig ladies of the bedchamber when the Tory, Robert Peel, was attempting to form a ministry caused the *Bedchamber Crisis (1839). Her close friendship with *Disraeli, who made her Empress of India (1876), contrasted with her strained relations with his rival *Gladstone. In the last years of her reign she enjoyed enormous popularity.

Victoria, Lake (*or* Victoria Nyanza)   The largest lake in Africa, in Uganda, Tanzania, and Kenya. It was discovered for Europeans in 1858 by Speke. Area: 69 485 sq km (26 826 sq mi).

Victoria and Albert Museum   A London museum founded in 1853 to house examples of applied arts of all periods and cultures. Originally at Marlborough House, it moved to South Kensington in 1857.

Victoria Cross (VC)   The highest British decoration for "bravery . . . in the presence of the enemy." Instituted by Queen Victoria in 1856, VCs were until 1945 cast from the metal of Russian guns taken during the Crimean War (1854–56).

Victoria Falls   17 55S 25 52E A waterfall in the Zambezi River on the border of Zimbabwe and Zambia. The river drops 128 m (420 ft), and then flows through a gorge known as the **Boiling Pot.**

vicuna   A hoofed mammal, *Vicugna vicugna*, found on high plateaus of the Andes (South America). Resembling a small camel, it is 75 cm high and has a brown coat with white underparts. It is valued for its wool.

video recording   The storage of a *television programme on magnetic tape. Because the demodulated video (vision) signal can have frequencies in the megahertz range, the signal is recorded diagonally on the tape (each diagonal line representing one line of the picture) and the tape is run slowly over a drum on which the recording and reading heads rotate at high speeds. Video discs include those in which the signal can be retrieved by a laser system.

Vienna (German name: Wien) 48 12N 16 20E The capital of Austria, on the River Danube. Most of the chief buildings lie on or within the Ringstrasse, the boulevard built in 1857 to replace the old city ramparts. *Economy*: commerce, industry, and tourism are important. *History*: seat of the Habsburgs (1278–1918) and residence of the Holy Roman Emperor (1558–1806), Vienna became an important cultural centre in the 18th and 19th centuries. It suffered considerable damage during World War II and was jointly occupied by the Allied Powers (1945–55). Population (1987): 1 506 201.

Vienna, Congress of (1814–15) A conference of European powers following the fall of *Napoleon. Its Final Act created a kingdom of the Netherlands, a German confederation of 39 states, Lombardy-Venetia subject to Austria, and the Congress Kingdom of Poland. Monarchs were restored in Spain, Naples, Piedmont, Tuscany, and Modena, and *Louis XVIII was confirmed as King of France.

Vienna Circle The group of philosophers who developed the doctrine of *logical positivism. Founded by Moritz Schlick (1882–1936) in 1924, the Vienna Circle flourished until 1939. Members included Rudolf *Carnap.

Vientiane 18 06N 102 30E The capital of Laos, a port on the River Mekong. Founded in the 13th century, it came under Siamese control in the 18th century and was destroyed (1828) following a revolt against Siamese rule. It became capital of the French protectorate of Laos in the late 19th century. Population (1984 est): 120 000.

Viet Cong Communist guerrillas who fought in the *Vietnam War (1954–75). In 1960 they established the National Liberation Front, coordinating opposition to the South Vietnamese Government.

Viet Minh The Vietnam League for Independence, formed in 1941 by *Ho Chi Minh to create an independent Vietnamese republic. After World War II, the Viet Minh played an important role in the *Indochina war against France (1946–54).

Vietnam, Socialist Republic of A country in SE Asia, occupying the E part of the Indochina peninsula. *Economy*: mainly agricultural. Teak and bamboo are the chief products and fishing is important. Industrial developments have been concentrated mainly in the N. Exports include coal, rubber, wood, tea, and coffee. *History*: the northern kingdom of Nam Viet was conquered in 111 BC by the Chinese. In 939 AD it broke free, resisting further Chinese invasions until the 15th century. Its southward expansion culminated (1802) in a united Vietnamese empire, which lasted until the French established (1887) the Union of *Indochina. France's refusal in 1945 to recognize Ho Chi Minh's government led to war (1946–54); after the defeat at Dien Bien Phu, the French withdrew. The Geneva Conference (1954) divided Vietnam into communist North Vietnam and noncommunist South Vietnam, between which civil war ensued (*see* Vietnam War). In 1976, the victorious North proclaimed the reunited Socialist Republic of

Vietnam. Deteriorating relations between Vietnam and China led to Vietnam's invasion of Cambodia (December 1978–January 1979). The Chinese invasion of Vietnam (February–March, 1979) led to a massive increase in the number of refugees, known as the Boat People. In the 1980s there were border clashes with Thailand. Vietnam withdrew from Cambodia in 1989. President: Vo Chi Cong (1914–). Official language: Vietnamese. Official currency: dong of 100 hao. Area: 329 466 sq km (127 180 sq mi). Population (1989): 62 000 000. Capital: Hanoi. Main port: Haiphong.

Vietnam War (1954–75) The war between communist North Vietnam and South Vietnam which was aided from 1961 by the USA. It resulted in communist victory and the union (1976) of North and South Vietnam. Some 900 000 Viet Cong and North Vietnamese, 50 000 Americans, and 400 000 South Vietnamese died. *See also* Indochina.

Vigo 42 15N 8 44W A port and naval base in NW Spain, on the Atlantic coast. In 1702 an English-Dutch fleet sank a Spanish treasure fleet here. Population (1988): 275 580.

Viking probes Two identical US spacecraft sent into orbit around Mars in 1976. The Lander sections landed on the surface in July and September and performed various experiments. The Orbiter sections took measurements and photographs of Mars' surface.

Vikings Scandinavian warriors active from the late 8th to the mid-11th centuries, who established settlements in the British Isles (especially at York and Dublin), founding an Anglo-Danish dynasty (1016; *see* Canute). They also established settlements in Normandy, the E Baltic, *Vinland, and Greenland. Viking literature (the sagas) and art are noted for their vitality.

Villa, Pancho (Francesco V.; 1878–1923) Mexican revolutionary. Villa supported successive revolts against Mexican governments and came to dominate the north. In 1916 he raided Texas and New Mexico. After an agreement with the Mexican Government in 1920, he disbanded his army. He was later assassinated.

Villa-Lobos, Heitor (1887–1959) Brazilian composer. He toured Brazil collecting folksongs and in 1945 founded the Brazilian Academy of Music. His output includes 12 symphonies, *Bachianas Brasileiras* (1930–45), *Rudepoema* (1921–26), and the ballet *Uirapurú* (1917).

villein An unfree peasant of medieval Europe, holding land from the lord of the *manor in return for labour. Many gained ownership of their holdings following the *Peasants' Revolt.

Villon, François (1431–?1463) French poet. Condemned to be hanged (1463) for vagrancy and crime, he was banished instead. The ballades and other poems in his *Lais* and *Grand Testament* are compassionate, ironical, and preoccupied with death.

Vilnius (Polish name: Wilno) 54 40N 25 19E A city in the W Soviet Union, on the River Neris. *History*: handed to Russia in 1795, it was given to Lithuania after World War I, but seized by Poland in 1922. Restored to Lithuania in 1940, and occupied by the Germans during World War

II, it became part of the Soviet Union after the war. Its large Jewish population was virtually exterminated by the Germans. Population (1987): 566 000.

Vimy. *See* World War I.

vinegar A dilute solution of acetic acid, produced from soured wine, beer (malt vinegar), or other dilute alcoholic liquids. It is used in salad dressings, preserving, etc.

vingt-et-un. *See* pontoon.

Vinland The Viking name for the area of NE America, probably Newfoundland, discovered, explored, and briefly settled by *Leif Eriksson (c. 1000).

vinyl resins. *See* polyvinyl chloride.

viol A bowed stringed instrument, common from the 15th until the early 18th centuries, when it was superseded by the *violin. Viols have six strings (tuned in fourths), a shallow bridge, gut frets, and a flat back. They are held between the knees; the bass viol acquired the name **viola da gamba** from the Italian *gamba*, leg.

viola A musical instrument similar to the *violin, but having a larger body, thicker strings, and a heavier bow. It has a range of over four octaves from the C below middle C; its strings are tuned C, G, D, A.

violet A flowering plant that grows up to 40 cm tall, with blue or white flowers. Garden violets are derived from the Eurasian sweet violet (*Viola odorata*). The dog violet (*V. canina*) is another common species. *Pansies are closely related to violets.

violin A bowed string instrument, the highest member of the family that includes the viola, cello, and double bass. It has four strings tuned in fifths (G, D, A, E), an arched bridge, and a smooth fingerboard. It has a range of four octaves from the G below middle C. The design of the violin was perfected by the Amati, Guarneri, and Stradivari families in Italy between the mid-16th and early 18th centuries.

violoncello. *See* cello.

viper A venomous snake occurring in Europe, Asia, and Africa. 0.3–3 m long, vipers have hollow fangs that can be erected to inject venom. They feed on small animals. American vipers are known as **pit vipers.**

Virgil (Publius Vergilius Maro; 70–19 BC) Roman poet. His *Eclogues* (42–37 BC) describe an idealized pastoral landscape. His interest in agriculture led to a more practical vision of Italy in the *Georgics* (36–29 BC). The *Aeneid*, a national epic in 12 books, describes the wanderings of Aeneas and the founding of Rome. He died of fever after returning from Greece. He was the supreme poet of imperial Rome.

virginals A keyboard instrument of the 16th and 17th centuries, the earliest form of the *harpsichord. Often made in the form of a box, which could be set on the table, the single strings run parallel to the keyboard.

Virginia A state on the mid-Atlantic coast of the USA. The principal industries are chemicals and tobacco processing. Fishing, tourism, and mining are also significant. Produce includes tobacco, corn, apples, and peaches. *History*: one of the 13 original colonies, it was named after Eliza-

beth I, the Virgin Queen. It became a state in 1788. Area: 105 716 sq km (40 817 sq mi). Population (1986 est): 5 787 000. Capital: Richmond.

Virginia creeper A cultivated climbing shrub, *Parthenocissus tricuspidata* of SE Asia or *P. quinquefolia* of North America, also called woodbine. It clings by means of tendrils and suckers and has red foliage in autumn.

Virgin Islands A West Indian group of approximately one hundred islands in the Lesser Antilles. **The British Virgin Islands** consist of about 40 islands, the largest, Tortola. They became a crown colony in 1956. Area: 153 sq km (59 sq mi). Population (1987): 13 246. Capital: Road Town. **The Virgin Islands of the United States** consist of three main islands, the largest being *St Croix, and about 50 smaller ones. They were purchased from Denmark in 1917. Area: 344 sq km (133 sq mi). Population (1985): 110 800. Capital: Charlotte Amalie.

virus A microorganism that can reproduce only in living cells. Viruses consist of a core of either *DNA or *RNA, surrounded by a protein coat (capsule) and, in some types, an enclosing envelope. After entering a host cell the viral DNA (or RNA), which contains its genes, directs the host cell to assemble numbers of identical viruses. When these are liberated, they may damage or kill the host cell. Viruses are responsible for many diseases in plants and animals.

viscacha A South American *rodent, *Lagostomus maximus*, related to *chinchillas. Over 50 cm in length, viscachas live in warrens. They are nocturnal and feed on grasses and seeds.

Visconti, Luchino (1906–76) Italian film director. Born into a noble family, he became a committed Marxist. His films include *The Leopard* (1963), *The Damned* (1970), and *Death in Venice* (1971). He also directed many opera and drama productions.

viscosity A measure of the degree to which a fluid resists a deforming force. Viscosity is defined by Newton's law of viscosity: if two layers of a fluid, area A and distance x apart, flow with a relative velocity v, there is a force between them equal to vAv/x. v is called the coefficient of viscosity. Viscosity is measured in newton seconds per square metre. The **kinematic viscosity** is the coefficient of viscosity divided by the density of the fluid.

Vishakhapatnam 17 42N 83 24E A city in India, on the Bay of Bengal. An important port, India's first steamer was launched here in 1948. Population (1981): 594 000.

Vishnu The second member of the Hindu trinity, the *Trimurti. He is known as the Preserver and is married to *Lakshmi. His ten manifestations (avatars), include Rama and *Krishna. He is often portrayed as sleeping on a seven-headed snake.

Visigoths A branch of the *Goths. Forced by the *Huns across the Danube (376 AD), they destroyed a Roman army at Adrianople (378) and, under Alaric I (c. 370–410 AD), sacked Rome in 410.

Vistula, River (Polish name: Wisła) The longest river of Poland, rising in the Carpathian Mountains and flowing N and NW to enter the

Baltic Sea near Gdańsk. Length: 1090 km (677 mi).

vitamin An organic compound, other than a protein, fat or carbohydrate, required in small amounts by living organisms for normal health and growth. Vitamins function as *coenzymes in many of the body's chemical reactions.

vitamin A (*or* retinol) A fat-soluble vitamin required for the formation of the visual pigments of the eyes. It also functions in the maintenance of healthy mucous membranes. Sources include liver, fish-liver oils, and egg yolk.

vitamin B complex A group of water-soluble vitamins that are constituents of *coenzymes in the body's chemical reactions. Thiamine (B_1) occurs in cereal grains, beans, peas, and pork. Deficiency leads to *beriberi. Riboflavin (B_2) is found in yeast, liver, milk, and leafy plants. Nicotinamide (nicotinic acid *or* niacin) can be manufactured from the amino acid tryptophan; liver is a rich source of the vitamin and milk and eggs of tryptophan. Vitamin B_6 (pyridoxine) is widely distributed in yeast, liver, milk, beans, and cereals. Other members of the vitamin B complex are: pantothenic acid, a constituent of coenzyme A found in many plant and animal tissues; biotin, manufactured by bacteria in the intestine and also occurring in meat, leafy vegetables, etc.; choline, found in most foods; folic acid and vitamin B_{12} (cyanocobalamin). The latter two can both be manufactured by bacteria in the intestine, and liver is a good source of vitamin B_{12}.

vitamin C (*or* ascorbic acid) A water-soluble compound required especially for the maintenance of healthy connective tissue. It cannot be manufactured in the body by man and certain animals. Fruit and vegetables, especially citrus fruits, are good sources. Deficiency leads to scurvy, a now rare disease.

vitamin D A fat-soluble vitamin consisting of several related sterols, principally cholecalciferol (D_3) and ergocalciferol (D_2). Vitamin D is important in calcium and phosphorus metabolism, and hence for healthy bones and teeth. Vitamin D_3 is produced by the action of sunlight on skin. Fish and fish-liver oils are the main sources; vitamin D_2 is added to margarine. Deficiency in infants causes *rickets.

vitamin E A vitamin consisting of related compounds that function as antioxidants by preventing the formation in tissues of reactive peroxides. The most potent form is alpha-tocopherol, found in leafy plants, cereals, and eggs.

vitamin K A vitamin consisting of compounds necessary for the formation of prothrombin, important in blood clotting. Vitamin K occurs in vegetables, cereals, and egg yolk and can be manufactured by bacteria in the intestine.

Viti Levu The largest Fijian island. Mount Victoria rises to 1302 m (4341 ft). Sugar, pineapples, cotton, and rice are produced. Area: 10 386 sq km (4010 sq mi). Population (latest est): 445 422. Chief settlement: Suva.

Vitoria 42 51N 2 40W A city in N Spain. Wellington defeated the French here (1813). Population (1981): 192 773.

Vitruvius (Marcus Vitruvius Pollio; 1st century BC) Roman architect and engineer. His *De architectura* strongly influenced architects in Renaissance Italy.

Vivaldi, Antonio (1678–1741) Italian composer and violinist. Besides operas and sacred music, Vivaldi wrote over 450 concertos, including a set of four violin concertos entitled *The Four Seasons*.

viviparity A form of reproduction in which the embryo develops within the mother's body. Viviparity occurs in most mammals–the embryos being nourished through the placenta–and in some snakes, lizards, and sharks.

vivisection The use of live animals for experiments to discover the effects of drugs, cosmetics, food additives, and other chemicals on living organisms. They are also used in medical and biological research. In the UK experimenters are licensed by the Home Office. Alternatives to live animals include the use of test-tube (*in vitro*) techniques, tissue cultures, and computer-based mathematical models.

Vladivostok 43 09N 131 53E A port of the SE Soviet Union, on the Sea of Japan. It is the terminus of the Trans-Siberian Railway and a major Soviet naval base. Population (1987): 615 000.

vocal cords. *See* larynx.

vodka An alcoholic drink distilled from potatoes, rye, barley, or malt, usually in E Europe. Colourless and without a distinctive flavour, vodka is used in many mixed drinks.

voiceprint A graphic record of the sounds produced during speech. The record shows the range of frequencies and harmonics produced and can be used to identify an individual voice.

volcanoes Vents in the earth's surface through which magma from the earth's interior erupts as lava, gases, and solid or molten fragments. Basaltic lava tends to produce gently sloping cones, the lava flowing over a wide area, whereas the more viscous acid lava produces a steeper-sided cone. Volcanic cones are often topped by craters, created by volcanic explosions. The world's highest volcano (extinct) is Aconcagua (6959 m) in the Andes.

vole A widely occurring short-tailed *rodent, ranging in size from 7 to 35 cm. They have blunt noses and their cheek teeth grow continuously. The field vole eats nearly its own weight in seeds, roots, and leaves every 24 hours. *See also* water vole.

Volga, River A river in the W Soviet Union, the longest river in Europe. Rising in the Valdai Range, it flows mainly E and S to the Caspian Sea. Length: 3690 km (2293 mi).

Volgograd (name until 1925: Tsaritsyn; name from 1925 until 1961: Stalingrad) 48 45N 44 30E A city in the Soviet Union, on the River Volga. It was redeveloped after World War II (*see* Stalingrad, Battle of). Population (1987): 988 000.

volleyball A six-a-side court game invented in the USA in 1895, in which an inflated ball is hit with the hands or arms. After the service each team is allowed to hit the ball three times before it crosses the net. A rally ends when the ball touches the ground or is not returned correctly. A game goes to 15 points and a 2-point lead is required to win.

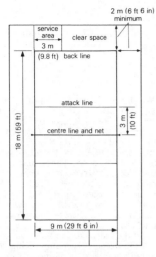

VOLLEYBALL *The height of the ceiling is a minimum of 7 m (23 ft). The top of the net is 2.43 m (8 ft) above the floor for men or 2.24 m (7 ft 4 in) for women.*

volt (V) The *SI unit of potential, potential difference, or electromotive force equal to the potential difference between two points on a conductor carrying a steady current of one ampere when the power dissipated is one watt. Named after Alessandro *Volta (1745–1827).

Volta, River A river in West Africa. The Black Volta and White Volta join in central Ghana to form the River Volta, which flows S to enter the Bight of Benin. Length: 480 km (300 mi).

Voltaire (François-Marie Arouet; 1694–1778) French philosopher and moralist of the age of Enlightenment. He conducted a lifelong campaign against injustice and intolerance. His writings include the satirical fable *Candide* (1759), *Traité de la tolérance* (1763), the *Dictionnaire philosophique* (1764), and histories of Peter the Great and Louis XV.

voltmeter A device for measuring *potential difference. In the direct-current moving-coil voltmeter the magnetic force on a coil in a magnetic field is used to deflect a needle, the high impedance needed being provided by a high resistance in series with the coil. *Cathode-ray oscilloscopes and digital voltmeters are used for both direct and alternating current.

Volturno, River A river in S central Italy, flowing SE and SW to the Tyrrhenian Sea. In 1860 it was the scene of a battle in which Garibaldi defeated the Neapolitans (*see* Risorgimento). Length: 175 km (109 mi).

Voluntary Service Overseas (VSO) A British organization founded in 1958 to send volunteers overseas to work as teachers and doctors or on agricultural, industrial, or business schemes.

von Braun, Wernher (1912–77) US *rocket engineer, born in Germany. He was director of the German Rocket Test Centre at Peenemünde during World War II, when the *V-2 rocket was built. After the war von Braun worked on US space rockets.

voodoo Magical cults of West African origin, practised in the Caribbean and in parts of South America. Rituals include trances induced by spirit possession, animal sacrifice, drum beating, and dancing.

Voronezh 51 40N 39 13E A city in the central Soviet Union. It is at the centre of an agricultural region. Population (1987): 872 000.

Voroshilovgrad (name until 1935: Lugansk) 48 35N 39 20E A city in the SW Soviet Union. It lies in the coal-producing Donets Basin. Population (1987): 509 000.

Vorster, Balthazar Johannes (1915–83) South African statesman; prime minister (1966–78) and briefly president (1978). Known for his strict enforcement of racial policies, he retired during investigations of financial irregularities.

Vosges A range of mountains in NE France. It extends roughly N–S to the W of the River Rhine, rising to 1423 m (4672 ft).

Voyager probes Two US spacecraft launched in 1977 to obtain information and pictures of the outer planets. Voyager 1 approached Jupiter in 1979 then flew towards Saturn, which it reached in 1980. Voyager 2 flew past Jupiter in 1979, Saturn in 1981, Uranus in 1986, and Neptune in August, 1989.

VSO. *See* Voluntary Service Overseas.

Vulcan The Roman god of fire. He became patron of metalworkers after his identification with the Greek god of fire and crafts, Hephaestus.

vulcanization A process in which heating natural rubber with sulphur creates sulphur bridges (–S–S–) between the polymer chains, making it harder. An inert filler is incorporated at the same time.

Vulgate The Latin translation of the Bible made by St Jerome in the 4th century AD. The oldest surviving translation of the whole Bible, it was adopted by the Council of *Trent (1546) as the official version of the Roman Catholic Church.

vulture A large carrion-eating bird with a naked head; they are 60–100 cm long with a wingspan up to 3 metres. American vultures, such as the *condor, have a hooked bill, large feet, and are voiceless. Vultures are also found in temperate and tropical regions of Europe, Asia, and Africa. They have a feathered ruff at the base of the neck. *See also* griffon vulture; lammergeier.

W

wadi A dry valley in a desert that will occasionally contain water after a violent downpour of rain.

Wagner, (Wilhelm) Richard (1813–83) German composer. His early operas *Rienzi* (1842) and *The Flying Dutchman* (1843) led to his appointment as conductor at the Dresden opera house, where *Tannhäuser* was successfully performed (1845). During the composition of *Der Ring des Nibelungen*, an operatic treatment of German mythology, he fell in love with Mathilde Wesendonck (1828–1902), who inspired the opera *Tristan und Isolde*. Wagner later married (1870) Cosima von Bülow (1837–1930), Liszt's daughter. In 1868 he produced *Die Meistersinger von Nürnberg* and began building a theatre in Bayreuth for the first performance of *The Ring* (1876). His last opera, *Parsifal*, was produced in Bayreuth in 1882.

Wagram, Battle of (5–6 July, 1809) The battle in which Napoleon finally defeated the Austrians, fought NE of Vienna.

wagtail A widely distributed songbird noted for its constantly bobbing tail. The pied wagtail (*Motacilla alba*) is black, grey, and white, about 18 cm long, and often roosts in large numbers.

Waikato River The longest river in New Zealand, in North Island. Rising in Mount Ruapehu, it flows NW to the Tasman Sea. Length: 350 km (220 mi).

Waitangi, Treaty of (1840) A treaty between the British and 46 Maori chiefs in New Zealand, giving the Maori full rights and confirmed possession of their lands. The Treaty was later broken by European settlers.

Wakamatsu. *See* Kitakyushu.

Wakashan languages A group of *North American Indian languages of the NW Pacific coast, including *Nootka and Kwakiutl.

Wakefield 53 42N 1 29W A city in N England, the administrative centre of West Yorkshire on the River Calder. A battle was fought here in 1460 during the Wars of the Roses. Population (1988 est): 75 500.

Walachia (*or* Wallachia) A principality in SE Europe, founded in 1290. In the late 14th century it came under Turkish domination. In 1859 Walachia united with *Moldavia to form Romania, whose independence was recognized in 1878.

Walcheren An island in the SW Netherlands, in the Scheldt estuary. Protected from the sea by dykes, it produces sugar beet and vegetables. Area: 212 sq km (82 sq mi). Chief towns: Flushing and Middelburg.

Waldheim, Kurt (1918–) Austrian diplomat; secretary general of the UN (1972–81), president of Austria (1986–). He became president despite controversy over his war record as a Nazi officer in the Balkans.

Wales (Welsh name: Cymru) A principality in the W of Great Britain, comprising a political division of the *United Kingdom. The Isle of Anglesey lies off the NW coast. *Economy*: the valleys and coastal plain in the S were highly industrialized—the coalfields in the valleys and the steel industry on the coast. The decline of both the coal and steel industries has brought a switch to newer industries on the coast. The Royal Mint is situated at Llantrisant. In Milford Haven, in the SW, oil is refined and there are associated petrochemical industries here and near Swansea. Tourism, forestry, and sheep rearing are important. *History*: the Celts living in Wales were little affected by the Roman occupation. King *Offa of Mercia built a great dyke (8th century), providing a frontier behind which the Welsh kingdoms were contained. Temporary unity was achieved under Hywel the Good (d. 950). Edward I of England's defeat of *Llywelyn ap Gruffud (d. 1282) established English supremacy. Owen *Glendower's revolt in the early 14th century was crushed and English rule was imposed with the Acts of *Union (1536–43). Welsh nationalism has been a powerful force in recent years, although *devolution plans were rejected in a referendum in 1979. Area: 20 767 sq km (8016 sq mi). Population (1986 est): 2 821 000. Capital: Cardiff.

Walesa, Lech (1943–) Polish statesman; president of Poland (1990–). As leader of the trade union *Solidarity, he was awarded the 1983 Nobel Peace Prize for his efforts to ensure workers' rights. In 1989 he helped to form Poland's first noncommunist government since World War II.

walking (*or* race walking) In athletics, a form of racing in which a particular gait is used; the advancing foot must touch the ground before the other leaves it. Races are held on a track or on roads.

wallaby A plant-eating marsupial closely related to the *kangaroo. Hare wallabies are the smallest, measuring up to 90 cm in length. Rock wallabies have rough feet for negotiating rocky ground. Scrub wallabies inhabit the open forest.

Wallace, Alfred Russel (1823–1913) British naturalist, who formulated a theory of evolution by natural selection independently of *Darwin. He also proposed an imaginary line (known as Wallace's line) dividing the wildlife of Asia and Australia.

Wallachia. *See* Walachia.

wallcreeper A songbird, *Tichodroma muraria*, of Europe and Asia. About 17 cm long, it has a grey plumage with black wings patched with red. It climbs rock faces with its sharp claws, probing crevices for insects.

Waller, (Thomas) Fats (1904–1943) US Black jazz musician. An exceptional pianist, his compositions included "Honeysuckle Rose" and "Ain't Misbehavin'".

wallflower A widespread plant of the mustard family, with yellow or brown flowers. Many varieties of *Cheiranthus cheiri* are cultivated as garden plants.

Wallis, Sir Barnes (Neville) (1887–1979) British aeronautical engineer, who designed the airship R100 and the Wellington bomber. He also invented the bouncing bomb (1943) and the swing-wing aircraft.

Wallis and Futuna A French overseas territory in the SW Pacific Ocean comprising two small groups of islands. The chief of the **Wallis Islands** is Uvéa, while the **Futuna Islands** (*or* Iles de Horne) consist of Futuna and Alofi. Copra and timber are produced. Area: 275 sq km (106 sq mi). Population (1988 est): 15 400. Capital: Matautu, on Uvéa.

Walloons The French-speaking inhabitants of Belgium, living mainly in the S and E of the country. They are descended from the northernmost group of *Franks who adopted the *Romance speech. *Compare* Flemings.

Wall Street The centre of the financial district in New York City, in which the Stock Exchange is situated.

walnut A Eurasian tree, *Juglans regia*, grown for its nuts and for ornament. Up to 30 m tall, it has plum-sized green fruits each containing an edible kernel enclosed in a wrinkled shell. The timber of this species and of the American black walnut (*J. nigra*) is valued for furniture.

Walpole, Sir Hugh (Seymour) (1884–1941) British novelist. Born in New Zealand, he wrote *The Dark Forest* (1916), *The Cathedral* (1922), and a family saga, *The Herries Chronicle* (1930–33).

Walpole, Sir Robert, 1st Earl of Orford (1676–1745) British statesman, regarded as the first prime minister (1721–42). He became a Whig MP in 1700 and was secretary for war (1708–10) and treasurer of the navy (1710–11). In 1712 he was charged with corruption but returned to government in 1715 as first lord of the treasury and chancellor of the exchequer. Losing office in 1717, he became paymaster general in 1720; after his handling of the *South Sea Bubble he again became (1721) first lord of the treasury and chancellor of the exchequer. Conflict with Spain led to the War of Jenkins' Ear and Walpole was forced to resign. His fourth son **Horace Walpole, 4th Earl of Orford** (1717–97) was the author of the gothic novel, *The Castle of Otranto* (1765) and numerous letters.

walrus A large *seal, *Odobenus rosmarus*, of coastal Arctic waters. Males are up to 3.7 m long and weigh about 1400 kg. Walruses have tusks up to 1 m long used to dig for molluscs and for fighting.

Walton, Ernest Thomas Sinton (1903–) Irish physicist, who shared the 1951 Nobel Prize with Sir John *Cockcroft for their invention in 1929 of the first particle accelerator.

Walton, Izaak (1593–1683) English writer. His best-known work is *The Compleat Angler* (1653), on fishing. He also wrote biographies of

John Donne (1640), George Herbert (1670), and other churchmen.

Walton, Sir William (Turner) (1902–83) British composer. *Façade* (1922), a setting of poems by Edith Sitwell, was followed by two symphonies (1932–35, 1960), the opera *Troilus and Cressida* (1954), concertos for viola (1929), violin (1939), and cello (1957), the oratorio *Belshazzar's Feast* (1931), and music for Laurence Olivier's Shakespearean films.

wandering Jew. *See* tradescantia.

Wapping A former dockland area in E London, in Tower Hamlets. Transfer of several newspaper offices from Fleet Street to Wapping in the mid-1980s and increased use of technology led to job losses and strikes.

waratah An Australian shrub, *Telopea speciosissima*: the floral emblem of New South Wales. Up to 2 m tall, it has scarlet flowers.

Warbeck, Perkin (c. 1474–99) Flemish-born impostor in a plot against Henry VII of England. Pretending to be the Duke of York (presumed murdered in 1483) he landed in Cornwall in 1497 but he and his 6000 followers fled in the face of Henry's troops. Captured at Beaulieu, he was hanged.

warble fly A parasitic fly widespread in Europe and North America. Some species attack cattle: eggs are laid on the legs and the larvae burrow into the tissue. When mature the larvae leave the host and form pupas in the ground.

warbler A small widely distributed songbird. 9–25 cm long, they have brown plumage and feed on insects and berries. *See* blackcap; chiffchaff; reed warbler; whitethroat.

Ward, Sir Joseph George (1856–1930) New Zealand statesman; Liberal (1906–12) and United Party (1928–30) prime minister. He advocated greater unity within the British Empire in foreign affairs.

Wardrobe In medieval England, the room in which the king kept his clothes and jewels; it became a government department in the late 12th century, owing to the king's need for cash while travelling. It declined in importance during the 14th century.

Warhol, Andy (Andrew Warhola; 1926–87) US pop artist and film producer. He achieved notoriety in the early 1960s with paintings of soup cans and portraits of film stars. His controversial films include *The Chelsea Girls* (1966).

War of 1812 (1812–14) The war declared on Britain by the USA when Britain forced sailors from US ships into service and cut off US shipping during the Napoleonic Wars. The USA was also angered by British assistance to Indians harassing NW settlements. The war had no clear outcome but helped forge US unity.

War of Independence, American. *See* American Revolution.

Warsaw (Polish name: Warszawa) 52 15N 21 00W The capital of Poland, on the River Vistula. It became the capital in 1611. It was occupied by Russia in 1794 and later by France and Prussia. After German occupation in World War I, it became the capital again on independence (1918). During the German occupation in World War II, the survivors (about 100 000) of a Jewish ghetto staged an uprising (1943), after which they were murdered. Population (1985): 1 649 000.

Warsaw Pact (*or* Warsaw Treaty Organization) A military treaty signed in 1955 by the Soviet Union, Albania (until 1968), Bulgaria, Czechoslovakia, East Germany (until 1990), Hungary, Poland, and Romania, as a communist counterpart to NATO.

Wars of Religion (1562–98) French civil wars between the Huguenots (French Protestants) and the Roman Catholics. The wars ended with the Edict of *Nantes, which gave the Huguenots religious freedom.

wart (*or* verruca) A small growth on the skin, caused by viruses. Warts are commonest in children and usually appear on the hands and feet. They appear suddenly and may disappear without treatment. Persistent warts can be treated by cauterization, freezing, or with drugs.

warthog A wild pig, *Phocochoerus aethiopicus*, of tropical Africa. Short-legged, with a large head, bulging eyes, and curved tusks, warthogs grow to about 75 cm high. They are greyish, with sparse hair.

Warwick 52 17N 1 34W A town in central England, the administrative centre of Warwickshire on the River Avon. It is a historic town with a 14th-century castle. Population (1981): 21 936.

Warwick, Richard Neville, Earl of (1428–71) English statesman, known as the Kingmaker. A supporter of the Yorkists in the Wars of the Roses, he was responsible for the seizure of the Crown in 1461 by Edward, Duke of York (Edward IV). In 1470, he changed sides and briefly restored Henry VI to the throne. After the Lancastrians were defeated (1471), he was killed, at Barnet.

Warwickshire A county in the Midlands of England. It is predominantly agricultural. Area: 1981 sq km (765 sq mi). Population (1987 est): 484 200. Administrative centre: Warwick.

Wash, the A shallow inlet of the North Sea, in E England between Lincolnshire and Norfolk. Length: about 30 km (19 mi). Width: 24 km (15 mi).

Washington One of the Pacific states in NW USA. The major industry is the construction of aircraft. Minerals extracted include gold, silver, and uranium. Tourism is growing. *History*: the British Hudson Bay Company dominated the area until the 1840s. In 1846 the boundary between Washington and Canada was agreed and the state (1889) was named after George Washington. Area: 176 616 sq km (68 192 sq mi). Population (1987 est): 4 481 100. Capital: Olympia.

Washington, DC 38 55N 77 00W The capital of the USA, on the Potomac River and coextensive with the District of Columbia. Its landmarks include the Washington Monument, the Lincoln Memorial, the Capitol, the White House, the *Pentagon, and the Smithsonian Institution. Planned by the French engineer, Pierre L'Enfant (1754–1825), it dates from 1793. Population (1986 est): 626 000.

Washington, George (1732–99) US statesman; the first president of the USA (1789–97).

Washington gained his military reputation in the French and Indian War before becoming an opponent of British rule. On the outbreak of the *American Revolution (1775–83) he became commander of the American forces. After the final victory at Yorktown (1781), Washington presided over the Constitutional Convention (1787) and was unanimously elected president.

wasp A stinging insect, 6–40 mm long, related to bees. European wasps form colonies consisting of a queen, males, and workers. The adults feed on nectar, insects, etc. New colonies are established by young fertilized queens–the only individuals to survive the winter. Certain parasitic wasps lay their eggs in the nests of other wasps. *See also* hornet; potter wasp.

Wasserman, August von (1866–1925) German bacteriologist, who invented a test for detecting *syphilis, a test for tuberculosis, and an antitoxin against diphtheria.

watch A timepiece worn by a person. Watches first came into use in the 16th century with the invention by Peter Henlein (1480–1542) of the mainspring. Using a verge escapement, they were bulky devices worn on the girdle. The invention of the balance spring (claimed by both *Hooke and *Huygens) in 1675 enabled it to be concealed in the pocket. At the beginning of the 20th century wrist watches were introduced, mainly as a convenience in World War I. In the early 1950s the first electromagnetic watches were developed (powered by tiny batteries), but it was not until the 1960s that electronic watches appeared. In the 1970s quartz watches without moving parts were developed, using a digital display. The circuits can be so small that some digital wrist watches incorporate additional functions (e.g. calculators).

water (H_2O) A colourless tasteless liquid consisting of eight parts of oxygen to two parts of hydrogen by weight. Water covers 72% of the earth's surface and is found in all living matter and as a small constituent of the atmosphere. The solid form of water (ice) is less dense (916.8 kg/m^3) than the liquid at 0°C (999.84 kg/m^3), which is why ice floats and frozen water pipes burst. The maximum density (999.97 kg/m^3) occurs at 3.98°C, unlike most liquids in which the maximum density occurs at the melting point. Water molecules are polar (positively charged at one end, negative at the other), making water an excellent solvent. See pages 574–575.

water boatman A widely distributed insect that lives on fresh or brackish water. It has a boat-shaped body with oarlike hind legs and feeds on vegetation, scooped up by the front legs.

waterbuck An African antelope, *Kobus ellipsiprymnus*. About 130 cm high, waterbucks have a wiry brown coat with a white rump patch and spreading horns.

water buffalo A large buffalo, *Bubalus bubalis*, also called Asiatic buffalo or carabao, found in swampy parts of SE Asia and domesticated throughout Asia for their milk and for pulling loads. Up to 180 cm high and heavily built, they are greyish with backward-curving horns.

water chestnut A Eurasian aquatic plant, *Trapa natans*, with floating leaves, feathery sub-

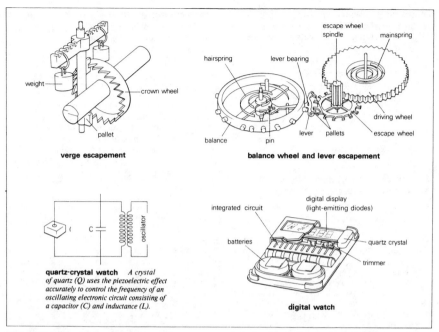

WATCH *Early watches used the verge escapement of clocks. The balance wheel and lever escapement dominated watch design until the quartz crystal and digital watch emerged in the 20th century.*

merged leaves, and white flowers. The spiny fruit, up to 5 cm across, contains edible seeds. The Chinese water chestnut is the edible tuber of an E Asian sedge, *Eleocharis tuberosa.*

watercress   Either of two plants, *Nasturtium officinale* or *N. microphyllum* × *officinale*, of the mustard family, native to Eurasia and widely cultivated for the young shoots, used in salads. Watercress grows in streams or on mud.

water flea   A widely distributed freshwater *crustacean. Usually 1–3 mm long, it has a transparent carapace, which encloses 4–6 pairs of limblike appendages.

Waterford (Irish name: Port Lairge)   52 15N 7 06W A city and port in the Republic of Ireland, the county town of Co Waterford. It has Protestant and Roman Catholic cathedrals and is famous for glass making. Population (1986): 39 516.

Waterford (Irish name: Contae Port Lairge) A county in the Republic of Ireland. Area: 1838 sq km (710 sq mi). Population (1986): 91 098. County town: Waterford.

water gas   A mixture of equal amounts of hydrogen and carbon monoxide made by passing steam over red hot coke: $H_2O + C \rightarrow H_2 + CO$. The mixture is a useful fuel gas, but has now been largely replaced by natural gas.

Watergate   A building in Washington, DC, that gave its name to a political scandal leading to the resignation of the president, Richard Nixon, in 1974. The *Washington Post* exposed the involvement of presidential officials during the

1972 presidential election in a burglary of the headquarters of the Democratic Party at the Watergate, and in subsequent arrangements (the "coverup") to buy off the burglars.

water glass (*or* sodium silicate)   A mixture of silicates with the formula $xNa_2O.ySiO_2$, forming a viscous solution in water. It is made by fusing *sodium carbonate and sand in an electric furnace and is used in making silica gel, detergents, and textiles.

Waterhouse, Alfred (1830–1905) British architect of the *gothic revival. His work included the Manchester Town Hall (1868) and the romanesque Natural History Museum (1881) in London.

water lily   A widely distributed freshwater plant with round floating wax-coated leaves arising from creeping stems buried in the mud. The large white or coloured flowers are cup-shaped.

Waterloo, Battle of (18 June, 1815) The battle in which *Napoleon Bonaparte was finally defeated by British, Dutch, Belgian, and German forces commanded by Wellington and the Prussians under von Blücher. Napoleon caught Wellington near the village of Waterloo (Belgium) and attempted to smash his army. However, British lines held until the Prussians arrived, when a concerted charge brought victory.

watermark   A distinctive mark produced in *paper during manufacture by making it slightly thinner in some places than in others. In hand-made paper, it is formed by wires in the bottom

The compound Water consists of two hydrogen atoms bonded to an oxygen atom (H_2O). As a gas (steam), the water molecules move about independently of each other.

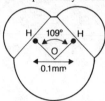

As a liquid, some of the molecules are held together by hydrogen bonds. As a solid (ice), the molecules form a rigid crystal.

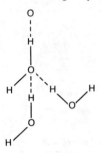

Some 6.7% of the world's electricity is produced by hydroelectric power in which reservoirs provide a flow of water to turn water turbines, which drive the generators.

The life supporter Water is essential to all living things. Plants (the producers) depend on water for their food, producing organic compounds from water and carbon dioxide in photosynthesis:

$$2H_2O + CO_2 = [CH_2O] + H_2O + O_2$$

They in turn provide food for animals (the consumers). The water in lakes, rivers, and oceans provides the living medium for fish and other aquatic animals, many of which supply food for man. The human body contains 65-70% water by weight (about 40 litres). A healthy adult male requires 2.5 litres of water per day to compensate for water loss.

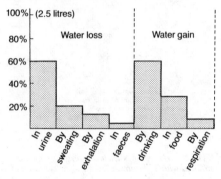

The water cycle Water evaporates from the sea into the atmosphere, the clouds in the sky produce rain and snow, which fall onto the land, some soaking into the earth as groundwater and some flowing back into the sea in rivers. Water from the land is also returned to the atmosphere by transpiration by trees and other plants.

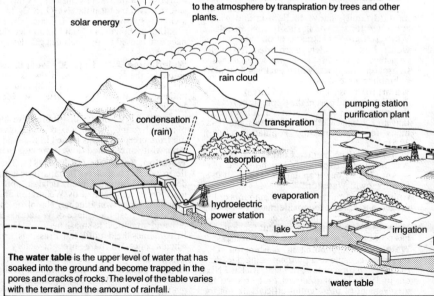

The water table is the upper level of water that has soaked into the ground and become trapped in the pores and cracks of rocks. The level of the table varies with the terrain and the amount of rainfall.

The cleanser Water is the universal cleanser. In religion it is a symbolic cleanser, purifying the body of the infant Christian in baptism and sanctifying the body of the dying Hindu, seen here in the Ganges at Benares (Varanasi).

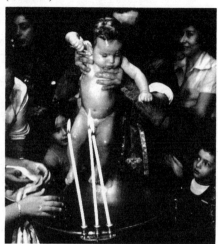

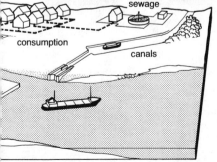

The transporter About 70% of the earth's surface is covered with oceans, which are inhabited at various depths by a wide variety of aquatic plants and animals. These oceans have also provided humans with a means of transporting themselves and their goods from one continent to another.

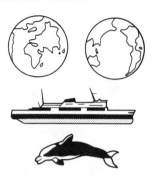

The enemy Floods have drowned and starved millions of people throughout history - from the probably apocryphal inundation of Genesis to the recent disasters in Bangladesh seen here (1985).

Droughts, too, have terrible results, especially in densely populated areas relying on agriculture, such as India and Africa (illustrated here by a failed rice crop in Mali).

of the mould. In machine-made paper the mark is put in by a roller.

watermelon The fruit of a climbing plant, *Citrullus vulgaris*, of the gourd family, native to Africa but widely cultivated. The large fruits, up to 25 cm across, have green rind and red or yellow sweet flesh.

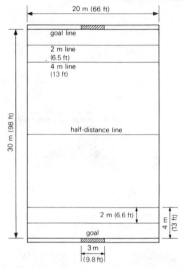

WATER POLO *The dimensions of the field of play. The water must be at least 1 m deep.*

water polo A seven-a-side (with four substitutes) ball game played in a swimming pool. It developed in England in the 1870s, with players riding barrels to resemble horses and hitting the ball with paddles; in the modern game players swim.

water rat A large aquatic *rodent found in Australia, New Guinea, and the Philippines. The Australian water rat (*Hydromys chrysogaster*) is about 35 cm long and has otter-like fur and a white-tipped tail. *Water voles and *muskrats are also known as water rats.

water snake. *See* grass snake.

water spider A European *spider, *Argyroneta aquatica*, that lives under water in a bell-shaped structure constructed from silk and plant material and filled with bubbles of air. It feeds inside on small animals. The male (15 mm long) is larger than the female (10 mm long).

waterspout A funnel-shaped cloud extending from the base of a cumulonimbus cloud to the surface of the sea. It is a small-scale low-pressure system, characterized by rotating winds.

water table The level of the water that has trickled through the ground and become trapped in permeable rocks. The level varies with surface features and rainfall. *See also* artesian well.

water vole A large *vole, *Arvicola terristris*, of Europe and Asia. 15–20 cm long, it has brown fur, burrows into river banks, and feeds on vegetation.

water wheel. *See* turbine.

Watford 51 40N 0 25W A town in SE England, in Hertfordshire. In addition to printing and other industry, it is a commuter town for London. Population (1986): 76 500.

Watling Street The Roman road that traversed Britain from London to Wroxeter, with a branch to the legionary fortress at Chester.

Watson, James Dewey (1928–) US geneticist, who (with Francis *Crick) proposed a model for the molecular structure of *DNA (1953). Watson later investigated aspects of the *genetic code. He received a Nobel Prize (1962) with Crick and Maurice *Wilkins.

Watson-Watt, Sir Robert Alexander (1892–1973) British physicist. From 1935 he pioneered the development of *radar, enabling it to be used by the Allies in World War II ahead of the Germans.

watt (W) The *SI unit of power equal to one joule per second. It is the energy per second expended by a current of one ampere flowing between points separated by a potential difference of one volt. Named after James *Watt.

Watt, James (1736–1819) British engineer, whose efficient steam engine (1769) replaced the earlier Newcomen engine. By 1800 some 500 Watt engines were in use, contributing to the *industrial revolution. He later invented the centrifugal governor. Watt devised the unit "horsepower" and the SI unit of power is named after him.

Watteau, (Jean) Antoine (1684–1721) French rococo painter. His *fêtes galantes* (scenes of gallantry) and paintings of comedians, notably *L'Embarquement pour l'île de Cythère* and the portrait of the clown *Gilles* (both Louvre) brought fame before his death from tuberculosis.

wattle An Australian *acacia tree or shrub used for fencing, woodwork, etc. The commonest species are the black wattle (*Acacia binervata*), the golden or green wattle (*A. pycnantha*), and the silver wattle (*A. dealbata*). *See also* mimosa.

Waugh, Evelyn (Arthur St John) (1903–66) British novelist. With *Decline and Fall* (1928), *Vile Bodies* (1930), and *The Loved One* (1948), he established his reputation. After his conversion to Roman Catholicism in (1930), religious themes appeared in his novels, especially *Brideshead Revisited* (1945) and his war trilogy *Men at Arms* (1952), *Officers and Gentlemen* (1955), and *Unconditional Surrender* (1961).

wave A periodic change in a system that is propagated through a medium (or through space). If the graph of the wave is shaped like a

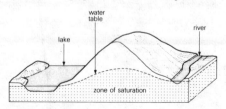

WATER TABLE

sine curve, it is known as a sine (or sinusoidal) wave. Examples include electromagnetic waves and sound waves. A wave is characterized by its amplitude (maximum displacement), *wavelength, and *frequency. A travelling wave transmits energy; a standing or stationary wave does not.

waveguide A hollow conductor for transmitting microwaves over short distances; usually filled with air, it occasionally has some other *dielectric.

wavelength The distance between successive peaks (or troughs) of a *wave. It is equal to the speed of the wave divided by its frequency.

Wavell, Archibald Percival, 1st Earl (1883–1950) British field marshal. After service in World War I he became *Allenby's chief of staff in Palestine. In World War II, as commander in the Middle East, he defeated the Italians in Africa. After his unsuccessful offensive against Rommel in June, 1941, he was transferred to SE Asia. He was viceroy of India (1943–47).

wave power The use of the energy of sea waves to generate electricity. Various types of generator have been developed; the "nodding-duck" type consists of a string of floats that bob up and down in the waves, the bobbing motion turning a generator. It is estimated that the waves off the coast of Britain could generate a total of 120 gigawatts.

wax A smooth substance of low melting point (40–80°C) obtained from plants (e.g. carnauba wax) or animals (e.g. *beeswax, *lanolin) or made synthetically. Mineral waxes include paraffin wax, obtained by distilling petroleum. Waxes are used in polishes, candles, modelling, etc.

waxwing A broad-billed songbird, *Bombycilla garrulus*, occurring in N coniferous forests. Its plumage is liver-coloured above with a reddish crest and it has a black throat and eyestripe. The red tips of the flight feathers resemble sealing wax.

Wayland (or Weland) In Teutonic mythology, a smith, who was captured and lamed by a Swedish king, Nidudr. Nidudr kept him on an island, forcing Wayland to work for him. Wayland secretly murdered the king's sons, made ornaments of their skulls, raped the king's daughter, and revealed all to Nidudr before escaping. In England his forge, "Wayland's Smithy," is associated with a site near White Horse Hill on the Berkshire Downs.

Wayne, John (Marion Michael Morrison; 1907–79) US film actor. Following his success in *Stagecoach* (1939), his classic westerns included *Red River* (1948), *Rio Bravo* (1959), and *True Grit* (1969).

weak interaction See particle physics.

weasel A widely occurring carnivorous mammal, *Mustela nivalis*. Growing to about 25 cm long, it has short legs and is brown above with white underparts. Weasels feed on small rodents, etc.

weather. See meteorology.

weaverbird A small songbird of tropical Africa and Asia. Most species build elaborate domed nests. The communal nest of the sociable weaver

(*Philetairus socius*) houses 20–30 pairs of birds. Weavers are seed eaters with conical bills and coloured plumage.

weaverfinch A small finchlike tropical seed-eating songbird. They have conical bills and are usually brightly coloured. See zebra finch.

weaving The interlacing of two or more yarns at right angles on a loom to produce a fabric. The loom is set up with a series of longitudinal threads (warp). In plain weave, alternate warp threads are raised and lowered by means of wires or cords (heddles) to allow the crosswire threads (weft), wound onto a bobbin (shuttle), to pass between them. Different weaves, such as twill and herringbone, are made by altering the interlacing pattern. Power looms were invented by Edmund *Cartwright in 1786.

Webb, Sidney (James), Baron Passfield (1859–1947) British socialist economist. He helped to found the *Fabian Society (1884) and the London School of Economics (1895). He initiated many educational reforms while he was a member of the London County Council (1892–1910), entering parliament in 1922. He collaborated with his wife **Beatrice (Potter) Webb** (1858–1943) on several books, including *The History of Trade Unionism* (1894) and *Industrial Democracy* (1897).

weber (Wb) The *SI unit of magnetic flux equal to the flux linking a circuit of one turn that produces an electromotive force of one volt when reduced uniformly to zero in one second. Named after Wilhelm Weber (1804–91).

Weber, Carl Maria von (1786–1826) German composer. His most successful opera, *Der Freischütz* (1821) is based on a German fairy story.

Weber, Max (1864–1920) German sociologist, one of the founders of modern *sociology. His best-known work, *The Protestant Ethic and the Spirit of Capitalism* (1904), relates the emergence of a particular type of economic system to the effects of religious values. His *Methodology of the Social Sciences* (1904) remains a major text. He served on the committee that drafted the constitution of the *Weimar Republic.

Webern, Anton von (1883–1945) Austrian composer. His compositions, using serialism, include a concerto for nine instruments (1934) and a string quartet (1938).

Webster, John (c. 1580–c. 1625) English dramatist. His plays include *The White Devil* (1612) and *The Duchess of Malfi* (c. 1613).

Weddell Sea A large inlet of the S Atlantic Ocean in Antarctica, between the Antarctic Peninsula and Coats Land. It is named after British explorer James Weddell (1787–1834).

Wedgwood, Josiah (1730–95) British potter. He opened his factory at Burslem, Staffordshire (England) in 1759. In 1769 he opened a new factory (Etruria), including a village for his workmen. His high-quality ceramics, **Wedgwood ware**, perfected creamware and developed basalt and jasperware.

weevil A widely distributed beetle, also called snout beetle. Most weevils are less than 6 mm long with mouthparts at the tip of a beaklike part (rostrum). Many species are serious pests.

weight. *See* mass and weight.

weight lifting A sport in which competitors lift weighted barbells. Contestants usually make three attempts in each of two styles, the snatch and the clean and jerk.

Weil, Simone (1909–43) French philosopher. An active socialist in the 1930s, after a mystical experience she became a Roman Catholic, although she refused baptism. During World War II she worked for the Free French in London. Her writings, published after her death, include *Waiting for God* (1951) and *The Need for Roots* (1952).

Weill, Kurt (1900–50) German composer. His collaboration with Bertolt *Brecht produced the operas *The Rise and Fall of the City of Mahagonny* (1927) and *The Threepenny Opera* (1928), a modern version of *The Beggar's Opera* (*see* Gay, John).

Weimar 50 59N 11 15E A city in central Germany, on the River Ilm. It was the capital of the grand duchy of Saxe-Weimar-Eisenach (1815–1918). In 1919 the German National Assembly met in Weimar and drew up the constitution of the *Weimar Republic. Population (1983 est): 63 900.

Weimaraner (*or* Weimeraner) A breed of dog developed in Weimar, Germany, for hunting game. It has drooping ears and a short tail. The short coat is silverish. Height: 61–69 cm (dogs); 56–64 cm (bitches).

Weimar Republic The state of Germany from 1919 to 1933. Named after the town in which its constitution was formulated; it faced persistent crises and was finally overthrown by Hitler.

Weismann, August Friedrich Leopold (1834–1914) German biologist and a founder of genetics. In 1883 he proposed that heredity was based upon the transfer, from generation to generation, of germ plasm with a definite molecular constitution.

Weizmann, Chaim (Azriel) (1874–1952) Russian-born Israeli statesman; the first president of Israel (1949–52). Working in England, he discovered (1916) a process for making acetone. This contribution to the British war effort helped the negotiations that led to the *Balfour Declaration (1917). His moderate policies as president (1920–31, 1935–46) of the World Zionist Movement were important in the establishment of Israel.

Welles, (George) Orson (1915–85) US film actor and director. Arriving in Hollywood in 1940, he made his first film, *Citizen Kane* (1941), which became a classic. Other films include *The Magnificent Ambersons* (1942), *Macbeth* (1948), and *Chimes at Midnight* (1966). He also acted in *The Third Man* (1949).

Wellington 41 17S 174 47E The capital of New Zealand, a port in North Island. It became the seat of central government in 1865 and is now the commercial centre of New Zealand. Population (1988): 325 200.

Wellington, Arthur Wellesley, 1st Duke of (1769–1852) British general and statesman, known as the Iron Duke; prime minister (1828–30). Born in Dublin, he went to India in 1799,

becoming governor of Mysore. He was responsible for victory (1814) in the *Peninsular War and at Waterloo (1815), where he and Marshal Blücher (1742–1819) finally defeated Napoleon. He served in Lord Liverpool's Tory government, and as prime minister supported *Catholic emancipation. His opposition to parliamentary reform brought about his resignation. Under Peel he served as foreign secretary (1834–35) and was commander in chief of the British army (1827–28; 1842–52).

wellingtonia. *See* sequoia.

Wells, H(erbert) G(eorge) (1866–1946) British novelist. *The Time Machine* (1895) and other science-fiction novels were followed by the social novels, including *Kipps* (1905) and *The History of Mr Polly* (1910). Non-fiction included *The Outline of History* (1920) and *The Shape of Things to Come* (1933).

Welsh Nationalist Party. *See* Plaid Cymru.

Welsh pony Either of two breeds of pony originating in Wales. The Welsh Mountain pony, for riding and draught work, has short legs and a profuse mane. The larger Welsh riding pony is a popular children's mount. Height: Mountain pony: up to 1.22 m (12 hands); riding pony: up to 1.37 m (13½ hands).

Welwyn Garden City 51 48N 0 13W A town in SE England, in Hertfordshire. Founded in 1919 by Sir Ebenezer Howard, it became a new town in 1948. Population (1981): 40 496.

Wenceslas, St (d. 929 AD) Duke of Bohemia (?924–29). Wenceslas' unpopular submission to the German king Henry the Fowler led to his assassination. He became Bohemia's patron saint.

wentletrap A widely distributed sea snail, 2–10 cm long, having shells with long spires; that of the precious wentletrap (*Epitonium scalare*) is prized by collectors. Some species produce a purple dye.

werewolf In folklore, a man who becomes a wolf by night and preys on humans. Belief in werewolves is ancient and widespread; some were regarded as hereditary, others only change form during a full moon, a transformation known as lycanthropy.

wergild The sum payable as compensation in Anglo-Saxon England to the family of a slain man by his assassin or the latter's kin. The amount depended on the status and nationality of the victim.

Weser, River A river in NW Germany. It flows NW from Münden to the North Sea. Length: 477 km (296 mi).

Wesker, Arnold (1932–) British dramatist. His first successful trilogy was *Chicken Soup with Barley* (1958), *Roots* (1959), and *I'm Talking about Jerusalem* (1960). Later plays include *Chips with Everything* (1962), *The Merchant* (1978), and *Shoeshine* (1988).

Wesley, John (1703–91) British religious leader, founder of *Methodism. Wesley and his younger brother **Charles Wesley** (1707–88) belonged to a group nicknamed "Methodists" because of their disciplined religious lives. The brothers sailed to Georgia as missionaries in 1735, but returned disillusioned in 1738, both experiencing a revelation that sent them round the country preaching repentance, faith, and love. The Wesleyan Methodist Church was organized after their death. Charles was the author of many hymns.

Wessex The kingdom of the West *Saxons, under which Anglo-Saxon England was united in the 9th century. Egbert, King of Wessex (802–39), destroyed *Mercian dominance in 825 and made possible the union of England under Alfred the Great.

West, Mae (1892–1980) US actress, who became a sex symbol during the 1930s. Her films included *She Done Him Wrong* (1933), *I'm No Angel* (1933), and *My Little Chickadee* (1939).

West, Dame Rebecca (Cicely Isabel Fairfield, 1892–1983) British writer. Her books include the novels *The Thinking Reed* (1936) and *The Birds Fall Down* (1966) and the political journalism *The Meaning of Treason* (1949) and *A Train of Powder* (1955).

West Atlantic languages A subgroup of the *Niger-Congo family, spoken in Guinea and Senegal. It includes the languages Wolof and *Fulani.

West Bank A territory in Israel, on the W bank of the River Jordan. It comprises the hills of Judaea and Samaria and part of *Jerusalem. Formerly part of *Palestine, it remained in Arab hands after 1948, became part of Jordan following the ceasefire of 1949, and was occupied by Israel in 1967. Israel has since been under pressure to withdraw and allow a Palestinian state (declared by the PLO in 1988) to be set up. *See* Camp David. Area: about 6000 sq km (2320 sq mi). Population (1988): 866 000.

westerlies The chief winds blowing between 30° and 70° latitude. In the N hemisphere winds blow mainly from the SW and in the S hemisphere, from the NW.

Western Australia The largest state of Australia, bordering on the Indian Ocean, Timor Sea, and Great Australian Bight. Agricultural activities include dairy farming, lumbering, and the cultivation of citrus fruits, wheat, and vines. Mineral resources include bauxite, nickel, oil, gold, and ferrous minerals. Industrial activity is chiefly around Perth. Area: 2 527 621 sq km (975 920 sq mi). Population (1986): 1 440 607. Capital: Perth.

Western Sahara (name until 1975: Spanish Sahara) A territory in NW Africa, bordering on the Atlantic Ocean, Mauritania, and Morocco. It consists chiefly of desert. *History*: in 1884 Spain claimed a protectorate over the coastal zone of Río de Oro and in 1958 Spanish Sahara became a province of Spain with its capital at El Aaiún. In 1976 the province was divided between Mauritania and Morocco. Morocco occupied the S Western Sahara when Mauritania withdrew in 1979. Area: 266 000 sq km (102 680 sq mi). Population (1986 est): 180 000.

Western (Wailing) Wall. *See* Temple of Jerusalem.

West Germany. *See* Germany.

West Glamorgan A county of South Wales, bordering on the Bristol Channel. Area: 815 sq km (315 sq mi). Population (1987 est): 363 200. Administrative centre: Swansea.

West Indies A group of islands extending for over 2400 km (1500 mi) from Florida to Venezuela enclosing the Caribbean Sea. It is often subdivided into the *Greater Antilles, the *Lesser Antilles, and the *Bahamas. *Economy*: sugar-cane cultivation has been important since colonization began. Many islands also grow tobacco, bananas, spices, or coffee. Mineral deposits include asphalt and bauxite. *History*: Columbus discovered the islands in 1492 and named them believing he had found the west route to India. The Spanish, the first Europeans to settle, introduced the cultivation of sugar and imported African slaves to work the plantations. The Federation of the West Indies within the Commonwealth was formed in 1958 and dissolved in 1962. Many islands are now independent within the Commonwealth. Area: over 235 000 sq km (91 000 sq mi).

Westmeath (Irish name: Contae Na Hiarmhidhe) A county in the central Republic of Ireland. Area: 1764 sq km (681 sq mi). Population (1986): 63 306. County town: Millingar.

West Midlands A metropolitan county in the West Midlands of England, created in 1974 from SE Staffordshire, NW Warwickshire, and part of NE Worcestershire. Area: 899 sq km (347 sq mi). Population (1987 est): 2 624 300. Administrative centre: Birmingham.

Westminster, City of A borough of central Greater London, on the N bank of the River Thames. Among its historic buildings are *Buckingham Palace, the Palace of Westminster, and *Westminster Abbey. It also contains St James's Park, Green Park, Hyde Park, and Regent's Park. Population (1987 est): 173 400.

Westminster, Statutes of 1. (1275, 1285, 1290) Laws introduced by Edward I of England. The first Statute dealt mainly with criminal law and procedures for the improvement of royal justice, the second dealt with rights of inheritance, and the third prohibited subinfeudation of land (i.e. the granting of portions of a knight's estate), which had caused loss of feudal dues to the King. **2.** (1931) The Statute that established the *Commonwealth of Nations.

Westminster Abbey A historic abbey church at Westminster, London. The present building, begun (1245) by Henry III, replaces one dedicated (1065) by Edward the Confessor, whose shrine is in the abbey. Since William I, every English monarch (except Edward V and Edward VIII) has been crowned in Westminster Abbey and many are buried there. The Coronation Chair, first used in 1307, contains the Stone of Scone, captured by Edward I from the Scots in 1296. Other notable features include Poets' Corner, where Chaucer and many others are buried or have memorials.

Westphalia A region of NW Germany. In the 18th century Westphalia came largely under Prussian control. During the period 1807–13 the region became the kingdom of Westphalia, under the rule of Napoleon's brother Jérôme Bonaparte. The Congress of Vienna (1815) restored most of Westphalia to Prussia.

Westphalia, Peace of (1648) The agreements, negotiated in Osnabrück and Münster

(Westphalia), that ended the *Thirty Years' War. It recognized the independence of the German states, the Swiss Confederation, and the Netherlands. Lutherans, Calvinists, and Roman Catholics were given equal rights.

West Point 41 23N 73 58W A military reservation in the USA, in New York state. It is the site of the United States Military Academy (1802).

West Sussex A county of S England, formerly part of Sussex, bordering on the English Channel. It is predominantly agricultural. Tourism is important in the coastal resorts. Area: 2016 sq km (779 sq mi). Population (1989 est): 714 100. Administrative centre: Chichester.

West Virginia A state in the E central USA. Although predominantly a rural state, manufacturing and mining (especially of coal) are important. Originally part of Virginia, it joined the Union as a separate State in 1863. Area: 62 628 sq km (24 181 sq mi). Population (1986 est): 1 919 000. Capital: Charleston.

West Yorkshire A metropolitan county of NE England, created in 1974. Coalmining and wool textiles are important. Area: 2039 sq km (787 sq mi). Population (1987 est): 2 052 400. Administrative centre: Wakefield.

wet rot The decay that affects timber containing a relatively large amount of moisture. It is caused by the cellar fungus (*Coniophora cerebella*) and characterized by the formation of a dark mass on the surface. Treatment is by drying affected timbers. *Compare* dry rot.

Wexford (Irish name: Contae Loch Garman) A county in the SE Republic of Ireland. It was the first Irish county to be colonized from England (1169). Cattle rearing is important. Area: 2352 sq km (908 sq mi). Population (1986): 102 456. County town: Wexford.

Weyden, Rogier van der (c. 1400–64) Flemish painter of portraits and religious altarpieces. The influence of the Master of *Flémalle is evident in The Deposition (Prado). In 1450 he visited Italy and paintings from this period, for example the Entombment (Uffizi), show Italian influences.

Weymouth 50 36N 2 28W A town in S England, on the coast of Dorset. It is a resort and port with ferries to the Channel Islands and Cherbourg. Population (1985 est): 57 400, with Melcombe Regis.

whale A large marine mammal that lacks hind limbs; its forelimbs are flippers and its tail is flattened to form a pair of paddle-like flukes. Whales breathe through a blowhole on top of the head and are insulated by a thick layer of blubber under the skin. Whalebone whales, including the *rorquals and *blue whale, are large and feed on shrimplike crustaceans. Toothed whales, including the *dolphins, *narwhal, and *sperm whale, are smaller and feed on fish and squid. *See also* whaling.

whaling The hunting of whales for their carcasses, which are a source of meat, fats, oils, and other chemicals. Whaling has reduced whale populations to the point that some species are in danger of extinction. The International Whaling Commission has attempted to ban whaling completely, but certain countries, such as Japan, persist in slaughtering these magnificent creatures.

Whangarei 35 43S 174 20E A city in New Zealand, in North Island. It is the site of New Zealand's only oil refinery (1964). Population (1988): 43 800.

wheat A *cereal grass that is native to W Asia but widely cultivated. The stems, up to 1 m high, each bear a cylindrical head of up to a hundred flower clusters. The grain of bread wheat (*Triticum aestivum*) is milled to produce flour. Hard or durum wheat (*T. durum*) is used to make pasta and semolina.

wheel animalcule. *See* rotifer.

whelk A widely distributed sea snail. 4–12 cm long, whelks feed on molluscs and worms. The common northern whelk (*Buccinum undatum*), 5 cm long, has a drab yellow-brown shell and edible flesh. Tropical species are more colourful.

whidah. *See* whydah.

Whigs A British political group that dominated politics in the first half of the 18th century. Identifying with industrialist, Nonconformist, and reforming interests, they became the *Liberal Party under *Gladstone, after about 1868.

whimbrel A *curlew, *Numenius phaeopus*, that breeds on Arctic tundra and winters in Africa, South America, and S Asia. 40 cm long, it has a streaked brown plumage and a dark crown with a pale central stripe.

whinchat A migratory songbird, *Saxicola rubetra*, that winters in Africa and breeds in Europe and Asia, feeding on flies and moths. The male has a streaked brown plumage, pale chestnut breast, white wingbars, and a white eyestripe; the female is duller.

whip In the UK, an official of a political party responsible for ensuring that the party's MPs vote according to its leadership's policies. The term also refers to the summons to vote sent by whips to MPs.

whippet A breed of slender dog developed in England during the 19th century from terrier and greyhound stock and used for coursing and racing. The fine short coat can be any mixture of colours. Height: 46 cm (dogs); 43 cm (bitches).

whip snake A slender tree-dwelling snake. The common European speckled grey whip snake (*Zamenis gemonensis*) feeds on other snakes and lizards. The green whip snakes occur in tropical Asia and Australasia.

whirligig A dark shiny widely distributed water beetle. It spins around on the surface of still fresh water, feeding on insects or other small animals. If disturbed, it exudes a foul-smelling milky liquid.

whirlwind A small revolving column of air, which whirls around a low-pressure centre produced by local heating and convectional uprising. In desert areas it may cause *sandstorms.

whisky An alcoholic drink, a spirit, obtained from malted (germinated) barley or other grain. The word comes from the Gaelic *uisgebeatha*, water of life. The malted grain is dried, ground, and mixed with water to form a mash; this is then fermented and distilled, and the resulting spirit is aged in the cask for at least three years.

The main types are Scotch whisky and US and Irish whiskey (spelt with an 'e').

Whistler, James (Abbott) McNeill (1834–1903) US painter. He specialized in portraits and landscapes dominated by one or two colours, the best known being *The Artist's Mother* (Louvre) and *Nocturne in Blue and Gold* (Tate Gallery).

Whitby, Synod of (663 AD) A council summoned at Whitby by King Oswy of Northumbria to decide whether to adopt Roman or Celtic Church practices in Britain. The Roman view triumphed.

White, T(erence) H(anbury) (1906–64) British novelist. He lived as a recluse in Ireland and in the Channel Isles. His books include a retelling of the Arthurian legend, *The Once and Future King* (1958).

white ant. *See* termite.

whitebait The young of *herrings and *sprats. They are highly valued as food.

whitebeam A tree, *Sorbus aria*, of the rose family, up to 15 m tall and found mainly in S and central Europe. Swedish whitebeam, a hybrid between whitebeam and *mountain ash, is often planted in parks.

white dwarf A very small faint low-mass star (less than 1.44 solar masses) that has undergone *gravitational collapse following exhaustion of its nuclear fuel. Electrons are stripped from the constituent atoms, and it is the pressure exerted by these densely packed electrons that eventually halts the star's contraction. The density is then 10^7–10^{11} kg m^{-3}.

Whitehall A street in Westminster, London, where many government offices are located. The Cenotaph is also in Whitehall.

Whitehead, A(lfred) N(orth) (1861–1947) British philosopher and mathematician. Whitehead's first major work, the *Principia Mathematica* (1910–13), was written with Bertrand *Russell. In *Principles of Natural Knowledge* (1919) and *The Concept of Nature* (1920), he explored the relationships between concepts and sense perception.

White House The official residence of the president of the USA. In Washington, DC, the building was burnt (1814) by the British during the *War of 1812 but was later restored, being painted white to hide the smoke stains.

Whitelaw, William (Stephen Ian), 1st Viscount (1918–) British Conservative politician; leader of the House of Lords (1983–88). He was leader of the House of Commons (1970–72), secretary of state for Northern Ireland (1972–73) and employment (1973–74), and home secretary (1979–83).

White Russians The Russians who fought against the Soviet Red Army in the civil war (1917–21) that followed the *Russian Revolution. The name comes from that of the royalist opponents to the French Revolution, who adopted the white flag of the French *Bourbon dynasty.

White Sea (Russian name: Beloye More) A gulf of the Arctic Ocean in the NW Soviet Union. It gives access to Archangel and Kandalaksha.

white shark A dangerous man-eating shark, *Carcharodon carcharias*, that occurs in tropical and temperate seas. Up to 11 m long, it is grey-brown to slate-blue with light-grey undersides.

whitethroat A *warbler, *Sylvia communis*, that breeds in N Europe and Asia and winters in central Africa. It is about 14 cm long. The male is russet brown with a greyish head and white throat; the female is a duller brown.

white whale A small Arctic toothed *whale, *Delphinapterus leucas*, also called beluga. Young white whales are blue-grey, but change to white as they mature. About 4.5 m long with a rounded head, they feed mainly on fish.

whiting A marine food and game fish, *Merlangius merlangus*, found in shallow European waters. Up to 70 cm long, it is olive, sandy, or bluish above and silvery white below.

Whitlam, (Edward) Gough (1916–) Australian statesman; Labor prime minister (1972–75). He ended conscription, relaxed rules on immigration, and tried to lessen US influence.

Whitman, Walt (1819–92) US poet. *Leaves of Grass* (1855) contains revolutionary free-verse poems expressing his democratic idealism.

Whit Sunday (*or* Pentecost) The seventh Sunday after Easter, a Christian festival commemorating the descent of the Holy Spirit on the Apostles on the 50th day after Easter (Acts 2.1). Whit Sunday became a time for baptisms, hence its name ("White" Sunday), referring to the white baptismal robes.

Whittington, Dick (Richard W.; d. 1423) English merchant, who was three times Lord Mayor of London (1397–98, 1406–07, 1419–20). The legend of Whittington and his cat dates from the early 17th century.

Whittle, Sir Frank (1907–) British aeronautical engineer who designed and flew the first British jet aircraft. The engine was fitted into a specially constructed Gloster E28/39; its maiden flight took place on 15 May, 1941.

WHO. *See* World Health Organization.

whooping cough An infection of the air passages of children caused by the bacterium *Bordetella pertussis*. It is characterized by violent bouts of coughing accompanied by a whooping sound and may be complicated by pneumonia or convulsions. A vaccine is available.

whooping crane A rare bird, *Grus americana*, that breeds in NW Canada and winters in SE Texas. 150 cm tall with a wingspan of 210 cm, it has a white plumage with black-tipped wings, black legs, and a bare red face and has a loud whooping call.

whortleberry. *See* bilberry.

whydah (*or* whidah) A small *weaverbird, also called widowbird, occurring in open grassy regions of Africa. The males have long tail feathers used in the courtship display.

Wichita 37 43N 97 20W A city in the USA, in Kansas. It is the state's largest city, with railway workshops, oil refineries, and an aircract industry. Population (1986 est): 288 070.

Wicklow (Irish name: Contae Chill Mhantáin) A county in the E Republic of Ireland. Agriculture is the chief occupation. Area: 2025 sq km

(782 sq mi). Population (1986): 94 482. County town: Wicklow.

Wien. *See* Vienna.

Wiener, Norbert (1894–1964) US mathematician. A child prodigy, Wiener developed an interest in the mathematics of information and communication, which he called *cybernetics. After World War II, Wiener wrote about the social problems resulting from automation.

Wiesbaden 50 05N 8 15E A spa city in SW Germany, on the River Rhine. Its hot saline springs have made it a popular resort since Roman times. Population (1987): 266 500.

Wigan 53 33N 2 38W A town in NW England, in Greater Manchester. It is an industrial and market town in a coalmining area. Population (1981): 79 535.

wigeon A *duck, *Anas penelope*, that breeds in N Europe and Asia and winters as far south as Africa and S Asia. 45 cm long, males have a chestnut head with a yellowish crown and grey back; females are brown with a white belly and white shoulders.

Wight, Isle of (Latin name: Vectis) 50 40N 1 15W An island and county in S England, separated from the mainland by the Solent and Spithead. Tourism and yachting (with the annual Cowes Regatta Week) are important. Area: 380 sq km (147 sq mi). Population (1989 est): 132 000. Administrative centre: Newport.

Wilberforce, William (1759–1833) British philanthropist. As an MP (1780–1825) he led the parliamentary campaign to abolish *slavery (achieved in 1807) and then to free existing slaves (achieved a month after his death).

wildcat A *cat, *Felis sylvestris*, inhabiting dense woodland of Europe and W Asia. About 75 cm long, it has a bushy rounded tail and thick striped coat. Wildcats may breed successfully with domestic cats.

Wilde, Oscar (Fingal O'Flahertie Wills W.; 1854–1900) British dramatist and poet, born in Dublin. He dazzled London society with his wit and became a leading figure of the *Aesthetic movement. His works include the novel *The Picture of Dorian Gray* (1891) and a series of brilliant social comedies: *Lady Windermere's Fan* (1892), *A Woman of No Importance* (1893), *An Ideal Husband* (1895), and *The Importance of Being Earnest* (1895). Socially and financially ruined by a trial in 1895 arising from his homosexual relationship with Lord Alfred Douglas (1870–1945), he was imprisoned for two years. In exile in France he produced his best-known poem, *The Ballad of Reading Gaol* (1898).

wildebeest. *See* gnu.

Wilder, Billy (Samuel W.; 1906–) US film director, born in Austria. His films include *The Lost Weekend* (1945), *Some Like It Hot* (1959), *Front Page* (1974), and *Buddy Buddy* (1981).

Wilder, Thornton (1897–1975) US novelist and dramatist. His best-known plays are *Our Town* (1938) and *The Skin of Our Teeth* (1942); his novels include *The Bridge of San Luis Rey* (1927).

Wilhelmina (1880–1962) Queen of the Netherlands (1890–1948), who encouraged

Dutch resistance in World War II. She abdicated in favour of her daughter Juliana.

Wilkes, John (1725–97) British journalist and politician. He founded the weekly *North Briton*, in which he attacked George III's ministers. The famous issue No 45 (1763) accused the government of lying in the king's speech and Wilkes was arrested for libel. Outlawed in 1764 and three times expelled from the House of Commons, he was at last permitted to take his seat in 1774.

Wilkins, Maurice Hugh Frederick (1916–) New Zealand physicist. He developed a technique that assisted James *Watson and Francis *Crick in determining the structure of DNA. These three scientists shared the 1962 Nobel Prize.

Willemstad 12 12N 68 56W The capital and main port of the *Netherlands Antilles, on the SE coast of Curaçao. Population (1983): 50 000.

William (I) the Conqueror (c. 1028–1087) Duke of Normandy (1035–87) and the first Norman King of England (1066–87). When Harold II succeeded Edward the Confessor, William invaded England, defeated and killed his rival at the battle of Hastings, and became king. In 1085 William commissioned the *Domesday Book.

William (I) the Silent (1533–84) Prince of Orange and leader of the *Revolt of the Netherlands against Spanish rule. In 1579 the northern Protestant provinces declared independence with William as their first stadholder (chief magistrate). He was assassinated by a Spanish agent.

William II Rufus (c. 1056–1100) King of England (1087–1100), succeeding his father William the Conqueror. His harsh rule aroused opposition, notably from *Anselm. He was killed by an arrow while hunting in the New Forest.

William III (1650–1702) King of England (1689–1702) and stadholder (chief magistrate) of the United Provinces (1672–1702), known as William of Orange. Grandson of Charles I of England, in 1677 he married James II of England's daughter Mary. In 1688 he was invited by the opposition to his father-in-law to invade England and in 1689 was proclaimed joint sovereign with his wife, Mary II (*see* Glorious Revolution). William defeated the former king at the *Boyne in 1690.

William IV (1765–1837) King of England and Hanover (1830–37), succeeding his brother George IV. Known as the Sailor King or Silly Billy, he served in the Royal Navy (1778–1790) and married (1818) Adelaide of Saxe-Meiningen (1792–1849).

William and Mary style An English derivative (1689–1702) of the *Louis XIV style of furniture. The cabriole leg was a typical innovation and rich gilding was common. Cabinet furniture was finely veneered with marquetry or lacquered and gilded.

William of Ockham. *See* Ockham's Razor.

William of Orange. *See* William III (King of England).

William of Wykeham (1324–1404) English churchman and statesman. Bishop of Winchester from 1366 and Lord Chancellor

(1367–71, 1389–91), he founded New College, Oxford (1379), and Winchester College (1382).

Williams, John (1941–) Australian guitarist, living in the UK. A virtuoso of the classical guitar, he also composes and performs music influenced by pop and jazz.

Williams, Tennessee (1911–83) US dramatist. *The Glass Menagerie* (1945), his first major success, introduced his recurrent themes of family tensions and sexual frustration, which characterized *A Streetcar Named Desire* (1947) and *Cat on a Hot Tin Roof* (1955).

Williamson, Malcolm (1931–) Australian composer, living in the UK since 1953. His works include seven symphonies, an organ concerto (1961), the operas *Our Man in Havana* (1963) and *The Violins of St Jacques* (1966), and *Mass of Christ the King* (1977).

willow A tree or shrub that is native to temperate and arctic regions. Male and female catkins are borne on separate trees and open before the leaves. Willows are common in wet places and some are grown as ornamentals, especially the weeping willow (*Salix babylonica*). Cricket bats are made from willow wood. *See also* osier.

willow pattern A *chinoiserie pattern attributed to Thomas Minton and introduced about 1780. The elements are a willow tree, pagoda, figures on a river bridge, and two flying birds in an elaborate border.

Wilson, Charles Thomson Rees (1869–1959) British physicist, who won the 1927 Nobel Prize for his invention of the *cloud chamber.

Wilson, (James) Harold, Baron (1916–) British statesman; Labour prime minister (1964–70, 1974–76). He became an MP in 1945 and president of the Board of Trade in 1947, succeeding Gaitskill as Labour leader in 1963. His statutory incomes policy and plans for industrial-relations reform were unpopular and he lost the 1970 election. During his second term of office the UK's terms of membership of the EC were renegotiated. In 1976 Wilson unexpectedly resigned. He was made a life peer in 1983.

Wilson, (Thomas) Woodrow (1856–1924) US statesman; Democratic president (1913–21). In his first term as president he introduced progressive reforms. In World War I, Wilson declared war on Germany (1917) in response to its unrestricted submarine campaign. Wilson's Fourteen Points (1918) contained a plan for a League of Nations that became part of the Treaty of Versailles.

Wiltshire A county of S England. It is predominantly agricultural. Prehistoric sites include *Stonehenge and *Avebury. Area: 3481 sq km (1344 sq mi). Population (1986 est): 545 200. Administrative centre: Trowbridge.

Winchester 51 04N 1 19W A city in S England, the administrative centre of Hampshire. Capital of Saxon Wessex, its cathedral was built in the 11th century on Saxon foundations. Winchester College (1382), founded by *William of Wykeham, is England's oldest public school. Population (1981): 30 642.

Windermere The largest lake in England, in Cumbria in the Lake District. It is extensively used for watersports. Length: 17 km (10.5 mi).

Windhoek 22 34S 17 06E The capital of Namibia. It is the centre of the world's karakul (Persian lamb) skin industry. Population (1988 est): 114 500.

windmills Machines that enable useful work to be obtained from *wind power. The wind turns a set of vanes or sails mounted on a horizontal shaft, the rotation of which is transmitted by gearing to working machinery. Windmills had appeared by 1150 in NE Europe and were used for grinding corn, pumping water, and powering light industry. The modern metal windmill with multiple-bladed sails is found world wide in rural areas.

wind power The use of wind energy to generate electricity. Because of the world shortage of conventional energy resources, wind-power generators (aerogenerators), like other *alternative energy sources, have now become more attractive economically. Wind power is free from pollution, uses no fuel, and the times of peak output are likely to coincide with peak demand. There are several different designs of aerogenerator, including the *windmill. In the UK about 12 wind turbines feed the national grid, mainly using Atlantic winds on the W coast. By 2005 1% of UK energy may be provided by wind power.

Windsor 51 29N 0 38W A town in SE England, in Berkshire on the River Thames. *Windsor Castle, a royal residence, dominates the town. Population (1983 est): 27 886.

Windsor, House of The name of Britain's royal family since 1917, when it replaced Saxe-Coburg-Gotha, the family name of Prince *Albert. In 1960 Elizabeth II declared that those of her descendants in the male line who were not princes or princesses would take the surname Mountbatten-Windsor. See p. 584.

Windsor Castle A royal residence in Windsor, Berkshire. It was begun by William the Conqueror as a stockaded earthwork. Additions made by subsequent monarchs include the keep by Henry III, St George's Chapel by Edward IV, and the Albert Memorial Chapel (so called by Queen Victoria) by Henry VII. Many monarchs are buried in these chapels.

Windward Islands (Spanish name: Islas de Barlovento) A West Indian group of islands forming part of the S Lesser Antilles. They comprise the islands of Martinique, St Lucia, St Vincent, the N Grenadines, and Grenada.

wine An alcoholic drink made from fermented grape juice. The grapes are crushed, traditionally by treading, now generally by machine, to bring the yeast ("bloom") on the grapeskins into contact with the sugar in the juice, which it then converts into ethanol (ethyl alcohol). Depending upon when the fermentation is stopped, the resulting wine is dry, medium, or sweet. Table wines contain about 9–13% alcohol. Fortified wines (e.g. *port, *sherry) contain about 16–23% alcohol. The bubbles in sparkling wines are caused by a secondary fermentation in the bottle (*see also* champagne). Red wines are made from whole grapes; for white wines the grapeskins are removed at an early stage in production. The word "vintage" is now used to designate a wine of outstanding quality. See p. 585.

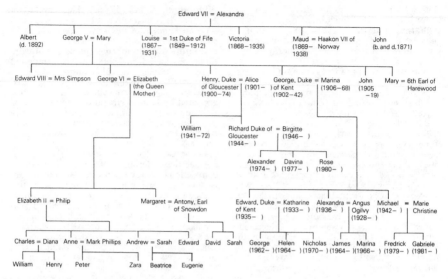

Edward VII = Alexandra

Albert (d. 1892)

George V = Mary

Louise = 1st Duke of Fife (1867–1931) (1849–1912)

Victoria (1868–1935)

Maud = Haakon VII of (1869–1938) Norway

John (b. and d.1871)

Edward VIII = Mrs Simpson

George VI = Elizabeth (the Queen Mother)

Henry, Duke = Alice of Gloucester (1901–) (1900–74)

George, Duke = Marina of Kent (1906–68) (1902–42)

John (1905 –19)

Mary = 6th Earl of Harewood

William (1941–72)

Richard Duke of = Birgitte Gloucester (1946–) (1944–)

Alexander (1974–)

Davina (1977–)

Rose (1980–)

Elizabeth II = Philip

Margaret = Antony, Earl of Snowdon

Edward, Duke = Katharine of Kent (1933–) (1935–)

Alexandra = Angus Ogilvy (1936–) (1928–)

Michael = Marie (1942–) Christine

Charles = Diana

Anne = Mark Phillips

Andrew = Sarah

Edward

David

Sarah

George (1962–)

Helen (1964–)

Nicholas (1970–)

James (1964–)

Marina (1966–)

Fredrick (1979–)

Gabriele (1981–)

William

Henry

Peter

Zara

Beatrice

Eugenie

HOUSE OF WINDSOR

Wingate, Orde Charles (1903–44) British soldier. A Zionist, he organized Jewish guerrillas in Palestine (1936–39). In World War II, after taking Addis Ababa from the Italians (1941), he formed the Chindits (the 77th Indian Brigade) to disrupt communications behind the Japanese lines in Burma. He was killed in an aircrash.

Winnipeg 49 53N 97 10W A city in W Canada, capital of Manitoba. Established as a fur-trading post (1806), it is now the distribution, financial, and manufacturing centre of the Canadian prairies. Population (1986): 594 551.

Winnipeg, Lake A lake in W Canada, in S Manitoba. Emptying into Hudson Bay, it drains much of the Canadian prairies. Area: 24 514 sq km (9465 sq mi).

wintergreen An evergreen creeping plant or small shrub found in N temperate and arctic regions. The flowers are white or pale-pink. **Oil of wintergreen** comes from the leaves of the winterberry (*Gaultheria procumbens*), a North American shrub.

Winterhalter, Franz Xavier (1806–73) German painter and lithographer, famous for his portraits of European royalty. These included King Louis Philippe, Napoleon III, and Queen Victoria.

Winter War. *See* Russo-Finnish War.

wireworm. *See* click beetle.

Wisconsin A state in the N central USA. The manufacturing of machinery, paper, and electrical and transport equipment is the major economic activity; dairy products and livestock are also important. *History*: handed over to the USA by the British in 1783, it became a territory in 1836 and a state in 1848. Area: 145 438 sq km (56 154 sq mi). Population (1988 est): 4 815 502. Capital: Madison.

wisent. *See* bison.

wisteria A woody vine of the pea family, native to E Asia and North America and grown for ornament. The most common species, the Japanese *Wisteria floribunda*, may grow to 30 m.

witan A body of 30 to 40 high-ranking people, which advised Anglo-Saxon kings on foreign policy, taxation, etc. It met at the king's will and had no fixed procedure.

witchcraft The attempt to influence natural events by persons using supernatural means. In Europe the biblical command "Thou shalt not suffer a witch to live" was used to justify widespread persecution, especially in the 16th and 17th centuries. Witches were accused of worshipping the devil at night-time orgies (sabbaths), keeping evil spirits (familiars), killing livestock, wrecking crops, and causing barrenness, impotence, and fits. Many traditional African communities hold witchcraft accountable for similar misfortunes.

witch hazel A shrub or small tree native to E Asia and North America. The most common species, the American *Hamamelis virginiana*, is the source of witch-hazel lotion used in pharmacy.

Wittenberg 53 00N 11 41E A town in E Germany, on the River *Elbe. The *Reformation began here on 31 October, 1517. Population (1983 est): 54 043.

Wittgenstein, Ludwig (1889–1951) Austrian philosopher. His two major works are the *Tractatus Logico-philosophicus* (1921) and *Philosophical Investigations* (1953). His preoccupation with language as a social phenomenon has been extremely influential among European philosophers.

Witwatersrand (*or* the Rand) A ridge of hills in NE South Africa. It extends about 160 km (99

WINE *The major French wine-producing regions and some standard bottle shapes.*

Champagne   Bordeaux   Burgundy   Alsatian white

mi) chiefly W of Johannesburg. It has been worked for gold since the 1880s.

woad A rare branching plant, *Isatis tinctoria*, of the mustard family, native to Europe. Up to 120 cm tall, it has yellow flowers and was formerly cultivated for the dye extracted from its leaves.

Wodehouse, Sir P(elham) G(renville) (1881–1975) British-born writer, who became a US citizen in 1955. His comic novels featuring Bertie Wooster and his manservant Jeeves, include *The Inimitable Jeeves* (1923) and *The Code of the Woosters* (1938).

Woden. *See* Odin.

wolf A wild *dog, *Canis lupus*, of Europe, Asia, and North America. Wolves are 140–190 cm long and live in packs of 5–30; they feed mainly on fish and animal remains but also attack deer. In colder climates they are larger and shaggier.

Wolfe, James (1727–59) British soldier. After the outbreak of the Seven Years' War he was sent to Canada, where he captured Louisberg (1758) and in 1759 besieged the Marquis de Montcalm (1712–59) in Quebec. His forces scaled the Heights of Abraham and the following victory established British supremacy in Canada, although both commanders were killed.

wolfhound. *See* borzoi; Irish wolfhound.

wolfram. *See* tungsten.

wolframite The principal ore of tungsten, $(Fe,Mn)WO_4$. It is found particularly in quartz veins associated with granitic rocks.

Wolfram von Eschenbach (c. 1170–c. 1220) German poet. His *Parzifal* (c. 1212) was the first German work to use the story of the Holy Grail and is the basis of Wagner's opera.

wolf spider A widespread *spider, also called hunting spider. Up to 25 mm long, wolf spiders are brown with long legs and are usually active at night, hunting prey rather than trapping it in webs. The female carries the eggs and young.

Wollongong, Greater 34 25S 150 52E A city in Australia, in New South Wales. It includes the towns of Wollongong, Bulli, and Port Kembla. Population (1985 est): 237 600.

Wollstonecraft, Mary (1759–97) British writer. In 1797 she married the social philosopher William Godwin (1756–1836). Her best-known work, *A Vindication of the Rights of Women* (1792) argued for equal opportunities. She died giving birth to her daughter Mary, who married *Shelley.

Wolsey, Thomas, Cardinal (c. 1475–1530) English churchman and statesman; Lord Chancellor (1515–29) under Henry VIII. Wolsey's attempts to raise taxes to pay for his policies encountered opposition. He fell from power after failing to persuade the pope to annul Henry's marriage to Catherine of Aragon, dying on his way to face trial.

Wolverhampton 52 36N 2 08W A town in central England, in the West Midlands. Metalworking and engineering are the principal industries. Population (1984): 254 000.

wolverine A carnivorous mammal, *Gulo gulo*, also called glutton, inhabiting northern forests. About 1 m long, it weighs about 25 kg, and hunts lemmings and hares.

womb (*or* uterus) A hollow muscular organ in women in which the fetus develops. It is connected by the vagina to the outside and to the ovaries by the Fallopian tubes. In a nonpregnant woman the lining of the womb is shed at monthly intervals (*see* menstruation). During pregnancy the womb becomes enlarged (about 30 cm long) and undergoes strong contractions at childbirth to force the baby out through the vagina.

wombat A bearlike *marsupial of Australia. The coarse-haired wombat (*Phascolomis ursinus*), about 1 m long, has strong claws used for tunnelling. It feeds on grass, roots, and bark.

Women's Institutes, National Federation of A British organization founded in 1915 to develop the quality, chiefly through further education, of rural life for women. Local institutes meet monthly to hear talks on a wide range of subjects.

Women's Royal Voluntary Service A British organization founded in 1938 as the Women's Voluntary Service (WVS). Its members provide many welfare services, including Meals on Wheels.

wood The hard tissue of the stems and branches of trees and shrubs. It consists of *xylem cells strengthened with lignin. The central part of the trunk–heartwood–consists of dead xylem. The wood (softwood) of conifers is less dense than the wood (hardwood) from broad-leaved trees, which contain more fibres and are therefore stronger.

Wood A family of English architects who worked in Bath, which **John Wood the Elder**

(1704–54) began to develop in the late 1720s. His work was continued by his son **John Wood the Younger** (1728–81), who designed the famous Royal Crescent (1767–75) and the Assembly Rooms (1769–71).

Wood, Sir Henry (Joseph) (1869–1944) British conductor. He established the London Promenade concerts at the Queen's Hall; they have continued at the Albert Hall since the Queen's Hall was bombed in World War II.

woodbine. *See* honeysuckle; Virginia creeper.

woodchuck. *See* marmot.

woodcock A long-billed gamebird, *Scolopax rusticola*, of Europe and Asia. 34 cm long, it has red-brown plumage with a dark-barred head and underparts and a white-tipped tail. Woodcocks feed on worms and insect larvae.

woodcut A *printing technique. The design is drawn on a block of wood, all the undrawn parts being cut away. The block is inked and pressed onto paper to transfer the design. The woodcut was used in China (c. 5th century AD) for textile design but its history in Europe dates from the 14th century. Leading 16th-century German woodcut artists include *Dürer and *Holbein.

woodlouse A widely distributed crustacean found in damp shady places under stones, logs, etc. Woodlice have a body covering of armour-like plates. A common species is the *Armadillidium vulgare*, about 17 mm long, which rolls into a ball when disturbed.

woodpecker A bird occurring worldwide except Madagascar, Australia, and New Zealand. 9–57 cm long, woodpeckers have multicoloured plumage, often barred or spotted. They chisel through tree bark with their long straight bills in search of insects.

wood pigeon A *pigeon, *Columba palumbus*, which is a serious pest on farmland in Europe and Asia. 40 cm long, it has a mainly grey plumage with a black-tipped tail, white wing patches, and a green, purple, and white neck patch.

wood sorrel A European plant, *Oxalis acetosella*, with white flowers and clover-like leaves. It is common in woodland.

woodwind instruments Musical instruments in which a column of air is made to vibrate either by blowing across a mouth hole, as in the flute, or by making a single or a double reed vibrate, as in the oboe, bassoon, clarinet, and saxophone.

woodworm The larva of the furniture beetle (*Anobium punctatum*) which damages furniture and old buildings. The larvae bore into wood and emerge when adult.

wool Fibres obtained from the fleeces of domestic sheep. Elastic and absorbent, it is also an excellent insulator. *Merino wool is the best in quality; garments labelled "Pure New Wool" are 100% merino. British and New Zealand wools are used in tweeds, blankets, etc. The strong coarse wool of Asian sheep and mountain breeds is used chiefly for carpets.

Woolf, (Adeline) Virginia (*born* Stephen; 1882–1941) British novelist; a central figure of the *Bloomsbury group. Her novels include *Mrs Dalloway* (1925), *To the Lighthouse* (1927), and

The Waves (1931), written in an impressionistic style to convey the fluidity of existence. She also wrote biographies and criticism. She committed suicide by drowning. Her husband **Leonard (Sidney) Woolf** (1880–1969), whom she married in 1912 and with whom she founded the Hogarth Press in 1917, wrote five volumes of autobiography (1960–69).

woolly bear. *See* tiger moth.

woolly rhinoceros An extinct rhinoceros that inhabited Europe, Asia, and North Africa during the Pleistocene epoch (2.5 million to 10 000 years ago). Well-preserved specimens show that it had a shaggy coat and two horns.

woolsack A large red cushion, stuffed with wool, on which the Lord Chancellor sits as speaker of the House of Lords. It dates from the middle ages, when the wool trade was important.

Woomera 31 11S 136 54E A town in central South Australia. It is the site of the Long Range Weapons Establishment and a launching base for space satellites. Population (1984): 1800.

Worcester 52 11N 2 13W A city in W central England, the administrative centre of Hereford and Worcester on the River Severn. The cathedral (begun 1084) is mainly 14th-century. Worcester is famous for its porcelain. Population (1987 est): 79 000.

word processor A computer system enabling documents, letters, etc., to be keyboarded, edited, printed, and stored. A typical word processor consists of a keyboard, visual-display unit, a disk backing store, and a high-quality printer.

Wordsworth, William (1770–1850) British poet, born in Cumberland. In 1795 he met S. T. *Coleridge, with whom he collaborated on *Lyrical Ballads* (1798). In 1799 he settled in the Lake District with his wife Mary and sister Dorothy; here he wrote his verse autobiography *The Prelude* (completed 1805; published 1850).

work The product of a force and the distance through which it causes a body to move in the direction of the force. Work, like energy, is measured in *joules.

workhouses Institutions set up in the 17th century in Britain and elsewhere to provide employment and shelter for poor people. The 1834 Poor Law Amendment Act made it necessary for anyone seeking assistance to enter a workhouse; their inhuman rules made them extremely unpopular.

Working Men's Club and Institute Union A club founded in 1862, now having over 4000 branches throughout the UK providing educational and recreational facilities.

World Bank. *See* International Bank for Reconstruction and Development.

World Council of Churches An organization of more than 200 Protestant and Orthodox churches (but not the Roman Catholic church). A product of the ecumenical movement to re-establish unity among Christian Churches, it was founded at Amsterdam in 1948, with headquarters at Geneva.

World Health Organization (WHO) A specialized agency of the *United Nations established in 1948. It supports work to abolish specific diseases, carries out and finances research into epidemics, trains health workers, strengthens national health services, and has established international health regulations; it also provides aid in emergencies. Its headquarters are in Geneva.

WORLD WAR I *The Eastern Front.*

World War I (1914–18) The Great War between the Allied Powers including the British Empire, France, Russia, Belgium, Japan, Serbia, Italy (from May, 1915), Portugal (from March, 1916), Romania (from August, 1916), the USA (from April, 1917), and Greece (from July, 1917) on one side, and the Central Powers, including Germany, Austria-Hungary, Turkey (from November, 1914), and Bulgaria (from October, 1915) on the other. Its causes included fear of German territorial ambitions; tensions among European powers were expressed by the *Triple Alliance and the *Triple Entente. The immediate cause was conflict of interests between Russia and Austria-Hungary in the Balkans. On 28 June, 1914, the heir to the Austro-Hungarian throne, Archduke Francis Ferdinand, was assassinated at Sarajevo by a Serbian nationalist; on 28 July Austria-Hungary, with German support, declared war on Serbia. Russia's mobilization led Germany to declare war on Russia and on France. Germany's invasion of Belgium brought the UK into the war on 4 August.

Western Front: The German forces advanced rapidly through Belgium until they were forced by the British Expeditionary Force (BEF) and the French under Joffre, at the first battle of the Marne (5–9 Sept), to retreat. Germany was prevented from reaching the Channel at the first battle of Ypres (12 Oct–11 Nov). On 21 February, 1916, the Germans attacked the French at

Verdun but on 1 July Haig, now commander of the BEF, opened the battle of the Somme, during which *tanks were used (by the British) for the first time. With the USA (enraged by German *submarine warfare) now participating, on 31 July Britain launched the third battle of Ypres and by 6 November had taken Passchendaele. In spring 1918 Germany pushed back the Allied line, but in September the Hindenburg line was broken. In October Germany sued for peace.

Eastern Front and Balkans: in August, 1914, the Russians were defeated at Tannenburg. When Turkey attacked Russia in the Caucasus Mountains, the Allies launched the **Gallipoli campaign**, in which Australian and New Zealand forces played a major part. It failed to break through the Dardanelles and by January, 1916, had withdrawn. The Allies landed at Salonika and the **Macedonian campaign** continued until Bulgaria surrendered in September, 1918. Russia collapsed following the *Russian Revolution (March, 1917) and made peace with the Central Powers (1918).

Middle East: the **Mesopotamian campaign**, intended to protect oil installations, was launched on 6 November, 1914; in March, Baghdad fell. Meanwhile the Allies had invaded Palestine, Allenby taking Jerusalem in December, 1917; the Turks were finally crushed by September 1918.

Italy: in 1917 the Italians were defeated by Austria-Hungary at Caporetto (Oct-Nov). In October, 1918, however, Austria-Hungary was defeated at Vittorio-Veneto and in November finally surrendered.

War at sea and in the air: at **sea** the British navy was dominant until the battle of Jutland in May, 1916. Victory in December 1914 off the Falkland Islands eased the capture of the German colonies in Africa and the Pacific. German raids on the English coast were repelled by Beatty's victory at Dogger Bank in January, 1915, but the German U-boats sunk some 6000 ships during the war. World War I was the first to use **aircraft**: in 1915 German Zeppelins, and in 1917 German aircraft, attacked British cities. Some air combat took place on the Western and Eastern Fronts and towards the end of the war the new Royal Air Force bombed German cities.

Conclusion: with the defeat of Germany on the Western Front and Austria-Hungary in Italy, revolt broke out in Germany. On 9 November the German emperor, William II, fled and on 11 November Germany signed the armistice. On 18 January, 1919, the Allies met at the Paris Peace Conference to decide the peace settlement, which was signed by Germany (the Treaty of Versailles) on 28 June. The Allies lost some 5 million lives (3 million French and Russians) and the Central Powers, some 3.5 million (3 million Germans and Austro-Hungarians).

World War II (1939–45) The war between the Allied Powers, including the Commonwealth, France, the Soviet Union (from June, 1941), the USA (from December, 1941), and China (from December, 1941) on one side, and the *Axis Powers, including Germany, Italy (from June, 1940), and Japan (from December, 1941) on the other. The war was caused by the failure of the

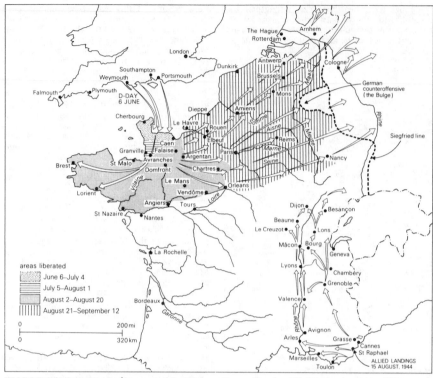

WORLD WAR II *The development of the Western Front after the Allied D-day invasion of Normandy.*

Paris Peace Conference (after World War I) and by the territorial ambitions of Germany under Adolf Hitler. In March, 1938, Germany annexed Austria (*see* Anschluss) and in September the *Sudetenland. In March, 1939, Hitler occupied the rest of Czechoslovakia. Hitler's agreements with Mussolini (May) and Stalin (August) led Britain, France, and Poland to make an agreement of mutual assistance on 25 Aug. On 1 September Germany invaded Poland; two days later Britain and France declared war on Germany.

Western Europe (1939–41): Polish defeat (September) was followed by the Soviet invasion of Finland (*see* Russo-Finnish War), and in April Germany invaded Denmark and Norway. The Allied failure in Scandinavia led to Chamberlain's resignation and on 10 May, the day that Germany invaded Belgium and the Netherlands, Churchill became Britain's prime minister. The Germans advanced round the *Maginot line, splitting the Allied forces; between 29 May and 4 June, some 338 226 Allied troops were rescued from Dunkirk. On 22 June Pétain signed the French armistice with Germany, after which French resistance was directed by de Gaulle from London.

In August and September, 1940, the German *Luftwaffe attacked London and other British cities but the RAF's defeat of the Luftwaffe in the Battle of Britain (RAF lost 915 aircraft, Luft-

waffe 1733), made it impossible for Germany to invade Britain.

Africa and the Middle East (1940–43): in September, 1940, Italy advanced from Libya into Egypt but was forced to retreat by Wavell's troops. In February 1941 Rommel and the German Afrika Corps arrived in N. Africa. In March Wavell's force, weakened by sending troops to aid Greece, retreated to the Egyptian border. By January 1942 Auchinleck (who had replaced Wavell), had been forced to take up a defensive position at El-Alamein. In August Auchinleck was replaced by Alexander and Montgomery became commander of the Eighth Army, defeating Rommel at the battle of Alamein (23 Oct–4 Nov). On 8 November an Anglo-US force under Eisenhower landed in French N Africa. The French surrendered and the Allies advanced through Tunisia to meet (7 April, 1943) Montgomery's Eighth Army. The Allies took Bizerta and Tunis and on 13 May the Axis forces surrendered (some 248 000 troops were captured).

In **East Africa**, Wavell took Addis Ababa from the Italians in April, 1941, and secured Ethiopia and British Somaliland (captured by Italy in 1940). In the **Middle East**, Britain and the Allies occupied Iraq, Lebanon, Syria, and Iran in 1948.

Italy (1943–45): on 10 July, 1943, the Eighth Army under Montgomery and the US Fifth Army under the supreme command of Eisenhower, landed in Sicily. On 25 July Mussolini fell, on 3 Sept the Italian armistice was signed, and the Allies landed on the Italian mainland. The Germans held back the Allies at the Ortona-Garigliano line until an Allied offensive broke through to Rome (4 June 1944). Bologna and then Milan were taken in April, 1945.

Eastern Front (1941–45): Germany, with Finland, Hungary, and Romania, invaded the Soviet Union on 22 June, 1941. They took the Crimea and the Ukraine, besieged Leningrad, and by November were in sight of Moscow. After the Soviet victory at the battle of *Stalingrad (August, 1942) the Germans launched a new offensive in July but were forced back and finally expelled from Soviet soil in August, 1944. In October Soviet troops invaded Germany and in January, 1945, launched a final offensive, taking Poland, Austria, and Hungary and entering Czechoslovakia. Berlin fell on 2 May, shortly after Hitler's suicide.

Western Front (1944–45): on 6 June, 1944, D-Day, the Allied invasion of Normandy began under Eisenhower. By 2 July one million US and British troops had landed. On 25 August Paris fell to the Allies, who now advanced into the Ruhr.

At the battle of Arnhem in September, however, airborne troops were withdrawn after sustaining heavy losses. In December the Germans launched a counteroffensive (the battle of the Bulge) in the Ardennes region of S Belgium. US troops forced the Germans to retreat in January, 1945, and the final Allied offensive was launched. On 4 May, Montgomery accepted the surrender of German forces in NW Germany at Lüneburg Heath. On 7 May the Germans signed a general surrender at Reims.

War at sea: the **battle of the Atlantic**, began in December, 1939, with the battle of the River Plate in the S Atlantic. In November, 1940, a successful naval air attack was launched on Taranto and in March, 1941, at Cape Matapan the British Mediterranean fleet stopped an Italian attempt to prevent the transfer of British troops from Egypt to Greece. In May HMS *Hood* was sunk by the *Bismarck* and, three days later, the *Bismarck* was sunk by the *Dorsetshire*. However, the major threat was the German U-boats; by summer 1943 37 had been sunk and the battle of the Atlantic was over.

Asia (1941–45): the Japanese attack on Pearl Harbor on 7 December, 1941, brought the USA into the war. On 10 December Germany and Italy declared war on the USA and the second *Sino-Japanese War became part of the wider conflict.

Japan invaded Malaya on 8 December and captured Hong Kong (25 Dec), Manila (3 January, 1942), and Singapore (15 Feb). The Dutch East Indies fell on 10 March and the Philippines and Burma in May. However, the US naval and air victories of the Coral Sea (4–8 May) and *Guadalcanal (Aug) halted Japan's eastward expansion. In October, 1944, the Japanese fleet was decisively defeated at Leyte Gulf and the Allied conquest of Manila (February, 1945), the Philippines (June), and Borneo (May-June) fol-

lowed. Burma was reconquered in May, 1945. Japanese resistance finally ended by the atomic bombing of Hiroshima (6 Aug, 1945) and Nagasaki three days later; Japan surrendered on 14 August.

Conclusion: the postwar settlement was decided at the *Potsdam Conference in July and August, 1945 (*see also* Tehran Conference; Yalta Conference).

The war cost Germany some 3.5 million combatants and 780 000 civilians. In contrast the UK lost 264 443 soldiers and 92 673 civilians. The Soviet Union lost 11 million combatants and 7 million civilians; the Japanese 1.3 million and 672 000 respectively; and the USA, 292 131 and 6000. In addition some 5.7 million Jews died in Nazi concentration camps.

World Wide Fund for Nature (WWFN) An international organization, formerly called the World Wildlife Fund, dedicated to the conservation of endangered species and their natural habitats. Founded in 1961, the WWFN has financed projects both in Britain and abroad. The international president is HRH the Duke of Edinburgh.

worm An *invertebrate animal. The term is applied especially to *earthworms and various parasites.

Worms 49 38N 8 23E A town in SW Germany, on the River Rhine. It has an 11th-century cathedral and synagogue (1034). *History*: in the 5th century AD it was the capital of Burgundy. Among the imperial diets (assemblies) held here was that of 1521 at which Luther refused to recant. Population (1984): 73 000.

wormwood An aromatic herb or shrub, *Artemisia absinthium*, of the daisy family, found in grasslands and the source of the alcoholic drink absinthe. Up to 80 cm high, it has yellow flowers.

Wotan. *See* Odin.

Wounded Knee A creek in South Dakota (USA) in which US troops on 29 December, 1890, fearing an uprising among the Sioux, killed over 200 men, women, and children.

wrack Brown *seaweed found worldwide on rocky shores. Branching fronds arise from a rootlike anchor (holdfast). Some common species are bladderwrack (*Fucus vesiculosus*) and serrated wrack (*F. serratus*).

wrasse A fish found near rocks or coral reefs in shallow seas. It has a slender coloured body, 5–200 cm long, long dorsal and anal fins, and thick lips.

wreckfish A carnivorous fish, *Polyprion americanus*, also called stone bass, found in Mediterranean and Atlantic offshore waters. It has a heavy body, up to 2 m long, brown above and yellowish below and a jutting lower jaw.

wren A small brown bird, *Troglodytes troglodytes*, found in Europe and Asia. About 10 cm long, it has reddish plumage with barring on the wings and tail. Related birds occurring in South America, Australia, and New Zealand are also called wrens.

Wren, Sir Christopher (1632–1723) English architect. A founder member of the Royal Society, he later became its president (1680–82). His first architectural designs were for Pembroke College chapel, Cambridge (1663), and the

Sheldonian Theatre, Oxford (1664). After the *Fire of London Wren produced a plan for rebuilding the City. This was rejected but Wren was commissioned to rebuild 51 City churches, some 36 company halls, and *St Paul's Cathedral. Later buildings include the Greenwich Hospital (begun 1694) and additions to Hampton Court (1698).

wrestling A form of unarmed combat, in which two people attempt to throw and hold each other down. It became an Olympic sport in 704 BC. In **Graeco-Roman wrestling** body holds below the waist and using legs to hold or trip are not allowed. They are, however, allowed in **freestyle wrestling**. In both styles a wrestler wins a match by throwing his opponent onto his back and pinning both shoulders to the mat for one second or by winning points according to a complex system. **Sambo wrestling** developed in the Soviet Union. **Sumo** is a Japanese style in which the wrestlers, usually weighing around 130 kg (20 stone), attempt to force each other out of the ring. *See also* judo.

Wrexham 53 03N 3 00W A town in North Wales, in Clwyd. It is a market town and coalmining centre. Population (1983 est): 40 357.

Wright, Frank Lloyd (1869–1959) US architect. He attracted attention with his Chicago houses, especially the Robie house (1909). Later buildings include the Johnson Wax factory at Racine, Wisconsin (1936–39), Taliesin West (1938), his home in Arizona, and the Guggenheim Museum (1959) in New York.

Wright, Orville (1871–1948) US aviator, who with his brother **Wilbur Wright** (1867–1912) made the first powered and controlled flights, on 17 December, 1903, at Kitty Hawk, North Carolina; the aircraft covered 250 metres.

Wrocław (German name: Breslau) 51 05N 17 00E A city in SW Poland, on the River Oder. Founded during the 10th century, it was damaged in World War II under siege from the Soviet armies (1945). Population (1985): 636 000.

wrought iron Iron containing less than 0.1% carbon. It was originally produced by repeatedly hammering and folding hot *pig iron to squeeze out the impurities. The puddling process has now superseded hand working.

Wuhan 30 35N 114 19E A port in E central China, where the Yangtze and Han Rivers meet. Formed by the amalgamation (1950) of the ancient cities of Hankou (*or* Hankow), Hanyang, and Wuchang, it is a commercial and industrial centre. Population (1986): 3 400 000.

Wu-hsi. *See* Wuxi.

Wuppertal 51 05N 7 10E A city in NW Germany, in the *Ruhr. It was formed in 1929 from six towns, including Elberfeld, and was heavily bombed in World War II. Population (1989): 3 400 000.

Wuxi (*or* Wu-hsi) 31 35N 120 19E A city in E China, on the *Grand Canal. A grain market since the 7th century, it is also an industrial centre. Population (1987 est): 696 300.

Wycherley, William (1640–1716) English dramatist. His satirical comedies include *The Country Wife* (1675) and *The Plain Dealer* (1676), adapted from Molière's *Le Misanthrope*.

Wycliffe, John (c. 1329–84) English religious reformer. His criticisms of the Church resulted in his condemnation as a heretic. He attacked the doctrine of transubstantiation and emphasized the importance of the Bible, of which he supervised the first English translation. Wycliffe's followers, the *Lollards, were forerunners of English Protestantism.

Wye, River A river in E Wales and W England. Flowing mainly SE from Plynlimmon it joins the River Severn near Chepstow. Length: 210 km (130 mi).

Wyoming A mountain state in the NW USA. Resources include oil, natural gas, uranium, coal, trona, bentonite clay, and iron ore. Livestock production dominates farming. Its Yellowstone National Park attracts considerable tourism. *History*: part of the Louisiana Purchase (1803), the arrival of the Union Pacific Railway (1867–69) brought settlement in the S; the area became a state in 1890. Area: 253 596 sq km (97 914 sq mi). Population (1988 est): 477 097. Capital: Cheyenne.

X

xenon (Xe) A *noble gas, present in the atmosphere and discovered in 1898 by Sir William Ramsay and M. W. Travers (1872–1961). Xenon is used in special lamps and the radioactive isotope ^{133}Xe is produced in nuclear reactors. It is a "poison", i.e. a neutron absorber, and is a crucial factor in the control of the chain reaction (*see* nuclear energy). At no 54; at wt 131.3; mp −111.9°C; bp −107°C.

Xenophon (c. 430–c. 354 BC) Greek historian and soldier, who became a disciple of Socrates. In 410 he successfully led a group of 10 000 Greek mercenaries in a retreat through the Persian Empire after their former commander, Cy-rus, was killed in battle. This feat formed the subject of his best-known work, the *Anabasis*. His other works include *Memorabilia*, *Apology*, and *Symposium*, which deal with Socrates.

xerography A technique for producing black-and-white copies (photocopies) of documents, drawings, etc. In the photocopying machine a pattern of electric charge is induced by light falling on a layer of semiconductor material on a conducting surface. Toner powder is sprayed or rolled onto this material, so that it sticks to the highly charged areas. The image so formed is printed onto charged paper.

xerophyte A plant that lives in a hot dry climate and is adapted for conserving water. Cacti, for example, often have spiny leaves (to prevent water loss) and succulent stems (in which water is stored).

Xerxes I (d. 465 BC) King of Persia (486–465). He invaded Greece (*see* Greek-Persian Wars) in 480. However, defeat at Salamis (480), Plataea and Mycale (479), and the consequent revolt of the Asiatic Greeks forced him to withdraw. This tyrannous ruler was assassinated in a court plot.

Xhosa A Bantu people of the *Transkei (South Africa), many of whom work in other areas of South Africa. Their language employs click sounds borrowed from the *Khoisan languages.

Xi An (Hsi-an *or* Sian) 34 16N 108 54E A city in central China. It contains many Tang pagodas and a noted museum and is an important industrial centre. As a Tang capital (618–906 AD) it attracted many Buddhist, Muslim, and Christian missionaries. After 1935 it was a Guomindang (Nationalist) base. Population (1986): 2 330 000.

Xi Jiang (*or* Hsi Chiang) The most important river in S China, rising in Yunnan province and flowing E to form the densely populated Canton delta and the Zhu Jiang River. Length: about 1900 km (1200 mi).

Xiong Nu (*or* Hsiung-nu) Turkish and Mongol tribes on the N and NW borders of China, which threatened Chinese security from about 500 BC. The Chinese attempted to control them by building the Great Wall of China, marrying their daughters to Xiong Nu leaders, and trading with them.

X-ray astronomy The study of celestial objects by the X-rays they emit. As X-rays are absorbed by the earth's atmosphere, observations have to be made above 150 km by rocket or satellite. The first X-ray source, Scorpius X-1, was discovered in 1962.

X-rays *Electromagnetic radiation lying between ultraviolet radiation and gamma rays in the electromagnetic spectrum. X-rays may have wavelengths between 10^{-9} metre and 10^{-11} metre. Discovered by Wilhelm *Roentgen in 1895, they are produced when heavy metal atoms are struck by sufficiently energetic electrons, as in an X-ray tube. X-rays cause ionization in gases and penetrate matter. X-rays have many uses in medical diagnosis, *radiotherapy, and the study of crystals (X-ray diffraction), etc.

xylem A plant tissue specialized for the transport of water and salts. The main cells are tube-like, with their walls strengthened by deposits of *lignin. In trees and shrubs the lignin eventually blocks the tubes completely: this tissue forms *wood.

xylene (*or* dimethyl benzene; $C_6H_4(CH_3)_2$) A colourless toxic flammable liquid obtained by fractional *distillation of petroleum. It is used as an aviation fuel and as a solvent.

xylophone A percussion instrument, consisting of a frame on which wooden bars in the pattern of a keyboard are fixed, each with a resonating metal tube beneath it. It is played with two sticks. Orchestral xylophones usually have a range of three octaves.

Y

Yahweh The pronunciation of YHWH, one of the Hebrew names of God, which occurs often in the Bible. "Jehovah" is another pronunciation of this name.

yak A shaggy-coated wild ox, *Bos grunniens*, inhabiting mountain pastures of central Asia. Domesticated yaks are kept for pulling and carrying loads and for their milk. Wild yaks, up to 2 m high with long upward-curving horns, are larger than domestic yaks and are always black.

Yale University One of the oldest universities in the USA (founded 1701), situated at New Haven, Connecticut. It is named after Elihu Yale (1648–1721), who donated his books to the college.

Yalta Conference (1945) The conference, held at the Black Sea port of Yalta, towards the end of World War II, attended by Roosevelt (USA), Stalin (Soviet Union), and Churchill (UK). They agreed upon the postwar occupation of Germany by the USA, Soviet Union, UK, and France and decided that German surrender must be unconditional.

yam A twining plant cultivated in wet tropical regions for its edible tubers. These can reach a length of 2.6 m; they are prepared as potatoes.

Yamasaki, Minoru (1912–86) US architect. His earliest buildings, such as Missouri's St Louis airport (1953–55), were simple but elegant. However, later works, such as the World Trade Center in New York (1970–77), used controversial pseudo-Gothic elements.

Yamoussoukro 6 49N 5 17W The capital of Côte d'Ivoire. Yamoussoukro was chosen as an inland replacement for the old capital of Abidjan in 1983. Population (1983 est): 70 000.

Yangon. *See* Rangoon.

Yangtze River (Chinese name: Chang Jiang *or* Ch'ang Chiang) The longest river in China and the third longest in the world. Rising in a mountain range on the Tibetan borders, it flows roughly E to enter the East China Sea. The Yangtze is one of China's main transport routes. Length: 6380 km (3964 mi).

Yaoundé (*or* Yaunde) 3 51N 11 31E The capital of Cameroon. Founded in 1888, it has been capital of Cameroon since 1922 (except during World War II). Population (1985 est): 583 500.

yard An Imperial unit of length originally defined as the distance between two gold plugs on a bronze bar. In 1963 the yard was redefined as 0.9144 metre (*see* metric system).

Yawata. *See* Kitakyushu.

yaws A chronic tropical disease caused by a *spirochaete bacterium, Treponema pertenue. It occurs mostly among poor children and is spread by skin contact, and is characterized by growths all over the skin. Treatment with penicillin is highly effective.

year The time taken by the earth to complete one revolution around the sun. This is equal to the period of the sun's apparent motion around the ecliptic. The **tropical year**, of 365.2422 days, is the interval between two successive passages of the sun through the vernal *equinox. The **sidereal year**, of 365.2564 days, refers to successive passages of the sun through a point relative to the background stars. *See also* calendar.

yeast A single-celled fungus that ferments carbohydrates (*see* fermentation). Strains of *Saccharomyces cerevisiae* are used in baking, brewing, etc. Yeast extracts are used as a food for their high vitamin B content.

Yeats, William Butler (1865–1939) Irish poet and dramatist. His best-known poems appeared in *The Tower* (1928) and *The Winding Stair* (1929); among them are 'Easter, 1916', 'The Second Coming', and 'Sailing to Byzantium'. With Lady Gregory (1852–1932), in 1904 he founded the Abbey Theatre, Dublin, for which he wrote many plays. He was a senator of the Irish Free State (1922–28) and won the Nobel Prize in 1923.

yellow fever An acute virus infection transmitted by female *Aëdes* mosquitoes, which occur in tropical rain forests. In severe cases the virus affects the liver causing *jaundice (hence the name), the kidneys, and the heart. There is no specific treatment but two kinds of vaccine can prevent it.

yellowhammer A *bunting, *Emberiza citrinella*, that occurs in Europe and Asia. About 16 cm long, the male has a bright-yellow head and underparts, chestnut rump, and a brown-streaked back; females are less colourful.

Yellow River (Chinese name: Huang He *or* Huang Ho) A river in China, rising in the W and flowing roughly E to enter the Gulf of Chihli via a fertile delta. Length: about 4350 km (2700 mi).

Yellow Sea (Chinese name: Huang Hai) A large shallow inlet of the W Pacific Ocean, bordered by China and Korea. It is so called because of the yellowish silt deposited by the Chinese rivers.

Yellowstone National Park The largest national park in the USA, chiefly in NW Wyoming but extending into S Montana and E Idaho. Its many active geysers include Old Faithful. Area: 8956 sq km (3458 sq mi).

Yeltsin, Boris (1931–) Soviet politician. He was first secretary of the Moscow Communist Party from 1985 until his removal by Gorbachov in 1987. In 1990 he was elected president of the Russian SSR and left the Communist Party. He is seen as the chief rival to Gorbachov, whom he has criticized for slowness in implementing reform.

Yemen Republic A country in the Middle East, in S *Arabia bordering on the Red Sea, the Gulf of Aden, and the Arabian Sea. *Economy:* chiefly agricultural. Cotton is the main crop: others include cereals, coffee, fruit and vegetables, tobacco, and the narcotic quat. Livestock are kept. Sardine fishing and handicrafts are important and salt is mined. There is an oil refinery and light industry in Aden. The economy relies on foreign aid and money from Yemenis working abroad. *History:* ruled by imams (priest-kings) from the 9th century, Yemen was nominally part of the Ottoman Empire from the 16th century to 1918. Aden was captured from the Turks in 1839 and occupied by the British East India Company. The British made treaties with other local rulers, finally uniting them under the Aden Protectorate (1937). The state of North Yemen, in the NW of present-day Yemen and with its capital at Sana'a, was established in 1934. In 1963 the Aden Protectorate and adjoining sheikdoms formed the Federation of South Arabia. This collapsed in 1967 and South Yemen became independent with its capital at Aden. In North Yemen civil war (1962–70) ended with the recognition of a republican regime. Successive heads of state were assassinated in 1977 and 1978. The history of South Yemen was dominated by border disputes with North Yemen (1967–72, 1978, and 1989) and with Oman (until 1976). In 1986 there was a violent coup; Haider Abu Bakr al Attas became president in the subsequent elections. Plans for union between the two Yemens were announced in 1989 and implemented in 1990. President: Ali Abdullah Saleh. Prime minister: Haider Abu Bakr al Attas. Official currencies: riyal and dinar. Official language: Arabic. Area: 531 870 sq km (205 311 sq mi). Population (1990 est): 13 000 000. Capital: Sana'a (administrative) and Aden (commercial).

Yenisei, River A river in the central Soviet Union, rising in the Sayan Mountains and flowing N to **Yenisei Bay** on the Kara Sea. Length: about 4000 km (2485 mi).

Yeomen of the Guard The bodyguard of the British sovereign established by Henry VII in 1485. They are often confused with the Yeoman Warders of the Tower of London, who wear a similar red and gold uniform. The nickname Beefeaters is applied to both but disliked by the Yeoman of the Guard.

Yerevan (Russian name: Erevan) 40 10N 44 31E The capital of the Armenian SSR. It dates from at least the 7th century AD. A commercial centre, it has chemical, textile, and food-processing industries. Population (1987): 1 168 000.

Yeti. *See* Abominable Snowman.

yew A coniferous tree or shrub native to the N hemisphere. The bright red berries are sweet-tasting and attractive to birds, but the seeds and leaves are poisonous. The most widespread species is the common yew (*Taxus baccata*), of Europe, SW Asia, and N Africa.

Yezo. *See* Hokkaido.

Yggdrasill In Norse mythology, an evergreen ash tree embracing the whole universe. Its three roots join the underworld, the land of giants, and the home of the gods (Asgard).

Yiddish A language used by *Ashkenazim (East European) Jews and based on a dialect of High German. It emerged during the 9th century and is written in the *Hebrew alphabet.

yield point The point at which a body becomes permanently deformed when subjected to a sufficiently large stress. Below the yield point the body is elastic, above the yield point it becomes plastic.

YIN AND YANG *The symbols are interlocked and each contains a tiny portion of the other.*

yin and yang Contrasting but complementary principles at the root of traditional Chinese cosmology. Yin is the negative feminine mode, associated with the earth, darkness, and passivity. Yang is the positive dynamic principle of masculine energy associated with heaven and light.

ylang-ylang A slender evergreen tropical Asian tree, *Cananga odorata*, also called perfume tree. An oil distilled from the fragrant greenish-yellow flowers is used in perfumery, cosmetics, and soaps.

YMCA. *See* Young Men's Christian Association.

yoga The principles and practice of self-training associated with all Indian philosophical traditions. Physical control is stressed in Hindu yoga, meditation in the Buddhist practice, and self-denial in Jainism. Usually the aim is a state of release and liberation from the material world.

yogurt. *See* dairy products.

Yokohama 35 28N 139 28E A port and second largest city of Japan, in SE Honshu. Together with Tokyo it forms Japan's greatest urban area. Population (1987): 3 072 000.

Yokosuka 35 18N 139 39E A port in Japan, in SE Honshu on Tokyo Bay. It has a major naval base and its chief industry is shipbuilding. Population (1985): 427 000.

Yom Kippur (Hebrew: Day of Atonement) A Jewish holy day, falling nine days after *Rosh Hashanah. A day of penitence, it is marked by 24 hours' total fast.

Yom Kippur War. *See* Israel.

York (Latin name: Eboracum) 53 58N 1 05W A city in N England, in North Yorkshire on the River Ouse. It was the principal Roman garrison in Britain. The cathedral (Minster) was begun in 1154. There is a university (founded 1963) and the Yorvig Viking Centre opened in 1984. Industries include chocolate, sugar, glass and railway engineering; tourism is important. Population (1981): 99 787.

York A ruling dynasty of England descended from Edmund, Duke of York (1342–1402), the fourth son of Edward III. Richard Plantaganet, Duke of *York, led the Yorkist opposition to Henry VI in the Wars of the *Roses (1455–85), in which the Yorkist emblem was the white rose. The Yorkist kings were Edward IV, Edward V, and Richard III.

York, Archbishop of The second of the two archbishops of England and head of the northern province of the Church of England. The Archbishop of York is styled Primate of England. He ranks next to the Lord Chancellor. The present (95th) archbishop is John Habgood (1983–).

York, Prince Andrew, Duke of (1960–) Second son of Elizabeth II and fourth in succession to the throne. A helicopter pilot in the Royal Navy, he married Sarah Ferguson in July, 1986. Their daughters are Princess Beatrice (1988–) and Princess Eugenie (1990–).

York, Richard Plantagenet, 3rd Duke of (1411–60) English nobleman. His claim to the throne against Henry VI resulted in the Wars of the *Roses in 1455. He was killed in a skirmish at Wakefield. His sons became Edward IV and Richard III.

Yorkshire A former county in NE England. It was reorganized in 1974 to form the counties of *North Yorkshire and *Humberside and the metropolitan counties of *West Yorkshire and *South Yorkshire.

Yorkshire terrier A breed of toy dog developed in N England during the 19th century. It is small and compact with a very long straight coat that trails on the ground. This is black at birth but matures to steel-blue with tan on the head and chest. Height: 20–23 cm.

Yosemite National Park A national park in the USA, in central California. The scenic Yosemite Valley contains the world's three largest monoliths of exposed granite. There are also many lakes, rivers, and waterfalls. Area: 3061 sq km (1182 sq mi).

Young, Brigham (1801–1877) US Mormon leader, who succeeded Joseph *Smith. A former Methodist, Young joined the new church in 1832. After Smith's death he led the major migration to Salt Lake City, Utah (1846–47).

Young, Thomas (1773–1829) British physician and physicist. He identified astigmatism, demonstrated the interference of light, and suggested a wave theory of light in opposition to *Newton's theory. As a result of his work on elasticity, the ratio of stress to strain is known as Young's modulus. Also an Egyptologist, he helped decipher the *Rosetta Stone.

Young Men's Christian Association (YMCA) A Christian organization for young men and, since 1971, for young women, founded in 1844 by George Williams (1821–1905). Its aim is to encourage Christian morality and qualities of leadership.

Young Women's Christian Association (YWCA) A Christian organization for women (to which men may now also belong). It was founded in 1855 by Emma Robarts and Mary Jane Kinnaird to promote unity among Christians and understanding between different faiths.

Youth Hostels Association (YHA) A British organization, founded in 1930, to encourage a greater understanding of the countryside, especially by providing hostels where young people may stay inexpensively.

Ypres (Flemish name: Ieper) 50 51N 2 53E A town in W Belgium, on the River Yperlee. Its many medieval buildings were almost completely destroyed during *World War I. Population (1985 est): 35 000.

ytterbium (Yb) A *lanthanide element, named after the village of Ytterby in Sweden. Its compounds include the oxide (Yb$_2$O$_3$) and trihalides (for example YbCl$_3$). At no 70; at wt 173.04; mp 819°C; bp 1194°C.

yttrium (Y) A *lanthanide element, discovered in 1794 by J. Gadolin (1760–1852). It is widely used as the oxide (Y$_2$O$_3$) to make red television-tube phosphors. At no 39; at wt 88.906; mp 1522 ± 8°C; bp 3338°C.

Yucatán A peninsula of Central America, chiefly in SE Mexico, separating the Gulf of Mexico from the Caribbean Sea. It was a centre of Maya civilization. Area: about 181 300 sq km (70 00 sq mi).

yucca A fleshy plant native to S North America. Yuccas vary from small shrubs to 15-m-high trees, with stiff sword-shaped leaves on a stout trunk and white bell-shaped flowers. Several species are grown as pot plants.

Yugoslavia, Socialist Federal Republic of (Serbo-Croat name: Jugoslavia) A country in SE Europe, on the Adriatic Sea. *Economy*: livestock is especially important and the principal crops are wheat, maize, sugar beet, sunflowers, and potatoes. There are thriving wine, forestry, and fishing industries. Mineral resources include coal, iron ore, copper, lead, and some oil. Development of heavy and light industry has been rapid

since World War II and tourism is important. *History*: Yugoslavia was formed in 1918 by the federation of Serbia, Montenegro, Croatia, Slovenia, and Bosnia-Herzegovina. Alexander I assumed absolute power in 1929 and was assassinated by Croatian nationalists in 1934. In World War II Yugoslavia was occupied by the Germans, with resistance divided between the Chetniks and the Partisans. After the war the Partisans' leader *Tito became head of a communist government. Since Tito's death a new premier is chosen each year. In 1990 the Communists gave up their monopoly of power and multi-party elections were promised. Nationalist movements in Serbia, Slovenia, and Croatia now threaten the unity of the country. Official languages: all national languages, with Serbo-Croat serving as the lingua franca. Official currency: dinar of 100 para. Area: 255 804 sq km (98 725 sq mi). Population (1988): 23 411 000. Capital: Belgrade. Main port: Rijeka.

Yukawa, Hideki (1907–81) Japanese physicist, who suggested (1935) the existence of virtual particles. Confirmation came in 1947, when the British physicist Cecil Powell (1903–69) discovered the pion. Yukawa was awarded a Nobel Prize in 1949.

Yukon A territory of NW Canada, on the Beaufort Sea. It is covered by tundra in the N. The population is concentrated on the central plateau, where silver, lead, zinc, copper, and asbestos are mined. There is some lumbering, and tourism is growing. The Yukon was opened up by the *Klondike gold rush (1897–99). Area: 531 844 sq km (205 345 sq mi). Population (1986 est): 26 166. Capital: Whitehorse.

Yukon River A river in NW North America. Rising in NW Canada, it flows N through Alaska then SW into the Bering Sea. Length: 3185 km (1979 mi).

YWCA. *See* Young Women's Christian Association.

Z

Zagreb 45 48N 15 58E The second largest city of Yugoslavia and capital of Croatia, on the River Sava. It possesses a gothic cathedral and a university (1669). Industries include textiles, machinery, and paper manufacture. Population (1981): 1 174 512.

Zaïre, Republic of (name from 1960 until 1971: Congo) A large country in central equatorial Africa, with a short coastline on the Atlantic Ocean. *Economy*: the chief cash crops are coffee, cotton, palm oil, and rubber. Zaïre exports copper from the Shaba mines and is the world's chief producer of industrial diamonds and cobalt. Other minerals include manganese, zinc, uranium, and oil. The rivers, especially the Zaïre River, are important for hydroelectricity and transport. *History*: when the Portuguese penetrated the region in the late 15th century it was dominated by the

kingdom of the Kongo. Leopold II of the Belgians established personal rule over the Congo Free State, which was recognized by the European powers at the Conference of Berlin (1884–85). In 1908 it became the colony of the Belgian Congo. Independence was obtained in 1960, as the Republic of the Congo. The almost immediate withdrawal of Katanga province under Moise Tshombe (1919–69) resulted in civil war. In 1965 *Mobutu Sese Seko seized power and in 1971 the Congo was renamed Zaïre. In 1978 Zaïre became a one-party state; multi-party elections were promised in 1990. Official language: French. Official currency, since 1967: zaïre of 100 makuta. Area: 2 345 409 sq km (895 348 sq mi). Population (1987 est): 31 780 000. Capital: Kinshasa. Main port: Matadi.

Zaïre River (former name: Congo R.) The second longest river in Africa. It is formed from the confluence of the Rivers Lualaba and Chambezi (later the River Luvua), which flow N as the Lualaba until the Boyoma Falls, where it becomes the Zaïre River. It flows generally W then SW to enter the Atlantic Ocean at Boma. Length: 4820 km (3000 mi).

Zambezi River A river in S Africa. Rising in NW Zambia, it flows generally S then E to form the Zambia–Zimbabwe border, the *Victoria Falls and Kariba Dam being located along this course, before flowing SE to enter the Indian Ocean. It has a drainage area of about 1 347 000 sq km (520 000 sq mi). Length: 2740 km (1700 mi).

Zambia (name until 1964: Northern Rhodesia) A country in S central Africa. *Economy*: copper accounts for about 96% of the total mineral production. Lead and zinc are also important, and some coal is mined. The chief subsistence crop is maize. Cash crops include tobacco, groundnuts, cotton, and sugar. Livestock and forestry are also important. *History*: the area was occupied by Bantu peoples when it was raided by Arab slave traders in the 18th century. In the 19th century Cecil *Rhodes made the region part of a territory named Rhodesia and administered by the British South Africa Company. It became Northern Rhodesia in 1911 and a British protectorate in 1924. It formed part of the Federation of Rhodesia and Nyasaland (1953–63), obtaining full independence within the British Commonwealth as the Republic of Zambia (1964). *Kaunda has been president since independence. In 1972 a new constitution led to one-party (the United National Independence Party) rule. Official language: English. Official currency, since 1968: kwacha of 100 ngwee. Area: 752 262 sq km (290 586 sq mi). Population (1987 est): 7 120 000. Capital: Lusaka.

Zanzibar An island in Tanzania, off the NE coast of the mainland. A sultanate from 1856 to 1964, it was under British rule from 1890 until it became independent within the British Commonwealth in 1963. In 1964 the Sultan was exiled and Zanzibar united with Tanganyika to form Tanzania. It exports mainly cloves and copra. Area: 1658 sq km (640 sq mi). Population (1985 est): 571 000. Chief town: Zanzibar.

Zapata, Emiliano (?1877–1919) Mexican revolutionary, who championed the cause of land reform against the president Porfirio Diaz (1830–1915) and succeeding governments. By late 1911 he controlled the state of Morelos, where he chased out the estate owners and divided their land amongst the peasants. In 1919 he was assassinated.

Zaporozhye (name until 1921: Aleksandrovsk) 47 50N 35 10E A city in the SW Soviet Union, on the River Dnepr. There is a large hydroelectric station and important iron and steel industries. Population (1987): 875 000.

Zaragoza (English name: Saragossa) 41 39N 0 54W A city in NE Spain, in Aragon on the River Ebro. During the Peninsular War it heroically resisted a French siege (1808–09). An industrial centre, Zaragoza produces paper and wine. Population (1986): 596 080.

Zarathustra. *See* Zoroaster.

Zealots A Jewish political party of the 1st century AD. Bitterly opposed to Roman rule in Judaea, they played a leading part in the revolt of 66 AD. Their last stronghold, *Masada, fell in 73.

zebra An African wild horse having black and white stripes covering part or all of the body. Species include the plains zebra (*Equus burchelli*), the mountain zebra (*E. zebra*), and Grévy's zebra (*E. grevyi*), the largest species, standing over 1.5 m at the shoulder.

zebra finch An Australian *weaverfinch, *Taeniopyga castanotis*. It has a red bill and the males are grey above with white underparts, reddish flanks, and black-and-white barred throat, breast, and tail. Zebra finches are popular cagebirds.

zebra fish A tropical freshwater fish, *Brachydanio rerio*, also called zebra danio, found in E India and popular in aquaria. It has a shiny blue body, up to 4.5 cm long, with four yellowish stripes along its sides. *See also* scorpion fish.

zebu The domestic *cattle of Asia and Africa, *Bos indicus*, also called Brahmin (*or* Brahman). Larger and leaner than western cattle, zebus have a distinctive hump, a large dewlap, and long horns. They have been exported to many hot countries for crossbreeding with beef breeds because of their tolerance to heat and their insect resistance.

Zeebrugge 51 20N 3 13E A small port in NW Belgium, on the North Sea, connected by ship canal (1907) to Bruges. In 1987 the British ferry *Herald of Free Enterprise* capsized outside the harbour with the loss of 193 lives.

Zeeman, Pieter (1865–1943) Dutch physicist, who discovered (1886) the splitting of the spectral lines of a substance when placed in a magnetic field (**Zeeman effect**). He shared the 1902 Nobel Prize with the Dutch physicist Hendrik Lorentz (1853–1928).

Zeffirelli, G. Franco (1923–) Italian director and stage designer. His films include *The Taming of the Shrew* (1966), *Romeo and Juliet* (1968), *Jesus of Nazareth* (1975), *La Traviata* (1983), and *Otello* (1986). He has also worked on numerous operas and his many stage productions include *Othello* (Stratford-upon-Avon, 1961) *Hamlet* (Old Vic, 1964), and *Filumena* (1977).

Zen Buddhism (Japanese *Zen*, meditation) In China and Japan, a Buddhist school emphasizing the passing on of enlightenment (*see* Buddhism) from master to disciple without relying on the scriptures. One of the two major sects, Soto, stresses meditation. Much of Japanese and Chinese art, music, and literature, and culture express the Zen attitude to life.

zenith The point in the sky lying directly above an observer and 90° from all points on his horizon. The (unobservable) point diametrically opposite the zenith is the **nadir**.

Zenobia (3rd century AD) The wife of Odaenathus of Palmyra, whom she may have murdered (267) and whom she succeeded as regent for their son. Zenobia occupied Syria,

Egypt, and much of Asia Minor before the Roman emperor Aurelian (c. 215–275 AD) defeated and captured her in 272.

Zeno of Citium (c. 335–262 BC) Greek philosopher, who was born in Cyprus of Phoenician origin, came to Athens in 313 BC, and attended lectures at *Plato's Academy. He evolved his own doctrine of *Stoicism.

Zeno of Elea (born c. 490 BC) Greek philosopher. Zeno's paradoxes are the first logical arguments, eliciting contradictory conclusions from an opponent's hypotheses. They support the doctrines that reality is indivisible and reason is at variance with the senses.

zeolites A group of complex silicate minerals mostly occurring in cavities in basic volcanic rocks. They are usually colourless or white and are relatively soft. Formerly used as water softeners, they are used as molecular sieves in the petroleum industry and as drying agents.

Zeppelins. See airships.

Zetland. See Shetland Islands.

Zeus The Greek sky and weather god, the supreme deity, identified with the Roman *Jupiter. He was the son of Cronus and Rhea, and brother of Poseidon and Hades. His defeat of Cronus and the *Titans represents the triumph of the Olympian deities over their predecessors. His offspring included *Athena, *Apollo, and *Dionysus; his wife was *Hera.

Zeus, statue of The statue designed by the Greek sculptor *Phidias in about 430 BC for the temple of Zeus at Olympia. One of the *Seven Wonders of the World, it was 12 m (40 ft) high and covered with jewels, ivory, and gold. It was destroyed in the 5th century AD.

Zhangjiakou (or Chang-chia-k'ou; Mongolian name: Kalgan) 40 51N 114 59E A city in NE China, in Hebei province near the *Great Wall. It was historically important for defence against and trade with the Mongols and is the site of two forts (1429, 1613). Population (1980 est): 1 094 000.

Zhengzhou (or Cheng-chou) 34 35N 113 38E A city in E China, the capital of Henan province. An old administrative centre, it has many industries developed since 1949. Population (1986 est): 1 590 000.

Zhou (?1027–221 BC) The earliest Chinese dynasty of which there is accurate knowledge. Feudal rulers weakened Zhou authority in the socalled Warring States period (481–221), after which the *Qin emerged to unite China. The late Zhou was the great period of Chinese philosophy, when Taoist and Confucian thought first emerged.

Zhukov, Georgi Konstantinovich (1896–1974) Soviet marshal. Becoming chief of the army general staff in 1941, he planned or commanded almost every major Soviet military operation in World War II, including the Soviet occupation force in Germany. Under Khrushchev he became defence minister and then a member of the presidium of the Communist Party.

Ziegfeld, Florenz (1867–1932) US theatrical producer. His lavish revues were modelled on the *Folies-Bergère. The Ziegfeld Follies, billed as "An American Institution," appeared annually

from 1907 until his death. He created such hits as Sally (1920), Show Boat (1927), and Bitter Sweet (1929).

Ziegler, Karl (1898–1973) German chemist, who shared the 1963 Nobel Prize with Giulio Natta (1903–) for their work on plastics and polymers. Ziegler showed that certain compounds (**Ziegler catalysts**) could be used to produce tough polymers with high melting points.

ziggurat An ancient Mesopotamian brick-built temple tower. Ziggurats were constructed of rectangular units of diminishing size, generally with a shrine for the god on top. They existed in every major Sumerian, Babylonian, and Assyrian centre.

Zimbabwe, State of (name until 1979: Rhodesia) A country in SE Africa. It is bounded in the N by the Zambezi River and in the S by the Limpopo River. Economy: cash crops include cotton, sugar, tea, and citrus fruit. The chief subsistence crops are maize, millet, and groundnuts. Forestry and fishing are important. Zimbabwe's rich mineral resources include copper, asbestos, gold, chrome, and nickel. History: there was a medieval Bantu civilization in the region. In 1889 Cecil *Rhodes obtained a charter for the British South Africa Company, and the region was named Rhodesia (1895). In 1911 it was divided into Northern Rhodesia (now *Zambia) and Southern Rhodesia, the latter becoming a self-governing British colony in 1922. The two parts of Rhodesia were reunited in the Federation of *Rhodesia and Nyasaland (1953–63); in 1963 the Whites demanded independence for Southern Rhodesia (Rhodesia from 1964). The UK's refusal to permit independence without a guarantee of majority rule led the prime minister Ian *Smith to issue a unilateral declaration of independence (UDI) in 1965. In 1970 Rhodesia declared itself a republic. In 1974 the Rhodesian government opened negotiations with the leaders of the Zimbabwe African People's Union (ZAPU) and the Zimbabwe African National Union (ZANU), which had pursued guerrilla activities since the 1960s. In 1978 agreement was reached on a transitional government leading to Black majority rule. Lord Soames (1920–87) was appointed governor to supervise the disarming of guerrillas, the holding of elections (which brought Robert *Mugabe to power), and the granting of independence to Zimbabwe as a member of the Commonwealth (1980). In 1987 ZAPU and ZANU united under Mugabe's leadership. Official language: English; the most important African languages are Ndebele and Shona. Official currency, since 1979: Zimbabwe dollar of 100 cents. Area: 390 622 sq km (150 820 sq mi). Population (1989 est): 9 120 000. Capital: Harare.

zinc (Zn) A bluish-white metal occurring principally in the ores calamine ($ZnCO_3$), zincite (ZnO), and zinc blende (ZnS). Zinc is used to make *galvanized steel and forms a number of alloys, including *brass. The sulphide (ZnS) is a phosphor and is used in making television screens and fluorescent tubes. Zinc oxide (ZnO) is widely used as a pigment and in medicines, batteries, and other products. At no 30; at wt 65.37; mp 419.58°C; bp 907°C.

zinnia A plant of the daisy family, mostly native to North America. Zinnias have stiff hairy stems and daisy-like flowers of various colours. Cultivated zinnias are hybrids derived from a Mexican species and have double flowers, about 11 cm across.

Zion (*or* Sion) A stronghold (II Samuel 5.6–7) on the SE hill of Jerusalem, captured by David, who made it the centre of his capital (Jerusalem). It is also described throughout the Old Testament as the place in which God lives and reigns. In the New Testament and in later Christian writings, it symbolizes heaven.

Zionism A Jewish nationalist movement. It emerged during the 19th century and was formally established at the First Zionist Congress (Basle, 1897), when the World Zionist Organization was established. Its political aim was the establishment of a Jewish national home in Palestine; Jewish immigration into Palestine (*aliyah*) was encouraged. It was supported by the *Balfour Declaration. After World War II, the *holocaust provided Zionism with an unanswerable case. Since the establishment of *Israel in 1948 the Zionist movement has continued to foster *aliyah* and support for Israel.

zircon A mineral consisting of zirconium silicate. It is usually colourless or yellowish. Gem varieties include hyacinth (red) and jargoon (colourless or smoky grey). It is the chief ore of zirconium.

zirconium (Zr) A grey high-melting-point transition metal, isolated by J. J. Berzelius in 1824. It occurs as zircon (zirconium silicate; $ZrSiO_4$). The dioxide (zirconia; ZrO_2) has a high melting point (2715°C) and is used in materials subjected to high temperatures. The metal is used in nuclear reactors since it is a good neutron absorber. At no 40; at wt 91.22; mp 1852°C; bp 4377°C.

zither A plucked stringed instrument of ancient origin, consisting of a flat resonating box fitted with 30 to 40 strings, approximately 5 of which lie across a fretted fingerboard for playing the melody. The rest are used for playing accompanying chords.

zodiac A zone of the heavens extending about 8° on either side of the ecliptic. Within it lies the apparent annual path of the sun, as seen from the earth, and the orbits of the moon and major planets (apart from Pluto). The 12 constellations in the zodiac are known as "signs" or "houses" to astrologers (*see* astrology). The 12 signs and their astrologically effective dates are: Aries, the Ram 21 Mar–19 Apr; Taurus, the Bull 20 Apr–20 May; Gemini, the Twins 21 May–21 June; Cancer, the Crab 22 June–22 July; Leo, the Lion 23 July–22 Aug; Virgo, the Virgin 23 Aug–22 Sept; Libra, the Scales 23 Sept–23 Oct; Scorpio, the Scorpion 24 Oct–21 Nov; Sagittarius, the Archer 22 Nov–21 Dec; Capricornus, the Goat 22 Dec–19 Jan; Aquarius, the Water-carrier 20 Jan–18 Feb; and Pisces, the Fish 19 Feb–20 Mar.

zodiacal light A faint glow that is visible in the western sky just after sunset and the eastern sky just before sunrise, especially in the tropics. It can be seen along the direction of the ecliptic, tapering upwards from the horizon. It is sunlight reflected from interplanetary dust particles.

Zog I (1895–1961) King of Albania (1928–39). Zog was proclaimed king after serving as prime minister (1922–24) and president (1925–28). He let Albania fall under Italian economic domination and when Mussolini invaded Albania (1939), he fled into exile.

Zohar (Hebrew: splendour) The classical text of the *kabbalah. It claims to be a mystical commentary on the *Torah and a collection of theosophical discussions dating from the time of the *Mishnah. It was actually written about 1280 by the Spanish kabbalist Moses de Leon, although it contains some later additions.

Zola, Émile (1840–1902) French novelist. Originally a journalist and clerk, he dedicated himself to a literary career after the success of his first major novel, *Thérèse Raquin* (1867). His series of 20 novels entitled *Les Rougon-Macquart* (1871–93) includes *L'Assommoir* (1877), describing the effects of drink on a working-class family; *Nana* (1880), concerning a girl from the slums; and *Germinal* (1885), about a mining community. He defended *Dreyfus in an open letter, *J'accuse* (1898).

Zollverein A customs union of 18 German states formed under Prussian control in 1834. By 1867 all German states except Hamburg and Bremen had joined. It paved the way for German unification under Prussian leadership (1871).

zoology The branch of biological sciences specializing in the scientific study of animals. This includes their classification, anatomy, physiology, ecology, behaviour, evolution, etc. The importance of animals as food producers, pests, etc., makes many aspects of zoology economically significant. *See also* ornithology.

Zoroaster (*or* Zarathustra; c. 628–c. 551 BC) Iranian prophet, founder of *Zoroastrianism. Probably born near Tehran, he is believed to have been a priest in the ancient religion when he received a vision urging him to preach a new faith.

Zoroastrianism The religion of Persia before Islam, founded by *Zoroaster, surviving there in some areas and in India among the Parsees (*see* Parseeism). It recognizes two principles, good and evil, as personified by Ahura Mazda and Ahriman. Ahura Mazda will eventually triumph, resurrecting the dead and creating a paradise on earth. Death corrupts—hence the custom of exposing corpses to be devoured by vultures.

Zuccari Two Italian painters, leading figures in Roman *mannerism. **Taddeo Zuccari** (1529–66) is known for his frescoes. His brother and pupil **Federico Zuccari** (c. 1540–1609) painted Elizabeth I in England (1575) and decorated the dome of the Duomo, Florence, and the high altar in the *Escorial.

zucchini. *See* courgette.

Zuider Zee A former inlet of the SE North Sea, within the Netherlands. The N part, the Waddenzee, is separated from the S part (now the IJsselmeer) by a huge dam (completed 1932).

Zululand An area of South Africa, in NE Natal. The home of the *Zulu people, it became a powerful state during the 1820s. In 1879 the Zulus were defeated by the British and Zululand was incorporated into Natal in 1897. It comprises part of the *Bantu Homeland of KwaZulu.

Zulus A Bantu people of Natal (South Africa). In the 19th century under Shaka (c. 1787–1828), the Zulus conquered an extensive empire until eventually defeated in wars with the Europeans. In their highly efficient military organization, warriors could not marry until they attained a certain grade.

Zürich 47 23N 8 33E The largest city in Switzerland, on Lake Zürich. It is the commercial and industrial centre of Switzerland; tourism is also important. The Romans occupied the site in the 1st century BC. During the middle ages it became the most important Swiss town and joined the Swiss confederation in 1351. Population (1987): 346 500.

zygote. *See* fertilization.

PRIME MINISTERS
GREAT BRITAIN (from 1721)

Name	Sovereign	Term
Robert Walpole	George I, II	1721-42
Spencer Compton, Earl of Wilmington	George II	1742-43
Henry Pelham	George II	1743-54
Thomas Pelham-Holles, Duke of Newcastle	George II	1754-56
William Cavendish, Duke of Devonshire	George II	1756-57
Thomas Pelham-Holles, Duke of Newcastle	George II, III	1757-62
John Stuart, Earl of Bute	George III	1762-63
George Grenville	George III	1763-65
Charles Watson-Wentworth, Marquis of Rockingham	George III	1765-66
William Pitt, Earl of Chatham	George III	1766-68
Augustus Henry Fitzroy, Duke of Grafton	George III	1768-70
Frederick North	George III	1770-82
Charles Watson-Wentworth, Marquis of Rockingham	George III	1782
William Petty, Earl of Shelburne	George III	1782-83
William Henry Cavendish Bentinck, Duke of Portland	George III	1783
William Pitt (son of Earl of Chatham)	George III	1783-1801
Henry Addington	George III	1801-04
William Pitt	George III	1804-06
William Wyndham Grenville, Baron Grenville	George III	1806-07
William Bentinck, Duke of Portland	George III	1807-09
Spencer Perceval	George III	1809-12
Robert Banks Jenkinson, Earl of Liverpool	George III, IV	1812-27
George Canning	George IV	1827
Frederick John Robinson, Viscount Goderich	George IV	1827-28
Arthur Wellesley, Duke of Wellington	George IV, William IV	1828-30
Charles Grey, Earl Grey	William IV	1830-34
William Lamb, Viscount Melbourne	William IV	1834
Robert Peel	William IV	1834-35
William Lamb, Viscount Melbourne	William IV, Victoria	1835-41
Robert Peel	Victoria	1841-46
John Russell	Victoria	1846-52
Edward George Geoffrey Smith Stanley, Earl of Derby	Victoria	1852
George Hamilton Gordon, Earl of Aberdeen	Victoria	1852-55
Henry John Temple, Viscount Palmerston	Victoria	1855-58
Edward Stanley, Earl of Derby	Victoria	1858-59
Henry Temple, Viscount Palmerston	Victoria	1859-65
John Russell, Earl Russell	Victoria	1865-66
Edward Stanley, Earl of Derby	Victoria	1866-68
Benjamin Disraeli	Victoria	1868
William Ewart Gladstone	Victoria	1868-74
Benjamin Disraeli, Earl (1876) of Beaconsfield	Victoria	1874-80
William Ewart Gladstone	Victoria	1880-85
Robert A. T. Gascoyne-Cecil, Marquis of Salisbury	Victoria	1885-86
William Ewart Gladstone	Victoria	1886
Robert Gascoyne-Cecil, Marquis of Salisbury	Victoria	1886-92
William Ewart Gladstone	Victoria	1892-94
Archibald Philip Primrose, Earl of Rosebery	Victoria	1894-95
Robert Gascoyne-Cecil, Marquis of Salisbury	Victoria, Edward VII	1895-1902
Arthur James Balfour	Edward VII	1902-05
Henry Campbell-Bannerman	Edward VII	1905-08
Herbert Henry Asquith	Edward VII, George V	1908-16
David Lloyd George	George V	1916-22
Andrew Bonar Law	George V	1922-23
Stanley Baldwin	George V	1923-24
James Ramsay MacDonald	George V	1924
Stanley Baldwin	George V	1924-29
James Ramsay MacDonald	George V	1929-35
Stanley Baldwin	George V, Edward VIII, George VI	1935-37
Neville Chamberlain	George VI	1937-40
Winston Churchill	George VI	1940-45
Clement Richard Attlee	George VI	1945-51
Winston Churchill	George VI, Elizabeth II	1951-55
Anthony Eden	Elizabeth II	1955-57
Harold Macmillan	Elizabeth II	1957-63
Alec Douglas-Home	Elizabeth II	1963-64
Harold Wilson	Elizabeth II	1964-70
Edward Heath	Elizabeth II	1970-74
Harold Wilson	Elizabeth II	1974-76
James Callaghan	Elizabeth II	1976-79
Margaret Thatcher	Elizabeth II	1979–90
John Major	Elizabeth II	1990–

AUSTRALIA

Edmund Barion	1901-03
Alfred Deakin	1903-04
John C. Watson	1904
George Houstoun Reid	1904-05
Alfred Deakin	1905-08
Andrew Fisher	1908-09
Alfred Deakin	1909-10
Andrew Fisher	1910-13
Joseph Cook	1913-14
Andrew Fisher	1914-15
William M. Hughes	1915-23
Stanley M. Bruce	1923-29
James H. Scullin	1929-31
Joseph A. Lyons	1932-39
Robert Gordon Menzies	1939-41
Arthur William Fadden	1941
John Curtin	1941-45
Joseph Benedict Chifley	1945-49
Robert Gordon Menzies	1949-66
Harold Edward Holt	1966-67
John Grey Gorton	1968-71
William McMahon	1971-72
Gough Whitlam	1972-75
J. Malcolm Fraser	1975-83
Robert Hawke	1983-

CANADA

John A. Macdonald	1867-73
Alexander Mackenzie	1873-78
John A. Macdonald	1878-91
John J. C. Abbott	1891-92
John S. D. Thompson	1892-94
Mackenzie Bowell	1894-96
Charles Tupper	1896
Wilfrid Laurier	1896-1911
Robert L. Borden	1911-20
Arthur Meighen	1920-21
W.L. Mackenzie King	1921-26
Arthur Meighen	1926
W. L. Mackenzie King	1926-30
Richard B. Bennett	1930-35
W. L. Mackenzie King	1935-48
Louis Stephen St. Laurent	1948-57
John George Diefenbaker	1957-63
Lester B. Pearson	1963-68
Pierre Elliott Trudeau	1968-79
Joseph Clark	1979-80
Pierre Elliott Trudeau	1980-84
John Turner	1984
Brian Mulroney	1984-

NEW ZEALAND

Henry Sewell	1856
William Fox	1856
Edward William Stafford	1856-61
William Fox	1861-62
Alfred Domett	1862-63
Frederick Whitaker	1863-64
Frederick Aloysius Weld	1864-65
Edward William Stafford	1865-69
William Fox	1869-72
Edward William Stafford	1872
George Marsden Waterhouse	1872-73
William Fox	1873
Julius Vogel	1873-75
Daniel Pollen	1875-76
Julius Vogel	1876
Harry Albert Atkinson	1876-77
George Grey	1877-79
John Hall	1879-82
Frederick Whitaker	1882-83
Harry Albert Atkinson	1883-84
Robert Stout	1884
Harry Albert Atkinson	1884
Robert Stout	1884-87
Harry Albert Atkinson	1887-91
John Ballance	1891-93
Richard John Seddon	1893-1906
William Hall-Jones	1906
Joseph George Ward	1906-12
Thomas Mackenzie	1912
William Ferguson Massey	1912-25
Francis Henry Dillon Bell	1925
Joseph Gordon Coates	1925-28
Joseph George Ward	1928-30
George William Forbes	1930-35
Michael J. Savage	1935-40
Peter Fraser	1940-49
Sidney G. Holland	1949-57
Walter Nash	1957-60
Keith J. Holyoake	1960-72
John R. Marshall	1972
Norman Kirk	1972-74
Wallace Rowling	1974-75
Robert D. Muldoon	1975-84
David Lange	1984–89
Geoffrey Palmer	1989–90
Michael Moore	1990
James Bolger	1990–

UNITS OF MEASUREMENT

SI units (Système International d'Unités) are now widely used throughout the world, especially for scientific purposes. SI units are metric units, based on the metre, kilogram, and second.

The base units are:

quantity	SI unit	symbol
length	metre	m
mass	kilogram	k
time	second	s
current	ampere	A
temperature	kelvin	K
luminous intensity	candela	c
amount of substance	mole	mol
plane angle	radian	rad
solid angle	steradian	sr

The derived units with special names are:

quantity	SI unit	symbol
frequency	hertz	Hz
energy	joule	J
force	newton	N
power	watt	W
pressure	pascal	Pa
electric charge	coulomb	C
potential difference	volt	V
electric resistance	ohm	Ω
electric conductance	siemens	S
electric capacitance	farad	F
magnetic flux	weber	Wb
inductance	henry	H
magnetic flux density	tesla	T
luminous flux	lumen	lm
illuminance	lux	lx
absorbed dose	gray	Gy
activity	becquerel	Bq
dose equivalent	sievert	Sv

SI units are used in decimal multiples, e.g. 1 km = 1000 metres, often written 10^3 m ($1 \times 10^3 = 10 \times 10 \times 10 = 1000$); 1 cm = 1/100 of a metre, often written 10^{-2} m ($1 \times 10^{-2} = 1 \div (10 \times 10) = 1/100$). The following prefixes are used:

submultiple	prefix	symbol	multiple	prefix	symbol
10^{-1}	deci-	d	10^1	deca-	da
10^{-2}	centi-	c	10^2	hecto-	h
10^{-3}	milli-	m	10^3	kilo-	k
10^{-6}	micro-	μ	10^6	mega-	M
10^{-9}	nano-	n	10^9	giga-	G
10^{-12}	pico-	p	10^{12}	tera-	T
10^{-15}	femto-	f	10^{15}	peta-	P
10^{-18}	atto-	a	10^{18}	exa-	E

These prefixes are used with all SI units.

length
SI base unit: metre
Imperial units: inch, foot, yard, mile

1 cm = 0.3937 in	1 in = 2.54 cm
1 m = 3.2808 ft = 1.09361 yds	1 ft = 0.3048 m
1 km = 0.62137 mile	1 mile = 1.60934 km

Examples
The radius of an electron is about 3 femtometres (3×10^{-15} m).
The distance between the sun and its nearest neighbour (Proxima Centauri) is about 40 petametres (4×10^{16} m).

mass
SI base unit: kilogram
Imperial units: ounce, pound, ton

1 g = 0.03527 oz	1 oz = 28.3495 g
1 kg = 2.20462 lb	1 lb = 0.45359 kg
1 tonne (1000 kg) = 0.9842 ton	1 ton = 1.01605 tonnes

Examples
The mass of a carbon atom is about 20 millionths of an attogram (2×10^{-23} g).
The mass of the earth is about six thousand million exagrams (6×10^{27} g).

time
SI base unit: second
Other units: minute, hour, day, year

Examples
The time between collisions of oxygen molecules at 0°C (760mmHg) is about 0.2 nanosecond (2×10^{-10}s).
The earth was created about 145 000 teraseconds ago (1.45×10^{17}s).

temperature
SI base unit: kelvin (K)
Other units: degree Celsius (centigrade), degree Fahrenheit

1 kelvin = 1°C
1 kelvin = 1.8°F

Examples
Absolute zero is a temperature of 0 kelvin.
The temperature inside the hottest stars is about 1 gigakelvin (10^9 K).

energy
SI unit: joule (J)
Other units: calorie, British thermal unit

1 joule = 0.2388 cal	1 cal = 4.1868 joules
1000 joules = 0.9478 Btu	1 Btu = 1055.06 joules

Examples
The energy released by a single disintegrating uranium atom is 40 picojoules (4×10^{-11} J).
The Hiroshima atom bomb released 84 terajoules (8.4×10^{12} J).